k_M	Required rate of return on "the market"
k_p	Cost of preferred stock
k_{RF}	Rate of return on a riskless asset
k_s	Cost of retained earnings
k_{sL}	Cost of equity of a levered firm
k_{sU}	Cost of equity of an unlevered firm
M/B	Market to book ratio
MCC	Marginal cost of capital
n	(1) Number of periods or years
	(2) Number of shares outstanding
NPV	Net present value
NWC	Net working capital
P	(1) Price of a share of stock
	(2) Price per unit of output
	(3) Probability of occurrence
P/E	Price/earnings ratio
PI	Profitability index
PV	Present value
Q	Unit sales
r	(1) Rate of return on new investment
	(2) IRR of a project
	(3) Correlation coefficient
ROA	Return on assets
ROE	Return on equity
RP	Risk premium
S	(1) Dollar sales
	(2) Total market value of equity
SML	Security Market Line
Σ	Summation sign (capital sigma)
σ	Standard deviation (lower case sigma)
T	Tax rate
t	Time
TIE	Times-interest-earned ratio
V	(1) Value
	(2) Variable cost per unit
V_L	Total market value of a levered firm
V_U	Total market value of an unlevered firm
YTM	Yield to maturity

INTERMEDIATE FINANCIAL MANAGEMENT

SECOND EDITION

EUGENE F. BRIGHAM
UNIVERSITY OF FLORIDA

LOUIS C. GAPENSKI
UNIVERSITY OF FLORIDA

The Dryden Press

Chicago   New York   Philadelphia   San Francisco   Montreal   Toronto
London   Sydney   Tokyo   Mexico City   Rio de Janeiro   Madrid

Acquisitions Editor: Ann Heath
Developmental Editor: Judy Sarwark
Project Editor: Cate Rzasa
Design Director: Alan Wendt
Production Manager: Mary Jarvis
Director of Editing, Design, and Production: Jane Perkins

Text and Cover Designer: C. J. Petlick
Copy Editor: Susan Thornton
Compositor: The Clarinda Company
Text Type: 10/12 I.T.C. Garamond

Library of Congress Cataloging-in-Publication Data
Brigham, Eugene F., 1930–
    Intermediate financial management.

    Includes bibliographies and index.
    1. Business enterprises—Finance.   2. Corporations—
    Finance.   I. Gapenski, Louis C.   II. Title.
HG4026.B6694   1987   658.1′5   86-19765
ISBN 0-03-009774-6

Printed in the United States of America
789-039-987654321

Address orders:
383 Madison Avenue
New York, NY 10017

Address editorial correspondence:
One Salt Creek Lane
Hinsdale, IL 60521

THE DRYDEN PRESS
HOLT, RINEHART AND WINSTON
SAUNDERS COLLEGE PUBLISHING

The Dryden Press Series in Finance

Brigham
Financial Management: Theory and Practice,
Fourth Edition

Brigham
Fundamentals of Financial Management,
Fourth Edition

Brigham and Gapenski
Intermediate Financial Management,
Second Edition

Campsey and Brigham
Introduction to Financial Management

Clayton and Spivey
The Time Value of Money

Cretien, Ball, and Brigham
Financial Management with Lotus 1-2-3®

Crum and Brigham
Cases in Managerial Finance,
Sixth Edition

Fama and Miller
The Theory of Finance

Gitman and Joehnk
Personal Financial Planning,
Fourth Edition

Harrington
Case Studies in Financial Decision Making

Johnson
Issues and Readings in Managerial Finance,
Third Edition

Johnson and Johnson
Commercial Bank Management

Kidwell and Peterson
Financial Institutions, Markets, and Money,
Third Edition

Lorie and Brealey
**Modern Developments
in Investment Management,**
Second Edition

Mayo
Finance: An Introduction,
Second Edition

Mayo
Investments: An Introduction

Myers
**Modern Developments in Financial
Management**

Pettijohn
PROFIT

Reilly
**Investment Analysis and
Portfolio Management,**
Second Edition

Reilly
Investments,
Second Edition

Tallman and Neal
Financial Analysis and Planning Package

Weston and Brigham
Essentials of Managerial Finance,
Eighth Edition

Weston and Copeland
Managerial Finance,
Eighth Edition

PREFACE

Several years ago, when the body of knowledge of financial management was smaller, the essential principles and analytical techniques could be covered in a one-term lecture course, then reinforced in a case course the following term. This approach is no longer feasible. The body of essential knowledge has expanded beyond what can be covered in one term, and it is inefficient to try to cover the remainder exclusively with cases—they are best suited for applying and discussing principles that students have already studied.

As this situation was developing, we at the University of Florida (and others elsewhere) were experiencing increasing difficulties in structuring our financial management curriculum. Finally, we reached these conclusions: (1) The introductory course should provide all business students with an overview of finance. (2) Finance majors need a second course that provides more depth on such topics as capital budgeting, capital structure theory, cost of capital, working capital management, mergers, and leasing. (3) A pure case course can be taught efficiently only after students have taken the first two courses.

When we attempted to teach finance in this three-course sequence, we had a problem. The first and third courses worked well, but no second-course book was available that covered the topics the way we thought they should be addressed. We tried books that emphasized financial theory, but they did not work well because students could not see the usefulness of the theory and consequently were not motivated to learn it. We tried books that were designed as introductory MBA texts, but they were far from optimal. Finally, we concluded that we needed a new text, one designed specifically for the second finance course as it should be taught in the 1980s. That conclusion led to this book.

CONCEPT OF THE BOOK

As we began work on *Intermediate Financial Management (IFM)*, we concluded that it should incorporate the following features:

1. Completeness. Since *IFM* is designed for finance majors, it should be both self-contained and suitable for reference purposes. Therefore, we specifically and purposefully included some material that overlaps with basic finance texts. We included relatively brief reviews of most first-course topics, both because we wanted to put *IFM* on a stand-alone basis and also because many students experience a delay between the introductory course and the second financial management course, and they need a review to "get up to speed" before tackling new materials. This is particularly true of certain "special topics" materials such as mergers, lease analysis, and convertibles, and perhaps even working capital management, which because of time pressures, are often only skimmed over in the introductory course.

2. Blend of theory and applications. Financial theory is useful to financial decision makers, both for the general insights it provides and also for its direct application in several important decision areas. However, theory can seem sterile and pointless unless its usefulness is made clear. Therefore, in *IFM* we present theory in a decision-making context designed to motivate students by showing them how theory can lead to better decisions.

3. Computer orientation. Rapid advancements in computer hardware and software are revolutionizing financial management. Powerful microcomputers are now affordable to any business that can hire a business student, and new software makes it easy to do things that were not feasible several years ago. Today, a business that does not use microcomputers in its financial planning process is about as competitive as a student who tries to take a finance exam without a financial calculator. Therefore, we provide many examples of how computers can be used to help make better financial decisions. This orients students toward the kind of business environment they will face upon graduation; moreover, students can often understand key financial concepts better after working through a computer model of the problem.

Obviously, not everyone has access to a personal computer or a mainframe terminal, so the text includes only a limited number of problems that require computer solutions. However, we do provide a good bit of computer output and, throughout the text, we discuss computer applications with an emphasis on *Lotus 1-2-3*®. In addition, we provide *Lotus 1-2-3* models both for a number of end-of-chapter problems and for a series of cases.

INTENDED MARKET AND USE

As noted above, *IFM* is designed for use in the second finance course. At the University of Florida, we cover most of the book in a one-term course, along with some cases which summarize major topic areas and provide insights into the complex decisions faced by practicing financial managers. To assist instructors in selecting cases, we highlight some applicable ones in the reference sections of appropriate chapters. Also, in the *Instructor's Manual*, we provide seven cases that were written specifically to illustrate parts of *IFM* and which utilize *Lotus 1-2-3* models; these cases can be reproduced and distributed to students for use in the course.

MAJOR CHANGES IN THE SECOND EDITION

Since the first edition was published, we have used the text in four courses, and we have also obtained numerous valuable comments from users at other schools. The reaction of our students, other professors, and the market in general has been overwhelmingly positive—everything indicates that our concept for the book was sound. Even so, virtually everything can be improved, especially first edition books. The most important changes are listed on the next page.

1. The second edition and all its ancillary materials incorporate fully the provisions of the new (1986) tax law, including (1) the new, lower marginal rates; (2) elimination of the capital gains benefit; (3) elimination of the investment tax credit; and (4) new depreciation rates. These changes have significant policy implications for dividend policy, capital structure decisions, capital budgeting, and lease analysis, and they required major changes in text discussions, end-of-chapter problems and cases, and all material in the *Instructor's Manual*.

2. Although we wanted the book to be complete enough to serve as a reference, the sheer bulk of the first edition intimidated many students. Thus, we have reduced the size of the book by 200 pages, primarily by streamlining the discussion but also by eliminating some relatively unimportant material.

3. Important works on both asymmetric information and signaling theory have appeared in recent years. We have incorporated this work into relevant sections of the book, especially in the areas of capital structure and dividend policy.

4. Chapter 1 was beefed up and recast to focus on fundamental concepts which influence managerial decisions, including the goals of the firm, agency theory, and the nature and effects of efficient markets.

5. Chapter 2, Risk and Return, was streamlined significantly.

6. In our treatment of capital structure, we reduced the coverage of early capital structure theories, but we also expanded the discussion of both the Miller model and signaling/asymmetric information theory.

7. Part IV, Long-Term Financing Decisions, was reorganized. Dividend policy is now in a separate chapter; materials from the old Chapter 15, The Timing of Financing Policy, were incorporated into other chapters; and our coverage of financial futures and their implications for financial management were expanded.

8. Our discussion of cash management was updated to reflect current practices.

9. The bankruptcy material was condensed and placed in an appendix to the long-term debt chapter.

10. Multiple discriminant analysis is now covered in the financial analysis chapter, where it is used to synthesize ratio analysis.

11. Multinational finance concepts have been integrated into the various chapters of the book, through the use of sections entitled "The International Perspective."

12. The set of end-of-chapter problems was expanded by approximately 20 percent, and more discussion questions were added.

13. Computerized problems, modeled with *Lotus 1-2-3*, were added to most chapters, and a diskette containing the models is available to instructors. These problems, which are identified by a diskette logo below the problem number (for example, see Problem 2-11 on Page 71), are designed (1) to show students the power of computers in financial analysis, and (2) to help students understand basic finance concepts. Very little knowledge of computers, and no knowledge of *1-2-3*, are required to use the models, but they can serve both as an aid to learning *1-2-3* and as a building block in the development of more complex models. Thus, the end-of-chapter *1-2-3* problems provide a good lead-in to the *1-2-3* oriented cases contained in the *Instructor's Manual*.

ORGANIZATION OF THE BOOK

We begin *IFM* with an introduction to financial management plus a review and extension of risk analysis, basic valuation concepts, and cost of capital (Chapters 1–4). Next, we focus on the firm's strategic, long-term decisions, which include capital structure (Chapters 5–6) and capital budgeting (Chapters 7–10). We then discuss various types of long-term capital (Chapters 11–15). Next, we take up tactical, operating decisions, or working capital policy and management (Chapters 16–19). At this point, students have seen how the decisions that affect individual asset and liability accounts are analyzed, and hence how financial ratios are determined, so we are in a position to examine the combined effects of such decisions in the section on financial analysis, planning, and control (Chapters 20–21). We conclude with a discussion of mergers and pension fund management (Chapters 22 and 23).

This organization fits well with the way our course has evolved at the University of Florida. However, the ordering of topics can be changed to suit other instructors' preferences without difficulty, because the various chapters and parts can be treated as modules.

ANCILLARY MATERIALS

A number of additional items are available as aids to both students and instructors:

Instructor's Manual. A comprehensive manual is available to instructors who adopt the book. The manual includes a suggested course outline, suggested lectures for each chapter, solutions to all end-of-chapter problems, and additional end-of-chapter problems that can be used for homework, lectures, or exams. In addition, the manual includes seven *Lotus 1-2-3* cases and solutions that were written specifically for use in the course. These cases cover the following topics: (1) capital structure analysis, (2) capital budgeting, (3) bond refunding, (4) lease analysis, (5) cash budgeting, (6) financial analysis, and (7) financial forecasting.

Diskette with Models. The diskette, which The Dryden Press will provide free to adopters, contains the *Lotus 1-2-3* models for both the computerized end-of-chapter problems and the cases provided in the *Instructor's Manual*. This selection of computer material permits instructors to incorporate *Lotus 1-2-3* into the course at two levels: (1) the end-of-chapter problem models, which introduce students to the power of *Lotus 1-2-3* without requiring them to learn how to model, and (2) cases which require students to do some actual *1-2-3* modeling and hence which require a basic understanding of *1-2-3*. To obtain the diskette, complete the insert card found at the front of the *Instructor's Manual*.

Casebooks. Two casebooks are available as supplements to the text: *Cases in Managerial Finance*, sixth edition (1987, Dryden Press), by Roy L. Crum and Eugene F. Brigham, which provides a set of structured cases that focus on single financial decisions, and *Case Studies in Financial Decision Making* (1985, Dryden Press), by Diana Harrington, which provides a set of new Harvard-type cases.

Readings Books. A number of readings books can be used as a supplement to this text, including *Issues and Readings in Managerial Finance*, third edition (1987, Dryden Press), by Ramon E. Johnson.

Microcomputer Books. Paul D. Cretien, Susan E. Ball, and Eugene F. Brigham have written a supplemental book, *Financial Management with Lotus 1-2-3* (1987, Dryden Press), designed to teach students how to use *1-2-3* for financial modeling, taking them from formatting and copying diskettes to the development of macros and other complex procedures. This supplement also provides a series of "template models" that address many types of financial management decisions.

ACKNOWLEDGMENTS

A great many people participated, directly or indirectly, in the preparation of this book. We would like to acknowledge the help of Edward Altman, Roger Bey, Keith Boles, Mary Broske, B. J. Campsey, Severin Carlson, Stephen Celec, William W. Damon, Sankar De, Myles S. Delano, Susan Fischer, Steven L. Flint, Michael Garlington, Sam Hadaway, Roger Hill, Ronald Hoffmeister, Keith Johnson, Joseph Kiernan, Dorothy Koehl, Joan Lamm, Edward C. Lawrence, Charles Linke, Judy E. Maese, Terry Maness, D. J. Masson, Chris J. Muscarella, Timothy Nantell, Thomas O'Brien, James Pettijohn, Richard Pettway, William Rentz, Pietra Rivoli, John Settle, Neil Sicherman, Clay Singleton, Steve Smith, Don Stevens, Glen Strassburg, Paul Swink, Gary Tallman, Russell Taussig, David Upton, Steve Vinson, Sue L. Visscher, J. B. Welch, and Dennis Zocco. In addition, the following professors provided comments and suggestions for improving the second edition:

Bruce Anderson	Ralph Hocking
Ronald Anderson	James LePage
Gregory Brauer	Gene Morris
David Cary	Robert Olsen
Antony Chang	Jaye Smith
Jay Choi	Ted Teweles
John Cotner	Paul Vanderheiden
James Desreumaux	Norm Williams
James Filkins	Michael Yonan
Rudyard Goode	

We also extend our gratitude to Tom Berry, De Paul University, who both worked with us on the manuscript and reviewed all the end-of-chapter problems and solutions.

Special thanks are due to Fred Weston, Myron Gordon, Merton Miller, and Franco Modigliani, who have done much to help develop the field of financial management and who provided us with instruction and inspiration; to Roy Crum, who coauthored the multinational finance sections; to Russ Fogler, who coauthored the pension fund chapter; to Art Herrmann, who coauthored the bankruptcy appendix; to Dilip Shome, who coauthored the capital structure theory chapter; to Dana Aberwald, Susan Ball, Mary Alice Hanebury, and Kay Mangan, who helped us develop the *Lotus 1-2-3* models; and to Steve Ambrose, Bob Karp, and Terry Sicherman, who cheerfully typed and revised the manuscript countless times.

Both our colleagues and our students at the University of Florida gave us many useful suggestions, and The Dryden Press staff—especially Ann Heath, Mary Jarvis, Jane Perkins, Cate Rzasa, Judy Sarwark, Bill Schoof, Betsy Webster, and Alan Wendt—helped greatly with all phases of the text development and production.

ERRORS IN THE TEXT

At this point in the preface, authors generally say something like this: "We appreciate all the help we received from the people listed above, but any remaining errors are, of course, our own responsibility." And in many books, there are plenty of remaining errors. Having experienced difficulties with errors ourselves, both as students and as instructors, we resolved to avoid this problem in *Intermediate Financial Management*. As a result of our error detection procedures, we are convinced that the book is relatively free of mistakes.

Partly because of our confidence that few errors remain, but primarily because we want very much to detect any errors that may have slipped by so we can correct them in subsequent printings, we decided to offer a reward of $5 per error (conceptual error, misspelled word, arithmetic mistake, and the like) to the first person who reports it to us. (Any error that has follow-through effects is counted as two errors only.) Two accounting students have set up a foolproof audit system to make sure we pay off. Accounting students tend to be skeptics!

CONCLUSION

Finance is, in a real sense, the cornerstone of the enterprise system. Good financial management is therefore vitally important to the economic health of business firms, and hence to the nation and the world. Because of its importance, financial management should be thoroughly understood, but this is easier said than done. The field is relatively complex, and it is undergoing constant change in response to shifts in economic conditions. All of this makes financial management stimulating and exciting, but also challenging and sometimes perplexing. We sincerely hope that the second edition of *Intermediate Financial Management* will help you understand the financial problems faced by businesses today, as well as the best ways to solve those problems.

Eugene F. Brigham
Louis C. Gapenski

College of Business Administration
University of Florida
Gainesville, Florida 32611

January 1987

CONTENTS IN BRIEF

CONTENTS

 # I

THE FRAMEWORK OF FINANCIAL MANAGEMENT

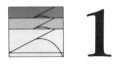

1

INTRODUCTION TO FINANCIAL MANAGEMENT

In the introductory finance course, students are generally given an overview of financial markets and institutions plus an introduction to the decisions and tasks faced by practicing financial managers in their daily activities. In this text, we cover the same topics, but in greater depth. We review and reinforce the basic concepts, but we also (1) discuss in detail the key theoretical underpinnings of financial management and (2) present an in-depth treatment of the tools and techniques necessary to implement the theory in the "real world."

This chapter begins with the results of a survey of how financial managers allocate their time among different tasks. Then we discuss five key concepts that are critical to the various decision models that form the basis of financial management: (1) the goals of the firm, (2) agency relationships, (3) the efficient markets hypothesis, (4) discounted cash flow analysis, and (5) the trade-off between risk and return. Failure to consider any one of these concepts can lead to an improper specification of a decision process, and hence to an incorrect decision. Therefore, it is important that you understand each of the concepts, and that you ask yourself how each applies to the particular decision at hand.

We close the main body of the chapter with a discussion of the organization of the text, and then, after the summary, we include a section entitled "The International Perspective." Business is becoming increasingly international in scope, and this section is designed to give you a "feel" for how the topics in the chapter are affected by the global environment. Other chapters include similar sections on the international environment.

THE PRACTICING FINANCIAL MANAGER

This book is designed to help you become a financial manager. If you do go into financial management, what will you actually do? Larry Gitman and Charles Maxwell (G-M) surveyed the financial managers of the 1,000 largest industrial companies in the United States—the Fortune 1000—and asked how they spent most of their time. Here are the results:[1]

Financial Activity	Percent of Time Spent
Financial planning and budgeting	35%
Managing working capital	32
Managing capital expenditures	19
Raising long-term funds	14
	100%

G-M went on to examine the time spent on various activities in more detail. Here is a summary:

Financial Activity	Percent of Time Spent
Asset management	58%
Liability management	42
	100%
Short-term activities	60%
Long-term activities	40
	100%

We see that managers, in general, spent more time managing assets than managing liabilities. Apparently, the greater frequency and complexity involved in acquiring, operating, and maintaining current and fixed assets required more time than did liability management. Also, responding managers spent more time on short-term than long-term activities. The dynamic and highly volatile short-term markets, the daily nature of short-term financial activities, and the fact that long-term funds are raised infrequently (but in large amounts) may explain this breakdown.[2]

G-M also asked the financial managers to rank their activities by importance, and these rankings generally follow the time allocation reported above. However, we must be careful when defining "importance," because comparing the relative importance of the activities listed is a bit like asking you to compare the relative importance of air, water, food, clothing, and shelter. Note also that the percentages refer to the time of the chief financial officer (CFO) of very large corporations. Lower level members of the financial staff would find their duties much more concentrated—for example, if you got a job as a financial analyst with a large firm, you would probably be assigned primarily to planning and budgeting, or working

---

[1]See Lawrence J. Gitman and Charles E. Maxwell, "Financial Activities of Major U.S. Firms: Survey and Analysis of Fortune's 1000," *Financial Management*, Winter 1985, 57-65.

[2]G-M pointed out that the survey was taken in March 1983, and at the time the financial markets were extremely volatile and the economy was weak. Thus, it is possible that firms were limiting capital investment and financing activities, and concentrating on the activities necessary to ensure survival.

capital, or capital expenditure analysis. Still, you would be unable to function well in any one field without a good knowledge of what is going on in the other areas, and you could also expect to be rotated into other areas both as part of your career development and as the company's focus changes in response to changes in its operating environment.

GOALS OF THE FIRM

Decisions are not made in a vacuum but, rather, with some objective in mind. Throughout this book, we operate on the assumption that management's primary goal is to maximize the wealth of its stockholders, which translates into *maximizing the price of the common stock*. There are, of course, other objectives—managers, who make the actual decisions, are interested in their own personal satisfaction, in employees' welfare, and in the good of both their communities and society at large. Still, for the reasons set forth below, *stock price maximization is the most important goal of most firms,* and it is a reasonable operating objective upon which to build financial decision rules.

Social Responsibility

An issue that deserves consideration is social responsibility: Should businesses operate strictly in the stockholders' best interests, or are firms also partly responsible for the welfare of employees, creditors, customers, the communities in which they operate, and indeed for society at large? In tackling this question, consider first those firms whose rates of return on investment are close to normal, that is, close to the average for all firms. If some of these companies attempt to be social do-gooders, thereby increasing their costs over what they otherwise would have been, and if the other businesses in the industry do not follow suit, then the socially oriented firms would probably be forced by competition to abandon their efforts. Thus, any socially responsible act that raises costs will be difficult, if not impossible, in industries subject to keen competition.

What about oligopolistic firms with profits above normal levels—can they not devote resources to social projects? Undoubtedly, they can; many large, successful firms do engage in community projects, employee benefit programs, and the like to a greater degree than would appear to be called for by pure wealth maximization goals.[3] Still, publicly owned firms are constrained in such actions by capital market factors. Suppose a saver who has funds to invest is considering two alternative firms. One firm devotes a substantial part of its resources to social actions, while the other concentrates on profits and stock prices. Most investors are likely to shun the socially oriented firm, and its management would be highly exposed

---

[3]Even firms such as these find it necessary to justify such programs at stockholder meetings by stating that these programs contribute to long-run profit maximization.

to a takeover. After all, why should the stockholders of one corporation subsidize society to a greater extent than stockholders of other businesses? For this reason, even highly profitable firms (unless their managers own more than 50 percent of the stock) are constrained against taking unilateral cost-increasing social actions.

Does all this mean that firms should not exercise social responsibility? Not at all—it simply means that most cost-increasing actions may have to be put on a *mandatory* rather than a voluntary basis, at least initially, to ensure that the burden of such action falls uniformly across all businesses. Thus, social benefit programs such as fair hiring practices, minority training, product safety, pollution abatement, and antitrust actions are most likely to be effective if realistic rules are established initially and then enforced by government agencies. Of course, it is critical that industry and government cooperate in establishing the rules of corporate behavior, that the costs as well as the benefits of such actions be accurately estimated and taken into account, and that firms follow the spirit as well as the letter of the law in their actions. In such a setting, the rules of the game become constraints.

Stock Price Maximization and Social Welfare

If firms attempt to maximize stock prices, is this good or bad for society? In general, it is good. Aside from such illegal actions as attempting to form monopolies, violating safety codes, and failing to meet pollution control requirements—all of which are constrained by the government—*the same actions that maximize stock prices also benefit society*. First, stock price maximization requires efficient, low-cost operations that produce the desired quality and quantity of output at the lowest possible cost. Second, stock price maximization requires the development of products that consumers want and need, so the profit motive leads to new technology, new products, and new jobs. Finally, stock price maximization necessitates efficient and courteous service, adequate stocks of merchandise, and well-located business establishments, because these factors are all necessary to make sales, and sales are necessary for profits. *Therefore, the types of actions that help a firm increase the price of its stock are also directly beneficial to society at large.* This is why profit-motivated, free-enterprise economies have been so much more successful than socialistic and other types of economic systems. Since financial management plays a crucial role in the operations of successful firms, and since successful firms are absolutely necessary for a healthy, productive economy, it is easy to see why finance is important from a social standpoint.[4]

---

[4]People sometimes argue that firms, in their efforts to raise profits and stock prices, increase product prices and gouge the public. In a reasonably competitive economy, which we have, prices are constrained by competition and consumer resistance. If a firm raises its prices beyond reasonable levels, it will simply lose its market share. Even giant firms like General Motors lose business to the Japanese and Germans, as well as to Ford and Chrysler, if they do not set prices that merely cover production costs plus a "normal" profit. Of course, firms *want* to earn more, and they constantly try to cut costs, develop new products, and so on, and thereby earn above-normal profits. Yet, if they are successful and do earn above-normal profits, these very profits will attract competition and eventually drive prices down, so the main beneficiary is the consumer.

AGENCY RELATIONSHIPS

In a very important article, Michael Jensen and William Meckling defined an *agency relationship* as a contract under which one or more persons (the principals) hire another person (the agent) to perform some service on their behalf, and then delegate some decision-making authority to the agent.[5] Within the financial management framework, agency relationships exist (1) between stockholders and managers and (2) between bondholders (or creditors generally) and stockholders. These relationships are discussed in the following sections.

Stockholders Versus Managers

Jensen and Meckling contend that a potential conflict arises whenever a manager owns less than 100 percent of the firm's common stock. If a firm is solely owned and managed by a single individual, we can assume that the owner-manager will take every possible action to increase his or her own welfare. Most of the actions taken would probably be to increase personal wealth, but some could also lead to increases in leisure or expenditures on perquisites.[6] If the owner-manager relinquishes a portion of his or her ownership by selling some of the firm's stock to outsiders, a potential conflict of interests will arise. For example, the manager may now decide (1) to lead a more relaxed life and not work as strenuously to maximize shareholder wealth, because less of this wealth will go to him or her, or (2) to consume more perquisites, because part of the costs of the perquisites now fall on the outside stockholders. Thus, a potential conflict exists between the two parties, the principals (outside shareholders) and the agent (manager).

Yet another potential conflict situation can arise when one firm seeks to acquire another. Suppose General Motors wanted to acquire Burroughs Corporation to gain access to the computer industry. Burroughs' managers own less than 1 percent of its stock, but they earn high salaries and have a great deal of power. Suppose further that Burroughs stock sells for $60 per share, but GM offered $80 per share. Should Burroughs' managers support the merger or resist it? The managers' own self-interest might be best served by defeating the merger attempt, yet the stockholders might be better off if the merger went through.

To ensure that managers act in the best interests of the outside shareholders, these shareholders will have to incur *agency costs*, which take several forms: (1) expenditures to monitor managerial actions, (2) expenditures to bond the managers, (3) expenditures to structure the organization so that the possibility of undesirable managerial behavior is limited, and (4) opportunity costs associated with lost profit opportunities because the organizational structure does not permit man-

[5]See Michael C. Jensen and William H. Meckling, "Theory of the Firm: Managerial Behavior, Agency Costs, and Ownership Structure," *Journal of Financial Economics*, October 1976, 350-360. The discussion of agency theory which follows draws heavily from their work.

[6]*Perquisites* are executive fringe benefits such as luxurious offices, use of corporate planes and yachts, personal assistants, and so on.

agers to take actions on as timely a basis as would be possible if the managers were also the owners.

There are two extreme positions regarding how to deal with this agency relationship. First, if managers were compensated only with shares of stock, then agency costs would be low, because managers would have less incentive to take excessive leisure or perquisites. However, it would be difficult to hire managers under these terms. At the opposite extreme, owners could monitor closely every managerial activity, but this solution would be extremely costly and inefficient. The optimal solution lies somewhere between the extremes, where executive compensation is tied to performance, but some monitoring is also done. Several mechanisms which tend to force managers to act in the shareholders' best interests are discussed next. These are (1) the managerial labor market, (2) the threat of firing, (3) the threat of takeover, and (4) the proper structuring of managerial incentives.

Managerial Labor Market

It has been argued that the managerial labor market exerts a great deal of influence on managerial behavior, perhaps even enough to make the agency problem unimportant and not worth worrying about.[7] The argument goes like this: Managers' wealth is composed of both current wealth and the present value of future income. The better the managerial performance, as measured by stock prices, the higher will be the salary the manager will command, both in his or her current employment and in future employment. Thus, if the capital markets (stock prices) provide efficient signals concerning managerial performance, and if the managerial labor market correctly values managerial performance, then the manager's own desire for personal wealth will provide a strong incentive for him or her to act in the shareholders' best interests.

The Threat of Firing

Until recently, the probability of a large firm's management being ousted by its stockholders was so remote that little threat was posed. This situation existed because ownership of most firms was so widely distributed, and management's control over the proxy mechanism so strong, that it was almost impossible for dissident stockholders to gain enough votes to overthrow the managers. However, stock ownership is being increasingly concentrated in the hands of large institutions rather than individuals, and the institutional money managers have the clout, if they choose to use it, to exercise considerable influence over a firm's operations. To illustrate, consider the case of GAF Corporation, a leading producer of building materials and industrial chemicals, with 1985 sales of $724 million. Its stock price was as high as $41 in 1965, after which it began a long slide, and by 1980 it was selling at below $8. At that point, institutions began to buy heavily, and their ownership increased from 15 to 40 percent. Many bought shares on the expectation

---

[7]See Eugene F. Fama, "Agency Problems and the Theory of the Firm," *Journal of Political Economy*, April 1980, 288-307.

that GAF's chairman, Jesse Werner, would retire at the end of 1981 and that the company would be broken up or taken over. This expectation was fueled by the fact that Mr. Werner, who had been chairman since 1964, announced in 1980 that GAF would sell eight marginally profitable businesses representing about half its sales. Analysts figured that this would make the company cash-rich and a likely takeover candidate and that the price of its stock would rise. Indeed, the stock price did more than double, from $7.75 in 1980 to $16.375 in 1981.

But Mr. Werner decided to keep his job. He obtained a new five-year contract and announced that the firm would reinvest internally most of the $212 million it had received from the sale of several unprofitable divisions. These actions caused GAF's stock price to drop back below $9.

All this prompted Samuel Heyman, a Connecticut shopping center owner who held 4.2 percent of GAF's stock, to wage a *proxy fight*. On April 28, 1983, at the annual meeting, Mr. Heyman received proxies representing about 60 percent of the shares, so he was able to oust Mr. Werner. The victory for the dissidents was made possible because of the support of large institutional holders. "You've got to outperform the market," explained one money manager. "If your clients have many money managers, and you're performing poorly, the meter starts running, and pretty soon you get cut from the list." Another money manager said, "There is little patience with poor management." So, whereas individual investors may be uninformed, lazy, or simply willing to "vote with their feet" by selling shares in companies whose performance is sub-par, institutional investors are more likely to work actively to oust an inefficient management. Recognizing this fact, people like Mr. Heyman are now more likely to "run against" an entrenched management than would have been true some years ago.

The Threat of Takeover

Hostile takeovers (where management does not want the firm to be taken over) are most likely to occur when a firm's stock is undervalued relative to its potential, reflecting poor managerial decisions. In a hostile takeover, the managers of the acquired firm are generally fired, and even if any are able to stay on, they lose the autonomy that they had prior to the acquisition. For example, in 1986, San Francisco based Wells Fargo acquired Crocker National, another large California bank. Coincident with the acquisition, Wells Fargo fired 70 percent of Crocker's 75 top executives. As stated in a press release, these executives, mostly senior vice-presidents and above, "will not have a future" in the combined organization. Such action gets the attention of other managers, and causes those managers to strive to maximize their firms' share prices. In the words of one company president, "If you want to keep control, don't let your company's stock sell at a bargain price."

Actions to increase the firm's stock price and to keep it from being a bargain are obviously good from the standpoint of the stockholders, but other tactics that managers can take to ward off a hostile takeover may not be. Two examples of questionable tactics are (1) poison pills and (2) greenmail. A *poison pill* is an action that a firm can take which practically kills it and thus makes it unattractive to potential suitors. Examples include Scott Industries' sale of its most attractive assets and Rubbermaid's threat to issue its stockholders rights which would give them the right to buy stock in any firm that acquired Rubbermaid at half price. *Greenmail*, which is like blackmail, occurs when this sequence of events takes place: (1) a potential acquirer (firm or individual) buys a block of stock in a company, (2) the target company's management becomes frightened that the acquirer will make a tender offer and take control of the company, and (3) to head off a possible takeover, management offers to pay greenmail, buying the stock of the potential raider at a price above the existing market price without offering the same deal to other stockholders. A good example of greenmail was Texaco's buy-back of 13 million shares of its stock from the Bass Brothers organization at a price of $50 at a time when the stock sold in the market at less than $40. Currently, the courts and Congress are taking a hard look at poison pills, greenmail, and the like.

Structuring Managerial Incentives

More and more, firms are tying managers' compensation to the company's performance, and research suggests that this motivates managers to operate in a manner consistent with stock price maximization.[8]

Performance plans are now widely used as part of executive compensation programs. In the 1950s and 1960s, most of these plans involved stock options on the theory that allowing management to purchase stock at a fixed price would provide an incentive for managers to take actions that would maximize the stock's price. However, this type of managerial incentive lost favor during the 1970s because the options generally did not pay off. The whole stock market was relatively flat, and stock prices did not necessarily reflect companies' earnings growth. It was recognized that good incentive plans must be based on factors over which managers have control, and since they cannot control the general stock market, stock option plans proved to have a weakness as an incentive device. Therefore, although 61 of the 100 largest U.S. firms used stock options as their sole incentive compensation in 1970, by 1985 not even one of the largest 100 companies relied exclusively on a stock option plan.

The main tool now is *performance shares*, which are shares of stock given to executives on the basis of performance as measured by earnings per share, return on assets, return on equity, and the like. For example, Honeywell uses growth in earnings per share as its primary performance measure. The firm has two overlapping four-year performance periods, beginning two years apart. At the beginning of each period, the participating executives are allocated a certain number of performance shares, say 10,000 shares for the president down to 1,000 shares for a lower-ranking manager. If the company achieves its targeted 13 percent annual average growth in earnings per share, the managers will earn 100 percent of their shares. If corporate performance is above the target, managers can earn even more shares, up to a maximum of 130 percent, which requires a 16 percent growth rate. However, if growth is below 13 percent, they get less than 100 percent of the shares, and below a 9 percent growth rate, they get zero.

---

[8]See Wilbur G. Lewellen and Blaine Huntsman, "Managerial Pay and Corporate Performance," *American Economic Review*, September 1970, 710-720.

Notice that performance shares have a value even if the company's stock price remains constant because of a poor general stock market, whereas under similar conditions stock options would have no value even though managers had been successful in boosting earnings. Of course, the *value* of the shares received is dependent on market price performance, because 1,000 shares of Honeywell stock are a lot more valuable if the stock sells for $200 than if it sells for only $100. Other firms are using different measures for their performance plans, since there is mounting evidence that growth in earnings per share is not perfectly correlated with growth in a firm's stock price, and also because inflation has a large effect on earnings growth. For example, Sears, Roebuck & Company now bases its compensation package on real return on equity, and Combustion Engineering, Inc., gives bonuses based on the spread between its cost of equity and its return on equity.

All incentive compensation plans—executive stock options, performance shares, profit-based bonuses, and so forth—are supposed to accomplish two purposes. First, they offer executives an incentive to act on those factors under their control so as to contribute to stock price maximization. Second, the existence of such performance plans helps companies attract and retain top-level executives.

Stockholders Versus Creditors

A second agency relationship occurs between stockholders and creditors, and potential conflicts can also arise here. Creditors lend funds to the firm at rates based on (1) the riskiness of the firm's existing assets; (2) expectations concerning the riskiness of future asset additions; (3) the firm's existing capital structure, that is, the amount of debt financing it uses; and (4) expectations concerning future capital structure changes. These factors determine the riskiness of the firm's cash flows, and hence the safety of its debt issues.

Now suppose the stockholders, acting through their elected managers, decide to have the firm take on new projects that are exposed to more risk than was anticipated by creditors. This would cause the required rate of return on the firm's debt to increase, which in turn would cause the value of the outstanding debt to fall. If the riskier capital investments turn out to be successful, all of the benefits would go to the stockholders, because the creditors receive only a fixed return. What we would have, from the stockholders' point of view, is a game of "heads I win, tails you lose," which is not a good game from the creditors' standpoint. Similarly, if the firm increases its leverage in an effort to boost profits, then the value of the old debt will decrease because the old debt's bankruptcy protection will be lessened by the issuance of the new debt. In both of these situations, stockholders would be expropriating wealth from the firms' creditors.

Does this mean that stockholders, through their managers/agents, should try to expropriate wealth from the firm's creditors? In general, the answer is no. First, because such attempts have been made in the past, creditors today protect themselves against such stockholder actions through restrictions in credit agreements. Second, if creditors perceive that the firm is using devious means to maximize shareholder wealth at the creditors' expense, they will either refuse to deal further with the firm or else require much higher than normal rates of return to compensate for the risks of such possible exploitation. Thus, firms which try to deal unfairly with creditors either lose access to the debt markets or are saddled with higher interest rates and consequently lower returns on equity, and generally with a decrease in the long-run value of the stock.

In view of these constraints, it follows that the goal of maximizing shareholder wealth must also be consistent with fair play with creditors. Stockholder wealth depends on continued access to capital markets, and access depends on fair play and abiding by both the letter and the spirit of contracts and agreements. There-fore, the managers, as agents of both the creditors and the shareholders, must act in a manner that is fairly balanced between the interests of both classes of security holders. Still, creditors must anticipate that if conditions require management to make hard choices, those choices will be tilted toward stockholders, not creditors.

Additionally, because of other constraints and sanctions, management actions that would expropriate wealth from the firm's employees, customers, suppliers, or community will ultimately be to the detriment of shareholders. We conclude, then, that in our society the goal of shareholder wealth maximization in the long run also implies the fair treatment of all other groups whose economic position is affected by the performance, and hence value, of the firm.

THE EFFICIENT MARKETS HYPOTHESIS

A body of theory called the *Efficient Markets Hypothesis (EMH)* holds (1) that stock prices reflect all current information and hence are always in equilibrium and (2) that it is impossible for an investor to consistently "beat the market." Essentially, the EMH notes that there are some 100,000 or so full-time, highly trained, professional analysts and traders operating in the market and following some 3,000 major stocks. If each analyst followed only 30 stocks, there would still be 1,000 analysts following each stock. Further, these analysts work for organiza-tions such as Merrill Lynch and Prudential Insurance, which have billions of dollars available to take advantage of bargains. As new information about a stock becomes available, these 1,000 analysts all receive and evaluate it at approximately the same time, and the price of the stock should adjust almost immediately to reflect the new information.

Financial theorists generally define three forms, or levels, of market efficiency:

1. *Weak-form* efficiency implies that all information contained in past price move-ments is fully reflected in current market prices. Therefore, information about re-cent trends in a stock's price is of no use in selecting stock—the fact that a stock has risen for the past three days, for example, gives us no useful clues as to what it will do today or tomorrow. People who believe that weak-form efficiency exists also believe that "tape watchers," "chartists," and other technical analysts are wast-ing their time.[9]

---

[9]Tape watchers are people who watch the NYSE tape, while chartists plot past patterns of stock price movements. Both are classified as *technical analysts* as distinguished from *fundamental analysts* who concentrate on financial statement analysis, industry sales trends, R&D expenditures, and so on. The technicians believe that they can see from past stock price movements if something is happening to the stock that will cause its price to move up or down in the near future.

Note that the EMH is a *hypothesis*, not a proven law, so it may or may not be correct. In fact, weak-form efficiency does appear to exist—past movements in stock prices (and interest rates) give few reliable clues as to the future direction of either the market or of individual securities. There have been some spectacularly successful "calls" by technical analysts who predicted either increases or decreases based on past trends, but there have been equally spectacular errors. Even when a technician predicts a rise or fall, and the market does rise or fall immediately thereafter, one must wonder if the prediction was not a self-fulfilling prophecy. In any event, all careful studies have concluded that the weak form of the EMH is essentially correct. Therefore, looking at past trends in stocks (or bond) prices is not likely to be useful for purposes of predicting future price movements.

2. *Semistrong-form* efficiency implies that current market prices reflect all *publicly available* information. If this is true, no abnormal returns can be gained by acting on publicly available information.[10] Thus, if semistrong efficiency exists, it would do no good to pore over annual reports or other published data, because market prices would have adjusted to any good or bad news contained in such reports as soon as they came out. However, insiders (say, the president of a company) could, even under semistrong efficiency, still make abnormal returns on their own companies' stocks.

Empirical tests have also been conducted to test the validity of semistrong-form efficiency, but the evidence is mixed. One group of tests has theorized that if it is possible to glean information that is not already reflected in stock prices from an analysis of data, then certain analysts and organizations would emerge as superior in terms of their portfolio returns vis-à-vis the returns on others' portfolios. However, it is difficult to get data on analysts' performance, and it is difficult to compare performance results because of differences in risks among portfolios. Also, results are clouded by the fact that it is hard to tell if superior performance is based on superior analysis of public information or an ability to ferret out information that has not yet become generally available, such as preliminary results of R&D tests, new orders, and the like. Indeed, it is not really clear if a good analyst is good because he or she can analyze information better than others or because he or she is better at getting information in the first place.

A poll of academicians would probably indicate that they are split evenly on the validity of semistrong efficiency, and few would have a very strong opinion either way. In other words, most would feel that fundamental analysis could occasionally uncover an undervalued or overvalued security, but, generally speaking, stock prices would reflect all publicly available information. Regardless of what academicians think, most Wall Streeters do not believe in semistrong efficiency, at least judging by their actions. The vast majority of institutional money is under the control of portfolio managers who hire analysts (at up to $500,000 per year) and listen to them, and the major brokerage houses compete for top analysts like the New York Yankees competes for free agent ballplayers.

---

[10]An abnormal return exceeds that return which is justified by the riskiness of the investment.

In our view, both the academicians and the Wall Streeters are correct. Good security analysts can ferret out and process information so as to identify undervalued or overvalued securities, but competition among the many excellent analysts keeps the gains from such activities small vis-à-vis picking stocks at random. Still, even a very small advantage can be worth the cost to the manager of a $10 billion portfolio. So, while it might not pay a finance professor with a few thousand dollars to pore over financial statements to get a somewhat higher rate of return on his or her portfolio, it probably would pay IBM's pension fund managers to hire security analysts.

3. *Strong-form* efficiency implies that current market prices reflect all pertinent information, whether publicly available or privately held. If this form held, then even insiders would find it impossible to earn abnormal returns in the stock market. Almost no one believes that strong-form efficiency is valid—studies of legal sales and purchases by corporate officers and directors indicate that when these insiders sell, the stocks are likely to underperform the market, and vice versa when they buy. It is even more apparent that insiders can make abnormal profits if they trade illegally on specific information that has not been disclosed to the public, such as a takeover offer, an R&D breakthrough, and the like.[11]

What effect does the EMH have on the decisions faced by financial managers? First, since security prices do appear to generally reflect all public information, most securities would seem to be fairly valued.[12] This does not mean that new information could not cause a security's price to soar or to plummet, but it does mean that stocks and bonds, in general, are neither overvalued nor undervalued— they are fairly priced, and in equilibrium. Certainly there are cases where financial managers do have some special information not known to outsiders, but for the larger, actively traded firms, which are followed by literally hundreds of full-time security analysts backed by billions of dollars of capital, the market quickly reacts to all new developments. Therefore, an investor can only expect to receive a return that approximately compensates him or her for the risks involved, and a firm must expect to bear a cost that is commensurate with the riskiness of the security being issued.

The EMH has significant implications for managerial decisions, especially those pertaining to bond and stock issues, stock repurchases, bond refunding, and tender

---

[11]In summer 1986, Dennis Levine, a managing director of Drexel Burnham Lambert, Inc., pleaded guilty to a charge filed by the SEC of making $12.6 million in profits using nonpublic information. Levine, a senior member of Drexel's mergers and acquisitions department, was accused of illegally trading in the securities of 54 companies from 1980 to 1985 while possessing "material nonpublic information" about actual or proposed tender offers, mergers, leveraged buyouts, and other business combinations. His sentencing was delayed for six months during which time he was reported to be cooperating with the authorities to help convict others involved with insider trading fraud in return for a lighter sentence. Already, several senior executives in other leading investment banking houses have been arrested. Unfortunately, the Levine case suggests that the illegal use of insider information to reap large profits may not be all that unusual, and it certainly disproves the strong-form EMH.

[12]For additional information on the efficient markets hypothesis and the resultant empirical testing, see Eugene F. Fama, "Efficient Capital Markets: A Review of Theory and Empirical Work," *Journal of Finance*, May 1970, 383-417.

offers. Financial assets are, in general, fairly valued, and decisions based on a security being undervalued or overvalued must be approached with great caution. Similarly, the stock and bond markets as a whole embody all public information. Thus, it is impossible to predict whether stock prices or bond prices (or interest rates) are going to go up or down in the future. Bond and stock price movements will reflect new information that is unknown now, and this new information could move the markets in either direction.[13]

DISCOUNTED CASH FLOW ANALYSIS

The value of a 1925 Rolls-Royce once owned by Al Capone is an elusive quantity. One person might be willing to pay $100,000 for the car, while another might think it is worth only $20,000. The car's value is based on such tangible factors as what other cars of similar vintage are selling for, maintenance cost, gas mileage, and so on, plus such intangible factors as pure snob appeal. On the other hand, the values of many assets, including all securities, stem solely from the cash flows the asset is expected to produce, and hence the value of such an asset is clear cut—it is the present value of the asset's expected future cash flows. The process of valuing future cash flows is called *discounted cash flow analysis*, and since virtually all financial decisions involve future cash flows, virtually all financial decisions involve discounted cash flow analysis.

The rationale for discounted cash flow analysis is the time value of money: A dollar in hand today is worth more than a dollar due some time in the future. You should already be familiar with time value concepts, so we will not cover them here.[14] To perform a discounted cash flow analysis, we need (1) estimates of future cash flows and (2) a discount rate. Estimating future cash flows for some assets, such as bonds, is relatively easy—since the flows are fixed by contract, then unless default occurs, the contracted flows will be realized. On the other hand, estimating future cash flows for other assets can be extremely difficult; for example, when IBM decided to go into personal computers in 1979, no one had more than a hazy idea of how much the project would cost, or the levels of sales, profits, and cash flows that would be generated in the future. Even when future cash flows have been estimated, this is only the first step in discounted cash flow analysis—we still need a discount rate, and the discount rate must correctly reflect both the riskiness of the expected cash flows and other investment opportunities in the economy. Assessing the riskiness of the flows, and then picking the right discount rate, can be as difficult as estimating the level of the cash flows.

---

[13]Our discussion here is somewhat simplified. Stock prices are generally expected to trend up because of the reinvestment of earnings. Similarly, yield curves contain information about expected interest rate movements. But this information is already embodied in security prices, and thus it cannot be used by investors to make abnormal profits or by firms to lower their capital costs by "proper" timing of securities offerings with respect to general market trends.

[14]Appendix A provides a review of time value concepts. If you feel weak in this area, we *strongly* suggest that you read that appendix now.

Since most important financial decisions involve discounted cash flow analysis, that topic will be addressed throughout the book. For now, remember that discounted cash flow analysis involves (1) estimating the future flows and (2) choosing a discount rate which reflects both the riskiness of the expected flows and returns available on other investment opportunities.

THE RISK/RETURN TRADE-OFF

Most financial decisions involve alternative courses of action. For example, should we set the firm's credit terms at 2/10, net 30, or at 1/15, net 60? Should we buy a replacement machine now or should we wait until next year? Or should we set the debt-to-assets ratio at 20 percent, 40 percent, or what? In general, the alternative courses of action will have different returns—the expected return on the replacement machine now might be 20 percent versus a 25 percent return if we wait a year.

In all such situations, one might be tempted to accept the alternative with the higher expected return, but this would be wrong—if markets are efficient, then those alternatives that offer higher returns will normally also have higher risk. The correct question, then, is not which alternative has the higher return, but which alternative has the higher return after adjusting for risk? In other words, which alternative has the higher return over and above the return that is required when the riskiness of the alternatives is considered? To illustrate, suppose IBM's stock has an expected rate of return of 14 percent, while its bonds yield 9 percent. Does this mean that investors should flock to buy the stock and ignore the bonds? Of course not—the higher expected return on the stock merely reflects the fact that the stock is riskier than the bonds. Those investors who are not able or willing to assume much risk will choose the bonds, while those who are less risk averse will buy IBM's stock. From IBM's perspective, financing with stock is less risky than using debt, so IBM is willing to pay the higher cost of equity to hold down the firm's exposure to risk. Assuming that IBM's managers believe that the stock and bond markets are efficient and in equilibrium, then if the company needed to raise capital, it would be indifferent between issuing debt and issuing stock in the sense that each has a cost commensurate with the risks involved.

The moral of this story is simple. There are three key questions in every financial decision: (1) What is the return involved? (2) What is the risk involved? (3) Do expected returns adequately compensate for the perceived risk? For decisions that involve the capital markets, expected returns will virtually always be just sufficient to compensate for the risks. However, product markets (that is, markets for real assets ranging from machine tools to toothpaste to shopping centers) are not necessarily efficient, and hence excess returns can be earned in these markets. However, when excess returns are available, take them and run, because market efficiency will generally not permit the opportunity to last for long, even in product markets. The personal computer market can again be used to illustrate the point. When IBM analyzed the market in the late 1970s, it appeared that a void existed, and that high profit margins and good volumes would combine to produce high returns on the investment needed to go into the personal computer business. However, by 1986 the high rates of return earned by IBM and other early entrants into this market had attracted entry by Japanese, Korean, and British firms, plus many American businesses, and as a result profit margins and consequently returns on investment were down to "normal" levels. Thus, product markets tend to be efficient, but long lags may be involved. Capital markets, in contrast, are generally instantaneously efficient. Thus, it definitely pays businesses to look for profit opportunities in their product markets, but the expected payoff for time invested searching for gains in capital markets is much lower.

FINANCIAL THEORY VERSUS FINANCIAL PRACTICE

The study of financial management, and thus this textbook, includes both normative and positive concepts. For the most part, the theory which we discuss is *normative* in the sense that it tells financial managers what they "ought to do." However, we also discuss *positive* finance, which includes empirical studies of investors' reactions to various managerial decisions as well as surveys designed to find out what financial managers are actually doing in practice.

Both normative and positive concepts are important, but in practice financial decision makers do not always follow the normative prescriptions developed by financial theorists. Does this mean that the theory is incorrect, that financial managers are acting incorrectly, or what? The answer varies. In some instances, financial theories contain simplifying assumptions that are not representative of the actual financial environment in which firms operate, resulting in decision rules that are not always valid in the much more complex "real world." In other cases, it is virtually impossible to apply finance theory as developed because it is impossible to obtain inputs necessary to implement the theoretical models. In these cases, the theory may be right, but it can only be used indirectly, to provide insights into judgmental decisions. In still other situations, the theory may be correct, and it may also be possible to apply it, but the inertia of doing things the old way may still predominate.

Where unreconciled differences exist either between theory and practice or between alternative theories, we proceed as follows: (1) First, we present the relevant finance theory or theories, along with their major assumptions. (2) We then discuss the empirical evidence which supports and refutes the theories. (3) Finally, we present some insights into how practicing financial managers actually make decisions in the face of conflicting evidence. This approach will allow you to see all sides of the issue and will increase your ability to make correct financial decisions when required in the future.

A NOTE ON TAX LAWS

The details of U.S. tax law are changed fairly often—indeed, a nontrivial change has occurred, on average, every 1.5 years since 1913, when our federal income tax system began. Further, certain parts of our tax system are tied to the rate of inflation, so changes occur automatically each year, depending on the rate of inflation during the previous year.

Every ten years or so, major tax law changes have occurred; the most recent was in October 1986. Most parts of the 1986 tax law will take effect in 1987, but to reduce adverse effects on individuals and corporations who had laid plans under the old law, parts of the new law will be phased in over a two-to-three year transition period. To avoid unnecessary detail, we will, in this text, focus on the tax system as it will exist once the 1986 changes have been fully implemented.

The 1986 tax law changes that are most significant for financial management decisions include the following:

1. The top marginal rates for both individuals and corporations have been drastically lowered. The top rate for individuals is now 28 percent, compared to 50 percent under the old law. However, state and local income taxes, and federal surtaxes, can raise the top individual rate to about 40 percent. The highest marginal rate for corporations is now 34 percent, while under the old law it was 46 percent. Note again, though, that state income taxes and federal surtaxes can push the effective corporate rate well above 40 percent.

2. Capital gains are now taxed at the same rate as ordinary income, both to individuals and corporations. From 1921 through 1986, long-term capital gains were taxed at substantially lower rates than ordinary income. For example, in 1986, long-term capital gains were taxed at only 40 percent of the tax rate on ordinary income. However, the 1986 tax law eliminates this differential, and capital gains income will henceforth be taxed as if it were ordinary income.

3. The investment tax credit has been eliminated, and the depreciation schedules under the Accelerated Cost Recovery System (ACRS) have been changed. These particular tax law changes will have an impact on capital investment and leasing decisions, and we will discuss them in more detail in Chapters 8 and 14.

4. Interest income received by a corporation is taxed as ordinary income at regular corporate rates. However, dividends received by one corporation from another, in recent years, have been taxed at considerably lower rates to ease the burden of triple taxation. In 1986, 85 percent of the dividends received by a corporation were excluded from taxable income. Under the new tax law, the exclusion is lowered slightly, to 80 percent.

We have incorporated the major provisions of the new tax law throughout the text, and in several sections, we specifically discuss the impact of the new law on financial management decisions. However, to illustrate the decision-making process, we use several "real-world" examples which occurred over the last few years. In these examples, we apply the actual tax law that was in effect at the time the decisions were made.

ORGANIZATION OF THE BOOK

Part I consists of three chapters that contain fundamental background information that is necessary to understand the remainder of the book. Included is a discussion of the financial environment, risk, rates of return, and valuation models. In Part II, we cover cost of capital and capital structure. After studying these three chapters, you should be able (1) to estimate a firm's cost of capital, (2) to understand the principal theories of capital structure, and (3) to make judgments about a firm's optimal capital structure, given its operating characteristics.

In Part III, we take a detailed look at the process of identifying and evaluating potential capital budgeting projects. The primary emphasis here is on (1) alternative capital budgeting decision techniques, (2) cash flow estimation, (3) risk analysis in capital budgeting, and (4) the determination of the optimal capital budget.

Part IV focuses on the process of raising long-term capital: How much of its income should a firm pay out as dividends versus plow back into the business? What are the principal sources and forms of external long-term capital? How does the choice of type of financing affect the value of the firm? And how does a firm choose among the alternate types of capital and then establish the optimal set of terms for the type of capital it plans to use?

In Part V, we examine short-term financial policy and operations, or working capital management. We first consider working capital policy in general; then we consider how current assets should be financed; and, finally, we analyze the management of cash, marketable securities, receivables, and inventories.

Part VI deals with financial analysis, planning, and control. Prior sections of the book provide a detailed knowledge of specific topics, but in Part VI we tie these separate topics together and discuss the interdependencies between capital budgeting, working capital management, and so on. Our emphasis is on both the analysis of historical financial statements to see where the firm has been, where it is now, and what changes are needed, and on the construction of pro forma financial statements designed to show where the firm is heading and what future results can be expected under alternative operating plans.

Finally, in Part VII, we consider some subjects that, while important, are best studied within the general framework of financial management as developed in Parts I through VI. Included here are mergers and pension fund management.

SUMMARY

Our primary task in this chapter was to define the environment in which financial management decisions are made. We concluded that the primary goal of most publicly owned firms is *stock price maximization*. Managers do have other goals, both personal and social, but in a competitive economy, where managers serve at the pleasure of stockholders, stock price maximization must be the dominant goal.

There does exist, however, the potential for conflicts of interest between shareholders and managers, and between shareholders and creditors. These conflicts arise because of *agency relationships*. A number of incentives motivate managers to act in the best interests of stockholders, including (1) the managerial labor market, (2) the threat of firing, (3) the threat of takeovers, and (4) properly structured managerial compensation packages. We also concluded that it is generally in the best interest of stockholders to treat creditors fairly, but that creditors must recognize that in times of stress managers will make decisions that favor stockholders over bondholders, and debt contracts should be written to minimize the possibility of such adverse actions.

We also discussed the *Efficient Markets Hypothesis (EMH)*, which postulates (1) that securities are always in equilibrium and (2) that it is impossible for investors who do not have inside information to consistently earn abnormal returns. The EMH, which comes in three forms, has significant implications for managerial decision making. Basically, security prices reflect all public information, and decisions that are predicated on the existence of undervalued or overvalued securities must be approached with extreme caution.

We also noted that many of the decisions faced by financial managers involve *discounted cash flow (DCF) analysis.* DCF analysis requires two steps: (1) estimating future cash flows and (2) choosing the discount rate which reflects the riskiness of the flows. Note, though, that all financial decisions involve a *risk/return trade-off*: Alternatives must be evaluated both in terms of relative returns and in terms of relative risks.

The International Perspective

In theory, the models and analytical procedures developed throughout the text are valid for both domestic and multinational operations. However, problems uniquely associated with the international environment increase the complexity of the manager's task and often force us to alter the way alternative courses of action are evaluated and compared. Five major factors complicate the situation and distinguish financial management as practiced by firms operating entirely in a single country in comparison to those that operate in several different countries:

1. Cash flows in various parts of a multinational corporate system will be denominated in different currencies. Hence, an analysis of exchange rates and the effects of changing currency values must be included in all types of financial analyses.

2. Each country in which the firm operates will have its own unique political and economic institutions. Institutional differences among countries can cause significant problems when the corporation tries to coordinate and control the worldwide operations of its subsidiaries. For example, differences in tax laws among countries can cause a given economic transaction to have strik-

ingly dissimilar after-tax consequences depending on where it occurred. Similarly, differences in legal systems of host nations, such as the Common Law of Great Britain versus the French Civil Law, complicate matters ranging from the simple recording of a business transaction to the role played by the judiciary in resolving conflicts. Such differences can restrict the flexibility of multinational corporations to deploy resources as they wish, and even preclude procedures in one part of the company that are required in another part. These differences also make it difficult for executives trained under one system to control operations effectively in another.

3. Even within geographic regions that have long been considered relatively homogeneous, different countries have their own unique cultural heritages which shape their values and define the role of business in the society. Multinational corporations find that such matters as defining the appropriate goals of the firm, attitudes toward risk-taking, dealings with employees, the ability to curtail unprofitable operations, and so on, can vary dramatically from one country to the next.

4. Most traditional models in finance assume the existence of a competitive marketplace, in which the terms of competition are determined through the actions of participants. The government, through its power to establish basic ground rules, is only slightly involved in this process. Thus, the market provides both the primary barometer of success and an indicator of actions that need to be taken to remain competitive. This view of the process is reasonably correct for the United States and a few other major Western industrialized nations, but it does not accurately describe the situation in the majority of countries. Frequently, the terms under which companies compete, actions that must be taken or avoided, and the terms of trade on various transactions are determined not in the marketplace but by direct negotiation between the host government and the multinational corporation. This is essentially a political process, and it must be treated as such. Thus, our traditional financial models must be recast to include political and other non-economic facets of the decision.

5. The distinguishing characteristic of a nation state that differentiates it from a multinational corporation is that the nation state exercises sovereignty over people and property in its territory. Hence, a nation state can place constraints on the transfer of corporate resources and even expropriate, without compensation, the assets of the firm. This is a political risk, and it tends to be largely a given rather than a variable which can be changed by negotiation. Political risk varies from country to country, and it must be addressed explicitly in financial analyses.

These five factors complicate financial management within the multinational firm, and they clearly increase the business risk of the firms involved. However, the higher profitability often makes it well worthwhile for firms to accept these risks, and to learn how to minimize or at least live with them.

Questions and Problems

1-1   If you were running a large, publicly owned corporation, would you make decisions to maximize stockholders' welfare or your own? What are some actions stockholders could take to ensure that your interests and theirs coincided? Are there other factors which influence managers to act in the best interests of the firms' shareholders?

1-2   The managers of U.S. firms have been criticized for making decisions based on short-term results rather than long-term goals. Is this criticism valid? What might motivate managers to focus on short-term results? Should stockholder wealth maximization be thought of as a long-run or short-run goal?

1-3   Would the management of a firm in an oligopolistic or a competitive industry be more likely to engage in what might be called "socially conscious" practices? Explain your reasoning.

1-4   Would the "normal" rate of return on investment be the same in all industries? Would normal rates of return change over time? Explain.

1-5   What is meant by an agency relationship? What parties to financial management are involved in agency relationships?

1-6   What are the three forms of market efficiency? Which forms do you believe to hold in the U.S. capital markets? In product markets?

1-7   What are the two major tasks involved in discounted cash flow analysis?

1-8 The Berry Company is evaluating two mutually exclusive capital investment opportunities. Project L has an expected rate of return of 15 percent, while Project H has an expected return of 18 percent. Which project should be chosen? Why?

1-9 Some economists have argued that trading on insider information should be legalized. List the pros and cons of this proposal.

Selected Additional References

For a good summary of financial management, see

Pogue, Gerald A., and Kishore Lall, "Corporate Finance: An Overview," *Sloan Management Review*, Spring 1974, 19-38.

For alternative views on firms' goals and objectives, see the following articles:

Anthony, Robert N., "The Trouble with Profit Maximization," *Harvard Business Review*, November-December 1960, 126-134.

Donaldson, Gordon, "Financial Goals: Management versus Stockholders," *Harvard Business Review*, May-June 1963, 116-129.

Elliot, J. W., "Control, Size, Growth, and Financial Performance in the Firm," *Journal of Financial and Quantitative Analysis*, January 1972, 1309-1320.

Meckling, William H., and Michael C. Jensen, "Reflections on the Corporation as a Social Invention," *Midland Corporate Finance Journal*, Fall 1983, 6-15.

Seitz, Neil, "Shareholder Goals, Firm Goals and Firm Financing Decisions," *Financial Management*, Autumn 1982, 20-26.

For a thorough discussion of the agency problem, see

Barnea, Amir, Robert A. Haugen, and Lemma W. Senbet, *Agency Problems and Financial Contracting* (Englewood Cliffs, N.J.: Prentice-Hall, 1985).

For a general review of the state of the art in academic finance, together with an extensive bibliography of key research articles, see

Beranek, William, "Research Directions in Finance," *Quarterly Review of Economics and Business*, Spring 1981, 6-24.

Cooley, Philip L., and J. Louis Heck, "Significant Contributions to Finance Literature," *Financial Management*, Tenth Anniversary Issue 1981, 23-33.

Weston, J. Fred, "Developments in Finance Theory," *Financial Management*, Tenth Anniversary Issue 1981, 5-22.

For more information on managerial compensation, see

Cooley, Philip L., and Charles E. Edwards, "Ownership Effects on Managerial Salaries in Small Business," *Financial Management*, Winter 1982, 5-9.

Lambert, Richard A., and David F. Larker, "Executive Compensation, Corporate Decision-Making and Shareholder Wealth: A Review of the Evidence," *Midland Corporate Finance Journal*, Winter 1985, 6-22. The Winter 1985 issue of the *Midland Corporate Finance Journal* contains several other articles which pertain to executive compensation plans.

For Wall Street's view on market efficiency, see

"A Discussion of Corporate Financial Communication," *Midland Corporate Finance Journal*, Spring 1984, 40-72.

2

RISK AND RETURN

Virtually all financial decisions have one thing in common—they require an estimate of both an expected result and the risk that the expected result will not be achieved. Generally, the expected result translates into "expected return," and risk means the probability of not achieving that return. If the expected return is high enough to compensate for the risk involved, then the decision is "go," and the action is taken. Otherwise, the action is not undertaken.

Risk analysis is critically important, so it is essential to understand how risk is analyzed before moving on to specific types of financial decisions. In this chapter, we will see that risk can be defined in two ways: (1) *total risk*, which focuses on a single asset and which involves the dispersion of outcomes around the expected return on that asset, and (2) *systematic*, or *market, risk*, which focuses on a portfolio of assets and which shows how the risk of the portfolio is affected by an individual asset.

Risk analysis alone is not very useful. We must be able to relate risk to expected returns, and to answer this question: How much return is required to compensate for a given degree of risk? As we shall see, the Capital Asset Pricing Model (CAPM) provides one neat, precise answer to this question. However, the CAPM has not been and indeed cannot be confirmed empirically—it may or may not represent the way investors actually behave; hence, a CAPM-based analysis may or may not lead to decisions that will maximize the value of the firm. This fact does not by itself invalidate the CAPM, but it does raise a caution flag which forces us to consider alternative ways of specifying both how risk should be measured and how the additional expected return required to compensate for a given degree of risk should be established.

PROBABILITY DISTRIBUTIONS

In general, risk refers to the probability that some unfavorable event will occur. To illustrate, suppose you are the financial manager of a firm which has $100,000 to invest for a period of one year. Four investment alternatives as shown in Table 2-1 are being considered:

1. One-year U.S. Treasury bills (T-bills) offering an 8 percent rate of return. The T-bills would be bought at a discount and would return their par value at maturity.

2. Corporate bonds with a 9 percent coupon and a 10-year maturity. However, our firm will sell the bonds at the end of 1 year. Therefore, the rate of return

Table 2-1
Four Alternative Investments

State of the Economy	Probability of Occurrence	Investment's Rate of Return if State Occurs			
		T-Bills	Corporate Bonds	Project 1	Project 2
Deep recession	0.05	8.0%	12.0%	−3.0%	−2.0%
Mild recession	0.20	8.0	10.0	6.0	9.0
Average economy	0.50	8.0	9.0	11.0	12.0
Mild boom	0.20	8.0	8.5	14.0	15.0
Strong boom	0.05	8.0	8.0	19.0	26.0
	1.00				
Expected rate of return =		8.0%	9.2%	10.3%	12.0%

Notes:
a. The probabilities of occurrence must sum to 1.0 when all states are considered.
b. You should think of the returns under different states of the economy as being ranges, and the given returns as being points within those ranges. For example, think of the 10 percent return on corporate bonds during a mild recession as being the most likely return under that state of the economy, where 10 percent is used for convenience.

realized on the bonds will depend on the interest rate level that prevails at the end of the year. This interest rate level, in turn, will depend on the state of the economy at the end of the year: A strong economy would probably lead to higher interest rates, which would decrease the market value of the bonds, although the opposite would be true if the economy were weak.

3. Capital budgeting Project 1, which has a net cost of $100,000, zero cash flows during the year, and a payoff at the end of 1 year which depends on the state of the economy.

4. An alternative capital project, Project 2, which also has a cost of $100,000 and a payoff at year-end, but its payoff distribution differs from that of Project 1.

A *probability distribution* is defined as a set of possible outcomes, with a probability of occurrence attached to each outcome. Thus, Table 2-1 contains four probability distributions, one for each of the four investment alternatives. The T-bills' rate of return is known with certainty—it is 8 percent irrespective of the state of the economy. Thus, T-bills have zero risk.[1] However, the actual, or realized, rates of return on the other three investments will not be known until the end of

---

[1] Note that the T-bill investment is riskless only in the sense that *nominal* returns are assured for one period. The *real* return on a T-bill is risky, as the real rate of return depends on the rate of inflation realized over the 1-year holding period. Further, T-bills can present a problem to an investor who relies upon his or her portfolio for continuing income: When the T-bills mature, they must be reinvested, and if interest rates have declined, the portfolio's income will drop. This risk, which is called *reinvestment rate* risk, is not a problem in our example since the firm's holding period matches the maturity of the bills. Finally, note that the relevant return on any investment is the return after taxes have been paid, and hence the rates listed in Table 2-1 should be after-tax rates of return.

the holding period. Since their outcomes are not known with certainty, these three investments are defined as being risky.

Probability distributions may be either *discrete* or *continuous*.[2] A discrete probability distribution has a finite number of outcomes; thus, Table 2-1 contains discrete probability distributions. There is only one possible value, or outcome, for the T-bills' rate of return, although for the other three alternatives, there are five possible outcomes. Each outcome has a corresponding probability of occurrence. For example, the probability of the T-bills having an 8.0 percent rate of return is 1.0, and the probability of the corporate bonds having a 9.0 percent rate of return is 0.50.

If we multiply each possible outcome by its probability of occurrence and then sum these products, we have a weighted average of outcomes. The weights are the probabilities, and the weighted average is defined as the *expected value*. Since our outcomes are rates of return, our expected values are *expected rates of return*. The expected rate of return, $\hat{k}$, called "k-hat," is expressed in equation form as follows:

$$\text{Expected rate of return} = \hat{k} = \sum_{i=1}^{n} k_i P_i. \tag{2-1}$$

Here k_i is the *i*th possible outcome, P_i is the probability that the *i*th outcome will occur, and n is the number of possible outcomes.

Using Equation 2-1, we find Project 2's expected rate of return to be 12.0 percent:

$$\hat{k} = \sum_{i=1}^{5} k_i P_i$$

$$= k_1(P_1) + k_2(P_2) + k_3(P_3) + k_4(P_4) + k_5(P_5)$$

$$= -2.0\%(0.05) + 9.0\%(0.20) + 12.0\%(0.50) + 15.0\%(0.20) + 26.0\%(0.05)$$

$$= 12.0\%.$$

The expected rates of return on the other three investment alternatives were calculated similarly and are shown in Table 2-1.

Discrete probability distributions can be expressed in graphic as well as tabular form. Figure 2-1 shows bar graphs (or histograms) for Projects 1 and 2. The range of possible rates of return for Project 1 is from −3.0 to +19.0 percent, and the range for Project 2 is from −2.0 to +26.0 percent. Note that the height of each bar represents the probability of occurrence, and that the sum of the probabilities for each alternative equals 1.00. Also, note that the distribution of rates of return for Project 2 is symmetric, whereas the distribution for Project 1 is skewed to the left. Similar graphs for the T-bills and the corporate bonds would show the returns

---

[2]We will concentrate on discrete distributions, because they are better for illustrating basic risk and return concepts. However, continuous distributions are also used extensively in financial analysis, so we discuss them in Appendix 2A.

Figure 2-1
Graphic Discrete Probability Distributions

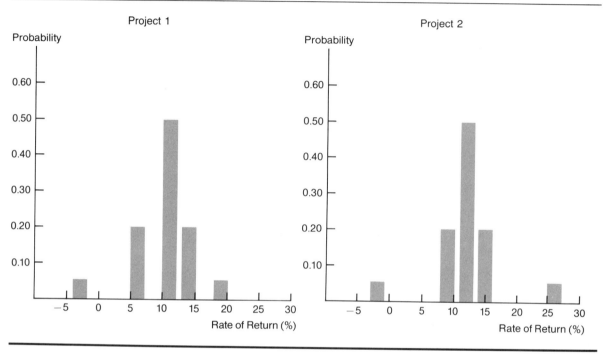

on the T-bills represented by a single spike, while the returns on the corporate bonds would have a graph that is skewed to the right.

TOTAL RISK ANALYSIS

We can use the concepts of discrete probability distributions and expected values to help measure risk. We know that risk is present when the estimated distribution has more than one possible outcome, but how should risk be measured and quantified? Some answers are provided in the remainder of this chapter.

Variance and Standard Deviation

Variance is a measure of the dispersion of a distribution around its expected value: The larger the variance, the greater the dispersion. To calculate the variance of a discrete distribution, we use the following formula:

$$\text{Variance} = \sigma^2 = \sum_{i=1}^{n} (k_i - \hat{k})^2 P_i. \qquad (2\text{-}2)$$

To illustrate, we will calculate the variance of the rate of return on Project 2. We know that its expected rate of return, $\hat{k}$, is 12.0 percent. Thus, its variance is calculated by using Equation 2-2 plus data from Table 2-1 as follows:

$$
\begin{aligned}
\sigma^2 &= \sum_{i=1}^{5} (k_i - \hat{k})^2 P_i \\
&= (-2.0 - 12.0)^2(0.05) + (9.0 - 12.0)^2(0.20) + (12.0 - 12.0)^2(0.50) \\
&\quad + (15.0 - 12.0)^2(0.20) + (26.0 - 12.0)^2(0.05) \\
&= (-14.0)^2(0.05) + (-3.0)^2(0.20) + (0.0)^2(0.50) \\
&\quad + (3.0)^2(0.20) + (14.0)^2(0.05) \\
&= 9.8 + 1.8 + 0.0 + 1.8 + 9.8 \\
&= 23.2.
\end{aligned}
$$

Variance is measured in the same units as the outcomes, in this case percentages, but squared.

Since it is difficult to attach meaning to a squared percentage, the standard deviation is often used as an alternative measure of dispersion about the mean. The *standard deviation (SD or σ)* is found by taking the square root of the variance:

$$
SD = \sigma = \sqrt{\sigma^2} = \sqrt{\sum_{i=1}^{n} (k_i - \hat{k})^2 P_i}. \tag{2-3}
$$

Thus, the standard deviation of Project 2's rate of return can be found by using Equation 2-3 as follows:

$$
\sigma = \sqrt{23.2} = 4.82\%.
$$

Since the standard deviation is a measure of dispersion, we can draw some conclusions about the distribution of outcomes if the expected value and standard deviation are known. If the distribution is approximately normal, we can state that 68.3 percent of the outcomes will fall within one standard deviation of the expected value, that 95.5 percent will fall within two standard deviations, and that almost all outcomes (99.7 percent) will fall within three standard deviations.[3]

Table 2-2 contains the expected rates of return, variances, and standard deviations of all four investment alternatives, along with their coefficients of variation (CV), which we will discuss in the next section. We see that the T-bills have the smallest variance and standard deviation, while Project 2 has the largest.

At this point, one might be tempted to say that the T-bills are the least risky alternative and that Project 2 is the most risky. However, this may or may not be true; before reaching a definite conclusion, we must consider some other factors

---

[3]See Appendix 2A for a review of continuous distributions, including the normal distribution. Also, note that even if a distribution is not close to normal, we can evoke Tchebysheff's theorem and state that for *any* distribution, at least 89 percent of all outcomes will lie within three standard deviations of the expected value. See William Mendenhall, Richard L. Scheaffer, and Dennis D. Wackerly, *Mathematical Statistics with Applications* (Boston: Duxbury, 1981).

Table 2-2
Return and Risk Measures for the Table 2-1 Investment Alternatives

Expected Rate of Return or Risk Measure		Investment Alternatives		
	T-Bills	Corporate Bonds	Project 1	Project 2
Expected return ($\hat{k}$)	8.00%	9.20%	10.30%	12.00%
Variance (Var or σ^2)	0.00	0.71	19.31	23.20
Standard deviation (SD or σ)	0.00%	0.84%	4.39%	4.82%
Coefficient of variation (CV)	0.00	0.09	0.43	0.40

such as the magnitudes of the expected rates of return, the skewness of the distributions, our confidence in the specification of the distributions, and the relationship between each asset and other assets that might be held in the investment portfolio.[4]

Coefficient of Variation

As a general rule, investments with higher expected returns have larger standard deviations than investments with smaller expected returns. Thus, some Project X with a 30 percent expected rate of return might have a standard deviation of 10

---

[4]It seems logical, in a risk analysis, to be more concerned about the probabilities of returns being less than expected rather than greater than expected. If the distribution is symmetric, the variance and standard deviation do provide true measures of the downside risk: it is simply half the total risk. However, if the distribution is skewed, halving the variance or standard deviation yields a distorted picture of the actual risk. If the distribution is skewed to the right, the variance and standard deviation overstate the downside risk; if the distribution is skewed to the left, the opposite occurs. A statistic which eliminates this distortion is the *semivariance (SV)*, defined as follows:

$$SV = \sum_{i=1}^{m} (k_i - \hat{k})^2 P_i. \tag{2-2a}$$

Here m is the set of outcomes that fall *below* the expected value. For example, look at the corporate bond alternative in Table 2-1. Remembering that its expected rate of return is 9.2 percent, the semivariance is calculated by using Equation 2-2a as follows:

$$SV = \sum_{i=1}^{3} (k_i - \hat{k})^2 P_i$$
$$= (8.0 - 9.2)^2(0.05) + (8.5 - 9.2)^2(0.20) + (9.0 - 9.2)^2(0.50)$$
$$= 0.19.$$

The semivariances of all four alternatives listed in Table 2-1 are as follows: 0.00, 0.19, 12.54, and 11.60. In a symmetric distribution, we would find that the semivariance is one-half the variance. This occurs for Project 2. However, the semivariance of Project 1 is more than one-half the variance—because Project 1's returns are skewed to the left, its variance understates the downside risk. The corporate bond's semivariance is less than one-half the variance—because the bond's distribution is skewed right, its variance overstates its downside risk. Because financial data are generally not precise enough to warrant the use of highly refined analytical techniques, and because most distributions we deal with are relatively symmetrical, we concentrate in this book on the variance and standard deviation as measures of dispersion.

percent, while some Project Y might have an expected rate of return of 10 percent and standard deviation of 5 percent. However, if the returns of Projects X and Y are approximately normal, then Project X would have only a 0.13 percent probability of a negative return in spite of its high σ; while Project Y, even with a standard deviation only half as large as that of Project X, would have a much higher probability of a loss. Thus, to interpret properly the implications of standard deviations as measures of the relative risks of investments whose expected returns are different, we should standardize the standard deviation and calculate the risk per unit of return. This is accomplished by using the *coefficient of variation (CV)*, which is defined as the standard deviation divided by the expected value:

$$\text{Coefficient of variation} = CV = \frac{\sigma}{\hat{k}}. \tag{2-4}$$

$$\text{Project X: } CV_X = 10/30 = 0.33.$$
$$\text{Project Y: } CV_Y = 5/10 = 0.50.$$

Thus, we see Project Y actually has more risk per unit of expected return than Project X. Therefore, one could argue that Y is riskier than X in spite of the fact that X's standard deviation is larger.

Table 2-2 contains the coefficients of variation of our four original investment alternatives. We see that the rankings using the coefficient of variation as the risk measure are not the same as the rankings based on the standard deviation: Project 2 is riskier than Project 1 using the standard deviation, but the opposite is true when we correct for size and measure risk by the coefficient of variation.

Subjective Versus Objective Probability Distributions

Thus far, we have used subjectively estimated probability distributions in all of our examples of expected, or *ex ante*, risk and return measures. We could apply the same techniques to historical, or *ex post*, data to obtain *objective* as opposed to *subjective* distributions, provided (1) historical data are available and (2) the future is likely to repeat the past. For example, suppose Project 2, a capital investment project, did not represent a new venture; rather, similar investments have been made in each of the last 10 years. In this case, we would have 10 historical, or realized, rates of return ($\bar{k}$, pronounced "k-bar") available on these projects. We could use this set of data to determine Project 2's historical average, or *mean, rate of return; its variance; and its standard deviation. We would have 10 sample points, and we could use this procedure to evaluate them:

1. Calculate the average historical return, $\bar{k}_{Avg}$:

$$\bar{k}_{Avg} = \frac{\sum_{t=1}^{n} \bar{k}_t}{n}.$$

2. Historical variance $= \sigma^2 = \dfrac{\sum_{t=1}^{n} (\bar{k}_t - \bar{k}_{Avg})^2}{n-1}.$

3. Historical standard deviation $= \sigma = \sqrt{\dfrac{\sum\limits_{t=1}^{n}(\bar{k} - \bar{k}_{Avg})^2}{n - 1}}.$

This is the standard statistical procedure for handling sample data, and we would be treating the 10 years of data as if they were drawn from a larger universe of data. Of course, to be useful as a forecast of future results, we must have reason to believe that conditions during the next year will be similar to conditions over the last 10 years. If we do, then we could use the historical distribution as a proxy for the future, or ex ante, distribution, and the derived rate of return, variance, and standard deviation could be used to evaluate Project 2. Of course, this type of analysis is possible only for certain types of investments—if the project is an entirely new venture, then historical data cannot be used.

This discussion of subjective versus objective probability distributions illustrates an important point—in financial analysis, we generally face *two* sources of risk: (1) The risk associated with uncertain outcomes, given a known probability distribution, and (2) the additional risk that results from the fact that our assumed distribution may itself be incorrect. Historical data are often unavailable, and even where such data are available, the distribution itself may be changing over time. Therefore, the second source of risk is quite important. Risk analysis may appear to be quite precise, but a great deal of judgment always lies behind the analysis.

The Mean-Variance Criterion

Thus far we have looked at several measures of risk, but at this point we have no way of choosing among the four alternatives. The *mean-variance criterion* is one possible decision rule that can be used to choose among possible investment alternatives. This criterion is based on two assumptions: (1) The decision maker is risk averse, and (2) the distributions being evaluated are approximately normal.[5] The first assumption is certainly true for the average investor; the second condition generally holds reasonably well for securities such as stocks and bonds, but it does not always hold for physical asset investments.

The mean-variance criterion is based on a comparison of expected returns ($\hat{k}_i$) and standard deviations (σ_i), and it can be stated symbolically as follows:

Alternative X is preferred to Alternative Y if and only if either

$$\hat{k}_X \geq \hat{k}_Y \quad \text{and} \quad \sigma_X^2 < \sigma_Y^2,$$

or

$$\hat{k}_X > \hat{k}_Y \quad \text{and} \quad \sigma_X^2 \leq \sigma_Y^2.$$

---

[5]Risk aversion means that if two investment alternatives of equal expected return but differing risk are being considered, the less risky alternative will be chosen. Most investors are indeed risk averse, and certainly the average investor is averse to risk with his or her "serious money." Firms' managers may or may not be personally averse to risk, but they should recognize investors' risk aversion and its effects on market prices, and thus run the firm accordingly. Since all of this is a well-documented fact, we shall assume risk aversion through the remainder of the book.

Applying this criterion to our four investment alternatives, we find that no one alternative is necessarily preferred to any other alternative, because the alternatives with the higher variances also have higher expected rates of return.

Although the mean-variance criterion can sometimes be useful for screening alternative investments, it must be used with care if the normality assumption is not met. Application of the mean-variance criterion to nonnormal distributions may result in an anomaly called the *mean-variance paradox,* a situation in which the mean-variance criterion leads to incorrect conclusions. In our examples, the paradox occurs when choosing between Projects 1 and 2. We have already concluded that neither is clearly preferred under the mean-variance criterion. Nevertheless, if you look back at Table 2-1, you will see that Project 2 is actually better than 1, because it has a higher outcome for each possible state of the economy. Thus, regardless of which state of the economy occurs, we would always get a higher rate of return from Project 2 than from 1. In other words, Project 2 *dominates* 1 as an investment.[6]

Summary on Total Risk

We were able to eliminate one of our four illustrative investment alternatives, Project 1, but we were unable to make a clear choice among the other three. Theoretically, the choice should be made on the basis of the risk aversion of the owners of the firm. However, financial managers generally cannot measure stockholders' risk aversion, so managers often substitute their own preferences, along with other, more tangible, factors. For example, Project 2 has a probability, albeit low, of a rate of return of −2.0 percent, that is, a loss. Perhaps the financial manager is unwilling to accept any chance of a loss, and hence would reject that alternative. Also, the financial manager must consider his or her confidence in the estimated rates of return. Is he or she equally confident of the accuracy of the probability distributions of all four alternatives, or is there reason to be more confident in one alternative than another? If the decision maker "doesn't trust the numbers," then he or she may well reject what seems on paper to be the best alternative.

PORTFOLIO THEORY

Thus far, we have considered the riskiness of four investment alternatives on the assumption that they are each held in isolation. Now we analyze the riskiness of assets held in *portfolios,* or combinations of assets. As we shall see, an asset held

---

[6]There is another approach to decision rules called *stochastic dominance* which does not require the normality assumption, and hence is more powerful than the mean-variance criterion. However, the application of stochastic dominance requires that each alternative's probability distribution be specified completely, rather than summarized by an expected value and standard deviation. For this reason, stochastic dominance is seldom used explicitly in financial management decisions. For a complete discussion of stochastic dominance, see Haim Levy and Marshall Sarnat, *Portfolio and Investment Selection* (Englewood Cliffs, N. J.: Prentice-Hall, 1984).

as part of a portfolio is normally less risky than the same asset held in isolation. Moreover, an asset that would be relatively risky if held in isolation may not be risky at all if it is held in a well-diversified portfolio. Thus, considering risk in a portfolio context could completely change a decision based on our earlier analysis. In the remainder of this chapter, we focus on financial assets such as stocks and bonds rather than real assets. However, the principles of portfolio theory are equally applicable to both types of assets, as we shall see in Chapter 9, where we discuss capital budgeting risk analysis.

Expected Return on a Portfolio

The expected rate of return on a portfolio is simply a weighted average of the expected returns of the individual securities in the portfolio:[7]

$$\hat{k}_p = \sum_{i=1}^{n} x_i \hat{k}_i. \tag{2-5}$$

Here $\hat{k}_p$ is the expected rate of return on the portfolio; x_i is the proportion of the portfolio invested in the ith asset; $\hat{k}_i$ is the expected rate of return on the ith asset; and n is the number of assets in the portfolio. For example, suppose Stock A has an expected return of $\hat{k}_A = 10\%$, Stock B has $\hat{k}_B = 15\%$, and you plan to invest your money in A, in B, or in a combination of the two. If you put all your money in A, your one-stock portfolio will have an expected return of $\hat{k}_p = \hat{k}_A = 10\%$. If you invest only in B, your expected return will be $\hat{k}_p = \hat{k}_B = 15\%$. If you put half your money in each stock, then your expected portfolio return will be $\hat{k}_p = 0.5(10\%) + 0.5(15\%) = 12.5\%$, a weighted average of the two stocks' returns. Of course, after the fact and a year later, the realized rates of return on Stocks A and B, the $\bar{k}_i$ values, will probably be different from their expected values, so $\bar{k}_p$ will be somewhat different from $\hat{k}_p = 12.5\%$.

Portfolio Risk

As we just saw, the expected return on a portfolio is simply a weighted average of the expected returns on the individual stocks in the portfolio, and each stock's contribution to the expected portfolio return is $x_i\hat{k}_i$. However, unlike for returns, the standard deviation of a portfolio, σ_p, is generally *not* a weighted average of the standard deviations of the individual securities in the portfolio, and each stock's contribution to the portfolio's standard deviation is *not* $x_i\sigma_i$. Indeed, it is theoretically possible to combine two stocks which are, individually, quite risky as measured by their standard deviations, and to form from these risky assets a portfolio

---

[7] Similarly, the realized rate of return on a portfolio, $\bar{k}_p$, is

$$\bar{k}_p = \sum_{i=1}^{n} x_i \bar{k}_i,$$

where $\bar{k}_i$ is the realized rate of return on the ith asset.

which is completely riskless, with σ_p = 0%. To illustrate, consider the situation in Figure 2-2, where we present data on realized rates of return for Stocks W and M and for a portfolio invested 50 percent in each stock. (These stocks are called W and M because their returns graphs in Figure 2-2 resemble a W and an M.) Panel A plots realized returns in a time series format, while Panel B plots probability distributions of returns, assuming the distributions are approximately normal. The two stocks, each with σ_i = 22.6%, would be quite risky if they were held in isolation, but when they are combined to form Portfolio WM, with σ_p = 0.0%, they are not risky at all.

The reason Stocks W and M can be combined to form a riskless portfolio is that their returns move countercyclically to one another—when W's returns fall, those of M rise, and vice versa. In statistical terms, we say that the returns on Stocks W and M are *perfectly negatively correlated*, with r = correlation coefficient = -1.0.[8]

The opposite of perfect negative correlation, with r = -1.0, is perfect positive correlation, with r = $+1.0$. Returns on two perfectly positively correlated stocks would move up and down together, and a portfolio consisting of two such stocks would be just as risky as the individual stocks. This point is illustrated in Figure 2-3, where we combine Stocks M and M′, which are perfectly positively correlated. We see that the portfolio's standard deviation is equal to that of the individual stocks, indicating that diversification does nothing to reduce risk if the portfolio consists of perfectly positively correlated stocks.

Figures 2-2 and 2-3 demonstrate that (1) when stocks are perfectly negatively correlated (r = -1.0), all risk can be diversified away, but (2) when stocks are perfectly positively correlated (r = $+1.0$), diversification does no good whatever in terms of reducing risk. In reality, most stocks are positively correlated, but not perfectly so. For New York Stock Exchange stocks, the correlation coefficient for the returns on two randomly selected stocks would be about $+0.6$, and for most pairs of stocks, r would lie in the range of $+0.5$ to $+0.7$. *Under such conditions, combining stocks into portfolios reduces risk but does not eliminate it completely.* Figure 2-4 illustrates this point with two stocks whose correlation coefficient is r = $+0.65$. The portfolio's average realized return is 15.0 percent, which is exactly the same as the average return for each of the two stocks, but the portfolio's standard deviation is 20.6 percent, which is less than the standard deviation of either stock. Thus, the portfolio's risk is *not* an average of the risks of its component stocks—diversification has reduced, but not eliminated, risk.

From these examples, we can see that in one extreme case (r = -1.0), risk can be completely eliminated, while in the other extreme case (r = $+1.0$), diversification does no good whatever. In between these extremes, combining two

---

[8]*Correlation* is defined as the tendency of two variables to move together. The *correlation coefficient, r,* measures this tendency, and it can range from $+1.0$, denoting that the two variables move up and down in perfect synchronization, to -1.0, denoting that the variables always move in exactly opposite directions. A correlation coefficient of zero suggests that the two variables are not related to one another; that is, changes in one variable are *independent* of changes in the other. We will discuss correlation in more detail in the next section.

Figure 2-2
Rate of Return Distributions for Two Perfectly Negatively Correlated Stocks (r = −1.0) and for Portfolio WM

A. Rate of Return

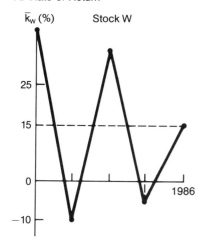
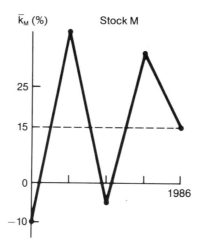
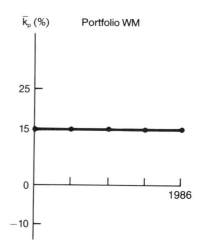

B. Probability Distribution of Returns

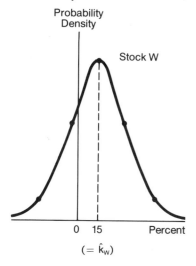
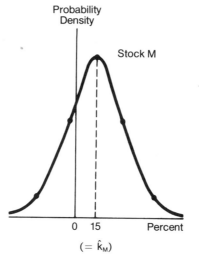
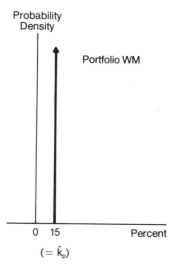

Year	Stock W k_w	Stock M k_M	Portfolio WM k_p
1982	40%	−10%	15%
1983	−10	40	15
1984	35	−5	15
1985	−5	35	15
1986	15	15	15
Average return =	15%	15%	15%
Standard deviation =	22.6%	22.6%	0.0%

Figure 2-3
Rate of Return Distributions for Two Perfectly Positively Correlated Stocks (r = +1.0) and for Portfolio MM'

A. Rate of Return

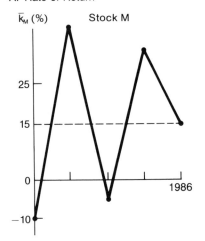

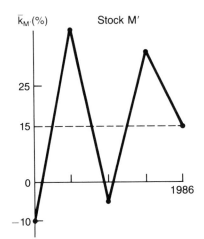

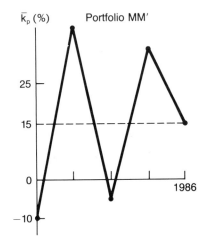

B. Probability Distribution of Returns

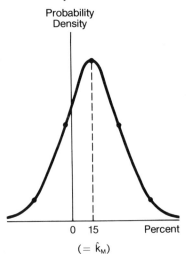

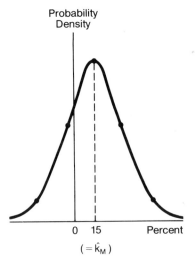

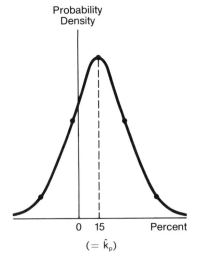

Year	Stock M k_M	Stock M' k_M'	Portfolio MM' k_p
1982	−10%	−10%	−10%
1983	40	40	40
1984	−5	−5	−5
1985	35	35	35
1986	15	15	15
Average return =	15%	15%	15%
Standard deviation =	22.6%	22.6%	22.6%

Figure 2-4

**Rate of Return Distributions for Two Partially Correlated
Stocks (r = +0.65) and for Portfolio WY**

A. Rate of Return

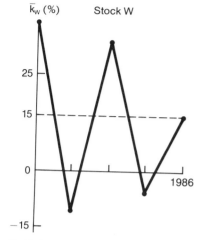

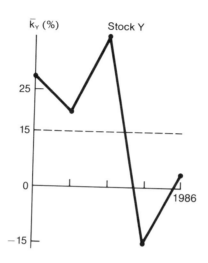

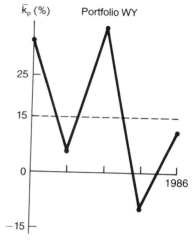

B. Probability Distribution of Returns

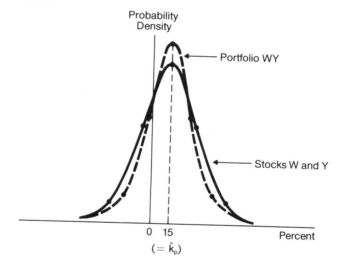

Year	Stock W $\bar{k}_W$	Stock Y $\bar{k}_Y$	Portfolio WY $\bar{k}_p$
1982	40%	28%	34%
1983	−10	20	5
1984	35	41	38
1985	−5	−17	−11
1986	15	3	9
Average return =	15%	15%	15%
Standard deviation =	22.6%	22.6%	20.6%

stocks into a portfolio reduces but does not eliminate the riskiness inherent in the individual stocks.[9]

Measuring Portfolio Risk

In the preceding section, we examined portfolio risk at an intuitive level. With that base, we now describe how portfolio risk is actually measured and dealt with in practice. First, as noted previously, the riskiness of a portfolio is measured by the standard deviation of its expected returns.[10] Equation 2-6 is used to calculate the standard deviation of a portfolio containing n assets:

$$\sigma_p = \sqrt{\sum_{i=1}^{n}(k_{pi} - \hat{k}_p)^2 P_i}.$$
(2-6)

Here σ_p is the standard deviation of the portfolio's expected return; k_{pi} is the return on the portfolio under the *i*th state of the economy; $\hat{k}_p$ is the expected rate of return on the portfolio; and P_i is the probability of occurrence of the *i*th state of the economy. This equation is exactly the same as Equation 2-3, for the standard deviation of a single asset, except that here the asset is a portfolio of assets (for example, a mutual fund share).

Covariance and the Correlation Coefficient

Two key concepts in portfolio analysis are (1) *covariance* and (2) *correlation coefficients*. First, covariance is a measure of the general movement relationship between two variables. For example, if the price of Stock A tends to increase as the economy moves from a recession to a boom, the covariance between Stocks A and B tells us whether the price of Stock B tends to increase, to decrease, or to stay the same, and how strong the movement relationship is between A and B. Equation 2-7 defines the covariance (Cov) between two variables such as Stocks A and B:

$$Cov(AB) = \sum_{i=1}^{n}(k_{Ai} - \hat{k}_A)(k_{Bi} - \hat{k}_B)P_i.$$
(2-7)

The first term in parentheses after the Σ is the deviation of Stock A's return from its expected value under the *i*th state of the economy; the second term is Stock B's deviation under the same state; and P_i is the probability of the *i*th state occurring. Before going through an example, note these points:

[9]For ease of illustration, our examples in this section showed stocks which had the same realized average return and standard deviation. The implications would be the same if we had used stocks with differing returns and standard deviations.

[10]Alternative risk measures, such as the coefficient of variation or semivariance, could also be used to measure the risk of a portfolio, but since portfolio returns (1) are approximately normally distributed and (2) have reasonably similar mean values, these refinements are generally not necessary and hence are not used.

1. If A and B tend to move together, the terms in parentheses will both be positive or both be negative for any state of the economy; that is, if k_{Ai} is above its average, $\hat{k}_A$, then k_{Bi} generally will be above $\hat{k}_B$, and vice versa. Therefore, if the assets move together, the terms in parentheses will both be positive or both be negative, hence the product $(k_{Ai} - \hat{k}_A)(k_{Bi} - \hat{k}_B)$ will be positive, while if the assets move counter to one another, the products will tend to be negative. However, if the two stocks' returns fluctuate randomly, then the products will sometimes be positive and sometimes be negative, and the sum of these products will be close to zero.

2. Therefore, if Stocks A and B tend to move together, their covariance, Cov(AB), will be positive, while if they tend to move counter to one another, Cov(AB) will be negative. If they fluctuate randomly, Cov(AB) could be either positive or negative, but in either event, it will be close to zero.

3. If either A or B is highly uncertain, that is, if it has a high standard deviation, then its parentheses' terms will tend to be large, the products will tend to be large, and the absolute size of Cov(AB) also will tend to be large. However, the size of Cov(AB) will be small, even if σ_A and/or σ_B is large, if A and B move randomly.

4. If either stock has a zero standard deviation, and hence is riskless, then its deviations $(k_i - \hat{k})$ always will be zero, and Cov(AB) also will be zero. Similarly, if one asset is not completely riskless, but it does have a relatively low risk, then its deviations will tend to be small, and this will hold down the size of Cov(AB).

5. Therefore, Cov(AB) will be large and positive if two assets which have large standard deviations and which tend to move together are combined; it will be large and negative if two high σ assets which move counter to one another are combined; and it will be small if the two assets' returns move randomly, rather than up or down with one another, or if either of the assets has a small standard deviation.

To illustrate the calculation process, first look at Table 2-3, which presents the probability distributions of the rates of return on four stocks, and at Figure 2-5, which plots scatter diagrams between returns on several pairs of returns. We can use Equation 2-7 to calculate the covariance between Stocks F and G as follows:

Table 2-3
Probability Distributions of Stocks E, F, G, and H

Probability of Occurrence	Rate of Return Distribution			
	E	F	G	H
0.1	10.0%	6.0%	14.0%	2.0%
0.2	10.0	8.0	12.0	6.0
0.4	10.0	10.0	10.0	9.0
0.2	10.0	12.0	8.0	15.0
0.1	10.0	14.0	6.0	20.0
$\hat{k} =$	10.0%	10.0%	10.0%	10.0%
$\sigma =$	0.0%	2.2%	2.2%	5.0%

Figure 2-5
Scatter Diagrams

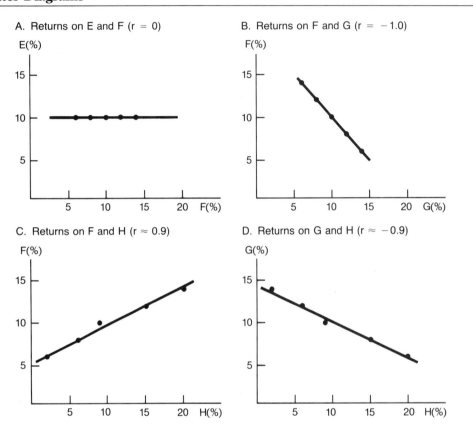

Notes:
a. The lines shown in each graph are called *regression lines;* they will be discussed in detail later in the chapter.
b. These graphs are drawn as if each point had an equal probability of occurrence.

$$\text{Cov(FG)} = \sum_{i=1}^{5}(k_{Fi} - \hat{k}_F)(k_{Gi} - \hat{k}_G)P_i$$

$$= (6 - 10)(14 - 10)(0.1) + (8 - 10)(12 - 10)(0.2)$$
$$+ (10 - 10)(10 - 10)(0.4) + (12 - 10)(8 - 10)(0.2)$$
$$+ (14 - 10)(6 - 10)(0.1)$$
$$= -4.8.$$

The negative sign indicates that the rates of return tend to move in opposite directions, which is consistent with the pattern shown in Panel B of Figure 2-5. However, if we calculated the covariance between Stocks F and H, we would find $\text{Cov(FH)} = +10.8$, indicating that these assets tend to move together, as Panel C shows. A zero covariance, as between Stocks E and F, indicates that there is no relationship between the variables; that is, the variables are independent. (E's return is always 10 percent; therefore, $\sigma_E = 0\%$, so the covariance of E with any other asset must be zero.)

We can also measure the degree of co-movement between each pair of stocks by the correlation coefficient, which standardizes the covariance by dividing by a product term; this facilitates comparisons by putting things on a similar scale. The correlation coefficient, r, is calculated as follows:

$$r_{AB} = \frac{\text{Cov(AB)}}{\sigma_A \sigma_B}. \tag{2-8}$$

The sign of the correlation coefficient is the same as the sign of the covariance; a positive sign means that the variables move together, while a negative sign indicates that they move in opposite directions. Moreover, the standardization process confines the correlation coefficient to values between -1.0 and $+1.0$.

Using Equation 2-8, we find the correlation coefficient between Stocks F and G to be -1.0 (except for a rounding error):

$$r_{FG} = \frac{-4.8}{(2.2)(2.2)} \approx -1.0.$$

These two stocks are said to be perfectly negatively correlated. As Panel B of Figure 2-5 shows, the regression line for these two assets' rates of return is negatively sloped, and all points lie exactly on the line.

The correlation coefficient between Stocks F and H is $+0.9$. Thus, there is a strong positive relationship—their regression is upward sloping, but all points are not exactly on the line.

The Two-Asset Case

Under the assumption that the distributions of returns on the individual securities are normal, a complicated looking but operationally simple equation can be used to determine the total risk of a two-asset portfolio:[11]

$$\sigma_p = \sqrt{x^2 \sigma_A^2 + (1-x)^2 \sigma_B^2 + 2x(1-x)r_{AB}\sigma_A\sigma_B}. \tag{2-9}$$

---

[11]Equation 2-9 is derived from Equation 2-6 in standard statistics books. Notice that if $x = 1$, all of the portfolio is invested in Security A, and Equation 2-9 reduces to σ_A:

$$\sigma_p = \sqrt{\sigma_A^2} = \sigma_A.$$

The portfolio contains but a single asset, so the risk of the portfolio and that of the asset are identical. Note also that Equation 2-9 could be expanded to include any number of assets by adding additional terms, but we shall not do so here.

Here x is the fraction of the portfolio invested in Security A, so $(1 - x)$ is the fraction invested in Security B. Also, note that the term $r_{AB}\sigma_A\sigma_B$ is equal to the covariance between Securities A and B:

$$r_{AB} = \frac{Cov(AB)}{\sigma_A\sigma_B},$$

so

$$Cov(AB) = r_{AB}\sigma_A\sigma_B.$$

The primary use of the statistical relationships we have discussed thus far is to select *efficient* portfolios—defined as those portfolios which provide the highest expected return for any degree of risk, or the lowest degree of risk for any expected return. To illustrate the concept, assume that two investment securities, A and B, are available, and that we have a specific amount of money to invest. We can allocate our funds between the securities in any proportion. Suppose Security A has an expected rate of return of $\hat{k}_A = 5\%$ and a standard deviation of returns $\sigma_A = 4\%$; for Security B, the expected return is $\hat{k}_B = 8\%$ and the standard deviation is $\sigma_B = 10\%$. Our task is to determine the set of *attainable* portfolios, and then from this attainable set to select the *efficient* subset.

To construct the attainable set, we need data on the degree of correlation between the two securities' expected returns, r_{AB}. Let us work with three different assumed degrees of correlation, $r_{AB} = +1.0$, $r_{AB} = 0$, and $r_{AB} = -1.0$, and using them, develop the portfolios' expected returns, $\hat{k}_p$, and standard deviations of returns, σ_p. (Of course, only one correlation can exist; our example simply shows three alternative situations.)

To calculate $\hat{k}_p$, we use Equation 2-5. First, substitute in the given values for $\hat{k}_A$ and $\hat{k}_B$, and then solve for $\hat{k}_p$ at different values of x. For example, when x equals 0.75, then $\hat{k}_p = 5.75\%$:

$$\hat{k}_p = x_A\hat{k}_A + x_B\hat{k}_B$$
$$= 0.75(5\%) + 0.25(8\%) = 5.75\%.$$

Other values of $\hat{k}_p$ were found similarly and are shown in Table 2-4.

Next, we use Equation 2-9 to find σ_p with different fractions of A and B in the portfolio. Substitute in the given values for σ_A, σ_B, and r_{AB}, and then solve Equation 2-9 for σ_p at different values of x. For example, in the case where $r_{AB} = 0$ and x $= 0.75$, then $\sigma_p = 3.9\%$:

$$\sigma_p = \sqrt{x^2\sigma_A^2 + (1 - x)^2\sigma_B^2 + 2x(1 - x)r_{AB}\sigma_A\sigma_B}$$
$$= \sqrt{(0.5625)(16) + (0.0625)(100) + 2(0.75)(0.25)(0)(4)(10)}$$
$$= \sqrt{9.00 + 6.25} = \sqrt{15.25} = 3.9\%.$$

The $\hat{k}_p$ and σ_p equations can be solved for other values of x, and for the three cases, $r_{AB} = +1.0$, 0, and -1.0. Table 2-4 gives the solution values for x = 1.0,

Table 2-4
$\hat{k}_p$ and σ_p under Various Assumptions

Proportion of Portfolio in Security A (Value of x)	Proportion of Portfolio in Security B (Value of 1 − x)	$r_{AB} = +1.0$		$r_{AB} = 0$		$r_{AB} = -1.0$	
		$\hat{k}_p$	σ_p	$\hat{k}_p$	σ_p	$\hat{k}_p$	σ_p
1.00	0.00	5.00	4.0	5.00	4.0	5.00	4.0
0.75	0.25	5.75	5.5	5.75	3.9	5.75	0.5
0.50	0.50	6.50	7.0	6.50	5.4	6.50	3.0
0.25	0.75	7.25	8.5	7.25	7.6	7.25	6.5
0.00	1.00	8.00	10.0	8.00	10.0	8.00	10.0

0.75, 0.50, 0.25, and 0.0, and Figure 2-6 gives plots of $\hat{k}_p$, σ_p, and the attainable set of portfolios, for each case. In both the table and the graphs, note the following points:

1. The three graphs across the top row of Figure 2-6 designate Case I, where the two assets are perfectly positively correlated, that is, $r_{AB} = +1.0$. The three graphs in the middle row are for the zero correlation case, and the three in the bottom row are for perfect negative correlation.

2. All three cases are theoretical in the sense that we would rarely encounter $r_{AB} = -1.0$, 0.0, or $+1.0$. Generally, in the real world, r_{AB} would be in the range of $+0.5$ to $+0.7$ for stocks, although r_{AB} is approximately equal to $+1.0$ for high quality bonds. Case II (zero correlation) produces graphs which, pictorially, most closely resemble most real-world examples.

3. The left column of graphs shows how the expected portfolio returns vary with different combinations of A and B; the middle column shows how risk is affected by the portfolio mix in the three cases; and the right column shows the attainable set of risk/return combinations.

4. The graphs in the left column are identical in each of the three cases: the portfolio return, $\hat{k}_p$, is a linear function of x, and it does not depend on the correlation of the assets in the portfolio.

5. In the middle column of graphs, we see that portfolio risk, σ_p, is linear in Case I, where $r_{AB} = +1.0$; it is nonlinear in Case II; and Case III shows that risk can be completely diversified away if $r_{AB} = -1.0$. Thus, σ_p does depend on correlation, although $\hat{k}_p$ does not.

6. The right column of graphs shows the *attainable,* or *feasible, set* of portfolios constructed with different mixes of Securities A and B. Each graph was plotted from pairs of $\hat{k}_p$ and σ_p as shown in Table 2-4. For example, Point A in the upper right graph is the point $\hat{k}_p = 5$, $\sigma_p = 4$ from the columns of Table 2-4 under the heading $r_{AB} = +1.0$. All other points on the curves were plotted similarly. With only two securities, the attainable set is a curve or line.

Figure 2-6
Illustrations of Portfolio Returns, Risk, and the Attainable Set of Portfolios

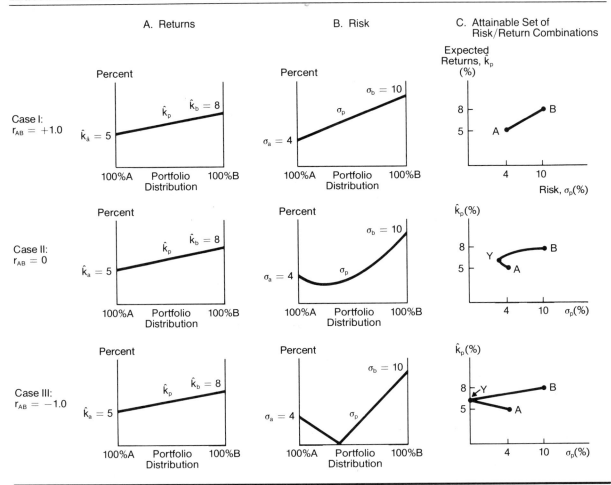

7. Are all portfolios on the attainable set equally good? The answer is no: only that part of the attainable set from Y to B in Cases II and III is defined to be *efficient*, while the part from A to Y is inefficient, because for any degree of risk on the line segment AY, a higher return can be found on segment YB. Thus, no rational investor would hold a portfolio that lay on segment AY. In Case I, however, the entire feasible set is also efficient—no combination of the securities can be ruled out in that case.

From these examples, we can see that in one extreme case (r = −1.0), risk can be completely eliminated, while in the other extreme case (r = +1.0), diversification does no good whatever. In between these extremes, combining two stocks into a portfolio reduces but does not eliminate the riskiness inherent in the individual stocks.[12]

The Multi-Asset Case

What would happen if we added more and more stocks to the portfolio? As a rule, the riskiness of a portfolio will decline as the number of stocks in the portfolio increases. If we added enough stocks, could we completely eliminate risk? In general, the answer is no, but the extent to which adding stocks to a portfolio reduces the portfolio's risk depends on the degree of correlation among the stocks. The smaller the correlation coefficient, the lower will be the remaining risk in a large portfolio. Indeed, if we could find enough stocks whose correlation coefficients were zero or negative, all risk could be eliminated. However, in the typical case, where the correlations among the individual stocks are positive but less than $+1.0$, some but not all risk can be eliminated.

As noted previously, it is very difficult, if not impossible, to find stocks whose expected returns are negatively correlated—most stocks tend to do well when the national economy is strong and poorly when it is weak.[13] Thus, even very large portfolios end up with a certain degree of risk. Consider, for example, Figure 2-7, which shows how portfolio risk is affected by forming larger and larger portfolios of New York Stock Exchange (NYSE) stocks. Standard deviations are plotted for an average one-stock portfolio, an average two-stock portfolio, and so on, up to a portfolio consisting of all $1,500+$ common stocks listed on the Exchange. The graph illustrates that the riskiness of a portfolio consisting of NYSE stocks tends to decline and to approach a limit asymptotically as the size of the portfolio increases.

According to data accumulated in recent years, σ_1, the standard deviation of an average one-stock portfolio (or an average stock), is approximately 28 percent, whereas a portfolio consisting of all stocks, which is called the *market portfolio*, would have a standard deviation of about 15.1 percent. The market portfolio's standard deviation is given the symbol σ_M, so $\sigma_M = 15.1\%$.

Since an average stock held in isolation would have a riskiness of $\sigma_i \approx 28\%$, and a very large portfolio would have $\sigma_M = 15.1\%$, almost half of the riskiness inherent in stock investments can be eliminated by holding stocks in portfolios. Further, it is not necessary to hold all stocks—a portfolio consisting of about 40 randomly selected stocks will have σ_p close to σ_M. Some risk will always remain, however,

---

[12]If we differentiate Equation 2-9, set the derivative equal to zero, and then solve for x, we obtain the fraction of the portfolio that should be invested in Security A if we wish to form the least-risky portfolio. Here is the equation:

$$x = \frac{\sigma_B(\sigma_B - r_{AB}\sigma_A)}{\sigma_A^2 + \sigma_B^2 - 2r_{AB}\sigma_A\sigma_B}.$$

As a rule, we limit x to the range 0 to $+1.0$; that is, if the solution value is $x > 1.0$, set $x = 1.0$, and if x is negative, set $x = 0$. A negative x would imply short sales, and $x > 1.0$ would imply borrowing.

[13]It is not too hard to find a few stocks that happened to decline because of a particular set of circumstances in the past while most other stocks were advancing; it is much harder to find stocks that could logically be *expected* to decline in the future when other stocks are rising.

Figure 2-7
Effect of Portfolio Size on Portfolio Risk

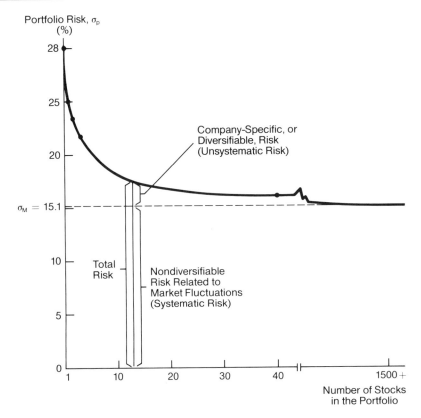

Note: At this point we are interested in general concepts, not exact technical precision. However, it should be noted (1) that the graph shown would result if the one-stock, two-stock, and so on, portfolios were formed by random selection of stocks from the NYSE list, but (2) that if NYSE stocks were, before the random selection, partitioned into "high risk," "average risk," and "low risk" groups, then the curve for the high-risk group would be above, and the one for the low-risk group below, the line shown above. Various experiments have demonstrated this to be the case for almost any reasonable grouping criteria.

even in the largest of portfolios, because it is virtually impossible to diversify away the effects of broad stock market declines that affect essentially all stocks.

Components of Total Risk

That part of the risk of an average stock which can be eliminated is called *diversifiable*, or *company-specific*, *risk*. Diversifiable risk is caused by such company-specific events as lawsuits, strikes, successful and unsuccessful marketing programs, and winning and losing major contracts. Since occurrences that are unique to a particular firm (or to its industry) are essentially random, their effects on a portfolio can be eliminated by diversification—bad events in one firm will be offset by good events in another. *Systematic*, or *market, risk*, on the other hand, stems from such external events as war, inflation, recessions, and high interest rates, which have an impact on all firms. Since all firms are affected simultaneously by these factors, systematic risk cannot be eliminated by diversification.

We know that investors demand a premium for bearing risk; that is, the higher the riskiness of a security, the higher its expected return must be to induce investors to buy (or hold) the security. However, if investors are primarily concerned with *portfolio risk* rather than the risk of the individual securities in the portfolio, how should the riskiness of the individual stocks be measured? The answer is this: *The relevant riskiness of an individual stock is its contribution to the riskiness of a well-diversified portfolio.* In other words, the riskiness of Stock X to a doctor who has a portfolio of 40 stocks, or to a trust officer managing a 150-stock portfolio, is the contribution that Stock X makes to the portfolio's riskiness. The stock might be quite risky if held by itself, but if most of its risk can be eliminated by diversification, the stock's relevant risk, which is its contribution to the portfolio's risk, might be small.

With only two assets, the feasible set of portfolios is a line or curve as shown in the third column of graphs in Figure 2-6. However, if we were to increase the number of assets, we would obtain an area, such as the shaded area in Figure 2-8. The points A, H, G, and F represent single securities (or portfolios containing only one security). All the other points in the shaded area, including its boundaries, represent portfolios of two or more securities. The shaded area is called the *feasible,* or *attainable, region*. Each point in this area represents a particular portfolio with a risk of σ_p and an expected return of $\hat{k}_p$. For example, point X represents one such portfolio's risk and expected return, as do B, C, D, and E.

The Efficient Frontier

Given the full set of potential portfolios that could be constructed from the available assets, which portfolio should actually be constructed? This choice involves two separate decisions: (1) determining the *efficient set* of portfolios and (2) choosing from the efficient set the single portfolio that is best for the individual investor.

In Figure 2-8, the boundary line BCDE defines the efficient set of portfolios.[14] Portfolios to the left of the efficient set are not possible because they lie outside the attainable set. Portfolios to the right of the boundary line (interior portfolios) are inefficient because some other portfolio would provide either a higher return with the same degree of risk or a lower risk for the same rate of return. For example, Portfolio X is dominated by Portfolios C and D.

---

[14]A computational procedure for determining the efficient set of portfolios was developed by Harry Markowitz and first reported in his article, "Portfolio Selection," *Journal of Finance*, March 1952, 77-91. In this article, Markowitz developed the basic concepts of portfolio theory.

Figure 2-8
The Efficient Set of Investments

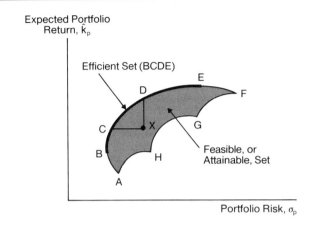

Risk/Return Indifference Curves

Given the efficient set of portfolio combinations, which specific portfolio should an investor choose? To determine the optimal portfolio for a particular investor, we must know the investor's attitude toward risk as reflected in his or her risk/return trade-off function, or *indifference curve*.

An investor's risk/return trade-off function is based on the standard economic concepts of utility theory and indifference curves, which are illustrated in Figure 2-9. The curves labeled I_A and I_B represent the indifference curves of Individuals A and B. Ms. A is indifferent with regard to the riskless 5 percent portfolio, a portfolio with an expected return of 6 percent but with a risk of $\sigma_p = 1.4\%$, and so on. Mr. B is equally well satisfied with a riskless 5 percent return, an expected 6 percent return with risk of $\sigma_p = 3.3\%$, and so on.

Notice that Ms. A requires a higher expected rate of return to compensate for a given amount of risk than does Mr. B; thus, Ms. A is said to be more *risk averse* than Mr. B. Her higher risk aversion causes Ms. A to require a higher *risk premium*—defined here as the difference between the 5 percent riskless return and the required return associated with any specific amount of risk—than does Mr. B. Thus, Ms. A requires a risk premium (RP_A) of 2.5 percent to compensate for a risk of $\sigma_p = 3.3\%$, while Mr. B's risk premium for this degree of risk is only $RP_B = 1.0\%$. As a generalization, the steeper the slope of the indifference curve, the more risk averse is the investor. Thus, Ms. A is more averse to risk than is Mr. B.

Each individual has a "map" of indifference curves; the indifference maps for Ms. A and Mr. B are shown in Figure 2-10. The higher curves denote a greater

Figure 2-9
Indifference Curves for Risk and Expected Rate of Return

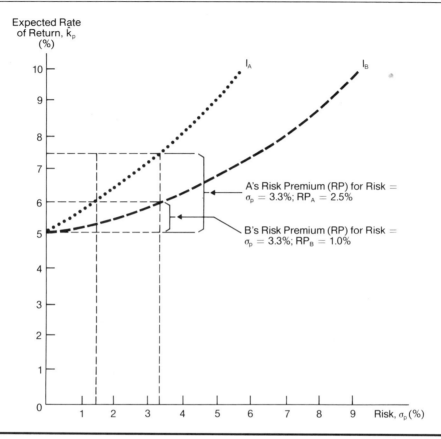

level of satisfaction (or utility). Thus, I_{B2} is better than I_{B1} because, for any level of risk, Mr. B has a higher expected return, hence greater utility. An infinite number of indifference curves could be drawn for each individual, and each individual has a unique set of curves.

The Optimal Portfolio for an Investor

Figure 2-10 also shows the feasible set of portfolios for the two-asset case, under the assumption that $r_{AB} = 0$, as it was developed in Figure 2-6. The optimal portfolio for each investor is found at the tangency point between the efficient set of portfolios and one of the investor's indifference curves. This tangency point marks the highest level of satisfaction the investor can attain. Ms. A, who is more risk

Figure 2-10
Selecting the Optimal Portfolio of Risky Assets

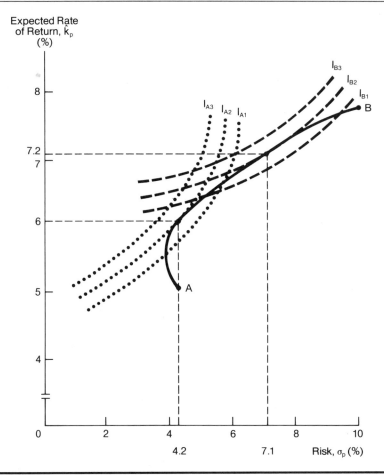

averse than Mr. B, chooses a portfolio with a lower expected return (about 6 percent) but a riskiness of only $\sigma_p = 4.2\%$. Mr. B picks a portfolio that provides an expected return of about 7.2 percent, but it has a risk of about $\sigma_p = 7.1\%$. Ms. A's portfolio is more heavily weighted with the less risky security, while Mr. B's portfolio contains a larger proportion of the more risky security.[15]

---

[15]Ms. A's portfolio would contain 67 percent of Security A and 33 percent of Security B, whereas Mr. B's portfolio would consist of 27 percent of Security A and 73 percent of Security B. These percentages can be determined with Equation 2-5 by simply seeing what percentage of the two securities is consistent with $\hat{k}_p = 6.0\%$ and 7.2%. For example, $x(5\%) + (1 - x)(8\%) = 7.2\%$, and solving for x, we obtain $x = 0.27$ and $(1 - x) = 0.73$.

THE CAPITAL ASSET PRICING MODEL

As we saw in the preceding section, the riskiness of a portfolio as measured by its standard deviation of returns is generally less than the average risk of the individual assets in the portfolio. This phenomenon, in turn, has important implications for the required rate of return on any given security. Investors should (and generally do) hold portfolios of securities, not just one security, so it is reasonable to consider the riskiness of any security in terms of its contribution to the riskiness of a portfolio rather than in terms of its riskiness if held in isolation. The *Capital Asset Pricing Model (CAPM)* specifies the equilibrium relationship between risk and required rates of return on assets when they are held in well-diversified portfolios.

Basic Assumptions of the CAPM

As in all financial theories, a number of assumptions were made in the development of the CAPM; they are summarized in the following list:[16]

1. All investors are single-period expected utility of terminal wealth maximizers who choose among alternative portfolios on the basis of each portfolio's expected return and standard deviation.

2. All investors can borrow or lend an unlimited amount at a given risk-free rate of interest, k_{RF}, and there are no restrictions on short sales of any asset.[17]

3. All investors have identical estimates of the means, variances, and covariances of returns among all assets; that is, investors have homogeneous expectations.

4. All assets are perfectly divisible and perfectly liquid (that is, marketable at the going price), and there are no transactions costs.

5. There are no taxes.

6. All investors are price takers (that is, all investors assume that their own buying and selling activity will not affect stock prices).

7. The quantities of all assets are given and fixed.

Theoretical extensions in the literature have attempted to relax the basic CAPM assumptions, and in general these extensions have yielded results that are reasonably consistent with the basic theory. However, even the extensions contain assumptions which are both strong and unrealistic. Therefore, the validity of the model can only be established through empirical tests. More will be said later in this chapter about the empirical validity of the CAPM, but first we discuss its basic properties and conclusions.

---

[16]See Michael C. Jensen, "Capital Markets: Theory and Evidence," *Bell Journal of Economics and Management Science*, Autumn 1972, 357-398.

[17]In a short sale, one borrows a stock, and then sells it, expecting to buy it back later (at a lower price) in order to repay the person from whom the stock was borrowed. If you sell short and the stock price rises, you lose; you gain if the stock price falls after you go short.

The Capital Market Line

Figure 2-10 showed the set of portfolio opportunities for the two-asset case and illustrated how indifference curves can be used to select the optimal portfolio from the feasible set. In Figure 2-11, we have constructed a similar diagram for the multi-asset case, but here we also include a risk-free asset with a return k_{RF}. The riskless asset by definition has zero risk, and hence $\sigma = 0\%$, so it is plotted on the vertical axis.

Figure 2-11 shows the feasible set of portfolios of risky assets (the shaded area) and a set of indifference curves (I_1, I_2, I_3), which represent the tradeoff between risk and expected return for a particular investor. Point N, where indifference curve I_1 is tangent to the efficient set, represents a possible portfolio choice; it is the point on the efficient set of risky portfolios where the investor obtains the highest possible return for a given amount of risk, σ_p, and the smallest degree of risk for a given expected return, $\hat{k}_p$.

However, the investor can do better than Portfolio N; he or she can reach a higher indifference curve. In addition to the feasible set of risky portfolios, we now have a risk-free asset that provides a certain return, k_{RF}. Given the additional alternative of investing in the risk-free asset, investors can create new portfolios that combine the risk-free asset with a portfolio of risky assets. This enables them to

Figure 2-11
Investor Equilibrium: Combining the Risk-Free Asset with the Market Portfolio

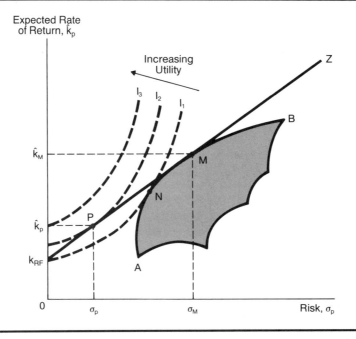

achieve any combination of risk and return that lies along the straight line connecting k_{RF} with M, the point of tangency of that straight line and the stock portfolio efficient set curve.[18] All portfolios on the line $k_{RF}MZ$ are preferred to the other risky portfolio opportunities on curve ANMB; the points on the line $k_{RF}MZ$ represent the best attainable combinations of risk and return.

Given the new opportunity set $k_{RF}MZ$, our investor will move from Point N to Point P, which is on his or her highest attainable risk/return indifference curve. Note that line $k_{RF}MZ$ dominates the opportunities that could have been achieved from the stock portfolio opportunities curve alone. In general, since investors can include both the risk-free security and a fraction of the risky portfolio, M, in a portfolio, it will be possible to move to a point such as P. In addition, if the investor can borrow as well as lend (lending is equivalent to buying risk-free debt securities) at the riskless rate k_{RF}, it is possible to move out the line segment MZ, and one would do so if his or her utility indifference curve were tangent to $k_{RF}MZ$ to the right of Point M.[19]

All investors should hold portfolios lying on the line $k_{RF}MZ$ under the conditions assumed in the CAPM. This implies that they would hold only efficient portfolios that are combinations of the risk-free security and the risky portfolio M. Thus, the addition of the risk-free asset totally changes the efficient set. Now, the efficient set lies along line $k_{RF}MZ$ rather than along the curve ANMB. Also, note

---

[18]The risk/return combinations between a risk-free asset and a risky asset (a single stock or a portfolio of stocks) will always be linear. To see this, consider the equations for return, $\hat{k}_p$, and risk, σ_p, for any combination x and $(1 - x)$:

$$\hat{k}_p = xk_{RF} + (1 - x)\hat{k}_M, \tag{2-5a}$$

and

$$\sigma_p = \sqrt{x^2\sigma_{RF}^2 + (1 - x)^2\sigma_M^2 + 2x(1 - x)r_{RF/M}\sigma_{RF}\sigma_M}. \tag{2-9a}$$

Equation 2-5a is obviously linear. For Equation 2-9a, we know that k_{RF} is the risk-free asset, so $\sigma_{RF} = 0$; hence, σ_{RF}^2 is also zero. Using this information, we can simplify Equation 2-9a as follows:

$$\sigma_p = \sqrt{(1 - x)^2\sigma_M^2}$$
$$= (1 - x)\sigma_M.$$

Thus, σ_p is also linear when a riskless asset is combined with a portfolio of risky assets.

If expected returns as measured by $\hat{k}_p$ and risk as measured by σ_p are both linear functions of x, then the relationship between $\hat{k}_p$ and σ_p when graphed as in Figure 2-11 must also be linear. For example, if 100 percent of the portfolio is invested in k_{RF} with a return of 8 percent, the portfolio return will be 8 percent and σ_p will be 0. If 100 percent is invested in M, with $\hat{k}_M = 12\%$ and $\sigma_M = 10\%$, then $\sigma_p = 1.0(10\%) = 10\%$, and $\hat{k}_p = 0(8\%) + 1.0(12\%) = 12\%$. If 50 percent of the portfolio is invested in M and 50 percent in the risk-free asset, then $\sigma_p = 0.5(10\%) = 5\%$, and $\hat{k}_p = 0.5(8\%) + 0.5(12\%) = 10\%$. Plotting these points will reveal the linear relationship given as $k_{RF}PMZ$ in Figure 2-11.

[19]An investor who is relatively averse to risk will have a steep indifference curve and will end up at a point such as P, holding some of the risky market portfolio and some of the riskless asset. An investor less averse to risk will have a relatively flat indifference curve, and hence will move out beyond M toward Z, borrowing to do so. The risk-prone investor might buy stocks on margin and use personal leverage. If individuals' borrowing rates are higher than k_{RF}, then the line $k_{RF}MZ$ will tilt down (that is, be less steep) beyond M. This condition would invalidate the basic CAPM, or at least require it to be modified. Therefore, the assumption of equal lending and borrowing rates is crucial to CAPM theory.

that if the capital market is to be in equilibrium, M must be a portfolio that contains every asset in exact proportion to that asset's fraction of the total market value of all assets; that is, if Security i is x percent of the total market value of all securities, x percent of the market portfolio M must consist of Security i. In summary, all investors will hold efficient portfolios having standard deviation and return combinations along the line $k_{RF}MZ$, with the particular location of a given individual on the line being determined by the point at which his or her indifference curve is tangent to the line.

The line $k_{RF}MZ$ in Figure 2-11 is defined as the *Capital Market Line (CML)*. It has an intercept of k_{RF} and a slope of $(\hat{k}_M - k_{RF})/\sigma_M$.[20] Therefore, the equation for the capital market line may be expressed as follows:

$$\text{CML: } \hat{k}_p = k_{RF} + \left(\frac{\hat{k}_M - k_{RF}}{\sigma_M}\right)\sigma_p. \tag{2-10}$$

In words, the expected rate of return on any efficient portfolio is equal to the riskless rate plus a risk premium, and the risk premium is equal to $(\hat{k}_M - k_{RF})/\sigma_M$ times the portfolio's standard deviation, σ_p. Thus, the CML prescribes a linear relationship between expected return and risk, and it can be rewritten as follows:

$$\text{CML: } \hat{k}_p = k_{RF} + \lambda\sigma_p. \tag{2-10a}$$

Here

$$\lambda = \text{Market price per standard deviation of risk}$$

$$= (\hat{k}_M - k_{RF})/\sigma_M = \text{slope of the CML.}$$

For example, suppose $k_{RF} = 10\%$, $\hat{k}_M = 15\%$, and $\sigma_M = 15\%$.

Then, $\lambda = (15\% - 10\%)/15\% = 0.33$. Therefore, if a particular portfolio has $\sigma_p = 10\%$, then its $\hat{k}_p$ will be

$$\hat{k}_p = 10\% + 0.33(10\%) = 13.3\%.$$

A riskier portfolio with $\sigma_p = 20\%$ will have $\hat{k}_p = 10\% + 0.33(20\%) = 16.6\%$. Both Equations 2-10 and 2-10a state that the expected return on an efficient portfolio in equilibrium is equal to a risk-free return plus a risk premium which is equal to the market price of risk multiplied by the standard deviation of the portfolio's returns. This relationship is graphed in Figure 2-12. The CML is drawn as a straight line with an intercept at k_{RF}, the risk-free return, and a slope equal to the market price of risk, λ, which is the market risk premium $(\hat{k}_M - k_{RF})$ divided by σ_M. The market price of risk, or the slope of the CML, reflects the aggregate attitude of investors toward risk.

---

[20]Recall that the slope of any line is measured as $\Delta Y/\Delta X$, or the change in height associated with a given change in horizontal distance. k_{RF} is at 0 on the horizontal axis, so $\Delta X = \sigma_M - 0 = \sigma_M$. The vertical axis difference associated with a change from k_{RF} to $\hat{k}_M$ is $\hat{k}_M - k_{RF}$. Therefore, slope $= \Delta Y/\Delta X = (\hat{k}_M - k_{RF})/\sigma_M$.

Figure 2-12
Expected Return on an Efficient Portfolio

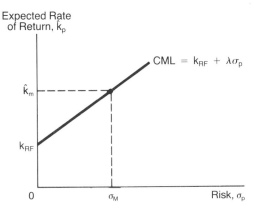

Note: We did not draw it in, but you can visualize the shaded space shown in Figure 2-11 in this graph, and the CML as the line formed by connecting k_{RF} with the tangent to the shaded space.

The Security Market Line

The next step in the development of the CAPM takes us from risk and returns on efficient portfolios to risk and returns on individual securities. Under the CAPM theory, the riskiness of a security is measured by its beta coefficient ("b," discussed in the next section), and the relationship between securities' risk and return is known as the *Security Market Line (SML)*:

$$\text{SML: } k_i = k_{RF} + b_i(k_M - k_{RF}). \tag{2-11}$$

Here

k_i = the required rate of return on the ith stock. ($\hat{k}_i$ = expected rate of return. In equilibrium, $k_i = \hat{k}_i$.)

k_{RF} = the riskless rate of return, generally measured by the rate of return on U.S. Treasury securities.

k_M = the required rate of return on an average (b = 1.0) stock. k_M is also the required rate of return on a portfolio consisting of all stocks, or the market portfolio. In equilibrium, $k_M = \hat{k}_M$.

$(k_M - k_{RF})$ = RP_M = the market risk premium, or the price of risk for an average stock.[21] It is the additional return over the riskless rate required to compensate investors for assuming an "average" amount of risk.

---

[21]The term "average stock" is a bit like "average U.S. family." The average family has 2.73 members, its head is 34.6 years old, its income is $28,362, and so on. No one family actually conforms to average, but each family can be compared to the statistical average. Similarly, the "average stock" is a statistical concept measured in terms of its expected rate of return, standard deviation of returns, and covariance with other stocks. By definition, if A denotes "average" and M denotes "the market," then $k_A = k_M$, $b_A = b_M = 1.0$, and $RP_A = RP_M = (k_A - k_{RF}) = (k_M - k_{RF})$.

b_i = the beta coefficient of the ith stock.

$b_i(k_M - k_{RF})$ = RP_i = the risk premium on the ith stock. The stock's risk premium is less than, equal to, or greater than the premium on an average stock depending on whether its beta is less than, equal to, or greater than 1.0.

Thus, if k_{RF} = 8%, b_i = 0.5, and k_M = 12%, then by Equation 2-11, k_i = 10%:

$$k_i = 8\% + 0.5(12\% - 8\%)$$
$$= 8\% + 0.5(4\%)$$
$$= 10\%.$$

Figure 2-13 shows the SML when k_{RF} = 8% and k_M = 12%. Several features of the graph are worth noting:

1. Required rates of return are shown on the vertical axis, and risk as measured by beta is shown on the horizontal axis.

2. Riskless securities have b_i = 0; therefore, k_{RF} appears as the vertical axis intercept.

3. The slope of the SML [$\Delta Y/\Delta X$ = $(k_M - k_{RF})/(1.0 - 0.0)$ = $(k_M - k_{RF})$ = 12% − 8% = 4 percentage points] reflects the degree of risk aversion in the economy—the greater the average investor's aversion to risk, then (1) the steeper the slope of the SML, (2) the greater the risk premium for any risky asset, and (3) the higher the required rate of return on risky assets in general. Note that beta is *not* the slope of the SML; the slope of the line in Figure 2-13 is the market risk

Figure 2-13
The Security Market Line (SML)

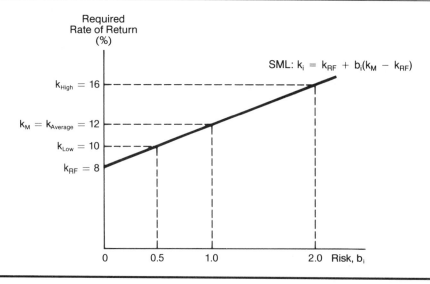

premium, a constant 4 percentage points, while beta in the graph can vary from zero to over 2.0.

4. Required rates of return are shown for stocks with $b_i = 0.5$, $b_i = 1.0$, and $b_i = 2.0$.

As we can see from the SML, required rates of return depend not only on market risk as measured by beta, but also on the risk-free rate and the market risk premium. Since these variables change, the SML is not normally stable over time. For example, increases in inflationary expectations would increase the risk-free rate, thus causing a parallel shift upward in the SML in Figure 2-13; however, an increase in aggregate risk aversion would cause the slope of the SML to increase.

The Concept of Beta

An *average stock* is defined as one which tends to move up and down in step with the general market as measured by some index such as the Dow Jones Industrial Average or the New York Stock Exchange Index. Such a stock will, by definition, have a beta (b) of 1.0, which indicates that if the market moves up by 10 percentage points, the stock will also tend to move up by 10 percentage points; if the market falls by 10 percentage points, the stock will likewise fall by 10 percentage points. A portfolio of such b = 1.0 stocks will move up and down with the broad market averages, and this portfolio will be just as risky as the averages. If b = 0.5, the stock is only half as volatile as the market—it will rise and fall only half as much as the indices—and a portfolio of such stocks is only half as risky as a portfolio of b = 1.0 stocks. On the other hand, if b = 2.0, the stock is twice as volatile as an average stock, so a portfolio of such stocks will be twice as risky as an average portfolio.

Betas are calculated and published by Merrill Lynch, Value Line, and numerous other organizations. The beta coefficients of some well-known companies, as calculated by Merrill Lynch, are shown in Table 2-5.[22] Most stocks have betas in the range of 0.50 to 1.50, and the average for all stocks is 1.0 by definition.

Portfolio Beta Coefficients

A portfolio consisting of low-beta securities will itself have a low beta, as the beta of any set of securities is the weighted average of the individual securities' betas:

$$b_p = \sum_{i=1}^{n} x_i b_i. \tag{2-12}$$

Thus, if a high-beta stock (one whose beta is greater than 1.0) is added to an average risk portfolio ($b_p = 1.0$), then the beta and consequently the riskiness of

---

[22]These betas are called "historical," or "ex post," betas because they are based strictly on historical, or past, data. Other types of betas, such as adjusted and fundamental betas, are also in wide use today. The different types of betas will be discussed in Chapter 4.

Table 2-5
Illustrative List of Beta Coefficients

Stock	Beta
El Torito Restaurants	2.1
National Semiconductor	1.4
Sperry Corporation	1.3
Dow Chemical	1.3
General Electric	1.0
Polaroid	1.0
Chevron	0.9
IBM	0.8
Anheuser-Busch	0.7
Hershey Foods	0.5

Source: Merrill Lynch, May 1986.

the portfolio will increase. Conversely, if a low-beta stock (one whose beta is less than 1.0) is added to an average risk portfolio, the portfolio's beta and risk will decline. *Therefore, since a stock's beta measures its contribution to the riskiness of a portfolio, beta is the appropriate measure of the stock's riskiness.*

To illustrate, if an investor holds a $100,000 portfolio consisting of $10,000 invested in each of ten stocks, and if each stock has a beta of 0.8, then the portfolio will have $b_p = 0.8$. Thus, the portfolio is less risky than the market, and it should experience relatively narrow price swings and have relatively small rate of return fluctuations.

Now suppose one of the existing stocks is sold and replaced by a stock with $b = 2.0$. This action will increase the riskiness of the portfolio from $b_{p1} = 0.8$ to $b_{p2} = 0.92$. This is calculated by using Equation 2-12 as follows:

$$b_{p2} = \sum_{i=1}^{n} x_i b_i = 0.9(0.8) + 0.1(2.0) = 0.92.$$

Had a stock with $b = 0.6$ been added, the portfolio beta would have declined from 0.8 to 0.78.

Calculating Beta Coefficients: The Characteristic Line

Professor William F. Sharpe developed the concept of beta coefficients and pioneered their use for separating the risk of an individual stock into diversifiable and market risk components.[23] Sharpe noted that the market risk of a given stock

[23]See William F. Sharpe, "Capital Asset Prices: A Theory of Market Equilibrium under Conditions of Risk," *Journal of Finance*, September 1964, 425-442. It should be noted that beta analysis in practice is much more difficult than our discussion makes it sound. We will see this in Chapter 4.

can be measured by its tendency to move with the general market. His procedure for determining market risk is illustrated in Figure 2-14, which is explained in the following paragraphs. First, however, familiarize yourself with the definitions of the terms used in Figure 2-14:

$\bar{k}_J$ = the historical realized rate of return on Stock J. (Recall that $\hat{k}_J$ and k_J are defined as Stock J's expected and required returns, respectively.)

Figure 2-14
Calculating Beta Coefficients

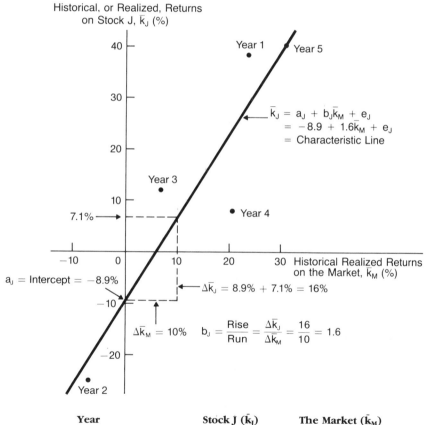

Year	Stock J ($\bar{k}_J$)	The Market ($\bar{k}_M$)
1	38.6%	23.8%
2	−24.7	−7.2
3	12.3	6.6
4	8.2	20.5
5	40.1	30.6
Average $\bar{k}$ =	14.9%	14.9%
$\sigma_{\bar{k}}$ =	26.5%	15.1%

$\bar{k}_M$ = the historical realized rate of return on the market.

a_J = the vertical axis intercept term for Stock J.

b_J = the slope, or beta coefficient, for Stock J.

e_J = the random error, reflecting the difference between the actual return on Stock J in a given year and the return predicted by the regression line.

The historical returns on Stock J are given in the lower section of Figure 2-14, along with historical returns on the market, $\bar{k}_M$. Notice that when returns on the market are high, returns on Stock J likewise tend to be high, and when the market is down, Stock J's returns are low. This general relationship is expressed more precisely in the regression line shown in Figure 2-14.

Recall what the term *regression line* or *regression equation* means: The equation $Y = a + bX + e$ is the standard form of a simple linear regression. It states that the dependent variable, Y, is equal to a constant, a, plus b times X, where X is the "independent" variable, plus a random error term. Thus, the rate of return on Stock J during a given time period depends on what happens to the general stock market, which is measured by $\bar{k}_M$, plus random events that affect Stock J but do not affect most other stocks.

The regression equation can be obtained by plotting the data points on graph paper and then drawing a line through the scatter of points "by eye." There is a mathematical line of best fit, the *least squares regression line*, and unless the data points all line up neatly, the "by eye" regression line will differ somewhat from the least squares line, and different students will draw in somewhat different lines.[24] In the 1964 article in which he developed the CAPM, Sharpe called the regression line the *characteristic line*. Thus, a stock's beta is the slope of its characteristic line.

Once the regression, or characteristic, line has been drawn on the graph paper, we can estimate its intercept and slope, the a and b values in $Y = a + bX$. The intercept, a, is simply the point where the line cuts the vertical axis. The slope coefficient, b, can be estimated by the "rise over run" method. This involves calculating the amount by which $\bar{k}_J$ increases for a given increase in $\bar{k}_M$. For example, we observe (in Figure 2-14) that $\bar{k}_J$ increases from -8.9 to $+7.1$ percent (the rise) when $\bar{k}_M$ increases from 0.0 to 10.0 percent (the run). Thus, b, the beta coefficient, can be measured as follows:

$$b_J = \frac{\text{Rise}}{\text{Run}} = \frac{\Delta Y}{\Delta X} = \frac{7.1 - (-8.9)}{10.00 - 0.00} = \frac{16.0}{10.00} = 1.6.$$

Note that rise over run is a ratio, and it would be the same if measured by using any two arbitrarily selected points on the line.

Although the "by eye" approach is useful for visualizing what the beta concept is all about, an in-depth understanding as well as efficient application of the concept require the use of statistics. Basic statistics courses set forth the following

---

[24]In practical applications, the regression equation would always be fitted by the method of least squares, using a hand-held calculator with statistical functions or a computer.

procedure for calculating the slope of any simple regression equation (this is also the formula that is programmed into the statistical functions on a calculator):

$$b_j = \frac{\text{Covariance between Stock J and the market}}{\text{Variance of market returns}} = \frac{\text{Cov}(\bar{k}_J, \bar{k}_M)}{\sigma_M^2}$$

$$= \frac{r_{JM}\sigma_J\sigma_M}{\sigma_M^2} = r_{JM}\left(\frac{\sigma_J}{\sigma_M}\right).$$

Here we see that a stock's beta depends on (1) its correlation with the stock market as a whole, r_{JM}; (2) its own variability, σ_J; and (3) the variability of the market, σ_M. In the Figure 2-14 example, $r_{JM} = 0.91$, $\sigma_J = 26.5\%$, and $\sigma_M = 15.1\%$. Therefore, $b_J = 0.91(26.5\%/15.1\%) = 1.60$.

Some Observations about Betas

Now that we have plotted Stock J's historical rates of return and estimated its beta coefficient, we can note the following points: First, the *future* returns on Stock J are assumed to bear a linear relationship of the following form to those of the market:

$$\hat{k}_J = a_J + b_J\hat{k}_M + e_J \qquad (2\text{-}13)$$

$$= -8.9 + 1.6\hat{k}_M + e_J.$$

In other words, the historical relationship between Stock J and the market as a whole, as given by the characteristic line, is assumed to continue on into the future.[25]

Second, in addition to general market movements, each firm also faces events that are peculiar to it and independent of the general economic climate. Such events cause the returns on any Firm J's stock to move somewhat independently of those for the market as a whole, and these random events are accounted for by the random error term, e_J. Before the fact, the expected value of the error term is zero; after the fact, it generally will be either positive or negative.

Third, the regression coefficient, b (the beta coefficient), is a market sensitivity index; it measures the relative volatility of a given stock (J) versus the average stock, or "the market." This tendency of an individual stock to move with the market constitutes a risk, because the market does fluctuate, and these fluctuations

---

[25]The characteristic line equation is also called the *Market Model*. The market model asserts that the relationship between the returns on individual stocks and the returns on the market is linear and can be expressed by Equation 2-13. The Capital Asset Pricing Model (CAPM) states that, in equilibrium, returns on individual stocks can be expressed by the Security Market Line, Equation 2-11. The two models require different assumptions, and hence acceptance of one model does not necessarily imply acceptance of the other. We will use the market model, or characteristic line, only to estimate betas for use in the Security Market Line of the CAPM. For more information on the Market Model and the differences between the two models, see Sid Mittra and Chris Gassen, *Investment Analysis and Portfolio Management* (New York: Harcourt Brace Jovanovich, 1981).

cannot be diversified away. This component of total risk is the stock's *market, or nondiversifiable, risk.*

Finally, the relationship between a stock's total risk, market risk, and diversifiable risk can be expressed as follows:

$$\text{Total risk} = \text{Variance} = \text{Market risk} + \text{Diversifiable risk}$$
$$\sigma_J^2 = b_J^2 \sigma_M^2 + \sigma_{e_J}^2.$$

Here σ_J^2 is the variance or total risk of Stock J, σ_M^2 is the variance of the market, b_J is Stock J's beta coefficient, and $\sigma_{e_J}^2$ is the variance of Stock J's regression error term.

Several points about total and market risk should be noted:

1. If, in a graph such as Figure 2-14, all the points plotted exactly on the regression line, then the variance of the error term, $(\sigma_{e_J}^2)$ would be zero and all of the stock's risk would be market related. On the other hand, if the points were widely scattered about the regression line, much of the stock's risk would be diversifiable. The shares of a large, well-diversified mutual fund would plot very close to the regression line, as would those of a broadly diversified conglomerate corporation.

2. If the stock market never fluctuated, then stocks would have no market risk. Of course, the market does fluctuate, so market risk is present; even if you hold an extremely well-diversified portfolio, you will still suffer losses if the market falls. In recent years, the standard deviation of market returns, σ_M, has generally run about 15 percent. Back in the "wild" days of the 1920s, before regulation and other forces helped stabilize the market, fluctuations were even greater.

3. Beta is a measure of market risk, and the actual market risk of Stock J is $b_J^2 \sigma_M^2$. Market risk can also be expressed in standard deviation form, as $b_J \sigma_M$. Stock J's market risk is thus $b_J \sigma_M = 1.6(15.1\%) = 24.2\%$, while its total risk is $\sigma_J = 26.5\%$. For any given level of market volatility as measured by the market's standard deviation, σ_M, the higher a stock's beta, the higher its market risk. If beta were zero, the stock would have no market risk, while if beta were 1.0, the stock would be exactly as risky as the market—assuming the stock is held in a diversified portfolio—and the stock's market risk would be σ_M.

4. The diversifiable risk should be eliminated by diversification, so the *relevant* risk is not total risk, but market risk. If Stock J had b = 0.5, then the stock's relevant risk would be $b_J \sigma_M = 0.5(15.1\%) = 7.55\%$. A portfolio of such low-beta stocks would have a standard deviation of expected returns of $\sigma_p = 7.55\%$, or one-half the standard deviation of expected returns of a portfolio of average (b = 1.0) stocks. Had Stock J been a high-beta stock (b = 2.0), then its relevant risk would have been $b_J \sigma_M = 2.0(15.1\%) = 30.2\%$. A portfolio of b = 2.0 stocks would have $\sigma_p = 30.2\%$, so such a portfolio would be twice as risky as a portfolio of average stocks.

5. A stock's risk premium depends only on its market risk, not its total risk: $RP_J = b_J(k_M - k_{RF})$. Mr. A might have only one stock, hence be concerned with total risk and seek a return based on that risk. However, if Ms. B has a well-diversified portfolio, she would face less risk from Stock J. Therefore, if Stock J offered a return high enough to satisfy Mr. A, it would represent a bargain for Ms. B. She would then buy it, pushing its price up and its yield down in the process. Since most financial assets are held by diversified investors, and since any given security can have only one price and hence only one rate of return, market action drives each stock's risk premium to the level specified by its relevant, or market, risk.

EMPIRICAL TESTS OF THE CAPM

As noted earlier, the CAPM was developed on the basis of a set of assumptions that are not realistic. If those assumptions were all true, then the CAPM would also have to be true. However, since the assumptions are not completely correct, the basic SML equation, $k_i = k_{RF} + b_i(k_M - k_{RF})$, might or might not represent an accurate description of how investors behave and how rates of return are established in the marketplace. For example, if many investors are not fully diversified, hence have not eliminated all diversifiable risk from their portfolios, then (1) beta would not be an adequate measure of risk and (2) the SML would not explain how required returns are set. Also, if the interest rate that investors must pay to borrow money is greater than the risk-free rate (that is, if the borrowing rate is greater than the lending rate), then the CML would not continue in a straight line beyond Point M as it does in Figure 2-11, and this too would invalidate the SML. And, of course, taxes and brokerage costs do exist, and their presence could distort the CAPM relationships.

For all these reasons, it is entirely possible that the CAPM is not completely valid, in which case the SML will not produce accurate estimates of k_i. Therefore, the CAPM must be tested empirically and validated before it can be used with any real confidence. The literature dealing with empirical tests of the CAPM is quite extensive, so we can give here only a brief synopsis of some of the key work.

Tests of the Stability of Beta Coefficients

According to the CAPM, the beta that should be used to estimate a stock's market risk reflects investors' estimates of the stock's *future* volatility in relation to that of the market. Obviously, we do not know now how a stock will be related to the market in the future, nor do we know how the average investor views this expected future relative volatility. All we have are data on past volatility, which we can use to plot the characteristic line and to calculate *historical betas*. If historical betas are stable over time, then there would seem to be reason for investors to use past betas as estimators of future volatility. For example, if Stock J's beta had been stable in the past, then its historical b_J would probably be a good proxy for its *ex ante*, or expected, b_J. By "stable," we mean that if b_J were calculated by using data from the period of, say, 1982 to 1986, then this same beta (approximately) should be found from 1987 to 1991.

Robert A. Levy, Marshall E. Blume, and others have studied the question of beta stability in depth.[26] Levy calculated betas for individual securities, as well as for

---

[26]See Robert A. Levy, "On the Short-Term Stationarity of Beta Coefficients," *Financial Analysts Journal*, November-December 1971, 55-62, and Marshall E. Blume, "Betas and Their Regression Tendencies," *Journal of Finance*, June 1975, 785-796.

portfolios of securities, over a range of time intervals. He concluded (1) that the betas of individual stocks are unstable, hence that past betas for *individual securities* are *not* good estimators of their future risk, but (2) that betas of portfolios of ten or more randomly selected stocks are reasonably stable, hence that past *portfolio* betas are good estimators of future portfolio volatility. In effect, the errors in individual securities' betas in a portfolio tend to offset one another. The work of Blume and others supports Levy's position.

The conclusion that follows from the beta stability studies is that the CAPM is a better concept for structuring investment portfolios than it is for purposes of estimating the cost of capital for individual securities. We will address this issue in Chapter 4, when we discuss cost of capital estimation procedures.

Estimating the Slope of the SML

As we have seen, the CAPM states that a linear relationship exists between a security's required rate of return and its beta. Further, when the SML is graphed, the vertical axis intercept should be k_{RF}, and the required rate of return for a stock (or portfolio) with $b = 1.0$ should be k_M, the required rate of return on the market. Various researchers have attempted to test the validity of the model by calculating betas and realized rates of return, plotting these values in graphs such as Figure 2-15, and then observing whether or not (1) the intercept is equal to k_{RF}, (2) the regression line is linear, and (3) the line passes through the

Figure 2-15
Tests of the CAPM

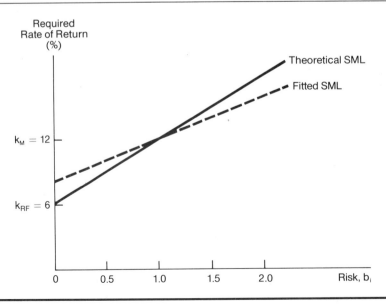

point b $= 1.0$, k_M. Monthly historical rates of return are generally used for the stocks, and both 30-day Treasury bill rates and long-term Treasury bond rates have been used to estimate the value of k_{RF}. Also, most of the studies actually analyze portfolios rather than individual securities because security betas are so unstable.

Before discussing the actual results of the tests, it is critical to recognize that although the CAPM is an ex ante, or forward-looking model, the data used to test it are entirely historical. There is no reason to believe that realized rates of return over past holding periods necessarily reflect expected rates of return such as the model should deal with. Also, historical betas may or may not reflect either current or expected future risk. This lack of ex ante data makes it extremely difficult to test the true CAPM. Still, for what it is worth, here is a summary of the key empirical tests:

1. The evidence generally shows a significant positive relationship between realized returns and systematic risk. However, the slope of the relationship is usually less than that predicted by the CAPM.

2. The relationship between risk and return appears to be linear. Empirical studies give no evidence of significant curvature in the risk/return relationship.

3. Tests that attempt to assess the relative importance of market and company-specific risk do not yield definitive results. The CAPM suggests that company-specific risk is not relevant, yet both kinds of risk appear to be positively related to security returns; that is, higher returns are required to compensate for both diversifiable and market risk. However, it may be that the observed relationships may be at least partly spurious; that is, they may reflect statistical problems rather than the true nature of capital markets.

4. In a very important paper, Richard Roll has questioned whether it is even conceptually possible to test the CAPM.[27] Roll showed that the linear relationship which prior researchers had observed in graphs like Figure 2-15 resulted from the mathematical properties of the models being tested, and hence that a finding of linearity proved nothing whatever about the validity of the CAPM. Roll's work did not disprove the CAPM theory, but he did show that it is virtually impossible to prove that investors behave in accordance with the theory.

5. If the CAPM were completely valid, it should apply to all financial assets, including bonds. In fact, when bonds are introduced into the analysis, they *do not* plot on the SML. This is worrisome, to say the least.

Current Status of the CAPM

The CAPM is extremely appealing at an intellectual level; it is logical and rational, and once someone works through and understands the mathematics, his or her reaction is usually to swallow it hook, line, and sinker. However, doubts begin to arise when one thinks about the assumptions upon which the model is based, and

---

[27]See Richard Roll, "A Critique of the Asset Pricing Theory's Tests," *Journal of Financial Economics*, March 1977, 129-176.

these doubts are as much reinforced as allayed by the empirical tests. Our own views as to the current status of the CAPM are as follows:

1. The CAPM framework, with its focus on market as opposed to total risk, is clearly useful as a way of thinking about the riskiness of assets in general. Thus as a conceptual model the CAPM is of truly fundamental importance.

2. Although the CAPM appears to provide neat, precise answers to important questions about risk and required rates of return, the answers are really quite fuzzy. The simple truth is that we do not know precisely how to measure any of the inputs required to implement the CAPM. These inputs should all be ex ante, yet we have available only ex post data. Further, as we shall see in Chapter 4, historical data such as $\bar{k}_M$, k_{RF}, and betas vary greatly depending on the time period studied and the methods used to estimate them. Thus, although the CAPM may appear precise, its inputs cannot be estimated with any precision at all, and hence estimates of k_i found through use of the CAPM are subject to large errors.

3. Because the CAPM is logical in the sense that it represents the way people who want to maximize returns while minimizing risk ought to behave, assuming they can get all the necessary data, the model is definitely here to stay. Attempts will, of course, be made to improve it and to make it more operational.

4. It is appropriate to think about many financial problems in a CAPM framework. However, it is equally important to recognize the limitations of the CAPM when using it in practice. Again, this point will be made clear in Chapter 4.

ARBITRAGE PRICING THEORY AND OTHER MODELS

The CAPM is a single-factor model. That is, it specifies that risk is a function of only one factor, the covariance between a security's returns and the market returns, or, equivalently, the security's beta coefficient. Perhaps the risk/return relationship is more complex. If so, we might expect a stock's required return to be a function of more than one factor. For example, what if investors, because personal taxes on capital gains are deferred until the stock is sold, value capital gains income more highly than dividend income? Then, for two stocks with the same market risk, the stock paying the higher dividend would have a higher required rate of return. In that case, required return would be a function of both market risk and dividend yield, or two factors.

Going on, what if many factors are required to specify the equilibrium risk/return relationship rather than just one or two? Stephen Ross has proposed an approach called the *Arbitrage Pricing Theory (APT).*[28] The APT can include any number of risk factors, so the required return could be a function of three, four, or even more factors. Unfortunately, the APT does not specify which factors are relevant to the model. Thus, the specification of the model must be determined

---

[28]See Stephen A. Ross, "The Arbitrage Theory of Capital Asset Pricing," *Journal of Economic Theory,* December 1976, 341-360.

empirically, and much of the current APT research is devoted to factor identification. The APT shows promise, and at this point some people consider it to be a leading contender to replace the CAPM. However, much more work is required before the APT can be applied to financial management decisions. We discuss it in more depth in Appendix 2B.

SUMMARY

This chapter concentrated on the concept of risk, especially on its proper definition and measurement. We began by examining *total risk*, which is measured by the degree of dispersion of outcomes around the expected value. The greater the dispersion, the greater the total risk. We introduced several specific total risk measures, including *variance*, *standard deviation*, and *coefficient of variation*. We then looked at the *mean-variance criterion*, which is a method of choosing among risky alternatives when total risk is considered to be the most relevant type of risk. Note, though, that if the screening process does not eliminate all but one alternative, the decision maker must make the final decision on the basis of his or her (or the stockholders') degree of risk aversion. The total risk model gave no precise method for deciding among nondominant alternatives.

Next, we looked at the concept of *market risk*. We saw that the riskiness of an asset held as part of a well-diversified portfolio is not the same as the riskiness of that asset held in isolation. We concentrated on the riskiness of common stocks, but the market risk concept is equally applicable to any asset held in a portfolio. We saw that the riskiness of a given stock can be split into two components: (1) *market risk*, which is caused by changes in the broad stock market and which cannot be eliminated by diversification, and (2) *company-specific*, or *diversifiable, risk*, which can be eliminated by holding a diversified portfolio.

Finally, we examined the *Capital Asset Pricing Model (CAPM)*. Under a very restrictive set of assumptions, the CAPM tells us that market risk, which is the relevant risk, can be measured by the *beta coefficient*, a measure of the tendency of a stock to move with the market. Further, the beta coefficient can be determined by a regression line called the *characteristic line*. Once the beta coefficient is estimated, the *Security Market line (SML)* is used to determine the required rate of return on that asset. Thus, the CAPM provides a specific decision rule by which to evaluate financial decisions: Simply compare the expected rate of return, $\hat{k}_i$, with the required rate of return, k_i, as given by the SML, and buy the stock (or accept the project) if $\hat{k}_i > k_i$. However, we noted (1) that the CAPM has not been verified empirically, and (2) that it requires ex ante, not ex post, data, and ex ante data can only be obtained in a subjective, judgmental manner. Therefore, the CAPM should be used with a great deal of caution.

Problems with the CAPM have lead financial theorists to seek other models to explain the risk/return relationship; the *Arbitrage Pricing Theory (APT)* is one important new development. However, APT has not yet been developed to the point where it can be applied in practice.

The International Perspective

Chapter 2 implicitly focused on the risk and return of domestic investments. Although the same concepts are involved when we move to the international scene, some important differences must also be observed. For example, an international investor must be concerned with sovereign risk and exchange rate risk. *Sovereign risk* is the risk that the sovereign country in which the real assets backing an investment are located will take some action, such as nationalization without adequate compensation, that decreases the value of the investment. InterNorth Corporation, a multibillion dollar U.S.-based energy company, experienced exactly this situation when Peru nationalized an InterNorth subsidiary in 1985, resulting in a sharp drop in InterNorth's stock price.

Sovereign risk is clearly diversifiable, but the second type of international risk, *exchange rate risk*, is less easy to classify. Exchange rate risk refers to the fact that different countries use different currencies, and the values of currencies in relation to one another—exchange rates, or the rates at which U.S. dollars, for example, can be converted into Japanese yen—change over time. To illustrate, in May 1985, the exchange rate between yen and dollars was 251:1, meaning that one dollar could buy 251 yen. In February 1986, just eight months later, the exchange rate had dropped to 180:1. This change, defined as a *decline in the dollar* because a dollar would now buy fewer yen, had a major effect on both U.S. and Japanese firms and investors. First, think of a U.S. investor who had bought $1,000 worth of Sony or Toyota stock, with a yen value of 1,000 × 251 = 251,000. If the yen value of the stock had remained constant at 251,000, its dollar value would have risen from $1,000 to 251,000/180 = $1,394.44, a 39.4 percent increase. Since the dollar fell against most other major currencies, this same experience was repeated in other international capital markets, and as a result, those

U.S. investors who weighted their portfolios heavily with foreign stocks did extremely well in 1985.

Exchange rate fluctuations also affect the real investment returns of U.S. and foreign multinational corporations. For example, IBM has a huge investment in Japan. Let us assume that IBM Japan earned 125 billion yen in 1985, that the exchange rate was 251 yen to the dollar, and hence that the yen profit was *translated* into 125,000,000,000/251 = $498 million, which IBM would report as part of its 1985 net income. Now suppose IBM Japan earned the same yen profit in 1986, but the exchange rate was 180; now the Japanese subsidiary would contribute 125,000,000,000/180 = $694 million, a 39 percent increase. Similar increases would be experienced by IBM's operations in Europe and elsewhere around the globe. Of course, if the value of the dollar returned in 1987 to its 1985 level, IBM's reported profits would decline.

Consider also how exchange rates affect real goods, and hence sales and profits. The decline in the dollar from 251 to 180 yen means that Toyota's yen earnings on a $10,000 auto would decline from 251(10,000) = 2,510,000 to 180(10,000) = 1,800,000. To keep yen income per car constant, Toyota would have to raise the price of its U.S. exports to 2,510,000/180 = $13,944. Thus, the exchange rate shift means that Toyota will either have to boost sharply the price of cars sold in the U.S. or else experience a profit decline. Of course, U.S. auto companies, and other U.S. exporters, will gain from the dollar's decline, as that decline makes U.S. goods more competitive in world markets.

The ability of investors to purchase international financial assets also affects risk/return relationships. To see what is involved, consider Figure 2-16, which shows the Capital Market Line (CML) as we developed it in Figure 2-11. The heavily shaded area represents the feasible set of portfolios

Figure 2-16
Portfolio Analysis with Global Diversification

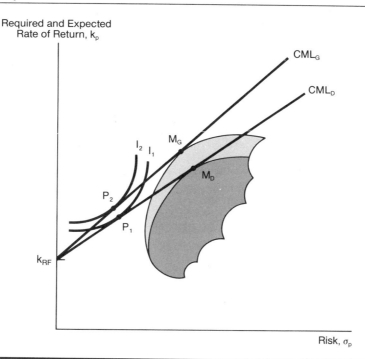

of domestic risky assets; the lightly shaded area represents the addition to the feasible set when international assets are included; k_{RF} represents the rate of return on domestic riskless assets; M_D is the domestic market portfolio; and M_G is the *global market portfolio*, which contains foreign as well as domestic securities. Note that there are no riskless foreign assets: even foreign treasury bills are risky because of exchange rate risk. Since returns on foreign securities are not perfectly correlated with those on domestic securities, the inclusion of foreign assets in the portfolio shifts the boundary (or feasible) set of portfolios upward and to the left. This has the effect of rotating the CML upward, from CML_D to CML_G. This, in turn, permits an investor to move from portfolio P_1, on indifference curve I_1, to portfolio P_2, on the higher indifference curve I_2. P_2 contains a combination of domestic and foreign stocks, plus riskless domestic government securities, and it is better than P_1 in that it provides both a higher expected return and a lower level of risk.

Questions and Problems

2-1   (Basic risk concepts) Suppose you are offered (1) $1 million or (2) a gamble in which you get $2 million if a head is flipped but zero if a tail comes up.

    a. What is the expected value of the gamble?

    b. Would you take the sure $1 million or the gamble?

c. If you take the sure $1 million, are you a risk averter or a risk seeker?

d. Suppose you actually take the $1 million. You can invest it in either a U.S. Treasury bond that will return $1,075,000 at the end of a year or common stock that has a 50-50 chance of being either worthless or worth $2,300,000 at the end of the year.

(1) What is the expected rate of return on the stock investment? The expected rate of return on the bond investment is 7.5 percent.

(2) Would you invest in the bond or the stock?

(3) Just how large would the expected profit and the expected rate of return on the stock investment have to be to make *you* invest in the stock?

(4) How might your decision be affected if, rather than buying one stock for $1 million, you could construct a portfolio consisting of 100 stocks with $10,000 in each? Each of these stocks has the same return characteristics as the one stock, that is, a 50-50 chance of being worth either zero or $23,000 at year end. Would the correlation of returns on these stocks matter?

2-2 (Basic risk concepts) A life insurance policy is a financial asset with the premium paid being the cost of the asset. In a term policy, you buy pure protection: if you die, your beneficiary collects the face amount of the policy. Assume that you buy a one-year term policy.

a. How do you calculate the expected return on the policy?

b. Suppose the policyholder has no other assets other than his or her "human capital," or future earnings capacity. What is the correlation between returns on the policy and returns on the holder's human capital?

c. Life insurance companies have administrative costs to cover; hence, the expected return to the holder must be low or even negative. Use the portfolio concept to explain why people still buy life insurance.

2-3 (Total risk analysis) The Miller Corporation is considering three possible capital projects for next year. Each project has a 1-year life, and project returns depend on next year's state of the economy. The estimated rates of return are shown in the table:

State of the Economy	Probability of Each State Occurring	Rates of Return If State Occurs		
		A	B	C
Recession	0.25	10%	9%	14%
Average	0.50	14	13	12
Boom	0.25	16	18	10

a. Find each project's expected rate of return, variance, standard deviation, and coefficient of variation.

b. Apply the mean-variance criterion to the alternative projects. Do any of the projects dominate any of the others according to this criterion?

2-4 (Portfolio effects and market risk analysis) Refer to the three alternative projects contained in Problem 2-3. Assume that the Miller Corporation is going to invest one-third of its available funds in each project. That is, Miller will create a portfolio of three equally weighted projects.

a. What is the expected rate of return on the portfolio?

b. What are the variance and standard deviation of the portfolio?

c. What are the covariance and correlation coefficient between Projects A and B? Between Project A and C?

      d. Assume that Project A in Problem 2-3 represents "the market." What is the beta of Project B? Of Project C?

2-5 **(Total and market risk analysis)** As a financial analyst at White Electronics you are conducting an analysis of four investment alternatives. Each alternative has a holding period of one year. The estimated rates of return for the three alternative states of the economy are shown in the table:

State of the Economy	Probability of Each State Occurring	Rates of Return If State Occurs			
		A	B	C	M
Recession	0.20	10%	6%	22%	5%
Average	0.60	10	11	14	15
Boom	0.20	10	31	−4	25

      a. Determine each alternative's expected rate of return, variance, standard deviation, and coefficient of variation.

      b. Is Alternative A riskless?

      c. Your boss, the firm's financial manager, has asked you to assess the *total risk* of the four investment alternatives. Also, he requested that you apply the mean-variance criterion to determine whether any of the alternatives can be eliminated. What is your response?

      d. After performing the preceding analyses, you realize that the entire risk analysis was based on the total risk of the proposed alternatives. You believe it is appropriate to perform a market, or systematic, risk analysis. Alternative M is a broadly diversified mutual fund, so M can be used as a proxy for the market. Find the beta of each alternative, and then use the SML to evaluate the alternatives.

2-6 **(Market risk analysis)** The Little Company has developed the following data regarding the rates of return available on a potential project and the market:

State of the Economy	Probability of Each State Occurring	Rates of Return If State Occurs	
		Market	Project
Deep recession	0.05	−20%	−30%
Mild recession	0.25	10	5
Average	0.35	15	20
Mild boom	0.20	20	25
Strong boom	0.15	25	30

Further, Little's financial analysts estimate the risk-free rate at 8 percent.

      a. What are the expected rates of return on the market and the project?

      b. What is the market's beta? The project's?

      c. What is the required rate of return on the project according to the CAPM?

      d. Should the project be accepted?

2-7 **(Market versus total risk)** Your eccentric uncle just died and you inherited $100,000. However, the will stipulated that the entire amount must be invested in common stocks. Specifically, $50,000 must be invested in a single stock (1-stock portfolio) and the other $50,000 must be invested in a 100-stock portfolio. You are very risk averse, and hence want to minimize the riskiness of each $50,000 investment.

a. How would you choose your single-stock portfolio?

b. How would you choose the stocks in your 100-stock portfolio?

c. Should you view the riskiness of your one-stock portfolio in isolation, or should you consider the fact that you actually own 101 stocks?

2-8 **(Realized rates of return and portfolio effects)** Stocks A and B have the following historical dividend and price data:

Year	Stock A		Stock B	
	Dividend	Year-End Price	Dividend	Year-End Price
1981	—	$22.50	—	$43.75
1982	$2.00	16.00	$3.40	35.50
1983	2.20	17.00	3.65	38.75
1984	2.40	20.25	3.90	51.75
1985	2.60	17.25	4.05	44.50
1986	2.95	18.75	4.25	45.25

a. Calculate the realized rate of return (or holding period return) for each stock in each year. Then assume that someone had held a portfolio consisting of 50 percent of A and 50 percent of B. What would be the realized rate of return on the portfolio in each year from 1982 through 1986? What are the average returns for each stock and for the portfolio?

b. Now calculate the standard deviation of returns for each stock and for the portfolio.

c. On the basis of the extent to which the portfolio has a lower risk than the stocks held individually, would you guess that the correlation coefficient between returns on the two stocks is closer to 0.9, 0.0, or -0.9?

d. If you added more stocks at random to the portfolio, what is the most accurate statement of what would happen to σ_p?

　　(1) σ_p would remain constant.

　　(2) σ_p would decline to somewhere in the vicinity of 15 percent.

　　(3) σ_p would decline to zero if enough stocks were included.

2-9 **(Security Market Line)** Suppose $k_{RF} = 10\%$, $k_M = 14\%$, and $b_A = 1.4$.

a. What is k_A, the required rate of return on Stock A?

b. Now suppose k_{RF} (1) increases to 11 percent or (2) decreases to 9 percent. The slope of the SML remains constant. How will this affect k_M and k_A?

c. Now assume k_{RF} remains at 10 percent, but k_M (1) increases to 15 percent or (2) falls to 12 percent. The slope of the SML does *not* remain constant. How will this affect k_A?

d. Now assume that k_{RF} remains at 10 percent and k_M at 14 percent, but beta (1) rises to 1.6 or (2) falls to 0.75. How will this affect k_A?

2-10 **(Portfolio beta and Security Market Line)** The Super Growth Investment Fund has a total investment of $400 million in five stocks:

Stock	Investment	Stock's Beta Coefficient
A	$120 million	0.5
B	100 million	2.0
C	60 million	4.0
D	80 million	1.0
E	40 million	3.0

The beta coefficient for a fund such as this can be found as a weighted average of the betas of the fund's investments. The current risk-free rate is 7 percent, and the expected market return, $\hat{k}_M$, has the following probability distribution for the next period:

Probability	Market Return
0.1	8%
0.2	10
0.4	12
0.2	14
0.1	16

a. What is the estimated equation for the Security Market Line (SML)?

b. Compute the required rate of return on the Super Growth Fund for the next period.

c. Suppose management receives a proposal for a new stock. The investment needed to take a position in the stock is $50 million; it will have an expected return of 16 percent; and its estimated beta coefficient is 2.5. Should the new stock be purchased? At what expected rate of return would management be indifferent to purchasing the stock?

2-11 (Characteristic line and Security Market Line) You are given the following set of data:

	Historical Rates of Return	
Year	Stock X	NYSE
1	−14.0%	−26.5%
2	23.0	37.2
3	17.5	23.8
4	2.0	−7.2
5	8.1	6.6
6	19.4	20.5
7	18.2	30.6

a. Use a calculator with a linear regression function (or the computerized diskette) to determine Stock X's beta coefficient, or plot these data points on a scatter diagram, draw in the regression line, and then estimate the value of the beta coefficient.

b. Determine the arithmetic average rates of return for Stock X and the NYSE over the period given. Calculate the standard deviation of returns for both Stock X and the NYSE.

c. Assuming (1) that the situation during Years 1 to 7 is expected to hold true in the future (that is, $\hat{k}_X = \bar{k}_X$; $\hat{k}_M = \bar{k}_M$; and both σ_X and b_X in the future will equal their past values), and (2) that Stock X is in equilibrium (that is, it plots on the Security Market Line), what is the risk-free rate?

d. Plot the Security Market Line.

e. Suppose you hold a large, well-diversified portfolio and are considering adding to the portfolio either Stock X or another stock, Stock Y, that has the same beta as Stock X but a higher standard deviation of returns. Stocks X and Y have the same expected returns; that is, $\hat{k}_X = \hat{k}_Y = 10.6\%$. Which stock should you choose?

2-12 (Characteristic line) You are given the following set of data:

	Historical Rates of Return	
Year	NYSE	Stock Y
1	4.0%	3.0%
2	14.3	18.2
3	19.0	9.1
4	−14.7	−6.0
5	−26.5	−15.3
6	37.2	33.1
7	23.8	6.1
8	−7.2	3.2
9	6.6	14.8
10	20.5	24.1
11	30.6	18.0
Mean =	9.8%	9.8%
σ =	19.6%	13.8%

a. Construct a scatter diagram showing the relationship between returns on Stock Y and the market, and then draw a freehand approximation of the regression line. What is the approximate value of the beta coefficient? If you have a calculator with a linear regression function or the computerized diskette, check the approximate value of beta obtained from the graph.

b. Give a verbal interpretation of what the regression line and the beta coefficient show about Stock Y's volatility and relative riskiness as compared to those of other stocks.

c. Suppose the scatter of points had been more spread out, but the regression line was exactly where your present graph shows it. How would this affect (1) the firm's risk if the stock is held in a one-asset portfolio and (2) the actual risk premium on the stock if the CAPM holds exactly?

d. Suppose the regression line had been downward-sloping and the beta coefficient had been negative. What would this imply about (1) Stock Y's relative riskiness, (2) its correlation with the market, and (3) its probable risk premium?

e. Construct an illustrative probability distribution graph of returns on portfolios consisting of (1) only Stock Y, (2) 1 percent each of 100 stocks with beta coefficients similar to that of Stock Y, and (3) all stocks (that is, the distribution of returns on the market). Use as the expected rate of return the arithmetic mean as given previously for both Stock Y and the market and assume that the distributions are normal. Are the expected returns "reasonable"; that is, is it reasonable for $\hat{k}_Y = \hat{k}_M = 9.8\%$?

2-13 (Efficient frontier) An investor plans to invest in Stock A, Stock B, or some combination of the two stocks. The expected rate of return for A is 9 percent and $\sigma_A = 4\%$; the expected rate of return for B is 10 percent and $\sigma_B = 5\%$; $r_{AB} = 0.5$.

a. Construct a table giving $\hat{k}_p$ and σ_p for 100 percent, 75 percent, 50 percent, 25 percent, and 0 percent investment in Stock A. (Hint: For x = 75%, $\hat{k}_p$ = 9.25% and σ_p = 3.78%; for x = 50%, $\hat{k}_p$ = 9.5% and σ_p = 3.91%.)

b. Use your calculated $\hat{k}_p$ and σ_p values to graph the attainable set of portfolios, and indicate which part of the attainable set is efficient.

c. Using hypothetical indifference curves, show how an investor might choose a portfolio consisting of Stocks A and B.

2-14 (Capital Market Line) Stock A has an expected rate of return $\hat{k}_A = 10\%$ and $\sigma_A = 10\%$. Stock B has $\hat{k}_B = 14\%$ and $\sigma_B = 15\%$. $r_{AB} = 0$. The rate of return on riskless assets is 6 percent.

    a. Construct a graph that shows the feasible and efficient sets, giving consideration to the existence of the riskless asset.

    b. Explain what would happen to the CML if the two stocks had (1) a positive correlation coefficient or (2) a negative correlation coefficient. Assume everything else is held constant.

    c. Suppose these were the *only* three securities (A, B, and riskless) in the economy, and *everyone's* indifference curves were such that they were tangent to the CML *to the right* of the point where the CML was tangent to the efficient set of risky assets. Would this represent a stable equilibrium? If not, how would an equilibrium be produced?

2-15 (SML and CML comparison) The beta coefficient of an asset can be expressed as a function of the asset's correlation with the market as follows:

$$b_i = \frac{r_{iM}\sigma_i}{\sigma_M}.$$

    a. Substitute this expression for beta into the Security Market Line (SML), Equation 2-11. This results in an alternate form of the SML.

    b. Compare your answer to Part a with the Capital Market Line (CML), Equation 2-10. What similarities are observed? What conclusions can be drawn?

2-16 (Capital Asset Pricing Model) You are planning to invest $200,000. Two securities, A and B, are available, and you can invest in either of them or in a portfolio with some of each. Returns on A and B have a correlation coefficient of $r_{AB} = -0.5$. You estimate that the following probability distributions of returns are applicable for A and B:

Security A		Security B	
P_A	k_A	P_B	k_B
0.1	-10%	0.1	-30%
0.2	5	0.2	0
0.4	15	0.4	20
0.2	25	0.2	40
0.1	40	0.1	70

    a. The expected return for Security B is $\hat{k}_B = 20\%$, and $\sigma_B = 25.7\%$. Find $\hat{k}_A$ and σ_A.

    b. Find the value of x that produces the minimum risk portfolio. (Hint: Use the formula given in Footnote 12.)

    c. Construct a table giving $\hat{k}_p$ and σ_p for portfolios with x = 1.00, 0.75, 0.50, 0.25, 0.0, and the minimum risk value of x. (Hint: for x = 0.75, $\hat{k}_p = 16.25\%$ and $\sigma_p = 8.5\%$; for x = 0.50, $\hat{k}_p = 17.5\%$ and $\sigma_p = 11.1\%$; for x = 0.25, $\hat{k}_p = 18.75\%$ and $\sigma_p = 17.9\%$.)

    d. Graph the feasible set of portfolios and identify the efficient section of the feasible set.

    e. Suppose your risk/return trade-off function, or indifference curve, is tangent to the efficient set at the point where $\hat{k}_p = 18\%$. Use this information, plus the graph constructed in Part d, to locate (approximately) your optimal portfolio. Draw in a reasonable indifference curve, indicate the percentage of your funds invested in each security, and determine the optimal portfolio's σ_p and $\hat{k}_p$. (Hint: Estimate σ_p and $\hat{k}_p$ graphically and then use the equation for $\hat{k}_p$ to determine x.)

f. Now suppose a riskless asset with a return $k_{RF} = 10\%$ becomes available. How would this change the investment opportunity set? Explain why the investment opportunity set becomes linear.

g. Given the indifference curve in Part e, would you change your portfolio? If so, how? (Hint: Assume the indifference curves are parallel.)

h. What are the beta coefficients of Stocks A and B? [Hints: (1) Recognize that $k_i = k_{RF} + b_i(k_M - k_{RF})$ and solve for b_i and (2) assume that your preferences match those of most other investors.]

Selected Additional References

Probably the best sources of additional information on probability distributions and single-asset risk measures are statistics textbooks. For example, see

McClave, James T., and P. George Benson, *Statistics for Business and Economics* (San Francisco: Dellen, 1982).

Mendenhall, William, Richard L. Schaeffer, and Dennis D. Wackerly, *Mathematical Statistics with Applications* (Boston: Duxbury, 1981).

For an excellent discussion of the mean-variance criterion and stochastic dominance, see

Levy, Haim, and Marshall Sarnat, *Portfolio and Investment Selection* (Englewood Cliffs, N. J.: Prentice-Hall, 1984).

Probably the best place to find an extension of portfolio theory concepts is one of the investments textbooks. These are some good recent ones:

Francis, Jack C., *Investments: Analysis and Management* (New York: McGraw-Hill, 1980).

Radcliffe, Robert C., *Investment: Concepts, Analysis, and Strategy* (Glenview, Ill.: Scott, Foresman, 1987).

Reilly, Frank K., *Investment Analysis and Portfolio Management* (Hinsdale, Ill.: Dryden, 1985).

Sharpe, William F., *Investments* (Englewood Cliffs, N.J.: Prentice-Hall, 1985).

Those who want to start at the beginning in studying portfolio theory and the CAPM should see

Lintner, John, "Security Prices, Risk, and Maximal Gains from Diversification," *Journal of Finance*, December 1965, 587-616.

Markowitz, Harry M., "Portfolio Selection," *Journal of Finance*, March 1952, 77-91.

Mossin, Jan, "Security Pricing and Investment Criteria in Competitive Markets," *American Economic Review*, December 1969, 749-756.

Sharpe, William F., "Capital Asset Prices: A Theory of Market Equilibrium under Conditions of Risk," *Journal of Finance*, September 1964, 425-442.

Literally thousands of articles providing theoretical extensions and tests of the CAPM theory have appeared in finance journals. Some of the more important earlier papers are contained in a book compiled by Jensen:

Jensen, Michael C., ed., *Studies in the Theory of Capital Markets* (New York: Praeger, 1972).

However, the validity of the empirical tests has been questioned; see

Roll, Richard, "A Critique of the Asset Pricing Theory's Tests," *Journal of Financial Economics*, March 1977, 129-176.

Wallace, Anise, "Is Beta Dead?" *Institutional Investor*, July 1980, 23-30.

For a very readable discussion of Arbitrage Pricing Theory, see

Bower, Dorothy H., Richard S. Bower, and Dennis E. Logue, "A Primer on Arbitrage Pricing Theory," *Midland Corporate Finance Journal*, Fall 1984, 31-40.

Additional references concerning the use of the CAPM are given in Chapters 4 and 9.

# 2A
CONTINUOUS PROBABILITY DISTRIBUTIONS

In Chapter 2, we illustrated risk/return concepts using discrete distributions, and we assumed that only five states of the economy could exist. In reality, however, the state of the economy can range from a deep recession to a fantastic boom, and there are an infinite number of possibilities in between. It is inconvenient to work with a large number of outcomes using discrete distributions, but it is relatively easy to deal with such situations with *continuous distributions*, since they can be completely specified by only two or three summary statistics such as the mean, standard deviation, and a measure of skewness. In the past, financial managers did not have the tools necessary to use continuous distributions in practical risk analyses. Now, however, most firms except very small ones have access to computers and powerful software packages, such as the *Interactive Financial Planning System (IFPS)*, which can analyze continuous distributions. Thus, if financial risk analysis is computerized, as is increasingly the case, it is often preferable to use continuous distributions to express the distribution of outcomes.[1]

Uniform Distribution

One continuous distribution that is often used in financial planning models is the *uniform distribution*, in which each possible outcome has the same probability of occurrence as any other outcome; hence, there is no clustering of values. Figure 2A-1 shows two uniform distributions.

Distribution A of Figure 2A-1 has a range of -5 to $+15$ percent. Therefore, the absolute size of the range is 20 units. Since the entire area under the density function must equal 1.00, the height of the distribution, h, must be 0.05: 20h = 1.0, so h = 1/20 = 0.05. We can use this information to find the probability of different outcomes. For example, suppose we want to find the probability that the rate of return will be less than zero. The probability is the area under the density function from -5 to 0 percent; that is, the shaded area:

$$\text{Area} = [\text{Right point} - \text{Left point}][\text{Height of distribution}]$$
$$= [0 - (-5)][0.05] = 0.25 = 25\%.$$

Similarly, the probability of a rate of return between 5 and 15 is 50 percent:

$$\text{Probability} = \text{Area} = [15 - 5][0.05] = 0.50 = 50\%.$$

The expected rate of return is the midpoint of the range, or 5 percent, for both Distribution A and Distribution B in Figure 2A-1. Since there is a smaller probability of the actual return falling very far below the expected return in Distribution B, we would say that Distribution B depicts a less risky situation.

---

[1]Computerized risk analysis techniques are discussed in detail in Chapter 9.

Figure 2A-1
Uniform Probability Distributions

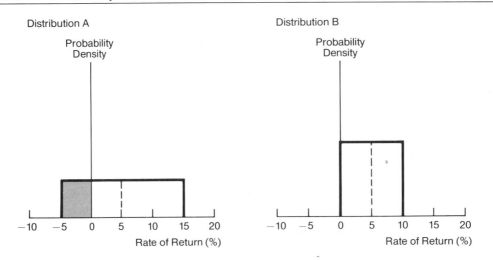

Note: The expected rate of return for both distributions is $\hat{k}$ = 5%.

Triangular Distribution

Another useful continuous distribution is the *triangular distribution*. This type of distribution, which is illustrated in Figure 2A-2, has a clustering of values around the most likely outcome, and the probability of occurrence declines in each direction from the most likely outcome. Distribution C has a range of −5 to +15 percent and a most likely return of +10 percent. Distribution D has a most likely return of 5 percent, but its range is only from 0 to +10 percent. Note that Distribution C is skewed to the left, while Distribution D is symmetrical. The expected rate of return for Distribution C could be calculated, and it would turn out to be 7.25 percent, whereas that of D is only 5 percent.[2] However, it is obvious by inspection that Distribution C is riskier: its dispersion about the mean is greater than that for Distribution D, and it has a significant chance of actual losses, whereas losses are not possible in Distribution D.

Normal Distribution

Because it is discussed so much in statistics courses, is so easy to use, and conforms well to so many real-world situations, the most commonly used continuous distribution is the *normal distribution*. It is symmetric about the expected value, and its tails extend out to plus and minus infinity. Figure 2A-3 is a normal distribution with an

---

[2]Note that the most likely outcome equals the expected outcome only when the distribution is symmetric. If the distribution is skewed to the left, the expected outcome falls to the left of the most likely outcome, and vice versa.

Figure 2A-2
Triangular Probability Distributions

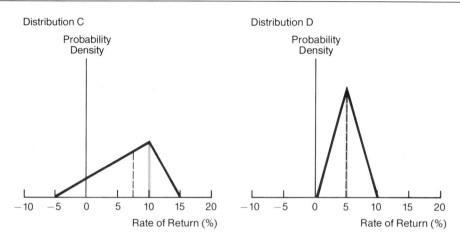

Note: The most likely rate of return is 10 percent for Distribution C and 5 percent for Distribution D; the expected rates of return are $\hat{k}_C = 7.25\%$ and $\hat{k}_D = 5\%$.

Figure 2A-3
Normal Probability Distribution

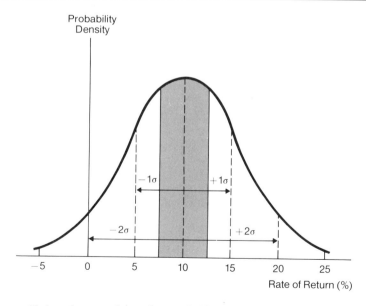

Note: The most likely and expected rate of return is 10 percent.

expected, or mean (μ, pronounced "mu"), rate of return of 10 percent and a standard deviation (σ, or sigma) of 5 percent. Approximately 68.3 percent of the area under any normal curve lies within $\pm 1\sigma$ of its mean, 95.5 percent lies within $\pm 2\sigma$, and 99.7 percent lies within $\pm 3\sigma$. Therefore, the probability of actually achieving a rate of return within the range of 5 to 15 percent ($\mu \pm 1\sigma$) is 68.3 percent, and so forth. Obviously, the smaller the standard deviation, the smaller the probability of the actual outcome deviating very much from the expected value, hence the smaller the risk of the investment.

If we want to find the probability that an outcome will fall between 7.5 and 12.5 percent, we must calculate the area beneath the curve between these points, or the shaded area in Figure 2A-3. This area can be determined by integration or, more easily, by the use of statistical tables of the area under the normal curve.[3] To use the tables, we first use the following formula to standardize the distribution:

$$z = \frac{x - \mu}{\sigma}. \tag{2A-1}$$

Here z is the standardized variable, or the number of standard deviations from the mean; x is the outcome of interest; and μ and σ are the mean and standard deviation of the distribution, respectively.[4] In our example, we are interested in the probability that an outcome will fall between 7.5 and 12.5 percent. Since the mean of the distribution is 10, and it is between the two points of interest, we must evaluate and then combine two probabilities, one to the left and one to the right of the mean. We first normalize these points by using Equation 2A-1:

$$z_{\text{Left}} = \frac{7.5 - 10}{5} = -0.5; \; z_{\text{Right}} = \frac{12.5 - 10}{5} = +0.5.$$

The areas associated with these z values as found in Table 2A-1 are 0.1915 and 0.1915.[5] This means that the probability is 0.1915 that the actual outcome will fall between 7.5 and 10 percent and also 0.1915 that it will fall between 10 and 12.5 percent. Thus, the probability that the outcome will fall between 7.5 and 12.5 percent is 0.1915 + 0.1915 = 0.3830, or 38.3 percent.

Suppose we are interested in determining the probability that the actual outcome will be less than zero. We first determine that the probability is 0.4773 that the outcome will be between 0 and 10 percent and then observe that the probability of an outcome less than the mean, 10, is 0.5000. Thus, the probability of an outcome less than zero is 0.5000 − 0.4773 = 0.0227, or 2.27 percent.

---

[3]The equation for the normal curve is tedious to integrate, thus making the use of tables much more convenient. The equation for the normal curve is

$$f(x) = \frac{1}{\sqrt{2\pi\sigma^2}} e^{-(x - \mu)^2/2\sigma^2},$$

where π and e are mathematical constants; μ and σ denote the expected value, or mean, and standard deviation of the probability distribution; and x is any possible outcome.

[4]Note that if the point of interest is 1σ away from the mean, then $x - \mu = \sigma$, so $z = \sigma/\sigma = 1.0$. Thus, when $z = 1.0$, the point of interest is 1σ away from the mean; when $z = 2$, the deviation is 2σ; and so forth.

[5]Note that the negative sign on z_{Left} is ignored. Since the normal curve is symmetric around the mean, the minus sign merely indicates that the point of interest lies to the left of the mean.

Table 2A-1
Area under the Normal Curve

z	Area from the Mean to the Point of Interest
0.0	0.0000
0.5	0.1915
1.0	0.3413
1.5	0.4332
2.0	0.4773
2.5	0.4938
3.0	0.4987

Note: Here z is the number of standard deviations from the mean. Some area tables are set up to indicate the area to the left or right of the indicated z values, but in our table, we indicate the area between the mean and the z value. Thus, the area from the mean to either $+0.5$ or -0.5 is 0.1915, or 19.15 percent of the total area or probability. A more complete set of values can be found in Table A-5 at the end of the book.

Using Continuous Distributions

Continuous distributions are generally used in financial analysis in the following manner:

1. Someone with a good knowledge of a particular situation is asked to specify the most applicable type of distribution and its parameters. For example, a company's marketing manager might be asked to supply this information for sales of a given product, or an engineer might be asked to estimate the construction costs of a capital project.

2. A financial analyst could then use these input data to help evaluate the riskiness of a given decision. For example, the analyst might conclude that the probability is 50 percent that the actual rate of return on a project will be between 5 and 10 percent, that the probability of a loss (negative rate of return) on the project is 15 percent, or that the probability of a return greater than 10 percent is 25 percent. Generally, such an analysis would be done by using a computer program. We shall return to this topic in Chapter 9.

Since the normal distribution is symmetric, we could use the normal curve to approximate the distribution of Project 2 in Table 2-1 in Chapter 2; this is given in Figure 2A-4. Here we show an expected rate of return of 12.0 percent, with the bulk of the distribution lying between 0 and 24.0 percent. Although outcomes less than -6 percent or more than 30 percent have a very low probability of occurrence, there is still some chance that they will occur in our normal distribution approximation.

Figure 2A-5 contains triangular distribution approximations for Projects 1 and 2, whose discrete distributions are also given in Table 2-1 in Chapter 2. We constructed the triangular distributions such that the most likely value is 10.3 percent for Project 1 and 12.0 percent for Project 2. Note that triangular distributions can be used to approximate either symmetrical or skewed distributions. Also, in contrast to the normal distribution, we see that values exceeding certain limits, say below -5.0 percent or above 21 percent for Project 1, are not permitted. Thus, using a symmetric triangular distribution as an alternative to a normal distribution enables us to place absolute limits on the set of attainable values.

Figure 2A-4
Project 2 as a Normal Distribution

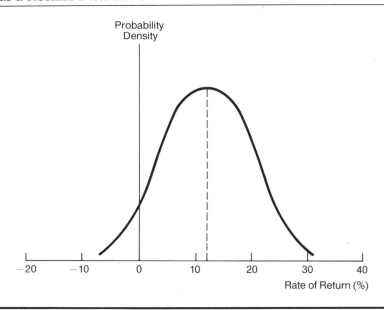

Figure 2A-5
Projects 1 and 2 as Triangular Distributions

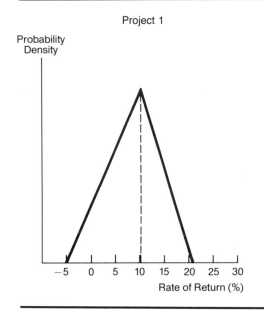

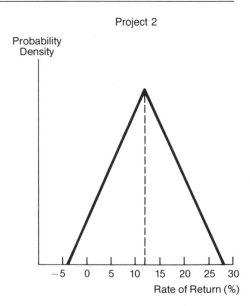

In theory, we should use the specific distribution that best represents the true situation. Sometimes the true distribution is known, but with most financial data, it is not known. For example, we might think that interest rates could range from 8 to 15 percent next year, with a most likely value of 10 percent. This suggests a triangular distribution. Or we might think that interest rates next year can best be represented by a normal distribution, with a mean of 10 percent and a standard deviation of 2.5 percent. The point is, there is simply no type of distribution that is always "best"; you need to be familiar with different types of distributions and their properties, and then you must select the best distribution for the problem at hand.

 # 2B

ARBITRAGE PRICING THEORY

As noted in Chapter 2, the CAPM has several weaknesses, including (1) the fact that it is based on some unrealistic assumptions, (2) the argument raised by Roll that it cannot be tested empirically, and (3) the fact that the CAPM assumes that a stock's required return is based on only one factor (the general stock market) whereas in fact other factors, such as relative sensitivity to inflation and dividend payout, may also influence a stock's returns relative to those of other stocks. The *Arbitrage Pricing Theory (APT)* is designed to help overcome these weaknesses. We should note at the outset that the APT is based on complex mathematical and statistical theory which goes far beyond the scope of this text. However, the APT model is widely discussed in the current academic literature, and it is being recommended in practitioner-oriented journals for such uses as measuring the cost of equity. Actual usage to date is extremely limited, but it may increase, so students of finance should at least have an intuitive idea of what APT is all about.

The CAPM states that each stock's required return is equal to the risk-free rate plus its beta coefficient times the market risk premium:

$$k_i = k_{RF} + b_i(k_M - k_{RF}). \qquad \text{(2B-1)}$$

The realized return, $\bar{k}_i$, will actually turn out to be

$$\bar{k}_i = \hat{k}_i + b_i(\bar{k}_M - \hat{k}_M) + e_i; \qquad \text{(2B-2)}$$

that is, the realized return, $\bar{k}_i$, will be equal to the expected return, $\hat{k}_i$, plus an increment or decrement, $b_i(\bar{k}_M - \hat{k}_M)$, whose magnitude depends on the stock's sensitivity to market returns, b_i, and the realized excess or shortfall in the market return, plus a random error term, e_i.

The market return, $\bar{k}_M$, is actually determined by a number of factors, including economic activity as measured by gross national product (GNP), the strength of the world economy, the level of inflation, changes in tax laws, and so forth. Further, different groups of stocks are affected in different ways by these fundamental factors. Thus, rather than specifying the stock's returns as a function of one factor (returns on the market), one could specify required and realized returns of individual stocks to be a function of various fundamental economic factors. If this were done, we would transform Equation 2B-2 into 2B-3:

$$\bar{k}_i = \hat{k}_i + b_{i1}(\bar{F}_1 - \hat{F}_1) + \cdots + b_{ij}(\bar{F}_j - \hat{F}_j) + e_i, \qquad \textbf{(2B-3)}$$

where

$\bar{k}_i$ = the realized rate of return on Stock i.

$\hat{k}_i$ = the expected rate of return on Stock i.

b_{ij} = the sensitivity of Stock i to economic Factor j.

$\bar{F}_j$ = the realized value of economic Factor j.

$\hat{F}_j$ = the expected value of Factor j.

e_i = the effect of unique events on the realized return of Stock i.

Equation 2B-3 shows that the realized return on any stock is equal to the stock's expected return plus increments or decrements which depend on (1) changes in fundamental economic factors, (2) the sensitivity of the stock to these changes, plus (3) a random term which reflects changes in those factors unique to the firm or industry.

Certain stocks or groups of stocks are most sensitive to Factor 1, others to Factor 2, and so forth, and every portfolio's returns would depend on what happened to the different fundamental factors. Theoretically, one could construct a portfolio such that (1) the portfolio was riskless and (2) its net investment was zero (some stocks were sold short, with the proceeds from the short sales being used to buy the stocks held long). Such a portfolio would have to have a zero expected return, or else arbitrage operations would occur, which in turn would cause the prices of the underlying assets to change until the portfolio's expected return was zero. Using some complex mathematics and assumptions similar to those used to derive the CAPM relationships, plus the short sales assumption, the APT equivalent of the CAPM's Security Market Line can be developed from Equation 2B-3:[1]

$$\hat{k}_i = k_i = k_{RF} + b_{i1}(\lambda_1 - k_{RF}) + \cdots + b_{ij}(\lambda_j - k_{RF}). \qquad \textbf{(2B-4)}$$

Here λ_j is the required rate of return on a portfolio with unit sensitivity to the jth economic factor ($b_j = 1.0$) and zero sensitivity to all other factors. Thus, for example, ($\lambda_2 - k_{RF}$) is the risk premium on a portfolio with $b_2 = 1.0$ and all other $b_j = 0.0$. Note that Equation 2B-4 is identical in form to the SML, but it permits a stock's required return to be a function of multiple factors.

The APT has several advantages over the CAPM:

1. It requires fewer and less restrictive assumptions about the distribution of returns on stocks. (CAPM assumes that expected returns on stocks are normally distributed; APT permits any returns distribution.)

2. APT does not require strong assumptions about investors' utility functions.

---

[1]See Thomas E. Copeland and J. Fred Weston, *Financial Theory and Corporate Policy* (Reading, Mass.: Addison-Wesley, 1983).

3. It is not necessary to measure the return on the market portfolio (which gets around Roll's argument that the CAPM is untestable because the market portfolio is not measurable).

However, the APT also has some disadvantages:

1. In addition to many of the CAPM's assumptions about perfect markets, APT also assumes the possibility of unlimited short sales and the ability to net short sale proceeds against long purchases of stocks, and hence to create a portfolio with zero investment.

2. The fundamental factors are not actually specified. Researchers use a complex statistical procedure (factor analysis) to categorize stocks into groups whose returns (1) move up and down together but (2) are uncorrelated with returns movements in other stock groups. Presumably, the stocks in each group are affected by some "factor," but this factor cannot be identified with real precision.

3. The CAPM has been around a long time, and its implementation problems (for example, difficulties in measuring ex ante betas and in testing the model for empirical validity) are well known. The APT is new, and hence it has not been examined as closely, but when it is, the same kinds of implementation problems are likely to surface.

4. Finally, the CAPM is intuitively appealing, but the APT is not intuitively clear, and no one (to our knowledge) has figured out a way to explain it to practitioners. Until a clear explanation is forthcoming, the APT is not likely to be used by real-world decision makers.

3
VALUATION CONCEPTS AND MODELS

The primary goal of management is to maximize the value of the firm's stock, and because of this, the valuation process lies at the heart of financial management. We discussed in Chapter 2 how risk and return are measured and how they influence security prices. Now we extend our analysis to show how investors estimate future cash flows and then use them to help find the value of the firm's securities. Because corporate managers make decisions which influence cash flows to investors, they must understand how investors evaluate securities and, hence, respond to managerial actions.

GENERAL VALUATION MODEL

Since the values of all financial assets stem from streams of expected cash flows, all such assets are valued in essentially the same way: (1) The cash flow stream must be estimated; this involves finding both the expected cash flow for each period and the riskiness of each cash flow. (2) The required rate of return for each cash flow is established; these rates could be constant over time, or different rates might be required for each cash flow. (3) Each cash flow is discounted by its required rate of return, and these present values are then summed to find the value of the asset. Equation 3-1 formalizes this process:[1]

$$V_0 = \frac{CF_1}{(1 + k_1)^1} + \frac{CF_2}{(1 + k_2)^2} + \ldots + \frac{CF_t}{(1 + k_t)^t} + \ldots + \frac{CF_n}{(1 + k_n)^n} \quad (3\text{-}1)$$

$$= \sum_{t=1}^{n} \frac{CF_t}{(1 + k_t)^t}.$$

Here V_0 is the current, or present, value of the asset; CF_t is the expected cash flow at Time t; k_t is the required rate of return for each period's cash flow; and n is the number of periods over which cash flows are expected to be generated. If the cash

---

[1]Equation 3-1 is presented in *risk-adjusted discount rate* format. Later, in Chapter 9, we will see that assets can also be valued by the *certainty equivalent* method.

flow stream exhibits certain regularities, and if the required rate of return is constant, then Equation 3-1 can be reduced to simpler forms. We will examine both the general case set forth in Equation 3-1 and several simpler reduced forms later in the chapter.

We should note that the basic valuation model can be applied to physical assets as well as to securities. *Physical assets* are such properties as land, buildings, equipment, and even whole businesses. *Securities* are pieces of paper which represent claims against physical assets. Moreover, business securities are generally broken down into three primary classes: (1) *debt*, which is a contractual obligation calling for specific payments; (2) *preferred stock*, which is also contractual in nature but which has a claim to income and assets after the firm's debt; and (3) *common stock*, which represents ownership and which has a residual claim to all income and assets after the claims of debtholders and preferred stockholders have been satisfied.

There are also variations within each of the primary types of business securities. For example, there is long-term and short-term debt, and some debt calls for periodic interest payments during its life and then a return of the principal in a lump sum at maturity, whereas other debt calls for amortization of the principal over the life of the debt. Some debt calls for fixed interest payments; other debt calls for a variable rate of interest, or even for payment in gold, silver, or oil rather than money. Some debt (and preferred stock) is convertible into common stock; some is backed by a mortgage on specific assets; and some is backed only by the firm's general credit strength.

Each of these variations calls for a somewhat different application of Equation 3-1. Indeed, since firms (and investment bankers) have created an almost limitless variety of securities, with new ones being created every day, one could spend his or her career developing variations of the basic equation. However, at this point, we shall deal with models for the three basic securities—bonds, preferred stock, and common stock. Later in the book, we shall go on to physical asset valuation (capital budgeting) and also to such special cases as option securities and leases.

BOND VALUATION

A *bond* generally provides a fixed stream of interest payments, payable semiannually, plus a lump sum equal to the amount originally borrowed at maturity. As is true of all securities, a bond's value is the present value of an expected cash flow stream, and in this case, we have the present value of an annuity plus the present value of a lump sum. Therefore, Equation 3-1 can be modified to find the value of a bond, V, as shown in Equation 3-2:[2]

$$V = \sum_{t=1}^{2n} \frac{I}{2}\left(\frac{1}{1 + k_d/2}\right)^t + M\left(\frac{1}{1 + k_d/2}\right)^{2n}. \qquad (3\text{-}2)$$

---

[2]The valuation formula presented here is for a bond with semiannual coupon payments, because this is the most common method of payment. Equation 3-2 could be adjusted for other coupon payment periods.

Here

I = annual coupon payment; we divide I by 2 to determine the semiannual interest payment. Note that we assume the first interest payment will be received in 6 months.

M = par value, which is the amount to be repaid at maturity.

k_d = required rate of return on the debt issue in question; we divide k_d by 2 to adjust for semiannual compounding.

n = number of years to maturity; multiplying n by 2 again adjusts for semiannual compounding.

To illustrate, we would find the value of a 12 percent, $1,000 par value bond with semiannual payments and 10 years to maturity, when k_d is 10 percent, as follows:

$$V = \sum_{t=1}^{20} \frac{\$120}{2}\left(\frac{1}{1 + 0.10/2}\right)^t + \$1,000\left(\frac{1}{1 + 0.10/2}\right)^{20}$$

$$= \sum_{t=1}^{20} \$60\left(\frac{1}{1.05}\right)^t + \$1,000\left(\frac{1}{1.05}\right)^{20}$$

$$= \$1,124.62.$$

We used a financial calculator to solve this equation, proceeding as follows: Enter PMT = 60, FV = 1,000, n = 20, and k = i = 5; then press the PV button to solve for V. Without a financial calculator, we would proceed as follows, using interest factor tables:

$$V = \$60(PVIFA_{5\%,20}) + \$1,000(PVIF_{5\%,20})$$

$$= \$60(12.4622) + \$1,000(0.3769)$$

$$= \$1,124.63.$$

The penny difference is due to rounding.[3]

Yield to Maturity

The valuation model set forth in Equation 3-2 can also be used to find the bond's *yield to maturity*. Given the current market value of the bond and its coupon payment, par value, and number of years to maturity, Equation 3-2 can be solved for the yield to maturity, YTM = k_d, which is the bond's expected rate of return.[4]

---

[3]Here $PVIFA_{5\%,20}$ is the present value interest factor for a 20-period annuity discounted at 5 percent and $PVIF_{5\%,20}$ is the interest factor for a lump sum discounted for 20 periods at 5 percent. Appendix A, at the end of the book, contains a review of time value of money plus interest factor tables. However, serious finance students should have a financial calculator, and our illustrations and problems utilize calculator solutions. Of course, the illustrations and problems could also be solved using the interest factor tables in Appendix A, but in many cases this procedure would be inordinately time consuming.

[4]Actually, the bond's YTM is the *promised* rate of return if it is held to maturity. If there is some possibility that the interest and principal will not be paid, or will not be paid on time, then the expected rate of return would be less than the YTM. Further, if it is likely that the bond will be called before its maturity, then the YTM will not represent the expected return. We discuss calls in the next section.

The YTM is that discount rate which causes the present value of the promised payment stream to equal the current price of the bond. Yield to maturity can be easily determined using a financial calculator; otherwise, one must use a trial-and-error process.

As an example, what is the yield to maturity on a 20-year, 12 percent, semiannual bond which is now selling at its par value of $1,000?[5]

$$\$1,000 = \sum_{t=1}^{40} \frac{\$120}{2}\left(\frac{1}{1 + k_d/2}\right)^t + \$1,000\left(\frac{1}{1 + k_d/2}\right)^{40}.$$

Using a financial calculator with a bond valuation function, we find the annual yield to maturity to be 12 percent. Here is the process: Enter PMT $= 120/2 = 60$, PV $= 1,000$ (or $-1,000$ on some calculators), FV $= 1,000$, and n $= 40$; and then press the k $=$ i key to find the semiannual yield. Finally, multiply by 2 to obtain the annual YTM, $k_d = 2(6.0\%) = 12.0\%$. Thus, the yield to maturity, k_d, is 12.0 percent.[6]

The yield to maturity for a bond that sells at par, as in this example, consists entirely of an interest yield. However, if the bond sells at a price other than its par value, the yield to maturity has both an interest component and a capital gain (or loss) component. One who purchases a bond and holds it until maturity will receive, assuming no default occurs, the yield to maturity that existed on the purchase date. However, the bond's price, and thus its yield to maturity, will change almost daily, reflecting fluctuating interest rates in the economy.

Yield to Call

If a bond is *callable*, that is, if the issuer can redeem the bond prior to maturity, the purchaser may not have the opportunity to hold the bond until maturity. For example, if a firm has callable 12 percent coupon bonds outstanding, and if interest rates fall from 12 to 8 percent, then the company could call in the 12 percent bonds, replace them with newly issued 8 percent bonds, and save $(0.12 - 0.08)(\$1,000) = \$40$ of interest per bond per year. The decision to call (or to *refund*) the issue is discussed fully in Chapter 13. For now, our concern is the effect of a potential call on a bond's expected return.

If the going rate of interest is well below a callable bond's coupon rate, then the bond is likely to be called. In this case, investors should estimate the expected rate of return on the bond as the *yield to call (YTC)* rather than as the yield to maturity. To calculate the yield to call, we must modify Equation 3-2. This time, we are concerned with the call price and number of periods to the call date rather than the par value and number of periods to maturity. The result is Equation 3-3:

$$V = \sum_{t=1}^{2n} \frac{I}{2}\left(\frac{1}{1 + k_d/2}\right)^t + \text{Call price}\left(\frac{1}{1 + k_d/2}\right)^{2n}. \qquad (3\text{-}3)$$

---

[5]Note that we used a par value of $1,000 in our example. A bond may actually have a par value of any size. A $1,000 par value is very common, but so are other par values, such as $5,000.

[6]The same answer would result if we used tables; the factors for 6 percent would solve the equation, so 6% $\times$ 2 $=$ 12% is the YTM. The tables are easy to use as long as all the interest rates work out to even numbers, but it is quite difficult to evaluate a bond whose k_d value is not an even number. Here financial calculators are essential for practical purposes.

Here n = the number of years until the bond is expected to be called, V is the current market price, call price is the price the company must pay in order to call the bond (often the par value plus one year's interest), and k_d is the yield to call.

For example, if the 12 percent bonds described previously were expected to be called in 5 years at a call price of $1,120, the yield to call would be found by solving for k_d in the following equation:

$$\$1,000 = \sum_{t=1}^{10} \frac{\$120}{2}\left(\frac{1}{1 + k_d/2}\right)^t + \$1,120\left(\frac{1}{1 + k_d/2}\right)^{10}.$$

In this example, the yield to call is 13.75 percent.

Although it might at first glance appear that an investor would benefit from the call, this is not correct. The investor who had been receiving $120 per year per bond would now receive a lump sum payment of $1,120, which would presumably be reinvested for the remaining 15 years at the current prevailing rate of 8 percent. Therefore, the annual cash flow would drop from 0.12($1,000) = $120 to 0.08($1,120) = $89.60, so our investor would have an income reduction of $120 − $89.60 = $30.40 per year for the next 15 years, but he or she would now receive $1,120 at original maturity rather than $1,000. The present value of the lost income, which is about $260, exceeds the present value of the $120 call premium, which is about $38, so the investor would lose by the call.

Viewed another way, as a result of the call the investor would get a high rate of return, 13.75 percent, but only for five years, after which the return would drop to 8 percent. A 12 percent return for 20 years is better than 13.75 percent for 5 years followed by 8 percent for 15 years. We can quantify this conclusion by solving for k_d in the following equation. This gives us the expected rate of return over the original 20-year holding period, assuming the bonds were called after 5 years and the investor reinvested the $1,120 call price in new 8 percent bonds:

$$\$1,000 = \sum_{t=1}^{10} \frac{\$120}{2}\left(\frac{1}{1 + k_d/2}\right)^t + \sum_{t=11}^{40} \frac{\$89.60}{2}\left(\frac{1}{1 + k_d/2}\right)^t + \$1,120\left(\frac{1}{1 + k_d/2}\right)^{40}.$$

Again, with a financial calculator, but this time using the IRR function, we find the expected rate of return to be 10.55 percent.[7] Thus, if the bond were called, the investor's return over the original holding period would be reduced from 12 to 10.55 percent, or by 1.45 percentage points.

Personal Tax Effects

If an investor pays personal income taxes, then his or her *relevant cash flows* are the after-personal-tax cash flows produced by the security, and the relevant rate of return to the investor is the after-tax rate of return. This distinction is quite important, because different types of income are subject to different tax treatments, and it is necessary for investors to compare after-tax returns if they are to make valid choices among alternative investment opportunities.

---

[7]To find k_d using the IRR function of a financial calculator, be sure to treat the second interest stream as an annuity of $44.80 for 29 periods, and treat the last cash flow as $44.80 + $1,120 = $1,164.80.

To illustrate tax effects, consider again the 12 percent coupon, semiannual, 20-year bonds discussed in the preceding section. If the bonds were not callable, then an investor in the 28 percent tax bracket who bought them at par would receive an after-tax return, k_{dAT}, found by solving this equation:

$$\$1,000 = \sum_{t=1}^{40} \frac{\$120}{2} (1 - 0.28)\left(\frac{1}{1 + k_{dAT}/2}\right)^t + \$1,000\left(\frac{1}{1 + k_{dAT}/2}\right)^{40}$$

$$= \sum_{t=1}^{40} \$43.20\left(\frac{1}{1 + k_{dAT}/2}\right)^t + \$1,000\left(\frac{1}{1 + k_{dAT}/2}\right)^{40}.$$

The after-tax yield to maturity is 8.64 percent, only $1 - T = 1 - 0.28 = 0.72 = 72$ percent of the before-tax yield. Thus, the 12.0 percent before-tax return is reduced sharply by taxation.[8]

Other Points

Before concluding our discussion of bonds, we should note five additional points.

Other Models

First, we have not presented a complete set of models, but on the basis of the analysis set forth previously, you should be able to develop a valuation model for any particular type of bond you might encounter. In Chapter 13, we will examine zero coupon bonds, and in Chapter 15, we will discuss convertibles. The principles developed in this chapter will be applied to develop models for those securities.

Call Protection

Second, we noted earlier that callable bonds are less desirable than noncallable bonds, and also that the danger of a call is greater if the market interest rate is below the coupon rate, as it would be for a bond selling at a premium. Note also that if interest rates have risen, causing a bond to sell at a discount, the bond is not likely to be called, even if the issuer has the legal right to call it. Therefore, because of the effects of call provisions, callable discount bonds will, other things held constant, sell on a lower yield basis than callable premium bonds because

---

[8]Several points related to the taxation of bonds should be noted:

1. The interest on bonds issued by state and local governments (municipal bonds, or "munis") is normally exempt from federal taxes. However, munis issued to support revenue-producing activities may be taxable.

2. If a bond was issued at a discount below its par value (an "original issue discount, or OID, bond"), the discount must be amortized over the bond's remaining life, and the annual amortization charge must be added to the coupon interest on an annual basis to determine taxable income. Note also that any bond issued after July 18, 1984, and subsequently purchased at discount, must be treated in the same manner as an OID bond.

3. If a bond is bought at a premium above its par value, the premium may be amortized over the bond's remaining life, and the annual amortization charge may be used to reduce the coupon interest, and hence taxable income.

4. If you buy a security (stock or bond) at one price and sell it at another price, the difference is defined as a capital gain or a capital loss. Before 1987, long-term capital gains (gains on assets held for more than six months) were taxed at rates that were only 40 percent of the rates on ordinary income. That situation no longer exists.

investors recognize that the premium bond is likely to be called, whereas the discount bond is not.

Effective Annual Rate

Third, we should clarify our definition of yield to maturity. In determining a bond's yield to maturity, we solved for $k_d/2$ and then multiplied this value by 2 to obtain k_d = YTM. This is in accord with convention, and k_d is indeed the nominal, or stated, annual yield to maturity as Wall Street uses the term. Since we generally compare a bond with other bonds, and since most bonds pay interest semiannually, this definition presents no problems.

However, a problem arises if one attempts to compare bond yields calculated in this manner with yields on other securities which call for annual, quarterly, monthly, or any other non-semiannual compounding period. In those cases, it would be necessary to convert the yields on all the securities being compared to their *effective annual rates*, using Equation 3-4:

$$\text{Effective annual rate} = \left(1 + \frac{k_{Nom}}{m}\right)^m - 1.0. \qquad \text{(3-4)}$$

Here k_{Nom} is the nominal, or stated, annual yield, and m is the number of compounding periods per year. Note that k_{Nom}/m is the periodic rate of return, which is $k_d/2$ in our semiannual bond examples.

Applying Equation 3-4 to our semiannual bond with a nominal annual yield of 12.0 percent, we find

$$\text{Effective annual rate} = (1 + 0.12/2)^2 - 1.0 = (1.06)^2 - 1.0$$
$$= 1.1236 - 1.0 = 0.1236 = 12.36\%.$$

Thus, the effective annual yield to maturity is 0.36 percentage points higher than the nominal, or stated, yield to maturity.[9]

Timing of First Payment

Fourth, throughout our discussion of bond valuation we assumed that the first interest payment would be received in exactly 6 months. In other words, we assumed that the last coupon payment was made yesterday. Of course, this condition is only met twice a year, and the models would have to be modified to account for different time periods to receipt of first payment. This refinement would be essential for investors to use the models, but it is generally not required for financial management purposes.

---

[9]Occasionally, it is useful to ask what periodic rate is required to attain a particular effective annual rate. Equation 3-4 can be rearranged to answer such a question:

$$(1 + \text{Effective annual rate})^{1/m} - 1.0 = \frac{k_{Nom}}{m} = \text{Periodic rate}.$$

For example, what semiannual rate will yield an effective annual rate of 12%? The answer is 5.83%:

$$(1 + 0.12)^{1/2} - 1.0 = (1.12)^{1/2} - 1.0 = 1.0583 - 1.0 = 0.0583 = 5.83\%.$$

Corporate Viewpoint

Finally, although we have discussed bond valuation from the investor's viewpoint, our primary interest is the cost of capital to a firm which issues bonds. In Chapter 4, we will use the concepts developed in this chapter, plus flotation cost and corporate tax considerations, to develop the firm's cost of debt.

PREFERRED STOCK VALUATION

Preferred stocks offer the promise of a fixed dividend, often forever but sometimes for a fixed term. *Perpetual preferreds* are those preferreds that promise an indefinitely long, constant cash flow stream, and Equation 3-1 can be modified to find their value:[10]

$$V_0 = \sum_{t=1}^{\infty} \frac{CF}{(1 + k)^t} = \frac{CF}{k}.$$

Expressed in preferred stock symbols, we have Equation 3-5:

$$P_0 = \frac{D}{k_p}. \tag{3-5}$$

Here P_0 is the current value of the preferred stock, D is the constant expected periodic dividend payment, and k_p is the periodic required rate of return on the preferred stock. For example, if a preferred stock pays a $2.00 annual dividend and investors require a 10 percent rate of return, the value of the stock is $20.00:

$$P_0 = \frac{\$2.00}{0.10} = \$20.00.$$

Most preferred stocks pay dividends quarterly, and we can also use quarterly values to find the price of the preferred issue: $P_0 = \$0.50/0.025 = \$20.00$.

We can solve Equation 3-5 for the expected rate of return on a share of preferred stock:

$$\hat{k}_p = \frac{D}{P_0}. \tag{3-5a}$$

Note that the k in Equation 3-5a has a "hat," indicating that we are estimating an expected rate of return. In Equation 3-5, the absence of a hat indicates that k is a required rate of return.[11] Ordinarily, markets are in equilibrium, so $k_p = \hat{k}_p$.

For our preferred stock selling for $20.00, Equation 3-5a can be used to find the expected rate of return:

$$\hat{k}_p = \frac{\$2.00}{\$20.00} = 0.10 = 10.0\%.$$

---

[10]The proof of Equation 3-5 is given in Appendix 3A.

[11]As with bonds, $\hat{k}_p$ is actually the promised rate of return. If there is some probability that dividends will not be paid forever, or that a dividend could be late, the expected rate of return would be less than that obtained from Equation 3-5a.

This is the nominal expected rate of return. To find the effective annual return, we must first find the expected periodic yield,

$$\text{Quarterly } \hat{k}_p = \frac{\$0.50}{\$20.00} = 0.025 = 2.5\%,$$

and then, using Equation 3-4, find the effective annual yield:

$$\text{Effective annual rate} = (1.025)^4 - 1.0 = 1.1038 - 1.0 = 0.1038 = 10.38\%.$$

If we were comparing yields on quarterly preferred stocks with those on semiannual bonds, we would need to convert both to an effective annual basis before making the comparison.

Personal Tax Effects

We also need to consider the effects of personal income taxes. In an *ex ante* sense, all of the yield expected on a share of perpetual preferred stock, or its total return, is a dividend yield.[12] For an individual investor, the dividend is taxed at the investor's marginal tax rate, so the after-tax yield is merely

$$\hat{k}_{pAT} = \hat{k}_p(1 - T). \tag{3-6}$$

Here $\hat{k}_{pAT}$ is the after-tax yield, $\hat{k}_p$ is the before-tax yield, and T is the investor's marginal personal tax rate.[13] If an investor in the 28 percent marginal tax bracket bought the preferred stock described previously, his or her after-tax nominal rate of return would be 7.2 percent:

$$\hat{k}_{pAT} = 10\%(1 - 0.28) = 10\%(0.72) = 7.2\%.$$

Corporate Ownership of Preferred Stock

If the owner of the preferred stock had been a corporation, 80 percent of the dividend would have been exempt from income taxes. Thus, the after-tax yield to a corporate owner of preferred stock is found as follows:[14]

---

[12]Ex post, interest rates in the economy can change, causing a change in the value of the preferred stock and hence a capital gain or loss, but the *expected* gain or loss is zero because the expected future value of k_p is the current value.

[13]Note that Equation 3-6, with k_d in place of $\hat{k}_p$, can also be used to find the after-tax yield to maturity on a bond which sells at par, because the entire yield is in the form of interest payments.

[14]The corporate owner of a share of preferred stock would receive this after-tax dividend from the stock:

$$\text{After-tax dividend} = D - 0.2(T)D = D(1 - 0.2T).$$

Divide by P_0 to put on a yield basis:

$$\hat{k}_{pAT(Corp)} = \frac{D}{P_0}(1 - 0.2T) = \hat{k}_p(1 - 0.2T). \tag{3-6a}$$

Note, though, that if a corporation purchases preferred stock with debt, the exclusion is reduced by the interest deductions.

$$\hat{k}_{pAT(Corp)} = \hat{k}_p(1 - 0.2T). \qquad\qquad (3\text{-}6a)$$

Assuming the corporation is in the 34 percent marginal tax bracket, this 10 percent pre-tax preferred would provide an after-tax yield of

$$\hat{k}_{pAT(Corp)} = 10\%[1 - (0.2)(0.34)] = 10\%(0.932) = 9.32\%.$$

This 9.32 percent for the corporate owner compares with a 7.2 percent after-tax yield for an individual in the 28 percent tax bracket. Thus, on an after-tax basis, preferred stocks offer higher returns to corporations than to individual investors when both are taxed at the top marginal tax rate. No such advantage exists for bonds. Thus, most nonconvertible preferred stocks in the United States are owned by corporations, not by individuals.

Other Points about Preferred Stock

We should make four additional points before moving to common stock valuation. (1) Most recently issued preferred stocks contain *sinking funds*; frequently, two percent of the issue must be retired each year. Such a preferred would have a maximum maturity of 50 years at time of issue, and an average maturity of 25 years. The average maturity would decline after issue, and the expected rate of return on such an issue should be determined in the same way as the yield on a bond. (2) As with bonds, our primary interest is the cost of capital to a firm which issues preferred stock, and in the next chapter, we shall use the concepts developed here to help estimate the cost of preferred stock. (3) Our valuation formulas are based on the assumption that the first dividend is received three months from today. Adjustments can easily be made to account for different times to receipt of first dividend.[15] (4) Recently, companies have begun to issue adjustable rate, or floating rate, preferred stocks. We shall discuss these securities in Chapter 12.

COMMON STOCK VALUATION

The expected cash flows from a share of common stock consist of two components: (1) the dividend expected in each year and (2) the price an investor expects to receive from the sale of the stock. In this section, we analyze several models for determining the value of a share of stock under different conditions. First, however, it is useful to define the following terms:

---

[15]For example, assume that a preferred issue has a perpetual annual dividend of $2.00 paid quarterly, and that the required rate of return on this stock is 10 percent. Further, assume that the first $0.50 dividend will be received in one month. The value of the stock immediately after the next dividend payment will be $2/0.10 = $20, but a purchaser will also receive the $0.50 quarterly dividend in 30 days, so the value of the stock 30 days hence will be $20 + $0.50 = $20.50. The value today is $20.50 discounted back for one month, or 1/12 year, at 10 percent, which is $20.33.

D_t = dividend the stockholder expects to receive in Year t.[16] Note that D_0, the dividend which has just been paid, is known with certainty, but all future dividends are expected values, so the estimate of D_t may differ among investors. However, there is a consensus estimate of D_t, which we call "the D_t value estimated by the representative, or marginal, investor."

$\hat{P}_t$ = price of the stock expected at the end of Year t. $\hat{P}_0$ is the calculated, or intrinsic, value of the stock today, as determined by a particular investor on the basis of his or her cash flow expectations and perceptions of the risk inherent in the stock.

P_0 = market value of the stock today. For any individual investor, $\hat{P}_0$ may differ from P_0. However, for investors in the aggregate, and also for the representative, or marginal, investor, $\hat{P}_0$ must equal P_0.

g_t = expected dividend growth rate in Year t; g_t may differ among individual investors, but the g_t value of concern to us here is that of the representative investor. Further, g_t can follow any pattern over time. If the dividend growth rate is constant, that is, if $g_{t+1} = g_t$ for all t, then the stock is called a *constant growth* stock, and in this case g can be used without the time subscript.

k_s = required rate of return on the stock, considering both its riskiness and the returns available on other investments. Again, k_s may differ among investors, depending on how they view the company's risk, but the k_s of primary concern is that of the representative investor.

$\hat{k}_s$ = rate of return which the investor actually expects to receive. For any individual investor, $\hat{k}_s$ could be equal to, above, or below k_s, but for the stock to be in equilibrium, $\hat{k}_s$ must equal k_s for the marginal investor.

The first equation presented in this chapter, Equation 3-1, can be used to value any financial asset. For example, if you purchase a share of stock with the intention of having it passed on to your heirs forever, the intrinsic value of the stock, $\hat{P}_0$, would be calculated as the present value of an infinite stream of expected dividends:

$$\hat{P}_0 = \frac{D_1}{(1 + k_s)^1} + \frac{D_2}{(1 + k_s)^2} + \frac{D_3}{(1 + k_s)^3} + \ldots + \frac{D_\infty}{(1 + k_s)^\infty}. \tag{3-7}$$

For practical purposes, it would not be necessary to extend the dividend stream beyond, say, 40 years, because the contribution to the present value of dividends after that point would be negligible.

Suppose, though, that you expect to hold the stock for a finite period, say five years, and then to sell it. How then would you calculate the stock's value? The value should still be determined by Equation 3-7. To see why this is so, recognize that when you sell the stock, the person who buys it from you will base its price on the present value of the expected cash flows from that point on. But his or her cash flows consist of expected dividends plus an expected sale price. That sale price, in turn, is based on dividends in the still more distant future. By extension, we must conclude that the value of any stock today is equal to the present value of the stock's expected future dividends, regardless of the length of the holding period.

---

[16]Since most common stocks pay quarterly dividends, we could speak here of periods (quarters) rather than years. However, in common stock valuation, we generally work on an annual basis, primarily because the data used are not precise enough to warrant refinement on a quarterly basis. See Footnote 17.

Equation 3-7 is a generalized stock valuation model in the sense that the time pattern of D_t can be anything. For many purposes, however, it is useful to assume a particular time pattern for D_t and then to develop simplified versions of the generalized model. Some specific models are presented in the following sections.

Constant Growth

If one believes that a stock's dividends will grow at a constant rate on into the indefinite future, that is, $g_{t+1} = g_t$ for all t, then Equation 3-7 may be simplified as follows:[17]

$$\hat{P}_0 = \frac{D_0(1 + g)}{k_s - g} = \frac{D_1}{k_s - g}. \tag{3-8}$$

The constant growth model expressed in Equation 3-8 is often called the Gordon model, after Myron J. Gordon, who did much to develop and popularize it.

Note that the Gordon model is sufficiently general to be used to value a zero growth stock, including a share of perpetual preferred stock. If growth is zero, Equation 3-8 reduces to the form of Equation 3-5. Note also that to use the Gordon model, k_s must be greater than g.

Here is an example which illustrates both the Gordon model and the Security Market Line (SML) concept. Assume that Johnson Foods Corporation just paid a dividend of $2.00 (that is, $D_0 = \$2.00$), that an investor expects Johnson's dividends to grow at a constant rate of 6 percent, that the estimated beta coefficient of the stock is 1.2, that the risk-free rate is 8 percent, and that the investor requires a 14 percent return on an average risk stock. Assuming that the SML properly describes the risk/return relationship, it can be used to determine the investor's required rate of return on Johnson's stock:

$$k_s = k_{RF} + b(k_M - k_{RF}) = 8\% + 1.2(14\% - 8\%)$$
$$= 8\% + 7.2\% = 15.2\%.$$

Now, Equation 3-8 can be used to value Johnson's stock:

$$\hat{P}_0 = \frac{\$2.00(1.06)}{0.152 - 0.06} = \frac{\$2.12}{0.092} = \$23.04.$$

---

[17]The proof of Equation 3-8 is shown in Appendix 3A. Note that constant dividend growth implies (1) that earnings also grow at a constant rate and (2) that the payout ratio is a constant. Also, it is not difficult to modify Equation 3-8 to account for the fact that dividends are actually paid quarterly. If we assume quarterly dividend payments, with an annual dividend increase, then Equation 3-8 becomes

$$\hat{P}_0 = \frac{D_{q1}(1 + k_s)^{0.75} + D_{q2}(1 + k_s)^{0.50} + D_{q3}(1 + k_s)^{0.25} + D_{q4}(1 + k_s)^0}{k_s - g}. \tag{3-8a}$$

Here D_{qt} is the quarterly dividend in Quarter t, k_s is the annual required rate of return, and g is the annual dividend growth rate. As with Equation 3-8, Equation 3-8a assumes that the analysis is performed on a dividend payment date, so that the first dividend will be received exactly one period hence. Further, the quarterly model assumes that four constant quarterly dividends will be received, then the dividend will be increased and four more constant quarterly dividends will be received, and so on. For more on the quarterly model, see the Linke-Zumwalt article cited in the end of chapter references.

Thus, the intrinsic value of Johnson's stock, as seen by this investor, is $23.04. If the market price of the stock is below $23.04, he or she should buy it.

Other investors would go through a similar process to evaluate the stock. Of course, many investors rely on the advice of such financial service firms as Merrill Lynch and E. F. Hutton, but analysts for these firms perform the same types of calculations that we have described, so they serve as proxies for final investors. If the majority of investors conclude that a stock's intrinsic value exceeds its current market price, its market price will be bid up to the point where its market value equals its intrinsic value. The reverse would hold if the stock were overvalued. Only when market value and intrinsic value are equal for the marginal investor will the stock be in equilibrium. Once equilibrium has been reached—and this is the general situation—the stock's price will be relatively stable: it will trade within a narrow range until something happens, such as an announcement of higher-than-expected earnings.

We can rearrange Equation 3-8 to solve for k_s:

$$\hat{k}_s = \frac{D_1}{P_0} + g. \tag{3-9}$$

Notice that we added a "hat" to the k and deleted the one over P_0, because here we use the known current market price to find the expected rate of return. For the stock to be in equilibrium, P_0 must equal $\hat{P}_0$ and k_s must equal $\hat{k}_s$ for the marginal investor. Also, we see that the total expected rate of return is equal to the expected dividend yield, D_1/P_0, plus the expected growth rate, g. Under constant growth conditions, g also represents the expected capital gains yield, and this percentage yield is expected to remain constant each year. Thus, for a constant growth stock, investors expect earnings, dividends, and consequently the stock's price all to grow at the same rate, g. Finally, note that if P and D both increase at the same rate, then the dividend yield, D_t/P_{t-1}, will remain constant.

Nonconstant Growth

Although the dividend streams of some stocks are expected to grow at a constant rate, for many others the constant growth assumption is not appropriate. For example, many new technology stocks are expected to grow rapidly for a few years but then to slow down as they approach maturity. The value of such stocks is found by following these three steps:

1. Partition the dividend stream into two parts; a beginning period of nonconstant growth followed by a period of permanent constant growth. Then, find the present value of the dividends expected during the nonconstant growth period.

2. Use the constant growth model to find the expected value of the stock at the end of the nonconstant growth period; that is, at the beginning of the constant growth period, and then discount this value back to the present.

3. Add these two components to find the current intrinsic value of the stock, $\hat{P}_0$.

This process is summarized in Equation 3-10 or, equivalently, 3-10a:

$$\hat{P}_0 = \sum_{t=1}^{n} \frac{D_0(1 + g_t)^t}{(1 + k_s)^t} + \frac{D_{n+1}}{k_s - g}\left[\frac{1}{1 + k_s}\right]^n. \qquad (3\text{-}10)$$

$$\hat{P}_0 = \sum_{t=1}^{n} \frac{D_1(1 + g_t)^{t-1}}{(1 + k_s)^t} + \frac{D_{n+1}}{k_s - g}\left[\frac{1}{1 + k_s}\right]^n. \qquad (3\text{-}10a)$$

Here

   n = expected number of years of nonconstant growth.

   g_t = growth rate expected in each Year t of the nonconstant growth phase. g_t could vary from year to year, or it could be stable.

   g = expected constant growth rate once the company reaches a mature, steady-state condition.

D_{n+1} = first expected dividend after the constant growth phase has been reached.

   D_0 = last dividend paid.

   D_1 = next dividend expected.

   k_s = required rate of return on the stock.

To illustrate how nonconstant growth stocks are evaluated, assume the following facts for Solar Laser Technology (SLT):

$n = 3$.

g_t = 30% for each year during the stock's rapid growth period, 3 years.

g = 10%.

D_0 = $1.82.

k_s = 16%.

Step 1. Find the present value of SLT's expected dividends during the nonconstant growth phase, PV D_n:

$$\text{PV } D_n = \sum_{t=1}^{3} \frac{\$1.82(1.30)^t}{(1.16)^t} = \frac{\$1.82(1.30)^1}{(1.16)^1} + \frac{\$1.82(1.30)^2}{(1.16)^2} + \frac{\$1.82(1.30)^3}{(1.16)^3}$$

$$= \frac{\$2.366}{1.160} + \frac{\$3.076}{1.346} + \frac{\$3.999}{1.561} = \$2.040 + \$2.285 + \$2.562 = \$6.887.$$

Step 2. Find SLT's expected stock value at the beginning of its constant growth phase, $\hat{P}_n$, and then discount this value back to the present to obtain PV $\hat{P}_n$:

$$\text{PV } \hat{P}_n = \frac{\$3.999(1.10)}{0.16 - 0.10}\left[\frac{1}{1.16}\right]^3 = \frac{\$4.399}{0.06}\left[\frac{1}{1.16}\right]^3$$

$$= \$73.317\left[\frac{1}{1.16}\right]^3 = \$46.971.$$

Step 3. Add these two components to find the intrinsic value of SLT's stock, $\hat{P}_0$:

$$\hat{P}_0 = \$6.887 + \$46.971 = \$53.858 \approx \$53.86.$$

Figure 3-1 shows the solution to the SLT stock price problem worked out on a time line. Use of a time line helps to set up the calculations, especially when the growth rates during the nonconstant period are irregular.

Many new high technology stocks currently pay no dividends. In order to evaluate such a stock, we must recognize that although initially the company plans to retain all of its income to finance growth, it will eventually start paying dividends. Hewlett-Packard, IBM, and many other companies paid no dividends early in their lives but do pay them today. Apple Computer pays no dividends currently, but at some point investors expect it to start declaring dividends. For a company with $D_0 = \$0$, it is necessary to break down Equation 3-10 into three segments, as follows:

$$P_0 = \sum_{t=1}^{L} \frac{\$0}{(1 + k_s)^t} + \sum_{t=L+1}^{M} \frac{D_{L+1}(1 + g_t)^{t-(L+1)}}{(1 + k_s)^t} + \frac{D_{M+1}}{k_s - g}\left[\frac{1}{1 + k_s}\right]^M. \quad \textbf{(3-10b)}$$

The first term simply recognizes that no dividends will be paid for L years. The second term assumes that an initial dividend of D_{L+1} will be paid at Year $L+1$ and that the dividend will grow at a nonconstant rate during the period L to M. Finally, the third term finds the present value of the expected stock price once it reaches maturity and becomes a constant growth stock.

Personal Tax Effects

As with bonds, the relevant cash flow for an investor who must pay personal taxes is the *after-tax cash flow*, and the relevant rate of return for decision purposes is the *after-tax rate of return*.

Figure 3-1
Nonconstant Growth: Solar Laser Technology

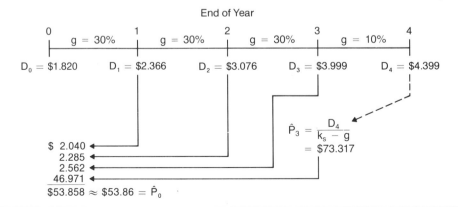

Constant Growth

Recall that a constant growth stock's expected total return, $\hat{k}_s$, consists of an expected dividend yield plus an expected capital gains yield. To find the expected total after-tax return, we must adjust both the dividend and the capital gains components for taxes. To illustrate, assume that an individual investor in the 28 percent marginal tax bracket is choosing between the stocks of these two constant growth companies: (1) High-Yield Corporation, with $P_0 = \$30$, $D_1 = \$3.60$, and $g = 3\%$ and (2) High-Growth Company, with $P_0 = \$30$, $D_1 = \$0.90$, and $g = 12\%$. The stock that is selected will be held for one year and then sold. What are the expected before-tax and after-tax rates of return on the two stocks?

Before-tax returns:

$$\text{High-Yield: } \hat{k}_s = \frac{D_1}{P_0} + g = \frac{\$3.60}{\$30} + 3\% = 12\% + 3\% = 15\%.$$

$$\text{High-Growth: } \hat{k}_s = \frac{D_1}{P_0} + g = \frac{\$0.90}{\$30} + 12\% = 3\% + 12\% = 15\%.$$

After-tax returns:

Prior to 1987, long-term capital gains were taxed at a lower rate than dividend income, and this made high-growth stocks much more attractive than those with high yields to stockholders in high tax brackets. Now that capital gains are taxed at the same rate as dividends, the tax advantage of capital gains has been significantly reduced but not eliminated. The reason why capital gains are still better than dividends from a tax standpoint is that the taxes on gains are deferred until the stock is sold, whereas taxes on dividends must be paid each year.

The advantage of the capital gains tax deferral depends upon the investor's time horizon, or the expected holding period. If an investor expects to sell within one year, there is no tax advantage, because taxes will be paid on the capital gains at the same time they are paid on the dividends. On the other hand, if the stock will be held forever (or, really, until the stockholder dies), then no capital gains taxes will ever be paid.[18]

For the High-Yield and the High-Growth Corporations, here are the expected after-tax yields for the two extreme holding periods for an investor in the 28 percent tax bracket:

1-Year H. P.:

$$\text{High-Yield: } \hat{k}_{SAT} = \text{Dividend yield } (1 - T) + \text{Capital gains yield } (1 - T) \quad \textbf{(3-11)}$$

$$= 12\%(1 - 0.28) + 3\%(1 - 0.28)$$

$$= 8.64\% + 2.16\% = 10.80\%.$$

---

[18]When a stockholder dies, his or her estate must pay estate taxes. However, if stock held by the deceased has risen in value, no capital gains tax liability is due, and the basis of the stock (or other asset) to the beneficiary is the stock's value at the time of death. Therefore, one can escape capital gains taxes by dying. Actually, it generally makes little sense for an elderly or seriously ill stockholder to sell stock that has appreciated greatly in price for precisely this reason.

High-Growth: $\hat{k}_{sAT} = 3\%(1 - 0.28) + 12\%(1 - 0.28) = 10.80\%$.

∞ *H. P.*:

High-Yield: $\hat{k}_{sAT}$ = Dividend yield $(1 - T)$ + Capital gains yield   **(3-11a)**

$$= 12\%(1 - 0.28) + 3\%$$

$$= 8.64\% + 3.00 = 11.64\%.$$

High-Growth: $\hat{k}_{sAT} = 3\%(1 - 0.28) + 12\%$

$$= 2.16\% + 12.00\% = 14.16\%.$$

For holding periods greater than one year but less than forever, it is necessary to solve this equation for $\hat{k}_{sAT}$:[19]

$$P_0 = \sum_{t=1}^{n} \frac{D_0(1 + g)^t(1 - T)}{(1 + k_{sAT})^t} + \frac{[P_0(1 + g)^n - P_0](1 - T) + P_0}{(1 + k_{sAT})^n} \qquad \textbf{(3-11b)}$$

Using *Lotus 1-2-3*, we evaluated Equation 3-11b for several different holding periods. Here are the after-tax expected rates of return for 5- and 10-year holding periods:

	Expected Rate of Return	
Holding Period	**High-Yield**	**High-Growth**
5-year	10.96%	11.42%
10-year	11.13	12.04

Had the investor been in a zero tax bracket, as are pension funds, many foundations, and some students and retirees, the before- and after-tax returns would have been identical, 15 percent. But for tax-paying investors, more capital gains income than dividend income results in a higher after-tax rate of return.

Because of the deferral of capital gains taxes, stockholders might be expected to prefer corporations that retain earnings, plow them back into the business, and thus provide capital gains instead of paying out dividends. Before accepting this as gospel, however, we must consider many other factors which affect dividend policy. This will be done in Chapter 11. Nevertheless, from a tax standpoint, an investor in a high tax bracket is better off if a high percentage of his or her total return comes as long holding return capital gains rather than as dividend income.

Nonconstant Growth

What about the after-tax expected rate of return on a nonconstant growth stock? Since the dividend yield and capital gains yield components are not constant, we cannot apply Equation 3-11b. Instead, we must revert to our generalized model,

---

[19]The after-tax expected rate of return to a corporation which holds a limited amount of another firm's stock is found in a like manner except only 20 percent of the dividends received are taxable.

Figure 3-2
After-Tax Rate of Return: Solar Laser Technology

1. Before-Tax Cash Flows, End of Year:

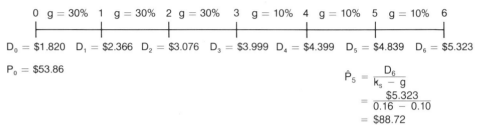

$$\hat{P}_5 = \frac{D_6}{k_s - g}$$
$$= \frac{\$5.323}{0.16 - 0.10}$$
$$= \$88.72$$

2. After-Tax Cash Flows, End of Year:

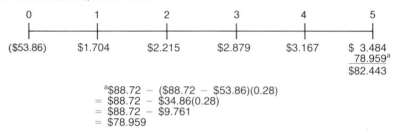

[a]$88.72 − ($88.72 − $53.86)(0.28)
= $88.72 − $34.86(0.28)
= $88.72 − $9.761
= $78.959

3. Insert indicated after-tax cash flows into a financial calculator and solve for IRR. IRR = $\hat{k}_{sAT}$ = 12.12%.

Equation 3-10 or 3-10a, and again, we must specify a holding period. We then proceed by (1) placing the expected before-tax cash flows on a time line consistent with the assumed holding period, (2) converting the cash flows to an after-tax stream, and (3) then calculating the internal rate of return on this stream. The IRR is the expected after-tax rate of return.

To illustrate, we can determine the expected after-tax yield on the Solar Laser Technology (SLT) stock, which was described in an earlier section. Assume that the investor in question has a marginal tax rate, T, of 28 percent and a holding period of five years, and that SLT's current market price is $53.86. Figure 3-2 shows the time line solution; the expected after-tax rate of return is 12.12 percent.

SECURITY MARKET EQUILIBRIUM

Investors (1) calculate intrinsic values for stocks, (2) compare the calculated value for each stock with its current market price, and (3) make buy or sell decisions based on whether a stock's intrinsic value is greater or less than its market price. Only if its market price is equal to its intrinsic value as calculated by a "representative" investor will a stock be in equilibrium, and if it is not in equilibrium, buy or sell orders will quickly push it to an equilibrium.

Now suppose good news regarding a stock comes out—say the firm strikes oil. The announcement will be sent over the Dow Jones news tape, immediately causing investors to revise upward their estimate of the company's future growth rate. Assume also that the news lowers the company's perceived risk and hence lowers its required k. These actions will cause the stock's intrinsic value to rise above its last market price. Buy orders will hit the market within minutes, pushing the stock's price up to its equilibrium price.

Stock prices are *not* constant; they regularly fluctuate as random buy and sell orders come in from people who have cash to invest or who need cash, and they also undergo violent changes at times, because many different events can and do occur to cause changes in equilibrium prices. However, as we discussed in Chapter 1, the capital markets are efficient in the sense that stock prices (and bond prices) fully and instantaneously reflect all publicly available information. Consequently, equilibrium ordinarily exists for any given stock, and in general required and expected returns are equal, as are market prices and intrinsic values. There are, of course, times when a stock, or even the whole market, continues to react for several months to a favorable or unfavorable development, but this does not signify inefficiency; rather, it simply indicates that as more new bits of information about the situation become available, the market adjusts to them.[20]

SUMMARY

Each corporate decision should be analyzed in terms of how the decision will affect the value of the firm's stock. It is obviously necessary for management to know how stock prices are established before attempting to measure how a given decision will affect their own firm's stock price. Additionally, since firms use other securities, such as bonds and preferred stock, investors' valuation processes in general are important to the financial manager.

All financial assets are valued in the same way: The value of any financial asset is merely the present value of its expected cash flows. Several different valuation models were developed for bonds, preferred stocks, and common stocks. Since investors are primarily concerned with after-tax cash flows, we looked at after-tax, as well as before-tax, cash flows and rates of return.

---

[20]In 1986, complex transactions called *programmed trades* have increased the short-run volatility of the stocks that are included in the major indexes. Program trading is done by professional traders, and each trade involves $10 million or more. Computers are used to keep track of the price of a futures contract on the index and of the prices of each stock in the index. If larger than normal deviations appear between the price of the index future and the prices of the underlying stocks, then traders can buy one and short sell the other, and earn a profit on the transaction. What happens, though, is that dozens of traders, backed by billions of dollars of capital, all have the same information in their computers, and their programs give all of them buy and sell signals at about the same time. As a result, a massive number of buy or sell orders hits the floor of the exchanges at about the same time, and the result is a substantial rise or fall in the prices of the stocks in the index. The stocks are temporarily driven away from equilibrium. However, even as the program traders are perfecting their art, others are working to take advantage of the temporary disequilibrium, and their actions quickly restore stocks to their equilibrium prices.

We also saw that in equilibrium, intrinsic values equal market prices, and that expected returns are equal to required returns, as seen by the marginal investor. Further, since capital markets are efficient, securities are constantly in equilibrium. New information can and does cause major shifts in equilibrium prices, but the adjustment period is short.

In the remainder of the book, we will use the concepts and models presented here to develop corporate decision rules.

Questions and Problems

3-1   (Bond valuation) The Microware Company's bonds pay $100 in interest semiannually ($50 every six months), mature in 15 years, and pay $1,000 at maturity.

> **a.** What is the value of these bonds when the going rate of interest is (1) 6 percent, (2) 9 percent, and (3) 12 percent?
> **b.** Now suppose Microware has some other bonds that also pay $50 interest every six months, $1,000 at maturity, and mature in one year. What is the value of these bonds at a going rate of interest of (1) 6 percent, (2) 9 percent, and (3) 12 percent?
> **c.** Why do the longer-term bonds fluctuate more when interest rates change than do the shorter-term bonds (the one-year bonds)?

3-2   (Yield to maturity) The McCulloch Company issued a new series of bonds on January 1, 1966. The bonds were sold at par ($1,000), had a 12 percent coupon, and had an original maturity of 30 years. Coupon payments are made semiannually (on June 30 and December 31).

> **a.** What was the yield to maturity of the bond on January 1, 1966?
> **b.** What was the price of the bond on January 1, 1971, 5 years later, assuming that the level of interest rates had fallen to 10 percent?
> **c.** Find the current yield and the capital gains yield on the bond on January 1, 1971, given the price as determined in Part b. (Note: The current yield on a bond is the annual coupon payment divided by the current price. The capital gains yield is the YTM minus the current yield.)
> **d.** On July 1, 1986, the bonds sold for $896.64. What was the YTM at that date? What was the effective annual rate?
> **e.** What was the current yield and capital gains yield on July 1, 1986?
> **f.** What was the after-tax yield on July 1, 1986, for an investor in the 40 percent state-plus-federal tax bracket?

3-3   (Discount bond valuation) In February 1961, the Miami Transportation Authority issued a series of 3.4 percent, annual coupon payment, 30-year bonds. Interest rates rose substantially in the years following the issue, and as rates rose, the price of the bonds declined. In February 1974, 13 years later, the price of the bonds had dropped from $1,000 to $650.

> **a.** Each bond originally sold at its $1,000 par value. What was the yield to maturity of these bonds at their time of issue?
> **b.** Calculate the yield to maturity in February 1974.
> **c.** Assume that interest rates stabilized at the 1974 level and remain at this level for the remainder of the life of the bonds. What will be their price in February 1986, when they have 5 years remaining to maturity?
> **d.** What will the price of the bonds be the day before they mature in 1991?

e. In 1974, the Miami Transportation Authority bonds were called "discount bonds." What happens to the price of discount bonds as they approach maturity? Is there a "built-in capital gain" on discount bonds?

f. The coupon interest divided by the market price of a bond is defined as the bond's *current yield*. What is the current yield of a Transportation Authority bond (1) in February 1974 and (2) in February 1986? What are its expected annual capital gains yields and total yields (total yield equals yield to maturity) on those same two dates?

3-4 **(Yield to call)** It is now January 1, 1987, and you are considering the purchase of an outstanding bond that was issued on January 1, 1985. The bond has a 10.5 percent annual coupon and a 30-year original maturity (it matures in 2015). There was originally a 5-year call protection (until December 31, 1989), after which time the bond could be called at 110 (that is, at 110 percent of par, or for $1,100). Interest rates have declined since the bond was issued, and the bond is now selling at 115.174 percent, or $1,151.74. You want to determine both the yield to maturity and the yield to call for this bond.

   a. What is the yield to maturity on January 1, 1987, for this bond? What is its yield to call?

   b. If you bought this bond, which return do you think you would actually earn? Explain your reasoning.

   c. Suppose the bond had sold at a discount. Would the yield to maturity or the yield to call have been more relevant?

   (Do Parts d and e only if you are using the computerized diskette.)

   d. Suppose the bond's price suddenly jumps to $1,250. What is the yield to maturity now, and the yield to call?

   e. Suppose the price suddenly falls to $800; now what would the YTM and YTC be?

3-5 **(Callable bonds)** Assume that on January 1, 1982, Barbizon Industries (BI) issued semiannual payment, A-rated bonds with an annual coupon of 18 percent, call protection for 10 years, a 30-year maturity, and a $1,000 par value. The bonds are callable at $1,120 on January 1, 1992, the first call date, and the call price declines thereafter at the rate of $6 per year until maturity. By January 1, 1987, interest rates on A-rated bonds had fallen to these levels: 5-year maturity: 8 percent; 20- to 30-year maturity: 10 percent.

   a. Within what general price range do you think the bonds would sell on January 1, 1987?

   b. Toward which end of this range do you think the actual price would lie?

   c. If the bonds actually sold at a price of $1,500 on January 1, 1987, what pre-tax rate of return could a pension fund expect if it bought the bonds?

   d. Suppose, on January 1, 1987, you were the pension fund's investment manager, and you had a choice between the BI bonds at a price of $1,500 and a new issue of 5-year, noncallable, 7.75 percent coupon, semiannual payment, $1,000 par bonds also issued by BI that sell at par. Which would you prefer, the 18 percent bonds of 2012 or the 7.75 percent bonds of 1992?

   e. Does your answer to Part d suggest that you might want to change your answer to Part a?

3-6 **(After-tax yield to maturity)** It is now January 1, 1987. The Kamco Corporation has a 15 percent, semiannual coupon, noncallable bond issue outstanding which matures on December 31, 2006. Each bond currently sells for 112 percent of its $1,000 par value.

    a. What is the bond's before-tax yield to maturity?

    b. What is the bond's *effective* annual YTM?

    c. What is the bond's after-tax yield to maturity to an investor in the 28 percent marginal tax bracket?

        (1) Assume that the premium is treated as a long-term capital loss at maturity.

        (2) Assume that the premium is amortized over the life of the issue and used to offset the interest income.

3-7 **(Preferred stock valuation)** The Casey Company has a perpetual preferred stock issue outstanding that pays a 10 percent dividend. The par value of each share is $100 and the dividend is paid quarterly. The shares are currently trading for $85.

    a. What is the expected nominal rate of return on the issue?

    b. What is the expected effective annual rate of return?

    c. What is the expected after-tax return (1) to an individual investor in the 28 percent marginal tax bracket? (2) To a corporate investor in the 34 percent marginal tax bracket?

    d. Now assume that the issue has a sinking fund provision whereby the firm redeems 10 percent of the issue in each year over the next 10 years at a share price equal to par value, or $100. What is the expected pre-tax rate of return with a sinking fund provision? (Hint: No investor knows when his or her shares will be redeemed, but the expected time to redemption is 5 years.)

3-8 **(Bond and preferred stock tax effects)** Preferred stock is riskier for investors than bonds because interest payments are a contractual obligation which must be met, whereas preferred dividends can be omitted without the risk of bankruptcy. But most firms can issue preferred stock having a slightly lower dividend yield than the interest rate required on roughly comparable bond issues. For example, a firm might need to offer a 12 percent coupon payment on new bonds, but it may be able to issue new preferred stock with an 11 percent dividend yield.

    a. Why can riskier preferred stock be offered at a lower expected rate of return than can less risky bonds?

    b. What type of investor normally buys preferred stock?

    c. Most firms do not use preferred stock financing, in spite of your answer to Part a. Why?

3-9 **(Declining firm valuation)** Nevada Silver Company's ore reserves are being depleted, and its costs of recovering a declining quantity of ore are rising each year. As a result, the company's earnings and dividends are declining at the rate of 10 percent per year.

    a. If $D_0 = \$6$ and $k_s = 15\%$, what is the value of Nevada Silver's stock?

    b. Explain why anyone would be willing to buy a stock whose price is expected to fall over time.

3-10 **(Constant growth stock valuation)** Grover Laboratories' next annual dividend is forecast to be $2.00, and the firm is expected to grow at a constant annual rate of 6 percent indefinitely. Investors require a return of 15 percent on this stock.

    a. What is the stock's intrinsic value?

    b. Refer to Footnote 17. What is Grover's intrinsic value using the quarterly growth model?

    c. Explain why your answers to Parts a and b are different.

3-11 **(Value of dividends)** Nathan Peterson, the president of Bennett Chemical, recently made the following statement: "Our firm has virtually unlimited growth opportunities. Thus, we will be retaining all earnings within the firm, and hence paying no dividends. In fact, I can't see us ever paying any dividends. Let the stockholders get their returns by price appreciation. Heck, they should like that better anyway." Evaluate the impact of this statement on Bennett's stock price.

3-12 **(Zero dividend stock valuation)** It is now January 1, 1987. Last year, Blue Ridge Coal suffered a major strike which had a disastrous effect on the firm's financial condition, forcing management to temporarily suspend dividend payments. It is expected that the firm will not pay a dividend in 1987 or 1988, but it will declare a $0.50 per share dividend in 1989. Dividend growth is expected to be 3 percent in 1990 and 1991, and thereafter dividends are expected to grow indefinitely at the same rate as the national economy, 6 percent. The required rate of return on the stock, k_s, is 15 percent.

   a. Calculate the expected dividends for 1987 through 1992.

   b. Find the value of the stock today.

   c. Calculate the current dividend yield, D_1/P_0, the capital gains yield expected in 1987, $(\hat{P}_1 - P_0)/P_0$, and the expected total return (dividend yield plus capital gains yield) for 1987. Also, calculate these same three yields for 1988 and 1989. Assume that the stock is in equilibrium; thus, $\hat{P}_0 = P_0$.

   d. What is the impact of zero dividends on the return mix; that is, on the relative values of dividend yield versus capital gains yield? Would an investor's tax situation influence the value of such stocks?

3-13 **(Nonconstant growth stock valuation)** Jamaica Bauxite Company (JBC) has been growing at a rate of 25 percent per year in recent years. This same growth rate is expected to last for another 2 years, after which growth will drop to the normal long-run rate of 6 percent. JBC's last dividend was $2, and the stock's required rate of return is 14 percent.

   a. What is JBC's stock worth today? What is its current dividend yield and capital gains yield?

   b. Now assume that JBC's period of supernormal growth is 5 years rather than 2 years. How does this affect its price, dividend yield, and capital gains yield?

   c. What will JBC's dividend yield and capital gains yield be the year after its period of supernormal growth ends? (Hint: These values will be the same regardless of whether you examine the case of 2 or 5 years of supernormal growth.)

   d. Of what interest to investors is the changing relationship between dividend yield and capital gains yield over time?

3-14 **(Nonconstant growth stock valuation)** It is now January 1, 1987. Solana Engineering has just developed a solar panel capable of generating 200 percent more electricity than any solar panel currently on the market. As a result, Solana is expected to experience a 30 percent annual growth rate for the next 5 years. By the end of 5 years other firms will have developed comparable technology, and Solana's growth rate will slow to 8 percent per year indefinitely. Stockholders require a return of 12 percent on Solana stock. The most recent annual dividend (D_0), which was paid yesterday, was $1.50 per share.

   a. Calculate the expected dividends for 1987, 1988, 1989, 1990, 1991, and 1992.

   b. Calculate the value of the stock today, $\hat{P}_0$. Proceed by finding the present value of the dividends expected at the end of 1987, 1988, 1989, 1990, and 1991 plus the present value of the stock price which should exist at the end of 1991.

   c. Calculate the current dividend yield, D_1/P_0, the capital gains yield expected in 1987 and the expected total return (dividend yield plus capital gains yield) for 1987. (Assume that $\hat{P}_0 = P_0$, and recognize that the capital gains yield is equal to the total return minus the dividend yield.) Also, calculate these same three yields for 1991.

d. How might an investor's tax situation affect his or her decision to purchase stocks of companies in the early stages of their lives, when they are growing rapidly, versus stocks of older, more mature firms? When does Solana Engineering stock become "mature" in this example?

(Do Parts e and f only if you are using the computerized diskette.)

e. Suppose your boss tells you that she believes that Solana's annual growth rate will be only 15 percent over the next 5 years, and that the firm's normal growth rate is only 6 percent. Calculate the expected dividend stream and the value of the stock today under these assumptions.

f. Suppose your boss also tells you that she regards Solana as being quite risky, and that she feels that the required rate of return is 15 percent, not 12 percent. Calculate the value of Solana's stock. Do the calculations with k_s values of 20 percent and 25 percent to see how k_s affects the stock price.

3-15 (After-tax security valuation) On January 1, 1987, you are considering buying stock in GenStar Corporation, which has just announced a new type of biodegradable container. Earnings per share in 1986 were $1.20. The company's expected earnings growth rate is 50 percent for 1987 and 1988, 25 percent for the following 2 years, and 10 percent thereafter. Its payout ratio is expected to be zero in 1987 and 1988, to rise to 20 percent for the following 2 years, and then to stabilize at 50 percent. $k_M = 15\%$, $k_{RF} = 10\%$, and GenStar's b = 1.2.

   a. What is GenStar's market price, if the assumptions set forth previously are those of a "representative" investor?

   b. Suppose that the investor was offered the opportunity to purchase a "junk bond" issued by TeleTech Company, a competitor of GenStar. The issue has four years remaining until maturity, and carries a coupon rate of 12%. What price could the investor pay for this bond and earn the same *before-tax* return as the GenStar stock (16%)? What is the after-tax yield to an investor with a 40% state-plus-federal marginal tax rate?

   c. Assume that you (1) are in the 40 percent tax bracket, (2) can buy GenStar stock for $22.26, and (3) can buy the TeleTech Company junk bond for $888.07. Your investment horizon is four years hence, as you would like to buy a house. (Remember that the TeleTech bond had 4 years to maturity.) Which investment would be a better choice for you?

(Do Parts d and e only if you are using the computerized diskette.)

   d. Try varying the purchase price of the TeleTech bond, while keeping the tax rate at 40%. How low must the price of the bond drop before you would consider choosing it over the GenStar stock?

   e. Suppose Congress reinstated the capital gains tax preference, making the tax rate on long-term capital gains only 40 percent of the rate on ordinary income. How would this affect the after-tax return of the two investment alternatives? Would this alter the decision you made for Part c?

   f. In general, what can you conclude about the type of clientele which would be attracted to each alternative?

3-16 (After-tax security valuation) Assume that you are in the 40 percent federal-plus-state marginal tax bracket and that capital gains taxes are deferred until maturity. Assuming equal investment risk and a horizontal yield curve, rank the following investment opportunities on the basis of their effective annual yields:

   a. A $100 par value perpetual preferred stock with an annual coupon of 12 percent, quarterly payments, and selling at $105.

b. A 20-year, noncallable, semiannual bond with a coupon of 12 percent currently selling at $1,050 versus a $1,000 par value.

c. A 20-year, noncallable, semiannual bond with a coupon of 6 percent selling at a price of $637 versus a $1,000 par value.

d. How would the situation change if the ranker had been (1) a pension fund investment manager or (2) a corporation that is in the 40 percent federal-plus-state bracket? Explain in words but demonstrate that you could quantify your answer.

Selected Additional References

Many investments textbooks cover stock and bond valuation models in depth and detail. Some of the better ones are listed in the Chapter 2 references.

The seminal work on stock valuation models is

Williams, John Burr, *The Theory of Investment Value* (Cambridge, Mass.: Harvard University Press, 1938).

The following classic articles extend J. B. Williams's works:

Durand, David, "Growth Stocks and the Petersburg Paradox," *Journal of Finance*, September 1957, 348-363.

Gordon, Myron J., and Eli Shapiro, "Capital Equipment Analysis: The Required Rate of Profit," *Management Science*, October 1956, 102-110.

The quarterly stock valuation model is discussed in

Linke, Charles M. and J. Kenton Zumwalt, "Estimation Biases in Discounted Cash Flow Analyses of Equity Captial Cost in Rate Regulation," *Financial Management*, Autumn 1984, 15-21.

 # 3A

DERIVATION OF VALUATION EQUATIONS

The derivation of the formulas for the value of a perpetuity and the value of a constant growth stock are presented here.

Value of a Perpetuity

The value of a perpetual preferred stock is given by

$$P_0 = \frac{D}{(1 + k_p)^1} + \frac{D}{(1 + k_p)^2} + \ldots + \frac{D}{(1 + k_p)^\infty}. \qquad \text{(3A-1)}$$

Equation 3A-1 may be rewritten as follows:

$$P_0 = D\left[\frac{1}{(1 + k_p)^1} + \frac{1}{(1 + k_p)^2} + \ldots + \frac{1}{(1 + k_p)^n}\right]. \qquad \text{(3A-2)}$$

Multiply both sides of Equation 3A-2 by $(1 + k_p)$:

$$P_0(1 + k_p) = D\left[1 + \frac{1}{(1 + k_p)^1} + \frac{1}{(1 + k_p)^2} + \ldots + \frac{1}{(1 + k_p)^{n-1}}\right]. \qquad \text{(3A-3)}$$

Subtract Equation 3A-2 from Equation 3A-3, obtaining

$$P_0(1 + k_p - 1) = D\left[1 - \frac{1}{(1 + k_p)^n}\right]. \tag{3A-4}$$

As $n \to \infty$, $1/(1 + k_p)^n \to 0$, so Equation 3A-4 approaches

$$P_0(k_p) = D,$$

and thus we obtain Equation 3-5,

$$P_0 = \frac{D}{k_p}.$$

Although we used preferred stock notation, Equation 3-5 is valid for any perpetuity.

Value of a Constant Growth Stock

The proof for Equation 3-8, the formula for the value of a constant growth stock, $\hat{P}_0 = D_1/(k_s - g)$, is developed as follows. Rewrite Equation 3-7 as

$$\hat{P}_0 = \frac{D_0(1 + g)^1}{(1 + k_s)^1} + \frac{D_0(1 + g)^2}{(1 + k_s)^2} + \frac{D_0(1 + g)^3}{(1 + k_s)^3} + \cdots + \frac{D_0(1 + g)^n}{(1 + k_s)^n}$$

$$= D_0\left[\frac{(1 + g)^1}{(1 + k_s)^1} + \frac{(1 + g)^2}{(1 + k_s)^2} + \frac{(1 + g)^3}{(1 + k_s)^3} + \cdots + \frac{(1 + g)^n}{(1 + k_s)^n}\right]. \tag{3A-5}$$

Multiply both sides of Equation 3A-5 by $(1 + k_s)/(1 + g)$:

$$\left[\frac{(1 + k_s)}{(1 + g)}\right]\hat{P}_0 = D_0\left[1 + \frac{(1 + g)^1}{(1 + k_s)^1} + \frac{(1 + g)^2}{(1 + k_s)^2} + \cdots + \frac{(1 + g)^{n-1}}{(1 + k_s)^{n-1}}\right]. \tag{3A-6}$$

Subtract Equation 3A-5 from Equation 3A-6 to obtain

$$\left[\frac{(1 + k_s)}{(1 + g)} - 1\right]\hat{P}_0 = D_0\left[1 - \frac{(1 + g)^n}{(1 + k_s)^n}\right].$$

$$\left[\frac{(1 + k_s) - (1 + g)}{(1 + g)}\right]\hat{P}_0 = D_0\left[1 - \frac{(1 + g)^n}{(1 + k_s)^n}\right].$$

Assuming $k_s > g$, as $n \to \infty$ the term in brackets on the right-hand side of the equation $\to 1.0$, leaving

$$\left[\frac{(1 + k_s) - (1 + g)}{(1 + g)}\right]\hat{P}_0 = D_0,$$

which simplifies to Equation 3-8,

$$(k_s - g)\hat{P}_0 = D_0(1 + g) = D_1$$

$$\hat{P}_0 = \frac{D_1}{k_s - g}. \tag{3-8}$$

 **II**

COST OF CAPITAL AND
CAPITAL STRUCTURE

4

THE COST OF CAPITAL

A firm's cost of capital is critically important in finance for three reasons: (1) Maximizing the value of a firm requires that the costs of all inputs, including capital, be minimized, and to minimize the cost of capital we must be able to estimate it. (2) Proper capital budgeting decisions require an estimate of the cost of capital. (3) Many other types of decisions, including those related to leasing, bond refunding, and working capital policy, require estimates of the cost of capital.[1]

Although in theory a cost of capital estimate is easy to develop, in practice it is an extremely difficult process. Our discussion in this chapter focuses on the actual estimation process, and we proceed in three steps: (1) We identify those capital components which should be included in the cost of capital, (2) we determine the cost of each capital component, and then (3) we bring together the component costs to form a weighted average, or overall, cost of capital to the firm.

CAPITAL COMPONENTS AND COSTS

In developing the firm's overall cost of capital, we first identify and then determine the cost of each component, and then we combine the component costs to form the *weighted average cost of capital (WACC)*. *Capital*, as we use the term, represents the funds used to finance the firm's assets and operations. The operations which produce sales and profits are not possible without the assets that are shown on the left side of the balance sheet, and those assets must be financed from the sources shown on the right side. Thus, capital constitutes the entire right-hand side of the balance sheet, including both short-term and long-term debt, preferred stock, and common equity.

Capital Components

Our first task is to decide which capital sources should be included in the WACC estimate. Since the cost of capital is used primarily in the process of making long-term investment decisions, our discussion will focus on the development of the

---

[1]Additionally, the cost of capital is vitally important in regulated industries, including electric, gas, telephone, and water companies. In essence, regulatory commissions first measure a utility's cost of capital, and then they set prices so that the company will just earn this rate of return. If the cost of capital estimate is too low, then the company will not be able to attract sufficient capital to meet long-run demands for service, and the public will suffer. If the estimated cost of capital is too high, customers will pay too much for service.

cost of capital for capital budgeting purposes. First, consider the firm's short-term, non-interest-bearing liabilities: accounts payable, accrued wages, and accrued taxes. All of these items arise from normal operations; if sales increase, then funds are spontaneously (automatically) generated from these sources. In capital budgeting analyses, the dollar amount of the spontaneously generated liabilities associated with a given project is subtracted from the amount that would otherwise be required to finance the project. To illustrate, assume that a potential project has a total cost of $2,000,000, consisting of $1,500,000 of fixed assets and $500,000 of required new current assets, say inventories. However, if payables and accruals will spontaneously increase by $200,000 if the project is undertaken, then these funds serve to offset the increase in current assets. Thus, the project's net current assets (or net working capital) would be only $300,000, and the net funds required for the project would be only $1,800,000. It is the cost of this $1,800,000 that concerns us; will the return on the project be high enough to cover the cost of the $1,800,000 of nonspontaneous capital required to undertake it? Since we are concerned with the cost of the nonspontaneous capital, spontaneously generated liabilities are not included when the WACC is calculated.

We must also decide how to treat short-term notes payable, often bank loans, which are not generated spontaneously. The answer depends on whether the firm deliberately uses short-term debt to finance long-term investments. If short-term debt is generally used as temporary financing to support cyclical or seasonal fluctuations in assets, it should not be considered when the WACC is calculated. However, if the firm does use short-term debt as part of its permanent financing, then such debt should be included in the cost of capital calculation. As we will show in Chapter 16, the use of nonspontaneous short-term debt to finance long-term assets is a highly risky procedure, and it is not common among well-managed firms. Therefore, in this chapter, we shall assume that interest-bearing, short-term debt is used to support cyclical or seasonal working capital, and since our primary focus is on developing a cost of capital for use in capital budgeting, we shall exclude short-term debt when we calculate the WACC unless otherwise noted. Long-term debt, preferred stock, and common equity (including retained earnings) are the primary sources of capital for capital expansion, so they are all included in the WACC calculation.

In summary, the relevant capital components for cost of capital purposes are (1) that portion of short-term interest-bearing debt that is considered to be permanent financing; (2) all long-term debt; (3) all preferred stock; and (4) all common equity. Non-interest-bearing liabilities such as accounts payable are netted out in the capital budgeting process and are excluded from the cost of capital calculations.

Taxes

In developing the costs for the different capital components, the issue of taxes arises: Should we use a before- or an after-tax cost? In considering this question, remember that stockholders are concerned primarily with the cash flows that are available for their use, namely, those cash flows available to common shareholders after corporate taxes have been paid. Therefore, if management is to maximize stockholder well-being and thereby maximize the price of the stock, all cash flow/ rate of return calculations must be done on an after-tax basis. *For this reason, the WACC must be developed on an after-tax basis, so we must consider corporate tax effects when we determine the cost of each relevant capital component.*

Historical Versus New, or Marginal, Costs

Another issue is this: Is the historical, or embedded, cost of capital raised in the past relevant, or should we focus on the cost of new, marginal funds? Embedded costs are important for some decisions. For example, the average cost of all the debt raised in the past and still outstanding is relevant to regulators who determine the allowed rate of return for a public utility. However, in financial management, the WACC is used primarily to make capital budgeting decisions, and these decisions hinge on the cost of new capital. *Thus, for our purposes in this chapter, the relevant costs are not historical costs but, rather, the marginal costs of new funds to be raised during the planning period.*

COST OF DEBT

As discussed just above, the relevant cost of debt is the after-tax cost of new debt. Although estimating this cost is conceptually straightforward, some problems arise in practice. First, as noted in an earlier section, it is necessary to decide whether or not short-term debt should be included in the WACC. Second, not all long-term debt has a fixed and known payment schedule: companies use both fixed and floating rate debt, straight and convertible debt, and debt both with or without sinking funds. Each form of debt generally has a somewhat different cost, and large firms normally use several different types.

It is unlikely that the financial manager will know at the start of a planning period the exact types and amounts of debt that will be used during the planning period: the type of debt actually used will depend on the specific assets to be financed and on capital market conditions as they develop over time. Even so, the financial manager does know what types of debt are typical for his or her firm. For example, National Computer Corporation (NCC), a full line computer manufacturer, typically sells commercial paper to raise short-term money to finance cyclical working capital needs and 30-year bonds to raise long-term debt capital. Thus, for planning purposes, NCC's managers include only long-term debt in their WACC estimate, and they assume that this debt will consist of 30-year bonds.

Assume that it is January 1987. NCC's financial managers are developing the firm's WACC estimate for 1987. How should they determine the component cost of debt? Most financial managers would begin by discussing current and prospective interest rates with their firms' investment bankers. Assume that NCC's banker stated that a new 30-year, noncallable, straight bond issue would require a 12 percent coupon rate, with semiannual payments, and that it would be offered to the public at a $1,000 par value. Flotation costs are estimated to be 1 percent of the issue, or $10 for every $1,000 par value bond. Thus, the net proceeds from each bond would be $1,000 less a $10 flotation cost, or $990. NCC's marginal tax rate is 34 percent.

With this information, we would estimate the cost of debt in two steps:

1. Find the *before-tax cost to the company* using this equation:

$$\begin{aligned}
\text{Net proceeds of bond} &= \sum_{t=1}^{2n} \frac{\text{Semiannual interest payment}}{(1 + k_d/2)^t} + \frac{\text{Par value}}{(1 + k_d/2)^n} \qquad (4\text{-}1) \\[2mm]
\$990 &= \sum_{t=1}^{60} \frac{\$60}{(1 + k_d/2)^t} + \frac{\$1{,}000}{(1 + k_d/2)^{60}}.
\end{aligned}$$

Using a financial calculator, we find $k_d/2 = 6.06\%$, and hence the flotation-adjusted $k_d = 12.12\%$.

2. Adjust for taxes using this equation:

$$\begin{aligned}
\text{After-tax cost of debt} &= \text{Pre-tax cost}(1 - T) \\
&= (\text{Flotation-adjusted } k_d)(1 - T) \qquad (4\text{-}2) \\
&= 12.12\%(0.66) = 8.00\%.
\end{aligned}$$

Note that most public offerings of debt have flotation costs of less than one percentage point, and flotation costs are even lower on private placements. Thus, if flotation costs were simply ignored, and the component cost of debt were found as $k_d(1 - T)$, the error would not be very large.[2] In our own example, $k_d(1 - T) = 12\%(0.66) = 7.92\%$, and hence the error would be eight basis points.[3]

Before closing our discussion of the cost of debt, we should note one additional point regarding the tax adjustment. In our example, we used a marginal tax rate of 34 percent. Therefore, we were implicitly assuming that NCC's marginal tax rate over the next 30 years will remain at 34 percent. However, there are three potential problems with this assumption: (1) The value of the tax deduction depends on the taxable income for each year, and a change in taxable income might lead to a change in the marginal tax rate, and hence to a change in the after-tax cost of debt. (2) Tax losses can only be carried back for three years; therefore, several years of consecutive losses would mean that the benefits of tax deductibility could not be realized in the year the interest is paid. Instead, this benefit would

---

[2]Several other points should be made. First, if the bond is callable, then we might want to analyze the yield to call. However, for newly issued bonds, expected yield to call is equal to yield to maturity. Second, it is sometimes suggested that the effective annual rate cost of debt should be used in the WACC. In our example, the flotation-adjusted effective annual rate is $(1.0606)^2 - 1.0 = 0.1249 = 12.49\%$. That position would be correct only if the cost of common stock were based on a quarterly compounding model and if, in capital budgeting, an attempt were made to determine exactly when, during the year, cash flows would come in rather than assuming end-of-year flows. In view of the uncertainties inherent in cost of equity estimation, and the even greater uncertainties about the cash flows of projects over their operating lives, we (and most people in industry) think it would be pointless to attempt to estimate effective rates and intra-year cash flows; it would even be misleading in that such calculations would imply greater accuracy than exist in the basic data. Further, it would be inconsistent to use an effective bond yield with an annual return on equity—the bond's cost would be inflated vis-à-vis that of the equity. Finally, note that the flotation cost can be amortized over the life of the bond ($\$10/30 = \$0.33$ per year, or $\$0.167$ per semiannual period). This saves taxes in the amount of $\$0.167(T) = \$0.167(0.34) = \$0.057$ per period. Theoretically, we should take this tax savings into account, but ignoring it does not introduce a material error.

[3]A basis point is 1/100 of a percentage point. Investment bankers in particular use this term.

be delayed until the firm becomes profitable, and this would raise the after-tax cost of debt. (3) Congress could, as they just did in 1986, raise or lower the applicable tax rate, which would also have an effect on the after-tax cost of debt. For all these reasons, we should recognize that firms cannot be certain of the true effects of tax deductibility, so the true cost of debt could be higher or lower than the calculated after-tax cost.

COST OF PREFERRED STOCK

A number of firms, including National Computer Company, use preferred stock as part of their permanent financing mix. To determine this cost, we first note that preferred dividends, like common dividends, are not tax deductible. *Therefore, no tax adjustment is necessary when calculating the cost of preferred stock.* Second, most preferred is issued without a stated maturity date, although almost all preferred issued in recent years does have a call feature and/or a sinking fund. Finally, although it is not mandatory that preferred stock dividends be paid, firms do generally have every intention of meeting their preferred dividend payments, because if they fail to do so (1) they cannot pay dividends on their common stock, (2) they will find it very difficult to raise additional funds in the capital markets, and (3) in some cases preferred stockholders have the right to assume control of the firm.

With these points in mind, assume that NCC's investment banker indicated that the firm could sell 12 percent preferred stock. If the stock had a par value of $100, then the annual dividend would be $12. Additionally, the investment banker stated that the flotation costs would amount to 2.5 percent of the par value. Thus, the firm would net $97.50 from each share sold, and it would have an obligation to pay $12 of dividends per share per year. Thus, we calculate the component cost of preferred stock as follows:

$$\text{Component cost of preferred stock} = k_p = \frac{D_p}{P_n}. \tag{4-3}$$

Here D_p is the annual preferred dividend and P_n is the price the firm receives net of flotation costs. Applying Equation 4-3 to our example, we find NCC's cost of preferred stock to be 12.31 percent:[4]

$$k_p = \frac{D_p}{P_n} = \frac{\$12}{\$97.50} = 0.1231 = 12.31\%.$$

[4]Most preferred stocks pay quarterly dividends, so we could calculate an effective return based on quarterly compounding. However, for the same reasons we discussed in Footnote 2 in connection with debt, it would be inappropriate (or at least not worthwhile) to do so. We should also note that firms have begun to issue variable, or floating rate, bonds and preferred stocks. Since future capital market rates are difficult, if not impossible, to predict, future interest payments and preferred dividends are normally estimated on the basis of current rates, and hence the expected costs of floating rate securities are the same as for fixed rate securities. However, the realized cost on a floating rate issue can be higher or lower than expected, depending on the actual rates over the life of the security, whereas the realized cost of a fixed rate security is known with relative certainty. Finally, note that current tax laws do not permit either preferred or common stock flotation costs to be expensed against taxable income.

COST OF COMMON EQUITY

A firm can raise common equity capital in two ways: (1) by retaining earnings and (2) by issuing new common stock. Thus, when we consider NCC's component cost of equity, we are really considering the costs of two different types of equity.

COST OF RETAINED EARNINGS

The costs of debt and preferred stock are based on the return that investors require on these securities, and the cost of equity obtained by retaining earnings can be defined similarly: *It is k_s, the rate of return stockholders require on the firm's common stock.*

The reason why we must assign a cost of capital to retained earnings involves the *opportunity cost principle*. The firm's net income after taxes and after preferred dividends are paid literally belongs to its common stockholders. Bondholders are compensated by interest payments; preferred stockholders are compensated by fixed dividend payments; and the firm's remaining income belongs to its common stockholders and serves to "pay the rent" on stockholders' capital.

Management may either pay out earnings in the form of dividends or retain earnings for reinvestment in the business. If part of the earnings is retained, an *opportunity cost* is incurred: stockholders could have received these earnings as dividends and then invested this money in stocks, bonds, real estate, and so on. *Thus, the firm should earn on its retained earnings at least as much as its stockholders themselves could earn on alternative investments of equivalent risk.*

What rate of return can stockholders expect to earn on other investments of equivalent risk? The answer is k_s: they can get a return of k_s in the market by buying the stock of the firm in question or the stocks of similar firms. Therefore, if the firm cannot invest retained earnings and earn at least k_s, then it should pay these earnings to its stockholders so that they can invest the money themselves in assets that do provide this return.

Whereas debt and preferred stock are contractual obligations which have easily determined costs, it is not at all easy to measure k_s. Three methods can be used to estimate k_s: (1) the Capital Asset Pricing Model (CAPM), (2) the Discounted Cash Flow (DCF) model, and (3) the bond yield plus risk premium approach. These methods should not be regarded as mutually exclusive, for none of them dominates the others, and all are subject to error when used in practice. When faced with the task of estimating a company's cost of equity, we generally use all three and then choose among them on the basis of how we judge the validity of the data used for each one in the specific case at hand.

THE CAPM APPROACH

As we saw in Chapter 2, the Capital Asset Pricing Model is based on some unrealistic assumptions, and it has not been empirically verified. Still, the model is often used in the cost of capital estimation process because of its logical appeal.

Under the CAPM we assume that common stockholders view only market risk as being relevant. Thus, the risk premium that investors demand is assumed to be based solely on the stock's beta coefficient and the market risk premium as set forth in the Security Market Line (SML) equation:

$$k_s = k_{RF} + b_i(k_M - k_{RF}).$$

Given an estimate of (1) the risk-free rate, k_{RF}; (2) the beta of the firm's stock, b_i; and (3) the required rate of return on the market, k_M, we can estimate the required rate of return on the firm's stock, k_s. This required return can then be used as an estimate of the cost of retained earnings.

Estimating the Risk-Free Rate

The starting point for the CAPM cost of equity estimate is k_{RF}, the risk-free rate. There is really no such thing in the U.S. economy as a riskless asset. Treasury securities are essentially free of default risk, but long-term T-bonds are subject to capital losses if interest rates rise, and a portfolio invested in short-term T-bills will provide a volatile earnings stream because the rate paid on T-bills varies over time.

Since we cannot in practice find a truly riskless rate upon which to base the CAPM, what rate should we use? Our preference—and this preference is shared by most practitioners—is to use the rate on long-term Treasury bonds. Our reasons follow:

1. Capital market rates include a pure rate (generally thought to vary from 2 to 4 percent) plus a premium for expected inflation. This premium reflects the inflation rate expected over the life of the asset, be it 30 days or 30 years. The rate of inflation is likely to be relatively high during booms and low during recessions. Therefore, during booms T-bill rates tend to be high to reflect the high current inflation rate, whereas in recessions T-bill rates are generally low. T-bond rates, on the other hand, reflect expected inflation rates over a long period, hence they are far less volatile than T-bill rates.

2. Common stocks are long-term securities, and although a particular stockholder may not have a long investment horizon, a majority of stockholders do invest on a long-term basis. Therefore, it seems more reasonable to think that stock returns would embody long-term inflation expectations similar to those embodied in bonds rather than the short-term inflation expectations in bills. On this account, the cost of equity should be more highly correlated with T-bond rates than with T-bill rates.

3. Treasury bill rates are subject to more random disturbances than are Treasury bond rates. For example, bills are used by the Federal Reserve System to control the money supply, and bills are also used by foreign governments, firms, and individuals as a temporary safe-house for money. Thus, if the Fed decides to stimulate the economy, it drives down the bill rate, and the same thing happens if trouble erupts somewhere in the world and money flows into the United States seeking a temporary haven. T-bond rates are also influenced by Fed actions and by international money flows, but not to the same extent as T-bill rates. This is another reason why T-bill rates are more volatile than T-bond rates and, we think, more volatile than k_s.

4. We have seen the CAPM used to estimate a particular firm's cost of equity over time. When T-bill rates were low, in 1977 and 1978, the CAPM cost of equity estimate was about 11 percent. When T-bill rates shot up in 1979 and 1980, the CAPM estimate more than doubled, to 23 percent. The company's bond yields, meanwhile, only rose from 9 to 14 percent. Neither we nor the company's management believed that the cost of equity rose by 12 full percentage points while the cost of long-term debt was rising by only 5 percentage points. CAPM estimates based on T-bond yields produced much more reasonable results.[5]

In view of the preceding discussion, it is our view that common equity costs are more logically related to Treasury bond rates than to T-bill rates. This leads us to favor T-bonds as the base rate, or k_{RF}, in a CAPM cost of equity analysis.[6] T-bond rates can be found in *The Wall Street Journal* or the *Federal Reserve Bulletin*. Generally, we use the yield on a 20-year T-bond as the proxy for the risk-free rate. Assuming that this rate was 9.7 percent in January 1987, we would use this as our estimate for k_{RF} in a January 1987 CAPM cost of equity estimate.

Estimating the Market Risk Premium

The market risk premium, $RP_M = k_M - k_{RF}$, can be estimated in one of two major ways: (1) an analysis based on ex post, or historical, returns and (2) an analysis based on ex ante, or forward-looking, returns.

Ex Post Risk Premiums

The most thorough and widely publicized ex post risk premium study is conducted annually by Ibbotson Associates, who examine market data over long periods of time to find the average annual rates of return on stocks, T-bills, T-bonds,

---

[5]All of this can be illustrated by a true but not-very-funny story. A particular state public utility commission hired a professor who used T-bill rates as the base rate in his CAPM analysis to estimate the cost of capital for the state's utilities. Each utility's cost of capital in turn was built into its electric, gas, or telephone rates. Therefore, the lower the cost of capital, the lower the utility service rates, and the lower the service rates, the less political heat the commission faced. This particular commission was very politically sensitive—so much so that one of its staff members admitted privately that the commission had selected its cost of capital expert on the basis of who could produce the lowest number.

The commission hired the professor in 1978, when T-bill rates were very low, as were his CAPM cost of equity estimates based on the T-bill rate. But the rate cases did not come up until 1979, and by then, the bill rate had gone through the roof. As a result, the professor's cost of equity estimates were even higher than the companies were asking permission to earn! At that point, the commission rejected the CAPM approach and sent the professor home. We have not heard much about him lately, but with short-term rates now below long-term rates, he may attempt a comeback.

[6]Astute students will note that the T-bond rate is not a true risk-free rate because long-term bond rates contain a maturity premium which compensates investors for interest rate risk. However, this premium is very difficult to measure at any point in time, and its impact on stocks and bonds is probably similar. We are willing, therefore, to accept the T-bond rate as a proxy for k_{RF}.

Table 4-1
Ibbotson Associates Risk Premiums

Risk Premium	Arithmetic Mean	Standard Deviation
Stocks over T-bills	8.2%	21.3%
Stocks over T-bonds	7.6	a
Stocks over corporate bonds	7.0	a

[a]Ibbotson Associates did not report a standard deviation for risk premiums of stocks over T-bonds or corporate bonds. However, we made several estimates and concluded that their magnitudes are comparable to that of the stocks-over-T-bills risk premium.

and a set of high-grade corporate bonds.[7] For example, Table 4-1 summarizes some results from their 1985 study, which covers the period 1926-1984. They first subtracted the historical, or realized, return on the various debt securities from the historical realized return on stocks, in each of the 59 years. They then obtained the average risk premiums of stocks over T-bills, T-bonds, and corporate bonds, and the standard deviations of those risk premiums.

Ibbotson Associates found the average risk premium of stocks over T-bonds to be 7.6 percentage points.[8] However, these premiums have large standard deviations, so one must use them with caution. Also, it should be noted that the choice of the beginning and ending periods can have a major impact on the calculated risk premiums. Ibbotson Associates used the longest period available to them, but had their data begun some years earlier or later, or ended earlier, their results would have been seriously affected. Indeed, over many periods their data would indicate *negative* risk premiums, which would lead to the conclusion that Treasury securities have a higher required return than common stocks, which in turn is contrary to both financial theory and common sense. All this suggests that historical risk premiums should be approached with a great deal of caution. As one businessman muttered after listening to a professor give a lecture on the CAPM, "Beware of academicians bearing gifts!"

Ex Ante Risk Premiums

The ex post approach to risk premiums assumes that investors expect future results, on average, to equal past results. However, as noted previously, the estimated risk premium varies depending on the period selected, and, in any event, investors

---

[7]See *Stocks, Bonds, Bills, and Inflation: 1985 Yearbook* (Chicago: Ibbotson Associates, 1985).

[8]It is worth noting that Ibbotson Associates calculated average returns on two bases: (1) by taking each of the 59 annual holding period returns during the years 1926-1984 and deriving the arithmetic average of these annual returns and (2) by finding the compound annual rate of return over the whole period, which amounts to a geometric average. The risk premium as measured by arithmetic averages is 2.2 percentage points higher than the geometric mean risk premium. This leads to the question of which average to use. The arithmetic average is most consistent with the standard CAPM; under the CAPM, investors are supposed to be concerned with returns during the next period (say one year) and to focus on the expected return and the standard deviation of this return.

in the 1980s probably expect results in the future to be different from those achieved during the Great Depression of the 1930s, the World War II of the 1940s, and the peaceful boom years of the 1950s, all of which are included (and given equal weight to more recent results) in the Ibbotson data. The highly questionable assumption that future expectations are equal to past realizations, together with the sometimes nonsensical results obtained in historical risk premium studies, has led to a search for ex ante risk premiums.

The most fruitful approach to ex ante premiums uses the Discounted Cash Flow (DCF) model to estimate the expected market rate of return. In other words, use DCF to develop a current estimate of $\hat{k}_M = k_M$; then find RP_M as $k_M - k_{RF}$; and finally use this estimate of RP_M in the CAPM model. This procedure recognizes that, in equilibrium, the expected rate of return on the market is also its required rate of return. Thus, if we can estimate $\hat{k}_M$, we also have an estimate of k_M:

$$\hat{k}_M = \frac{D_1}{P_0} + g = k_{RF} + RP_M = k_M.$$

Since D_1 for the market, say the S&P 500, can be predicted quite accurately, and since the current market value of the index (used for P_0) is known, the major task is to estimate g, the average expected long-term growth rate for the market index. Even here, however, the estimation task is simplified, because one can reasonably assume a constant long-term growth rate for a market proxy such as the S&P 500, whereas the constant growth assumption is generally less appropriate for a single stock.

Financial services companies such as Merrill Lynch publish, on a regular basis, a forecast based on DCF methodology for the expected rate of return on the market, $\hat{k}_M$. For example, Merrill Lynch puts out such a forecast in its bimonthly publication *Quantitative Analysis*. One can subtract the current T-bond rate from such a market forecast to obtain an estimate of the current market risk premium, RP_M. To illustrate, assume that Merrill Lynch's reported expected return on the market in January 1987 was 14.0 percent. The T-bond rate, as mentioned earlier, is assumed to be 9.7 percent. Thus, Merrill Lynch's implied market risk premium over T-bonds would be 4.3 percentage points.

Two potential problems arise when we attempt to use data from organizations such as Merrill Lynch. First, what we really want is *investors'* expectations, and not those of security analysts. However, this is probably not a major problem, since several studies have proved beyond much doubt that investors, on average, form their own expectations on the basis of professional analysts' forecasts. The second problem is that there are a number of investments organizations besides Merrill Lynch, and, at any given time, their forecasts of future market returns are generally somewhat different. This suggests that it would be most appropriate to obtain a number of forecasts of $\hat{k}_M$, and then to use the average value to estimate RP_M for use in the CAPM. A service (Institutional Brokers Estimate System, or IBES) publishes data on the forecasts of essentially all widely followed analysts, so one can use the IBES aggregate growth rate forecast along with an aggregate dividend yield to develop a consensus RP_M forecast, and hence avoid potential bias from the use of only one organization's analysts. However, we have followed the forecasts of several of the larger organizations over a period of several years, and we have rarely found them to differ by more than ± 0.3 percentage points from one another. Therefore, for present purposes, the Merrill Lynch $\hat{k}_M = k_M = 14.0\%$ and $RP_M = 4.3$ percentage points may be considered to be a "reasonable" proxy for the expectations of an average (or marginal) investor.

Note, though, that risk premiums are not stable: they vary over time. Therefore, in CAPM estimates of the cost of equity it is essential to use current estimates of RP_M. Further, neither logic nor empirical data support the use of historical, or ex post, premiums, so when we do cost of capital studies, we obtain estimates of $\hat{k}_M$ as published by a number of brokerage houses and then use the average $\hat{k}_M$ as the basis for $RP_M = k_M - k_{RF}$.

Estimating Beta

The last parameter needed for a CAPM cost of equity estimate is the beta coefficient. Recall from Chapter 2 that a stock's beta is a measure of its volatility relative to that of an average stock, and that betas are generally estimated from the stock's characteristic line; that is, estimated by running a linear regression between past returns on the stock in question and past returns on some market index. We will define betas developed in this manner as *historical betas*.

Note, however, that historical betas show how risky a stock was *in the past*, whereas investors are interested in *future* risk. It may be that a given company appeared to be quite safe in the past, but that things have changed, and its future risk is judged to be higher than its past risk, or vice versa. AT&T is a good example. Historically, AT&T was among the bluest of the blue chips, but investors today recognize that the Bell System was recently broken up, and that the surviving AT&T now faces far more intense competition than it ever faced in the past. Chrysler, on the other hand, was practically bankrupt a few years ago, but it now appears to be quite healthy. Therefore, one would think that Chrysler's risk had declined while AT&T's had increased.

Now consider the use of beta as a measure of a company's risk. If we use a historical beta in a CAPM framework to measure the firm's cost of equity, we are implicitly assuming that its future risk is the same as its past risk. This would be a troublesome assumption for a company like Chrysler or AT&T in 1987. But what about most companies in most years: As a general rule, is future risk sufficiently similar to past risk to warrant the use of historical betas in a CAPM framework? For individual firms, past risk is *not* a good predictor of future risk, and historical betas of individual firms are not very stable.

Since historical betas are not very good predictors of future risk, researchers have sought ways to improve them. This has led to the development of two different types of betas: (1) adjusted historical betas and (2) fundamental betas. *Adjusted betas* grew largely out of the work of Marshall E. Blume, who showed that true betas tend to move toward 1.0 over time.[9] One begins with a firm's pure historical statistical beta, makes an adjustment for the expected future movement toward 1.0, and produces an adjusted beta which will, on average, be a better predictor of the future beta than would the unadjusted historical beta. The adjustment process involves some complex statistics, so we shall not cover it here.

Other researchers have extended the adjustment process to include such fundamental risk variables as financial leverage, sales volatility, and the like. The end product here is a *fundamental beta*.[10] These betas are constantly adjusted to reflect changes in a firm's operations and capital structure, whereas with historical betas (including adjusted ones) such changes might not be reflected until several years after the company's "true" beta had changed.

Adjusted historical betas are obviously heavily dependent on unadjusted betas, and so are fundamental betas as they are actually calculated. Therefore, the plain old historical beta, calculated as the slope of the characteristic line, is important even if one goes on to develop a more exotic version. With this in mind, it should be noted that several different sets of data can be used to calculate historical betas, and the different data sets produce different results. Here are some points to note:

1. Betas can be based on historical periods of different lengths. For example, data for the past one, two, three, and so on years may be used. Most people who calculate betas today use five years of data, but this choice is arbitrary, and different lengths of time usually alter significantly the calculated beta for a given company.[11]

2. Returns may be calculated on holding periods of different lengths—a day, a week, a month, a quarter, a year, and so on. For example, if it has been decided to analyze data on NYSE stocks over a five-year period, then we might obtain $52 \times 5 = 260$ weekly returns on each stock and on the market index. We could also use $12 \times 5 = 60$ monthly returns, or $1 \times 5 = 5$ annual returns, and so on. The set of returns on each stock, however large it turns out to be, would then be regressed on the corresponding market returns to obtain the stock's beta. In statistical analysis, it is generally better to have more rather than fewer observations, because using more observations generally leads to greater statistical confidence. This suggests the use of weekly returns, and say five years of data, for a sample size of 260, or even daily returns for a still larger sample size. However, the shorter the holding period, the more likely the data are to exhibit random "noise," and the greater the number of years of data, the more likely it is that the company's basic risk position will have changed (for example, see the preceding comments

---

[9]See Marshall E. Blume, "Betas and Their Regression Tendencies," *Journal of Finance*, June 1973, 785-796.

[10]See Barr Rosenberg and James Guy, "Beta and Investment Fundamentals," *Financial Analysts Journal*, May-June 1976, 60-72. Rosenberg, a professor at the University of California at Berkeley, later set up a company which calculated fundamental betas by a proprietary procedure and then sold them to institutional investors.

[11]A commercial provider of betas once told the authors that his firm and others did not know what was the right period to use, but they decided to use five years in order to reduce the apparent differences between various services' betas, because large differences reduced everyone's credibility!

on Chrysler and AT&T). Thus, the choice of both number of years of data and length of the holding period for calculating rates of return involves trade-offs between a desire to have many observations versus a desire to have recent and consequently more relevant data.

3. The value used to represent "the market" is also an important consideration, and one that can have a significant effect on the calculated beta. Most beta calculators today use the New York Stock Exchange Composite Index (based on about 1,700 stocks, weighted by the value of each company), but others use the S&P 500 Index or some other group, up to one (the Wilshire Index) with over 5,000 stocks. In theory, the broader the index, the better the beta: indeed, the index should really include returns on all stocks, bonds, leases, private businesses, real estate, and even "human capital." As a practical matter, however, we cannot get accurate returns data on most types of assets, so measurement problems largely restrict us to stock indices.

The bottom line of all this is that one can calculate betas in many different ways, and depending on the method used, different betas, and hence different costs of capital, will result. To illustrate this point, consider Table 4-2 which contains the January 1986 beta coefficients for five well-known companies as reported by Merrill Lynch and Value Line. Merrill Lynch uses the S&P 500 as the market index, while Value Line uses the New York Stock Exchange Composite Index. Further, Value Line betas are adjusted, while the Merrill Lynch betas reported are pure historical betas. Merrill Lynch uses five years of monthly returns, or 60 observations; Value Line uses 260 weekly observations.

Where does this leave financial managers regarding the proper beta? They must "pay their money and take their choice." Some managers will calculate their own betas, using whichever procedure seems most appropriate under the circumstances. Others will use betas calculated by organizations such as Merrill Lynch or Value Line, perhaps using one service or perhaps averaging the betas of several services. The choice is a matter of judgment and data availability, for there is no "right" beta. With luck, the betas derived from different sources will, for a given company, be close together. If they are not, then our confidence in the CAPM cost of capital estimate will be diminished.

Table 4-2
Beta Coefficients for Five Companies, January 1986

	Merrill Lynch	Value Line
Apple Computer	1.5	1.7
General Motors	0.8	1.1
IBM	0.8	1.0
Safeway Stores	0.8	0.8
San Diego Gas & Electric	0.6	0.6

Illustration of the CAPM Approach

We are now in a position to estimate National Computer's cost of equity from retained earnings by the CAPM method. We use as the risk-free rate the assumed T-bond rate in January 1987, which is 9.7 percent, and Merrill Lynch's assumed estimate of the expected return on the market, $\hat{k}_M = k_M = 14.0\%$. Thus, we can write the SML equation for January 1987 as follows:

$$k_s = k_{RF} + b_i(k_M - k_{RF})$$
$$= 9.7\% + b_i(14.0\% - 9.7\%) = 9.7\% + b_i(4.3\%).$$

Therefore, if we know a company's beta, we can insert it into the SML equation and estimate the company's cost of retained earnings, k_s. For example, we have obtained two estimates of NCC's beta: One service reported an adjusted beta of 1.05, and the other estimated an unadjusted beta of 1.20. Using the adjusted beta, we obtain $k_{NCC} = 14.2\%$:

$$k_{NCC} = 9.7\% + 1.05(4.3\%) \approx 14.2\%.$$

Using the unadjusted beta, we obtain an estimate of 14.9 percent. Therefore, on the basis of this CAPM analysis, National Computer Corporation's cost of retained earnings falls in the range of 14.2 to 14.9 percent.

Rather than picking single values, we could have developed high and low estimates for both the risk-free rate and the market risk premium. Then, by combining all of the low estimators and all of the high estimators, we could have estimated the extreme low and high values of NCC's cost of retained earnings. Obviously, this expected range would have been greater than 14.2 to 14.9 percent.

THE DCF APPROACH

The second major procedure for estimating the cost of retained earnings is the Discounted Cash Flow (DCF) approach. We know that the intrinsic value of a stock, $\hat{P}_0$, is the present value of its expected dividend stream:

$$\hat{P}_0 = \frac{D_1}{(1 + k_s)^1} + \frac{D_2}{(1 + k_s)^2} + \frac{D_3}{(1 + k_s)^3} + \cdots + \frac{D_\infty}{(1 + k_s)^\infty}.$$

Also, we know that we can recast this equation, given the market price of the stock, P_0, and solve for $\hat{k}_s$, the implied expected return:

$$P_0 = \frac{D_1}{(1 + \hat{k}_s)^1} + \frac{D_2}{(1 + \hat{k}_s)^2} + \frac{D_3}{(1 + \hat{k}_s)^3} + \cdots + \frac{D_\infty}{(1 + \hat{k}_s)^\infty}.$$

Finally, we know that in equilibrium, $\hat{k}_s = k_s$, so if a stock is in equilibrium, as it generally is, then an estimate of the expected rate of return also provides us with an estimate of the required rate of return.

If a stock is expected to grow at a constant rate, we can use the Gordon model to estimate $\hat{k}_s$:

$$\hat{k}_s = \frac{D_1}{P_0} + g.$$

Here P_0 is read from *The Wall Street Journal*, and next year's annual dividend, D_1, can be estimated relatively easily. Unfortunately, it is not easy to estimate g, the growth rate expected by the marginal investor. However, there are several ways to estimate growth rates; we will examine three of them.

Historical Growth Rates

First, if earnings and dividend growth rates have been relatively stable in the past, and if investors expect these trends to continue, then the past realized growth rate may be used as an estimate of the expected future growth rate. To illustrate, consider Figure 4-1, which gives EPS and DPS data from 1972 to 1986 for NCC, along with a plot of these data on a semilog scale. Note these points:

1. Time period. We show 15 years of data in Figure 4-1. However, we could have used 25 years, 5 years, or 10 years. There is no rule as to the appropriate number of years to analyze when calculating historic growth rates.

2. Compound growth rate, point-to-point. The easiest historical growth rate to calculate is the compound rate between two dates. For example, EPS grew at an annual rate of 7.5 percent from 1972 to 1986, and DPS grew at a 4.8 percent rate during this same period.[12] Note that the point-to-point growth rate could change radically if we used two other points. For example, if we calculated the 5-year EPS growth rate from 1980 to 1985, we would obtain 2.6 percent, but the 5-year rate one year later, from 1981 to 1986, is 11.0 percent. This radical change occurs because the point-to-point rate is extremely sensitive to the base and terminal years.

3. Compound growth rate, average-to-average. To alleviate the problem of base and terminal year sensitivity, some analysts use an average-to-average calculation. For example, to calculate NCC's EPS growth rate over the period 1980 to 1985, the Value Line analysts would (1) get the average EPS over the years 1979 to 1981 and use this value ($3.33) as the base year, (2) get the average EPS over the years 1984 to 1986 and use this value ($4.97) as the terminal year, and (3) calculate a growth rate of 8.3 percent based on these data. This procedure is superior to the simple point-to-point calculation for purposes of a DCF analysis.

4. Least squares regression. A third way, and in our view the best way, to esti-

---

[12]To obtain g_{EPS} using a financial calculator, enter 2.08 as PV, 5.73 as FV, 14 as n (because, with 15 data points, we have 14 growth periods), and then press i to obtain the growth rate, 7.5 percent.

Figure 4-1
National Computer Corporation:
Semi-Log Plot of EPS and DPS, 1972-1986

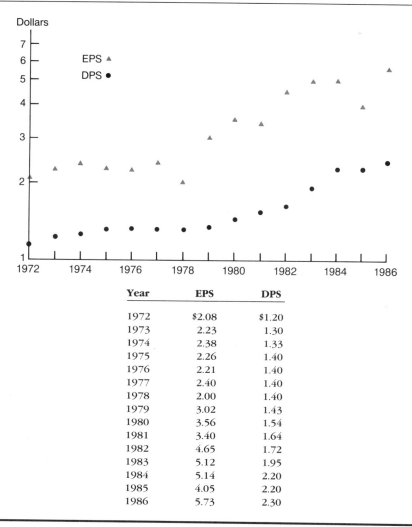

Year	EPS	DPS
1972	$2.08	$1.20
1973	2.23	1.30
1974	2.38	1.33
1975	2.26	1.40
1976	2.21	1.40
1977	2.40	1.40
1978	2.00	1.40
1979	3.02	1.43
1980	3.56	1.54
1981	3.40	1.64
1982	4.65	1.72
1983	5.12	1.95
1984	5.14	2.20
1985	4.05	2.20
1986	5.73	2.30

mate historical growth rates is by log-linear least squares regression.[13] The regression method gives consideration to all data points in the series, and hence it is the least likely to be biased by a randomly high or low beginning or ending year. The

---

[13]Log-linear regression is a standard time-series linear regression in which the data points are plotted as natural logarithms. The advantage of a log-linear regression is that the slope of the regression line is the average annual growth rate. In a standard time-series linear regression of EPS or DPS, the slope of the regression line is the average annual dollar change. For a more complete discussion of log-linear regression, see Robert C. Radcliffe, *Investment: Concepts, Analysis, and Strategy* (Glenview, Ill.: Scott, Foresman, 1987).

Table 4-3
National Computer Corporation:
Historical Growth Rates

	EPS	DPS	Average
Point-to-point (1981-1986)	11.0%	7.0%	9.0%
Point-to-point (1972-1986)	7.5	4.8	6.2
Average-to-average (1980-1985)	8.3	7.7	8.0
Average-to-average (1973-1985)	6.9	4.7	5.8
Least squares regression (1981-1986)	6.6	7.6	7.1
Least squares regression (1972-1986)	7.9	4.6	6.3

only practical way to estimate a least squares growth rate is with a computer or a financial calculator.

5. Earnings versus dividends. If earnings and dividends are growing at the same rate, there is no problem, but if these two growth rates are unequal, we do have a problem. First, the DCF model calls for the expected *dividend* growth rate. However, if EPS and DPS are growing at different rates, something is going to have to change: these two series cannot grow at two different rates indefinitely. There is no rule for handling differences in historic g_{EPS} and g_{DPS}, and where they differ, this simply demonstrates in yet another way the problems with using historical growth as a proxy for expected future growth. Like many aspects of finance, judgment is required when estimating growth rates.

Table 4-3 summarizes the historical growth rates we have just discussed. It is obvious that one can take a given set of historical data and, depending on the years and the calculation method used, obtain a large number of quite different growth rates. Now recall our purpose in making these calculations: We are seeking the future dividend growth rate that investors expect, and we reasoned that, if past growth rates have been stable, then investors might base future expectations on past trends. This is a reasonable proposition, but, unfortunately, one never finds very much historical stability. Therefore, the use of historical growth rates in a DCF analysis must be applied with judgment, and also used (if at all) in conjunction with other growth estimation methods as discussed next.

Retention Growth

Another method for estimating the growth rate is to use Equation 4-4:

$$g = b(r). \tag{4-4}$$

Here r is the expected future return on equity, and b is the fraction of its earnings that a firm is expected to retain.[14] Equation 4-4 produces a constant growth rate,

---

[14]Since there are more terms for which symbols are needed than there are letters in the alphabet, some letters are used to denote several different things. This is one of those instances, and *b* is standard notation for both the beta coefficient and the retention rate. Note also that the retention rate is the complement of the payout rate, that is, retention rate = (1 − payout ratio).

and when we use it we are, by implication, making four important assumptions: (1) that we expect the retention ratio, b, to remain constant; (2) that we expect the return on equity on new investment, r, to equal the firm's current ROE, which implies that we expect the return on equity to remain constant; (3) that the firm is not expected to issue new common stock or, if it does, that this new stock will be sold at a price equal to its book value; and (4) that future projects are expected to have the same degree of risk as the firm's existing assets.

NCC has had an average return on equity of about 15 percent over the past 15 years. The ROE has been relatively steady, but even so it has ranged from a low of 11.0 percent to a high of 17.6 percent during this period. In addition, NCC's dividend payout ratio has averaged 0.52 over the past 15 years, so its retention rate, b, has averaged $1.0 - 0.52 = 0.48$. Using Equation 4-4, we estimate g to be 7.2 percent:

$$g = 0.48(15\%) = 7.2\%.$$

This figure, together with the historical EPS and DPS growth rates examined earlier, might lead us to conclude that National Computer's expected growth rate is in the range of 6.5 to 7.5 percent. Therefore, if we forecasted NCC's next annual dividend to be $2.40, and if we determined that its current stock price is $32, then its dividend yield would be $D_1/P_0 = \$2.40/\$32 = 0.075$ or 7.5%, and its DCF cost of capital would be in the range of 14.0 to 15.0 percent:

$$\text{Lower end: } \hat{k}_{NCC} = k_{NCC} = 7.5\% + 6.5\% = 14.0\%.$$

$$\text{Upper end: } \hat{k}_{NCC} = k_{NCC} = 7.5\% + 7.5\% = 15.0\%.$$

This is about the same as the 14.2 to 14.9 percent estimate obtained by the CAPM method.

Analysts' Forecasts

A final method of estimating g is to use analysts' forecasts. However, these forecasts seldom assume constant growth. For example, in January 1987, analysts were forecasting that NCC would have a 10.4 percent annual growth rate in earnings and dividends over the next 5 years, or from 1987 through 1991. Additionally, they were forecasting a steady-state growth rate beyond 1991 of 6.5 percent. On the basis of the current $32 market price and a D_1 of $2.40, we can use the nonconstant growth stock valuation equation developed in Chapter 3 to find the expected rate of return:

$$P_0 = \sum_{t=1}^{5} \frac{D_1(1 + g_s)^{t-1}}{(1 + \hat{k}_s)^t} + \left(\frac{D_6}{\hat{k}_s - g_n}\right)\left(\frac{1}{1 + \hat{k}_s}\right)^5.$$

$$\$32 = \sum_{t=1}^{5} \frac{\$2.40(1.104)^{t-1}}{(1 + \hat{k}_s)^t} + \left(\frac{\$3.80}{\hat{k}_s - 0.065}\right)\left(\frac{1}{1 + \hat{k}_s}\right)^5.$$

Solving for $\hat{k}_s$ is no trivial matter—we used a *Lotus 1-2-3* model and found $\hat{k}_s = k_s$ to be about 15.0 percent.

As an alternative, the nonconstant growth forecasts could be used to develop a proxy constant growth rate. Computer simulations indicate that dividends beyond Year 50 contribute very little to the value of any stock; the PV of dividends beyond Year 50 is virtually zero, so for practical purposes, we can ignore anything beyond 50 years. If we consider only a 50-year horizon, we can develop a weighted average growth rate and use it as a constant growth rate for cost of capital purposes. In the NCC case, we assumed a growth rate of 10.4 percent for 5 years followed by a growth rate of 6.5 percent for 45 years, which produces an average growth rate of $0.10(10.4\%) + 0.90(6.5\%) = 6.9\%$. This constant growth rate proxy results in $k_s = \hat{k}_s = 14.4\%$:

$$k_s = \hat{k}_s = \frac{\$2.40}{\$32} + 6.9\%$$

$$= 7.5\% + 6.9\% = 14.4\%.$$

These calculations suggest a range for k_s of perhaps 14.4 to 15.0 percent.

BOND YIELD PLUS RISK PREMIUM APPROACH

The last method we will discuss for estimating the required rate of return on retained earnings calls for adding an assumed risk premium to the company's own bond yield:

$$k_s = \text{Bond yield} + \text{Risk premium.}$$

A corporate treasurer can easily look up his or her own firm's bond yield if the bond is publicly traded or ask an investment banker for k_d if the bonds are not traded. The real problem occurs when trying to estimate the appropriate risk premium for the firm.

Table 4-1 presented historical risk premiums as reported by Ibbotson Associates. If risk premiums were stable over time, or if they fluctuated randomly about a stable mean, then the average historical premium could be used as an estimate of the current and prospective future risk premium. However, risk premiums are not stable, so it is necessary to estimate risk premiums on a current basis, and more reliance should be placed on the current level of the risk premium than on its historical average. Studies suggest that risk premiums are reasonably stable during periods when interest rates are stable, but that they become volatile during periods in which interest rates are volatile.

There are two common methods of estimating current risk premiums: a survey approach and a DCF-based approach, similar to the method we discussed earlier in connection with the market risk premium. One example of the survey approach is the work of Charles Benore, a security analyst with Paine Webber. Benore has for several years surveyed a large number of institutional investors, asking them what premium above the return on the company's bonds would make them indifferent to the choice of investing in the stock or the bonds. In one recent study, Benore found that most investors required a premium of from 2 to 4 percentage points on stock over the company's bond yield, with a mean value of 3.6 percentage points. This mean could be used as an estimate of the risk premium. Benore's survey analyzes only public utility companies, but the approach is applicable to any company or industry. Note, though, that Benore has, in some recent years, reported average risk premiums as high as 6 percent, and in other years he found values closer to 3 percent, so his studies confirm that risk premiums are not stable, and hence that recent survey data should be used.

The second method for estimating risk premiums is based on the DCF model. To illustrate, we assumed earlier that in January 1987 Merrill Lynch, using the DCF approach, estimated that the required rate of return on the market, as measured by the S&P 500, was 14.0 percent. At the same time, assume that the *Federal Reserve Bulletin* reported that the yield on an average corporate long-term bond was 11.2 percent. Using these data, we would estimate the market risk premium of an average stock over an average bond to be $14.0 - 11.2 = 2.8$ percentage points, or 280 basis points. However, one should recognize that the figure of 2.8 percentage points is not precise; we would, ourselves, conclude that the risk premium of an average company's stock over its own bonds, in January 1987, was somewhere between 2.3 and 3.3 percentage points.

We can apply the DCF-based risk premium approach to estimate the required rate of return for NCC. The company has been experiencing some problems from lower-cost foreign producers, and its bonds are only rated Baa. Therefore, whereas the *Federal Reserve Bulletin* reported that an average corporate bond yielded 11.2 percent in January 1987, NCC's relatively risky bonds yielded 12.0 percent, ignoring flotation costs. (Our studies indicate that the average NYSE company's bonds are rated A; NCC's bonds are rated below A.) Assuming that every company's required equity return exceeds its cost of debt by the risk premium amounts estimated previously, we would determine the high and low values of NCC's cost of equity as follows:

$$\text{Low: } k_{NCC} = 12.0\% + 2.3\% = 14.3\%.$$

$$\text{High: } k_{NCC} = 12.0\% + 3.3\% = 15.3\%.$$

Had NCC had a higher bond rating, its cost of debt and consequently its estimated cost of equity would have been lower.[15]

Note again, however, that risk premiums have not been stable over time, so it is not appropriate as a general rule to add 2.3 to 3.3 percentage points to a company's bond yield to indicate its cost of equity. In recent years, our work suggests

---

[15]Other variations on this theme could be employed. We could, for example, develop DCF cost of capital estimates for different industries and for firms with similar bond ratings. Also, note that if you know a company's bond rating, or can estimate from an analysis of its financial statements what rating it would have if its debt were rated, then you could find its approximate k_d in Moody's or Standard & Poor's bond yield publications. This procedure is useful for outsiders analyzing companies that have no publicly traded debt. The company's own treasurer would always know, or could quickly find out, the value of k_d from the firm's investment banker.

that the over-own-debt risk premium has ranged from about 1.5 to about 4.5 percentage points. (The low premium occurred when interest rates were quite high and people were reluctant to invest in long-term bonds because of a fear of runaway inflation, further increases in interest rates, and losses on investments in bonds. The high premiums occur in periods when interest rates are relatively low.) Therefore, we repeat our earlier warning: use a current risk premium when estimating equity capital costs by the bond yield plus risk premium method.

COMPARISON OF THE CAPM, DCF, AND RISK PREMIUM METHODS

We have discussed three methods for estimating the required rate of return on retained earnings—CAPM, DCF, and bond yield plus risk premium. Table 4-4 summarizes the results for National Computer Corporation. We see that the estimates range from 14.0 to 15.3 percent, that the average highs and average lows produce a range of 14.2 to 15.1 percent, and that the overall average is 14.6 percent. In our view, there is sufficient consistency in the results to warrant the use of 14.6 percent as an estimate of the cost of retained earnings for National Computer. If the methods produced widely varied estimates, then the financial manager would have to use his or her judgment as to the relative merits of each estimate, and then choose the estimate which seemed most reasonable under the circumstances.

COST OF NEWLY ISSUED COMMON EQUITY

The cost of retained earnings, as estimated in the preceding section, is appropriate when retained earnings are being used to finance expansion. However, if the firm is expanding so rapidly that its retained earnings have been exhausted, then it must raise equity by selling newly issued common stock, and common equity has a higher cost than retained earnings. Specifically, the sale of new common equity, as with the sale of preferred equity and debt, involves flotation costs. These costs lower the net usable dollars produced by new stock issues, and this in turn increases the cost of the funds. We took account of flotation costs in our estimations of the costs of debt and preferred stock, and the same general approach can be used with common equity.

When the firm sells new common stock, it nets $P_0(1 - F)$, where F is the percentage flotation cost expressed in decimal form. Note that F consists of underwriting expenses such as printing costs and investment banker commissions, as well as price effects resulting from market pressure and information asymmetries. These topics will be discussed in detail in Chapters 5 and 12. If the firm is in a constant growth situation, the Gordon model, with flotation costs, can be used:

$$\text{Net proceeds} = P_0(1 - F) = \frac{D_1}{\hat{k}_e - g}. \qquad (4\text{-}5)$$

Table 4-4
**Estimated Required Rates of Return
for National Computer Corporation**

Method	Estimate	
	Low	High
CAPM	14.2%	14.9%
DCF (constant growth)	14.0	15.0
DCF (nonconstant growth)	14.4	15.0
Bond yield plus risk premium	14.3	15.3
Average	14.2%	15.1%
Overall average	14.6%	

Here $\hat{k}_e$ is the cost of equity raised by selling new stock. Solving Equation 4-5 for $\hat{k}_e$ produces this expression:

$$\hat{k}_e = \frac{D_1}{P_0(1 - F)} + g. \qquad (4\text{-}5a)$$

This procedure recognizes that the purchaser of a share of newly issued stock will expect the same dividend stream as the holder of an old share, but the company will, because of flotation expenses, receive less money from the sale of the new share, $P_0(1 - F)$, than the value of the old share, P_0. Therefore, the money raised from the sale of new stock will have to "work harder" to produce the earnings needed to provide the dividend stream. As a result, $k_e > k_s$.

Note also that we could rewrite Equation 4-5a as follows:

$$\hat{k}_e = \frac{D_1/P_0}{(1 - F)} + g = \frac{\text{Dividend yield}}{(1 - F)} + g. \qquad (4\text{-}5b)$$

Equations 4-5a and 4-5b are equivalent, and either can be used, depending on the form of the available data.

Thus far, we have discussed the flotation adjustment only in the constant growth case. In situations where the constant growth model is not appropriate, the flotation adjustment is a bit more complicated. No change in principle is involved, but we do have to use the nonconstant growth model. Again, we reduce the current market price by the flotation cost per share. To illustrate, consider the DCF model for the cost of retained earnings for National Computer Corporation as developed in an earlier section:

$$P_0 = \$32 = \sum_{t=1}^{5} \frac{\$2.40(1.104)^{t-1}}{(1 + \hat{k}_s)^t} + \left(\frac{\$3.80}{\hat{k}_s - 0.065}\right)\left(\frac{1}{1 + \hat{k}_s}\right)^5.$$

When we solved this equation, we found $\hat{k}_s$ to be about 15.0 percent. To find the cost of new equity, assuming that total flotation costs are 15 percent of gross proceeds, we must multiply P_0 times $(1 - F)$ and then solve for $\hat{k}_e$ in the following equation:

$$P_0(1 - F) = \$32(1 - 0.15) = \sum_{t=1}^{5} \frac{\$2.40(1.104)^{t-1}}{(1 + \hat{k}_e)^t} + \left(\frac{\$3.80}{\hat{k}_e - 0.065}\right)\left(\frac{1}{1 + \hat{k}_e}\right)^5$$

$$\$27.20 = \sum_{t=1}^{5} \frac{\$2.40(1.104)^{t-1}}{(1 + \hat{k}_e)^t} + \left(\frac{\$3.80}{\hat{k}_e - 0.065}\right)\left(\frac{1}{1 + \hat{k}_e}\right)^5.$$

The solution value for $\hat{k}_e = k_e$ is about 16.4 percent versus $\hat{k}_s = k_s = 15.0\%$ for retained earnings, so the flotation cost adjustment is about $+1.4$ percentage points, meaning that new outside equity costs about 1.4 percentage points more than retained earnings.

Notice that only one method (DCF) is commonly used to estimate the flotation cost adjustment, whereas three methods are used to estimate k_s. The flotation cost adjustment is then added to the final estimate of the cost of retained earnings. For National Computer, the final estimate of the cost of retained earnings was 14.6 percent. Thus, NCC's cost of new equity is estimated to be $14.6\% + 1.4\% = 16.0\%$.

WEIGHTED AVERAGE COST OF CAPITAL

Thus far, we have discussed how to determine the costs of the various capital components. Now we must combine them to form a weighted average cost of capital, WACC $= k_a$. Each firm has in mind a target capital structure, defined as that mix of debt, preferred, and common equity which causes its stock price to be maximized. Further, when the firm raises new capital, it generally tries to keep the actual capital structure reasonably close to the target over time. Here is the general formula for the weighted average cost of capital:

$$\text{WACC} = k_a = w_d k_d(1 - T) + w_p k_p + w_s(k_s \text{ or } k_e). \tag{4-6}$$

Here w_d, w_p, and w_s are the weights used for debt, preferred stock, and common stock, respectively. The cost of the debt component of the WACC would itself be an average of several items if the firm uses several types of debt for its permanent financing; the common equity used in the calculation will be either the cost of retained earnings, k_s, or the cost of new common stock, k_e.

One point should be made immediately: *k_a is the weighted average cost of each new dollar of capital raised at the margin*—it is not the average cost of all the dollars the firm has raised in the past, nor is it the average cost of all the dollars the firm will raise during the current year. We are primarily interested in obtaining a cost of capital for use in capital budgeting, and for such purposes, a *marginal cost* is required.[16] That means, conceptually, that we must estimate the cost of

---

[16]The only use we can think of for the average cost of all the capital a firm has raised, as opposed to the marginal cost of capital, is in public utility rate making, where utility commissions are supposed to set rates such that customers pay for all costs of service, including the cost of the capital that was used to buy the assets that are used to provide service.

Table 4-5
National Computer Corporation:
Capital Components on December 31, 1986
(Millions of Dollars)

Component	Book Value
Long-term debt	$ 736
Preferred stock	100
Common stock	1,421
Total	$2,257

each dollar the firm raises during the year. Each of those dollars will consist of some debt, some preferred, and some common equity, and the equity will be either retained earnings or new common stock.

Consider the weights used in Equation 4-6. These weights are based on each component's fraction of the firm's total relevant capital, where all capital values are *market values*, not book, or balance sheet, values. How could we estimate these weights for a given firm? If we worked for the firm, or if we had access to its planning documents, we would know its target capital structure, and hence we would know the appropriate component weights. If we did not have this information, we would generally assume that the firm is currently at its target, or optimal, capital structure, and then determine the weights from its financial statements. For example, Table 4-5 presents a simplified statement of NCC's capital components as of December 31, 1986. We assumed that National Computer does not use short-term debt as a permanent part of its capitalization; therefore, we need to consider only the long-term components.

The book values in Table 4-5 could be used directly to determine book value weights. However, since we want to use market value weights to determine the overall cost of capital, we must convert each of the book values into market values. First, an examination of NCC's 1986 income statement shows that interest on its long-term debt is approximately $72 million. This long-term debt, on average, has a coupon yield of about $72/$736 = 0.0978, or 9.78 percent. However, as we saw earlier, the current required return on NCC's 30-year bonds is 12.0 percent. NCC's debt shown on the balance sheet has an average maturity that is closer to 20 than to 30 years. However, the yield curve is fairly flat over the 20- to 30-year range, so we can assume that NCC's 20-year debt would also have a cost of 12.0 percent. A 20-year bond with a 9.78 percent coupon yield and a required rate of return of 12.0 percent would sell for $834.18 (assuming annual coupons), or at about 83.4 percent of par value. Thus, if we assume that NCC's long-term debt has an average of 20 years to maturity, the market value of this debt is 83.4 percent of book value, or 0.834($736) ≈ $614 million. (Usually cost of capital calculations are made by members of a company's financial staff, and they would know things that outsiders must assume.)

Table 4-6
National Computer Corporation:
Book Value and Market Value Weighting
on December 31, 1986
(Millions of Dollars)

	Book Value		Market Value	
	Dollars	**Percent**	**Dollars**	**Percent**
Long-term debt	$ 736	33%	$ 614	26%
Preferred stock	100	4	85	4
Common stock	1,421	63	1,664	70
Total	$2,257	100%	$2,363	100%

To find the market value of the preferred stock, we merely multiply the stock price by the number of preferred shares outstanding. NCC had one million shares of preferred outstanding, and each share had a current market price of $85, so the market value of NCC's preferred stock was $85(1) = $85 million. The market value of NCC's common stock is found in a similar manner. NCC's stock price was about $32, and 52 million shares were outstanding. Therefore, the market value of its common stock was $32(52) = $1,664 million.

Table 4-6 presents the market value weights and compares them to the book value weights. We can use the market value weights, along with the calculated component costs, to estimate NCC's WACC. Here we will assume a before-tax cost rate of 12.0 percent on debt, a 34 percent marginal tax rate, a cost of preferred of 12.3 percent, and a 14.6 percent cost of equity from retained earnings:

$$\text{WACC} = k_a = w_d k_d (1 - T) + w_p k_p + w_s k_s$$
$$= 0.26(12.0\%)(1 - 0.34) + 0.04(12.3\%) + 0.70(14.6\%)$$
$$= 2.06\% + 0.49\% + 10.22\% \approx 12.8\% = \text{WACC}.$$

Note that if we incorrectly used book value weights, we would obtain an incorrect WACC, 12.3 percent versus the correct 12.8 percent. The difference is not large in this case, because NCC's stock price is reasonably close to its book value. However, for a company such as IBM, whose stock sells at about three times book, the book and market capital structures would be quite different, and that would lead to major differences in the WACC based on book versus market weights, and hence a major error if book weights were used.

NCC's 12.8 percent WACC assumes that equity is obtained as retained earnings. If the equity is raised by selling new common stock, then flotation costs would increase NCC's cost of equity from 14.6 to 16.0 percent, and hence increase the WACC from 12.8 to 13.8 percent:

$$\text{WACC} = k_a = w_d k_d (1 - T) + w_p k_p + w_s k_e$$
$$= 0.26(12.0\%)(0.66) + 0.04(12.3\%) + 0.70(16.0\%) \approx 13.8\%.$$

The WACC is actually a function of the amount of new capital raised. As long as NCC's equity requirements can be met by retaining earnings, its WACC is 12.8 percent. However, if the firm's capital expenditures are so large that new equity must be sold, then its WACC will be 13.8 percent. We will extend the concept of the WACC in Chapter 10, where we discuss in detail the firm's marginal cost of capital (MCC) schedule and show how this schedule is used to help determine the optimal capital budget.

OTHER ISSUES IN THE COST OF CAPITAL

Before concluding this chapter, we must discuss some other items that affect the cost of capital. The purpose here is as much to raise questions as to answer them. Still, the material does have important practical implications, so anyone engaged in financial management should be aware of the issues and understand how they impact the practical, rule-of-thumb procedures that financial managers are necessarily forced to follow.

The Effects of Personal Taxes

Whenever a firm retains a portion of its net income rather than paying all earnings out in dividends, there is an *opportunity cost* to the stockholders. National Computer has a required rate of return on equity (retained earnings) of 14.6 percent. This suggests that shareholders could invest retained earnings, if they were paid out in dividends, in the stock market in firms of similar risk and receive a 14.6 percent return. Therefore, NCC should retain and reinvest earnings only if the projects in which the retained earnings are invested yield 14.6 percent or more on the equity invested. The value $k_s = 14.6\%$ is defined as the opportunity cost of retained earnings. However, note that we have implicitly assumed that the stockholders (1) pay no income tax on dividends received and (2) incur no brokerage costs when they reinvest dividends. To the extent that these assumptions are not met, the opportunity cost of retained earnings might be lower than the required rate of return, k_s. The following example illustrates this point.

The ABC Company has net earnings of $1 million; all of its stockholders are in the 30 percent marginal federal-plus-state tax bracket, and they are net savers as opposed to people who live on investment income. Management estimates that, under present conditions, the stockholders' required rate of return is $k_s = 12\%$; that is, they could invest in firms of similar risk and receive a return of 12 percent. On earnings paid out as dividends, the recipients will first pay income taxes. Then, since they are net savers, they will reinvest the after-tax proceeds in the stock of the same or a similar firm and receive a 12 percent return. Brokerage costs incurred to reinvest dividends will average 3 percent of the value of the newly purchased stock. What rate of return must be earned on retained earnings to provide ABC's stockholders with incremental earnings equal to what they would receive externally?

1. $\dfrac{\text{After-tax proceeds}}{\text{of dividend payment}}$ $= \$1,000,000 - \text{Personal taxes}$

$$= \$1,000,000 - \$300,000 = \$700,000.$$

2. $\dfrac{\text{Net investment}}{\text{after brokerage costs}}$ $= \$700,000 - \text{Brokerage costs}$

$$= \$700,000 - \$21,000 = \$679,000.$$

3. Earnings on net investment $= (\$679,000)(0.12) = \$81,480.$

4. Internal rate of return, k_r, necessary to provide stockholders with incremental income of $81,480:

$$\$81,480 = (\$1,000,000)(k_r)$$

$$k_r = 0.08148 \approx 8.1\%.$$

Therefore, if the firm were able to earn 8.1 percent on retained earnings, its stockholders would be as well off as they would be if all earnings were paid out and then reinvested to yield 12 percent. Thus, the internal opportunity cost, or the required rate of return on retention-financed investments, k_r, is less than the stockholders' required rate of return, k_s.

Combining the steps set forth above, k_r may be calculated as follows:

$$k_r = k_s(1 - T)(1 - B). \tag{4-7}$$

Here k_r is the required return on retention-financed investments, k_s is the stockholders' required rate of return, T is the stockholders' marginal tax rate, and B is the percentage brokerage cost. In the example being considered,

$$k_r = (12\%)(0.7)(0.97) \approx 8.1\%.$$

Thus, Equation 4-7 gives the same value for k_r as we developed earlier.

This procedure, although it appears reasonable at first glance, is generally not correct. If the firm repurchases shares of its own stock in the marketplace, it can earn a return of $k_s = 12\%$ on funds so invested. Thus, assuming it can repurchase its own shares at the current market price, the firm should not make a physical asset investment that has a risk-adjusted expected return on equity that is less than k_s.[17]

Most publicly owned firms do have the opportunity to invest in their own shares. Indeed, as we shall see in Chapter 11, open market stock repurchases are fairly common for firms whose internal investment opportunities are limited. However, closely held firms do not normally have the opportunity to repurchase shares. For such firms, a major repurchase would be deemed by the IRS to be an attempt on the part of the controlling stockholders to avoid personal income taxes; hence, the firm would be subject to severe penalties. This too is discussed in Chapter 11, but our major conclusion is this: *Equation 4-7 is not applicable for any publicly owned firm. Such firms should never invest internally to earn risk-adjusted eq-*

---

[17]In reality, the company would have to pay brokerage costs on the repurchase. Thus, the net return on money invested to repurchase stock is slightly less than k_s.

uity returns of less than k_s, because they have the opportunity to earn k_s on stock repurchases. However, personal tax effects are important for closely held firms, and Equation 4-7 should be used to estimate the cost of retained earnings in such cases.

Cost of Depreciation-Generated Funds

The very first increment of internal funds used to finance any year's investments in new assets, or the capital budget, is depreciation-generated funds. Further, in their statements of sources and uses of funds, corporations generally show depreciation charges to be one of the most important, if not the most important, source of funds.[18] Of course, depreciation is an allowance for the annual reduction in value of a firm's fixed assets. Thus, for an ongoing firm, depreciation-generated funds would be used to replace worn-out and obsolete assets.

For capital budgeting purposes, should depreciation be considered "free" capital, should it be ignored completely, or should a charge be assessed against it? *The answer is that a charge should indeed be assessed against depreciation-generated funds, and the cost used should be the weighted average cost of capital before outside equity is used.* The reasoning here is that the firm could, if it so desired, distribute the depreciation-generated funds to its stockholders and creditors, the parties who financed the assets in the first place, so these funds definitely have an opportunity cost. For example, suppose a firm has $10 million of depreciation-generated funds available. Its equity has a cost of $k_s = 15\%$, and its debt has an after-tax cost of $k_d(1 - T) = 12\%(1 - T) = 12\%(0.66) = 7.92\%$. If it has a 50-50 capital structure and it uses no preferred stock, then its WACC would be $k_a = 0.5(7.92\%) + 0.5(15\%) = 11.46\%$.

Now suppose the firm has no projects available to it, not even projects which replace worn-out equipment, that return 11.46 percent or more. It obviously should not raise new capital, and it should not even retain any earnings for internal investment, because stockholders would be better off receiving the earnings as

---

[18]Depreciation is a noncash charge. To illustrate, suppose a company reports the following income statement:

Sales	$100.0
Costs: Operating	60.0
Depreciation	20.0
Taxable income	$ 20.0
Taxes (34%)	6.8
Net income	$ 13.2

If sales are all collected during the year, and if all costs except depreciation are paid in cash during the year, then cash flow from operations available for dividends or reinvestment will be $33.2:

$$\text{Cash flow} = \text{Net income} + \text{Depreciation} = \$13.2 + \$20 = \$33.2.$$

This point is discussed in greater depth in Chapter 8.

dividends and investing them themselves at k_s = 15%, or having the company repurchase its stock. Going on, this firm should not even invest its depreciation-generated $10 million. If it did keep and invest this money, it would receive a return of less than 11.46 percent. If it distributed the $10 million to its investors, with $5 million going to stockholders and $5 million to bondholders so as to maintain the target capital structure, then the stockholders could buy the stock of companies with similar risk and earn 15 percent on their money. (Such a distribution would, under certain conditions, be a return of capital, and hence not taxable. If the distribution were taxable, then the company could repurchase its shares rather than make a direct distribution to stockholders.) *The conclusion from all this is that depreciation has a cost which is approximately equal to the weighted average cost of capital before external equity is used.* This cost is based on the opportunity cost to existing investors rather than the required rate of return of new investors, but opportunity costs are just as real as other costs.

Since depreciation-generated funds have the same cost as the firm's WACC when retained earnings are used for the equity component, it is not necessary to consider them when estimating the firm's WACC. However, these funds do influence the point at which the WACC increases due to flotation costs on new stock sales. This point will be discussed further in Chapter 10.

Cost of Deferred Taxes

Most companies show "deferred taxes" as a liability item on their balance sheets. Deferred taxes arise principally from accelerated tax depreciation, which causes delays in payments of regular taxes. For example, suppose the XYZ Company uses ACRS depreciation for tax purposes but straight line for book (or stockholder reporting) purposes. Its ACRS depreciation for 1986 might be $20 million versus $10 million had it used straight line. The company's tax and book income statements are given in Table 4-7. As a result of using ACRS depreciation, the company writes off assets for tax purposes over a period which is shorter than their economic lives. Therefore, in the early years of an asset's life, tax depreciation is high, so actual taxes are low. Later on, tax depreciation will be low, so actual taxes will be high relative to the taxes that would result from the use of straight line depreciation. The deferred taxes represent the taxes that do not have to be paid currently but which will have to be paid at some future date.

Companies keep a "running total" of the accumulated deferred taxes that have accrued over time, and the net balance is reported on the balance sheet as a "reserve for deferred taxes." Thus, XYZ Company would add $3.4 million to the accumulated deferred tax figure reported on its 1985 balance sheet. In later years, when tax depreciation falls below straight line depreciation, the "reserve for deferred taxes" will be drawn down, and a credit will appear on the income statement seen by investors.[19]

---

[19]When we were working on this section, we looked at how several companies reported taxes in their financial statements. Three patterns were noted. First, most industrial companies reported income in their annual reports to stockholders as we show in Column 2 of Table 4-7. However, two other situations were found. First, IBM and several other extremely strong firms used accelerated (ACRS) depre-

Table 4-7
**Illustration of XYZ Company's 1986 Deferred Taxes
(Millions of Dollars)**

	Tax Books (1)	Stockholder Books (2)
Sales	$100.0	$100.0
Costs except depreciation	60.0	60.0
Depreciation (noncash charge)	20.0	10.0
Operating income	$ 20.0	$ 30.0
Taxes:		
Current (34%)	6.8	6.8[a]
Deferred (noncash charge)	—	3.4[b]
Net income	$ 13.2	$ 19.8
Cash flow[c]	$ 33.2	$ 33.2

[a]Taken from tax books.
[b]Deferred taxes represent the difference between taxes actually paid and taxes that would have been paid had straight line been used for tax purposes:

$$\text{Deferred taxes} = \$30(0.34) - \$6.8 = \$3.4.$$

[c]Cash flow = Net income + Noncash expenses
       = Net income + Depreciation + Deferred taxes.

Deferred taxes represent a noncash charge; hence, they constitute a source of funds in a cash flow sense. In effect, deferred taxes represent a tax-free loan from the federal government, so they represent zero cost capital. However, just like depreciation, deferred taxes have an opportunity cost. The deferred tax cash flow, $3.4 million for XYZ Company in 1986, could be turned over to the firm's investors, and hence deferred taxes, like depreciation, have a cost equal to the firm's WACC using retained earnings as the equity component. Indeed, deferred taxes arise solely because a firm records a different depreciation expense on its tax books than the expense on the books used to report income to shareholders. To see this, note that the shareholder books show deferred taxes of $3.4 million and a net income that is $19.8 − $13.2 = $6.6 million greater than shown on the tax books. The deferred taxes and incremental net income sum to $10 million, which

ciation for book and tax purposes. Thus, in effect, IBM would not have a Column 2 and would simply report Column 1 to stockholders. This is a very conservative accounting practice, as it lowers reported earnings substantially for any growing company. At the other extreme, some public utilities reported income as shown in Column 2 but *without subtracting the deferred taxes*. In this case, reported income would be $30.0 − $6.8 = $23.2 million. This treatment is very *unconservative*, since it disregards the fact that future taxes will rise as tax depreciation falls. The regulatory commissions of these utilities force them to report this way to make their profits look higher without the need to raise utility service rates in the short run.

The main point is that otherwise identical companies can report very different levels of earnings. Security analysts, and investors generally, need to be aware of the accounting procedures of different companies. A rose is a rose is a rose, but a dollar of reported profits for one company is not necessarily equal to a dollar reported by another.

is the same as the difference in the depreciation expense between the two sets of books. Thus, the tax books show $10 million in depreciation cash flow while the shareholder books show $10 million more in net income and deferred taxes cash flow.

Since the cash flow from deferred taxes stems from depreciation cash flows, it is treated in the same way: deferred taxes are not included when estimating the firm's WACC. The WACC is based strictly on the firm's target capital structure, which does not explicitly include depreciation or deferred taxes. However, the deferred taxes cash flow does affect the point at which the WACC increases due to the increased cost of new common equity sales. This point will also be discussed further in Chapter 10.

Alternative Approach to Flotation Cost Adjustments

Throughout this chapter, we have incorporated flotation costs in the component costs of capital. The inclusion of flotation costs raises component costs, and hence increases the firm's WACC. An alternate approach to handling flotation costs is to ignore such costs when estimating the firm's WACC. Then, in the capital budgeting process, the dollar flotation costs are allocated to the firm's new projects, and hence increase project costs rather than capital costs. Although the alternative approach has some theoretical superiority, it is not generally used by firms today.[20]

SUMMARY

This chapter focused on the estimation of a firm's *weighted average cost of capital (WACC)*. We first discussed the relevant components and costs. If a capital component is part of the firm's permanent financing mix, then it should be included in the firm's WACC. The relevant cost of each component is the after-tax cost of new money.

We found that it is relatively easy to estimate a firm's costs of debt and preferred stock. Generally, market data from a firm's existing debt and preferred stock issues can be used to estimate these costs. However, we found that estimating the cost of equity is much more difficult. Three approaches can be used: *CAPM, Discounted Cash Flow (DCF)*, and *bond yield plus risk premium*. Each of these methods requires parameters which are themselves very difficult to estimate, so the cost of equity estimations, although perhaps expressed as point values, are really better described as ranges of values. We would have the most confidence in our cost of equity estimate if we used all three techniques and the three estimates were in general agreement.

---

[20]For a more complete discussion of the alternative approach, see Carl M. Hubbard, "Flotation Costs in Capital Budgeting: A Note on the Tax Effect," *Financial Management*, Summer 1984, 38-40; and John P. Ezzell and R. Burr Porter, "Flotation Costs and the Weighted Average Cost of Capital," *Journal of Financial and Quantitative Analysis*, September 1976, 403-413.

Once the component costs are estimated, we use *market value* weights to construct the firm's WACC. The firm's cost of capital is important to the financial manager both because it establishes the cutoff rate for capital projects and it helps the financial manager to identify the optimal capital structure, and hence it will be a key parameter in the next six chapters. The cost of capital does not remain constant: it increases when retained earnings are exhausted and the firm must turn to new common equity financing.

Finally, we discussed the implications of personal income taxes and deferred taxes. We concluded that personal income taxes may be ignored when estimating the cost of capital for publicly owned firms, although personal taxes lower the cost of retained earnings, k_s, for privately held companies whose owners are in positive tax brackets. We also concluded that deferred taxes represent an interest-free loan from the federal government. However, deferred taxes arise solely from differences between accounting conventions, and there is no need to include them when calculating the firm's WACC.

Questions and Problems

4-1 **(Cost of equity)** The Penrose Construction Company's EPS in 1986 was $2.00. EPS in 1981 was $1.36. The company pays out 40 percent of its earnings as dividends, and the stock currently sells for $21.60. Its optimal market value proportion of debt is 60 percent, and the firm does not use preferred stock financing.

    a. Calculate the growth rate in earnings per share.

    b. Assume that the growth rate calculated in Part a will continue. Calculate the dividend per share expected in 1987.

    c. What is the cost of retained earnings, k_s, estimate according to the DCF approach?

    d. The sale of new stock would net the company $18.36 per share. What is Penrose's percentage flotation cost, F? What is the cost of new common stock, k_e?

4-2 **(WACC calculation)** Conway Corporation's present market value capital structure, shown in the table, is considered to be optimal. Short-term debt is only used to finance seasonal and cyclical working capital needs.

Long-term debt	$20,000,000
Common equity	40,000,000
Total capital	$60,000,000

New bonds will have an 8 percent coupon rate and will be sold at par. Common stock, currently selling at $30 a share, can be sold to net the company $27 a share. The next expected annual dividend is $1.20, and shareholders expect dividends to grow at a constant rate of 10 percent. Conway's marginal tax rate is 34 percent.

    a. Estimate the cost of retained earnings using the DCF approach.

    b. What is the cost of new common equity?

    c. Estimate the firm's WACC using (1) the cost of retained earnings and (2) the cost of new equity.

4-3   **(Growth rates and WACC)** The following tabulation gives earnings per share figures for Monroe Manufacturing during the preceding 10 years. The firm's common stock, 140,000 shares outstanding, is now selling for $50 a share, and the expected dividend for the coming year (1987) is 50 percent of the 1987 EPS. Investors expect past trends to continue, so g may be based on the earnings growth rate.

Year	EPS	Ln EPS
1977	$2.00	0.69
1978	2.28	0.82
1979	2.57	0.94
1980	2.88	1.06
1981	3.20	1.16
1982	3.36	1.21
1983	3.56	1.27
1984	3.85	1.35
1985	4.19	1.43
1986	4.53	1.51

The current interest rate on new debt is 8 percent. The firm's marginal tax rate is 34 percent. The firm's market value capital structure, considered to be optimal, is as follows:

Debt	$ 3,000,000
Common equity	7,000,000
Total capital	$10,000,000

a. What is the historic growth rate in EPS for the years 1978-1985, using the average-to-average technique?
b. Estimate the firm's WACC assuming the growth rate obtained in Part a will continue into the indefinite future.
(Do Parts c, d, e, and f only if you are using the computerized diskette.)
c. Use log-linear regression to determine the 1978-1985 historic growth rate. Compare this to the historic growth rate using the average-to-average technique.
d. Determine the 1979-1985 and 1980-1985 historic growth rate using the average-to-average technique and log-linear regression. Compare the results.
e. Use the three log-linear growth rates to estimate the firm's WACC.
f. Assume that flotation costs are 5 percent on each new share sold. What is the cost of new common equity for each log-linear growth rate? What is the WACC when the equity component consists of new stock sales for each growth rate?

4-4   **(Market value weights)** Suppose the Solvang Company has this *book value* balance sheet:

Current assets	$30,000,000	Current liabilities	$10,000,000
Fixed assets	50,000,000	Long-term debt	30,000,000
		Common equity:	
		Common stock	
		(1 million shares)	1,000,000
		Retained earnings	39,000,000
Total assets	$80,000,000	Total claims	$80,000,000

The current liabilities consist entirely of notes payable to banks, and the interest rate on this debt is 10 percent, the same as the rate on new bank loans. The long-term debt consists of 30,000 annual coupon bonds, each of which has a par value of $1,000; carries a coupon interest rate of 6 percent; and matures in 20 years. The going rate of interest on new long-term debt, k_d, is 10 percent, and this is the present yield to maturity on the bonds. The common stock sells at a price of $60 per share. Estimate Solvang's market value capital structure. (Assume that Solvang uses short-term financing in its permanent capital structure.)

4-5 **(Component cost factors)** How would each of the following affect a firm's after-tax cost of debt, $k_d(1 - T)$; its cost of equity, k_s; and its average cost of capital, k_a? Indicate by a plus (+), a minus (−), or a zero (0) whether the factor would raise, lower, or have an indeterminate effect on the items in question. Assume other things are held constant. Be prepared to justify your answer but recognize that several of the parts probably have no single correct answer; these questions are to stimulate thought and discussion.

	Probable Effect on		
	$k_d(1 - T)$	k_s	k_a
a. The corporate tax rate is lowered.	_____	_____	_____
b. The Federal Reserve tightens credit.	_____	_____	_____
c. The firm uses more debt; that is, it increases the debt/assets ratio.	_____	_____	_____
d. The dividend payout ratio is increased.	_____	_____	_____
e. The firm doubles the amount of capital it raises during the year.	_____	_____	_____
f. The firm expands into a risky new area.	_____	_____	_____
g. The firm merges with another firm whose earnings are countercyclical to those of the first firm and to the stock market.	_____	_____	_____
h. The stock market falls drastically, and our firm's stock falls along with the rest.	_____	_____	_____
i. Investors become more risk averse.	_____	_____	_____
j. The firm is an electric utility with a large investment in nuclear plants. Several states propose a ban on nuclear power generation.	_____	_____	_____

4-6 **(Cost of equity estimation methods)** You have just estimated the cost of equity for Freeway Shipping Company using all three estimation techniques. The results are summarized in the table:

Method	k_s Estimate
CAPM	12.1%
DCF	14.0
Bond yield plus risk premium	15.4

The inconsistency of the results are worrisome, but you must still develop your equity cost estimate. What factors might you consider as you attempt to place confidence in the above estimates?

4-7 **(WACC estimation)** Laser Communications, Inc. (LCI), has the following capital structure, which it considers to be optimal:

Debt	25%
Preferred stock	15
Common stock	60
Total capital	100%

LCI's net income expected this year is $17,142.86; its established dividend payout ratio is 30 percent; its marginal tax rate is 34 percent; and investors expect earnings and dividends to grow at a constant rate of 9 percent in the future. LCI paid a dividend of $3.60 per share last year (D_0), and its stock currently sells at a price of $60 per share. Treasury bonds yield 11 percent; an average stock has a 14 percent expected rate of return; and LCI's beta is 1.51. These terms would apply to new security offerings:

Common: New common stock would have a flotation cost of 10 percent.
Preferred: New preferred could be sold to the public at a price of $100 per share, with a dividend of $11. Flotation costs of $5 per share would be incurred.
Debt: Debt could be sold at an interest rate of 12 percent.

a. Estimate the component costs of debt, preferred stock, retained earnings, and new common stock. Use both the CAPM and DCF methods to estimate k_s.
b. What is LCI's WACC?

4-8 **(Integrative problem)** A summary of the balance sheet of Travellers Inn, Inc. (TII), a company which was formed by merging a number of regional motel chains and which hopes to rival Holiday Inn on the national scene, is shown in the table:

Travellers Inn
December 31, 1986
(Millions of Dollars)

Cash	$ 10	Accounts payable		$ 10
Accounts receivable	20	Accruals		10
Inventories	20	Short-term debt		5
Current assets	$ 50	Current liabilities		$ 25
Net fixed assets	50	Long-term debt		30
		Preferred stock		5
		Common equity:		
		Common stock	$10	
		Retained earnings	30	
		Total common equity		40
Total assets	$100	Total claims		$100

These facts are also given for TII:

(1) Short-term debt consists of bank loans which currently cost 10 percent, with interest payable quarterly. These loans are used to finance receivables and inventories on a seasonal basis, so in the off-season, bank loans are zero.

(2) The long-term debt consists of 20-year, semiannual payment mortgage bonds with a coupon rate of 8 percent. Currently, these bonds provide a yield to investors of $k_d = 12\%$. If new bonds were sold, they would yield investors 12 percent, but a flotation cost of 5 percent would be required to sell new bonds.

(3) TII's perpetual preferred stock has a $100 par value, pays a quarterly dividend of $2, and has a yield to investors of 11 percent. New preferred

would have to provide the same yield to investors, and the company would incur a 5 percent flotation cost to sell it.

(4) The company has 4 million shares of common stock outstanding. $P_0 = \$20$, and the stock has recently traded in a range of \$17 to \$23. $D_0 = \$1$, and $EPS_0 = \$2$. ROE based on average equity was 24 percent in 1986, but management expects to increase this return on equity to 30 percent; however, security analysts are not aware of management's optimism in this regard.

(5) Betas, as reported by security analysts, range from 1.3 to 1.7; the T-bond rate is 10 percent; and k_M is estimated by various brokerage houses to be in the range of 14.5 to 15.5 percent. Brokerage house reports forecast growth rates in the range of 10 to 15 percent over the foreseeable future. However, some analysts do not explicitly forecast growth rates, but they indicate to their clients that they expect TII's historic trends as shown in the table to continue.

(6) At a recent conference, TII's financial vice president polled some pension fund investment managers on the minimum rate of return they would have to expect on TII's common to make them willing to buy the common rather than TII bonds, when the bonds yielded 12 percent. The responses suggested a risk premium over TII bonds of 4 to 6 percent.

(7) TII is in the 40 percent federal-plus-state tax bracket. Its dominant stockholders are in the 28 percent bracket.

(8) New common stock would have a 10 percent flotation cost.

(9) TII's principal investment banker, Henry, Kaufman & Company, predicts a decline in interest rates, with k_d falling to 10 percent and the T-bond rate to 8 percent, although Henry, Kaufman & Company acknowledges that an increase in the expected inflation rate could lead to an increase rather than a decrease in rates.

(10) Here is the historic record of EPS and DPS:

Year	EPS[a]	DPS[a]
1972	$0.09	$0.00
1973	−0.20	0.00
1974	0.40	0.00
1975	0.52	0.00
1976	0.10	0.00
1977	0.57	0.00
1978	0.61	0.00
1979	0.70	0.00
1980	0.78	0.00
1981	0.80	0.00
1982	1.20	0.20
1983	0.95	0.40
1984	1.30	0.60
1985	1.60	0.80
1986	2.00	1.00

[a]Adjusted for a 2:1 stock split in 1977, a 3:1 split in 1985, and 10 percent stock dividends in 1974 and 1982.

Assume that you are a recently hired financial analyst, and your boss, the treasurer, has asked you to estimate the company's WACC for both retained earnings and new common stock sales. Your cost of capital figures at each level should be appropriate for use in evaluating projects which are in the same risk class as the firm's average assets now on the books.

Selected Additional References

The following articles provide some valuable insights into the CAPM approach to estimating the cost of equity:

Beaver, William H., Paul Kettler, and Myron Scholes, "The Association between Market Determined and Accounting Determined Risk Measures," *Accounting Review*, October 1970, 654-682.

Bowman, Robert G., "The Theoretical Relationship between Systematic Risk and Financial (Accounting) Variables," *Journal of Finance*, June 1979, 617-630.

Cooley, Philip L., "A Review of the Use of Beta in Regulatory Proceedings," *Financial Management*, Winter 1981, 75-81.

Chen, Carl R., "Time-Series Analysis of Beta Stationarity and Its Determinants: A Case of Public Utilities," *Financial Management*, Autumn 1982, 64-70.

The weighted average cost of capital as described in this chapter is widely used in both industry and academic circles. It has been criticized on several counts, but to date it has withstood the challenges. See the following articles:

Arditti, Fred D., and Haim Levy, "The Weighted Average Cost of Capital as a Cutoff Rate: A Critical Examination of the Classical Textbook Weighted Average," *Financial Management*, Fall 1977, 24-34.

Beranek, William, "The Weighted Average Cost of Capital and Shareholder Wealth Maximization," *Journal of Financial and Quantitative Analysis*, March 1977, 17-32.

Boudreaux, Kenneth J., and Hugh W. Long; John R. Ezzell and R. Burr Porter; Moshe Ben Horim; and Alan C. Shapiro, "The Weighted Average Cost of Capital: A Discussion," *Financial Management*, Summer 1979, 7-23.

Reilly, Raymond R., and William E. Wacker, "On the Weighted Average Cost of Capital," *Journal of Financial and Quantitative Analysis*, January 1973, 123-126.

Some other works that are relevant include the following:

Alberts, W. W., and Stephen H. Archer, "Some Evidence on the Effect of Company Size on the Cost of Equity Capital," *Journal of Financial and Quantitative Analysis*, March 1973, 229-242.

Chen, Andrew, "Recent Developments in the Cost of Debt Capital," *Journal of Finance*, June 1978, 863-883.

Myers, Stewart C., "Interactions of Corporate Financing and Investments Decisions—Implications for Capital Budgeting," *Journal of Finance*, March 1974, 1-25.

Nantell, Timothy J., and C. Robert Carlson, "The Cost of Capital as a Weighted Average," *Journal of Finance*, December 1975, 1343-1355.

For some insights into the cost of capital techniques used by major firms, see

Gitman, Lawrence J., and Vincent A. Mercurio, "Cost of Capital Techniques Used by Major U.S. Firms: Survey and Analysis of Fortune's 1000," *Financial Management*, Winter 1982, 21-29.

Additional references on the cost of capital are cited in Chapters 5 and 9.

5

CAPITAL STRUCTURE THEORY

One of the most perplexing issues facing financial managers is the relationship between capital structure and firm value. Several theories of capital structure have been proposed, and we will discuss them in some detail. We begin by presenting some key terms and equations. Then we briefly discuss three early (pre-1958) theories: the net income (NI) approach, the net operating income (NOI) approach, and the traditional approach. Next, we consider the classic 1958 Modigliani and Miller (MM) analysis, which marked the beginning of "modern capital structure theory." We then go on to expand the basic MM analysis to include the effects of corporate and personal taxes, financial distress, and agency costs. Finally, we present the asymmetric information (or signaling) theory, an alternative capital structure hypothesis which has recently been proposed and which is in many respects consistent with the capital structures one actually observes in practice.

Our conclusions are as follows: (1) There does exist an optimal capital structure, or at least an optimal range of structures, for every firm. (2) However, financial theory is not powerful enough at this point to enable us to locate a firm's optimal structure with any degree of precision. (3) Still, financial theory does help us identify the key factors which influence the value-maximizing structure, so an understanding of the material in this chapter will aid a firm that is choosing its target capital structure.

KEY TERMS AND EQUATIONS

Several theories have been set forth regarding how *leverage*, or the use of debt, affects the value of a firm and its cost of capital. These theories address two basic questions: Can a firm increase the wealth of its stockholders by replacing some of its equity with debt, and, if so, exactly how much debt should the firm use? As we

---

This chapter was coauthored with Dilip K. Shome of Virginia Polytechnic Institute and State University.   149

explore these two questions, we will utilize several valuation equations; the key terms used in these equations are as follows:

S = market value of the firm's common stock (price per share times number of shares outstanding).

D = market value of its debt. For simplicity, we shall ignore preferred stock and assume that the firm uses only one class of debt, which is a perpetuity. (Assuming perpetual debt simplifies the analysis.)

V = D + S = total market value of the firm.

EBIT = earnings before interest and taxes, also called net operating income (NOI). Again, for simplicity we shall assume that the expected value of EBIT is a constant over time. EBIT could rise or fall, but the best estimate for the EBIT in any future year is the same as that for any other year.

k_d = interest rate on the firm's single class of perpetual debt.

k_s = cost of equity, or required rate of return on the firm's common stock.

k_a = weighted average cost of capital.

T = corporate tax rate.

We assume that the firm is in a zero-growth situation; that is, EBIT is expected to remain constant, and all earnings are paid out as dividends. Therefore, the total market value of its common stock, S, is a perpetuity whose value is found as follows:

$$S = \frac{\text{Dividends}}{k_s} = \frac{\text{Net income}}{k_s} = \frac{(\text{EBIT} - k_d D)(1 - T)}{k_s}. \qquad (5\text{-}1)$$

Equation 5-1 is merely the value of a perpetuity, with the numerator being the net income available to common stockholders, which we assume is all paid out as dividends, while the denominator is the cost of common equity. We shall use Equation 5-1 to show how changes in the amount of debt financing would affect the value of the firm's stock under the different capital structure theories. Also, note that we can solve Equation 5-1 for k_s, the cost of equity:

$$k_s = \frac{(\text{EBIT} - k_d D)(1 - T)}{S}. \qquad (5\text{-}1a)$$

We will use this form of the equation when we discuss the effects of leverage on the cost of equity.

Another basic required equation is that for the weighted average cost of capital as developed in Chapter 4:

$$k_a = \text{WACC} = w_d k_d (1 - T) + w_s k_s = \left(\frac{D}{V}\right) k_d (1 - T) + \left(\frac{S}{V}\right) k_s. \qquad (5\text{-}2)$$

We will use Equation 5-2 to examine how changes in the debt ratio affect the firm's average cost of capital.

A third basic equation is that for the total market value of the firm, V. Note that we could find V by first using Equation 5-1 to find the value of the equity and then adding the value of the debt: $V = S + D$. However, another expression for the value of the firm is required in our analysis.[1]

$$V = \frac{EBIT(1 - T)}{k_a}. \tag{5-3}$$

Equation 5-3 shows that V can be found as the value of a perpetuity which capitalizes the constant after-tax operating income, $EBIT(1 - T)$, at the firm's WACC, k_a. Note that Equation 5-1 capitalizes the earnings available to common stockholders, and Equation 5-3 capitalizes after-tax operating cash flows, which must service both debtholders and stockholders. Note also that we could solve Equation 5-3 for k_a to obtain an alternative expression for the WACC:

$$k_a = WACC = \frac{EBIT(1 - T)}{V}. \tag{5-3a}$$

We will use Equations 5-1, 5-1a, 5-2, 5-3, and 5-3a to examine the way changes in capital structure affect the firm's value and cost of capital under the different capital structure theories. This is our next task.

EARLY THEORIES OF CAPITAL STRUCTURE

One of the earliest formal works on the theory of capital structure was David Durand's 1952 study, which identified the three positions that had been taken by writers up to that time:[2] (1) the net income (NI) approach, (2) the net operating

---

[1]Equation 5-3 is derived as follows:

Step 1. Solve Equation 5-2 for V:

$$V = \frac{(D)k_d(1 - T) + (S)k_s}{k_a}.$$

Step 2. Substitute Equation 5-1 for S in the Step 1 equation:

$$V = \frac{(D)k_d (1 - T) + \left[\dfrac{(EBIT - k_dD)(1 - T)}{k_s}\right]k_s}{k_a}.$$

Step 3. Cancel the k_s values in the numerator and then modify the equation to produce this expression:

$$V = \frac{k_dD(1 - T) + EBIT(1 - T) - k_dD(1 - T)}{k_a}.$$

Step 4. Cancel the $k_dD(1 - T)$ terms, producing this important new equation:

$$V = \frac{EBIT(1 - T)}{k_a}. \tag{5-3}$$

[2]See David Durand, "Costs of Debt and Equity Funds for Business: Trends and Problems of Measurement," *Conference on Research in Business Finance* (New York: National Bureau of Economic Research, 1952). Although Durand's work is dated, we include it in the text to provide historical perspective.

income (NOI) approach, and (3) a middle-ground position Durand called the traditional approach. The differences among the three approaches result solely from
differing assumptions about how investors establish the value of a firm's debt and
equity. For convenience, we examine the three approaches under the assumption
of zero taxes.

The Net Income (NI) Approach

The *NI approach* assumes (1) that investors capitalize, or value, the firm's net
income at a constant rate (k_s = constant) and (2) that firms can raise all the debt
they want at a constant rate (k_d = constant). With both k_s and k_d constant, as the
firm uses more and more debt, the weighted average cost of capital, k_a as given by
Equation 5-2, declines, because debt is cheaper than equity. Further, if k_a declines
as debt is increased, then, because of the Equation 5-3 relationship, the firm's value
must increase as its use of debt increases.

The situation as viewed under the NI approach is shown on the left side of
Figure 5-1: as the firm moves from zero toward 100 percent debt, its overall cost
of capital decreases continuously, and its value increases continuously. Thus, if the
NI assumptions are correct, firms should use (almost) 100 percent debt in order
to maximize value.

The Net Operating Income (NOI) Approach

The *NOI approach*, graphed in the middle section of Figure 5-1, assumes that
investors have an entirely different reaction to corporate debt. Specifically, the NOI
approach assumes that investors value NOI (or EBIT) at a constant rate (k_a =
constant). As in the NI approach, NOI advocates assume that k_d is a constant.
Notice (1) that a constant k_a results in a constant value for the firm regardless of
its use of debt (this follows when Equation 5-3 is applied), and (2) that a constant
k_a, along with a constant k_d, implies that k_s increases with leverage (Equation 5-2),
and hence that stockholders regard the use of leverage as increasing the riskiness
of the equity cash flows. If the NOI assumptions were true, then capital structure
decisions would be unimportant—one capital structure would be as good as any
other.[3]

The Traditional Approach

Most academicians and practitioners at the time of Durand's work took a middle-
of-the-road approach, somewhere between NI and NOI, which Durand called the
traditional approach. The graphs on the right side of Figure 5-1 illustrate the

---

[3]The NI and NOI theories, as they were originally set forth, assumed away corporate income taxes.
However, Durand did examine the two approaches including corporate income taxes, and he found
that under the NOI approach, the firm's value does increase with leverage due to the tax deductibility
of interest. However, the firm's value under the NI approach increases at an even faster rate. Thus, in a
world with corporate taxes, both approaches would indicate that the optimal capital structure calls for
virtually 100 percent debt.

Figure 5-1
Effects of Leverage:
NI, NOI, and Traditional Approaches

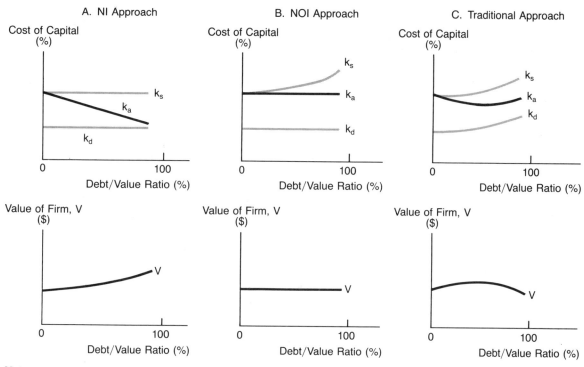

Notes:
a. Under the NI approach, the plot of value versus D/V is slightly bowed. A plot of value versus dollars of debt would be linear.
b. The graphs do not extend all the way to a 100 percent debt/value ratio because at that point the creditors become the equity holders. See Footnote 5 for a discussion.

traditionalists' view, which suggested that up to some "moderate" amount of leverage, risk does not increase noticeably on either the debt or the equity, so k_d and k_s are both relatively constant out to some point. However, beyond that critical debt ratio, both debt and equity costs begin to rise, and these increases more than offset the advantages of cheaper debt. The result is (1) a U-shaped weighted average cost of capital curve and (2) a value of the firm which first rises, then hits a peak, and finally declines as the debt ratio increases. Thus, according to the traditionalists, there is some capital structure with less than 100 percent debt which maximizes the value of the firm.

Whereas the NI and NOI theories as set forth by Durand are mathematically precise, the traditional approach was more judgmental in nature. Moreover, a review of the literature of the time offers little in the way of an explanation for the assumed shape of the traditional curves; they were drawn on the basis of judgment rather than statistical evidence. We will return to a discussion of the traditional view later in the chapter, but first we must examine the Modigliani-Miller models and their extensions.

THE MODIGLIANI-MILLER MODELS

The capital structure theories presented thus far were based on assertions about investor behavior rather than on either a carefully constructed formal proof or formal statistical studies. In what has been called the most influential financial research ever published, Franco Modigliani and Merton Miller (MM) addressed the capital structure issue in a rigorous, scientific fashion, and they set off a chain of research that continues to this day.[4]

Assumptions

To begin, MM made the following assumptions, some of which were later relaxed:

1. Firms' business risk can be measured (by σ_{EBIT}), and firms with the same degree of business risk are said to be in a *homogeneous risk class*.

2. All present and prospective investors have identical estimates of each firm's future EBIT; that is, investors have *homogeneous expectations* about expected future corporate earnings and the riskiness of these earnings. This assumption is comparable to our use of a "representative investor" in earlier chapters when we discussed the DCF model and market equilibrium ($\hat{k}_s = k_s$).

3. Stocks and bonds are traded in *perfect capital markets*. This assumption implies, among other things, (1) that there are no brokerage costs and (2) that investors (both individuals and institutions) can borrow at the same rate as corporations.

4. The debt of firms and individuals is riskless, so the interest rate on debt is the risk-free rate. Further, this situation holds regardless of how much debt a firm (or an individual) issues.

5. All cash flows are perpetuities; that is, the firm is a zero-growth firm with an "expectationally constant" EBIT, and its bonds are perpetuities. "Expectationally

---

[4]See Franco Modigliani and Merton H. Miller, "The Cost of Capital, Corporation Finance and the Theory of Investment," *American Economic Review*, June 1958, 261-297; "The Cost of Capital, Corporation Finance and the Theory of Investment: Reply," *American Economic Review*, September 1958, 655-669; "Taxes and the Cost of Capital: A Correction," *American Economic Review*, June 1963, 433-443; and "Reply," *American Economic Review*, June 1965, 524-527. In a 1979 survey of Financial Management Association members, the original MM article was judged to have had the greatest impact on the field of finance of any work ever published. See Philip L. Cooley and J. Louis Heck, "Significant Contributions to Finance Literature," *Financial Management*, Tenth Anniversary Issue 1981, 23-33.

constant" means that investors expect EBIT to be constant, but the realized level could be different from the expected level.

MM without Corporate Taxes

MM first performed their analysis under the assumption that there are no corporate income taxes. On the basis of the preceding assumptions, and in the absence of corporate taxes, MM stated and algebraically proved three propositions:

Proposition I

The value of any firm is established by capitalizing its expected net operating income (NOI = EBIT) at a constant rate which is appropriate for the firm's risk class:

$$V_L = V_U = \frac{EBIT}{k_a} = \frac{EBIT}{k_{sU}}. \tag{5-4}$$

The constant rate, k_{sU} is the required rate of return for an unlevered, or all-equity, firm in a given risk class.

Since V is established by the Proposition I equation, *under the MM theory, the value of the firm is independent of its leverage.* This also implies that the weighted average cost of capital to any firm, leveraged or not, is (1) completely independent of its capital structure and (2) equal to the cost of equity to an unlevered firm in the same risk class. Thus, MM's Proposition I is identical to the NOI hypothesis as expressed in Figure 5-1.

Proposition II

The cost of equity to a levered firm is equal to (1) the cost of equity to an unlevered firm in the same risk class plus (2) a risk premium whose size depends on the differential between the costs of equity and debt to an unlevered firm and the amount of leverage used:

$$k_{sL} = k_{sU} + \text{Risk premium} = k_{sU} + (k_{sU} - k_d)(D/S). \tag{5-5}$$

Here the subscripts L and U designate levered and unlevered firms in a given risk class, and Proposition II states that as the firm's use of debt increases, its cost of equity also rises, and in a mathematically precise manner.

Taken together, the two MM propositions imply that the inclusion of more debt in the capital structure will not increase the value of the firm, because the benefits of cheaper debt will be exactly offset by an increase in the cost of equity. *Thus, the basic MM theory states that in a world without taxes, both the value of a firm and its cost of capital are unaffected by its capital structure.*

Proposition III

A firm should invest only in those projects with rates of return (IRRs) greater than or equal to $k_a = k_{sU}$:

$$IRR \geq k_a = k_{sU}. \tag{5-6}$$

This proposition is well accepted in finance, and we will discuss it more fully in Chapter 7, on capital budgeting.

Proof of the MM Propositions without Corporate Taxes

Proof of Proposition I

MM used an *arbitrage proof* to support their propositions. They showed that, under their assumptions, if two companies differed only (1) in the way they are financed and (2) in their total market values, then investors would sell shares of the overvalued firm, buy those of the undervalued firm, and continue this process until the companies had exactly the same market value. To illustrate, assume that two firms, Firm L (for levered) and Firm U (for unlevered), are identical in all important respects except financial structure. Firm L has $4,000,000 of 7.5 percent debt, while Firm U uses only equity. Both firms have EBIT = $900,000, and σ_{EBIT} is the same for both firms, so they are in the same business risk class.

In the initial situation, before any arbitrage occurs, assume that both firms have the same equity capitalization rate: $k_{sU} = k_{sL} = 10\%$. Under this condition, according to Equation 5-1, the following situation would exist:

Firm U:

$$\text{Value of Firm U's stock} = S_U = \frac{EBIT - k_d D}{k_{sU}} = \frac{\$900,000 - \$0}{0.10} = \$9,000,000.$$

$$\text{Total market value of Firm U} = V_U = D_U + S_U = \$0 + \$9,000,000 = \$9,000,000.$$

Firm L:

$$\text{Value of Firm L's stock} = S_L = \frac{EBIT - k_d D}{k_{sL}}$$

$$= \frac{\$900,000 - 0.075(\$4,000,000)}{0.10} = \$6,000,000.$$

$$\text{Total market value of Firm L} = V_L = D_L + S_L = \$4,000,000 + \$6,000,000 = \$10,000,000.$$

Thus, before arbitrage, the value of the levered company, Firm L, exceeds that of unlevered Firm U.

MM argue that this is a disequilibrium situation which cannot persist. To see why, suppose you owned 10 percent of L's stock, so the market value of your investment was $600,000. According to MM, you could increase your total investment income without increasing your exposure to risk. For example, suppose you

(1) sold your stock in L for $600,000, (2) borrowed an amount equal to 10 percent of L's debt ($400,000), and then (3) bought 10 percent of U's stock for $900,000. Notice that you would receive $1 million from the sale of your 10 percent of L's stock plus your borrowing, and you would be spending only $900,000 on U's stock, so you would have an extra $100,000, which MM assumed you would invest in riskless debt to yield 7.5 percent, or $7,500 annually.

Now consider your income position:

Old Income:	10% of L's $600,000 equity income		$60,000
New Income:	10% of U's $900,000 equity income	$90,000	
	Less 7.5% interest on $400,000 loan	(30,000)	60,000
	Plus 7.5% interest on extra $100,000		7,500
	New net income		$67,500

Thus, your net investment income from common stock would be exactly the same as before, $60,000, but you would have $100,000 left over for investment in riskless debt, which would increase your income by $7,500. Therefore, the total return on your $600,000 net worth would rise. Further, your risk, according to MM, would be the same as before; you would have simply substituted $400,000 of "homemade" leverage for your 10 percent share of Firm L's $4 million of corporate leverage, and hence neither your "effective" debt nor your risk would have changed. Thus, you would have increased your income without raising your risk, which is obviously a desirable thing to do. (We could have assumed that you used the extra $100,000 to reduce your debt. This would have lowered your income, but also lowered your debt and hence your risk exposure. This would put you in a position with the same income but with less risk, so again, you would benefit by switching out of Firm L's stock and into that of U.)

MM argue that this arbitrage process would actually occur, with sales of L's stock driving its price down, and purchases of U's stock driving its price up, until the market values of the two firms were equal. Until this equality was established, gains could be obtained by switching from one stock to the other, so the profit motive would force the equality to be reached. When equilibrium was established, the values of Firms L and U, and their weighted average costs of capital, would be equal. Thus, according to Modigliani and Miller, V and k_a must be independent of capital structure under equilibrium conditions.

Proofs of Propositions II and III
The proofs of these propositions are relatively straightforward. See the first two proofs in Appendix 5A.

MM with Corporate Taxes

MM also derived a second set of propositions which include the effect of corporate taxes. Most importantly, with corporate income taxes, they concluded that leverage will increase a firm's value, because interest on debt is a deductible expense, and hence more of a leveraged firm's operating income flows through to investors. The MM propositions when corporations are subject to income taxes follow.

Proposition I

The value of a levered firm is equal to the value of an unlevered firm in the same risk class plus the value of the tax savings, which is equal to the corporate tax rate (T) times the amount of debt the firm uses:

$$V_L = V_U + TD. \tag{5-4a}$$

The important point here is that when corporate taxes are introduced, the value of the levered firm exceeds that of the unlevered firm. Additionally, the differential increases as the use of debt increases, so a firm's value is maximized at virtually 100 percent debt financing. (Note: The value of the unlevered firm is found by using Equation 5-3, with $k_a = k_{sU}$.)

Proposition II

The cost of equity to a levered firm is equal to (1) the cost of equity to an unlevered firm in the same risk class plus (2) a risk premium whose size depends on the differential between the costs of equity and debt to an unlevered firm, the amount of financial leverage, and the corporate tax rate:

$$k_{sL} = k_{sU} + (k_{sU} - k_d)(1 - T)(D/S). \tag{5-5a}$$

Notice that Equation 5-5a is identical to the corresponding without-tax equation, 5-5, except for the term $(1 - T)$ in 5-5a. Since $(1 - T)$ is less than 1.0, the imposition of corporate taxes causes the cost of equity to rise at a slower rate than it did in the absence of taxes. It is this characteristic that produces the Proposition I result, namely, the increase in firm value as leverage increases.

Proposition III

A firm should invest only in those projects with a rate of return which meets the following condition:

$$IRR \geq k_{sU}[1 - T(D/V)]. \tag{5-6a}$$

The term $k_{sU}[1 - T(D/V)]$ is the "cut-off rate" for new investment, and only those projects with returns equal to or above this rate should be accepted.

The proofs of MM's Propositions I, II, and III with corporate taxes are given in Appendix 5A.

Illustration of the MM Model with Corporate Taxes

To illustrate the MM model with corporate taxes, assume that the following data and conditions hold for Mid-State Water Company, an old, established firm that supplies water to business and residential customers in several low-growth midwestern metropolitan areas.

1. Mid-State currently has no debt; it is an all-equity company.

2. Expected EBIT = $4,000,000. EBIT is not expected to increase over time, so Mid-State is in a no-growth situation.

3. Mid-State has a 40 percent federal-plus-state tax rate, so T = 40%.

4. Mid-State pays out all of its income as dividends.

5. If Mid-State begins to use debt, it can borrow at a rate k_d = 8%. This borrowing rate is constant, and it is independent of the amount of debt used. Any money raised by selling debt would be used to retire common stock, so Mid-State's assets would remain constant.

6. The risk of Mid-State's assets, and thus its EBIT, is such that its shareholders require a rate of return, k_{sU}, of 12 percent if no debt is used.

When Mid-State has zero debt, Equation 5-3 can be used to find its value, $20 million:

$$V_U = \frac{EBIT(1 - T)}{k_{sU}} = \frac{\$4 \text{ million}(0.6)}{0.12} = \$20.0 \text{ million}.$$

With $10 million of debt, we see by the Proposition I equation (5-4a) that total market value rises to $24 million:

$$V_L = V_U + TD = \$20 \text{ million} + 0.4(\$10 \text{ million}) = \$24 \text{ million}.$$

Therefore, the value of Mid-State's stock must be $14 million:

$$S = V - D = \$24 \text{ million} - \$10 \text{ million} = \$14 \text{ million}.$$

We can also find Mid-State's cost of equity, k_{sL}, and its weighted average cost of capital, k_a, at a debt level of $10 million. First, we use Equation 5-5a, Proposition II, to find k_{sL}, the leveraged cost of equity:

$$\begin{aligned} k_{sL} &= k_{sU} + (k_{sU} - k_d)(1 - T)(D/S) \\ &= 12\% + (12\% - 8\%)(0.6)(\$10 \text{ million}/\$14 \text{ million}) \\ &= 12\% + 1.71\% = 13.71\%. \end{aligned}$$

Now we can find the company's weighted average cost of capital, k_a:

$$\begin{aligned} WACC = k_a &= (D/V)(k_d)(1 - T) + (S/V)k_s \\ &= (\$10/\$24)(8\%)(0.6) + (\$14/\$24)(13.71\%) = 10\%. \end{aligned}$$

Alternatively, we could find k_a by using Equation 5-3a as follows:

$$k_a = \frac{EBIT(1 - T)}{V} = \frac{\$4 \text{ million}(0.6)}{\$24 \text{ million}} = 0.10 = 10\%.$$

Mid-State's value and cost of capital based on the MM model at various debt levels are shown in Figure 5-2. Here we see that in an MM world with corporate

Figure 5-2
Effects of Leverage:
MM with Taxes (Millions of Dollars)

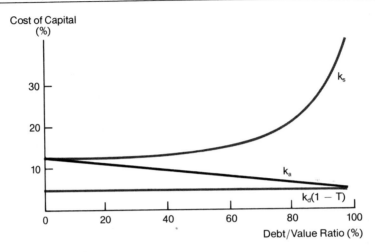

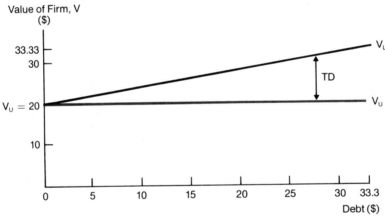

D (1)	V (2)	S (3)	D/V (4)	k_d (5)	k_s (6)	k_a (7)
$ 0	$20.00	$20.00	0.00%	8.0%	12.00%	12.00%
5	22.00	17.00	22.73	8.0	12.71	10.91
10	24.00	14.00	41.67	8.0	13.71	10.00
15	26.00	11.00	57.69	8.0	15.27	9.23
20	28.00	8.00	71.43	8.0	18.00	8.57
25	30.00	5.00	83.33	8.0	24.00	8.00
30	32.00	2.00	93.75	8.0	48.00	7.50
33.33[a]	33.33	0.00	100.00	12.0	—	12.00

[a]The case of 100 percent debt is the theoretically limiting case. See Footnote 5 for a discussion.

taxes, financial leverage does matter: the value of the firm is maximized, and its cost of capital is minimized, if it uses virtually 100 percent debt financing.[5]

Relationship of Proposition III to the Weighted Average Cost of Capital

MM propose, in Proposition III with corporate taxes, that new projects should be accepted if and only if

$$\text{IRR} \geq k_{sU}[1 - T(D/V)]. \tag{5-6a}$$

We do not discuss capital budgeting until Chapter 7. However, readers may recall from introductory texts that a new project which has the same risk as the firm's existing projects should be accepted only if its IRR is greater than the firm's marginal cost of capital, which is based on the WACC as expressed in Equation 5-2. The MM criterion, which is based on the cost of equity to an unlevered firm, can be consistent with a decision rule based on the WACC. It is relatively easy to show that the right side of Equation 5-6a is equivalent to Equation 5-2, provided that the Equation 5-2 cost of debt is a constant and that the cost of equity is specified by Equation 5-5a; this is proved in Appendix 5A.

THE MILLER MODEL

Although MM included *corporate* taxes in the second version of their model, they did not extend the model to analyze the effects of *personal* taxes. However, in his 1976 presidential address to the American Finance Association, Merton Miller did introduce a model designed to show how leverage affects firms' values when both personal and corporate taxes are taken into account.[6] To explain Miller's model,

---

[5]In the limiting case, where the firm used 100 percent debt financing, the bondholders would own the entire company, and hence they would have to bear all the business risk. (Up until this point, MM assume that the stockholders bear all the risk.) If the bondholders bear all the risk, then the capitalization rate on the debt should be equal to the equity capitalization rate at zero debt, $k_d = k_{sU} = 12\%$.

The income stream to the stockholders in the all-equity case was $CF_U = \$4,000,000(1 - T) = \$2,400,000$, and the value of the firm was

$$V_U = \frac{\$2,400,000}{0.12} = \$20,000,000.$$

With all debt, the entire $4,000,000 of EBIT would be used to pay interest charges. k_d would be 12%, so $I = 0.12(\text{Debt}) = \$4,000,000$. Taxes would be zero, and investors (bondholders) would get the entire $4,000,000 of operating income; they would not have to share it with the government. Thus, at 100 percent debt, the value of the firm would be

$$V_L = \frac{\$4,000,000}{0.12} = \$33,333,333 = D.$$

There is, of course, a transition problem in all this—MM assume that $k_d = 8\%$ regardless of how much debt the firm has until debt reaches 100 percent, at which point k_d jumps to 12 percent, the cost of equity. As we shall see later in the chapter, k_d realistically rises as the use of financial leverage increases.

[6]See Merton H. Miller, "Debt and Taxes," *Journal of Finance*, May 1977, 261-275.

let us begin by defining T_c as the corporate tax rate, T_s as the personal tax rate on income from stocks, and T_d as the personal tax rate on income from debt. Note that stock returns come partly as dividends and partly as capital gains, so T_s is a weighted average of the effective tax rates on dividends and capital gains, while essentially all debt income comes from interest, which is effectively taxed at an investor's top rate.

With personal taxes included, *and under the same set of assumptions used in the earlier MM models*, the value of an unlevered firm is found as follows:

$$V_U = \frac{\text{EBIT}(1 - T_c)(1 - T_s)}{k_{sU}}. \tag{5-7}$$

The $(1 - T_s)$ term adjusts for personal taxes. Therefore, the numerator shows how much of the firm's operating income is left after the unlevered firm itself pays corporate income taxes and its investors subsequently pay personal taxes on their equity income. Since the introduction of personal taxes lowers the usable income to investors, these taxes reduce the value of the unlevered firm, other things held constant.

Miller's results can be obtained from an arbitrage proof similar to the one we presented earlier. However, we shall use an alternative approach here. To begin, we first partition the levered firm's annual cash flows, CF_L, into those going to the stockholders and those going to the bondholders:

$$CF_L = \text{Net CF to stockholders} + \text{Net CF to bondholders} \tag{5-8}$$
$$= (\text{EBIT} - I)(1 - T_c)(1 - T_s) + I(1 - T_d).$$

Here I is the annual interest payment. Equation 5-8 can be rearranged as follows:

$$CF_L = \text{EBIT}(1 - T_c)(1 - T_s) - I(1 - T_c)(1 - T_s) + I(1 - T_d). \tag{5-8a}$$

The first term in Equation 5-8a is identical to the after-tax cash flow of an unlevered firm, and its present value is found by discounting the perpetual cash flow by k_{sU}. The second and third terms, which reflect leverage, result from the cash flows associated with interest payments. These two cash flows are assumed to have a risk equal to that of the basic interest payment stream, and hence their present values are obtained by discounting at the cost of debt, k_d. (Remember, these are all perpetual cash flows, so the basic perpetuity valuation model, $V = CF/k$, applies.) Combining the present values of the three terms, we obtain this value for the levered firm:

$$V_L = \frac{\text{EBIT}(1 - T_c)(1 - T_s)}{k_{sU}} - \frac{I(1 - T_c)(1 - T_s)}{k_d} + \frac{I(1 - T_d)}{k_d}. \tag{5-9}$$

The first term in Equation 5-9 is identical to V_U as set forth in Equation 5-7, and we can consolidate the second two terms as follows:

$$V_L = V_U + \frac{I(1 - T_d)}{k_d}\left[1 - \frac{(1 - T_c)(1 - T_s)}{(1 - T_d)}\right]. \tag{5-9a}$$

Now recognize that the after-tax perpetual interest payment divided by the required rate of return on debt, $I(1 - T_d)/k_d$, equals the market value of the debt, D. Substituting D into the preceding equation, and rearranging, we obtain this very important expression:

$$V_L = V_U + \left[1 - \frac{(1 - T_c)(1 - T_s)}{(1 - T_d)} \right] D. \qquad (5\text{-}10)$$

Equation 5-10 is the Miller Model for the value of a levered firm in a world with both corporate and personal taxes.

The Miller Model has several important implications:

1. The term in brackets,

$$\left[1 - \frac{(1 - T_c)(1 - T_s)}{(1 - T_d)} \right],$$

multiplied by D, represents the gain from leverage. The bracketed term replaces the factor $T = T_c$ in the earlier MM model with corporate taxes, $V_L = V_U + TD$.

2. If we ignore all taxes, that is, if $T_c = T_s = T_d = 0$, then the bracketed term reduces to zero, which is the same as the original MM model without corporate taxes.

3. If we ignore personal taxes, that is, if $T_s = T_d = 0$, then the bracketed term reduces to $[1 - (1 - T_c)] = T_c$, which is the same as the MM model with corporate taxes.

4. If the effective personal tax rates on stock and bond incomes were equal, that is, if $T_s = T_d$, then $(1 - T_s)$ and $(1 - T_d)$ would cancel, and the bracketed term would again reduce to T_c.

5. Note that if $(1 - T_c)(1 - T_s) = (1 - T_d)$, then the bracketed term would go to zero, and the value of using leverage would also be zero. This implies that the tax advantage of debt to the firm would be exactly offset by the personal tax advantage of equity. Under this condition, capital structure would have no effect on a firm's value or its cost of capital, and hence we would be back to MM's original zero-tax theory. In his article, Miller took this position, but others have questioned it.

We can illustrate the Miller model and, at the same time, consider the effects of the 1986 Tax Reform Act on the value of leverage as measured by this model. Recall that before 1987 the top statutory rates were $T_c = 46\%$ and $T_d = 50\%$, and T_s was based on a rate of 50 percent on dividends and 20 percent, but deferred, on long-term capital gains. If we assume that half of stock returns come from dividends and half from capital gains, and that the tax on gains was deferred for 5 years, then the effective rate on stock income would be approximately $T_s = 30\%$.[7]

---

[7] $T_s = 0.5(50\%) + 0.5(\text{PV of } 20\%)$. Note that in a follow-on article, Miller and Scholes describe how investors could, theoretically, shelter or delay income from stock to the point where the effective personal tax rate on such income is essentially zero. See Merton H. Miller and Myron S. Scholes, "Dividends and Taxes," *Journal of Financial Economics*, December 1978, 333-364. However, the 1986 changes in the tax law eliminated most of the shelters Miller and Scholes discussed.

Using these values in the Miller model indicates that a levered firm's value increases over that of an unlevered firm by 24.4 percent of the amount of corporate debt:

$$\text{Gain from leverage} = \left[1 - \frac{(1 - T_c)(1 - T_s)}{(1 - T_d)} \right] D$$

$$= \left[1 - \frac{(1 - 0.46)(1 - 0.30)}{(1 - 0.50)} \right] D$$

$$= 0.244 \ D.$$

Note that the MM model with corporate taxes would indicate a gain from leverage of $T_c D = 0.46 \ D$.

Now, under the new tax law, $T_c = 34\%$, $T_d = 28\%$, and no differential exists between the tax rate on dividends and capital gains, although the tax on gains is deferred. If we again assume a 50 percent payout and a 5-year deferral of the capital gains, then $T_s = 25.4\%$. Inserting these tax rates into the Miller model, we find the gain from leverage to be 0.316 D:

$$\text{Gain from leverage} = \left[1 - \frac{(1 - 0.34)(1 - 0.254)}{(1 - 0.28)} \right] D$$

$$= 0.316 \ D.$$

As we note in the next section, there are a number of problems with the Miller model, so one should not put much trust in results such as those we just obtained. However, the Miller model does point out clearly (and correctly) that the MM model with corporate taxes overstates the advantage of corporate debt financing. In effect, personal taxes offset, to some extent, the benefit from the tax deductibility of corporate interest payments.

Criticisms of the MM and Miller Theories

The conclusions of each of the various capital structure theories follow logically from their initial assumptions: if their assumptions are correct, then their conclusions must be reached. However, both academicians and financial executives have voiced concern over the validity of the MM and Miller theories because of the fact that virtually no firms follow their recommendations. Both the MM model with corporate taxes and the Miller model with "reasonable" tax rates lead to the conclusion that firms should use 100 percent debt. That situation is not observed in practice except by firms such as Frontier Airlines whose equity has been eroded by operating losses. People who disagree with the MM and Miller theories and their suggestions for financial policy generally attack them on the grounds that their assumptions do not reflect actual market conditions. Some of the main objections are listed next:

1. The MM and Miller analyses imply that personal and corporate leverage are perfect substitutes. However, an individual investing in a levered firm has less loss exposure, which means a more *limited liability*, than if he or she used "home-made" leverage. For example, in our earlier illustration of the MM arbitrage argument, it should be noted that only the $600,000 our investor had in Firm L would be lost if that firm went bankrupt. However, if the investor engaged in arbitrage transactions and employed "homemade" leverage to invest in Firm U, then he or she could lose $900,000—the original $600,000 investment plus the $400,000 loan less the $100,000 investment in riskless bonds. This increased personal risk exposure would tend to restrain investors from engaging in arbitrage, and that could cause the equilibrium values of V_L, V_U, k_{sL}, and k_{sU} to be different from those specified by the equations. Restrictions on institutional investors, who dominate capital markets today, may also retard the arbitrage process, because most institutional investors cannot legally borrow to buy stocks, and hence they are prohibited from engaging in homemade leverage.

2. Brokerage costs were assumed away by MM and Miller, making the switch from L to U costless. However, brokerage and other transactions costs do exist, and they too impede the arbitrage process.

3. MM initially assumed that corporations and investors can borrow at the risk-free rate. Although risky debt has been introduced into the analysis by others, to reach the MM and Miller conclusions it is still necessary to assume that both corporations and investors can borrow at the same rate. Although major institutional investors probably can borrow at the corporate rate, many institutions are not allowed to borrow to buy securities. Further, most individual investors probably must borrow at higher rates than those paid by large corporations.

4. In his article, Miller concluded that an equilibrium would be reached, but his equilibrium requires that the tax benefit from corporate debt (1) be constant across firms, and (2) be constant for an individual firm regardless of the amount of leverage used. However, we know that the tax benefit varies from firm to firm: Highly profitable companies gain the maximum tax benefit from leverage, while the benefits to firms that are struggling are much smaller. Further, some firms have other tax shields such as high depreciation and pension plan contributions, and these shields reduce the tax savings value of interest payments.[8] It also appears simplistic to assume that the expected tax shield is unaffected by the amount of debt financing used. Higher leverage increases the probability that the firm cannot effectively use the full tax shield in the future, because higher leverage increases the probability of future unprofitability and consequently lower tax rates. All things considered, it appears likely that the corporate tax shield is more valuable to some firms than to others.

5. MM and Miller assume that there are no costs associated with financial distress. Further, they ignore agency costs. These topics are discussed in the next section.

---

[8]For a discussion of the impact of tax shields other than debt financing, see Harry DeAngelo and Ronald W. Masulis, "Optimal Capital Structure under Corporate and Personal Taxation," *Journal of Financial Economics*, March 1980, 3-30.

FINANCIAL DISTRESS AND AGENCY COSTS

Some of the assumptions inherent in the MM and Miller models can be relaxed, and when this is done, the basic conclusions remain unchanged.[9] However, as we discuss below, when financial distress and agency costs are added, the results are altered significantly.

Financial Distress Costs

A number of firms experience financial distress each year, and some of them are forced into bankruptcy. When financial distress, including but not restricted to bankruptcy, occurs, several things can happen:

1. Arguments between claimants often delay the liquidation of assets, thus leading to physical deterioration and/or obsolescence of inventories and fixed assets. Bankruptcy cases can take many years to settle, and during this time machinery rusts, buildings are vandalized, inventories become obsolete, and the like.

2. Lawyer's fees, court costs, and administrative expenses can absorb a large part of the firm's value. Together, the costs of physical deterioration plus legal fees and expenses are called the *direct costs* of bankruptcy.

3. Managers and other employees generally lose their jobs when a firm fails. Knowing this, the management of a firm that is in financial distress may take actions which keep it alive in the short run but which also dilute long-run value. For example, the firm may defer maintenance of machinery, sell off valuable assets at bargain prices to raise cash, or cut costs so much that the quality of its products is impaired and the firm's long-run market position is eroded.

4. Both customers and suppliers of companies that are experiencing financial difficulties are aware of the problems that can arise, and they often take "evasive action" that further damages the troubled firm. For example, Frontier Air Lines, as it struggled to avoid bankruptcy in 1986, was having trouble making sales because potential customers were worried about buying a seat for a future flight and then have the company shut down before they could take the trip. Some potential customers were also worried that the company might cut back on maintenance expenditures, and its suppliers were reluctant to grant normal credit terms, or to gear up to supply Frontier with parts and other materials on a long-term basis. Further, Frontier was having great difficulty obtaining capital. Finally, Frontier had trouble attracting and retaining the highest quality workers, as most workers with a choice prefer employment with a more stable airline to one that could go bankrupt any day. Eventually, Frontier did go bankruput, and thousands of employees lost their jobs.

---

[9]For example, see Robert A. Haugen and James L. Pappas, "Equilibrium in the Pricing of Capital Assets, Risk-Bearing Debt Instruments, and the Question of Optimal Capital Structure," *Journal of Financial and Quantitative Analysis*, June 1971, 943-954; Joseph Stiglitz, "A Re-Examination of the Modigliani-Miller Theorem," *American Economic Review*, December 1969, 784-793; and Mark E. Rubenstein, "A Mean-Variance Synthesis of Corporate Financial Theory," *Journal of Finance*, March 1973, 167-181.

Table 5-1
Expected Costs of Financial Distress

		Amount of Debt			
	$0	$5 Million	$10 Million	$20 Million	$30 Million
Probability of financial distress	0.0	0.05	0.15	0.50	0.95
PV of expected costs of financial distress ($5 million times the indicated probability)	$0	$250,000	$750,000	$2,500,000	$4,750,000

Nonoptimal managerial actions associated with financial distress, as well as the costs imposed by customers, suppliers, and capital providers, are called the *indirect costs* of financial distress. Of course, these costs may be incurred by a firm in financial distress even if it does not go into bankruptcy: bankruptcy is just one point on the continuum of financial distress.

All things considered, the direct and indirect costs associated with financial distress are high.[10] Further, financial distress occurs only if a firm has debts: debt-free firms do not experience financial distress. *Therefore, the greater the use of debt financing, and the larger the fixed interest charges, the greater the probability that a decline in earnings will lead to financial distress and, hence, the higher the probability that the costs of financial distress will be incurred.*

An increase in the probability of financial distress lowers the current value of a firm and raises its cost of capital. To see why, suppose we estimate that Mid-State Water will incur financial distress costs of $7 million if it fails at some future date, and that the *present value* of this possible future cost is $5 million. Further, the probability of financial distress increases with leverage, causing the expected present value cost of financial distress to rise from zero at zero debt to $4.75 million at $30 million of debt as shown in Table 5-1.

These expected costs of financial distress must be subtracted from the values we previously calculated in the lower section of Figure 5-2 to find the firm's value at various amounts of leverage: they would reduce the values of V and S in Columns 2 and 3 and, as a result, would raise k_s and k_a in Columns 6 and 7. For example, at $20 million of debt, we would obtain the values in Table 5-2.[11] These

---

[10]See Edward I. Altman, "A Further Empirical Investigation of the Bankruptcy Cost Question," *Journal of Finance*, September 1984, 1067-1089. On the basis of a recent sample of 26 bankrupt companies, Altman found that bankruptcy costs often exceeded 20 percent of firm value.

[11]To find k_s and k_a in Table 5-2, apply Equations 5-1a and 5-2, respectively:

$$k_s = \frac{(EBIT - k_d D)(1 - T)}{S} = \frac{[\$4 - 0.08(\$20)](1 - 0.4)}{\$5.5} = 26.18\%.$$

$$k_a = WACC = (D/V)(k_d)(1 - T) + (S/V)(k_s)$$
$$= (20/25.5)(8\%)(0.6) + (5.5/25.5)(26.18\%)$$
$$= 3.76\% + 5.65\% = 9.41\%.$$

Table 5-2
Effects of Financial Distress
(Millions of Dollars)

	Figure 5-2 Values at D = \$20 Million with Financial Distress Effects Ignored: Pure MM	Figure 5-2 Values at D = \$20 Million with Financial Distress Effects Considered: Modified MM
V	\$28.00	\$28.00 − \$2.5 = \$25.5
S	\$8.00	\$8.00 − \$2.5 = \$5.5
k_s	18.00%	26.18%
k_a	8.57%	9.41%

changes would, of course, then have carry-through effects on the graphs in Figure 5-2—most important, they would (1) reduce the decline of the k_a line and (2) reduce the slope of the V_L line.

The effects of financial distress are also felt by a firm's bondholders. Firms experiencing financial distress have a higher probability of defaulting on debt payments, and hence the expectation of financial distress influences bond investors' required rates of return: The higher the probability of financial distress, the higher the required yield on debt. Thus, as firms use more and more debt financing, and hence increase the probability of distress, the value of k_d also increases, causing several elements in Figure 5-2 to change.

Agency Costs

We introduced the concept of agency costs in Chapter 1. One type of agency cost is associated with the use of debt, and it involves the relationship between a firm's stockholders and its bondholders. In the absence of any restrictions, a firm's management would be tempted to take actions that would benefit stockholders at the expense of bondholders. For example, if Mid-State Water were to sell only a small amount of debt, then this debt would have relatively little risk, and hence a high bond rating and a low interest rate. Yet, having sold the low-risk debt, Mid-State could then issue more debt secured by the same assets as the original debt. This would raise the risks faced by *all bondholders*, cause k_d to rise, and consequently cause the original bondholders to suffer capital losses. Similarly, suppose that after issuing a substantial amount of debt, Mid-State decided to restructure its assets, selling off assets with low business risk and acquiring assets that were more risky but that also had higher expected rates of return. If things worked out well, the stockholders would benefit. If things went sour, most of the loss in a highly leveraged firm would fall on the bondholders. In other words, the stockholders would be playing a game of "heads, I win; tails, you lose" with the bondholders.

Because of the possibility that stockholders might try to take advantage of bondholders in these and other ways, bonds are protected by restrictive covenants.

These covenants hamper the corporation's legitimate operations to some extent. Further, the company must be monitored to insure that the covenants are being obeyed, and the costs of monitoring are passed on to the stockholders in the form of higher debt costs. The costs of lost efficiency plus monitoring are what we mean here by the term *agency costs*, and the existence of these costs increases the cost of debt to the firm and thus reduces the advantage of debt.[12]

Firm Value and the Cost of Capital with Financial Distress and Agency Costs

If the MM model with corporate taxes were correct, a firm's value would rise continuously as it moved from zero debt toward 100 percent debt: the equation $V_L = V_U + TD$ shows that TD, and hence V_L, is maximized if D is at a maximum. Recall that the rising component of value, TD, results directly from the shelter provided by the debt interest. However, the following factors, which were ignored by MM, could cause V_L to decline with increases in debt: (1) the present value of costs associated with potential future financial distress and (2) the present value of agency costs. Therefore, MM's relationship between a firm's value and its use of leverage should look like this:

$$V_L = V_U + TD - \begin{pmatrix} \text{PV of} \\ \text{expected} \\ \text{financial} \\ \text{distress costs} \end{pmatrix} - \begin{pmatrix} \text{PV of} \\ \text{agency} \\ \text{costs} \end{pmatrix}. \qquad (5\text{-}11)$$

The relationship expressed in Equation 5-11 is graphed in Figure 5-3. The tax shelter effect totally dominates until the amount of debt reaches Point A. After Point A, financial distress and agency costs become increasingly important, offsetting some of the tax advantages. At Point B, the marginal tax shelter benefits of additional debt are exactly offset by the disadvantages of debt, and beyond Point B, the disadvantages outweigh the tax benefits.

Equation 5-10, the Miller Model, can also be modified to reflect financial distress and agency costs. The equation would be identical to Equation 5-11, except that the gain from leverage term, TD, would reflect the addition of personal taxes. In either the MM or Miller models, the gain from leverage can at least be roughly estimated, but the value reduction resulting from potential financial distress and agency costs is almost entirely subjective. We know that these costs must increase as leverage rises, but we simply do not know the specific functional relationship.

---

[12]Jensen and Meckling point out that there are also agency costs between outside equity holders and management. See "Theory of the Firm: Managerial Behavior, Agency Costs, and Ownership Structure," *Journal of Financial Economics*, October 1976, 305-360. Their study further suggests that (1) bondholder agency costs increase as the debt ratio increases, but (2) outside stockholder agency costs move in reverse fashion, falling with increased use of debt.

Figure 5-3
Net Effects of Leverage on the Value of the Firm

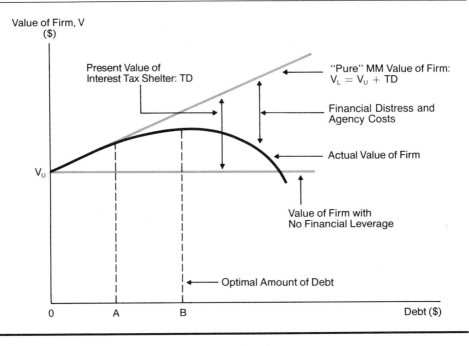

REVIEW OF THE TRADEOFF MODELS

Implications of the Models

Both the MM with corporate taxes and the Miller models as modified to reflect financial distress and agency costs can be described as *tradeoff* models. That is, the optimal capital structure is found by balancing the tax shield benefits of leverage against the financial distress and agency costs of leverage, and hence the costs and benefits are "traded off" against one another. The tradeoff models are not capable of specifying precise optimal capital structures, but they do lead to three qualitative statements about financing behavior:

1. Risky firms, as measured by the variability of returns on the firm's assets, ought to borrow less, other things equal. The greater this variability, the greater the probability of financial distress at any level of debt, and hence the greater the expected costs of distress. Thus, firms with lower business risk can borrow more before the expected costs of distress offset the tax advantages of borrowing.

2. Firms that employ tangible assets such as real estate and standard production machinery should borrow more than firms whose value is derived either from intangible assets such as patents and goodwill or from growth opportunities. The costs of financial distress depend not only on the probability of incurring distress, but also on what happens if distress occurs. Specialized assets, intangible assets, and growth opportunities are more likely to lose value if financial distress occurs than are standardized, tangible assets.

3. Firms that are currently paying taxes at the highest rate, and that are likely to continue to do so in the future, should carry more debt than firms with current and/or prospectively lower tax rates. High corporate tax rates produce greater benefits from debt financing, and hence high-rate firms can carry more debt, other factors held constant, before the tax shield is offset by financial distress and agency costs.

According to the tradeoff models, each firm should set a target capital structure which balances the costs and benefits of leverage, because such a structure will maximize its value. We would expect to find actual target structures that are consistent with the three points just raised. Further, we would generally expect to find that firms within an industry have similar capital structures, because such firms have roughly the same types of assets, business risks, and profitability.

The Empirical Evidence

The tradeoff models have intuitive appeal because they lead to the conclusion that both no debt and all debt are bad, while a "moderate" debt level is good. However, we must ask ourselves whether these models explain actual behavior. If they do not, then we must search for other explanations or else assume that managers, and hence investors, are acting irrationally, an assumption that we are unwilling to make.

The tradeoff models do have some empirical support.[13] For example, firms that have tangible assets in place tend to borrow more heavily than firms whose value stems from intangibles and/or growth opportunities. However, there is other empirical evidence which refutes the tradeoff models. First, several studies have examined models of financing behavior to see if firms' financing decisions reflect adjustment toward a target capital structure. These studies provide some evidence that this occurs, but the explanatory power of the models is very low, suggesting that tradeoff models capture only a small part of actual behavior. Second, no study has clearly demonstrated that a firm's tax rate has a predictable, material effect on its capital structure. In fact, firms used debt financing long before corporate income taxes even existed. Finally, actual debt ratios tend to vary widely across apparently similar firms, whereas the tradeoff models suggest that debt usage should be relatively consistent within industries.

All in all, the empirical support for the tradeoff models is not very convincing. This leads to the conclusion that firms either take extended excursions away from their optimal structures or that the tradeoff models do not tell the full story.

---

[13]For examples of the empirical research in this area, see Robert Taggart, "A Model of Corporate Financing Decisions," *Journal of Finance*, December 1977, 1467-1484; and Paul Marsh, "The Choice Between Equity and Debt: An Empirical Study," *Journal of Finance*, March 1982, 121-144.

ASYMMETRIC INFORMATION THEORY

In the early 1960s, Professor Gordon Donaldson of Harvard University conducted an extensive survey of how corporations actually establish their capital structures.[14] Here is a summary of his findings:

1. Firms prefer to finance with internally generated funds; that is, retained earnings and depreciation.

2. Firms set their target dividend payout ratios based on their expected future investment opportunities and expected future cash flows. The target payout ratio is set at a level such that under normal conditions retained earnings plus depreciation will meet capital expenditure requirements.

3. Dividends are "sticky" in the short run—firms are reluctant to make major changes in the dollar dividend, and they are especially reluctant to cut the dividend. Thus, in any given year, depending on realized cash flows and actual investment opportunities, a firm may or may not have sufficient internally generated funds to cover its capital expenditures.

4. If the firm has excess retained earnings, it will invest in marketable securities or use the funds to retire debt. If it has insufficient retained earnings to finance non-postponable new projects, it will draw down its marketable securities portfolio.

5. If external funds are required, firms first issue debt, then convertible bonds, and then common stock only as a last resort. Thus, Donaldson observed a "pecking order" of financing, not the balanced approach that is called for under the tradeoff theories.

Professor Stewart Myers noted the inconsistency between Donaldson's findings and the MM/Miller theories, and that led him to propose a new theory.[15] First, Myers noted that Donaldson's pecking order findings led away from rather than toward a well-defined capital structure. Equity is raised in two forms, and one, retained earnings, is at the top of the pecking order, while the other, new common stock, is at the bottom.

Next, Myers noted that the tradeoff theories assume that all market participants have homogeneous expectations, which implies (1) that all participants have the same information set and (2) that any changes in operating income are purely random as opposed to anticipated by some parties. Myers had the insight to see that if the homogeneous expectations assumption is relaxed, and asymmetric (or different) information by different groups of market participants is admitted, Don-

---

[14]Gordon Donaldson, *Corporate Debt Capacity: A Study of Corporate Debt Policy and the Determination of Corporate Debt Capacity* (Boston: Harvard Graduate School of Business Administration, 1961).

[15]Stewart C. Myers, "The Capital Structure Puzzle," *Journal of Finance*, July 1984, 575-592. It is interesting to note that, like the Miller Model, Myers' paper was presented as a presidential address to the American Finance Association.

aldson's results could be explained in a logical manner. Myers' work resulted in what is now called the *asymmetric information theory* of capital structure.

The basis for the theory, as articulated by Myers, rests on the existence of asymmetric information. To illustrate, assume that a firm has 10,000 common shares outstanding at a current price of $19 per share, so the market value of its equity is $190,000. However, its managers have better information about the firm's prospects than stockholders, and the managers believe that the actual share value based on existing assets is $21, giving the equity a total "true" market value of $210,000. Such information asymmetry could easily exist, for managers often know more about their firms' prospects than do current and potential investors.[16]

Suppose further that the firm now identifies a new project which requires external financing of $100,000 and which has an estimated net present value (NPV) of $5,000. (Remember that a project's NPV is a residual value over its costs, and that this residual accrues to the shareholders.) This project is unanticipated by the firm's investors, and hence its $5,000 NPV has not been incorporated into the firm's $190,000 equity market value. Should the firm accept the project? To begin, assume that the firm plans to sell new equity to raise the $100,000 to finance the project. Several possibilities are set forth next:

1. Symmetric information. First, as a point of departure, consider the situation where all investors *do* have the same information as management regarding existing asset values. Under these conditions, the stock would be selling at $21 per share, so the firm would have to sell $100,000/$21 = 4,762 new shares to finance the project. Acceptance of the project would result in a new stock price of $21.34:

$$\text{New stock price} = \frac{\text{Original market value} + \text{New money raised} + \text{NPV}}{\text{Original shares} + \text{New shares}}$$

$$= \frac{\$210,000 + \$100,000 + \$5,000}{10,000 + 4,762} = \$21.34.$$

Clearly, both old and new shareholders would benefit if the project were accepted.

2. Asymmetric information prior to stock issue. Consider now the situation where our firm's management can in no way inform investors about the stock's "true" value. Perhaps it is necessary to hold back such information to maintain a competitive edge, or perhaps SEC regulations cause management to refrain from "touting" the stock price prior to the new issue (if things did not work out as expected, new shareholders might sue the managers who had provided the rosy forecast). In this situation, new stock would fetch only $19 per share, so the company would have to sell $100,000/$19 = 5,263 shares in order to raise the re-

---

[16]This assumption is contrary to the strong-form efficient markets hypothesis (EMH) presented in Chapter 1, but few observers—including people who believe ardently in weak and semistrong efficiency—are willing to accept strong-form efficiency.

quired $100,000. If this were done, this new price would result if the project were accepted *and then the asymmetric information situation was removed*:

$$\text{New stock price} = \frac{\text{New market value} + \text{New money raised} + \text{NPV}}{\text{Original shares} + \text{New shares}}$$

$$= \frac{\$210,000 + \$100,000 + \$5,000}{10,000 + 5,263} = \$20.64.$$

Under this condition, the project should not be undertaken. If the project were not accepted, and hence new shares not sold, then the price of the stock would rise to $21 when the information asymmetry is removed. The sale of new stock at $19 per share leads to a $0.36 loss to the firm's existing shareholders and a $1.64 gain to the new shareholders.

3. A more profitable project. Suppose now that the project had an NPV of $20,000, and other conditions were unchanged. Now the firm's stock price would rise to $21.62 if it undertook the project.

$$\text{New stock price} = \frac{\$210,000 + \$100,000 + \$20,000}{10,000 + 5,263} = \$21.62.$$

Under these conditions, the firm should take on the project. Note, though, that most of the positive NPV will go to the new stockholders, who will pay $19 per share and thus enjoy a capital gain of $2.62 versus a gain of only $0.62 for the original stockholders.

4. Dark clouds on the horizon. Now suppose an entirely different situation faced the firm. Stockholders think the firm is worth $19 per share, but the firm's managers think (1) that outside investors are entirely too optimistic about the firm's growth opportunities, (2) that investors are not properly recognizing proposed legislation which will require large, nonearning investments in pollution control equipment, and (3) that investors do not fully anticipate the need for new R&D expenditures which may be required to keep the firm's products competitive. If all of these bad events materialize, profit margins will be under pressure, cash flows will be down, and the company will not be able to carry safely its present level of debt. Moreover, the stock price will fall sharply, and it will be extremely difficult to raise the capital that will be necessary to assure the firm's survival.

Faced with these conditions, management might well conclude that the "true" value of the firm's stock is only $17 per share, and further decide to sell a new issue of 10,000 shares at a price of $19, raising $190,000 and using the funds to retire debt or to support this year's capital budget. This action would increase the "true" value of the stock from $17 to $18:

$$\text{New "true" value} = \frac{\text{Old "true" equity value} + \text{New money}}{\text{Original shares} + \text{New shares}}$$

$$= \frac{\$170,000 + \$190,000}{10,000 + 10,000} = \$18.00.$$

Current stockholders will, if management's expectations come true, suffer a loss when the bad news becomes known, but the sale of new stock would reduce that loss. (Note: Management would have to word the prospectus for the new issue carefully, pointing out the potential problems. However, virtually all prospectuses are filled with cautionary language, so investors cannot tell from them what management really expects.)

5. Finance the original project with debt. If the firm used debt to finance the original $100,000 project, *and then the information asymmetry was removed*, the new stock price would be $21.50:

$$\text{New stock price} = \frac{\text{New market value} + \text{NPV}}{\text{Original shares}}$$

$$= \frac{\$210,000 + \$5,000}{10,000} = \$21.50.$$

Thus, if debt financing is used, all of the residual value of the new project accrues to the old shareholders. Further, the information asymmetry will have little effect on the value of the firm's debt, assuming that debt is secured by collateral and also has various restrictive covenants which tend to stabilize its value. Myers called debt financing "safe" financing because debt value is little affected by information asymmetry.

What does all this suggest about corporate financial policy? First, in a world where asymmetric information exists, corporations should issue new shares only if they have extraordinarily profitable investments that cannot be postponed or financed by debt, or if management thinks the shares are overvalued. Second, investors recognize this and tend to mark down a company's share prices when it announces plans to issue new shares, because chances are that the announcement is signaling bad news, not good news. Third, the financing pecking order that Donaldson observed is rational when asymmetric information exists—it pays to retain a large fraction of earnings, and to keep the equity ratio up and the debt ratio down, so as to maintain some "reserve borrowing capacity" which can be used to support the capital budget if and when an unusually large volume of positive NPV projects come along, or if problems arise which require outside capital.[17]

OUR VIEW OF CAPITAL STRUCTURE THEORY

The great contribution of the tradeoff models of MM, Miller, and their followers is that these models identified the specific benefits and costs of using debt—the tax effects, financial distress costs, and so on. Prior to these models, no capital struc-

---

[17]Flotation costs also play a role in capital structure theory. In general, flotation costs are smaller on debt issues than on equity issues, and this provides an additional rationale for using debt rather than outside equity. We will discuss this issue in more detail in Chapter 12.

Figure 5-4
**Effects of Leverage:
The Tradeoff View**

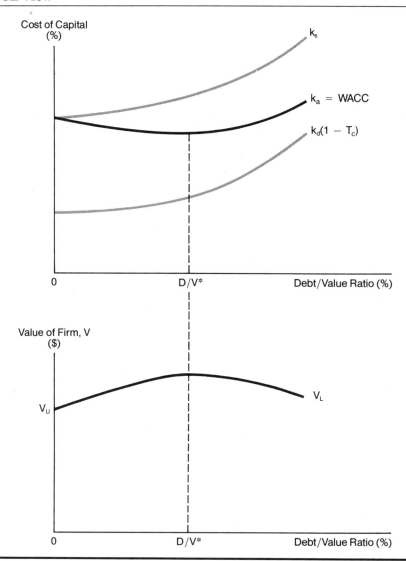

ture theory existed, and we had no systematic way of analyzing the effects of debt financing.

The tradeoff view is summarized graphically in Figure 5-4. The top graph shows the relationships between the debt ratio and the costs of debt, equity, and the WACC. Both k_s and $k_d(1 - T_c)$ rise steadily with increases in leverage, but the rate of increase accelerates at higher debt levels, reflecting agency costs and the increased probability of financial distress and its attendant costs. The WACC first declines, then hits a minimum at D/V*, and then begins to rise. It is interesting to note that Figure 5-4 looks very much like the graphs on the right side of Figure 5-1, which represent the traditional position prior to MM's work. Although the traditionalists did not state very clearly why they believed the graphs took their assumed shapes, we can use the tradeoff models, when the effects of financial distress and agency costs are included, to help with this explanation. Also, note that the general shapes of the curves apply regardless of whether we are using the MM with corporate taxes model, the Miller model, or a variant of these models.

Unfortunately, it is extremely difficult for financial managers to actually quantify the costs and benefits of debt financing to their firms, and hence it is virtually impossible to pinpoint D/V*, the capital structure that truly maximizes the firm's value. Most experts believe such a structure exists for every firm, but that it changes substantially over time as the nature of the firm and the capital markets change. Most experts also believe that, as shown in Figure 5-4, the relationship between firm value and leverage is relatively flat, and hence that relatively large deviations from the optimum can occur without materially affecting a firm's value.

Now consider the asymmetric information theory. Because of asymmetric information, investors know less about a firm's prospects than do its managers. Further, managers try to maximize value for current stockholders, not new ones, so if the firm has excellent prospects, management will not want to issue new shares, but if things look bleak, then a new stock offering may be sold. Therefore, investors take a stock offering to be a signal of bad news, so stock prices tend to decline when new issues are announced. As a result, new equity financing is especially expensive, and this fact must be incorporated into the capital structure decision. Its effect is to motivate firms to maintain a reserve borrowing capacity, so that future investment opportunities can be financed by debt when internal funds are insufficient.

By combining the two theories, we obtain this possible explanation for firms' behavior: (1) Debt financing provides benefits because of the tax deductibility of interest. Hence, firms should have some debt in their capital structures. (2) However, financial distress and agency costs place limits on debt usage—beyond some point, these costs offset the tax advantage of debt. (3) Finally, because of asymmetric information, firms maintain some reserve borrowing capacity in order to take advantage of good investment opportunities or to avoid having to issue stock in troubled times and at distressed prices.

Of course, all this sounds reasonable, but how should financial decisions be made in practice? The answer is rather fuzzy, and many factors must be considered when actually choosing a capital structure. This topic will be covered in the next chapter.

SUMMARY

This chapter presented the major elements of the theory of capital structure. We saw that three early theories—*net income (NI)*, *net operating income (NOI)*, and *traditional*—were advanced to explain the relationship between leverage and the firm's value and cost of capital. However, these theories were more speculations than true theories. Then, in 1958, Franco Modigliani and Merton Miller (MM) startled the financial community by proposing, and proving, that under a certain set of assumptions capital structure is irrelevant. This was MM's famous zero tax article. But firms do pay taxes, and MM went on to expand their model to include corporate taxes. Here, capital structure is relevant, and firms maximize value by using almost 100 percent debt financing.

Finally, Miller went one step further and added personal taxes to the model. The interpretation of the *Miller model* is somewhat controversial, but most professionals believe that the addition of personal taxes reduces, but does not eliminate, the value of debt financing. Miller's model still prescribes that firms should use virtually all debt financing. However, both the MM and Miller analyses ignored financial distress and agency costs. The addition of these costs results in a tradeoff framework. Here the costs and benefits of debt financing are balanced against one another, resulting in an optimal capital structure that falls somewhere between zero debt and 100 percent debt.

An alternative theory, called the *asymmetric information theory*, was recently proposed by Stewart Myers. This theory, which is based on managers having better information than investors, postulates that there is a preferred order of financing: (1) retained earnings, (2) debt, and (3) new common stock. Firms finance according to this "pecking order," and hence observed capital structures reflect the cumulative need for external financing over time. We believe that there is some benefit to debt financing, and further that firms probably try to maintain a borrowing reserve. Thus, firms use debt based on their tax rates, asset structures, and inherent riskiness, but they also try to maintain the ability to issue new debt if it becomes necessary to raise external capital.

Establishing a target capital structure in practice is more a matter of informed judgment than of quantitative analysis. In the next chapter, we discuss the many factors that influence this important corporate decision.

Questions and Problems

5-1 **(MM without taxes)** Companies U and L are identical in every respect except that U is unlevered while L has $10 million of 5 percent bonds outstanding. Assume (1) that all of the MM assumptions are met, (2) that there are no corporate or personal taxes, (3) that EBIT is $2 million, and (4) that the cost of equity to Company U is 10 percent.
   a. What value would MM estimate for each firm?
   b. What is k_s for Firm U? For Firm L?
   c. Find S_L, and then show that $S_L + D = V_L = 20 million.
   d. What is k_a for Firm U? For Firm L?
   e. Suppose $V_U = 20 million and $V_L = 22 million. According to MM, do these values represent an equilibrium? If not, explain the process by which equilibrium will be restored.

5-2 **(MM with corporate taxes)** Refer to Problem 5-1. Assume that all the facts hold, except that the firms are subject to a 40 percent federal-plus-state corporate tax rate.
   a. What value would MM now estimate for each firm? (Use Proposition I.)

b. What is k_s for Firm U? For Firm L?

c. Find S_L, and then show that $S_L + D = V_L$ results in the same value as obtained in Part a.

d. What is k_a for Firm U? For Firm L?

e. Use Proposition III to find the cut-off rates for Firm U and for Firm L. How does this rate compare with the WACCs determined in Part d?

5-3 (Miller model) Refer to Problems 5-1 and 5-2. Assume that all facts hold, except that both corporate and personal taxes apply. Assume that both firms must pay a federal-plus-state corporate tax rate of $T_c = 40\%$, and that investors in both firms face a tax rate of $T_d = 28\%$ on debt income and $T_s = 20\%$, on average, on stock income.

a. What is the value of the unlevered firm, V_U? (Note that V_U is now reduced by the tax on stock income, and hence $V_U \neq \$12$ million as in Problem 5-2a.)

b. What is the value of V_L?

c. What is the gain from leverage in this situation? Compare this with the gain from leverage in Problem 5-2.

d. Set $T_c = T_s = T_d = 0$. What is the value of the firm? The gain from leverage?

e. Now suppose $T_s = T_d = 0$. What are the value of the levered firm and the gain from leverage?

f. Assume that $T_d = 28\%$, $T_s = 28\%$, and $T_c = 40\%$. Now what are the value of the levered firm and the gain from leverage?

5-4 (MM with and without taxes) Far East Unlimited (FEU) is just about to commence operations as an international trading company. The firm will have book assets of $10 million, and it expects to earn a 16 percent return on these assets before taxes. However, because of certain tax arrangements with foreign governments, FEU will not pay any taxes; that is, its tax rate will be zero. Management is trying to decide how to raise the required $10 million. It is known that the capitalization rate for an all-equity firm in this business is 11 percent; that is, $k_{sU} = 11\%$. Further, FEU can borrow at a rate $k_d = 6\%$. Assume that the MM assumptions apply.

a. According to MM, what will be the value of FEU if it uses no debt and it uses $6 million of 6 percent debt?

b. What are the values of k_a and k_s at debt levels of $D = \$0$, $D = \$6$ million, and $D = \$10$ million? What effect does leverage have on firm value? Why?

c. Assume the initial facts of the problem ($k_d = 6\%$, EBIT = \$1.6 million, $k_{sU} = 11\%$), but now assume that a 40 percent federal-plus-state corporate tax rate exists. Find the new market values for FEU with zero debt and with \$6 million of debt, using the MM formulas.

d. What are the values of k_a and k_s at debt levels of $D = \$0$, $D = \$6$ million, and $D = \$10$ million, assuming a 40 percent corporate tax rate? Plot the relationships between the value of the firm and the debt ratio, and between capital costs and the debt ratio.

e. What is the maximum dollar amount of debt financing that can be used? What is the value of the firm at this debt level? What is the cost of this debt?

f. How would each of the following factors tend to change the values you plotted in your graph?

   (1) The interest rate on debt increases as the debt ratio rises.

   (2) At higher levels of debt, the probability of financial distress rises.

5-5 (Agency costs) Explain why agency costs would probably be higher for a large, publicly owned firm that uses both debt and equity capital than for a small, unleveraged, owner-managed firm.

5-6 **(Agency costs)** Until recently, the Anderson Company carried a triple-A bond rating and was strong in every respect. However, a series of problems has afflicted the firm: It is currently in severe financial distress, and its ability to make future payments on outstanding debt is questionable. If the firm were forced into bankruptcy at this time, the common stockholders would almost certainly be wiped out. Although Anderson has limited financial resources, its cash flows (primarily from depreciation) are sufficient to support one of two mutually exclusive investments, each costing $150 million and having a 10 year expected life. These projects have the same market (or systematic) risk, but different total risk as measured by the variance of returns. Each project has the following after-tax cash flows for 10 years:

	Annual Cash Inflows	
Probability	Project A	Project B
0.5	$30,000,000	$10,000,000
0.5	35,000,000	50,000,000

Assume that both projects have the same market risk as the firm's "average" project. Anderson's weighted average cost of capital is 15 percent.

a. What is the expected annual cash inflow from each project?

b. Which project has the greater total risk?

c. Which project would you choose if you were an Anderson stockholder? Why?

d. Which project would the bondholders prefer to see management select? Why?

e. If the choices conflict, what "protection" do the bondholders have against the firm's making a decision that is contrary to their interests?

f. Who bears the cost of this "protection"? How is this cost related to leverage and the optimal capital structure?

5-7 **(Information asymmetry)** The stock of Gentech Company is currently selling at its low for the year, but management believes that the stock price is only temporarily depressed because of investor pessimism. The firm's capital budget this year is so large that the firm requires external financing. However, management does not want to sell new stock at the current low price and is therefore considering a temporary departure from its "optimal" capital structure by borrowing the funds it would otherwise have raised in the equity markets. Does this seem to be a wise move? Does this action conform to the theories presented in the chapter?

5-8 **(MM with financial distress costs)** Concord, Inc., currently has no debt. An in-house research group has just been assigned the job of determining whether the firm should change its capital structure. Because of the importance of the decision, management has also hired the investment banking firm of Stanley Morgan & Company to conduct a parallel analysis of the situation. Mr. Smith, the in-house analyst, who is well versed in modern finance theory, has decided to carry out the analysis using the MM framework. Mr. Jones, the Stanley Morgan consultant, who has a good knowledge of capital market conditions and is confident of his ability to predict the firm's debt and equity costs at various levels of debt, has decided to estimate the optimal capital structure as that structure which minimizes the firm's weighted average cost of capital. The following data are relevant to both analyses:

$$\text{EBIT} = \$4 \text{ million per year, in perpetuity.}$$
$$\text{Federal-plus-state tax rate} = 40\%.$$
$$\text{Dividend payout ratio} = 100\%.$$
$$\text{Current required rate of return on equity} = 12\%.$$

The cost of capital schedule predicted by Mr. Jones follows:

	At a Debt Level of (Millions of Dollars)							
	$0	$2	$4	$6	$8	$10	$12	$14
Interest rate (%)	—	8.0	8.3	9.0	10.0	11.0	13.0	16.0
Cost of equity (%)	12.0	12.25	12.75	13.0	13.15	13.4	14.65	17.0

Mr. Smith estimated the present value of financial distress costs at $8 million. Additionally, he estimated the following probabilities of financial distress:

	At a Debt Level of (Millions of Dollars)							
	$0	$2	$4	$6	$8	$10	$12	$14
Probability of financial distress	0	0	0.05	0.07	0.10	0.17	0.47	0.90

    a. What level of debt would Mr. Jones and Mr. Smith recommend as optimal?
    b. Comment on the similarities and differences in their recommendations.

5-9 **(Theory comparisons)** A utility company is supposed to be allowed to charge prices high enough to cover all costs, including its cost of capital. Public service commissions are supposed to take actions to stimulate companies to operate as efficiently as possible in order to keep costs, and hence prices, as low as possible. In the mid-1960s, AT&T's debt ratio was about 33 percent. Some people (Myron J. Gordon in particular) argued that a higher debt ratio would lower AT&T's cost of capital and permit it to charge lower rates for telephone service. Gordon thought an optimal debt ratio for AT&T was about 50 percent. Do the theories presented in the chapter support or refute Gordon's position?

5-10 **(MM with financial distress costs)** The Wallace Corporation is an unlevered firm, and it has constant expected operating earnings (EBIT) of $2 million per year. Wallace's federal-plus-state tax rate is 40 percent, its cost of equity is 10 percent, and its market value is V = S = $12 million. Management is considering the use of debt. (Debt would be issued and used to buy back stock, so the size of the firm would remain constant.) Since interest expense is tax deductible, the value of the firm would tend to increase as debt is added to the capital structure, but there would be an offset in the form of rising risk of financial distress. The firm's analysts have estimated, as an approximation, that the present value of any future financial distress costs is $8 million, and that the probability of distress would increase with leverage according to the following schedule:

Value of Debt	Probability of Distress
$ 0	0.0%
2,500,000	2.5
5,000,000	5.0
7,500,000	10.0
10,000,000	25.0
12,500,000	50.0
15,000,000	75.0

a. According to the "pure" MM with corporate taxes model, what is the optimal level of debt? (Consider only those debt values listed above.)

b. What is the optimal capital structure when financial distress costs are included? *(Do Parts c, d, e, and f only if you are using the computerized diskette.)*

c. Plot the value of the firm, with and without distress costs, as a function of the level of debt.

d. Assume that the firm's unlevered cost of equity is 8 percent. What is the firm's optimal capital structure now? (From this point on, include distress costs in all your analyses.)

e. Return to the base case k_{sU} of 10 percent. Now assume that the firm's tax rate increases to 60 percent. What effect does this change have on the firm's optimal capital structure?

f. Return to the base case tax rate of 40 percent. Assume that the estimated present value of financial distress costs is only $5 million. Now what is the firm's optimal capital structure?

Selected Additional References

The body of literature on capital structure—and the number of potential references—is huge. Therefore, only a sampling can be given here. For an extensive review of the recent literature, as well as a detailed bibliography, see

Beranek, William, "Research Directions in Finance," *Quarterly Review of Business and Economics*, Spring 1981, 6–24.

The major theoretical works on capital structure theory are discussed in an integrated framework in

Fama, Eugene F., and Merton H. Miller, *The Theory of Finance* (New York: Holt, Rinehart and Winston, 1972).

In addition to Miller's work, the effect of personal taxes on capital structure decisions has been addressed by

Gordon, Myron J., and Lawrence I. Gould, "The Cost of Equity Capital with Personal Income Taxes and Flotation Costs," *Journal of Finance*, September 1978, 1201–1212.

Some other references of note include the following:

Conine, Thomas E., Jr., "Debt Capacity and the Capital Budgeting Decision: Comment," *Financial Management*, Spring 1980, 20–22.

Ferri, Michael, and Wesley H. Jones, "Determinants of Financial Structure: A New Methodological Approach," *Journal of Finance*, June 1979, 631–644.

Flath, David, and Charles R. Knoeber, "Taxes, Failure Costs, and Optimal Industry Capital Structure," *Journal of Finance*, March 1980, 89–117.

Lee, Wayne Y., and Henry H. Barker, "Bankruptcy Costs and the Firm's Optimal Debt Capacity: A Positive Theory of Capital Structure," *Southern Economic Journal*, April 1977, 1453–1465.

Martin, John D., and David F. Scott, "Debt Capacity and the Capital Budgeting Decision: A Revisitation," *Financial Management*, Spring 1980, 23–26.

Schneller, Meir I., "Taxes and the Optimal Capital Structure of the Firm," *Journal of Finance*, March 1980, 119–127.

Taggart, Robert A., Jr., "Taxes and Corporate Capital Structure in an Incomplete Market," *Journal of Finance*, June 1980, 645–659.

There has been considerable discussion in the literature concerning a financial leverage clientele effect. Many theorists postulate that firms with low leverage are favored by high-tax bracket investors and vice versa. Two recent articles on this subject are

Harris, John M., Jr., Rodney L. Roenfeldt, and Philip L. Cooley, "Evidence of Financial Leverage Clienteles," *Journal of Finance*, September 1983, 1125–1132.

Kim, E. Han, "Miller's Equilibrium, Shareholder Leverage Clienteles, and Optimal Capital Leverage," *Journal of Finance*, May 1982, 301–319.

For a very readable discussion of the many issues involved in capital structure theory, see "A Discussion of Corporate Capital Structure," *Midland Corporate Finance Journal*, Fall 1985, 19–48.

5A
PROOFS TO ACCOMPANY CHAPTER 5

In Chapter 5 we presented the proof for MM's Proposition I under the assumption of no corporate taxes. However, the remaining propositions were presented without proofs. We present those proofs in this appendix.

Proof of MM Proposition II without Corporate Taxes

We noted in Chapter 5 that Equation 5-1a could be used to find the cost of equity for a zero-growth company. Here is Equation 5-1a with $T = 0$, and substituting k_{sL} for k_s to denote the use of leverage:

$$k_{sL} = \frac{EBIT - k_dD}{S}. \qquad (5\text{-}1a)$$

From the Proposition I equation, plus the fact that $V = S + D$, we can write

$$V = S + D = \frac{EBIT}{k_{sU}}.$$

This equation can be rearranged as follows:

$$EBIT = k_{sU}(S + D).$$

Now, substitute this expression for EBIT in Equation 5-1a:

$$k_{sL} = \frac{k_{sU}(S + D) - k_d D}{S} = \frac{k_{sU}S}{S} + \frac{k_{sU}D}{S} - \frac{k_d D}{S}.$$

Simplifying, we obtain this expression:

$$k_{sL} = k_{sU} + (k_{sU} - k_d)(D/S). \qquad (5\text{-}5)$$

This is the Proposition II equation we sought to prove.

Proof of MM Proposition III without Corporate Taxes

A firm should invest in new projects only if the value of the firm is increased by at least as much as the cost of the investment. Thus, if ΔV is the change in firm value, and ΔI is the cost of the investment, then the firm should make the investment only if ΔV exceeds ΔI, which implies

$$\frac{\Delta V}{\Delta I} \geq 1.$$

But from Proposition I,

$$V = \frac{EBIT}{k_{sU}}.$$

Therefore, $\Delta V = \Delta EBIT / k_{sU}$. Thus, a firm should invest in a new project only if

$$\frac{\frac{\Delta EBIT}{k_{sU}}}{\Delta I} \geq 1$$

or

$$\frac{\Delta EBIT}{\Delta I} \geq k_{sU}.$$

Since the cash flows are perpetuities, and since there are no corporate taxes, then $\Delta EBIT / \Delta I$ is the rate of return on the new investment, or the IRR. Thus, invest only if $IRR \geq k_{sU} = k_a$.

Proof of MM Proposition I with Corporate Taxes

MM originally used an arbitrage proof similar to the one we gave in Chapter 5 to prove Proposition I without corporate taxes, but their points can be confirmed with a simpler alternate proof. First, assume that two firms are identical in all respects except capital structure. Firm U has no debt in its capital structure, while L uses debt. Expected EBIT and σ_{EBIT} are identical for each firm.

Under these assumptions, the operating cash flows available to Firm U's investors, CF_U, are

$$CF_U = EBIT(1 - T), \qquad\qquad (5A\text{-}1)$$

and the cash flows to Firm L's investors (stockholders and bondholders) are

$$CF_L = (EBIT - k_dD)(1 - T) + k_dD. \qquad\qquad (5A\text{-}2)$$

Equation 5A-2 can be rearranged as follows:

$$CF_L = EBIT(1 - T) - k_dD + Tk_dD + k_dD$$
$$= EBIT(1 - T) + Tk_dD = CF_U + Tk_dD. \qquad\qquad (5A\text{-}2a)$$

The first term in Equation 5A-2a, $EBIT(1 - T)$, is identical to Firm U's net income, CF_U, while the second term, Tk_dD, represents the tax savings, and hence the additional operating income, that is available to Firm L's investors because of the fact that interest is deductible.

The value of the unlevered firm, V_U, may be determined by capitalizing its annual net income after corporate taxes, $CF_U = EBIT(1 - T)$, at its cost of equity:

$$V_U = \frac{CF_U}{k_{sU}} = \frac{EBIT(1 - T)}{k_{sU}}. \qquad\qquad (5A\text{-}3)$$

The value of the levered firm, on the other hand, is found by capitalizing both parts of its after-tax cash flows as expressed in Equation 5A-2a. MM argue that because L's "regular" earnings stream is precisely as risky as the income of Firm U, it should be capitalized at the same rate, k_{sU}. However, they argue that the tax savings are more certain—these savings will occur as long as interest on the debt is paid, so the tax savings are exactly as risky as the firm's debt, which MM assume to be riskless. Therefore, the cash flows represented by the tax savings should be discounted at the risk-free rate, k_d. Thus, we obtain Equation 5A-4 for Firm L's value:

$$V_L = \frac{EBIT(1 - T)}{k_{sU}} + \frac{Tk_dD}{k_d} = \frac{EBIT(1 - T)}{k_{sU}} + TD. \qquad\qquad (5A\text{-}4)$$

Since the first term in Equation 5A-4, $EBIT(1 - T)/k_{sU}$, is identical to V_U in Equation 5A-3, we may also express V_L as follows:

$$V_L = V_U + TD. \qquad\qquad (5A\text{-}4a)$$

Equation 5A-4a is MM's Proposition I with taxes. Thus, we see that the value of the levered firm exceeds that of the unlevered company, and the differential increases as the use of debt, D, goes up.

Proof of MM Proposition II with Corporate Taxes

The value of a levered firm's equity may be found by use of Equation 5-1 in Chapter 5 as follows:

$$S_L = \frac{(EBIT - k_dD)(1 - T)}{k_{sL}}. \qquad\qquad (5\text{-}1)$$

Solving for k_{sL}, we obtain

$$k_{sL} = \frac{(EBIT - k_d D)(1 - T)}{S_L}, \qquad (5\text{-}1a)$$

which can be rewritten as

$$k_{sL} = \frac{EBIT(1 - T) - k_d D(1 - T)}{S_L}. \qquad (5A\text{-}5)$$

From Proposition I, Equation 5A-4, we know that

$$V_L = \frac{EBIT(1 - T)}{k_{sU}} + TD,$$

which can be rewritten as

$$V_L k_{sU} = EBIT(1 - T) + k_{sU}TD,$$

and hence as

$$EBIT(1 - T) = (V_L - TD)k_{sU}.$$

Now substitute this expression for $EBIT(1 - T)$ in Equation 5A-5:

$$k_{sL} = \frac{(V_L - TD)k_{sU} - k_d D(1 - T)}{S_L}$$

$$= \frac{V_L k_{sU} - TDk_{sU} - k_d D + TDk_d}{S_L}.$$

Now recognize that $V_L = S_L + D$, and substitute for V_L in the preceding equation:

$$k_{sL} = \frac{(S_L + D)k_{sU} - TDk_{sU} - k_d D + TDk_d}{S_L}$$

$$= \frac{S_L k_{sU} + Dk_{sU} - TDk_{sU} - k_d D + TDk_d}{S_L}$$

$$= \frac{S_L k_{sU}}{S_L} + \frac{Dk_{sU} - TDk_{sU} - k_d D + TDk_d}{S_L}$$

$$= k_{sU} + (k_{sU} - Tk_{sU} - k_d + Tk_d)\frac{D}{S_L},$$

or

$$k_{sL} = k_{sU} + (k_{sU} - k_d)(1 - T)(D/S). \qquad (5\text{-}5a)$$

This last expression is the equation set forth in MM's Proposition II, and hence we have proved the proposition.

Proof of MM Proposition III with Corporate Taxes

As in the no-tax case, a firm should invest in new projects if and only if

$$\frac{\Delta V}{\Delta I} \geq 1.$$

We know from Equation 5A-4 that

$$\Delta V_L = \frac{(1 - T)\Delta EBIT}{k_{sU}} + T\Delta D.$$

Substituting for ΔV in $(\Delta V/\Delta I) \geq 1.0$ gives this expression:

$$\frac{\Delta V}{\Delta I} = \frac{\dfrac{(1 - T)\Delta EBIT}{k_{sU}} + T\Delta D}{\Delta I} \geq 1$$

$$\frac{(1 - T)\Delta EBIT}{\Delta I} + \frac{k_{sU}T\Delta D}{\Delta I} \geq k_{sU}$$

$$\frac{(1 - T)\Delta EBIT}{\Delta I} \geq k_{sU} - k_{sU}\left(\frac{T\Delta D}{\Delta I}\right)$$

$$\frac{(1 - T)\Delta EBIT}{\Delta I} \geq k_{sU}\left[1 - T\left(\frac{\Delta D}{\Delta I}\right)\right].$$

The left-hand side is the after-tax rate of return on new investment, or the IRR. How do we interpret the factor $\Delta D/\Delta I$ on the right-hand side? MM proposed that all projects will be financed using the long-term target capital structure. Thus, the factor $\Delta D/\Delta I$ should represent the target market value debt ratio of the firm, D/V. This interpretation results in

$$IRR \geq k_{sU}[1 - T(D/V)], \tag{5-6a}$$

which is Proposition III.

Proof of Equivalency Between MM Proposition III and WACC

To prove equivalency, we must compare the MM Proposition III definition of the cut-off rate with the WACC, which is defined as follows:

$$WACC = k_a = (D/V)k_d(1 - T) + (S/V)k_s. \tag{5-2}$$

However, from Proposition II, we know that

$$k_{sL} = k_{sU} + (k_{sU} - k_d)(1 - T)(D/S). \tag{5-5a}$$

The MM expression for k_s can be substituted into the WACC equation and then simplified as follows:

$$k_a = (D/V)k_d(1 - T) + (S/V)[k_{sU} + (k_{sU} - k_d)(1 - T)(D/S)]$$

$$= (D/V)k_d(1 - T) + (S/V)k_{sU} + (k_{sU} - k_d)(1 - T)(D/V)$$

$$= (D/V)k_d(1 - T) + (S/V)k_{sU} + k_{sU}(1 - T)(D/V) - (D/V)k_d(1 - T).$$

The first and last terms cancel, and recognizing that $S = V - D$, we obtain

$$k_a = \frac{V - D}{V}k_{sU} + k_{sU}(1 - T)(D/V)$$

$$= (V/V)k_{sU} - (D/V)k_{sU} + k_{sU}(D/V) - k_{sU}T(D/V) \qquad \text{(5-6a)}$$

$$= k_{sU} - k_{sU}T(D/V)$$

$$= k_{sU}[1 - T(D/V)].$$

Since this last expression is the cut-off rate in MM's Proposition III, we see that MM's definition of the cost of capital, or cut-off rate, is indeed equivalent to the weighted average cost of capital.

6

THE TARGET CAPITAL STRUCTURE

In Chapter 5, we saw that the tax benefit/financial distress tradeoff models imply that each firm has an optimal, or value-maximizing, capital structure which exactly balances the costs and the benefits of debt financing. However, as we also noted in Chapter 5, it is virtually impossible to pinpoint this value-maximizing capital structure. Still, it is possible to identify the factors that influence capital structure, and then to establish a *target capital structure*. This target may actually be set as a range, and it will change over time as conditions vary, but at any given moment, the firm's management should have a specific capital structure in mind, and financing decisions over time should be consistent with this target. If the actual debt ratio is below the prescribed ratio, expansion capital should be raised by issuing debt, while stock should be sold if the debt ratio is above the target level.

Some of the factors which affect the optimal capital structure are related to the firm's industry; other factors are unique to individual firms. Empirical evidence shows that definite industry patterns exist, and this and other evidence reinforces our conclusion that an optimal capital structure does exist for each firm. However, the evidence also reinforces our conclusion that actually establishing the proper target structure is an imprecise process at best, and it involves a combination of quantitative analysis and informed judgment.

BUSINESS AND FINANCIAL RISK: TOTAL RISK PERSPECTIVE

In Chapter 2, when we examined risk from the viewpoint of the individual investor, we distinguished between *market risk*, which is measured by the firm's beta coefficient, and *total risk*, which includes both market risk and an element of risk which can be eliminated by diversification. Now we introduce two new dimensions of risk: (1) *business risk*, or the riskiness of the firm's assets if it used no debt, and (2) *financial risk*, the additional risk placed on the common stockholders as a result of the firm's decision to use debt.[1] Conceptually, the firm has a

---

[1] Using preferred stock also adds to financial risk. To simplify matters somewhat, we shall consider only debt and common equity in this chapter.

certain amount of risk inherent in its operations: this is its business risk. Part of this business risk is company-specific and can be eliminated by diversification, while the remaining business risk is market risk. If the firm uses debt, then it in effect partitions its business risk and concentrates most of it on one class of investors—the common stockholders. However, the common stockholders are compensated for their higher risk by a higher expected return.

Business Risk

Business risk, in a total risk sense, is defined as the uncertainty inherent in projections of future *operating income*, or *earnings before interest and taxes (EBIT)*, and it is the single most important determinant of a firm's capital structure. Figure 6-1 gives some clues about Porter Electronics Company's business risk. The top graph shows the trend in EBIT from 1976 through 1986; this graph gives both security analysts and Porter's management an idea of the degree to which EBIT has varied in the past and might vary in the future. Note that Porter is growing, and the relevant variation of EBIT is the dispersion about its trend line. The bottom graph shows the beginning of year subjectively estimated probability distribution of Porter's EBIT for 1986 based on the trend line in the top section of Figure 6-1. As the graphs indicate, actual EBIT in 1986 was only $266 million, compared to an expected value of $275 million.

Porter's past fluctuations in EBIT were caused by many factors—booms and recessions in the national economy, successful new products introduced both by Porter and by its competitors, labor strikes, price controls, a fire in Porter's major plant, and so on. Similar events will doubtless occur in the future, and when they do, the realized EBIT will be higher or lower than the projected level. Further, there is always the possibility that a long-term disaster might strike, permanently depressing the company's earning power; for example, a competitor might introduce a new product that would permanently lower Porter's earnings. This uncertainty regarding Porter's future operating income is defined as the company's *basic business risk*.

Business risk varies not only from industry to industry but also among firms in a given industry. Further, business risk can change over time. For example, the electric utilities were regarded for years as having little business risk, but a combination of events in the 1970s and 1980s altered the utilities' situation, producing sharp declines in their operating income, and greatly increasing the industry's business risk. Now, food processors and grocery retailers are frequently given as examples of industries with low business risk, while cyclical manufacturing industries such as steel are regarded as having especially high business risk. Also, smaller companies, and those that are dependent on a single product, are often regarded as having a high degree of business risk.[2]

---

[2]We have avoided any discussion of market versus company-specific risk in this section. We note now (1) that any action which increases business risk in the total risk sense will generally also increase a firm's beta coefficient, and (2) that a part of business risk as we define it here will generally be company-specific, and hence subject to elimination by diversification by the firm's stockholders. This point is discussed at some length in the next major section.

Figure 6-1
Porter Electronics Company:
Trend in EBIT, 1976-1986 and
Subjective Probability Distribution of EBIT, 1986

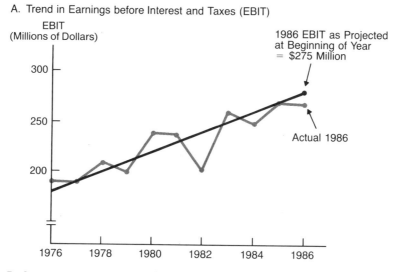

A. Trend in Earnings before Interest and Taxes (EBIT)

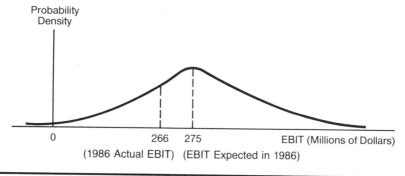

B. Subjective Probability Distribution of EBIT

Business risk depends on a number of factors; the more important ones are listed below:

1. Demand variability. The more stable the demand for a firm's products, other things held constant, the lower its business risk.

2. Sales price variability. Firms whose products are sold in highly volatile markets are exposed to more business risk than similar firms whose output prices are more stable.

3. Input cost variability. Firms whose input costs are highly uncertain are exposed to a high degree of business risk.

4. Ability to adjust output prices for changes in input costs. Some firms are better able to raise their own output prices when input costs rise than are others. The greater the ability to adjust output prices to reflect cost conditions, the lower the degree of business risk, other things held constant.

5. The extent to which costs are fixed: operating leverage. If a high percentage of a firm's costs are fixed, and hence do not decline when demand falls off, then it is exposed to a relatively high degree of business risk. This factor is called *operating leverage*, and it is discussed at length in the next section.

Each of these factors is determined partly by the firm's industry characteristics, but each of them is also controllable to some extent. For example, most firms can, through their marketing policies, take actions to stabilize both unit sales and sales prices. However, this stabilization may require firms to spend a great deal on advertising and/or price concessions in order to get commitments from their customers to purchase fixed quantities at fixed prices in the future. Similarly, firms such as Porter Electronics can reduce the volatility of future input costs by negotiating long-term labor and materials supply contracts, but they may have to agree to pay prices above the current spot price level to obtain these contracts.[3]

Operating Leverage

As we have noted, business risk depends in part on the extent to which a firm builds fixed costs into its operations—if fixed costs are high, even a small decline in sales can lead to a large decline in EBIT, so, other things held constant, the higher a firm's fixed costs, the greater is its business risk. Higher fixed costs are generally associated with more highly automated, capital intensive firms and industries. Also, businesses that employ highly skilled workers who must be retained and paid even during recessions have relatively high fixed costs.

If a high percentage of a firm's total costs are fixed, then the firm is said to have a high degree of *operating leverage*. In physics, leverage implies the use of a lever to raise a heavy object with a small force. In politics, if people have leverage, their smallest word or action can accomplish a lot. *In business terminology, a high degree of operating leverage, other factors held constant, implies that a relatively small change in sales results in a large change in operating income.*

Figure 6-2 illustrates the concept of operating leverage by comparing the results that a new firm would achieve if it uses different degrees of operating leverage. Plan A calls for a relatively small amount of fixed charges, $20,000—here the firm would not have much automated equipment, so its depreciation, maintenance, property taxes, and so on would be low. Note, however, that under Plan A the total operating costs line has a relatively steep slope, indicating that variable costs per unit are higher than they would be if the firm used more operating leverage. Plan B calls for a higher level of fixed costs, $60,000. Here the firm uses automated equipment (with which one operator can turn out a few or many units at the same

---

[3]For example, in 1986 utilities could buy coal in the spot market for about $30 per ton. Under a 5-year contract, coal cost about $50 per ton. Clearly, the price for reducing uncertainty was high!

Figure 6-2
Illustration of Operating Leverage

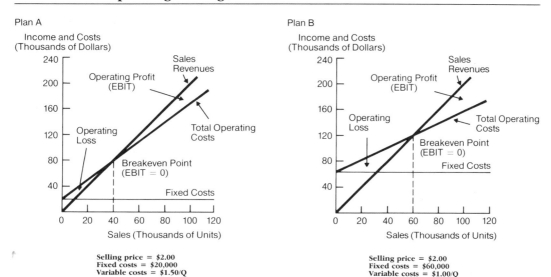

Plan A

Income and Costs
(Thousands of Dollars)

Selling price = $2.00
Fixed costs = $20,000
Variable costs = $1.50/Q

Probability of Sales, P (1)	Units Sold, Q (2)	Sales (3)	Operating Costs (4)	Operating Profit, EBIT (3) − (4) = (5)
0.02	0	$ 0	$ 20,000	($20,000)
0.03	20,000	40,000	50,000	(10,000)
0.05	40,000	80,000	80,000	0
0.15	60,000	120,000	110,000	10,000
0.50	110,000	220,000	185,000	35,000
0.15	160,000	320,000	260,000	60,000
0.05	180,000	360,000	290,000	70,000
0.03	200,000	400,000	320,000	80,000
0.02	220,000	440,000	350,000	90,000
	Expected value $220,000			$35,000
	Standard deviation $ 94,021			$23,505

Plan B

Income and Costs
(Thousands of Dollars)

Selling price = $2.00
Fixed costs = $60,000
Variable costs = $1.00/Q

Probability of Sales, P (1)	Units Sold, Q (2)	Sales (3)	Operating Costs (4)	Operating Profit, EBIT (3) − (4) = (5)
0.02	0	$ 0	$ 60,000	($ 60,000)
0.03	20,000	40,000	80,000	(40,000)
0.05	40,000	80,000	100,000	(20,000)
0.15	60,000	120,000	120,000	0
0.50	110,000	220,000	170,000	50,000
0.15	160,000	320,000	220,000	100,000
0.05	180,000	360,000	240,000	120,000
0.03	200,000	400,000	260,000	140,000
0.02	220,000	440,000	280,000	160,000
	Expected value $220,000			$ 50,000
	Standard deviation $ 94,021			$ 47,011

labor cost) to a much larger extent. The breakeven point is higher under Plan B: Breakeven occurs at 60,000 units under Plan B versus only 40,000 units under Plan A.

We can calculate the breakeven quantity by recognizing that breakeven occurs when EBIT = 0:

$$\text{EBIT} = 0 = PQ - VQ - F. \tag{6-1}$$

Here P is average sales price per unit of output, Q is units of output, V is variable cost per unit, and F is fixed operating costs.[4] We can solve Equation 6-1 for the breakeven quantity, Q_{BE}:

---

[4]This definition of breakeven does not include fixed financial costs. If there are fixed financial costs, the firm will suffer an accounting loss at the operating breakeven point. Thus, Equation 6-1 defines the *operating* breakeven level of sales. We will introduce financial costs shortly.

$$Q_{BE} = \frac{F}{P - V}. \tag{6-1a}$$

Thus, for Plan A,

$$Q_{BE} = \frac{\$20,000}{\$2.00 - \$1.50} = 40,000 \text{ units,}$$

and for Plan B,

$$Q_{BE} = \frac{\$60,000}{\$2.00 - \$1.00} = 60,000 \text{ units.}$$

How does operating leverage affect business risk? *Other things held constant, the higher a firm's operating leverage, the higher is its business risk.* This point is demonstrated in Figure 6-3, where we show how probability distributions for EBIT under Plans A and B are developed.

The top section of Figure 6-3 graphs the probability distribution of sales that was presented in tabular form in Figure 6-2. The sales probability distribution depends on how demand for the product varies, and not on whether the product is manufactured by Plan A or by Plan B. Therefore, the same sales probability distribution applies to both production plans; this distribution has expected sales of $220,000, and it ranges from zero to about $450,000.

We use the sales probability distribution, together with the operating costs at each sales level, to develop graphs of the EBIT probability distributions under Plans A and B. These are shown in the lower section of Figure 6-3. Plan B has a higher expected EBIT, but this plan also entails a much higher probability of large losses. Clearly, Plan B, the one with more fixed costs and a higher degree of operating leverage, is riskier. *In general, holding other factors constant, the higher the degree of operating leverage, the greater the business risk as measured by variability of EBIT.*

To what extent can firms control their operating leverage? To a large extent, operating leverage is determined by technology. Electric utilities, telephone companies, airlines, steel mills, and chemical companies simply *must* have heavy investments in fixed assets; this results in high fixed costs and operating leverage. Grocery stores, on the other hand, generally have significantly lower fixed costs, and hence lower operating leverage. Still, although industry factors do exert a major influence, all firms do have some control over their operating leverage. For example, an electric utility can expand its generating capacity by building either a nuclear reactor or a coal-fired plant. The nuclear generator would require a larger investment, and hence higher fixed costs, but its variable operating costs would be relatively low. The coal plant, on the other hand, would require a smaller investment and would have lower fixed costs, but the variable costs (for coal) would be high. Thus, by its capital budgeting decisions, a utility (or any other company) can influence its operating leverage, and hence its basic business risk.

The concept of operating leverage was, in fact, originally developed for use in making capital budgeting decisions. Mutually exclusive projects which involve alternative methods for producing a given product often have different degrees of

Figure 6-3
Analysis of Business Risk

A. Sales Probability Distribution

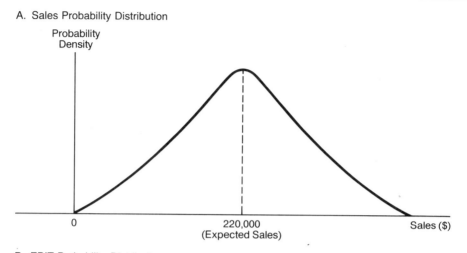

B. EBIT Probability Distribution

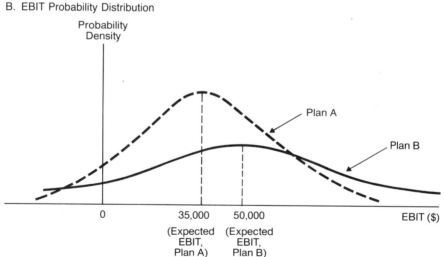

Note: We are using continuous distributions to approximate the discrete distributions contained in Figure 6-2.

operating leverage, and hence different breakeven points and different degrees of risk. Porter Electronics and many other companies regularly undertake a type of breakeven analysis (the sensitivity analysis discussed in Chapter 9) for each proposed project as a part of their regular capital budgeting process. Still, once a corporation's operating leverage has been established, this factor influences its capital structure decisions. This point is covered next.

Financial Risk

Financial risk is the additional risk placed on the common stockholders as a result of financial leverage. Conceptually, the firm has a certain amount of risk inherent in its operations—this is its business risk, which is defined as the uncertainty inherent in projections of future EBIT. If a firm uses debt and preferred stock (financial leverage), this concentrates its business risk on the common stockholders. To illustrate, suppose 10 people decide to form a corporation to manufacture steel roof trusses. There is a certain amount of business risk in the operation. If the firm is capitalized only with common equity, and if each person buys 10 percent of the stock, then each investor shares equally in the business risk. However, suppose the firm is capitalized with 50 percent debt and 50 percent equity, with five of the investors putting up their capital as debt and the other five putting up their money as equity. In this case, those investors who put up the equity will have to bear all of the business risk, so the common stock will be twice as risky as it would have been had the firm been financed only with equity. Thus, the use of debt, or *financial leverage*, concentrates the firm's business risk on its stockholders.

To illustrate the concentration of business risk, consider a new firm which expects an EBIT of $4 million, requires assets of $20 million, and has a zero tax rate.[5] To begin the analysis, divide the $4 million expected EBIT by the $20 million of assets to obtain the expected *basic earning power (BEP)* of those assets, which in this case is BEP $= \$4/\$20 = 0.20 = 20\%$. If the company used no debt, then these conditions would exist:

1. Its assets would be equal to its equity.
2. Its return on equity (ROE) would be equal to its basic earning power (BEP).
3. Its equity would be exactly as risky as its assets.

Now suppose the firm decides to change its capital structure by issuing $10 million of debt which carries a 15 percent interest rate, substituting these funds for $10 million of equity. Its expected return on equity (which would now be only $10 million) would rise from 20 to 25 percent:

Expected EBIT (unchanged)	$4,000,000
Interest (15% on $10 million of debt)	1,500,000
Income available to common (zero taxes)	$2,500,000

Expected ROE $= \$2,500,000/\$10,000,000 = 25\%$.

Thus, the use of debt would "leverage up" the expected ROE from 20 percent to 25 percent.

---

[5] We assume a zero tax rate to simplify the illustration. However, the same conclusions would be reached had we used a positive tax rate.

Financial leverage increases risk as well as expected return to the equity investors. For example, suppose EBIT actually turned out to be $2 million rather than the expected $4 million, so the basic earning power (BEP) ratio turned out to be 10 percent rather than 20 percent. If the firm used no debt, then ROE would decline from 20 to 10 percent. However, with debt financing, ROE would fall from 25 to only 5 percent:

	BEP = 10%	
	Zero Debt	**$10 Million of Debt**
Actual EBIT	$2,000,000	$2,000,000
Interest (15%)	0	1,500,000
Income available to common (zero taxes)	$2,000,000	$ 500,000
Actual ROE: $2,000,000/$20,000,000 =	10%	
$500,000/$10,000,000 =		5%
Expected ROE =	20%	25%

A more complete analysis of the effects of leverage on this firm's ROE is illustrated in Figure 6-4. The two lines in the top graph show the level of ROE that would exist at different levels of basic earning power under the two different capital structures. The lines were plotted from data developed as described previously, and they show that the greater the use of financial leverage, the more sensitive ROE is to changes in the basic earning power of assets.[6]

The lower panel of Figure 6-4 shows the effects of leverage on the firm's ROE probability distribution. With zero debt, the company would have an expected ROE of 20 percent, the same as its expected BEP, and a relatively tight distribution. With $10 million of debt, the expected ROE would be 25 percent, but the ROE distribution would be much flatter, indicating a larger standard deviation of returns (σ_{ROE}) and a more risky situation for the equity investors.

Our conclusions from this analysis may be stated as follows:

1. The use of debt generally increases the expected ROE; this situation occurs whenever the expected basic earning power exceeds the cost of debt.

---

[6]If still more debt—say $15 million—were used, the ROE line would be even steeper, while if $5 million of debt were used, the new line would be between the two lines now shown in Figure 6-4. The lines would all intersect at the point where ROE = BEP = 15%, showing that if BEP = k_d, then leverage has no effect on ROE. Note also that the vertical axis intercept reflects the fixed interest cost that must be borne by the stockholders; that is, at the intercept, the BEP is zero, but interest must be paid, and this interest must come out of the stockholders' share of the business, and hence it produces an accounting loss and a 15 percent negative return to stockholders. The stockholders' loss would be greater or smaller if the firm uses a greater or lesser amount of debt. For example, if the firm uses only $5 million of debt, then the stockholders would have a 7.5 percent negative return if BEP were zero.

Note also that we have assumed away taxes. If taxes were introduced, the effect would be to lower the ROE. For example, if the tax rate were 50 percent, then the ROE for any BEP would be half the level currently shown in Figure 6-4, and the ROE lines in the top panel of the figure would shift downward so that the lines intersected at BEP = 15%, ROE = 7.5%.

Figure 6-4
Effects of Financial Leverage on ROE

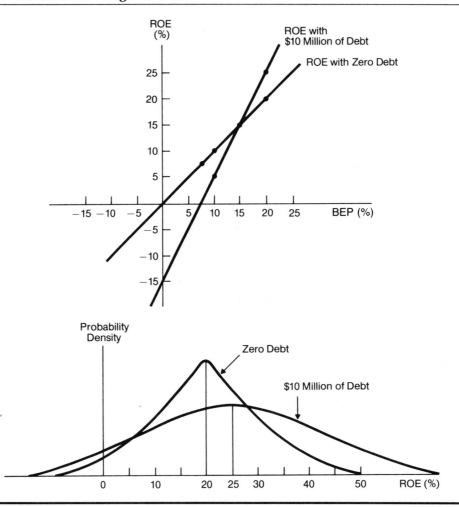

2. σ_{BEP} is a measure of business risk, and σ_{ROE} is a measure of the risk borne by stockholders. $\sigma_{ROE} = \sigma_{BEP}$ if the firm does not use any debt, or financial leverage, but if the firm does use debt, then $\sigma_{ROE} > \sigma_{BEP}$ because business risk is being concentrated on the stockholders.

3. The difference between σ_{BEP}, the risk that stockholders would bear if no financial leverage were used, and σ_{ROE}, the risk stockholders actually face, is a measure of the risk-increasing effects of financial leverage:

$$\text{Risk from financial leverage} = \sigma_{ROE} - \sigma_{BEP}.$$

BUSINESS AND FINANCIAL RISK: MARKET RISK PERSPECTIVE

Thus far, our discussion of business and financial risk has focused on total risk. We have used σ_{BEP} as the measure of business risk and σ_{ROE} as the measure of the total risk borne by the stockholders. Thus, in the total risk sense, $\sigma_{ROE} - \sigma_{BEP}$ is a measure of financial risk. Now we shift our focus from total risk to *market,* or *systematic, risk.*

In an important article, Robert Hamada combined the CAPM with the MM after-tax model to obtain this expression for k_{sL}, the cost of equity to a leveraged firm:[7]

$$
\begin{aligned}
k_{sL} &= \begin{array}{c}\text{Risk-free}\\ \text{rate}\end{array} + \begin{array}{c}\text{Business risk}\\ \text{premium}\end{array} + \begin{array}{c}\text{Financial risk}\\ \text{premium}\end{array} \qquad\qquad (6\text{-}2)\\
&= k_{RF} + b_U(k_M - k_{RF}) + b_U(k_M - k_{RF})(1 - T)(D/S).
\end{aligned}
$$

Here b_u is the beta coefficient the firm would have if it used no financial leverage, and the other terms are as defined in Chapter 5. In effect, Equation 6-2 partitions the required rate of return to a leveraged firm into three components: k_{RF}, the risk-free rate, which compensates shareholders for the time value of money; a premium for business risk as reflected by the term $b_U(k_M - k_{RF})$; and a premium for financial risk as reflected by the third term, $b_U(k_M - k_{RF})(1 - T)(D/S)$. If a firm has no financial leverage ($D = 0$), then the financial risk premium term would be zero, so the third term would drop out and equity investors would be compensated only for business risk.

As we saw in the last chapter, the MM model with corporate taxes does not hold exactly, and we also know that the CAPM does not fully describe investor behavior. Therefore, Equation 6-2 must be regarded as an approximation. Nevertheless, Equation 6-2 can provide financial managers with some useful insights. As an illustration, assume that Firm U, an unlevered company with $b_U = 1.5$ and \$100,000 of equity ($S = \$100,000$), is considering replacing \$20,000 of equity with debt. If $k_{RF} = 10\%$, $k_M = 15\%$, and $T = 34\%$, then Firm U's current unlevered required rate of return on equity would be 17.5 percent:

$$
\begin{aligned}
k_{sU} &= 10\% + 1.5(15\% - 10\%)\\
&= 10\% + 7.5\% = 17.5\%.
\end{aligned}
$$

This shows that the business risk premium is 7.5 percentage points. If the firm were to add \$20,000 of debt to its capital structure, then its new value according to MM would be $V_L = V_U + TD = \$100,000 + 0.34(\$20,000) = \$106,800$, and its k_s, using Equation 6-2, would rise to 18.64 percent:

$$
\begin{aligned}
k_{sL} &= 10\% + 1.5(15\% - 10\%) + 1.5(15\% - 10\%)(1 - 0.34)(\$20,000/\$86,800)\\
&= 10\% + 7.5\% + 1.14\% = 18.64\%.
\end{aligned}
$$

---

[7]See Robert S. Hamada, "Portfolio Analysis, Market Equilibrium, and Corporation Finance," *Journal of Finance*, March 1969, 13-31.

Thus, adding $20,000 of debt to the capital structure would result in a financial risk premium of 1.14 percentage points, which would be added to the business risk premium of 7.5 percentage points.

Hamada also showed that Equation 6-2 can be used to analyze the effect of its financial leverage on a firm's beta. We know that under the CAPM, the SML can be used to determine a firm's required rate of return on equity:

$$\text{SML: } k_{sL} = k_{RF} + b_L(k_M - k_{RF}).$$

Now, by equating the SML equation with Equation 6-2, we obtain:

$$k_{RF} + b_L(k_M - k_{RF}) = k_{RF} + b_U(k_M - k_{RF}) + b_U(k_M - k_{RF})(1 - T)(D/S)$$

$$b_L(k_M - k_{RF}) = b_U(k_M - k_{RF}) + b_U(k_M - k_{RF})(1 - T)(D/S)$$

$$b_L = b_U + b_U(1 - T)(D/S), \tag{6-3}$$

or

$$b_L = b_U[1 + (1 - T)(D/S)]. \tag{6-3a}$$

Thus, under the MM and CAPM assumptions, the beta of a levered firm is equal to the beta the firm would have if it used zero debt, adjusted upward by a factor that depends on (1) the corporate tax rate and (2) the amount of financial leverage employed. Therefore, the firm's relevant (or market) risk, which is measured by b_L, depends on both the firm's business risk as reflected in b_U and financial risk as reflected in the leverage ratio, D/S.

To continue our illustration, if Firm U were to replace $20,000 of equity with debt, its beta would increase to 1.73 according to Equation 6-3a:

$$b_L = b_U [1 + (1 - T)(D/S)]$$

$$= 1.5 [1 + (1 - 0.34)(\$20,000/ \$86,800)]$$

$$= 1.5 (1.152) = 1.728.$$

We can confirm the Equation 6-2 value of $k_{sL} = 18.64\%$ by using $b_L = 1.728$ in the SML:

$$k_{sL} = k_{RF} + b_L (k_M - k_{RF})$$

$$= 10\% + 1.728 (15\% - 10\%) = 18.64\%.$$

These relationships can be used to help estimate a company's cost of equity. They are especially useful when the firm does not have publicly traded common stock, and, as we shall see in Chapter 9, to help establish the cost of equity for a division of a diversified company. In both instances, we proceed by obtaining betas for similar publicly traded firms and then "lever them up or down" to make them consistent with our own firm's (or division's) capital structure and tax rate. The result is an estimate of our firm's (or division's) beta, given its business risk as measured by the betas of other firms in the same industry and its financial risk as measured by its own capital structure and tax rate.

ESTIMATING THE TARGET CAPITAL STRUCTURE: A SIMPLIFIED EXAMPLE

We saw in Chapter 5 that the tax benefit/financial distress tradeoff theory leads to the conclusion that each firm has an optimal capital structure, one which maximizes its value and minimizes its weighted average cost of capital. In this section, we present an illustration which demonstrates many important points that we discussed in Chapter 5.

Forman Software Systems

Forman Software Systems (FSS) was founded in 1980 to develop and market a new type of operating system for personal computers. The basic program was written and patented by Charles Forman, FSS's founder. Forman owns a majority of the stock, although a significant portion is held by institutional investors. The company has no debt. FSS's key financial data are shown in Table 6-1. Assets are carried at a book value of $1 million; hence, the common equity also has a balance sheet value of $1 million. However, these balance sheet figures are not very meaningful be-

---

Table 6-1
Data on Forman Software Systems

Balance Sheet as of December 31, 1986

Current assets	$ 500,000	Debt	$ 0
Net fixed assets	500,000	Common equity (1.0 million shares outstanding)	1,000,000
Total assets	$1,000,000	Total claims	$1,000,000

Income Statement for 1986

Sales		$20,000,000
Fixed operating costs	$ 4,000,000	
Variable operating costs	12,000,000	16,000,000
Earnings before interest and taxes (EBIT)		$ 4,000,000
Interest		0
Taxable income		$ 4,000,000
Taxes (40% federal-plus-state)		1,600,000
Net income		$ 2,400,000

Other Data

1. Earnings per share = EPS = $2,400,000/1,000,000 shares = $2.40.
2. Dividends per share = DPS = $2,400,000/1,000,000 shares = $2.40. Thus, the company has a 100 percent payout ratio.
3. Book value per share = $1,000,000/1,000,000 shares = $1.
4. Market price per share = P_0 = $20. Thus, the stock sells at 20 times its book value.
5. Price/earnings ratio = P/E = $20/2.40 = 8.33 times.
6. Dividend yield = DPS/P_0 = $2.40/$20 = 12%.

cause (1) the asset figures do not include any value for patents and (2) the fixed assets were purchased several years ago at lower than today's prices.

Charles Forman will retire shortly, and he is planning to sell a major part of his interest in the company to the public, using the proceeds of the sale to diversify his personal portfolio. As a part of the planning process, the question of capital structure has arisen. Should the firm continue its policy of using no debt, or should it recapitalize? And if it does decide to substitute debt for equity, how far should it go? As in all such decisions, the correct answer is that *it should choose that capital structure which maximizes the value of the company.* If the company's total market value is maximized, so will be the price of its stock, and its cost of capital will simultaneously be minimized.

To simplify the analysis, we assume that the long-run demand for FSS's products is not expected to grow; hence, its EBIT is expected to continue at $4 million. (However, future sales may turn out to be different from the expected level, so realized EBIT may be more or less than the expected $4 million.) Also, since the company has no need for new capital, all of its income will be paid out as dividends.

Now assume that FSS's financial manager consults with investment bankers and learns that debt can be sold, but the more debt used, the riskier the debt and the higher the interest rate, k_d. Also, the bankers state that the more debt FSS uses, the greater the riskiness of its stock, and hence the higher its required rate of return on equity, k_s. Estimates of k_d, beta, and k_s at different debt levels are given in Figure 6-5, along with a graph of the relationship between k_s and debt.

Given the data in Table 6-1 along with those in Figure 6-5, we can determine FSS's total market value, V, at different capital structures, and we can then use this information to establish the company's stock price as a function of its capital structure. These equations, which were developed in Chapter 5, are used in the analysis:[8]

$$V = D + S. \tag{6-4}$$

$$S = \frac{\text{Net income after taxes}}{k_s} = \frac{(\text{EBIT} - k_dD)(1 - T)}{k_s}. \tag{6-5}$$

$$P_0 = \frac{\text{DPS}}{k_s} = \frac{\text{EPS}}{k_s}. \tag{6-6}$$

$$k_a = (D/V)(k_d)(1 - T) + (S/V)(k_s). \tag{6-7}$$

We first substitute values for k_d, D, and k_s into Equation 6-5 to obtain values for S, the market value of common equity, at each level of debt, D, and we then sum S and D to find the total value of the firm. Table 6-2 and Figure 6-6, which plots selected data from the table, were developed by this process. The values shown in Columns 1, 2, and 3 of the table were taken from Figure 6-5, while those in

---

[8]Note that Equations 6-4 through 6-7 do not stem from a particular capital structure theory—they do not require acceptance of MM, Miller, or any other theory. Rather, they are definitions and basic DCF valuation equations for perpetual cash flows.

Figure 6-5
FSS's Cost of Debt and Equity and Beta

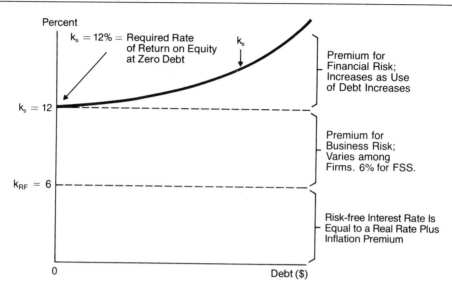

Amount Borrowed[a] (1)	Interest Rate on all Debt, k_d (2)	Estimated Beta Coefficient of Stock, b (3)	Required Rate of Return on Stock, k_s[b] (4)
$ 0	—	1.50	12.0%
2,000,000	8.0%	1.55	12.2
4,000,000	8.3	1.65	12.6
6,000,000	9.0	1.80	13.2
8,000,000	10.0	2.00	14.0
10,000,000	12.0	2.30	15.2
12,000,000	15.0	2.70	16.8
14,000,000	18.0	3.25	19.0

[a]FSS is unable to borrow more than $14 million because of limitations on interest coverage in its corporate charter.
[b]We assume that $k_{RF} = 6\%$ and $k_M = 10\%$. Therefore, at zero debt, $k_s = 6\% + 1.5(10\% - 6\%) = 12\%$. Other values of k_s are calculated similarly.

Column 4 were obtained by solving Equation 6-5 at different debt levels. The values for the firm given in Column 5 were obtained by summing Columns 1 and 4, $D + S = V$.

To see how the stock prices shown in Column 6 were developed, visualize this series of events:

1. Initially, FSS has no debt. The firm's value is $20 million, or $20 for each of its 1 million shares. (See the top line of Table 6-2.)

Table 6-2
FSS's Value, Stock Price, and Cost of Capital at Different Debt Levels

Value of Debt, D (in Millions) (1)	k_d (2)	k_s (3)	Value of Stock, S (in Millions) (4)	Value of Firm, V (in Millions) (1) + (4) = (5)	Stock Price, P_0 (6)	D/V (7)	k_a = WACC (8)
$ 0.0	—	12.0%	$20.000	$20.000	$20.00	0.0%	12.0%
2.0	8.0%	12.2	18.885	20.885	20.89	9.6	11.5
4.0	8.3	12.6	17.467	21.467	21.47	18.6	11.2
6.0	**9.0**	**13.2**	**15.727**	**21.727**	**21.73**	**27.6**	**11.0**
8.0	10.0	14.0	13.714	21.714	21.71	36.8	11.1
10.0	12.0	15.2	11.053	21.053	21.05	47.5	11.4
12.0	15.0	16.8	7.857	19.857	19.86	60.4	12.1
14.0	18.0	19.0	3.160	17.160	17.16	81.6	12.3

Notes:
a. The data in Columns 1 through 3 were taken from Figure 6-5.
b. The values for S in Column 4 were found by use of Equation 6-5:

$$S = \frac{\text{Net income}}{k_s} = \frac{(\text{EBIT} - k_d D)(1 - T)}{k_s}.$$

For example, at D = $0,

$$S = \frac{(\$4.0 - 0)(0.6)}{0.12} = \frac{\$2.4}{0.12} = \$20.0 \text{ million},$$

and at D = $6.0,

$$S = \frac{[\$4.0 - 0.09(\$6.0)](0.6)}{0.132} = \frac{\$2.076}{0.132} = \$15.727 \text{ million}.$$

c. The values for V in Column 5 were obtained as the sum of D + S. For example, at D = $6.0, V = $6.0 + $15.727 = $21.727 million.
d. The stock prices shown in Column 6 are equal to the value of the firm as shown in Column 5 divided by the original number of shares outstanding, which in this case is 1 million. The logic behind this procedure is explained in the text.
e. Column 7 is found by dividing Column 1 by Column 5. For example, at D = $6, D/V = $6/$21.727 = 27.6%.
f. Column 8 is found by use of Equation 6-7. For example, at the optimal capital structure,

$$k_a = (D/V)(k_d)(1 - T) + (S/V)(k_s)$$
$$= (0.276)(9\%)(0.6) + (0.724)(13.2\%) = 11.0\%.$$

2. Management announces a decision to change the capital structure; legally, the firm *must* make an explicit announcement or run the risk of having stockholders sue the directors.

3. The values shown in Columns 1 through 5 of Table 6-2 are estimated as described previously. The major institutional investors, and the large brokerage companies which advise individual investors, have analysts just as capable of making

Figure 6-6
**Relationship between FSS's Capital Structure,
Cost of Capital, and Stock Price**

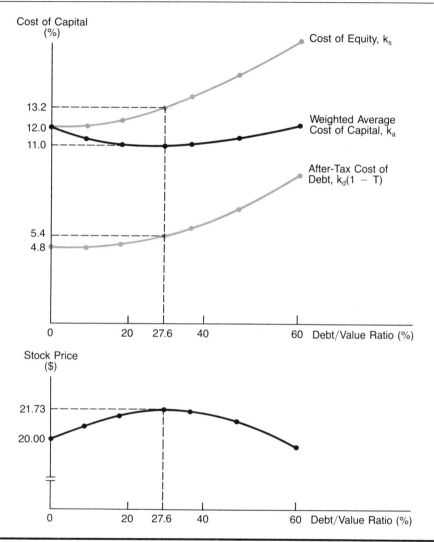

these estimates as the firm's management. These analysts would start making their own estimates as soon as FSS announced the planned change in leverage, and they would presumably reach the same conclusions as the FSS analysts.

4. FSS's stockholders initially own the entire company. (There are not yet any bondholders.) They see, or are told by their advisor-analysts, that very shortly the value of the enterprise will rise from $20 million to some higher amount, presumably the maximum attainable, or $21,727,000. Thus, they anticipate that the value of the firm will increase by $1,727,000.

5. This additional $1,727,000 will accrue to the firm's current stockholders. Since there are 1 million shares of stock, each share will rise in value by $1.73, or from $20 to $21.73.

6. This price increase will occur *before* the transaction is completed. Suppose, for example, that the stock price remained at $20 after the announcement of the recapitalization plan. Shrewd investors would immediately recognize that the stock's price will soon go up to $21.73, and they would place orders to buy at any price below $21.73. This buying pressure would quickly run the price up to $21.73, at which point it would remain constant. Thus, $21.73 is the *equilibrium stock price* for FSS once the decision has been made to recapitalize.

7. The firm sells $6 million of bonds at an interest rate of 9 percent. This money is used to buy stock at the market price, which is now $21.73, so 276,116 shares are repurchased:

$$\text{Shares repurchased} = \frac{\$6,000,000}{\$21.73} = 276,116.$$

8. The value of the stock after the 276,116 shares have been repurchased is $15,727,000, as shown in Column 4 of Table 6-2. There are $1,000,000 - 276,116 = 723,884$ shares still outstanding, so the value per share of the remaining stock is

$$\text{Value per share} = \frac{\$15,727,000}{723,884} = \$21.73.$$

This confirms our earlier calculation of the equilibrium stock price.

9. The same process was used to find stock prices at other capital structures; these prices are given in Column 6 of Table 6-2 and plotted in the lower graph of Figure 6-6. *Since the maximum price occurs when FSS uses $6 million of debt, its optimal capital structure calls for $6 million of debt.* Note that $6 million of debt corresponds to a firm value of $21.727 million. Thus, the optimal market value capital structure, D/V*, is $6/$21.727 = 27.6%.

10. In this example, we assume that EBIT would decline from $4 million to $3.52 million if the firm's debt rose to $14 million. The reason for the decline is that, at this very high level of debt, managers and employees would be worried about the firm's failing and about losing their jobs; suppliers would not sell to the firm on normal credit terms; orders would be lost because of customers' fears that the company might go bankrupt and thus be unable to deliver; and so on. EBIT is independent of financial leverage at "reasonable" debt levels, but at extreme degrees of leverage, EBIT is adversely affected.

11. Quite obviously, the situation in the real world is much more complex, and less exact, than this example suggests. Most important, different investors will have different estimates for EBIT and k_s, and hence will form different expectations about the equilibrium stock price. This means that FSS might have to pay more than $21.73 to repurchase its shares, or perhaps that the shares could be bought at a lower price. These changes would cause the optimal amount of debt to be somewhat higher or lower than $6 million. Still, $6 million represents our best estimate as to the optimal debt level; hence, it is the level we should use as our target capital structure.

12. The WACC for the various levels of debt is shown in Column 8 of Table 6-2. It can be seen that the minimum cost of capital, 11.0%, corresponds to the level of debt at which the value of the firm and its stock price are maximized, $6.0 million.

The stock price and cost of capital relationships developed in Table 6-2 are graphed in Figure 6-6. Here we see that FSS's stock price is maximized, and its weighted average cost of capital is minimized, at the same D/V ratio, 27.6 percent.

Extensions of the Example

In the preceding section, we examined the effects of debt on its stock price if FSS went from zero debt to some positive level of debt. Now we will examine the general effects of a change from one debt level to some other level, using this equation:

$$P_1 = \frac{\text{Ending value of firm} - \text{Beginning value of debt}}{\text{Beginning number of shares}}. \tag{6-8}$$

Note that the beginning value of debt could be zero, so Equation 6-8 is general in the sense that it could apply to any analysis, zero initial debt or not. In this section, we explain the logic of Equation 6-8, and we illustrate it with three different cases.

Example 1

Suppose we wish to determine what would happen to FSS's stock price if it went from zero debt to $4 million of debt. This requires us to find V_1 and P_1 with $4 million of debt:

$$V_1 = D_1 + S_1 = D_1 + \frac{(\text{EBIT} - k_d D)(1 - T)}{k_s}$$

$$= \$4,000,000 + \frac{(\$4,000,000 - \$332,000)(0.6)}{0.126}$$

$$= \$4,000,000 + \$17,466,667 = \$21,466,667.$$

$$P_1 = \frac{\text{Ending value} - \text{Beginning debt}}{\text{Beginning shares}} = \frac{\$21,466,667 - \$0}{1,000,000}$$

$$= \$21.47, \text{ versus } P_0 = \$20 \text{ with zero debt.}$$

As explained previously, this stock price would exist *as soon as investors learned of the recapitalization plans, before the plans were actually carried out.* Stockholders would recognize that the company will have a value of $21,466,667 very shortly, and this value will belong entirely to them because they will receive the $4,000,000 brought in by the sale of bonds as payment for shares repurchased. Note also that management must inform all stockholders of the planned recapitalization. If you were a stockholder, you would certainly not be willing to sell your stock back to the company at $20 per share if you expected to see the stock price rise to $21.47. You and the other stockholders would insist on receiving as much if you sold your stock back to the company as you would end up with if you chose not to sell it.[9]

Once the plan had been carried out, the shares outstanding would decline from 1,000,000 to 813,694:

$$\text{New shares} = \text{Old shares} - \text{Shares repurchased}$$
$$n_1 = n_0 - \text{Shares repurchased}$$
$$= n_0 - \frac{\text{Incremental debt}}{\text{Price per share}}$$
$$= 1,000,000 - \frac{\$4,000,000}{\$21.47}$$
$$= 1,000,000 - 186,306$$
$$= 813,694 \text{ shares after repurchase.}$$

Check on stock price:

$$P_1 = \frac{\text{New value of equity}}{\text{New shares outstanding}} = \frac{S_1}{n_1} = \frac{\$17,466,667}{813,694} = \$21.47.$$

Had we made similar calculations, but used $6 million of debt, the resulting stock price would have been $21.73 as shown in Table 6-2.

Example 2

Now assume that FSS actually made the move to $4 million of debt, and management is now considering another increase in leverage. What would happen to FSS's stock price if it increased its leverage from $4 million to $6 million of debt? Assume that its old debt must be retired if new debt is issued, so the entire $6 million of debt will have a cost of 9 percent (from Figure 6-5). Now the analysis will begin with these initial values:

---

[9]Indeed, if you and other stockholders were silly enough to sell at $20 per share, then the $4 million of debt could be used to buy and retire even more shares, so the remaining shares would be worth even more than $21.47. In fact, the stock would, under these conditions, be worth $21.83:

$$P_1 = \frac{S_1}{n_1} = \frac{\$17,466,667}{1,000,000 - (\$4,000,000/\$20)} = \$21.83.$$

Of course, you might be afraid that the recapitalization plan would fall through, so you might be willing to sell out for slightly less than $21.47, say for $21, figuring that $21 in the hand is better than $21.47 in the bush.

$$\text{Initial debt value} = D_0 = \$4,000,000.$$
$$\text{Initial stock value} = S_0 = \$17,466,667.$$
$$\text{Initial total value} = V_0 = \$21,466,667.$$
$$\text{Initial stock price} = P_0 = \$21.47.$$
$$\text{Initial number of shares} = n_0 = 813,694.$$

The new equilibrium total value will be

$$V_1 = D_1 + S_1$$

$$= \$6,000,000 + \frac{(\$4,000,000 - \$540,000)(0.6)}{0.132}$$

$$= \$6,000,000 + \$15,727,272 = \$21,727,272,$$

and the new equilibrium stock price will be

$$P_1 = \frac{V_1 - D_0}{n_0} = \frac{\$21,727,272 - \$4,000,000}{813,694}$$

$$= \frac{\$17,727,272}{813,694} = \$21.79.$$

Thus, FSS could increase the value of its stock from $21.47 to $21.79 by increasing its leverage from $4 million to $6 million.[10] This second round of debt financing would increase the stockholders' gain by ($21.79 − $21.47)813,694 = $260,382.

Example 3

Now assume that FSS again plans to increase its leverage from $4 million to $6 million, but that the old debt need not be retired. Here, the $4 million in old debt would remain in force, carrying a coupon rate of 8.3 percent. As before, assume that the new debt issue of $2 million would have a cost of 9 percent. Assuming the same initial values as in Example 2, the new equilibrium values are calculated as follows:

$$\textbf{1. } S_1 = \frac{\left[\text{EBIT} - \binom{\text{Cost of}}{\text{old debt}}\binom{\text{Amount of}}{\text{old debt}} - \binom{\text{Cost of}}{\text{new debt}}\binom{\text{Amount of}}{\text{new debt}}\right](1 - T)}{k_s}$$

$$= \frac{[\$4,000,000 - (0.083)(\$4,000,000) - (0.09)(\$2,000,000)](0.6)}{0.132}$$

$$= \frac{(\$3,488,000)(0.6)}{0.132} = \$15,854,545.$$

---

[10]Notice the slight difference in equilibrium stock prices at $6 million of debt: $21.73 in the first example versus $21.79 now. This difference demonstrates two points: (1) If FSS could move to its optimal capital structure in stages, it could repurchase shares at a lower average price than the equilibrium price of $21.73, and (2) if it could buy back shares at a lower price, its final price would be higher because more shares could be repurchased for a given expenditure (debt raised), and hence fewer shares would be outstanding in the end.

2. The old debt has a book value of $4,000,000. However, because more debt is to be issued, the risk of the old debt will rise and consequently its market value will fall to $3,688,889:

$$D_0' = \frac{0.083(\$4,000,000)}{0.09} = \$3,688,889.$$

3. The loss suffered by the old bondholders is $311,111:

$$D_0 - D_0' = \$4,000,000 - \$3,688,889 = \$311,111.$$

4. The new value of the firm will be

$$V_1 = D_1 + S_1 = D_0' + \text{New debt} + S_1$$
$$= \$3,688,889 + \$2,000,000 + \$15,854,545$$
$$= \$21,543,434.$$

5. The new equilibrium stock price will be

$$P_1 = \frac{\$21,543,434 - \$3,688,889}{813,694} = \$21.943.$$

6. The stockholders will have an aggregate gain calculated as follows:

$$\text{Stockholders' gain} = (P_1 - P_0)n_0$$
$$= (\$21.943 - \$21.467)(813,694)$$
$$= \$387,318.$$

7. Of the stockholders' $387,318 gain, $311,111 will have "come out of the hides of the old bondholders," while $76,207 will have come as a "true gain from leverage" as a result of tax savings net of costs associated with financial distress:

$$\text{True gain from leverage} = V_1 - V_0$$
$$= \$21,543,434 - \$21,466,667$$
$$= \$76,767.$$

(There are rounding errors in these calculations.)

Thus, FSS could increase the value of its stock from $21.47 to $21.94 by increasing its leverage from $4 million to $6 million if it did not have to refund its initial lower-cost debt. Of course, this gain to stockholders would come mostly at the expense of the old bondholders. The addition of $2 million of new debt would increase the riskiness of all the firm's securities. The stockholders would be compensated, as would the new bondholders, but the old bondholders would still be receiving coupon payments of only 8.3 percent, even though the new debt increased the riskiness of FSS's bonds to the point where $k_d = 9\%$.[11] Therefore, the value of the old debt would fall, and there would be a transfer of wealth from the old bondholders to FSS's stockholders. Because of the possibility of such events, bond indentures generally limit the amount of debt a firm can issue.

The Effect of Financial Leverage on EPS

Thus far we have focused on the impact of leverage on a firm's total value and its stock price. Before we leave the FSS illustration, we should also take a look at how leverage affects earnings per share (EPS); this is done in Table 6-3. The top third of the table gives operating income data. It begins by recognizing that FSS's future EBIT is not known with certainty. Expected EBIT is $4 million, but the realized EBIT could be less than or greater than $4 million. To simplify matters, we have assumed a discreet distribution of sales, and hence EBIT, with only three possible outcomes. Notice that here EBIT is assumed not to depend on financial leverage.[12]

The middle third of Table 6-3 shows the situation that would exist if FSS continues to use no debt. Net income after taxes is divided by the 1 million shares outstanding to calculate EPS. If sales were as low as $10 million, EPS would be zero, but EPS would rise to $4.80 at sales of $30 million.

The EPS at each sales level is next multiplied by the probability of that sales level to obtain the expected EPS, which is $2.40 if FSS uses no debt. We also calculate the standard deviation of EPS and its coefficient of variation to get an idea of the firm's total risk at a zero debt ratio: $\sigma_{EPS} = \$1.52$, and $CV_{EPS} = 0.63$.

The lower third of Table 6-3 shows the financial results that would occur if the company decided to use $10 million of debt. The interest rate on the debt, 12 percent, is taken from Figure 6-5. With $10 million of 12 percent debt outstanding, the company's interest expense is $1.2 million per year. This is a fixed cost, and it is deducted from EBIT as calculated in the top section. Next, taxes are taken out, and we work on down to the EPS figures that would result at each sales level. With $10 million of debt, EPS would be $-\$1.37$ if sales were as low as $10 million; it

---

[11]The $2 million of additional debt might actually have a cost somewhat below 9 percent. This is because retention of the old debt at 8.3 percent would result in lower total interest payments at the new debt level than if the entire $6 million of debt had cost 9 percent. Given equal business risk, the lower interest payments would lower the probability of financial distress, and thus lower the riskiness of the new debt. Additionally, lower distress risk would mean that equity holders might have a required return somewhat less than the 13.2 percent indicated in Table 6-2. However, these gains all come at the expense of the existing bondholders—the addition of new debt makes the old debt more risky, yet the old debtholders will not be compensated for the additional risk. Our analysis does not include these effects; they would, of course, be extremely hard to measure with any degree of confidence.

[12]As we discussed earlier, capital structure does affect EBIT at very high debt levels. For example, we assumed that FSS's EBIT would fall from $4 million to $3.52 million if the level of debt rose to $14 million. However, debt in Table 6-3 is limited to $10 million, so the "excessive leverage effect on EBIT" is not present in this particular example.

Table 6-3
FSS's EPS at Different Amounts of Debt
(Millions of Dollars Except per Share Figures)

Operating Income (EBIT)

Probability of indicated sales	0.2	0.6	0.2
Sales	$10.00	$20.00	$30.00
Fixed costs	4.00	4.00	4.00
Variable costs (60% of sales)	6.00	12.00	18.00
Total costs (except interest)	$10.00	$16.00	$22.00
Earnings before interest and taxes (EBIT)	$ 0.00	$ 4.00	$ 8.00

Zero Debt

Less interest	$ 0.00	$ 0.00	$ 0.00
Earnings before taxes	0.00	4.00	8.00
Less taxes (40%)	0.00	1.60	3.20
Net income	$ 0.00	$ 2.40	$ 4.80
Earnings per share on 1 million shares (EPS)	$ 0.00	$ 2.40	$ 4.80
Expected EPS		$ 2.40	
Standard deviation of EPS[a]		$ 1.52	
Coefficient of variation of EPS[a]		0.63	

$10 Million of Debt

Less interest (0.12 × $10,000,000)	$ 1.20	$ 1.20	$ 1.20
Earnings before taxes	(1.20)	2.80	6.80
Less taxes (40%)[b]	(0.48)	1.12	2.72
Net income	($ 0.72)	$ 1.68	$ 4.08
Earnings per share on 524,940 shares (EPS)[c]	($ 1.37)	$ 3.20	$ 7.77
Expected EPS		$ 3.20	
Standard deviation of EPS[a]		$ 2.90	
Coefficient of variation of EPS[a]		0.91	

[a]Procedures for calculating the standard deviation and the coefficient of variation were discussed in Chapter 2.

[b]Assume tax credit on losses. If credits were not available, expected EPS would be lower, and risk higher, at high debt levels.

[c]Shares outstanding is determined as follows:

$$\text{Shares} = \text{Original shares} - \frac{\text{Debt}}{\text{Stock price}} = 1,000,000 - \frac{\text{Debt}}{\text{Stock price}},$$

where the stock price is taken from Table 6-2, Column 6. With $10 million of debt, P = $21.05. After the recapitalization, 524,940 shares will remain outstanding:

$$\text{Shares} = 1,000,000 - \frac{\$10,000,000}{\$21.05} = 524,940.$$

EPS figures can also be calculated using this formula:

$$\text{EPS} = \frac{(\text{EBIT} - k_d D)(1 - T)}{\text{Original shares} - \text{Debt/Price}}.$$

For example, at D = $10 million,

$$\text{EPS} = \frac{[\$4,000,000 - (0.12)(10,000,000)](0.6)}{1,000,000 - \$10,000,000/\$21.05} = \frac{\$1,680,000}{524,940} = \$3.20.$$

Figure 6-7
**Probability Distribution of EPS for FSS with
Different Amounts of Financial Leverage**

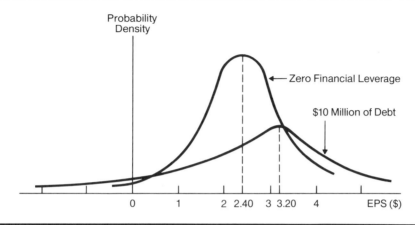

would rise to $3.20 if sales were $20 million; and it would soar to $7.77 if sales were as high as $30 million.

Continuous approximations of the EPS distributions under the two financial structures are graphed in Figure 6-7. Although expected EPS is much higher if the firm uses financial leverage, the graph makes it clear that the risk of low or even negative EPS is also higher if debt is used. Figure 6-7 shows clearly that using leverage involves a risk/return tradeoff—higher leverage increases expected earnings per share, but using more leverage also increases the firm's risk. It is this increasing risk that causes k_s and k_d to increase at higher amounts of financial leverage.

The relationship between expected EPS and financial leverage is plotted in the top section of Figure 6-8. Here we see that expected EPS first rises as the use of debt increases—interest charges rise, but a smaller number of shares outstanding as debt is substituted for equity still causes EPS to increase. However, EPS peaks when $12 million of debt is used. Beyond this amount, interest rates rise rapidly, and EBIT begins to fall, so EPS is depressed in spite of the falling number of shares outstanding. Risk, as measured by the coefficient of variation of EPS shown in column 4 of the data in Figure 6-8, rises continuously, and at an increasing rate, as debt is substituted for equity.

Does the same amount of debt maximize both price and EPS? The answer is *no*. As we can see from the lower graph in Figure 6-8, FSS's stock price is maximized with $6 million of debt, while expected EPS is maximized by using $12 million of debt. *Since management is primarily interested in maximizing the value of the stock, the optimal capital structure calls for the use of $6 million of debt.*

Figure 6-8
**Relationship between FSS's
Expected EPS and Stock Price**

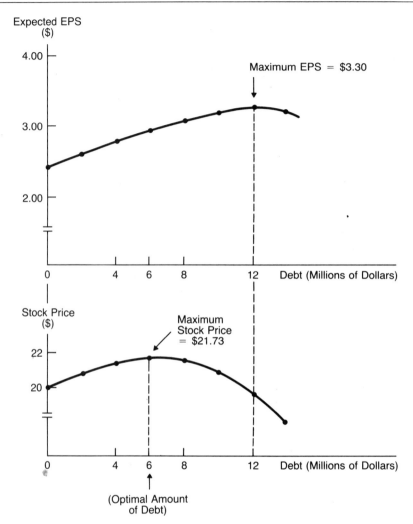

Debt	Expected EPS	Standard Deviation of EPS	Coefficient of Variation	Stock Price
$ 0	$2.40[a]	$1.52[a]	0.63[a]	$20.00
2,000,000	2.55	1.68	0.66	20.89
4,000,000	2.70	1.87	0.69	21.47
6,000,000	2.87	2.09	0.73	21.73
8,000,000	3.04	2.40	0.80	21.71
10,000,000	3.20[a]	2.90[a]	0.91[a]	21.05
12,000,000	3.30	3.83	1.16	19.86
14,000,000	3.26	5.20	1.60	17.16

[a]These values are taken from Table 6-3. Values at other debt levels were calculated similarly. Stock prices are from Table 6-2.

Problems with the FSS Analysis

The Forman Software Systems example illustrated the effects of leverage on firm value, stock prices, earnings per share, and debt values. However, the example was obviously simplified to facilitate the discussion, and we cannot overemphasize the difficulties that are encountered when one attempts to use this type of analysis in practice. First, the capitalization rates (k_d and especially k_s) are very difficult to estimate. The cost of debt at different debt levels can generally be estimated with some degree of confidence, but cost of equity estimates must be viewed as very rough approximations.[13]

Second, the mathematics of the valuation process make the outcomes very sensitive to the input estimates. Thus, fairly small errors in the estimates of k_d, k_s, and EBIT can lead to large errors in estimated EPS and stock price.

Third, our example was restricted to the case of a no-growth firm. In view of the input requirements to model even a simple no-growth situation, and the still greater requirements for the growth model, it is unrealistic to think that a precise optimal capital structure can really be identified.

Finally, many firms are not publicly owned, and that causes still more difficulties. If a privately held firm's owner never plans to have his or her firm go public, then potential market value data are really irrelevant. However, an analysis based on market values for a privately owned firm is very useful if the owner is interested in knowing how the firm's market value would be affected by leverage should the decision be made to go public.

SOME CONSIDERATIONS IN THE CAPITAL STRUCTURE DECISION

Since one cannot determine precisely the optimal capital structure, managers must apply judgment along with quantitative analysis. The judgmental analysis involves several different factors, and in one situation a particular factor might have great importance, while the same factor might be relatively unimportant in another situation. This section discusses some of the more important judgmental issues that should be taken into account.

Long-Run Viability

Managers of large firms, especially those providing vital services such as electricity or telephone service, have a responsibility to provide *continuous* service, so they must refrain from using leverage to the point where the firm's long-run viability is

---

[13]The statistical relationship between k_s and financial leverage has been studied extensively by using both cross-sectional and time series data. In the cross-sectional studies, a sample of firms is analyzed, with multiple regression techniques used in an attempt to "hold constant" all factors other than financial leverage that might influence k_s. The general conclusion of the cross-sectional studies is that k_s rises as leverage increases, but statistical problems preclude us from specifying the functional relationship with much confidence.

In the time series studies, a single firm's k_s is analyzed over time in an attempt to see how k_s changes in response to changes in its debt ratio. Here again, "other factors" do not remain constant, so it is impossible to specify exactly how k_s is affected by financial leverage.

endangered. Long-run viability may conflict with short-run stock price maximization and cost of capital minimization.[14]

Managerial Conservatism

Well-diversified investors have eliminated most, if not all, of the diversifiable risk from their portfolios. Therefore, the typical investor can tolerate some chance of financial distress, because a loss on one stock would probably be offset by random gains on other stocks in his or her portfolio. However, managers generally view potential distress with more concern—they are typically not well diversified, and their careers, thus the present value of their expected earnings, can be seriously affected by the onset of financial distress. Thus, it is not difficult to imagine that managers might be more "conservative" in their use of leverage than the average stockholder would desire. If this is true, then managers would set somewhat lower target capital structures than the ones which maximize the expected stock prices. The managers of a publicly owned firm would never admit this, for unless they owned voting control, they would quickly be removed from office. However, in view of the uncertainties about what constitutes the value-maximizing structure, management could always say that the target capital structure employed is, in its judgment, the value-maximizing structure, and it would be difficult to prove otherwise.[15]

Lender and Rating Agency Attitudes

Regardless of a manager's own analysis of the proper leverage for his or her firm, there is no question but that lenders' and rating agencies' attitudes are frequently important determinants of financial structures. In the majority of cases, the corporation discusses its financial structure with lenders and rating agencies, and gives much weight to their advice. Also, if a particular firm's management is so confident of the future that it seeks to use leverage beyond the norms for its industry, its lenders may be unwilling to accept such debt increases, or may do so only at a high price.

One of the primary measures of the risk of financial distress used by lenders and rating agencies is *coverage ratios*. Accordingly, managements give considerable weight to such ratios as the *times-interest-earned (TIE) ratio*, which is defined as EBIT divided by total interest charges. The lower this ratio, the higher is the probability that a firm will encounter financial distress.

---

[14]Recognizing this fact, most public service commissions require utilities to obtain their approval before issuing long-term securities, and Congress has empowered the SEC to supervise the capital structures of public utility holding companies. However, in addition to concern over the firms' safety, which suggests low debt ratios, both managers and regulators recognize a need to keep all costs as low as possible, including the cost of capital. Since a firm's capital structure affects its cost of capital, regulatory commissions and utility managers try to select capital structures that minimize utilities' cost of capital, subject to the constraint that a firm's ability to finance needed construction projects is not endangered.

[15]It is, of course, possible for a particular manager to be less conservative than his or her firm's average stockholder. However, this condition is less likely to occur than is excessive managerial conservatism, which is just another manifestation of the agency problem. If excessive conservatism exists, then managers, as agents of the stockholders, are not acting in the best interests of their principals.

Table 6-4
**FSS's Expected Times-Interest-Earned Ratio
at Different Amounts of Debt**

Amounts of Debt (in Millions)	Expected TIE[a]
$ 0	Undefined
2	25.0
4	12.1
6	7.4
8	5.0
10	3.3
12	2.2

[a]TIE = EBIT/Interest. Example: TIE = $4,000,000/$1,200,000 = 3.3 at $10 million of debt. Data are from Table 6-1 and Figure 6-5.

Table 6-4 shows how FSS's expected TIE ratio declines as its use of debt increases. When only $2 million of debt is used, the expected TIE is a high 25 times, but the interest coverage ratio declines rapidly as debt rises. Note, however, that these coverages are expected values—the actual TIE will be higher if sales exceed the expected $20 million level, but lower if sales fall below $20 million.

The variability of the TIE ratio is highlighted in Figure 6-9, which shows the probability distributions of the ratio at $8 million and $12 million of debt. The expected TIE is much higher if only $8 million of debt is used. Even more important, with less debt there is a much lower probability of a TIE of less than 1.0, the level at which the firm is not earning enough to meet its required interest payment and thus becomes seriously exposed to the threat of bankruptcy.

Another ratio that is often used by lenders and rating agencies is the *fixed charge coverage (FCC) ratio*. This is a more precise measure than the TIE ratio because it recognizes that there are fixed charges other than interest payments which could lead to financial distress. The FCC ratio is defined as follows:

$$FCC = \frac{EBIT + \text{Lease payments}}{Interest + \left(\begin{array}{c}\text{Lease} \\ \text{payments}\end{array}\right) + \left(\dfrac{\text{Sinking fund payments}}{1 - T}\right)}.$$

Note that this definition "grosses up" the sinking fund payments in recognition of the fact that these payments must be made with after-tax dollars (net income) because sinking fund payments are not tax deductible.

If FSS had $1 million of lease payments and $1 million of sinking fund payments, its FCC ratio at a debt level of $10 million would be 1.3:

$$FCC = \frac{\$4,000,000 + \$1,000,000}{\$1,200,000 + \$1,000,000 + \dfrac{\$1,000,000}{0.6}}$$

$$= \frac{\$5,000,000}{\$3,866,667} = 1.3.$$

Figure 6-9
**Probability Distributions of Times-Interest-Earned Ratio
for FSS with Different Capital Structures**

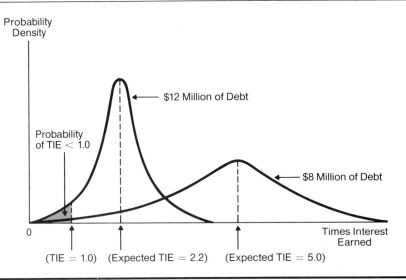

Thus, the coverage of total fixed charges is considerably less than the 3.3 times-interest-earned coverage at the $10 million debt level.

Business Risk

We have seen that a firm's overall risk is a function of both business risk and financial risk. If management decides that overall risk should not exceed certain limits, then the company can take on more financial risk if it lowers its business risk, and vice versa. Accordingly, factors such as sales stability and operating leverage, which influence business risk, also influence firms' optimal capital structures.

Reserve Borrowing Capacity

When we discussed the information asymmetry theory in Chapter 5, we noted that firms should attempt to maintain the capacity to issue debt at all times. For example, suppose Firm Y had just successfully completed an R&D program, and its internal projections showed much higher earnings in the immediate future. However, the new earnings are not yet anticipated by investors, and hence are not reflected in the price of its stock. Firm Y would not want to issue stock—it would prefer to finance with debt until the higher earnings materialized and were reflected in the stock price, at which time it could sell an issue of common stock, retire the debt, and return to its target capital structure. Similarly, if the financial manager felt that interest rates were temporarily low, but likely to rise fairly soon, he or she might want to issue long-term bonds and thus "lock in" the favorable rates for many years. To maintain this reserve borrowing capacity, firms generally tend to use less debt under "normal" conditions, and hence to present a stronger financial picture, than they otherwise would. This is not suboptimal from a long-run standpoint, although it might appear so if viewed strictly on a short-run basis.

Note too that firms' debt contracts often specify that no new debt can be issued unless certain ratios exceed minimum levels. Very frequently, the TIE ratio is required to exceed 2 or 2.5 times as a condition for the issuance of additional debt. With this in mind, look back at Figure 6-9 and note that, if it used $12 million of debt, FSS's TIE would be less than 2.0 almost half the time, whereas the probability of a coverage less than 2.0 would be quite small if it used only $8 million of debt.

Control

The effect that its choice of securities has on a management's control position may also influence its capital structure decision. If a firm's management just barely has majority control (just over 50 percent of the stock), but it is not in a position to buy any more stock, debt may be the choice for new financings. On the other hand, a management group that is not concerned about voting control may decide to use equity rather than debt if the firm's financial situation is so weak that the use of debt might subject the company to serious risk of default. If the firm gets into serious difficulties, the creditors (through covenants in the debt agreements) will assume control and perhaps force a management change. This has happened to Chrysler, International Harvester (now Navistar International), Braniff, Continental Illinois Bank, and a number of other companies in recent years. However, if too little debt is used, management runs the risk of a takeover, where some other company or management group tries to persuade stockholders to turn over control to the new group, which may plan to boost earnings and stock prices by using financial leverage. This recently happened to Lenox, the china company. In general, control considerations do not necessarily suggest the use of debt or of equity, but if management is at all insecure, the effects of capital structure on control will certainly be taken into account.

Additional Considerations

In addition to those factors just listed, the following considerations, which were discussed in detail in Chapter 5, are also relevant to the capital structure decision:

Asset Structure
Firms whose assets are suitable as security for loans tend to use debt rather heavily. Thus, real estate companies tend to be highly leveraged, but companies involved in technological research employ relatively little debt.

Growth Rate
Other factors the same, faster growing firms must rely more heavily on external capital—slow growth can be financed with retained earnings, but rapid growth generally requires the use of external funds. As postulated in the information asym-

metry theory, firms first turn to debt financing to meet external funding needs. Further, the flotation costs involved in selling common stock exceed those incurred when selling debt. Thus, rapidly growing firms tend to use somewhat more debt than do slower-growth companies.

Profitability
One often observes that firms with very high rates of return on investment use relatively little debt. This behavior is consistent with the information asymmetry theory, and the practical reason seems to be that highly profitable firms such as IBM, 3M, and Kodak simply do not need to do much debt financing—their high rates of return enable them to do most of their financing with retained earnings.

Taxes
Interest is a deductible expense, while dividends are not deductible; hence, the higher a firm's corporate tax rate, the greater is the advantage of using corporate debt.

AN APPROACH TO SETTING THE TARGET CAPITAL STRUCTURE

Thus far in Chapters 5 and 6, we have discussed (1) several theories of capital structure, (2) a method of analysis based on these theories (including a discussion of the very severe problems one encounters with such an application of the theory), and (3) a myriad of factors which influence the capital structure decisions of most firms. In this section, we describe a pragmatic approach to setting the target capital structure. Our approach requires judgmental assumptions, but it also allows managers to see how alternative capital structures would affect future profitability, coverage, and external financing requirements under a variety of assumptions.

The starting point for the analysis is a *Lotus 1-2-3* forecasting model that is set up to test the effects of capital structure changes. Here is a brief description of the model and how it has been used. Basically, the model generates forecasted data based on historical, or base year, data plus additional inputs supplied by the financial manager. Each data item can be fixed, or it can be allowed to vary from year to year. The required additional data, all of which represent either expectations or policy variables, include the following:

1. Annual growth rates in unit sales
2. Annual inflation rates
3. Corporate tax rate
4. Variable costs as a percentage of sales
5. Fixed costs
6. Interest rate on already outstanding (or embedded) debt
7. Marginal cost of common equity
8. Marginal cost of debt

9. Capital structure ratios
10. Dividend growth rate
11. Long-term dividend payout ratio

The model uses the input data to forecast balance sheets and income statements for some specified number of years. Further, the model calculates and displays selected other information such as external financing requirements, ROE, EPS, DPS, times interest earned, stock price, and WACC on an annual basis.

The financial manager begins by entering base year values and data on expected unit sales growth rates, expected inflation rates, and so on. This input is used by the model to forecast operating income and asset requirements which, in general, will be independent of the financing decision. Next, the financial manager must consider the financing mix. Our model permits as inputs both the debt/equity mix and the debt maturity mix. By debt maturity mix, we mean the proportion of short-term versus long-term debt. Further, the manager must consider the effects of the capital structure on the component costs, and then must enter those cost rates. We would expect that a higher debt ratio would increase the costs of all components, and vice versa if less debt were used. With all inputs entered, the model then completes the forecasted financial statements and generates projected stock prices.

Then, the model's output must be reviewed and analyzed. Since we are focusing on the capital structure decision, we would pay particular attention to the forecasted EPS, coverage, and external funding requirements as well as the projected stock price. Finally, the model is used to analyze alternative scenarios. This analysis takes two forms: (1) changing the financing inputs to get some idea of how the financing mix affects the key outputs, and (2) changing the operating inputs to see how the basic business risk of the firm affects the key outputs under various financing strategies.

The model can generate the output from the scenario analyses quite easily, but it remains up to the financial manager to assign input values, to interpret the output, and finally to set the target capital structure. The final decision is based on all the factors we have discussed in Chapters 5 and 6, and the decision-maker must judge which factors are most relevant to his or her firm. Reaching a decision is not easy, but a capital structure forecasting model such as the one we use at least permits the analysis of the effects of alternative courses of action, which is an essential element of good decision making.

It should be noted that, although capital structure decisions do affect the prices of companies' stocks, those effects are relatively small in comparison to the effects of operating decisions. A company's ability to identify (or create) market opportunities, and to produce and sell products efficiently, determine its success. Its financial arrangements can facilitate or hamper operations, but the best of financial plans cannot overcome deficiencies in the operations area. These statements are supported by empirical studies, which generally find a weak statistical relationship between capital structure and stock prices. The statements are also supported by runs of our computer model, which shows stock prices to be affected significantly by changes in unit sales, sales prices, fixed costs, and variable costs, but not affected much by changes in capital structure. This last point can also be seen from the FSS example discussed above. Refer again to Table 6-2. Forman Software Systems' stock price is maximized at a D/V ratio of 27.6 percent. However, at a much lower D/V of 18.6 percent, the firm's stock price drops only from $21.73 to $21.47, or by a slight 1.2 percent, while if D/V rises to 36.8 percent, FSS's stock price hardly drops at all. Thus, FSS could set its target D/V ratio anywhere in the range from 18.6 to 36.8 percent and still be very close to maximizing firm value. That appears to be a typical situation.

SOME ADDITIONAL INSIGHTS INTO CAPITAL STRUCTURE DECISIONS

At this point, one might have an uneasy feeling regarding both how to establish an optimal capital structure and its effect. We know that we can construct models which generate projected earnings, stock prices, coverage ratios, and so on under different capital structures. However, our confidence in these results is limited, because we do not know for sure how k_d and k_s, and hence P_0, will really change with changes in the capital structure. We also know that in practice a myriad of more or less subjective factors also influence the decision. Therefore, to complete our discussion of the target capital structure, it seems appropriate to take a look at how managers say they actually establish target capital structures.

Professors David Scott and Dana Johnson surveyed a group of large firms to find out how management attempts to locate the optimal capital structure, or even whether management believes that one can be determined.[16] Scott and Johnson sent questionnaires to the chief financial officer (CFO) of each Fortune 1,000 firm. Although only 212 financial managers replied, the sample was still large enough to provide useful insights into the operational decision process.

First, the respondents did report a belief that capital structure decisions matter—in general, financial managers believe that the prudent use of debt can lower the firm's overall cost of capital, and that excessive use of debt can increase the required rate of return on equity. Second, the most popular measures of financial leverage are (1) the long-term debt to total capitalization ratio,[17] (2) the times-interest-earned (TIE) ratio, and (3) the long-term debt to common equity ratio. However, when computing these ratios, accounting (or book) values rather than market values were almost always used. Third, 64 percent of the responding managers indicated that their firms' target long-term debt to total capitalization ratios were in the range of 26 to 40 percent, and the most popular reported target range was 26 to 30 percent. (Because stock market values generally exceed book values, the debt ratio measured in market value terms would be quite a bit lower than the reported book value figures.)

---

[16]See David F. Scott and Dana J. Johnson, "Financing Policies and Practices in Large Corporations," *Financial Management*, Summer 1982, 51-59.

[17]Total capitalization is defined as long-term debt plus preferred stock plus common equity. Therefore, current liabilities are excluded.

The survey also gathered data on the influence of various parties on the capital structure decision. The data indicate that the firm's own managers give the greatest weight to their own internal analyses, but that investment bankers and bond rating agencies also have a significant influence. Additionally, firms do consider industry averages when setting their target capital structures, but they are quite willing to depart from these averages if their own conditions suggest that a departure is warranted.

VARIATIONS IN CAPITAL STRUCTURES AMONG FIRMS

As might be expected, wide variations in the use of financial leverage occur both among industries and among the individual firms in each industry. Table 6-5 illustrates differences for selected industries, ranked in descending order of common equity ratios as shown in Column 5.[18]

The drug and electronics companies do not use much debt; these companies have generally been quite profitable, and hence able to finance through retained earnings, and the uncertainties inherent in industries that are oriented toward research and subject to huge product liability suits render the heavy use of leverage unwise. Retailers, steel, and utility companies, on the other hand, use debt relatively heavily, but for different reasons. Retailers use short-term debt to finance inventories and long-term debt secured by mortgages on their stores. The steel companies have been losing money in recent years, and these losses have eroded their equity positions and also made it difficult for them to sell new common stock. Therefore, the steel companies have been forced to borrow (at relatively high interest rates) to modernize their plants, and the result is a high debt ratio and an average coverage of less than 1.0. The utilities have traditionally used large amounts of debt—their fixed assets make good security for mortgage bonds, and their relatively stable sales make it safe for them to carry more debt than would be true for firms with more business risk.

Particular attention should be given to the times-interest-earned ratio. This ratio is a function of (1) financial leverage and (2) profitability. Generally, the least-levered industries, such as the drug companies, have the highest coverage ratios, while industries such as steel, which had profit problems in 1984, have low ratios.

Wide variations in capital structures also exist among firms within given industries—for example, although the average common equity ratio in 1984 for the drug industry was 78.4 percent, Upjohn's equity ratio was only 66.4 percent, but Bristol-Myers' ratio was near 90 percent. Thus, factors unique to individual firms, including managerial attitudes, do play an important role in setting target capital structures.

---

[18]Information on capital structures and financial strength is available from a multitude of sources. We used the *Compustat* data tapes to develop Table 6-5, but other published sources include *The Value Line Investment Survey, Robert Morris Associates Annual Studies*, and *Dun & Bradstreet Key Business Ratios*.

Table 6-5
Capital Structure Percentages, 1984:
Selected Industries Ranked by Common Equity Ratios

Industry	Short-Term Debt (1)	Long-Term Debt (2)	Total Debt (3)	Preferred Stock (4)	Common Equity (5)	Times-Interest-Earned Ratio (6)
Drugs	9.0%	12.5%	21.5%	0.1%	78.4%	9.1 ×
Electrical/electronics	7.8	15.4	23.2	1.5	75.3	6.9
Automotive	5.0	19.0	24.0	2.0	74.0	7.6
Retailing	14.7	32.1	46.8	1.4	51.8	3.1
Utilities (electric, gas and telephone)	2.5	45.9	48.4	6.8	44.8	3.2
Steel	4.5	48.5	53.0	3.0	44.0	0.9
Composite (average of all industries, not just those listed above)	18.3%	31.8%	50.1%	2.7%	47.2%	2.3 ×

Note: These ratios are based on accounting (or book) values. Stated on a market value basis, the equity percentages would rise because most stocks sell at prices that are much higher than their book values.

Source: *Compustat* Industrial Data Tape, 1985.

BOOK WEIGHTS VERSUS MARKET WEIGHTS

In Chapter 4, we calculated the weighted average cost of capital with market value rather than book value weights. Further, in our discussions of capital structure in Chapter 5 we continued to focus on market value, not book value. However, survey data indicate that financial managers generally focus on book value structures. Thus, there seems to be a conflict between academic theory and business practice. Here are some thoughts on this issue:

1. If stocks and bonds do not sell exactly at book value—and they almost never do—then it is impossible for a growing firm to establish and maintain at constant levels a target book value and a target market value capital structure. The firm could stay on its book value target or on its market value target, but not on both. To illustrate, assume that a company has, at book value, $50 million of debt and $50 million of equity, for a total book value of $100 million. However, its stock sells at twice book. Here is the capital structure situation, with dollars in millions:

	Book Value		Market Value	
Debt	$ 50	50%	$ 50	33%
Equity	50	50	100	67
Total	$100	100%	$150	100%

Now suppose the company needs to raise an additional $50 million. If it sells $25 million of debt and $25 of common stock, it will add these amounts to its balance sheet, so its book value capital structure will remain constant. However, adding $25 million to both debt and equity will cause its market value capital structure to change. On the other hand, if it raises $16.7 million as debt and $33.3 million as equity, its market value capital structure will remain constant, but its book value structure will change. Thus, it can maintain either its book value or its market value capital structure, but not both.

2. Book values, as reported on balance sheets, reflect the historical cost of assets. At times, historical costs have little to do with assets' current earning power, with the actual value of these assets, or with their ability to produce cash flows which can be used to service debt. Market values would, almost always, better reflect earning power, cash generation, and debt service ability.

3. As we have repeatedly noted throughout this chapter and the last one, the point of capital structure analysis is to find that capital structure which maximizes the firm's market value, and hence its stock price. Since this optimum is defined in terms of stock prices, it can only be determined by an analysis of market values.

4. Now suppose a firm found its optimal market value structure, but then financed so as to maintain a constant book value structure. This would lead to a departure from value maximization. Therefore, if a firm is growing, it must finance so as to hold constant its market value structure. That will, as we just saw, normally lead to a change in the book value structure.

5. Since the firm should, to keep its value at a maximum, finance so as to hold its market value structure constant, the weighted average cost of capital, k_a, should be found using market value weights.

6. Business executives prefer stability and predictability to volatility and uncertainty. Book values are far more predictable than market values. Further, a financial manager can set a target book value capital structure and then attain it, right on the money. It would be virtually impossible to maintain a target market value structure because of bond and stock price fluctuations. This is one reason why executives focus on book value structures rather than more logical market value structures. Also, many financial executives have accounting backgrounds, and accountants focus on accounting numbers. However, as financial executives gain a knowledge of financial (as opposed to accounting) theory, the focus should shift more toward market values.

7. For purposes of developing the weighted average cost of capital, we strongly recommend the use of market value weights. However, if a company does focus on a book value capital structure, and does seek to maintain that structure, then it will finance in accordance with book value weights, and in this case its weighted average cost of capital should be based on book weights.

8. Some executives have argued against the use of market value weights on the grounds that as stock prices change, so would capital structure weights, with the result being a volatile cost of capital. This argument is incorrect. The cost of capital should be based on *target* weights, and not the actual capital structure, and there is no reason to think that a target market value structure would be any less stable than a target book value structure. In fact, as we discuss later, target market value weights are probably more stable than target book weights.

9. Now consider a fairly typical situation. Firm X currently has a 50/50 debt/equity ratio at book, and a 33/67 ratio at market. It targets on the book value ratio. Several years go by. Inflation occurs, so new assets cost more. Output prices are based on marginal costs, which have risen because of inflation. With the new, higher prices, the rate of return on old assets increases, as does the value of the old assets, and the firm's stock price rises. Book values per share are relatively stable, so the increasing stock price leads to an increase in the market/book ratio. Debt values, on the other hand, remain close to book. Rising stock prices, when combined with stable bond prices, could cause the market value debt/equity ratio to remain constant at the 33/67 level, or even to increase, even though the firm finances on a 50/50 basis.

10. Note also that, under our scenario, the rising ROE will lead to improved coverages. This fact, together with analysts' knowledge that the firm's book asset values are understated, will support an increase in the debt ratio measured at book.

11. The situation just described has been occurring in the United States in recent years. ROEs have moved up sharply (from about 13 percent in the early 1970s to well over 15 percent in the 1980s). Debt/equity ratios at book have gone up from about 33/67 to close to 50/50, while debt/equity ratios at market have remained fairly constant. Thus, it appears that companies have actually been keeping their market value capital structures stable, in spite of the fact that executives say they target on book value ratios.

What can we conclude from all this? We are absolutely convinced that the procedures we recommend are correct—namely, firms should focus on market value capital structures and base their cost of capital calculations on market value weights. Because market values do change, it would be impossible to keep the capital structure on target at all times, but this fact in no way detracts from the validity of market value targets.

SUMMARY

In this chapter, we examined the way in which firms actually establish target capital structures. We began by defining (1) *business risk*, which is the riskiness of the firm if it uses no debt, and (2) *financial risk*, which is the additional risk placed on the common stockholders as a result of debt financing. Business risk and financial risk can be viewed from either a total risk or market risk standpoint; we examined both.

We next examined the effects of financial leverage on stock prices, earnings per share, and the cost of capital. Our analysis suggests that an *optimal capital structure*—one which simultaneously maximizes the firm's total market value and stock price while minimizing its average cost of capital—exists for each firm. However, although it is theoretically possible to determine the optimal capital structure, as a practical matter we cannot estimate this structure with precision. Accordingly, financial executives generally treat the optimal capital structure as a range—for example, 40 to 50 percent debt—rather than as a precise point, such as 45 percent debt. Also, we saw that financial executives analyze the effects of different capital structures on expected earnings per share and interest coverage ratios, and they also tend to analyze such factors as business risk, asset structure, effects on control, and so on. Finally, the optimal capital structure should be thought of in market value rather than book value terms, even though managers often seem to pay more attention to book than to market values. In the final analysis, the final target capital structure is more judgmentally than rigorously determined.

The International Perspective

In recent years, there has been considerable discussion in the popular press concerning the competitiveness of U.S. versus Japanese corporations. One factor that is often cited as an advantage to Japanese firms is their lower overall cost of capital. The key factor here is the fact that Japanese firms, on average, use far more debt than do their U.S. counterparts. This has led some critics of U.S. industry to suggest that our companies would be more competitive if they used significantly more debt. Why do firms in different countries employ different capital structures, and what effects do these differences have on economic efficiency?

Recent statistics reported by the Organization for Economic Cooperation and Development (OECD) show that, on average, Japanese firms have 85 percent debt-to-total assets ratios (in book value terms), German firms use 63 percent debt, and U.S. firms use only 37 percent. Of course, different countries have somewhat different accounting conventions, and hence it is difficult to draw definitive conclusions from the OECD statistics. The main problems arise from intercountry differences in accounting for historical costs, for the use of lease financing, and for pension plan funding. However, even after adjusting for these differences, we still find that companies in Japan and Germany use significantly more leverage than do U.S. companies.

Why do these leverage differences exist? The first candidate to come to mind is differential tax structures among the countries; there are significant intercountry differences in corporate and personal tax structures. However, interest payments on corporate debt are tax deductible in all three countries, and individuals in all countries must pay taxes on both stock and bond income, except that there are no capital gains taxes in either Germany or Japan. When one uses the Miller model to compare relative tax effects, it appears that the overall tax advantage of debt is greater for U.S. firms than for either Japanese or German firms. Thus, tax effects cannot explain why U.S. firms use so much less debt than their Japanese or German counterparts.

A second potential explanation for the observed capital structure difference is agency costs. In Chapter 1 we learned that agency costs arise from two agency relationships: (1) the relationship between shareholders and managers, and (2) the relationship between bondholders and shareholders. In the United States, equity agency costs are comparatively low—corporations produce quarterly reports, pay quarterly

dividends, and must comply with relatively stringent audit requirements. These equity features are not common to the other countries. Conversely, debt agency costs are probably lower in Germany and Japan than in the United States. In Germany and Japan, most debt consists of secured bank loans as opposed to publicly-issued bonds, and the banks are closely linked to their debtor corporations. Indeed, German and Japanese banks often (1) hold major equity positions in their debtor corporations, (2) hold in trust, and vote, the shares of many individual shareholders, and (3) have bank officers sit on the boards of the debtor corporations. Given these close relationships, the banks are directly involved in the operations of the debtor firms, and they would be hurt if the stocks plunged even if the debt remained secure. This suggests that German and Japanese banks might be more willing to bear with debtors in the event of financial distress than would bondholders in the United States, which in turn would enable German and Japanese firms to use more debt than their U.S. counterparts.

In summary, there are major differences in the ownership structures of firms in different countries, and these differences are reflected in the capital markets. There is no evidence that one structure is better or worse than another, but it is clear that institutional differences cause major differences in capital structures.

Questions and Problems

6-1 **(Business and financial risk: total)** Here are the estimated ROE distributions for Firms A, B, and C:

	Probability				
	0.1	0.2	0.4	0.2	0.1
Firm A: ROE_A	0.0%	5.0%	10.0%	15.0%	20.0%
Firm B: ROE_B	(2.0)	5.0	12.0	19.0	26.0
Firm C: ROE_C	(5.0)	5.0	15.0	25.0	35.0

a. Calculate the expected value and standard deviation for Firm C's ROE. $ROE_A = 10.0\%$, $\sigma_A = 6.3\%$, $ROE_B = 12.0\%$, $\sigma_B = 7.7\%$.

b. Discuss the relative riskiness of the three firms' returns. (Assume that these distributions are expected to remain constant over time.)

c. Now suppose all three firms have the same standard deviation of basic earning power (EBIT/Total assets), $\sigma_A = \sigma_B = \sigma_C = 6.3\%$. What can we tell about the financial risk of each firm?

6-2 **(Business and financial risk: market)** Air Tampa has just been incorporated, and its new board of directors is currently grappling with the question of optimal capital structure. The company plans to offer commuter air services between Tampa and smaller surrounding cities. Jaxair has been around for a few years, and it has about the same basic business risk as Air Tampa would have. Jaxair's market-determined beta is 1.8, and it has a current market value debt ratio (total debt/total assets) of 50 percent and a federal-plus-state tax rate of 40 percent. Air Tampa expects only to be marginally profitable at start up, and hence its tax rate would only be 25 percent. Air Tampa's owners expect that the total book and market value of the firm's stock, if it uses zero debt, would be $10 million.

    a. Estimate the beta of an unlevered firm in the commuter airline business based on Jaxair's market-determined beta. (Hint: Jaxair's market-determined beta is a levered beta. Use Equation 6-3a and solve for b_U.)

    b. Now assume that $k_{RF} = 10\%$ and $k_M = 15\%$. Find the required rate of return on equity for an unlevered commuter airline. What is the business risk premium for this industry?

    c. Air Tampa is considering three capital structures: (1) $2 million debt, (2) $4 million debt, and (3) $6 million debt. Estimate Air Tampa's k_s for these debt levels. What is the financial risk premium at each level?

    d. Calculate Air Tampa's k_s and financial risk premium at $6 million debt assuming its federal-plus-state tax rate is now 40 percent. Compare this with your corresponding answer to Part c. (Hint: The increase in the tax rate causes V_U to drop to $8 million.)

6-3 **(Capital structure analysis)** The following data reflect the current financial conditions of Davis Corporation:

Value of debt (book = market)	$1,000,000
Market value of equity	$5,257,143
Sales, last 12 months	$12,000,000
Variable operating costs (50% of sales)	$6,000,000
Fixed operating costs	$5,000,000
Tax rate, T (federal-plus-state)	40%

At the current level of debt, the cost of debt, k_d, is 8 percent and the cost of equity, k_s, is 10.5 percent. Management questions whether or not the capital structure is optimal, so the financial vice president has been asked to consider the possibility of issuing $1 million of additional debt and using the proceeds to repurchase stock. It is estimated that if the leverage were increased by raising the level of debt to $2 million, the interest rate on new debt would rise to 9 percent and k_s would rise to 11.5 percent. The old 8 percent debt is senior to the new debt, and it would remain outstanding, continue to yield 8 percent, and have a market value of $1 million. Davis is a zero-growth firm, with all of its earnings paid out as dividends.

    a. Should Davis increase its debt to $2 million?

b. If the firm decided to increase its level of debt to $3 million, its cost of the additional $2 million of debt would be 12 percent and k_s would rise to 15 percent. The original 8 percent of debt would again remain outstanding, and its market value would remain at $1 million. What level of debt should the firm choose: $1 million, $2 million, or $3 million?

c. The market price of Davis Corporation's stock was originally $20 per share. Calculate the new equilibrium stock prices at debt levels of $2 million and $3 million.

d. Calculate the firm's earnings per share if it uses debt of $1 million, $2 million, and $3 million. Assume that the firm pays out all of its earnings as dividends. If you find that EPS increases with more debt, does this mean that the firm should choose to increase its debt to $3 million, or possibly higher?

e. What would happen to the value of the old bonds if Davis uses more leverage and the old bonds are not senior to the new bonds?

6-4   **(Operating leverage)** Savannah Systems Inc., produces satellite earth stations, which sell for $100,000 each. Savannah's fixed costs are $2,000,000; 50 earth stations are produced and sold each year; profits total $500,000; and Savannah's assets (all equity financed) are $5,000,000. Savannah estimates that it can change its production process by increasing its fixed assets by $4,000,000. This change will (1) add $500,000 to fixed operating costs, (2) reduce variable costs per unit, V, by $10,000, and (3) increase output by 20 units, but (4) the sales price on all units will have to be lowered to $95,000 to permit sales of the additional output. Savannah has tax loss carry-forwards that cause its tax rate to be zero, and its cost of capital is 15 percent. Savannah uses no debt.

a. Should Savannah make the change?

b. Would Savannah's operating leverage increase or decrease if it made the change? What about its breakeven point?

c. Would the new situation have more or less business risk than the old one?

6-5   **(Capital structure analysis)** Suppose, some years later, Savannah Systems is in this situation:

EBIT	$4,000,000
Value of debt, D	$2,000,000
Cost of equity, k_s	15%
Cost of debt, k_d	10%
Shares outstanding, n_0	600,000
Tax rate, T	34%

The firm's market is stable, and it expects no growth, so all earnings are paid out as dividends. The debt consists of perpetual bonds.

a. What is the total market value of Savannah's stock, S, its price per share, P_0, and the firm's total market value, V?

b. What is Savannah's weighted average cost of capital, k_a?

c. The firm can increase its debt by $8 million, to a total of $10 million, using the new debt to buy back and retire some of its shares. Its interest rate on all debt will be 12 percent (it will have to call and refund the old debt), and its cost of equity will rise from 15 percent to 17 percent. EBIT will remain constant. Should the firm change its capital structure?

d. If Savannah did not have to refund the $2 million of old debt, how would this have affected things? Assume the new and the old debt are equally risky, with k_d = 12%, but the coupon rate on the old debt is 10 percent.

e. What is the firm's TIE ratio under the original condition and under the conditions in Part c?

6-6 **(Capital structure analysis)** ABC, Inc., has no debt outstanding, and its financial position is given by the following data:

Assets (book = market)	$3,000,000
EBIT	$500,000
Cost of equity, k_s	10%
Stock price, P_0	$15
Shares outstanding, n	200,000
Tax rate, T (federal-plus-state)	40%

The firm is considering selling bonds and simultaneously repurchasing some of its stock. If it uses $900,000 of debt, its cost of equity, k_s, will increase to 11 percent to reflect the increased risk. Bonds can be sold at a cost, k_d, of 7 percent. ABC is a no-growth firm. Hence, all its earnings are paid out as dividends, and earnings are expectationally constant over time.

a. What effect would this use of leverage have on the value of the firm?

b. What would be the price of ABC's stock?

c. What happens to the firm's earnings per share after the recapitalization?

d. The $500,000 EBIT given above is actually the expected value from the following probability distribution:

Probability	EBIT
0.10	($ 100,000)
0.20	200,000
0.40	500,000
0.20	800,000
0.10	1,100,000

What is the probability distribution of EPS with zero debt and with $900,000 of debt? Which EPS distribution is riskier?

e. Determine the probability distributions of times interest earned for each debt level. What is the probability of not covering the interest payment at the $900,000 debt level?

6-7 **(Capital structure analysis)** Stead Printing, Inc., has a total market value of $100 million, consisting of 1 million shares selling for $50 per share and $50 million of 10 percent perpetual bonds now selling at par. The company's EBIT is $13.24 million, and its tax rate is 15 percent. Stead can change its capital structure by either increasing its debt to $70 million or decreasing it to $30 million. If it decides to *increase* its use of leverage, it must call its old bonds and issue new ones with a 12 percent coupon. If it decides to *decrease* its leverage, it will call in its old bonds and replace them with new 8 percent coupon bonds. The company will sell or repurchase stock at the new equilibrium price to complete the capital structure change.

Stead pays out all earnings as dividends; hence, its stock is a zero growth stock. If it increases leverage, k_s will be 16 percent. If it decreases leverage, k_s will be 13 percent.

a. What is the cost of equity to Stead at present?

b. Should the firm change its capital structure?

c. Suppose the tax rate is changed to 34 percent. This would lower after-tax income and also cause a decline in the price of the stock and the value of the equity, other things held constant. Calculate the new stock price (at $50 million of debt).

d. Continue the scenario of Part c, but now re-examine the question of the optimal amount of debt. Does the tax rate change affect your decision about the optimal use of financial leverage?

e. Go back to Part b; that is, assume T = 15%. How would your analysis of the capital structure change be modified if the firm's presently outstanding debt could not be called, and it did not have to be replaced, that is, if the $50 million of 10 percent debt continued even if the company issued new 12 percent bonds?

f. Suppose these probabilities for EBIT exist: P[EBIT = $5 million] = 0.2; P[EBIT = $15 million] = 0.6; and P[EBIT = $25 million] = 0.2. Under the assumptions of Part e, what is (1) expected EPS and σ_{EPS}, and (2) expected TIE and σ_{TIE}, assuming an increase in book value of debt to $70 million?

6-8 (Pro forma analysis) The C.S. Grant Company is currently all-equity financed, but the firm is considering a change to 50 percent debt financing. The debt would cost 12 percent, and would be used to repurchase shares currently selling at $25 per share. Grant now has 40,000 shares outstanding and $1,000,000 in total assets. Its pro forma income statement for 1987, assuming zero debt usage, is as follows:

Sales	$900,000
Operating costs	750,000
EBIT	$150,000
Taxes (40%)	60,000
Net income	$ 90,000

Note: The 40 percent tax rate includes federal and state taxes.

a. What is the expected EPS for 1987 using zero debt? At a debt level of $500,000?

b. Assume that operating costs remain at 83.33 percent of sales over a wide range of sales levels. Further, the 1987 pro forma income statement is based on expected sales of $900,000, but the actual sales distribution is as follows:

Probability	Sales
0.10	$ 500,000
0.15	700,000
0.50	900,000
0.15	1,100,000
0.10	1,300,000

Find the EPS at each sales level for both zero debt and 50 percent debt financing.

c. Make a plot of EPS versus sales level for both financing alternatives. Place the plots on the same set of axes. Interpret this graph.

(Do Parts d and e only if you are using the computerized diskette.)

d. At a zero debt level, Grant's expected ROE = $90,000/$1,000,000 = 9.0%, while at $500,000 of debt, expected ROE = $54,000/$500,000 = 10.8%. Determine the firm's ROE at each debt level for every possible sales level. Plot the two ROE distributions.

e. Now, assume that the $500,000 debt financing would cost 15 percent. Repeat the Part d analysis. Is there a significant difference? Why?

6-9 **(Subjective analysis)** You have been hired as a financial consultant by two firms, Alpha Industries (Firm A) and Zed Corporation (Firm Z). Firm A is in the fast-growing microcomputer retail sales industry, while Firm Z manufactures office equipment such as pencil sharpeners, staplers, and tape dispensers. Your task is to recommend the optimal capital structure for the two firms. Discuss the factors that would influence your decision, and specifically how each of these factors applies to each firm. Here are some additional points about the two firms:

(1) Firm A generally leases its stores, while Firm Z purchases its plants.

(2) Firm A's stock is widely held, while the family of Firm Z's founder holds 40 percent of its stock.

(3) Firm Z has a significant amount of accelerated depreciation expense each year, while Firm A has almost none.

(4) Firm A has demonstrated high growth and profitability over the last few years. On the other hand, Firm Z's growth has averaged a modest 5 percent per year, and its profit margins and ROEs have been unspectacular.

Selected Additional References and Cases

Chapter 5 provided references on the theory of capital structure; the references listed here are oriented more toward applications than theory.

Donaldson's work on the setting of debt targets is old but still relevant:

Donaldson, Gordon, "New Framework for Corporate Debt Capacity," *Harvard Business Review*, March-April 1962, 117-131.

————, "Strategy for Financial Emergencies," *Harvard Business Review*, November-December 1969, 67-79.

Definitive references on the empirical relationship between capital structure and (1) the cost of debt, (2) the cost of equity, (3) earnings, and (4) the price of a firm's stock are virtually nonexistent—statistical problems make the precise estimation of these relationships extraordinarily difficult, if not impossible. One good way to get a feel for the issues involved is to obtain a set of the cost of capital testimonies filed in a major utility rate case—such testimony is available from state public utility commissions, the Federal Communications Commission, the Federal Energy Regulatory Commission, and utility companies themselves. For an academic discussion of the issues, see

Caks, John, "Corporate Debt Decisions: A New Analytical Framework," *Journal of Finance*, December 1978, 1297-1315.

Gordon, Myron J., *The Cost of Capital to a Public Utility* (East Lansing, Mich.: Division of Research, Graduate School of Business Administration, Michigan State University, 1974).

Hamada, Robert S., "The Effect of the Firm's Capital Structure on the Systematic Risk of Common Stocks," *Journal of Finance*, May 1972, 435-452.

Masulis, Ronald W., "The Impact of Capital Structure Change on Firm Value: Some Estimates," *Journal of Finance*, March 1983, 107-126.

Shalit, Sol S., "On the Mathematics of Financial Leverage," *Financial Management*, Spring 1975, 57-66.

Shiller, Robert J., and Franco Modigliani, "Coupon and Tax Effects on New and Seasoned Bond Yields and the Measurement of the Cost of Debt Capital," *Journal of Financial Economics*, September 1979, 297-318.

To learn more about the link between market risk and operating and financial leverage, see

Gahlon, James M., and James A. Gentry, "On the Relationship between Systematic Risk and the Degrees of Operating and Financial Leverage," *Financial Management*, Summer 1982, 15-23.

See the following three articles for additional insights into the relationship between industry characteristics and financial leverage:

Bowen, Robert M., Lane A. Daley, and Charles C. Huber, Jr., "Evidence on the Existence and Determinants of Inter-Industry Differences in Leverage," *Financial Management*, Winter 1982, 10-20.

Scott, David F., Jr., and John D. Martin, "Industry Influence on Financial Structure," *Financial Management*, Spring 1975, 67-73.

Long, Michael, and Ileen Malitz, "The Investment-Financing Nexus: Some Empirical Evidence," *Midland Corporate Finance Journal*, Fall 1985, 53-59.

For a more thorough discussion of the international implications of capital structure, see

Rutterford, Janette, "An International Perspective on the Capital Structure Puzzle," *Midland Corporate Finance Journal*, Fall 1985, 60-72.

The following cases contain many of the concepts we present in Chapters 5 and 6:

Crum, Roy L., and Eugene F. Brigham, *Cases in Managerial Finance* (Hinsdale, Ill.: Dryden, 1987):

Case 29, "Floral Fancy Plant Company," which shows the effect of leverage on EPS and stock price.

Case 31, "Sanitary Solutions," which concentrates on the effect of financial leverage on firm value and WACC.

Case 30, "Elektra Aerospace Corporation," which illustrates how operating and financial leverage interact to affect firm value.

Harrington, Diana, *Cases in Financial Decision Making* (Hinsdale, Ill.: Dryden, 1985):

"Marriott," which illustrates several ways to measure debt capacity when determining the optimal capital structure.

III

CAPITAL BUDGETING

7

INTRODUCTION TO CAPITAL BUDGETING

In the three preceding chapters, we discussed the cost of capital and the target capital structure. Now we turn to investment decisions involving fixed assets, or *capital budgeting*. The term *capital* refers to fixed assets used in production, while a *budget* is a plan which details projected inflows and outflows during some future period. Thus, the *capital budget* outlines the planned expenditures on fixed assets, and *capital budgeting* is the whole process of analyzing projects and deciding whether they should be included in the capital budget. This process is of fundamental importance to the success or failure of the firm, for its fixed asset investment decisions chart the course of a company for many years into the future. Indeed, these decisions *determine* the future.

Since the primary goal of the firm is shareholder wealth maximization, the appropriate goal for a firm's capital budgeting program is also maximization of shareholder wealth, or maximization of firm value. If an individual investor identifies and purchases a stock or bond whose market price is less than its intrinsic value, the value of the investor's portfolio will increase when the market recognizes the stock's true value. Similarly, if a firm identifies (or creates) investment opportunities with present values greater than their costs, the value of the firm will increase. This increase in firm value from capital budgeting will be reflected in the growth of the stock's price: the more effective the firm's capital budgeting procedures, the higher its earnings, and hence the higher the price of its stock.

Our treatment of capital budgeting is divided into four parts. First, Chapter 7 gives an overview and explains the basic techniques used in capital budgeting analysis. Chapter 8 goes on to consider how cash flows are estimated. Chapter 9 discusses risk analysis in capital budgeting, and then Chapter 10 explains how the optimal capital budget is established.

Table 7-1
Cash Flows for Projects S and L

Year (t)	Expected After-Tax Net Cash Flow, CF_t	
	Project S	Project L
0	($1,000)[a]	($1,000)[a]
1	500	100
2	400	300
3	300	400
4	100	600

[a]Represents the net investment outlay, or initial cost. The parentheses indicate a negative number, or cash outflow.

CAPITAL BUDGETING DECISION RULES

Five major methods are used to rank projects and to decide whether or not they should be accepted for inclusion in the capital budget: (1) payback, (2) accounting rate of return (ARR), (3) net present value (NPV), (4) internal rate of return (IRR), and (5) profitability index (PI). We first explain how each ranking criterion is calculated, and then we evaluate how well each performs in terms of identifying those projects which will maximize the firm's value.

We use the cash flow data shown in Table 7-1 for Projects S and L to illustrate each method, and throughout this chapter we assume that the projects are equally risky. Note that the cash flows, CF_t, are expected values, and that they are adjusted for tax, depreciation, and salvage value effects. Also, since many projects require an investment in both fixed assets and working capital, the investment outlays shown as CF_0 include any necessary changes in net working capital.[1] Finally, we assume that all cash flows occur at the end of the designated year. Incidentally, the S stands for *short* and the L for *long*: Project S is a short-term project in the sense that its cash inflows tend to come in sooner than L's.

Payback Period

The *payback period*, defined as the expected number of years required to recover the original investment, was the first formal method used to evaluate capital bud-

---

[1]Perhaps the most difficult part of the capital budgeting process is the estimation of the relevant cash flows. For simplicity, the net cash flows are treated as a given in this chapter, which allows us to focus on our main area of concern, the capital budgeting decision rules. However, in Chapter 8 we will discuss cash flow estimation in detail. Also, note that *working capital* is defined as the firm's current assets, and that *net working capital* is current assets minus current liabilities.

geting projects. When applied to Projects S and L, the payback period is 2 1/3 years for S and 3 1/3 years for L:[2]

$$\text{Payback}_S: \text{2 1/3 years.}$$

$$\text{Payback}_L: \text{3 1/3 years.}$$

If the firm required a payback of three years or less, Project S would be accepted, but Project L would be rejected. If the projects were *mutually exclusive*, S would be accepted over L because S has the shorter payback.[3] Thus, the payback method ranks S over L.

Some firms use a variant of the regular payback, the *discounted payback period*, which is similar to the regular payback period except that the expected cash flows are discounted by the project's cost of capital.[4] Thus, the discounted payback period is defined as the number of years required to recover the investment from *discounted* net cash flows. Table 7-2 contains the discounted net cash flows for Projects S and L, assuming a project cost of capital of 10 percent. To construct Table 7-2, each cash inflow in Table 7-1 is divided by $(1 + k)^t = (1.10)^t$, where t is the year in which the cash flow occurs and k is the project's cost of capital. After 3 years, Project S will have generated $1,011 in discounted cash inflows. Since the cost is $1,000, the discounted payback is just under 3 years or, to be precise, $2 + (\$214/\$225) = 2.95$ years. Project L's discounted payback is 3.88 years:

$$\text{Discounted payback}_S = 2.0 + 214/225 = 2.95 \text{ years.}$$

$$\text{Discounted payback}_L = 3.0 + 360/410 = 3.88 \text{ years.}$$

---

[2]The easiest way to calculate the payback period is to accumulate the project's net cash flows and see when they sum to zero. For example, the annual and cumulative net cash flows of Project S are shown below:

	Cash Flow	Cumulative Cash Flow
Year 0	($1,000)	($1,000)
Year 1	500	(500)
Year 2	400	(100)
Year 3	300	200
Year 4	100	300

Thus, the investment is recovered by the end of Year 3. Assuming that cash flows occur evenly during the year, the recovery actually occurs one-third of the way into Year 3: $100 remains to be recovered at the end of Year 2, and since Year 3 produces $300 in net cash flow, the payback period for Project S is 2 1/3 years.

[3]*Mutually exclusive* means that if one project is taken on, the other must be rejected. For example, the installation of a conveyor-belt system in a warehouse and the purchase of a fleet of forklift trucks for the same warehouse would be mutually exclusive projects—accepting one implies rejection of the other. *Independent* projects are projects whose cash flows are independent of one another.

[4]The project's cost of capital reflects (1) the marginal cost of capital to the firm and (2) the differential risk between the firm's existing projects and the project being evaluated. This concept will be discussed in detail in Chapter 9.

Table 7-2
Discounted Cash Flows for Projects S and L

Year (t)	Discounted Net Cash Flow			
	Project S		Project L	
	Annual	Cumulative	Annual	Cumulative
0	($1,000)	($1,000)	($1,000)	($1,000)
1	455	(545)	91	(909)
2	331	(214)	248	(661)
3	225	11	301	(360)
4	68	79	410	50

For Projects S and L, the rankings are the same regardless of which payback method is used; that is, Project S is preferred to Project L, and Project S would still be selected if the firm were to require a payback of three years or less. Often, however, the regular and the discounted paybacks produce conflicting rankings.

Note that the payback is a type of "breakeven" calculation in the sense that if cash flows come in at the expected rate until the payback year, then the project will break even. However, the regular payback does not take account of the cost of capital—no cost for the debt or equity used to undertake the project is reflected in the cash flows or the calculation. The discounted payback does take account of capital costs—it shows the breakeven year after covering debt and equity costs. However, as we shall see, both payback methods have some serious deficiencies, and other procedures are less likely to lead to errors in project selection. Therefore, we will not dwell on the finer points of payback analysis.

It should be noted, however, that the payback period does provide information on how long funds will be tied up in a project. Thus, the shorter the payback period, other things held constant, the greater is the project's liquidity. Also, since cash flows expected in the distant future are generally regarded as being riskier than near-term cash flows, the payback is often used as a rough measure of liquidity and project riskiness.

Accounting Rate of Return (ARR)

The *accounting rate of return (ARR)*, which looks at a project's contribution to net income rather than its cash flow, is the second oldest evaluation technique. In its most commonly used form, the ARR is measured as the ratio of the project's average annual expected net income to its average investment. If we assume that Projects S and L will both be depreciated by the straight line method to a book value of zero, then each will have a total depreciation expense of $1,000/4 = $250 per year. The average cash flow minus the average depreciation charge is the average annual income. For Project S, average annual income is $75:

$$\text{Average annual income} = \text{Average cash flow} - \text{Annual depreciation}$$
$$= (\$1,300/4) - \$250 = \$75.$$

The average investment is the beginning investment minus one-half the total depreciation, or $500:

$$\text{Average investment} = \text{Cost} - 0.5(\text{Depreciation})$$
$$= \$1,000 - \$500 = \$500.$$

This $500 is also the book value of the asset halfway through its life.

Combining the average annual income with the average investment, we obtain an ARR for Project S of 15 percent:

$$\text{ARR}_S = \frac{\text{Average annual income}}{\text{Average investment}} = \frac{\$75}{\$500} = 15\%.$$

By a similar calculation, we determine ARR_L to be 20 percent.[5] Thus, the ARR method ranks Project L over Project S. If the firm required an ARR of 16 percent or more, Project L would be accepted, but Project S would be rejected. Note also that in this case the project rankings under the ARR method are the opposite of the project rankings using either payback method. One could argue about which method is better, and hence which set of rankings should be used. However, this would really be a hollow argument, because both the payback and ARR methods are badly flawed. The regular payback and the ARR both ignore the time value of money, and the discounted payback ignores cash flows that are expected after the payback year. Since none of these procedures provides adequate information on the contribution of the project to the firm's value, they could all lead to incorrect capital budgeting decisions.

Net Present Value (NPV)

As the flaws in the payback and the ARR methods were recognized, people began to search for methods to improve the effectiveness of project evaluations. One such method is the *net present value (NPV)* method. To implement this approach, one proceeds as follows:

1. Find the present value of each cash flow, including both inflows and outflows, discounted at the project's cost of capital.
2. Sum these discounted cash flows; this sum is defined as the project's NPV.
3. If the NPV is positive, the project should be accepted; if the NPV is negative, it should be rejected; and if two projects are mutually exclusive, the one with the higher positive NPV should be chosen.

The NPV can be expressed as follows:

$$NPV = \sum_{t=0}^{n} \frac{CF_t}{(1 + k)^t}. \tag{7-1}$$

---

[5]Actually, there are many ways to calculate ARRs. Since all of them have major deficiencies, we see no point in extending the discussion.

Here CF_t is the expected net cash flow at Period t, and k is the project's cost of capital.[6] Cash outflows (expenditures on the project, such as the cost of buying equipment or building factories) are treated as *negative* cash flows. In evaluating Projects S and L, only CF_0 is negative, but for many large projects such as the Alaska Pipeline, an electric generating plant, or IBM's new portable computer, outflows occur for several years before operations begin and cash flows turn positive. Also, note that Equation 7-1 is quite general, so inflows and outflows could occur on any basis, say quarterly or monthly, and t could represent quarters or months rather than years.[7]

At a 10 percent cost of capital, the NPV of Project S is $78.82:

$$NPV_S = \frac{-\$1,000}{(1.10)^0} + \frac{\$500}{(1.10)^1} + \frac{\$400}{(1.10)^2} + \frac{\$300}{(1.10)^3} + \frac{\$100}{(1.10)^4}$$

$$= -\$1,000 + \$454.55 + \$330.58 + \$225.39 + \$68.30$$

$$= \$78.82.$$

By a similar process, we find $NPV_L = \$49.18$. On this basis, both projects should be accepted if they are independent, but S should be the one chosen if they are mutually exclusive.

Rationale for the NPV Method

The rationale for the NPV method is straightforward. The value of a firm is the sum of the values of its parts. If a firm takes on a zero-NPV project, the position of the original investors remains constant—the firm becomes larger, but the price of its stock remains unchanged. However, if the firm takes on a project with a positive NPV, the position of the original investors is improved. In our example, the original shareholders' wealth would increase by $78.82 if the firm takes on Project S, but

---

[6]In Equation 7-1, we assume that the project's cost of capital, k, is constant across all periods. Later in the chapter we discuss the situation in which k varies from period to period.

[7]If t represents any period other than years, then the cost of capital should be adjusted to reflect the periodic rate. For example, if the annual cost of capital were 10 percent, but we were evaluating a project on the basis of quarterly cash flows, the approximate periodic rate would be $10\%/4 = 2.5\%$, and the precise periodic rate, k/4, would be 2.41 percent:

$$(1 + k/4)^4 - 1.0 = 0.10$$

$$(1 + k/4)^4 = 1.10$$

$$(1 + k/4) = (1.10)^{1/4} = 1.0241$$

$$k/4 = 0.0241 = 2.41\%.$$

For most projects, calculation of the precise periodic rate is unwarranted because of the degree of uncertainty in the cash flows. However, there are projects—for example, the construction of a building for lease to the U.S. Postal Service on a long-term basis—for which the precise adjustment might be warranted.

by only $49.18 if it takes on Project L. Viewed in this manner, it is easy to see why S is preferred to L, and it is also easy to see the logic of the NPV approach.[8]

Internal Rate of Return (IRR)

In Chapter 3, we reviewed procedures for finding the yield to maturity, or rate of return, on a bond—if you invest in the bond and hold it to maturity, you will earn the YTM on the money you invested. Exactly the same concepts are employed in capital budgeting when the IRR method is used. The IRR is defined as that discount rate, r, which equates the present value of a project's expected cash inflows to the present value of the project's expected costs:

$$PV(\text{Inflows}) = PV(\text{Investment costs}),$$

or, equivalently,

$$\sum_{t=0}^{n} \frac{CF_t}{(1 + r)^t} = 0. \tag{7-2}$$

For our Project S, here is the set-up:

$$\frac{-\$1,000}{(1 + r)^0} + \frac{\$500}{(1 + r)^1} + \frac{\$400}{(1 + r)^2} + \frac{\$300}{(1 + r)^3} + \frac{\$100}{(1 + r)^4} = 0.$$

Here we know the value of each CF_t, but we do not know the value of r. Thus, we have an equation with one unknown, and we can solve for the value of r. *The solution value of r is defined as the IRR.*

Notice that the internal rate of return formula, Equation 7-2, is simply the NPV formula, Equation 7-1, solved for the particular discount rate that forces the NPV to equal zero. Thus, the same basic equation is used for both methods, but in the NPV method the discount rate, k, is specified and the NPV is found, whereas in the IRR method the NPV is specified to equal zero and the value of r = IRR that forces this equality is determined.

Internal rates of return can be calculated very easily by computers, and many firms have now computerized their capital budgeting processes and automatically

---

[8]This description of the process is somewhat oversimplified. Both analysts and investors anticipate that firms will identify and accept positive NPV projects, and stock prices reflect these expectations. Thus, stock prices react to announcements of new capital projects only to the extent that such projects were not already expected. In this sense, we may think of a firm's value as consisting of two parts: (1) the value of its existing assets and (2) the value of its "growth opportunities," or projects with positive NPVs. AT&T is a good example of this: the company has the world's largest long-distance network plus telephone manufacturing facilities, both of which provide earnings and cash flows, and it has Bell Labs, which has the *potential* for coming up with new products in the computer/telecommunication area that could be extremely profitable. Security analysts (and investors) thus analyze AT&T as a company with a set of cash-producing assets plus a set of growth opportunities that will materialize if and only if it can come up with a number of positive NPV projects through its capital budgeting process.

generate IRRs, NPVs, and paybacks for all projects. (See Problem 7-6 at the end of this chapter.) Even many hand-held calculators have built-in functions for calculating IRRs. Thus, business firms have no difficulty whatever with the mechanical side of capital budgeting, and a serious business student should have a financial calculator capable of finding IRRs. All IRRs reported hereafter in this and the following chapters were obtained by using a financial calculator (or a PC). By keying in the cash flows and then hitting the IRR button, we find that Project S has $IRR_S = 14.5\%$, while $IRR_L = 11.8\%$. If both projects have a cost of capital of 10 percent, the internal rate of return rule indicates that if the projects are independent, both should be accepted—they both are expected to earn more than the cost of the capital needed to finance them. If they are mutually exclusive, S ranks higher and should be accepted, while L should be rejected. If the cost of capital is more than 14.5 percent, both projects should be rejected.

Rationale for the IRR Method

Why is the particular discount rate that equates a project's cost with the present value of its receipts (the IRR) so special? To answer this question, let us first assume that our illustrative firm obtains the $1,000 needed to take on Project S by borrowing from a bank at an interest rate of 14.5 percent. Since the internal rate of return was calculated to be 14.5 percent, the same as the cost of the bank loan, the firm can invest in the project, use the cash flows generated by the investment to pay off the principal and interest on the loan, and come out exactly even on the transaction. This point is demonstrated in Table 7-3, which shows that Project S provides cash flows that are just sufficient to pay 14.5 percent interest on the unpaid balance of the bank loan, retire the loan over the life of the project, and end up with a balance that differs from zero only by a rounding error of 32 cents.

If the internal rate of return exceeds the cost of the funds used to finance a project, a surplus remains after paying for the capital, and this surplus accrues to the firm's stockholders. Therefore, taking on a project whose IRR exceeds its cost of capital increases the value of the firm's stock. On the other hand, if the internal rate of return is less than the cost of capital, then taking on the project imposes a

Table 7-3
Analysis of Project S's IRR as a Loan Rate

Investment (1)	Cash Flow (2)	Interest on the Loan at 14.5% $0.145 \times (1) = (3)$	Repayment of Principal $(2) - (3) = (4)$	Ending Loan Balance $(1) - (4) = (5)$
$1,000.00	$500	$145.00	$355.00	$645.00
645.00	400	93.53	306.47	338.53
338.53	300	49.09	250.91	87.62
87.62	100	12.70	87.30	0.32

cost on existing stockholders. It is this "breakeven" characteristic that makes the IRR useful in evaluating capital projects.[9]

Profitability Index

Another method used to evaluate projects is the *profitability index (PI)*, or the *benefit/cost ratio*, as it is sometimes called:

$$PI = \frac{PV \text{ benefits}}{PV \text{ costs}} = \frac{\sum\limits_{t=0}^{n} \dfrac{CIF_t}{(1 + k)^t}}{\sum\limits_{t=0}^{n} \dfrac{COF_t}{(1 + k)^t}}. \tag{7-3}$$

Here CIF_t represents the expected cash inflows, or benefits, and COF_t represents the expected cash outflows, or costs. The PI shows the *relative* profitability of any project, or the present value of benefits per present value dollar of costs. The PI for Project S, based on a 10 percent cost of capital, is 1.079:

$$PI_S = \frac{\$1,078.82}{\$1,000} = 1.079.$$

Similarly, $PI_L = 1.049$. A project is acceptable if its PI is greater than 1.0, and the higher the PI, the higher is the project's ranking. Therefore, both S and L would be accepted by the PI criterion if they were independent, and S would be ranked ahead of L if they were mutually exclusive.

Mathematically, the NPV, the IRR, and the PI methods must always lead to the same accept/reject decisions for independent projects: If a project's NPV is positive, its IRR must exceed k and its PI must be greater than 1.0. However, NPV, IRR, and PI can give conflicting rankings for mutually exclusive projects. This point will be discussed in more detail later in the chapter.

EVALUATION OF THE DECISION RULES

We have presented five possible capital budgeting rules, all of which are used to a greater or lesser extent in practice. However, the methods can lead to different capital budgeting decisions, so we need to answer this question: Which method is best, where "best" is defined as the method that selects the set of projects which maximizes firm value and hence shareholder wealth. If more than one method does this, then the best method would be the one that is easiest to use in practice.

Here are three properties that must be exhibited by a selection method if it is to lead to consistently correct capital budgeting decisions:

---

[9]This example illustrates the logic of the IRR method, but for technical correctness, the capital used to finance the project should be assumed to come from both debt and equity, and not from debt alone.

1. The method must consider all cash flows throughout the entire life of a project.

2. The method must consider the time value of money; that is, it must reflect the fact that dollars which come in sooner are more valuable than distant dollars.

3. When the method is used to select from a set of mutually exclusive projects, it must choose that project which maximizes the firm's stock value.

How do the five methods stand in regard to the required properties? Both the regular and the discounted paybacks violate Property 1—they do not consider all cash flows. Additionally, the undiscounted payback also violates Property 2. The accounting rate of return also violates Property 2—it uses accounting income rather than cash flow, and it does not differentiate between early and late dollars. The NPV, IRR, and PI methods all satisfy Properties 1 and 2, and all three lead to identical and correct accept/reject decisions for independent projects. However, only the NPV method satisfies Property 3 under all conditions: There are certain conditions under which the IRR and the PI methods fail to identify correctly that project, in a set of mutually exclusive projects, which maximizes the firm's stock price. This point is explored in depth in the following sections.

COMPARISON OF THE NPV AND IRR METHODS

We have noted that the NPV method exhibits all the desired decision rule properties and, as such, is the best method for evaluating projects. Because the NPV method is better than IRR and PI, we were tempted to explain NPV only, to state that it should be used as the acceptance criterion, and to go on to the next topic. However, the IRR and PI methods are familiar to many corporate executives, and they are widely entrenched in industry. Therefore, it is important that finance students thoroughly understand the IRR and PI methods and be prepared to explain why, at times, a project with a lower IRR or PI may be preferable to one with a higher IRR or PI. Also, it is often useful to compare alternatives in terms of their IRRs or PIs, but when such comparisons are made, it is essential that the analyst be fully aware of how the IRR and the PI are developed, and when they can be used in a rational manner.

NPV Profiles

A graph which relates a project's NPV and the discount rate used to calculate the NPV is defined as the project's *net present value profile*; profiles for Projects L and S are shown in Figure 7-1. To construct the profiles, we first note that at a zero discount rate, the NPV is simply the total of the undiscounted cash flows of the project; thus, at a zero discount rate $NPV_S = \$300$, and $NPV_L = \$400$. These values are plotted as the vertical axis intercepts in Figure 7-1. Next, we calculate the projects' NPVs at three discount rates, say 5, 10, and 15 percent, and plot these values. The four points plotted on our graphs are shown at the bottom of the figure.

Figure 7-1
Net Present Value Profiles:
NPVs of Projects S and L at Different Discount Rates

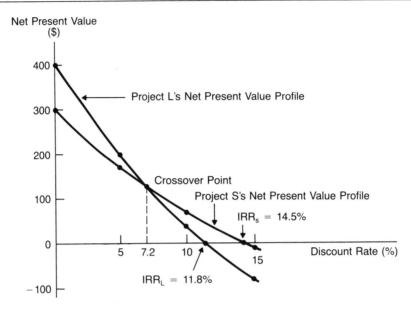

Discount Rate	NPV$_S$	NPV$_L$
0%	$300.00	$400.00
5	180.42	206.50
10	78.80	49.15
15	(8.33)	(80.13)

Recall that the IRR is defined as the discount rate at which a project's NPV equals zero. Therefore, *the point where its net present value profile crosses the horizontal axis indicates a project's internal rate of return.* Since we calculated IRR$_S$ and IRR$_L$ in an earlier section, we have two other points which we can use in plotting the projects' NPV profiles.

When we connect the plot points, we have the net present value profiles.[10] NPV profiles can be very useful in project analysis, and we will use them often in the remainder of the chapter.

---

[10]Notice that the NPV profiles are curved—they are *not* straight lines. Also, the NPVs approach the t = 0 cash flow (the cost of the project) as the discount rate increases without limit. The reason is that, at an infinitely high discount rate, the PV of the inflows would be zero, so NPV = CF$_0$, which in our example is − $1,000. We should also note that under certain conditions the NPV profiles can cross the horizontal axis several times, or never cross it. This point is discussed later in the chapter.

NPV Rankings Depend on the Discount Rate

We saw in Figure 7-1 that the NPV profiles of both Project L and Project S decline as the discount rate increases. But notice in the figure that Project L has the higher NPV at low discount rates, although NPV_S exceeds NPV_L if the discount rate is above 7.2 percent. Notice also that Project L's NPV is "more sensitive" to changes in the discount rate than is NPV_S; that is, Project L's net present value profile has the steeper slope, indicating that a change in k has a larger effect on NPV_L than on NPV_S.

To see why L has the greater sensitivity, recall first that the cash flows from S are received faster than those from L; in a payback sense, S is a short-term project, while L is a long-term project. Next, recall the equation for the NPV:

$$NPV = \frac{CF_0}{(1 + k)^0} + \frac{CF_1}{(1 + k)^1} + \frac{CF_2}{(1 + k)^2} + \frac{CF_3}{(1 + k)^3} + \frac{CF_4}{(1 + k)^4}.$$

Now notice that the denominators of the terms in this equation increase as k and t increase, and the increase is exponential; that is, the effect of a higher k is more pronounced if t is larger. To understand this point more clearly, consider the following data:

PV of a $100 cash flow due in 1 year, discounted at 5%	$95.24
PV of a $100 cash flow due in 1 year, discounted at 10%	$90.91
Percentage decline in PV resulting from a 5% increase in k when t = 1	−4.5%
PV of a $100 cash flow due in 10 years, discounted at 5%	$61.39
PV of a $100 cash flow due in 10 years, discounted at 10%	$38.55
Percentage decline in PV resulting from a 5% increase in k when t = 10	−37.2%

A doubling of the discount rate causes only a slight decline in the PV of a Year 1 cash flow, but the same discount rate increase causes the PV of a Year 10 cash flow to fall by 37 percent. Thus, if a project has most of its cash flows coming in the early years, its NPV will not be lowered very much if the discount rate increases, but a project whose cash flows come later will be severely penalized by high discount rates. Accordingly, Project L, which has its largest cash flows in the later years, is hurt badly when the discount rate is high, while Project S, which has relatively rapid cash flows, is affected less by rising discount rates.

Independent Projects

If two projects are *independent*, then the NPV and IRR criteria always lead to the same accept/reject decision: if NPV says accept, IRR also says accept. To see why this is so, look back at Figure 7-1 and notice (1) that the IRR criterion for acceptance is that the project's cost of capital is less than (or to the left of) the IRR, and (2) that whenever the project's cost of capital is less than the IRR, its NPV is positive. Thus, for any cost of capital less than 11.8 percent, Project L is acceptable by both the NPV and the IRR criteria, while both methods reject the project if the cost of capital is greater than 11.8 percent. Project S—and all other independent projects under consideration—could be analyzed similarly, and it will always turn out that if IRR > k, then NPV > 0.

Mutually Exclusive Projects

Now assume that Projects S and L are *mutually exclusive*, rather than independent. That is, we can choose either Project S or Project L, or we can reject both, but we cannot accept both projects. Notice in Figure 7-1 that, as long as the cost of capital is *greater than* the crossover rate of 7.2 percent, NPV_S is greater than NPV_L, and also that IRR_S is greater than IRR_L. Therefore, for k greater than the crossover rate of 7.2 percent, the two methods lead to the selection of the same project. However, if the cost of capital is *less than* the crossover rate, the NPV method ranks Project L higher, but the IRR method always indicates that Project S is better. Thus, a conflict exists. NPV says choose mutually exclusive L, while IRR says take S. Which answer is correct? Logic suggests that the NPV method is best, since it selects that project which adds the most to shareholder wealth.

Conditions for Conflict

There are two basic conditions which cause NPV profiles to cross, and thus which lead to potential conflicts between NPV and IRR: (1) when *project size (or scale) differences* exist, meaning that the cost of one project is larger than that of the other, or (2) when *timing differences* exist, meaning that the timing of cash flows from the two projects differs such that most of the cash flows from one project come in the early years and most of the cash flows from the other project come in the later years, as occurred with Projects L and S.[11]

When either size or timing differences occur, the firm will have different amounts of funds to invest in the various years, depending on which of the two mutually exclusive projects it chooses. For example, if one project costs more than the other, then the firm will have more money at t = 0 to invest elsewhere if it selects the smaller project. Similarly, for projects of equal size, the one with the larger early cash inflows provides more funds for reinvestment in the early years. Given this situation, the assumed rate of return at which differential cash flows can be invested is an important consideration. This point is illustrated in the following sections.

Project Scale

Mutually exclusive projects often differ in size. For example, suppose a firm has the opportunity to buy a copper mine for $600,000. If it buys the mine, the company can get the ore to its smelter in two different ways. Plan S (the smaller

---

[11]Of course, it is possible for mutually exclusive projects to differ with respect to both scale and timing. Also, if mutually exclusive projects have different lives (as opposed to different cash flow patterns over a common life), this introduces further complications, and for meaningful comparisons, some mutually exclusive projects must be evaluated over a common life. This point will be discussed in detail in the next chapter.

project) calls for buying a fleet of trucks for $400,000, resulting in a total project cost of $600,000 + $400,000 = $1,000,000. Plan L (the larger project) calls for spending $4.4 million to install a conveyor-belt system for moving the ore, making the total cost $600,000 + $4,400,000 = $5,000,000. If trucks are used, then fuel, labor, and other operating costs will be much higher than with the conveyor system. For simplicity, assume that the project will operate for only one year, after which the ore body will be exhausted. Assume also that after-tax expected net cash inflows, which occur at the end of the year, will be $1.28 million under Plan S but $6.0 million under Plan L.

Assuming that both projects' cost of capital is 10 percent, we can find each project's NPV as follows:

$$NPV_S = -\$1,000,000 + \$1,280,000/(1.10) = \$163,636.$$

$$NPV_L = -\$5,000,000 + \$6,000,000/(1.10) = \$454,545.$$

We can also find each project's IRR:

$$IRR_S: -\$1,000,000 + \$1,280,000/(1 + r) = 0$$

$$\$1,280,000/(1 + r) = \$1,000,000$$

$$1 + r = \$1,280,000/\$1,000,000 = 1.28$$

$$IRR_S = r = 0.28 = 28\%.$$

$$IRR_L: -\$5,000,000 + \$6,000,000/(1 + r) = 0$$

$$\$6,000,000/(1 + r) = \$5,000,000$$

$$1 + r = \$6,000,000/\$5,000,000 = 1.20$$

$$IRR_L = r = 0.20 = 20\%.$$

Thus, there is a conflict: $NPV_L > NPV_S$, but $IRR_S > IRR_L$.

Given this conflict, which project should be accepted? If we assume that the cost of capital is constant, meaning that the firm can raise all the capital it wants at a cost of 10 percent, then the answer is L, the project with the higher NPV. The differential between the initial outlays on the two projects ($4 million) can be looked upon as an investment itself, Project Δ. That is, Project L can be broken down into two components, one equal to Project S and the other a "residual project" equal to a hypothetical Project Δ. The hypothetical investment has a "cost" of $4 million and a net present value equal to the differential between the NPVs of the first two projects, or $290,909. This is shown below:

Project	Cost	NPV
L	$5,000,000	$454,545
S	1,000,000	163,636
Δ	$4,000,000	$290,909

Since the hypothetical Project Δ has a positive net present value, it should be accepted. This amounts to accepting Project L.

To put it another way, Project L can be split into two components, one costing $1 million and having a net present value of $163,636 and the other costing $4 million and having a net present value of $290,909. Since each of the two components has a positive net present value, both should be accepted. But if Project S is accepted, the second component of Project L, the hypothetical Project Δ, is rejected. Since the IRR method selects Project S, whereas the NPV method selects Project L, we conclude that the NPV method is better.[12]

NPV profiles for these two projects are shown in Panel A of Figure 7-2. The crossover point for the two profiles is 18 percent, indicating that no NPV/IRR conflict occurs unless the cost of capital is less than 18 percent. In our example, k = 10%, and this is why the conflict occurred.[13]

Timing of Cash Flows

Conflicts between NPV and IRR can also arise because of differences in the timing of projects' cash flows, even when the two projects have exactly the same initial investment cost. To illustrate, suppose we were considering the purchase of timber rights in a forest for $1 million. If we were to log the property immediately according to Plan S (which is a short-term project), our expected cash flow would be $1.28 million at the end of Year 1. Alternatively, if we were to delay logging the property for 10 years according to Plan L (which is a long-term project), the larger trees would produce a net cash inflow of $4,046,000 at the end of Year 10.

---

[12]The matter of project size can be considered in more dramatic terms: Would a business that is able to raise all the capital it wants at a cost of 10 percent rather have a 20 percent rate of return on a $1,000 investment or a 15 percent return on a $1 million investment? The answer is obvious here, and the same principle applies in more realistic situations. Notice also that, under the assumption of unlimited capital at a constant cost, the existence of other projects is irrelevant to the choice between L and S. Any other projects that are "good" can be accepted and financed regardless of whether or not L or S is selected.

[13]The exact crossover point between the NPV profiles of Projects S and L can be calculated by finding Project Δ's IRR. First, note that Δ's cash flows are as follows:

	t = 0	t = 1
CF_L	($5,000,000)	$6,000,000
$- CF_S$	$-$ (1,000,000)	$-$ 1,280,000
CF_Δ	($4,000,000)	$4,720,000

Then, find Project Δ's IRR:

$$- \$4,000,000 + \$4,720,000/(1 + r) = 0$$

$$IRR_\Delta = r = 0.18 = 18\%.$$

If we developed an NPV profile for Project Δ and plotted it on Panel A of Figure 7-2, its vertical axis intercept would be at + $720,000, and it would decline and cross the horizontal axis at 18 percent, directly below the crossover point.

As we shall see later in the chapter, the cost of capital, k, is the proper reinvestment rate. If k, and hence reinvestment rates, are low, then Project Δ has a positive NPV. However, as k rises, then Project Δ becomes less attractive. At a rate of 18 percent, Δ's NPV = 0, and NPV_Δ becomes negative as the assumed reinvestment rate rises above 18 percent.

Figure 7-2
**NPV Profiles of Mutually Exclusive Projects
That Differ in Size and Timing**

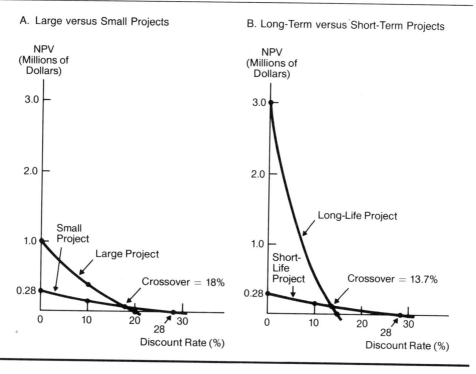

A. Large versus Small Projects

B. Long-Term versus Short-Term Projects

Assuming that each project's cost of capital is 10 percent, we can find each project's NPV as follows:

$$NPV_S = -\$1,000,000 + \$1,280,000/(1.10)^1 = \$163,636.$$

$$NPV_L = -\$1,000,000 + \$4,046,000/(1.10)^{10} = \$559,908.$$

We can also find each project's IRR:

$$IRR_S: -\$1,000,000 + \$1,280,000/(1 + r)^1 = 0$$

$$IRR_S = r = 0.28 = 28\%.$$

$$IRR_L: -\$1,000,000 + \$4,046,000/(1 + r)^{10} = 0$$

$$IRR_L = r = 0.15 = 15\%.$$

Again, we have a conflict: Because of timing differences, $NPV_L > NPV_S$, but $IRR_S > IRR_L$.

We know that high discount rates impose a greater penalty on distant cash flows than on near-term cash flows. Therefore, long-term projects such as Project L have NPV profiles which decline quite steeply relative to the NPV profiles of projects such as S. Panel B of Figure 7-2 illustrates this point for the two projects under consideration here. If the cost of capital is to the left of the crossover point, 13.7 percent, then a conflict occurs between NPV and IRR. In this case, k = 10%, so a conflict does exist.

Earlier, where our two projects differed in scale but had no difference in the timing of cash flows, we set up a hypothetical Project Δ, which had a positive NPV, to show why the project with the larger basic NPV should be accepted. We can illustrate timing differences similarly. Project S provides a cash flow of $1,280,000 at the end of Year 1, while Project L has a cash flow of $4,046,000 at the end of Year 10. If we accept Project S, we get a cash flow of $1,280,000 at t = 1. If we accept Project L, we give up this Year 1 cash flow, which amounts to making an investment, in order to get $4,046,000 at t = 10. Thus, our "timing difference" Project Δ has a cost of $1,280,000 at the end of Year 1 and a cash inflow of $4,046,000 at the end of Year 10, and its NPV is $396,272:

$$NPV = -\$1,280,000/(1.10)^1 + \$4,046,000/(1.10)^{10}$$
$$= -\$1,163,636 + \$1,559,908 = \$396,272.$$

If we accept Project S, we are rejecting Project Δ, with its positive NPV of $396,272. Since we would be foregoing a $396,272 increase in the value of the firm if we accepted S, we should reject it and accept Project L.

Causes of Conflict

In both our differential size and differential timing examples, we found that *cash flow differentials* existed. In the size example, we would have had an extra $4 million at t = 0 if we had taken the smaller project, but our cash flow at t = 1 would have been smaller by $4.72 million. In the timing example, we would have had an extra $1.28 million in Year 1 if we had taken the shorter-term project, but $4.046 million less at t = 10. The critical issue in resolving conflicts between mutually exclusive projects is this: What is the value of generating the cash flows earlier rather than later, or to put it another way, at what opportunity rate can we reinvest differential early years' cash flows? *The use of the NPV method implicitly assumes that the opportunity rate at which cash flows generated by a project can be reinvested is the cost of capital, whereas use of the IRR method implies that the firm has the opportunity to reinvest at the IRR.* These assumptions are inherent in the mathematics of the discounting process. Thus, the NPV method evaluates the cash flows at the cost of capital, while the IRR method evaluates cash flows at the project's IRR. The cash flows may actually be withdrawn as dividends by the stockholders and spent on beer and pizza, but the assumption of a reinvestment opportunity is still implicit in the calculations.

Which is the better assumption, reinvestment at the cost of capital or reinvestment of each project's cash flows at that project's IRR? We can answer the question as follows:

1. Assume that the firm's cost of capital is 10 percent. Management can obtain all the funds it wants at this rate. This condition is expected to hold in the foreseeable future. Further, assume that all potential projects have the same risk as the firm's current projects.

2. The capital budgeting process calls for all potential projects to be evaluated at $k = 10\%$. All projects with NPV > 0 are accepted. Plenty of capital is available to finance these projects, both now and in the future.

3. As cash flows come in from past investments, what will be done with them? These cash flows can either (a) be paid out to the equity and debt investors who, on average, require a 10 percent rate of return, or (b) be used as a substitute for outside capital that costs 10 percent. Thus, since the cash flows are expected to save the firm 10 percent, this is their value to the firm, and hence their opportunity cost reinvestment rate.

4. The IRR method implicitly assumes reinvestment at the internal rate of return itself. Given (a) ready access to capital markets and (b) a constant expected future cost of capital, the appropriate reinvestment rate is the opportunity cost of capital, or 10 percent. Even if the firm takes on projects in the future whose IRRs average some high rate, say 30 percent, this is irrelevant—those projects could always be financed with new external capital costing 10 percent, so cash flows from past projects have an opportunity cost reinvestment rate which is only equal to the cost of capital.

Therefore, we simply must come to the conclusion that *the correct reinvestment rate assumption is the cost of capital, which is implicit in the NPV method.* This, in turn, leads us to prefer the NPV method, at least for firms willing and able to obtain capital at a cost reasonably close to their current cost of capital. In Chapter 10, when we discuss capital rationing, we will see that under certain conditions the NPV rule may be questionable, but for most firms at most times, NPV is without a doubt conceptually better than IRR.

We should reiterate that, when projects are independent, the NPV and IRR methods both make exactly the same accept/reject decision. However, *when evaluating mutually exclusive projects, the NPV method should be used.* We should also note that there is one other situation in which the IRR approach may not be usable—this is when evaluating nonnormal projects. A *normal* capital project is one that has one or more cash outflows (costs) followed by a series of cash inflows. If, however, a project calls for a large cash outflow either sometime during or at the end of its life, then it is a *nonnormal* project. Nonnormal projects can present unique difficulties when evaluated by the IRR method. The most common problem encountered when evaluating nonnormal projects is multiple IRRs, which we discuss later in the chapter.

COMPARISON OF THE NPV AND PI METHODS

We can illustrate the conflict between NPV and PI with our earlier example which compared Project L (for large), which called for investing $5 million in a mine equipped with a conveyor-belt system for handling ore, with Project S (for small), which called for an expenditure of only $1 million to do the same thing by employing a fleet of trucks. Recall that the conveyor-belt system had lower operating costs, so its cash flows were larger, and the net present values were found to be $454,545 for L and $163,636 for S. Therefore, on the basis of the NPV criterion, we would select Project L. However, if we compute the ratio of the present value of the returns (or benefits) of each project divided by its cost, we find S's profitability index to be $PI_S = \$1,163,636/\$1,000,000 = 1.16$, and L's index to be $PI_L = \$5,454,545/\$5,000,000 = 1.09$. Thus, the NPV method suggests that we should accept Project L because $NPV_L > NPV_S$, but the PI method suggests acceptance of Project S, because $PI_S > PI_L$.

Given this conflict, which project should be accepted? Alternatively stated: Is it better to use the net present value approach on an absolute basis (NPV) or on a relative basis (PI)? *For a firm that seeks to maximize stockholders' wealth, the NPV method is better.* Recall that the differential between the initial outlays of the two projects ($4,000,000) can itself be looked upon as an investment, Project Δ, whose NPV is equal to the differential in the NPVs of the two projects ($290,909). Thus, Project L can be broken down into two projects, one equal to Project S and one a residual project equal to the hypothetical Project Δ. Since both Project S and Project Δ contribute positively to the value of the firm, they should both be accepted. This amounts to accepting Project L, the one chosen by the NPV method. Thus, we conclude that the NPV method leads to better decisions than does the PI method.

PRESENT VALUE OF FUTURE COSTS

Often, firms make accept/reject decisions on mutually exclusive projects on the basis of the present value of future costs rather than on the basis of the projects' NPVs. For example, Du Pont recently evaluated several different methods for disposing of wastes at one of its processing plants. The disposal system chosen would have no effect on either the prices or the quantity of products produced by the plant—these would be set in the competitive marketplace. Therefore, the revenue stream would be the same regardless of which waste disposal process is used, so revenues are irrelevant to this capital budgeting decision.

Since the revenue stream will be the same, Du Pont could make the decision on the basis of expected future costs alone, choosing the process that does the job for the lowest cost. Table 7-4 contains the expected net costs for the best two processes over their 5-year expected lives. Process A requires a lower expenditure on capital equipment than B, but A is more labor intensive. Therefore, A's Year 0 cost is relatively low, but its operating costs are relatively high.

Du Pont's analysts judged the processes to both have the same risk as the company's average project, and thus they used the firm's overall cost of capital, 12 percent, to discount the flows of each project. As shown in Table 7-4, Process A has a lower present value of future costs, so it was chosen. We will have more to say about discounting costs (or outflows) in Chapter 9, where we discuss risk adjustments.

Table 7-4
Production Costs for Processes A and B

	Expected Net Cost	
Year	Process A	Process B
0	($50,000)	($100,000)
1	(22,000)	(10,000)
2	(22,000)	(10,000)
3	(22,000)	(10,000)
4	(22,000)	(10,000)
5	(22,000)	(10,000)
PV(12%)	($129,305)	($136,048)

CHANGING CAPITAL COSTS

Up to this point, we have assumed that the firm expects its cost of capital to remain constant in the future. However, suppose the firm expects the cost of capital to change over time, either because it forecasts a general rise or fall in economy-wide capital costs or because it expects a change in its own situation. In this case, the NPV calculation should recognize that the project's cost of capital is not constant. To illustrate, suppose Project W has a cost of $10,000 and expected net cash inflows of $4,100 at the end of each of the next three years. If the project's cost of capital is expected to be a constant 10 percent, then $NPV_W = \$196$:

$$NPV_W = -\$10,000 + \frac{\$4,100}{(1.10)^1} + \frac{\$4,100}{(1.10)^2} + \frac{\$4,100}{(1.10)^3}$$
$$= -\$10,000 + \$10,196 = \$196.$$

However, what if the firm expects capital costs to increase over the next three years?[14] Assume that the first year's weighted average cost of capital, k_1, is 10 percent, but k_2 is expected to rise to 12 percent and k_3 to 14 percent. In this situation, the calculated NPV is $-\$26$:

$$NPV_W = -\$10,000 + \frac{\$4,100}{(1.10)} + \frac{\$4,100}{(1.12)(1.10)} + \frac{\$4,100}{(1.14)(1.12)(1.10)}$$
$$= -\$10,000 + \$3,727 + \$3,328 + \$2,919 = -\$26.$$

---

[14]If the debt used to help finance the project has a maturity equal to the life of the project, then the cost of debt can be taken as a constant. However, the cost of equity would still change from year-to-year if the general level of interest rates moves up and down. Potential changes in equity costs could, theoretically, be estimated from information contained in the term structure of interest rates.

Thus, Project W would be accepted if capital costs were constant, but the project would be rejected if they were expected to increase.[15]

This simple example illustrates several points: (1) If capital costs are expected to change over time, then the NPV should be calculated using multiple costs of capital. (2) A project's acceptability can be reversed by changing capital costs. (3) Regardless of our assumption regarding capital costs, $IRR_W = 11.1\%$, so if capital costs are nonconstant, the rate to which the IRR must be compared to determine project acceptability is unclear. These points reinforce our preference for the NPV method over the IRR method.

Should firms predict future capital costs and then use them in the capital budgeting process? If they are able to forecast these costs, then changes in capital costs should be considered. However, predicting future capital costs is a most difficult undertaking, so firms normally use today's capital costs as the best estimate of future capital costs, which results in a constant cost of capital.

MULTIPLE IRRs

A fairly common problem when one uses the IRR method is that in solving Equation 7-2,

$$\sum_{t=0}^{n} \frac{CF_t}{(1 + r)^t} = 0, \qquad (7\text{-}2)$$

it is possible to obtain more than one positive value of r, which means that multiple IRRs occur. Notice that Equation 7-2 is a polynomial of degree n, so it has n different roots, or solutions. All except one of the roots either are imaginary numbers or are negative when investments are normal (one or more cash outflows followed by cash inflows), so in the normal case, only one positive value of r appears. However, the possibility of multiple real roots, hence multiple IRRs, arises when the project is nonnormal (negative net cash flows occur during some year after the project has been placed in operation).

To illustrate this problem, suppose a firm is considering the expenditure of $1.6 million to develop a strip mine (Project M). The mine will produce a cash flow of $10 million at the end of Year 1. Then, at the end of Year 2, $10 million must be

---

[15]Another specification if capital costs are expected to change over time is

$$NPV = \sum_{t=0}^{n} \frac{CF_t}{(1 + k_t)^t}.$$

Note that here k is a constant when discounting a single cash flow, but that different cash flows can have different discount rates. The proper specification depends on the facts of the case. See Philip L. Cooley, It-Keong Chew, M. Chapman Findlay, III, Alan W. Frankle, and Rodney L. Roenfeldt, "Capital Budgeting Procedures under Inflation: Cooley, Roenfeldt and Chew vs. Findlay and Frankle," *Financial Management*, Autumn 1976, 83-90.

expended to restore the land to its original condition. Therefore, the project's expected net cash flows are as follows (in millions of dollars):

Project	Expected Net Cash Flow		
	Year 0	End of Year 1	End of Year 2
M	− $1.6	+ $10	− $10

These values can be substituted into Equation 7-2 to derive the IRR for the investment:

$$NPV = \frac{- \$1.6 \text{ million}}{(1 + r)^0} + \frac{\$10 \text{ million}}{(1 + r)^1} + \frac{- \$10 \text{ million}}{(1 + r)^2} = 0.$$

When solved, we find that NPV = 0 when r = 25% and also when r = 400%.[16] Therefore, the IRR of the investment is both 25 and 400 percent. This relationship is depicted graphically in Figure 7-3.[17] Note that no dilemma would arise if the NPV method were used; we would simply use Equation 7-1, find the NPV, and use this to evaluate the project. If Project M's cost of capital is 10 percent, then its NPV is − $0.77 million and the project should be rejected.

The authors encountered another example of multiple internal rates of return when a major California bank *borrowed* funds from an insurance company and then used these funds (plus an initial investment of its own) to buy a number of jet engines, which it then leased to a major airline. The bank expected to receive positive net cash flows (lease payments plus tax savings minus interest on the insurance company loan) for a number of years, then several large negative cash flows as it repaid the insurance company loan, and, finally, a large inflow from the sale of the engines when the lease expired.[18]

The bank discovered two IRRs and wondered which was correct. It could not ignore the IRR and use the NPV method, since the lease was already on the books, and the bank's senior loan committee, as well as Federal Reserve bank examiners, wanted to know the return on the lease. The bank's solution called for compounding the cash flows—both positive and negative—at an assumed reinvestment rate of 9 percent, its average return on loans, to arrive at a compounded terminal value for the operation. Then the interest rate that equated this terminal sum to the

---

[16]If you attempted to find the IRR of Project M with most financial calculators, you would get an error message. This same message would be given for all projects with multiple IRRs. We found Project M's IRRs by first calculating NPVs using several different values for k and then plotting the NPV profile. The intersections with the X-axis give a rough idea of the IRR values. Finally, we used trial and error to find the exact values of k which forced NPV = 0.

[17]Does Figure 7-3 suggest that the firm should try to *raise* its cost of capital to about 100 percent in order to maximize the NPV of the project? Certainly not. As we know, the firm should seek to *minimize* its cost of capital; this will cause the price of its stock to be maximized. Actions taken to raise the cost of capital might make this particular project look good, but those actions would be terribly harmful to the firm's more numerous normal projects. Only if the firm's cost of capital is high, in spite of efforts to keep it down, will the illustrative project have a positive NPV.

[18]The situation described here is a *leveraged lease*. See Chapter 14 for more on leveraged leases.

Figure 7-3
NPV Profile for Project M

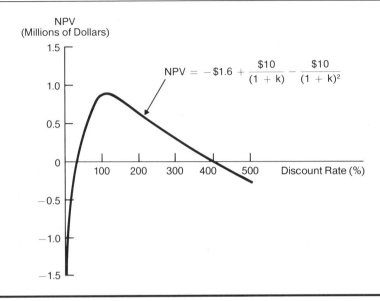

bank's initial cost was called the IRR, or the rate of return on the lease. This procedure satisfied both the loan committee and the bank examiners.[19]

The examples just presented illustrate one problem, multiple IRRs, that can arise when the IRR criterion is used with a project that has nonnormal cash flows. Use of the IRR method on nonnormal cash flow projects could produce other problems such as no IRR or an IRR which leads to an incorrect accept/reject decision. In all such cases, the NPV criterion could be easily applied, and this method leads to conceptually correct capital budgeting decisions.

CAPITAL BUDGETING METHODS IN PRACTICE

We have analyzed various capital budgeting selection criteria and concluded that the NPV method is conceptually superior. We also know that the NPV and IRR methods will result in the same decision except in certain cases involving mutually exclusive projects or nonnormal cash flows, and when conflicts arise, the NPV ranking should be used. Thus, companies should rely on the NPV method, but do

---

[19]For additional insights into the multiple root problem, see William H. Jean, "On Multiple Rates of Return," *Journal of Finance*, March 1968, 187-192.

Table 7-5
Capital Budgeting Methods Used

Method	Primary		Secondary	
	Number	Percent	Number	Percent
IRR	60	53.6%	13	14.0%
ARR	28	25.0	13	14.0
NPV	11	9.8	24	25.8
Payback period	10	8.9	41	44.0
PI	3	2.7	2	2.2
Total	112	100.0%	93	100.0%

they? Lawrence Gitman and John Forrester conducted a survey to help answer this question.[20]

Gitman and Forrester received 103 usable responses from a survey sent to 268 major companies known to make large capital expenditures. They found that the responsibility for capital budgeting analysis generally rests with the finance department. The respondents also stated that identifying projects and estimating their cash flows were the most difficult and the most critical steps in the capital budgeting process.

Table 7-5 summarizes the capital budgeting methods used by the respondent firms. The results indicate a strong preference for discounted cash flow (DCF) capital budgeting techniques, that is, NPV, IRR, and PI, with the dominant method being IRR rather NPV. However, the heavy use of ARR and payback as primary ranking techniques indicates that not all U.S. firms are technologically up to par in an economic sense.

Note also that almost all the respondents used at least two methods in their analysis, and as evidenced by 112 primary methods from 103 respondents, some firms use more than one primary method. Although the questionnaire did not bring out this point, we suspect that many of the analysts of firms which use the IRR as the primary method (1) recognize its drawbacks, yet use it anyway because it is easy to explain to nonfinancial executives, but (2) use NPV as a check on IRR when evaluating mutually exclusive or nonnormal projects. We also suspect that the payback method is used as a liquidity and/or risk indicator to help choose among competing projects whose NPVs and/or IRRs are close together.[21] Note also that virtually all firms of any size have computerized their capital budgeting analysis process, so they generally calculate all of the indicators discussed in this chap-

---

[20]See Lawrence J. Gitman and John R. Forrester, Jr., "A Survey of Capital Budgeting Techniques Used by Major U.S. Firms," *Financial Management*, Fall 1977, 66-71.

[21]See David Durand, "Comprehensiveness in Capital Budgeting," *Financial Management*, Winter 1981, 7-13, for an interesting view of why payback period remains popular.

ter. Finally, it is interesting (and encouraging) to note that when compared with earlier surveys, Gitman and Forrester found that the discounted cash flow methods are gaining in usage.

SUMMARY

Capital budgeting is similar in principle to security valuation—future cash flows are estimated, risks are appraised and reflected in a project's cost of capital discount rate, all cash flows are put on a present value basis, and if a project's *net present value (NPV)* is positive, it is accepted. Alternatively, if a project's *internal rate of return (IRR)* is greater than its cost of capital, it is accepted. Because of differing reinvestment rate assumptions, the NPV and IRR methods can lead to conflicts when evaluating *mutually exclusive* projects. When conflicts exist, they should, in general, be resolved in favor of the project with the higher NPV.

In outline form, the capital budgeting process centers around the following steps:

1. The expected future cash flows from a project are estimated. This involves estimating (a) the investment outlay required for the project and (b) the cash inflows over the project's projected life. Cash flow estimation is the most important, yet the most difficult, step in the capital budgeting process. It will be discussed in detail in the next chapter.

2. The riskiness inherent in the project is appraised. This important subject is taken up in Chapter 9.

3. The next step is to rank projects by their NPVs or IRRs, accepting those with NPV > 0 or IRR > the cost of capital. Conflicts between NPV and IRR rankings should be resolved in favor of the NPV. Some firms also calculate projects' *payback periods, accounting rates of return (ARRs)*, and *profitability indices (PIs)*. The payback does provide an indication of a project's risk and liquidity, because it shows how long the original capital will be "at risk." Therefore, firms often calculate projects' NPVs, IRRs, and PIs as measures of profitability, and paybacks as a risk/liquidity indicator.

Although this chapter has presented the basic elements of the capital budgeting process, there are many other aspects of this crucial topic. Some of the more important ones are discussed in the following three chapters.

Questions and Problems

7-1 **(Capital budgeting methods)** Project S has a cost of $10,000 and is expected to produce benefits (cash flows) of $3,000 per year for five years. Project L costs $25,000 and is expected to produce cash flows of $7,400 per year for five years. Calculate the two projects' NPVs, IRRs, and PIs, assuming a cost of capital of 12 percent. Which project would be selected, assuming they are mutually exclusive, using each ranking method? Which should actually be selected?

7-2 **(Capital budgeting methods)** You are a financial analyst for Wingate Manufacturing Company. The director of capital budgeting has asked you to analyze two proposed capital investments, Projects X and Y. Each project has a cost of $10,000, and the cost of capital for both projects is 12 percent. The projects' expected net cash flows are

	Expected Net Cash Flow	
Year	Project X	Project Y
0	($10,000)	($10,000)
1	6,500	3,500
2	3,000	3,500
3	3,000	3,500
4	1,000	3,500

    a. Calculate each project's payback, accounting rate of return, net present value (NPV), internal rate of return (IRR), and profitability index (PI). (To determine the accounting rate of return, assume that the depreciation expense is $500 per year for both projects.)

    b. Which project, or projects, should be accepted if they are independent?

    c. Which project should be accepted if they are mutually exclusive?

    d. How might a change in the cost of capital produce a conflict between the NPV and the IRR rankings of these two projects? At what values of k would this conflict exist?

    e. Why does the conflict exist?

7-3 **(Reinvestment rate assumption)** In what sense is a reinvestment rate assumption embodied in NPV and IRR calculations? What is the implicitly assumed reinvestment rate of each method? Which assumption is correct? Why?

7-4 **(NPV versus IRR)** Assume that a firm has no mutually exclusive projects, only independent ones; that its cost of capital is constant; and that all of its projects are normal in the sense of having an outflow followed by a stream of inflows. Under these conditions, the NPV and the IRR methods will always result in identical capital budgets. Discuss the statement.

7-5 **(NPV versus IRR versus PI)** For independent projects, is it true that if PI > 1.0, then NPV > 0 and IRR > k? Prove it.

7-6 **(NPV and IRR analysis)** Fuller Products Company (FPC) is considering two mutually exclusive investments. The projects' expected net cash flows are as follows:

	Expected Net Cash Flow	
Year	Project A	Project B
0	($300)	($405)
1	(387)	134
2	(193)	134
3	(100)	134
4	600	134
5	600	134
6	850	134
7	(180)	0

a. Construct NPV profiles for Projects A and B.

b. What is each project's IRR?

c. If you were told that each project's cost of capital is 10 percent, which project should be selected? If the cost of capital were 17 percent, what would the proper choice be?

d. What is the crossover rate, and what is its significance?

(Do Parts e and f only if you are using the computerized diskette.)

e. FPC's management is confident of the project's cash flows in Years 0 to 6 but is uncertain as to what the Year 7 cash flows will be for the two projects. Under a worst case scenario, Project A's Year 7 cash flow will be − $300 and B's will be − $150, while under a best case scenario, the cash flows will be − $70 and + $120 for Projects A and B, respectively. Answer Parts b and c using these new cash flows. Which project should be selected under each scenario?

f. Put the Year 7 cash flows back to − $180 for A and zero for B. Now change the cost of capital and observe what happens to NPV at k = 0%, 5%, 20%, and 400% (input as 4.0).

7-7   **(Timing differences)** The Texas Exploration Company is considering two mutually exclusive plans for extracting oil on property for which it has mineral rights. Both plans call for the expenditure of $10,000,000 to drill development wells. Under Plan A, all the oil will be extracted in one year, producing a cash flow at t = 1 of $12,000,000, while under Plan B, cash flows will be $1,750,000 per year for 20 years.

a. What are the annual cash flows that will be available to Texas Exploration if it undertakes Plan B rather than Plan A?

b. If Texas Exploration accepts Plan A, then invests the extra cash generated at the end of Year 1, what rate of return (reinvestment rate) would cause the cash flows from reinvestment to equal the cash flows from Plan B?

c. Suppose a company has a cost of capital of 10 percent. Is it logical to assume that it would take on all available independent projects (of average risk) with returns greater than 10 percent? Further, if all available projects with returns greater than 10 percent have been taken, would this mean that cash flows from past investments would have an opportunity cost of only 10 percent, because all the firm could do with these cash flows would be to replace money that has a cost of 10 percent? Finally, does this imply that the cost of capital is the correct rate to assume for the reinvestment of a project's cash flows?

d. Construct NPV profiles for Plans A and B, identify each project's IRR, and indicate the crossover rate of return.

7-8   **(Scale differences)** The Damon Publishing Company is considering two mutually exclusive expansion plans. Plan A calls for the expenditure of $50 million on a large-scale, integrated plant which will provide an expected cash flow stream of $8 million per year for 20 years. Plan B calls for the expenditure of $15 million to build a somewhat less efficient, more labor intensive plant which has an expected cash flow stream of $3.4 million per year for 20 years. Damon's cost of capital is 10 percent.

a. Calculate each project's NPV and IRR.

b. Set up a Project Δ by showing the cash flows that will exist if Damon goes with the large plant rather than the smaller plant. What are the NPV and the IRR for this Project Δ?

c. Graph the NPV profiles for Project A, Project B, and Project Δ.

d. Give a logical explanation, based on reinvestment rates and opportunity costs, as to why the NPV method is better than the IRR method when the firm's cost of capital is constant at some value such as 10 percent.

7-9 **(Multiple rates of return)** The Utah Uranium Company is deciding whether or not it should open a strip mine, the net cost of which is $4.4 million. Net cash inflows are expected to be $27.7 million, all coming at the end of Year 1. The land must then be returned to its natural state at a cost of $25 million, payable at the end of Year 2.

a. Plot the project's NPV profile.

b. Should the project be accepted if k = 8%? If k = 14%? Explain your reasoning.

c. Can you think of some other capital budgeting situations where negative cash flows during or at the end of the project's life might lead to multiple IRRs?

7-10 **(Multiple rates of return)** The Sacramento Development Company (SDC) has many excellent investment opportunities, but it has insufficient cash to undertake them all. Now SDC is offered the chance to borrow $2 million from the Pacific City Retirement Fund at 10 percent, the loan to be repaid at the end of one year. Also, a "consulting fee" of $700,000 will be paid to Pacific City's mayor at the end of one year for helping to arrange the credit. Of the $2 million received, $1 million will be used immediately to buy an old city-owned hotel and to convert it to a gambling casino. The other $1 million will be invested in other lucrative SDC projects that otherwise would have to be foregone because of a lack of capital. For two years, all cash generated by the casino will be plowed back into the casino project. At the end of the two years, the casino will be sold for $2 million.

Assuming that (1) the deal has been worked out in the sunshine and is completely legal and (2) cash from other SDC Company operations will be available to make the required payments at the end of Year 1, under what rate of return conditions should SDC accept the offer? Disregard taxes.

7-11 **(Present value of costs)** The Fogler Coffee Company is evaluating the within-plant distribution system for its new roasting, grinding, and packing plant. The two alternatives are (1) a conveyor system with a high initial cost, but low annual operating costs, and (2) several forklift trucks, which cost less, but have considerably higher operating costs. The decision to construct the plant has already been made, and the choice here will have no effect on the overall revenues of the project. The cost of capital for the plant is 8 percent, and the projects' expected net costs are listed in the table:

| | Expected Net Cost | |
Year	Conveyor	Forklift
0	($500,000)	($200,000)
1	(120,000)	(160,000)
2	(120,000)	(160,000)
3	(120,000)	(160,000)
4	(120,000)	(160,000)
5	(20,000)	(160,000)

a. What is the IRR of each alternative?

b. What is the present value of costs of each alternative? Which method should be chosen?

Selected Additional References

For an in-depth treatment of capital budgeting techniques, see

Bierman, Harold, Jr., and Seymour Smidt, *The Capital Budgeting Decision* (New York: Macmillan, 1984).

Grant, Eugene L., William G. Ireson, and Richard S. Leavenworth, *Principles of Engineering Economy* (New York: Ronald, 1976).

Levy, Haim, and Marshall Sarnat, *Capital Investment and Financial Decisions* (Englewood Cliffs, N. J.: Prentice-Hall, 1982).

Osteryoung, Jerome S., *Capital Budgeting: Long-Term Asset Selection* (Columbus, Ohio: Grid, 1979).

For a discussion of strategic considerations in capital budgeting, see

Crum, Roy L., and Frans G. J. Derkinderen, eds., *Readings in Strategies for Corporate Investments* (New York: Pitman, 1981).

The following articles present interesting comparisons of four different approaches to finding NPV:

Brick, Ivan E., and Daniel G. Weaver, "A Comparison of Capital Budgeting Techniques in Identifying Profitable Investments," *Financial Management*, Winter 1984, 29-39.

Greenfield, Robert L., Maury R. Randall, and John C. Woods, "Financial Leverage and Use of the Net Present Value Investment Criterion," *Financial Management*, Autumn 1983, 40-44.

Three articles related directly to the topics in Chapter 7 are

Bacon, Peter W., "The Evaluation of Mutually Exclusive Investments," *Financial Management*, Summer 1977, 55-58.

Kim, Suk H., and Edward J. Farragher, "Current Capital Budgeting Practices," *Management Accounting*, June 1981, 26-30.

Lewellen, Wilbur G., Howard P. Lanser, and John J. McConnell, "Payback Substitutes for Discounted Cash Flow," *Financial Management*, Summer 1973, 17-23.

Additional capital budgeting references are provided in Chapters 8, 9, and 10.

8

CASH FLOW ESTIMATION AND OTHER TOPICS IN CAPITAL BUDGETING

The basic principles of capital budgeting were covered in Chapter 7. Now we examine some additional issues, including (1) cash flow estimation, (2) replacement decisions, (3) mutually exclusive projects with unequal lives, (4) abandonment value, (5) alternative NPV methods, and (6) effects of inflation on capital budgeting analysis.

CASH FLOW ESTIMATION

The most important, but also the most difficult, step in the analysis of a capital project is estimating its cash flows—both the investment outlays that will be required and the annual net cash inflows after the project goes into operation. Many variables are involved in cash flow forecasting, and many individuals and departments participate in the process. For example, the forecasts of unit sales and sales prices are normally made by the marketing department, based on its knowledge of price elasticity, advertising effects, the state of the economy, competitors' reactions, and trends in consumers' tastes. Similarly, the capital outlays associated with a new product are generally obtained from the engineering and product development staffs, while operating costs are estimated by cost accountants, production experts, personnel specialists, purchasing agents, and so forth.

Obtaining accurate estimates of the costs and revenues associated with a large, complex project can be exceedingly difficult, and forecast errors can be quite large. For example, when several major oil companies decided to build the Alaska Pipeline, the original cost forecasts were in the neighborhood of $700 million. The final cost was closer to $7 billion. Similar, or even worse, miscalculations are common in product design cost estimates, such as the costs to develop a new personal computer. Further, as difficult as plant and equipment costs are to estimate, sales revenues and operating costs over the life of the project are generally even harder to forecast. For example, when AT&T developed the Picturephone, it envisaged   265 large sales in both the residential and business markets, yet it turned out that virtually no one was willing to pay the price required to cover the project's costs. Because of its financial strength, AT&T was able to absorb losses on the project with no problem, but the Picturephone venture would surely have forced a weaker firm into bankruptcy.

The financial staff's role in the forecasting process includes (1) coordinating the efforts of the other departments, such as engineering and marketing, (2) ensuring that everyone involved with the forecast uses a consistent set of economic assumptions, and (3) making sure that no biases are inherent in the forecasts. This last point is extremely important, because division managers often become emotionally involved with pet projects and/or develop empire-building complexes, leading to cash flow forecasting biases which make bad projects look good on paper. The AT&T Picturephone project is an example of this problem.

Unbiased point estimates of the key variables are not sufficient—as we shall see in the next chapter, data on probability distributions or other indications of the likely ranges of errors are also essential. Moreover, it is useful to have an idea of the relationship between each input variable and some basic economic variable such as gross national product, for if all production and sales variables are related to such a variable, then the financial manager will have an idea of how the project will do under different economic conditions.

It is almost impossible to overstate the difficulties that are encountered in cash flow forecasts. It is also difficult to overstate the importance of these forecasts. We cover next certain principles which, if observed, will help to minimize forecast errors.

IDENTIFYING THE RELEVANT CASH FLOWS

Cash flows for a project are defined as the differences in cash flows for each period if the project is undertaken versus if it is not undertaken:

$$\text{Project CF}_t = \frac{\text{CF}_t \text{ for corporation}}{\text{with project}} - \frac{\text{CF}_t \text{ for corporation}}{\text{without project}}. \tag{8-1}$$

Thus, project cash flows are *incremental cash flows*. In this section, we discuss the measurement of the incremental cash flows attributable to a project.

Cash Flow Versus Accounting Income

Accounting income statements are in some respects a mix of apples and oranges. For example, accountants deduct labor costs, which are cash outflows, from revenues, which may or may not be entirely cash (some sales may be on credit). At the same time, accountants do not deduct capital outlays, which are cash outflows, but they do deduct depreciation expenses, which are not cash outflows. In capital budgeting, it is critical that we base decisions strictly on cash flows, the actual dollars that flow into and out of the company during each time period.

As noted above, the relevant cash flows for capital budgeting purposes are the incremental cash flows attributable to a project. It would be possible to construct for the corporation pro forma cash flow statements with and without a project for each year of the project's life, and then to measure the annual project cash flows as the differences in cash flows between the two sets of statements. If this were done, the following formula would result:

$$\text{NOCF}_t = [(R_{1t} - R_{0t}) - (OC_{1t} - OC_{0t}) - (D_{1t} - D_{0t})](1 - T) + (D_{1t} - D_{0t}). \quad \text{(8-2)}$$

Here NOCF_t is the project's net operating cash flow in Period t; R_1 is the corporation's revenue if the project is undertaken, while R_0 is the sales revenue if it is not accepted; OC_1 and OC_0 are the operating costs with and without the project; and D_1 and D_0 are the respective depreciation charges.[1]

To illustrate, assume that a firm is considering a new project that has a cost of $1 million and a 10-year life. If the project is undertaken, the income/cash flow statement in the left column of the following table is expected to result. If the project is not undertaken, the middle column is projected. The third column shows the key changes the project is expected to produce, so the project's projected net operating cash flow is $298,000 per year for 10 years:

	With Project	Without Project	Change
Sales (R)	$1,600,000	$1,000,000	$600,000
Operating costs (OC)	600,000	400,000	200,000
Depreciation (D)	200,000	100,000	100,000
Pre-tax income	$ 800,000	$ 500,000	$300,000
Taxes (34%)	272,000	170,000	102,000
Net income (NI)	$ 528,000	$ 330,000	$198,000
NOCF (NI + D)	$ 728,000	$ 430,000	$298,000

Substituting values into Equation 8-2 would produce exactly the same net operating cash flow, $298,000.

As we will see later in the chapter, there are times when new projects affect the sales and costs associated with the firm's original assets, and in such cases it is useful to think in terms of Equation 8-2 and comparative income statements. However, new projects often do not affect the firm's existing cash flows, and in such cases we can use a short-cut cash flow formula:

$$\text{NOCF}_t = [R_t - OC_t - D_t](1 - T) + D_t. \quad \text{(8-3)}$$

Here R, OC, and D represent the sales, operating costs, and depreciation of the project itself. To illustrate, suppose a project has a cost of $1 million, it will increase sales by $600,000 per year for 10 years, its operating costs will be $200,000 per year, and the project cost will be depreciated by the straight line method

---

[1]Here we are concentrating on operating cash flows since these are the flows to be discounted by the WACC to find the project's NPV. As we demonstrate later in the chapter, an alternate procedure can be used which subtracts financing costs to determine cash flows after interest expenses. If this were done, the discount rate used to calculate the NPV would be the cost of common equity, not the WACC.

toward a zero salvage value over 10 years. If the firm's marginal tax rate is 34 percent, then Equation 8-3 may be solved as follows:

$$\text{NOCF}_t = (\$600{,}000 - \$200{,}000 - \$100{,}000)(0.66) + \$100{,}000 = \$298{,}000.$$

Going through some algebra, we can transform Equation 8-3 into

$$\text{NOCF}_t = (R_t - C_t)(1 - T) + TD_t. \qquad \text{(8-3a)}$$

Equation 8-3a demonstrates that the net operating cash flow, NOCF_t, during a given period consists of two terms: (1) sales revenues minus cash operating costs, reduced by taxes, and (2) a depreciation cash flow equal to the amount of depreciation taken during the period times the tax rate. In this form, it is clear that the basic effect of depreciation on cash flows is the reduction in taxes caused by the depreciation expense, and the higher the firm's tax rate, the greater the value of depreciation. Equations 8-3 and 8-3a are equivalent methods for calculating net operating cash flows, and either method can be used in capital budgeting analysis, depending on the form in which data are available.

Cash Flow Timing

In financial analysis, we must be careful to account properly for the timing of cash flows. Accounting income statements are for periods such as years or months, so they do not reflect exactly when, during the period, revenues or expenses occur. However, because of the time value of money, capital budgeting cash flows should in theory be analyzed as they actually occur. Of course, there must be a compromise between accuracy and simplicity. A time line with daily cash flows would in theory provide the most accuracy, but daily cash flow estimates would be costly to construct, unwieldy to use, and probably no more accurate than annual cash flows because our ability to forecast is simply not good enough to warrant this degree of detail. Therefore, in most cases, we simply assume that all cash flows occur at the end of every year. However, for some projects, it may be useful to assume that cash flows occur at midyear, or even to forecast quarterly or monthly cash flows. In any event, it is important to specify the timing of cash flows on some reasonable basis.

Incremental Cash Flows

As noted previously, in capital budgeting we are concerned only with those cash flows that result directly from the project; that is, the project's incremental cash flows. Three special problems that can occur when estimating incremental cash flows are discussed next.

Sunk Costs
Sunk costs are not incremental costs, and they should not be included in the analysis. A *sunk cost* refers to an outlay that has already occurred (or been committed); hence, it is an outlay that is not affected by the accept/reject decision under

consideration. Suppose, for example, that in 1987 Northeast BankCorp were evaluating the establishment of a branch office in a newly developed section of Boston. To help perform the analysis, Northeast had, back in 1986, hired a consulting firm to perform a site analysis at a cost of $100,000; this $100,000 was expensed for tax purposes in 1986. Is this 1986 expenditure a relevant cost with respect to the 1987 capital budgeting decision? The answer is no. The $100,000 is a sunk cost; Northeast cannot recover it regardless of whether or not the new branch is built. It often turns out that a particular project looks bad (it has a negative NPV, or an IRR less than the cost of capital) when all the associated costs, including sunk costs, are considered. However, on an incremental basis, the project may be a good one, because the incremental cash flows are large enough to produce a positive NPV on the incremental investment. Thus, the correct treatment of sunk costs is critical to a proper capital budgeting analysis.[2]

Opportunity Costs

The second potential problem relates to *opportunity costs*: All relevant opportunity costs must be included in a correct capital budgeting analysis. For example, suppose Northeast BankCorp already owns a piece of land that is suitable for the branch location. When evaluating the prospective branch, should the cost of the land be disregarded because no additional cash outlay would be required? No, because there is an opportunity cost inherent in the use of the property. For example, suppose the land could be sold to yield $150,000 after taxes. Use of the site for the branch would require foregoing this inflow, so the $150,000 must be charged as an opportunity cost against the project. Note, though, that the proper land cost in this example would be the $150,000 market-determined value, irrespective of whether Northeast had paid $50,000 or $500,000 for the property when it was acquired.

Effects on Other Parts of the Firm (Externalities)

The third potential problem involves the effects of a project on other parts of the firm. For example, suppose some of Northeast's customers who would use the new branch are already banking with Northeast's downtown office. The loans and deposits, and hence profits, generated by these customers would not be new to the bank, but, rather, they would represent a transfer from the main office to the branch. Thus, the net revenues produced by these customers should not be treated as incremental income in the capital budgeting decision. On the other hand, having a suburban branch might actually attract new customers to the downtown office, because some potential customers would like to be able to make transactions both from home and from work. In this case, the additional revenues that would flow to the downtown office should be attributed to the branch.

---

[2]For an excellent example of the improper treatment of sunk costs by a major corporation, see U. E. Reinhardt, "Break-Even Analysis for Lockheed's TriStar: An Application of Financial Theory," *Journal of Finance*, September 1973, 821-838.

Although often difficult to determine, "externalities" such as these must be considered. They should, if possible, be quantified, or at least noted, so the final decision maker will be aware of their existence.

TAX EFFECTS

Tax effects can have a major impact on cash flows, and in many cases tax effects can make or break a project. Therefore, it is critical that taxes be dealt with correctly in capital budgeting decisions. However, as financial analysts, we encounter two problems: The tax laws are extremely complex, and these laws are subject to interpretation and change. Fortunately, the financial staff can get assistance from the firm's internal or external accountants and tax lawyers. Even so, it is necessary for financial managers to have at least a working knowledge of the current tax laws and their effects on cash flows.[3]

Depreciation is calculated for tax purposes by a procedure known as the *Accelerated Cost Recovery System* (*ACRS,* which is pronounced "acres"). We now describe the highlights of ACRS as it existed in 1987 under the Tax Reform Act of 1986, as well as some other relevant tax code features.

Tax Depreciation Life

The cost of an asset is expensed gradually over its depreciable life for tax purposes. Historically, an asset's depreciable life was determined by its estimated useful economic life on the theory that an asset should be fully depreciated at approximately the same time that it reached the end of its useful economic life. Such an approach is still correct for accounting purposes, but our tax laws are as much reflective of economic policy motives—for example, stimulating business investment—as of accounting theory. Therefore, ACRS totally abandoned the relationship between tax life and economic life, and it set simpler guidelines which created several classes of assets, each with a more-or-less arbitrarily prescribed life, called a *recovery period*, or *class life*.

Table 8-1 describes what types of property fit into the different class life groups. The first column of Table 8-1 gives the ACRS class life, and the second column describes the types of assets which fall into each category.

Computing ACRS Depreciation

Under earlier depreciation methods, the rate at which the value of an asset actually declined was estimated, and this rate was then used as the basis for tax depreciation. Thus, different assets were depreciated along different paths over time. The

---

[3]It is difficult for textbook authors to decide how much detail to include on corporate taxes, primarily because tax laws change virtually every year. Even so, the best way to learn about tax effects is to work with examples based on the current tax law. However, you should recognize that many aspects of the law will probably change before you actually perform an on-the-job cash flow analysis.

Table 8-1
ACRS Classes and Asset Lives under the Tax Reform Act of 1986

Class	Type of Property
3-year	Computers and equipment used in research.
5-year	Automobiles, tractor units, light-duty trucks, computers, and certain special manufacturing tools.
7-year	Most industrial equipment, office furniture, and fixtures.
10-year	Certain longer-lived types of equipment.
27.5-year	Residential rental real property such as apartment buildings.
31.5-year	All nonresidential real property, including commercial and industrial buildings.

ACRS method, however, prescribes a specific procedure for calculating depreciation rates, or *recovery allowances,* for all assets within each class. The annual depreciation expense is then determined by multiplying the asset's *depreciable basis* by the applicable recovery allowance. Table 8-2 contains our best estimates of the recovery allowances prescribed by the Tax Reform Act of 1986. However, as we write this, negotiations are still going on between the Senate and the House, and the final procedures may vary considerably from those we used. Nevertheless, the Table 8-2 allowances were used in all applicable examples, end-of-chapter problems, and cases, and hence students should use these percentages when working with text material.

Half-Year Convention
The ACRS recovery allowances as shown in Table 8-2 employ the *half-year convention*; that is, they assume that all assets are put into service at midyear, and hence generate a half-year's depreciation, irrespective of when the asset actually goes into service. This feature hurts companies that put assets into service early in the year, but it is beneficial to companies that acquire assets late in the year. To understand why this is so, consider two firms which purchase depreciable assets in 1986. Firm J places its new asset into service on January 1, while Firm D's asset goes into service on December 31. Prior to 1981, depreciation for the first year was based on the actual portion of the year the asset was in service. Therefore, Firm J would have obtained a full year's depreciation, but Firm D could have expensed only one day's depreciation for 1986. However, under the ACRS method, each firm receives six months' depreciation. Clearly, this convention hurts Firm J, since it receives only six months' depreciation for an asset that is in service for a full year, but it helps Firm D since it receives six months' depreciation even though its asset is in service only one day. Note, however, that the recovery allowances for 27.5-year and 31.5-year class life property reflect the actual month that the asset was placed in service.

Depreciable Basis
The *depreciable basis* is a critical element of ACRS because each year's allowance (depreciation expense) depends on the asset's depreciable basis and its ACRS class life. The depreciable basis under ACRS is not adjusted for salvage value. Thus,

Table 8-2
ACRS Recovery Allowance Estimates (1986 Rates)

Ownership Year	Class of Investment			
	3-Year	5-Year	7-Year	10-Year
1	34%	20%	15%	10%
2	33	32	25	18
3	33	20	18	15
4		14	12	12
5		14	10	9
6			10	8
7			10	7
8				7
9				7
10				7
	100%	100%	100%	100%

Notes:
a. We developed these recovery allowance percentages based on the double (200 percent) declining balance method, with a switch to straight-line depreciation at some point in the asset's life. For example, consider the 10-year recovery allowances. The straight-line allowance would be 10 percent per year, so the 200 percent declining balance multiplier is $2.0 \times 10\% = 20\%$. However, the half-year convention applies, so the ACRS allowance for Year 1 is 10 percent. In Year 2, there is 90 percent of the depreciable basis remaining to be depreciated, so the recovery allowance is $0.20(90\%) = 18\%$. After 6 years, straight-line depreciation exceeds the double declining balance depreciation, so a switch is made to straight line. This switch gives an allowance of $28\%/4 = 7\%$.
b. The half-year convention can be applied in two ways: (1) The remaining half year of depreciation can be pro rated over the remaining class life; this is done under the pre-1987 law. (2) The half year can be taken in the year following the class life. We assumed that Method 1 will be used, but the new tax bill might go to Method 2.

salvage value is not deducted from an asset's capitalized cost to determine its depreciable basis. To illustrate, assume that a company pays $80,000 for a new computer system, which has an expected salvage value of $20,000. In addition, the freight charges are $5,000, and $15,000 must be spent for installation. Thus, the capitalized cost, which is also the depreciable basis, is $80,000 + $5,000 + $15,000 = $100,000. This number, multiplied by the Table 8-2 percentages, would produce the annual depreciation allowances.

Investment Tax Credit
An *investment tax credit (ITC)* provides for a direct reduction of taxes, and it is designed to stimulate business investment.[4] ITCs were first introduced in the Kennedy administration, in 1961, and they have been put in and taken out of the tax system depending on how Congress perceives the need to stimulate business investment versus the need for federal revenues. For example, under 1981 tax law,

---

[4]In addition to investment tax credits, there are also tax credits for research and development, job-training and employment programs, and other specific expenditures which will not be discussed in this text.

the ITC was 6 percent for assets in the 3-year class and 10 percent for assets in the 5-year or longer classes. The dollar tax deduction was determined by multiplying the capitalized cost of the asset by the applicable ITC percentage. ITCs were eliminated by the Tax Reform Act of 1986. However, Congress could reinstate them at any time, so you should be familiar with the concept.

ACRS Illustration

Assume that the computer system that we previously discussed falls into the 5-year class and it is placed into service on March 1, 1987. Its depreciable basis is $100,000, and each year's dollar recovery allowance (depreciation expense) is determined by multiplying the depreciable basis by the applicable Table 8-2 percentage allowance. Thus, its depreciation expense for 1987 is 0.20 ($100,000) = $20,000. Similarly, its depreciation expense is 0.32 ($100,000) = $32,000 for 1988, $20,000 for 1989, and $14,000 for 1990 and 1991. Note that the depreciation expense over the entire 5-year class life totals the depreciable basis, $100,000.

Straight-Line Option

Firms may elect to use the straight-line method for tax depreciation in place of the recovery allowances listed in Table 8-2. However, under most circumstances, it is advantageous to use the accelerated allowances and hence we will not discuss the straight-line procedures.

Salvage Value

We have already mentioned that salvage value has no effect on the depreciable basis, and hence on the depreciation expense taken under ACRS. Still, when performing a cash flow analysis, we must estimate the market value of the asset at the end of the project's economic life, as this is an expected cash inflow. Tax effects on the salvage value must be taken into account, and any difference between the asset's salvage value and its book value is treated as ordinary income and is taxed at the firm's marginal tax rate. Since the ACRS class life is normally less than the economic life of the asset, the book value will often be zero when the asset is sold, in which case the entire salvage value will be taxed as corporate income.[5]

CHANGES IN NET WORKING CAPITAL

In Chapter 4, when we discussed the relevant WACC components, we ignored spontaneous liabilities on the grounds that capital from these sources would simply reduce the expenditures required to finance projects. Normally, additional inventories are required to support a new operation, and the new sales will also produce additional accounts receivable. Thus, both inventories and receivables will increase

---

[5]In this case, the tax depreciation charges exceeded "true" depreciation, and the excess depreciation is "recaptured". Since depreciation reduced ordinary income, its recapture is treated as ordinary income.

as a result of capital budgeting decisions, so the "investment outlay" of a new project must include the associated current assets as well as the fixed assets involved.[6] However, accounts payable and accruals will also increase spontaneously as a result of the expansion, and this will reduce the need to raise capital to finance the project. The difference between the projected increases in current assets and current liabilities is defined as a *change in net working capital*. If the change associated with a project is positive, as it generally is for expansion projects, this indicates that additional financing, over and above the cost of the fixed assets, is needed to fund the change in current assets. Conversely, if in some situation the change in net working capital were negative, then the project would be generating a cash inflow from the change in net working capital.

Net working capital changes may occur over several periods, so the increase (or decrease) could be reflected in cash flows for several periods. However, once the operation has stabilized, working capital should also stabilize at the new level, and beyond this time no changes will occur until the project is terminated. At the end of the project's life, we generally assume that the firm's total working capital requirements revert to prior levels. Thus, the firm will experience an end-of-project cash flow that is equal, but opposite in sign, to the total net working capital change that occurred in the project's early years. This point is illustrated in the next section.

CASH FLOW ANALYSIS EXAMPLE

Up to this point, we have discussed several important aspects of cash flow analysis, but we have not seen how they relate to one another and affect the capital budgeting decision. In this section, we illustrate all this by examining a capital budgeting decision that faces Robotics International Corporation (RIC). RIC, a world leader in the robotics industry, produces a line of industrial robots and peripheral equipment which perform many routine assembly line tasks. The company enjoyed much success in the late 1970s and early 1980s, when automobile manufacturers and other durable goods producers sought to cut costs by automating the production process. However, by 1986, increased competition, particularly from Japanese firms, had caused RIC's management to be concerned about the company's growth potential. RIC's research and development department had been applying industrial robot technology to develop a line of office maintenance robots. (The maintenance robot is designed to function as a janitor, performing such tasks as vacuuming, dusting, and emptying trash cans. A floor plan of the office is programmed into the robot to enable it to move freely about the facility.) This effort has now reached the stage where a decision on whether or not to go forward with production must be made.

RIC's marketing department has plans to target sales of the robots to the larger office complexes, and if they are successful there, then the robots could be mar-

---

[6]Actually, the entire change in net working capital does not have to be financed. Some of the increase in receivables represents profits which do not require financing. This topic is discussed in Chapter 19.

keted to a wide variety of businesses, including schools, hospitals, and eventually even to households. The marketing vice-president believes that annual sales would be 25,000 units if the robots were priced at $2,200 each. The engineering department has estimated that the firm would need a new manufacturing plant; this plant could be built and made ready for production in 2 years, once the "go" decision is made. The plant would require a 25-acre site, and RIC currently has an option to purchase a suitable tract of land for $1.2 million. Building construction would begin in early 1988 and continue through 1989. The building, which would fall into the ACRS 31.5-year class, would cost an estimated $8 million, and a $4 million payment would be due to the contractor on December 31, 1988, and another $4 million payable on December 31, 1989.

The necessary manufacturing equipment would be installed late in 1989 and would be paid for on December 31, 1989. The equipment, which would fall into the ACRS 7-year class, would have a cost of $9.5 million, including transportation, plus another $500,000 for installation. To date, the company has spent $10 million on research and development associated with the office robot. The company has expensed $2.5 million of the R&D costs, and the remaining $7.5 million has been capitalized and will be amortized over the life of the project. However, if RIC decides not to go forward with the project, the capitalized R&D expenditures could be written off on December 31, 1987.[7]

The project would also require an initial investment in net working capital equal to 12 percent of the estimated sales in the first year. The initial working capital investment would be made on December 31, 1989, and on December 31 of each following year, net working capital would be increased by an amount equal to 12 percent of any sales increase expected during the coming year. The project's estimated economic life is 6 years. At that time, the land is expected to have a market value of $1.7 million, the building a value of $1.0 million, and the equipment a value of $2 million. The production department has estimated that variable manufacturing costs would total 65 percent of dollar sales, and that fixed overhead costs, excluding depreciation, would be $8 million for the first year of operations. Sales prices and fixed overhead costs, other than depreciation, are projected to increase with inflation, which is expected to average 6 percent per year over the 6-year life of the project.

RIC's marginal federal-plus-state tax rate is 40 percent; its weighted average cost of capital is 10 percent; and the company's policy, for capital budgeting purposes, is to assume that cash flows occur at the end of each year. Since the plant would begin operations on January 1, 1990, the first operating cash flows would thus occur on December 31, 1990.

As an RIC financial analyst, you have been assigned the task of conducting the initial capital budgeting analysis. For now, you are to assume that the project has the same risk as the firm's current average project, and to use the corporate WACC, 10 percent, for this project. (However, the departments that have provided input

---

[7]The tax laws concerning the expensing versus amortization of R&D expenditures are relatively complex. Our treatment is merely intended to illustrate how such costs might be handled.

to the analysis have been directed to provide additional information concerning the probability distributions of their estimates for use in a second-stage analysis. These distribution estimates will be used in Chapter 9, where we assess the riskiness of the project. At this point, you should simply recognize that all of the cash flow estimates are expected values based on estimated probability distributions.)

Analysis of the Cash Flows

The first step in the analysis is to summarize the investment outlays required for the project; this is done in Table 8-3. Note that the land cannot be depreciated, and hence we show its depreciable basis to be $0. Also, since the project will require an increase in net working capital during 1989, this is shown as an investment requirement for that year. Finally, note that the $2,500,000 of already expensed R&D costs is not relevant to the analysis, since it is a sunk cost. However, if the project is not undertaken, the entire $7.5 million of capitalized R&D expenses can be written off in 1987, and it will then produce a tax savings in that year. On the other hand, if RIC accepts the project, this immediate write-off will not be available. Consequently, the value of the tax shelter ($7,500,000 $\times$ 0.40 = $3,000,000) must be included as an investment opportunity cost assigned to 1987.

Having estimated the capital requirements, we must now estimate the cash flows (operating cash flows and net working capital outlays) which will occur once production begins; these are set forth in Table 8-4. The cash inflow estimates are based on information received from RIC's various departments. Note that the sales

Table 8-3
RIC: Investment Requirements, 1987-1989

Fixed Assets	1987	1988	1989	Total Costs, 1987-1989	Depreciable Basis
Land	$1,200,000	$ 0	$ 0	$ 1,200,000	$ 0
Building	0	4,000,000	4,000,000	8,000,000	8,000,000
Equipment	0	0	10,000,000	10,000,000	10,000,000
Total fixed assets	$1,200,000	$4,000,000	$14,000,000	$19,200,000	
Net working capital[a]	0	0	6,600,000	6,600,000	
R&D opportunity cost[b]	3,000,000	0	0	3,000,000	
Total investment	$4,200,000	$4,000,000	$20,600,000	$28,800,000	

[a]12 percent of first year's sales, or 0.12($55,000,000) = $6,600,000.

[b]R&D expenditures of $10 million were made prior to 1987; $2.5 million of these costs have been expensed, and $7.5 million were capitalized. If the project is abandoned, then the $7.5 million of capitalized R&D costs can be expensed immediately, producing a tax saving of 0.40($7,500,000) = $3,000,000. If the project is accepted, the company will not get this immediate tax saving (it would, in that case, amortize the R&D costs and receive the associated tax savings over the life of the project). Thus, the $3,000,000 is an opportunity cost which must be charged to the project in 1987.

Table 8-4
RIC: Operating and Net Working Capital Cash Flows, 1990-1995

	1990	1991	1992	1993	1994	1995
Unit sales	25,000	25,000	25,000	25,000	25,000	25,000
Sale price[a]	$ 2,200	$ 2,332	$ 2,472	$ 2,620	$ 2,777	$ 2,944
Net sales[a]	$55,000,000	$58,300,000	$61,800,000	$65,500,000	$69,425,000	$73,600,000
Variable costs[b]	35,750,000	37,895,000	40,170,000	42,575,000	45,126,250	47,840,000
Fixed costs (overhead)[a]	8,000,000	8,480,000	8,988,800	9,528,128	10,099,816	10,705,805
Amortization of R&D expense[c]	1,250,000	1,250,000	1,250,000	1,250,000	1,250,000	1,250,000
Depreciation (building)[d]	240,000	240,000	240,000	240,000	240,000	240,000
Depreciation (equipment)[d]	1,500,000	2,500,000	1,800,000	1,200,000	1,000,000	1,000,000
Earnings before taxes	$ 8,260,000	$ 7,935,000	$ 9,351,200	$10,706,872	$11,708,934	$12,564,195
Taxes (40%)	3,304,000	3,174,000	3,740,480	4,282,749	4,683,574	5,025,678
Project NOI	$ 4,956,000	$ 4,761,000	$ 5,610,720	$ 6,424,123	$ 7,025,360	$ 7,538,517
Noncash expenses[e]	2,990,000	3,990,000	3,290,000	2,690,000	2,490,000	2,490,000
Cash flow from operations[f]	$ 7,946,000	$ 8,751,000	$ 8,900,720	$ 9,114,123	$ 9,515,360	$10,028,517
Addition to NWC[g]	(396,000)	(420,000)	(444,000)	(471,000)	(501,000)	8,832,000
Net operating and NWC cash flows	$ 7,550,000	$ 8,331,000	$ 8,456,720	$ 8,643,123	$ 9,014,360	$18,860,517

[a]1990 estimate increased by an assumed 6 percent inflation rate.

[b]65 percent of net sales.

[c]If the project is accepted, RIC will amortize the $7.5 million of capitalized R&D costs over 6 years, so it will have a noncash, deductible expense of $7,500,000/6 = $1,250,000 per year.

[d]ACRS recovery allowances were estimated as follows:

Year	1	2	3	4	5	6
Building	3%	3%	3%	3%	3%	3%
Equipment	15%	25%	18%	12%	10%	10%

Allowances for the equipment were taken from Table 8-2. Allowances for the building are representative of those for long-lived assets. These percentages were multiplied by the depreciable basis to obtain the depreciation expense for each year.

[e]Sum of amortized R&D expense plus depreciation on building and equipment.

[f]Net operating income plus noncash expenses.

[g]12 percent of next year's increase in sales. For example, 1991 sales are $3.3 million larger than 1990 sales, so the addition to NWC in 1990 to prepare for the 1991 sales increase is (0.12)($3,300,000) = $396,000. The cumulative working capital investment will be recovered in 1995.

price and fixed costs are projected to increase each year by the 6 percent inflation rate, and since variable costs are 65 percent of sales, they too will rise by 6 percent per year. The reported R&D expenses represent the amortization of the $7.5 million of capitalized R&D costs; this is a deduction for tax purposes, but it is also a noncash charge, so it must be added to depreciation and net income to obtain cash flows from operations. The changes in net working capital (NWC) represent the additional investments required by sales increases (12 percent of the next year's increase, all of which results from inflation) during 1990-1994, and the recovery of the cumulative net working capital investment in 1995. The depreciation amounts were obtained by multiplying the depreciable basis by the appropriate ACRS recovery allowance rate.

The analysis also requires an estimation of the cash flows generated by salvage values; Table 8-5 summarizes this analysis. First, we compare the projected 1995 market values against the 1995 book values and initial costs. The land cannot be depreciated, and it has an estimated 1995 salvage value greater than the initial purchase price. Thus, RIC would have to pay taxes on the profit. The building has an estimated salvage value less than the book value—it will be sold at a loss for tax purposes. The loss will reduce ordinary income and thus generate a tax savings; in effect, the company has been depreciating the building too slowly, so it would write off the loss against ordinary income. On the other hand, the equipment will be sold for more than book value, but for less than its original depreciable basis,

Table 8-5
RIC: Projected Net Salvage Values, 1995

	Land	Building	Equipment
Salvage (ending market) value	$1,700,000	$1,000,000	$ 2,000,000
Initial cost	1,200,000	8,000,000	10,000,000
Depreciable basis	0	8,000,000	10,000,000
Book value (1995)[a]	1,200,000	6,560,000	1,000,000
Capital gains income	$ 500,000	$ 0	$ 0
Ordinary income (loss)[b]	0	($5,560,000)	$ 1,000,000
Taxes[c]	(200,000)	2,224,000	(400,000)
Net salvage value	$1,500,000	$3,224,000	$ 1,600,000

Total cash flow from salvage value = $1,500,000 + $3,224,000 + $1,600,000 = $6,324,000.

[a]Book value for building in 1995 equals depreciable basis minus accumulated ACRS depreciation of $1,440,000. The accumulated depreciation on the equipment is $9,000,000. See Table 8-4.
[b]Building: $6,560,000 book value − $1,000,000 market value = $5,560,000 depreciation shortfall treated as an operating expense in 1995.
Equipment: $1,000,000 book value − $2,000,000 market value = $1,000,000 depreciation recapture treated as ordinary income in 1995.
[c]Since capital gains are now taxed at the ordinary income rate, all taxes are based on RIC's 40 percent marginal federal-plus-state rate.

so RIC will have to pay ordinary taxes on the $1 million profit. In all cases, the book value is the depreciable basis less accumulated depreciation, and the total cash flow from salvage is merely the sum of the land, building, and equipment components.

Making the Decision

To summarize the analysis and get the data ready for evaluation, it is useful to combine all of the net cash flows on a time line such as the one shown in Table 8-6. The table also shows the payback period, IRR, NPV (at the 10 percent cost of capital), and the PI. The project appears to be acceptable using the IRR, NPV, or PI methods, and it would also be acceptable if RIC required a payback of six years or less. Note, however, that the analysis thus far has been based on the assumption that the project has the same degree of risk as RIC's average project. If the project is riskier than an average project, then it would be necessary to increase the cost of capital, which in turn might cause the NPV to become negative, the IRR to fall below k, and the PI to be less than 1.0. In Chapter 9, we will extend the evaluation of this project to include the necessary risk analysis.

At this point in the analysis, before going on to take risk into account, it is useful to sit back and take a hard look at the estimated cash flows and the resulting IRR. Sometimes things look better than they really are. For example suppose the project had a relatively long life and an IRR which was significantly above the firm's cost of capital. The very fact that the project is so profitable might attract other firms into the market, and new entry might cause the actual cash flows to fall far below those originally estimated. Thus, the financial analyst should view long-term, high-profitability projects with some skepticism, for only if the firm has some type of cost or marketing advantage over other firms can above-normal rates of return be sustained over time. In the case of the office robot project, management does not think that competitors would be able to develop and produce office robots within the next 8 years. Additionally, even though the IRR is relatively high, we shall see in Chapter 9 that the project is also relatively risky, and a 21.6 percent return on a risky project is not likely to cause competitors to embark on crash programs.

Table 8-6
RIC: Time Line of Consolidated Cash Flows

			End-of-Year Net Cash Flows					
1987	1988	1989	1990	1991	1992	1993	1994	1995
($4,200,000)	($4,000,000)	($20,600,000)	$7,550,000	$8,331,000	$8,456,720	$8,643,123	$9,014,360	$25,184,517

Payback period: 5.5 years from first outflow.
IRR: 21.6% versus a 10% cost of capital.
NPV: $13,005,785.
PI: 1.5.

REPLACEMENT ANALYSIS

RIC's office robot project was used to show how an expansion project is analyzed. RIC and other companies also make *replacement decisions*, and the analysis relating to replacements is somewhat different from that for expansion projects because the cash flows from the old asset must be considered. Replacement analysis is illustrated with another RIC example, this time from the company's plastics division.

A lathe for trimming molded plastics was purchased 10 years ago at a cost of $7,500. The machine had an expected life of 15 years at the time it was purchased, and management originally estimated, and still believes, that the salvage value will be zero at the end of the 15-year life. The machine is being depreciated on a straight-line basis; therefore, its annual depreciation charge is $500, and its present book value is $2,500.[8]

The division manager reports that a new special purpose machine can be purchased for $12,000 (including freight and installation), which over its 5-year life, will reduce labor and raw materials usage sufficiently to cut operating costs from $7,000 to $4,000. This reduction in costs will cause before-tax profits to rise by $7,000 − $4,000 = $3,000 per year.

It is estimated that the new machine can be sold for $2,000 at the end of 5 years; this is its estimated salvage value. The old machine's actual current market value is $1,000, which is below its $2,500 book value. If the new machine were acquired, the old lathe would be sold to another company rather than exchanged for the new machine. RIC's marginal federal-plus-state tax rate is 40 percent, and the replacement project is of average risk. Net working capital requirements will also increase by $1,000 at the time of replacement. The new machine falls into the 5-year ACRS class, and RIC's cost of capital is 10 percent. Should the replacement be made?

Table 8-7 shows the worksheet format that RIC uses to analyze replacement projects. A line-by-line description of the table follows.

Line 1. The top section of the table, Lines 1 through 5, sets forth the cash flows which occur at (approximately) t = 0, the time the investment is made. Line 1 shows the purchase price of the new machine, including any installation and freight charges.

Line 2. Here we show the price received from the sale of old equipment.

Line 3. Since the old equipment would be sold at less than book value, this creates a loss which reduces RIC's taxable income, and hence its next quarterly income tax payment. The tax saving is equal to (Loss)(T) = ($1,500)(0.40) = $600, where T is the marginal corporate tax rate. The Tax Code defines this loss as an operating loss, because it reflects the fact that inadequate depreciation was taken on the old asset. If there had been a profit on the sale (that is, if the sales

---

[8]This machine was purchased prior to the Economic Recovery Tax Act of 1981, so the Accelerated Cost Recovery System was not in place at the time. RIC chose to depreciate the lathe on a straight line basis.

Table 8-7
Replacement Analysis Worksheet

I. Net Outflows at the Time the Investment is Made (t = 0)

1. Cost of new equipment	$12,000
2. Market value of old equipment	(1,000)
3. Tax effect of sale of old equipment	(600)
4. Increase in net working capital	1,000
5. Total initial outflow	$11,400

II. Operating Inflows over the Project's Life

	t = 0	t = 1	t = 2	t = 3	t = 4	t = 5
6. After-tax decrease in costs		$1,800	$1,800	$1,800	$1,800	$1,800
7. Depreciation on new machine		2,400	3,840	2,400	1,680	1,680
8. Depreciation on old machine		500	500	500	500	500
9. Change in depreciation		1,900	3,340	1,900	1,180	1,180
10. Tax savings from depreciation		760	1,336	760	472	472
11. Net operating cash flow (6 + 10)		$2,560	$3,136	$2,560	$2,272	$2,272

III. Terminal Year Cash Flows

12. Estimated salvage value of new machine	$1,200
13. Return of working capital	1,000
14. Total termination cash flow	$2,200

IV. Net Cash Flows

	t = 0	t = 1	t = 2	t = 3	t = 4	t = 5
15. Total net cash flow	($11,400)	$2,560	$3,136	$2,560	$2,272	$4,472

V. Results

Payback period: 4.2 years.
IRR: 9.3% versus a 10% cost of capital.
NPV: − $229.06.
PI: 0.98.

---

price had exceeded book value), Line 3 would have shown taxes *paid*, a positive cash outflow. In the actual case, the equipment would be sold at a loss, so no taxes would be paid, and RIC would realize a tax savings of $600.[9]

Line 4. The investment in additional net working capital (new current asset requirements less increases in accounts payable and accruals) is shown here. This investment will be recovered at the end of the project's life (see Line 13). No taxes are involved.

Line 5. Here we show the total net cash outflow at the time the replacement is made. RIC writes a check for $12,000 to pay for the machine, and another $1,000

---

[9]If the old asset were being exchanged for the new asset, rather than being sold to a third party, the tax consequences would be different. In an exchange of similar assets, no gain or loss is recognized. If the market value of the old asset is greater than its book value, the depreciable basis of the new asset is decreased by the excess amount. Conversely, if the market value of the old asset is less than its book value, the depreciable basis is increased by the shortfall.

is invested in net working capital. However, these outlays are partially offset by the items on Lines 2 and 3.

Line 6. Section II of the table shows the *incremental operating cash flows*, or benefits, that are expected if the replacement is made. The cash flows for each year are based on Equation 8-2 as set forth earlier in the chapter. The first of these benefits is the reduction in operating costs shown on Line 6, which (1) increases cash flows because operating costs are reduced by $3,000, but (2) also raises taxable income, and hence income taxes payable. Therefore, the after-tax benefit is $3,000(1 − T) = $3,000(1 − 0.40) = $3,000(0.60) = $1,800. Note that had the replacement resulted in an increase in sales in addition to the reduction in costs (if the new machine had been both larger and more efficient), then this amount would also be reported on Line 6 (or a separate line could be added). Finally, note that the $3,000 cost savings is constant over Years 1-5; had the annual savings been expected to change over time, this fact would have to be built into the analysis.

Line 7. The depreciable basis of the new machine, $12,000, is multiplied by the appropriate ACRS recovery allowance for 5-year class property to obtain the depreciation figures shown on Line 7. Note that Line 7 totals $12,000, the depreciable basis.

Line 8. Line 8 shows the $500 straight-line depreciation on the old machine.

Line 9. The depreciation expense on the old machine as shown on Line 8 will not be available if the replacement is made, but the new machine's depreciation will be available. Therefore, the $500 depreciation of the old machine is subtracted from that on the new machine to show the net change in annual depreciation. The change is positive in this case, but it could have been negative.

Line 10. The net increase in depreciation results in a tax savings which is equal to the change in depreciation multiplied by the tax rate: Depreciation savings = T (Change in depreciation) = 0.40($1,900) = $760 for Year 1. Note that the relevant cash flow is the tax savings on the *net change* in depreciation, and not the depreciation on the new equipment. Capital budgeting decisions are based on *incremental* cash flows, and since we lose $500 of depreciation if we replace the old machine, that fact must be taken into account.

Line 11. Here we show the net operating cash flows over the project's 5-year life. These flows are found by summing the after-tax cost decrease and the depreciation tax savings, Line 6 plus Line 10.

Line 12. Part III shows the cash flows associated with the termination of the project. The estimated salvage value of the new machine at the end of its 5-year life is $2,000. Since the book value of the new machine at the end of 5 years is zero, RIC will have to pay taxes on the proceeds. Thus, the after-tax salvage value cash flow is $2,000(1 − 0.40) = $2,000(0.60) = $1,200.[10]

---

[10]In this analysis, the salvage value of the old machine is zero. However, if the old machine could be sold at the end of five years, then replacing the old machine now would deprive the firm of this cash flow. Thus, the after-tax salvage value of the old machine would represent an opportunity cost to the firm, and it would be included as a Year 5 cash outflow in the terminal cash flow section of the worksheet.

Line 13. An investment of $1,000 in net working capital was shown as an outflow at t = 0. This investment, like the new machine's salvage value, will be recovered when the project is terminated at the end of Year 5. Accounts receivable will be collected, inventories will be drawn down and not replaced, and this will produce an inflow of $1,000 at t = 5.

Line 14. Here we show the total cash flows resulting from terminating the project.

Line 15. Part IV shows, on Line 15, the total net cash flows in a form suitable for capital budgeting evaluation.

Part V of the table, "Results," shows the replacement project's payback, IRR, NPV, and PI. The project is assumed to be of similar risk to the old project, and the old project is assumed to be about as risky as RIC's average project. Therefore, a 10 percent project cost of capital is appropriate. At this cost of capital, the project is not acceptable, and hence the old lathe should not be replaced.

EVALUATING PROJECTS WITH UNEQUAL LIVES

Note that a replacement decision involves two mutually exclusive projects: (1) The firm can either retain the old asset or (2) it can replace it with a new asset. To simplify matters, in our replacement example we assumed that the new machine had a life equal to the remaining life of the old machine. If, however, we were choosing between two mutually exclusive alternatives that had significantly different lives, it would be necessary to take this into account. We now discuss two procedures—(1) replacement chains and (2) equivalent annual annuities—that illustrate both the problem and approaches to dealing with it.

Suppose RIC is planning to modernize its production facilities, and as a part of the process, it is considering either a conveyor system (Project C) or a forklift truck (Project F) for moving industrial robot components from the parts department to its main assembly line. Table 8-8 shows both the expected net cash flows and the NPV for each of these mutually exclusive alternatives. We see that Project

Table 8-8
Expected Net Cash Flows for Projects C and F

Year	Project C	Project F
0	($40,000)	($20,000)
1	8,000	7,000
2	14,000	13,000
3	13,000	12,000
4	12,000	—
5	11,000	—
6	10,000	—
NPV at 10%	$9,281	$6,123

C, when discounted at a 10 percent cost of capital, has the higher NPV and hence appears to be the better project.

Replacement Chain (Common Life) Approach

Although the analysis in Table 8-8 suggests that Project C should be selected, this analysis is incomplete, and the decision to choose Project C is actually incorrect. If we choose Project F, we will have an opportunity to make a similar investment after 3 years, and if cost conditions continue at the Table 8-8 levels, this second investment will also be profitable. However, if we choose Project C, we will not have this second investment opportunity. Therefore, to make a proper comparison of Projects C and F, we must find the NPV of Project F over a 6-year period and then compare this extended NPV with the NPV of Project C over the same 6 years.

The NPV for Project C, as calculated in Table 8-8, is already over a 6-year life. For Project F, however, we must take three additional steps: (1) determine the NPV of a second Project F three years hence, (2) discount this NPV back to the present, and (3) sum these two component NPVs:

1. If we make the assumption that Project F's cost and annual cash flows will not change if the project were repeated in three years, and that RIC's cost of capital will remain at 10 percent, then Project F's second-stage NPV would remain the same as its first-stage NPV, $6,123. However, the second NPV would not accrue for three years, and hence it would represent a present value at t = 3.

2. The present value (at t = 0) of the replicated Project F is determined by discounting the second NPV (at t = 3) back three years at 10 percent to determine its value at t = 0: $6,123/(1.10)^3 = $4,600.

3. The "true" NPV of Project F is $6,123 + $4,600 = $10,723. This is the value which should be compared with the NPV of Project C, $9,281. Since the "true" NPV of Project F is greater than the NPV of Project C, Project F should be selected.

Equivalent Annual Annuity Approach

Although the preceding example illustrates why a chain analysis is necessary if mutually exclusive projects have different lives, the arithmetic is generally more complex in practice. For example, one project might have an 8-year life versus an 11-year life for the other. This would require an analysis over 88 years, the lowest common denominator of the two lives. In such a situation, it is often simpler to use a second procedure, the equivalent annual annuity method, which involves three steps:

1. Find each project's NPV over its original life. In the previous example, we found $NPV_C = $9,281$ and $NPV_F = $6,123$.

2. Find the annuity cash flow that has the same present value as each project's NPV. For example, for Project C, enter $9,281 as the PV, k = i = 10%, and n = 6 in your calculator and solve for PMT. The answer is $2,131. This annuity, when discounted back 6 years at 10 percent, has a present value equal to Project C's original NPV, $9,281. The value $2,131 is called the project's *equivalent annual annuity (EAA)*. The EAA for Project F was found similarly to be $2,462. Thus, Project C has an NPV which is equivalent to an annuity of $2,131 per year for 6 years, while Project F's NPV is equivalent to an annuity of $2,462 for 3 years.

3. Assuming that continuous replacements will be made when each project's life ends, these EAAs will continue on out to infinity; that is, they will constitute perpetuities. Recognizing that the value of a perpetuity is V = Annual receipt/k, we can find the net present values of the infinite EAAs of Projects C and F as follows:

$$\text{Infinite horizon NPV}_C = \$2,131/0.10 = \$21,310.$$

$$\text{Infinite horizon NPV}_F = \$2,462/0.10 = \$24,620.$$

Since the infinite horizon NPV of F exceeds that of C, Project F should be accepted. Therefore, the EAA method leads to the same decision rule as the simple chain method—accept Project F.

Computationally, the EAA method is often easier to apply than the chain method. However, the chain method is often easier to explain to decision makers, and it does not require the assumption of an infinite time horizon. Also, note that Step 3 above is not really necessary to make the decision—we could have stopped after Step 2, because the project with the higher EAA will have the higher NPV over any common life.

When should we worry about unequal life analysis? As a general rule, the unequal life issue (1) does not arise for independent projects but (2) can arise if mutually exclusive projects with significantly different lives are being evaluated. However, even for mutually exclusive projects, it is not always appropriate to extend the analysis to a common life. This should only be done if there is a high probability that the projects will actually be replicated beyond their initial lives.

We should note several potentially serious weaknesses of our unequal life analysis: (1) If inflation is expected, then replacement equipment will have a higher price, and sales prices will probably change, and thus the static conditions built into the analysis would be invalid. (2) Replacements that occur down the road would doubtless employ new technology, which in turn would change the cash flows, yet replacement chain analysis and the EAA approach both assume constant technology. (3) It is difficult enough to estimate the life of most projects, so estimating the lives of a series of projects is often just speculation.

In view of these problems, no experienced financial analyst would be too concerned about comparing mutually exclusive projects with lives of, say, 8 years and 10 years. Given all the uncertainties in the estimation process, such projects could, for all practical purposes, be assumed to have the same lives. Still, it is important for you to recognize that a problem does exist if mutually exclusive projects have substantially different lives. When we encounter such problems in practice, we build expected inflation and/or possible efficiency gains directly into the cash flow estimates, and then use the replacement chain approach (but not the equivalent annual annuity method). The cash flow estimation is more complicated, but the concepts involved are exactly the same as in our example.

ABANDONMENT VALUE

Customarily, projects are analyzed as though the firm will definitely operate each project over its assumed useful life. However, this may not be the best course of action—it may be best to abandon a project prior to its potential life, and this possibility can materially affect the project's calculated NPV and IRR.[11] The situation in Table 8-9 can be used to illustrate the abandonment value concept and its effects on capital budgeting. The abandonment values are equivalent to salvage values, except that they have been estimated for each year of Project A's life.

Using a cost of capital of 10 percent, the expected NPV over the 3-year estimated life is $-\$117$:

$$NPV = -\$4,800 + \$2,000/(1.10)^1 + \$1,875/(1.10)^2 + \$1,750/(1.10)^3$$

$$= -\$117.$$

Thus, Project A would not be accepted if we considered the single alternative of a 3-year life with a zero salvage (abandonment) value. However, what would its NPV be if the project were abandoned after 2 years? In this case, we would receive operating cash flows in Years 1 and 2, plus the abandonment value at the end of Year 2, and the NPV would be $138:

$$NPV = -\$4,800 + \$2,000/(1.10)^1 + \$1,875/(1.10)^2 + \$1,900/(1.10)^2$$

$$= \$138.$$

Thus, Project A becomes acceptable if we plan to operate it for 2 years and then abandon it. To complete the analysis, we note that if the project were abandoned after 1 year, its NPV would be $-\$255$. Thus, the optimal project life is 2 years.

As a general rule, any project should be abandoned when the abandonment value is greater than the present value of all cash flows beyond the abandonment year, discounted to the abandonment decision point. For example, if we accept Project A and operate it for one year, then the abandonment value would be $3,000, but the present value at Year 1 of cash flows beyond Year 1 would be $\$1,875/(1.10)^1 + \$1,750/(1.10)^2 = \$3,151$, assuming the project continues through Year 3; and $\$1,875/(1.10)^1 + \$1,900/(1.10)^1 = \$3,432$, assuming abandonment at the end of Year 2. Thus, the Year 1 abandonment value is less than the Year 1 present values of the expected future cash flows under either of the two alternative longer lives, so the project should not be abandoned at this point. However, a similar analysis at Year 2 would show that the abandonment value of $1,900 is greater than the discounted value of future cash flows of $\$1,750/(1.10)^1 = \$1,591$, so our decision rule would tell us to abandon the project in Year 2. This is, of course, the same conclusion that we reached from the NPV calculations.

Abandonment value should be considered in the capital budgeting process because, as our example illustrates, there are cases in which recognition of abandon-

---

[11]See Alexander A. Robichek and James C. Van Horne, "Abandonment Value and Capital Budgeting," *Journal of Finance*, December 1967, 577-589.

Table 8-9
Investment, Net Operating, and Abandonment Cash Flows for Project A

Year	Initial Investment and Operating Cash Flow	Abandonment Value in Year t
0	($4,800)	$4,800
1	2,000	3,000
2	1,875	1,900
3	1,750	0

ment can make an otherwise unacceptable project acceptable. Indeed, this type of analysis is required to determine a project's economic life. For Project A, the *economic life* is actually two years rather than the three-year *physical life*, with the economic life being defined as that project life which maximizes the project's NPV and thus maximizes shareholder wealth.

Two very different types of abandonment occur: (1) sale by the original user of a still-valuable asset to some other party who can obtain greater cash flows from the asset and (2) abandoning an asset because the project is losing money. The first type situation often occurs in real estate, where tax considerations make it more profitable for one party to sell property to another, because the second party can obtain higher depreciation tax shelters if the property is bought at a price greater than its book value. Similarly, corporations often sell whole divisions to other companies that think they can operate the division more efficiently.

The second type of abandonment—the ability to close down money losing operations—can greatly reduce the riskiness of a project. This aspect of abandonment is discussed in Chapter 9. The main point for you to understand now is that the cash flows from a project can be materially different if it is abandoned (or sold off) at some point rather than operated to the end of its physical life, and if abandonment possibilities are not considered when in fact they exist, then the cash flows from the project can be badly misspecified.

ALTERNATIVE NPV METHODS

We have focused on using the weighted average cost of capital (WACC) to estimate a project's NPV. However, we should note that this procedure is just one of several different NPV methods that can be used in project evaluation. In this section, we compare the WACC method with two alternative NPV procedures: (1) the equity residual method, and (2) the adjusted present value (APV) method.[12]

---

[12]For a more detailed discussion of alternative NPV methods, see Donald R. Chambers, Robert S. Harris, and John J. Pringle, "Treatment of Financing Mix in Analyzing Investment Opportunities," *Financial Management*, Summer 1982, 24-41.

WACC Method

Before we discuss the alternative methods, let us briefly review the WACC approach to estimating a project's NPV. Table 8-10 contains the net operating income and cash flows for Project D, a two-year, average risk project with no end-of-project cash flows. The net investment outlay, or cost, for the project is $100,000. For simplicity, we assume that the project is depreciated by the straight-line method over its two-year life, resulting in a depreciation expense of $50,000 per year.

Now assume (1) that the firm's target capital structure is 50 percent debt and 50 percent equity, (2) that $k_d = 10\%$ and $k_s = 16\%$, and (3) that the marginal federal-plus-state tax rate is $T = 40$ percent. According to the WACC method, the project's NPV is estimated by discounting the project's net operating cash flows by the firm's WACC:

$$WACC = k_a = w_d k_d (1 - T) + w_s k_s$$
$$= 0.5(10\%)0.60 + 0.5(16\%) = 11.0\%.$$
$$NPV = -\$100,000 + \$74,000/1.11 + \$74,000/(1.11)^2$$
$$= -\$100,000 + \$66,667 + \$60,060 = \$26,727.$$

Since Project D's NPV is positive, the firm would accept the project.

Note two important points about the way we calculated Project D's NPV: (1) The net operating cash flows do not include any financing effects—there is no interest expense deduction, and hence no recognition of the tax deductibility of interest payments. Thus, the net operating cash flows must provide a return to both the firm's equityholders and to its debtholders. (2) The discount rate (WACC) includes adjustments for the basic operating risk of the project, the financial risk of the project, and the tax deductibility of interest. Thus, the operating cash flows do not take account of interest and its effects on taxes, but the WACC does adjust for these effects.

Table 8-10
Net Operating Income and Cash Flows for Project D

	Year 1	Year 2
Revenues (R)	$150,000	$150,000
Operating costs (OC)	60,000	60,000
Depreciation expense (D)	50,000	50,000
Operating income	$ 40,000	$ 40,000
Taxes (40%) (T)	16,000	16,000
Net operating income (NOI)	$ 24,000	$ 24,000
Depreciation expense (D)	50,000	50,000
Net operating cash flow (NOI+D)	$ 74,000	$ 74,000

Cost at t = 0: $100,000

Equity Residual Method

While the WACC method focuses on operating cash flows, and the financing mix is accounted for in the discount rate, in the equity residual method, the NPV analysis focuses on the cash flows that accrue solely to the equityholders. Refer again to the operating cash flows for Project D given in Table 8-10. To convert these to equity flows, we must include both the interest payments and the principal repayments on the funds used to finance the project.

Note that the $100,000 project cost would be constructively financed using $50,000 debt and $50,000 equity in accordance with the firm's target capital structure. Now, assume that the debt financing consists of a 2-year balloon note, wherein interest will be paid annually, and the entire principal amount will be repaid at the end of the second year. Table 8-11 starts with Project D's operating income as developed in Table 8-10, and then adds the debt servicing requirement to estimate the net cash flows to equityholders. Since these flows accrue solely to equityholders, the appropriate discount rate is the cost of equity, 16 percent.

Recognizing that the equity investment is only $50,000, Project D's NPV using the equity residual approach is $26,813:

$$NPV = -\$50,000 + \$71,000/1.16 + \$21,000/(1.16)^2$$
$$= -\$50,000 + \$61,207 + \$15,606 = \$26,813.$$

Note these points. First, the WACC and the equity residual methods result in NPVs that are approximately equal. Actually, the methods are equivalent provided that project debt in any year equals a constant fraction of the present value of the future cash flows, a condition necessary to maintain the capital structure at the target level giving consideration to the fact that taking on the project increases the value of the equity. (If the company raises $50,000 of debt and $50,000 of equity to finance the project, but the value of the stock rises by the amount of the NPV of the project, then the market value capital structure will depart from the target

Table 8-11
Net Cash Flow to Equityholders

	Year 1	Year 2
Operating income	$40,000	$40,000
Interest expense	5,000	5,000
Earnings before taxes	$35,000	$35,000
Taxes (40%)	14,000	14,000
Net income	$21,000	$21,000
Depreciation	50,000	50,000
Net cash flow	$71,000	$71,000
Principal repayment	0	50,000
Net to equityholders	$71,000	$21,000

50-50 level. This point has been discussed in the financial literature.[13]) We could alter the debt repayment schedule to keep the capital structure exactly on target, and if we did, the equity residual and WACC methods would produce identical NPVs. Thus, the only difference between the WACC and the equity residual methods is the way in which the financing mix is incorporated into the analysis. In the equity residual method, interest payments and their tax benefits are incorporated into the cash flows. In the WACC method, financing effects are incorporated into the discount rate. Normally, analysts find it easier to use the WACC method, but there are situations in which it is easier to use the equity residual method. One example is when evaluating merger candidates, which we discuss in Chapter 22.

Adjusted Present Value

A third method of NPV evaluation which has been proposed in the academic literature is the *adjusted present value (APV)* approach.[14] This method separates the net present value of a project into two components: (1) the NPV which the project would produce if it were all-equity financed and (2) the PV of the "financing-related cash flows." Thus, we can express APV as follows:

$$\text{APV} = \sum_{t=0}^{n} \frac{\text{NOCF}_t}{(1 + k_{sU})^t} + \begin{array}{c} \text{PV of} \\ \text{financing-related,} \\ \text{cash flows} \end{array} \tag{8-4}$$

where k_{sU} is the cost of capital to an all-equity firm.

As an illustration of APV, consider Project D, whose net operating cash flows were given in Table 8-10. If the cost of equity to an all-equity firm were 13 percent for a project of this risk, then the first term of Equation 8-4 would be

$$-\$100{,}000 + \$74{,}000/1.13 + \$74{,}000/(1.13)^2 = \$23{,}440.$$

Thus, the value of the project to an all-equity firm is $23,440. However, the project is being evaluated by a firm which uses 50 percent debt with a before-tax cost of 10 percent. The firm would use $50,000 in debt financing, and its interest payments would be $5,000 per year, as shown in Table 8-11. This results in an annual tax savings of T($5,000) = 0.40($5,000) = $2,000. The present value of the tax savings is $3,471:

$$\$2{,}000/1.10 + \$2{,}000/(1.10)^2 = \$3{,}471.$$

We discount the tax savings by the cost of debt because these cash flows are generated by the debt, and hence have the same riskiness as debt. (Note that if the asset and consequently the debt used to finance it had been perpetuities, then the present value of the tax savings would have been (Tax rate)(Debt level) = TD, as

---

[13]See Eugene F. Brigham and T. Craig Tapley, "Financial Leverage and Use of the Net Present Value Criterion: A Reexamination," *Financial Management*, Summer 1985, 48-52.

[14]See Stewart C. Myers, "Interactions of Corporate Financing and Investment Decisions—Implications for Capital Budgeting," *Journal of Finance*, March 1974, 1-25.

described by Modigliani and Miller in their equation for the value of a levered firm, $V_L = V_U + TD$.)

Now we can combine the two elements to find the project's adjusted present value:

$$APV = \$23,440 + \$3,471 = \$26,911.$$

Thus, the project's value when financing-related cash flows are considered is $26,911.

The major advantage of the APV approach is that it permits the financing effects specific to a particular project to be incorporated into the analysis of that project. For example, suppose RIC were considering the construction of an electric generating plant which would supply power for its own operations but would also provide some surplus power which could be sold to Mid-State Electric Company for general distribution. Suppose, further, that the proposed generating station would be established by RIC as a separate subsidiary corporation. The subsidiary would be financed with 20 percent equity and 80 percent debt. RIC would own all of the equity, but the debt would be guaranteed in part by Mid-State Electric and in part by the federal government. These guarantees, plus the fact that the generating plant's revenues would be more predictable than would revenues from RIC's other operations, would permit the use of far more debt for this project than for RIC's other operations. This type of arrangement is called a "project financing arrangement," or "off balance sheet financing," because (1) it involves raising capital which is dedicated to a specific project and (2) the debt associated with the project is not shown on the sponsoring company's balance sheet.[15] (RIC would show its equity investment in the project as an asset.)

The APV method is well suited for dealing with those projects where (1) the debt used to support the project can be specifically identified, (2) the project will be financed with a debt/equity mix different from the one the firm normally uses, and (3) the use of a differential debt/equity mix on one project does not alter the firm's optimal debt/equity mix used to finance the firm's other projects. The other NPV methods do, of course, also recognize the tax benefits of debt. However, the WACC and equity residual methods tend to allocate the tax benefits of debt uniformly across all projects, whereas the APV method allocates these benefits to the specific projects which produce the benefits. Thus, the WACC and equity residual methods implicitly assume that all projects are financed with the same debt/equity mix, whereas the APV method provides a neat way to recognize differential debt-carrying capacities of different assets.

A major drawback of the APV for use in normal, ongoing capital budgeting procedures is the fact that use of the APV requires the specification of (1) the cost of equity for a leverage-free firm in a risk class equal to that of *each asset* under consideration and (2) the amount and cost of debt that will be used to finance *each asset*. Such specifications may be possible for large, stand-alone projects, such as RIC's proposed electric generating plant, but they are not feasible for the vast

---

[15]We discuss project financing further in Chapter 13.

majority of capital projects. As a general rule, a firm can estimate its WACC, given its existing capital structure, far more accurately than it can estimate the leverage-free cost of equity for an assembly line or a group of lathes. Moreover, as we shall see in the next chapter, it is generally necessary to use different costs of capital to evaluate different projects, because projects differ in riskiness. Therefore, since the WACC is being adjusted anyway, it is possible to make a further adjustment in the WACC to recognize that projects with greater debt-carrying capacity have a lower effective cost of capital. For these reasons, financial managers have not, in general, adopted the APV approach. However, you should be familiar with it, with the circumstances in which its use should be considered, and with the insights it provides with respect to the need to adjust the WACC for projects whose debt capacity differs significantly from that of the firm as a whole.

ADJUSTING FOR INFLATION

Inflation is a fact of life in the United States and most other nations, so it must be considered in any sound capital budgeting analysis.[16]

The Cost of Capital under Inflation

Note that *in the absence of inflation*, where the real rate, k_r, and the nominal rate, k_n, are equal (as are the real and nominal expected net operating cash flows— $RNOCF_t$ and $NOCF_t$, respectively), a project's NPV is calculated as follows:[17]

$$\text{NPV (no inflation)} = \sum_{t=0}^{n} \frac{RNOCF_t}{(1 + k_r)^t}. \qquad (8\text{-}5)$$

Now suppose the expected rate of inflation becomes positive, and we expect both sales prices and input costs to rise at the rate i. Further, this same inflation rate, i, is built into the market cost of capital. In this event, the nominal net operating cash flow, $NOCF_t$, will increase annually at the rate i percent, producing this situation:

$$NOCF_t = RNOCF_t(1 + i)^t.$$

For example, if we expected a net operating cash flow of $100 in Year 5 in the absence of inflation, then with a 5 percent rate of inflation, $NOCF_5 = \$100(1.05)^5 = \$127.63$.

---

[16]For a formal discussion of this subject, see James C. Van Horne, "A Note on Biases in Capital Budgeting Introduced by Inflation," *Journal of Financial and Quantitative Analysis*, January 1971, 653-658; Philip L. Cooley, Rodney L. Roenfeldt, and It-Keong Chew, "Capital Budgeting Procedures under Inflation," *Financial Management*, Winter 1975, 18-27; and "Cooley, Roenfeldt, and Chew vs. M. C. Findlay and A. W. Frankle," *Financial Management*, Autumn 1976, 83-90.

[17]Remember that the nominal rate of return includes an inflation premium that reflects investors' expectations about future inflation rates, while the real rate of return does not. If expected inflation is zero, then the inflation premium is also zero, and real and nominal rates are equal.

Now if net operating cash flows increase at the rate i percent per year, and if this same inflation factor is built into the firm's cost of capital, then the NPV is calculated as follows:

$$\text{NPV (with inflation)} = \sum_{t=0}^{n} \frac{RNOCF_t \ (1 \ + \ i)^t}{(1 \ + \ k_r)^t \ (1 \ + \ i)^{t}} \tag{8-6}$$

Since the $(1 \ + \ i)^t$ terms in the numerator and denominator cancel, we are left with Equation 8-5:

$$NPV = \sum_{t=0}^{n} \frac{RNOCF_t}{(1 \ + \ k_r)^{t}}.$$

Thus, whenever both costs and sales prices, and hence annual cash flows, are expected to rise at the same inflation rate that investors have built into the cost of capital, then the inflation-adjusted NPV determined using Equation 8-6 is identical to the inflation-free NPV found using Equation 8-5.

However, firms occasionally use base year, or constant, dollars throughout the analysis—say 1988 dollars if the analysis is done in 1987—along with a cost of capital as determined in the market place. This is wrong: *If the cost of capital includes an inflation premium, as it typically does, but the cash flows are all stated in constant dollars, then the calculated NPV will be downward biased.* The denominator will reflect inflation, but the numerator will not, producing a downward bias in NPV. If sales prices and all costs are expected to rise at exactly the same rate, then the bias can be corrected by (1) increasing cash flows in the numerator at the inflation rate and (2) using the nominal cost of capital, k_n, as the discount rate. Alternatively, we could leave $RNOCF_t$ in the numerator but use k_r rather than k_n in the denominator. Either procedure will insure consistency and thus eliminate the bias.

Adjusting for Nonneutral Inflation

With nonneutral inflation (which means a situation where input costs, output prices, and/or the cost of capital have different inflation rates), it is necessary to develop annual net operating cash flows, $NOCF_t$, which specifically account for inflation. This is what we did earlier in our RIC example as summarized in Table 8-4. There we assumed that sales prices, variable costs, and fixed overhead costs would all increase at a rate of 6 percent per year, but that depreciation charges would not be affected by inflation. Of course, we could have assumed different rates of inflation for sales prices, for variable costs, and for fixed overheads. For example, RIC might have long-term labor contracts which cause wage rates to rise with the Consumer Price Index (CPI), but its raw materials might be purchased under a fixed price contract, with the net result that variable costs are expected to rise by a smaller percentage than sales prices. In any event, one should build inflation into the capital budgeting analysis, with the specific adjustment reflecting as accurately as possible the most likely set of circumstances.[18]

---

[18]See Problem 8-10 for a specific example of how inflation affects capital budgeting analyses.

Our conclusions about inflation may be summarized as follows. First, inflation is critically important, for it can and does have major effects on businesses. Therefore, it must be recognized and dealt with. Second, there is really no simple, easy way to bring inflation into the decision process. The only effective way of dealing with it is to build inflation estimates into each cash flow element, using the best available information on how each element will be affected. Third, since we cannot estimate future inflation rates with precision, errors are bound to be made. Thus, inflation adds to the uncertainty, or riskiness, of capital budgeting as well as to its complexity. Fortunately, computers are available to help with inflation analysis, but an awareness of the nature of the problem is essential for financial analysis.

SUMMARY

This chapter has dealt with six issues in capital budgeting: cash flow estimation, replacement decisions, unequal life analyses, abandonment value, alternative NPV methods, and inflation adjustments.

The most important, yet most difficult, step in capital budgeting analysis is *cash flow estimation*. The key to cash flow estimation is to consider only *incremental* after-tax cash flows. *Replacement analysis* is conceptually similar to new project analysis, except that replacement cash flow estimation requires consideration of the fact that the old asset could continue to generate additional cash flows. Additionally, if the replacement asset has a life different than that remaining on the old asset, it may be necessary to adjust to a common life. This adjustment can be made either by *replacement chains* or by *equivalent annual annuities*. Adjusting for unequal lives may be necessary for analyzing any set of mutually exclusive projects when (1) different lives are involved and (2) the projects are expected to continue beyond the assets' initial lives.

If a project does not have a clearly defined economic life, part of the project evaluation is the determination of the project's optimal life. One method for accomplishing this is to estimate the project's *abandonment values*, and then to use these to find that life which maximizes the project's NPV.

In this text, we focus on the WACC method for determining a project's NPV. However, there are several alternative approaches to calculating NPVs, including the *equity residual method* and the *adjusted present value (APV) method*. The approaches differ in their method of incorporating the effects of debt financing. The WACC method incorporates these effects into the discount rate; the equity residual method incorporates debt financing effects into the cash flows; and the APV method separates project values into two components: (1) the value of the project to an all-equity firm, and (2) the value added by debt financing.

Inflation exists in the United States and most other economies, and it must be dealt with in capital budgeting analysis. If inflation is ignored, then (1) the cash flows in the numerator of the NPV equation are not adjusted for expected inflation, but (2) an adjustment is automatically (and generally unconsciously) made in the denominator because market forces build inflation into the cost of capital. Thus, the net result is to create a downward bias in evaluating projects. The best way of correcting for this bias is to build price increases based on expected inflation rates directly into the expected cash flows.

This chapter has considered a number of important issues which financial managers must deal with in their capital budgeting procedures. In Chapter 9, we will discuss risk analysis in capital budgeting, and in Chapter 10 we will discuss the optimal capital budget.

Questions and Problems

8-1 **(Depreciation effects)** Ronald Clay, great grandson of the founder of Clay Tile Products and current president of the company, believes in simple, conservative accounting. In keeping with his philosophy, he has decreed that the company shall use alternative straight line depreciation, based on the ACRS class lives, for all newly acquired assets. Your boss, the financial vice president and the only non-family officer, has asked you to develop an exhibit which shows how much this policy costs the company in terms of market value. Mr. Clay is interested in increasing the value of the firm's stock because he fears a family stockholder revolt which might remove him from office. For your exhibit, assume that the company spends $50 million each year on new capital projects, that the projects have on average a 10-year class life, that the company has a 10 percent cost of debt, and that its tax rate is 34 percent. (Hint: Show how much the NPV of projects in an average year would increase if Clay used the standard ACRS recovery allowances.)

8-2 **(New project analysis)** You have been asked by the president of your company to evaluate the proposed acquisition of a new spectrometer for the firm's R & D department. The equipment's basic price is $50,000, and it will cost another $10,000 to modify it for special use by your firm. The spectrometer, which falls into the ACRS 3-year class, will be sold after 3 years for $20,000. Use of the equipment will require an increase in net working capital (spare parts inventory) of $2,000. The equipment will have no effect on revenues, but it is expected to save the firm $20,000 per year in before-tax operating costs, mainly labor. The firm's marginal federal-plus-state tax rate is 40 percent.

    a. What is the net cost of the spectrometer? (That is, what is the Year 0 net cash flow?)

    b. What are the net operating cash flows in Years 1, 2, and 3?

    c. What are the additional (nonoperating) cash flows in Year 3?

    d. If the project's cost of capital is 10 percent, should the spectrometer be purchased?

8-3 **(New project analysis)** You have been asked by the president of your company to evaluate the proposed acquisition of a new milling machine. The machine's base price is $180,000, and it will cost another $25,000 to modify it for special use by your firm. The machine falls into the ACRS 3-year class. The machine will be sold after 3 years for $80,000. Use of the machine will require an increase in net working capital (inventory) of $7,500. The machine will have no effect on revenues, but it is expected to save the firm $75,000 per year in before-tax operating costs, mainly labor. The firm's marginal tax rate is 34 percent.

    a. What is the net cost of the machine for capital budgeting purposes? (That is, what is the Year 0 net cash flow?)

    b. What are the operating cash flows in Years 1, 2, and 3?

c. What are the additional (nonoperating) cash flows in Year 3?

d. If the project's cost of capital is 10 percent, should the machine be purchased? *(Do Parts e, f, g, and h only if you are using the computerized diskette.)*

e. Determine the NPV if the cost of capital were (1) to rise to 12 percent or (2) fall to 8 percent.

f. There is some uncertainty about the salvage value. It could be as low as $50,000 or as high as $90,000. What would the NPV be at those two salvage value levels (assume k = 10 percent)? Should this uncertainty affect the decision to invest? What salvage value (to the nearest thousand) would make you indifferent to the project?

g. Return to the original salvage value of $80,000. What would be the project's NPV if the corporate tax rate were increased to 46 percent?

h. Return the tax rate to 34 percent. Now assume that the manufacturer of the machine calls you with bad news: The base price of the machine has increased to $200,000. What does this do to the project's NPV? At what price (to the nearest hundred) would you be indifferent to the project?

8-4 **(Replacement analysis)** The Diamond Equipment Company purchased a machine 5 years ago at a cost of $100,000. It had an expected life of 10 years at the time of purchase and an expected salvage value of $10,000 at the end of the 10 years. It is being depreciated by using the straight-line method toward a salvage value of $10,000, or by $9,000 per year.

A new machine can be purchased for $150,000, including installation costs. Over its 5-year life, it will reduce cash operating expenses by $50,000 per year. Sales are not expected to change. At the end of its useful life, the machine is estimated to be worthless. ACRS depreciation will be used, and it will be depreciated over its 3-year class life rather than its 5-year economic life.

The old machine can be sold today for $65,000. The firm's marginal tax rate is 34 percent. The appropriate discount rate is 15 percent.

a. If the new machine is purchased, what is the amount of the initial cash flow at Year 0?

b. What incremental operating cash flows will occur at the end of Years 1-5 as a result of replacing the old machine?

c. What incremental nonoperating cash flow will occur at the end of Year 5 if the new machine is purchased?

d. What is the NPV of this project? Should Diamond replace the old machine?

8-5 **(Replacement analysis)** The Orange Fizz Company is contemplating the replacement of one of its bottling machines with a newer and more efficient one. The old machine has a book value of $500,000 and a remaining useful life of 5 years. The firm does not expect to realize any return from scrapping the old machine in 5 years, but it can sell it now to another firm in the industry for $200,000. The old machine is being depreciated toward a zero salvage value, or by $100,000 per year, using the straight line method.

The new machine has a purchase price of $1.2 million, an estimated useful life and ACRS class life of 5 years, and an estimated salvage value of $175,000. It is expected to economize on electric power usage, labor, and repair costs, and also to reduce the number of defective bottles. In total, an annual saving of $275,000 will be realized if it is installed. The company is in the 40 percent federal-plus-state tax bracket, and it has a 10 percent cost of capital.

a. What is the initial cash outlay required for the new machine?

b. Calculate the annual depreciation allowances for both machines, and compute the change in the annual depreciation expense if the replacement is made.

c. What are the operating cash flows in Years 1 to 5?

d. What is the cash flow from the salvage value in Year 5?

e. Should the firm purchase the new machine? Support your answer.

f. In general, how would each of the following factors affect the investment decision, and how should each be treated?

    1. The expected life of the existing machine decreases.

    2. The cost of capital is not constant but is increasing.

(Do Parts g, h, and i only if you are using the computerized diskette.)

g. The firm may be able to purchase an alternative new bottling machine from another supplier. Its purchase price would be $1,050,000, and its salvage value would be $250,000. This machine has a lower annual operating savings of $210,000. Should the firm purchase this machine?

h. If the salvage value on the alternative new machine were $200,000 rather than $250,000, how would this affect the decision?

i. With everything as in Part h, assume that the cost of capital declined from 10 percent to 8 percent. How would this affect the decision?

8-6 (Unequal lives) Toddler Clothes, Inc., is considering the replacement of its old, fully depreciated knitting machine. Two new models are available: Machine 190-3, which has a cost of $190,000, a 3-year expected life, and after-tax cash flows (labor savings and depreciation) of $87,000 per year; and Machine 360-6, which has a cost of $360,000, a 6-year life, and after-tax cash flows of $98,300 per year. Knitting machine prices are not expected to rise, because inflation will be offset by cheaper components (microprocessors) used in the machines. Assume that Toddler's cost of capital is 14 percent.

    a. Should the firm replace its old knitting machine, and, if so, which new machine should it use?

    b. Suppose the firm's basic patents will expire in 9 years, and the company expects to go out of business at that time. Assume further that the firm depreciates its assets using the straight line method, that its marginal federal-plus-state tax rate is 40 percent, and that the used machines can be sold at their book values. Under these circumstances, should the company replace the old machine and, if so, which new model should the company purchase?

8-7 (Abandonment value) The Motown Milk Company recently purchased a new delivery truck. The new truck cost $22,500, and it is expected to generate net after-tax cash flows, including depreciation, of $6,250 per year. The truck has a 5-year expected life. The expected abandonment values (in this case, salvage values after tax adjustments) for the truck are given below. The company's cost of capital is 10 percent.

Year	Annual Cash Flow	Abandonment Value
0	($22,500)	$22,500
1	6,250	17,500
2	6,250	14,000
3	6,250	11,000
4	6,250	5,000
5	6,250	0

a. Should Motown operate the truck until the end of its 5-year life, or, if not, what is its optimal economic life?

b. Would the introduction of abandonment values, in addition to operating cash flows, ever *reduce* the expected NPV and/or the IRR of a project?

8-8 **(Adjusted present value)** The Richfield Company is considering a new investment project. The project will cost $29,000 initially, and it has expected net cash flows of $9,400 each year for four years. The project will be terminated at the end of four years. The project will be financed with 25 percent debt which bears a 9 percent interest rate and 75 percent equity. If Richfield did not use debt, its equity would cost 12 percent. Its marginal federal-plus-state tax rate is 40 percent. Assume that debt for the project will remain outstanding throughout the project's life; it will not be amortized.

a. What is the adjusted present value of the project? What would the APV be if the project were expected to be renewed every four years, indefinitely?

b. To what extent is the validity of the APV approach as described in the text dependent on the MM leverage theory?

8-9 **(Inflation adjustments)** The Roth Company is considering an average risk investment in a mineral water spring project that has a cost of $150,000. The project will produce 1,000 cases of mineral water per year indefinitely. The current sales price is $138 per case, and the current cost per case (all variable) is $105. Roth is taxed at a rate of 34 percent. Both prices and costs are expected to rise at a rate of 6 percent per year. Roth uses only equity, and it has a cost of capital of 15 percent. Assume that cash flows consist only of after-tax profits, since the spring has an indefinite life and will not be depreciated.

a. Should Roth accept the project? (Hint: The project is a perpetuity, so you must use the formula for a perpetuity to find the NPV.)

b. If total costs consisted of a fixed cost of $10,000 per year and variable costs of $95 per unit, and if only the variable costs were expected to increase with inflation, would this make the project better or worse? Continue with the assumption that the output price will rise with inflation.

8-10 **(Inflation adjustments)** The Aronson Company is evaluating an average-risk capital project having both a 3-year economic and ACRS class life. The net investment outlay at Time 0 is $18,800. The expected end-of-year cash flows, expressed in Time 0 dollars, are listed below:

	Year 1	Year 2	Year 3
Revenues	$30,000	$30,000	$30,000
Variable costs	15,000	15,000	15,000
Fixed costs	6,500	6,500	6,500
Depreciation	6,392	6,204	6,204

The firm has a marginal federal-plus-state tax rate of 40 percent. Aronson's current cost of debt is 12 percent, and its cost of equity is 16 percent. These costs include an estimated inflation premium of 6 percent. The firm's target capital structure is 50 percent debt and 50 percent equity.

a. What is Aronson's nominal WACC? Its real WACC?

b. What are the project's relevant real cash flows? What discount rate should be utilized when calculating a project's NPV based upon real cash flows? Why?

c. What is the NPV for this project? Should this project be accepted? What might have occurred if you had used the *nominal* WACC with *real* cash flows?

d. Now assume that all revenues and costs, except depreciation, are expected to increase at the inflation rate of 6 percent. What are the project's nominal cash flows and NPV based on these flows? Why is this NPV different from the NPV calculated in Part c?

(Do Part e only if you are using the computerized diskette.)

e. Assume that the firm's management anticipates a rate of inflation resulting in a 6 percent inflation premium for Year 1 through Year 3. Based upon this assumption, the firm accepts the project. However, suppose the firm actually experiences nonneutral inflation such that revenues increase by only 6 percent, while variable and fixed costs increase by 7.5 percent. What are the actual after-tax cash flows in this case? What effect would the acceptance of the project coupled with unanticipated nonneutral inflation have had upon the value of the firm?

f. If a company, in its capital budgeting process, bases its cash flows on sales prices and unit costs as of the time it analyzes the project, (1) would this tend to produce systematic errors in its capital budgeting evaluations, (2) would any such error be more serious for long-term or short-term projects, and (3) if you do think that systematic errors are likely to occur, how could they be corrected?

Selected Additional References and Cases

Several articles have been written regarding the implications of the Accelerated Cost Recovery System (ACRS). Among them are the following:

Angell, Robert J., and Tony R. Wingler, "A Note on Expensing Versus Depreciating Under the Accelerated Cost Recovery System," *Financial Management*, Winter 1982, 34-35.

McCarty, Daniel E., and William R. McDaniel, "A Note on Expensing Versus Depreciating Under the Accelerated Cost Recovery System: Comment," *Financial Management*, Summer 1983, 37-39.

For further information on replacement analysis, as well as other aspects of capital budgeting, see the texts by Bierman and Smidt, by Grant, Ireson, and Leavengood, and by Levy and Sarnat referenced in Chapter 7.

Three additional papers on the impact of inflation on capital budgeting are the following:

Bailey, Andrew D., and Daniel L. Jensen, "General Price Level Adjustments in the Capital Budgeting Decision," *Financial Management*, Spring 1977, 26-32.

Mehta, Dileep R., Michael D. Curley, and Hung-Gay Fung, "Inflation, Cost of Capital, and Capital Budgeting Procedures," *Financial Management*, Winter 1984, 48-54.

Rappaport, Alfred, and Robert A. Taggart, Jr., "Evaluation of Capital Expenditure Proposals Under Inflation," *Financial Management*, Spring 1982, 5-13.

For additional insights into unequal life analysis, see

Emery, Gary W., "Some Guidelines for Evaluating Capital Investment Alternatives with Unequal Lives," *Financial Management*, Spring 1982, 15-19.

For an interesting discussion on cash flow estimation biases, see

Statman, Meir, and Tyzoon T. Tyebjee, "Optimistic Capital Budgeting Forecasts: An Experiment," *Financial Management*, Autumn 1985, 27-33.

For more information on alternative NPV formulations, see

Brick, Ivan E., and Daniel G. Weaver, "A Comparison of Capital Budgeting Techniques in Identifying Profitable Investments," *Financial Management*, Winter 1984, 29-39.

The Crum-Brigham casebook contains the following cases which focus on Chapter 7 and 8 material:

Case 12, "Granville Pump Company," which focuses on the replacement decision.

Case 13, "Sugar Lake Refining and Processing Company," which illustrates the difference between accounting income and economic cash flow.

Case 14, "Narwhal Sports Industries, Inc.," which emphasizes the determination of relevant costs.

Case 17, "Composite Technologies Corporation," which illustrates the need to use replacement chains when alternatives with unequal lives are being compared.

The Harrington casebook contains the following relevant cases:

"Ing. C. Olivetti & Co. S.p.A.," which describes alternative plant investments.

"R. G. Barry Corporation," which focuses on the introduction of a new product.

"Massalin Particulares," which illustrates capital budgeting in an inflationary environment.

 9

RISK ANALYSIS IN CAPITAL BUDGETING

Risk analysis is important in all financial decisions, especially those relating to capital budgeting. As we saw in Chapter 2, the higher the risk associated with an investment, the higher is the rate of return needed to compensate investors for assuming the risk. This is also true when the investor is a corporation and the investment is a capital project. This chapter discusses procedures both for measuring risk in a capital budget context and for incorporating it into the firm's capital expenditure decisions.

RISK ADJUSTMENT

There are two basic approaches to risk adjustment: (1) The *risk-adjusted discount rate (RADR)* method, which adjusts the denominator of the present value equation—the higher the riskiness of the cash flows, the higher the discount rate and consequently the lower the present value of the asset. (2) The *certainty equivalent (CE)* method, which adjusts for risk by altering the numerator of the present value equation, reducing the value of expected cash inflows to adjust for risk—the riskier a cash flow, the more it is reduced and consequently the lower the present value of the asset. Although the RADR method is most commonly used, the CE method does have some advantages. Also, a study of the CE method will help you understand better some aspects of risk-adjusted discount rates.

The Certainty Equivalent Method

The certainty equivalent (CE) method follows directly from the concept of utility theory. Under the CE approach, the decision maker must first evaluate a cash flow's risk and then specify how much money he or she would require, with certainty, to produce an indifference between this riskless sum and the risky cash flow's expected value. To illustrate, suppose a rich eccentric offered you the following two choices:

1. Flip a fair coin. If a head comes up, you receive $1 million, but if a tail comes up, you get nothing. The expected value of the gamble is (0.5)($1,000,000) +

$(0.5)($0) = $500,000$, but the actual outcome will be either $0 or $1 million, so it is risky.

2. Do not flip the coin and simply pocket $300,000 cash.

If you find yourself indifferent to the two alternatives, then $300,000 is defined to be your certainty equivalent for this particular risky $500,000 expected cash flow. The certain (or riskless) $300,000 amount thus provides you with exactly the same utility as the risky $500,000 expected return.

Now ask yourself this question: In the example, exactly how much cash-in-hand would it actually take to make *you* indifferent to the choices of a certain sum and the risky $500,000 expected return on the coin flip? If you are like most people, your certainty equivalent would be significantly less than $500,000, indicating that you are risk averse. In general, risk aversion is present if the certainty equivalent is less than the expected value of a cash flow, and the lower the certainty equivalent, the greater the degree of risk aversion.

The certainty equivalent concept is illustrated in Figure 9-1. The curve shows a series of risk/return combinations to which this particular individual is indifferent. For example, Point A represents an investment with a perceived degree of risk as measured by the risk coefficient, b_A, and with an expected dollar return of $2,000. The individual with the risk/return trade-off function, or indifference curve, shown here is indifferent to the alternatives of a sure $1,000, an expected $2,000 with risk b_A, and an expected $3,000 with risk b_B.[1]

The certainty equivalent concept can be applied to the capital budgeting decision as an alternative to the use of risk-adjusted discount rates. We proceed as follows:

1. Estimate the certainty equivalent cash flow in each Year t, CE_t, based on the expected cash flow in that year and its riskiness.

2. Once we have expressed each risky cash flow as a certainty equivalent, we can discount by the risk-free rate to obtain the project's NPV:

$$NPV = \sum_{t=0}^{n} \frac{CE_t}{(1 + k_{RF})^{t}} \qquad (9\text{-}1)$$

To illustrate, suppose Project A, whose expected net cash flows are shown in Table 9-1, is to be evaluated using the certainty equivalent method. Assume that the initial net cost, $2,000, is fixed by contract and hence known with certainty. Further, assume that the capital budgeting analyst estimates that the cash inflows in Years 1-4 all have the same risk (average), and that the appropriate certainty equivalent is $700. The project's NPV, found using a risk-free discount rate of 5 percent, is approximately $482:

---

[1]If the investor were *risk neutral*, his or her indifference curve would be a horizontal line. A *risk-seeker*'s indifference curve would slope downward. The curve shown in Figure 9-1 shows risk aversion, and specifically *increasing risk aversion*; an upward sloping straight line would show *constant risk aversion*.

Figure 9-1
Certainty Equivalent Concept

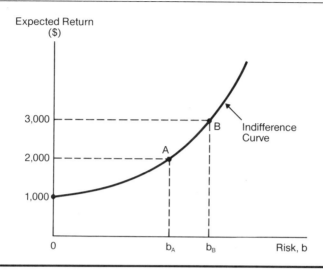

$$NPV_A = -\$2,000 + \frac{\$700}{(1.05)^1} + \frac{\$700}{(1.05)^2} + \frac{\$700}{(1.05)^3} + \frac{\$700}{(1.05)^4}$$

$$= \$482.17.$$

Since the risk-adjusted NPV is positive, the project should be accepted.

The certainty equivalent method is simple and neat. Further, it can easily accommodate differential risk among cash flows. For example, if the Year 4 expected net cash flow of $1,000 included a very risky estimated salvage value, we could simply reduce the certainty equivalent, say from $700 to $500, and recalculate the project's NPV. Unfortunately, there is no practical way to estimate a risky cash flow's certainty equivalent. Each individual would have his or her own estimate, and these could vary significantly. To further complicate matters, certainty equiv-

Table 9-1
Project A's Certainty Equivalent Analysis

Year	Expected Net Cash Flow	Degree of Risk	Certainty Equivalent
0	($2,000)	Zero	($2,000)
1	1,000	Average	700
2	1,000	Average	700
3	1,000	Average	700
4	1,000	Average	700

alents should reflect shareholders' risk preferences rather than those of management. For these reasons, the certainty equivalent method is not used to any extent in corporate decision-making. However, it is conceptually a powerful tool, and in the next section we will use certainty equivalents to explain the risk assumptions that are embodied in constant risk-adjusted discount rates.

Certainty Equivalents Versus Risk-Adjusted Discount Rates

As noted previously, investment risk can be handled by making adjustments either to the numerator of the present value equation (the certainty equivalent, or CE, method) or to the denominator of the equation (the risk-adjusted discount rate, or RADR, method). The RADR method is most frequently used in practice because it is far easier to estimate suitable discount rates based on current market data than it is to derive certainty equivalent cash flows. Some financial theorists have suggested that the certainty equivalent approach is theoretically superior,[2] but other theorists have shown that if risk is perceived to be an increasing function of time, then using a risk-adjusted discount rate is a valid procedure.[3]

Risk-adjusted rates lump together the pure time value of money as represented by the risk-free rate and risk as represented by a risk premium: $k = k_{RF} + RP$. On the other hand, the certainty equivalent approach keeps risk and the time value of money separate. This separation gives an advantage to certainty equivalents. To see why, suppose we are comparing two investments, A and B. Our analysis of these projects' risk suggests that their required rates of return are 5 percent for A because it is riskless ($k_{RF} = 5\%$), and 10 percent for B ($k = k_{RF} + RP = 5\% + 5\% = 10\%$). To estimate the value of each project, we discount its expected cash flows by its risk-adjusted discount rate. Since the riskless rate is 5 percent, the risk premium for Project A is zero and for B it is 5 percent. Does B's constant risk premium, and hence its constant RADR, imply that the relative riskiness of its cash flows over time is also perceived to be constant? In other words, is the implied riskiness of CF_1 the same as that of CF_{10} in view of the fact that $k = RADR = 10\%$ for both cash flows? The answer is no; and to see why, we must first look at the assumptions inherent in the risk-adjusted discount rate.

Consider the particular assumptions that are implicit in the choice of a constant discount rate over time. The present value of a cash flow in Year t, using the CE approach, is

$$PV_t = \frac{CE_t}{(1 + k_{RF})^t}$$

The present value of a Year t cash flow, using the RADR approach, is

---

[2]See Alexander A. Robichek and Stewart C. Myers, "Conceptual Problems in the Use of Risk-Adjusted Discount Rates," *Journal of Finance*, December 1966, 727-730.

[3]See Houng-Yhi Chen, "Valuation under Uncertainty," *Journal of Financial and Quantitative Analysis*, September 1967, 313-326.

$$PV_t = \frac{CF_t}{(1 + k)^{t'}}$$

For the two methods to lead to the same NPV, and hence to be equivalent, the present values must be equal. Therefore, we must have

$$\frac{CE_t}{(1 + k_{RF})^t} = \frac{CF_t}{(1 + k)^{t'}}$$

Rearranging, we can solve for the ratio of the certainty equivalent to the expected cash flow:

$$\frac{CE_t}{CF_t} = \frac{(1 + k_{RF})^t}{(1 + k)^t}. \qquad (9\text{-}2)$$

Now suppose we are calculating CE_{10}/CF_{10}, the ratio for a cash flow expected after 10 years, when the riskless rate is 5 percent and the risky rate is 10 percent. Substituting these values into Equation 9-2, the ratio is found as follows:

$$\frac{CE_{10}}{CF_{10}} = \frac{(1 + k_{RF})^{10}}{(1 + k)^{10}} = \frac{(1.05)^{10}}{(1.10)^{10}}$$

$$= \frac{1.6289}{2.5937} = 0.6280 = \begin{array}{l} \text{Certainty equivalent} \\ \text{adjustment factor} \end{array}$$

This is the only ratio, or certainty equivalent adjustment factor, that is consistent with $k_{RF} = 5\%$, $RP = 5\%$, and $t = 10$. Thus, if the expected cash flow in Year 10 is \$1,000, its certainty equivalent must be $0.6280(\$1,000) = \$628$; otherwise, the two methods will not produce identical PVs.

Equation 9-2 has some interesting implications that can be seen in Figure 9-2, where we work out certainty equivalent values for a \$1,000 expected cash flow and our particular pair of interest rates over time and then plot these values. Note that with k_{RF}, RP, and k all set at constant values, then risk, as reflected in the certainty equivalent of the \$1,000 expected cash flow, is an increasing function of time. This phenomenon occurs because the risk premium embodied in $k = k_{RF} + RP$ is compounded.

The relationship between k, risk, and time is graphed in Figure 9-3. A constant value of k implies increasing risk; this condition is shown in Panel A. However, if the riskiness of returns is no higher for distant than for close-at-hand returns, then distant returns should be discounted at a lower k than are close returns; this condition is shown in Panel B. This result occurs because the risk premium component of k is being compounded: $k = R_F + k_{RF}$, so $(1 + k)^t = (1 + k_{RF} + RP)^t$.

Implications

A firm using the risk-adjusted discount rate approach for its capital budgeting decisions will have an overall cost of capital that reflects its overall market-determined riskiness. This rate should be used for "average" projects, that is, projects

Figure 9-2
Changes in Perceived Risk over Time

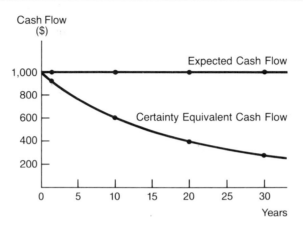

Illustrative Calculations of Certainty Equivalents

Year	$(1 + k_{RF})^t =$ $(1.05)^t$	$(1 + k)^t =$ $(1.10)^t$	Certainty Equivalent Adjustment Factor = $CE_t/CF_t =$ $(1.05)^t/(1.10)^t$	Cash Flow (CF_t)	Certainty Equivalent Adjustment Factor × $1,000 = CE_t$
0	1.0000	1.0000	1.0000	$1,000	$1,000.00
1	1.0500	1.1000	0.9545	1,000	954.50
10	1.6289	2.5937	0.6280	1,000	628.00
20	2.6533	6.7275	0.3944	1,000	394.40
30	4.3219	17.4494	0.2477	1,000	247.70

Notes:
a. This table calculates the certainty equivalent for an expected cash flow of $1,000 to be received in the future. The calculation forces equivalency between the certainty equivalent and risk-adjusted discount rate methods based on a risk-free discount rate of 5 percent and a risky rate of 10 percent.
b. The expected cash flows are constant over time, yet their certainty equivalents decline over time. This implies that the risk of the flows must be increasing over time.
c. The calculations were based on a constant risky rate of 10 percent. *Therefore, use of a constant risk-adjusted discount rate implies increasing risk over time.*

which have the same risk as the firm's existing projects. Lower rates should be used for less risky projects, and higher rates should be used for riskier projects. To facilitate the decision process, corporate headquarters generally prescribes rates for different classes of investments (for example, replacement, expansion of existing lines, and expansion into new lines). Then, investments of a given class within a given division are analyzed in terms of the prescribed rate. For example, replacement decisions in the retailing division of an oil company might all be evaluated with a 10 percent discount rate.

Consciously or unconsciously, such use of a constant k assumes that risk increases with time, and it therefore imposes a relatively severe burden on long-

Figure 9-3
Relationship between Risk and Time

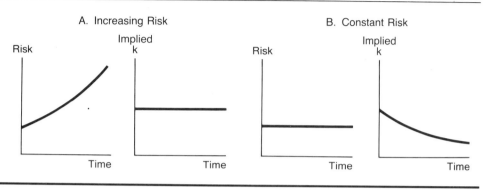

term projects. This means that short-payoff alternatives will tend to be selected over those with longer payoffs when, for example, there are alternative ways of performing a given task.

However, there may be a substantial number of projects for which distant returns are *not* more risky than near-term returns. For example, the estimated returns on a water pipeline serving a developing community may be quite uncertain in the short run, because the rate of growth of the community is uncertain. However, the water company may be quite sure that in time the community will be fully developed and will utilize the full capacity of the pipeline. Similar situations could exist in many public projects—water projects, highway programs, schools, and so forth; in public utility investment decisions; and when industrial firms are building plants or retailers stores to serve growing geographic markets.

To the extent that the implicit assumption of rising risk over time reflects the facts, then a constant discount rate may be appropriate. Indeed, in the vast majority of business situations, risk undoubtedly is an increasing function of time, so a constant risk-adjusted discount rate is generally reasonable. However, one should be aware of the relationships described in this section and avoid the pitfall of unwittingly penalizing long-term projects when they are not, in fact, more risky than short-term projects.

INTRODUCTION TO RISK ASSESSMENT

Regardless of how risk is incorporated into the capital budgeting decision, the first step in the process must be to assess the riskiness of the project. Two separate and distinct types of risk can be measured: (1) *market*, or *beta*, *risk*, which measures project risk from the standpoint of an investor who holds a highly diversified portfolio, and (2) *total*, or *corporate*, *risk*, which looks at a project's risk without considering the effects of the stockholders' own personal diversification. In both cases, the relevant risk is incremental risk, that is, the impact of the project on the firm's risk. As we shall see, a particular project might have highly uncertain returns, yet taking it on might not affect the firm's risk at all because of portfolio effects.

A project's corporate risk is measured by the project's impact on the firm's earnings variability, while the project's market risk is measured by its effect on the firm's beta coefficient. Taking on a project with a high degree of corporate, or total, risk will not necessarily affect the firm's beta to any great extent. However, if the project has highly uncertain returns, and if those returns are highly correlated with those of most other assets in the economy, then the project will have a high degree of both corporate and market risk. For example, suppose General Motors decides to undertake a major expansion to build solar-powered autos. GM is not sure how its technology will work on a mass production basis, so there are great risks in the venture. Suppose management also estimates that the project will have a higher probability of success if the economy is strong, for then people will have money to spend on the new autos. This means that the project will tend to do well if other companies are also doing well and to do badly if others do badly; hence, the project's beta coefficient will be high. A project like this would have a high degree of both corporate risk and market risk.

Market risk is important because of its direct impact on stock price. Corporate risk is also important for three primary reasons:

1. Undiversified stockholders, including the owners of small businesses, are more concerned about total risk than about market risk.

2. Many financial theorists argue that investors, even those who are well diversified, consider factors other than market risk when setting required returns. As noted in Chapter 2, empirical studies of the determinants of required rates of return generally find both market and total risk to be important.

3. The firm's stability is important to its managers, workers, customers, suppliers, and creditors, and also to the community in which it operates. Firms that are in serious danger of bankruptcy, or even of suffering low profits and reduced output, have difficulty attracting and retaining good managers and workers. Also, both suppliers and customers are reluctant to depend on weak firms, and such firms have difficulty borrowing money except at high interest rates. These factors will tend to reduce risky firms' profitability, and hence the prices of their stocks.

For these reasons, corporate risk is also important, even to well-diversified stockholders.

TECHNIQUES FOR MEASURING CORPORATE RISK

The starting point for analyzing corporate risk involves determining the uncertainty inherent in a project's cash flows. This analysis can be handled in a number of ways, ranging from informal judgments to complex economic and statistical analyses involving large-scale computer models. To illustrate what is involved, let's refer back to Robotics International's office robot project as described in Chapter 8. Most of the elements in Tables 8-3, 8-4, and 8-5, which produced the expected

Figure 9-4
Probability Distributions for Units Sold in 1990

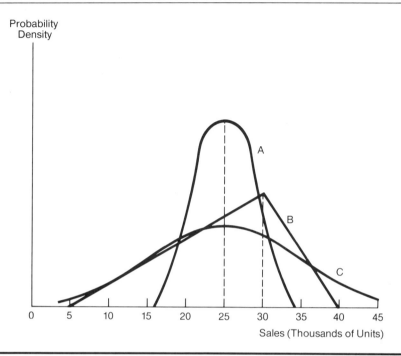

net cash flows for the project as set forth in Table 8-6, are subject to uncertainty. For example, sales for 1990 were projected at 25,000 units to be sold at a net price of $2,200 per unit, or $55 million in total. However, unit sales would almost certainly be somewhat higher or lower than 25,000, and the sales price would probably be different from $2,200 per unit. In effect, the sales volume and price estimates are really expected values taken from probability distributions, as are many of the other values listed in Tables 8-3 through 8-5. The distributions could be relatively "tight," reflecting small standard deviations and low risk, or they could be "flat," denoting a great deal of uncertainty about the variable in question and hence a high risk. For example, the 25,000 unit sales estimate for 1990 could have come from a distribution such as A, B, or C in Figure 9-4. The more peaked the distribution, the higher the probability that actual sales will be close to the predicted level, and hence the smaller the risk of the project.[4]

---

[4]In Figure 9-4, Distribution A is symmetric about the expected value, but it is not normal since the tails do not extend to plus and minus infinity. Distribution B is triangular, and it is skewed left from the most likely value. Distribution C is approximately normal. Distributions A and C both have expected values and most likely values (modes) of 25,000. Distribution B has an expected value of 25,000 but a most likely value of 30,000.

Sensitivity Analysis

Intuitively, we know that many of the variables which determine a project's cash flows are based on some type of probability distribution such as the ones shown in Figure 9-4. We also know that if a key input variable such as units sold changes, so will the project's NPV. *Sensitivity analysis is a technique which indicates exactly how much the NPV will change in response to a given change in an input variable, other things held constant.*

Sensitivity analysis begins with a *base case* situation based on expected input values. To illustrate the procedure, we shall consider the data given in Table 8-4 in Chapter 8, where projected income statements for RIC's office robot project were shown. The values for unit sales, sales price, fixed costs, and variable costs are the *expected*, or *base case*, values, and the resulting $13,005,785 NPV shown in Table 8-6 is called the *base case NPV*. Now we ask a series of "what if" questions: "What if unit sales falls 20 percent below the expected level?" "What if the sales price per unit falls?" "What if variable costs are 70 percent of dollar sales rather than the expected 65 percent?" *Sensitivity analysis is designed to provide the decision maker with answers to questions such as these.*

In a sensitivity analysis, we change each variable by specific percentages above and below the expected value, holding other things constant, then calculate new NPVs, and then plot the derived NPVs against the variable that was changed. Figure 9-5 shows the office robot project's sensitivity graphs for three of the key input

Figure 9-5
Sensitivity Analysis for RIC
(Thousands of Dollars)

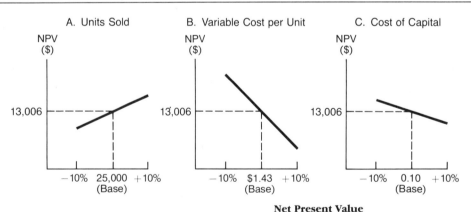

Change from Base Value	Net Present Value		
	Units Sold	**Variable Cost per Unit**	**Cost of Capital**
−10%	$ 8,522	$21,652	$14,744
−5	10,764	17,329	13,858
0	13,006	13,006	13,006
+5	15,248	8,683	12,185
+10	17,489	4,360	11,395

variables. The table below the graphs gives the NPVs that were used to construct the graphs. The slopes of the lines in the graphs show how sensitive NPV is to changes in each of the inputs: the steeper the slope, the more sensitive the NPV is to the change in the variable. Here we see that the project's NPV is very sensitive to changes in variable costs, fairly sensitive to changes in sales volume, and relatively insensitive to changes in the cost of capital.

If we were comparing two projects, then, other things held constant, the one with the steeper sensitivity lines would be regarded as riskier—a relatively small error in estimating variables such as the variable cost per unit or demand for the product would produce a large error in the project's projected NPV. Thus, sensitivity analysis provides useful insights into the relative riskiness of different projects.

Before we move on, note these two additional points about sensitivity analysis. First, spreadsheet computer models are ideally suited for performing sensitivity analysis, because the model automatically recalculates NPV when an input value is changed. We used a *Lotus 1-2-3* model to conduct the analyses represented in Figure 9-5, both the tabular data and the graphs. Second, we could have plotted the sensitivity lines on one graph, with percentage deviations from the base case shown on the horizontal axis. This would facilitate direct comparison of the sensitivities among different input variables.

Scenario Analysis

Although sensitivity analysis is probably the most widely used risk analysis technique, it does have limitations. Consider, for example, a proposed coal mine whose NPV is highly sensitive to changes in both output and sales prices. However, if a utility company has contracted to buy most of the mine's output at a fixed price per ton, plus inflation adjustments, then the mining venture may not be very risky in spite of its steep sensitivity lines. *In general, a project's corporate risk depends on both (1) its sensitivity to changes in key variables and (2) the range of likely values of these variables as reflected in their probability distributions.* Because sensitivity analysis considers only the first factor, it is incomplete.

A risk analysis technique which considers both the sensitivity of NPV to changes in key variables and also the range of likely variable values is *scenario analysis*. Here, the operating executives pick a "bad" set of circumstances (low unit sales, low sales price, high variable cost per unit, high construction cost, and so on) and a "good" set. The NPV under the "bad" and "good" conditions would be calculated and compared to the expected, or base case, NPV.

As an example, let us return to the RIC office robot project. Assume that RIC's executives are fairly confident of their estimates of all the project's cash flow variables except price and unit sales. Further, suppose they regard a drop in unit sales below 5,000, or a rise above 40,000 units, as being extremely unlikely. Similarly, they expect sales price as set in the marketplace to fall within the range of $1,700 to $2,700. Thus 5,000 units at a price of $1,700 defines the lower bound or the worst case scenario, while 40,000 units at a price of $2,700 defines the upper bound or the best case scenario. Remember that the expected, or base case, values

Table 9-2
Scenario Analysis Results Summary

Scenario	Probability of Outcome	Sales (Volume (Units)	Sales Price	NPV (Thousands)
Worst case	0.25	5,000	$1,700	($24,901)
Base case	0.50	25,000	2,200	13,006
Best case	0.25	40,000	2,700	56,222

Expected NPV = $14,333,000.

σ_{NPV} = $28,712,000.

Note: Variables other than unit sales and sales prices were set at their expected values.

are 25,000 units sold at a price of $2,200. Also, note that the indicated sales prices are for 1990, with future years' prices expected to rise because of inflation.

To carry out the scenario analysis, we use the worst case variable values to obtain the worst case NPV and the best case variable values to obtain the best case NPV.[5] We actually performed the analysis using our *Lotus* model, and Table 9-2 summarizes the results of our analysis. We see that the base case forecasts a positive NPV; the worst case produces a negative NPV; and the best case results in a very large positive NPV. We can use the results of the scenario analysis to determine the expected NPV, standard deviation of NPV, and coefficient of variation (and also IRR, PI, and payback values, along with their standard deviations). To begin, we need an estimate of the probabilities of occurrence of the three scenarios. Suppose management estimates that there is a 25 percent probability of the worst case occurring, a 50 percent probability of the base case, and a 25 percent probability of the best case. Of course, it is *very difficult* to estimate accurately scenario probabilities.

Now we have a discrete probability distribution of returns just like those we used in Chapter 2, except that the return is measured in dollars (NPV) rather than in percentages. The expected NPV (in thousands of dollars) is

$$0.25(-\$24,901) + 0.50(\$13,006) + 0.25(\$56,222) = \$14,333.$$

Note that the expected NPV is *not* the same as the base case NPV, $13,006 (in thousands), which was based on the expected values of all the input variables. This is because the two uncertain variables, sales volume and sales price, are multiplied together to get dollar sales, and this process causes the NPV distribution to be

---

[5]We could have included worst and best case values for fixed and variable costs, the inflation rate, salvage values, and so on. For illustrative purposes, we limit the changes to only two variables. Also, note that we are treating sales price and quantity as independent variables; that is, a low sales price could occur when unit sales were low, and a high sales price could be coupled with high unit sales, or vice versa. As we discuss in the next section, it is relatively easy to vary these assumptions if the facts of the situation suggest a different set of assumptions.

skewed to the right. (A big number times another big number produces a very big number, which in turn causes the average, or expected value, to be increased.) The standard deviation of NPV (in thousands of dollars) is $28,712:[6]

$$\sigma_{NPV} = \sqrt{0.25(-\$24,901 - \$14,333)^2 + 0.50(\$13,006 - \$14,333)^2 + 0.25(\$56,222 - \$14,333)^2}$$
$$= \$28,712.$$

Scenario analysis does provide information about a project's corporate risk. However, it is limited in that it only considers a few discrete outcomes (NPVs) for the project, although there are in reality an infinite number of possibilities. In the next section, we describe a more realistic method of assessing a project's corporate risk.

Monte Carlo Simulation

Monte Carlo simulation, so named because this type of analysis grew out of work on the mathematics of casino gambling, ties together sensitivities and input variable probability distributions.[7] However, simulation requires a mainframe computer, coupled with an efficient financial planning software package, while scenario analysis can be done using a PC with a spreadsheet program, or even with a calculator.

The first step in a computer simulation is to specify a probability distribution for each of the key variables in the analysis. To illustrate, suppose we have esti-

---

[6]If we had a probability distribution for the net cash flow for each year of a project's life, then we could calculate the expected cash flow for each year, CF_t, and the variance of that cash flow, σ_t^2. We could then calculate the expected NPV as

$$E(NPV) = \sum_{t=0}^{n} \frac{CF_t}{(1 + k)^t}. \tag{9-3}$$

If the net cash flow distributions across time were normal and were not correlated with one another (independent) then the standard deviation of the NPV would be calculated as follows:

$$\text{Independent cash flow case: } \sigma_{NPV} = \left[\sum_{t=0}^{n} \frac{\sigma_t^2}{(1 + k)^{2t}}\right]^{1/2}. \tag{9-4}$$

If the net cash flow distributions from one year to the next were normal and were completely dependent on one another such that the correlation coefficient between them is 1.0, then σ_{NPV} is calculated as

$$\text{Dependent cash flow case: } \sigma_{NPV} = \sum_{t=0}^{n} \frac{\sigma_t}{(1 + k)^t}. \tag{9-5}$$

See Frederick S. Hillier, "The Derivation of Probabilistic Information for the Evaluation of Risky Investments," *Managerial Science*, April 1963, 443-457. Although Hillier's approach to finding projects' standard deviations is relatively simple, it is rarely used in practice because (1) many project cash flow distributions are not normal and (2) most project cash flow distributions over time are neither independent nor perfectly positively correlated. Still, Hillier's model does show that if a project's cash flows are independent across time (that is, fluctuate randomly from year to year), this indicates a less risky situation than if cash flows are dependent, because for a given set of σ_t, Equation 9-4 produces a lower σ_{NPV} than Equation 9-5.

[7]The concept of simulation analysis in capital budgeting was first reported by David B. Hertz, "Risk Analysis in Capital Investments," *Harvard Business Review*, January-February 1964, 95-106.

Table 9-3
Probability Distribution for Robot Sales Price

Sales Price (1)	Probability (2)	Associated Random Numbers (3)
$1,700	0.05	00-04
2,000	0.20	05-24
2,200	0.50	25-74
2,400	0.20	75-94
2,700	0.05	95-99

mated the probability distribution of the RIC office robot's sales price as represented by Columns 1 and 2 of Table 9-3.[8] The expected sales price is $2,200, but the price can range from $1,700 to $2,700. The third column gives a set of random numbers associated with each price estimate. Notice that in Column 2, there is a 5 percent probability that sales price will be as low as $1,700; therefore, 5 digits (0, 1, 2, 3, and 4) are assigned to this price. Twenty digits are assigned to a price of $2,000, and so on for the other possible prices. Once the distributions and associated random numbers have been specified for all the key variables—in other words, once a table such as 9-3 has been set up for sales quantity, unit variable costs, construction costs, and so on—the computer simulation can begin. These are the steps involved:

1. Computers have stored in them, or they can generate, random numbers. First, on Trial Run 1, the computer will select a different random number for each uncertain variable. For example, it might select 44 for units sold, 17 for the sales price, and 16 for labor costs.

2. Depending on the random number selected, a value is determined for each variable. The 17 associated with the sales price indicates in Table 9-3 that the appropriate sales price for use in the first run is $2,000. Values for all the other variables are set in like manner.[9]

3. Once a value has been established for each of the variables, the computer generates a set of income statements and cash flows. These cash flows are then dis-

---

[8]Here we assume that sales price is a discrete variable which can take on only five values. This simplification is purely for illustrative purposes; actual simulation models need not have such restrictions. In fact, the simulation model which we used to generate data for this section allows the variable values to be specified either as continuous distribution parameters or as any number of discrete values.

[9]Simulation models can handle either independence or dependence among variables. In this simple example, we assume independence; however, in many simulations, it is more realistic to assume dependence. Thus, it might be assumed that if demand is weak and the figure for units sold is relatively low, then prices will also be weak. Similarly, the sales price in one year can be completely independent of or dependent on the price in the preceding year, or it can be somewhat correlated with the previous year's price. Simulation programs can handle these issues, although decision makers often have trouble specifying exactly how the different variables are related to one another.

counted at the cost of capital (which may also be treated as a random variable), and the result is the net present value of the project on the computer's first run.[10]

4. The NPV generated on Run 1 is stored in memory, and the computer then goes on to Run 2. Here, a different set of random numbers, and hence cash flows, is used. The NPV generated in Run 2 is again stored, and the model proceeds on for perhaps 500 runs. Modern computers can complete this operation almost instantaneously for a cost of less than a dollar.

5. The stored NPVs (all 500 of them) are then printed out in the form of a frequency distribution, together with the expected NPV and the standard deviation of this NPV, and the IRR, PI, and payback period.

Using this procedure, we can perform a simulation analysis on RIC's office robot project. As in our scenario analysis, we have simplified the illustration by specifying the distributions for only two key variables, unit sales and the sales price. For all the other variables, we merely specify their expected values.

In our simulation analysis, we assume that sales prices can be represented by a continuous normal distribution.[11] Further, suppose the expected value is $2,200 and the actual sales price is not likely to vary by more than $500 from the expected value, that is, to fall below $1,700 or rise above $2,700. We know that in a normal distribution, the expected value plus or minus three standard deviations will encompass virtually the entire distribution. Thus, three standard deviations of the sales price would be about $500, so as a reasonable approximation, we may assume that $\sigma_{\text{Sales price}}$ = $500/3 = $166.67 $\approx$ $167. Therefore, we tell the computer to assume that the sales price distribution is normal with an expected value of $2,200 and a standard deviation of $167.

Next, we assume that the estimated distribution of unit sales is also symmetric with an expected value of 25,000 units, but sales could be as high as 40,000 units, given our production capacity, while if public acceptance is poor, sales could be as low as 10,000 units. Again, we could have specified a normal distribution, but in the case of unit sales, management feels that a triangular distribution, with an expected value of 25,000, a lower limit of 10,000, and an upper limit of 40,000 is most appropriate.

---

[10]An alternative procedure is to use as the discount rate in simulation analysis the risk-free rate rather than the cost of capital. The logic behind this approach is the fact that in simulation analysis, we are trying to assess a project's risk as reflected by the uncertainty inherent in its cash flows and then to use this observed uncertainty as a basis for establishing a risk-adjusted discount rate. Thus, under the risk-free discounting procedure, one finds the NPV distribution based on k_{RF}, which reflects only the time value of money, and then uses the variability inherent in this NPV distribution as the basis for setting the project's cost of capital. Finally, the project's NPV is calculated using the project's own risk-adjusted cost of capital to determine if the project should be accepted or rejected.

One can certainly argue that the approach based on k_{RF} is more logical than the one based on the average cost of capital. However, as we discuss later in the chapter, both procedures—and indeed the entire simulation approach—are only aids to informed judgmental decisions, so one discount rate is probably as good as another. The key thing is to maintain consistency among the methods being used to analyze different projects.

[11]See Appendix 2A for a discussion of continuous distributions including both normal and triangular distributions.

We used the *Interactive Financial Planning System (IFPS)* to conduct a simulation analysis of the office robot project. Most large corporations have *IFPS* or similar software either on their own computer or available through a time sharing system, and the same is true of many universities. The key results of our simulation are presented in Table 9-4. The top line of the table shows the cumulative probability distribution. Suppose someone asks, "What is the probability that the project will have an NPV greater than $10,000,000?" The answer is, "Almost 60 percent," because NPV = $10,000,000 lies between 50 and 60 percent, but much closer to 60 percent.

Notice that the mean, or expected, NPV is $12,862,000. This value is not the same as the NPV we calculated earlier in the scenario analysis because the sales price and quantity distribution assumptions are different. Also, again note that even though both input distributions (price and quantity) are symmetric, the distribution of NPV is not symmetric—it is skewed slightly to the right, as indicated by a skewness coefficient of +0.1. This is because our two uncertain variables, sales price and quantity, are multiplied together to get dollar sales. The multiplication process skews the resulting dollar sales distribution to the right, and this skewness is reflected in the NPV distribution.

The primary advantage of simulation is that it shows us a range of possible outcomes, with attached probabilities, and not just point estimates of the NPV. The expected NPV can be used as a measure of the project's profitability, while the variability of this NPV as measured by σ_{NPV} can be used to measure risk. To illustrate, the office robot project's expected NPV is $12,862,000, and the standard deviation of this NPV, as calculated by the computer in the simulation, is $\sigma_{NPV} = $10,124,000.[12] If we assume that RIC's average project has an expected NPV of $975,000 and $\sigma_{NPV} = $370,000, then we can calculate the *coefficient of variation (CV)* for the office robot project and compare it with the CV of the average project as follows:

$$\text{Coefficient of variation} = CV = \frac{\text{Standard deviation}}{\text{Expected value}} = \frac{\sigma_{NPV}}{\text{Expected NPV}}.$$

$$CV_{\text{Office robot}} = \frac{\$10,124,000}{\$12,862,000} = 0.79.$$

$$CV_{\text{Average project}} = \frac{\$370,000}{\$975,000} = 0.38.$$

Since the coefficient of variation is a standardized risk measure, it can be used to compare the relative riskiness of projects which differ in size. We see that the CV of the office robot project is much larger than the CV of RIC's average project. To account for risk, RIC adds two percentage points to the cost of capital of such high-risk projects as the office robot.

---

[12]Since this distribution is only approximately normal, the standard deviation cannot be used to make precise statements about risk, as it could be if the distribution of NPV were actually normal. Nevertheless, the standard deviation and the coefficient of variation can still be used to gain insights into the relative total risk of different projects.

Table 9-4
Summary of Simulation Results

				Probability of NPV or IRR being Greater than the Indicated Value (Thousands of Dollars)					
	0.90	0.80	0.70	0.60	0.50	0.40	0.30	0.20	0.10
NPV	−$322	$3,363	$6,682	$9,935	$12,931	$15,221	$18,054	$21,177	$26,824
IRR	0.090	0.129	0.161	0.189	0.214	0.231	0.252	0.273	0.309

NPV Sample Statistics (Thousands of Dollars)		
Mean	Standard Deviation	Skewness Coefficient
$12,862	$10,124	0.1

Our analysis thus far was based on RIC's average cost of capital, 10 percent. Therefore, we must now reevaluate the project using a risk-adjusted project cost of capital of 12 percent. When evaluated at a cost of capital of 12 percent, the NPV of the office robot project, using expected values of all variables, is $9,901,507. Thus, even at the high risk-adjusted cost of capital, the office robot project still has a large positive NPV. Thus, it appears to be acceptable.

Limitations of Simulation Analysis

In spite of its obvious appeal, simulation analysis has not been as widely used in industry as one might think.[13] Several major reasons for this lack of general acceptance have been advanced. First, the simulation process described above assumes that the variables are independent of one another. However, it may be that such variables as unit sales and sales prices are correlated. For example, if demand is weak, sales prices may also be depressed, which suggests that if unit sales is low, then a low sales price should also be used.[14] Similarly, the simulation process described above assumes that the values of each variable, and hence the bottom line cash flows, are independent over time. However, in many situations, it seems more reasonable to assume that high sales in the early years imply market acceptance, and hence high sales in future years, rather than to assume that sales in one year are not correlated with sales levels in other years.

---

[13]For an interesting discussion on the pros and cons of simulation analysis, see Wilbur G. Lewellen and Michael S. Long, "Simulation Versus Single-Value Estimates in Capital Expenditure Analysis," *Decision Sciences*, October 1972, 19-33.

[14]This statement implies a *downward (or left) shift* in the demand curve for the product. One can also visualize *movement along the demand curve*, which would imply that low sales prices would be associated with high demand. This relationship would be built into the simulation by the analyst. For example, if RIC decided to price office robots at a base price of $2,000 rather than $2,200, then the base case expected sales level would probably be somewhat above 25,000 units.

It is easy enough to incorporate any type of correlation among variables into a simulation analysis; for example, *IFPS* permits us to specify both intervariable and intertemporal correlations. However, it is *not* easy to specify what the correlations should be. Indeed, people who have tried to obtain such relationships from the operating executives who must estimate them have eloquently emphasized the difficulties involved.[15] Clearly, the problem is not insurmountable, as simulation is used in business. Still, it is important not to underestimate the difficulty of obtaining valid estimates of probability distributions and correlations among the variables.

A second problem with simulation analysis is that even when a simulation analysis has been completed, no clear-cut decision rule emerges. We end up with an expected NPV and a distribution about this expected value, which we can use to judge the project's risk. However, the analysis has no mechanism to indicate whether the profitability as measured by the expected NPV is sufficient to compensate for the risk as indicated by σ_{NPV} or CV_{NPV}.

Finally, simulation analysis, as well as scenario and sensitivity analysis, ignores the effects of diversification, both among projects within the firm and by investors in their personal investment portfolios. Thus, an individual project may have highly uncertain returns, but if those returns are not correlated with the returns on the firm's other assets, then the project may not be very risky in terms of either corporate or market risk. Indeed, if the project's returns are negatively correlated with the returns on the firm's other assets, then it may decrease the firm's corporate risk, and the larger its σ, the more it will reduce the firm's overall risk. Similarly, if a project's returns are not correlated with the stock market, then even a project with highly variable returns might not be regarded as risky by well-diversified stockholders, who are probably more concerned with market risk than with total risk.

Decision Tree Analysis

If a decision could result in one of several specific outcomes, it is often useful to think of it in terms of a *decision tree* such as the one shown here:

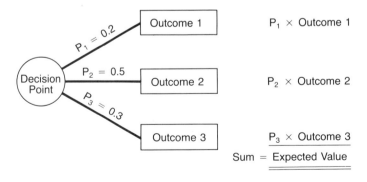

[15]For an excellent discussion of this problem, see K. Larry Hastie, "One Businessman's View of Capital Budgeting," *Financial Management*, Winter 1974, 36-43. Hastie was treasurer of Bendix Corporation.

Decision tree analysis is especially useful in situations where a series of decisions, over a period of time, are involved. For example, suppose RIC is considering the production of industrial robots for the television manufacturing industry. The capital budgeting decision for this project will be broken down into three stages, as set forth in Figure 9-6:

Stage 1. At t = 0, conduct a $500,000 study of the market potential for robot use in the television assembly-line process.

Stage 2. If it appears that a sizable market for robotics does exist, then at t = 1 spend $1,000,000 to design and fabricate several prototype robots. These robots would then be evaluated by television industry engineers, and their reactions would determine whether RIC should proceed with the project.

Stage 3. If reaction to the prototype robots is good, then at t = 2 build a production plant at a net cost of $10,000,000. If this stage were reached, the cash flow at t = 3 is expected to be either $13,000,000 or $16,000,000, depending on the state of the economy, competition, and so forth.

A decision tree such as the one in Figure 9-6 is often used to analyze multistage, or sequential, decisions. In Figure 9-6, we assume that one year goes by between decisions and that a single net cash inflow from the project would occur one year after the final decision if we go into production. Each circle represents a

Figure 9-6
RIC Decision Tree
(Thousands of Dollars)

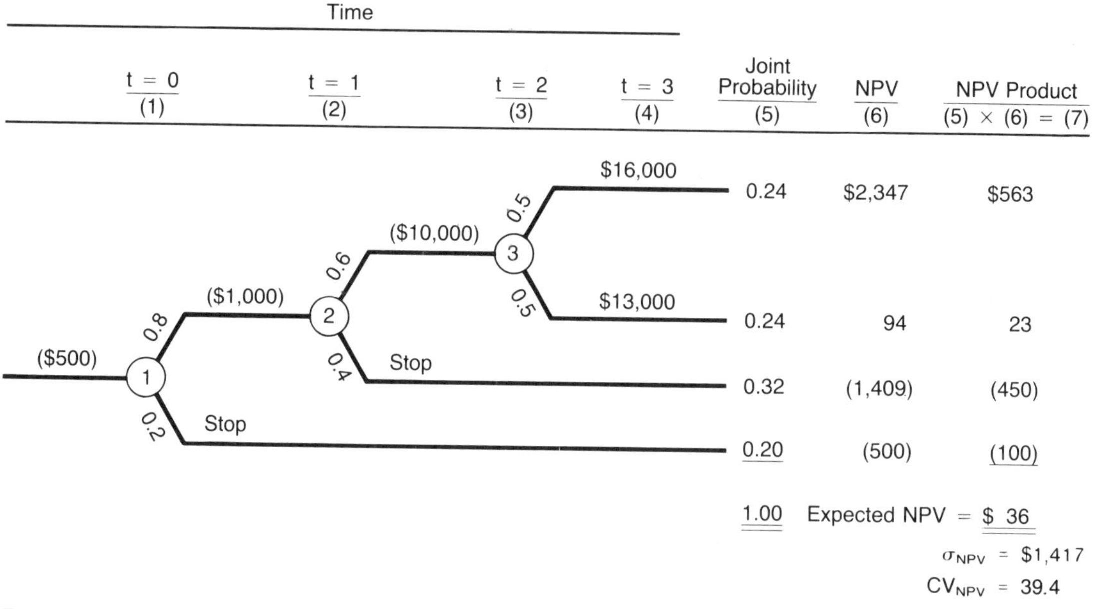

decision point, or stage. The dollar value to the left of each decision point represents the investment required if the decision is "go" at that point. Each diagonal line represents a branch of the decision tree, and each branch has an estimated probability. For example, if RIC decides to "go" with the project at Decision Point 1, it will have to spend $500,000 on a marketing study. Management estimates that there is a probability of 0.8 that the study will produce favorable results, leading to the decision to move on to Stage 2, and a 0.2 probability that the marketing study will produce negative results, indicating that the project should be canceled after Stage 1. If the project is stopped here, the cost to RIC will be $500,000 for the initial marketing study.

If the marketing study is undertaken, and if it does yield positive results, then RIC will go on to Decision Point 2 and spend $1,000,000 on the prototype robot. Management estimates (before even making the initial $500,000 investment) that there is a 60 percent probability that the television engineers will find the robot useful and a 40 percent probability that they will not like it. These are conditional probabilities; that is, they are conditioned upon reaching Decision Point 2. If the engineers accept the robot, RIC would then spend the final $10,000,000, while if the engineers do not like it, the project would be dropped. Finally, if RIC does go into production, the payoff is assumed to be either $16,000,000 or $13,000,000, with each outcome having a 50 percent probability. (Although we used only two production outcomes for simplicity, we could have used any number of outcomes or even a continuous distribution of outcomes. Similarly, we could have specified the outcomes at t = 3 in terms of net cash flows per year for n subsequent years and then found the present value of these future cash flows rather than specifying a lump sum cash flow.)

Column 5 of Figure 9-6 gives the joint probability of occurrence of each final outcome. Each joint probability is obtained by multiplying together all probabilities on a particular branch. For example, the probability that RIC will, if Stage 1 is undertaken, move through Stages 2 and 3, and that a strong demand will produce a $16,000,000 net cash inflow, is (0.8)(0.6)(0.5) = 0.24.

Column 6 of Figure 9-6 gives the NPV of each final outcome. RIC has a cost of capital of 10 percent, and management assumes initially that all projects have average risk. The NPV of the top (most favorable) outcome is about $2.35 million:

$$NPV = \frac{\$16,000,000}{(1.10)^3} - \frac{\$10,000,000}{(1.10)^2} - \frac{\$1,000,000}{(1.10)^1} - \$500,000 = \$2,347,483.$$

Other NPVs were calculated similarly.

Column 7 of Figure 9-6 gives the product of the NPVs in Column 6 times the joint probabilities in Column 5. The sum of the NPV products is the expected NPV of the project. Based on the expectations set forth in Figure 9-6, and a cost of capital of 10 percent, the expected NPV is approximately $36,000.

Since the expected NPV is positive, should RIC initiate Stage 1? Not necessarily. Recall that management assumed that the project is of average risk, and hence used the unadjusted cost of capital to evaluate it. However, the company should now reconsider and decide whether this project is more, less, or as risky as an average project. The expected NPV is only $36,000, and its standard deviation is $1,417,000, so the coefficient of variation is quite large. This suggests that the project is highly risky in terms of corporate risk. Note also that there is a probability of 0.52 of losing money and a probability of 0.32 of losing $1.4 million. With those high loss probabilities, chances are good that the project would be rejected.

THE IMPACT OF ABANDONMENT VALUE ON CORPORATE RISK

In Chapter 8 we introduced the concept of abandonment value. We now show how the possibility of abandonment can affect a project's risk as well as its expected NPV. Suppose RIC has analyzed a new project which calls for the expenditure of $2 million on a new plant. If the economy is good over the next 10 years, then the plant will provide a net cash flow of $450,000 per year for 10 years. If the economy is average, the annual cash flow is expected to be $400,000 per year, but if the economy is poor, the cash flow from operations will be only $100,000. There is a 0.3 probability of a good economy, a 0.4 probability of an average economy, and a 0.3 probability of a bad economy. The project cost of capital is 10 percent.

The top section of Figure 9-7 gives in decision tree format an analysis of the project. Its expected NPV is negative, − $3,016, and it has a high standard deviation and coefficient of variation. This suggests that the project should be rejected. However, suppose the possibility exists that the project can be abandoned if results are poor. Specifically, suppose the plant and equipment can be sold, and a tax loss (and hence a tax credit) established, with the result being an immediate abandonment value of $1,000,000. This situation is shown in the lower section of Figure 9-7. The NPV under bad economic conditions is still negative, but less so than if the plant were kept in operation, and the result is a positive expected NPV ($112,647 versus − $3,016) and lower risk. Thus, when abandonment possibilities are considered, the project becomes acceptable.

MARKET RISK

The types of corporate risk analysis discussed thus far in the chapter provide insights into projects' risk which help us make better accept/reject decisions. However, as noted, they do not take account of portfolio risk, and they are subjective rather than objective in the sense that they do not state specifically which projects should be accepted and which rejected. In this section, we show how the CAPM has been proposed to help overcome those shortcomings. Of course, the CAPM has shortcomings of its own, but it does nevertheless offer some useful insights into risk analysis in capital budgeting.

To begin, recall that the Security Market Line expresses the risk/return relationship as follows:

$$k_s = k_{RF} + b(k_M - k_{RF}).$$

Figure 9-7
Effects of Abandonment on NPV and σ_{NPV}

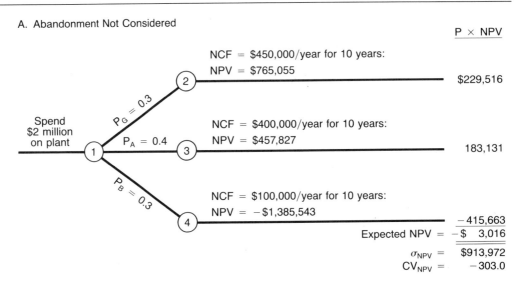

A. Abandonment Not Considered

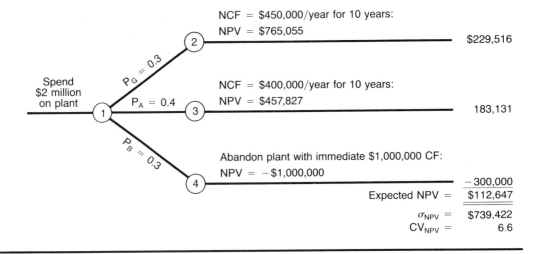

B. Abandonment Considered

For example, if RIC stock's beta = 1.2, k_{RF} = 8%, and k_M = 13%, then RIC's cost of equity is 14 percent:

$$k_s = 8\% + 1.2(13\% - 8\%)$$
$$= 8\% + 1.2(5\%) = 14.0\%.$$

Further, if RIC's cost of debt is 10 percent, its marginal federal-plus-state tax rate is 40 percent, and its target capital structure calls for 50 percent debt and 50 percent common equity, then its WACC is 10 percent:

$$\text{WACC} = k_a = w_d k_d (1 - T) + w_s k_s$$
$$= 0.5(10\%)(0.60) + 0.5(14\%)$$
$$= 3.0\% + 7.0\% = 10.0\%.$$

This suggests that investors would be willing to give RIC money to invest in average-risk projects if the company could earn 10 percent or more on this money. Here again, the term "average risk" means projects which have risk similar to that of the firm's existing assets.

Suppose, however, that taking on a particular project will cause a change in RIC's 1.2 beta coefficient, and hence change the company's cost of equity. For example, the office robot project might have a beta, if financed at the corporate capital structure, of 2.0. Since the firm itself may be regarded as a "portfolio of assets," and since the beta of any portfolio is a weighted average of the betas of its individual assets, taking on the office robot project would cause the overall corporate beta to rise, and it will end up somewhere between the original beta of 1.2 and the office robot project's beta of 2.0. The new corporate beta will depend on the relative size of the investment in office robots versus RIC's investment in other assets. If 80 percent of RIC's total funds would end up in other assets with an average beta of 1.2, and 20 percent in office robots with a beta of 2.0, then the new corporate beta would be 1.36:

$$\text{New b} = 0.8(1.2) + 0.2(2.0) = 1.36.$$

This increase in RIC's beta coefficient would cause the stock price to decline *unless the increased beta were offset by a higher expected rate of return*. Specifically, taking on the new project would cause the required rate of return on equity to rise to 14.8 percent,

$$k_s = 8\% + 1.36(5\%) = 14.8\%,$$

and the overall corporate cost of capital would rise to 10.4 percent:

$$k_a = 0.5(10\%)(0.60) + 0.5(14.8\%) = 10.4\%.$$

Therefore, to keep the office robot investment from lowering the value of the firm, RIC's overall expected rate of return would have to rise from 10.0 to 10.4 percent.

If investments in RIC's other assets must earn 10.0 percent, how much must the office robot investment earn in order for the new overall rate of return to equal 10.4 percent? We know that if it completes the office robot investment, RIC would have 80 percent of its assets invested in other assets earning 10.0 percent, that 20 percent of its assets would be in office robots earning X percent, and that the average required rate of return would be 10.4 percent. Therefore,

$$0.8(10.0\%) + 0.2X = 10.4\%.$$

Solving for X, we find that the office robot project must have an overall expected return of 12.0 percent if the corporation is to earn its new cost of capital.

In summary, if RIC takes on the office robot project, the corporate beta would rise from 1.2 to 1.36; the cost of equity would increase from 14.0 to 14.8 percent; the weighted average cost of capital would rise from 10.0 to 10.4 percent; and the office robot investment would have to earn at least 12.0 percent in order for RIC to earn its overall cost of capital.

This line of reasoning leads to the conclusion that if the beta coefficient for each project, b_i, could be determined, then individual projects' weighted average costs of capital, k_{ai}, could be found as follows:

1. Find Project i's required rate of return on equity, k_{si}:

$$k_{si} = k_{RF} + b_i(k_M - k_{RF}).$$

2. Use k_{si} to find the project's overall required rate of return, k_{ai}, or $WACC_i$:

$$k_{ai} = w_d k_d (1 - T) + w_s k_{si}.$$

Applying these two steps to RIC's office robot decision gives this result:

$$k_{si} = 8\% + 2.0(5\%) = 18.0\%.$$

$$k_{ai} = 0.5(10\%)(0.60) + 0.5(18.0\%) = 12.0\%.$$

We see that the required rate of return on the office robot project is the same using this "short-cut" method as it was when we developed the project's cost of capital by solving for X in the equation $10.4\% = 0.8(10\%) + 0.2X$. Note, however, that both solutions disregard any effects of the new project on either the firm's capital structure or its cost of debt; implicitly, we assumed that the new project's debt cost and financing mix would be the same as for all other projects. Potential effects of capital projects on debt capacity and the cost of debt are taken up next.

RELATIONSHIP AMONG FIRM BETAS, ASSET BETAS, AND CAPITAL STRUCTURE

Betas as developed in Chapter 2 show how returns on a firm's stock co-vary with returns on the market. Moreover, the beta of the firm is based on the betas of its individual assets. Therefore, we can think of each project, or asset, as a "minifirm," and of the firm itself as a portfolio of minifirms. If a firm were financed only with common equity, and if it consisted of only one asset, then the beta of the firm and that of the asset (or project) would be identical. In this sense, we can regard a "project beta" as being equal to the beta of an unleveraged, single-asset minifirm.

The beta of a firm with an all-equity capital structure (which means that the firm has zero financial leverage) is defined as an "unlevered beta." If the firm then begins to use debt, the riskiness inherent in its equity, and also its "levered beta," will begin to rise. In Chapter 6, we presented Robert Hamada's formula for the relationship between levered and unlevered betas:

$$\text{Hamada's formula: } b_L = b_U[1 + (1 - T)(D/S)]. \qquad (9\text{-}6)$$

If we were dealing with an unlevered, single-project firm, then its beta, b_U, would also be the beta of the firm's single asset. Thus, b_U can be thought of as an unlevered asset's beta.

The beta of the *equity* of a single-asset firm is a function of both the asset's business risk as measured by b_U, and how the asset is financed, and it can be approximated by the Hamada equation. We stated earlier that the beta on RIC's stock before it takes on the office robot project (its levered beta) is 1.2. This value was determined by regressing historic returns of the company on those of the market. RIC's debt financing, that is, its capital structure, was already reflected in its market-determined stock beta. However, what is the average underlying beta of RIC's existing assets, that is, the beta the company would have if it used no debt? To find this average asset beta, we must remove the financing effect; this can be approximated by solving Equation 9-6, the Hamada formula, for b_U:

$$b_U = \frac{b_L}{1 + (1 - T)(D/S)}. \qquad (9\text{-}6a)$$

For RIC, with a debt/equity ratio of 0.50/0.50, we obtain an asset beta of 0.75:

$$b_U = \frac{1.2}{1 + (0.60)(0.50/0.50)} = \frac{1.2}{1.6} = 0.75.$$

Thus, the beta of RIC's existing assets (which consist primarily of plant and equipment used to produce commercial robots) is equal to the beta the company would have if it used no debt, 0.75. Financial leverage has pushed the stock beta up from 0.75 to 1.20.

Equations 9-6 and 9-6a enable us to convert asset betas to firm betas, and vice versa, which is to say between unlevered betas and levered betas. However, recall our discussion in Chapter 6, where we noted that Equations 9-6 and 9-6a were derived under some very restrictive assumptions. Therefore, our results must be viewed as rough approximations. Nevertheless, we will use these equations in the next section, when we discuss the "pure play" method for estimating project betas.

TECHNIQUES FOR MEASURING BETA RISK

In Chapter 4, when we discussed the estimation of firms' betas, we indicated that it is difficult to estimate "true future betas" for common stocks. The estimation of project betas is even more difficult and more fraught with uncertainty, primarily because individual assets pay no dividends and have no quoted market prices; hence, we cannot calculate historic betas and use them as a starting point. However, two approaches have been used for the estimation of individual assets' betas: (1) the pure play method and (2) the accounting beta method.

The Pure Play Method

In the *pure play approach*, the company tries to find one or more nonintegrated, single product companies in the same line of business as the project being evaluated.[16] For example, suppose RIC could find several existing single-product firms that manufacture office robots. Further, suppose it believes that its office robot project would be subject to the same risks as those of the other firms. It could then determine betas of these firms by the regular regression process, average them, and use this average as a proxy for the office robot project's beta.

To illustrate, assume that RIC's analysts have identified three publicly owned companies engaged only in the production and distribution of office robots. Further, assume that the average beta of these firms is 1.79; that their average debt-to-equity ratio, D/S, is 0.4/0.6 = 0.67; and that their average federal-plus-state tax rate is 36 percent. We cannot, however, conclude that the office robot project's appropriate leverage-adjusted beta is 1.79, because RIC has a capital structure and tax rate different from those of the proxy firms.

To adjust for the difference in financial leverage and tax rates, we can employ Equations 9-6 and 9-6a, using the following four steps:

Step 1. Note that the proxy firms' average beta of 1.79 reflects their average D/S ratio of 0.67 and their average tax rate of 36 percent.

Step 2. We can insert these values into Equation 9-6a to determine the proxy firms' underlying asset beta:

$$b_U = \frac{1.79}{1 + (0.64)(0.67)} = 1.25.$$

Step 3. Now we can use Equation 9-6 to find what the proxy firms' asset betas would have been if they had had the same capital structure and tax rate as RIC:

$$b_L = 1.25[1 + (0.60)(0.50/0.50)]$$
$$= 2.0.$$

Step 4. Determine the office robot project's cost of equity and its weighted average cost of capital, using RIC's capital structure:

$$k_{si} = 8\% + 2.0(13\% - 8\%) = 18.0\%.$$
$$k_{ai} = 0.5(10\%)(0.60) + 0.5(18.0\%) = 12.0\%.$$

These values are consistent with those we calculated earlier.

The pure play approach is often difficult to implement because it is difficult to find pure play proxy firms. For our illustration, we assumed the existence of three

---

[16]See Russell J. Fuller and Halbert S. Kerr, "Estimating the Divisional Cost of Capital: An Analysis of the Pure-Play Technique," *Journal of Finance*, December 1981, 997-1009, for a more thorough discussion of the pure play method. Fuller and Kerr used the method to estimate divisional betas and then tested the results empirically. They concluded that the pure play method is a valid technique for estimating the betas of major sub-parts of a firm.

pure play proxies. In reality, there is no pure play office robot manufacturer. In fact, most robots are made by GM, GE, IBM, Westinghouse, and other large, multidivisional firms, and their robot operations are combined with their other operations in a manner that makes it impossible to ascertain market betas for their robots. However, there are times when the method is feasible. For example, when IBM was considering going into personal computers, it was able to get data on Apple Computer and several other essentially pure play personal computer companies. Similarly, Pillsbury is able to employ this technique when it is considering capital budgeting decisions in its Burger King, Godfather's Pizza, Steak and Ale, and Bennigan's divisions. More will be said about this subject in the section on divisional costs of capital.

The Accounting Beta Method

As previously noted, it is generally not possible to find single product, publicly traded firms suitable for the pure play approach. When this is the case, companies often use the *accounting beta method*. As you know, betas are normally found by regressing the returns of a particular company's stock against returns on a stock market index. However, one could run a regression of the company's basic earning power (EBIT/Total assets) over time against the average basic earning power for a large sample of stocks such as the NYSE or the S&P 500. Such data are readily available from Standard & Poor's Compustat tapes. Betas determined in this way, that is, by using accounting data rather than stock market data, are called *accounting betas*.

Historic accounting betas can be calculated for all types of companies (publicly owned or privately held), for divisions, or even for single projects. (The Compustat tapes provide data by product lines for most companies.) How good are accounting betas as proxies for market betas? Many studies have addressed this issue.[17] Although the results vary, most studies do support the conclusion that firms with high accounting betas tend to have high market betas, whereas firms with low accounting betas tend to have low market betas. However, the correlations are generally only in the 0.5 to 0.6 range, so accounting-determined betas provide only rough approximations for market-determined betas, systematic risk, and consequently the cost of capital.

To illustrate the use of accounting betas, suppose RIC went forward with the office robot project, and several years later, the results of this decision were embedded in the corporation's operating results. Now, suppose the company was considering a major expansion in office robotics (or in its other divisions), so it wanted an update on the cost of capital in the office robot division versus that in other segments of the firm. The financial staff could now use the historic operating

---

[17]For example, see William H. Beaver and James Manegold, "The Association between Market-Determined Measures of Systematic Risk: Some Further Evidence," *Journal of Financial and Quantitative Analysis*, June 1975, 231-284. Additionally, many of the accounting versus market beta studies are summarized in George Foster, *Financial Statement Analysis* (Englewood Cliffs, N.J.: Prentice-Hall, 1984).

data on office robots that was now available to calculate accounting betas for office robots (and for other product lines). These betas could then be used to establish risk-adjusted costs of capital for use in the capital budgeting decision process. This point will be explored in more detail later in the chapter.

PORTFOLIO EFFECTS WITHIN THE FIRM

As we noted in Chapter 2, a stock might be quite risky if held in isolation but not very risky if held as part of a well-diversified portfolio. The same thing is true of capital projects—the returns on an individual project might be highly uncertain, but if the project is small relative to the total firm, and if its returns are not highly correlated with the firm's other assets, then the project may not be very risky in either the corporate or the beta sense.

Many firms do make serious efforts to diversify; often, this is a specific objective of the long-run strategic plan. For example, Exxon and other oil companies have diversified into both coal and other forms of energy to broaden their operating bases; the major real estate developers have diversified geographically to lessen the impact of a slowdown in one region; and defense contractors such as Mc-Donnell-Douglas are seeking acquisitions in nondefense areas to reduce the effects of swings in the defense budget. The major objective of such moves as these is to stabilize earnings, reduce corporate risk, and thereby raise the value of the firm's stock.

However, the wisdom of corporate diversification designed to reduce risk has been questioned—why should a firm diversify when its stockholders could so easily diversify on their own? In other words, it may be true that if the returns on GE and on RCA are not perfectly positively correlated, then merging the companies (as happened in 1986) will reduce their risks somewhat, but would it not be just as easy for investors to carry out this risk-reducing diversification directly without all the trouble and expense of a merger?

As you might suspect, the answer is not so simple. While stockholders could accomplish directly some of the risk-reduction benefits from corporate diversification, other benefits can only be gained by diversification at the corporate level. A relatively stable corporation may be able to attract a better work force, and also to use more low-cost debt, than could two less stable firms. And, of course, there may also be spillover effects from diversification: For example, GE could provide RCA with technical assistance in the production of TV sets, RCA could give GE a stable market for some of its products; and the two companies' research departments might be able to gain economies of scale from combined operations. More will be said about this subject in Chapter 22.

PROBLEMS WITH PROJECT RISK ASSESSMENT

We have discussed two types of risk normally considered in capital budgeting analyses—corporate risk and market risk—and we have discussed ways of assessing each. However, two important questions remain: (1) Is it correct for a firm to consider both corporate risk and market risk in its capital budgeting decisions? (2) What do we do when the corporate risk and market risk assessments lead to different conclusions?

These questions do not have easy answers. From a theoretical standpoint, well-diversified investors should be concerned only with market risk, managers should be concerned only with stock price maximization, and these two factors should lead to the conclusion that market, or beta, risk ought to be given virtually all the weight in capital budgeting decisions. However, if investors are not well diversified, if as a result of market imperfections or other factors the CAPM does not really operate as theory says it should, or if measurement problems keep us from implementing the CAPM approach in capital budgeting, then it might be appropriate to give total risk more weight than financial theorists would suggest. Note also that the CAPM ignores financial distress costs, even though such costs can be significant, and that the probability of financial distress depends on a firm's total risk, not on its beta risk. Therefore, one could easily conclude that even well-diversified investors should want a firm's management to give at least some consideration to total risk rather than concentrating entirely on market risk.

Although it would be desirable to reconcile these problems and to measure project risk on some absolute scale, the best we can do in practice is to determine project risk in a somewhat nebulous, relative sense. For example, we might be able to say, with a fair degree of confidence, that Project A has less total risk than the firm's average project. Then, assuming that market risk and corporate risk are highly correlated (as studies suggest), a project with more total risk than average will also have more market risk.[18]

What does all this mean to the financial manager? He or she should make as good an assessment as possible of projects' relative total risk and market risk. If each type of risk is higher than average for a given project, then that project's cost of capital should be increased relative to the firm's overall cost of capital. If both relative risks are below average, then the adjustment should be reversed. Unfortunately, it is impossible to specify exactly how large the adjustment should be. This topic is pursued in the following section.

INCORPORATING PROJECT RISK INTO CAPITAL BUDGETING DECISIONS

Thus far, we have seen that capital budgeting can affect a firm's market risk, its corporate risk, or both. We have also seen that it is exceedingly difficult to quantify either effect. In other words, it may be possible to reach the general conclusion that one project is riskier than another (in either the market or the corporate sense), but it is difficult to develop a really good *measure* of project risk. Further,

---

[18]For example, see M. Chapman Findlay III, Arthur E. Gooding, and Wallace Q. Weaver, Jr., "On the Relevant Risk for Determining Capital Expenditure Hurdle Rates," *Financial Management*, Winter 1976, 9-16.

this lack of precision in measuring project risk makes it difficult to specify risk-adjusted rates of return, or project costs of capital, with which to evaluate individual projects. As we saw in Chapter 4, it is possible to estimate a firm's overall cost of capital reasonably well. Moreover, it is generally agreed that riskier projects should be evaluated with a higher cost of capital than the overall corporate cost, while a lower discount rate should be used for lower-risk projects. Unfortunately, there is no good way of specifying exactly *how much* higher or lower these discount rates should be; given the present state of the art, risk adjustments are necessarily judgmental and somewhat arbitrary.

Capital structure must also be taken into account. For example, one division might have a lot of real estate, which is well suited as collateral for loans, whereas some other division might have most of its capital tied up in special purpose machinery, which is not good collateral. As a result, the division with the real estate might have a higher *debt capacity* than the machinery division. In this case, the first division might calculate its WACC using a higher debt ratio than the second division.

Although the process is not exact, RIC and many other companies develop risk-adjusted discount rates for use in capital budgeting in a two-step process: (1) *Divisional costs of capital* are established for each of the major operating divisions on the basis of the divisions' estimated betas and capital structures, and (2) within each division, all projects are classified into three categories—high risk, average risk, and low risk. Each of RIC's divisions then uses its basic divisional cost of capital as the discount rate for average-risk projects, reduces the divisional WACC by one percentage point when evaluating low-risk projects, and raises the WACC by two percentage points for high-risk projects. For example, if a division's basic WACC is estimated to be 10 percent, then a 12 percent discount rate would be used for high-risk projects and a 9 percent rate for low-risk projects. Average-risk projects, which constitute about 80 percent of most of its divisions' capital budgets, would be evaluated at the 10 percent divisional cost of capital. This procedure is not very elegant, but it does at least recognize that different divisions have different characteristics, and hence different costs of capital, and it also acknowledges differential project riskiness within divisions. RIC's financial staff feels that these adjustments are in the right direction, and that the company makes better decisions than would be obtained if no adjustments were made.

RISKY CASH OUTFLOWS

In Chapter 7 we stated that some mutually exclusive projects are evaluated on the basis of minimizing the present value of future costs rather than on the basis of the projects' NPVs. This is done because (1) it is often impossible to allocate revenues to a particular project and (2) it is easier to focus on costs when two projects will generate identical incremental output. For example, suppose Duke Power must build a new generating plant to provide electricity to western North Carolina. Several alternative types of plants are available, and they have different initial costs, different lives, and different operating costs. There is no question about building some type of plant, because Duke Power's franchise agreement with the state requires it to supply power to the region. In this case, the decision will be based on the *minimization of the PV of expected future costs*.

Some projects also have large cash outflows which occur at the end of the projects' lives. For example, in 1986 Toronto Development Company (TDC) was offered the opportunity to use a large city-owned warehouse in the northern part of the city, and to lease space to others for a period of 10 years. During the 10 years, TDC would obtain large cash inflows. However, at the end of the 10-year period, TDC would be required to raze the building and to develop the site as a park, at a cost estimated at $5 million, but the cost could be much higher or lower, depending on conditions at the time.

In either the case of Duke Power's generating plant or TDC's warehouse-to-park project, the decision maker must apply risk adjustments to future cash outflows, and *the risk adjustment for a risky cash outflow is the exact opposite of that for an inflow, or a "normal" risk adjustment*.

Consider again the Duke Power example. Suppose Duke is choosing between a coal-fired plant and a nuclear plant. The coal plant has a lower initial cost but much higher operating costs during the plant's life. Also, the coal plant has a zero salvage value—removal costs equal the scrap value of the plant. However, the costs of disassembling and disposing of a radioactive nuclear plant are quite high, and very uncertain. Further, nuclear plants are less reliable than coal plants, and hence costly repairs may be necessary. There is also more uncertainty about the construction cost, the in-service timing, and the life of a nuclear plant. For all these reasons, there is good reason to regard the nuclear plant as being riskier than the coal plant.

Both nuclear and coal plants generally take a number of years to build, and they have expected lives of about 30 years. However, for simplicity, we shall assume that both plants have a 1-year construction period and a 5-year operating life. Further, we shall disregard inflation, and we also assume that the two plants have an equal capacity and that the outputs of both plants would be sold at the same price per unit.

Table 9-5 gives the projected costs associated with the two power plants: the investment costs at Year 0 and the operating costs plus decommissioning cost during Years 1 to 5. We assume that Duke Power's overall WACC, before it announces plans for a new generating plant, is 10 percent. If this discount rate were used to find the PV of future costs, we see from Table 9-5 that the plants would be judged equal. However, if Duke recognizes that the nuclear plant is more risky, and it therefore evaluates this project with a 12 percent cost of capital, then the nuclear plant's PV of future costs declines to $2,973 million, while at a still higher cost of 15 percent, the nuclear plant's costs drop to only $2,916 million. Thus, the riskier the nuclear plant is judged to be, the better it looks!

Something is obviously wrong. Clearly, if two alternative investments have the same expected revenue stream and the same PV of future costs, then a risk-averse decision maker would favor the less risky alternative. Therefore, if we want to penalize a cash outflow for higher-than-average risk, then that outflow must have a *higher* absolute present value, not a *lower* value. *Therefore, a stream of cash out-*

Table 9-5
Expected Costs:
Coal Versus Nuclear Power Plants
(Millions of Dollars)

Year	Coal Plant	Nuclear Plant
0	($1,500)	($2,500)
1	(400)	(10)
2	(400)	(10)
3	(400)	(10)
4	(400)	(10)
5	(400)	(10) + (770) = (780)
PV of costs at: 10%	($3,016)	($3,016)
12%	—	(2,973)
15%	—	(2,916)

Correct analysis: PV_{Coal} (at 10%) = ($3,016).
$PV_{Nuclear}$ (at 7%) = ($3,090).
Therefore, build the coal plant.

flows that has higher-than-average risk must be evaluated with a lower-than-average cost of capital.

Recognizing this situation, Duke Power might discount the nuclear plant's costs at a 7 percent rate versus a 10 percent rate for the coal plant. In this case, the coal plant, with a PV cost of $3,016 million versus $3,090 million for the nuclear plant, would be chosen. This example illustrates both the problem that negative cash flows cause and an approach for dealing with the problem.[19]

RISK ANALYSIS IN PRACTICE

As in several past chapters, we close this chapter by taking a brief look at what is currently being done in practice. The Gitman and Forrester study referenced in Chapter 7 addressed the issue of how firms treat risk and uncertainty in the capital

---

[19]The negative cash flow problem could arise in a conventional NPV analysis as well as a PV of future cost analysis. For example, in the Toronto Development Company example, if the cash outflow at the end of the project's life were judged to be more risky than the cash inflows during the project's life, and if the outflow were discounted at a higher risk-adjusted discount rate, then this would incorrectly bias the evaluation toward acceptance of the project.

For more on the effects of negative cash flows, see Wilbur G. Lewellen, "Some Observations on Risk-Adjusted Discount Rates," *Journal of Finance*, September 1977, 1331-1337; and a comment on that paper by Stephen E. Celec and Richard H. Pettway, plus a reply by Lewellen, in the September 1979 issue of the *Journal*, 1061-1066.

budgeting process. A total of 71 percent of their questionnaire respondents indicated that they explicitly considered project risk. The survey did not reveal the percentages using specific risk measurement techniques, but a number of respondents did volunteer that they used sensitivity analysis, and simulation was also mentioned. The most popular method of adjusting for risk—employed by 43 percent of the respondents—was to increase or decrease the firm's cost of capital. Other risk adjustment techniques that were mentioned included certainty equivalents, some subjective downward adjustments of cash flows, and changes in the required minimum payback period.

Financial managers clearly recognize that assessing project risk and adjusting for it is an important part of capital budgeting analysis. The Gitman-Forrester results confirm this fact. However, their study also confirmed that risk cannot be measured precisely, and that risk assessment in practice involves judgment as well as quantitative analysis.

SUMMARY

Our analysis of risk has focused on two important issues: (1) the effects of a given project on the firm's beta coefficient (market risk) and (2) the project's effect on the variability of the firm's cash flows (corporate risk). *Market risk* should, in theory, affect the value of the stock. *Corporate risk* affects the financial strength of the firm, and this, in turn, influences its ability to use debt, to maintain smooth operations over time, and to avoid crises that might consume the energy of the firm's managers and disrupt its employees, customers, suppliers, and community.

There are several analytical techniques available to help measure a project's corporate risk. Among these are (1) *sensitivity analysis*, (2) *scenario analysis*, (3) *Monte Carlo simulation*, and (4) *decision tree analysis*. However, the final decision regarding a project's corporate risk is always judgmental. The major difficulty in determining a project's market risk is to establish the project's beta coefficient. The beta of an asset such as a truck or a machine may be meaningless, but the betas of divisions that are large enough to be operated as independent firms may be quite important. In practice, market risk is generally estimated for large divisions of firms and then used to establish divisional costs of capital. There are two approaches to measuring market risk: (1) the *pure play* method and (2) the *accounting beta* method.

Once a project's risk has been estimated, this risk must then be incorporated into the analysis (1) by adjusting the project's cash flows (*certainty equivalent* method) or (2) by adjusting the project's cost of capital (*risk-adjusted discount rate* method). Regardless of which method is used, risk adjustments for risky cash outflows require a reversal of the "normal" adjustment process.

Both the measurement of risk and its incorporation into capital budgeting decisions involve judgment. It is possible to use quantitative techniques such as simulation and decision trees as an aid to judgment, but in the final analysis, the assessment of risk in capital budgeting will always remain a judgmental process.

Questions and Problems

9-1 **(Certainty equivalents)** You are the director of capital budgeting for Sun Berry Company (SBC), a producer of frozen cranberry juice. SBC uses the certainty equivalent approach to capital budgeting decisions. You are evaluating the acquisition of a new juice press with the following *expected* net cash flows. Further, you estimate the certainty equivalent cash flows, CE_t, as listed:

Year	Cash Flow	CE_t
0	($20,000)	($20,000)
1	5,000	4,500
2	5,000	4,500
3	5,000	4,500
4	15,000	10,500

You view the Year 4 cash flow as being more risky than Years 1-3 because a large proportion of the Year 4 cash flow is salvage value, and SBC's engineering estimates of salvage value are very uncertain. Conversely, you know the cost of the machine with certainty, since its manufacturer has given SBC a fixed bid for a 90-day period.

   a. Assume that the risk-free rate is 4 percent. What is the project's NPV using the certainty equivalent (CE) method?

   b. The project has the same risk as the firm's average project, and SBC's WACC is 12 percent. What is the project's NPV using the risk-adjusted discount rate (RADR) method?

   c. What intertemporal risk assumption is inherent in the constant RADR method? Which method do most firms use? Why?

9-2 **(Corporate risk)** The staff of Art Deco Graphics has estimated the following net cash flows and probabilities for a new printing process:

Year	Net Cash Flows		
	P = 0.2	**P = 0.6**	**P = 0.2**
0	($100,000)	($100,000)	($100,000)
1	20,000	30,000	40,000
2	20,000	30,000	40,000
3	20,000	30,000	40,000
4	20,000	30,000	40,000
5	20,000	30,000	40,000
5*	0	20,000	30,000

Line 0 is the cost of the process, Lines 1-5 are operating cash flows, and Line 5* contains the estimated salvage value. Art Deco's cost of capital for an average risk project is 10 percent.

   a. Assume that the project has average risk. Find the project's base case NPV. (Hint: Use the expected net cash flow in each year as the base case.)

   b. Your boss is worried about the project's sensitivity of NPV to salvage value. Construct a salvage value sensitivity diagram. (Even though the estimated salvage values are discrete, assume that salvage value could vary from the base case by plus or minus 10 percent, 20 percent, and 30 percent.)

c. Assume that all the cash flows are perfectly positively correlated. That is, that there are only three possible cash flow streams over time: (1) the worst case, (2) the most probable case, and (3) the best case, with probabilities of 0.2, 0.6, and 0.2, respectively. Find the project's expected NPV, its standard deviation, and its coefficient of variation.

d. The coefficient of variation of the firm's average project is in the range 0.8 to 1.0. If the coefficient of variation of a project being evaluated is greater than 1.0, 2 percentage points are added to the firm's cost of capital. Similarly, if the coefficient of variation is less than 0.8, 1 percentage point is deducted from the cost of capital. What is this project's cost of capital? Should the firm accept or reject the project?

9-3   **(Pure play approach)** QuickCopy Company (QCC) has a target capital structure of 40 percent debt and 60 percent equity. Its beta, which is an average of five estimates by financial service firms, is 1.5. QCC is evaluating a new project which is totally unrelated to its existing line of business. However, it has identified two proxy firms exclusively engaged in this business line. They, on average, have a beta of 1.2 and a debt ratio of 50 percent. QCC's new project has an estimated IRR of 13.5 percent. The risk-free rate is 10 percent, and the market risk premium is 5 percent. All three firms have a marginal tax rate of 34 percent. QCC's before-tax cost of debt is 14 percent.

a. What is the project's beta, b_U?

b. What is the beta of the project if undertaken by QCC?

c. Should QCC accept the project?

9-4   **(Risky cash outflows)** Cal State Utilities is deciding if it should build an oil or a coal generating plant. Its WACC is 8 percent for low-risk projects, 10 percent for projects of average risk, and 12 percent for high-risk projects. Management believes that an oil plant is of average risk, but that a coal plant is of high risk due to the problem of acid rain. The cash *outflows* required to construct each plant are listed below. The revenues, fuel costs, and other operating costs are expected to be the same under both plans:

Year	Construction Costs (Thousands of Dollars)	
	Coal Plant	Oil Plant
0	($ 100)	($ 400)
1	(500)	(1,000)
2	(1,500)	(1,000)
3	(1,500)	(1,000)
4	(1,500)	(1,500)
5	(1,000)	(1,000)
6	(500)	(200)

Which type plant should be constructed?

9-5   **(Sequential decisions)** The Horgan Yacht Company (HYC), a prominent sailboat builder in Florida, may design a new 30-foot sailboat based on the "winged" keel used by Australia II that won the America's Cup after 132 years of dominance by the United States.

First, HYC would have to invest $10,000 at t = 0 for the design and model tank testing of the new boat. HYC's managers believe that there is a 60 percent probability that this phase will be successful and the project will continue. If Stage 1 is not successful, the project will be abandoned with zero salvage value.

The next stage, if undertaken, would consist of making the molds and producing two prototype boats. This would cost $500,000 at t = 1. If the boats test well, HYC would go into production. If they do not, the molds and prototypes could be sold for $100,000. The managers estimate that the probability is 80 percent that the boats will pass testing, and that Stage 3 will be undertaken.

Stage 3 consists of changing over one current production line to produce the new design. This would cost $1,000,000 at t = 2. If the economy is strong at this point, the net value of sales would be $3,000,000, while if the economy is weak, the net value would be $1,500,000. Both net values occur at t = 3, and each state of the economy has a probability of 0.5. HYC's cost of capital is 12 percent.

  a. Assume that this project has average risk. Construct a decision tree and determine the project's expected NPV.

  b. Find the project's standard deviation of NPV and coefficient of variation (CV) of NPV. If HYC's average project had a CV of between 1.0 and 2.0, would this project be of high, low, or average corporate risk?

9-6 **(Divisional cost of capital)** Suppose Lima Locomotive Company, which has a high beta and also a great deal of corporate risk, merged with Homestake Mining, which has a low beta but relatively high corporate risk. What would the merger do to the cost of capital in the consolidated company's locomotive division and its gold mining division?

9-7 **(Divisional market risk adjustments)** SureGrip Rubber Company has two divisions: (1) the tire division, which manufactures tires for new autos; and (2) the recap division, which manufactures recapping materials that are sold to independent tire recapping shops throughout the United States. Since auto manufacturing fluctuates with the general economy, the tire division's earnings contribution to SureGrip's stock price is highly correlated with returns on most other stocks. If the tire division were operated as a separate company, its beta coefficient would be about 1.60. The sales and profits of the recap division, on the other hand, tend to be counter-cyclical, since recap sales boom when people cannot afford to buy new tires. The recap division's beta is estimated to be 0.40. Approximately 75 percent of SureGrip's corporate assets are invested in the tire division and 25 percent are in the recap division.

Currently, the rate of interest on Treasury securities is 10 percent, and the expected rate of return on an average share of stock is 15 percent. SureGrip uses only common equity capital, and hence it has no debt outstanding.

  a. What is the required rate of return on SureGrip's stock?

  b. What discount rate should be used to evaluate capital budgeting projects? Explain your answer fully, and in the process, illustrate your answer with a project which costs $100,000, has a ten-year life, and provides expected after-tax net cash flows of $20,000 per year.

9-8 **(Scenario and sensitivity analysis)** Your firm, Agrico, is considering the purchase of a tractor which will have a net cost of $30,000, will increase pre-tax operating cash flows exclusive of depreciation effects by $10,000 per year, and will be depreciated on a straight line basis to zero over 5 years at the rate of $6,000 per year, beginning the first year. (Annual cash flows will be $10,000, reduced by taxes, plus the tax savings that result from $6,000 of depreciation.) The board of directors, however, is having a heated debate as to whether the tractor will actually last 5 years. Specifically, Charles

Cornwell insists that he knows of some that have lasted only 4 years. Jim Adams agrees with Cornwell, but he argues that most tractors do give 5 years of service. Jane Wright, on the other hand, says she has seen some last as long as 8 years.

a. Given this discussion, the board asks you to prepare a scenario analysis to ascertain the importance of the uncertainty about the tractor's life. Assume a 40 percent marginal federal-plus-state tax rate, a zero salvage value, and a cost of capital of 10 percent. (Hint: Here straight-line depreciation is based on the ACRS class life of the tractor and is not affected by the actual life. Also, ignore the half-year convention for this problem.)

(Do Parts b and c only if you are using the computerized diskette.)

b. The board would also like to know how changes in the cost of capital affect the analysis. Assume that the machine's life is 5 years, and analyze the effects of a change in the cost of capital to 8 percent or to 12 percent. Is the project very sensitive to changes in the cost of capital?

c. The board would like to determine the sensitivity of the project's NPV to changes in certain variables. First, they would like to examine the effect of changes in pre-tax operating revenues upon NPV. Calculate the project's NPV at plus 10, 20, and 30 percent of the estimated $10,000 pre-tax revenues, as well as minus 10, 20, and 30 percent of this figure. (Hold all other variables constant.) Second, calculate the effect upon NPV of various project lives. (Hint: Hold all other variables constant, and try lives ranging from 1 to 10 years.) Finally, examine NPV while changing the cost of capital. (Once again, hold all other variables constant at their original levels.) Plot a separate sensitivity diagram for each variable examined above.

9-9 **(Simulation)** Hospital Supplies Corporation (HSC) manufactures medical products for hospitals, clinics, and nursing homes. HSC may introduce a new type of X-ray scanner designed to identify certain types of cancers in their early stages. There are a number of uncertainties about the proposed project, but the following data are believed to be reasonably accurate.

	Probability	Value	Random Numbers
Developmental costs	0.3	$2,000,000	00-29
	0.4	4,000,000	30-69
	0.3	6,000,000	70-99
Project life	0.2	3 years	00-19
	0.6	8 years	20-79
	0.2	13 years	80-99
Sales in units	0.2	100	00-19
	0.6	200	20-79
	0.2	300	80-99
Sales price	0.1	$13,000	00-09
	0.8	13,500	10-89
	0.1	14,000	90-99
Cost per unit (excluding developmental costs)	0.3	$5,000	00-29
	0.4	6,000	30-69
	0.3	7,000	70-99

HSC uses a cost of capital of 15 percent to analyze average-risk projects, 12 percent for low-risk projects, and 18 percent for high-risk projects. These risk adjustments reflect primarily the uncertainty about each project's NPV and IRR as measured by the coefficients of variation of NPV and IRR. HSC is in the 40 percent federal-plus-state income tax bracket.

a. What is the expected IRR for the X-ray scanner project? Base your answer on the expected values of the variables. Also, assume the after-tax "profits" figure you develop is equal to annual cash flows. All facilities are leased, so depreciation may be disregarded. Can you determine the value of σ_{IRR} short of actual simulation or a fairly complex statistical analysis?

b. Assume that HSC uses a 15 percent cost of capital for this project. What is the project's NPV? Could you estimate σ_{NPV} without either simulation or a complex statistical analysis?

c. Show the process by which a computer would perform a simulation analysis for this project. Use the random numbers 44, 17, 16, 58, 1; 79, 83, 86; and 19, 62, 6 to illustrate the process with the first computer run. Actually calculate the first-run NPV and IRR. Assume that the cash flows for each year are independent of cash flows for other years. Also, assume that the computer operates as follows: (1) A developmental cost and a project life are estimated for the first run. (2) Next, sales volume, sales price, and cost per unit are estimated and used to derive a cash flow for the first year. (3) Then, the next three random numbers are used to estimate sales volume, sales price, and cost per unit for the second year, and hence the cash flow for the second year. (4) Cash flows for other years are developed similarly, on out to the first run's estimated life. (5) With the developmental cost and the cash flow stream established, NPV and IRR for the first run are derived and stored in the computer's memory. (6) The process is repeated to generate perhaps 500 other NPVs and IRRs. (7) Frequency distributions for NPV and IRR are plotted by the computer, and the distributions' means and standard deviations are calculated.

d. Does it seem a little strange to conduct a risk analysis such as the one here *after* having already established a cost of capital for use in the analysis? What might be done to improve this situation?

e. In this problem, we assumed that the probability distributions were all independent of one another. It would have been possible to use conditional probabilities where, for example, the probability distribution for cost per unit would vary from trial to trial, depending on the unit sales for the trial. Also, it would be possible to construct a simulation model such that the sales distribution in Year t would depend on the sales level attained in Year $t - 1$. Had these modifications been made in this problem, do you think the standard deviation of the NPV distribution would have been larger (riskier) or smaller (less risky) than where complete independence is assumed?

f. Name two *major* difficulties not mentioned above that occur in the kind of analysis discussed in this problem.

Selected Additional References and Cases

The literature on risk analysis in capital budgeting is vast; here is a small but useful selection of additional references that bear directly on the topics covered in this chapter:

Ang, James S., and Wilbur G. Lewellen, "Risk Adjustment in Capital Investment Project Evaluations," *Financial Management*, Summer 1982, 5-14.

Bower, Richard S., and Jeffrey M. Jenks, "Divisional Screening Rates," *Financial Management*, Autumn 1975, 42-49.

Fama, Eugene F., "Risk-Adjusted Discount Rates and Capital Budgeting under Uncertainty," *Journal of Financial Economics*, August 1977, 3-24.

Gehr, Adam K., Jr., "Risk-Adjusted Capital Budgeting Using Arbitrage," *Financial Management*, Winter 1981, 14-19.

Gup, Benton E., and S. W. Norwood III, "Divisional Cost of Capital: A Practical Approach," *Financial Management*, Spring 1982, 20-24.

Lessard, Donald R., and Richard S. Bower, "An Operational Approach to Risk Screening," *Journal of Finance*, May 1973, 321-338.

Myers, Stewart C., and Samuel M. Turnbull, "Capital Budgeting and the Capital Asset Pricing Model: Good News and Bad News," *Journal of Finance*, May 1977, 321-333.

Robichek, Alexander A., "Interpreting the Results of Risk Analysis," *Journal of Finance*, December 1975, 1384-1386.

The Crum-Brigham casebook contains the following cases which focus on capital budgeting under uncertainty:

Case 15, "Egret Printing & Publishing Company," which illustrates alternative expansion paths.

Case 16, "Lotis Electronics," which focuses on sequential investment strategies.

Case 18, "Wayland Control & Instrument Corporation," which illustrates project evaluation under uncertainty.

The Harrington casebook contains the following applicable cases:

"Interchemical Consumer Products Division," which focuses on simulation analysis.

"Alaska Interstate," which illustrates a variety of ways to measure the riskiness of a conglomerate's subsidiaries.

"The Jacobs Division," which focuses on the riskiness of mutually exclusive alternatives.

10
THE OPTIMAL
CAPITAL BUDGET

In Chapter 4, we developed the concept of the weighted average cost of capital (WACC), and in Chapters 7, 8, and 9, we saw how capital projects are evaluated. However, capital budgeting and the cost of capital are actually interrelated—we cannot determine the cost of capital unless we know the size of the capital budget, and we cannot determine the size of the capital budget unless we know the cost of capital. Therefore, as we show in this chapter, the cost of capital and the capital budget must be determined simultaneously.

THE INVESTMENT OPPORTUNITY SCHEDULE (IOS)

Carson Foods Company, a relatively small Midwestern grocery wholesaler, is used to illustrate the concepts involved. Consider first Figure 10-1, which gives some information on Carson's potential capital projects for next year. The tabular data show each project's cash flows, IRR, and payback. The graph is defined as the firm's *Investment Opportunity Schedule (IOS)*, which is a plot of each project's IRR, in descending order, versus the dollars of new capital required to finance it (or the cash flow at t = 0). For example, Project B has an IRR of 38.5 percent, shown on the vertical axis, and a cost of $100,000, shown on the horizontal axis. Notice also that Projects A and B are mutually exclusive. Thus, Carson Foods has two possible IOS schedules: the one defined by the solid line, which contains Project B plus C, D, E, and F, and the one defined by the dotted line, which contains Project A plus C, D, E, and F. Beyond $600,000, the two IOS schedules are identical. Thus, the two alternative schedules differ only in that one contains B and has C ranked second while the other contains A, in which case C ranks first because $IRR_C >$ IRR_A. For now, we assume that all six projects have the same risk as Carson's "average" project.

Figure 10-1
Carson Foods:
Investment Opportunity Schedules

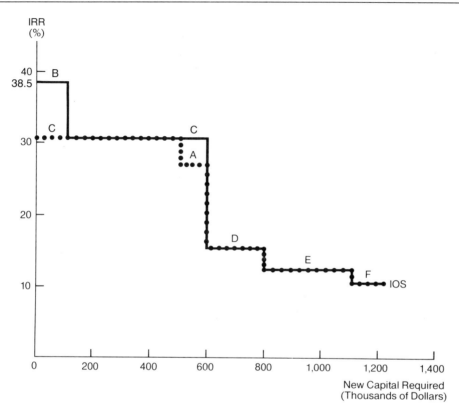

	Cash Flows from Potential Capital Projects					
Year	A[a]	B[a]	C	D	E	F
0	($100,000)	($100,000)	($500,000)	($200,000)	($300,000)	($100,000)
1	10,000	90,000	190,000	52,800	98,800	58,781
2	70,000	60,000	190,000	52,800	98,800	58,781
3	100,000	10,000	190,000	52,800	98,800	—
4	—	—	190,000	52,800	98,800	—
5	—	—	190,000	52,800	—	—
6	—	—	190,000	52,800	—	—
IRR	27.0%	38.5%	30.2%	15.0%	12.0%	11.5%
Payback	2.2	1.2	2.6	3.8	3.0	1.7

[a]Projects A and B are mutually exclusive.

THE MARGINAL COST OF CAPITAL (MCC) SCHEDULE

In Chapter 4, we discussed the concept of the weighted average cost of capital (WACC). However, the exact value of the WACC depends on the amount of new capital raised—the WACC will, at some point, rise if more and more capital is raised during a given year. This increase occurs because (1) flotation costs (including any "signaling" costs associated with stock issues) cause the cost of new equity to be higher than the cost of retained earnings, and (2) higher rates of return on debt, preferred stock, and common stock may be required to induce additional investors to supply capital to the firm.

To illustrate this concept, consider Carson Foods' WACC. Carson's market value target capital structure, together with other data needed to calculate the WACC, are given in Table 10-1. Carson has been growing at a constant 7 percent rate, a growth rate that is expected to remain stable into the future. Thus, we can use the constant growth (Gordon) model to estimate its cost of retained earnings:

$$k_s = \hat{k}_s = \frac{D_1}{P_0} + g = \frac{\$1.60}{\$20} + 0.070$$

$$= 0.080 + 0.070 = 0.150 = 15.0\%.$$

Now we can calculate Carson's WACC, which is 12 percent:

$$WACC = k_a = w_d k_d (1 - T) + w_p k_p + w_s k_s$$

$$= 0.3(10\%)(1 - 0.40) + 0.1(12\%) + 0.6(15\%)$$

$$= 1.8\% + 1.2\% + 9.0\% = 12.0\%.$$

Since the firm's optimal capital structure calls for 30 percent debt, 10 percent preferred, and 60 percent equity, each new (or marginal) dollar will be raised as

---

Table 10-1
Carson Foods: Cost of Capital Data

Market Value Capital Structure

Debt	$ 3,000,000	30%
Preferred stock	1,000,000	10
Common stock (300,000 shares)	6,000,000	60
Total market value	$10,000,000	100%

Other Data

Stock price = P_0 = $20.
Next expected dividend = D_1 = $1.60.
Expected constant growth rate = g = 7%.
Current interest rate on debt = k_d = 10%.
Current cost of preferred stock = k_p = 12%.
Federal-plus-state tax rate = T = 40%.
Flotation cost for equity = F = 10%.[a]

[a]F includes both underwriting expenses and the expected impact on stock price of a new stock offering.

30 cents of debt, 10 cents of preferred, and 60 cents of common equity; otherwise, the capital structure would not stay on target.[1] As long as Carson's after-tax cost of debt is 6 percent, its preferred cost is 12 percent, and its common equity cost is 15 percent, then its WACC will hold constant at 12 percent. Thus, we may assume for planning purposes that each new dollar will be raised as 30 cents of debt, 10 cents of preferred, and 60 cents of equity, and that each new (or marginal) dollar will have a weighted average cost of 12 percent.

Raising Equity by Issuing Common Stock

Can Carson raise an unlimited amount of new capital at the 12 percent cost? The answer is no. If Carson wanted to raise $1 million in new capital, the company would need $300,000 of debt, $100,000 of preferred stock, and $600,000 of common equity. The new equity could come from two sources: (1) that part of this year's profits which management decides to retain in the business rather than use for dividends (but not from earnings retained in the past, for they have already been invested in plant, equipment, inventories, and so on) or (2) selling an issue of common stock.

On the basis of the data in Table 10-1, the debt will have an interest rate of 10 percent, or an after-tax cost of 6 percent, while the preferred stock will have a cost of 12 percent. The cost of common equity will be k_s as long as the equity is obtained by retained earnings, *but the cost of equity will rise to k_e if the company uses up all of its retained earnings and must therefore sell new common stock.* Consider first the case where all the new equity comes from retained earnings. As we saw above, the cost of these retained earnings is 15 percent, and the resulting WACC is 12.0 percent. Now suppose the company expands so rapidly that its retained earnings for the year are not sufficient to meet its needs for new equity, forcing it to sell new common stock in order to keep the capital structure in balance. According to Table 10-1, the flotation cost on new stock is 10 percent, so we can use Equation 4-5a from Chapter 4 to find Carson's cost of external equity:

$$k_e = \frac{D_1}{P_0(1 - F)} + g = \frac{\$1.60}{\$20(0.9)} + 7\% = 15.9\%.$$

Thus, Carson's cost of external equity is 15.9 percent, up from the 15.0 percent cost of retained earnings, and this increase in the cost of equity causes the WACC to increase from 12.0 to 12.5 percent:

$$\begin{aligned} \text{New WACC} = k_a &= w_dk_d(1 - T) + w_pk_p + w_sk_e \\ &= 0.3(10\%)(0.60) + 0.1(12\%) + 0.6(15.9\%) \\ &= 1.8\% + 1.2\% + 9.5\% = 12.5\%. \end{aligned}$$

---

[1]Of course, Carson Foods does not really sell 30 cents of debt, 10 cents of preferred, and 60 cents of common equity for every $1 of capital raised. In fact, most of the financing for a year, or even for two years, might be done using a single source of funds, say a large stock offering. Still, over the long run, Carson does tend to raise capital using a mix of all three sources, and on average, it raises capital in accordance with its target capital structure.

How much new capital can Carson raise before it exhausts its retained earnings and is forced to sell new common stock; that is, at what amount of capital will it have to switch from k_s with a cost of 15 percent to k_e with a cost of 15.9 percent, and thus cause the WACC to rise from 12 percent to 12.5 percent? Assume that the company expects to have total earnings of $840,000 for the year and that it has a policy of paying out half of its earnings as dividends. Thus, the addition to retained earnings will be $420,000 during the year. How much total financing—debt and preferred, along with this $420,000 of retained earnings—can be done before the retained earnings are exhausted and the firm is forced to sell new common stock? In effect, we are seeking some amount, X, defined as a *break point*, which represents the total financing that can be done before Carson is forced to sell new common stock.

We know that 60 percent of the total capital raised, X, will be equity from the new retained earnings, which will amount to $420,000. Therefore,

$$\text{Retained earnings} = 0.6(\text{Total capital}) = 0.6X = \$420,000.$$

Solving for X, which is the *retained earnings break point*, we obtain

$$\begin{matrix} \text{Break point} \\ \text{for} \\ \text{retained earnings} \end{matrix} = X = \frac{\text{Retained earnings}}{0.6} = \frac{\$420,000}{0.6}$$

$$= \$700,000 = \begin{matrix} \text{Total capital at} \\ \text{which retained} \\ \text{earnings are exhausted} \end{matrix}$$

Thus, Carson Foods can raise a total of $700,000, consisting of $420,000 of retained earnings and 0.3($700,000) = $210,000 of new debt and 0.1($700,000) = $70,000 of new preferred stock supported by the $420,000 of retained earnings, without altering its capital structure:

New debt supported by retained earnings	$210,000	30%
Preferred stock supported by retained earnings	70,000	10
Retained earnings	420,000	60
Total expansion supported by retained earnings, or break point for retained earnings	$700,000	100%

Figure 10-2 plots Carson Foods' WACC against dollars of new capital required. The graph is called the *marginal cost of capital (MCC) schedule* because each point on the schedule shows the cost of obtaining another dollar of new capital, that is, the cost at the margin. Each dollar has a weighted average cost of 12 percent until the company has raised a total of $700,000. This $700,000 will consist of $210,000 of new debt with an after-tax cost of 6 percent, $70,000 of preferred stock with a cost of 12 percent, and $420,000 of retained earnings with a cost of 15 percent. However, if Carson raises $700,001 or more, each dollar over $700,000 will contain 60 cents of equity obtained by selling new common equity at a cost of 15.9 percent, so its k_a = WACC will be 12.5 percent rather than 12.0 percent.

Figure 10-2
Carson Foods:
Marginal Cost of Capital Schedule

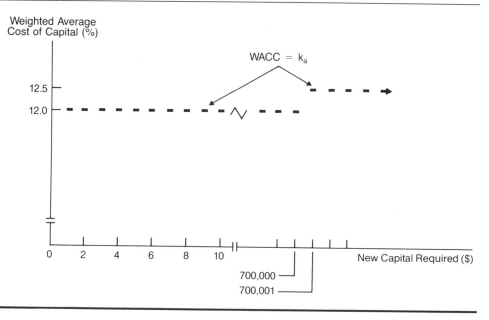

Other Increases in Component Costs

There is a jump, or break, in Carson's MCC schedule at $700,000 of new capital. Could there be other breaks in the schedule? Yes, there could be. The cost of capital could rise due to further increases in the cost of common equity, or because of increases in the costs of debt or preferred stock as the firm issues more and more securities. Some theorists have argued that the costs of capital components other than common stock should not rise. Their argument is that as long as the capital structure does not change, and presuming that the firm uses new capital to invest in profitable projects with the same degree of risk as its existing projects, investors should be willing to invest unlimited additional capital at the same rate. However, this argument assumes an infinitely elastic demand for a firm's securities, which in turn assumes an infinite supply of investors with the same opinions and attitudes about the firm as its current set of investors. For most firms, especially smaller ones but also for larger ones, these assumptions do not seem to hold. Therefore, the demand curve of investors for a given firm's securities seems to be downward sloping, and the more securities sold during a given period, the lower the price received for the securities and thus the higher the required rate of return. As a result, beyond some point, the more new financing required, the higher the typical firm's WACC.

Here are some additional points to consider concerning this subject:

1. Firms often establish lines of credit with lenders, and even if formal lines of credit are not established, a firm will usually have business relationships with certain lenders. These lenders will have already conducted credit checks and risk analyses of the company, and thus they can lend additional funds without incurring significant fixed costs. Once a firm reaches its lending limit with a given source of capital, however, it will be forced to borrow from other creditors, who in turn will have to incur investigation costs. Thus, as the firm borrows more and more, and is forced to turn to additional loan sources, it may find that its debt costs increase.

2. There may exist a "clientele," or group of investors, that is particularly attracted to a firm's common stock. This could be the firm's existing stockholders, investors in its operating area, or others who know and respect its managers. At any rate, as more and more new common stock is sold in any period, some current investors may be willing and able to buy additional shares, but at some point new investors will surely have to be brought in. If these new investors did not view the firm's stock as being attractive at its original price, then additional sales can only occur if the stock price is lowered, and this action has the effect of increasing the firm's flotation costs, and hence its cost of equity.

3. Both debt and equity investors base their required rates of return on the perceived riskiness of the firm. That perceived risk embodies a number of factors, one of which is the rate at which the firm expands its operations. At low expansion rates, proven managers can continue to control operations, finances will not be strained, and so on. However, if the expansion rate exceeds a moderate level, then investors begin to worry that the firm's risk may be increasing. Such perceptions of increasing risk, whether justified or not, would cause the costs of both debt and equity to increase as more and more funds are required.

4. As we discussed in Chapters 5 and 6, in connection with the asymmetric information theory of capital structure, (1) managers generally have better information regarding a firm's prospects than do its stockholders, (2) there are good reasons for firms to finance with debt when prospects are good and with stock when the reverse is true, so (3) investors are consequently leery (and rightly so) when a company announces a new offering of common stock. That line of reasoning affects the capital structure decision, making companies use equity during "normal" times so that they will have "reserve borrowing capacity" available in times of financial stress and thus be able to avoid new stock offerings.

When we apply asymmetric information effects to cost of capital considerations, the implications are straightforward—if the firm needs so much capital that it must sell new common stock, then investors will worry that the stock sale is a signal that things are bad, not good, and thus will mark the price of the stock down and cause the cost of equity, and hence the WACC, to rise. This is yet another reason for thinking that k_e is larger than k_s, and asymmetric information/signaling price effects may well be larger (but less quantifiable) than underwriting costs.

For these reasons, most experts believe that the marginal cost of capital rises as a firm raises larger and larger amounts of capital. However, because of difficulties in estimating the effects of capital requirements on k_d, k_p, and k_e, firms do not, in general, attempt to define precisely the MCC schedule beyond the retained earnings break point as we are about to do. Thus, the following illustration is intended more to provide a conceptual view of the complete MCC schedule than to serve as a prescription for use in practice.

To illustrate how the MCC schedule might be constructed, suppose Carson could obtain only $300,000 of debt at a 10 percent interest rate, with additional debt costing 12 percent. This would result in a second break, where the $300,000 of 10 percent debt is exhausted. At what amount of *total financing* would the 10 percent debt be used up? If we let Y represent the total financing at this second break point, then

$$0.3(\text{Total financing}) = 0.3Y = \$300,000,$$

and solving for Y, we obtain

$$Y = \frac{10\% \text{ debt}}{0.3} = \frac{\$300,000}{0.3} = \$1,000,000 = \begin{array}{l}\text{Break point} \\ \text{for 10\% debt}\end{array}.$$

Thus, there will be a second break in the MCC schedule, at the point where Carson Foods has raised a total of $1 million. Beyond $1 million, the WACC rises from 12.5 to 12.9 percent as a result of the increase in k_d from 10 to 12 percent:

$$\text{WACC} = k_a = w_d k_d (1 - T) + w_p k_p + w_s k_e$$
$$= 0.3(12\%)(0.60) + 0.1(12\%) + 0.6(15.9\%)$$
$$= 2.2\% + 1.2\% + 9.5\% = 12.9\%.$$

In other words, the next dollar beyond $1 million will consist of 30 cents of 12 percent debt (7.2 percent after taxes), 10 cents of 12 percent preferred, and 60 cents of new common stock (retained earnings were used up back at $700,000 of new capital); and this marginal dollar will have an average cost of 12.9 percent.

The effect of this new WACC increase is shown in Figure 10-3. We now have two break points, one caused by using up all the retained earnings and the other caused by exhausting all the 10 percent debt. With the two breaks, we have three different WACCs: $\text{WACC}_1 = 12\%$ for the first $700,000 of new capital; $\text{WACC}_2 = 12.5\%$ in the interval between $700,001 and $1 million; and $\text{WACC}_3 = 12.9\%$ for all new capital beyond $1 million. Together, these three segments define Carson Foods' marginal cost of capital schedule.[2]

---

[2]When we use the term *weighted average cost of capital*, we are referring to k_a, which is the cost of one dollar raised partly as debt, partly as preferred, and partly as equity. One could also calculate the average cost of *all* capital the firm raises during a given year. For example, if Carson Foods raised $2 million, then the first $700,000 would have a cost of 12.0 percent, the next $300,000 would have a cost of 12.5 percent, and the last $1 million would have a cost of 12.9 percent. The entire $2 million would have an average cost of

$$(\$0.7/\$2)(12.0\%) + (\$0.3/\$2)(12.5\%) + (\$1.0/\$2)(12.9\%) = 12.53\%.$$

This particular cost of capital should not generally be used for financial decisions; normally it has no relevance in finance. The only exception we can think of is if Carson were considering a large, all-or-nothing project, say one with a cost of $2 million. In this case, it would raise $2 million or nothing, so for decision purposes, we would need to evaluate the project at the 12.53% average cost of the $2 million needed to finance it, not at the 12.9% marginal cost.

Figure 10-3
Carson Foods:
Marginal Cost of Capital Schedule Using Retained Earnings,
New Common Stock, and Higher-Cost Debt

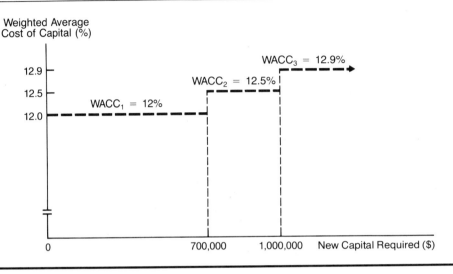

There could, of course, be still more break points. For example, the interest rate on debt might rise again, from 12 to 14 percent, after the firm had used $400,000 of the 12 percent debt. In this case, the 14 percent debt would be used after a total of $700,000 of lower-cost debt had been used: $300,000 of 10 percent debt plus $400,000 of 12 percent debt. Therefore, another break would occur at $2,333,333:

$$\text{Break point} \atop \text{for 12\% debt} = \frac{\$300,000 + \$400,000}{0.3} = \frac{\$700,000}{0.3} = \$2,333,333.$$

Other break points would occur if the interest rate continued to increase, if the cost of preferred stock rose, or if, as larger and larger amounts of common stock were sold, market pressure lowered the offering price of the stock and, consequently, raised the cost of common equity. In general, a break point will occur whenever the cost of one of the capital components rises, and the break point can in theory be determined by this equation:

$$\text{Break point} = \frac{\begin{array}{c}\text{Total amount of lower-cost}\\ \text{capital of a given type}\end{array}}{\begin{array}{c}\text{Fraction of this type of capital}\\ \text{in the capital structure}\end{array}}. \qquad (10\text{-}1)$$

The break point for the 12 percent debt was found by applying this generalized formula.

We see, then, that in theory numerous break points can occur. At the limit, we can even think of an MCC schedule with so many break points that it rises continuously beyond some given level of new financing. Note also that the first break point is not necessarily the point where retained earnings are used up—it is possible that low-cost debt could be exhausted *before* retained earnings have been used up. For example, if Carson Foods had available only $150,000 of 10 percent debt, then Point Y would have occurred at

$$Y = \frac{\$150,000}{0.3} = \$500,000 = \begin{array}{l} \text{Break point} \\ \text{for 10\% debt} \end{array}$$

This is well before the break point for retained earnings, which occurs at $700,000.

The easiest method for calculating MCC schedules is as follows:

1. Identify the points where breaks occur. A break will occur any time the cost of one of the capital components rises. (However, it is possible that two capital components could both increase at the same point.) Use Equation 10-1 to determine the exact break points, and then make a list of these breaks.

2. Determine the cost of capital for each component in the intervals between each break.

3. Calculate the WACC in each interval. The WACC is constant within each interval, but it rises at each break point.

Notice that if there are n separate breaks, there will be n + 1 different WACCs. For example, in Figure 10-3 we see two breaks and three different WACCs.

Depreciation-Generated Funds

We discussed the cost of depreciation-generated funds in Chapter 4, and we concluded that these funds have a cost equal to the lowest WACC, which is normally the WACC using retained earnings as the equity source. For Carson Foods, the cost of depreciation-generated funds is thus $WACC_1 = 12\%$. Now consider the effect of depreciation on the MCC schedule. It is a source of funds available for capital budgeting, so $WACC_1$ should be extended by the amount of depreciation as shown on the pro forma income statement.[3] For example, if Carson's depreciation expense will be $300,000 next year, then all the break points shown in Figure 10-3 would be pushed to the right by $300,000. Thus, the WACC would remain at 12

---

[3]We assume here that Carson Foods uses ACRS depreciation to compute income for both tax and stockholder reporting purposes. If it used ACRS for tax and straight line for stockholder reporting, then, as we discussed in Chapter 4, an item called "deferred taxes" would appear on the income statement. Like depreciation, deferred taxes represents a noncash charge, so it, along with depreciation, must be added to net income to determine cash flows from operations. The cash flow from deferred taxes is available for distribution to investors (at least for several years) or for reinvestment in the business, so it has an opportunity cost equal to that of depreciation cash flows. Therefore, if deferred taxes are present, they too should be used to extend $WACC_1$.

percent until $1,000,000 of new capital is required, and the $WACC_2$ to $WACC_3$ break point would occur at $1,300,000.

What difference does all this make, and should we be concerned with a MCC schedule that includes or excludes depreciation? If we are developing the net capital budget (that is, new projects less replacements financed with depreciation), then the MCC schedule without depreciation is appropriate. However, if we are concerned with the gross capital budget—including replacement as well as expansion projects—then depreciation should be included in the MCC schedule. For purposes of illustration, we assume that Carson Foods has already made its replacement decisions, and these projects require an investment approximately equal to the firm's depreciation. Thus, the investment opportunity schedule shown in Figure 10-1 is a net investment schedule, and hence the MCC schedule shown in Figure 10-3, which excludes depreciation, should be used in the analysis.

COMBINING THE MCC AND IOS SCHEDULES

Now that we have estimated the MCC schedule, we can use it to determine the discount rate for the capital budgeting process, *that is, we can use the MCC schedule to find the cost of capital for use in determining projects' net present values (NPVs)*. To do this, we combine the IOS and MCC schedules on the same graph, as in Figure 10-4, and then analyze this consolidated figure.

Finding the Marginal Cost of Capital

Just how far down its IOS curve should Carson go? That is, which of its available projects should it accept? *First, Carson Foods should accept all independent projects which have rates of return in excess of the cost of the capital that will be used to finance them, and it should reject all others.* Projects E and F should be rejected, because they would have to be financed with capital that has a cost of 12.5 and 12.9 percent, and at that cost of capital, we know that these projects must have negative NPVs since their IRRs are below their costs of capital. Therefore, Carson's capital budget should consist of either Project A or B, plus C and D, and the firm should thus raise and invest a total of $800,000.

The preceding analysis, as summarized in Figure 10-4, reveals a very important point: *The cost of capital used in the capital budgeting process is actually determined at the intersection of the IOS and MCC schedules. This cost is called the firm's marginal cost of capital, and if it is used, then the firm will make correct accept/reject decisions, and its level of financing and investment will be optimal. If it uses any other rate, its capital budget will not be optimal.*[4]

If Carson had fewer good investment opportunities, then its IOS schedule would be shifted to the left, possibly causing the intersection to occur at a lower level on

---

[4]The only exception to this general rule is situations where a large project is at the margin, and this project will require capital at different rates. We would then have to obtain the average cost of capital needed for the marginal project. Footnote 2 contains one example of this situation, and we will consider another example shortly.

Figure 10-4
Carson Foods:
Combined IOS and MCC Schedules

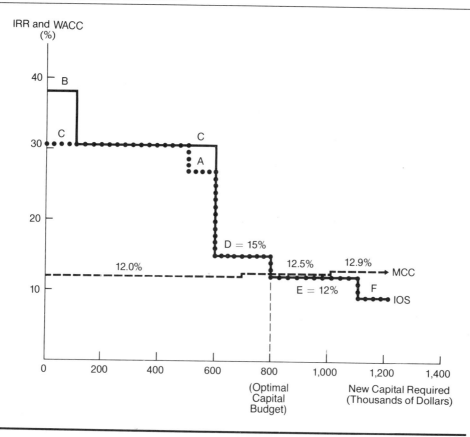

the MCC curve. Conversely, if the firm had more and better investment opportunities, its IOS would be shifted to the right, and the intersection could have occurred at a higher WACC. Thus, we see that the discount rate used in capital budgeting is influenced by the set of projects that is available. We have, of course, abstracted from differential project riskiness in this section, because we assumed that all of Carson's projects are equally risky. We will discuss the impact of differential risk on the optimal capital budget in a later section.

Choosing between Mutually Exclusive Projects

We have not, at this point, actually determined Carson's optimal capital budget. We know that it should total $800,000, and that Projects C and D should be included, but we do not know which of the mutually exclusive projects, A or B, should be made part of the final budget. How can we choose between A and B?

We know that in general the final set of projects should be the one which has the highest total NPV, as this set will increase the value of the firm by the largest amount. We also know that Projects C and D should be included in the final set, so their contributions to the total NPV will be the same regardless of whether we choose Project A or Project B. This narrows our analysis to the NPVs of A and B. The project with the higher NPV should be chosen.

Notice that Figure 10-1 contained the projects' paybacks and IRRs, but no NPVs. We were not able to determine the NPVs at that point, because we did not know the correct marginal cost of capital. Now, in Figure 10-4, we see that the last dollar raised will cost 12.5 percent, so Carson's marginal cost of capital is 12.5 percent. Therefore, assuming the projects are equally risky, we can use a 12.5 percent discount rate to find $NPV_A = \$34,431$ and $NPV_B = \$34,431$. Thus, in our example, Carson should be indifferent between the two mutually exclusive projects, according to the NPV criterion. To break the tie, assume for the sake of argument that Project B is selected because of its faster payback and higher IRR.

Evaluating the Marginal Project

With the MCC and IOS schedules contained in Figure 10-4, it is easy to decide where to stop accepting projects. With that particular set of data, Projects C and D are clearly acceptable, Projects E and F should be rejected, and the firm's marginal cost of capital is 12.5 percent. Now, consider another situation, where the analysis is not so clear-cut. Figure 10-5 contains exactly the same IOS schedules as before, but here we assume that Carson's treasurer found an error in the original cost of capital data and has developed a new MCC schedule. Under these revised cost conditions, the WACC is 11.0 percent for the first $900,000 of new capital and 13.0 percent beyond $900,000.

Clearly, Project F remains unacceptable, but the revised MCC schedule now cuts through Project E. Should Carson accept or reject Project E? First, note that if Project E could be accepted in part, then Carson would take on only part of it. That is, if Project E were completely divisible, then Carson should invest only $100,000 in the project, as this level of investment would have a marginal cost of capital of 11.0 percent but a 12.0 percent rate of return, hence a positive NPV.

Most projects, however, are not infinitely divisible. If Project E were completely indivisible, meaning that Carson would have to accept it in its entirety or else reject it, should it be accepted? To answer this question, we must determine Project E's average cost of capital, proceeding as follows. First, note that Project E requires an initial investment of $300,000. Next, we see in Figure 10-5 that the first $100,000 of capital raised for Project E has a cost of 11.0 percent and that the remaining $200,000 has a cost of 13.0 percent. Thus, one-third of the capital required has a cost of 11.0 percent, and two-thirds has a cost of 13.0 percent. Therefore, the average cost of capital for Project E is 12.3 percent:

$$k_{aE} = \left(\frac{\$100,000}{\$300,000}\right)(11.0\%) + \left(\frac{\$200,000}{\$300,000}\right)(13.0\%) = 12.3\%.$$

Figure 10-5
Carson Foods:
Revised Combined IOS and MCC Schedules

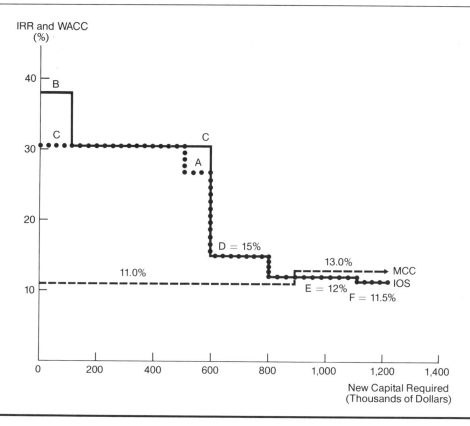

Now recall that $IRR_E = 12.0\%$. Thus, Project E's average cost of capital exceeds its IRR, its NPV must be negative, and hence Project E should be rejected. Therefore, with the revised MCC schedule, Carson's optimal capital budget appears to be \$800,000, and its marginal cost of capital is 11.0 percent. However, rejection of Project E produces a major change in the IOS schedules. With E gone, the IOS shifts to the left, and Project F, which has an IRR of 11.5 percent, can now be financed at a cost of capital of 11.0 percent. Therefore, at a MCC of 11 percent, F becomes acceptable.

Note also that with the original MCC schedule and MCC of 12.5 percent, Projects A and B had identical NPVs, but B was selected because of its faster payback and higher IRR. However, with the new MCC of 11 percent, A's NPV exceeds that of B:

$$NPV_A = \$38,942 > NPV_B = \$37,090.$$

Thus, A should be chosen over B because it adds the most to the value of the firm.[5] In summary, under the revised MCC conditions, Carson's optimal capital budget should include A, C, D, and F, for a total of $900,000.

Risk Adjustments

There are two ways to incorporate differential project risk into the capital budgeting process. First, we can adjust the firm's marginal cost of capital up or down to account for differential risk. For riskier-than-average projects we would use a discount rate that is higher than the firm's MCC, and vice versa. Alternatively, we could adjust the IOS schedule, lowering the IRRs of high risk projects and raising the IRRs of low risk projects. However, the whole process of finding the optimal capital budget could become circular at this point because risk adjustments might cause the IOS/MCC intersection to shift, which could in turn result in a new marginal cost of capital, which would require new risk-adjusted discount rates, and so on. Further, the Carson Foods illustration only considered six capital projects. It would be impossible to conduct this type of analysis when hundreds of projects are involved. For these reasons, firms generally use a less sophisticated, but more realistic, approach to finding the optimal capital budget, as we explain below.

ESTABLISHING THE OPTIMAL CAPITAL BUDGET IN PRACTICE

The procedures set forth above are conceptually correct, and it is important that you understand the logic of this process. However, Carson Foods and most other companies actually use a more judgmental, less quantitative process for establishing its final capital budget:

Step 1. The financial vice president obtains a reasonably good fix on the firm's IOS from the director of capital budgeting, and a reasonably good estimate of the MCC schedule from the treasurer. These two schedules are then combined, as in Figures 10-4 and 10-5 above, to get a reasonably good approximation to the cor-

---

[5] Note that the choice between mutually exclusive Projects A and B depends on Carson's MCC. However, this brings up another issue—what will the actual cost of capital for Carson Foods be over the next three years, when the cash flows from Projects A and B will be realized? As we saw in Chapter 7, under the NPV method, we usually assume that the cost of capital is expected to remain constant in the future. Thus, in terms of the analysis in this chapter, use of the NPV method implies an expectation that the MCC and IOS curves will in the future be similar to the ones that exist today. Although the MCC schedule will surely change, for most firms the best estimate of future capital costs is today's MCC schedule. A constant IOS is probably appropriate for a large firm whose product markets are growing at a steady rate, but probably not for a firm whose markets are cyclical or one which expands fixed assets at irregular intervals (for example, a paper company that builds a new mill every four or five years). A fluctuating IOS schedule would mean different intersections with the MCC schedule, hence a changing marginal cost of capital and consequently a changing cash flow opportunity cost over time. In such a case, Carson Foods would need to estimate its marginal cost of capital for each year of the three-year life of Projects A and B, then use the nonconstant capital cost model presented in Chapter 7 to evaluate the choice between A and B.

poration's marginal cost of capital or the cost of capital at the intersection. This will probably be done without graphs.

Step 2. The corporate MCC is scaled up or down by each division to reflect the division's capital structure and risk characteristics. Carson Foods, for example, assigns a factor of 0.9 to its stable, low-risk canned vegetables division but a factor of 1.1 to its more risky gourmet frozen foods group. Therefore, if the corporate cost of capital is determined to be 12 percent, the cost for the canned vegetables division is $0.9(12\%) = 10.8\%$, while that for the gourmet frozen foods division is $1.1(12\%) = 13.2\%$.

Step 3. Each project within each division is classified into one of three groups—high-risk, average-risk, and low-risk—and the same 0.9 and 1.1 factors are used to adjust the divisional costs. For example, a low-risk project in the canned vegetables division would have a cost of capital of $0.9(10.8\%) = 9.7\%$ if the corporate cost of capital were 12 percent, while a high-risk project in the gourmet frozen foods division would have a cost of $1.1(13.2\%) = 14.5\%$.

Step 4. Each project's NPV is then determined, using its risk-adjusted project cost of capital. The optimal capital budget consists of all independent projects with positive risk-adjusted NPVs plus those mutually exclusive projects with the highest positive risk-adjusted NPVs.

These steps implicitly assume that, in total, the projects taken on have, on average, about the same risk characteristics and consequently the same average cost of capital as the firm's existing assets. If this is not true, then the corporate MCC determined in Step 1 will not be correct, and it will have to be adjusted. However, given all the measurement errors and uncertainties inherent in the entire cost of capital/capital budgeting process, it does not pay to push the adjustment process very far.

All of this may seem rather arbitrary, and we agree. Nevertheless, the procedure does force the firm to think carefully about each division's relative risk, about each project's risk within the division, and about the relationship between the total amount of capital raised and the cost of that capital. Further, the procedure forces the firm to adjust its capital budget to conditions in the capital markets—if the cost of debt and equity rises, this fact will be reflected in the cost of capital used to evaluate projects, and projects that would be marginally acceptable when capital costs were low would (correctly) be ruled unacceptable when capital costs were high.

CAPITAL RATIONING

Under ordinary circumstances, capital budgeting is, in essence, an application of this classic economic principle: A firm should expand to the point where its marginal revenue is just equal to its marginal cost. When this rule is applied to the capital budgeting decision, marginal revenue is taken to be the risk-adjusted rate of return on projects, while marginal cost is the firm's marginal cost of capital. A simplified view of the concept is shown in Figure 10-6. Here we assume that the

Figure 10-6
The Typical Capital Budgeting Situation

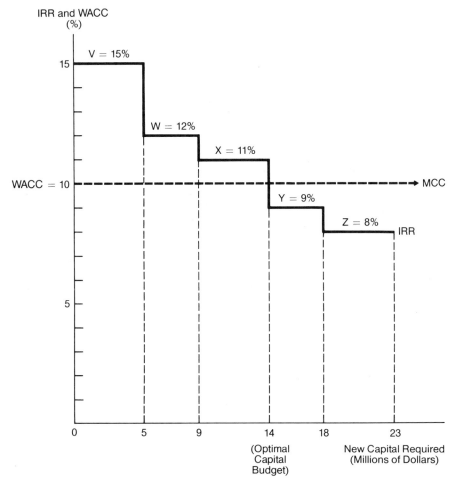

Note: If IRR > 10%, NPV is positive. Therefore, Projects V, W, and X have NPV > 0, and Y and Z have NPV < 0.

firm has five equally risky and independent investment opportunities which cost in total $23 million. Its cost of capital is assumed to be constant at 10 percent, implying that the firm can raise all the money it wants at a cost of 10 percent. Under these conditions, the firm should accept Projects V, W, and X, since they all have IRRs greater than the cost of capital, and hence NPVs greater than zero. It should reject Y and Z because they have IRRs less than k, indicating negative NPVs. This decision would maximize the value of the firm and the wealth of its stockholders.

Firms ordinarily operate in the manner depicted in the graph—they accept all independent projects having positive NPVs, reject those with negative NPVs, and choose between mutually exclusive investments on the basis of the higher NPV. However, some firms set an absolute limit on the size of their capital budgets such that the size of the budget is less than the level of investment called for by the NPV (or IRR) criterion. This is called *capital rationing*.

Reasons for Capital Rationing

The principal reason for capital rationing is that some firms are reluctant to engage in external financing (either borrowing or selling stock). One management, recalling the plight of firms with substantial amounts of debt during recent credit crunches, may simply refuse to use debt. Another management, which has no objection to selling debt, may not want to issue common stock for fear of losing some measure of voting control. Still others may refuse to use any form of outside financing, considering safety and control to be more important than additional profits. These are all cases of capital rationing, and they result in limiting the rate of expansion to a slower pace than would be dictated by "purely rational wealth-maximizing behavior."

We should make three points here. First, a decision to hold back on expansion is not necessarily irrational. If the owners/managers of a privately held firm have what they consider to be plenty of income and wealth, then it might be quite rational for them to "trim their sails," relax, and concentrate on enjoying what they have already earned rather than on earning still more. Such behavior would not, however, be appropriate for a publicly owned firm.

Second, it is not correct to interpret as capital rationing a situation where the firm is willing to sell additional securities at the going market price but finds that it cannot because the market simply will not absorb more of its issues. Rather, such a situation indicates that the MCC curve is rising. If more acceptable investments are indicated than can be financed, then the cost of capital being used is too low, and it should be raised.

Third, firms sometimes set a limit on capital expenditures, not because of a shortage of funds, but because of limitations on other resources, especially managerial talent. A firm might, for example, feel that its personnel development program is sufficient to handle an expansion of no more than 10 percent a year and then set a limit on the capital budget to insure that expansion is held to that rate. This is not capital rationing—rather, it involves a downward reevaluation of project returns if growth exceeds some limit; that is, expected rates of return are, after some point, a decreasing function of the level of expenditures.

Project Selection under Capital Rationing

How should projects be selected under conditions of true capital rationing? First, note that if a firm truly rations capital, its value is not being maximized: If management were maximizing, then they would move to the point where the marginal project's NPV was zero, and capital rationing as defined would not exist. So, if a firm uses capital rationing, it has ruled out value maximization. The firm may, how-ever, want to maximize value *subject to the constraint that the capital ceiling not be exceeded*. Constrained maximization behavior will, in general, result in a lower value than following unconstrained maximization, but some type of constrained maximization may produce reasonably satisfactory results. *Linear programming* is one method of constrained maximization that has been applied to capital rationing. Much work has been done in this area, and linear programming may, in the future, be widely applied in capital budgeting.[6]

If the firm does face capital rationing, and if the constraint cannot be lifted, what can the financial manager do? The objective should be to select projects, subject to the capital rationing constraint, such that the sum of the projects' NPVs is max-imized. Linear programming can be used, or if there are not too many projects involved, the financial manager can simply enumerate all possible sets of projects that meet the budget constraint and then select the set with the largest total NPV.

The complexities involved in a capital rationing situation are illustrated in Table 10-2. Here we assume that the firm is considering a total of eight potential projects; all are independent and equally risky. The firm has a 10 percent cost of capital, but management has decided to limit capital expenditures during the year to the amount of money that can be generated internally, $500,000. In the table, the projects are listed in the order of their NPVs, but their IRRs and profitability in-dexes (PIs) are also shown.

If it is to maximize the value of the firm, management must choose that set of projects whose NPVs sum to the greatest total, but subject to the constraint that total expenditures must not exceed $500,000. With only eight projects in total, we can try all different combinations and, by "brute force," determine the set which maximizes NPV. This set is optimal:[7]

Project	Cost	NPV
2	$250,000	$ 87,951
3	100,000	28,038
4	75,000	16,273
5	75,000	3,395
Totals	$500,000	$135,657

This analysis seems simple enough, but there are three factors which complicate it greatly in realistic situations:

1. Number of projects. In the example, we have only eight projects, so it is easy to simply list all the combinations whose costs do not exceed $500,000 and then see which combination provides the greatest total NPV. For a large firm with thou-

[6]For one interested in programming solutions to capital budgeting problems, a good starting point for further study is James C. T. Mao, *Quantitative Analysis of Financial Decisions* (New York: Macmillan, 1969).

[7]Note that in capital rationing our goal in project selection is to get the "biggest bang for the buck." Since this is measured by the profitability index (PI), one way to determine the optimal set is by accepting projects in descending order of PIs, but recognizing that some high-PI projects might have to be rejected because insufficient funds are available.

Table 10-2
Illustration of Capital Rationing

Project Number	Project Cost, or Outlay at t = 0	Project Life (Years)	Cash Flow per Year	NPV at the 10% Cost of Capital	IRR	Profitability Index
1	$400,000	20	$58,600	$98,895	13.5%	1.25
2	250,000	10	55,000	87,951	17.7	1.35
3	100,000	8	24,000	28,038	17.3	1.28
4	75,000	15	12,000	16,273	13.7	1.22
5	75,000	6	18,000	3,395	11.5	1.05
6	50,000	5	14,000	3,071	12.4	1.06
7	250,000	10	41,000	1,927	10.2	1.01
8	250,000	3	99,000	(3,802)	9.1	0.98

sands of projects, this would be a tedious process, although computer programs are available to solve such problems. However, the other problems listed below are more serious.

2. Project risk. In our example, we assumed that the eight projects are equally risky, and hence have the same cost of capital. If this were not the case, and if the number of projects were so large as to preclude hand analysis, then it would be difficult, if not impossible, to reach an optimal solution, because the computer programs currently available cannot deal efficiently with projects having differential risks.

3. Multiple time constraints. Our example also assumed a single-time-period capital constraint. However, when capital rationing is practiced, (1) the constraints usually extend out for several years, and (2) the funds available in future years depend on cash throw-offs from investments made in earlier years. Thus, the constraint in Year 2 depends on the investments made in Year 1, and so on. For example, we might have investment funds of $500,000 per year available from external sources for 1987 through 1991, plus the cash inflows in each year from investments made in previous years. To solve this type of multiperiod problem, we need information on both investment opportunities and funds availability in future years, not just on the situation in the current year. Also, the NPV we seek to maximize in that case is the sum of the present values of the NPVs in each year over the time horizon being analyzed, say 1987 through 1991. In such a situation, we might even choose Project 8 in Table 10-2, in spite of its negative NPV, because it has rapid cash throw-offs. In fact, if excellent investment opportunities are expected to be available in 1988, 1989, and 1990, taking Project 8 might be part of the best long-run strategy.

A Better Approach to Capital Rationing

Our main conclusion thus far about capital rationing—which means deliberately foregoing projects with positive NPVs—is that practicing it is irrational for any firm which seeks to maximize its stockholders' wealth. Also, while mathematical programming methods are available to help solve the simpler cases of capital rationing and enable management to make the best of a bad situation, programming methods are not capable of dealing with all the complexities encountered in the real world.

Fortunately, there is a better method for handling the types of situations that give rise to capital rationing. Usually, capital rationing occurs when the firm believes that it will encounter severe problems if it attempts to raise capital beyond some specified amount. For example, the interest rate it would have to pay might rise sharply if it attempted to increase its existing lines of credit. Such situations can be rationally handled by increasing the assigned cost of capital as the amount of capital raised increases. In effect, in terms of Figure 10-6, the marginal cost of capital schedule would begin to rise sharply beyond some amount of capital, and this higher MCC should be used as the discount rate when determining a project's NPV.

OTHER FACTORS WHICH INFLUENCE THE OPTIMAL CAPITAL BUDGET

We have seen that the optimal capital budget calls for accepting independent projects with a positive risk-adjusted NPV, and when evaluating mutually exclusive projects, the project with the highest positive risk-adjusted NPV should be selected. Do firms actually follow this rule? By and large they do, but over the years, both practitioners and financial theorists have noted that other factors also influence the decision. Some of them are noted below.

Stable Earnings per Share Growth

Eugene Lerner and Alfred Rappaport have proposed that managers should select projects based on an NPV evaluation, but subject to an earnings growth constraint.[8] Lerner and Rappaport contend that investors can see better what is developing in terms of reported EPS as opposed to the more nebulous NPV, so stock prices are influenced by the observed pattern of EPS growth. Firms which exhibit stable, predictable EPS growth rates will command higher prices than otherwise equivalent firms whose growth rates are erratic. Therefore, project selection should be influenced by effects on EPS growth stability.

To illustrate, suppose a company is considering two capital projects for this planning period, Projects L and M. Both projects have the same initial investment at t = 0, but Project L's expected net income in the first year is $10,000 versus an expected loss of $20,000 for Project M under existing accounting procedures. These values represent *accounting income, not cash flows*. However, when we consider the projects' cash flows over their entire lives, Project L has the higher NPV, although both NPVs are positive. The company's existing assets are expected

---

[8]See Eugene M. Lerner and Alfred Rappaport, "Limit DCF in Capital Budgeting," *Harvard Business Review*, July-August 1968, 133-139.

to generate a net income of $100,000 this year, and those assets will sustain that level of income over the foreseeable future. In the recent past, the company has grown at a 10 percent rate, and investors expect this growth rate to be maintained.

According to the NPV rule, both Projects L and M should be accepted. However, acceptance of both projects would cause next year's reported net income to be $100,000 + $10,000 − $20,000 = $90,000. Thus, if management's expectations are correct, the firm's net income (and its EPS) would fall by 10 percent. This would disappoint stockholders, and it would probably lead to a decline in the stock price. Note, however, that if only Project L were accepted, then income next year would increase by the expected 10 percent.

This simple example could be extended to many projects, and to a multiple year horizon, but the point would remain the same: If managers strive to maximize the present value of investment projects subject to the constraint that the earnings of the company should grow at a specified rate, then the set of projects selected may not necessarily be the set that maximizes the firm's long-run value. This behavior implies the existence of asymmetric information, that is, a situation where investors do not correctly perceive the true long-term value of investment projects. There is probably some truth in this notion.

Project Maturity

Suppose the term structure of interest rates is sharply upward sloping; does this mean that the cost of capital is higher for long-term projects than for short-term projects? Perhaps, but very often projects with specific lives are really part of continuous investment programs, which really means that capital commitments are for periods that are longer than the life of the specific project. For example, if a retail chain opens a new store in a new shopping center, the store's computer equipment might have a five-year life, yet replacement will almost certainly occur at the end of five years, and hence the capital commitment is really for a longer term. Thus, all the capital raised to invest in the new store will be "permanent" capital, and hence raised from long-term sources. Our conclusion is that, for most capital budgeting projects, term structure considerations are not important—the relevant cost of capital is the long-term cost, even if the project has a relatively short physical life. Of course, if some particular project were truly short-term, and would be financed with short-term funds, then its capital cost might well be different from that used for more typical capital projects.

Strategic Considerations

A great deal of corporate investment is made on the basis of strategic considerations. For example, several years ago General Motors analyzed the feasibility of battery-powered electric autos and concluded that they would not be profitable in the foreseeable future. Nevertheless, GM went ahead and spent several hundred million dollars to develop a prototype electric car. Management felt that such an investment was necessary to gain technological expertise, which in turn it deemed necessary to protect its basic position in the transportation industry.

In 1984 and 1985, GM made some other major strategic investments, even though standard NPV analyses might have suggested rejection. Specifically, GM spent approximately $2.5 billion to acquire Electronic Data Systems (EDS) Corporation and another $5 billion to buy Hughes Aircraft Company. Management wanted the EDS expertise to help tie together GM's fragmented data processing system, while Hughes was acquired to provide technological expertise in the area of electronic controls, which could help GM develop better autos that would be more competitive in world markets. When announcing the Hughes purchase, GM's managers declared "We're rebuilding our company for the 21st century."

Still other companies have invested in Japan for strategic reasons. Japanese manufacturing processes are superior to those of U.S. companies in many areas, so U.S. companies are investing in Japan "to learn how the Japanese do it." Generally, such investments involve the purchase of a minority interest in a Japanese company, along with a joint venture arrangement between the Japanese and the U.S. firms. General Motors varied the pattern recently when it joined with Toyota to produce autos in Fremont, California. GM hoped to have its Japanese partners train GM managers and employees in Japanese production procedures, while Toyota wanted to establish additional production facilities in the United States because of import quota restrictions. So far, the joint venture, which produces Nova automobiles, has been a resounding success for both parties.

Strategic investments, including many mergers, are designed to accomplish a variety of goals. Still, these investments do generally have two common elements: (1) Immediate cash flow benefits are hard to identify, and those that can be identified are often insufficient to justify the project, and (2) strategic investments offer insurance against the chance that "the regular way of doing business" will not be viable in the future.

SUMMARY

This chapter described how *MCC* and *IOS schedules* are developed and then combined to help determine the optimal capital budget. Capital typically has a higher cost if the firm expands beyond certain limits, which means that the MCC schedule turns up beyond some point. We used the *break point concept* to develop a step-function MCC schedule, which we then combined with the IOS schedule to determine the *marginal cost of capital (MCC)*, which is then used to determine the firm's optimal capital budget.

We noted, however, that most firms actually use a judgmental four-step process for establishing the optimal capital budget: (1) The treasurer develops an estimate of the firm's marginal cost of capital, say 11 percent. (2) The corporate MCC is scaled up or down by each division to reflect the division's capital structure and risk characteristics. (3) Each project within each division is classified as high-risk, average-risk, or low-risk, and the divisional cost of capital is then adjusted to determine each project's cost of capital. (4) Those independent projects with positive risk-adjusted NPVs are then included in the firm's optimal capital budget.

Capital rationing exists whenever a firm sets a specific limit on the size of its capital budget rather than expanding the capital budget to the point where all projects with NPV > 0 are included. If capital rationing exists, then management should attempt to maximize the sum of the individual projects' NPVs, subject to the constraint that investment does not exceed the available capital. Methods have been devised for dealing with capital rationing, but the best solution to this problem is simply to avoid it by adjusting the MCC schedule upward rather than imposing a limitation on new capital.

Other considerations such as a project's effect on reported profits and earnings growth rates, and strategic policy decisions, also affect the capital budget, but in general, a firm should accept all projects with marginal benefits exceeding marginal costs.

The International Perspective

Although the same basic principles of capital budgeting analysis apply to both foreign and domestic operations, there are three crucial differences: (1) Cash flow estimation is generally much more difficult for overseas investments. (2) Foreign cash flows are in foreign currencies, so exchange rate risk fluctuations add to the riskiness of overseas investments. (3) The possibility of deliberate government acts that truncate or divert cash flows adds another dimension to risk analysis for foreign investments. In this section, we briefly discuss the analysis of foreign capital projects.

The first issue to be addressed in foreign project analysis is defining the relevant cash flows: Is the relevant flow the net cash generated by the foreign subsidiary, or is it the incremental cash flows that will be sent back to the U.S. parent? As long as there are no restrictions on the repatriation of cash flows, these two cash flow streams will be the same. However, if there are local withholding taxes on dividends, restrictions on return of capital, or other blockages of international cash flows, both the timing and magnitude of the cash flows back to the parent will be different from the operating cash flows of the project. The parent corporation cannot use cash flows blocked in a foreign country to pay current dividends to its shareholders, nor does it have the flexibility to reinvest the capital in its other subsidiaries. Hence, from the perspective of the parent organization, *the relevant capital budgeting cash flows are the financial cash flows that are expected to be repatriated to the parent.*

The foreign currency cash flows to be repatriated must be converted into U.S. dollar values by translating them at expected future exchange rates. However, sensitivity or simulation analyses should be conducted to ascertain the effects of exchange rate variations, and based on these analyses, an exchange rate premium should be added to the cost of capital to reflect the *exchange rate risk* inherent in the investment. Note that exchange rate risk may be reduced by hedging, and an alternative to the exchange rate risk premium approach is to incorporate the cost of hedging into the project's cash flows. However, it is not always possible to hedge cash flows expected in the distant future, and unless the foreign operation uses a currency which is actively traded on the exchange markets, it may not be possible to hedge even short-run cash flows.

Sovereignty risk also differentiates international investment decisions from domestic capital budgeting. Sovereignty refers to the supreme and independent political authority of a nation state to do as it pleases within its own borders. Since foreign subsidiaries are physically located within the jurisdiction of the host country, they are subject to rules and regulations established by local government authorities, no matter how arbitrary or apparently unfair such requirements may be. Sovereignty risk includes both the possibility of expropriation or nationalization without adequate compensation, and of unanticipated restrictions of cash flows to the parent company, such as tighter controls on repatriation of dividends or higher taxes. The risk of expropriation of U.S. assets abroad is small in traditionally friendly and stable countries such as the United Kingdom or Switzerland. However, in Eastern Bloc countries, and in most developing nations in Latin America, Africa, and the Far East, the risk may be substantial. Past expropriations include those of ITT and Anaconda Copper in Chile, Gulf Oil in Bolivia, Occidental Petroleum in Libya, InterNorth Corporation in Peru, and many companies in both Cuba and Iran.

Generally, sovereignty risk premiums are not added to the cost of capital to adjust for sovereignty risk. If corporate management has a serious concern that a given country might expropriate foreign assets, it simply will not make significant investments in that country. Expropriation is viewed as a catastrophic or ruinous event, and managers have been shown to be extraordinarily risk averse in the presence of ruinous loss possibilities. However, companies can take steps to reduce the potential loss from expropriation in three major ways: (1) by financing the subsidiary with local sources of capital, (2) by structuring operations so that the subsidiary has value only as a part of the integrated corporate system, and (3) by obtaining insurance against economic losses from expropriation from a source such as the Overseas Private Investment Corporation (OPIC). In the latter case, insurance premiums would have to be added to the project's cost.

Questions and Problems

10-1 (Simple optimal capital budget) The Singleton Corporation's present capital structure, which is also its target capital structure, calls for 50 percent debt and 50 percent common equity. The firm has only one potential project, an expansion program with a 10.2 percent IRR and a cost of $20 million but which is completely divisible; that is, Singleton can invest any amount up to $20 million. The firm expects to retain $3 million of earnings next year. It can raise up to $5 million in new debt at a before-tax cost of 8 percent, and all debt after the first $5 million will have a cost of 10 percent. The cost of retained earnings is 12 percent and Singleton can sell any amount of new common stock desired at a constant cost of new equity of 15 percent. The firm's marginal federal-plus-state tax rate is 40 percent. What is Singleton's optimal capital budget?

10-2 (Optimal capital budget) The management of Tampa Phosphate Company (TPC) is planning next year's capital budget. TPC expects its net income to be $10,500 next year, and its payout ratio is 40 percent. The company's earnings and dividends are growing at a constant rate of 5 percent; the last dividend, D_0, was $0.90; and the current equilibrium stock price is $8.59. TPC can raise up to $10,000 of debt at a 12 percent before-tax cost, the next $10,000 will cost 14 percent, and all debt after $20,000 will cost 16 percent. If TPC issues new common stock, a 10 percent underwriting cost will be incurred. TPC can sell the first $16,000 of new common stock at the current market price, but to sell any additional new stock, TPC must lower the price to $7.63. TPC is at its optimal capital structure, which is 40 percent debt and 60 percent equity, and the firm's marginal federal-plus-state tax rate is 40 percent. TPC has the following independent, indivisible, and equally risky investment opportunities:

Project	Cost	IRR
A	$15,000	17%
B	20,000	14
C	15,000	16
D	12,000	15

What is TPC's optimal capital budget?

10-3 (Risk adjustments) Refer to Problem 10-2. Management neglected to incorporate project risk differentials into the analysis. TPC's policy is to add 2 percentage points to the cost of capital of those projects significantly more risky than average and to subtract 2 percentage points from the cost of capital of those projects which are substantially less risky than average. Management judges Project A to have high risk, Projects C and D to have average risk, and Project B to have low risk. What is the optimal capital budget after adjustment for project risk?

10-4 (MCC and IOS schedule uncertainty) The MCC and IOS schedules can be thought of as "bands" rather than as lines to show that they are not known with certainty but, rather, are merely estimates of the true MCC and IOS schedules.

   a. Do you think that the bands would be wider for the MCC or for the IOS schedule? In answering this question, visualize each point on the MCC and IOS schedules as being the expected value of a probability distribution.

   b. For the IOS schedule, would the band, or confidence interval, associated with each project be identical? If not, what would this imply, and how might it affect the firm's capital budgeting analysis?

10-5 (Optimal capital budget) The Melrose Company has a target capital structure of 30 percent debt and 70 percent common equity. For the coming year, management expects to realize net earnings of $105,000. The past dividend policy of paying out 50 percent of earnings will continue. Present commitments from its banker will allow Melrose to borrow according to the following schedule:

Loan Amount	Interest Rate
$0 to $42,000	8%
$42,001 and above	12

The company's federal-plus-state tax rate is 40 percent; the current market price of its stock is $50 per share; its *last* dividend was $1.85 per share; and the expected growth rate is a constant 8 percent. External equity (new common) can be sold at a flotation cost of 15 percent.

The firm has the following investment opportunities for the next period:

Project	Cost	Expected Annual Net Cash Flows	Project Life	IRR
A	$ 75,000	$15,629	8 years	13.0
B	100,000	15,582	10 years	9.0
C	50,000	15,775	4 years	
D	25,000	14,792	2 years	12.0
E	50,000	12,858	6 years	

Management asks you to help them determine what projects (if any) should be under-taken. You proceed with this analysis by answering the following questions:

   a. How many breaks are there in the MCC schedule?

   b. At what dollar amounts do the breaks occur, and what causes them?

   c. What is the weighted average cost of capital, k_a, in each of the intervals be-tween the breaks?

   d. What are the IRR values for Projects C and E?

   e. Graph the IOS and MCC schedules.

   f. Which projects should the firm accept?

   g. What implicit assumptions about project risk are embodied in this problem? If you learned that Projects E, A, and D were of above-average risk, yet the firm chose the projects which you indicated in Part f, how would this affect the situation?

10-6 (Mutually exclusive projects) In October 1986, Sharp Corporation executives were working on their capital budget for 1987. Sharp expects to have the following *book value* capital structure on December 31, 1986:

Debt	$12,000,000
Preferred stock (25,000 shares)	2,500,000
Common stock (1,000,000 shares)	5,000,000
Retained earnings	10,000,000
Total capital	$29,500,000

Earnings per share have grown steadily over the past seven years, from $1.65 in 1979 to $3.00 projected for 1986. The investment community expects growth to continue but at a slower rate; the average past growth rate of 9 percent has recently dropped to 5 percent, and it is expected to remain constant at this level. On the basis of a 5 percent growth rate, the stock now sells at a price/earnings ratio of 6×. The last divi-dend, D_0, was $1.88; it is expected to increase at the new 5 percent growth rate.

Sharp's preferred stock, which was issued several years ago, has a book value of $100 per share, and it pays a dividend of $9. The yield currently on preferred stock of this degree of risk is 11.25 percent.

The debt consists of $12,000,000 of $1,000 par, 20-year bonds with a 4.135 percent coupon, payable semiannually. These bonds were issued 7 years ago, and hence have 13 years remaining to maturity. The yield-to-maturity for these bonds is currently 6.00 percent.

The addition to retained earnings projected for 1986 is $1,026,000:

$$1986 \text{ DPS} = D_1 = (\$1.88)(1.05) = \$1.974.$$

$$\text{Retained earnings} = (\text{EPS} - \text{DPS})(1,000,000 \text{ shares})$$

$$= (\$3.00 - \$1.974)(1,000,000) = \$1,026,000.$$

These funds will be available during the 1987 budget year. The corporate tax rate, including state income taxes, is 40 percent.

Assuming that the market value capital structure relationships developed in Part a are maintained, new securities can be sold at the following costs:

● **Debt:** Up to $3 million of new bonds can be sold at a cost of 6.67 percent (after flotation adjustment). Debt in the range of $3 to $5 million would cost 7.00 percent, while all debt over $5 million would cost Sharp 9.33 percent.

• **Preferred:** Additional preferred stock can be sold to investors at a price of $100 per share (which is par value) with a coupon of 11.25 percent, but the company will incur a 5 percent flotation cost, and hence will net only $95 per share.

• **Common:** Up to $3 million of new common stock can be sold at the current market price, with an underwriting cost of 5 percent. All common stock over $3 million would also have underwriting costs of 5 percent, but the offering price must be lowered to $16.11.

On the basis of these data, answer the following questions:

a. Find Sharp's market value capital structure, rounded to the nearest million dollars.

b. At what dollar amounts of new capital will breaks occur in the MCC schedule?

c. Calculate the WACC in the interval between each of these breaks and then plot the MCC schedule.

d. Assume that the company has the following investment opportunities. They are all indivisible; that is, they must be accepted in total or else rejected. In addition, Projects A and A' are mutually exclusive; that is, only one, if either, may be accepted. All of the projects have a 1-year life.

Project	Cost at t = 0	Expected Year-End After-Tax Cash Flow at t = 1
A	$ 4,000,000	$ 4,600,000
A'	2,000,000	2,336,000
B	3,000,000	3,420,000
C	15,000,000	16,995,000
D	1,000,000	1,130,000
E	1,000,000	1,115,000

Develop the Investment Opportunity Schedule and determine which projects will be accepted. [Hints: (1) Draw an MCC schedule and two IOS schedules (one including A and the other A') on the same graph; (2) draw a graph with NPV profiles for A and A'; and (3) consider the choice between A and A' in the light of these two graphs, noting that the corporation's MCC (the cost of the last dollar raised, which is a *point* on the MCC *schedule*) is constant at 13.4 percent regardless of whether A or A' is chosen.]

e. Sharp receives some new information which leads management to revise downward the expected cash inflow on Project C from $16,995,000 to $16,800,000. How will this affect the ranking of projects and the accept/reject decision? (Hint: You need to construct new IOS schedules on a graph which also shows the MCC schedule.)

10-7 (Optimal capital budget) The Gladstone Company has the following capital structure, which it considers to be optimal:

Debt	25%
Preferred stock	15
Common equity	60
Total capital	100%

Gladstone's expected net income this year is $17,142.86; its established dividend pay-out ratio is 30 percent; its federal-plus-state tax rate is 40 percent; and investors expect earnings and dividends to grow at a constant rate of 9 percent in the future. Gladstone paid a dividend of $3.60 per share last year, and its stock currently sells at a price of $60 per share. Treasury bonds yield 11 percent; an average stock has a 14 percent expected rate of return; and the firm's beta is 1.51.

Gladstone can obtain new capital as indicated below:

• **Debt:** Up to $2,500 of debt can be sold at an interest rate of 12 percent; debt in the range of $2,501 to $5,000 must carry an interest rate of 14 percent; and all debt over $5,000 will have an interest rate of 16 percent.

• **Preferred:** New preferred can be sold at a price of $100 per share, with a dividend of $11. Flotation costs of $5 per share would be incurred for up to $3,750 of preferred, while these costs would rise to $10, or 10 percent, on all preferred over $3,750.

• **Common:** New common stock would have a flotation cost of 10 percent for up to $6,000 of stock, and 20 percent for all common over $6,000.

The firm has the following average-risk investment opportunities:

Project	Cost at t = 0	Expected Annual Net Cash Flow	Project Life	IRR
A	$ 5,000	$1,095.60	7 years	12.0%
B	5,000	1,577.21	5 years	17.4
C	5,000	1,085.09	8 years	14.2
D	10,000	1,894.74	10 years	13.7
E	10,000	2,713.92	6 years	

a. Find the break points in the MCC schedule.
b. Determine the component costs of capital for each capital structure component.
c. Calculate the weighted average cost of capital in the interval between each break in the MCC schedule.
d. Calculate the IRR for Project E.
e. Construct a graph showing the MCC and IOS schedules.
f. Which projects should Gladstone accept?

10-8 (Depreciation-generated funds) Here are some data on Mitchell Mining Company (MMC):

(1) Target capital structure: 40 percent debt, 10 percent preferred stock, and 50 percent equity.

(2) Projected net income available to common stockholders for next year is $10 million, and the dividend payout ratio is 40 percent. Preferred stock consists of $10 million face value of 10 percent preferred. Depreciation for next year is expected to be $1 million.

(3) The firm is a constant growth company, with $D_0 = \$2$, $P_0 = \$20$, and $g = 5\%$.

(4) The yield to investors is 12 percent on all new preferred stock. Flotation costs are 20 percent on all new common stock and 5 percent on all new preferred stock.

(5) $k_d = 10\%$ for up to $1 million of debt, and $k_d = 14\%$ for all debt over $1 million.

(6) T = 40%. (Includes federal and state income taxes.)

(7) The four projects listed below are being considered for next year's capital budget:

Project	Cost (Millions of Dollars)	IRR
A	$2.5	12.0%
B	5.0	13.6
C	7.5	15.0
D	2.5	12.8

These projects include replacement of worn-out equipment as well as expansion projects.

a. Calculate the required data and then plot the firm's MCC schedule.

b. Plot the IOS schedule.

c. Assuming that the projects are perfectly divisible and have average risk, what projects should the firm accept, and how large should its capital budget be? If any project is accepted in part, what percentage would be accepted?

d. Assuming that the projects are nondivisible and have average risk, which projects should be accepted, and what is the size of the optimal capital budget?

e. *Assume* that Mitchell's MCC is 13.0 percent. The firm adjusts its MCC for risk by multiplying by a factor of 1.1 for high-risk projects and a factor of 0.9 for low-risk projects. The director of capital budgeting has determined that C is a high-risk project, that A is a low-risk project, and that Projects B and D have average risk. What is the risk-adjusted cost of capital for each project? Which projects should the firm accept after adjusting for risk?

10-9 (Optimal capital budget) Shome Enterprises has a target capital structure of 40 percent debt and 60 percent common equity. For the coming year, management expects after-tax earnings of $1.25 million. The past dividend policy of paying out 40 percent of earnings will continue. Present commitments from its banker will allow the firm to borrow according to the following schedule:

Loan Amount	Interest Rate
$0 to $400,000	10% on this increment of debt
$400,001 to $750,000	12% on this increment of debt
$750,001 and above	14% on this increment of debt

The company's tax rate is 34 percent, the current market price of its stock is $20 per share, its *last* dividend was $1.10 per share, and the expected constant growth rate is 9 percent. External equity (new common) can be sold at a flotation cost of 15 percent. The firm has the following investment opportunities for the next year:

Project	Cost	Annual Cash Flows	Project Life	IRR
1	$1,000,000	$206,901	10 years	
2	925,000	244,419	6	15.0%
3	475,000	288,463	2	
4	850,000	273,977	4	12.0
5	625,000	117,153	8	11.0

Management asks you to help determine which projects (if any) should be undertaken. You proceed with this analysis by answering the following questions as posed in a logical sequence:

    a. How many breaks are there in the MCC schedule?

    b. At what dollar amounts do the breaks occur, and what causes them?

    c. What is the weighted average cost of capital, k_a, in each of the intervals between the breaks?

    d. What are the IRR values for Projects 1 and 3?

    e. Graph the IOS and MCC schedules.

    f. Which projects should the firm accept?

    g. What assumptions about project risk are implicit in this problem? If you learned that Projects 1, 2, and 3 were of above-average risk, yet the firm chose the projects which you indicated in Part f, how would this affect the situation?

    h. The problem stated that the firm pays out 40 percent of its earnings as dividends. In words, how would the analysis change if the payout ratio were changed to zero, to 100 percent, or somewhere in between?

    (Do the remaining parts only if you are using the computerized diskette.)

    i. Suppose the tax rate fell to zero, with other variables remaining constant. How would that affect the MCC schedule?

    j. Return the tax rate to 34 percent. Now assume the debt ratio is increased to 70 percent. That causes all interest rates to rise by 1 percentage point, to 11 percent, 13 percent, and 15 percent, and g to increase from 9 percent to 10 percent. What happens to the MCC schedule and the capital budget?

    k. New information becomes available. Change the Part j scenario to assume earnings of only $750,000, but a growth rate of 12 percent. How does that affect the capital budget?

    l. Would it be reasonable to use the model to analyze the effects of a change in the payout ratio without changing other variables?

Selected Additional References and Cases

Chapter 4 contains numerous references related to the cost of capital and its use in capital budgeting decisions. For additional insights into the capital rationing problem, see

Weingartner, H. Martin, "Capital Rationing: n Authors in Search of a Plot," *Journal of Finance*, December 1977, 1403-1431.

NPV criterion superiority rests on the assumption that the cost of capital is the appropriate opportunity cost of future project cash flows. For a discussion of this issue, see

Bacon, Peter W., "The Evaluation of Mutually Exclusive Projects," *Financial Management*, Summer 1977, 55-58.

The following cases from the Crum-Brigham casebook are suitable for use at this point:

Case 32, "Sub Contractor," which illustrates many of the techniques used in marginal cost of capital calculations.

Case 33, "Osborne Abrasives Manufacturing Corporation," which illustrates divisional hurdle rates.

 # IV
LONG-TERM FINANCING DECISIONS

11
DIVIDEND POLICY

Dividend policy involves the decision to pay out earnings versus retaining them for reinvestment in the firm. An examination of the constant growth stock price model, $\hat{P}_0 = D_1/(k_s - g)$, indicates that a policy of paying out more cash dividends, which raises D_1, will tend to increase the price of the stock. However, if cash dividends are raised, then less money will be available for reinvestment; this will reduce the expected growth rate, which in turn will depress the price of the stock. Thus, a change in dividends has two opposing effects. *The optimal dividend policy for a firm strikes the balance that investors in the aggregate want between current dividends and future growth, thereby maximizing the price of the stock.*

A firm that pays out some of its earnings as dividends is limiting its retained earnings, and hence the asset expansion it can finance with relatively cheap internal equity. Further expansion is possible, of course, but it will have to be supported by the sale of more expensive new common stock. Thus, for any given rate of asset expansion, decisions on dividend policy also imply decisions on new stock sales, if the optimal capital structure is to be maintained. In this chapter, we examine the factors which affect the optimal dividend policy for the firm.

DIVIDEND POLICY THEORIES

A number of factors influence dividend policy, including the number of good investment opportunities available to the firm, the availability and cost of alternative sources of capital, and stockholders' preferences for current versus future income. Our major goal in this section is to show how these and other factors interact to influence a firm's optimal dividend policy. We begin by examining three theories of dividend policy: (1) The dividend irrelevance theory, (2) the "bird-in-the-hand" theory, and (3) the tax differential theory.

Dividend Irrelevance

In the first important theoretical work on dividend policy, Merton Miller and Franco Modigliani (MM) argued that dividend policy has no effect on either the price of a firm's stock or its cost of capital—MM stated that dividend policy is *irrelevant.*[1] They reasoned that the value of the firm is determined by its basic earnings power and its risk class, and therefore that the firm's value depends on its asset investment policy rather than on how earnings are split between dividends and retained earnings. MM demonstrated, under a particular set of assumptions, that if firms pay higher dividends, then they must sell more stock to new investors, and that the share of the value of the company given up to new investors is exactly equal to the dividends paid out. For example, if IBM's capital budget calls for the expenditure of $1 billion in 1987, and if the company expects $1 billion of earnings, then (1) it could pay all its earnings out as dividends and finance the capital budget by selling $1 billion of new stock, (2) retain the entire $1 billion of earnings, sell no new stock, and provide stockholders with a capital gain of $1 billion, or (3) pick a payout anywhere between 0 and 100 percent and thus provide stockholders with a total of $1 billion in dividends and capital gains.

MM proved their proposition theoretically, but only under these five assumptions: (1) There are no personal or corporate income taxes. (2) There are no stock flotation or transaction costs. (3) Dividend policy has no effect on the firm's cost of equity. (4) Firms' capital investment policy is independent of their dividend policy. (5) Investors and managers have the same set of information (symmetric information) regarding future investment opportunities. We show how MM proved their dividend irrelevance hypothesis under these assumptions in Appendix 11A.

The MM assumptions are very strong, and they obviously do not hold precisely. Firms and investors do pay income taxes, firms do incur flotation costs, investors do incur transactions costs, both taxes and transactions costs could cause k_s to be affected by dividend policy, and managers often have better information than outside investors. Thus, the MM conclusions on dividend irrelevancy may not be valid under real world conditions, so shortly after their article appeared in 1961, other theories were put forth.

"Bird-in-the-Hand" Theory

One critical assumption inherent in MM's dividend irrelevance theory is that dividend policy does not affect investors' required rate of return on equity, k_s. This issue has been hotly debated in academic circles. Myron Gordon and John Lintner, on the one hand, argued that k_s increases as the dividend payout is reduced because investors can be more sure of receiving dividend payments than income from the capital gains which should result from retained earnings.[2] They say, in effect, that investors value a dollar of expected dividends more highly than a dollar of expected capital gains because the dividend yield component, D_1/P_0, is less risky than the g component in the total expected return equation, $\hat{k}_s = D_1/P_0 + g$.

---

[1] See Merton H. Miller and Franco Modigliani, "Dividend Policy, Growth, and the Valuation of Shares," *Journal of Business*, October 1961, 411-433.

[2] See Myron J. Gordon, "Optimal Investment and Financing Policy," *Journal of Finance*, May 1963, 264-272; and John Lintner, "Dividends, Earnings, Leverage, Stock Prices, and the Supply of Capital to Corporations," *Review of Economics and Statistics*, August 1962, 243-269.

Figure 11-1
The Miller-Modigliani and Gordon-Lintner Dividend Hypotheses

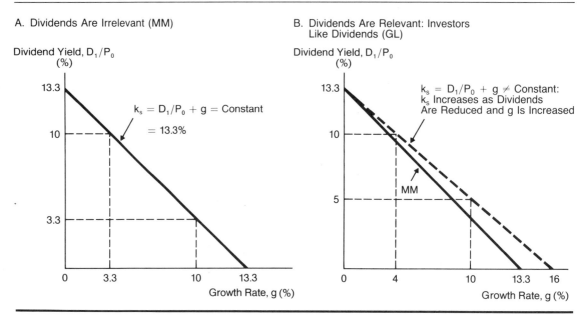

A. Dividends Are Irrelevant (MM)

B. Dividends Are Relevant: Investors Like Dividends (GL)

On the other hand, MM argued that investors are indifferent between D_1/P_0 and g, and hence that k_s is not affected by dividend policy. MM call the Gordon-Lintner argument "the bird-in-the-hand fallacy" because, in MM's view, many if not most investors are going to reinvest their dividends in the same or similar firms anyway, and, in any event, the riskiness of the firm's cash flows to investors in the long run is determined only by the riskiness of its asset cash flows, not by its dividend payout policy.[3]

Figure 11-1 presents two graphs which highlight the MM versus Gordon-Lintner arguments. The left panel shows the Miller-Modigliani position. Here the company has $\hat{k}_s = D_1/P_0 + g = k_s =$ a constant $= 13.3\%$ for any dividend policy. Thus, the equilibrium total return, k_s, is assumed to be a constant whether it comes entirely as a dividend yield (the vertical axis intercept), entirely as expected capital gains (the horizontal axis intercept), or as a combination of the two.

The dashed line in the right panel adds the Gordon-Lintner view. Gordon-Lintner argued that a possible capital gain in the bush is riskier than a dividend in the hand, so investors require a larger and larger total return, k_s, as capital gains are substituted for dividends. In other words, Gordon-Lintner argued that *more than 1 percent* of additional g is required to offset a 1 percent reduction of dividend

---

[3]Academicians other than MM have also rebutted the "bird-in-the-hand" theory. For example, see Michael Brennan, "A Note on Dividend Irrelevance and the Gordon Valuation Model," *Journal of Finance*, December 1971, 1115-1121.

yield. We will shortly discuss empirical tests designed to see whether the MM or the Gordon-Lintner view is correct.

Tax Differential Theory

In Chapter 3, we discussed the effects of personal taxes on stock and bond valuation. We pointed out that up until 1986, only 40 percent of long-term capital gains were taxed. Thus, an investor in the 48 percent marginal tax bracket paid a 48 percent tax rate on his or her dividend income, but only $(0.4)(0.48) = 19.2\%$ on long-term capital gains. Further, by not selling stock, the investor could defer realization of the capital gains and hence payment of the tax, and since a dollar paid in the future is less valuable than a dollar paid today, the deferral feature provides yet another advantage to capital gains. Under current tax laws, capital gains and dividend income are taxed at the same statutory rate, but the deferral feature still exists.

To illustrate, suppose an individual investor in the 28 percent tax bracket is considering the purchase of two stocks: Stock G, which is a growth stock with a 10 percent capital gains yield and a 5 percent dividend yield, and Stock Y, which is a yield stock with a 5 percent capital gains yield and a 10 percent dividend yield. Both stocks sell for $10, have the same risk, and are constant growth stocks, and hence $\hat{k}_G = \hat{k}_Y$ = Dividend yield + Capital gains yield = 15% on a before-tax basis. Table 11-1 contains the expected after-tax rates of return on Stocks G and Y for selected holding periods.[4] For all holding periods except one year, the after-tax yield on Stock G is greater than the after-tax yield on Stock Y. Further,

Table 11-1
After-Tax Rates of Return: Stock G and Stock Y

Stock	Holding Period in Years					
	1	2	3	4	5	∞
G	10.80%	10.94%	11.07%	11.20%	11.32%	13.60%
Y	10.80	10.87	10.94	11.00	11.07	12.20
Yield Differential	0.00	0.07	0.13	0.20	0.25	1.40

[4]The after-tax rates of return in Table 11-1 were calculated as follows: (1) determine the after-tax dollar dividend for each year during the holding period; (2) calculate the after-tax capital gain and the end-of-holding-period cash flow; and (3) calculate the IRR of the resulting cash flow stream, which is the expected after-tax rate of return. For example, Stock G's after-tax rate of return for a two-year holding period was found in this way: (1) Stock G sells for $10 and has a 5 percent dividend yield. Thus, $D_1 = \$10(0.05) = \$0.50$ and $D_2 = D_1(1 + g) = \$0.50(1.10) = \$0.55$. T = 28% and hence $(1 - T) = 0.72$, so the after-tax dividend stream is $D_{1AT} = \$0.50(0.72) = \$0.36$ and $D_{2AT} = \$0.55(0.72) = \$0.396$; (2) $\hat{P}_{2AT} = P_0(1 + g)^2 = \$10(1.10)^2 = \$12.10$. Thus, the Year 2 capital gain is $12.10 − $10.00 = $2.10, the tax is $2.10(0.28) = \$0.588$, and the after-tax proceeds from the sale are $12.10 − $0.588 = \$11.512$. (3) The after-tax cash flows are $CF_0 = -\$10.00$, $CF_1 = \$0.36$ and $CF_2 = \$0.396 + \$11.512 = \$11.908$. The IRR of this stream, which is Stock G's expected after-tax rate of return, is 10.94%.

the after-tax yield differential increases as the holding period increases. Stock G has the higher after-tax yield because a larger percentage of its return comes from capital gains, and these taxes are deferred until the end of the holding period. Of course, under the old tax laws, in which capital gains were taxed at a lower rate as well as deferred, the yield differentials were even more pronounced.

Tax paying investors with long holding periods would recognize that Stock G offers a higher after-tax return than Stock Y, and hence bid up the price of G relative to Y. Thus, Stock G's price might rise to $10.25, while Stock Y's might fall to $9.75. The end result would be a higher before-tax yield on Stock Y than on Stock G. If investors behave in this way, they would require higher pre-tax rates of return on high dividend yield stocks than they do on low dividend yield stocks to account for tax effects.

TESTS OF DIVIDEND THEORIES

In the preceding section, we presented three theories of dividend policy:

1. MM argued that dividend policy is irrelevant; that is, dividend policy does not affect a firm's value or its cost of capital. Thus, according to MM, there is no optimal dividend policy—one dividend policy is as good as any other.

2. Gordon and Lintner disagreed with MM, arguing that dividends are less risky than capital gains, so a firm should set a high dividend payout ratio and offer a high dividend yield to minimize its cost of capital. MM called this the "bird-in-the-hand fallacy."

3. A third group, whose position is the reverse of Gordon-Lintner, stated that since dividends are effectively taxed at higher rates than capital gains, investors require higher rates of return on stocks with high dividend yields. According to this theory, a firm should pay a low (or zero) dividend in order to minimize its cost of capital and maximize its value.

These three theories offer contradictory advice to corporate managers. MM say it doesn't matter, Gordon-Lintner say set a high payout, and the tax differential advocates say set a low payout. Which theory should we believe?

Two primary types of empirical tests have been conducted in an attempt to determine the true relationship between dividend policy and required returns. First, researchers have attempted to test the alternative theories along the lines set forth in Figure 11-1.[5] In theory, one could take a sample of companies which have different dividend policies, and hence different dividend yield and growth rate components, and plot them in graphs such as those shown in Figure 11-1. If the points all fell on the line in the left graph, so that the slope of the resulting regression line was − 1.0, this would support the MM irrelevance hypothesis. If the

---

[5]The earliest such test was Eugene F. Brigham and Myron J. Gordon, "Leverage, Dividend Policy, and the Cost of Capital," *Journal of Finance*, March 1968, 85-104. In work done in conjunction with writing this chapter, we reexamined the issue and reached the conclusions reported herein.

points all fell on the dashed line in the right graph, so that the slope was less negative (less steep) than -1.0 (say -0.5), this would support the Gordon-Lintner hypothesis. If the slope was more negative (steeper) than -1.0 (say -1.5), this would support the tax differential position.

In fact, when such tests have been conducted with reasonably good data, the slope of the regression line is found to be about -1.0. This seems to refute both Gordon-Lintner and tax differential advocates, and to support MM. However, statistical problems prevent us from saying that these tests *prove* that MM are right and that dividend policy does not affect k_s. The two statistical problems are these: (1) For a valid statistical test, things other than dividend policy must be held constant; that is, the sample companies must differ only in their dividend policies. (2) We must be able to measure with a high degree of accuracy the expected growth rates for the sample firms. Neither of these two conditions actually holds. We cannot find a set of publicly owned firms that differ only in their dividend policies, nor can we obtain precise estimates of the growth rates which the marginal investor expects. Therefore, we cannot determine with much precision what effect, if any, dividend policy has on the cost of equity. Our conclusion is that this particular type of test is not capable of solving the dividend policy dilemma.

Researchers have also studied the dividend yield effect from a CAPM perspective. They hypothesize that required returns are a function of both market risk, as measured by beta, and dividend yield. If so, then a stock's required return could be expressed as follows:

$$k_i = k_{RF} + b_i(k_M - k_{RF}) + \lambda_i(D_i - D_M). \qquad \textbf{(11-1)}$$

Here, D_i is the dividend yield of Stock i, D_M is the dividend yield of an average stock, and λ_i is the dividend impact coefficient. Researchers have tested Equation 11-1 by regressing historic values of k_{RF}, k_M, D_i, and D_M against historic values of k_i. If the coefficient of λ_i turns out to be zero, dividend yield would not appear to affect required returns. If λ_i were positive, then investors would appear to require a higher return on stocks with high dividend yields, as the tax differential theory predicts, and vice versa if λ_i were negative.

The results of this line of research have been mixed. Litzenberger and Ramaswamy showed, using NYSE data from 1936 through 1977, that stocks with high dividend yields did have higher total yields than did stocks with low dividend yields, after adjusting for market risk.[6] Their study indicates that investors' required rates of return increased about 0.24 percentage points for every percentage point increase in dividend yield. However, other studies have reached contradictory conclusions; namely, that the λ_i term is zero and consequently that dividend yield has no effect on required returns.[7] (Of course, when these studies were conducted, capital gains and dividend income were taxed at different rates.) The major

---

[6]See Robert H. Litzenberger and Krishna Ramaswamy, "The Effect of Personal Taxes and Dividends on Capital Asset Prices," *Journal of Financial Economics*, June 1979, 163-196.

[7]For example, see Fischer Black and Myron Scholes, "The Effects of Dividend Yield and Dividend Policy on Common Stock Prices and Returns," *Journal of Financial Economics*, May 1974, 1-22.

problem with all of these studies is that they used historical earned rates of return as proxies for expected future returns, and with such a poor proxy, the tests are almost bound to have mixed results. Thus, these CAPM empirical tests, like the pure DCF-based tests, have not led to definitive conclusions as to which dividend theory is most correct. Unfortunately, the issue is still unresolved.

OTHER DIVIDEND POLICY ISSUES

Before we discuss dividend policy in practice, we need to examine two other theoretical issues that could affect our views toward the three theories presented earlier. These issues are (1) the information content, or signaling, hypothesis, and (2) the clientele effect.

Information Content, or Signaling, Hypothesis

The MM dividend irrelevance theory assumes, among other considerations, that everyone—all investors and managers—has an identical opinion about the firm's investment opportunities and hence about the distributions of its expected future dividend stream. In reality, however, investors have conflicting opinions on both the level of future dividend payments and the degree of uncertainty inherent in those payments, and managers often have better information about future prospects than public stockholders.

It has been observed that an increase in the dividend (for example, the annual dividend per share is raised from $2.00 to $2.50) is often accompanied by an increase in the price of the stock, while a dividend cut generally leads to a stock price decline. This could suggest that investors, in the aggregate, prefer dividends to capital gains. However, MM argued differently. They noted the well-established fact that corporations are always reluctant to cut dividends, and hence do not raise dividends unless they anticipate higher, or at least stable, earnings in the future. Thus, MM argued that a higher-than-normal dividend increase is a "signal" to investors that the firm's management forecasts good future earnings.[8] Conversely, a dividend reduction, or a smaller-than-normal increase, signals that management is forecasting poor earnings in the future. Thus, MM claim that investor reactions to changes in dividend policy do not necessarily show that investors prefer dividends to retained earnings. Rather, the fact that price changes follow dividend actions

---

[8]Stephen Ross has suggested that managers can use capital structure as well as dividends to give signals concerning firms' future prospects. For example, a firm with good earnings prospects can carry more debt than a similar firm with poor earnings prospects. This theory, called "incentive-signaling," rests on the premise that signals based on cash-based variables (either debt interest or dividends) cannot be mimicked by unsuccessful firms because such firms do not have the future cash-generating power to maintain the announced interest or dividend payment. Thus, investors are more likely to believe a glowing verbal report when it is accompanied by a dividend increase or a debt-financed expansion program. See Stephen A. Ross, "The Determination of Financial Structure: The Incentive-Signaling Approach," *The Bell Journal of Economics*, Spring 1977, 23-40.

simply indicates to MM that there is an important *information,* or *signaling, content* in dividend announcements.

Like most other aspects of dividend policy, empirical studies on this topic have been inconclusive. There clearly is some information content in dividend announcements. However, it is difficult to tell whether stock price changes that follow increases or decreases in dividends reflect only signaling effects or both signaling and dividend preference effects, because these increases or decreases typically include both a change in the percentage payout ratio and a change in the dollars of dividends paid.

Clientele Effect

Different groups, or *clienteles*, of stockholders prefer different dividend payout policies. For example, stockholders such as retired individuals and university endowment funds often prefer current income, so they would want the firm to pay out a higher percentage of its earnings. Such investors are often in a low or even zero tax bracket, so taxes are of no concern. Other stockholders prefer reinvestment, because they have no need for current investment income and would simply reinvest any dividends received, after first paying income taxes on the dividend income.

If the firm retains and reinvests income, rather than paying dividends, those stockholders who need current income would be disadvantaged. They would receive capital gains, but they would be forced to go to the trouble and expense of selling off some of their shares to obtain cash. Also, some institutional investors (or trustees for individuals) may be precluded from selling stock and then "spending capital." The other group, the stockholders who are saving rather than spending dividends, would favor the low dividend policy, for the more the firm pays out in dividends, the more these stockholders will have to pay in current taxes and the more trouble and expense they will have to go through to reinvest their after-tax dividends. Thus, investors who desire current investment income should own shares in high dividend payout firms, while investors with no need for current investment income should own shares in low dividend payout firms.

To the extent that stockholders can shift their investments among firms, a firm can set the specific policy that seems appropriate to its management and then stockholders who do not like this policy can sell to other investors who do. However, switching may be inefficient because of (1) brokerage costs, (2) the likelihood that stockholders who are selling will have to pay capital gains taxes, and (3) a possible shortage of investors in the aggregate who like the firm's newly adopted dividend policy. Thus, management might be reluctant to change its dividend policy, because such changes might cause current shareholders to sell their stock, forcing the stock price down. Such a price decline might be temporary or it might be permanent—if few investors were attracted by the new dividend policy, then the stock price would remain depressed. Of course, it is possible that the new policy would attract an even larger clientele than the firm had previously, and if so, the stock price would rise.

Evidence from several studies suggests that there is in fact a clientele effect.[9] However, MM and others have argued that one clientele is as good as another, thus the existence of a clientele effect does not imply that one dividend policy is better than any other dividend policy. However, neither MM nor anyone else has offered proof that the aggregate makeup of investors permits firms to disregard clientele effects. This issue, like many others in the dividend arena, is still up in the air.

DIVIDEND POLICY IN PRACTICE

We noted above that there are three conflicting theories as to what type of dividend policy firms *should* follow. We also noted that empirical tests do not answer the question of which theory is correct. In this section, we present four alternative dividend payment policies that firms actually *do* follow. As a part of this discussion, we discuss a multitude of factors which are not generally discussed by the theorists but which appear to influence dividend policy in practice.

Residual Dividend Policy

In practice, dividend policy is influenced by both investment opportunities and the availability of funds to finance those opportunities. This fact has led to the development of the *residual dividend payment policy*, which states that a firm should follow these four steps when deciding its payout ratio: (1) Determine the optimal capital budget; (2) determine the amount of equity needed to finance that budget; (3) use retained earnings to supply this equity to the extent possible; and (4) pay dividends only if more earnings are available than are needed to support the optimal capital budget. The word *residual* implies "left over," and the residual policy implies that dividends should only be paid out of "leftover" earnings.

We saw in Chapter 4 that the cost of retained earnings is an *opportunity cost* which reflects rates of return available to equity investors. If a firm's stockholders could buy other stocks of equal risk and obtain a 12 percent dividend-plus-capital-gains yield, then 12 percent is the firm's cost of retained earnings. The cost of new outside equity raised by selling common stock is higher because of the costs of floating the issue, including both underwriting costs and any downward price pressure resulting from "negative signals" investors might get from the announcement of a stock offering.

Also, most firms have a target capital structure that calls for at least some debt, so new financing is done partly with debt and partly with equity. As long as the firm finances with the optimal mix, using the proper amounts of debt and equity, and provided it uses only internally generated equity (retained earnings), its marginal cost of each new dollar of capital will be minimized. Internally generated equity is available for financing a certain amount of new investment, but beyond

[9]For example, see R. Richardson Pettit, "Taxes, Transactions Costs and the Clientele Effect of Dividends," *The Journal of Financial Economics*, December 1977, 419-436.

Figure 11-2
Dallas Oil Company:
Marginal Cost of Capital Schedule

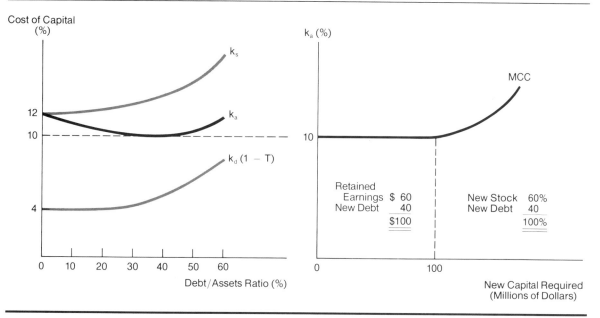

that amount, the firm must turn to more expensive new common stock. At the point where new stock must be sold, the cost of equity, and consequently the weighted average cost of capital (WACC), rises.

These concepts, which were developed in Chapters 4 and 10, are illustrated in Figure 11-2 with data from the Dallas Oil Company (DOC). DOC has a WACC of 10 percent as long as retained earnings are available, but its MCC schedule begins to rise at the point where new stock must be sold. DOC has $60 million of earnings and a 40 percent optimal debt ratio. Provided it does not pay cash dividends, DOC can make net investments (investments in addition to asset replacements financed from depreciation) of $100 million, consisting of $60 million from retained earnings plus $40 million of new debt supported by the retained earnings, at a 10 percent cost of capital. Therefore, its WACC is constant at 10 percent up to $100 million of capital. Beyond $100 million, the WACC rises as the firm begins to use more expensive new common stock.

Of course, if DOC does not retain all of its earnings, its WACC will begin to rise before $100 million. For example, if DOC retained only $30 million, then its WACC would begin to rise at $30 million retained earnings + $20 million debt = $50 million.

Now suppose DOC's director of capital budgeting constructs several investment opportunity schedules and plots them on a graph. The investment opportunity schedules for three different years—a good year (IOS_G), a normal year (IOS_N), and

Figure 11-3
**Dallas Oil Company:
Investment Opportunity (IRR) Schedules**

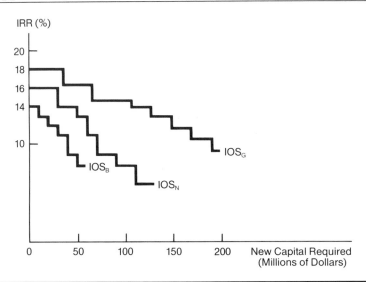

a bad year (IOS_B)—are shown in Figure 11-3. DOC can invest the most money, and at the highest rates of return, when the investment opportunities are as given by IOS_G.

In Figure 11-4, we combine these investment opportunity schedules with the cost of capital schedule. The point where the relevant IOS curve cuts the MCC curve defines the firm's marginal cost of capital and its optimal level of new investment. When investment opportunities are relatively bad (IOS_B), the optimal level of investment is $40 million; when opportunities are normal (IOS_N), $70 million should be invested; and when opportunities are relatively good (IOS_G), DOC should make new investments in the amount of $150 million.

If IOS_G is the appropriate schedule, the company should raise and invest $150 million. DOC has $60 million in earnings and a 40 percent target debt ratio. Thus, it can finance $100 million, consisting of $60 million of retained earnings plus $40 million of new debt, at an average cost of 10 percent if it retains all of its earnings. The remaining $50 million will include external equity and thus have a higher cost. If DOC pays out part of its earnings in dividends, it will have to begin to use costly new common stock earlier than need be, so its MCC schedule will rise earlier than it otherwise would. *This suggests that under the conditions of IOS_G, DOC should retain all of its earnings. According to the residual policy, DOC's payout ratio should be zero if IOS_G applies.*

Under the conditions of IOS_N, however, DOC should invest only $70 million. How should this investment be financed? First, notice that if DOC retained all of its earnings, $60 million, it would need to sell only $10 million of new debt.

Figure 11-4
Dallas Oil Company:
Combined IOS and MCC Schedules

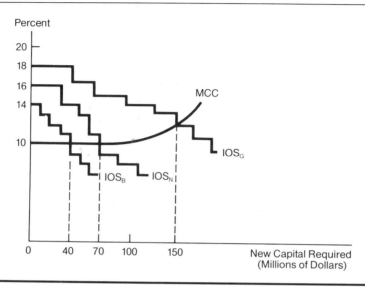

However, if DOC retained $60 million and sold only $10 million of new debt, it would move away from its target capital structure. To stay on target, DOC must finance 60 percent of the required $70 million by equity—retained earnings—and 40 percent by debt; this means DOC must retain $42 million and sell $28 million of new debt. If DOC retains only $42 million of its $60 million total earnings, it must distribute the residual, $18 million, to its stockholders. Thus, its optimal pay-out ratio under IOS_G is $18/$60 = 30\%$.

Under the conditions of IOS_B, DOC should invest only $40 million. Because it has $60 million in earnings, it could finance the entire $40 million out of retained earnings and still have $20 million available for dividends. Should this be done? Under our assumptions, this would not be a good decision, because DOC would move away from its optimal capital structure. To stay at the 40 percent target debt/assets ratio, DOC must retain $24 million of earnings and sell $16 million of debt. When the $24 million of retained earnings is subtracted from the $60 million total earnings, DOC is left with a residual of $36 million, the amount that should be paid out in dividends. Thus, the payout ratio as prescribed by the residual policy is $36/$60 = 60 percent.

If either the IOS schedule or earnings level varies from year to year, strict adherence to the residual dividend policy would result in dividend variability—one year, when investment opportunities are good, the firm would declare zero dividends, whereas the next year the same firm, with poor investment opportunities facing it, might declare a large dividend. Similarly, fluctuating cash flows would lead to variable dividends, even if investment opportunities were stable over time. As we will see shortly, such fluctuations could lead to an increase in k_s. As a result, few if any follow the residual theory exactly. However, as we also discuss, many firms do use the residual theory concept to help establish a long-run target payout ratio.

Constant or Steadily Increasing Dividends

In the past, many firms set a specific annual dollar dividend per share and then maintained it, increasing the annual dividend only if it seemed clear that future earnings would be sufficient to allow the new dividend to be maintained. A corollary of the policy was this rule: *Try to avoid ever having to reduce the annual dividend.*

More recently, inflation has tended to push up earnings, so most firms that would otherwise have followed the stable dividend payment policy have switched over to what is called the "stable growth rate" policy. Here the firm sets a target growth rate for dividends, say 6 percent per year, and strives to increase dividends by this amount each year. Obviously, earnings must be growing at a reasonably steady rate for this to be feasible.

Both a stable payment policy and a stable growth rate policy, using data for Morris Pharmaceuticals, Inc., over a 37-year period, are illustrated in Figure 11-5. Initially, earnings were $2 a share and dividends were $1 a share, so the payout ratio was 50 percent. During most of the 1950s, earnings fluctuated, but no clear trend was evident, so the dividend was kept at the $1 level. However, by the early 1960s, earnings had increased above earlier levels, causing the payout ratio to drop below 50 percent. Further, management believed the new earnings would be sustained, so the company raised the dividend in three steps to $1.50 to reestablish the 50 percent payout. During 1965 a strike caused earnings to fall below the regular dividend. Expecting the earnings decline to be temporary, management maintained the $1.50 dividend. Earnings fluctuated on a fairly high plateau from 1966 through 1973, during which time dividends remained constant.

Due in large part to inflation, earnings grew rather steadily during the 1970s and early 1980s, and investors came to expect most successful companies to increase dividends at a rate which, they hoped, would offset inflation. Therefore, after 1973 management adopted the policy of increasing the dividend annually. Inflation, and hence Morris' earnings growth, began to subside in the mid-1980s, and, in 1985, management made the decision to revert back to a constant dividend policy, with dividend increases occurring only after earnings gains.

There are several logical reasons for following a stable, predictable dividend policy. First, given the existence of the information content (or signaling) hypothesis, a fluctuating payment policy might lead to greater uncertainty, a higher k_s, and consequently a lower stock price than would exist under a stable policy. Second, stockholders who use dividends for current consumption want to be able to count on receiving dividends on a regular basis, so irregular dividends might lower demand for the stock and cause its price to decline. Therefore, even though the optimal payout prescribed by the residual policy might vary somewhat from year

Figure 11-5
Morris Pharmaceuticals, Inc.:
Dividends and Earnings over Time

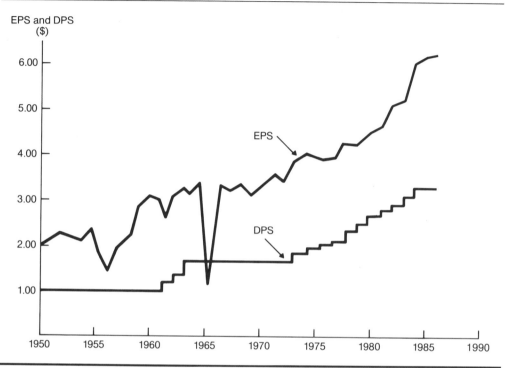

to year, a mix of actions such as delaying some investment projects, departing from the target capital structure during a particular year, or even selling common stock would be preferable to cutting the dividend or reducing the growth rate investors expect.

Constant Payout Ratio

A very few firms follow a policy of always paying out a constant percentage of earnings. Earnings will surely fluctuate, so following this policy necessarily means that the dollar amount of dividends will fluctuate. For reasons discussed in the preceding section, this policy is not likely to maximize a firm's stock price. Before its bankruptcy, Penn Central Railroad did follow the policy of paying out one-half its earnings: "A dollar for the stockholders and a dollar for the company," as one director put it. Logic like this could drive any company to bankruptcy!

Note, though, that many companies do have *target payout ratios* that are based on the residual theory. For example, Morris Pharmaceuticals has, over the period 1950-1986, paid out an average of about 50 percent of its earnings, even though the payout ratio is not constant on a year-to-year basis. The 50 percent long-run target payout is based on investment opportunities and capital availability as determined in a residual analysis study.

Low Regular Dividend plus Extras

A policy of paying a low regular dividend plus a year-end extra in good years is yet another commonly encountered policy. It gives the firm flexibility, yet investors can count on receiving at least a minimum dividend. Therefore, if a firm's earnings and cash flows are quite volatile, this policy may well be its best choice. The directors can set a relatively low regular dividend—low enough so that this dividend can be maintained even in low-profit years or in years when a considerable amount of retained earnings is needed—and then supplement it with an extra dividend in years when excess funds are available. General Motors, whose earnings fluctuate widely from year to year, has long followed such a policy, declaring the extra dividend toward the end of the year, when its profits and investment requirements are known. Eastman Kodak Company has also followed this policy. In November 1985, Kodak declared an extra $0.25 per share dividend along with its regular $0.55 quarterly dividend.

Payment Procedures

Dividends are normally paid quarterly. For example, Consolidated Insurance Company (CIC) paid dividends of $3.00, $0.75 each quarter, during 1986. In common financial language, we say that CIC's *regular quarterly dividend* is $0.75 or that its *regular annual dividend* is $3.00. The actual payment procedure is as follows:

1. Declaration Date. CIC's directors meet each quarter and declare the regular dividend. On the basis of their August 15, 1986 meeting the directors issued the following statement: "On August 15, 1986, the directors of CIC met and declared the regular quarterly dividend of 75 cents per share, payable to holders of record on September 15, payment to be made on October 2, 1986."

2. Holder-of-Record Date. At the close of business on the *holder-of-record date*, September 15, the company closes its stock transfer books and makes up a list of the shareholders as of that date. If CIC is notified of the sale and transfer of some stock before 5 p.m. on September 15, the new owner receives the dividend. However, if notification is received on or after September 16, the previous owner of the stock gets the dividend check.

3. Ex-Dividend Date. Suppose Jean Buyer buys 100 shares of CIC stock from John Seller on September 12. Will the company be notified of the transfer in time to list Buyer as the new owner and thus pay the dividend to her? To avoid conflict, the stock brokerage business has set up a convention of declaring that the right to the dividend remains with the stock until the close of business four *business days* prior to the holder-of-record date; on the fourth day before the record date, the right to the dividend no longer goes with the shares. The date when the right to the dividend leaves the stock is called the *ex-dividend date*. In this case, the ex-dividend date is six days prior to September 15, or September 8, because September 13 and 14, 1986 are nonbusiness days:

	September 8
Ex-dividend date:	September 9
	September 10
	September 11
	September 12
Holder-of-record date:	September 15

Therefore, if Buyer is to receive the dividend, she must buy the stock by September 8. If she buys it on September 9 or later, Seller will receive the dividend.

The CIC dividend amounts to $0.75, so the ex-dividend date is important. Barring fluctuations in the stock market, we would normally expect the price of a stock to drop by approximately the amount of the dividend on the ex-dividend date. Thus, if CIC closed at $30 3/4 on September 8, it would probably open at about $30 on September 9.[10]

4. Payment Date. The company actually mails the checks to the holders of record on October 2, the payment date.

Dividend Reinvestment Plans

During the 1970s, most of the larger companies instituted *dividend reinvestment plans*, or *DRPs*, whereby stockholders can automatically reinvest dividends received in the stock of the paying corporation.[11] Today it is estimated that about 1,000 companies offer DRPs and, although participation rates vary considerably, on average about 10 percent of the firms' shareholders are enrolled. There are two

---

[10]Tax effects actually cause the price decline, on average, to be less than the full amount of the dividend. Suppose you were an investor in the 50 percent tax bracket. If you bought CIC's stock on September 8, you would receive the dividend but almost immediately pay half of it out in taxes. Thus, you would want to wait until September 9 to buy the stock, if you thought you could get it for $0.75 per share less. Your reaction, and that of others, would influence stock prices around dividend payment dates. Here is what would happen:

1. Other things held constant, a stock's price should rise during the quarter, with the daily price increase (for CIC) equal to $0.75/90 = $0.0083. Therefore, if it started at $30 just after its last ex-dividend date, it would rise to $30.75 on September 8.

2. In the absence of taxes, the stock's price would fall to $30 on September 9, and it would then start moving up again as the next dividend accrual period began. Thus, over time, if everything else were held constant, the stock's price would follow a sawtooth pattern, with the depth of each tooth being $0.75.

3. Because of taxes, the stock's price will not rise by the full amount of the dividend, or fall by the full dividend amount when it goes ex dividend.

4. The amount of the rise and subsequent fall depends on the average investor's marginal tax rate. See Edwin J. Elton and Martin J. Gruber, "Marginal Stockholder Tax Rates and the Clientele Effect," *Review of Economics and Statistics,* February 1970, 68-74, for an interesting discussion of these topics.

[11]See Richard H. Pettway and R. Phil Malone, "Automatic Dividend Reinvestment Plans," *Financial Management*, Winter 1973, 11-18, for an excellent discussion of the subject.

types of DRPs: (1) plans which involve only "old stock" that is already outstanding, and (2) plans which involve newly issued stock. In either case, the stockholder must pay income taxes on the amount of the dividends, even though stock rather than cash is received.

Under both types of DRP, the stockholder elects either to continue receiving dividend checks or to use the dividends to buy more stock in the corporation. Under the "old stock" type of plan, if the stockholder elects reinvestment, a bank, acting as trustee, takes the total funds available for reinvestment (less a fee), purchases the corporation's stock on the open market, and allocates the shares purchased to the participating stockholders' accounts on a pro rata basis. The transactions costs of buying shares (brokerage costs) are low because of volume purchases, so these plans benefit small stockholders who do not need cash dividends for current consumption.

The "new stock" type of DRP provides for dividends to be invested in newly issued stock; hence, these plans raise new capital for the firm. AT&T, Florida Power & Light, Union Carbide, and many other companies have had such plans in effect in recent years, using them to raise substantial amounts of new equity capital. No fees are charged to stockholders, and many companies offer stock at a discount of 5 percent below the actual market price. The companies absorb these costs as a trade-off against flotation costs that would be incurred if stock were sold through investment bankers rather than through the dividend reinvestment plans. Discussions with corporate treasurers suggest that many other companies are seriously considering establishing or switching to new-stock DRPs.[12]

SUMMARY OF FACTORS THAT INFLUENCE DIVIDEND POLICY

In earlier sections, (1) we described the major theories of how dividend policy affects the value of a firm, and (2) we discussed four alternative payment policies. Firms choose a particular policy based on managements' beliefs concerning the dividend theories, plus a host of other factors. All of the factors which are taken into account may be grouped into four broad categories: (1) constraints on dividend payments, (2) investment opportunities, (3) availability and cost of alternative sources of capital, and (4) effects of dividend policy on k_s. Each of these categories has several subparts. They are all discussed in the following paragraphs.

---

[12]One interesting aspect of DRPs is that they are forcing corporations to reexamine their basic dividend policies. A high participation rate in a DRP suggests that stockholders might be better off if the firm simply reduced cash dividends to save stockholders some personal income taxes. Quite a few firms are surveying their stockholders to learn more about their preferences and to find out how they would react to a change in dividend policy. A more rational approach to basic dividend policy decisions may emerge from this research.

Note that companies use or stop the use of new-stock DRPs depending on their need for equity capital. Thus, both Union Carbide and AT&T recently stopped offering a new-stock DRP with a 5 percent discount because their needs for equity capital declined.

Constraints

1. Bond Indentures. Debt contracts often restrict dividend payments to earnings generated after the loan was granted. Also, debt contracts frequently stipulate that no dividends can be paid unless the current ratio, the times-interest-earned ratio, and other safety ratios exceed stated minimums.

2. Impairment of Capital Rule. Dividend payments cannot exceed the balance sheet item "retained earnings." This legal restriction, known as the "impairment of capital rule," is designed to protect creditors. (*Liquidating dividends* can be paid out of capital, but they must be indicated as such and must not reduce capital below limits stated in the firm's debt contracts.)

3. Availability of Cash. Cash dividends can only be paid with cash. Thus, a shortage of cash in the bank can restrict dividend payments. However, unused borrowing capacity can offset this factor.

4. Penalty Tax on Improperly Accumulated Earnings. To prevent wealthy individuals from using corporations to avoid personal taxes, the Tax Code provides for a special surtax on improperly accumulated income. Thus, if the IRS can demonstrate that the dividend payout ratio is being deliberately held down to help stockholders avoid personal taxes, heavy penalties will be imposed on the firm. However, as a practical matter, this factor has been applied only to privately owned firms.

Investment Opportunities

1. Location of the IOS Schedule. If the relevant IOS schedule in Figure 11-4 is far to the right, this will tend to produce a low payout ratio, and conversely if the IOS is far to the left.

2. Possibility of Accelerating or Delaying Projects. The ability to accelerate or postpone projects will permit more flexibility in a firm's dividend policy.

Alternative Sources of Capital

1. Cost of Selling New Stock. If a firm needs to finance a given level of investment, it can obtain equity by retaining earnings or by selling new common stock. If flotation costs and downward price pressure are high, k_e will be well above k_s, making it much better to finance through retention than through sale of new common stock. On the other hand, if these costs are low, dividend policy will be less important. Flotation and downward pressure costs differ among firms. For example, these costs are generally higher for small than for large firms. Hence, the importance of equity issuance costs, and consequently the degree of flexibility in setting a dividend policy, varies among firms.

2. Control. If management is concerned about maintaining control, it may be reluctant to sell new stock, and hence may retain more earnings than it otherwise would. This factor is especially important for small, closely held firms.

3. Capital Structure Flexibility. As we have seen, if stock issuance costs are low, a more flexible dividend policy may be followed, because equity can be raised by retaining earnings or by selling new stock. A similar situation holds for debt policy. If the firm can adjust its debt ratio without seriously affecting its cost of capital, then it can maintain a constant dollar dividend or constant growth rate by using a variable debt ratio. The shape of the average cost of capital curve (left panel in Figure 11-2) determines the practical extent to which the debt ratio can be varied. If the average cost of capital curve is relatively flat over a wide range, then capital structure policy is less critical than it would be if the curve had a "V" shape with a distinct minimum, and consequently a relatively flat cost of capital curve makes it easier to follow a constant dollar dividend or constant growth rate dividend policy.

Effects of Dividend Policy on k_s

The effects of dividend policy on k_s may be considered in terms of these four factors: (1) deferral of capital gains taxes, (2) stockholders' desire for current versus future income, (3) perceived riskiness of dividends versus capital gains, and (4) the information content of dividends (signaling). Since we discussed each of these factors in detail earlier, we need only note here that the importance of each factor's effect on k_s varies from firm to firm, depending on the makeup of its stockholders. Management certainly ought to take its own stockholders into account when it sets its dividend policy.

It should be apparent from our discussion thus far that dividend policy decisions are truly exercises in informed judgment, not decisions that can be quantified precisely. However, to make rational dividend decisions, financial managers do need to consider each of the points we have raised in the preceding sections.

STOCK REPURCHASES

As an alternative to paying cash dividends, a firm may distribute income to stockholders by *repurchasing its own stock*, and stock that has been repurchased by a firm is called *treasury stock*. If some of the outstanding stock is repurchased and held as treasury stock, fewer shares will remain outstanding. Assuming the repurchase does not adversely affect the firm's earnings, the earnings per share on the remaining shares will increase, resulting in a higher market price per share, which means that capital gains will have been substituted for dividends.

Companies have been repurchasing their stock in record amounts in recent years. For example, in 1985 Phillips Petroleum repurchased about 81 million shares of common stock having a total value of over $4.1 billion, the largest repurchase on record. Also in 1985, Atlantic Richfield repurchased about 67 million shares valued at $4 billion. Other billion dollar repurchases in 1985 were made by Unocal, Exxon, Union Carbide, Allied-Signal, and Litton Industries.

Most of the very large repurchase programs were part of a general corporate restructuring, wherein certain major assets, such as whole divisions or subsidiaries, are sold off, and the debt ratio is increased substantially. The asset sales and the issuance of new debt both bring in additional capital, and this capital is then distributed to stockholders through a major, one-time stock repurchase. A repurchase that is part of a corporate restructuring is quite different from a "regular" repurchase, where the repurchase is merely a substitute for cash dividends as a method for distributing corporate income to shareholders.

The effects of a "regular" repurchase can be illustrated with data on American Development Corporation (ADC). The company expects to earn $4.4 million in 1987, and 50 percent of this amount, or $2.2 million, has been allocated for distribution to common shareholders. There are 1,100,000 shares outstanding, and the market price is $20 a share. ADC could use the $2.2 million to repurchase 100,000 of its shares through a tender offer for $22 a share, or it could pay a cash dividend of $2 a share.[13]

The effect of the repurchase on the EPS and market price per share of the remaining stock can be determined in the following way:

1. Current EPS $= \dfrac{\text{Total earnings}}{\text{Number of shares}} = \dfrac{\$4.4 \text{ million}}{1.1 \text{ million}} = \$4$ per share.

2. Current P/E ratio $= \dfrac{\$20}{\$4} = 5\times$, assumed to remain constant.

3. $\dfrac{\text{EPS after repurchase}}{\text{of 100,000 shares}} = \dfrac{\$4.4 \text{ million}}{1 \text{ million}} = \$4.40$ per share.

4. Expected market price after repurchase $= (\text{P/E})(\text{EPS}) = (5)(\$4.40)$

$$= \$22 \text{ per share.}$$

5. Expected capital gains per remaining share $= \$22 - \$20$
$$= \$2.00.$$

It should be noticed from this example that investors would receive benefits of $2 per share in any case, either in the form of a $2 cash dividend or a $2 increase in the stock price. This result occurs because we assumed (1) that shares could be repurchased at exactly $22 a share and (2) that the P/E ratio would remain constant. If shares could be bought for less than $22, the repurchase would be even better for *remaining* stockholders, but the reverse would hold if ADC paid more than $22 a share. Furthermore, the P/E ratio might change as a result of the

---

[13]Stock repurchases are commonly made in three ways. First, a publicly owned firm can simply buy its own stock through a broker on the open market. Second, it can issue a *tender*, under which it permits stockholders to send in (that is, "tender") their shares to the firm in exchange for a specified price per share. When tender offers are made, the firm generally indicates that it will buy up a specified number of shares within a particular time period (usually about two weeks); if more shares are tendered than the company wishes to purchase, then purchases are made on a pro rata basis. Finally, the firm can purchase a block of shares from one or more large holders on a negotiated basis. If a negotiated purchase is employed, care should be taken to insure that these stockholders do not receive preferential treatment not available to other stockholders.

repurchase, rising if investors viewed the repurchase favorably and falling if they viewed it unfavorably. Some factors that might affect P/E ratios are considered next.

Advantages of Repurchases from the Stockholder's Viewpoint

1. Repurchase announcements may be viewed as positive signals by investors because the repurchase could be motivated by management's belief that the firm's shares are undervalued. For example, Teledyne, a $3 billion conglomerate, earns about $400 million per year, yet it has not paid a cash dividend in over 20 years, and it is not expected to pay any dividends in the foreseeable future. Profits are, however, used to repurchase stock and thus to stimulate growth. Teledyne's stock rose from $4 in 1975 to $355 in 1986, so the company is clearly doing something right!

2. The stockholder has a choice—to sell or not to sell. On the other hand, one must accept a dividend payment and pay the tax. Thus, Teledyne stockholders who want cash can sell some of their shares, and those who do not need cash can simply retain their stock and defer their tax liabilities.

3. A qualitative advantage advanced by market practitioners is that repurchase can often remove a large block of stock which is overhanging the market and keeping the price per share down.

Advantages of Repurchases from Management's Viewpoint

1. As noted earlier, dividends are "sticky" in the short run because managements are reluctant to raise dividends if the new dividend cannot be maintained in the future—because of signaling effects, managements dislike cutting cash dividends. Hence, if the excess cash flow is thought to be only *temporary*, management may prefer to make the distribution in the form of a share repurchase rather than to declare a cash dividend which they believe cannot be maintained.

2. Repurchased stock can be used for acquisitions or released when stock options are exercised, when convertibles are converted, or when warrants are exercised. Discussions with financial managers indicate that they often like to use repurchased stock rather than newly issued stock for these purposes so as to avoid dilution of per share earnings. To illustrate the first two points, in March 1986 Rockwell International, a major manufacturer of aerospace, automotive, and electronic products, announced a $500 million stock repurchase program that reduced its common shares outstanding by about 8 percent. This buyback was financed from earnings from B1-B bomber sales, a source which will not continue indefinitely. Further, some analysts speculated that the repurchased stock will eventually be used to acquire another firm.

3. Repurchases are the only practical alternative when management has decided to undertake a major restructuring, such as a large asset sale, a substantial increase in the debt ratio, or a combination of the two. For example, at one time American

Standard (a major plumbing supply company) had virtually no long-term debt outstanding. The company decided that its optimal capital structure called for the use of considerably more debt, but even if it had financed only with debt, it would have taken years to get the debt ratio up to the new target. What should the company do? It decided to sell long-term debt and to use the proceeds to repurchase its common stock, thus producing an instantaneous change in its capital structure.

4. Treasury stock can be resold in the open market if the firm needs additional funds.[14]

Disadvantages of Repurchases from the Stockholder's Viewpoint

1. The price of the stock might benefit more from cash dividends than from repurchases, because cash dividends are generally thought to be relatively dependable, but repurchases are not. Further, if a firm announces a regular, dependable repurchase program, the improper accumulation tax would become more of a threat. Although Teledyne has apparently had no problems in this regard, Teledyne's repurchases are irregular, which makes a difference.

2. The *selling* stockholders may not be fully aware of all the implications of a repurchase, or they may not have all the pertinent information about the corporation's present and future activities. However, firms generally announce a repurchase program before embarking on it to avoid potential lawsuits from selling stockholders.

3. The corporation may pay too high a price for the repurchased stock, to the disadvantage of remaining stockholders. If the shares are inactively traded, and if the firm seeks to acquire a relatively large amount of its own stock, the price may be bid above its equilibrium price. If so, the price will fall after the firm ceases its repurchase operations.

Disadvantages of Repurchases from Management's Viewpoint

1. Some people have argued that firms which repurchase substantial amounts of stock often have poorer growth rates and fewer good investment opportunities than firms which do not engage in repurchases. If the announcement of a repurchase program is taken as a signal that the firm has especially unfavorable growth opportunities, then there could be an adverse impact on the price of its stock.

---

[14]Another interesting use of stock repurchases was St. Joe Minerals' strategy of repurchasing its own stock to thwart an attempted takeover. Seagram Company was attempting to acquire a controlling interest in St. Joe through a tender offer of $45 a share. St. Joe's management countered with a tender offer of its own for seven million shares at $60 per share, to be financed by the sale of several divisions plus borrowings. Similarly, Texaco recently bought back over $1 billion of its stock from the Bass Brothers of Texas, who were rumored to be planning a takeover of Texaco. Texaco paid the Bass brothers a premium of about 40 percent over the market price. Some Texaco stockholders sued management, arguing that Texaco's management was giving away corporate assets in order to preserve their own jobs. This type of payment is called "greenmail."

However, if the firm does not have good investment opportunities, then it would probably be better for management to distribute funds to investors, who could then redeploy the funds elsewhere in the market. There is, in our view, little empirical support for the position that stockholders dislike repurchases.[15]

2. Repurchases might involve some risk from a legal standpoint. If the Internal Revenue Service could establish that the repurchases were primarily for the avoidance of taxes on dividends, then penalties could be imposed on the firm under the improper accumulation of earnings provision of the Tax Code. Such actions have been brought against privately held companies, but we know of no case involving a publicly owned firm, even though some firms have retired over one-half of their outstanding stock.

3. The SEC could raise questions if it appears that the firm may be manipulating the price of its shares. This factor, in particular, keeps firms from doing much repurchasing if they plan offerings of other types of securities in the near future, or if they contemplate merger negotiations where their stock would be exchanged for that of the acquired company.

Conclusions on Stock Repurchases

When all the pros and cons on stock repurchases are totaled, where do we stand? Our conclusions may be summarized as follows:

1. Repurchases on a regular, systematic, dependable basis may not be feasible because of uncertainties both about the tax treatment of such a program and about such factors as the market price of the shares, how many shares would be tendered, and so forth.

2. However, repurchases do offer investors tax deferral advantages over dividends, so this procedure should be given careful consideration on the basis of the firm's unique situation.

3. Repurchases can be especially valuable to a firm that is restructuring and consequently wants to significantly increase its debt ratio within a short period or else to dispose of cash generated from the sale of assets.

STOCK DIVIDENDS AND STOCK SPLITS

Stock dividends and stock splits are related to the firm's cash dividend policy. The rationale for stock dividends and splits can best be explained through an example; we will use the Nashville Company, a large multimedia entertainment company specializing in country and western music, in our illustrations.

Nashville's markets are expanding, and as the company continues to grow and to retain earnings, its book value per share will also grow. More important, its

---

[15]In fact, there is some evidence that the stocks of companies which repurchased large quantities of their common stock in the 10 years from 1974 through 1983 had above-average stock price appreciation. See "Beating the Market By Buying Back Stock," *Fortune*, April 29, 1985, 42-48.

earnings per share and market price per share will also rise. The company began its life with only a few thousand shares outstanding. After some years of growth, each share had a very high EPS and DPS. When a "normal" P/E ratio was applied to the stock, the derived market price was so high that few people could afford to buy a "round lot" of 100 shares. This limited the demand for the stock, thus keeping the total market value of the firm below what it would have been if more shares, at lower prices, were outstanding. To correct this situation, Nashville "split its stock" as described next.

Stock Splits

Although there is little empirical evidence to support the contention, there is nevertheless a widespread belief in financial circles that an *optimal price range* exists for stocks. "Optimal" means that if the price is in this range, the price/earnings ratio, and hence the value of the firm, will be maximized. Many observers, including Nashville's management, believe that the best range for most New York Stock Exchange stocks is from $20 to $80 per share. Companies whose shares are owned largely by institutions tend to move toward the high end of the range, while those owned largely by individuals, such as the public utilities, generally operate in the lower end of the range. Companies with average institutional ownership, like Nashville Company, cluster in the $30 to $50 range. Accordingly, if the price of Nashville's stock rose to $80, management would probably declare a two-for-one stock split, thus doubling the number of shares outstanding, halving the earnings and dividends per share, and thereby lowering the price of the stock. Each stockholder would have more shares, but each share would be worth less. If the post-split price were $40, Nashville's stockholders would be exactly as well off as they were before the split. If the price of the stock were to stabilize above $40, stockholders would be better off. Stock splits can be of any size. For example, the stock could be split two-for-one, three-for-one, 1.5-for-one, or in any other way.[16]

Stock splits can also be used to increase the "float," or the number of shares held by outsiders. For example, Care Corporation, a nursing home operator, recently declared a 4-for-1 split, in large part because about 60 percent of the company's 500,000 shares outstanding were controlled by insiders and relatives, leaving only 200,000 shares for trading by others. The split increased the float to 800,000 which, according to the firm's management, increased the trading activity in the stock. Note, though, that academic studies have suggested that stock splits actually lower trading volume when measured on a proportional basis, primarily because brokerage commissions are increased.[17]

---

[16]*Reverse splits*, which reduce the shares outstanding, can even be used. For example, a company whose stock sells for $5 might employ a one-for-five reverse split, exchanging one new share for five old shares and raising the value of the shares to about $25, which is within the "acceptable" range. LTV Corporation did this after several years of losses had driven its stock price down below the optimal range.

[17]Commissions are generally higher on trades of, say, 75 shares at $10 per share than on a trade of 10 shares at $75 a share, even though the dollar value of the trades is the same. For a further discussion of the effects of stock splits on market liquidity, see Thomas E. Copeland, "Liquidity Changes Following Stock Splits," *Journal of Finance*, March 1979, 115-141.

Stock Dividends

Stock dividends are similar to stock splits in that they divide the pie into smaller slices without affecting the fundamental position of the current stockholders. On a 5 percent stock dividend, the holder of 100 shares would receive an additional five shares (without cost); on a 20 percent stock dividend, the same holder would receive 20 new shares; and so on. Again, the total number of shares is increased, so earnings, dividends, and price per share all decline.

If a firm wants to reduce the price of its stock, should a stock split or a stock dividend be used? Stock splits are generally used after a sharp price run-up, when a large price reduction is sought. Stock dividends are frequently used on a regular annual basis to keep the stock price more or less constrained. For example, if a firm's earnings and dividends are growing at about 10 percent per year, the price would tend to go up at about that same rate, and the price would soon be outside the desired trading range. For this company, a 10 percent annual stock dividend would maintain the stock price within the optimal trading range.

Although the economic effects of stock splits and stock dividends are virtually identical, accountants treat them somewhat differently. On a two-for-one split, the shares outstanding are doubled, and the stock's par value is halved. This treatment is shown in Table 11-2, Section 2, for Nashville Company, using a pro forma 1987 balance sheet.

With a stock dividend, the par value is not reduced, but an accounting entry is made transferring capital from the retained earnings account to the common stock and paid-in capital accounts. The transfer from retained earnings is calculated as follows:

$$\begin{pmatrix} \text{Dollars} \\ \text{transferred from} \\ \text{retained} \\ \text{earnings} \end{pmatrix} = \begin{pmatrix} \text{Number} \\ \text{of shares} \\ \text{outstanding} \end{pmatrix} \begin{pmatrix} \text{Percentage} \\ \text{of the} \\ \text{stock dividend} \end{pmatrix} \begin{pmatrix} \text{Market} \\ \text{price of} \\ \text{the stock} \end{pmatrix}.$$

For example, if Nashville, which had 5 million shares outstanding selling at $80 each, declared a 20 percent stock dividend, the transfer would be

$$\text{Dollars transferred} = (5 \text{ million})(0.2)(\$80) = \$80,000,000.$$

As shown in Section 3 of Table 11-2, $1 million of this $80 million transfer would be added to the common stock account and $79 million to the additional paid-in capital account. The retained earnings account would be reduced from $155 to $75 million.[18]

---

[18]Note that Nashville could not pay a stock dividend that exceeded 38.75 percent; a stock dividend of that percentage would exhaust the retained earnings. Thus, a firm's ability to declare stock dividends is constrained by the amount of its retained earnings. Of course, if Nashville had wanted to pay a 50 percent stock dividend, it could just switch to a 1.5-for-1 stock split and accomplish the same objective.

Table 11-2
Nashville Company:
Stockholders' Equity Accounts, Pro Forma 12/31/87

1. Before a stock split or a stock dividend

Common stock (6 million shares authorized, 5 million outstanding, $1 par)	$ 5,000,000
Additional paid-in capital	10,000,000
Retained earnings	155,000,000
Total common stockholders' equity	$170,000,000

2. After a two-for-one stock split

Common stock (12 million shares authorized, 10 million outstanding, $0.50 par)	$ 5,000,000
Additional paid-in capital	10,000,000
Retained earnings	155,000,000
Total common stockholders' equity	$170,000,000

3. After a 20 percent stock dividend

Common stock (6 million shares authorized, 6 million outstanding, $1 par)[a]	$ 6,000,000
Additional paid-in capital[b]	89,000,000
Retained earnings[b]	75,000,000
Total common stockholders' equity	$170,000,000

[a]Shares outstanding are increased by 20 percent, from 5 million to 6 million.
[b]A transfer equal to the market value of the new shares is made from the retained earnings account to the additional paid-in capital and common stock accounts: Transfer = (1 million shares)($80) = $80 million. Of this $80 million, (1 million shares)($1 par) = $1 million goes to common stock and $79 million to paid-in capital.

Price Effects

If a company splits its stock or declares a stock dividend, will this action increase the market value of its stock? Several empirical studies have sought to answer this question, and in general here are their findings:[19]

1. On average, the price of a company's stock rises shortly after it announces a stock split or dividend.

2. However, these price increases appear to be more the result of the fact that investors take stock splits/dividends as signals of higher earnings and dividends than of a desire for stock dividends/splits per se. Since only those companies whose

---

[19]See Eugene F. Fama, Lawrence Fisher, Michael C. Jensen, and Richard Roll, "The Adjustment of Stock Prices to New Information," *International Economic Review*, February 1969, 1-21; Mark S. Grinblatt, Ronald W. Masulis, and Sheridan Titman, "The Valuation Effects of Stock Splits and Stock Dividends," *Journal of Financial Economics*, December 1984, 461-490; C. Austin Barker, "Evaluation of Stock Dividends," *Harvard Business Review*, July-August 1958, 99-114; and Copeland op. cit.

managements think things look good tend to use stock splits/dividends, the announcement of a stock split is taken as a signal that earnings and cash dividends are likely to rise. Thus, the price increases that are associated with stock splits/dividends are the result of signals of favorable prospects for earnings and dividends, not with a like of stock splits/dividends per se.

3. It has been observed that if a company announces a stock split or dividend, its price will tend to rise. However, if during the coming months it does not announce earnings and dividends above the levels expected before the split/stock dividend, then its stock price will drop back to the earlier level.

4. As we noted earlier, brokerage commissions are higher in percentage terms on lower priced stocks. This means that it is more expensive to trade low-priced than high-priced stocks, and this in turn means that stock splits reduce the liquidity of a company's shares. This evidence suggests that stock splits/dividends are actually harmful.

What do we conclude from all this? From a pure economic standpoint, stock dividends and splits are just additional pieces of paper. However, they do provide management with a relatively low cost way of signaling that the firm's prospects look good. Further, we should note that since no large, publicly owned stocks sell at prices above several hundred dollars, we simply do not know what the effect would be if IBM, Xerox, Hewlett-Packard, and other highly successful firms had never split their stock and consequently sold at prices in the thousands or even tens of thousands of dollars. All in all, it probably makes sense to employ stock dividends/splits when a firm's prospects are favorable, especially if the price of its stock has gone beyond the normal trading range.

SUMMARY

Dividend policy reflects the firm's decision to pay out earnings versus retaining them for reinvestment in the firm. Any change in dividend policy has both favorable and unfavorable effects on the price of the firm's stock: Higher dividends mean higher near-term cash flows to investors, which is good, but lower future growth, which is bad. The optimal dividend policy balances these opposing forces and maximizes the price of the stock.

We first identified three dividend theories: (1) *dividend irrelevance*, (2) "*bird-in-the-hand*", and (3) *tax differential*. We then described a number of factors that affect dividend policy, including the following: *legal constraints* such as bond indenture provisions, the firm's *investment opportunities*, the *availability and cost of funds from other sources* (new stock and debt), *stockholders' desire for current income*, and the *information effect* of dividend changes. Because of the large number of factors that influence dividend policy, and also because the relative importance of these factors changes over time and across companies, it is impossible to develop a precise, generalized model for use in establishing dividend policy.

The *residual dividend policy* is used by most firms to set a long-run target payout, but most firms set their actual dividends either (1) as a *stable or contin-*

uously increasing dollar dividend per share or (2) as a *low regular dividend plus extras* that depends on annual earnings. Also, we noted that many firms today are using *dividend reinvestment plans* to help stockholders reinvest dividends at minimal brokerage costs, and some firms use stock repurchase plans in lieu of more cash dividends.

We also discussed *stock repurchases*, both as an element in corporate restructuring programs and also as an alternative to cash dividends. Repurchases have certain advantages—especially tax deferred—over dividends, but repurchases also have disadvantages. The volume of repurchase activity has been quite high in recent years, and barring adverse changes in our tax laws, this activity should continue or even increase.

Stock splits and *stock dividends* were also discussed. Our conclusion was that these actions may be beneficial if the firm's stock price is quite high, but otherwise they have little effect on the value of the firm.

Questions and Problems

11-1 (Dividend theories) Modigliani and Miller, on the one hand, and Gordon and Lintner, on the other, have expressed strong views regarding the effect of dividend policy on a firm's cost of capital and value.

    a. In essence, what are the MM and the GL views regarding the effect of dividend policy on cost of capital and value? Illustrate your answer with a graph.

    b. How does the tax differential model differ from the views of MM and GL?

    c. According to the text, which position (MM, GL, or tax differential) has received statistical confirmation from empirical tests?

    d. How could MM use the information content, or signaling, hypothesis to counter their opponents' arguments? If you were debating MM, how would you counter them?

    e. How could MM use the clientele effect concept to counter their opponents' arguments? If you were debating MM, how would you counter them?

11-2 (Residual dividend policy) One position expressed in the literature is that firms should set their dividends as a residual, after using income to support new investment.

    a. Explain what a residual dividend policy implies, illustrating your answer with a graph showing how different conditions could lead to different dividend payout ratios.

    b. Could the residual dividend policy be consistent with (1) a constant growth rate policy, (2) a constant payout policy, and/or (3) a low-regular-plus-extras policy? Explain.

    c. In Chapters 5 and 6, we considered the relationship between capital structure and the cost of capital. If the k_a = WACC versus debt ratio plot were shaped like a sharp V, would this have a different implication for the importance of setting dividends according to the residual policy than if the ratio relationship were shaped like a shallow bowl (or a U)?

    d. Companies A and B both have IOS schedules which intersect their MCC schedules at a point which, under the residual policy, calls for a 20 percent payout. In both cases, a 20 percent payout would require a cut in the annual dividend from $2 to $1. One company cut its dividend and accepted all projects, while the other did not cut its dividend and accepted less than the optimal number of projects. One company had a relatively steep IOS curve, while the other had a relatively flat IOS. Explain which company had the steep, and which the flat, IOS.

11-3 (Stock dividends and splits) More NYSE companies had stock dividends and stock splits during 1983 and 1984 than ever before. What events in these years could have made stock splits and dividends so popular? Explain the rationale that a financial vice president might give the board of directors to support a stock split/dividend recommendation.

11-4 (Residual dividend policy) Berry Manufacturing Corporation (BMC) has an all-equity capital structure which includes no preferred stock. It has 200,000 shares of $2 par value common stock outstanding.

When BMC's founder, who was also its research director and most successful inventor, died unexpectedly in late 1986, BMC was left suddenly and permanently with materially lower growth expectations and relatively few attractive new investment opportunities. Unfortunately, there was no way to replace the founder's contributions to the firm. Previously, BMC had found it necessary to plow back most of its earnings to finance growth, which has been averaging 12 percent per year. Future growth at a 5 percent rate is considered realistic, but that level would call for an increase in the dividend payout. Further, it now appears that new investment projects with at least the 14 percent rate of return required by BMC's stockholders ($k_s = 14\%$) would amount to only $800,000 for 1987 in comparison to a projected $2,000,000 of net income after taxes. If the existing 20 percent dividend payout were continued, retained earnings would be $1.6 million in 1987, but as noted, investments which yield the 14 percent cost of capital amount to only $800,000.

The one encouraging thing is that the high earnings from existing assets are expected to continue and net income of $2 million is still expected for 1987. Given the dramatically changed circumstances, BMC's management is reviewing the firm's dividend policy.

a. Assuming that the acceptable 1987 investment projects would be financed entirely by earnings retained during the year, calculate DPS in 1987 assuming BMC uses the residual payment policy.

b. What payout ratio does this imply for 1987?

c. If the increased payout ratio is maintained for the foreseeable future, what should be the present intrinsic value of the common stock? How does this compare with the price that should have prevailed under the assumptions existing just prior to the news about the death of the founder? If the two values of $\hat{P}_0$ are different, comment on why.

d. What are the implications of continuing the 20 percent payout? Assume that if this payout is maintained then the average rate of return on the retained earnings will be 7.5 percent and the new growth rate will be

$$g = (1.0 - \text{Payout ratio})(\text{ROE})$$
$$= (1.0 - 0.2)(7.5\%) = (0.8)(7.5\%) = 6.0\%.$$

11-5 (Stock dividends) The board of directors of Seaton Corporation declared a 4 percent stock dividend and a cash dividend of $0.40 per share in December 1986. The cash dividend will be paid on old shares *plus* shares received in the stock dividend. Construct a pro forma balance sheet that shows the effect of these actions; use one new balance sheet that incorporates both actions. The stock is selling for $25 per share. A condensed version of the Seaton's balance sheet as of December 31, 1986, before the dividends, follows (in millions of dollars):

Cash	$ 50	Debt	$1,000
Other assets	1,950	Common stock (60 million shares authorized, 50 million shares outstanding, $1 par)	50
		Paid-in capital	200
		Retained earnings	750
Total assets	$2,000	Total claims	$2,000

11-6 (Dividend policy and capital structure) The Tennessee Bourbon Company (TBC) has for many years enjoyed a moderate but stable growth in sales and earnings. However, bourbon consumption has been falling recently, primarily because of an increasing use of lighter alcoholic beverages such as vodka and wines. Anticipating further declines in sales for the future, TBC's management hopes eventually to move almost entirely out of the liquor business and into a newly developed, diversified product line in growth-oriented industries. The company is especially interested in the prospects for pollution-control devices, because its research department has already done much work in this area. Right now the company estimates that an investment of $24 million is necessary to purchase new facilities and to begin operations on these products, but the investment could be earning a return of about 18 percent within a short time. The only other available investment opportunity totals $9.6 million, is expected to return about 11.2 percent, and is indivisible, that is, it must be accepted in its entirety or else be rejected.

The company is expected to pay a $2.00 dividend on its 7 million outstanding shares, the same as its dividend last year. The directors might, however, change the dividend if there are good reasons for doing so. Net income for the year is expected to be $22.5 million; the common stock is currently selling for $45; the firm's target debt ratio (debt/assets ratio) is 45 percent; and its tax rate is 34 percent. The costs of various forms of financing are listed below:

New bonds, $k_d = 11\%$. This is a before-tax rate.

New common stock sold at $45 per share will net $41.

Required rate of return on retained earnings, $k_s = 14\%$.

a. Calculate TBC's expected payout ratio, the break point where its MCC schedule rises, and its marginal cost of capital above and below the point of exhaustion of retained earnings at the current payout. (Hint: k_s is given, and D_1/P_0 can be found. Then, knowing k_s and D_1/P_0, and assuming constant growth, g can be determined.)
b. How large should TBC's capital budget be for the year?
c. What is an appropriate dividend policy for the firm? How should the capital budget be financed?
d. How might risk factors influence TBC's cost of capital, capital structure, and dividend policy?
e. What assumptions, if any, do your answers to the above make about investors' preferences for dividends versus capital gains, that is, their preferences regarding the D_1/P_0 and g components of k_s?
(Do Part f only if you are using the computerized diskette.)
f. Assume that TBC's management is considering a change in its capital structure to include more debt, and thus it would like to analyze the effects of an increase

in the debt ratio to 60 percent. However, the treasurer believes that such a move would cause lenders to increase the required rate of return on new bonds to 12 percent and k_s would rise to 14.5 percent. How would this change affect the optimal capital budget? If k_s rose to 16 percent, would the low-return project be acceptable? Would the project selection be affected if the dividend were reduced to $1.25 from $2.00, still assuming k_s = 16 percent?

11-7 **(Stock repurchases)** Goldware, Inc., has earnings this year of $16.5 million, 50 percent of which is required to take advantage of the firm's excellent investment opportunities. The firm has 2,062,500 shares outstanding, selling currently at $32 per share. Greg Beaumont, a major stockholder (187,500 shares), has expressed displeasure with a great deal of managerial policy. Management has approached him about selling his holdings back to the firm, and he has expressed a willingness to do this at a price of $32 a share. Assuming that the market uses a constant P/E ratio of 4 in valuing the stock, should the firm buy Beaumont's shares? Assume that dividends will not be paid on Beaumont's shares if they are repurchased. (Hint: Calculate the ex-dividend price of the stock with and without the repurchase, and add to these values the dividends received to determine the remaining stockholders' value per share.)

Selected Additional References and Cases

Dividend policy has been studied extensively by academicians. The first major academic work, and still a classic that we recommend highly, is Lintner's analysis of the way corporations actually set their dividend payment policies:

Lintner, John, "Distribution of Incomes of Corporations among Dividends, Retained Earnings, and Taxes," *American Economic Review*, May 1956, 97-113.

The effects of dividend policy on stock prices and capital costs have been examined by many researchers. The classic theoretical argument that dividend policy is important, and that stockholders like dividends, was set forth by Gordon, while Miller and Modigliani (MM) developed the notion that dividend policy is not important. Many researchers have extended both Gordon's and MM's theoretical arguments, and have attempted to test the effects of dividend policy in a variety of ways. Although statistical problems have precluded definitive conclusions, the following articles, among others, have helped to clarify the issues:

Brennan, Michael, "Taxes, Market Valuation, and Corporate Financial Policy," *National Tax Journal*, Spring 1975, 417-427.

Hayes, Linda S., "Fresh Evidence That Dividends Don't Matter," *Fortune*, May 4, 1981, 351-354.

Lewellen, Wilbur G., Kenneth L. Stanley, Ronald C. Lease, and Gary G. Schlarbaum, "Some Direct Evidence on the Dividend Clientele Phenomenon," *Journal of Finance*, December 1978, 1385-1399.

Mukherjee, Tarun, and Larry M. Austin, "An Empirical Investigation of Small Bank Stock Valuation and Dividend Policy," *Financial Management*, Spring 1980, 27-31.

On stock dividends and stock splits, see

Baker, H. Kent, and Patricia L. Gallagher, "Management's View of Stock Splits," *Financial Management*, Summer 1980, 73-77.

Copeland, Thomas E., "Liquidity Changes Following Stock Splits," *Journal of Finance*, March 1979, 115-141.

On repurchases, see

Finnerty, Joseph E., "Corporate Stock Issue and Repurchase," *Financial Management*, Autumn 1975, 62-71.

Stewart, Samuel S., Jr., "Should a Corporation Repurchase Its Own Stock?" *Journal of Finance*, June 1976, 911-921.

Woolridge, J. Randall, and Donald R. Chambers, "Reverse Splits and Shareholder Wealth," *Financial Management*, Autumn 1983, 5-15.

For a survey of managers' views on dividend policy, see

Baker, H. Kent, Gail E. Farrelly, and Richard B. Edelman, "A Survey of Management Views on Dividend Policy," *Financial Management*, Autumn 1985, 78-84.

Other pertinent articles include

Brealey, Richard A., "Does Dividend Policy Matter?" *Midland Corporate Finance Journal*, Spring 1983, 17-25.

Woolridge, J. Randall, and Chinmoy Gosh, "Dividend Cuts: Do They Always Signal Bad News?" *Midland Corporate Finance Journal*, Summer 1985, 20-32.

The following cases from the Crum-Brigham casebook focus on the issues contained in this chapter:

Case 34, "Hansen Mineral Resources," which emphasizes the effect of dividend policy on stock prices.

Case 35, "Warner Body Works," which deals with virtually all the aspects of dividend policy.

The Harrington casebook contains the following applicable case:

"New Hampshire Savings Bank Corporation," which illustrates the traditional arguments set forth as the board of directors attempt to establish the company's dividend policy.

 11A

PROOF OF MILLER AND MODIGLIANI'S DIVIDEND IRRELEVANCE THEORY

Under the assumptions set forth in Chapter 11, MM developed an algebraic proof for their proposition that the value of a firm is independent of its dividend policy. That proof is presented in this appendix. Here are the terms used in the proof:

P_0 = stock price at $t = 0$.

P_1 = stock price at $t = 1$.

D_1 = dividend per share at $t = 1$.

 n = number of shares outstanding at $t = 0$.

m = number of new shares issued at $t = 1$.

 I = total new investment during Period 1

X = net income during Period 1

k_s = cost of retained earnings = cost of new equity (assumed to be constant).

Now, looking only at a one-period dividend decision, the price of the stock at the beginning of the period, P_0, is equal to the present value of the dividend paid at the end of the period, D_1, plus the present value of the stock price at the end of the period, P_1:

$$P_0 = \frac{D_1 + P_1}{(1 + k_s)}. \qquad \text{(11A-1)}$$

For simplicity, MM assume that the firm is all-equity financed, so we can obtain the firm's total market value by multiplying both sides of the equation by n, the shares outstanding at $t = 0$:

$$nP_0 = \frac{nD_1 + nP_1}{(1 + k_s)}. \tag{11A-2}$$

Now assume that m additional shares will be sold at $t = 1$ at a price P_1, bringing in mP_1 dollars. The m shares of new stock will not receive the D_1 dividend. We can add $+mP_1$ and $-mP_1$ to the numerator of Equation 11A-2 without changing its value:

$$nP_0 = \frac{nD_1 + nP_1 + mP_1 - mP_1}{(1 + k_s)}.$$

Then, rearranging terms, we obtain Equation 11A-2a:

$$nP_0 = \frac{nD_1 + (n + m)P_1 - mP_1}{(1 + k_s)}. \tag{11A-2a}$$

Equation 11A-2a shows that the value of the firm at $t = 0$ is equal to the present value of dividends to be paid at $t = 1$, plus the total value of the stock at $t = 1$, minus the value at $t = 1$ of the stock that will belong to the new stockholders.

If no debt is used, the sources and uses of funds at $t = 1$ are as follows:

$$\text{Sources of funds} = \text{Uses of funds}.$$

$$mP_1 + X = I + nD_1. \tag{11A-3}$$

Thus, the sources of funds are the money raised by selling stock plus the net income for the period, and the uses of these funds are for new investment and the dividend payment to the original shareholders.

Rearranging Equation 11A-3, we obtain this expression:

$$mP_1 = I + nD_1 - X. \tag{11A-3a}$$

Now, if we substitute Equation 11A-3a into Equation 11A-2a, we produce Equation 11A-4

$$nP_0 = \frac{nD_1 + (n + m)P_1 - (I + nD_1 - X)}{(1 + k_s)}$$

$$= \frac{(n + m)P_1 - I + X}{(1 + k_s)}, \tag{11A-4}$$

which is MM's basic expression for the current $(t = 0)$ value of the firm. Notice that the firm's value, nP_0, does not depend directly on the next period's dividend, for there is no D_1 term in Equation 11A-4. Thus, under the MM assumptions, the stock price is not affected by the firm's dividend decision—any gain in the current stock price which results from an increase in dividends is exactly offset by a decrease in the current price due to having to sell stock to finance new investment. Therefore, shareholders can receive their cash flows from the firm either as dividends or as capital gains (end-of-period price), and under the MM assumptions, the shareholder should be indifferent to the two alternatives.

MM extended their model to a multi-period setting by looking at subsequent dividend decisions. The results remain the same—under their assumptions, dividends are irrelevant.

12

COMMON AND PREFERRED STOCK FINANCING

When a firm's requirements for additional equity cannot be met by retained earnings, the company must sell new stock. In this chapter, we discuss (1) the market for common stock, (2) the decision to go public, (3) the decision to list a stock on an exchange, (4) procedures for selling new common stock, (5) preferred stock financing, and (6) the investment banking process.

THE MARKET FOR COMMON STOCK

Some companies are so small that their common stock is not actively traded—it is owned by only a few people, usually the companies' managers. Such companies are said to be *privately held*, or *closely held*, and the stock is said to be *closely held stock*. On the other hand, the stocks of most larger companies are owned by many investors, most of whom are not active in management. Such companies are said to be *publicly owned*, and their stock is said to be *publicly held stock*.

The stocks of smaller publicly owned firms are not listed on an exchange; they trade in the *over-the-counter (OTC)* market. The companies and their stocks are said to be *unlisted*. However, most larger publicly owned companies apply for listing on an exchange. These companies and their stocks are said to be *listed*. As a general rule, companies are first listed on a regional exchange, such as the Pacific Coast or Midwest, then they move up to the American (AMEX), and finally, if they grow large enough, to the "Big Board," the New York Stock Exchange (NYSE). Thousands of stocks are traded in the OTC market, but in terms of market value of both outstanding and daily transactions, the NYSE dominates, with about 60 percent of the business. However, as we discuss below, electronic hook-ups between OTC market participants are giving them many of the advantages formerly enjoyed by only the NYSE, so the OTC market has been growing more rapidly than the exchanges in recent years.

Institutional investors such as pension trusts, insurance companies, and mutual funds own about 35 percent of all common stocks. However, the institutions buy and sell relatively actively, so they account for about 75 percent of all transactions. Thus, the institutions have a heavy influence on the prices of individual stocks—in a real sense, institutional investors determine the price levels of individual stocks, and hence they set the tone of the market.

We can classify stock market transactions into three distinct categories:

1. New Public Offerings by Privately Held Firms: The Primary Market. In 1986, Microsoft Corporation, a major developer of computer software (including the operating system for the IBM PC line) decided to sell about $50 million of stock to raise capital needed for a major expansion program. At the time, Microsoft was owned by its management and a handful of private investors. Microsoft's action is defined as *going public*—whenever stock in a closely held corporation is offered to the public for the first time, the company is said to be going public. The market for stock that is in the process of going public is often called the *new issue market*.

2. Additional Shares Sold by Established, Publicly Owned Companies: The Primary Market. In 1986, the Boston Edison Company sold 2 million new shares at about $50 per share, netting about $100 million in new equity capital. At the time of the issue, the firm had over 16 million common shares outstanding and traded on the NYSE. Boston Edison's sale was a primary market offering, but not a new issue market offering.

3. Outstanding Shares of Established, Publicly Owned Companies: The Secondary Market. If the owner of 100 shares of AT&T sells his or her stock, the trade is said to have occurred in the *secondary market*. Thus, the market for outstanding shares, or *used shares*, is defined as the secondary market. Over 400 million shares of AT&T were bought and sold on the NYSE in 1985, and AT&T did not receive a dime from these transactions.

Firms can go public without raising any additional capital. For example, in its early days, the Ford Motor Company was owned exclusively by the Ford family. When Henry Ford died, he left a substantial part of his stock to the Ford Foundation. When the Foundation later sold some of this stock to the general public, the Ford Motor Company went public, even though the company raised no capital in the transaction.

THE DECISION TO GO PUBLIC

Most businesses begin life as proprietorships or partnerships and then, as the more successful ones grow, at some point they find it desirable to convert into corporations. Initially, these new corporations' stocks are generally owned by the firm's officers, key employees, and/or a very few investors who are not actively involved in management. However, if growth continues, at some point the company may decide to go public. As described earlier, Microsoft Corporation decided to take this step in 1986. The advantages and disadvantages of public ownership are discussed next.

Advantages of Going Public

1. Permits Diversification. As a company grows and becomes more valuable, its founders often have most of their wealth tied up in the company. By selling some of their stock in a public offering, they can diversify their holdings, thereby reducing somewhat the riskiness of their personal portfolios.

2. Increases Liquidity. The stock of a closely held firm is illiquid: it has no ready market. If one of the holders wants to sell some shares to raise cash, it is hard to find a ready buyer, and even if a buyer is located, there is no established price on which to base the transaction. These problems do not exist with publicly owned firms.

3. Facilitates Raising New Corporate Cash. If a privately held company wants to raise cash by a sale of new stock, it must either go to its existing owners, who may either not have any money or not want to put any more eggs in this particular basket, or shop around for wealthy investors. However, it is usually quite difficult to get outsiders to put money into a closely held company, because if the outsiders do not have voting control (over 50 percent of the stock), the inside stockholders/managers can run roughshod over them. The insiders can pay or not pay dividends, pay themselves exorbitant salaries, have private deals with the company, and so on. For example, the president might buy a warehouse and lease it to the company at a high rental, get the use of a Rolls Royce, and enjoy frequent all-the-frills travel to conventions. The insiders can even keep the outsiders from knowing the company's actual earnings, or its real worth. There are not many positions more vulnerable than that of an outside stockholder in a closely held company, and for this reason, it is hard for closely held companies to raise new equity capital. Going public, which brings with it both public disclosure of information and regulation by the Securities and Exchange Commission (SEC), greatly reduces these problems, making people more willing to invest in the company, and thus helping the firm to raise capital.

4. Establishes a Value for the Firm. For a number of reasons, it is often useful to establish a firm's value in the marketplace. For one thing, when the owner of a privately owned business dies, state and federal inheritance tax appraisers must set a value on the company for estate tax purposes. Often, these appraisers set too high a value, which creates an obvious problem. However, a company that is publicly owned has its value established, with little room for argument. Similarly, if a company wants to give incentive stock options to key employees, it is useful to know the exact value of those options. Also, for liquidity reasons employees much prefer to own stock, or options on stock, that is publicly traded.

Disadvantages of Going Public

1. Cost of Reporting. A publicly owned company must file quarterly and annual reports with the SEC and/or with various state agencies. These reports can be costly, especially for small firms.

2. Disclosure. Management may not like the idea of reporting operating data, because such data will then be available to competitors. Similarly, the owners of the company may not want people to know their net worth, and since a publicly owned company must disclose the number of shares owned by its officers, directors, and major stockholders, it is easy enough for anyone to multiply shares held by price per share to estimate the net worth of the insiders.

3. Self-Dealings. The owners/managers of closely held companies have many opportunities for various types of questionable but legal self-dealings, including the payment of high salaries, nepotism, personal transactions with the business (such as a leasing arrangement), and not-truly-necessary fringe benefits. Such self-dealings, which are often designed to minimize taxes, are much harder to arrange if a company is publicly owned.

4. Inactive Market/Low Price. If the firm is very small, and if its shares are not traded with much frequency, its stock will not really be liquid, and the market price may not be representative of the stock's true value. Security analysts and stockbrokers simply will not follow the stock, because there will just not be enough trading activity to generate enough sales commissions to cover the costs of following the stock.

5. Control. Because of the dramatic increase in tender offers and proxy fights in the 1980s, the managers of publicly owned firms who do not have voting control must be concerned about maintaining control. Further, there is pressure on such managers to produce annual earnings gains, even when it might be in the shareholders' best long-term interests to adopt a strategy that might penalize short-run earnings but benefit earnings in future years. These factors have led a number of public companies to "go private" in "leveraged buyout" deals where the managers borrow the money to buy out the nonmanagement stockholders.

Conclusions on Going Public

It should be obvious from this discussion that there are no hard-and-fast rules regarding if or when a company should go public. This is an individual decision that should be made on the basis of the company's and its stockholders' own unique circumstances.

If a company does decide to go public, either by the sale of newly issued stock to raise new capital or by the sale of stock by the current owners, the key issue is setting the price at which shares will be offered to the public. The company and its current owners want to set the price as high as possible—the higher the offering price, the smaller the fraction of the company the current owners will have to give up to obtain any specified amount of money. On the other hand, potential buyers will want the price set as low as possible.

THE DECISION TO LIST

The decision to go public is truly a milestone in a company's life—it marks a major transition in the relationship between the firm and its owners. The decision to list the stock and have it trade on an exchange rather than in the over-the-counter market, on the other hand, is not a major event. The company will have to file a few new reports with an exchange and to abide by the rules of the exchange; stockholders will generally purchase or sell shares through a stockbroker who acts as an *agent* rather than a *dealer*; and the stock's price will be quoted in the newspaper under a stock exchange rather than in the over-the-counter section. These are not very significant differences.

In order to have its stock listed, a company must apply to an exchange, pay a relatively small fee, and meet the exchange's minimum requirements. These requirements relate to the size of the company's net income as well as to the number of shares outstanding and in the hands of outsiders (as opposed to the number held by insiders, who generally do not trade their stock very actively). Also, the company must agree to disclose certain information to the exchange; this information is designed to help the exchange track trading patterns and thus to try to be sure that no one is attempting to manipulate the price of the stock.[1] The size qualifications increase as one moves from the regional exchanges to the AMEX and on to the NYSE.

Assuming a company qualifies, many people believe that listing is beneficial both to it and to its stockholders. Listed companies receive a certain amount of free advertising and publicity, and their status as a listed company enhances their prestige and reputation. This may have a beneficial effect on the sales of the products of the firm, and it probably is advantageous in terms of lowering the required rate of return on the common stock. Investors respond favorably to increased information, increased liquidity, and confidence that the quoted price is not being manipulated. By providing investors with these benefits in the form of listing their companies' stocks, a financial manager may be able to lower his or her firm's cost of equity and increase the value of its stock.[2]

PROCEDURES FOR SELLING NEW COMMON STOCK

If stock is to be sold to raise new capital, the new shares may be sold in one of five ways: (1) on a pro rata basis to existing stockholders through a rights offering, (2) through investment bankers to the general public in a public offering, (3) to a single buyer (or a very small number of buyers) in a private placement, (4) to employees through an employee stock purchase plan, or (5) through a dividend reinvestment plan. We discussed dividend reinvestment plans in Chapter 11; the other methods of selling stock are considered in the following sections.

---

[1]It is illegal for anyone to attempt to manipulate the price of a stock. During the 1920s, and earlier, syndicates would buy and sell stock back and forth at rigged prices so that the public would believe that a particular stock was worth more or less than its true value. The exchanges, with the encouragement and support of the SEC, utilize sophisticated computer programs to help spot any irregularities that suggest manipulation, and they require disclosures to help identify manipulators. This same system helps to identify illegal insider trading.

[2]As radical improvements take place in telecommunications and computer technologies, the differences between the OTC and the exchanges become less distinct. As a result, some very large companies such as MCI and Apple, which almost certainly would have been listed on the NYSE in earlier days, have elected to remain in the OTC market.

Rights Offerings

Common stockholders often have the right, called the *preemptive right*, to purchase any additional shares sold by the firm. The preemptive right may or may not be included in the corporate charter; this is a decision of the incorporators, but it can be changed by a later vote of stockholders. The purpose of the preemptive right is twofold. First, it protects the power of control of present stockholders. Second, and by far the more important reason for publicly owned companies, it protects stockholders against dilutions of value. These points will become clear in later sections.

If the preemptive right is contained in a particular firm's charter, the company must offer any newly issued common stock to existing stockholders. If the charter does not prescribe a preemptive right, the firm can choose to sell to its existing stockholders or to the public at large. If it sells to the existing stockholders, the stock flotation is called a *rights offering*. Each stockholder is issued an option to buy a certain number of new shares, and the terms of the option are listed on a certificate called a *stock purchase right*, or simply a *right*. Each stockholder receives one right for each share of stock held.

Several issues confront the financial manager who is setting the terms of a rights offering. The various considerations can be illustrated with data from Southeast Airlines, whose partial balance sheet and income statement are given in Table 12-1. Southeast earns $8 million after taxes, and it has 1 million shares outstanding, so earnings per share are $8. The stock sells at 12.5 times earnings, or for $100 a share. The company announces plans to raise $10 million of new equity capital through a rights offering, and it decides to sell the new stock to shareholders for $80 a share. The questions facing the financial manager are these:

1. How many rights will be required to purchase a share of the newly issued stock?

2. What is the value of each right?

3. What effect will the rights offering have on the price of the existing stock?

We will now analyze each of these questions.

Number of Rights Needed to Purchase One New Share

Southeast plans to raise $10 million in new equity and to sell the new stock at a price of $80 a share. Dividing the total funds to be raised by the subscription price gives the number of shares to be issued:

$$\text{Number of new shares} = \frac{\text{Funds to be raised}}{\text{Subscription price}} = \frac{\$10,000,000}{\$80} = 125,000 \text{ shares.}$$

The next step is to divide the number of previously outstanding shares by the number of new shares to get the number of rights required to subscribe to one share of the new stock. Note that stockholders always get one right for each share of stock they own, so

Table 12-1
Southeast Airlines: Financial Statements before Rights Offering

Partial Balance Sheet

		Total debt	$ 40,000,000
		Common stock	10,000,000
		Retained earnings	50,000,000
Total assets	$100,000,000	Total claims	$100,000,000

Partial Income Statement

Earnings before interest and taxes	$16,121,212
Interest on debt	4,000,000
Income before taxes	12,121,212
Taxes (34% assumed)	4,121,212
Net income	$ 8,000,000
Earnings per share (1,000,000 shares)	$8
Market price of stock (price/earnings ratio of 12.5)	$100

$$\frac{\text{Number of rights needed to}}{\text{buy a share of the stock}} = \frac{\text{Old shares}}{\text{New shares}} = \frac{1,000,000}{125,000} = 8 \text{ rights.}$$

Therefore, a stockholder will have to surrender 8 rights plus $80 to receive one of the newly issued shares. Had the subscription price been set at $95 a share, 9.5 rights would have been required to subscribe to each new share; at $10 a share, only one right would have been needed to buy a new share.

Value of a Right

It is clearly worth something to be able to buy for less than $100 a share of stock selling for $100. The right provides this privilege, so the right must have a value. To see how the theoretical value of a right is established, we continue with the example of Southeast Airlines, assuming that it will raise $10 million by selling 125,000 new shares at $80 a share.

First, notice that the *total market value* of the old stock was $100 million: $100 a share times 1 million shares. (The book value is irrelevant.) When the firm sells the new stock, it brings in an additional $10 million. As a first approximation, we assume that the total market value of the common stock increases by exactly this $10 million, to $110 million. Actually, the market value of all the common stock will go up by more than $10 million if investors think the company will be able to invest these funds at a return substantially in excess of the cost of equity capital, but it will go up by less than $10 million if investors are doubtful of the company's ability to put the new funds to work profitably in the near future.

Under the assumption that market value exactly reflects the new funds brought in, the total market value of the common stock after the new issue will be $110 million. Dividing this new value by the new total number of shares outstanding, 1.125 million, we obtain a new market value of $97.78 a share:

$$\text{New market value} = \frac{\$100,000,000 + \$10,000,000}{1,000,000 + 125,000} = \$97.78.$$

Since the rights give stockholders the privilege of buying for only $80 a share of stock that will end up being worth $97.78, thus saving $17.78, is $17.78 the value of each right? The answer is no, because eight rights are required to buy one new share. We must divide $17.78 by eight to get the value of each right. In the example, each right is worth $2.22.

Ex Rights

Southeast Airlines' rights have a very definite value, which accrues to the holders of the common stock. What will be the price of the stock if it is traded during the offering period? This depends on who will receive the rights, the old owners or the new. The standard procedure calls for the company to set a "holder-of-record date," then for the stock to go *ex rights* four trading days prior to the holder-of-record date. If the stock is sold prior to the ex-rights date, it is sold *rights on*; that is, the new owner will receive the rights. If the stock is sold on or after the ex-rights date, the old owner will receive them. The exact time at which the stock goes ex rights is at the close of business (say 5 p.m.) on the fifth trading day before the holder-of-record date, so the ex-rights day is the fourth trading day before the record date. The following tabulation indicates what is involved (November 8 is a Friday and the 11th is a Monday):

	Date	
Rights on:	November 7	$100.00
	November 8	100.00
Ex-rights date:	November 11	97.78
	November 12	97.78
	November 13	97.78
	November 14	97.78
Holder-of-record date:	November 15	97.78

On October 24, Southeast Airlines announced the terms of the new financing, stating that rights would be mailed out on December 1 to stockholders of record as of the close of business on November 15. Anyone who buys the old stock on or before November 8 will receive the rights; anyone who buys the stock on or after November 11 will not receive the rights. In the case of Southeast Airlines, the rights-on price is $100, whereas the ex-rights price is $97.78.

Formula Value of a Right before the Ex-Rights Date

To simplify the procedures described previously, equations have been developed to determine the value of rights. While the stock is still selling rights on, the value at which the rights will sell when they are issued can be found by use of the following formula:

$$\frac{\text{Value of}}{\text{one right}} = \frac{\text{Market value of stock, rights on} - \text{Subscription price}}{\text{Number of rights required to purchase one share} + 1}.$$

$$R = \frac{M_o - S}{N + 1}. \tag{12-1}$$

Here

R = value of one right.

M_o = rights-on market price of the stock.

S = subscription price.

N = number of rights required to purchase a new share of stock.

Substituting in the appropriate values for Southeast Airlines, we obtain

$$R = \frac{\$100 - \$80}{8 + 1} = \frac{\$20}{9} = \$2.22.$$

This agrees with the value of the rights we found by the long procedure.

Formula Value of a Right on or after the Ex Rights Date

Suppose you are a stockholder in Southeast Airlines. When you return to the United States from a trip to Europe, you read about the rights offering in the newspaper. The stock is now selling ex rights for $97.78 a share. How can you calculate the theoretical value of a right? Simply by using the following formula, which follows the logic described in preceding sections:[3]

---

[3]We developed Equation 12-2 directly from the verbal explanation given in the section "Value of a Right." Equation 12-1 can then be derived from Equation 12-2 as follows:

1. Note that

$$M_e = M_o - R. \tag{12-3}$$

2. Substitute Equation 12-3 into Equation 12-2, obtaining

$$R = \frac{M_o - R - S}{N}. \tag{12-4}$$

3. Simplify Equation 12-4 as follows, ending with Equation 12-1:

$$R = \frac{M_o - S}{N} - \frac{R}{N}$$

$$R + \frac{R}{N} = \frac{M_o - S}{N}$$

$$R\left(\frac{N + 1}{N}\right) = \frac{M_o - S}{N}$$

$$R = \frac{M_o - S}{N}\left(\frac{N}{N + 1}\right)$$

$$R = \frac{M_o - S}{N + 1}. \tag{12-1}$$

This completes the derivation.

$$\text{Value of} \atop \text{one right} = \frac{\text{Market value of stock, ex rights} - \text{Subscription price}}{\text{Number of rights required to purchase one share}}.$$

$$R = \frac{M_e - S}{N} \qquad\qquad (12\text{-}2)$$

$$= \frac{\$97.78 - \$80}{8} = \frac{\$17.78}{8} = \$2.22.$$

Here M_e is the ex-rights market price of the stock.

Effects on Position of Stockholders

Stockholders have the choice of exercising their rights or selling them. Those who have sufficient funds and a desire to own more shares of the company's stock will exercise their rights. Other investors can sell theirs. In either case, provided the formula value of the right holds true, the stockholders will neither benefit nor lose by the rights offering. This statement can be illustrated by the position of an individual stockholder in Southeast Airlines.

Assume the stockholder has eight shares of stock before the rights offering. Each share has a market value of $100 a share, so the stockholder has a total market value of $800 in the company's stock. If the rights are exercised, one additional share can be purchased at $80 a share, a new investment of $80. The total investment is now $880, and the investor owns nine shares of the company's stock, which has a value of $97.78 a share after the rights offering. The value of the stock is 9($97.78) = $880, exactly what is invested in it.

Alternatively, if the eight rights are sold at their value of $2.22 a right, the investor will receive $17.78, ending up with the original eight shares of stock plus $17.78 in cash. The original eight shares of stock now have a market price of $97.78 a share, or 8($97.78) = $782.24. This new $782.24 market value of the stock, plus the $17.78 in cash, is the same as the original $800 market value of the stock except for a rounding error. From a purely mechanical or arithmetical standpoint, stockholders neither gain nor lose from the sale of additional shares of stock through rights, irrespective of whether they exercise or sell their rights. Of course, if they forget either to exercise or to sell the rights, or if the brokerage costs of selling the rights are excessive, then stockholders can suffer losses. However, the issuing firm generally makes special efforts to minimize brokerage costs and to allow enough time for stockholders to take action, so such losses are minimal.

Notice that the price of the company's stock will be lower after a rights offering than prior to an offering. Stockholders have not suffered a loss, however, because they receive the value of the rights. Thus, the stock price decline is similar in nature to a stock split. The larger the underpricing in the rights offering, the greater the stock split effect, and the lower the final stock price. If a company wants to lower the price of its stock by a substantial amount, it will set the subscription price well below the current market price. If it does not want to lower the price very much, it will set the subscription price just far enough below the current price to ensure that the market price will remain above the subscription price during the offering period, assuring that the new shares will be purchased and the new funds will come into the corporation.

Public Offerings

If the preemptive right exists in a company's charter, it must sell new stock through a rights offering. If the preemptive right does not exist, the company can choose between a rights offering and a *public offering*. We discuss procedures for public offerings later in the chapter.

Private Placements

In a *private placement*, securities are sold to one or a few investors, generally institutional investors. Private placements are most common with bonds, but they also occur with stocks.

One particular type of private stock placement that is occurring with increasing frequency is the situation where a large company makes an equity investment in a smaller supplier. For example, in 1983, IBM invested close to $500 million in Rolm, a telecommunications equipment manufacturer, and a similar amount in Intel, a semiconductor manufacturer. In both instances, (1) the companies needed capital for expansion, (2) IBM was engaged in joint development ventures with the companies, and hence wanted them to be financially strong, and (3) the companies had strong, independent managements, who would probably have resisted an attempt by IBM to take full control. So, IBM (1) bought stock that gave it an ownership in the 15 to 25 percent range, (2) agreed to limit its ownership to no more than 30 percent, and (3) simultaneously executed operating contracts for joint ventures with Rolm and Intel.

Similar arrangements are quite common, and some of them go back many years. For example, Sears Roebuck has for many years supplied equity capital to some of its major suppliers, including Johnson Controls, which furnishes Sears with "DieHard" batteries, and with DeSoto Chemical, which supplies most of the paints that Sears sells. Such arrangements can be mutually beneficial, but they do have to be set up carefully to make sure future problems are minimized.

Employee Purchase Plans

Many companies have plans that allow employees to purchase stock on favorable terms. First, under executive incentive stock option plans, key managers are given options to purchase stock. These managers generally have a direct, material influence on the company's fortunes, so if they perform well, the stock will go up, and the options will become valuable. Second, there are plans for lower-level employees. For example, IBM permits employees who are not participants in its stock option plan to allocate up to 10 percent of their salaries to its stock purchase plan, and the funds are then used to buy newly issued shares at 85 percent of the market value on the purchase date. Often, the company's contribution (in IBM's case, the 15 percent discount) is not vested in an employee until five years after the purchase date. This type plan is designed to instill loyalty in the employees and to reduce turnover. A third type of plan is related to the second one, but here the stock bought for employees is purchased out of a share of the company's profits. Congress has sought to encourage such plans through tax policy—under a version of the *Employee Stock Ownership Plan (ESOP)*, companies can claim a tax credit equal to a percentage of wages, provided that the funds are used to buy newly issued stock for the benefit of employees. The amount of the credit varies from year to year, depending on the whims of Congress: currently it is 1/2 of 1 percent of total wages. Firms have been jumping on the ESOP bandwagon in record numbers in recent years. It has been estimated that over 7,000 companies now have ESOPs covering over 10 million employees.

Although all of these plans are designed more to provide incentives to help improve employee performance than to raise capital, the fact is that they do, for many companies, produce a surprisingly large amount of new equity. For example, in 1985, IBM sold over 5 million shares to its employees, raising about $560 million in the process. This is not a trivial sum, even for IBM.[4]

ADVANTAGES AND DISADVANTAGES OF COMMON STOCK FINANCING

In this section we briefly discuss the advantages and disadvantages of common stock financing.

Advantages of Common Stock Financing

1. Common stock does not entail fixed charges. If the company generates the earnings, it can pay common stock dividends. This is very much in contrast to interest on debt, which must be paid regardless of the level of earnings.

2. Common stock carries no fixed maturity date—it is permanent capital and does not have to be "paid back."

3. Since common stock provides a cushion against losses to the firm's creditors, the sale of common stock increases the credit-worthiness of the firm.

4. Common stock can, at times, be sold more easily than debt. It appeals to certain investor groups because (1) it typically carries a higher expected return than does preferred stock or debt, (2) it provides the investor with a better hedge against inflation than does straight preferred stock or bonds, and (3) returns from common stock in the form of capital gains are not taxed until the gains are realized.

Disadvantages of Common Stock Financing

1. The sale of common stock may extend voting rights or control to the additional stock owners who are brought into the company. For this reason, additional equity financing is often avoided by small firms, whose owner-managers may be unwilling to share control of their companies with outsiders. Note, though, that firms can use special classes of common stock that do not carry voting rights. For example, General Motors issued separate nonvoting Class E common stock in connection with

---

[4]Note, though, that IBM and other companies may choose to repurchase shares on the open market for redistribution to ESOP participants. The decision to use newly issued shares or repurchased shares depends upon the company's need for funds in a given year. Still, employee purchase plans provide the potential for raising equity regardless of whether they are actually used for this purpose each and every year.

its acquisition of Electronic Data Systems. For years, the NYSE had prohibited the listing of more than one class of common stock, and NYSE officials were especially vocal against listing nonvoting shares. However, some 22 Big Board-listed companies now have more than one class of common and, in 1986, the NYSE "reluctantly" agreed to list multiple classes of common stock.

2. Common stock gives more owners the right to share in income. The use of debt enables the firm to acquire funds at a fixed cost, whereas common stock gives equal rights to new stockholders to share in the net profits of the firm.

3. The costs of underwriting and distributing common stock are usually higher than those for underwriting and distributing preferred stock or debt.

4. As we discussed in Chapters 5 and 6, the sale of new common stock may be perceived by investors as a negative signal, and hence cause the stock price to fall.

PREFERRED STOCK FINANCING

Preferred stock is a hybrid—it is similar to bonds in some respects and to common stock in other ways. Accountants generally view preferred stock as equity and record it on the balance sheet as an equity account. However, financial managers view preferred stock as being somewhere between debt and common equity—it imposes a fixed charge and hence increases the firm's financial leverage, yet if the preferred dividend is not paid, this does not force the company into bankruptcy. We first describe the basic features of preferred, after which we describe some recent innovations in preferred stock financing.

Basic Features

Preferred stock generally has a par (or liquidating) value, usually either $25 or $100. The dividend is indicated either as a percentage of par, as so many dollars per share, or sometimes both ways. For example, several years ago Mississippi Power Company sold 150,000 shares of $100 par value preferred stock for a total of $15 million. This preferred had a stated annual dividend of $12 per share, so the preferred dividend yield was $12/$100 = 0.12, or 12 percent, at the time of issue. The dividend was set when the stock was issued; it will not be changed in the future. Therefore, if the market discount rate for the preferred, k_p, changes from 12 percent after the issue date—as it did—then the market price of the preferred stock will go up or down. Currently, k_p for Mississippi Power's preferred is 9 percent, and the price of the preferred has risen to $12/0.09 = $133.33.

If the preferred dividend is not earned, the company does not have to pay it. However, most preferred issues are *cumulative*, meaning that the cumulative total of all unpaid preferred dividends must be paid before dividends can be paid on the common stock. Unpaid preferred dividends are called *arrearages*.[5]

---

[5]Dividends in arrears do not earn interest; thus, arrearages do not increase in a compound interest sense. They only grow from continued nonpayment of the preferred dividend. Also, many preferred stocks accrue arrearages for only a limited number of years, not indefinitely. Often, only three years of arrearages accrue; the cumulative feature ceases after three years, but the dividends in arrears until that point continue in force.

Preferred stock normally has no voting rights. However, most preferred issues stipulate that the preferred stockholders can elect either a majority or a minority of the directors—say three out of 10—if the preferred dividend is passed (omitted). For example, Jersey Central Power & Light, one of the companies that owned a share of the Three Mile Island (TMI) nuclear plant, has preferred stock outstanding which can elect a *majority* of the directors if the preferred dividend is passed for four successive quarters. Jersey Central kept paying its preferred dividends even during the dark days following the TMI accident. Had the preferred only been entitled to elect a minority of the directors, the dividend would probably have been passed.

Even though nonpayment of preferred dividends will not bankrupt a company, corporations issue preferred with every intention of paying the dividends. Even if passing the dividend does not give the preferred stockholders control of the company, failure to pay a preferred dividend precludes payment of common dividends and, in addition, makes it difficult for a firm to raise capital by selling bonds, and virtually impossible to sell more preferred or common stock. However, having preferred stock outstanding does give the firm that experiences temporary problems a chance to overcome its difficulties; had bonds been used instead of preferred stock, the company might have been forced into bankruptcy before it could straighten out its problems. Thus, from the viewpoint of the issuing corporation, preferred stock is less risky than bonds.

Investors, on the other hand, regard preferred stock as being riskier than bonds for two reasons: (1) Preferred stockholders' claims are subordinated to those of bondholders in the event of liquidation, and (2) bondholders are more likely to continue receiving income during hard times than are preferred stockholders. Accordingly, investors require a higher after-tax rate of return on a given firm's preferred stock than on its bonds. However, recall that 80 percent of preferred dividends are exempt from the corporate tax; this makes preferred stock attractive to corporate investors. In recent years, high-grade preferred stock, on average, has sold on a lower pre-tax yield basis than have high-grade bonds. As an example, in April 1986, Du Pont's preferred stock had a market yield of about 7.3 percent, whereas its bonds provided a yield of 8.6 percent, or 1.3 percentage points *more* than its preferred. The tax treatment accounted for this differential; the *after-tax yield* to corporate investors was greater on the preferred stock than on the bonds.[6]

About half of all preferred stock issued in recent years has been convertible into common stock. For example, Enron Corporation issued preferred stock which stip-

---

[6]The after-tax yield on an 8.6 percent bond to a corporate investor that is paying a 46 percent marginal tax rate is $8.6\%(1 - T) = 8.6\%(0.54) = 4.6\%$. The after-tax yield on a 7.3 percent preferred stock is $7.3\%(1 - \text{Effective T}) = 7.3\%[1 - (0.15)(0.46)] = 6.8\%$. Also, note that the tax law prohibits firms from issuing debt and then using the proceeds to purchase another firm's preferred or common stock. If debt financing is used for stock purchases, then the 80 percent dividend exclusion is reduced. This provision is designed to prevent firms from engaging in "tax arbitrage," or the use of tax-deductible debt to purchase largely tax-exempt preferred stock. Finally, note that the dividend exclusion was 85 percent and the highest corporate tax bracket was 46 percent in 1986, and hence these values were used in our April 1986 example. Under the new tax law, these values are 80 and 34 percent, respectively.

ulated that one share of preferred could be converted into three shares of common, at the option of the preferred stockholder. Convertibles are discussed at length in Chapter 15.

Some preferred stocks are similar to perpetual bonds in that they have no maturity date. However, many preferred shares do have a sinking fund provision, often one which calls for the retirement of 2 percent of the issue each year, meaning that the issue will "mature" in a maximum of 50 years. Also, many preferred issues are callable by the issuing corporation. This feature, if exercised, can also limit the life of the preferred.[7]

Nonconvertible preferred stock is virtually all owned by corporations, which can take advantage of the 80 percent dividend exclusion to obtain a higher after-tax yield on preferred stock than on bonds. Individuals should not own preferred stocks (except convertible preferreds)—they can get higher yields on safer bonds, so it is simply not logical for them to hold preferreds. As a result of this ownership pattern, the volume of preferred stock financing is geared to the supply of money in the hands of insurance companies and other corporate investors who are looking for tax-favored investments. When the supply of such money is plentiful, the prices of preferred stocks are bid up, their yields fall, and investment bankers suggest to companies that they consider issuing preferred stock.

Recent Innovations

The 1980s have spawned several important innovations in preferred stock financing. We will discuss two new wrinkles here: (1) floating, or adjustable rate, preferred and (2) money market, or market auction, preferred.

Adjustable-rate preferred stocks (ARPs) were introduced in 1982. These stocks, instead of paying fixed dividends, have their dividends tied to the rate on Treasury securities. The ARPs, which are issued mainly by large commercial banks, were touted as nearly perfect short-term corporate investments since (1) only 20 percent of the dividends are taxable to corporations, and (2) the floating rate feature tends to keep the issue trading at near par. The new security proved to be so popular as a short-term investment for firms with idle cash that mutual funds which invest in these securities sprouted like weeds (the funds, in turn, are purchased by corporations). However, the ARPs still had some price volatility due (1) to changes in the riskiness of the issues (some big banks which had issued ARPs, such as Continental Illinois, ran into serious loan default problems) and (2) to the fact that Treasury yields exhibited significant fluctuations between dividend rate adjustments. Thus, even ARPs had too much price instability for the liquid asset portfolios of many corporate investors.

---

[7]Prior to the late 1970s, virtually all preferred stock was perpetual, and almost no issues had sinking funds. Then, insurance company regulators, worried about the unrealized losses the companies had been incurring on preferred holdings as a result of rising interest rates, put into effect some regulatory changes which essentially mandated that insurance companies buy only sinking fund preferreds. From that time on, virtually no new issues have been perpetuities. This example illustrates the way the nature of securities changes as a result of changes in the economic environment.

In 1984, Shearson Lehman Brothers introduced *money market, or market auction, preferred*. Here is how they work: The underwriter conducts an auction on the issue every seven weeks (to get the 80 percent exclusion from taxable income, buyers must hold the stock at least 46 days). Any holders who want to sell their shares can put them up for auction at par value. Buyers then submit bids in the form of the yields they are willing to accept over the next 7-week period. The yield that is set on the issue for the next period is the lowest yield necessary to sell all the shares being offered at that auction. The buyers pay the sellers the par value, and hence holders are virtually assured that their share can be sold at par. The issuer then has to pay the dividend rate over the next 7-week period as determined by the auction. From the holder's standpoint, market auction preferred is a low-risk, largely tax-exempt, 7-week maturity security which can be sold between auction dates at close to par value.

Adjustable-rate and market auction preferreds, although initially issued exclusively by banks, are also now being issued by nonfinancial corporations. For example, Texas Instruments issued $225 million of market auction preferred in March 1986. About the only thing investors do not seem to like about ARPs and auction market preferred is that, as stock, it is more vulnerable to an issuer's financial problems than debt would be.

Advantages and Disadvantages of Preferred Stock Financing

There are both advantages and disadvantages to selling preferred stock. Here are the major advantages from the issuers' standpoint:

1. In contrast to bonds, the obligation to make preferred dividend payments is not contractual in nature, and the passing (omission) of preferred dividends cannot force a firm into bankruptcy.

2. By selling preferred stock, the firm avoids the dilution of common equity that occurs when common stock is sold.

3. Since preferred stock typically has no maturity, and since preferred sinking fund payments, if present, are typically spread over a long period, preferred issues avoid the cash flow drain from repayment of principal inherent in debt issues.

These are the major disadvantages:

1. Preferred stock dividends are not deductible as a tax expense to the issuer, and hence the after-tax cost of preferred is typically higher than the after-tax cost of debt.

2. Although preferred dividends can be passed, investors expect them to be paid, and firms intend to pay the dividends if conditions permit. Thus, preferred dividends are truly a fixed payment, and the use of preferred stock, like debt, increases the financial risk of the firm and hence increases the cost of all financing.

THE INVESTMENT BANKING PROCESS

In this section, we describe the way securities are issued, and the role of investment bankers in the process.

Stage I Decisions

The decision to issue securities is made in two stages. At Stage I, the firm itself makes some initial, preliminary decisions, including the following:

1. **Dollars to Be Raised.** How much new capital is needed?

2. **Type of Securities Used.** Should common, preferred, bonds, or hybrid securities, or a combination, be used? Further, if common stock is to be issued, should it be done as a rights offering or by a direct sale to the general public?

3. **Competitive Bid Versus a Negotiated Deal.** Should the company simply offer a block of its securities for sale to the highest bidder, or should it negotiate a deal with an investment banker? These two procedures are called *competitive bids* and *negotiated deals*, respectively. Only about 100 of the largest firms listed on the NYSE, whose securities are already well known to the investment banking community, are in a position to use the competitive bidding process. The investment banks must do a large amount of investigative work in order to bid on an issue unless they are already quite familiar with the firm, and such costs would be too high to make it worthwhile unless the banker were sure of getting the deal. Therefore, except for the very largest firms, offerings of stock or bonds are generally on a negotiated basis.

4. **Selection of an Investment Banker.** If the issue is to be negotiated, the firm must select an investment banker. This can be an important decision for a firm that is going public. On the other hand, an older firm that has already "been to market" will have an established relationship with an investment banker. However, it is easy to change bankers if the firm is dissatisfied. Different investment banking houses are better suited for different companies. The older, larger "establishment houses" such as Morgan Stanley deal mainly with companies such as AT&T, IBM, and Exxon. Other bankers such as Drexel Burnham Lambert handle more speculative issues. Some houses specialize in new issues, while others are not well suited to handle such issues because their brokerage clients are relatively conservative. (Investment banking firms sell new issues largely to their own regular brokerage customers, so the nature of these customers has a major effect on the ability of the house to do a good job for a corporate client.) Table 12-2 lists the ten largest investment bankers for 1985 as measured by the dollar amount of securities underwritten for U.S. firms.

Stage II Decisions

Stage II decisions, which are made jointly by the firm and its selected investment banker, include the following:

1. **Reevaluating the Initial Decisions.** The firm and its banker will reevaluate the initial decisions regarding the size of the issue and the type of securities to

Table 12-2
Ten Largest Investment Bankers

	Total Amount Managed (In Billions of Dollars)	In U.S.		Outside U.S.
		Debt	Equity	
1. Salomon Brothers	$34.2	$23.9	$4.9	$5.4
2. First Boston	26.2	17.2	3.3	5.7
3. Goldman Sachs	19.9	10.9	5.0	4.1
4. Merrill Lynch	17.6	9.3	5.5	2.8
5. Drexel Burnham Lambert	13.3	9.9	3.3	0.1
6. Morgan Stanley	12.7	6.6	3.0	3.0
7. Shearson Lehman	10.3	5.1	4.4	0.8
8. Kidder Peabody	4.3	1.7	1.8	0.8
9. Union Bank of Switzerland	3.0	—	—	3.0
10. Paine Webber	2.9	1.9	1.0	—

Note: Some rows do not total because of rounding errors.
Source: *The Wall Street Journal*, January 2, 1986.

use. For example, the firm may have decided initially to raise $50 million by selling common stock, but the investment banker may convince management that it would be better off, in view of current market conditions, to limit the stock issue to $25 million and to raise the other $25 million as debt.

2. Best Efforts or Underwritten Issues. The firm and its investment banker must decide whether the banker will work on a *best efforts* basis or will *underwrite* the issue. In a best efforts sale, the banker does not guarantee that the securities will be sold or that the company will get the cash it needs, only that it will put forth its best efforts to sell the issue. On an underwritten issue, the company does get a guarantee. Therefore, the banker bears significant risks in underwritten offerings. For example, on IBM's $1 billion bond sales in 1979, interest rates rose sharply, and bond prices fell, after the deal had been set but before the investment bankers could sell the bonds to ultimate purchasers. The bankers lost somewhere between $10 million and $20 million. Had the offering been on a best efforts basis, IBM would have been the loser.

3.   Banker's Compensation; Other Expenses. The investment banker's compensation must be negotiated. Also, the firm must estimate the other underwriting expenses it will incur in connection with the issue—lawyers' fees, accountants' costs, printing and engraving, and so on. Usually, the banker will buy the issue from the company at a discount below the price at which the securities are to be offered to the public, with this "spread" being set to cover the banker's costs and to provide a profit.

Table 12-3 gives an indication of the issuance costs associated with public issues of bonds, preferred stock, and common stock. As the table shows, costs as a percentage of the proceeds are higher for stocks than for bonds, and costs are

Table 12-3

Issuance Costs for Underwritten, Nonrights Offerings (Expressed as Percentage of Gross Proceeds)

Size of Issue (Millions of Dollars)	Bonds			Preferred Stock			Common Stock		
	Underwriting Commission	Other Expenses	Total Costs	Underwriting Commission	Other Expenses	Total Costs	Underwriting Commission	Other Expenses	Total Costs
Under 1.0	10.0%	4.0%	14.0%	—	—	—	13.0%	9.0%	22.0%
1.0–1.9	8.0	3.0	11.0	—	—	—	11.0	5.9	16.9
2.0–4.9	4.0	2.2	6.2	—	—	—	8.6	3.8	12.4
5.0–9.9	2.4	0.8	3.2	1.9%	0.7%	2.6%	6.3	1.9	8.1
10.0–19.9	1.2	0.7	1.9	1.4	0.4	1.8	5.1	0.9	6.0
20.0–49.9	1.0	0.4	1.4	1.4	0.3	1.7	4.1	0.5	4.6
50.0 and over	0.9	0.2	1.1	1.4	0.2	1.6	3.3	0.2	3.5

Notes:

a. Small issues of preferred are rare, so no data on issues below $5 million are given.

b. Flotation costs tend to rise somewhat when interest rates are cyclically high, indicating that money is in relatively tight supply, and hence investment bankers will have a relatively hard time placing issues with permanent investors. Thus, the figures shown in Table 12-3 represent averages, as flotation costs actually vary somewhat over time.

Sources: Securities and Exchange Commission, *Cost of Flotation of Registered Equity Issues* (Washington, D.C.: U.S. Government Printing Office, December 1974); Pettway, Richard H., "A Note on the Flotation Costs of New Equity Capital Issues of Electric Companies," *Public Utilities Fortnightly*, March 18, 1982; Hansen, Robert, "Evaluating the Costs of a New Equity Issue," *Midland Corporate Finance Journal*, Spring 1986; and informal surveys of common stock, preferred stock, and bond issues conducted by the authors.

higher for small than for large issues. The relationship between size of issue and flotation cost is due primarily to the existence of fixed costs—certain costs must be incurred regardless of the size of the issue, so the percentage flotation cost is quite high for small issues.

Also, it should be noted that when relatively small companies go public to raise new capital, the investment bankers frequently take part of their compensation in the form of options to buy stock in the firm. For example, DEW Technologies, Inc., went public with a $10 million issue in 1986 by selling 1 million shares at a price of $10 per share. Its investment bankers bought the stock from the company at a price of $9.75 per share, so the direct underwriting fee was only 1,000,000($10.00 − $9.75) = $250,000, or 2.5 percent, but they also received a 5-year option to buy 200,000 shares at a price of $10 per share. If the stock should go up to $15 per share, which the bankers expected it to do, then the investment banking firm would make a $1 million profit, which would in effect be an additional underwriting fee.

4. Setting the Offering Price. If the company is already publicly owned, the offering price will be based upon the existing market price of the stock or the yield on the bonds. Typically, for common stock, the investment banker buys the securities at a prescribed number of points below the closing price on the last day of registration. For example, suppose that in October 1986, the stock of Microwave Telecommunications, Inc. (MTI) had a current price of $28.50 per share, and the stock had traded between $25 and $30 per share during the previous three months. Suppose further that MTI and its underwriter agreed that the investment banker would buy 10 million new shares at $1 per share below the closing price on the last day of registration. If the stock closed at $25 on the day the SEC released the issue, MTI would receive $24 per share. Typically, such agreements have an escape clause that provides for the contract to be voided if the price of the securities drops below some predetermined figure. In the illustrative case, this "upset" price might be set at $24 per share. Thus, if the closing price of the shares on the last day of registration had been $23.50, MTI would have had the option of withdrawing from the agreement.

The investment banker will have an easier job if the issue is priced relatively low, but the issuer of the securities naturally wants as high a price as possible. Some conflict of interest on price therefore arises between the investment banker and the issuer. If the issuer is financially sophisticated and makes comparisons with similar security issues, the investment banker will be forced to price close to the market.

As we discussed in Chapter 5, the announcement of a new stock offering by a mature firm is often taken as a negative signal—if the firm's prospects were very good, management would not want to issue new stock and thus share the rosy future with new stockholders, so the announcement of a new offering is taken as bad news. Consequently, the price will probably fall when the announcement is made, so the offering price will probably have to be set at a price substantially below the pre-announcement market price. Consider Figure 12-1, in which d_0 is the estimated market demand curve for MTI's stock and S_0 is the number of shares

Figure 12-1
Microwave Telecommunications, Inc.:
Estimated Common Stock Demand Curves

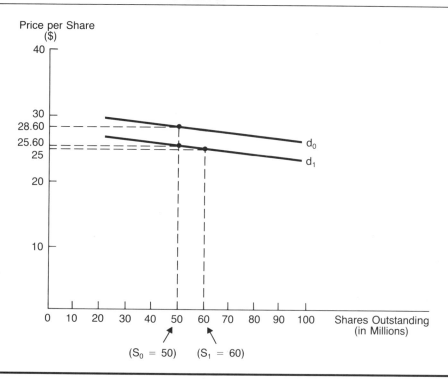

currently outstanding. Initially, there are 50 million shares outstanding, and the equilibrium price of the stock is $28.60 per share, determined as follows:

$$P_0 = \frac{D_1}{k_s - g} = \frac{\$2.00}{0.12 - 0.05} \approx \$28.60.$$

The values shown for D_1, k_s, and g are the *estimates of the marginal investor.* Investors who do not now own MTI's stock probably, on average, regard the stock as being more risky, and hence assign it a higher value for k_s, or perhaps they estimate the company's growth rate as being lower than do people who now own the stock, and so use g < 5 percent when calculating the stock's intrinsic value. Thus, people who do not now own the stock think the stock is worth less than $28.50.

When MTI announces that it is going to sell another 10 million shares, this is taken as a negative signal. Consequently, the demand curve for the stock drops from d_0 to d_1, and the price falls. The new equilibrium price, if 50 million shares were outstanding, and if the marginal investor now expects MTI's growth rate to be 4.2 percent, would be about $25.60:

$$P_0 = \frac{\$2.00}{0.12 - 0.042} \approx \$25.60.$$

However, if MTI is to sell another 10 million shares of stock, it will either have to attract investors who would not be willing to own the stock at the $25.60 per share price or else induce present stockholders to buy additional shares. There are two ways this can be accomplished: (1) by reducing the offering price of the stock or (2) by "promoting" or "advertising" the company and thus shifting the demand curve for its stock back to the right.[8] If the demand curve does not shift at all from d_1, we see from Figure 12-1 that the only way the 10 million additional shares could be sold would be by setting the offering price at about $25 per share. However, if the investment banker could promote the stock sufficiently to shift the demand curve back up to d_0, then the offering price could be set much closer to the pre-announcement equilibrium price of $28.60 per share.[9]

The extent to which the demand curve can be shifted depends primarily on two factors: (1) what investors think the company can do with the money brought in by the stock sale and (2) how effectively the brokers promote the issue. If investors can be convinced that the new money will be invested in highly profitable projects that will substantially raise earnings and the earnings growth rate, then the demand curve shift will occur, and the stock price might actually go above $28.50. Even if investors do not radically change their expectations about the company's fundamental factors, the fact that MTI's stock is brought to their attention may shift the demand curve. The extent to which this promotion campaign is successful in shifting the demand curve depends, of course, upon the effectiveness of the investment banking firm. Therefore, the effectiveness of different investment bankers, as perceived by MTI's financial manager, will be an important factor in the choice of an underwriter.

One final point is that *if pressure from the new shares and/or negative signaling effects drives down the price of the stock, all shares outstanding, not just the new shares, are affected.* Thus, if MTI's stock should fall from $28.60 to $25 per share as a result of the financing, and if the price should remain at that new level, then the company would incur a loss of $3.60 on each of the 50 million shares

---

[8] It should be noted that investors can buy newly issued stock without paying normal brokerage commissions, and brokers are careful to point this out to potential purchasers. Thus, if an investor were to buy MTI's stock at $28.50 per share in the regular market, the commission would be about 1 percent, or 28 cents per share. If the stock were purchased in an underwriting, this commission would be avoided.

It should also be noted that for years many academicians argued that the demand curve for a firm's stock is either horizontal or has an extremely slight downward slope, and that signalling effects are minimal. Most corporate treasurers, on the other hand, have long felt that both effects exist for mature companies, and recent empirical studies confirm the treasurers' position. For example, see Andrei Shleifer, "Do Demand Curves for Stocks Slope Down?" *Journal of Finance*, July 1986, 579-590.

[9] Note that the supply curve is a vertical line, first at 50 million and then, after the new issue, at 60 million.

previously outstanding, or a total market value loss of $180 million. This loss, like underwriting expenses, is a flotation cost, and hence should be considered as a cost associated with the stock issue. However, if the company's prospects really were poorer than investors thought, then the price decline would have occurred sooner or later anyway. On the other hand, if the company's prospects are really not all that bad (the signal was incorrect), then over time MTI's demand curve will move back to d_0, or even above d_0, so the company would not suffer a permanent loss anywhere close to $180 million on an issue such as this one.

If the company is "going public," there will be no established price or demand curve, so the bankers will have to estimate the *equilibrium price* at which the stock will sell after issue. Note that if the offering price is set below the true equilibrium price, the stock will rise sharply after the issue, and the company and its selling stockholders will have given away too much stock to raise the required capital. If the offering price is set above the true equilibrium price, either the issue will fail or, if the bankers succeed in selling the stock to their investment clients, these clients will be unhappy when the stock subsequently falls to its equilibrium level. Therefore, it is important that the equilibrium price be closely approximated, although it is hard to estimate this price. The methods and procedures set forth in Chapters 3 and 4 are used in such price estimations.

Selling Procedures

Once the company and its investment banker have decided how much money to raise, the types of securities to issue, and the basis for pricing the issue, they will prepare and file an SEC *registration statement* and a *prospectus*. It generally takes about 20 days for the issue to be approved by the SEC. The final price of the stock (or the interest rate on a bond issue) is set at the close of business the day the issue clears the SEC, and the securities are offered to the public the following day.

Investors are required to pay for securities within 10 days, and the investment banker must pay the issuing firm within four days of the official commencement of the offering. Typically, the banker sells the stock within a day or two after the offering begins, but on occasion, the banker miscalculates, setting the offering price too high, and thus is unable to move the issue. At other times, the market declines during the offering period, forcing the banker to reduce the price of the stock or bonds. In either instance, on an underwritten offering the firm receives the price that was agreed upon, and the banker must absorb any losses that may be incurred.

Because they are exposed to large potential losses, investment bankers typically do not handle the purchase and distribution of issues single-handedly unless the issue is a very small one. If the sum of money involved is large and the risk of a price fluctuation is substantial, investment bankers form *underwriting syndicates* in an effort to minimize the risk each banker carries. The banking house which sets up the deal is called the *lead*, or *managing, underwriter*.

In addition to the underwriting syndicate, on larger offerings still more investment bankers are included in the *selling group*, which handles the distribution of securities to individual investors. The selling group includes all members of the underwriting syndicate plus additional dealers who take relatively small participations, or shares of the total issue, from the members of the underwriting syndicate. Thus, the underwriters act as *wholesalers*, while members of the selling group act as *retailers*. The number of houses in a selling group depends partly upon the size of the issue. For example, the one set up when Communications Satellite Corporation (Comsat) went public consisted of 385 members.

A new selling procedure has recently emerged which does not require an underwriting syndicate. In this type of sale, called an *unsyndicated stock offering*, the managing underwriter, acting alone, sells the issue entirely to institutional investors, thus bypassing both retail stockbrokers and individual investors. In 1985, more than 30 percent of common stock issues, measured in dollars, were sold directly by the managing underwriters without retail distribution; back in 1981, only 2 percent of issues were unsyndicated. Behind this phenomenon is a simple motivating force: money. The fees that issuers pay on a syndicated offering, which includes commissions paid to retail brokers, can run at least a full percentage point higher than those on unsyndicated offerings. Further, although total fees are lower if there is no syndicate, managing underwriters usually come out ahead because they do not have to share the fees with an underwriting syndicate. Recent issuers of unsyndicated stock include Transamerica Corporation and Public Service Company of New Mexico. However, some types of stock do not appeal to institutional investors, and hence not all firms can use unsyndicated offers.

Shelf Registrations

The selling procedures described previously, including the 20-day minimum waiting period between registration with the SEC and sale of the issue, apply to most security sales. However, it should be noted that large, well-known public companies which issue securities frequently may file a *master registration statement* with the SEC and then update it with a *short-form statement* just prior to each individual offering. Further, the company can decide at 10 a.m. to sell securities and have the sale completed before noon. This procedure is known as *shelf registration* because, in effect, the company puts its new securities "on the shelf" and then sells them to investors when it feels the market is "right." Firms with less than $150 million in stock held by outside investors cannot use shelf registrations. The rationale for this distinction is to protect investors who may not be able to get adequate financial data about a little-known company in the short time between announcement of a shelf issue and its sale.

Maintenance of the Secondary Market

In the case of a large, established firm such as IBM or GM, the investment banking firm's job is finished after it has disposed of the stock and turned the net proceeds over to the issuing firm. However, in the case of a small company going public for the first time, the investment banker is under some obligation to maintain a market in the shares after the issue has been completed. Such stocks are typically traded in the over-the-counter market, and the lead underwriter generally agrees to "make a market" in the stock so as to keep it reasonably liquid. The company wants a good market to exist for its stock, as do the stockholders. Therefore, if the banking house wants to do business with the company in the future, to keep its own brokerage customers happy, and to have future referral business, it will hold an inventory and help to maintain an active secondary market in the stock.

SUMMARY

This chapter has focused on (1) common stock financing, (2) preferred stock financing, and (3) the investment banking process. Typically, firms begin as proprietorships or partnerships, and then, as they grow and prosper, convert to closely held corporations. If they continue to grow, they will eventually face two major decisions: (1) the decision to go public and (2) the decision to list the stock on an exchange.

If common stock is being sold, the shares may be sold in five ways: (1) through a rights offering, (2) by a public offering, (3) by a private placement, (4) through an employee stock purchase plan, and (5) through a dividend reinvestment plan.

Preferred stocks are similar to bonds in that they offer a fixed return. However, preferred stock is less risky than bonds from the corporation's viewpoint because the dividend does not have to be paid if it is not earned, so nonpayment of preferred dividends will not bankrupt the firm. From the investors' standpoint, however, preferred stocks are riskier than bonds, because firms are more likely to omit preferred dividends than to fail to pay interest, and bonds have priority over preferred stock in the event of bankruptcy.

Decisions related to security issues are made in two stages. In Stage 1, the firm decides on the types of securities to be offered and selects the investment banker. The details of the issue, including underwriting expenses, are worked out in Stage 2. One of the key Stage 2 decisions is setting the offering price. If a common stock issue results in a permanent lowering of the stock price, then this loss may be considered as part of the flotation cost.

Questions and Problems

12-1 (Rights versus public offerings) The Delaware Ferry Company needs to raise $50 million of new equity to support its shipbuilding program. The firm's stock currently sells for $100 per share, and it has 10 million shares outstanding. Its charter does not include the preemptive right, so the new equity can be raised by a public offering or a rights offering.

    a. What are the pros and cons of each type of offering?

    b. If a public offering is to be used, what would be the approximate price to the public and the percentage underwriting cost to the firm? (See Table 12-3.)

    c. If a rights offering is to be used,

        (1) What subscription price would you recommend, and at that price, what would be the value of each right and the ex-rights price of the stock?

        (2) How would the percentage flotation cost under the rights offering compare with that under the public offering?

12-2 (Rights offerings) United Appliance Company's common stock is priced at $72 a share in the market. Notice is given that stockholders may purchase one new share at a price of $40 for every 7 shares held. You hold 120 shares at the time of notice.
   a. At approximately what price will each right sell in the market?
   b. Why will this be the appropriate price?
   c. What effect will the issuance of rights have on the original market price? Why?

12-3 (Rights offerings) Sarah Stone has 300 shares of Piper Industries. The market price per share is $75. The company now offers stockholders one new share to be purchased at $60 for every four shares held.
   a. Determine the value of each right.
   b. Assume that Sarah (1) uses 80 rights and sells the other 220 or (2) sells 300 rights at the market price you have calculated. Prepare a statement showing the changes in her position in each case.

12-4 (Market pressure) Is it true that the "flatter," or more nearly horizontal, the demand curve for a particular firm's stock, the more important the role of the investment banker when the company sells a new issue of stock.

12-5 (Flotation costs) Company A has assets of $20 million, net income after taxes of $1 million, manufactures widgets, and is publicly owned. Company B is identical to A in every respect except that B's stock is all owned by its founder. If each firm sells stock to the public to raise $5 million of new money for corporate purposes, which would probably have the higher flotation cost? Why?

12-6 (Market regulation) The SEC attempts to protect investors who are purchasing newly issued securities by making sure that the information put out by a company and its investment banker is correct and is not misleading. However, the SEC *does not* provide any information about the real value of the securities; hence, an investor might pay too much for some new stock and consequently lose heavily. Do you think the SEC should, as a part of every new stock or bond offering, render an opinion to investors on the proper value of the securities being offered? Explain.

12-7 (New issue pricing) The Teweles Company is a small software development firm. The company has been successful and has grown. Now Teweles is planning to sell an issue of common stock to the public for the first time, and it faces the problem of setting an appropriate price on its common stock. The company and its investment banker feel that the proper procedure is to select firms similar to it with publicly traded common stock and to make relevant comparisons.

Several software manufacturers are reasonably similar to Teweles with respect to size, asset composition, and debt/equity proportions. Of these companies, GoodWrite and SpreadFast are most similar. Data are given on page 431. When analyzing these data, assume that 1981 and 1986 were reasonably "normal" years for all three companies; that is, these years were neither especially good nor especially bad in terms of sales, earnings, and dividends. At the time of the analysis, k_{RF} was 10 percent and k_M was 15 percent. GoodWrite is listed on the American Exchange and SpreadFast on the NYSE, while Teweles will be traded in the OTC market.
   a. Assume that Teweles has 100 shares of stock outstanding. Use this information to calculate earnings per share (EPS), dividends per share (DPS), and book value per share for Teweles.
   b. On the basis of your answer to Part a, do you think Teweles' stock would sell at a price in the same "ballpark" as that of GoodWrite and SpreadFast, that is, sell in the range of $25 to $100 per share?

1981 and 1986 Data	GoodWrite	SpreadFast	Teweles (Totals)
Earnings per share			
1986	$ 4.50	$7.50	$1,200,000
1981	3.00	5.50	816,000
Price per share			
1986	$36.00	$65.00	—
Dividends per share			
1986	$ 2.25	$ 3.75	$ 600,000
1981	1.50	2.75	420,000
1986 Data:			
Book value per share	$30.00	$55.00	$9,000,000
Market/book ratio	120%	118%	—
Total assets	$28 million	$ 82 million	$20 million
Total debt	$12 million	$ 30 million	$11 million
Sales	$41 million	$140 million	$37 million

c. Assuming that Teweles' management can split the stock so that the 100 shares could be changed to 1,000 shares, 100,000 shares, or any other number, would such an action make sense in this case? Why?

d. Now assume that Teweles did split its stock and has 400,000 shares. Calculate new values for EPS, DPS, and book value per share.

e. What can you say about the relative growth rates of the three companies?

f. What can you say about their dividend payout policies?

g. Return on equity (ROE) can be measured as EPS/book value per share, or as total earnings/total equity. Calculate ROEs for the three companies.

h. Calculate debt/total assets ratios for the three companies.

i. Calculate P/E ratios for GoodWrite and SpreadFast. Are these P/Es consistent with the growth and ROE data? If not, what other factors would explain the relative P/E ratios?

j. Now determine a range of values for Teweles' stock price, with 400,000 shares outstanding, by applying GoodWrite and SpreadFast P/E ratios, price/dividend ratios, and price/book value ratios to your data for Teweles.

k. Using the equation $\hat{k} = D_1/P_0 + g$, find approximate $\hat{k}$ values for GoodWrite and SpreadFast. Then use these values in the constant growth stock price model to find a price for Teweles' stock.

l. At what price do you think Teweles' shares should be offered to the public? You will want to find the *equilibrium price*, that is, a price that will be low enough to induce investors to buy the stock, but not so low that it will rise sharply immediately after it is issued. Think about relative growth rates, ROEs, dividend yields, and total returns.

m. Would your recommended price be different if the offering were by the Teweles family, selling some of their 400,000 shares, or if it were new stock authorized by the company? For example, another 100,000 shares could be authorized, which when issued would bring the outstanding shares up to 500,000, with 400,000 shares owned by the Teweles and 100,000 shares held by the public. If the Teweles sell their own shares, they receive the proceeds as their own personal funds. If the company sells newly issued shares, the company receives the funds and presumably uses the money to expand the business.

n. If the price you selected above were actually established as the price at which the stock would be offered to the public, approximately how much money, in total, would Teweles actually receive?

Selected Additional References and Cases

For a wealth of facts and figures on a major segment of the stock market, see New York Stock Exchange, *Fact Book* (New York: published annually).

For both a description of the stock markets and some further facts and figures, see the investment textbooks referenced in Chapter 2. For a discussion of the current state of investment banking and trends in the industry, see

Hayes, S. L., "The Transformation of Investment Banking," *Harvard Business Review*, January-February 1979, 153-170.

Rogowski, Robert, and Eric Sorensen, "The New Competitive Environment of Investment Banking: Transactional Finance and Concession Pricing of New Issues," *Midland Corporate Finance Journal*, Spring 1986, 64-71.

Other good references on specific aspects of equity financing include the following:

Block, Stanley, and Marjorie Stanley, "The Financial Characteristics and Price Movement Patterns of Companies Approaching the Unseasoned Securities Market in the Late 1970s," *Financial Management*, Winter 1980, 30-36.

Bowyer, John W.. and Jess B. Yawitz, "Effect of New Equity Issues on Utility Stock Prices," *Public Utilities Fortnightly*, May 22, 1980, 25-28.

Fabozzi, Frank J., "Does Listing on the AMEX Increase the Value of Equity?" *Financial Management*, Spring 1981, 43-50.

Hansen, Robert S., and John M. Pinkerton, "Direct Equity Financing: A Resolution to a Paradox," *Journal of Finance*, June 1982, 651-665.

Logue, Dennis, and Robert A. Jarrow, "Negotiation versus Competitive Bidding in the Sale of Securities by Public Utilities," *Financial Management*, Autumn 1978, 31-39.

For more information on shelf registration, see

Bhagat, Sanjai, "The Evidence on Shelf Registration," *Midland Corporate Finance Journal*, Spring 1984, 6-12.

For an excellent discussion of the various procedures used to raise capital, see

Smith, Clifford W., Jr., "Raising Capital: Theory and Evidence," *Midland Corporate Finance Journal*, Spring 1986, 6-22. Also, Pages 72-76 of the Spring 1986 issue of the *Midland Corporate Finance Journal* contain a bibliography of recent articles pertaining to investment banking and capital acquisition.

For an additional discussion of adjustable rate preferred stock, see

Winger, Bernard J., et al., "Adjustable Rate Preferred Stock," *Financial Management*, Spring 1986, 48-57.

The following cases from the Crum-Brigham casebook focus on the issues contained in this chapter:

Case 20, "Helios Engineering," which emphasizes the investment banking process.

Case 21, "Farnsworth Furniture Industries," which focuses on the analysis of a rights offering.

Case 22, "Grafton Timber Company," which illustrates the decision to go public.

The Harrington casebook contains the following applicable case:

"Hop-In Food Stores, Incorporated," which focuses on a firm's decision to go public.

13

LONG-TERM DEBT FINANCING

As noted in Chapters 5 and 6, the use of debt financing is generally required to maximize the value of the firm. In this chapter, we discuss long-term debt, including its different forms, typical provisions in debt contracts, bond ratings, refunding operations, and the various factors that influence a firm's decision to use debt financing at a particular point in time.

TRADITIONAL TYPES OF LONG-TERM DEBT

There are many types of long-term debt: amortized and nonamortized, publicly issued or privately placed, secured and unsecured, marketable and nonmarketable, callable and noncallable, and so on. In this section, we review briefly the traditional long-term debt instruments and then, in the next section, we discuss some important recent innovations in long-term debt financing.

Term Loans

A *term loan* is a contract under which a borrower agrees to make a series of interest and principal payments, on specific dates, to a lender.[1] Investment bankers are generally not involved: Term loans are negotiated directly between the borrowing firm and a financial institution—generally a bank, an insurance company, or a pension fund. Although the maturities of term loans vary from 2 to 30 years, most are for periods in the 3- to 15-year range.

Term loans have three major advantages over public offerings—*speed, flexibility*, and *low issuance costs*. Also, because they are negotiated directly between the lender and the borrower, formal documentation is minimized. The key provisions of the loan can be worked out much more quickly, and with more flexibility, than

---

[1]Most term loans are *amortized*, or paid off, in equal installments over the life of the loan. See Appendix A at the end of the book for a review of amortization. Also, if the interest and maturity payments required under a term loan agreement are not met on schedule, the borrowing firm is said to have *defaulted*, and it can then be forced into bankruptcy. See Appendix 13A for a discussion of bankruptcy.

can those for a public issue, and it is not necessary for a term loan to go through the Securities and Exchange Commission registration process. A further advantage of term loans over publicly held debt has to do with future flexibility: If a bond issue is held by many different bondholders, it is virtually impossible to obtain permission to alter the terms of the agreement, even though new economic conditions may make such changes desirable. With a term loan, the borrower can generally negotiate with the lender to work out modifications in the contract.

The interest rate on a term loan can be either fixed for the life of the loan or variable. If it is fixed, the rate used will be close to the rate on bonds of equivalent maturity for companies of comparable risk. If the rate is variable, it is usually set at a certain number of percentage points over the prime rate, the commercial paper rate, the T-bill rate, or the London Interbank Offered Rate (LIBOR). Then, when the index rate goes up or down, so does the rate on the outstanding balance of the term loan. In 1986, about 75 percent of the dollar amount of term loans made by banks had floating rates, up from virtually zero in 1970. Most of the money banks lend to corporations is "bought" in the certificate of deposit market, and if the CD rate rises along with other market rates, banks need to raise the rates they earn in order to meet their own interest costs. With the increased volatility of interest rates in recent years, banks have rightly become reluctant to make long-term, fixed rate loans.

Bonds

Like a term loan, a bond is a long-term contract under which a borrower agrees to make payments of interest and principal, on specific dates, to the holder of the bond. Although bonds are similar to term loans, a bond issue is generally advertised, offered to the public, and actually sold to many different investors. Indeed, thousands of individual and institutional investors may participate when a firm such as New York Telephone sells a bond issue, while there is generally only one lender in the case of a term loan.[2] Although bonds are generally issued with maturities in the range of 20 to 30 years, shorter maturities, such as 7 to 10 years, are occasionally used. Unlike term loans, a bond's interest rate is generally fixed, although in recent years, there has been an increase in the use of various types of floating rate bonds.

Mortgage Bonds

Under a *mortgage bond*, the corporation pledges certain real assets as security for the bond. To illustrate, suppose McLaughlin Container Company needs $10 million to purchase land and to build a plant. Bonds in the amount of $4 million, secured by a mortgage on the property, are issued. If McLaughlin defaults on the bonds, the bondholders could foreclose on the plant and sell it to satisfy their claims.

---

[2]However, for very large term loans, 20 or more financial institutions may form a syndicate to grant the credit. Also, it should be noted that a bond issue can be sold to one lender (or to just a few); in this case, the issue is said to be "privately placed." Companies that place bonds privately do so for the same reasons that they use term loans—speed, flexibility, and low issuance costs.

McLaughlin could, if it so chose, issue *second mortgage bonds* secured by the same $10 million plant. In the event of liquidation, the holders of these second mortgage bonds would have a claim against the property only after the first mortgage bondholders had been paid off in full. Thus, second mortgages are sometimes called *junior mortgages*, or *junior liens*, because they are junior in priority to claims of *senior mortgages*, or *first mortgage bonds*.

Most major corporations' first mortgage indentures (discussed in detail later in the chapter) were written 20, 30, 40, or more years ago. These indentures are generally "open ended," meaning that new bonds may be issued from time to time under the existing indenture. However, the amount of new bonds that can be issued is virtually always limited to a specified percentage of the firm's total "bondable property," which generally includes all plant and equipment. For example, Savannah Electric Company can issue first mortgage bonds in total up to 60 percent of its fixed assets. If fixed assets totaled $100 million, and if Savannah Electric had $50 million of first mortgage bonds outstanding, then it could, by the 60 percent of property test, issue another $10 million of bonds.

In recent years, Savannah Electric has at times been unable to issue any new first mortgage bonds because of another indenture provision: Its times-interest-earned (TIE) ratio was below 2.5, the minimum coverage that it must maintain in order to sell new bonds. Thus, Savannah Electric passed the property test but failed the coverage test; hence, it could not issue first mortgage bonds, and it had to finance with other securities. Since first mortgage bonds carry lower rates of interest than junior long-term debt, this restriction was a costly one.

Savannah Electric's neighbor, Georgia Power Company, has more flexibility under its indenture; its interest coverage requirement is only 2.0 versus Savannah's 2.5 requirement. In hearings before the Georgia Public Service Commission, it was suggested that Savannah Electric should change its indenture coverage to 2.0 so that it could issue more first mortgage bonds. However, this was simply not possible—the holders of the outstanding bonds would have to approve the change, and it is inconceivable that they would vote for a change that would seriously weaken their position.

Debentures

A *debenture* is an unsecured bond, and as such, it has no lien against specific property as security for the obligation. Debenture holders are, therefore, general creditors whose claims are protected by property not otherwise pledged. In practice, the use of debentures depends on the nature of the firm's assets and its general credit strength. If its credit position is exceptionally strong, the firm can issue debentures—it simply does not need specific security. AT&T and IBM have both financed mainly through debentures; they are such strong corporations that they do not have to put up property as security for their debt issues. Debentures are also issued by companies in industries where it would not be practical to provide security through a mortgage on fixed assets. Examples of such industries are the large mail-order houses and commercial banks, which characteristically hold most of their assets in the form of inventory or loans, neither of which is satisfactory security for a mortgage bond. Finally, companies that have used up their capacity to borrow in the mortgage market may be forced to use debentures. These companies' debentures will be quite risky, and their interest rate will be correspondingly high.

Subordinated Debentures

The term *subordinate* means "below," or "inferior." Thus, *subordinated debt* has claims on assets in the event of bankruptcy only after senior debt has been paid off. Debentures may be subordinated either to designated notes payable—usually bank loans—or to all other debt. In the event of liquidation or reorganization, holders of subordinated debentures cannot be paid until senior debt, as named in the debentures' indenture, has been paid. The subordinated debenture of a company that has used up its ability to employ mortgage bonds is normally quite risky, and these debentures carry interest rates that are four to five percentage points above the rate on top quality debt. Precisely how subordination works, and how it strengthens the position of senior debtholders, is shown in Appendix 13A.

Other Types of Bonds

Several other types of bonds are used sufficiently often to warrant mention. First, *convertible bonds* are securities that are convertible into shares of common stock, at a fixed price, at the option of the bondholder. Basically, convertibles provide their holders with a chance for capital gains in exchange for a lower coupon rate, while the issuing firm gets the advantage of the low coupon rate. Bonds issued with *warrants* are similar to convertibles. Warrants are options which permit the holder to buy stock for a stated price. Therefore, if the price of the stock rises, the holder of the warrant will earn a capital gain. Bonds that are issued with warrants, like convertibles, carry lower coupon rates than straight bonds. Both warrants and convertibles are discussed in detail in Chapter 15.

Income bonds pay interest only when the interest is earned. Thus, these securities cannot bankrupt a company, so from a corporation's standpoint, they are less risky than "regular" bonds. However, from an investor's standpoint, they are riskier than regular bonds. Another type of bond that has been discussed in the United States, but which has not yet been used here to any extent, is the *indexed,* or *purchasing power, bond*, which is popular in Brazil, Israel, and a few other countries long plagued by high inflation. The interest rate paid on these bonds is based on an inflation index such as the Consumer Price Index, and the interest paid rises when the inflation rate rises, thus protecting the bondholders against inflation. Mexico has used bonds whose interest rate is pegged to the price of oil to finance the development of its huge petroleum reserves; since oil prices and inflation are correlated, these bonds offer some protection to investors against inflation.

Some companies may be in a position to benefit from the sale of either *development bonds* or *pollution control bonds*. State and local governments may set up both *industrial development agencies* and *pollution control agencies*. These agencies are allowed, under certain circumstances, to sell *tax-exempt bonds*, then to make the proceeds available to corporations for specific uses deemed (by Congress) to be in the public interest. Thus, an industrial development agency in Florida might sell bonds to provide funds for a paper company to build a plant in the

Florida Panhandle, where unemployment is high. Similarly, a Pittsburgh pollution control agency might sell bonds to provide U.S. Steel with funds to be used to purchase pollution control equipment. In both cases, the income from the bonds would be tax exempt to the holders, so the bonds would sell at relatively low interest rates. Note, however, that these bonds are guaranteed by the corporation that will use the funds, not by a governmental unit, so their rating reflects the credit strength of the corporation. Note also that the 1986 tax law imposes tougher requirements to qualify for tax-exempt status than did the previous law.

RECENT INNOVATIONS IN BOND FINANCING

The 1980s witnessed several innovations in long-term debt financing. We will discuss five in this section. The first three—zero coupons bonds, floating rate bonds, and bonds that are redeemable at par—are a result of the extreme volatility in interest rates which has characterized the last decade. The fourth, so called "junk bonds," gained popularity (some observers might say notoriety) as a source of takeover financing. The fifth, project financing, permits a firm to tie a debt issue to a specific asset.

Zero (or Very Low) Coupon Bonds

Zero (or very low) coupon bonds are offered at a substantial discount below their par values; hence, they are also called *original issue discount bonds* (*OIDs*). This type of bond was first used in a major way in 1981, and in recent years IBM, Alcoa, J. C. Penney, ITT, Cities Service, GMAC, Martin-Marietta, and many other companies have used them to raise billions of dollars. We include a discussion of these securities both to illustrate how they are analyzed and also to demonstrate how quickly financial markets react to changes in the economic environment.

An example will help clarify what zero coupon bonds are and how they are analyzed. In 1985 Carson Foods issued $100 million (par value) of "zeroes." They have no coupons, pay no interest, and mature after 5 years, in 1990, at which time holders will be paid $1,000 per bond. The bonds were originally issued at a discount of 42.826 percent below par, or for $571.74 per $1,000 bond. The semiannual interest rate which causes $571.74 to grow to $1,000 over 5 years (10 periods) is 5.75 percent, which is equivalent to a nominal annual return of 11.50 percent. Since most bonds pay interest semiannually, and since people normally compare the yield on a zero with yields on "regular" bonds, it is important to calculate the zero's yield in the same manner as we would for a coupon bond— find the semiannual rate, $k_d/2$, and then multiply by 2 to obtain the nominal annual rate. Even though the effective annual rate, or APR, is $(1.0575)^2 - 1.0 = 0.1183 = 11.83\%$, 11.5 percent is the rate that should be used when comparing Carson's zeroes to reported yields on semiannual coupon bonds.

Carson received about $57 million, less underwriting expenses, for the issue, but it will have to pay back $100 million in 1990. The advantages to Carson include the following: (1) No cash outlays are required for either interest or principal until the bond matures; (2) the zeroes have a relatively low yield to maturity (Carson would have had to pay approximately 12 percent rather than 11.5 percent had it issued regular coupon bonds at par); and (3) Carson receives an annual tax deduction, which means that the bonds provide a positive cash flow in the form of tax savings over their life. However, there are also two disadvantages to Carson: (1) The bond is, in effect, simply not callable; since it would have to be called at its $1,000 par value, Carson cannot refund it if interest rates should fall. (2) Carson will have a very large, nondeductible cash outlay coming due in 1990.

There are two principal advantages to investors in zero coupon bonds: (1) They have no danger whatever of a call, and (2) investors are guaranteed a "life of bond" yield (11.5 percent in the Carson case) irrespective of what happens to interest rates—the holders of Carson's bonds do not have to worry about "reinvestment risk," which means having to reinvest coupons received at low rates if interest rates should fall, which would result in a realized yield to maturity of less than 11.5 percent.[3] This second feature is extremely important to pension funds, life insurance companies, and other institutions which make actuarial contracts based on assumed reinvestment rates. For such investors, the risk of declining interest rates, and hence an inability to reinvest cash inflows at the assumed rate, is greater than the risk of an increase in rates and the accompanying fall in bond values.

To illustrate, suppose an insurance company or pension fund administrator signed a contract to pay $100,000 in five years in exchange for a lump sum premium of $61,391 today. The premium was based on the assumption that the company could invest the $61,391 at a return of 10 percent. If the $61,391 were invested in regular coupon bonds paying a 10 percent coupon rate, then the accumulated value five years hence would be equal to the required $100,000 only if all coupon payments could be reinvested at 10 percent over the next five years. If interest rates were to fall, then the accumulated amount would fall short of the required $100,000. Note, however, that if the $61,391 were invested in a zero coupon bond with a 10 percent yield, the insurance company would be sure of ending up with the required $100,000 regardless of what happened to interest rates in the future. Thus, the insurance company or pension fund would have been "immunized" against a decline in interest rates.

One might think there would be a tax advantage to investors in zero coupon bonds in that income would come in the form of capital gains rather than interest income, and hence be taxed at maturity, but this is not true in the United States. The IRS has ruled that original-issue discounts must be amortized and treated as ordinary income. Further, all zero coupon bonds must be registered, and the issuing corporation must send both the registered owner and the IRS a Form 1099 each year indicating the amount of the amortized discount. However, according to

---

[3]Recently a number of municipal governments have begun using zeroes to obtain funds for low-income housing projects. However, unlike most corporate zeroes, the muni zeroes permit the issuers to pay them off in advance at a compounded amount equal to $X(1 + k)^n$, where X is the original purchase price, k is the original yield to maturity, and n is the number of periods since issue. There is no reason why corporations could not also issue such callable zeroes, except, of course, investors would insist on higher base yields because such callability would remove the main advantage of zeroes to investors.

Table 13-1
Calculation of Zero Coupon Bond Interest

Semiannual Period (1)	Beginning Investment Value (2)	Calculated Interest (3)	Tax Savings (4)
1	$571.74	$32.88	$15.12
2	604.62	34.77	15.99
3	639.38	36.76	16.91
4	676.14	38.88	17.88
5	715.02	41.11	18.91
6	756.14	43.48	20.00
7	799.61	45.98	21.15
8	845.59	48.62	22.37
9	894.21	51.42	23.65
10	945.63	54.37	25.01
		$428.26	

Notes:

a. The periodic interest rate is 5.749943 percent.

b. The amounts shown in Column 3 are found by multiplying the beginning investment value shown in Column 2 times 0.05749943.

c. The investment value shown in Column 2 is the previous period's investment value plus interest, Column 2 plus Column 3.

d. The sum of Column 3, $428.26, is the total calculated interest, and $428.26 + $571.74 = $1,000.00.

e. The tax savings shown in Column 4 is the interest, or amortization, charge multiplied by Carson's 1985 marginal tax rate of 46 percent.

investment bankers who have handled the underwritings, this is not a material issue, because taxable zeroes have been sold exclusively to tax-exempt organizations, principally pension funds and Individual Retirement Plans (IRAs).[4] Yet, since pension funds are by far the largest purchasers of corporate bonds, the potential market for zero coupon bonds is by no means small.

To analyze a zero coupon bond and to compare it with a coupon bond, a corporate treasurer (or pension fund administrator) must employ the valuation models developed in Chapter 3. Consider again Carson's bonds. Someone buying Carson's zeroes would pay $571.74 per bond at t = 0 and receive $1,000 ten semiannual periods later. The periodic interest rate is 5.749943 percent, the rate that causes $571.74 to grow to $1,000 over 10 periods as found with a financial calculator. Table 13-1 shows how interest charges associated with the bond are calculated. The values shown in Column 3 will be reported to the IRS by Carson for each bondholder, and the bondholders (if they pay taxes) must declare these

[4]This statement refers to sales within the United States. There was also a strong market for zero coupon bonds issued by U.S. companies in Europe and the Far East, especially in Japan, where the appreciation of the bonds was treated as capital gains income rather than as interest income. Japan subsequently modified its tax laws and now treats the amortized discount as interest.

amounts as income, even though they receive no cash each year. Carson, on the other hand, can deduct the amounts shown in Column 3, calling them "amortization of discount on bonds." Note particularly that the discount is not amortized using the straight line method; rather, amortization is calculated on the basis of the compound interest method. The periodic amortization is tax deductible, and hence will save Carson T(Amortization) = 0.46(Amortization) in taxes each six months. These savings are shown in Column 4 of Table 13-1.

Thus, Carson received $571.74 at Period 0; it must repay $1,000 after 5 years (Period 10); and it receives tax benefits during the interim. The after-tax cash flows look like this:

Period	After-Tax Cash Flows
0	$571.74
1	15.12
2	15.99
3	16.91
4	17.88
5	18.91
6	20.00
7	21.15
8	22.37
9	23.65
10	25.01 − 1,000 = −974.99

The discount rate which forces the NPV of the above cash flows to equal zero is the after-tax periodic cost of the zero coupon bond. This rate, $k_d/2$, is 3.105 percent, and hence the after-tax cost of the issue is 2(3.105%) = 6.21%.

If Carson had sold a semiannual payment coupon bond, its pre-tax cost would have been 12 percent. Its after-tax interest payments would have been (Coupon/2)(1 − T) = ($120/2)(0.54) = $32.40, and its after-tax cost of debt would have been k_d = 12%(1 − T) = 6.48%. Thus, on an after-tax basis, the zero coupon bond has a lower cost to Carson than would a regular coupon bond, 6.21 percent for the zero versus 6.48 percent for the coupon bond.[5] For a purchaser, of course, the reverse is true. A tax-exempt bond buyer would receive the yield to maturity, which is 11.5 percent for the zero coupon bond and 12.0 percent for the coupon bond. Purchasers apparently believed that call protection plus the interest rate immunization were worth the 0.5 percentage point cost.

In 1983, several brokerage houses introduced a new security based on separating, or "stripping," the interest coupons from the principal amount of a Treasury bond. Merrill Lynch first introduced the concept with its Treasury Investment

---

[5]Note that the compound interest method of amortization used on original issue discount bonds results in an after-tax cost to the issuer which is equal to the after-tax cost of a coupon bond with the same yield to maturity. A coupon bond with an 11.5 percent YTM has an after-tax cost of 0.54(11.5%) = 6.21%, which is the same as we calculated by looking at the actual cash flows.

Growth Receipts (TIGRs, or "tigers"). To back its first TIGRs, Merrill Lynch bought $500 million face value of 30-year Treasury bonds, which it placed in trust. Then, Merrill Lynch in effect stripped off the coupons that mature each six months over the next 30 years, and used the 2 × 30 = 60 sets of coupons to back 60 series of TIGRS that mature at six-month intervals as the coupon payments on the Treasury bonds come due. The investor receives nothing until the maturity date he or she selects, be it six months or 30 years away. Sold at a discount, the TIGR is redeemed at face value at maturity—the more distant the maturity, the deeper the discount. Thus, with the introduction of TIGRs, insurance companies and pension funds were offered a default-free substitute for zero coupon corporate bonds, and thus far, the substitute has proved more acceptable than the original product.

Floating Rate Debt

In the late 1970s and early 1980s, inflation pushed interest rates up to unprecedented levels. These rising interest rates caused sharp declines in the prices of long-term bonds. Even supposedly "risk-free" U.S. Treasury bonds lost fully half their value, and a similar situation occurred with corporate bonds, mortgages, and other fixed rate, long-term securities. The lenders who held the fixed rate debt were of course hurt very badly. Bankruptcies (or forced mergers to avoid bankruptcy) were commonplace in the banking and especially in the savings and loan industries. Pension fund asset values declined, requiring corporations to increase contributions to their plans, which in turn hurt profits. Insurance company reserves plummeted, causing those companies severe problems, including the bankruptcy of Baldwin-United, a $9 billion diversified insurance firm.

As a result of all this, many lenders became extremely reluctant to lend money at fixed rates on a long-term basis, and they would do so only at high rates. There is normally a *maturity risk premium* embodied in long-term interest rates—this is a risk premium designed to offset the risk of declining bond prices if interest rates rise. Prior to the 1970s, this maturity risk premium is estimated to have been about one percentage point, meaning that, under "normal" conditions, a firm might expect to pay about one percentage point more to borrow on a long-term basis than on a short-term basis. However, in the late 1970s and early 1980s, the maturity risk premium is estimated to have jumped to about 3 percentage points. This made long-term debt very expensive relative to short-term debt.

Lenders were able and willing to lend on a short-term basis, but corporations were rightly reluctant to borrow short-term to finance long-term assets—such action is, as we shall see in Chapter 16, extremely dangerous. Therefore, we had a situation where lenders did not want to lend on a long-term basis, but corporations had a need for long-term money. The problem was solved by the introduction of long-term, floating rate debt. A typical floating rate issue works like this. The coupon rate is set for, say, the first six months after issue, after which it is adjusted every six months on the basis of some market rate. For example, Gulf Oil sold a floating rate bond that was pegged at 35 basis points above the rate on 30-year Treasury bonds. Other issues are tied to short-term rates. Additional provisions have been included in floating rate issues; for example, some may, after several years, be converted to fixed rate debt, whereas others have both a stated minimum coupon rate and a cap on how high the rate can go.

Floating rate debt is advantageous to lenders because, since the interest rate moves up if market rates rise, (1) the market value of the debt is stabilized and (2) the lender receives an income level which permits it to meet its own obligations (for example, a bank which owns floating rate bonds can use the interest it earns to pay interest on its own floating rate deposits). Floating rate debt is also advantageous to borrowing corporations because, with this security, they can obtain debt with a long maturity yet not have to continue paying high rates if rates fall in the future. Of course, if interest rates increase after a floating rate note has been signed, then the borrower would have been better off issuing conventional, fixed-rate debt.[6]

Bonds That Are Redeemable at Par

Bonds that are *redeemable at par* at the holder's option also protect the holder against a rise in interest rates. If rates rise, the price of fixed-rate debt declines. However, if the holders have the option of turning their bonds in and having them redeemed at par, they are protected against rising rates. Examples of such debt include Transamerica's $50 million issue of 25-year, 8½ percent bonds. The bonds are not callable by the company, but holders can turn them in for redemption at par five years after the date of issue. If interest rates have risen, holders will turn in the bonds and reinvest the proceeds at a higher rate. This feature enabled Transamerica to sell the bonds with an 8½ percent coupon at a time when other similarly rated bonds had yields of 9 percent.

Junk Bonds

A *junk bond* is a high-risk, high-yield bond. There are two types of junk bonds: (1) Bonds that were originally sound, but the issuer got into financial trouble after the bond was issued. These bonds generally have "reasonable" coupons but sell at deep discounts and thus have high yields to maturity to reflect their now-high risk. (2) Bonds that were quite risky at the time of issue. These bonds are almost always debentures, are generally subordinated to other debt, and are either issued to finance a leveraged buyout or a merger, or are issued by a company that is in deep trouble. For example, when Ted Turner attempted to buy CBS, he planned to finance the acquisition by issuing junk bonds to CBS's stockholders in exchange for their shares. Similarly, Merrill Lynch helped Public Service of New Hampshire finance construction of its troubled Seabrook nuclear plant with junk bonds.

In all new issue junk bond deals, the debt ratio is extremely high, so the bondholders must bear as much risk as stockholders normally would. The bonds' yields

---

[6]For a general discussion of floating rate debt, see Kenneth R. Marks and Warren A. Law, "Hedging against Inflation with Floating-Rate Notes," *Harvard Business Review*, March-April 1980, 106–112.

reflect this fact—Ted Turner's bonds would have carried a coupon rate of about 16 percent, and Merrill Lynch had to set a coupon rate of over 20 percent to sell the Public Service of New Hampshire bonds.

The emergence of junk bonds as an important type of new debt is another example of the way the investment banking industry adjusts to—and facilitates—new developments in capital markets. In the 1980s, mergers and takeovers increased dramatically. People like T. Boone Pickens and Ted Turner thought that certain old-line, established companies were financed too conservatively and run inefficiently, and they wanted to take over these companies and restructure them. To help finance these takeovers, the investment banking firm of Drexel Burnham Lambert had the idea of persuading certain institutions to purchase high-yield bonds. Drexel developed expertise in putting together deals that would be attractive to the institutions yet feasible in the sense that cash flow projections indicated that the issuing firms could meet their required interest payments. The fact that interest on the bonds is tax deductible, combined with the much higher debt ratios of the restructured firms, also increased after-tax cash flows and helped make the whole deal feasible.

The development of junk bond financing has done as much as any single factor to reshape the U.S. financial scene. It has led directly to the takeovers of Gulf Oil and hundreds of other companies, and it has led to major shake-ups in such companies as CBS and Union Carbide. It also caused Drexel Burnham Lambert to leap from essentially nowhere in the 1970s to the number five investment banking firm in 1985.

Project Financing

In recent years, many large projects such as the Alaska pipeline have been financed by what is called *project financing*. We can only present an overview of the concept, for in practice it involves very complicated provisions and can take many forms.

Project financing has been used to finance energy explorations, oil tankers, refineries, and utility power plants. Generally, one or more firms will sponsor the project, putting up the required equity capital, while the remainder of the financing is furnished by lenders or lessors.[7] Most often, a separate legal entity is formed to operate the project. The single most important feature of project financing is that normally the project's creditors do not have full recourse against the sponsors. In other words, the lenders and lessors must be paid from the project's cash flows, plus the sponsors' equity in the project, for the creditors have no claims against the sponsors' other assets or cash flows. Often the sponsors write "comfort" letters, giving general assurance that they will strive diligently to make the project successful, but these letters are not legally binding and therefore represent only a moral commitment. Therefore, in project financing the lenders and lessors must

---

[7]A lessor is an individual or firm that owns buildings and equipment and then leases them to another firm. Leasing is discussed in Chapter 14.

focus their analysis on the inherent merits of the project plus the equity cushion provided by the sponsors.[8]

Project financing is generally characterized by large size and a high degree of complexity. However, since project financing is tied to a specific project, it can be tailored to meet the specific needs of both the creditors and the sponsors. In particular, both funds provided during the construction phase and the subsequent repayment schedule can be coordinated with projected cash flows.[9]

SPECIFIC DEBT CONTRACT PROVISIONS

A firm's managers are most concerned about (1) the effective cost of debt and (2) any provisions which might restrict the firm's future actions. In this section, we discuss features which could affect either the cost of the firm's debt or its future flexibility.

Bond Indentures

An *indenture* is a legal document that spells out the rights of both the bondholders and the issuing corporation, and a *trustee* is an official (usually of a bank) who represents the bondholders and makes sure that the terms of the indenture are carried out. The indenture may be several hundred pages in length, and it will include *restrictive covenants* that cover such points as the conditions under which the issuer can pay off the bonds prior to maturity, the level at which the issuer's times-interest-earned ratio must be maintained if the company is to issue additional debt, and restrictions against the payment of dividends unless earnings meet certain specifications. Overall, these covenants relate to the agency problem first discussed in Chapter 1, and they are designed to insure, insofar as possible, that the firm does not change its financial policies in a way that would cause the quality of its bonds to deteriorate after they are issued.

The trustee is responsible for trying to keep the covenants from being violated and for taking appropriate action if a violation does occur. What constitutes "appropriate action" varies with the circumstances. It might be that to insist on immediate compliance would result in bankruptcy and possibly large losses on the bonds. In such a case, the trustee might decide that the bondholders would be

---

[8]In another type of project financing, each sponsor guarantees its share of the project's debt obligations. Here the creditors would also consider the credit worthiness of the sponsors in addition to the project's own prospects. It should be noted that project financing with multiple sponsors in the electric utility industry has led to problems when one or more of the sponsors has gotten into financial trouble. For example, Long Island Lighting, one of the sponsors in the Nine Mile Point nuclear project, became unable to meet its commitments to the project, which forced other sponsors to shoulder an additional burden or else see the project cancelled and lose all their investment up to that point. Utility executives have stated that this default, and others, will make companies reluctant to enter into similar projects in the future.

[9]It should also be noted that companies whose earnings were too low to satisfy their bond indenture coverage requirements have used project financings. In these cases, the new project was deemed stronger (better assets in terms of ability to generate cash flows per dollar of book value) than the firm's existing assets.

better served by giving the company a chance to work out its problems and thus avoid forcing it into bankruptcy.

The Securities and Exchange Commission (1) approves indentures and (2) makes sure that all indenture provisions are met before allowing a company to sell new securities to the public. Also, it should be noted that the indentures of most larger corporations were actually written in the 1930s or 1940s, and that many issues of new bonds sold since then were covered by the same indenture. The interest rates on the bonds, and perhaps also the maturities, varied depending on market conditions at the time of each issue, but bondholders' protection as spelled out in the indenture was the same for all bonds of the same type.[10]

Call Provisions

A *call provision* gives the issuing corporation the right to call a bond (or preferred stock) for redemption. If it is used, the call provision generally states that the company must pay an amount greater than the par value for the bond. The additional sum required, defined as the *call premium*, is typically set equal to one year's interest if the bond is called during the first year, with the premium declining at a constant rate of I/n each year thereafter, where I = annual interest and n = original maturity in years. For example, the call premium on a $1,000 par value, 20-year, 10 percent bond would generally be $100 if it were called during the first year, $95 during the second year (calculated by reducing the $100, or 10 percent, premium by one-twentieth), and so on.

The call privilege is valuable to the firm but potentially detrimental to the investor, especially if the bond is issued in a period when interest rates are cyclically high. This point was illustrated in Chapter 3, and it causes the interest rate on a new issue of callable bonds to exceed that on a new issue of noncallable bonds. For example, on February 1, 1986, Great Falls Timber Company sold an issue of A rated bonds to yield 10.375 percent. These bonds were callable immediately. On the same day, Midwest Milling Company sold an issue of A rated bonds to yield 10 percent. Midwest's bonds were noncallable for 10 years. (This is known as a *deferred call*.) Investors were apparently willing to accept a 0.375 percent lower interest rate on Midwest's bonds for the assurance that the relatively high (by historic standards) rate of interest would be earned for at least 10 years. Great Falls, on the other hand, had to incur a 0.375 percent higher annual interest rate to obtain the option of calling the bonds in the event of a subsequent decline in interest rates. We discuss the analysis for determining when to call an issue later in this chapter.

Sinking Funds

A *sinking fund* is a provision that provides for the systematic retirement of a bond issue (or an issue of preferred stock). Typically, the sinking fund provision requires a firm to call and retire a portion of its bonds each year. On rare occasions, the

---

[10]A firm will have different indentures for each of the major types of bonds it issues. For example, one indenture will cover its first mortgage bonds, another its debentures, and a third its convertible bonds.

firm may be required to deposit money with a trustee, who invests the funds and then uses the accumulated sum to retire the entire bond issue when it matures. Sometimes the stipulated sinking fund payment is tied to the sales or earnings of the current year, but usually it is a mandatory fixed amount. If it is mandatory, a failure to meet the sinking fund requirement causes the bond issue to be thrown into default, which may force the company into bankruptcy.

In most cases, the firm is given the right to handle the sinking fund in either of two ways:

1. It may call in for redemption (at par value) a certain percentage of the bonds each year—for example, it might be able to call 2 percent of the total original amount of the issue at a price of $1,000 per bond. The bonds are numbered serially, and the ones called for redemption are determined by a lottery.

2. It may buy the required amount of bonds on the open market. The firm will choose the least cost method. Therefore, if interest rates have risen, causing bond prices to fall, the company will elect to use the option of buying bonds in the open market at a discount. Otherwise, it will call them. Note that a call for sinking fund purposes is quite different from a refunding call. A sinking fund call requires no call premium, but only a small percentage of the issue is callable in any one year.

Although the sinking fund is designed to protect the bondholders by assuring that the issue is retired in an orderly fashion, it must be recognized that the sinking fund may at times work to the detriment of bondholders. If, for example, the bond carries a 13 percent interest rate, and if yields on similar securities have fallen to 9 percent, then the bond will sell above par. A sinking fund call at par would thus greatly disadvantage those bondholders whose bonds were called. On balance, however, securities that provide for a sinking fund and continuing redemption are regarded as being safer than bonds without sinking funds, so adding a sinking fund provision to a bond issue will lower the interest rate on the bond.

BOND RATINGS

Since the early 1900s, bonds have been assigned quality ratings that reflect their probability of going into default. The two major rating agencies are Moody's Investors Service (Moody's) and Standard & Poor's Corporation (S&P). These agencies' rating designations are shown in Table 13-2.[11]

The triple and double A bonds are extremely safe. Single A and triple B bonds are strong enough to be called "investment grade," and they are the lowest rated bonds that many banks and other institutional investors are permitted by law to hold. Double B and lower bonds are speculations; they are junk bonds with a

---

[11]In the discussion to follow, reference to the S&P code is intended to imply the Moody's code as well. Thus, for example, triple B bonds means both BBB and Baa bonds; double B bonds, both BB and Ba bonds.

Table 13-2
Comparison of Bond Ratings

	High Quality		Investment Grade		Substandard		Speculative		
Moody's	Aaa	Aa	A	Baa	Ba	B	Caa	to	C
S&P	AAA	AA	A	BBB	BB	B	CCC	to	D

Note: Both Moody's and S&P use "modifiers" for bonds rated below triple A. S&P uses a plus and minus system; thus, A+ designates the strongest A rated bonds and A− the weakest. Moody's uses a 1, 2, or 3 designation, with 1 denoting the strongest and 3 the weakest; thus, within the double A category, Aa1 is the best, Aa2 is average, and Aa3 is the weakest. Triple A bonds have no modifiers in either system.

higher probability of going into default, and many financial institutions are prohibited from buying them.

Bond Rating Criteria

Although the rating assignments are subjective, they are based on both qualitative and quantitative factors, such as the debt ratio, the coverage ratio, and so forth. Analysts at the rating agencies have consistently stated that no precise formula is used to set a firm's rating—many are taken into account, but not in a mathematically precise manner. Statistical studies have borne out this contention. Researchers who have tried to predict bond ratings on the basis of quantitative data have had only limited success, indicating that the agencies do indeed use a good deal of subjective judgment to establish a firm's rating.[12]

Importance of Bond Ratings

Bond ratings are important both to firms and to investors. First, a bond's rating is an indicator of its risk, so the rating has a direct, measurable influence on the bond's interest rate and the firm's cost of debt capital. Second, most bonds are purchased by institutional investors, not by individuals, and many of these institutions are restricted to investment-grade securities. Thus, if a firm's bonds fall below BBB, it will have a difficult time trying to sell new bonds, since many potential purchasers will not be allowed to buy them.

Ratings also have an effect on the availability of debt capital. If an institutional investor buys BBB bonds, which are subsequently downgraded to BB or lower, then (1) the institution's regulators will reprimand or perhaps impose restrictions on the institution if it continues to hold the bonds, but (2) since many other institutional investors will no longer be able to purchase the bonds, the institution that owns them will probably not be able to sell them except at a sizable loss.

---

[12]See Robert S. Kaplan and Gabriel Urwitz, "Statistical Models of Bond Ratings: A Methodological Inquiry," *Journal of Business*, April 1979, 231-261; and Ahmed Belkaoui, *Industrial Bonds and the Rating Process* (London: Quorum Books, 1983).

Because of this fear of downgrading, many institutions restrict their bond portfolios to at least A, or even AA, bonds. Some even confine purchases to AAA bonds. Thus, the lower a firm's bond rating, the smaller the group of available purchasers for its new issues.

As a result of their higher risk and more restricted market, lower-grade bonds have much higher required rates of return, k_d, than do high-grade bonds. Figure 13-1 illustrates this point. Throughout the nearly 34 years shown on the graph, U.S. Government bonds have always had the lowest yields, AAAs have been next, and the BBB bonds have had the highest yields of the three types.

Figure 13-1 also shows that the gaps between yields on the three types of bonds vary over time; in other words, the cost differentials, or risk premiums, fluctuate from year to year.[13] This point is highlighted in Figure 13-2, which gives the yields on the three types of bonds, and the risk premiums for AAA and BBB bonds, in June 1963, in June 1975, and again in January 1986. Note first that the riskless rate, or vertical axis intercept, rose over 5 percentage points from 1963 to 1986, reflecting the increase in realized and anticipated inflation. Second, the slope of the line also rose, indicating increased investor risk aversion, from 1963 to 1986, but risk aversion declined from 1975 to 1986. Thus, the penalty for having a low credit rating varies over time. Occasionally, as in 1963, it is not too severe, but at other times, as in 1975, it is quite large.[14]

Changes in Ratings

A change in a firm's bond rating will have a significant effect on its ability to borrow long-term capital, and on the cost of that capital. Rating agencies review outstanding bonds on a periodic basis, occasionally upgrading or downgrading a bond

---

[13]The term *risk premium* ought to reflect only the difference in the expected (and required) returns between two securities that results from differences in their risk. However, the difference between *yields to maturity* on different types of bonds consist of (1) a true risk premium; (2) a liquidity premium, which reflects the fact that U.S. Treasury bonds are more readily marketable than most corporate bonds; (3) a call premium, because most Treasury bonds are not callable, while corporate bonds are; and (4) an expected loss differential, which reflects the probability of loss on the corporate bonds. As an example of the latter point, suppose the yield to maturity on a BBB bond were 10 percent versus 7 percent on government bonds, but there is a 5 percent probability of total default loss on the corporate bond. In this case, the expected return on the BBB bond would be 0.95(10%) + 0.05(0%) = 9.5%, and the risk premium would be 2.5 percent, not the full 3.0 percentage point difference in "promised" yields to maturity. Therefore, the risk premiums given in Figure 13-2 overstate somewhat the true (but unmeasurable) risk premiums.

[14]The relationship graphed here is akin to the Security Market Line developed in Chapter 2, although bond ratings rather than beta coefficients are used to measure risk. A word about the scaling of the horizontal axis and about the placement of the points is in order. (1) We have shown a linear fit, although there is no theoretical reason to think that yields plotted against bond ratings are necessarily linear. (2) We have shown the interval on the horizontal axis between AAA and BBB to be equal to that between U.S. Government bonds and AAA, but this is an arbitrary scaling. (3) Finally, on an accurate, large-scale graph, it would be clear that the plotted points for the AAA and BBB bonds are not precisely on the straight lines shown in the graph; however, they are sufficiently close to warrant our analysis.

Attempts have been made to calculate beta coefficients for bonds and to plot bonds on the same SML that is used for common stocks. However, these results have not been successful—bonds do not plot on the same linear SML as stocks.

Figure 13-1
Yields on Selected Long-Term Bonds, 1953-1986

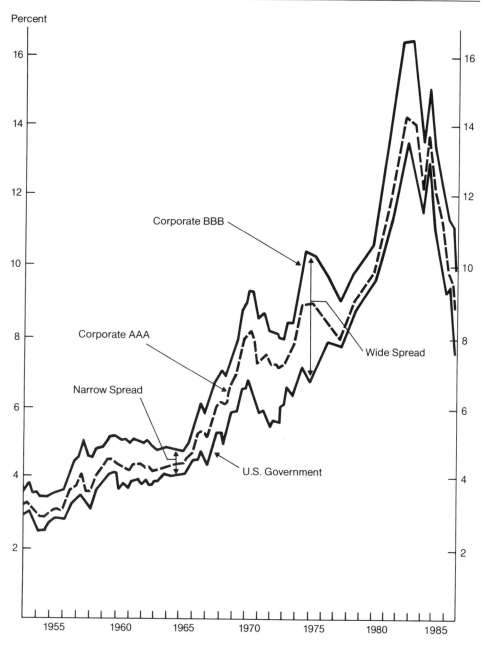

Sources: Federal Reserve Board, *Historical Chart Book,* 1983,
and *Federal Reserve Bulletin,* various issues.

Figure 13-2
**Relationship between Bond Ratings
and Bond Yields, 1963, 1975, and 1986**

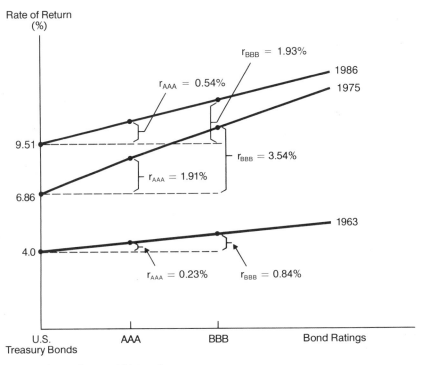

r_{AAA} = risk premium on AAA bonds

r_{BBB} = risk premium on BBB bonds

	Long-Term Government Bonds (Default-Free) (1)	AAA Corporate Bonds (2)	BBB Corporate Bonds (3)	Risk Premiums	
				AAA (4) = (2) − (1)	BBB (5) = (3) − (1)
June 1963	4.00%	4.23%	4.84%	0.23%	0.84%
June 1975	6.86	8.77	10.40	1.91	3.54
January 1986	9.51	10.05	11.44	0.54	1.93

Source: *Federal Reserve Bulletins.*

as a result of its issuer's changed circumstances. Also, an announcement that a company plans to sell a new debt issue, or to merge with another company and to pay for the acquisition by exchanging bonds for the stock of the acquired company, will trigger an agency review and possibly lead to a rating change. For example, in May 1986, when Burroughs announced plans to take over Sperry, S&P immediately placed the bonds of both companies on "CreditWatch" with "negative implications." CreditWatch is an S&P publication which lists bonds that it is actively reviewing for a possible rating change in response to some development, and investors are warned that the rating may be changed upon completion of the review. CreditWatch listings are published in the *Wall Street Journal*, and the publication itself may be subscribed to or read in many libraries. It spells out in detail what S&P sees as going on, and it is updated frequently.[15]

If a firm's situation has deteriorated somewhat, but its bonds have not been reviewed and downgraded, then it may choose to use a term loan or short-term debt rather than to finance through a public bond issue. This will perhaps postpone a rating agency review until the situation has improved. For example, a number of public utilities delayed bond issues in the early 1980s, financing with short-term debt until electric rate increases could be obtained to raise interest coverage ratios to acceptable levels. After rate increases were put into effect and coverages improved, the companies sold bonds and used the proceeds to retire the excess short-term debt.

ADVANTAGES AND DISADVANTAGES OF LONG-TERM DEBT FINANCING

From the issuer's viewpoint, there are several advantages and disadvantages to long-term, fixed-rate debt financing. The major advantages are as follows:

1. The cost of debt is fixed, so debtholders do not participate if profits soar. There is, however, a flip side to this argument—if profits fall, the bondholders must still be paid their interest.

2. The risk-adjusted component cost of debt is typically lower than that of common stock when corporate taxes are considered.

3. The owners of the corporation do not share their control when debt financing is used.

The major disadvantages are as follows:

1. Since debt service (interest plus scheduled principal repayments) is a fixed charge, a reduction in revenues may result in insufficient income to meet interest expenses. This can lead to bankruptcy.

2. As discussed in Chapters 5 and 6, financial leverage increases the firm's riskiness, and hence increases the costs of both debt and equity.

---

[15]Rating agencies do review ratings without being prompted by the company. However, most reviews associated with new issues are actually requested by the company, not because the company wants a review but because the investment bankers make such a review a condition of their handling the offering. Note also that a company must pay the agency to have its bonds rated. It has been suggested that such payments might lead to a favorable bias in ratings. However, there is no evidence whatever of any bias on the part of the major rating agencies. The value of their service, and hence the rating agencies' incomes, depends almost entirely on their credibility, so there is every reason to expect the agencies to maintain strict objectivity.

3. Debt normally has a fixed maturity, and hence the firm must repay the principal at some future time.

4. In a long-term contractual relationship, the indenture provisions are likely to be much more stringent than they are in a short-term credit agreement. Thus, the firm may be subject to more restrictions than if it had borrowed on a short-term basis or had issued common stock.

5. There is a limit to the amount of funds which can be raised at a "reasonable" rate. Widely accepted lending standards dictate that the debt ratio should not exceed certain limits, and when debt goes beyond these limits, its cost becomes exhorbitant.

REFUNDING OPERATIONS

Suppose a company sells bonds or preferred stock when interest rates are relatively high. Provided the issue is callable, as many are, the company could sell a new issue of low-yielding securities if and when interest rates drop. It could then use the proceeds to retire the high-rate issue and thus reduce its interest or preferred dividend expenses.[16] This is called a *refunding operation*. Refunding decisions actually involve two separate questions: (1) Is it profitable to call an outstanding issue in the current period and to replace it with a new issue, and (2) even if refunding is currently profitable, would the value of the firm be increased even more if the refunding were postponed to a later date? We consider both questions in this section.

First, note that the decision to refund a security is analyzed in much the same way as a capital budgeting expenditure. The costs of refunding—the investment outlays—are (1) the call premium paid for the privilege of calling the old issue and (2) the flotation costs incurred in selling the new issue. The annual benefits, in a capital budgeting sense, are the interest payments that are saved each year. For example, if the interest expense on the old issue is $1,000,000 and that on the new issue is $700,000, the $300,000 savings constitutes an annual benefit.

Discounted cash flow analysis is used to analyze the advantages of refunding—we must find the future cash flow savings, discount them back to the present, and then compare this discounted value with the cash outlays associated with the refunding. The firm should refund the bond if the present value of the cash savings exceeds the costs associated with the refunding, that is, if the NPV of the refunding operation is positive.

---

[16]During the early 1980s, there was a flurry of work on the pros and cons of refunding bond issues that had fallen to deep discounts as a result of rising interest rates. At such times, the company could go into the market, buy its debt at a low price, and retire it. The difference between the bonds' par value and the price the company paid would be reported as income, and taxes would have to be paid on it. The results of the research on the refunding of discount issues suggest that bonds should not, in general, be refunded after a rise in rates. See Andrew J. Kalotay, "On the Structure and Valuation of Debt Refundings," *Financial Management*, Spring 1982, 41-42; and Robert S. Harris, "The Refunding of Discounted Debt: An Adjusted Present Value Analysis," *Financial Management*, Winter 1980, 7-12.

In the discounting process, the after-tax cost of the new debt, k_d, should be used as the discount rate. The reasons for this are (1) there is relatively little risk to the savings—cash flows in a refunding are known with relative certainty, which is quite unlike the situation with cash flows in most capital budgeting decisions, and (2) the cash outlay required to refund the old issue is generally obtained by increasing the amount of the new issue (see Footnote 19).

The easiest way to examine the refunding decision is through an example. Microchip Computer Company has outstanding a $60 million bond issue which has a 15 percent annual coupon and 20 years remaining to maturity. This issue, which was sold 5 years ago, had flotation costs of $3 million, which the firm has been amortizing on a straight line basis over the 25-year original life of the issue. The bond has a call provision which makes it possible for the company to retire the bonds at this time by calling them in at a 10 percent call premium. Investment bankers have assured the company that it could sell an additional $60 million to $70 million worth of new annual coupon 20-year bonds at an interest rate of 12 percent. To insure that the funds required to pay off the old debt will be available, the new bonds would be sold one month before the old issue is called, so for one month, interest would have to be paid on two issues. Current short-term interest rates are 11 percent; for the one-month overlap period, proceeds from the new issue will be invested in short-term securities. Predictions are that long-term interest rates are unlikely to fall below 12 percent.[17] Flotation costs on a new refunding issue would amount to $2,650,000. Microchip's marginal tax rate is 34 percent. Should the company refund the $60 million of 15 percent bonds?

The following steps outline the decision process; the steps are summarized in worksheet form in Table 13-3.

Step 1. Determine the investment outlay required to refund the issue.

a. Call premium

$$\text{Before tax: } 0.10(\$60,000,000) = \$6,000,000.$$
$$\text{After tax: } \$6,000,000(1 - T) = \$6,000,000(0.66)$$
$$= \$3,960,000.$$

Although Microchip must expend $6 million on the call premium, this is a deductible expense in the year the call is made. Since the company is in the 34 percent tax bracket, it saves $6,000,000 − $3,960,000 = $2,040,000 in taxes. Therefore, the after-tax cost of the call is only $3.96 million. This amount is shown on Line 1 of Table 13-3.

b. Flotation costs on new issue
Flotation costs on the new issue are $2,650,000. For tax purposes, flotation costs must be amortized over the life of the new bond, or 20 years. Therefore, the annual tax deduction is

---

[17]The firm's management has estimated that there is a 75 percent probability that interest rates will remain at their present level of 12 percent or else rise; there is only a 25 percent probability that they will fall further.

Table 13-3
Worksheet for the Bond Refunding Decision

	Amount before Tax	Amount after Tax	Time Event Occurs	PV at 7.92%
Cost of Refunding: t = 0				
1. Call premium on old bond	$6,000,000	$3,960,000	0	$3,960,000
2. Flotation costs on new issue	2,650,000	2,650,000	0	2,650,000
3. Tax savings on new issue flotation cost amortization	(132,500)	(45,050)	1-20	(444,953)
4. Immediate tax savings on old flotation cost expense	(2,400,000)	(816,000)	0	(816,000)
5. Periodic tax benefits no longer received on old flotation costs	120,000	40,800	1-20	402,976
6. Extra interest on old issue	750,000	495,000	0	495,000
7. Interest on short-term investment	(550,000)	(363,000)	0	(363,000)
8. Total after-tax investment (PV of investment)				$5,884,023
Savings over the Life of the New Issue: t = 1 to 20				
9. Interest on old bond	$9,000,000	$5,940,000		
10. Interest on new bond	(7,200,000)	(4,752,000)		
11. Net savings of interest	$1,800,000	$1,188,000	1-20	$11,733,727

Refunding NPV

NPV = PV of interest savings − PV of investment
    = $11,733,727 − $5,884,023
    = $5,849,704.

$$\frac{\$2,650,000}{20} = \$132,500.$$

Since Microchip is in the 34 percent tax bracket, it has a tax savings of $132,500(0.34) = $45,050 a year for 20 years. This is an annuity of $45,050 for 20 years. In a refunding analysis, all cash flows should be discounted at the after-tax cost of new debt, in this case $12\%(1 - T) = 12\%(0.66) = 7.92\%$. The present value of the tax savings, discounted at 7.92 percent, is $444,953.

The net after-tax new flotation cost is $2,205,047:

Gross flotation costs on new issue	$2,650,000
PV of associated tax savings	(444,953)
Net (after-tax) flotation cost on new issue	$2,205,047

The gross costs and tax savings are reflected on Lines 2 and 3 of Table 13-3.

c. Flotation costs on old issue

The old issue has an unamortized flotation cost of $(20/25)(\$3,000,000) = \$2.4$ million at this time. If the issue is retired, the unamortized flotation cost may be recognized immediately as an expense, thus creating an after-tax savings of $\$2,400,000(0.34) = \$816,000$. The firm will, however, no longer receive a tax deduction of $\$120,000$ a year for 20 years, or an after-tax benefit of $\$40,800$ a year. The present value of this tax savings, discounted at 7.92 percent, is $\$402,976$.

The net after-tax effect of expensing the old flotation costs is a $\$413,024$ cash inflow:

Tax savings from immediate write-off of old flotation costs	($816,000)
PV of tax savings on old flotation costs had refunding not occurred	402,976
Net after-tax savings on old flotation costs	($413,024)

These figures are reflected on Lines 4 and 5 of the table. It is important to note that because of the refunding, the old flotation costs provide an immediate tax saving rather than annual savings over the next 20 years. Thus, the $\$413,024$ net savings simply reflects the difference between the present value of benefits received in the future without the refunding versus an immediate benefit if the refunding occurs.

d. Additional interest

One month "extra" interest on the old issue, after taxes, costs $\$495,000$:

$$(\text{Dollar amount})(1/12 \text{ of } 15\%)(1 - T) = \text{Interest cost}$$
$$(\$60,000,000)(0.0125)(0.66) = \$495,000.$$

However, the proceeds from the new issue can be invested in short-term securities for one month. Thus, $\$60$ million invested at a rate of 11 percent will return $\$363,000$ in after-tax interest:

$$(\$60,000,000)(1/12 \text{ of } 11\%)(1 - T) = \text{Interest earned}$$
$$(\$60,000,000)(0.009167)(0.66) = \$363,000.$$

The net after-tax additional interest cost is thus $\$132,000$:

Interest paid on old issue	$495,000
Interest earned on short-term securities	(363,000)
Net additional interest	$132,000

These figures are reflected in Lines 6 and 7.

e. Total after-tax investment

The total investment outlay required to refund the bond issue, which will be financed by debt, is thus $5,884,023:[18]

Call premium	$3,960,000
Flotation costs, new, net of tax savings	2,205,047
Flotation costs, old, net savings	(413,024)
Additional interest	132,000
Total investment	$5,884,023

This total is shown on Line 8 of the table.

Step 2. Calculate the PV of the annual interest savings.

a. Interest on old bond, after tax

The annual after-tax interest on the old issue is $5,940,000:

$$(\$60,000,000)(0.15)(0.66) = \$5,940,000.$$

This is shown on Line 9.

b. Interest on new bond, after tax

The new issue has an annual after-tax cost of $4,752,000:

$$(\$60,000,000)(0.12)(0.66) = \$4,752,000.$$

This is shown on Line 10.

c. Annual savings

Thus, the annual after-tax savings is $1,188,000:

Interest on old bond, after tax	$5,940,000
Interest on new bond, after tax	(4,752,000)
Annual net savings	$1,188,000

This is shown on Line 11.

d. PV of annual savings

The PV of $1,188,000 per year at 7.92 percent for 20 years is $11,733,727. This is also shown on Line 11.

---

[18]The net cash investment outlay (in this case, about $6 million) is usually obtained by increasing the amount of the new bond issue. Thus, the new issue would be about $66 million. However, the interest on the additional debt *should not* be deducted at Step 2 because the net investment outlay itself will be deducted at Step 3. If additional interest on the $6 million were deducted at Step 2, then interest would, in effect, be deducted twice. The situation here is exactly like that in regular capital budgeting decisions. Even though some debt may be used to finance a project, interest on that debt is not subtracted when developing the annual cash flows. Rather, the annual cash flows are *discounted* by the project's cost of capital.

Step 3. Determine the NPV of the refunding.

PV of benefits	$11,733,727
PV of costs	5,884,023
NPV from refunding	$ 5,849,704

Since the net present value of the refunding is positive, it would be profitable to refund the old bond issue.

Several other points should be noted. First, since the cash flows are based on differences between contractual obligations, their risk is the same as that of the underlying obligations. Therefore, the present values of the cash flows should be found by discounting at the firm's least risky rate—its after-tax cost of marginal debt. Second, since the refunding operation is advantageous to the firm, it must be disadvantageous to bondholders; they must give up their 15 percent bonds and reinvest in new ones that yield 12 percent. This points out the danger of the call provision to bondholders, and it also explains why bonds without a call provision command higher prices than callable bonds. Third, although it is not emphasized in the example, we assumed that the firm raises the investment required to under-take the refunding operation (the $5,884,023 shown on Line 8 of Table 13-3) as debt. This should be feasible, since the refunding operation will improve the inter-est coverage ratio even though, if the investment outlay is raised as debt, a larger amount of debt will be outstanding.[19] Fourth, we set up our example in such a way that the new issue had the same maturity as the remaining life of the old issue. Often, the old bonds have only a relatively short time to maturity (say, 5 to 10 years), while the new bonds would have a longer maturity (say, 25 to 30 years). In this situation, the analysis should only include cash flows up to the maturity of the old issue.[20] Fifth, refunding decisions are well suited for analysis with a spread-sheet program such as *Lotus 1-2-3*. The spreadsheet is easy to set up, and once it is, it is easy to vary the assumptions, especially the assumption about the interest rate on the new issue, and to see the way such changes affect the NPV.

---

[19]See Ahron R. Ofer and Robert A. Taggart, Jr., "Bond Refunding: A Clarifying Analysis," *Journal of Finance*, March 1977, 21-30, for a discussion of how the method of financing the refunding affects the analysis. Ofer and Taggart prove that (1) if the refunding investment outlay is to be raised as debt, the after-tax cost of debt is the proper discount rate, while (2) if these funds are to be raised as common equity, then the before-tax cost of debt is the proper rate. Since a profitable refunding will virtually always raise the firm's debt-carrying capacity (because total interest charges after the refunding will be lower than before the refunding), it is more logical to use debt than either equity or a combination of debt and equity to finance the operation. Therefore, firms generally do use additional debt to finance refunding operations, so we assume debt financing for the costs of refunding and discount at the after-tax cost of debt.

[20]It should also be noted that, to be exactly precise, the old bond should, in our example, have had a maturity of 20 years plus one month at the time the analysis was undertaken, so that the old issue would have exactly 20 years remaining when it is actually refunded.

One final point should be addressed: Although our analysis shows that the re-funding would increase the value of the firm, would refunding *at this time* truly maximize the firm's expected value? Note that if interest rates continue to fall, then the company might be better off waiting, for this could increase the NPV of the refunding operation even more. The mechanics of calculating the NPV of a refunding are simple, but the decision on *when* to refund is not a simple one at all, because it requires a forecast of future interest rates. Thus, refund now versus waiting for a possibly more favorable future refunding is a judgmental decision.

To illustrate the timing decision, assume that Microchip's managers forecast that long-term interest rates have a 50 percent probability of remaining at their present level of 12 percent over the next year. However, there is a 25 percent probability that rates could fall to 10 percent, and a 25 percent probability that they could rise to 14 percent. Further, assume that short-term rates are expected to remain one percentage point below long-term rates, and that the call premium would be reduced by one-twentieth if the call were delayed for one year.

The refunding analysis could then be repeated, as previously, but assuming it would take place one year from now. Thus, the old bonds would have only 19 years remaining to maturity. We performed the analysis and found the NPV distribution of refunding one year from now:

Probability	Long-Term Interest Rate	NPV of Refunding One Year from Now
25%	10%	$15,328,674
50	12	5,770,191
25	14	(2,158,208)

At first blush, it would seem reasonable to calculate the expected NPV of refunding next year in terms of the probability distribution. However, that would not be correct. If interest rates did rise to 14 percent, Microchip would not refund the issue; therefore, the actual NPV if rates rise to 14 percent would be zero. The expected NPV from refunding one year hence is, therefore, 0.25($15,328,674) + 0.50($5,770,191) + 0.25($0) = $6,717,264 versus $5,849,704 if refunding occurred today.

Even though the expected NPV of refunding in one year is higher, Microchip's managers would probably decide to refund today. The $5,849,704 represents a certain increase in firm value, whereas the $6,717,264 is only an expected increase, plus proper comparison requires that the $6,717,264 be discounted back one year to today. Microchip's managers should opt to delay refunding only if the expected NPV from later refunding is sufficiently above today's certain NPV to compensate for the risk and time value involved.

The refunding analysis could be extended by (1) including possible refunding at more than one future point in time, and (2) specifying future interest rates by a continuous rather than a discrete distribution. However, the essence of the timing decision would remain the same.

FACTORS THAT INFLUENCE LONG-TERM FINANCING DECISIONS

As we show in this section, many factors influence a firm's long-term financing decisions. It is impossible to rank the factors in order of importance, because their relative importance varies (1) among firms at any point in time and (2) for any given firm over time.

Capital Structure Considerations

One of the most important considerations in any financing decision is the way the firm's actual capital structure compares to its target capital structure. Remember that firms establish an optimal, or target, capital structure and, over time, finance in accordance with this target. Of course, in any one year, few firms finance exactly in accordance with their target capital structures, primarily because of flotation costs: Smaller issues of new securities have proportionally larger flotation costs, so firms tend to use debt one year and stock the next.

For example, assume that Consolidated Tools, Inc., a Cincinnati machine tool manufacturer, anticipates a requirement for $10 million of new external capital in each of the next 2 years. The target capital structure calls for 40 percent debt, so Consolidated, if it were to raise debt each year, would issue $4 million of new bonds each year for 2 years. The flotation costs, based on the data in Table 12-3 in Chapter 12, would be 6.2 percent of each $4 million issue. To net $4 million, Consolidated would have to sell $4 million/0.938 = $4,264,392 each year, and pay $264,392 in flotation costs on each issue, for a total of $528,784 in flotation costs over the 2 years.

Alternatively, Consolidated could elect to raise the total $8 million of debt in one year. The flotation cost for an $8 million issue would be 3.2 percent, so the firm would float an issue for $8 million/0.968 = $8,264,463 and pay $264,463 in total flotation costs. By issuing debt only once, Consolidated would cut its debt flotation costs almost in half. The same type of relationship would apply to sales of preferred stock and new common equity issues.

Note that making fewer, but larger, security offerings would cause Consolidated's capital structure to fluctuate about its the optimal level rather than stay right on target. However, (1) small fluctuations about the optimal capital structure have little effect on a firm's weighted average cost of capital, (2) investors would recognize that this action is prudent, and (3) the firm would save substantial amounts of flotation costs by financing in this manner. So, firms such as Consolidated tend, over the long haul, to finance in accordance with their target capital structures, but flotation costs plus the factors discussed in the following sections do influence the specific financing decisions in any given year.

We should also point out that firms such as Consolidated can, and often do, arrange financings in advance. Thus, if Consolidated concluded that it would need $8 million of debt over a 2-year period, it might arrange with one or more pension funds to lend it $4 million in each of the next 2 years, with the second $4 million being firmly committed by the lenders at the time the first $4 million is borrowed. Such financings can reduce flotation costs, because the lenders need make only one detailed credit analysis. Similarly, larger firms can use shelf registrations, which we discussed in Chapter 12, to hold down financing costs even while they sell relatively small blocks of securities. Both commitment financings and shelf registrations make it possible for firms to adhere reasonably closely to their optimal capital structures without incurring unduly high flotation costs.

Maturity Matching

Assume that Consolidated makes the decision to float a single $8 million nonconvertible bond issue, with a sinking fund. It must next choose a maturity for the issue, taking into consideration both the shape of the yield curve, management's own expectations about future interest rates, and the maturity of the assets being financed. To illustrate how asset maturities affect the choice of debt maturities, suppose Consolidated's capital projects over the next 2 years consist primarily of new, automated milling and stamping machinery for its Cincinnati plant. This machinery has an expected economic life of 10 years (even though it falls into the ACRS 5-year class life). Should Consolidated finance the debt portion of this equipment with 5-year, 10-year, 20-year, or 30-year debt, or some other maturity?

Note that some of the new capital for the machinery will come from common and preferred stock, both of which are generally considered to be perpetual securities with infinite maturities. Of course, preferred stock can have a sinking fund or be redeemable, and common stock can always be repurchased on the open market or by a tender offer, so the effective maturity of preferred and common stock can be reduced significantly. On the other hand, debt maturities can be specified at the time of issue. If Consolidated financed its capital budgets over the next 2 years with 10-year sinking fund bonds, it would be matching asset and liability maturities. The cash flows resulting from the new machinery could be used to make the interest and sinking fund payments on the issue, so the bonds would be retired as the machinery wore out. If Consolidated had used one-year debt, it would have to pay off this debt with cash flows derived from assets other than the machinery in question. Conversely, if it used 20-year or 30-year debt, it would have to service the debt long after the assets that were purchased with the debt had been scrapped and had ceased providing cash flows. This would worry the lenders.

Of course, the one-year debt could probably be rolled over year after year, out to the 10-year asset maturity. However, if interest rates rise, Consolidated would have to pay a higher rate when it rolled over its debt, or if the company experienced difficulties, it might even be unable to refund the debt at any reasonable rate. On the other hand, if Consolidated financed 10-year assets with 20-year or 30-year bonds, it would still have (1) a liability after the 10-year life of the asset, but (2) it would have generated some excess cash from the assets over their 10-year life. The question then would be, Can we reinvest the accumulated cash flows at a rate which will enable us to pay off the bonds over their remaining 20-year or 30-year life? This strategy clearly imposes uncertainty on the firm, since it cannot know at the time it sells the bonds if profitable capital investment opportunities will be available 10 years later.

For all these reasons, the least risky financing strategy is to match security maturities with asset maturities. In recognition of this fact, firms generally do place great emphasis on maturity matching, and this factor often dominates the debt portion of the financing decision.

Effects of Interest Rate Levels and Forecasts

Financial managers also consider interest rate levels and forecasts, both absolute and relative, when making financing decisions. For example, if long-term interest rates are high by historic standards and are expected to fall, managers will be reluctant to issue long-term debt and thus lock in those costs for long periods. We already know that one solution to this problem is for firms to use a call provision—callability permits refunding of the issue should interest rates drop, but there is a cost, because the firm must pay more for callable debt. Alternatively, the firm could finance with short-term debt whenever long-term rates were historically high, and then, assuming that interest rates subsequently fall, sell a long-term issue to replace the short-term debt. Of course, this strategy has its risks: If interest rates move even higher, the firm will be forced to renew its short-term debt at higher and higher rates, or to replace the short-term debt with a long-term bond which costs even more than it would have when the original decision was made.

One could argue, and many do, that capital markets are efficient. If so—and most evidence supports the efficient markets hypothesis—then it is impossible to predict what future interest rates will be because these rates will be determined by information which is not now known. Thus, under the efficient markets hypothesis, it would be unproductive for firms to try to "beat the market" by forecasting future capital costs and acting on such forecasts. According to this view, financial managers ought to arrange their capital structures in such a manner that they can ride out almost any economic storm, and this generally calls for (1) using some "reasonable" mix of debt and equity and (2) using debt with maturities which match the maturities of the assets being financed.

Although we personally support the view dictated by the efficient markets hypothesis, there is no question but that many managers disagree. They are influenced by current cost levels and forecasts, and they act accordingly. One manifestation of this behavior is the heavy use of shelf registrations. Some firms use shelf registrations because managers believe that financing "windows" exist. In the volatile interest rate environment that has characterized the 1980s, a company might decide to issue bonds when the rate is 12 percent but then find, 6 weeks later when it has SEC approval to go ahead with the issue, that rates are up to 13 percent. Had it had "bonds on the shelf," it could have gone ahead and sold the issue while the low-cost window was open. Another way to protect against rising rates is to hedge against this possibility by use of interest rate futures. We discuss futures markets and the use of futures in Chapter 15.

In early September of 1983, the interest rate on AAA corporate bonds was about 12.5 percent, up from 11.5 percent in April. Exxon's investment bankers advised the company to tap the Eurobond market for relatively cheap fixed-rate financing.[21] At the time, Exxon could issue its bonds in London at 0.4 percentage points *below* comparable maturity U.S. Treasury bonds. However, one of Exxon's officers was quoted as saying, "I say so what. The absolute level of rates is too high. Our people would rather wait." The managers of Exxon, as well as many other companies, were betting that the next move in interest rates would be down. This belief was also openly expressed by executives of ITT, Ontario Hydro, and RCA, among others.

These attitudes confirm that many firms base their financing decisions on expectations about future interest rates. It is easy to be right on one interest rate call—if you predict a decline in interest rates, you have a 50-50 chance of being correct. However, the success of a strategy based on forecasting rates requires that those forecasts be right more often than they are wrong, and it is very difficult to find someone with a long-term track record which is better than 50-50. Finance would be easy if we could predict future interest rates accurately. Unfortunately, predicting future interest rates with consistent accuracy is somewhere between difficult and impossible—people who make a living selling interest rate forecasts say it is difficult; many others say it is impossible.

Information Asymmetries

Earlier in the chapter, we discussed bond ratings and the effects of changes in ratings on the cost and availability of capital. If a firm's current financial condition is poor, its managers may be reluctant to issue new long-term debt because (1) a new debt issue would probably trigger a review by the rating agencies, and (2) debt issued when a firm is in poor financial condition would probably cost more and have more severe restrictive covenants than debt issued from strength. Further, in Chapters 5 and 6 we pointed out that firms are reluctant to use new common stock financing, especially when it might be regarded as a negative signal. Thus, a firm that is in a weakened condition, but which is forecasting a better time in the future, would be inclined to delay permanent financing of any type until things improved. Conversely, a firm that is strong now, but which forecasts a potentially bad time in the period just ahead, would be motivated to finance long term now rather than to wait. Each of these scenarios implies that the capital markets are either inefficient or that investors do not have the same information regarding the firm's future as does its financial manager. The second situation is undoubtedly true at times, and possibly the first one also in rare cases.

The firm's earnings outlook, and the extent to which forecasted higher earnings per share are reflected in stock prices, also has an effect on the choice of securities. If a successful R&D program has just been concluded, and management forecasts higher earnings than do most investors, then the firm would not want to issue common stock. It would use debt and then, once earnings rise and push up the stock price, sell common to restore the capital structure to its target level.

---

[21]See the section entitled "The International Perspective" at the end of this chapter for a discussion of Eurobonds.

Amount of Financing Required

Obviously, the amount of financing required will influence the financing decision. This is mainly due to flotation costs. A $1 million debt financing would most likely be done with a term loan or a privately placed bond issue, while a firm seeking $100 million of new debt would most likely use a public offering.

Availability of Collateral

Generally, secured debt will be less costly than unsecured debt. Thus, firms with large amounts of fixed assets which have a ready resale value are likely to use a relatively large amount of debt, especially mortgage bonds. Additionally, each year's financing decision would be influenced by the amount of qualified assets available as security for new bonds.

SUMMARY

This chapter described the characteristics, advantages, and disadvantages of the major types of long-term debt securities. The key difference between *bonds* and *term loans* is the fact that term loans are sold directly by a corporate borrower to between one and 20 lenders, whereas bonds are generally sold to many public investors through investment bankers.

Additionally, we discussed five recent innovations in long-term debt financing: (1) *zero coupon bonds*, (2) *floating rate bonds*, (3) *redeemable at par bonds*, (4) *junk bonds*, and (5) *project financing*. Finally, we discussed calling bonds and preferred stocks for *refunding*. In this discussion, we presented a method to evaluate the refunding decision, noting that the profitability of current refunding is relatively easy to ascertain, but the decision to refund now as opposed to waiting is much more complicated.

It is impossible to state, as a generalization, that either debt, preferred stock, or common equity is the "best" method of financing. Each has advantages and disadvantages vis-à-vis the other types of securities, and the relative importance of these advantages/disadvantages varies over time and from company to company. There are many factors that influence a firm's long-term financing decisions. Among the most important are (1) its target capital structure, (2) maturity matching, (3) current interest rate levels and forecasts of future rates, (4) information asymmetries, (5) the amount of financing required, and (6) the availability of collateral.

The International Perspective

Thus far, we have concentrated on the U.S. capital markets, where firms raise most of their long-term capital. However, many firms, both multinational and domestic, raise large sums of debt capital in the inter-national markets. For example, in early 1986, General Electric raised over $1 billion in the Eurobond market. These bonds were dollar denominated but issued in Europe to European holders of dollars. What was the big attraction that caused GE to look to Europe for its borrowing needs? As you might suspect, the answer is lower cost. To illustrate, GE's $300 million issue of April 30, 1986, cost the firm only 20 basis points more than the U.S. Treasury was paying on its bonds. Had it borrowed in the U.S. bond market, GE, a AAA-rated firm, would have paid at least 50 basis points over Treasury rates. In this section we briefly describe the international bond markets.

Any bond sold outside the country of the borrower is called an *international bond*, but it is necessary to distinguish further between two types of international bonds: (1) foreign bonds and (2) Eurobonds.

Foreign Bonds

Borrowers sometimes raise long-term debt capital in the domestic capital market of a foreign country. For instance, Bell Canada may need U.S. dollars to finance the operations of its subsidiaries located in the United States. If it decides to raise the needed capital in the domestic U.S. bond market, the bond would be underwritten by a syndicate of U.S. investment bankers, would be denominated in (that is, pays interest and principal in terms of) U.S. dollars, and would be sold to investors in the United States in accordance with SEC and applicable state regulations. Except for the foreign origin of the borrower—Canada—this bond would be indistinguishable from bonds issued by equivalent U.S. corporations. Since Bell Canada is a foreign corporation, though, this bond would be called a *foreign bond*. Formally, a foreign bond is a bond that is (1) issued by a foreign borrower, (2) underwritten by a syndicate whose members all come from the country where the funds are raised, (3) denominated in the currency of that same country, and (4) sold entirely within that country. Foreign bonds sold in the United States are sometimes called "Yankee bonds," while foreign bonds sold by U.S. and European

firms in Japan are often referred to as "Samurai bonds."

Eurobonds

The second type of international bond is the *Eurobond*, which is internationally syndicated and is denominated in a currency *other than* that of the country in which it is sold. For example, when GE sold U.S. dollar denominated bonds in Europe, through investment bankers who operate worldwide, to people who paid for the bonds with dollars, that was a Eurobond issue. The institutional arrangements by which Eurobonds are brought to market are different from those for most other bond issues. To a corporation issuing a Eurobond, perhaps the most important feature of the process is the far lower level of required disclosure than would usually be found for bonds issued in domestic markets, particularly in the United States. Also, governments tend not to apply as strict a set of regulations to securities denominated in foreign currencies but sold in domestic markets to investors holding foreign currencies as they would for home-currency securities. This often leads to lower total transaction costs for the issue.

Investors also like Eurobonds for several reasons. Generally, they are issued in bearer form rather than as registered bonds, so the names and nationalities of investors are not recorded. Individuals who desire anonymity, whether for privacy reasons or for less worthy motives such as tax avoidance, find Eurobonds to their liking. Similarly, most governments do not withhold tax on interest payments associated with Eurobonds. If the investor requires an effective yield of 10 percent, a Eurobond that is exempt from tax withholding would need a coupon rate of 10 percent. Another type of bond—for instance, a domestic issue subject to a 30 percent withholding tax on interest—would need a coupon rate of roughly 14.3 percent to yield an after-withholding rate of 10 percent. Investors who desire secrecy would not want to file for a refund of the tax, so they would prefer to hold the Eurobond.

Over half of all Eurobonds are denominated in dollars; bonds in German marks and Dutch guilders account for most of the rest. Although centered in Europe, Eurobonds are truly international. Their underwriting syndicates include investment bankers from all parts of the world, and the bonds are sold to investors not only in Europe but also in such faraway places as Bahrain and Singapore. Up to a few years ago, Eurobonds were issued solely by multinational firms, by international financial institutions, and by national governments. However, today the Eurobond market is also being tapped by purely domestic U.S. firms, such as electric utilities, that are going overseas to lower their debt costs.

Questions and Problems

13-1 (Long-term debt) How would each of the following actions affect the interest rate a firm must pay on a new issue of long-term debt? Indicate whether the action will tend to raise, lower, or have an indeterminate effect, then explain why.
   a. The firm uses bonds rather than a term loan.
   b. The firm uses nonsubordinated debentures rather than first mortgage bonds.
   c. The firm makes its bonds convertible into common stock.
   d. The firm makes its debentures subordinated to its bank debt. What will the effect be
      (1) on the debentures?
      (2) on the bank debt?
      (3) on average total debt?
   e. The firm sells income bonds rather than debentures.
   f. The firm must raise $100 million, all of which will be used to construct a new plant, and it is debating the sale of mortgage bonds or debentures. If it decides to issue $50 million of each type, as opposed to $75 million of mortgage bonds and $25 million of debentures, how would this affect
      (1) the debentures?
      (2) the mortgage bonds?
      (3) the average cost of the $100 million?
   g. The firm is planning to raise $25 million of long-term capital. Its outstanding bonds yield 9 percent. If it sells preferred stock, how will this affect the yield on the outstanding debt?
   h. The firm puts a call provision on its new issue of bonds.
   i. The firm includes a sinking fund on its new issue of bonds.
   j. The firm's bonds are downgraded from A to BBB.

13-2 (Risk and return) Suppose you work for the treasurer of a large, profitable corporation. Your company has some surplus funds to invest. You can buy these securities:
      (1) Twenty-year Aaa-rated Exxon bonds which sell at par and yield 12 percent.
      (2) Aa-rated Exxon preferred stock which yields 10 percent.
      (3) Ca-rated Eastern Airlines bonds which yield 16 percent.
      (4) C-rated Eastern Airlines preferred stock which yields 17 percent.
      (5) A-rated Alabama Power floating rate preferred stock which currently yields 9 percent.
      (6) Treasury bills which yield 8.5 percent.

a. Does it appear that these securities are in equilibrium; that is, do the yields reflect the relative riskiness of the securities?

b. If these were your only choices, which would you recommend?

13-3 (Sinking funds) A sinking fund can be set up in one of two ways:

1. The corporation makes annual payments to the trustee, who invests the proceeds in securities (frequently government bonds) and uses the accumulated total to retire the bond issue at maturity.

2. The trustee uses the annual payments to retire a portion of the issue each year, either calling a given percentage of the issue by a lottery and paying a specified price per bond or buying bonds on the open market, whichever is cheaper.

Discuss the advantages and disadvantages of each procedure from the viewpoint of both the firm and the bondholders.

13-4 (Sinking funds) The Reynolds Company has just sold a $100 million, 8 percent bond issue. A sinking fund will retire the issue over its 10-year life. Sinking fund payments are of equal amounts and will be made at the end of each year. The proceeds will be used to retire bonds as the payments are made. Bonds can be called at par for sinking fund purposes, or the funds paid into the sinking fund can be used to buy bonds in the open market. (For simplicity, assume that the bonds have an annual coupon.)

a. How large must each annual sinking fund payment be?

b. What will happen, under the conditions of the problem thus far, to the company's debt service requirements per year for this issue? Assume that the bonds are called for sinking fund purposes, and hence are retired at par. What effect does the call provision have on the expected cost of the issue?

c. Now suppose Reynolds had set its sinking fund so that *equal annual amounts*, payable at the end of each year, were paid into a sinking fund trust held by a bank, with the proceeds being used to buy government bonds that pay 6 percent interest. The payments, plus accumulated interest, must total $100 million at the end of 10 years, and the proceeds will be used to retire the bonds at that time. How large must the annual sinking fund payment now be?

d. What are the annual cash requirements to cover bond service costs under the trusteeship arrangement? What would be the expected cost of the issue with this type of sinking fund?

e. What would have to happen to interest rates to cause the company to buy bonds on the open market rather than call them under the original sinking fund plan? What impact would this have on the realized cost of the issue?

13-5 (Perpetual bond analysis) In 1936, the Canadian government raised $55 million by issuing perpetual bonds at a 3 percent annual rate of interest. Unlike most bonds issued today, which have a specific maturity date, these perpetual bonds can remain outstanding forever; they are, in fact, perpetuities.

At the time of issue, the Canadian government stated in the bond indenture that cash redemption was *possible* at face value ($100) on or after September 1966; in other words, the bonds were callable at par after September 1966. Believing that the bonds would in fact be called, many investors in the early 1960s purchased these bonds with expectations of receiving $100 in 1966 for each perpetual they had. In 1963, the bonds sold for $55, but a rush of buyers drove the price to just below the $100 par value by 1966. Prices fell dramatically, however, when the Canadian government announced that these perpetual bonds were indeed perpetual and would not be paid off. A new 30-year supply of coupons was sent to each bondholder, and the bonds' market price declined to $42 in December 1972.

Because of their severe losses, hundreds of Canadian bondholders formed the Perpetual Bond Association to lobby for face value redemption of the bonds. Government officials in Ottawa insisted that claims for face value payment were nonsense, that the bonds were clearly identified as perpetuals, and that they did not mature in 1966 or at any other time. One Ottawa official stated, "Our job is to protect the taxpayer. Why should we pay $55 million for less than $25 million worth of bonds?"

a. Would it make sense for a business firm to issue bonds such as the Canadian bonds described above? Would it matter if the firm was a proprietorship or a corporation?

b. If the United States government today offered a 5-year bond, a 50-year bond, a "regular" perpetuity, and a Canadian-type perpetuity, what do you think the relative order of interest rates would be (that is, rank the bonds from the one with the lowest to the one with the highest rate of interest)? Explain your answer.

c. **(1)** Suppose that because of pressure by the Perpetual Bond Association, you believe that the Canadian government would redeem this particular perpetual bond issue in five years. Which course of action would be more advantageous to you if you owned the bonds: (a) to sell your bonds today at $42 or (b) to wait five years and have them redeemed? Assume that similar risk bonds earn 8 percent today, and interest rates are expected to remain at this level for the next five years.

(2) If you had the opportunity to invest your money in bonds of similar risk, at what rate of return would you be indifferent to the choice of selling your perpetuals today or having them redeemed in five years; that is, what is the expected yield-to-maturity on the Canadian bonds?

d. Show, mathematically, the value of perpetuities that yield 7.15 percent, pay $3 interest annually, and are considered to be "regular" perpetuities. Show what would happen to the price of the bonds if the interest rate fell to 2 percent.

e. Are the Canadian bonds more likely to be valued as "regular" perpetuities if the going rate of interest is above or below 3 percent? Why?

f. Do you think the Canadian government would have taken the same action with regard to retiring the bonds if the interest rate had fallen rather than risen after they had been issued in 1936?

g. Do you think the Canadian government was "fair" or "unfair" in its actions? Give pros and cons, and justify your reason for thinking that one outweighs the other.

13-6 (Zero coupon bond) Suppose the Brauer Insurance Company needed to raise $400 million and its investment bankers indicated that 10-year zero coupon bonds could be sold at a YTM of 10 percent, whereas an 11 percent yield would be required on similar *annual* payment coupon bonds sold at par. Brauer's tax rate is 34 percent.

a. How many $1,000 par value bonds would the firm have to sell under each plan?

b. What would be the after-tax YTM on each type of bond (1) to a holder who is tax exempt and (2) to a taxpayer in the 28 percent bracket?

c. What would be the after-tax cost of each type of bond to Brauer?

d. Why would investors be willing to buy the zero coupon bonds?

e. Why might Brauer turn down the offer to issue zero coupon bonds?

(Do Part f only if you are using the computerized diskette.)

f. Redo Parts a, b, and c assuming that the YTM on zero coupon bonds falls to 8 percent and that on annual coupon bonds falls to 9 percent. As in the previous analysis, the after-tax yield to investors on the annual coupon bond exceeds that of the zero coupon bond. Has the differential between the annual and zero coupon bond yields changed? Would investors be more willing to purchase the zero coupon bond under the original assumptions or under the new assumptions? If the before-tax YTM were 8 percent on each type of bond, what would the after-tax YTMs be to zero and to 28 percent taxpayers, what would the after-tax cost be to the company, and what type of investors would be likely to hold the zeros and what type the regular coupon bonds?

13-7 (Bond refunding analysis) The Worldwide Company is considering whether to refund a $100 million, 15 percent coupon, 20-year bond issue which was sold 5 years ago. It is amortizing $4 million of flotation costs on the 15 percent bonds over the 20-year life of that issue. Worldwide's investment bankers have indicated that the company could sell a new $100 million, 15-year issue at an interest rate of 12.5 percent in today's market. The firm's management thinks the chances of an interest rate increase are about equal to the chances of a decrease. Specifically, it estimates a 0.25 probability of rates declining to 10 percent, a 0.5 probability of rates remaining at 12.5 percent, and a 0.25 probability of rates rising to 15 percent.

A call premium of 10 percent would be required to retire the old bonds, and flotation costs on the new issue would amount to $6 million. Worldwide's marginal federal-plus-state tax rate is 40 percent. The new bonds would be issued one month before the old bonds were called, with the proceeds of the new issue being invested in short-term government securities with a 9 percent coupon during the interim period.

    a. Calculate the NPV of the bond refunding.

    b. What factors would influence Worldwide's decision to refund now rather than later?

13-8 (Bond refunding analysis) Choi Industries is considering whether to refund a $75 million, 15 percent coupon, 30-year bond issue that was sold 5 years ago. It is amortizing $4.5 million of flotation costs on the 15 percent bonds over the 30-year life of that issue. The firm's investment bankers have indicated that the company could sell a new 25-year issue at an interest rate of 10.5 percent in today's market.

A call premium of 12.5 percent would be required to retire the old bonds, and flotation costs on the new issue would amount to $4.5 million. The firm's marginal tax rate is 34 percent. The new bonds would be issued one month before the old bonds were called, with the proceeds being invested in short-term government securities that return 7.5 percent annually.

    a. Perform a complete bond refunding analysis. What is the bond refunding's NPV? *(Do Parts b and c only if you are using the computerized diskette.)*

    b. Determine the interest rate on new bonds at which the firm would be indifferent to refunding today; that is, the interest rate at which the NPV of refunding would be zero.

    c. The firm's managers estimate the probability distribution of interest rates one year from now as follows:

Rate	Probability
8.5%	0.2
10.5	0.6
13.5	0.2

Find the NPV of refunding one year hence. Assume that (1) the new bond issue would have a 24-year maturity, (2) the call premium one year hence would be 12.0 percent, and (3) short-term rates remain at current levels. Should the firm refund the issue this year or wait until next year to make the decision? Why?

Selected Additional References and Cases

The investment textbooks listed in the Chapter 2 references provide useful information on bonds, as well as the markets in which they are traded. In addition, the following articles offer useful insights:

Backer, Morton, and Martin L. Gosman, "The Use of Financial Ratios in Credit Downgrade Decisions," *Financial Management*, Spring 1980, 53-56.

Clark, John J., with Brenton W. Harries, "Some Recent Trends in Municipal and Corporate Securities Markets: An Interview with Brenton W. Harries, President of Standard & Poor's Corporation," *Financial Management*, Spring 1976, 9-17.

Ferri, Michael G., "An Empirical Examination of the Determinants of Bond Yield Spreads," *Financial Management*, Autumn 1978, 40-46.

Kalotay, Andrew J. "Sinking Funds and the Realized Cost of Debt," *Financial Management*, Spring 1982, 43-54.

———, "Innovations in Corporation Finance: Deep Discount Private Placements," *Financial Management*, Spring 1982, 55-57.

Pinches, George E., J. Clay Singleton, and Ali Jahankhani, "Fixed Coverage as a Determinant of Electric Utility Bond Ratings," *Financial Management*, Summer 1978, 45-55.

Smith, Clifford W., and J. B. Warner, "On Financial Contracting: An Analysis of Bond Covenants," *Journal of Financial Economics*, June 1979, 117-161.

Weinsten, Mark I., "The Seasoning Process of New Corporate Bond Issues," *Journal of Finance*, December 1978, 1343-1354.

Zwick, Burton, "Yields on Privately Placed Corporate Bonds," *Journal of Finance*, March 1980, 23-29.

References on bond refunding include the following:

Ang, James S., "The Two Faces of Bond Refunding," *Journal of Finance*, June 1975, 869-874.

———, "The Two Faces of Bond Refunding: Reply," *Journal of Finance*, March 1978, 354-356.

Dyl, Edward A. and Michael D. Joehnk, "Refunding Tax Exempt Bonds," *Financial Management*, Summer 1976, 59-66.

Emery, Douglas R., "Overlapping Interest in Bond Refunding: A Reconsideration," *Financial Management*, Summer 1978, 19-20.

Finnerty, John D., "Refunding High-Coupon Debt," *Midland Corporate Finance Journal*, Winter 1986, 59-74.

Harris, Robert S., "The Refunding of Discounted Debt: An Adjusted Present Value Analysis," *Financial Management*, Winter 1980, 7-12.

Kalotay, Andrew J., "On the Advanced Refunding of Discounted Debt," *Financial Management*, Summer 1978, 14-18.

———, "On the Structure and Valuation of Debt Refundings," *Financial Management*, Spring 1982, 41-42.

Kraus, Alan, "An Analysis of Call Provisions and the Corporate Refunding Decision," *Midland Corporate Finance Journal*, Spring 1983, 46-60.

Laber, Gene, "The Effect of Bond Refunding of Discounted Debt," *Financial Management*, June 1979, 795-799.

———, "Implications of Discount Rates and Financing Assumptions for Bond Refunding Decisions," *Financial Management*, Spring 1979, 7-12

———, "Repurchases of Bonds through Tender Offers: Implications for Shareholder Wealth," *Financial Management*, Summer 1978, 7-13.

Livingston, Miles, "The Effect of Bond Refunding on Shareholder Wealth: Comment," *Journal of Finance*, June 1979, 801-804.

———, "Bond Refunding Reconsidered: Comment," *Journal of Finance*, March 1980, 191-196.

Mayor, Thomas H., and Kenneth G. McCoin, "Bond Refunding: One or Two Faces?" *Journal of Finance*, March 1978, 349-353.

Ofer, Ahron R., and Robert A. Taggart, Jr., "Bond Refunding Reconsidered: Reply," *Journal of Finance*, March 1980, 197-200.

Riener, Kenneth D., "Financial Structure Effects of Bond Refunding," *Financial Management*, Summer 1980, 18-23.

Yawitz, Jess B., and James A. Anderson, "The Effect of Bond Refunding on Shareholder Wealth," *Journal of Finance*, December 1977, 1738-1746.

———, "The Effect of Bond Refunding on Shareholder Wealth: Reply," *Journal of Finance*, June 1979, 805-809.

Zeise, Charles H., and Roger K. Taylor, "Advance Refunding: A Practitioner's Perspective," *Financial Management*, Summer 1977, 73-76.

For more information on Eurodollar bonds, see

Kidwell, David S., M. Wayne Marr, and G. Rodney Thompson, "Eurodollar Bonds: Alternative Financing for U.S. Companies," *Financial Management*, Winter 1985, 18-27; and the same authors' correction in the Spring 1986 issue of *Financial Management*.

The following Crum-Brigham cases focus on the topics covered in this chapter:

Case 19, "Seminole Gas and Electric," which illustrates the bond refunding decision.

Cases 23 and 24, "Environgard Corporation" and "Visual Imagery," which illustrate the stock versus bond decision.

The following Harrington cases are also relevant:

"Exxon Corporation," which describes three early 1980 debt/equity swaps.

"Treeline, Inc.," which illustrates the choice among various debt alternatives.

13A
BANKRUPTCY AND REORGANIZATION

Debtholders have a prior claim to a firm's income, and to its assets in the event of bankruptcy, over common and preferred stockholders. Also, different classes of debtholders are accorded different treatments in the event of bankruptcy, so it is important that one know who gets what if a firm fails. Finally, firms in financial distress can often survive "bad times" by a reorganization rather than resorting to a formal declaration of bankruptcy. These topics are discussed in this appendix.[1]

This appendix was coauthored by Arthur L. Herrmann of the University of Hartford.

[1] Much of the current work in this area is based on writings by Edward I. Altman. For a summary of his work, and that of others, see Edward I. Altman, "Bankruptcy and Reorganization," in *Financial Handbook*, Edward I. Altman, ed. (New York: Wiley, 1986), Chapter 35.

Federal Bankruptcy Laws

The bankruptcy process begins when a debtor is unable to meet scheduled payments to creditors or when the firm's cash flow projections indicate that it will soon be unable to do so. As the situation develops, these central issues arise:

1. Is the firm's inability to meet scheduled debt payments a temporary cash flow problem, or is it a permanent problem caused by long-term economic trends?

2. If the problem is a temporary one, then an agreement which gives the firm time to recover and to satisfy everyone will be worked out. However, if basic long-run asset values have declined, economic losses will have occurred. In this event, who should bear the losses?

3. Is the company "worth more dead than alive"—that is, would the business be more valuable if it were maintained and continued in operation or if it were liquidated and sold off in pieces?

4. Should the firm file for formal bankruptcy, or should it try to use informal procedures?

5. Who should control the firm while it is being rehabilitated or liquidated? Should the existing management be left in control, or should a trustee be placed in charge of operations?

Our bankruptcy laws were first enacted in 1898, modified substantially in 1938, changed again in 1978, and further fine-tuned in 1984. The 1978 act was a major revision designed to streamline and expedite proceedings, and it consists of eight odd-numbered chapters (the even-numbered chapters were deleted in the revision). Chapters 1, 3, and 5 contain general provisions applicable to the other chapters; Chapter 7 details the procedures to be followed when liquidating a firm; Chapter 9 deals with financially distressed municipalities; Chapter 11 is the business reorganization chapter; Chapter 13 covers the adjustment of debts for "individuals with regular income"; and Chapter 15 sets up a system of trustees who help administer proceedings under the new act. When you read in the paper that a firm, such as United Press International (UPI) in 1985, has "filed for court protection under Chapter 11," this means that the company is bankrupt and is trying to reorganize. Under Chapter 11, a company is protected from creditor lawsuits while it works out a court-approved plan to meet its debt obligations.

Our bankruptcy law is flexible, and it provides much scope for informal negotiations between a company and its creditors and stockholders. The case is opened by the filing of a petition with a federal district bankruptcy court. The petition may be either voluntary or involuntary—that is, it may be filed either by the firm's management or by its creditors. A committee of unsecured creditors is then appointed by the court to negotiate with management for a reorganization, which may include the restructuring (that is, lengthening maturities, reducing the interest rate, and/or reducing the principal) of debt and other claims against the firm. At the time of its Chapter 11 filing, UPI had about 1,500 creditors, with the largest unsecured creditor, AT&T, being owed $6.1 million. AT&T and the other creditors want to get as much of their claims as possible, but they may conclude that they will come out better if they accept less than the full amount owed them, because the alternative might be a "fire sale" liquidation rather than maintenance of the firm as a going concern. A trustee will be appointed by the court if that is deemed to be in the best interests of the creditors and stockholders; otherwise, the existing management will retain control. If no fair and feasible reorganization can be agreed to by the creditors and the company, and agreed to by the court, then the firm will be liquidated under the procedures spelled out in Chapter 7.

Liquidation Procedures

If a company is too far gone to be reorganized, it must be liquidated. Liquidation should occur if a business is worth more dead than alive, or if the possibility of restoring it to financial health is so remote that the creditors would face a high risk of even greater losses if operations were to continue.

Chapter 7 of the 1978 Bankruptcy Act is designed to accomplish these three objectives: (1) provide safeguards against the withdrawal of assets by the owners of the bankrupt firm; (2) provide for an equitable distribution of the assets among the creditors; and (3) allow insolvent debtors to discharge all their obligations and start over unhampered by a burden of prior debt.

The distribution of assets in a liquidation under Chapter 7 of the Bankruptcy Act is governed by the following priority of claims:

1. *Secured creditors, who are entitled to the proceeds of the sale of specific property pledged for a lien or a mortgage.* If the proceeds do not fully satisfy the secured creditors' claims, the remaining balance of such claims is treated as a general creditor claim. (See Item 9.)

2. *Trustee's costs to administer and operate the bankrupt firm.*

3. *Expenses incurred after an involuntary liquidation has begun but before a trustee is appointed.*

4. *Wages due workers if earned within three months prior to the filing of the petition in bankruptcy.* The amount of wages is limited to $2,000 per person.

5. *Claims for unpaid contributions to employee benefit plans that should have been paid within six months prior to filing.* However, these claims, plus wages in Item 4, may not exceed the $2,000 per wage-earner limit.

6. *Unsecured claims for customer deposits, not to exceed a maximum of $900 per individual.*

7. *Taxes due to federal, state, county, and any other government agency.*

8. *Unfunded pension plan liabilities.* Unfunded pension plan liabilities have a claim above that of the general creditors for an amount up to 30 percent of the book value of the common and preferred equity; any remaining unfunded pension claims rank with the general creditors.

9. *General, or unsecured, creditors.* Holders of trade credit, unsecured loans, the unsatisfied portion of secured loans and unfunded pension plan liabilities, and debenture bonds are classified as *general creditors.* Holders of subordinated debt also fall into this category, but they must turn over required amounts to the holders of senior debt, as discussed later in this section.

10. *Preferred stockholders, who can receive an amount up to the par value of the preferred stock.*

11. *Common stockholders, who receive the remaining funds, if any.*

To illustrate the way this priority system works, consider the balance sheet of Midwest Steel, Inc., shown in Table 13A-1. The assets have a book value of $90 million. The claims are indicated on the right-hand side of the balance sheet. Note that the

Table 13A-1
Midwest Steel, Inc.: Balance Sheet at Liquidation
(Thousands of Dollars)

Current assets	$80,000	Accounts payable	$20,000
Net fixed assets	10,000	Notes payable (to bank)	10,000
		Accrued wages, 1,400 @ $500	700
		U.S. taxes	1,000
		State and local taxes	300
		Current liabilities	$32,000
		First mortgage	$ 6,000
		Second mortgage	1,000
		Subordinated debentures[a]	8,000
		Total long-term debt	$15,000
		Preferred stock	$ 2,000
		Common stock	26,000
		Paid-in capital	4,000
		Retained earnings	11,000
		Total equity	$43,000
Total assets	$90,000	Total claims	$90,000

[a]Subordinated to $10 million in notes payable to the bank.

debentures are subordinate to the notes payable to banks. Midwest filed for bankruptcy under Chapter 11, and no fair and feasible reorganization could be arranged. Therefore, the trustee was ordered by the court to liquidate the firm under Chapter 7.

The assets as reported in the balance sheet in Table 13A-1 were greatly overstated; they were, in fact, worth much less than half of the $90 million at which they were carried. The following amounts were realized on liquidation:

From sale of current assets	$28,000,000
From sale of fixed assets	5,000,000
Total receipts	$33,000,000

The order of priority of the claims is shown in Table 13A-2. The first mortgage holders receive the $5 million in net proceeds from the sale of fixed assets. Since there were $6 million of first mortgage bonds, those bondholders are still owed $1 million. This unsatisfied claim is added to that of the other general creditors. After payment to the first mortgage bondholders come the fees and expenses of administration, which are typically about 20 percent of gross proceeds; in this example, they are $6 million. Next in priority are wages due workers, which total $700,000, and taxes due, which amount to $1.3 million.

Thus far, the priority claimants have been allocated $13 million of the $33 million of available cash, leaving $20 million for the general creditors. In this case, there were no claims for unpaid benefit plans or unfunded pension liabilities; if there had been, they would have had priority over the general creditors.

Table 13A-2
Midwest Steel, Inc.:
Order of Priority of Claims

Distribution to Priority Claimants

1.	Proceeds from sale of assets	$33,000,000
2.	First mortgage, paid from sale of fixed assets	5,000,000
3.	Fees and expenses of administration of bankruptcy	6,000,000
4.	Wages due workers earned within three months prior to filing of bankruptcy petition	700,000
5.	Taxes	1,300,000
6.	Available to general creditors	$20,000,000

Distribution to General Creditors

Claims of General Creditors	Claim[a] (1)	Application of 50 Percent[b] (2)	After Subordination Adjustment[c] (3)	Percentage of Original Claim Received[d] (4)
Unsatisfied portion of first mortgage	$ 1,000,000	$ 500,000	$ 500,000	92%
Unsatisfied portion of second mortgage	1,000,000	500,000	500,000	50
Notes payable	10,000,000	5,000,000	9,000,000	90
Accounts payable	20,000,000	10,000,000	10,000,000	50
Subordinated debentures	8,000,000	4,000,000	0	0
	$40,000,000	$20,000,000	$20,000,000	

[a]Column 1 is the claim of each class of general creditor. Total claims equal $40 million.
[b]From Line 6 in the upper section of the table, we see that $20 million is available for general creditors. This sum, divided by the $40 million of total claims, indicates that general creditors will initially receive 50 cents on the dollar; this is shown in Column 2.
[c]The debentures are subordinated to the notes payable, so $4 million must be reallocated from debentures to notes payable. This adjustment is made in Column 3.
[d]Column 4 shows the results of dividing the amount in Column 3 by the original claim amount given in Column 1, except for the first mortgage, where the $5 million received from the sale of fixed assets is included.

The claims of the general creditors total $40 million. Since $20 million is available, claimants would initially be allocated 50 percent of their claims, as shown in Column 2 of Table 13A-2, before the subordination adjustment. The subordination agreement requires the subordinated debentures to turn over to the notes payable all amounts received until the notes are satisfied. In this situation, the claim of the notes payable is $10 million, but only $5 million is available; the deficiency is therefore $5 million. After transfer of $4 million from the subordinated debentures, there remains a deficiency of $1 million on the notes; this amount will remain unsatisfied.

Note that 92 percent of the first mortgage bonds' claim and 90 percent of the bank claim is satisfied, whereas a maximum of 50 percent of other unsecured claims will be satisfied. These figures illustrate (1) the advantage of having a secured claim and (2) the usefulness of the subordination provision to the security to which the subordination is made. The claims of the subordinated debentures, the preferred stock, and the common stock are completely wiped out. Studies of bankruptcy liquidations reveal that unsecured creditors receive on the average about 15 cents on the dollar, whereas common stockholders generally receive nothing.

Informal Procedures

Both reorganization and liquidation can be accomplished without a formal bankruptcy court filing. In this section, we briefly discuss these informal procedures.

Informal Reorganization

In the case of a fundamentally sound company whose financial difficulties appear to be temporary, the creditors generally prefer to work directly with the company, helping it to recover and reestablish itself on a sound financial basis. Such voluntary plans usually require some type of restructuring of the firm's debt, which involves either postponing payment of debt obligations or reducing creditor claims, or both. These procedures are designed to keep the debtor in business and to avoid the court costs associated with formal bankruptcy. Although creditors may not obtain immediate payment and may even have to accept less than is owed them, they often recover more money, and sooner, than if formal bankruptcy is declared. Also, for both trade creditors and bankers, chances are good that a customer will be preserved.

We should point out that informal voluntary settlements are not reserved for small firms. International Harvester (now Navistar) avoided formal bankruptcy proceedings by getting its creditors to agree to restructure some $3.5 billion of debt. Likewise, Chrysler's creditors accepted both an extension of maturities and a reduction of accounts to help it through its bad years. As we write this, People Express is attempting to get its creditors to accept interest rates of about 9 percent versus coupon rates of up to 16 percent, and also to extend debt maturities by about 10 years.

Informal Liquidation

Assignment is an informal procedure for liquidating debts, and it usually yields creditors a larger amount than they would receive in a formal Chapter 7 liquidation. However, assignments are feasible only if the firm is small, and its affairs are not too complex. An assignment calls for title to the debtor's assets to be transferred to a third person, known as an *assignee* or *trustee*. The assignee is instructed to liquidate the assets through a private sale or a public auction, and then to distribute the proceeds among the creditors on a pro rata basis. The assignment does not automatically discharge the debtor's obligations. However, the debtor may have the assignee write on the check to each creditor the requisite legal language to make endorsement of the check acknowledgment of full settlement of the claim.

Assignment has some advantages over Chapter 7 liquidation, which involves more time, legal formality, and expense. The assignee has more flexibility in disposing of property than does a bankruptcy trustee. Action can be taken sooner, before the inventory becomes obsolete or the machinery rusts, and, since the assignee is often familiar with the channels of trade in the debtor's business, better results may be achieved. However, an assignment does not automatically result in a full and legal discharge of all the debtor's liabilities, nor does it protect the creditors against fraud.

Problem

13A-1 A firm has the following balance sheet:

Current assets	$1,500,000	Bank debt	$ 300,000
Fixed assets	1,500,000	Trade credit	600,000
		Subordinated debentures	600,000
		Total debt	$1,500,000
		Common equity	1,500,000
Total assets	$3,000,000	Total claims	$3,000,000

If the debentures are subordinated only to the bank debt and the firm goes bankrupt, how much will each class of investors receive under each of the following conditions?

a. A total of $2 million is received from sale of assets.

b. A total of $1.5 million is received from sale of assets.

(Do Parts c and d only if you are using the computerized diskette.)

c. A total of $1 million is received from sale of assets.

d. A total of $500,000 is received from sale of assets.

e. What is the significance of these findings for the banks, the trade creditors, the debenture holders, and the common stockholders?

14

LEASE FINANCING

Firms generally own fixed assets and report them on their balance sheets, but it is the *use* of buildings and equipment that is important, not their ownership per se. One way of obtaining the use of facilities and equipment is to buy them, but an alternative is to lease them. Prior to the 1950s, leasing was generally associated with real estate—land and buildings. Today, however, it is possible to lease virtually any kind of fixed asset, and in 1985 about 20 percent of all new capital equipment acquired by businesses was financed through lease arrangements. It is estimated that $200 billion worth of capital equipment is currently being leased.

TYPES OF LEASES

Leasing takes several different forms, the three most important of which are (1) sale-and-leaseback arrangements, (2) operating leases, and (3) straight financial, or capital, leases.

Sale and Leaseback

Under a *sale-and-leaseback* arrangement, a firm that owns land, buildings, or equipment sells the property to another firm and simultaneously executes an agreement to lease the property back for a specified period under specific terms. The capital supplier could be an insurance company, a commercial bank, a specialized leasing company, the finance arm of an industrial firm, or an individual investor. The sale-and-leaseback plan is an alternative to a mortgage.

Note that the seller, or *lessee*, immediately receives the purchase price put up by the buyer, or *lessor*.[1] At the same time, the seller-lessee retains the use of the property. The parallel to borrowing is carried over to the lease payment schedule. Under a mortgage loan arrangement, the lender would normally receive a series of equal payments just sufficient to amortize the loan while providing a specified rate of return on the outstanding loan balance. Under a sale-and-leaseback arrangement, the lease payments are set up in exactly the same manner—the payments are sufficient to return the full purchase price to the investor, plus a stated return on the lessor's investment.

---

[1]The term *lessee* is pronounced "less-ee," not "lease-ee," and *lessor* is pronounced "less-or."

In early 1986 over $3 billion of sale-and-leaseback deals were signed by electric utilities. For example, Tucson Electric sold its Springerville generating plant to a syndicate which included IBM and Philip Morris for $850 million and simultaneously leased it back. These deals took place because highly profitable lessors such as IBM and Philip Morris were better able to use the plants' tax benefits (ITC and accelerated depreciation) than could the utilities, many of which have accumulated large tax credit carry-forwards. We will have more to say about the tax benefits of leasing throughout the chapter.

Operating Leases

Operating leases, sometimes called *service leases*, provide for both *financing* and *maintenance*. IBM was one of the pioneers of the operating lease contract, and computers and office copying machines, together with automobiles and trucks, are the primary types of equipment involved in operating leases. Ordinarily, these leases require the lessor to maintain and service the leased equipment, and the cost of the maintenance is built into the lease payments.

Another important characteristic of operating leases is the fact that they are generally *not fully amortized*. In other words, the payments required under the lease contract are not sufficient to recover the full cost of the equipment. However, the lease contract is written for a period considerably less than the expected economic life of the leased equipment, and the lessor expects to recover all costs either in subsequent renewal payments, by leasing the equipment to other lessees, or by sale of the equipment.

A final feature of operating leases is that they frequently contain a *cancellation clause* which gives the lessee the right to cancel the lease and return the equipment before the expiration of the basic lease agreement. This is an important consideration to the lessee, for it means that the equipment can be returned if it is rendered obsolete by technological developments or if it is no longer needed because of a decline in the lessee's business.

Financial, or Capital, Leases

Financial leases, sometimes called *capital leases*, are differentiated from operating leases in that (1) they *do not* provide for maintenance service, (2) they *are not* cancellable, and (3) they *are* fully amortized (that is, the lessor receives rental payments equal to the full price of the leased equipment plus a return on investment). In a typical arrangement, the firm that will use the equipment (the lessee) selects the specific items it requires, and then it negotiates the price and delivery terms with the manufacturer. The user firm then arranges to have a leasing company (the lessor) buy the equipment from the manufacturer or the distributor. When the equipment is purchased, the user firm simultaneously executes an agreement to lease the equipment from the financial institution. The terms of the lease call for full amortization of the lessor's investment, plus a rate of return on the unamortized balance which is close to the percentage rate the lessee would have paid on a secured term loan. For example, if the lessee would have to pay 10 percent for a term loan, then a rate of about 10 percent would be built into the lease contract.

The lessee is generally given an option to renew the lease at a reduced rate upon expiration of the basic lease. However, the basic lease usually cannot be canceled unless the lessor is completely paid off. Also, the lessee generally pays the property taxes and insurance on the leased property. Since the lessor receives a return *after*, or *net of*, these payments, this type of lease is often called a "net, net" lease.

Financial leases are almost the same as sale-and-leaseback arrangements, the major difference being that the leased equipment is new and the lessor buys it from a manufacturer or a distributor instead of from the user-lessee. A sale and leaseback may, then, be thought of as a special type of financial lease. Both sale-and-leaseback arrangements and financial leases are analyzed in the same manner.

TAX EFFECTS

The full amount of the annual lease payment is a deductible expense for income tax purposes *provided that the Internal Revenue Service agrees that a particular contract is a genuine lease and not simply an installment loan called a lease.* This makes it important that a lease contract be written in a form acceptable to the IRS. The IRS considers any agreement to be a sale if (1) the total lease payments are made over a relatively short period and approximate the price of the property, (2) the lessee may continue to use the property over the remainder of its useful life for relatively nominal renewal payments, or (3) a purchase option at a favorable price is written into the lease contract.

The reason for the IRS's concern about these factors is that, without restrictions, a company could set up a "lease" transaction calling for very rapid payments, which would be tax deductions. The effect would be to depreciate the equipment over a much shorter period than its ACRS class life. For example, suppose a firm planned to acquire a $2 million printing press which had a 5-year ACRS class life. The annual depreciation allowances would be $400,000 in Year 1, $640,000 in Year 2, $400,000 in Year 3, and $280,000 in each of Years 4 and 5. If the firm were in the 34 percent tax bracket, the depreciation would provide a tax saving of $136,000 in Year 1, $217,600 in Year 2, $136,000 in Year 3, and $95,200 in each of Years 4 and 5, for a total savings of $680,000. At a 6 percent discount rate, the present value of these tax savings would be $582,700.

Now suppose the firm could acquire the press through a 3-year lease arrangement with a leasing company for payments of $666,666.67 per year with a one-dollar purchase option. If the $666,666.67 payments were treated as lease payments, they would be fully deductible, and hence would provide a tax saving of $0.34($666,666.67) = $226,666.67 per year for 3 years, with a present value of $605,883 versus a present value of only $582,700 for the depreciation shelters. Thus, the lease payments and the depreciation would both provide the same total amount of tax savings (34% of $2 million, or $680,000), but the savings would come in faster, and hence have a higher present value, with the 3-year lease. Therefore, if just any type of contract could be called a lease and given tax treatment as a lease, then the timing of the tax shelters could be speeded up as compared with ownership depreciation tax shelters. This speedup would benefit companies, but it would be costly to the government. For this reason, the IRS has established the rules described above for defining a lease for tax purposes.

Even though leasing can be used only within limits to speed up the effective depreciation schedule, there are still times when very substantial tax benefits can be derived from a leasing arrangement. For example, if a firm like Tucson Electric has a very large construction program which has generated so many investment tax credits and so much accelerated depreciation that it has no current tax liabilities, then depreciation shelters are not very useful. In this case, a leasing company set up by profitable companies like IBM and Philip Morris can buy the equipment, receive the depreciation shelters, and then share these benefits with the lessee by charging lower lease payments. This point will be discussed in detail later in the chapter, but the point to be made now is that if firms are to obtain tax benefits from leasing, the lease contract must be written in a manner that will qualify it as a true lease under IRS guidelines. If there is any question about the legal status of the contract, the financial manager must be sure to have the firm's lawyers and accountants check the latest IRS regulations.[2]

FINANCIAL STATEMENT EFFECTS

Lease payments are shown as operating expenses on a firm's income statement, but under certain conditions, neither the leased assets nor the liabilities under the lease contract appear on the firm's balance sheet. For this reason, leasing is often called *off balance sheet* financing. This point is illustrated in Table 14-1 by the balance sheets of two hypothetical firms, B and L. Initially, the balance sheets of both firms are identical, and they both have debt ratios of 50 percent. Next, each firm decides to acquire a fixed asset costing $100. Firm B borrows $100 and buys the asset, so both an asset and a liability go on its balance sheet, and its debt ratio rises from 50 to 75 percent. Firm L leases the equipment. The lease may call for fixed charges as high or even higher than the loan, and the obligations assumed under the lease may be equally or more dangerous from the standpoint of potential bankruptcy, but the firm's debt ratio remains at 50 percent.

To correct this problem, the Financial Accounting Standards Board issued FASB Statement 13, which requires that, for an unqualified audit report, firms that enter

---

[2]Under the Economic Recovery Tax Act of 1981, Congress relaxed the normal IRS rules to permit *safe harbor leases*, which had virtually no IRS restrictions and which were explicitly designed to permit the transfer of the tax benefits under the 1981 Act from low-profit companies which could not use them to high-profit companies which could. The point of safe harbor leases was to provide incentives for capital investment to companies which had little or no tax liability—under safe harbor leasing, companies with a low tax liability could sell the benefit to companies in a high marginal tax bracket. In 1981 and 1982, literally billions of dollars were paid by such profitable firms as IBM and Philip Morris for the tax shelters of such unprofitable ones as Ford and Eastern Airlines. However, in 1983, Congress sharply curtailed the use of safe harbor leases.

Table 14-1
Balance Sheet Effects of Leasing

Before Asset Increase				After Asset Increase							
Firms B and L				Firm B, which Borrows and Buys				Firm L, which Leases			
Current assets	$ 50	Debt	$ 50	Current assets	$ 50	Debt	$150	Current assets	$ 50	Debt	$ 50
Fixed assets	50	Equity	50	Fixed assets	150	Equity	50	Fixed assets	50	Equity	50
	$100		$100		$200		$200		$100		$100

into financial (or capital) leases must restate their balance sheets to report the leased asset as a fixed asset and the present value of the future lease payments as a debt. This process is called *capitalizing the lease*, and its net effect is to cause Firms B and L to have similar balance sheets, both of which will, in essence, resemble the one shown for Firm B.[3]

The logic behind Statement 13 is as follows. If a firm signs a lease contract, its obligation to make lease payments is just as binding as if it had signed a loan agreement—the failure to make lease payments can bankrupt a firm just as fast as the failure to make principal and interest payments on a loan. Therefore, for all intents and purposes, a financial lease is identical to a loan.[4] This being the case, if a firm signs a lease agreement, this has the effect of raising its true debt ratio, and thus its true capital structure is changed. Therefore, if the firm had previously established a target capital structure, and if there is no reason to think that the optimal capital structure has changed, then using lease financing requires additional equity support exactly like debt financing.

If disclosure of the lease in our Table 14-1 example were not made, then Firm L's investors could be deceived into thinking that its financial position is stronger than it really is. Thus, even before FASB Statement 13 was issued in 1976, firms were required to disclose the existence of long-term leases in footnotes to their financial statements. At that time, it was debated as to whether or not investors recognized fully the impact of leases and, in effect, would see that Firms B and L were in essentially the same financial position. Some people argued that leases

[3]FASB Statement 13, "Accounting for Leases," November 1976, spells out in detail the conditions under which the lease must be capitalized and the procedures for capitalizing it.

[4]There are, however, certain legal differences between loans and leases. In the event of liquidation in bankruptcy, a lessor is entitled to take possession of the leased asset, and if the value of the asset is less than the required payments under the lease, the lessor can enter a claim (as a general creditor) for one year's lease payments. In a reorganization, the lessor receives the asset plus three years' lease payments if needed to cover the value of the lease. The lender under a secured loan arrangement has a security interest in the asset, meaning that if it is sold, the lender will be given the proceeds, and the full unsatisfied portion of the lender's claim will be treated as a general creditor obligation. It is not possible to state, as a general rule, whether a supplier of capital is in a stronger position as a secured creditor or as a lessor. Usually, one position is regarded as being about as good as the other at the time the financial arrangements are being made.

were not fully recognized, even by sophisticated investors. If this were the case, then leasing could alter the capital structure decision in a really significant manner—a firm could increase its true leverage through a lease arrangement, and this procedure would have a smaller effect on its cost of conventional debt, k_d, and on its cost of equity, k_s, than if it had borrowed directly and reflected this fact on its balance sheet. These benefits of leasing would accrue to existing investors at the expense of new investors who would, in effect, be deceived by the fact that the firm's balance sheet did not reflect its true liability situation.

The question of whether investors were truly deceived was debated but never resolved. Those who believed strongly in efficient markets thought that investors were not deceived and that footnotes were sufficient, while those who questioned market efficiency thought that leases should be capitalized. Statement 13 represents a compromise between these two positions, though one that is tilted heavily toward those who favor capitalization.

A lease is classified as a capital lease, and hence is capitalized and shown directly on the balance sheet, if one or more of the following conditions exist:

1. Under the terms of the lease, ownership of the property is effectively transferred from the lessor to the lessee.

2. The lessee can purchase the property at less than its true market value when the lease expires.

3. The lease runs for a period equal to or greater than 75 percent of the asset's life. Thus, if an asset has a 10-year life and the lease is written for 8 years, the lease must be capitalized.

4. The present value of the lease payments is equal to or greater than 90 percent of the initial value of the asset.[5]

These rules, together with strong footnote disclosure rules for operating leases, are sufficient to insure that no one will be fooled by lease financing; thus, leases are regarded as debt for capital structure purposes, and they have the same effects as debt on k_d and k_s. Therefore, leasing is not likely to permit a firm to use more financial leverage than could be obtained with conventional debt.

EVALUATION BY THE LESSEE

Leases are evaluated by both the lessee and the lessor. The lessee must determine whether leasing an asset is less costly than buying the asset, and the lessor must decide what the lease payments must be to produce a reasonable rate of return. This section focuses on the analysis by the lessee.

In the typical case, the events leading to a lease arrangement follow the sequence described next. We should note that a degree of uncertainty exists regard-

---

[5]The discount rate used to calculate the present value of the lease payments must be the lower of (1) the rate used by the lessor to establish the lease payments (this rate is discussed later in the chapter) or (2) the rate of interest which the lessee would have to pay for new debt with a maturity equal to that of the lease.

ing the theoretically correct way to evaluate lease versus purchase decisions, and some very complex decision models have been developed to aid in the analysis. However, the simple analysis given here leads to the correct decision in all the cases we have ever encountered.

1. The firm decides to acquire a particular building or piece of equipment; this decision is based on regular capital budgeting procedures. The decision to acquire the machine is not at issue in the typical lease analysis—this decision was made previously as part of the capital budgeting process. In a lease analysis, we are concerned simply with whether to obtain the use of the machine by lease or by purchase. However, if the effective cost of capital obtained by leasing is substantially lower than the cost of debt, then the cost of capital used in capital budgeting would have to be recalculated, and perhaps projects formerly deemed unacceptable might become acceptable. We discuss a procedure for this reevaluation later in the chapter.

2. Once the firm has decided to acquire the asset, the next question is how to finance its acquisition. Well-run businesses do not have excess cash lying around, so capital to finance new assets must be obtained from some source.

3. Funds to purchase the asset could be obtained by borrowing, by retaining earnings, or by selling new equity. Alternatively, the asset could be leased. Because of the capitalization/disclosure provision for leases, leasing normally has the same capital structure effect as borrowing.

.   As indicated earlier, a lease is comparable to a loan in the sense that the firm is required to make a specified series of payments and that a failure to meet these payments could result in bankruptcy. Thus, the most appropriate comparison is the cost of lease financing versus the cost of debt financing.[6] The lease versus borrow-and-purchase analysis is illustrated with data on the Anderson Equipment Company. The following conditions are assumed:

1. Anderson plans to acquire an automated assembly line with a 5-year life and a cost of $10 million, delivered and installed.

2. Anderson can borrow the required $10 million on a 10 percent loan to be amortized over 5 years. Therefore, the loan will call for payments of $10,000,000/ $PVIFA_{10\%,5}$ = $2,637,974.81 per year. The exact payment was determined using a financial calculator, recognizing the fact that $10 million is the present value of a 5-year, 10 percent regular annuity.

3. The equipment's estimated salvage value is $1,000,000. Thus, if Anderson buys the equipment, it would expect to net $1,000,000 before taxes ($660,000 after taxes) when the equipment is sold after 5 years' use. Note that in leasing, the asset's salvage value is generally called *residual value*.

---

[6]Note that the analysis should compare the cost of leasing to the cost of debt financing *regardless* of how the asset is actually financed. The asset may be purchased with available cash if not leased, but since leasing is a substitute for debt financing, the appropriate comparison would still be to debt financing.

4. Anderson can lease the equipment for 5 years at a rental charge of $2,750,000, payable at the beginning of each year, but the lessor will own the equipment upon the expiration of the lease. (The lease payment schedule is established by the potential lessor, as described in the next major section, and Anderson can accept it, reject it, or negotiate.)

5. The lease contract stipulates that the lessor will maintain the equipment at no additional charge to Anderson. However, if Anderson borrows and buys, it will have to bear the cost of maintenance, which will be performed by the equipment manufacturer at a fixed contract rate of $500,000 per year, payable at the beginning of each year.

6. The equipment falls in the ACRS 5-year class life, and Anderson's marginal tax rate is 34 percent.

NPV Analysis

Table 14-2 shows the steps involved in an NPV lease analysis. Part I of the table is devoted to the costs of borrowing and buying. Here, Columns 2 through 5 give the loan amortization schedule; Column 6 shows the maintenance expense; and Column 7 gives depreciation charges. Tax-deductible expenses—interest, maintenance, and depreciation—are summed and shown in Column 8, while Column 9 gives the taxes saved due to these deductions. Column 10 summarizes the preceding columns, giving the annual net cash outflows that Anderson will incur if it borrows and buys the equipment. Further, if Anderson buys the equipment, it will net $660,000 after taxes from the sale of the equipment. This amount is shown as an inflow (negative cash outflow) in Column 10.[7]

---

[7]The logic behind the annual cash outflows if the asset is owned as developed in Table 14-2 is straightforward. Alternative methods which involve less arithmetic, but which are not as easy to understand, can also be used.

1. Recognize that the annual after-tax cash flows associated with the loan, when discounted at the after-tax cost of debt, must equal the amount borrowed $10,000,000. For example, the after-tax interest in the first year, $1,000,000(1 − 0.34) = $660,000, plus the principal payment, $1,638,000, is $2,298,000. Similar figures could be developed for the other years, and the PV of all those cash flows would be the amount borrowed, $10 million.

2. A second cash flow cost if the asset is purchased is the annual maintenance charge, after taxes: $500,000(1 − 0.34) = $330,000. The PV of those cash costs, discounted at 6.6 percent, is $1,457,948.

3. Depreciation provides a tax shelter—it saves taxes in the amount of T(Dep) each year. That amounts to a negative cash cost if the asset is purchased. The depreciation tax savings in Year 1 is $680,000, in Year 2 is $1,088,000, and so on. The PV of those tax shelters, discounted at 6.6 percent, is $2,871,116.

4. If the asset is owned, the lessee would receive the $660,000 after-tax residual value in Year 5. The PV of this flow is $479,466.

5. Putting these things together, we can produce a simplified formula for analyzing the PV cost of owning:

$$\begin{array}{ll} \text{PV cost} \\ \text{of owning} \end{array} = \begin{array}{l} \text{Amount} \\ \text{borrowed} \end{array} + \begin{array}{l} \text{PV of after-tax} \\ \text{maintenance costs} \end{array} - \begin{array}{l} \text{PV of dep.} \\ \text{tax savings} \end{array} - \begin{array}{l} \text{PV of after-tax} \\ \text{residual value} \end{array}$$

$$= \$10,000,000 + \$1,457,948 - \$2,871,116 - \$479,466$$

$$= \$8,107,366 \approx \$8,107,000.$$

We prefer the Table 14-2 approach because it is easier to explain to decision makers, and arithmetic is not a problem because the analysis would always be done with a computer.

Table 14-2
Anderson Equipment Company:
NPV Analysis
(Thousands of Dollars)

I. Cost of Owning

Year (1)	Loan Amortization Schedule				Maintenance Cost (6)	Depreciation (7)	Tax Deductible Expenses: (3)+(6)+(7) = (8)	Tax Savings: 0.34 × (8) = (9)	Net Cash Outflow If Owned: (2)+(6)−(9) = (10)
	Total Payment (2)	Interest (3)	Principal (4)	Remaining Balance (5)					
0					$500		$ 500	$ 170	$ 330
1	$ 2,638	$1,000	$ 1,638	$8,362	500	$ 2,000	3,500	1,190	1,948
2	2,638	836	1,802	6,560	500	3,200	4,536	1,542	1,596
3	2,638	656	1,982	4,578	500	2,000	3,156	1,073	2,065
4	2,638	458	2,180	2,398	500	1,400	2,358	802	2,336
5	2,638	240	2,398	0		1,400	1,640	558	2,080
5									(660)
	$13,190	$3,190	$10,000			$10,000			$8,107

PV cost of owning = $8,107

II. Cost of Leasing

Year (1)	Lease Payment (11)	Tax Savings: 0.34 × (11) = (12)	Net Cash Outflow If Leased: (11) − (12) = (13)
0	$2,750	$935	$1,815
1	2,750	935	1,815
2	2,750	935	1,815
3	2,750	935	1,815
4	2,750	935	1,815
5			

PV cost of leasing = $8,019

III. Cost Comparison

Net advantage to leasing (NAL) = PV cost of leasing − PV cost of owning = −$8,019 − (−$8,107) = $88.

Notes:

a. The net cash outflows are discounted at the lessee's after-tax cost of debt, 6.6 percent.

b. Two lines are shown in Part I for Year 5 in order to account for the residual value cash flow.

c. In practice, a lease analysis such as this would be done using an electronic spreadsheet such as Lotus 1-2-3. See Problems 14-5, 14-6, and 14-7.

Part II of Table 14-2 contains an analysis of the cost of leasing. The lease payments, shown in Column 11, are $2,750,000 per year; this rate, which includes maintenance, was established by the prospective lessor and offered to Anderson Equipment. If Anderson accepts the lease, the full amount will be a deductible expense, so the tax savings, shown in Column 12, is 0.34(Lease payment) = 0.34($2,750,000) = $935,000. Thus, the after-tax cost of the lease payment is Lease payment − Tax savings = $2,750,000 − $935,000 = $1,815,000. This amount is shown in Column 13, Years 0 through 4.

The next step is to compare the net cost of owning with the net cost of leasing. However, we must first put the annual cash flows of leasing and borrowing on a common basis. This requires converting them to present values, which brings up the question of the proper rate at which to discount the costs. In Chapter 2, we saw that the riskier the cash flows, the higher will be the discount rate used to find present values. This same principle was observed in our discussion of capital budgeting, and it also applies in lease analysis. Just how risky are the cash flows under consideration here? Most of them are relatively certain, at least when compared with the types of cash flow estimates that were developed in capital budgeting. For example, the loan payment schedule is set by contract, as is the lease payment schedule. The depreciation expenses are also established by law and not subject to change, and the $500,000 annual maintenance cost is fixed by contract as well. The tax savings are somewhat uncertain, but they will be as projected so long as Anderson's marginal tax rate remains at 34 percent. The residual value is the least certain of the cash flows, but even here, Anderson's management is fairly confident because the estimated residual value distribution is relatively tight.

Since the cash flows under the lease and under the borrow-and-purchase alternatives are both relatively certain, they should be discounted at a relatively low rate. Most analysts recommend that the company's cost of debt be used, and this rate seems reasonable in our example. Further, since all the cash flows are on an after-tax basis, *the after-tax cost of debt, which is 6.6 percent, should be used*. Accordingly, we discount the cash outflows in Columns 10 and 13 using a rate of 6.6 percent. The resulting present values are $8,107,000 for the cost of owning and $8,019,000 for the cost of leasing. The financing method that produces the smaller present value of costs is the one that should be selected. We define the net advantage to leasing (NAL) as follows:

$$NAL = PV \text{ cost of leasing} - PV \text{ cost of owning}.$$

Thus, the NAL for Anderson's lease is − $8,019,000 − (− $8,107,000) = $88,000. The NAL is actually the NPV of leasing versus borrowing and buying, and in this instance, it is to Anderson's advantage to lease.[8]

---

[8]The more complicated methods which exist for analyzing leasing generally focus on the issue of the discount rate that should be used to discount the cash flows. Conceptually, we could assign a separate discount rate to each individual cash flow component, then find the present values of each of the cash flow components, and finally sum these present values to determine the net advantage or disadvantage to leasing. This approach has been taken by Stewart C. Myers, David A. Dill, and Alberto J. Bautista (MDB) in "Valuation of Financial Lease Contracts," *Journal of Finance*, June 1976, 799-819, among

IRR Analysis

Anderson's lease versus purchase decision could also be analyzed using the IRR approach. Here we know the after-tax cost of debt, 6.6 percent, and we now find something called the *equivalent or after-tax cost rate implied in the lease contract*. Signing a lease is similar to signing a loan contract—the firm has the use of equipment, but it must make a series of payments, under either type of contract. We know the rate built into the loan; it is 10 percent for Anderson. There is an equivalent cost rate built into the lease. If the equivalent after-tax cost rate in the lease is less than the after-tax interest rate on the debt, then there is an advantage to leasing.

Table 14-3 sets forth the cash flows needed to determine the equivalent loan cost. Here is an explanation of the table:

1. The net cost to purchase the equipment, which is avoided if Anderson leases, is shown in Column 2 as a positive cash flow (an inflow) at Year 0. If Anderson leases, it avoids having to pay the net purchase price for the equipment—the lessor pays that cost, so Anderson saves $10 million. That is a positive cash flow at Year 0.

2. Next, we must determine what Anderson must give up (or "pay back") if it leases. As we saw in the last section, Anderson must make annual lease payments of $2,750,000, which amount to $1,815,000 on an after-tax basis. These amounts are reported as cash outflows in Column 3, Years 0-4.

3. If Anderson elects to lease, it will have to give up the right to depreciate the asset. The after-tax values of the depreciation tax shelters, which represent an opportunity cost of leasing, are shown as outflows in Column 4, Years 1-5.

4. If Anderson leases rather than borrows and buys the equipment, it will avoid the maintenance cost of $500,000 per year, or $330,000 after taxes. This is shown in Column 5 as an inflow, or benefit of leasing.

---

others. MDB correctly note that procedures like the one presented in this chapter are valid only if (1) leases and loans are viewed by investors as being equivalent and (2) all cash flows are equally risky, and hence appropriately discounted at the same rate. The first assumption is valid today for virtually all financial leases, and even where it is not, no one knows how to adjust properly for any capital structure effects that leases might have. (MDB, and others, have presented an adjustment formula, but it is based on the assumption that the Modigliani-Miller leverage argument, with no financial distress costs, is correct. Since even MM do not regard the pure MM model as being correct, the MDB formula cannot be correct.) Regarding the second assumption, it is generally believed that all of the cash flows in Table 14-2 except the residual value are of about the same degree of risk, at least to the extent that we are able to evaluate risk. Therefore, the procedures used in Table 14-2 normally meet the MDB assumption; hence, the Table 14-2 analysis is usually correct.

Regarding the residual value, advocates of multiple discount rates often point out that the salvage value is more uncertain than are the other cash flows and thus recommend discounting it at a higher rate. However, there is no way of knowing precisely how much to increase the after-tax cost of debt to account for the increased riskiness of the salvage value cash flow. Further, in a CAPM sense, all cash flows could be equally risky even though individual items such as the salvage value might have more or less total variability than others.

For all these reasons, many analysts use only one discount rate—the after-tax cost of debt—to evaluate the cash flows in a lease analysis.

Table 14-3
Anderson Equipment Company: IRR Analysis
(Thousands of Dollars)

Year (1)	Net Purchase Price (2)	After-Tax Lease Payment (3)	Depreciation Tax Saving (4)	Maintenance Cost after Taxes (5)	After-Tax Salvage (Residual) Value (6)	Net Cash Flow: (2)+(3)+(4)+(5)+(6) = (7)
0	$10,000	($1,815)		$330		$8,515
1		(1,815)	($ 680)	330		(2,165)
2		(1,815)	(1,088)	330		(2,573)
3		(1,815)	(680)	330		(2,165)
4		(1,815)	(476)	330		(1,961)
5			(476)		($660)	(1,136)

$$NPV = \sum_{t=0}^{5} \frac{NCF_t}{(1 + k_L)^t} = 0 \text{ when } k_L = IRR = 6.2\%.$$

5. If Anderson leases the equipment, it will give up the net after-tax salvage value of $660,000. This is also an opportunity cost of leasing, and it is shown in Column 6 as an outflow in Year 5.

6. Column 7 shows the annual net cash flows. There is an inflow at Year 0 followed by outflows in Years 1 to 5.

Given the cash flows in Column 7, we can find the IRR for the stream; it is 6.2 percent, and that is the equivalent after-tax cost rate implied in the lease contract. If Anderson leases, it is using up some of its debt capacity, and the implied cost rate is 6.2 percent. Since this cost rate is less than the 6.6 percent after-tax cost of a regular loan, this IRR lease analysis confirms the NPV analysis; Anderson should lease rather than buy the equipment. If the analysis is done correctly, the NPV and IRR approaches will always lead to the same decision. Thus, one method is as good as the other from a decision standpoint.[9] However, the NPV approach is more straightforward, and hence most people find it easier to follow and to explain to decision makers. On the other hand, the IRR approach is useful in situations where the financing method might influence the decision to acquire the asset in the first place. This last point is explored in the next section.

---

[9]Note that the net cash flows shown in Column 7 of Table 14-3 are the incremental cash flows to Anderson if it leases rather than borrows and buys. Thus, the NPV of these flows is the net advantage to leasing. When discounted at a rate of 6.6 percent, the NPV of the Column 7 flows is $88,652, which, except for a rounding error, is the same as we obtained in the Table 14-2 NPV analysis. Note also that if the loan rate had been IRR/(1 − T) = 6.2%/0.66 = 9.4% rather than 10%, the NAL in Table 14-2 would have been zero (except for rounding errors).

Feedback Effect on Capital Budgeting

Up to now, we have assumed that Anderson has already made a firm decision to acquire the new equipment. Thus, the lease analysis was conducted only to determine whether the equipment should be leased or purchased. But, as we stated earlier, if the cost of leasing is less than the cost of debt, it is possible for projects formerly deemed unacceptable to become acceptable.

To illustrate this point, assume that Anderson's target capital structure is 50 percent debt and 50 percent common equity, that Anderson's cost of debt, k_d, is 10 percent, and that its cost of equity, k_s, is 15 percent. Thus, Anderson's weighted average cost of capital is

$$k_a = 0.5(10\%)(0.66) + 0.5(15\%)$$
$$= 0.5(6.6\%) + 0.5(15\%) = 10.8\%.$$

Further, assume that the firm's initial capital budgeting analysis on this equipment, using a 10.8 percent project cost of capital, resulted in an NPV of $-\$50,000$. As we saw in the preceding section, the after-tax cost of leasing for this project is 6.2 percent, compared with Anderson's after-tax cost of debt of 6.6 percent. Thus, this project can be financed at a lower cost than other projects which involve equipment that cannot be leased.

What should we do now? There are two possible polar positions, depending on the firm's opportunity to substitute lease financing for regular debt financing:

1. *The debt component of all projects can be financed by leasing on similar lease terms.* In this case, the firm should never borrow—all of its "debt" financing should come from leasing. If it had a capital budget of $100 million, and if its optimal capital structure called for 50 percent debt, then it should lease assets with a cost of $50 million and finance the remainder with equity. All projects, regardless of how they will actually be financed, should be evaluated at a WACC based on the debt cost implied in the lease contracts, 6.2 percent in our example:

$$\text{WACC for use in capital budgeting} = 0.5(6.2\%) + 0.5(15\%) = 10.6\%.$$

Anderson's capital budgeting director should now recalculate the project's NPV using a cost of capital of 10.6 percent versus the average project cost of capital, ignoring leasing, of 10.8 percent. Assume that the project's NPV is now $+\$20,000$. The availability of lease financing has made the project acceptable, whereas the project would have been unacceptable if lease financing were not available.

2. *The project under consideration is unique in that it is the only one on which lease terms are available.* In this case, with the further assumption that the cost of the project does not exceed the company's debt financing for the year (or in total under certain circumstances), then the NPV of the project for capital budgeting purposes should be determined as follows:

$$\text{Adjusted NPV} = \frac{\text{NPV based on}}{\text{``regular'' WACC}} + \frac{\text{NAL from}}{\text{Table 14-2}}$$

$$= -\$50,000 + \$88,000 = \$38,000.$$

Here the firm has enough debt capacity to finance the project entirely by leasing, so the firm will get the entire NAL. (If all projects were suitable for leasing, they still could not be leased because of the total debt capacity constraint. Therefore, under the conditions of the preceding paragraph, this procedure is not appropriate.) The entire NAL should be allocated to this project. All other projects should be evaluated on the basis of the WACC with "regular" debt.

If neither polar position holds, or if different projects can be leased on different lease terms with different equivalent loan rates, then no simple rule can be used. Note, though, that as a practical matter we rarely need to go into the feedback effects of leasing on capital budgeting in the first place, because few projects that are not acceptable under one financing method would be acceptable under another. Given all the uncertainties about capital budgeting cash flows, few managers would change their minds about the acceptability of a project as a result of a few basis points change in the WACC. Still, for certain types of businesses, especially those where real estate is an important element, the availability of lease financing could make the difference in the go/no-go decision. Therefore, it is important for financial managers to know how leasing fits into capital budgeting analysis.

EVALUATION BY THE LESSOR

Thus far, we have considered leasing only from the lessee's viewpoint. It is also useful to analyze the transaction as the lessor sees it: Is the lease a good investment for the party who must put up the money? The lessor will generally be a specialized leasing company, a bank or bank affiliate, an individual or group of individuals, or a manufacturer such as IBM that uses leasing as a sales tool. The specialized leasing companies are often owned by profitable companies such as General Electric, which owns General Electric Credit Corporation (GECC), which is probably the largest leasing company in existence. Investment banking houses such as Merrill Lynch also set up and/or work with specialized leasing companies, where brokerage clients' money is made available to leasing customers in deals which permit the investors to share in the tax shelters provided by the lease.

Regardless of who the lessor is, any potential lessor needs to know the rate of return on the capital invested in the lease, and this information is also useful to the prospective lessee: Lease terms on large leases are generally negotiated, so the lessor and the lessee should know one another's position. The lessor's analysis involves (1) determining the net cash outlay, which is usually the invoice price of the leased equipment less any lease payments made in advance; (2) determining the periodic cash inflows, which consist of the lease payments minus both income taxes and any lessor's maintenance expense; (3) estimating the after-tax residual value of the property when the lease expires; and (4) determining whether the rate of return on the lease exceeds the lessor's opportunity cost of capital or, equivalently, whether the NPV of the lease exceeds zero.

To illustrate the lessor's analysis, we assume the same facts as for the Anderson Equipment Company lease, as well as this situation: (1) The potential lessor is a wealthy individual whose current income is in the form of interest, and whose marginal federal-plus-state income tax rate, T, is 40 percent. (2) The investor can buy bonds that have a 9 percent yield to maturity, providing an after-tax yield of $(9\%)(1 - T) = (9\%)(0.6) = 5.4\%$. This is the after-tax return that the investor can obtain on alternative investments of similar risk. (3) The before-tax salvage (or residual) value is $1,000,000. Since the asset will be fully depreciated at the end of the 5-year lease, this $1 million will be taxable at the 40 percent rate because of the recapture of depreciation rule, so the lessor will receive $600,000 after taxes from the sale of the equipment after the lease expires.

NPV Analysis

The lease analysis from the investor's standpoint is developed in Table 14-4. Here we see that the lease as an investment has a net present value of $33,000. On a present value basis, the investor who invests in the lease rather than in the 9 percent bonds (5.4 percent after taxes) is better off by this amount, indicating that the investor should be willing to write the lease. Since we saw earlier that the lease is also advantageous to Anderson Equipment Company, the transaction should be completed.

Table 14-4
Lease Analysis from the Lessor's Viewpoint
(Thousands of Dollars)

Year (1)	Net Equipment Cost (2)	Lease Payment (3)	Maintenance Expense (4)	Depreciation (5)	Taxes: [(3) − (4) − (5)]T = (6)	After-Tax Salvage (Residual) Value (7)	Net Cash Flow: (2) + (3) − (4) − (6) + (7) = (8)
0	($10,000)	$ 2,750	500		$900		($8,650)
1		2,750	500	$ 2,000	100		2,150
2		2,750	500	3,200	(380)		2,630
3		2,750	500	2,000	100		2,150
4		2,750	500	1,400	340		1,910
5				1,400	(560)	$600	1,160
		$13,750	$2,500	$10,000	$500		

$$NPV = \sum_{t=0}^{5} \frac{NCF_t}{(1 + k)^t} = \$33 \text{ when } k = 5.4\%.$$

IRR Analysis

IRR analysis for the lessor is less complicated than for the lessee. The lessor's net cash flows are shown in Column 8 of Table 14-4. The IRR of the lease is that discount rate which forces the NPV of the lease to zero:

$$NPV = 0 = \sum_{t=0}^{5} \frac{NCF_t}{(1 + k_L)^t}.$$

The solution value of k_L is 5.6 percent. Thus, the lease provides a 5.6 percent after-tax return to this 40 percent tax rate investor. This exceeds the 5.4 percent after-tax return on 9 percent bonds. So, using either the IRR or the NPV methods, the lease would appear to be a good investment.[10]

Setting the Lease Payment

In the preceding section, we evaluated the lease from the lessor's standpoint when the lease payment had already been specified. As a general rule, in large leases such as the one between Tucson Electric and the IBM/Philip Morris group, the parties will sit down and work out an agreement as to the size of the lease payments, with these payments being set so as to provide the lessor with some specific required rate of return. For smaller leases, the lessor does the analysis, again setting terms which provide a target rate of return, and then offers these terms to the potential lessee on a take-it-or-leave-it basis.

Competition among leasing companies forces lessors to build market-related returns into their lease payment schedules. To illustrate all this, suppose the potential lessor described above, after examining other alternative investment opportunities, decides that the 5.6 percent return on the Anderson Equipment Company lease is too low, and that the lease should provide an after-tax return of 6 percent. What lease payment schedule should be set?

To answer this question, note again that Table 14-4 contains the lessor's cash flow analysis. If we let X be the unknown lease payment, then the net after-tax cash flows in Years 0 through 5 are

$$CF(AT)_{0-5} = X + (2) - (4) - [X - (4) - (5)]T + (7),$$

where the numbers in parentheses are column numbers. We could algebraically set up the NPV equation to provide a 6 percent return and then solve for X. However, if the analysis is computerized it is very easy to change the lease payment until the lease's NPV = $0 or, equivalently, its IRR = 6.0 percent. We did this on our *Lotus 1-2-3* lease evaluation model, and found that the lessor must set the lease payment at $2,785,874 to obtain an expected after-tax rate of return of 6.0 percent. However, this lease payment may not be acceptable to the lessee,

---

[10]Note that the lease investment is actually slightly more risky than the alternative bond investment because the residual value cash flow is less certain than a principal repayment. Thus, the lessor would probably require an expected return somewhat above the 5.4 percent promised on a bond investment.

Anderson Equipment Company, in which case it may not be possible to strike a deal.

Leveraged Lease Analysis

Historically, only two parties have been involved in lease transactions—the lessor, who puts up the money, and the lessee. In recent years, however, a new type of lease, the *leveraged lease*, has come into widespread use. Under a leveraged lease, the lessor arranges to borrow part of the required funds, generally giving the lender a first mortgage on the plant or equipment being leased. The lessor still receives the tax shelter associated with accelerated depreciation. However, the lessor now has a riskier position, because the lessor's position is junior to that of the lender, who has a first mortgage on the plant or equipment.

Such leveraged leases, often with syndicates of wealthy individuals seeking tax shelters acting as owner-lessors, are an important part of the financial scene today. Incidentally, whether or not a lease is leveraged is not important to the lessee; from the lessee's standpoint, the method of analyzing a proposed lease is unaffected by whether or not the lessor borrows part of the required capital.

The example in Table 14-4 is not set up as a leveraged lease. However, it is easy enough to modify the analysis if the lessor borrows all or part of the required $10 million, making the transaction a leveraged lease. First, we would add a set of columns to Table 14-4 to show the financing cash flows. The interest component would represent another tax deduction, while the loan repayments would constitute additional cash outlays. The "initial cost" would be reduced by the amount of the loan. With these changes made, a new NPV and IRR could be calculated and used to evaluate whether or not the lease represents a good investment.

To illustrate, assume that the lessor can borrow $5 million of the $10 million net purchase price at a rate of 9 percent on a 5-year balloon loan. Table 14-5 contains the lessor's leveraged lease NPV analysis. The NPV of the leveraged lease investment based on the net cash flows shown in Column 4 is $33,000, which is the same as the $33,000 NPV for the unleveraged lease. Note, though, that the lessor has only spent $3.65 million on this lease. Therefore, the lessor could invest in 2.37 similar leveraged leases for the same $8.65 million investment required to finance a single unleveraged lease, producing a total net present value of 2.37($33,000) = $78,210.

The effect of leverage on the lessor's return is also reflected in the IRR. The IRR is that discount rate which equates the sum of the present values of the Column 4 cash flows to zero. We find the IRR of the leveraged lease to be about 9.3 percent, which is substantially higher than the 5.6 percent after-tax return on the unleveraged lease.[11]

---

[11]Note two additional points concerning the leveraged lease analysis. First, in this situation, leveraging had no impact on the lessor's per lease NPV. This is because the cost of leveraging (5.4 percent after taxes) equals the discount rate, and hence the leveraging cash flows are netted out on a present value basis. Second, the leveraged lease has multiple IRRs, one at 0.0 percent and another at approximately 9.3 percent.

Table 14-5
Leveraged Lease Analysis
(Thousands of Dollars)

Year (1)	Net Cash Flow from Table 14-4 (2)	Cash Flows from Leveraging[a] (3)	Net Cash Flow: (2) + (3) = (4)
0	($8,650)	$5,000	($3,650)
1	2,150	(270)	1,880
2	2,630	(270)	2,360
3	2,150	(270)	1,880
4	1,910	(270)	1,640
5	1,160	(5,270)	(4,110)

$$\text{NPV} = \sum_{t=0}^{5} \frac{\text{NCF}_t}{(1 + k)^t} = \$33 \text{ when k} = 5.4\%.$$

[a]The lessor borrows $5 million at $t = 0$ and repays it at $t = 5$. Interest expense, payable at the end of each year, is $0.09(\$5,000) = \$450$, but it is tax deductible, so the after-tax interest cash flow is $-\$450(1 - T) = -\$450(0.6) = -\$270$.

Typically, leveraged leases provide the lessor with higher expected rates of return (IRRs) and higher NPVs per dollar of invested capital than unleveraged leases. However, the riskiness of such leases is also higher for the same reason that any leveraged investment is riskier. Since leveraged leases are a relatively new development, no standard methodology has been developed for analyzing them in a risk/return framework. However, sophisticated lessors are now developing simulations similar to those described in Chapter 9. Then, given the apparent riskiness of the lease investment, the lessor can decide whether the returns built into the contract are sufficient to compensate for the risk involved.

OTHER ISSUES IN LEASE ANALYSIS

The basic methods of analysis for both the lessee and the lessor were presented in the previous sections. However, some other issues warrant discussion.

Estimated Residual Value

It is important to note that the lessor owns the property upon expiration of a lease, and hence the lessor has claim to the asset's salvage (or residual) value. Superficially, it would appear that if residual values are expected to be large, owning would have an advantage over leasing. However, this apparent advantage may not hold up. If expected residual values are large—as they may be under inflation for certain types of equipment and also if real property is involved—competition between leasing companies and other financial sources, as well as competition among leasing companies themselves, will force leasing rates down to the point where potential residual values are fully recognized in the lease contract. Thus, the existence of large residual values on equipment is not likely to result in materially higher costs for leasing.

Increased Credit Availability

As noted earlier, leasing is sometimes said to have an advantage for firms that are seeking the maximum degree of financial leverage. First, it is sometimes argued that firms can obtain more money, and for longer terms, under a lease arrangement than under a loan secured by a specific piece of equipment. Second, since some leases do not appear on the balance sheet, lease financing has been said to give the firm a stronger appearance in a *superficial* credit analysis and thus to permit the firm to use more leverage than would be possible if it did not lease.

There may be some truth to these claims for smaller firms. However, now that large firms are required to capitalize major leases and to report them on their balance sheets, this point is of questionable validity for any firm large enough to have audited financial statements.

Depreciation Tax Savings

If a firm is unprofitable, or if it is expanding so rapidly and generating so much depreciation expense that its taxable income is driven down to zero, then it may be worthwhile for it to enter a lease arrangement. Here the lessor (a bank, a leasing company, or a high-tax-bracket corporation or individual) will take the depreciation tax savings and give the lessee a corresponding reduction in lease charges. Railroads and airlines have been large users of leasing for this reason in recent years, as have unprofitable industrial companies such as U.S. Steel (now USX Corporation). Tax considerations are without question the dominant motives behind most financial leases that are written today.

Computer Models

Lease analysis, like capital budgeting analysis, is particularly well suited for computer analysis; see Problems 14-5, 14-6, and 14-7. Both the lessee and lessor could create computer models for their analyses. Setting the analysis up on a computer is especially useful when negotiations are underway, and when investment banking houses such as Merrill Lynch are working out a leasing deal between a group of investors and a company, the analysis would always be computerized.

Leasing under the 1986 Tax Act

The 1986 Tax Act contained three provisions that reduce the potential advantages of leasing: (1) The investment tax credit (ITC) was eliminated. Prior to 1987, many leases were signed for the primary purpose of transferring ITCs from zero tax bracket corporations such as U.S. Steel to high bracket investors such as IBM. (2) Under the 1986 Act, depreciation tax rates were effectively lowered. Thus, the depreciation benefits associated with owning buildings and equipment were lowered. (3) Tax rates were lowered, from a maximum of 46 percent to 34 percent for corporations, and from 50 percent to 28 percent for individuals. The first two factors lower the tax shelters that are available for transfer from low-bracket to high-bracket investors, while the third lowers the economic value of any such transfer (because the tax saving is equal to the deduction times the tax rate).

We used our lease analysis models to analyze a number of recent (1986) lease deals, but under the assumption the new tax laws were in effect. Invariably, the advantage of leasing fell sharply, often to the point where the lease deal would simply not be viable. We are tempted to predict, on the basis of that analysis, a reduction in the volume of leasing. It is more likely, however, that financial analysts will just sharpen their pencils (or their computers), come up with less profitable but not unprofitable deals, and continue expanding the volume of leasing business.

SUMMARY

This chapter discussed the three major types of leases: (1) *operating leases*, (2) *sale-and-leaseback plans*, and (3) *financial leases for new assets*. Operating leases generally provide both for the financing of an asset and for its maintenance, whereas both sale-and-leaseback plans and regular financial leases usually provide only financing and are alternatives to debt financing.

Financial leases (and sale-and leaseback plans) are evaluated by a cash flow analysis. We start with the assumption that an asset will be acquired, and that the acquisition will be financed either by debt or by a lease. Next, we develop the annual net cash outflows associated with each financing plan. Then we discount the two sets of outflows at the company's after-tax cost of debt. Finally, we choose the alternative with the lower present value of costs.

Leasing sometimes represents "off balance sheet" financing, which permits a firm to obtain more financial leverage if it leases than if it uses straight debt. This was formerly cited as a major reason for leasing. Today, however, taxes are the primary reason for the growth of financial leasing. Leasing permits depreciation tax savings to be transferred from the user of an asset to the supplier of capital, and if these parties are in different tax brackets, both can benefit from the lease arrangement.

Questions and Problems

14-1 (Tax law effects) Suppose Congress enacted new tax law changes that would (1) permit equipment to be depreciated over a shorter period, (2) lower corporate tax rates, and (3) increase the investment tax credit. Discuss how each of these potential changes would affect the relative volume of leasing (versus conventional debt) in the U.S. economy.

14-2 (Lessor incentives) Commercial banks moved heavily into equipment leasing during the early 1970s, acting as lessors. One major reason for this invasion of the leasing industry was to gain the benefits of accelerated depreciation and the investment tax credit on lease equipment. During this same period, commercial banks were investing heavily in municipal securities, and they were also making loans to real estate investment trusts (REITs). In the mid-1970s, these REITs had such serious difficulty that many banks suffered large losses on their REIT loans. Explain how its investments in municipal bonds and REITs could reduce a bank's willingness to act as a lessor.

14-3 (IRS restrictions) Suppose there were no IRS restrictions on what constituted a valid lease. Explain, in a manner that a legislator might understand, why some restrictions should be imposed. Illustrate your answer with numbers.

14-4 (Balance sheet effects) Two companies, Electroway and Lewis Corporation, began operations with identical balance sheets. A year later, both required additional manufacturing capacity at a cost of $50,000. Electroway obtained a 5-year, $50,000 loan at an 8 percent interest rate from its bank. Lewis, on the other hand, decided to lease the required $50,000 capacity for 5 years; an 8 percent return was built into the lease. The balance sheet for each company, before the asset increases, follows:

		Debt	$ 50,000
		Equity	100,000
Total assets	$150,000	Total claims	$150,000

a. Show the balance sheets for both firms after the asset increase and calculate each firm's new debt ratio.
b. Show how Lewis's balance sheet would look immediately after the financing if it capitalized the lease.
c. Would the rate of return (1) on assets and (2) on equity be affected by the choice of financing? How?

14-5 (Lease versus buy) Smith Industries must install $1 million of new machinery in its Texas plant. It can obtain a bank loan for 100 percent of the required amount. Alternatively, a Texas investment banking firm which represents a group of investors believes that it can arrange for a lease financing plan. *Assume* that these facts apply:

(1) The equipment falls in the ACRS 3-year class.
(2) Estimated maintenance expenses are $50,000 per year.
(3) Smith's tax rate is 34 percent.
(4) If the money is borrowed, the bank loan will be at a rate of 14 percent, amortized in 3 equal installments at the end of each year.
(5) The tentative lease terms call for payments of $320,000 at the end of each year for 3 years.
(6) Under the proposed lease terms, the lessee must pay for insurance, property taxes, and maintenance.
(7) Smith must use the equipment if it is to continue in business, so it will almost certainly want to acquire the property at the end of the lease. If it does, then under the lease terms it can purchase the machinery at its fair market value at that time. The best estimate of this market value is the $200,000 residual value, but it could be much higher or lower under certain circumstances.

To assist management in making the proper lease-versus-buy decision, you are asked to answer the following questions:
    a. Assuming that the lease can be arranged, should Smith lease or borrow and buy the equipment? Explain.

b. Consider the $200,000 estimated residual value. Is it appropriate to discount it at the same rate as the other cash flows? What about the other cash flows—are they all equally risky? (Hint: Riskier cash flows are normally discounted at higher rates, but when the cash flows are *costs* rather than *inflows*, the normal procedure must be reversed.)

(Do Parts c and d only if you are using the computerized diskette.)

c. Determine the lease payment at which Smith would be indifferent to buying or leasing, that is, the lease payment which equates the PV cost of leasing to that of buying. (Hint: Use trial-and-error.)

d. Using the $320,000 lease payment, what would be the effect if Smith's tax rate fell to zero?

14-6 (Lessor analysis) The Cary Company has decided to acquire some new R&D equipment. One alternative is to lease the equipment on a 4-year contract for a lease payment of $10,500 per year, payments to be made at the *beginning* of each year. The lease, which would include maintenance, is being offered by LePage Credit Corporation, a local leasing company. LePage would purchase the equipment outright for $40,000, and would have to pay the local dealer $1,000 at the beginning of each year to provide maintenance service. The equipment falls into the ACRS 3-year class; and it has a residual value of $10,000, which is the expected market value after 4 years. The lessor's marginal state-plus-federal tax rate is 40 percent. The analysts at LePage compare the returns on potential leases with returns available on comparable maturity commercial loans which the firm also writes. Currently, LePage is charging 9 percent on four year commercial loans.

a. What is the NPV on the lease investment?

b. What is the IRR on the lease investment? Should LePage write the lease? Why?

(Do Parts c, d, e, g, and h only if you are using the computerized diskette.)

c. Assume that interest rates rise, and LePage can now earn 14 percent (before taxes) on its commercial loans. How does this affect the lease analysis?

d. What lease payment must LePage charge to be indifferent between writing the lease and loaning at 14 percent?

e. Return to the original situation. Suppose there is a 25 percent chance that the residual value will be only $5,000, and another 25 percent probability that the residual value will be $15,000. There is a 50 percent probability that the residual value will be $10,000. What is LePage's best case and worst case NPVs? Suppose that the LePage analysts account for differential risk by increasing the residual value discount rate. What residual value discount rate forces NPV = $0 when the residual value is $10,000?

f. Now suppose that LePage can leverage the lease. LePage could borrow up to $30,000 using the truck as collateral on a term loan at an 8 percent rate. Should LePage leverage the lease? Should LePage leverage the lease at 9 percent?

g. Refer back to part f. Suppose that the loan for $30,000 may only be obtained at a rate of 10 percent. What is the new NPV to the lessor of the leveraged lease? Should LePage leverage the lease under these circumstances? Why?

h. If LePage was able to borrow only $15,000 for this project due to restrictive covenants contained in a previous loan agreement, would it be beneficial to leverage the lease at 8 percent? At 9 percent? At 10 percent?

14-7 (Lease analysis) As part of its overall plant modernization and cost reduction program, Southern Fabrics' management has decided to install a new automated weaving loom. In the capital budgeting analysis of this equipment, the IRR of the project was found to be 29 percent versus a project required return of 14 percent.

The loom has an invoice price of $100,000, including delivery and installation charges. The funds needed could be borrowed from the bank through a 4-year amortized loan at a 15 percent interest rate, with payments to be made at the end of each year. In the event the loom is purchased, the manufacturer will contract to maintain and service it for a fee of $8,000 per year paid at the end of each year. The loom falls in the ACRS 5-year class, and Southern's marginal federal-plus-state tax rate is 40 percent.

Brooks Automation, Inc., maker of the loom, has offered to lease the loom to Southern for $30,500 upon delivery and installation (at $t = 0$) plus 4 additional annual lease payments of $30,500 to be made at the end of Years 1 to 4. (Note that there are 5 lease payments in total.) The lease agreement includes maintenance and servicing. Actually, the loom has an expected life of 8 years, at which time its expected salvage value is zero; however, after 4 years, its market value is expected to equal its book value. Southern plans to build an entirely new plant in 4 years, so it has no interest in either leasing or owning the proposed loom for more than that period.

a. Should the loom be leased or purchased?

(Do the remainder of the problem only if you are using the computerized diskette.)

b. Southern's managers disagree on the appropriate discount rate to be used in the analysis. What effect would a discount rate change have on the lease-versus-purchase decision?

c. The salvage value is clearly the most uncertain cash flow in the analysis. What effect would a salvage value risk adjustment have on the analysis? (Assume that the appropriate salvage value pre-tax discount rate is 18 percent.)

d. The original analysis assumed that the firm would not need the loom after 4 years. Now assume that the firm will continue to use it after the lease expires. Thus, if it leased, Southern would have to buy the asset after 4 years at the then existing market value, which is assumed to equal the book value. What effect would this requirement have on the basic analysis?

e. Under the original lease terms, it was to Southern's advantage to purchase the loom. However, if you had analyzed the lease from the lessor's viewpoint, you would have found that it was more profitable for Brooks Automation to lease the machine than to sell it—in fact, the manager of Brooks has found that the company can lower the lease payment to $30,000 and still make more by leasing the machine than by selling it. With an annual lease payment of $30,000, should the loom be leased or bought?

f. Perform the lease analysis assuming that Southern's marginal tax rate is (1) 0 percent and (2) 50 percent. Assume a lease payment of $30,500 and a 15 percent pre-tax discount rate. What effect, if any, would the lessee's tax rate have on the lease-buy decision?

Selected Additional References and Cases

For a description of lease analysis in practice, as well as a comprehensive bibliography of the leasing literature, see

O'Brien, Thomas J., and Bennie H. Nunnally, Jr., "A 1982 Survey of Corporate Leasing Analysis," *Financial Management*, Summer 1983, 30-36.

Many of the theoretical issues surrounding lease analysis are discussed in the following articles:

Hockman, Shalom, and Ramon Rabinovitch, "Financial Leasing under Inflation," *Financial Management*, Spring 1984, 17-26.

Levy, Haim, and Marshall Sarnat, "Leasing, Borrowing, and Financial Risk," *Financial Management*, Winter 1979, 47-54.

Lewellen, Wilbur G., Michael S. Long, and John J. McConnell, "Asset Leasing in Competitive Capital Markets," *Journal of Finance*, June 1976, 787-798.

Miller, Merton H., and Charles W. Upton, "Leasing, Buying, and the Cost of Capital Services," *Journal of Finance*, June 1976, 761-786.

Schall, Lawrence D., "The Evaluation of Lease Financing Opportunities," *Midland Corporate Finance Journal*, Spring 1985, 48-65.

Leveraged lease analysis is discussed in these articles:

Athanasopoulos, Peter J., and Peter W. Bacon, "The Evaluation of Leveraged Leases," *Financial Management*, Spring 1980, 76-80.

Dyl, Edward A., and Stanley A. Martin, Jr., "Setting Terms for Leveraged Leases," *Financial Management*, Winter 1977, 20-27.

Grimlund, Richard A., and Robert Capettini, "A Note on the Evaluation of Leveraged Leases and Other Investments," *Financial Management*, Summer 1982, 68-72.

Perg, Wayne F., "Leveraged Leasing: The Problem of Changing Leverage," *Financial Management*, Autumn 1978, 47-51.

The Option Pricing Model (OPM) has recently been used in lease analysis by

Copeland, Thomas E., and J. Fred Weston, "A Note on the Evaluation of Cancellable Operating Leases," *Financial Management*, Summer 1982, 60-67.

Lee, Wayne Y., John D. Martin, and Andrew J. Senchack, "The Case for Using Options to Evaluate Salvage Values in Financial Leases," *Financial Management*, Autumn 1982, 33-41.

The Crum-Brigham casebook contains three cases which deal with lease analysis:

Case 25, "Biotech Services," which illustrates the standard lease-versus-purchase decision.

Case 26, "Sure Strike Tackle Company," which focuses on the analysis of sale-and-leaseback versus conventional mortgage financing.

Case 27, "Huysman Steel Corporation," which illustrates leveraged lease analysis and multiple IRRs.

15

OPTIONS, WARRANTS, CONVERTIBLES, AND FUTURES

Thus far our discussion of long-term financing has concentrated on common and preferred stock, on various types of debt, and on lease financing. In this chapter, we shall see how a company can use warrants and convertibles to make its securities attractive to a broader range of investors, thereby increasing the potential supply of capital. We also introduce options and futures markets, and illustrate how these markets provide a method for locking in future financing costs.

OPTIONS

Both warrants and convertibles are types of option securities, and options themselves represent an important part of today's financial scene. Therefore, we begin the chapter by discussing both the rapidly growing option markets and option pricing theory. An *option* is a contract which gives its holder the right to buy (or sell) an asset at some predetermined price within a specified period of time. "Pure options" are instruments that (1) are created by outsiders (generally investment banking firms) rather than the firm, (2) are bought and sold primarily by investors (or speculators), and (3) are of greater importance to investors than to financial managers. However, financial managers should understand option theory, because such an understanding will help them structure warrant and convertible financings. Additionally, option theory provides some useful insights into many other facets of corporate finance.

Option Types and Markets

There are many types of options and option markets.[1] To illustrate how options work, suppose you owned 100 shares of IBM, which, on April 23, 1986, sold for

---

[1]For an in-depth treatment of options, see Robert C. Radcliffe, *Investment Concepts, Analysis, and Strategy* (Glenview, Ill.: Scott, Foresman, 1987).

501

$155 per share. You could give (or sell) to someone else the right to buy the 100 shares at any time during the next 3 months at a price of, say, $160 per share. The $160 is called the *striking*, or *exercise, price.* Such options exist, and they are traded on a number of exchanges, with the Chicago Board Options Exchange (CBOE) being the oldest and the largest. This type of option is defined as a *call option*, because the purchaser has a "call" on 100 shares of stock. The seller of an option is defined as the *writer.* An investor who "writes" call options against stock held in his or her portfolio is said to be selling *covered options.* Options sold without the stock to back them up are called *naked options.* When the exercise price exceeds the current stock price, the option is said to be *out-of-the-money.* When the exercise price is less than the current price of the underlying stock, the option is *in-the-money.*

You can also buy an option which gives you the right to *sell* a stock at a specified price within some future period—this is called a *put option.* For example, suppose you think IBM's stock price is likely to decline from its current level of $155 sometime during the next 3 months. For $400 you could buy a 3-month put option giving you the right to sell 100 shares (which you would not necessarily own) at a price of $150 per share ($150 is the striking price). If you bought a 100-share contract for $400 and then IBM's stock actually fell to $140, your put option would be worth ($150 − $140)(100) = $1,000. After subtracting the $400 you paid for the option, your net profit (before taxes and commissions) would be $600.

Table 15-1 contains an extract from the April 24, 1986, *Wall Street Journal* Listed Option Quotations Table. This extract, which focuses on IBM, Exxon, and Sperry options, reflects the trading which occurred on the previous day. On April 23, 1986, Sperry's June (2-month), $55 call option sold on the CBOE for $2.375. Thus, for ($2.375)(100) = $237.50 you could buy an option that would give you the right to purchase 100 shares of Sperry at a price of $55 per share at any time during the next 2 months.[2] If the stock price stayed below $55 during that period, you would lose your $237.50, but if it rose to $75, then your $237.50 investment would have grown to ($75 − $55)(100) = $2,000. That translates into a very healthy annual rate of return. Incidentally, if the stock price did go up, you would probably not actually exercise your option and buy the stock—you would sell the options, which would then have a value of at least $2,000 versus the $237.50 you paid, to another option buyer.

Options trading is one of the hottest financial activities in the United States today. In addition to options on individual stocks, options are now available on several stock indexes such as the NYSE Index and the S&P 100 Index. The leverage involved makes it possible for speculators with just a few dollars to make a fortune almost overnight. Also, investors with sizable portfolios can sell options against their stocks and earn the value of the option (less brokerage commissions), even

---

[2]Actually, the *exercise date,* which is the last date that the option can be exercised, is the third Friday of the exercise month. Thus, the June options actually expire on June 20, 1986, so they have a term somewhat less than two months. Also, note that option contracts are generally written in 100-share multiples.

Table 15-1
April 23, 1986, Listed Option Quotations (CBOE)

NYSE Close	Strike Price	Calls—Last Quote			Puts—Last Quote		
		May	June	July	May	June	July
IBM							
155	150	$6\frac{3}{8}$	$8\frac{3}{4}$	$10\frac{3}{8}$	$1\frac{9}{16}$	$3\frac{1}{4}$	4
155	155	$3\frac{5}{8}$	$5\frac{3}{4}$	$7\frac{1}{2}$	$3\frac{3}{4}$	6	$6\frac{1}{2}$
155	160	$1\frac{11}{16}$	$3\frac{3}{4}$	$5\frac{1}{4}$	$8\frac{1}{4}$	r	10
Exxon							
$57\frac{5}{8}$	55	$2\frac{7}{8}$	$3\frac{1}{8}$	$3\frac{5}{8}$	$\frac{9}{16}$	$1\frac{1}{8}$	$1\frac{1}{2}$
Sperry							
$54\frac{1}{2}$	55	$1\frac{7}{16}$	$2\frac{3}{8}$	3	2	$2\frac{7}{8}$	r

Note: r means not traded on April 23.

if the stock's price remains constant. Further, options can be used to create hedges which protect the value of an individual stock or portfolio. We will discuss hedging strategies in more detail later in the chapter.[3]

Corporations such as Sperry and IBM, on whose stocks options are written, have nothing to do with the options market. The corporations do not raise money in the options market, nor do they have any direct transactions in it, and option holders do not vote for corporate directors (unless they exercise their options to purchase the stock, which few actually do). There have been studies by the SEC and others as to whether options trading stabilizes or destabilizes the stock market, and whether this activity helps or hinders corporations seeking to raise new capital. The studies have not been conclusive, but options trading does seem to be here to stay, and many regard it as the most exciting game in town.

Call Option Valuation

An analysis of Table 15-1 provides some insights into call option valuation. First, we see that there are at least three factors which affect a call option's value: (1) For a given striking price, the higher the stock's market price, the higher will be

---

[3]Illegal insider trading is very much in the news as we write this (Spring 1986). It should be noted that the recently caught insiders generally bought options rather than stock. Note also that in May, shortly after we prepared Table 15-1, Burroughs made an offer of $75 per share for Sperry. The Sperry June option jumped in price to $20. Thus, someone who bought Sperry stock in April would have made a gain of $75/$54.5 − 1.0 = 37.6%. A Sperry option would have provided a return of $20/$2.375 − 1.0 = 742.1%. Thus, if someone had knowledge that Burroughs planned to make a $75 offer for Sperry, a given dollar investment in options would provide a much larger payoff than the stock. Note, though, that it is illegal to use insider information for personal gain, and the insider in our example would be taking advantage of the option seller. Insider trading, in addition to being unfair and essentially equivalent to stealing, hurts the economy: Investors lose confidence in the capital markets and raise their required returns because of an increased element of risk, which raises the cost of capital and thus reduces the level of investment.

the call option price. Thus, Sperry's $55 July call option sells for $3, whereas Exxon's $55 July option sells for $3.625 because Exxon's current stock price is $57.625 versus $54.50 for Sperry. (2) For a given stock price, the higher the striking price, the lower will be the call option price. Thus, all of IBM's call options, regardless of exercise month, decline as the striking price increases. (3) The longer the option period, the higher will be the option price, because the longer the time before expiration, the greater chance that the stock price will climb substantially above the exercise price. Thus, for all striking prices, option prices increase as the expiration date is lengthened.

Floor Value Versus Option Price

How is the actual price of an option determined in the market? We shall, shortly, present a widely-used model (the Black-Scholes model) for pricing options, but first it is useful to establish some basic concepts. To begin, we define an option's *floor value* as follows:

$$\text{Floor value} = \frac{\text{Current price}}{\text{of the stock}} - \text{Striking price.}$$

For example, if a stock sells for $50, and its option has a striking price of $20, then the floor value is $30. The floor value can be thought of as the value of the option if it expired today. Note that the floor value of a call option cannot be negative, and hence the floor value of an out-of-the-money option is zero.

Now consider Figure 15-1, which presents some data on Space Technology, Incorporated (STI), a company which recently went public and whose stock has fluctuated widely during its short history. The third column in the tabular data shows the floor values for STI's options when the stock was selling at different prices; the fourth column gives the actual market prices for the option; and the fifth column shows the premium of the actual option price over its floor value. At any stock price below $20, the floor value is zero; above $20, each $1 increase in the price of the stock brings with it a $1 increase in the option's floor value. Note, however, that the actual market price of the option lies above the floor value at each price of the common stock, but the premium declines as the price of the common stock increases. For example, when the common stock sold for $20 and the option had a zero floor value, its actual price, and the premium, was $9. Then, as the price of the stock rose, the *floor value* matched the increase dollar for dollar, but the *market price* of the option climbed less rapidly, and the premium declined. The premium was $9 when the stock sold for $20 a share, but it declined to $1 by the time the stock price had risen to $73 a share. Beyond this point the premium virtually disappeared.

Why does this pattern exist? Why should the option ever sell for more than its floor value, and why does the premium decline as the price of the stock increases? The answer lies in the speculative appeal of options—they enable someone to gain a high degree of personal leverage when buying securities. To illustrate, *suppose STI's options sold for exactly their floor value.* Now suppose you were thinking

Figure 15-1
Option's Market Price and Floor Value: Space Technology, Inc.

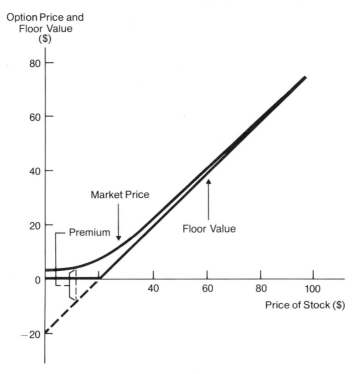

Price of Stock (1)	Striking Price (2)	Floor Value of Option: (1) − (2) = (3)	Market Price of Option (4)	Premium: (4) − (3) = (5)
$20.00	$20.00	$ 0.00	$ 9.00	$9.00
21.00	20.00	1.00	9.75	8.75
22.00	20.00	2.00	10.50	8.50
35.00	20.00	15.00	21.00	6.00
42.00	20.00	22.00	26.00	4.00
50.00	20.00	30.00	32.00	2.00
73.00	20.00	53.00	54.00	1.00
98.00	20.00	78.00	78.50	0.50

of investing in the company's common stock at a time when it was selling for $21 a share. If you bought a share and the price rose to $42, you would have made a 100 percent capital gain. However, had you bought the option at its floor value ($1 when the stock was selling for $21), your capital gain would have been $21 on a $1 investment, or 2,100 percent! At the same time, your total loss potential with the option would be only $1 versus a potential loss of $21 if you purchased the stock. The huge capital gains potential, combined with the loss limitation, is clearly worth something—the exact amount it is worth to investors is the amount of the premium.

But why does the premium decline as the price of the stock rises? Part of the answer is that both the leverage effect and the loss protection feature decline at high stock prices. For example, if you were thinking of buying STI stock when its price was $73 a share, the floor value of the option would be $53. If the stock price doubled to $146, the floor value of the option would go from $53 to $126. The percentage capital gain on the stock would still be 100 percent, but the percentage gain on the option would now be only 138 percent versus 2,100 percent in the earlier case. Notice also that the potential loss on the option is much greater when the option is selling at high prices. These two factors, the declining leverage impact and the increasing danger of losses, help explain why the premium diminishes as the price of the common stock rises.

In addition to the stock price and the exercise price, the price of an option depends on three other factors: (1) the option's time to maturity, (2) the variability of the stock price, and (3) the risk-free rate. We will explain precisely how these factors affect option prices in the next section, but for now, note these points:

1. The longer an option has to run, the greater is its value and the larger is its premium. If an option expires at 4 p.m. today, there is not much chance that the stock price will go way up, so the option must sell at close to its floor value, and its premium must be small. On the other hand, if the expiration date is a year away, the stock price could rise sharply, pulling the option's value up with it.

2. An option on an extremely volatile stock will be worth more than one on a very stable stock. If the stock price rarely moves, then there is a small chance of a large gain. However, if the stock price is highly volatile, the option could become very valuable. At the same time, losses on options are limited, so large declines in a stock's price do not have a corresponding bad effect on option holders. Therefore, the more volatile a stock, the higher is the value of its options.

Because of points (1) and (2), in a graph such as Figure 15-1, if everything else were constant, then the longer an option's life, the higher its market price line would be above the floor value line. Similarly, the more volatile the price of the underlying stock, the higher is the market price line. We will see, in the next section, precisely how these factors affect option values.

THE OPTION PRICING MODEL (OPM)

The *Black-Scholes Option Pricing Model (OPM)* was developed in 1973, just as the rapid growth in options trading began.[4] This model, which has actually been programmed into the permanent memories of some hand-held calculators, is

---

[4]See Fischer Black and Myron Scholes, "The Pricing of Options and Corporate Liabilities," *Journal of Political Economy*, May/June 1973, 637-659.

widely used by option traders. Our interest, however, lies in the insights that option theory provides in valuing all securities subject to contingent claims, including warrants, convertibles, and even the equity of a levered firm.

In deriving their option pricing model, which finds the value of a call option, Black and Scholes make the following assumptions:

1. The stock underlying the call option provides no dividends or other distributions during the life of the option.

2. There are no transactions costs in buying or selling either the stock or the option.

3. The short-term, risk-free interest rate is a known constant during the life of the option.

4. Any purchaser of a security may borrow any fraction of the purchase price at the short-term, risk-free interest rate.

5. Short selling is permitted without penalty, and the short seller will receive immediately the full cash proceeds of today's price for a security sold short.[5]

6. The call option can be exercised only on its expiration date.

7. Trading in all securities takes place in continuous time, and the stock price moves randomly in continuous time.[6]

The assumption that the option can only be exercised on the expiration date is characteristic of a *European* option. *American* options can be exercised at any time up to and including the expiration date. However, it has been shown that for nondividend paying stocks, the market price of an American call option is always greater than the value it would have if it were exercised immediately.[7] Hence, a rational investor would not exercise an American call option on a nondividend paying stock before it expired—the investor would sell the option on the open market. Therefore, the value of an American call option is the same as that of a European option.

The derivation of the Black-Scholes Option Pricing Model rests on the concept of the *riskless hedge*. By buying shares of a stock and simultaneously selling call options on that stock, an investor can create a risk-free investment position—gains on the stock will exactly offset losses on the option, and vice versa. This riskless hedged position must earn a rate of return equal to the risk-free rate; otherwise, an arbitrage opportunity would exist, and people trying to take advantage of this

---

[5]Suppose an investor (or speculator) does not now own any IBM stock. If the investor anticipates a rise in the stock price and consequently buys IBM stock, he or she is said to have *gone long* in IBM. On the other hand, if the investor thinks IBM's stock is likely to fall, he or she could *go short*, or *sell IBM short*. Since the short seller had no IBM stock, he or she would have to borrow the shares sold short from a broker. If the stock price falls, the short seller could, later on, buy shares on the open market and pay back the ones borrowed from the broker. The short seller's profit, before commissions and taxes, would be the difference in the price received from the short sale and the price paid later to purchase the replacement stock.

[6]See Appendix A for a brief review of continuous compounding and discounting.

[7]See Robert C. Merton, "The Theory of Rational Option Pricing," *Bell Journal of Economics and Management Science*, Spring 1973, 141-183.

opportunity would drive the price of the option to the equilibrium level specified by the Black-Scholes model.

The Black-Scholes model consists of the following three equations:

$$V = P[N(d_1)] - Xe^{-k_{RF}t}[N(d_2)].$$ (15-1)

$$d_1 = \frac{\ln(P/X) + [k_{RF} + (\sigma^2/2)]t}{\sigma\sqrt{t}}.$$ (15-2)

$$d_2 = d_1 - \sigma\sqrt{t}.$$ (15-3)

Here

V = current value of a call option with time t until expiration.

P = current price of the underlying stock.

$N(d_i)$ = probability that a deviation less than d_i will occur in a standard normal distribution. Thus, $N(d_1)$ and $N(d_2)$ represent areas under a standard normal distribution function.

X = exercise, or striking, price of the option.

e = exponential function ≈ 2.7183.

k_{RF} = risk-free interest rate.

t = time until the option expires (the option period).

$\ln(P/X)$ = natural logarithm of P/X.

σ^2 = variance of the instantaneous rate of return on the stock.

Note that the value of the option is a function of the variables we discussed earlier: (1) P, the stock's price; (2) t, the option's time to expiration; (3) X, the striking price; (4) σ^2, the price variance of the underlying stock; and (5) k_{RF}, the risk-free rate. We do not derive the Black-Scholes model—the derivation involves some extremely complicated mathematical statistics that go far beyond the scope of this text. However, it is not difficult to use the model, and under the assumptions set forth above, any option price different from the one found by Equation 15-1 would provide the opportunity for arbitrage profits, which would, in turn, force the option price back to the value indicated by the model. As we noted earlier, the Black-Scholes model is widely used by traders, so actual option prices do conform reasonably well to values derived from the model.

In essence, the first term of Equation 15-1, $P[N(d_1)]$, can be thought of as the expected present value of the terminal stock price, while the second term, $Xe^{-k_{RF}t}[N(d_2)]$, can be thought of as present value of the exercise price. However, rather than try to figure out exactly what the equations mean, it is more productive to work out some values and to see how changes in the inputs change the value of the option.

OPM Illustration

The current stock price, P, the exercise price, X, and the time to maturity, t, of the option can be obtained from a newspaper such as the *Wall Street Journal*. The risk-free rate, k_{RF}, used in the OPM is the yield on Treasury bills with a maturity date equal to the option expiration date. The stock price variance, σ^2, can be estimated by calculating the variance of the percentage change in daily stock prices for the past year, that is, the variance of $(P_t - P_{t-1})/P_t$ on a daily basis.

Assume that the following information has been obtained:

$$P = \$20.$$
$$X = \$20.$$
$$t = 3 \text{ months or } 0.25 \text{ years.}$$
$$k_{RF} = 12\% = 0.12.$$
$$\sigma^2 = 0.16.$$

Given this information, we can now use the OPM by solving Equations 15-1 through 15-3. Since d_1 and d_2 are required inputs for Equation 15-1, we solve Equations 15-2 and 15-3 first:

$$d_1 = \frac{\ln(\$20/\$20) + [0.12 + (0.16/2)](0.25)}{0.40(0.50)}$$

$$= \frac{0 + 0.05}{0.20} = 0.25.$$

$$d_2 = d_1 - 0.20 = 0.05.$$

Note that $N(d_1) = N(0.25)$ and $N(d_2) = N(0.05)$ represent areas under a standard normal distribution function. From Table A-5 in Appendix A at the end of the book, we see that the value $d_1 = 0.25$ implies a probability of $0.0987 + 0.5000 = 0.5987$, so $N(d_1) = 0.5987$. Similarly, $N(d_2) = 0.5199$. We can use those values to solve Equation 15-1:

$$V = \$20[N(d_1)] - \$20e^{-(0.12 \times 0.25)}[N(d_2)]$$

$$= \$20[N(0.25)] - \$20(0.9704)[N(0.05)]$$

$$= \$20(0.5987) - \$19.41(0.5199)$$

$$= \$11.97 - \$10.09 = \$1.88.$$

Thus, the value of the option, under the assumed conditions, is $1.88. Suppose the actual option price were $2.25. Arbitrageurs could simultaneously sell the option and buy the underlying stock, and earn a riskless profit. Such trading would occur until the price of the option were driven to $1.88. The reverse would occur if the option sold for less than $1.88. Thus, investors would be unwilling to pay more than $1.88 for the option, and they could not buy it for less.

To see how each of the five OPM factors affects the value of the option, V, consider Table 15-2. Here the top row shows the base case input values and the resulting option value, V = $1.88. The base case input values are those we used above to illustrate how to solve the OPM. In each of the subsequent rows, one factor is increased, while the values of the other four are held constant at their base case levels. The value of the call option is given in the last column. Now consider the effects of a change in each factor:

Table 15-2
Effects of OPM Factors on the Value of a Call Option

Case	P	X	t	k_{RF}	σ^2	V
Base case	$20	$20	0.25	12%	0.16	$1.88
Increase P by $5	**25**	20	0.25	12	0.16	5.81
Increase X by $5	20	**25**	0.25	12	0.16	0.39
Increase t to 6 months	20	20	**0.50**	12	0.16	2.81
Increase k_{RF} to 16%	20	20	0.25	**16**	0.16	1.99
Increase σ^2 to 0.25	20	· 20	0.25	12	**0.25**	2.27

1. **Current stock price.** As the current stock price, P, increases from $20 to $25, the option value increases from $1.88 to $5.81. Thus, the value of the call increases as the stock price increases, but not by as much as the stock price increases ($3.93 versus $5.00). Note, though, that the percentage increase in the option value ($5.81 − $1.88)/$1.88 = 209% far exceeds the percentage increase in the stock price ($25 − $20)/$20 = 25%.

2. **Exercise price.** As the exercise price, X, increases from $20 to $25, the value of the option declines. Again, though, the option value does not decrease in absolute amount by as much as the exercise price increases, but the percentage change in the option value, ($0.39 − $1.88)/$1.88 = −79%, exceeds the percentage change in the exercise price, ($25 − $20)/$20 = 25%.

3. **Option period.** As time to expiration increases from t = 3 months (or 0.25 years) to t = 6 months (or 0.50 years), the value of the option increases from $1.88 to $2.81. This result should not be surprising. The value of the option depends on the chances for an increase in the price of the underlying stock. Obviously, the longer the option runs, the higher the stock price may go. Thus, other factors held constant, a 6-month option is worth more than a 3-month option.

4. **Risk-free rate.** The next factor is the risk-free rate, k_{RF}. As the risk-free rate increases from 12 to 16 percent, the call option value increases slightly, from $1.88 to $1.99. Equations 15-1, 15-2, and 15-3 suggest that the principal effect of an increase in k_{RF} is the reduction of the present value of the exercise price of the option, $Xe^{-k_{RF}t}$, and hence an increase in the current value of the call option.[8] The risk-free rate also plays a role in determining the values of the normal distribution functions $N(d_1)$ and $N(d_2)$, but this effect is of secondary importance. Indeed, option prices in general are not very sensitive to interest rate changes, at least not to changes within the ranges normally encountered.

---

[8]At this point, you may be wondering why the first term in Equation 15-1, $P[N(d_1)]$, is not discounted. In fact, it has been, because the current stock price, P, already represents the present value of the expected expiration date stock price: P is a discounted value, and the discount rate used in the market to determine today's stock price includes the risk-free rate. Thus, Equation 15-1 can be thought of as the present value of the end-of-option-period spread between the stock price and the striking price, adjusted for the probability that the stock price will be higher than the striking price.

5. Variance. As the variance increases from the base case level of 0.16 to 0.25, the value of the call option increases from $1.88 to $2.27. That is, if all other factors are held constant, the riskier the underlying security, the more valuable will be the call option. This result is logical. First, if you bought an option to buy a stock that sells at its exercise price, and if $\sigma^2 = 0$, then there would be a zero probability of the stock price going up, and hence a zero probability of making any money on the option. On the other hand, if you bought an option on a high-variance stock, there would be a fairly high probability of the stock price going way up, and hence of making a high profit on the option. Of course, the price of a high-variance stock could go way down, but as an option holder, your losses would be limited to the price paid to buy the option—only the right-hand side of the stock's probability distribution counts. All of this makes options on risky stocks more valuable than those on safer, low-variance stocks. Put another way, an increase in the price of the stock helps options holders more than a decrease hurts them; thus, the greater the variance, the greater is the value of the option.

This concludes our brief discussion of options and option pricing theory. Appendix 15A discusses how option pricing theory can be used in financial decision making, while the next two sections describe warrants and convertibles, the major types of option securities issued by firms.

WARRANTS

A *warrant* is an option issued by a company which gives the warrant's owner the right to buy a stated number of shares of the company's stock at a specified price. Generally, warrants are distributed with debt, and they are used to induce investors to buy a firm's long-term debt at a lower interest rate than would otherwise be required. For example, when Infomatics Corporation, a rapidly growing high-tech company, wanted to sell $50 million of 20-year bonds in 1986, the company's investment banker informed the financial vice president that the bonds would be difficult to sell, and that an interest rate of 10 percent would be required. However, as an alternative, the banker suggested that investors might be willing to buy the bonds with a coupon rate of only 8 percent if the company would offer 20 warrants with each $1,000 bond, each warrant entitling the holder to buy one share of common stock at a price of $22 per share. The stock was selling for $20 per share at the time, and the warrants would expire in 1996 if they had not been exercised previously.

Why would investors be willing to buy Infomatics' bonds at a yield of only 8 percent in a 10 percent market just because warrants were also offered as part of the package? Because the warrants are long-term options which have value as discussed in the previous section, and this value offsets the low interest rate on the bonds and makes the package of low-yield bonds plus warrants attractive to investors.

Initial Market Price of Bond with Warrants

The Infomatics bonds, if they had been issued as straight debt, would have carried a 10 percent interest rate. However, with warrants attached, the bonds were sold to yield 8 percent. Someone buying the bonds at their $1,000 initial offering price would thus be receiving a package consisting of an 8 percent, 20-year bond plus 20 warrants. Since the going interest rate on bonds as risky as those of Infomatics was 10 percent, we can find the straight-debt value of the bonds, assuming an annual coupon, as follows:

$$\text{Value} = \sum_{t=1}^{20} \frac{\$80}{(1.10)^t} + \frac{\$1,000}{(1.10)^{20}}$$

$$= \$681.09 + \$148.64 = \$829.73.$$

Thus, a person buying the bonds in the initial underwriting would pay $1,000 and receive in exchange a straight bond worth about $830 plus 20 warrants presumably worth about $1,000 − $830 = $170:

Price paid for bond with warrants	=	Straight-debt value of bond	+	Value of warrants.
$1,000	=	$830	+	$170.

Since investors receive 20 warrants with each bond, each warrant has an implied value of $170/20 = $8.50.

The key issue in setting the terms of a bond-with-warrants offering is valuing the warrants. The straight-debt value of the bond can be estimated quite accurately. However, it is much more difficult to estimate the value of the warrants. Even the Black-Scholes OPM provides only a rough estimate because (1) its parameters are not easily estimated and (2) it assumes no dividends on the underlying stock, which is not generally a reasonable assumption for a long-term option. If, in setting the terms, the warrants are overvalued relative to their true market value, then it will be difficult to sell the issue at its par value. Conversely, if the warrants are undervalued, then investors who subscribe to the issue will receive a windfall profit since they can sell the warrants in the market for more than they implicitly paid for them. This windfall profit would come out of the pockets of Infomatics' stockholders.

Use of Warrants in Financing

In the past, warrants have generally been used by small, rapidly growing firms as "sweeteners" when they were selling either debt or preferred stock. Such firms are frequently regarded by investors as being highly risky. Their bonds could be sold only if they were willing to pay extremely high rates of interest and also to accept very restrictive indenture provisions. To avoid this, firms such as Infomatics often offered warrants along with the bonds. However, several years ago, AT&T raised $1.57 billion by selling bonds with warrants. This was the largest financing of any type ever undertaken by a business firm, and it marked the first use ever of warrants by a large, strong corporation.[9]

Getting warrants along with bonds enables investors to share in the company's growth, if it does in fact grow and prosper; therefore, investors are willing to accept a lower bond interest rate and less restrictive indenture provisions. A bond with warrants has some characteristics of debt and some characteristics of equity. It is a hybrid security that provides the financial manager with an opportunity to expand the firm's mix of securities and to appeal to a broader group of investors.

Virtually all warrants today are *detachable*. Thus, after a bond with attached warrants is sold, the warrants can be detached and traded separately from the bond. Further, when these warrants are exercised, the bond issue (with its low coupon rate) remains outstanding, so the warrants bring in additional funds to the firm while leaving its interest costs relatively low.

The exercise price is generally set at from 10 to 30 percent above the market price of the stock on the date the bond is issued. If the firm does grow and prosper, and if its stock price rises above the exercise price at which shares may be purchased, warrant holders could exercise their warrants and buy stock at the stated price. However, without some incentive, warrants would never be exercised prior to maturity—their value in the market would be greater than their floor, or exercise, value, and hence holders would sell rather than exercise. There are three conditions which would encourage holders to exercise their warrants: (1) Warrant holders will surely exercise warrants and buy stock if the warrants are about to expire with the market price of the stock above the exercise price. (2) Warrant holders will tend to exercise voluntarily and buy stock if the company raises the dividend on the common stock by a sufficient amount. No dividend is earned on the warrant, so it provides no current income. However, if the common stock pays a high dividend, it provides an attractive dividend yield. This induces warrant holders to exercise their option to buy the stock. (3) Warrants sometimes have *stepped-up exercise prices*, which prod owners into exercising them. For example, the Williamson Scientific Company has warrants outstanding with an exercise price of $25 until December 31, 1990, at which time, the exercise price rises to $30. If the price of the common stock is over $25 just before December 31, 1990, many warrant holders will exercise their options before the stepped-up price takes effect.

---

[9]It is interesting to note that before the AT&T issue, the New York Stock Exchange's stated policy was that warrants could not be listed because they were "speculative" instruments rather than "investment" securities. When AT&T issued warrants, however, the Exchange changed its policy, agreeing to list warrants that met certain requirements. Many other warrants have since been listed.

It is also interesting to note that, prior to the sale, AT&T's treasury staff, working with Morgan Stanley analysts, estimated the value of the warrants as a part of the underwriting decision. The package was supposed to sell for a total price in the neighborhood of $1,000. The bond value could be determined accurately, so the trick was to estimate the equilibrium value of the warrant under different possible exercise prices and years to expiration, and then use that exercise price and life that caused bond value + warrant value ≈ $1,000. Using the option pricing model, the AT&T/Morgan Stanley analysts set terms which caused the warrant to sell on the open market at within $0.35 of the estimated price.

Another desirable feature of warrants is that they generally bring in funds only if funds are needed. If the company grows, it will probably need new equity capital. At the same time, growth will cause the price of the stock to rise, the warrants to be exercised, and the firm to obtain additional cash. If the company is not successful and cannot profitably employ additional money, the price of its stock will probably not rise sufficiently to induce exercise of the warrants.

The Cost of Warrants

When Infomatics issued its debt with warrants, the firm received $50 million, or $1,000 for each bond. Simultaneously, the company assumed an obligation to pay $80 interest for 20 years plus $1,000 at the end of 20 years. The cost of the money would have been 8 percent if no warrants had been attached, but each Infomatics bond had 20 warrants, each of which entitles its holder to buy one share of Infomatics stock for $22. A cost rate must be assigned to the warrants to determine the total cost of the issue. As we shall see, the total cost is well above 8 percent.

Assume that Infomatics' stock price, which is now $20, is expected to grow, and does grow, at 10 percent per year. When the warrants expire 10 years from now, the stock price will be $20(1.10)^{10} = 51.87. Assuming the warrants had not been exercised during the 10-year period, the company would then have to issue one share of stock worth $51.87 for each warrant exercised, and in return, Infomatics would receive the exercise price, $22. Thus, a purchaser of the bonds, if he or she holds the complete package, will make a profit in Year 10 of $51.87 - $22 = 29.87 for each common share issued. Since each bond has 20 warrants attached, investors would have a gain of 20($29.87) = 597.40 per bond at the end of Year 10. Here is a time line of the cash flow stream to an investor:

0	1		9	10	11		20
− $1,000	+ $80	. . .	+ $80	+ $ 80	+ $80	. . .	+ $ 80
				+ 597.40			+ 1,000
				+ $677.40			+ $1,080

The IRR of this stream is 10.7 percent, which is the investor's overall rate of return on the issue. This return is 70 basis points higher than the return on straight debt, which reflects the fact that the issue is riskier to investors than a straight debt issue because some of the return is expected to come in the form of stock price appreciation, and that part of the return may not materialize.

The expected rate of return to investors is, of course, also the cost of the issue to the company—this was true of common stocks, straight bonds, and preferred stocks, and it is also true of bonds sold with warrants. In thinking about this, note that the investor's Year 10 gain of $597.40 does not just appear out of thin air—the company is giving the warrant holders the right to buy for $22 a share of stock with a market value of $51.87. That obviously dilutes the value of the stock, so Infomatics' original shareholders are incurring an opportunity cost which is exactly equal to the warrant holders' gain.

The cost of warrants can also be illustrated in terms of the effect on earnings per share (EPS). Suppose Infomatics had 1,000,000 common shares outstanding just prior to the expiration of the warrants. Further, assume that the company earns 13.5 percent on its market value equity, so earnings per share are 0.135($51.87) = $7, and total earnings are 1,000,000($7) = $7,000,000. Now, if there were 100,000 warrants outstanding at expiration, exercise of these warrants would bring in 100,000($22) = $2,200,000 of new equity funds, and the number of shares would increase by 100,000. Assuming that the earning power of the $2.2 million of new assets was also 13.5 percent, then 0.135($2,200,000) = $297,000 of new earnings would be produced, making the new total earnings $7,000,000 + $297,000 = $7,297,000. When that new total earnings figure is divided by the new total shares outstanding (1,000,000 + 100,000 = 1,100,000), we get a new EPS of $6.63:

$$\text{New EPS} = \$7{,}297{,}000/1{,}100{,}000 = \$6.63.$$

Thus, exercise of the warrants results in a dilution of EPS from $7 to $6.63, or by $0.37. This $0.37 EPS dilution is a real cost, it is borne by Infomatics' original shareholders, and it must be worked in when calculating the cost of the bonds-with-warrants.

CONVERTIBLES

Convertible securities are bonds or preferred stocks which, under specified terms and conditions, can be exchanged for common stock at the option of the holder. Unlike the exercise of warrants, which brings in additional funds to the firm, conversion does not bring in additional capital: Debt (or preferred stock) is simply replaced on the balance sheet by common stock. Of course, the reduction of the debt or preferred stock will improve the financial strength of the company and make it easier to raise additional fixed charge capital, but that requires a separate action.

Conversion Ratio and Conversion Price

One of the most important provisions of a convertible security is the *conversion ratio, R,* defined as the number of shares of stock a bondholder will receive upon conversion. Related to the conversion ratio is the *conversion price, P_c,* which is the effective price the company will receive for the common stock when conversion occurs. The relationship between the conversion ratio and the conversion price can be illustrated by the Silicon Valley Software Company's convertible debentures, issued at their $1,000 par value in July of 1986. At any time prior to maturity on July 1, 2006, a debenture holder can exchange a bond for 20 shares of common stock; therefore, the conversion ratio, R, is 20. The bond has a par value of $1,000, so the holder would be relinquishing the right to receive $1,000 at maturity upon conversion. Dividing the $1,000 par value by the 20 shares received gives a conversion price of $P_c = \$50$ a share:

$$\text{Conversion price} = P_c = \frac{\text{Par value of bond given up}}{\text{Shares received}}$$

$$= \frac{\$1,000}{R} = \frac{\$1,000}{20} = \$50.$$

Solving for R, we obtain the conversion ratio:

$$\text{Conversion ratio} = R = \frac{\$1,000}{P_c} = \frac{\$1,000}{\$50} = 20 \text{ shares.}$$

Once R is set, the value of P_c is established, and vice versa.

Like a warrant's exercise price, the conversion price is characteristically set at from 10 to 30 percent above the prevailing market price of the common stock at the time the convertible issue is sold. Exactly how the conversion price is established can best be understood after examining some of the reasons firms use convertibles.

Generally, the conversion price and conversion ratio are fixed for the life of the bond, although sometimes a stepped-up conversion price is used. For example, Breedon Industries' 1986 convertible debentures are convertible into 12.5 shares until 1996; into 11.76 shares from 1996 until 2006; and into 11.11 shares from 2006 until maturity in 2116. The conversion price thus starts at $80, rises to $85, and then goes to $90. Breedon's convertibles, like most, become callable after a 10-year call-protection period.

Another factor that may cause a change in the conversion price and ratio is a standard feature of almost all convertibles—the clause protecting the convertible against dilution from stock splits, stock dividends, and the sale of common stock at prices below the conversion price. The typical provision states that if common stock is sold at a price below the conversion price, then the conversion price must be lowered (and the conversion ratio raised) to the price at which the new stock was issued. Also, if the stock is split, or if a stock dividend is declared, the conversion price must be lowered by the percentage amount of the stock dividend or split. For example, if Breedon Industries were to have a two-for-one stock split during the first 10 years of its convertible's life, the conversion ratio would automatically be adjusted from 12.5 to 25, and the conversion price lowered from $80 to $40. If this protection were not contained in the contract, a company could completely thwart conversion by the use of stock splits and stock dividends. Warrants are similarly protected against dilution.

The standard protection against dilution from selling new stock at prices below the conversion price can, however, get a company into trouble. For example, assume that Breedon's stock was selling for $65 per share in 1986 at the time of the convertible issue. Further, suppose the market went sour, and Breedon's stock price dropped to $50 per share. A new common stock sale now would require lowering the conversion price on the convertible debentures from $80 to $50.

That would raise the value of the convertibles and, in effect, transfer wealth from the shareholders to the convertible holders. Potential problems such as this must be kept in mind by firms considering the use of convertibles or bonds with warrants.

Convertible Bond Model

In the spring of 1986, Silicon Valley Software was evaluating the use of the convertible bond issue described earlier. The issue would consist of 20-year convertible bonds which would sell at a price of $1,000 per bond; this $1,000 would also be the bond's par (and maturity) value. The bonds would pay a 10 percent annual coupon interest rate, or $100 per year. Each bond would be convertible into 20 shares of stock, so the conversion price would be $1,000/20 = $50. The stock was expected to pay a dividend of $2.80 during the coming year, and it sold at $35 per share. Further, the stock price was expected to grow at a constant rate of 8 percent per year. Therefore, $k_s = \hat{k}_s = D_1/P_0 + g = \$2.80/\$35 + 8\% = 8\% + 8\% = 16\%$. If the bonds were not made convertible, they would have to offer a yield of 13 percent, given their riskiness and the yields on other bonds. The convertible bonds would not be callable for 10 years, after which they could be called at a price of $1,050, with this price declining by $5 per year thereafter. If, after 10 years, the conversion value exceeds the call price by at least 20 percent, management would probably call the bonds.

Figure 15-2 shows the expectations of both an average investor and the company:[10]

1. The horizontal line at M = $1,000 represents the par (and maturity) value. Also, $1,000 is the price at which the bond is initially offered to the public.

2. The bond is protected against call for 10 years. It is initially callable at a price of $1,050, and the call price declines thereafter by $5 per year. Thus, the call price is represented by the solid section of the line V_0M''.

3. Since the convertible has a 10 percent coupon rate, and since the yield on a nonconvertible bond of similar risk was stated to be 13 percent, the "straight bond" value of the convertible, B_t, must be less than par. At the time of issue, assuming an annual coupon, B_0 is $789:

$$B_0 = \sum_{t=1}^{20} \frac{\$100}{(1.13)^t} + \frac{\$1,000}{(1.13)^{20}} = \$789.$$

Note, however, that the bond's straight debt value must be $1,000 just prior to maturity, so the bond's straight debt value rises over time. B_t follows the line B_0M'' in the graph.

---

[10]For a more complete discussion of how this model can be used to structure the terms of a convertible offering, see Eugene F. Brigham, "An Analysis of Convertible Debentures: Theory and Some Empirical Evidence," *Journal of Finance*, March 1966, 35-54; and M. Wayne Marr and G. Rodney Thompson, "The Pricing of New Convertible Bond Issues," *Financial Management*, Summer 1984, 31-37.

Figure 15-2
Model of a Convertible Bond

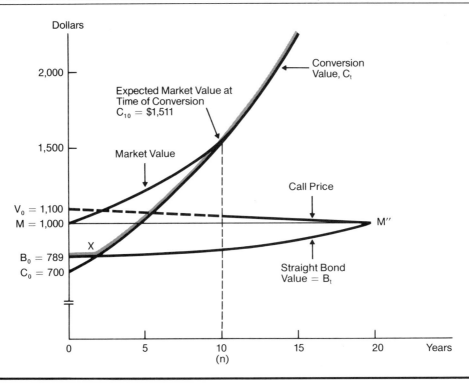

4. The bond's initial conversion value, or the value of the stock the investor would receive if the bonds were converted at $t = 0$, is \$700: The bond's conversion value is $P_t(R)$, so at $t = 0$, conversion value $= P_0(R) = \$35(20 \text{ shares}) = \$700$. Since the stock's price is expected to grow at an 8 percent rate, the conversion value of the bond should rise over time. For example, in Year 5 it should be $P_5(R) = \$35(1.08)^5(20) = \$1,029$. The expected conversion value over time is given by the line C_t in Figure 15-2.

5. The actual market price of the bond can never fall below the higher of its straight debt value or its conversion value. If the market price were below the straight bond value, those who wanted bonds would recognize the bargain and buy the convertible as a bond. If the market price were below the conversion value, people would buy the convertibles, turn them in for stock, and sell the stock at a profit. Therefore, the higher of the bond value and conversion value curves in the graph represents a *floor price* for the bond. In Figure 15-2, the floor price is represented by the thicker shaded line B_0XC_t.

6. In fact, the bond's market value will typically exceed its floor value. It will exceed the straight bond value because the option to convert is worth something—a 10 percent bond with conversion possibilities is worth more than a 10 percent bond without this option. The actual price will also exceed the conversion value because holding the convertible is safer than holding the common stock— the stock can fall to zero, but the convertible bond cannot fall below its straight bond value.[11] We cannot say exactly where the market value line will lie, but it will typically be above the floor set by the straight bond and conversion value lines.

7. At some point, the market value line will hit the conversion value line. This convergence will occur for two reasons. First, the stock should pay higher and higher dividends as the years go by, but the interest payments on the convertible are fixed. For example, Silicon's convertibles would pay $100 in interest annually, while the dividends on the 20 shares received upon conversion would initially be $20(\$2.80) = \$56$. However, at an 8 percent growth rate, the dividends after 10 years would be up to $120.90, while the interest would still be $100. Thus, at some point, rising dividends could be expected to push against the fixed interest payments, causing investors to convert voluntarily. Second, once the bond becomes callable, its market value cannot get very far above both the conversion value and the call price without exposing investors to the danger of a call. For example, suppose that 10 years after issue (when the bonds were callable), the market value of the bonds was $1,600, the conversion value was $1,500, and the call price was $1,050. If the company called the bonds the day after you bought 10 bonds for $16,000, you would be forced to convert into stock worth only $15,000, so you would suffer a loss of $100 per bond, or $1,000, in one day. Recognizing this danger, you and other investors would simply not pay much of a premium over the higher of the call price or the conversion value once the bond becomes callable. Therefore, in Figure 15-2, we assume that the market value line hits the conversion value line in Year 10, when the bond becomes callable.

8. We can let n represent the year when investors expect conversion to occur, either voluntarily because of rising dividends or because the company calls the convertibles to strengthen its balance sheet by substituting equity for debt. In our example, we assume that $n = 10$, the first call date. Had the company used a lower initial conversion value, or a lower expected growth rate for the stock, such that C_{10} was less than V_{10}, n would have been greater than 10, the first call date.

9. An investor can find the expected rate of return on the convertible bond, k_c, by solving for k_c in the following equation:

$$\begin{array}{c}\text{Price} \\ \text{paid for} \\ \text{bond}\end{array} = \$1,000 = \sum_{t=1}^{n} \frac{\$100}{(1+k_c)^t} + \frac{\begin{array}{c}\text{Expected market value} \\ \text{at time of conversion}\end{array}}{(1+k_c)^n}.$$

Since $n = 10$, the expected market value at Year 10 is $35(1.08)^{10}(20) = \$1,511$. We can substitute this value into the above equation and solve for k_c, the expected return on the convertible:

---

[11]Note, though, that the bond value line B_0M'' would fall later on if interest rates rose in the economy, or if the company's credit risk deteriorated and consequently its k_d rose.

$$\$1,000 = \sum_{t=1}^{10} \frac{\$100}{(1 + k_c)^t} + \frac{\$1,511}{(1 + k_c)^{10}}.$$

The solution value of k_c is 12.8 percent.

10. The return on a convertible is expected to come partly from interest income and partly from capital gains; in this case, the total return is 12.8 percent, with 10 percent representing interest income and 2.8 percent representing the expected capital gain. The interest component is relatively assured, while the capital gain component is more risky. On a new straight bond, all of the return is in the form of interest. Therefore, a convertible's expected yield is more risky than is that of a straight bond, so k_c should be larger than the cost of straight debt, k_d. Thus, it would seem that the expected rate of return on Silicon's convertibles, k_c, should lie between its cost of straight debt, k_d = 13%, and its cost of common stock, k_s = 16%.

Investment bankers use the type of model described here, plus a knowledge of the market, to set the terms on convertibles (the conversion ratio and the coupon interest rate) such that the security will just "clear the market" at its $1,000 offering price. In this example, the required conditions do not seem to hold—the calculated rate of return on the convertible is only 12.8 percent, which is less, rather than more, than the cost of straight debt. Therefore, it would appear that the terms on the bond must be made more attractive to investors. Silicon Valley Software would have to increase the coupon interest rate to a level above 10 percent, raise the conversion ratio above 20 (and thereby lower the conversion price from $50 to a level closer to the current $35 market price of the stock), or use a combination of these two such that the expected rate of return on the convertible ends up between 13 and 16 percent.

Use of Convertibles in Financing

Convertibles have two important advantages from the issuer's standpoint. (1) Convertibles, like bonds with warrants, offer a company the chance to sell debt with lower interest rates and less restrictive covenants in exchange for a chance to participate in the company's success if it does well. (2) Convertibles provide a way to sell common stock at prices higher than those currently prevailing. Many companies actually want to sell common stock, and not debt, but feel that the price of their stock is temporarily depressed. Management may know, for example, that earnings are depressed because of start-up costs associated with a new project, but they expect earnings to rise sharply during the next year or so, pulling the price of the stock up with them. Such management might think that if it sold stock now, it would be giving up more shares than necessary to raise a given amount of money. However, if it set the conversion price 20 to 30 percent above the present market price of the stock, then 20 to 30 percent fewer shares would be given up when the bonds were converted than would be required if stock were sold directly at the current time. Notice, however, that management is counting on the stock's price to rise above the conversion price to make the bonds attractive in conversion. If earnings do not rise and pull the stock price up, and hence conversion does not occur, then the company will be saddled with debt in the face of low earnings, which could be disastrous.

How can the company be sure that conversion will occur if the price of the stock rises above the conversion price? Typically, convertibles contain a call provision that enables the issuing firm to force bondholders to convert. Suppose the conversion price is $50, the conversion ratio is 20, the market price of the common stock has risen to $60, and the call price on the convertible bond is $1,050. If the company calls the bond, bondholders can either convert into common stock with a market value of 20($60) = $1,200 or allow the company to redeem the bond for $1,050. Naturally, bondholders prefer $1,200 to $1,050, so conversion occurs. The call provision therefore gives the company a way to force conversion, provided the market price of the stock is greater than the conversion price. Note, however, that most convertibles have a fairly long period of call protection—10 years is the general rule. Therefore, if the company wants to be able to force conversion fairly early, then it will have to set a short call protection period. This will, in turn, require that it set a higher coupon rate or a lower conversion price.

From the standpoint of the issuer, convertibles have three important disadvantages. (1) Although the use of a convertible security does give the issuer the opportunity to sell common stock at a price higher than the price at which it could be sold currently, if the common stock greatly increases in price, the issuing firm would probably find that it would have been better off if it had used straight debt in spite of its higher cost and then later sold common stock and refunded the debt. (2) If the company truly wants to raise equity capital, and if the price of the stock does not rise sufficiently after the bond is issued, then the company will be stuck with debt. This debt will, however, have a low interest rate. (3) Convertibles typically have a low coupon interest rate, and the advantage of this low-cost debt will be lost when conversion occurs.

REPORTING EARNINGS WHEN WARRANTS OR CONVERTIBLES ARE OUTSTANDING

If warrants or convertibles are outstanding, a firm could theoretically report earnings per share in one of three ways:

1. *Simple EPS*, where earnings available to common stockholders are divided by the average number of shares actually outstanding during the period.

2. *Primary EPS*, where earnings available are divided by the average number of shares that would have been outstanding if warrants and convertibles "likely to be converted in the near future" had actually been exercised or converted. Earnings are pro formed by "backing out" the interest on the convertibles. Accountants have a formula which basically compares the conversion or exercise price with the actual market value of the stock to determine the likelihood of conversion when deciding on the need to use this adjustment procedure.

3. *Fully diluted EPS*, which is similar to primary EPS except that *all* warrants and convertibles are assumed to be exercised or converted, regardless of the likelihood of exercise or conversion.

Simple EPS is virtually never reported by firms which have warrants or convertibles likely to be exercised or converted—the SEC requires that primary and fully diluted earnings be shown. For firms with large amounts of option securities outstanding, there can be a substantial difference between the primary and fully diluted EPS figures. The purpose of the provision is, of course, to give investors a more accurate picture of the firm's true profit position.

FUTURES

Recent years have been characterized by record capital markets volatility. To illustrate, in June 1982, AA bonds were yielding 15.3 percent, while the same bonds yielded only 8.9 percent in May 1986. Further, it is not unusual for long-term rates to move by over 100 basis points within a 2- or 3-month period; for example, AA rates fell from 10.4 percent in February 1986 to 8.9 percent in May 1986. At the same time, the level of stock prices has bounced around like a rubber ball. All this instability in the capital markets has made corporate financing much more difficult than it was in the 1950s, 1960s, and 1970s.

Although the evidence strongly indicates that managers can forecast their own firms' internal conditions better than outside investors, no one has been able to make consistent forecasts of interest rates and the general level of stock prices. If one believes that it is impossible to forecast future capital costs, then the major concern should be to minimize the adverse effects of changes in capital costs from today's "spot" costs. This can be done through transactions in the *futures markets*.[12]

Futures Markets and Contracts

Most financial and real asset transactions occur in what is known as the *spot*, or *cash*, *market*. Here, the asset is delivered immediately (or within a few days). *Futures*, or *futures contracts*, on the other hand, call for the purchase or sale of a financial or real asset at some future date, but at a price which is fixed today.

In 1986, futures contracts were available on more than 30 real and financial assets traded on 14 U.S. exchanges, the largest of which are the Chicago Board of Trade (CBT) and the Chicago Mercantile Exchange (CME). Futures contracts are divided into two classes, *commodity futures* and *financial futures*. Commodity futures, which cover various grains and oilseeds, livestock and meats, foods and fibers, metals, and wood, were first traded in the United States in the middle 1800s. Financial futures, which were first traded in 1975, include Treasury bills, Treasury notes and bonds, certificates of deposit, Eurodollar deposits, foreign currencies, and stock indexes.

To illustrate how futures contracts work, consider the CBT's contract on Treasury bonds. The basic contract is for $100,000 of a hypothetical 8 percent coupon,

---

[12]Our discussion of futures is necessarily limited in scope. For a more detailed description of futures and their use in financial management, see Robert W. Kolb, *Understanding Futures Markets* (Glenview, Ill.: Scott, Foresman, 1985).

Table 15-3
May 6, 1986, Futures Price

				Treasury Bonds (CBT)—$100,000; pts. 32nds of 100%		Yield		Open Interest (9)
(1)	Open (2)	High (3)	Low (4)	Settle (5)	Change (6)	Settle (7)	Change (8)	
June	100-20	101-11	100-07	100-16	−13	7.950	+.041	188,460
Sept	99-25	100-18	99-16	99-24	−11	8.025	+.034	42,622
Dec	99-00	99-24	98-24	98-30	−10	8.108	+.032	5,207

semiannual payment, Treasury bond with approximately 20 years to maturity. Table 15-3 shows an extract from the Treasury bond futures prices which appeared in the May 7, 1986, *Wall Street Journal.*

The first column gives the delivery month; the next three give the opening, high, and low prices on that contract for that day. The opening price for the June future, 100-20, means 100 and 20/32, or 100.625 percent of par. Column 5 gives the settlement price, which is typically the price at close of trading. Column 6 reports the change in settlement price from the preceding day—the June contract dropped by 13/32, or 0.4063 percent. Column 7 gives the yield on the 8 percent bonds at the settlement price, while Column 8 reports the change in the settlement yield from the previous trading day. Finally, Column 9 shows the "open interest," which is the number of contracts outstanding.

To illustrate, we focus on the Treasury bonds for December 1986 delivery. The settlement price on May 6 was 98-30, or 98 and 30/32 percent of the $100,000 contract value. Thus, the futures price closed at 98.9375 percent, or at 0.989375($100,000) = $98,937.50. The contract price declined by 10/32 of one percent of $100,000, or by $312.50, from the previous day. The settlement yield on the contract was 8.108 percent, and the yield increased by 0.032 percentage points from the previous day. Finally, there were 5,207 contracts outstanding on the December futures, representing a total value of about $520 million. Thus, on May 6, 1986, futures contracts for December 1986 delivery (7-month futures) of this hypothetical bond sold for $98,937.50 for 100 bonds with a par value of $100,000, which translates to a yield to maturity of about 8.1 percent.[13] This yield reflects investors' beliefs in May 1986 about the interest rate level which will prevail in December 1986. The spot yield on T-bonds on May 6 was about 7.9 percent, so the marginal participant in the futures market was predicting a 20 basis point increase in yields over the next 7 months.

---

[13]The yield is calculated by solving for k_d in the following equation:

$$\$989.375 = \sum_{t=1}^{40} \frac{\$40}{(1 + k_d/2)^t} + \frac{\$1,000}{(1 + k_d/2)^{40}}.$$

Recall that the hypothetical bond is assumed to be on a semiannual payment basis with an 8 percent coupon and a 20-year maturity.

Suppose now that three months later, on August 6, 1986, interest rates in the futures market had fallen from the May levels, say from 8.1 to 7.5 percent. Falling interest rates mean rising bond prices, so the December 1986 contract would now be worth about $105,138. Thus, the contract's value would have increased by $105,138 − $98,938 = $6,200.

When futures contracts are purchased, the purchaser does not have to put up the full amount of the purchase price; rather, the purchaser is required to post an initial *margin*, which for CBT Treasury bond contracts is $3,000 per $100,000 contract. However, investors are required to maintain a certain value in the margin account, called a *maintenance margin*. If the value of the contract declines, then the owner may be required to add additional funds to the margin account, and the more the contract value falls, the more money that must be added. The value of the contract is checked at the end of every working day, and margin account adjustments are made at that time. If an investor purchased a contract in May, and then sold it in August, he or she would have made a profit of $6,200 on a $3,000 investment, or a return of over 200 percent in only three months. It is clear, therefore, that futures contracts offer a considerable amount of leverage. Of course, if interest rates had risen, then the value of the contract would have declined, and the investor could easily have lost his or her $3,000, or more.

Commodity futures contracts are often settled by the actual delivery of the commodity—for example, a wheat farmer might sell in April a futures contract for 5,000 bushels of wheat for October delivery, and then deliver 5,000 bushels of wheat to satisfy the contract. The purchaser of the contract might be General Mills. The price would have been established in April, so the farmer would know how much he would get for his wheat, and General Mills would know its cost for flour. Financial futures, on the other hand, are virtually never settled by delivery of the securities involved. Rather, the transaction is completed by reversing the trade, which amounts to selling the contract back to the original seller.[14] The actual gains and losses on the contract are realized when the futures contract is closed.

Futures Versus Options

Futures contracts and options are similar to one another—so similar that people often confuse the two. Therefore, it is useful to compare the two instruments.

A *futures contract* is a definite agreement on the part of one party to buy something on a specific date and at a specific price, and the other party agrees to sell on the same terms. No matter how low or how high the price goes, the two parties must settle the contract at the agreed-upon price. An *option*, on the other hand, merely gives someone the right to buy (a call option) or sell (a put option), but the holder of the option does not have to complete the transaction.

---

[14]The buyers and sellers of financial futures contracts do not actually trade with one another, even though a contract cannot be bought without a seller, and vice versa. Each trader's contractual obligation is with the futures exchange. This feature helps to guarantee the fiscal integrity of the trade. Incidentally, commodities futures traded on the exchanges are settled in the same way as financial futures, but in the case of commodities much of the contracting is done off the exchange, between farmers and processors, and there actual deliveries occur.

Note also that options exist for individual stocks and for "bundles" of stocks such as those in the S&P or Value Line index, whereas futures are used for commodities, debt securities, and stock indexes. The two types of instruments can be used for the same purposes. One is not necessarily better or worse than another—they are simply different.

Hedging

Futures markets are used for both speculation and hedging. Speculation involves betting on future price movements, and futures are used because the inherent leverage in the contract enhances expected returns. Hedging, on the other hand, is done by a firm or individual engaged in a business where a price change could adversely affect profits. Of course, one party to a futures contract could be a speculator, the other a hedger. Thus, to the extent that they broaden the market and make hedging possible, speculators decrease risks in the economy. There are two basic types of hedges: (1) *long hedges*, in which futures contracts are bought in anticipation of (or to guard against) price increases, and (2) *short hedges*, where a firm or individual sells futures contracts to guard against price declines. Recall that rising interest rates lower bond prices and thus the value of bond futures contracts. Therefore, if a firm or individual needs to guard against an *increase* in interest rates, a futures contract that makes money if rates rise should be used. That means selling, or going short, on the futures contract. To illustrate, assume that Carson Foods plans to issue $10,000,000 of 10-year bonds in September 1986 to support a capital expenditure program. The interest rate would be 10 percent if the bonds were issued today, May 6, and at that rate, the project being financed has a positive NPV. However, Carson's financial manager fears that interest rates may rise over the next four months, and that, when the issue is actually sold, it may have a cost substantially above 10 percent, which would make the project a bad investment. Carson can protect itself against such a rise in rates by hedging in the futures market.

In this situation, Carson would be hurt by an increase in interest rates, and hence Carson would use a short hedge. It would choose a futures contract on the security most similar to the company's underlying security, long-term bonds. In this case, Carson would probably choose to hedge with Treasury bond futures. Since it has $10,000,000 in underlying securities, Carson would sell $10,000,000/$100,000 = 100 Treasury bond contracts for delivery in September. In doing so, Carson would have to put up 100($3,000) = $300,000 in margin money as well as pay brokerage commissions. We can see from Table 15-3 that each September contract has a value of 99 and 24/32 percent, so the total value of the 100 contracts is 0.9975($100,000)(100) = $9,975,000. Now suppose the interest rate on Carson's debt rises by 100 basis points, to 11 percent, over the next four months. Carson's own 10 percent coupon bonds would bring only about $920 per bond, because investors now require an 11 percent return. Thus, Carson would lose $80 per bond times 10,000 bonds, or $800,000, as a result of delaying the financing. However, the increase in interest rates has also brought about a change in the value of Carson's short position in the futures market. Since interest rates have increased, the futures contract value will fall, and if the interest rate on the futures contract also increased by a full percentage point, from 8.025 to 9.025 percent, the contract value would fall to $9,059,000. Carson would then close its position in the futures market by repurchasing for $9,059,000 the contracts which it sold short for $9,975,000, giving it a profit of $916,000, less commissions.

Thus, Carson has, if we ignore commissions and the opportunity cost of the margin money, offset the loss on the bond issue. In fact, Carson more than offset the loss, pocketing an additional $116,000 in our example. If futures contracts existed on Carson's own debt, then the firm could construct a *perfect hedge*, in which gains on the futures contract would exactly offset losses due to rising interest rates. In reality, it is virtually impossible to construct perfect hedges, because in most cases the underlying asset is not identical to the futures asset. Of course, if in our example interest rates had fallen, Carson would have lost on its futures position. However, this loss would have been offset by the fact that Carson could now sell its bonds at a lower yield.

Similarly, if Carson had been planning an equity offering, and if its stock tended to move fairly closely with one of the stock indexes on which futures are written, it could have hedged against falling stock prices by selling short the index future. Alternatively, if options on Carson Foods are traded in the option market, then options, rather than futures, could be used to hedge against falling stock prices. The futures and option markets permit flexibility in the timing of financial transactions, because the firm can be protected, at least partially, against changes that occur between the present and the time when a particular transaction will be completed. The cost of the protection is represented by commissions plus the opportunity cost of the margin money. Whether or not the protection is worth the cost is a matter of judgment, and it depends on management's risk aversion as well as the company's strength and ability to assume the risk of changing interest rates and stock prices. Clearly, many firms believe that hedging is worthwhile. Trammell Crow, a large Texas real estate developer, recently used T-bill futures to lock in interest costs on floating rate construction loans, while Dart & Kraft recently used Eurodollar futures to protect its marketable securities portfolio. Merrill Lynch, Salomon Brothers, and the other investment banking houses hedge in the futures and options markets to protect themselves when they are engaged in major underwritings. Similarly, commercial banks engage in hedging activities to protect their bond portfolios against interest rate increases. We will discuss the use of the futures market again when we examine inventory management.

SUMMARY

Both bonds with *warrants* and *convertibles* are forms of options used to finance business firms. The use of such securities is encouraged by an economic environment in which either recessions or booms can occur. The senior position of the fixed charge portion of those securities protects against recessions, while the option feature offers the opportunity for participation in rising stock markets.

The conversion of convertible securities does not provide additional funds to the company, but the exercise of warrants does bring in additional capital. In the past, larger and stronger firms tended to favor convertibles over bonds with warrants, so most warrants were issued by smaller, weaker concerns. However, AT&T's use of warrants in its $1.57 billion financing caused other large firms to reexamine their positions on warrants, and warrants have come into increasing use in recent years.

Partly because of investors' interest in warrants and convertibles, a new market in pure options was developed during the 1970s. Option contracts are created by investors, not by the firms whose securities are involved in option contracts. The corporations themselves do not raise capital from the sale of these options and, in fact, they have no direct involvement with this market. The *Black-Scholes Option Pricing Model (OPM)* can be used to estimate the value of a call option, and financial managers can use it when setting the terms on warrant and convertible issues. Also, as we explain in Appendix 15A, the stock of a firm can be viewed as a call option, and the OPM provides some insights into such traditional financial management issues as capital investment decisions.

Financial futures markets first appeared in the mid-1970s, although commodity futures have been traded since the 1850s. Futures permit firms to create hedge positions to protect themselves against the damage done by rising or falling interest rates. Futures markets are now used routinely by insurance companies and pension funds, and we expect that more and more nonfinancial firms will be using them in the future.

Questions and Problems

15-1 (Black-Scholes OPM) Cotner Software Corporation (CSC) options are actively traded on one of the regional exchanges. CSC's current stock price is $10, with a 0.16 instantaneous variance of returns. The current six-month risk-free rate is 12 percent.

    a. What is the value of CSC's six-month option with an exercise price of $10 according to the Black-Scholes model?

    b. What would be the effect on the option price if CSC redeployed its assets and thereby reduced its variance of returns to 0.09?

    (Do Parts c and d only if you are using the computerized diskette.)

    c. Assume that CSC returns to its initial asset structure; that is, its stock return variance is 0.16. Now assume that CSC's current stock price is $15. What effect does the stock price increase have on the option value?

    d. Return to base case (Part a) values. Now assume that the striking price is $15. What is the new option value?

15-2 (Convertible risk) Suppose a company simultaneously issues $50 million of convertible bonds with a coupon rate of 10 percent and $50 million of straight bonds with a coupon rate of 14 percent. Both bonds have the same maturity. Does the fact that the convertible issue has the lower coupon rate suggest that it is less risky than the straight bond? Explain.

15-3 (Warrants) Goode Industries, Inc., has warrants outstanding that permit the holders to purchase one share of stock per warrant at a price of $25.

    a. Calculate the floor value of Goode's warrants if the common sells at each of the following prices: (1) $20, (2) $25, (3) $30, (4) $100.

    b. At what approximate price do you think the warrants would actually sell under each condition indicated above? What premium is implied in your price? Your answer is a guess, but your prices and premiums should bear reasonable relationships to one another.

c. How would each of the following factors affect your estimates of the warrants' prices and premiums in Part b?

(1) The life of the warrant.

(2) Expected variability (σ_p) in the stock's price.

(3) The expected growth rate in the stock's EPS.

(4) The company announces a change in dividend policy: Whereas it formerly paid no dividends, henceforth it will pay out *all* earnings as dividends.

d. Assume Goode's stock now sells for $20 per share. The company wants to sell some 20-year, annual interest, $1,000 par value bonds. Each bond will have attached 50 warrants, each exercisable into one share of stock at an exercise price of $25. The firm's straight bonds yield 12 percent. Regardless of your answer to Part b above, assume that each warrant will have a market value of $3 when the stock sells at $20. What coupon interest rate, and dollar coupon, must the company set on the bonds-with-warrants if they are to clear the market? Round to the nearest dollar or percentage point.

15-4 (Convertible premiums) The Hocking Company was planning to finance an expansion in the summer of 1986. The principal executives of the company were agreed that an industrial company such as theirs should finance growth by means of common stock rather than by debt. However, they felt that the price of the company's common stock did not reflect its true worth, so they decided to sell a convertible security. They considered a convertible debenture but feared the burden of fixed interest charges if the common stock did not rise in price to make conversion attractive. They decided on an issue of convertible preferred stock, which would pay a dividend of $2.10 per share.

The common stock was selling for $42 a share at the time. Management projected earnings for 1986 at $3 a share and expected a future growth rate of 10 percent a year in 1987 and beyond. It was agreed by the investment bankers and the management that the common stock would sell at 14 times earnings, the current price/earnings ratio.

a. What conversion price should be set by the issuer? The conversion ratio will be 1.0; that is, each share of convertible preferred can be converted into one share of common. Therefore, the convertible's par value (and also the issue price) will be equal to the conversion price, which in turn will be determined as a percentage over the current market price of the common. Your answer will be a guess, but make it a reasonable one.

b. Should the preferred stock include a call provision? Why?

15-5 (Convertible bond analysis) In June 1976, U.S. Steel (now USX Corporation) sold $400 million of convertible bonds, the largest issue on record. The bonds had a 25-year maturity, a 5¾ percent coupon rate, and were sold at their $1,000 par value. The conversion price was set at $62.75 against a current price of $55 per share of common. The bonds were subordinated debentures, and they were given an A rating; straight nonconvertible debentures of the same quality yielded about 8¾ percent at the time.

a. Calculate the premium on the bonds, that is, the percentage excess of the conversion price over the current stock price.

b. What is U.S. Steel's annual interest savings on the convertible issue versus a straight debt issue?

c. Look up U.S. Steel's current stock price in the paper. On the basis of this price, do you think it likely that the bonds would have been converted? (Calculate the value of the stock one would receive by converting a bond.)

d. The bonds originally sold for $1,000. If interest rates on A-rated bonds had remained constant at 8¾ percent, what do you think would have happened to the price of the convertible bonds?

e. Now suppose the price of U.S. Steel's common stock had fallen from $55 on the day the bonds were issued to $20 at present. (At the time this problem was written, that is exactly what had happened.) Suppose also that the rate of interest had fallen from 8¾ to 5¾ percent. (This had not happened when the problem was being written—the interest rate on A-rated bonds was about 9 percent.) Under these conditions, what do you think would have happened to the price of the bonds?

f. Set up a graphic model to illustrate how investors valued the U.S. Steel convertibles in 1976. How well were these expectations realized?

15-6 (Warrant/convertible decisions) The Olsen Carpet Company has grown rapidly during the past 5 years. Recently its commercial bank urged the company to consider increasing permanent financing. Its bank loan under a line of credit has risen to $250,000, carrying an 8 percent interest rate. Olsen has been 30 to 60 days late in paying trade creditors.

Discussions with an investment banker have resulted in the decision to raise $500,000 at this time. Investment bankers have assured the firm that the following alternatives are feasible (flotation costs will be ignored):

- *Alternative 1*: Sell common stock at $8.

- *Alternative 2*: Sell convertible bonds at an 8 percent coupon, convertible into 100 shares of common stock for each $1,000 bond (that is, the conversion price is $10 per share).

- *Alternative 3*: Sell debentures at an 8 percent coupon, each $1,000 bond carrying 100 warrants to buy common stock at $10.

Jean Gilbert, the president, owns 80 percent of the common stock of Olsen and wishes to maintain control of the company. One hundred thousand shares are outstanding. The following are extracts of Olsen's latest financial statements:

Balance Sheet

		Current liabilities	$400,000
		Common stock, par $1	100,000
		Retained earnings	50,000
Total assets	$550,000	Total claims	$550,000

Income Statement

Sales	$1,100,000
All costs except interest	990,000
EBIT	$ 110,000
Interest	20,000
EBT	$ 90,000
Taxes (40%)	36,000
Net income	$ 54,000
Shares outstanding	100,000
Earnings per share	$0.54
Price/earnings ratio	15.83×
Market price of stock	$8.55

a. Show the new balance sheet under each alternative. For Alternatives 2 and 3, show the balance sheet after conversion of the bonds or exercise of the warrants. Assume that one-half of the funds raised will be used to pay off the bank loan and one-half to increase total assets.

b. Show Ms. Gilbert's control position under each alternative, assuming that she does not purchase additional shares.

c. What is the effect on earnings per share of each alternative, if it is assumed that profits before interest and taxes will be 20 percent of total assets?

d. What will be the debt ratio under each alternative?

e. Which of the three alternatives would you recommend to Gilbert, and why?

15-7 (Convertible bond model) Dynamics Incorporated needs to raise $25 million to construct production facilities for a new model diskette drive. The firm's straight non-convertible debentures currently yield 14 percent. Its stock sells for $30 per share; the last dividend was $2; and the expected growth rate is a constant 9 percent. Investment bankers have tentatively proposed that the firm raise the $25 million by issuing convertible debentures. These convertibles would have a $1,000 par value, carry a coupon rate of 10 percent, have a 20-year maturity, and be convertible into 20 shares of stock. The bonds would be noncallable for 5 years, after which they would be callable at a price of $1,075; this call price would decline by $5 per year in Year 6 and each year thereafter. Management has called convertibles in the past (and presumably it will call them again in the future), once they were eligible for call, when the bonds' conversion value was about 20 percent above the bonds' par value (not their call price).

a. Draw an accurate graph similar to Figure 15-2 representing the expectations set forth above. (Assume an annual coupon.)

b. What is the expected rate of return on the proposed convertible issue?

c. Do you think that these bonds could be successfully offered to the public at par? That is, does $1,000 seem to be an equilibrium price in view of the stated terms? If not, suggest the type of change that would have to be made to cause the bonds to trade at $1,000 in the secondary market, assuming no change in capital market conditions.

d. Suppose the projects outlined here work out on schedule for two years, but then the firm begins to experience extremely strong competition from Japanese firms. As a result, Dynamics' expected growth rate drops from 9 percent to zero. Assume that the dividend at the time of the drop is $2.38. The company's credit strength is not impaired, and its value of k_s is also unchanged. What would happen (1) to stock price and (2) to the convertible bond's price? Be as precise as you can.

Selected Additional References and Cases

The investment texts listed in Chapter 2 provide extended discussions of options, warrants, convertibles, and futures. The original Black-Scholes article tested the OPM to see how well predicted prices conformed to market values. For additional empirical tests, see

Galai, Dan, "Tests of Market Efficiency of the Chicago Board Options Exchange," *Journal of Business,* April 1977, 167-197.

Gultekin, N. Bulent, Richard J. Rogalski, and Seha M. Tinic, "Option Pricing Model Estimates: Some Empirical Results," *Financial Management,* Spring 1982, 58-69.

MacBeth, James D., and Larry J. Merville, "An Empirical Examination of the Black-Scholes Call Option Pricing Model," *Journal of Finance,* December 1979, 1173-1186.

Quite a bit of work has also been done on warrant pricing. Two of the more prominent articles are

Galai, Dan, and Mier I. Schneller, "The Pricing of Warrants and the Value of the Firm," *Journal of Finance*, December 1978, 1333-1342.

Schwartz, Eduardo S., "The Valuation of Warrants: Implementing a New Approach," *Journal of Financial Economics*, January 1977, 79-93.

For more insights into convertible pricing and use, see

Alexander, Gordon J., and Roger D. Stover, "Pricing in the New Issue Convertible Debt Market," *Financial Management*, Fall 1977, 35-39.

Alexander, Gordon J., Roger D. Stover, and D. B. Kuhnau, "Market Timing Strategies in Convertible Debt Financing," *Journal of Finance*, March 1979, 143-155.

Brennan, Michael, "The Case for Convertibles," *Issues in Corporate Finance* (New York: Stern Stewart Putnam & Macklis, 1983), 102-111.

Ingersoll, Jonathan E., "A Contingent Claims Valuation of Convertible Securities," *Journal of Financial Economics*, May 1977, 289-322.

————, "An Examination of Corporate Call Policies on Convertible Securities," *Journal of Finance*, May 1977, 463-478.

For additional insights into the use of financial futures for hedging, see

Bacon, Peter W., and Richard Williams, "Interest Rate Futures Trading: A New Tool for the Financial Manager," *Financial Management*, Spring 1976, 32-38.

McCabe, George M., and Charles T. Franckle, "The Effectiveness of Rolling the Hedge Forward in the Treasury Bill Futures Market," *Financial Management*, Summer 1983, 21-29.

The following cases cover issues presented in this chapter:

Case 28, "Biolog Development Corporation," in the Crum-Brigham casebook, which illustrates convertible bond valuation.

"FLX, Incorporated," in the Harrington casebook, which focuses on the retirement of convertible subordinated debentures which are selling below par.

15A
OPTION PRICING: IMPLICATIONS FOR CORPORATE FINANCIAL POLICY

The equity of a levered firm can be thought of as a call option. When a firm issues debt, this is in a sense equivalent to the shareholders selling the assets of the firm to the debtholders, who pay for the assets with cash plus an implied call option with a striking price equal to the principal value plus interest on the debt. If the company is successful, the stockholders will "buy the company back" by exercising their call and paying the principal and interest on the debt. Otherwise, they will default on the loan, which amounts to not exercising their call and thus giving the company to the creditors.

As an illustration, suppose the One-Shot Corporation is just being formed to make a 1-year investment in producing and marketing presidential campaign buttons. The firm requires an investment of $10,000, of which $7,500 will be obtained by selling debt with a 10 percent interest rate, and the other $2,500 will be raised by selling common stock. All cash distributions to debtholders and stockholders are to be made at the end of one year. After this year is over, the value of the firm will depend primarily on which candidates make it through the primary elections, plus perhaps some value in the collector's market. The estimated probability distribution of the firm's value is given next:

Probability	Value
0.7	$20,000
0.2	5,000
0.1	0

Thus, the expected value of the firm at the end of the year is $0.7(\$20,000) + 0.2(\$5,000) + 0.1(\$0) = \$15,000$. The expected value, if it were realized, would provide the shareholders with $6,750 before taxes on their $2,500 investment:

Expected value		$15,000
Less:		
Debt principal	$7,500	
Debt interest	750	8,250
		$ 6,750

Note that the expected value is not achievable: The value of the firm will be $0 or $5,000 or $20,000. If the value is either $0 or $5,000, the shareholders will not exercise their call option; instead, they will default. The debtholders would then be entitled to the value of the firm, and the equity holders would receive nothing. However, if the firm's value turns out to be $20,000, the shareholders will exercise the call option by paying off the $8,250 principal and interest, and then pocket the remaining $11,750 before taxes. Thus, equity ownership can be viewed as a call option. In this illustration, an equity investment of $2,500 (the current price of the call) entitles the shareholders to purchase the assets of the firm for $8,250 (the exercise price). This insight has been applied to several of the traditional issues of corporate finance.[1] We look at one issue here, investment decisions, and we will examine the implications of option analysis for mergers in Chapter 22.

Suppose a levered firm has a large portfolio of Treasury bills. Management could sell the bills (which are riskless) and use the proceeds to purchase a risky asset that would increase the firm's earnings variance, yet have no effect on the firm's systematic risk. Since the equity can be viewed as a call option, the increased variance would increase the market value of the equity without increasing its market risk. The risk of bankruptcy would increase, but shareholders would have increased their chances of greater gains while their losses would still be limited to the amount of their investment.

However, any gains to shareholders come at the expense of the debtholders. To illustrate, suppose the initial value of the firm's assets is $4 million, and it has $2 million of face (book) value of 2-year debt outstanding. (Interest, which is payable at maturity, is included in the face value of the debt, so the debt is a discount issue.) Further, assume that the variance, σ^2, of the rate of return on the firm's assets is 0.01, and that

---

[1] For example, see Dan Galai and Ronald Masulis, "The Option Pricing Model and the Risk Factor of Stock," *The Journal of Financial Economics*, January/March 1976, 53-82. Galai and Masulis combine the CAPM with the OPM. Thus, the assumptions of both models underlie their analysis.

the risk-free rate is 10 percent. If we view the stock as a call option on the firm's assets, then we would have:

V = current call option value, or current market value of the equity.
P = current value of the firm, or $4 million.
X = striking price, or face value of the $2 million of debt.

Then, using Equations 15-1 through 15-3, the market value of the firm's equity is found to be $2,362,538:

$$d_1 = \frac{\ln(\$4,000,000/\$2,000,000) + [0.10 + (0.01/2)](2)}{0.10 \sqrt{2}}$$

$$= \frac{\ln 2 + 0.2100}{0.1414} = 6.3872.$$

$$N(d_1) = 1.0.$$

$$d_2 = d_1 - \sigma\sqrt{t} = 6.3872 - 0.1414 = 6.2458.$$

$$N(d_2) = 1.0.$$

$$V = \$4,000,000[N(d_1)] - \$2,000,000e^{-(0.10)(2)}[N(d_2)]$$

$$= \$4,000,000(1) - \$1,637,462(1)$$

$$= \$2,362,538.$$

Given that the total value of the firm is $4,000,000, and that the market value of the equity using the OPM is $2,362,538, then the implied market value (or present value) of the $2,000,000 face value of debt must be $1,637,462.

Now suppose the firm uses some of its liquid assets to buy risky assets, increasing the variance of the firm's rate of return from 0.01 to 0.10. Thus, under the new situation, $\sigma^2 = 0.10$, and $\sigma = 0.3162$. Now we can recalculate the equity and debt values, assuming that the total value of the firm remains unchanged at $4 million:

$$d_1 = \frac{\ln 2 + [0.10 + (0.10/2)](2)}{0.3162 \sqrt{2}}$$

$$= \frac{0.6931 + 0.3000}{0.4472} = 2.2207.$$

$$N(d_1) = 0.9868.$$

$$d_2 = 2.2207 - 0.4472 = 1.7735.$$

$$N(d_2) = 0.9619.$$

$$V = \$4,000,000(0.9868) - \$1,637,462(0.9619)$$

$$= \$2,372,125.$$

The implied market value of the debt is now $4,000,000 - $2,372,125 = $1,627,875. Thus, under the assumptions of the OPM and CAPM (both of which must be invoked), and assuming a constant firm value, the equity holders have gained $2,372,125 - $2,362,538 = $9,587 at the expense of the debtholders. This illustration highlights the importance of restrictive covenants which debtholders can use to protect themselves against possible shareholder actions which would reduce the value of debt.

Options are important in the investments area, so students of finance need to have a knowledge of how they are used and priced in the market. The role of option theory in financial management is less clear. As we have seen, it is possible to use option theory to gain insights into the effects of asset investments on the value of the firm's debt and equity. However, these insights are really rather obvious, and one can see the general effects of asset risk changes more easily just by thinking about them than by working through the OPM. Still, it may be that the OPM approach can in the future lead to a more precise quantification of certain effects, which would be useful in structuring contracts and in other types of financial policy decisions. Those who advocate the use of the OPM in corporate finance would take that position. Others would argue that these applications may be all right in theory, but that they do not work in practice because, to obtain precise results, the model requires (1) all the assumptions of both the Black-Scholes OPM and the CAPM, plus (2) an estimate of the expected future returns on the firm's assets as seen by an average investor, and this combined set of assumptions and data requirements is just too restrictive for use in practical applications.

We are not ready to make a judgment on all this. We have seen some interesting practical attempts to apply the OPM to corporate finance, but it is not at all clear how things will work out. In any event, students of finance need to be aware of what is happening in the options area.

 **V**

WORKING CAPITAL POLICY AND MANAGEMENT

16

WORKING CAPITAL POLICY AND FINANCING

Working capital policy and management involves decisions relating to current assets, including decisions about financing them. Since about half of the typical firm's capital is invested in current assets, working capital policy is important to the firm and its shareholders. In fact, as we pointed out in Chapter 1, about 60 percent of a financial manager's time is devoted to short-term decision making, and many finance students' first assignment on the job will involve working capital management. For all these reasons, working capital is a vitally important topic. Chapter 16 provides an overview of working capital policy and financing, while Chapters 17, 18, and 19 focus on inventories, cash, and accounts receivable.

Most of the material in Chapter 16, and also much of that in Chapters 17, 18, and 19, is also covered in introductory finance texts. However, due to time pressures, working capital management is generally hurried through in most introductory courses. We concluded that the best way of dealing with this situation was to repeat most of the introductory level material before going on to more advanced working capital topics. If you covered some of the material in Chapters 16–19 in your introductory course, read it here as a review. In any event, the concepts and techniques are quite important, so be sure you understand them before going on.

WORKING CAPITAL TERMINOLOGY

It is useful to begin by reviewing some basic definitions and concepts:

1. *Working capital*, sometimes called *gross working capital*, simply refers to current assets.

2. *Net working capital* is defined as current assets minus current liabilities.

3. One key working capital ratio is the *current ratio*, which is computed by dividing current assets by current liabilities. This ratio measures a firm's liquidity, or its ability to meet current obligations.

Table 16-1
Foxcraft Printing Company:
Balance Sheets as of December 31, 1986, and June 30, 1987
(Thousands of Dollars)

	12/31/86	6/30/87		12/31/86	6/30/87
Cash	$ 20	$ 20	Accounts payable	$ 30	$ 50
Accounts receivable	80	20	Accrued wages	15	10
Inventories	100	200	Accrued taxes	15	10
			Notes payable	50	80
			Current portion of long-term debt	40	40
Current assets	$200	$240	Current liabilities	$150	$190
Fixed assets	500	500	Long-term debt	150	140
			Stockholders equity	400	410
Total assets	$700	$740	Total claims	$700	$740

---

4. The *quick ratio*, or *acid test*, which also measures liquidity, is current assets less inventories, divided by current liabilities. The quick ratio removes inventories from current assets because they are the least liquid of current assets. It is thus an "acid test" of a company's ability to meet its current obligations.

5. *Working capital policy* refers to basic policy decisions regarding (1) target levels for each category of current assets and (2) how current assets will be financed.

6. *Working capital management* involves the administration, within the policy guidelines, of current assets and current liabilities.

We must be careful to distinguish between (1) those current liabilities which are specifically used to finance current assets and (2) those which represent either current maturities of long-term debt or financing associated with a construction program which will, after the project is completed, be funded with the proceeds of a long-term security issue.

Table 16-1 contains the December 31, 1986, and projected June 30, 1987, balance sheets of Foxcraft Printing Company, a manufacturer of greeting cards. Note that, according to the definitions given, Foxcraft's December 31 working capital is $200,000, and its net working capital is $200,000 − $150,000 = $50,000. Also, Foxcraft's year-end current ratio is 1.33, and its quick ratio is 0.67. However, the total current liabilities of $150,000 includes the current portion of long-term debt, which is $40,000. This account is unaffected by changes in working capital policy, since it is a function of past long-term financing decisions. Thus, even though we define long-term debt coming due in the next accounting period as a current liability, it is not a working capital decision variable. Similarly, if Foxcraft were building a new factory and financing this construction with short-term loans which were to be converted to a mortgage bond when the building was completed, the construction loans would be segregated out with regard to working capital management.

THE REQUIREMENT FOR EXTERNAL WORKING CAPITAL FINANCING

The manufacture of greeting cards is a seasonal business. In June of each year, Foxcraft begins producing Christmas cards for sale in the July-November period, and by December 31, it has sold most of its Christmas and New Year cards, so its inventories are relatively low. However, most of its buyers purchase on credit, so the year-end receivables are at a seasonal high. Now look at Foxcraft's projected balance sheet for June 30, 1987. Here we see that Foxcraft's June inventories will be relatively high ($200,000 versus $100,000 the previous December), as will accounts payable ($50,000 versus $30,000), but receivables are projected to be relatively low ($20,000 versus $80,000).

Now consider what happens to Foxcraft's current assets and current liabilities over the period from December 1986 to June 1987. Current assets increase from $200,000 to $240,000, so the firm must raise $40,000—increases on the left side of the balance sheet must be financed by increases on the right-hand side. However, at the same time, the higher volume of both purchases and labor expenditures associated with increased production to build inventories will cause payables and accruals to increase *spontaneously*, on net, by $10,000: from $30,000 + $15,000 + $15,000 = $60,000 to $50,000 + $10,000 + $10,000 = $70,000. This leaves a $30,000 projected working capital financing requirement, which we assume will be obtained from the bank as a short-term loan. Therefore, on June 30, 1987, we show notes payable of $80,000, up from $50,000 on December 31, 1986.

These fluctuations for Foxcraft resulted from seasonal factors. Similar fluctuations in working capital requirements, and hence in financing needs, can occur over business cycles—typically, financing needs contract during recessions and expand during booms. In the next two sections, we examine (1) the working capital cash flow cycle and (2) alternative policies for establishing the level of current assets and the sources of funds to finance these assets.

THE WORKING CAPITAL CASH FLOW CYCLE

The concept of the *cash flow cycle* is important in working capital management. This cycle can be described for a typical manufacturing firm as follows. (1) The firm orders and then receives the raw materials it needs to produce the goods it expects to sell. Since firms usually purchase their raw materials on credit, this transaction creates an account payable. (2) Labor is used to convert the raw materials into finished goods. To the extent that wages are not fully paid at the time the work is done, accrued wages build up. (3) The finished goods are sold, usually on credit, which creates receivables. No cash has been received yet. (4) At some point during the cycle, accounts payable and accruals must be paid, usually before the receivables have been collected. At that point, a net cash drain occurs, and financing is required. (5) The working capital cash flow cycle is completed when the firm's receivables have been collected. At that point, the firm is ready to repeat the cycle and/or pay off the loans that were used to finance it.

Figure 16-1
The Cash Conversion Cycle

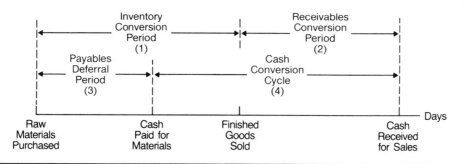

Verlyn Richards and Eugene Laughlin developed a useful approach to analyzing the working capital cash flow cycle.[1] Their approach centers on the conversion of operating events to cash flows, and it is thus called the *cash conversion cycle model*. Here are some terms used in the model:

1. *Inventory conversion period*, which is the average length of time required to convert raw materials into finished goods, and then to sell these goods. It might take, on average, 50 days from receipt of raw materials to manufacture and sale of the finished product.

2. *Receivables conversion period*, which is the average length of time required to convert the firm's receivables into cash, that is, to collect cash following a sale. That might take another 40 days.

3. *Payables deferral period*, which is the length of time between the purchase of raw materials and the cash payment for them. That would be 30 days if the firm buys on 30-day terms and pays on time.

4. *Cash conversion cycle*, which is the length of time between actual cash expenditures on productive resources (raw materials and labor) and actual cash receipts from the sale of products, that is, from the day labor and/or suppliers are paid to the day receivables are collected.

The concept is diagrammed in Figure 16-1. Each component is given a number, and the cash conversion cycle can be expressed by this equation:

$$\begin{matrix} \text{Inventory} \\ \text{conversion} \\ \text{period} \\ (1) \end{matrix} + \begin{matrix} \text{Receivables} \\ \text{conversion} \\ \text{period} \\ (2) \end{matrix} - \begin{matrix} \text{Payables} \\ \text{deferral} \\ \text{period} \\ (3) \end{matrix} = \begin{matrix} \text{Cash} \\ \text{conversion.} \\ \text{cycle} \\ (4) \end{matrix}$$

---

[1]See Verlyn D. Richards and Eugene J. Laughlin, "A Cash Conversion Cycle Approach to Liquidity Analysis," *Financial Management*, Spring 1980, 32-38. A similar approach was set forth earlier by Lawrence J. Gitman, "Estimated Corporate Liquidity Requirements: A Simplified Approach," *The Financial Review*, 1974, 79-88.

For our illustrative firm, it takes an average of 50 days to convert raw materials to inventory and to sell the goods, and 40 days to collect on receivables. However, 30 days normally lapse between receipt of goods and payment of the associated account payable, so the cash conversion cycle is 60 days:

$$50 \text{ days} + 40 \text{ days} - 30 \text{ days} = 60 \text{ days}.$$

Given these data, the firm knows when it receives an order that it will have to finance the costs of processing the order for a 60-day period. The firm's goal should be to shorten the cash conversion cycle as much as possible without hurting operations. This would improve profits, because the longer the cash conversion cycle, the greater the need for external financing, and such financing has a cost.

The cash conversion cycle can be shortened (1) by reducing the inventory conversion period, that is, by processing and selling goods more quickly, (2) by reducing the receivables conversion period, that is, by speeding up collections, or (3) by lengthening the payables deferral period, that is, by slowing down its own payments. To the extent that these actions can be taken *without increasing costs or depressing sales*, they should be carried out. You should keep the cash conversion cycle in mind as we go through both the remainder of this chapter and the other working capital chapters.

WORKING CAPITAL INVESTMENT AND FINANCING POLICIES

We should mention at the outset that working capital decisions are conceptually similar to long-term decisions such as capital structure and capital budgeting decisions in that they are made within a risk/return trade-off framework. However, finance theorists have not been totally successful in applying the goal of shareholder wealth maximization to working capital decisions in the sense of showing how a specific working capital decision affects stock values. Thus, there is no strong theoretical foundation which provides direction to financial managers.

Working capital policy involves two basic questions: (1) What is the appropriate level for current assets, both in total and by specific accounts? (2) How should current assets be financed?

Alternative Current Asset Investment Policies

Figure 16-2 shows three alternative policies regarding the total amount of current assets carried. Essentially, these policies differ in that different amounts of working capital are carried to support a given level of sales. The line with the steepest slope represents a "liberal" policy, where relatively large amounts of cash, marketable securities, and inventories are carried, and sales are stimulated by the use of a credit policy that provides liberal financing to customers and a corresponding high level of receivables. Conversely, with the "tight" policy, the holdings of cash, securities, inventories, and receivables are minimized. The moderate policy is between the two extremes.

Figure 16-2
Alternative Current Asset Investment Policies (Millions of Dollars)

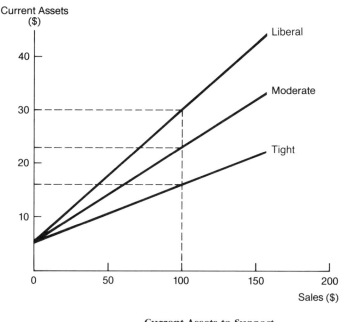

Policy	Current Assets to Support Sales of $100
Liberal	$30
Moderate	23
Tight	16

Note: The sales/current assets relationship is shown here as being linear. This is often not the case.

Under conditions of certainty—when sales, costs, lead times, payment periods, and so on, are known for sure—all firms would hold only minimal levels of current assets. Any larger amounts would increase the need for external funding without a corresponding increase in profits, while any smaller holdings would involve late payments to labor and suppliers, lost sales and production inefficiencies because of inventory shortages, and lost sales due to an overly restrictive credit policy.

However, the picture changes when uncertainty is introduced. Here the firm requires some minimum amount of cash and inventories based on expected payments, expected sales, expected order lead times, and so on, plus additional amounts, or *safety stocks*, which enable it to deal with ex post departures from the expected values. Similarly, accounts receivable levels are determined by credit terms, and the tougher the credit terms, the lower the receivables for any given level of sales. With a tight working capital policy, the firm would hold minimal levels of safety stocks for cash and inventories, and it would have a tight credit policy even though this meant running the risk of a decline in sales. A tight working capital policy often provides the highest expected return on investment, but it entails the greatest risk, while the converse is true under a liberal policy. The moderate policy falls in between the two extremes in terms of expected risk and return.

Corporate policy with regard to the level of current assets is never set all by itself—it is always established in conjunction with the firm's working capital financing policy, which we consider next.

Alternative Financing Policies

Most businesses experience seasonal and/or cyclical fluctuations. For example, construction firms have peaks in the spring and summer, retailers peak around Christmas, and the manufacturers who supply both construction companies and retailers follow similar patterns. Similarly, virtually all businesses must build up working capital when the economy is strong, but they then sell off inventories and have net reductions of receivables when the economy slacks off. Still, it is apparent that current assets rarely drop to zero, and this realization has led to the development of the idea of *permanent current assets.* Applying this idea to Foxcraft, Table 16-1 suggests that, at this stage in its life, Foxcraft's total assets fluctuate between $700,000 and $740,000. Thus, Foxcraft has $700,000 in permanent assets, composed of $500,000 of fixed assets and $200,000 in permanent current assets, plus *seasonal,* or *temporary, current assets* which fluctuate from zero to a maximum of $40,000. The manner in which the permanent and temporary current assets are financed defines the firm's *working capital financing policy.*

Maturity Matching

One policy is to match asset and liability maturities as shown in Panel A of Figure 16-3. This strategy minimizes the risk that the firm will be unable to pay off its maturing obligations. To illustrate, suppose Foxcraft borrows on a 1-year basis and uses the funds obtained to build and equip a plant. Cash flows from the plant (profits plus depreciation) would almost never be sufficient to pay off the loan at the end of only one year, so the loan must be renewed. If for some reason the lender refuses to renew the loan, then Foxcraft would have problems. Had the plant been financed with long-term debt, however, the required loan payments would have been better matched with cash flows from profits and depreciation, and the problem of renewal would not have arisen.

At the limit, a firm could attempt to match exactly the maturity structure of its assets and liabilities. Inventory expected to be sold in 30 days could be financed with a 30-day bank loan; a machine expected to last for 5 years could be financed by a 5-year loan; a 20-year building could be financed by a 20-year mortgage bond; and so forth. Actually, of course, uncertainty about the lives of assets prevents this exact maturity matching. For example, Foxcraft might finance inventories with a 30-day loan, expecting to sell the inventories and to use the cash generated to retire the loan. But if sales were slow, the cash would be not be forthcoming, and the use of short-term credit could end up causing a problem. Still, if Foxcraft makes

Figure 16-3
Alternative Current Asset Financing Policies

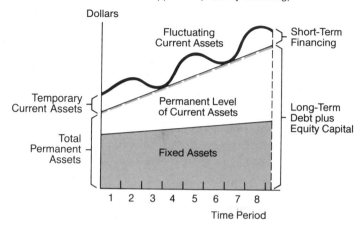

A. Moderate Approach (Maturity Matching)

Dollars

Fluctuating Current Assets

Short-Term Financing

Temporary Current Assets

Permanent Level of Current Assets

Long-Term Debt plus Equity Capital

Total Permanent Assets

Fixed Assets

1 2 3 4 5 6 7 8

Time Period

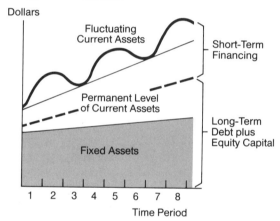

B. Aggressive Approach

Dollars

Fluctuating Current Assets

Short-Term Financing

Permanent Level of Current Assets

Long-Term Debt plus Equity Capital

Fixed Assets

1 2 3 4 5 6 7 8

Time Period

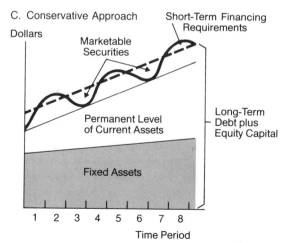

C. Conservative Approach

Dollars

Marketable Securities

Short-Term Financing Requirements

Permanent Level of Current Assets

Long-Term Debt plus Equity Capital

Fixed Assets

1 2 3 4 5 6 7 8

Time Period

an attempt to match asset and liability maturities, we would define this as a moderate working capital financing policy.

Aggressive Approach

Panel B of Figure 16-3 illustrates the situation for an aggressive firm which finances all of its fixed assets with long-term capital but part of its permanent current assets with short-term credit. A look back at Table 16-1 will show that Foxcraft actually follows this strategy. Assuming that the $40,000 current portion of long-term debt will be refinanced with new long-term debt, Foxcraft has $500,000 in fixed assets and $590,000 of long-term capital, leaving only $90,000 of long-term capital to finance $200,000 in permanent current assets. Additionally, Foxcraft has a minimum of $60,000 of "costless" short-term credit consisting of payables and accruals. Thus, Foxcraft uses $50,000 of short-term notes payable to help finance its permanent level of current assets.

Returning to Figure 16-3, the dashed line in Panel B could have been drawn *below* the line designating fixed assets, indicating that all of the current assets and part of the fixed assets were financed with short-term credit; this would be a highly aggressive, extremely nonconservative position, and the firm would be very much subject to dangers from rising interest rates as well as to loan renewal problems. However, short-term debt is often cheaper than long-term debt, and some firms are willing to sacrifice safety for the chance of higher profits.

Conservative Approach

As shown in Panel C of Figure 16-3, the dashed line could also be drawn *above* the line designating permanent current assets, indicating that permanent capital is being used to finance all permanent asset requirements and also to meet some or all of the seasonal demands. In the situation depicted in our graph, the firm uses a small amount of short-term credit to meet its peak requirements, but it also meets a part of its seasonal needs by "storing liquidity" in the form of marketable securities during the off-season. The humps above the dashed line represent short-term financing; the troughs below the dashed line represent short-term security holdings. Panel C represents a very safe, conservative working capital financing policy.

Working Capital Policy in Practice

We conclude our study of working capital policy by examining the results of a survey conducted by Keith Smith and Shirley Sell.[2] Smith and Sell surveyed a sample of the Fortune 1,000 companies to gain insights into working capital policy and management in practice. They found that 30 percent of the respondents had a formal, written working capital policy, and another 60 percent reported that they had an informal policy that is well known to the firm's executives. Also, the larger the firm, the higher is the probability of finding a formal policy.

---

[2]See Keith V. Smith and Shirley B. Sell, "Working Capital Management in Practice," in *Readings on the Management of Working Capital*, Keith V. Smith, ed. (St. Paul, Minn.: West, 1980).

In almost half of the responding firms, the vice president of finance has the primary responsibility for establishing the firm's overall working capital policy. The positions next most frequently mentioned were the president and the treasurer. Also, some firms indicated that a management committee had been established to set working capital policy, in which case the committee invariably included one or more of the officers previously mentioned. About half the firms indicated that working capital policy is reviewed on a specific periodic basis, the most frequent period being quarterly, while the other half indicated that working capital policy is reviewed whenever necessary.

ADVANTAGES AND DISADVANTAGES OF SHORT-TERM CREDIT

The three possible financing policies described previously were distinguished by the relative amounts of short-term debt used under each policy. The aggressive policy called for the greatest use of short-term debt, while the conservative policy called for the least. Maturity matching fell in between. Although using short-term credit is generally riskier than using long-term credit, short-term credit does have some significant advantages. The pros and cons of short-term financing are considered in this section.

Speed

A short-term loan can be obtained much faster than long-term credit. Lenders will insist on a more thorough financial examination before extending long-term credit, and the loan agreement will have to be spelled out in considerable detail because a lot can happen during the life of a 10- to 20-year loan. Therefore, if funds are needed in a hurry, the firm should look to the short-term markets.

Flexibility

If its needs for funds are seasonal or cyclical, a firm may not want to commit itself to long-term debt for three reasons: (1) Flotation costs are generally high when raising long-term debt but trivial for short-term credit. (2) While long-term debt can be repaid early, provided the loan agreement includes a prepayment provision, prepayment penalties can be expensive. Accordingly, if a firm thinks its need for funds may diminish in the near future, it should choose short-term debt for the flexibility it provides. (3) Long-term loan agreements always contain provisions, or covenants, which constrain the firm's future actions. Short-term credit agreements are generally much less onerous in this regard.

Cost of Long-Term Versus Short-Term Debt

The yield curve is normally upward sloping, indicating that generally interest rates are lower on short-term than on long-term debt. Thus, under normal conditions, interest expense at the time the funds are obtained will be lower if the firm borrows on a short-term rather than a long-term basis.

Risk of Long-Term Versus Short-Term Debt

Even though short-term debt is often less expensive than long-term debt, short-term credit subjects the firm to more risk than does long-term financing. This occurs for two reasons: (1) If a firm borrows on a long-term basis, its interest costs will be relatively stable over time, but if it uses short-term credit, its interest expense will fluctuate widely, at times going quite high. For example, the short-term rate banks charge large corporations more than tripled from the late 1970s to the early 1980s, rising from 6.25 to 21 percent. Many firms that had borrowed heavily on a short-term basis simply could not meet their rising interest costs, and as a result bankruptcies hit record levels in the early 1980s. (2) If a firm borrows heavily on a short-term basis, it may find itself unable to repay this debt, and it may be in such a weak financial position that the lender will not extend the loan; this too could force the firm into bankruptcy. Braniff Airlines, which failed during the credit crunch of 1982, is an example.

Another good example of the riskiness of short-term debt is provided by Transamerica Corporation, a major financial services company. Transamerica's chairman, Mr. Beckett, described how his company was moving to reduce its dependency on short-term loans whose costs vary with short-term interest rates. According to Mr. Beckett, Transamerica had reduced its variable-rate (short-term) loans by about $450 million over the past two years. "We aren't going to go through the enormous increase in debt expense again that had such a serious impact (on earnings)," he said. The company's earnings fell sharply because money rates rose to record highs. "We were almost entirely in variable-rate debt," he said, but currently "about 65 percent is fixed rate and 35 percent variable. We've come a long way, and we'll keep plugging away at it." Transamerica's earnings were badly depressed by the increase in short-term rates, but other companies were even less fortunate—they simply could not pay the rising interest charges, and this forced them into bankruptcy.

SOURCES OF SHORT-TERM FINANCING

Statements about the flexibility, cost, and riskiness of short-term versus long-term debt depend, to a large extent, on the type of short-term credit that is actually used. There are numerous sources of short-term funds, and in the following sections we describe four major types: (1) accruals, (2) accounts payable (trade credit), (3) bank loans, and (4) commercial paper.

ACCRUALS

Firms generally pay employees on a weekly, biweekly, or monthly basis, so the balance sheet will typically show some accrued wages. Similarly, the firm's own estimated income taxes, the social security and income taxes withheld from employee payrolls, and the sales taxes the firm collects are generally paid on a weekly, monthly, or quarterly basis, so the balance sheet will typically show some accrued taxes along with accrued wages.

Accruals increase automatically as a firm's operations expand. Further, this type of debt is "free" in the sense that no explicit interest is paid on funds raised through accruals. However, a firm cannot ordinarily control its accruals: Payrolls and the timing of wage payments are set by economic forces and industry custom, while tax payment dates are established by law. Thus, firms use all the accruals they can, but they have little control over the levels of these accounts.

ACCOUNTS PAYABLE, OR TRADE CREDIT

Firms generally make purchases from other firms on credit, recording the debt as an *account payable*. Accounts payable, or *trade credit*, is the largest single category of short-term debt, representing about 40 percent of the current liabilities of the average nonfinancial corporation. The percentage is somewhat larger for smaller firms: Because small companies often do not qualify for financing from other sources, they rely especially heavily on trade credit.[3]

Trade credit is a spontaneous source of financing in the sense that it arises from ordinary business transactions. For example, suppose a firm makes average purchases of $2,000 a day on terms of net 30, meaning that it must pay for goods 30 days after the invoice date. On average, it will owe 30 times $2,000, or $60,000, to its suppliers. If its sales, and consequently its purchases, were to double, then its accounts payable would also double, to $120,000. Simply by growing, the firm would have spontaneously generated an additional $60,000 of financing. Similarly, if the terms under which it bought were extended from 30 to 40 days, its accounts payable would expand from $60,000 to $80,000. Thus, lengthening the credit period, as well as expanding sales and purchases, generates additional financing.

The Cost of Trade Credit

Firms that sell on credit have a *credit policy* that includes certain *terms of credit*. For example, Microchip Electronics sells on terms of 2/10, net 30, meaning that a 2 percent discount is given if payment is made within 10 days of the invoice date, with the full invoice amount being due and payable within 30 days if the discount is not taken.

Suppose Personal Computer Company (PCC) buys an average of $12 million of electronic components from Microchip each year, less a 2 percent discount, for net purchases of $11,760,000/360 = $32,666.67 per day. For simplicity, suppose Microchip is PCC's only supplier. If PCC takes the discount, paying at the end of

---

[3]In a credit sale, the seller records the transaction as a receivable; the buyer, as a payable. We will examine accounts receivable as an asset investment in Chapter 19. Our focus in this chapter is on accounts payable, a liability item. We might also note that if a firm's accounts payable exceed its receivables, it is said to be *receiving net trade credit*, whereas if its receivables exceed its payables, it is *extending net trade credit*. Smaller firms frequently receive net credit; larger firms generally extend it.

the tenth day, its payables will average (10)($32,666.67) = $326,667; PCC will, on average, be receiving $326,667 of credit from its only supplier, Microchip Electronics.

Now suppose PCC decides *not* to take the discount; what will happen? First, PCC will begin paying invoices after 30 days, so its accounts payable will increase to 30($32,666.67) = $980,000.[4] Microchip will now be supplying PCC with an *additional* $653,333 of credit. PCC could use this additional credit to pay off bank loans, to expand inventories, to increase fixed assets, to build up its cash account, or even to increase its own accounts receivable.

Personal's new credit from Microchip has a cost—PCC is foregoing a 2 percent discount on its $12 million of purchases, so its costs will rise by $240,000 per year. Dividing this $240,000 by the additional credit, we find the implicit cost of the added trade credit as follows:

$$\text{Approximate percentage cost} = \frac{\$240,000}{\$653,333} = 36.7\%.$$

Assuming that PCC can borrow from its bank (or from other sources) at an interest rate less than 36.7 percent, it should not expand its payables by foregoing discounts.

The following equation can be used to calculate the approximate percentage cost, on an annual basis, of not taking discounts:

$$\begin{matrix} \text{Approximate} \\ \text{percentage} \\ \text{cost} \end{matrix} = \frac{\text{Discount percent}}{100 - \begin{matrix} \text{Discount} \\ \text{percent} \end{matrix}} \times \frac{360}{\begin{matrix} \text{Days credit is} \\ \text{outstanding} \end{matrix} - \begin{matrix} \text{Discount} \\ \text{period} \end{matrix}}. \qquad \text{(16-1)}$$

The numerator of the first term, discount percent, is the cost per dollar of credit, while the denominator in this term (100 − Discount percent) represents the funds made available by not taking the discount. The second term shows how many times each year this cost is incurred. To illustrate the equation, the approximate cost of not taking a discount when the terms are 2/10, net 30, is computed as follows:

$$\text{Approximate percentage cost} = \frac{2}{98} \times \frac{360}{20} = 0.0204(18)$$

$$= 0.367 = 36.7\%.$$

In effective annual interest terms, the rate is even higher. The discount amounts to interest, and with terms of 2/10, net 30, the firm gains use of the funds for 30 − 10 = 20 days, so there are 360/20 = 18 "interest periods" per year. The

---

[4]A question arises here: Should accounts payable reflect gross purchases or purchases net of discounts? Although generally accepted accounting practices permit either treatment on the grounds that the difference is not material, most accountants prefer to record both inventories and payables net of discounts, and then to report the higher payments that result from not taking discounts as an additional expense, called "discounts lost." Thus, *we show accounts payable net of discounts even if the company does not expect to take the discount.*

first term in Equation 16-1, (Discount percent)/(100 − Discount percent) = 0.02/0.98 = 0.0204, is the periodic interest rate. This rate is paid 18 times each year, so the effective annual rate cost of trade credit is

$$\text{Effective annual rate} = (1.0204)^{18} - 1.0 = 1.438 - 1.0 = 43.8\%.$$

Thus, the 36.7 percent approximate cost calculated with Equation 16-1 understates the true cost of trade credit.

Notice, however, that the cost of trade credit can be reduced by paying late. Thus, if PCC could get away with paying in 60 days rather than in the specified 30, then the effective credit period would become 60 − 10 = 50 days, and the approximate cost would drop from 36.7 percent to (2/98)(360/50) = 14.7%. The effective annual rate would drop from 43.8 to 15.7 percent:

$$\text{Effective annual rate} = (1.0204)^{7.2} - 1.0 = 1.157 - 1.0 = 15.7\%.$$

In periods of excess capacity, firms may be able to get away with late payments, but they will also suffer a variety of problems associated with "stretching" accounts payable and being branded a "slow payer" account. These problems are discussed later in the chapter.

The cost of the additional trade credit that results from not taking discounts can be worked out for other purchase terms. Some illustrative costs are shown below:

Credit Terms	Cost of Additional Credit if Cash Discount Not Taken	
	Approximate Cost	Effective Cost
1/10, net 20	36%	44%
1/10, net 30	18	20
2/10, net 20	73	107
3/15, net 45	37	44

As these figures show, the cost of not taking discounts can be substantial. Incidentally, throughout the chapter, we assume that payments are made either on the *last day* for taking discounts or on the *last day* of the credit period, unless otherwise noted. It would be foolish to pay, say, on the fifth day or on the twentieth day if the credit terms were 2/10, net 30.

Effects of Trade Credit on the Financial Statements

A firm's policy with regard to taking or not taking discounts can have a significant effect on its financial statements. To illustrate, let us assume that PCC is just beginning its operations. On the first day, it makes net purchases of $32,666.67. This amount is recorded on its balance sheet under accounts payable.[5] The second day it buys another $32,666.67. The first day's purchases are not yet paid for, so at the

---

[5]Inventories also increase by $32,666.67, but we are not now concerned with inventories.

end of the second day, accounts payable total $65,333.34. Accounts payable increase by another $32,666.67 on the third day, for a total of $98,000, and after 10 days, accounts payable are up to $326,667.

If PCC takes discounts, then on the 11th day it will have to pay for the $32,666.67 of purchases made on the first day, which will reduce accounts payable. However, it will buy another $32,666.67, which will increase payables. Thus, after the 10th day of operations, PCC's balance sheet will level off, showing a balance of $326,667 in accounts payable, assuming that the company pays on the 10th day in order to take discounts.

Now suppose PCC decides not to take discounts. In this case, on the 11th day, it will add another $32,666.67 to payables, but it will not pay for the purchases made on the 1st day. Thus, the balance sheet figure for accounts payable will rise to 11($32,666.67) = $359,333.37. This buildup will continue through the 30th day, at which point payables will total 30($32,666.67) = $980,000. On the 31st day, PCC will buy another $32,667 of goods, which will increase accounts payable, but it will also pay for the purchases made the 1st day, which will reduce payables. Thus, the balance sheet item accounts payable will stabilize at $980,000 after 30 days, assuming PCC does not take discounts.

Table 16-2, Part I, shows PCC's balance sheet, after it reaches a steady state, under the two trade credit policies. Total assets are unchanged by this policy decision, and we also assume that the accruals and common equity accounts are unchanged. The differences show up in accounts payable and notes payable; when PCC elects to take discounts and thus gives up some of the trade credit it otherwise could have obtained, it will have to raise $653,333 from some other source. It could have sold more common stock, or it could have used long-term bonds, but it chose to use bank credit, which has a 10 percent cost and is reflected in the notes payable account.

Part II of Table 16-2 shows PCC's income statement under the two policies. If the company does not take discounts, then its interest expense will be zero, but it will have a $240,000 expense for discounts lost. On the other hand, if it does take discounts, it will incur an interest expense of $65,333, but it will avoid the cost of discounts lost. Since discounts lost exceed the interest expense, the take-discounts policy results in the higher net income and, thus, in a higher stock price.

Components of Trade Credit: Free Versus Costly

On the basis of the preceding discussion, trade credit can be divided into two components: (1) *free trade credit*, which involves credit received during the discount period and which for PCC amounts to 10 days' net purchases, or $326,667, and (2) *costly trade credit*, which involves credit in excess of the free credit, and whose cost is an implicit one based on the foregone discounts.[6] PCC could obtain

[6]There is some question as to whether any credit is really "free," because the supplier will have a cost of carrying receivables which must be passed on to the customer in the form of higher prices. Still, where suppliers sell on standard terms such as 2/10, net 30, and where the base price cannot be negotiated downward for early payment, then for all intents and purposes, the 10 days of trade credit is indeed "free."

Table 16-2
**PCC's Financial Statements with
Different Trade Credit Policies**

I. Balance Sheets

	Take Discounts; Borrow from Bank	Do Not Take Discounts; Use Maximum Trade Credit
Cash	$ 500,000	$ 500,000
Receivables	1,000,000	1,000,000
Inventories	2,000,000	2,000,000
Fixed assets	2,980,000	2,980,000
Total assets	$ 6,480,000	$ 6,480,000
Accounts payable	$ 326,667	$ 980,000
Notes payable	653,333	0
Accruals	500,000	500,000
Common equity	5,000,000	5,000,000
Total claims	$ 6,480,000	$ 6,480,000

II. Income Statements

Sales	$15,000,000	$15,000,000
Less: Purchases	11,760,000	11,760,000
Labor	2,000,000	2,000,000
Interest	65,333	0
Discounts lost	0	240,000
Net income before tax	1,174,667	1,000,000
Tax (40%)	469,867	400,000
Net income	$ 704,800	$ 600,000

$653,333, or 20 days' net purchases, of non-free trade credit at a cost of approximately 37 percent. *Financial managers should always use the free component, but they should use the costly component only after analyzing the cost of this capital to make sure that it is less than the cost of funds which could be obtained from other sources.* Under the terms of trade found in most industries, the costly component will involve a relatively high percentage cost, so stronger firms will avoid using it.

We noted earlier that firms sometimes can and do deviate from the stated credit terms, thus altering the percentage cost figures cited above. For example, a California manufacturing firm that buys on terms of 2/10, net 30, makes a practice of paying in 15 days (rather than 10), but it still takes discounts. Its treasurer simply waits until 15 days after receipt of the goods to pay, and then writes a check for the invoiced amount less the 2 percent discount. The company's suppliers want its business, so they tolerate this practice. Similarly, a Wisconsin firm that also buys on terms of 2/10, net 30, does not take discounts, but it pays in 60 rather than in 30 days, thus "stretching" its trade credit. As we saw earlier, both practices reduce the cost of trade credit. Neither of these firms is "loved" by its suppliers, and neither could continue these practices in times when suppliers were operating at full capacity and had order backlogs, but these practices can and do reduce the costs of trade credit during times when suppliers have excess capacity.

SHORT-TERM BANK LOANS

Commercial banks, whose loans generally appear on firms' balance sheets under the notes payable account, are second in importance to trade credit as a source of short-term financing.[7] The banks' influence is actually greater than appears from the dollar amounts they lend, because banks provide *nonspontaneous* funds. As a firm's financing needs increase, it requests its bank to provide the additional funds. If the request is denied, the firm may be forced to abandon attractive growth opportunities.

Bank Loan Features

Some features of bank loans are discussed in the following paragraphs.

Maturity
Although banks do make longer-term loans, *the bulk of their lending is on a short-term basis*—about two-thirds of all bank loans mature in a year or less. Bank loans to businesses are frequently written as 90-day notes, so the loan must be repaid or renewed at the end of 90 days. Of course, if a borrower's financial position has deteriorated, the bank may well refuse to renew the loan. This can mean serious trouble for the borrower.

Promissory Note
When a bank loan is approved, the agreement is executed by signing a *promissory note*. The note specifies (1) the amount borrowed; (2) the percentage interest rate; (3) the repayment schedule, which can involve either a lump sum or a series of installments; (4) any collateral that might have to be put up as security for the loan; and (5) any other terms and conditions to which the bank and the borrower may have agreed. When the note is signed, the bank credits the borrower's checking account with the amount of the loan, while on the borrower's balance sheet, both cash and notes payable increase.

Compensating Balances
Banks typically require that a regular borrower maintain an average demand deposit (checking account) balance equal to from 10 to 20 percent of the face amount of the loan. This is called a *compensating balance*, and such balances raise the effective interest rate on the loans. For example, if a firm needs $80,000 to pay off outstanding obligations, but if it must maintain a 20 percent compensating bal-

---

[7]Although commercial banks remain the primary source of short-term loans, other sources are available. For example, in 1985 General Electric Credit Corporation (GECC) had over $2 billion in commercial loans outstanding. Firms such as GECC, which was initially established to finance consumers' purchases of GE's durable goods, often find business loans to be more profitable than consumer loans.

ance, then it must borrow $100,000 to obtain a usable $80,000. If the stated interest rate is 8 percent, the effective cost is actually 10 percent: $8,000 interest divided by $80,000 of usable funds equals 10 percent.[8]

Line of Credit

A *line of credit* is a formal or informal understanding between the bank and the borrower indicating the maximum credit the bank will extend to the borrower. For example, on December 31 a bank loan officer may indicate to a financial manager that the bank regards the firm as being "good" for up to $80,000 during the forthcoming year. If on January 10 the financial manager signs a promissory note for $15,000 for 90 days, this would be called "taking down" $15,000 of the total line of credit. This amount would be credited to the firm's checking account at the bank, and before repayment of the $15,000, the firm could borrow additional amounts up to a total of $80,000 outstanding at any one time.

Revolving Credit Agreement

A *revolving credit agreement* is a formal line of credit often used by large firms. To illustrate, in 1986 Fairmont Petroleum Company negotiated a revolving credit agreement for $100 million with a group of banks. The banks were formally committed for 4 years to lend Fairmont up to $100 million if the funds were needed. Fairmont, in turn, paid a commitment fee of one-quarter of 1 percent on the unused balance of the commitment to compensate the banks for making the commitment. Thus, if Fairmont did not take down any of the $100 million commitment during a year, it would still be required to pay a $250,000 fee. If it borrowed $50 million, the unused portion of the line of credit would fall to $50 million, and the fee would fall to $125,000. Of course, interest also had to be paid on the money Fairmont actually borrowed. As a general rule, the rate of interest on "revolvers" is pegged to the prime rate, so the cost of the loan varies over time as interest rates change.[9] Fairmont's rate was set at prime plus 0.5 percentage points.

---

[8]Note, however, that the compensating balance may be set as a minimum monthly *average*, and if the firm would maintain this average anyway, the compensating balance requirement would not raise the effective interest rate. Also, note that these *loan* compensating balances are added to any compensating balances that the firm's bank may require for *services performed*, such as clearing checks.

[9]Each bank sets its own prime rate, but, because of competitive forces, most banks' prime rates are identical. Further, most banks follow the rate set by the large New York City banks, and they, in turn, generally follow the rate set by Citibank, the world's largest. Citibank had a policy of setting the prime rate each week at 1¼ to 1½ percentage points above the average rate on large certificates of deposit (CDs) during the three weeks immediately preceding. CD rates represent the "price" of money in the open market, and they rise and fall with the supply and demand of money, so CD rates are "market-clearing" rates. By tying the prime rate to CD rates, the banking system insured that the prime rate would also be a market-clearing rate.

However, in recent years the prime rate has been held relatively constant even during periods when open market rates fluctuated. Also, in recent years many banks have been lending to the very strongest companies at rates below the prime rate. As we discuss later in this chapter, larger firms have ready access to the commercial paper market, and if banks want to do a significant volume of business with these larger companies, they must match or at least come close to the commercial paper rate. As competition in financial markets increases, as it has been doing because of the deregulation of banks and other financial institutions, "administered" rates such as the prime rate must give way to flexible, negotiated rates based on market forces.

Note that a revolving credit agreement is very similar to a line of credit. However, there is an important distinguishing feature: The bank has a *legal obligation* to honor a revolving credit agreement, and it receives a commitment fee. Neither the legal obligation not the fee exist under a less formal line of credit.

As an example of the types of short-term loans made by commercial banks, the *Federal Reserve Bulletin* reported that commercial banks made $35 billion of short-term loans to business during the first week of February 1986. Of the total, 14 percent were demand loans, with no stated maturity; 36 percent were overnight loans; 27 percent had maturities ranging from 1-30 days; and 23 percent had maturities ranging from 1 to 12 months. The weighted average maturity was 45 days. Also, 35 percent had a floating rate versus 65 percent with a fixed rate, and 77 percent were made under a formal commitment such as a revolving credit agreement, while only 23 percent were newly arranged credits.

COMMERCIAL PAPER

Commercial paper is a type of unsecured promissory note issued by large, strong firms, and it is sold primarily to other business firms, to insurance companies, to pension funds, to money market mutual funds, and to banks. Although the amount of commercial paper outstanding is smaller than bank loans outstanding, this form of financing has grown rapidly in recent years. At the end of January 1986, there was approximately $302 billion of commercial paper outstanding, versus about $495 billion of bank loans to businesses.

Maturity and Cost

Maturities of commercial paper generally vary from one to nine months, with an average of about five months.[10] The rates on commercial paper fluctuate with supply and demand conditions—they are determined in the marketplace, varying daily as conditions change. Recently, commercial paper rates have generally ranged from $1\frac{3}{4}$ to $2\frac{1}{2}$ percentage points below the stated prime rate, and about $\frac{1}{2}$ of a percentage point above the T-bill rate. For example, in February 1986, the average rate on 3-month commercial paper was 7.6 percent, the stated prime rate was 9.5 percent, and the 6-month T-bill rate was about 7.1 percent. Also, since compensating balances are not required for commercial paper, the *effective* cost differential is still wider.[11]

---

[10]The maximum maturity without SEC registration is 270 days. Also, commercial paper can only be sold to "sophisticated" investors; otherwise, SEC registration would be required even for maturities of 270 days or less.

[11]However, this factor is offset to some extent by the fact that firms issuing commercial paper are required by commercial paper dealers to have unused revolving credit agreements to back up their outstanding commercial paper, and fees must be paid on these lines. In other words, to sell $1 million of commercial paper, a firm must have revolving credit available to pay off the paper when it matures, and commitment fees on this unused credit line (about $\frac{1}{2}$ percent) increase the effective cost of the paper. Note also that commercial paper and T-bill rates are quoted on a discount basis, whereas the prime rate is on an annual yield basis.

Use of Commercial Paper

The use of commercial paper is restricted to a comparatively small number of concerns that are exceptionally good credit risks. Dealers prefer to handle the paper of firms whose net worth is $100 million or more and whose annual borrowing exceeds $10 million. One potential problem with commercial paper is that a debtor who is in temporary financial difficulty may receive little help, because commercial paper dealings are generally less personal than are bank relationships. Thus, banks are generally more able and willing to help a good customer weather a temporary storm than is a commercial paper dealer. On the other hand, using commercial paper permits a corporation to tap a wide range of credit sources, including financial institutions outside its own area and industrial corporations across the country, and this can reduce interest costs.

SECURED SHORT-TERM LOANS

Thus far, we have not addressed the question of whether or not loans are secured. Commercial paper loans are never secured by specific collateral, but all the other types of loans can be if this is deemed necessary or desirable. Given a choice, it is ordinarily better to borrow on an unsecured basis, since the bookkeeping costs of secured loans are often high. However, weak firms may find (1) that they can borrow only if they put up some type of security to protect the lender, or (2) that by using some security they can borrow at a much lower rate.

Several different kinds of collateral can be employed, including marketable stocks or bonds, land or buildings, equipment, inventory, and accounts receivable. Marketable securities make excellent collateral, but few firms hold portfolios of stocks and bonds. Similarly, both real property (land and buildings) and equipment are good forms of collateral, but they are generally used as security for long-term loans rather than for working capital loans. Therefore, most secured short-term business borrowing involves the use of either accounts receivable or inventories as collateral.

To understand the use of security, consider the case of an Orlando hardware dealer who wanted to modernize and expand his store. He requested a $200,000 bank loan. After examining his business's financial statements, the bank indicated (1) that it would lend him a maximum of $100,000, and (2) that the interest rate would be 13 percent. The owner had a substantial personal portfolio of stocks, so he offered to put up $300,000 of high-quality stocks to support the $200,000 loan. The bank then granted the full $200,000 loan, and at a rate of only 11 percent. The store owner might also have used his inventories or receivables as security for the loan, but processing costs would have been high.

In the past, state laws varied greatly with regard to the use of security in financing. Today, however, all states except Louisiana operate under the *Uniform Commercial Code*, which standardizes and simplifies the procedure for establishing loan security. The heart of the Uniform Commercial Code is the *Security Agreement*, a standardized document, or form, on which the specific assets that are pledged are stated. The assets can be items of equipment, accounts receivable, or inventories. Procedures under the Uniform Commercial Code for using accounts receivable and inventories as security for short-term credit are described in the following sections. Secured short-term loans involve quite a bit of paperwork and administrative costs, which makes them relatively expensive. However, this is often the only type of financing available to weaker firms.

ACCOUNTS RECEIVABLE FINANCING

Accounts receivable financing involves either the pledging of receivables or the selling of receivables (factoring). The *pledging of accounts receivable* is characterized by the fact that the lender not only has a claim against the receivables but also has recourse to the borrower: If the person or the firm that bought the goods does not pay, the selling firm must take the loss. Therefore, the risk of default on the accounts receivable pledged remains with the borrower. Also, the buyer of the goods is not ordinarily notified about the pledging of the receivables, and the financial institution that lends on the security of accounts receivable is generally either a commercial bank or one of the large industrial finance companies such as General Electric Credit Corporation (GECC).

Factoring, or *selling accounts receivable*, involves the purchase of accounts receivable by the lender, generally without recourse to the borrower. Under factoring, the buyer of the goods is typically notified of the transfer and is asked to make payment directly to the financial institution. Since the factoring firm assumes the risk of default on bad accounts, it must do a credit check. Accordingly, factors can provide not only money but also a credit department for the borrower. Incidentally, the same banks and other financial institutions that make loans against pledged receivables also serve as factors. Thus, depending on the circumstances and the wishes of the borrower, a financial institution will provide either form of receivables financing.

Procedure for Pledging Receivables

The financing of accounts receivable is initiated by a legally binding agreement between the seller of the goods and the financing institution. The agreement sets forth in detail the procedures to be followed and the legal obligations of both parties. Once the working relationship has been established, the seller periodically takes a batch of invoices to the financing institution. The lender reviews the invoices and makes credit appraisals of the buyers. Invoices of companies that do not meet the lender's credit standards are not accepted as collateral.

The financial institution seeks to protect itself at every step of the operation. First, selection of sound invoices is one way the financing institution safeguards itself. Second, if the buyer of the goods does not pay the invoice, the lender still has recourse against the seller. And third, the lender gets additional protection because the loan will generally be for less than 100 percent of the pledged receivables. For example, the lender may advance the selling firm only 75 percent of the amount of the pledged receivables.

Procedure for Factoring Receivables

The procedure for factoring is somewhat different from that for pledging. Again, an agreement between the seller and the factor specifies legal obligations and procedural arrangements. When the seller receives an order from a buyer, a credit approval slip is written and immediately sent to the factor for a credit check. If the factor approves the credit, shipment is made, and the invoice is stamped to notify the buyer to make payment directly to the factoring company. If the factor does not approve the sale, the seller generally refuses to fill the order, but if the sale is made anyway, the factor will not buy the account.

The factor normally performs three functions: (1) credit checking, (2) lending, and (3) risk bearing. However, the seller can select various combinations of these functions by changing provisions in the factoring agreement. For example, a small- or medium-sized firm can avoid establishing a credit department. The factor's service might well be less costly than a department that would have excess capacity for the firm's credit volume. At the same time, if the selling firm uses a noncredit specialist on a part-time basis to perform credit checking, then lack of education, training, and experience could result in excessive losses.

The seller may utilize the factor to perform the credit-checking and risk-taking functions without performing the lending function. The following procedure illustrates the handling of a $10,000 order under this arrangement. The factor checks and approves the invoices. The goods are shipped on terms of net 30. Payment is made to the factor, who remits to the seller. But if the buyer defaults, the $10,000 must still be remitted to the seller. If the $10,000 is never paid, the factor sustains a $10,000 loss. Note, though, that in this situation the factor does not remit funds to the seller until they are received from the buyer of the goods, or until the credit period has expired. Thus, the factor does not supply any credit.

Now consider the most typical situation, where the factor performs all three functions: credit analysis, lending, and risk bearing. The goods are shipped, and even though payment is not due for 30 days, the factor immediately makes funds available to the seller. Suppose $10,000 worth of goods are shipped. Further, assume that the factoring commission for credit checking and risk bearing is 2.5 percent of the invoice price, or $250, and that the interest expense is computed at a 9 percent annual rate on the invoice balance, or $75.[12] The selling firm's accounting entry is as follows:

Cash	$9,175	
Interest expense	75	
Factoring commission	250	
Reserve due from factor on collection of account	500	
Accounts receivable		$10,000

---

[12]Since the interest is only for one month, we multiply 1/12 of the stated rate (9 percent) by the $10,000 invoice price:

$$(1/12)(0.09)(\$10,000) = \$75.$$

Note that the effective rate of interest is really above 9 percent, because (1) the term is for less than 1 year and (2) a discounting procedure is used, so the borrower does not get the full $10,000. In many instances, however, the factoring contract would call for interest to be computed on the invoice price *less* both the factoring commission and the reserve account.

The $500 due from the factor on collection of the account is a reserve established by the factor to cover disputes between the seller and the buyers on damaged goods and on goods returned by buyers to the seller. The reserve is paid to the selling firm when the factor collects on the account.

Factoring is normally a continuous process instead of the single cycle just described. The firm receives orders; it transmits these orders to the factor for approval; upon approval, the goods are shipped and the factor advances money to the seller; the buyers pay the factor when payment is due; and the factor periodically remits any excess in the reserve to the seller of the goods. Once a routine is established, a continuous circular flow of goods and funds takes place between the seller, the buyers of the goods, and the factor. Thus, once the factoring agreement is in force, funds from this source are *spontaneous*.

Cost of Receivables Financing

Both accounts receivable pledging and factoring are convenient and advantageous, but they can be costly. The credit-checking and risk-bearing fee is generally 1 to 3 percent of the amount of invoices accepted by the factor, and even more if the buyers are poor credit risks. The cost of money charged on the unpaid balance of the funds advanced by the factor usually runs 2 to 3 percentage points over the prime rate.

Evaluation of Receivables Financing

It cannot be said categorically that accounts receivable financing is always either a good or a poor method of raising funds for an individual business. Among the advantages is, first, the flexibility of this source of financing: As the firm's sales expand, causing more financing to be needed, a larger volume of invoices, and hence collateral for loans, is generated automatically. Second, receivables can be used as security for a loan that might otherwise not be obtainable. Third, factoring can provide credit analysis that might otherwise be available only under much more expensive conditions.

Accounts receivable financing also has disadvantages. First, when invoices are numerous and relatively small in dollar amount, the administrative costs involved may be excessive. Second, when a firm uses receivables financing, its other creditors are placed at a severe disadvantage, because its most liquid asset other than cash is being used as collateral. For this reason, accounts receivable financing is often frowned upon by a firm's trade creditors, and using receivables financing may restrict the use of trade credit.

Future Use of Receivables Financing

We might make a prediction at this point: In the future, accounts receivable financing will probably increase in relative importance. Computer technology is rapidly advancing toward the point where the credit records of individuals and firms can be kept on disks and magnetic tapes. Systems have been developed such that a retailer can have an electronic box on hand, and when an individual's magnetic credit card is inserted into the box, the box gives a signal that the credit is "good" and that a bank is willing to "buy" the receivable created as soon as the store completes the sale. Such automated systems will greatly reduce the cost of handling invoices, making it feasible to use accounts receivable financing for very small sales and reducing the cost of all receivables financing. The net result will be a marked expansion of accounts receivable financing. In fact, when consumers use credit cards such as MasterCard or Visa, the seller is, in effect, factoring receivables: The store receives the amount of the purchase, less a percentage fee, the next working day, while the buyer receives 30 days (or so) credit, at which time he or she remits payment directly to the credit card company or sponsoring bank.

INVENTORY FINANCING

A substantial amount of credit is secured by business inventories. If a firm is a relatively good credit risk, the mere existence of the inventory may be a sufficient basis for receiving an unsecured loan. However, if the firm is a relatively poor risk, the lending institution may insist upon security, which often takes the form of a blanket lien against the inventory. Alternatively, trust receipts or warehouse receipts can be used to secure the loan. Various methods for using inventories as security are discussed in this section.

Blanket Liens

The *inventory blanket lien* gives the lending institution a lien against all the borrower's inventories. However, the borrower is free to sell inventories, so the value of the collateral can be reduced below the level that existed when the loan was granted.

Trust Receipts

Because of the inherent weakness of the blanket lien, another procedure for inventory financing was developed—the *trust receipt*, which is an instrument acknowledging that the goods are held in trust for the lender. When trust receipts are used, the borrowing firm, upon receiving funds from the lender, signs and delivers a trust receipt for the goods. The goods can be stored in a public warehouse or held on the premises of the borrower. The trust receipt acknowledges that the goods are held in trust for the lender and that any proceeds from the sale of trust goods must be transmitted to the lender at the end of each day. Automobile dealer financing is one of the best examples of trust receipt financing.

One problem with trust receipt financing is the requirement that a trust receipt must be issued for each specific item. For example, if the security is autos in a dealer's inventory, the trust receipts must indicate the cars by registration number. In order to validate its trust receipts, the lending institution must send someone to the premises of the borrower periodically to see that the auto numbers are correctly listed, because auto dealers who are in financial difficulty have been known to sell cars backing trust receipts and then use the funds obtained to meet payrolls and the like rather than to repay the bank. Problems are compounded if a borrower has geographically diversified operations, or if the borrower's operations are separated geographically from the lender. To offset these inconveniences, warehousing has come into wide use as a method of securing loans with inventory.

Warehouse Receipts

Like trust receipts, *warehouse receipt* financing uses inventory as security. A *public warehouse* is an independent third party operation engaged in the business of storing goods. Items which must age, such as tobacco and liquor, are often financed and stored in public warehouses. The borrower cannot remove the goods until the lender has been repaid, so the warehouse operator affords protection to the lender. However, at times a public warehouse is not practical because of the bulkiness of goods and the expense of transporting them to and from the borrower's premises. In such cases, a *field warehouse* may be established at the borrower's place of business. To provide inventory supervision, the lending institution employs a third party, a field warehousing company, which acts as an agent for the lending institution.

Field warehousing can be illustrated by a simple example. Suppose a firm which has steel reinforcing rods stacked in an open yard on its premises needs a loan. A field warehouse can be established if a field warehousing concern merely places a temporary fence around the rods, erects a sign stating: "This is a field warehouse supervised and operated by the Lawrence Field Warehousing Corporation," and assigns an employee to supervise and control the inventory.

The example illustrates the three essential elements for the establishment of a field warehouse: (1) public notification, (2) physical control of the inventory, and (3) supervision of the field warehouse by a custodian of the field warehouse concern. When the field warehousing operation is relatively small, the third condition is sometimes violated by hiring an employee of the borrower to supervise the inventory. This practice is viewed as undesirable by most lenders, because there is no control over the collateral by a person independent of the borrowing firm.[13]

Field warehouse financing is best illustrated by an actual case. A California tomato cannery was interested in financing its operations by bank borrowing. The cannery had sufficient funds to finance 15 to 20 percent of its operations during the canning season. These funds were adequate to purchase and process an initial

---

[13]This absence of independent control was the main cause of the breakdown that resulted in the $200 million plus losses connected with loans to the Allied Crude Vegetable Oil Company by Bank of America and other banks. American Express Field Warehousing Company was handling the operation, but it hired men from Allied's own staff as custodians. Their dishonesty was not discovered because of another breakdown—the fact that the American Express touring inspector did not actually take a physical inventory of the warehouses. As a consequence, the swindle was not discovered until losses running into the hundreds of millions of dollars had been suffered. See N. C. Miller, *The Great Salad Oil Swindle*, (Baltimore: Penguin Books, 1965, 72-77).

batch of tomatoes, but as the cans were put into boxes and rolled into the storerooms, the cannery needed additional funds for both raw materials and labor. Because of the cannery's poor credit rating, the bank decided that a field warehousing operation would be necessary to secure its loans.

A field warehouse was established, and the custodian notified the bank of the description, by number, of the boxes of canned tomatoes that had been placed in storage and under warehouse control. At that point, the bank established a deposit on which the cannery could draw, and from then on, the bank financed the operations. Farmers brought in more tomatoes; the cannery processed them; the cans were boxed; the boxes were put into the field warehouse; field warehouse receipts were drawn up and sent to the bank; the bank established further deposits for the cannery on the basis of the receipts; and the cannery drew on the deposits to continue the cycle.

Of course, the cannery's ultimate objective was to sell the canned tomatoes. As it received purchase orders, they were transmitted to the bank, and the bank directed the custodian to release part of the inventory. As remittances were received by the cannery, they were turned over to the bank to retire the loans.

Note that a seasonal pattern existed. At the beginning of the harvest season, the cannery's cash needs and loan requirements began to rise, and they reached a peak just as the canning season ended. It was expected that well before the new canning season begins, the cannery would have sold enough tomatoes to pay off the loan. If for some reason the cannery had a bad year, the bank might carry the loan over for another year to enable the company to work off its inventory.

Acceptable Products

In addition to canned foods, which account for about 17 percent of all field warehouse loans, many other types of products provide a basis for field warehouse financing. Some of these are miscellaneous groceries, which represent about 13 percent; lumber products, about 10 percent; and coal and coke, about 6 percent. These products are relatively nonperishable and are sold in well-developed, organized markets. Nonperishability protects the lender if it must take over the security. For this reason, a bank would not make a field warehousing loan on perishables such as fresh fish. However, frozen fish, which can be stored for a long time, can be field warehoused. An organized market makes it easier to obtain field warehouse financing: Banks are not interested in going into the canning or the fish business, so they want to be able to dispose of inventory with a minimum of time and effort.

Cost of Financing

The fixed costs of a field warehousing arrangement are relatively high; such financing is therefore not suitable for a very small firm. If a field warehouse company sets up the field warehouse itself, it will typically set a minimum charge of about $5,000 per year, plus 1 to 2 percent of the amount of credit extended to the borrower. Furthermore, the financing institution will charge an interest rate set at 2 to 3 percentage points over the prime rate. An efficient field warehousing operation requires a minimum inventory of at least $1 million.

Evaluation of Inventory Financing

Inventory financing, especially field warehouse financing, has many advantages. First, the amount of funds available is flexible because the financing is tied to the growth of inventories, which in turn is related directly to sales growth. Second, the field warehousing arrangement enhances the position of the lender and thus increases the acceptability of inventories as loan collateral. Third, the necessity for inventory control, safekeeping, and the use of specialists in warehousing has resulted in improved warehouse practice, which in turn saves handling costs, insurance charges, theft, and so on. Indeed, the services of the field warehouse companies have often saved money for firms in spite of the costs of such financing. The major disadvantages of a field warehousing operation are the paperwork and physical separation requirements and, for small firms, the fixed cost element.

SUMMARY

This chapter began with a discussion of the *working capital cash flow cycle* and alternative *working capital policies*. Working capital policy involves (1) the level of current assets and (2) the manner in which these assets are financed. We saw that because short-term credit offers greater flexibility and often a lower cost, most firms use at least some current debt in spite of the fact that short-term credit increases the firm's risk.

The chapter also examined the four major types of short-term credit available to a firm: (1) *accruals*, (2) *accounts payable (or trade credit)*, (3) *bank loans*, and (4) *commercial paper*. Companies use accruals on a regular basis, but this usage is not subject to discretionary actions. The other three types of credit are controllable, at least within limits.

Accounts payable may be divided into two components, *free trade credit* and *costly trade credit*. The cost of the latter is based on discounts lost, and it can be quite high. The financial manager should use all the free trade credit the firm can get, but costly trade credit should be used only if other credit is not available on better terms.

Bank loans may be negotiated on an individual basis as the need arises, or they may be obtained on a pre-arranged basis under a *line of credit* or *revolving loan agreement. Commercial paper* is an important source of short-term credit, but it is available only to large, financially strong firms. Interest rates on commercial paper are generally below the prime bank rate, and the relative cost of paper is even lower when compensating balances on bank loans are considered. However, commercial paper does have disadvantages—if a firm that depends heavily on commercial paper experiences problems, its source of funds will dry up immediately. Commercial bankers are much more likely to help their customers ride out bad times.

Short-term credit is often *secured* by accounts receivable, which may be either *pledged* as collateral or *factored* (sold). Inventories can also be used as collateral under (1) *blanket liens*, (2) *trust receipts*, or (3) *warehouse receipts*.

Questions and Problems

16-1 (Cost of trade credit) Suppose a firm makes purchases of $3,000,000 per year under terms of 2/10, net 30. It takes discounts.

    a. What is the average amount of accounts payable, net of discounts? (Assume the $3.0 million purchases are net of discounts; that is, gross purchases are $3,061,224, discounts are $61,224, and net purchases are $3.0 million. Also, use 360 days in a year.)

    b. Is there a cost of the trade credit it uses?

    c. If it did not take discounts, what would its average payables be, and what would be the cost of this nonfree trade credit?

    d. What would its cost of not taking discounts be if it "stretched" its payments to 40 days?

16-2 (Trade credit versus bank credit) Williams Corporation projects an increase in sales from $2 million to $2.5 million, but the company needs an additional $300,000 of current assets to support this expansion. The money can be obtained from the bank at an interest rate of 10 percent. Alternatively, Williams can finance the expansion by no longer taking discounts, thus increasing accounts payable. Williams purchases under terms of 1/10, net 30, but it can delay payment for an additional 30 days, paying in 60 days and thus becoming 30 days past due, without a penalty at this time.

    a. Based strictly on an interest rate comparison, how should Williams finance its expansion?

    b. What additional qualitative factors should be considered in reaching a decision?

16-3 (Accounts payable) The Bey Copper Corporation had sales of $1,950,000 last year and earned a 4 percent return, after taxes, on sales. Although its terms of purchase are 20 days, its accounts payable represent 60 days' purchases. The president of the company is seeking to increase the company's bank borrowings in order to become current (that is, have 20 days' payables outstanding) in meeting its trade obligations. The company's balance sheet is shown below (in thousands of dollars):

Cash	$ 25	Accounts payable	$ 300
Accounts receivable	125	Bank loans	250
Inventory	650	Accruals	125
Current assets	$ 800	Current liabilities	$ 675
Land and buildings	250	Mortgage on real estate	250
Equipment	250	Common stock, par 10¢	125
		Retained earnings	250
Total assets	$1,300	Total claims	$1,300

    a. How much bank financing is needed to eliminate past-due accounts payable?

    b. Would you as a bank loan officer make the loan? Why?

16-4 (Long-term versus short-term credit) From the standpoint of the borrower, is long-term or short-term credit riskier? Explain. Would it ever make sense to borrow on a short-term basis if short-term rates were above long-term rates?

16-5 (Factoring) The Singleton Company manufactures plastic toys. It buys raw materials, manufactures the toys in the spring and summer, and ships them to department stores and toy stores by late summer or early fall. Singleton factors its receivables. If it did not, Singleton's October 1986 balance sheet might appear as on page 564 (in thousands of dollars):

Cash	$ 40	Accounts payable	$1,200
Receivables	1,200	Notes payable	800
Inventory	800	Accruals	80
Current assets	$2,040	Current liabilities	$2,080
		Mortgages	200
		Common stock	400
Fixed assets	800	Retained earnings	160
Total assets	$2,840	Total claims	$2,840

Singleton provides advanced dating on its sales; thus, its receivables are not due for payment until January 31, 1987. Also, the firm would have been overdue on some $800,000 of its accounts payable if the above situation had actually existed.

Singleton has had an agreement with a finance company to factor the receivables for the period October 31 through January 31 of each selling season. The factoring company charges a flat commission of 2 percent, plus 6 percent per year interest on the outstanding balance; it deducts a reserve of 8 percent for returned and damaged materials. Interest and commissions are paid in advance. No interest is charged on the reserved funds or on the commission.

a. Show the balance sheet of Singleton on October 31, 1986, including the purchase of all the receivables by the factoring company and the use of the funds to pay accounts payable.

b. If the $1.2 million is the average level of outstanding receivables, and if they turn over four times a year (hence, the commission is paid four times a year), what are the total dollar costs of receivables financing (factoring) and the effective annual interest rate?

16-6 (Commercial paper versus bank credit) Suppose a firm can borrow at the prime rate or also sell commercial paper.

a. If the prime rate is 12 percent, what is a reasonable estimate for the cost of commercial paper?

b. If a substantial cost differential exists, why might a firm such as this one actually borrow some of its funds from both markets?

16-7 (Cash conversion cycle) A firm has an average age of accounts receivable of 53 days, an average age of accounts payable of 42 days, and an average age of inventory of 70 days.

a. What is the length of the firm's cash conversion cycle?

b. If the firm's annual sales are $1,323,000, what is its investment in accounts receivable?

16-8 (Alternative credit sources) Water Park, Incorporated (WPI), estimates that as a result of the seasonal nature of its business, it will require an additional $350,000 of cash for the month of July. WPI has the following four alternatives available for raising the needed funds:

(1) Establish a 1-year line of credit for $350,000 with a commercial bank. The commitment fee will be 0.5 percent per year on the unused portion, and the interest charge on the used funds will be 12 percent per year. Assume that the funds are needed only in July, and that there are 30 days in July and 360 days in the year.

(2) Forego the trade discount of 3/10, net 40, on $350,000 of purchases during July.

(3) Issue $350,000 of 30-day commercial paper at an 11.4 percent annual interest rate. The total transactions fee, including the cost of a backup credit line, on using commercial paper is 0.5 percent of the amount of the issue.

(4) Issue $350,000 of 60-day commercial paper at an 11.0 percent annual interest rate, plus a transactions fee of 0.5 percent. Since the funds are required for only 30 days, the excess funds ($350,000) can be invested in marketable securities for the month of August earning 10.8 percent annually. The total transactions cost of purchasing and selling the marketable securities is 0.4 percent of the amount of the issue.

    a. What is the cost of each financing arrangement?

    b. Is the source with the lowest expected cost necessarily the one to select? Why or why not?

16-9 **(Working capital financing policy)** Three companies—Aggressive, Between, and Conservative—have different working capital management policies as implied by their names. For example, Aggressive employs only minimal current assets, and it finances almost entirely with current liabilities plus equity. This "tight-ship" approach has a dual effect. It keeps total assets low, which tends to increase return on assets; but because of stock-outs and credit rejections, total sales are reduced, and since inventory is ordered more frequently and in smaller quantities, variable costs are increased. Condensed balance sheets for the three companies are presented below.

	Aggressive	Between	Conservative
Current assets	$150,000	$200,000	$300,000
Fixed assets	200,000	200,000	200,000
Total assets	$350,000	$400,000	$500,000
Current liabilities (cost = 12%)	$200,000	$100,000	$ 50,000
Long-term debt (cost = 10%)	0	100,000	200,000
Total debt	$200,000	$200,000	$250,000
Equity	150,000	200,000	250,000
Total claims on assets	$350,000	$400,000	$500,000
Current ratio	0.75:1	2:1	6:1

The cost of goods sold functions for the three firms are as follows:

$$\text{Cost of goods sold} = \text{Fixed costs} + \text{Variable costs.}$$

$$\textbf{Aggressive}: \text{Cost of goods sold} = \$200,000 + 0.70(\text{Sales}).$$

$$\textbf{Between}: \text{Cost of goods sold} = \$270,000 + 0.65(\text{Sales}).$$

$$\textbf{Conservative}: \text{Cost of goods sold} = \$385,000 + 0.60(\text{Sales}).$$

Because of the working capital differences, sales for the three firms under different economic conditions are expected to vary as indicated next:

	Aggressive	Between	Conservative
Strong economy	$1,200,000	$1,250,000	$1,300,000
Average economy	900,000	1,000,000	1,150,000
Weak economy	700,000	800,000	1,050,000

    a. Construct income statements for each company for strong, average, and weak economies using the following format:

        • Sales

        • Less cost of goods sold

- Earnings before interest and taxes (EBIT)
- Less interest expense
- Taxable income
- Less taxes (at 40%)
- Net income

b. Compare the basic earnings power (EBIT/assets) and return on equity for the companies. Which company is best in a strong economy? In an average economy? In a weak economy?

(Do Parts c, d, and e only if you are using the computerized diskette.)

c. Suppose, with sales at the normal-economy level, short-term interest rates rose to 25 percent. How would that affect the three firms?

d. Suppose that because of production slowdowns caused by inventory shortages, the aggressive company's variable cost ratio rises to 80 percent. What would happen to its ROE, assuming a normal economy and a short-term rate of 12 percent?

e. What considerations for management of working capital are indicated by this problem?

Selected Additional References and Cases

The following articles provide more information on overall working capital policy and management:

Lambrix, R. J., and S. S. Singhvi, "Managing the Working Capital Cycle," *Financial Executive*, June 1979, 32-41.

Maier, Steven F., and James H. Vander Weide, "A Practical Approach to Short-Run Financial Planning," *Financial Management*, Winter 1978, 10-16.

Merville, Larry J., and Lee A. Tavis, "Optimal Working Capital Policies: A Chance-Constrained Programming Approach," *Journal of Financial and Quantitative Analysis*, January 1973, 47-60.

Yardini, Edward E., "A Portfolio-Balance Model of Corporate Working Capital," *Journal of Finance*, May 1979, 535-552.

For more on trade credit, see

Brosky, John J., *The Implicit Cost of Trade Credit and Theory of Optimal Terms of Sale* (New York: Credit Research Foundation, 1969).

Schwartz, Robert A., "An Economic Analysis of Trade," *Journal of Financial and Quantitative Analysis*, September 1974, 643-658.

For more on bank lending and commercial credit in general, see

Campbell, Tim S., "A Model of the Market for Lines of Credit," *Journal of Finance*, March 1978, 231-243.

Stone, Bernell K., "Allocating Credit Lines, Planned Borrowing, and Tangible Services over a Company's Banking System," *Financial Management*, Summer 1975, 65-78.

For a discussion of effective yields, see

Glasgo, Philip W., William J. Landes, and A. Frank Thompson, "Bank Discount, Coupon Equivalent, and Compound Yields," *Financial Management*, Autumn 1982, 80-84.

Finnerty, John D., "Bank Discount, Coupon Equivalent, and Compound Yields: Comment," *Financial Management*, Summer 1983, 40-44.

The following case is appropriate for use with this chapter:

Case 9, "Conover Container Corporation," in the Crum-Brigham casebook, which illustrates how changes in working capital policy affect expected profitability and risk.

17

INVENTORY MANAGEMENT

Inventories, which may be classified as (1) *raw materials*, (2) *work-in-process*, and (3) *finished goods*, are an essential part of virtually all business operations. As is the case with accounts receivable, inventory levels depend heavily upon sales. However, whereas receivables build up *after* sales have been made, inventories must be acquired *ahead* of sales. This is a critical difference, and the necessity of forecasting sales before establishing target inventory levels makes inventory management a difficult task. Also, since errors in the establishment of inventory levels quickly lead either to lost sales or to excessive carrying costs, inventory management is as important as it is difficult.

Inventory management techniques are covered in depth in production management courses. Still, since financial managers have a responsibility both for raising the capital needed to carry inventory and for the overall profitability of the firm, it is essential that we cover the basics of inventory management.

TYPICAL INVENTORY DECISIONS

Two examples will make clear the types of issues involved in inventory management, and the problems poor inventory control can cause.

Retail Clothing Store

Chicago Discount Clothing Company (CDCC) must order in January swimsuits for summer sales, and it must take delivery by April to be sure of having enough suits to meet the heavy May-June demand. Bathing suits come in many styles, colors, and sizes, and if CDCC stocks incorrectly, either in total or in terms of the style-color-size distribution, then the store will have trouble. It will lose potential sales if it stocks too few suits, and it will be forced to lower prices and take losses if it stocks too many or the wrong types.

The effects of inventory changes on the balance sheet are important. For simplicity, assume that CDCC has a $10,000 base stock of inventories, financed by common stock. Its initial balance sheet is as follows:

Inventories (base stock)	$10,000	Common stock	$10,000
Total assets	$10,000	Total claims	$10,000

Now it anticipates that it will sell $5,000 worth of swimsuit inventory this summer. Dollar sales will actually be greater than $5,000, since CDCC makes about $200 in profits for every $1,000 of inventory sold. CDCC finances its seasonal inventory with bank loans, so its pre-summer balance sheet would look like this:

Inventories (seasonal)	$ 5,000	Notes payable to bank	$ 5,000
Inventories (base stock)	10,000	Common stock	10,000
Total assets	$15,000	Total claims	$15,000

If everything works out as planned, sales will be made, inventories will be converted to cash, the bank loan will be retired, and the company will earn a profit. The balance sheet, after a successful season, might look like this:

Cash	$ 1,000	Notes payable to bank	$ 0
Inventories (seasonal)	0	Common stock	10,000
Inventories (base stock)	10,000	Retained earnings	1,000
Total assets	$11,000	Total claims	$11,000

The company is now in a highly liquid position and is ready to begin a new season.
But suppose the season had not gone well, and CDCC had only sold $1,000 of its inventory. As fall approached, the balance sheet would look like this:

Cash	$ 200	Notes payable to bank	$ 4,000
Inventories (seasonal)	4,000	Common stock	10,000
Inventories (base stock)	10,000	Retained earnings	200
Total assets	$14,200	Total claims	$14,200

Now suppose the bank insists on repayment of the $4,000 outstanding on the loan, and it wants cash, not swimsuits. But if the swimsuits did not sell well in the summer, how will out-of-style suits sell in the fall? Assume that CDCC is forced to mark the suits down to half their cost in order to sell them to raise cash to repay the bank loan. The result will be as follows:

Cash	$ 2,200	Notes payable to bank	$ 4,000
Inventories (base stock)	10,000	Common stock	10,000
		Retained earnings	(1,800)
Total assets	$12,200	Total claims	$12,200

At this point, CDCC is in serious trouble. It does not have the cash to pay off the loan, and the firm's shareholders have lost $1,800 of their equity. If the bank will not extend the loan, and if other sources of cash are not available, CDCC will have to mark down its base stock prices in an effort to stimulate sales, and if this does not work, CDCC could be forced into bankruptcy. Clearly, poor inventory decisions can spell trouble.

Appliance Manufacturer

Now consider a different type of situation, that of Housepro Corporation, a well-established appliance manufacturer, whose inventory position, in millions of dollars, follows:

Raw materials	$ 200
Work-in-process	200
Finished goods	600
Total inventories	$1,000

Suppose Housepro anticipates that the economy is about to get much stronger and that the demand for appliances will rise sharply. If it is to share in the expected boom, Housepro will have to increase production. This means it will have to increase inventories, and, since the inventory build-up must precede sales, additional financing will be required—some liability account, perhaps notes payable, would have to be increased in order to support the additional inventory.

Proper inventory management requires close coordination among the sales, purchasing, production, and finance departments. The sales/marketing department is generally the first to spot changes in demand. These changes must be worked into the company's purchasing and manufacturing schedules, and the financial manager must arrange any financing that will be needed to support the inventory buildup. Improper coordination among departments, poor sales forecasts, or both, can lead to disaster.

ACCOUNTING FOR INVENTORY

When finished goods are sold, the firm must assign a cost of goods sold. The cost of goods sold appears on the income statement as an expense for the period, and the balance sheet inventory account is reduced by a like amount. Four methods can be used to value the cost of goods sold, and hence to value remaining inventory: (1) specific identification, (2) first-in, first-out (FIFO), (3) last-in, first-out (LIFO), and (4) weighted average.

Specific Identification

Under *specific identification*, a unique cost is attached to each item in inventory. Then, when an item is sold, the inventory value is reduced by that specific amount. This method is used only when the items are high cost and move relatively slowly, such as would be the case for an automobile dealer.

First-In, First-Out (FIFO)

In the *FIFO* method, the units sold during a given period are assumed to be the first units that were placed in inventory. As a result, the cost of goods sold is based on the cost of the older inventory items, and the remaining inventory consists of the newer goods. Note that this is purely an accounting convention—the actual physical units sold could be either the earlier or the later units placed in inventory, or some combination.

Last-In, First-Out (LIFO)

LIFO is the opposite of FIFO. The cost of goods sold is based on the last units placed in inventory, while the remaining inventory consists of the first goods placed in inventory.

Weighted Average

The *weighted average* method involves the computation of the weighted average unit cost of goods available for sale from inventory, and this average cost is then applied to the goods sold to determine the cost of goods sold. This method results in a cost of goods sold and an ending inventory value that falls somewhere between the ones obtained by the FIFO and LIFO methods.

Comparison of Inventory Accounting Methods

To illustrate these methods and their effects on a firm's financial statements, assume that Custom Furniture, Inc., manufactured five identical antique reproduction dining tables during a one-year accounting period. During the year, a new labor contract plus dramatically increasing mahogany prices caused manufacturing costs to almost double:

Table Number:	1	2	3	4	5	Total
Cost:	$10,000	$12,000	$14,000	$16,000	$18,000	$70,000

There were no tables in stock at the beginning of the period, and Tables 1, 3, and 5 were sold during the year.

If Custom used the specific identification method, the cost of goods sold would be reported as $10,000 + $14,000 + $18,000 = $42,000, while the end-of-period inventory value would be $70,000 − $42,000 = $28,000. If Custom used the FIFO method, its cost of goods sold would be $10,000 + $12,000 + $14,000 = $36,000, and ending inventory would be $70,000 − $36,000 = $34,000. If Custom used the LIFO method, its cost of goods sold would be $48,000, and its ending inventory would be $22,000. Finally, if Custom used the weighted average method of inventory valuation, its average cost per unit sold would be $70,000/5

= $14,000, its cost of goods sold would be 3($14,000) = $42,000, and its ending inventory would be $70,000 − $42,000 = $28,000.

If we assume that Custom's actual sales revenues from the tables totaled $80,000, or an average of $26,667 per unit sold, and that its other costs were minimal, the following is a summary of the effects of the four inventory methods:

Method	Sales	Cost of Goods Sold	Profit	Ending Inventory Value
Specific identification	$80,000	$42,000	$38,000	$28,000
FIFO	80,000	36,000	44,000	34,000
LIFO	80,000	48,000	32,000	22,000
Weighted average	80,000	42,000	38,000	28,000

Ignoring taxes, Custom's cash flows would not be affected by its choice of inventory accounting methods, yet its balance sheet and reported profits would vary with each method. In an inflationary period such as in our example, FIFO gives the lowest cost of goods sold and thus the highest reported net income. FIFO also shows the highest inventory value, so it produces the strongest apparent liquidity position as measured by net working capital or the current ratio. On the other hand, LIFO produces the highest cost of goods sold, the lowest reported profits, and the weakest apparent liquidity position. However, when taxes are considered, LIFO provides the greatest tax deductibility, and thus it results in the lowest tax burden. Consequently, after-tax cash flows are highest if LIFO is used.

Of course, these results only apply to periods in which costs are increasing. If costs were constant, all four methods would produce the same cost of goods sold, ending inventory, taxes, and cash flows. However, inflation has been a fact of life for most of the past 20 years, so most firms use LIFO to take advantage of its greater tax and cash flow benefits.[1]

INVENTORY MANAGEMENT

Inventory management focuses on four basic questions. (1) How many units should be ordered (or produced) at a given time? (2) At what point should inventory be ordered (or produced)? (3) What inventory items warrant special atten-

---

[1]Note also that inventory valuation methods have cumulative effects that build up over the years. As an example, Del Monte Corporation used LIFO for many years, so it had certain items which, from an accounting standpoint, had been produced back in the 1920s and were still carried on the balance sheet at production costs of that era. Thus, Del Monte had "1923 catsup" and other items whose value was greatly understated. (Of course, Del Monte had no 1923 catsup in storage; there is no necessary relationship between the dating of the physical and the accounting inventory items.) Then, if Del Monte happened to have a bad year, when profits would otherwise be depressed, it would sell off (for accounting purposes) some of the old, undervalued LIFO inventory. This would boost profits and help to "manage" earnings so as to produce a smooth pattern of growth over time.

tion? (4) Can inventory cost changes be hedged? The remainder of the chapter is devoted to providing answers to these four questions.

INVENTORY COSTS

The goal of inventory management is to provide at the lowest cost the inventories required to sustain operations. The first step in inventory management is to identify all the costs involved in purchasing and maintaining inventories. Table 17-1 gives a listing of the typical costs that are associated with inventories. In the table, we have broken down costs into three categories: those associated with carrying inventories, those associated with ordering and receiving inventories, and those associated with running short of inventories.

Although they may well be the most important element, we shall at this point disregard the third category of costs—the costs of running short. These costs are dealt with by adding safety stocks, as we will discuss later. Similarly, we shall discuss quantity discounts in a later section. The costs that remain for consideration at this stage, then, are carrying costs and ordering, shipping, and receiving costs.

Table 17-1
Costs Associated with Inventories

	Approximate Annual Percentage Cost
I. Carrying Costs	
Cost of capital tied up	15.0%
Storage and handling costs	0.5
Insurance	0.5
Property taxes	1.0
Depreciation and obsolescence	12.0
Total	29.0%
II. Ordering, Shipping, and Receiving Costs	
Cost of placing orders, including production and set-up costs	Varies
Shipping and handling costs	2.5%
Quantity discounts lost	Varies
III. Costs of Running Short	
Loss of sales	Varies
Loss of customer goodwill	Varies
Disruption of production schedules	Varies

Note: These costs vary from firm to firm, from item to item, and also over time. The figures shown are U.S. Department of Commerce estimates for an average manufacturing firm. Where costs vary so widely that no meaningful numbers can be assigned, we simply report "Varies."

Carrying Costs

Carrying costs generally rise in direct proportion to the average amount of inventory carried. Inventories carried, in turn, depend on the frequency with which orders are placed. To illustrate, if a firm sells S units per year, and if it places equal sized orders N times per year, then S/N units will be purchased with each order. If the inventory is used evenly over the year, and if no safety stocks are carried, then the average inventory, A, will be:

$$A = \frac{\text{Units per order}}{2} = \frac{\text{S/N}}{2}. \tag{17-1}$$

For example, if S = 120,000 units in a year, and N = 4, then the firm will order 30,000 units at a time, and its average inventory will be 15,000 units:

$$A = \frac{\text{S/N}}{2} = \frac{120,000/4}{2} = \frac{30,000}{2} = 15,000 \text{ units.}$$

Now assume the firm purchases its inventory at a price P = $2 per unit. The average inventory value is, thus, (P)(A) = $2(15,000) = $30,000. If the firm has a cost of capital of 10 percent, it will incur $3,000 in financing charges to carry the inventory for one year. Further, assume that each year the firm incurs $2,000 of storage costs (space, utilities, security, taxes, and so forth), that its inventory insurance costs are $500, and that it must mark down inventories by $1,000 because of depreciation and obsolescence. The firm's total costs of carrying the $30,000 average inventory is $3,000 + $2,000 + $500 + $1,000 = $6,500. Thus, the annual percentage cost of carrying the inventory for this firm is $6,500/$30,000 = 0.217 = 21.7%.

Defining the annual percentage carrying cost as C, we can, in general, find the annual total carrying cost, TCC, as the percentage carrying cost, C, times the price per unit, P, times the average number of units, A:

$$TCC = \text{Total carrying cost} = (C)(P)(A). \tag{17-2}$$

In our example,

$$TCC = (0.217)(\$2)(15,000) \approx \$6,500.$$

Ordering Costs

Although we assume that carrying costs are entirely variable and rise in direct proportion to the average size of inventories, ordering costs are usually fixed. For example, the costs of placing and receiving an order—interoffice memos, long-distance telephone calls, setting up a production run, and taking delivery—are essentially fixed regardless of the size of an order, so this part of inventory cost is simply the fixed cost of placing and receiving orders times the number of orders placed.[2] We define the fixed costs associated with ordering inventories as F, and if we place N orders per year, the annual total ordering cost is given by Equation 17-3:

$$\text{Total ordering cost} = \text{TOC} = (F)(N).$$ (17-3)

Here TOC = total ordering cost, F = fixed costs per order, and N = number of orders placed per year.

Equation 17-1 may be rewritten as N = S/2A, and then substituted into Equation 17-3:

$$\text{Total ordering cost} = \text{TOC} = F\left(\frac{S}{2A}\right).$$ (17-4)

To illustrate the use of Equation 17-4, if F = \$100, S = 120,000 units, and A = 15,000 units, then TOC, the total annual ordering cost, is \$400:

$$\text{TOC} = \$100 \left(\frac{120,000}{30,000}\right) = \$100(4) = \$400.$$

Total Inventory Costs

Total carrying cost, TCC, as defined in Equation 17-2, and total ordering cost, TOC, as defined in Equation 17-4, may be combined to find total inventory costs, TIC, as follows:

$$\text{Total inventory costs} = \text{TIC} = \text{TCC} \quad + \text{TOC}$$
$$= (C)(P)(A) + F\left(\frac{S}{2A}\right).$$ (17-5)

Recognizing that the average inventory carried is A = Q/2, or one-half the size of each order quantity, Q, we may rewrite Equation 17-5 as follows:

$$\text{TIC} = \text{TCC} \quad + \text{TOC}$$
$$= (C)(P)\left(\frac{Q}{2}\right) + (F)\left(\frac{S}{Q}\right).$$ (17-6)

---

[2]Note that, in reality, both carrying and ordering costs can have variable and fixed cost elements, at least over certain ranges of average inventory. For example, security and utilities charges are probably fixed in the short run over a wide range of inventory levels. Similarly, labor costs in receiving inventory could be tied to the quantity received and hence variable. To simplify matters, we treat all carrying costs as variable and all ordering costs as fixed. However, if these assumptions do not fit the situation at hand, the cost definitions can be changed. For example, one could add another term for shipping costs if there are economies of scale in shipping, such that the cost of shipping a unit is smaller if shipments are larger. However, in most situations, shipping costs are not sensitive to order size, so total shipping costs are simply the shipping cost per unit times the units ordered (and sold) during the year. Under this condition, shipping costs are not influenced by inventory policy, and hence they may be disregarded for purposes of determining the optimal inventory level and the optimal order size.

Here we see that total carrying cost equals average inventory in units, Q/2, multiplied by unit price, P, times the percentage annual carrying cost, C. Total ordering cost equals the number of orders placed per year, S/Q, multiplied by the fixed cost of placing and receiving an order, F. We will use this equation in the next section to develop the optimal inventory ordering quantity.

THE OPTIMAL ORDERING QUANTITY

Inventories are obviously necessary, but it is equally obvious that a firm will suffer if it has too much or too little inventory. How can we determine the optimal inventory level? One approach commonly used is based on the *economic ordering quantity (EOQ)* model as described next.

Derivation of the EOQ Model

Figure 17-1 illustrates the basic premise on which the EOQ model is built, namely, that some costs rise with larger inventories while other costs decline, and there is an optimal order size which minimizes the total costs associated with inventories. First, as noted earlier, the average investment in inventories depends on how frequently orders are placed and the size of each order—if we order every day, average inventories will be much smaller than if we order once a year. Further, as Figure 17-1 shows, the firm's carrying costs rise with larger orders: Larger orders mean larger average inventories, so warehousing costs, interest on funds tied up in inventory, insurance, and obsolescence costs will all increase. However, ordering costs decline with larger orders and inventories: The cost of placing orders, suppliers' production setup costs, and order handling costs will all decline if we order infrequently and consequently hold larger quantities.

If the carrying and ordering cost curves in Figure 17-1 are added, the sum represents total inventory costs, TIC. The point where the TIC is minimized represents the *economic ordering quantity (EOQ),* and this, in turn, determines the optimal average inventory level.

The EOQ is found by differentiating Equation 17-6 with respect to ordering quantity, Q, and setting the derivative equal to zero:

$$\frac{d(TIC)}{dQ} = \frac{(C)(P)}{2} - \frac{(F)(S)}{Q^2} = 0.$$

Now, solving for Q, we obtain:

$$\frac{(C)(P)}{2} = \frac{(F)(S)}{Q^2}$$

$$Q^2 = \frac{2(F)(S)}{(C)(P)}$$

$$EOQ = \sqrt{\frac{2(F)(S)}{(C)(P)}}. \tag{17-7}$$

Figure 17-1
Determination of the Optimal Order Quantity

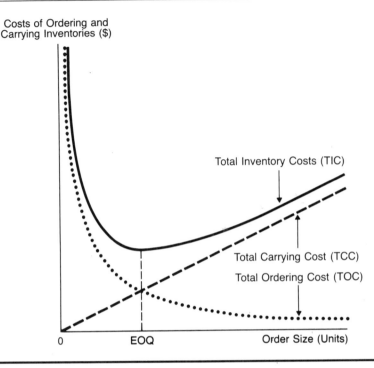

Here

EOQ = economic ordering quantity, or the optimum quantity to be ordered each time an
      order is placed.
  F = fixed costs of placing and receiving an order.
  S = annual sales in units.
  C = annual carrying costs expressed as a percentage of average inventory value.
  P = purchase price the firm must pay per unit of inventory.

Equation 17-7 is the EOQ model.[3] The assumptions of the model, which will be
relaxed shortly, include the following: (1) sales can be forecasted perfectly, (2)
sales are evenly distributed throughout the year, and (3) orders are received when
expected.

---

[3]The EOQ model can also be written as

$$EOQ = \sqrt{\frac{2(F)(S)}{C^*}},$$

where C^* is the annual carrying cost per unit expressed in *dollars*.

EOQ Model Illustration

To illustrate the EOQ model, consider the following data, supplied by Cotton Tops, Inc., a distributor of custom-designed T-shirts which sells to concessionaires at Daisy World:

S = sales = 26,000 shirts per year.

C = percentage carrying cost = 25 percent of inventory value.

P = purchase price per shirt = $4.92 per shirt. (The sales price is $9, but this is irrelevant for our purposes here.)

F = fixed cost per order = $1,000. Cotton Tops designs and distributes the shirts, but the actual production is done by another company. The bulk of this $1,000 cost is the labor cost for setting up the equipment for the production run, which the manufacturer bills separately from the $4.92 cost per shirt.

Substituting these data into Equation 17-7, we obtain an EOQ of 6,500 units:

$$EOQ = \sqrt{\frac{2(F)(S)}{(C)(P)}} = \sqrt{\frac{(2)(\$1,000)(26,000)}{(0.25)(\$4.92)}}$$

$$= \sqrt{42,276,423} \approx 6,500 \text{ units.}$$

With an EOQ of 6,500 shirts and annual usage of 26,000 shirts, Cotton Tops will place 26,000/6,500 = 4 orders per year. Notice that average inventory holdings depend directly on the EOQ: This relationship is illustrated graphically in Figure 17-2, where we see that average inventory = EOQ/2. Immediately after an order is received, 6,500 shirts are in stock. The usage rate, or sales rate, is 500 shirts per week (26,000/52 weeks), so inventories are drawn down by this amount each week. Thus, the actual number of units held in inventory will vary from 6,500 shirts just after an order is received to zero just before a new order arrives. With a 6,500 beginning balance, a zero ending balance, and a uniform sales rate, inventories will average one-half the EOQ, or 3,250 shirts, during the year. At a cost of $4.92 per shirt, the average investment in inventories will be (3,250)($4.92) ≈ $16,000. If inventories are financed by bank loans, the loan will vary from a high of $32,000 to a low of $0, but the average amount outstanding over the course of a year will be $16,000.

Notice that the EOQ, and hence average inventory holdings, rises with the square root of sales. Therefore, a given increase in sales will result in a less-than-proportionate increase in inventories, so the inventory/sales ratio will tend to decline as a firm grows. For example, Cotton Tops' EOQ is 6,500 shirts at an annual sales level of 26,000, and the average inventory is 3,250 shirts, or $16,000. However, if sales were to increase by 100 percent, to 52,000 shirts per year, the EOQ would rise only to 9,195 units, or by 41 percent, and the average inventory would rise by this same percentage. This suggests that there are economies of scale in holding inventories.[4]

---

[4]Note, however, that these scale economies relate to each particular item, not to the entire firm. Thus, a large distributor with $500 million of sales might have a higher inventory/sales ratio than a much smaller distributor if the small firm has only a few high-sales-volume items while the large firm distributes a great many low-volume items.

Figure 17-2
Inventory Position without Safety Stock

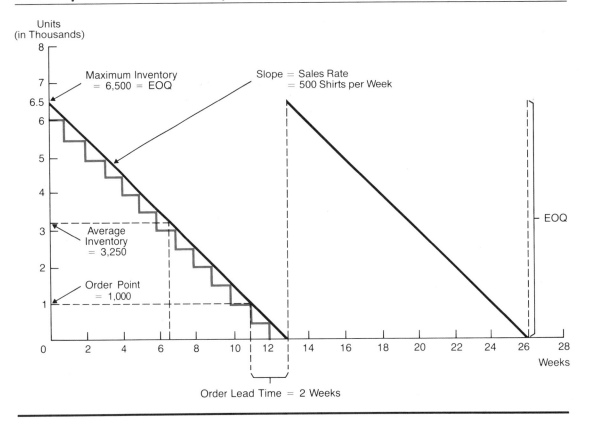

Finally, look at Cotton Top's total inventory costs for the year, assuming that the EOQ is ordered each time. Using Equation 17-6, we find total inventory costs are $8,000:

$$\text{TIC} = \text{TCC} + \text{TOC}$$

$$= (C)(P)\left(\frac{Q}{2}\right) + (F)\left(\frac{S}{Q}\right)$$

$$= 0.25(\$4.92)\left(\frac{6,500}{2}\right) + (\$1,000)\left(\frac{26,000}{6,500}\right)$$

$$\approx \$4,000 + \$4,000 = \$8,000.$$

Note these two points: (1) The $8,000 total inventory cost represents the total of carrying costs and ordering costs, but this amount does *not* include the 26,000($4.92) = $127,920 annual purchasing cost of the inventory itself. (2) As we see both in Figure 17-1 and in the numbers just preceding, at the EOQ, total carrying cost (TCC) equals total ordering cost (TOC). This property is not unique to our Cotton Tops illustration; it always holds.

Setting the Order Point

If a two-week lead time is required for production and shipping, what is Cotton Tops' order point level? If we use a 52-week year, Cotton Tops sells 26,000/52 = 500 shirts per week. Thus, if a two-week lag occurs between placing an order and receiving goods, Cotton Tops must place the order when there are 2(500) = 1,000 shirts on hand. During the two-week production and shipping period, the inventory balance will continue to decline at the rate of 500 shirts per week, and the inventory balance will hit zero just as the order of new shirts arrives.

If Cotton Tops knew for certain that both the sales rate and the order lead time would never vary, it could operate exactly as shown in Figure 17-2. However, sales do change, and production and/or shipping delays are frequently encountered; to guard against these events, the firm must carry additional inventories, or safety stocks, as discussed next.

EOQ MODEL EXTENSIONS

The basic EOQ model was derived under several restrictive assumptions. In this section, we relax some of these assumptions and, in the process, extend the model to make it more useful.

The Concept of Safety Stocks

The concept of a *safety stock* is illustrated in Figure 17-3. First, note that the slope of the sales line measures the expected rate of sales. The company *expects* to sell 500 shirts per week, but let us assume that the maximum likely sales rate is twice this amount, or 1,000 units each week. Further, assume that Cotton Tops sets the safety stock at 1,000 shirts, so it initially orders 7,500 shirts, the EOQ of 6,500 plus the 1,000 unit safety stock. Subsequently, it reorders the EOQ whenever the inventory level falls to 2,000 shirts, the safety stock of 1,000 shirts plus the 1,000 shirts expected to be used while awaiting delivery of the order.

Notice that the company could, over the two-week delivery period, sell 1,000 units a week, or double its normal expected sales. This maximum rate of sales is shown by the steeper dashed line in Figure 17-3. The condition that makes possible this higher maximum sales rate is the safety stock of 1,000 shirts.

The safety stock is also useful to guard against delays in receiving orders. The expected delivery time is two weeks, but with a 1,000 unit safety stock, the company could maintain sales at the expected rate of 500 units per week for an additional two weeks if production or shipping delays held up an order.

However, carrying a safety stock has costs. The average inventory is now EOQ/2 plus the safety stock, or 6,500/2 + 1,000 = 3,250 + 1,000 = 4,250 shirts, and the average inventory value is now (4,250)($4.92) = $20,910. This increase in

Figure 17-3
Inventory Position with Safety Stock Included

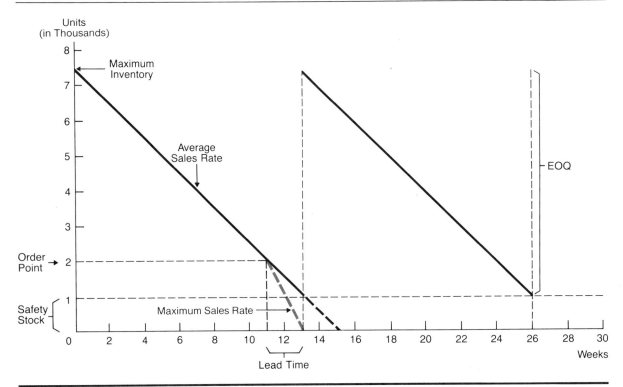

average inventory causes an increase in annual inventory carrying costs equal to (safety stock)(P)(C) = 1,000($4.92)(0.25) = $1,230.

The optimal safety stock varies from situation to situation, but, in general, it *increases* (1) with the uncertainty of demand forecasts, (2) with the costs (in terms of lost sales and lost goodwill) that result from inventory shortages, and (3) with the probability that delays will occur in receiving shipments. The optimum safety stock *decreases* as the cost of carrying this additional inventory increases.

Setting the Safety Stock Level

The critical question with regard to safety stocks is this: How large should the safety stock be? To answer this question, first examine Table 17-2, which contains the probability distribution of Cotton Tops' unit sales for an average 2-week period, the time it takes to receive an order of 6,500 T-shirts. Note that the expected sales over an average 2-week period is 1,000 units. Why do we focus on a 2-week period? Because shortages can occur only during the two weeks it takes an order to arrive.

Table 17-2
Two-Week Sales Probability Distribution

Probability	Unit Sales
0.1	0
0.2	500
0.4	1,000
0.2	1,500
0.1	2,000
1.0	Expected sales = 1,000

Cotton Tops' managers have estimated that the annual carrying cost is 25 percent of inventory value. Since each shirt has an inventory value of $4.92, the annual carrying cost per unit is 0.25($4.92) = $1.23, and the carrying cost for each 13-week inventory period is $1.23(13/52) = $0.308 per unit. Even though shortages can only occur during the 2-week order period, safety stocks must be carried over the full 13-week inventory cycle. Next, Cotton Tops' managers must estimate the cost of shortages. Assume that when shortages occur, 50 percent of Cotton Tops' buyers are willing to accept back orders, while 50 percent of its potential customers simply cancel their orders. Remembering that each shirt sells for $9.00, each one-unit shortage produces expected lost profits of 0.5($9.00 − $4.92) = $2.04. With this information, the firm can calculate the costs of different safety stock levels. This is done in Table 17-3.

For each safety stock level listed, we determine the expected cost of a shortage based on the sales probability distribution in Table 17-2. There is an expected shortage cost of $408 if no safety stock is carried; $102 if the safety stock is set at 500 units; and no expected shortage, hence no shortage cost, if a safety stock of 1,000 units is used. The cost of carrying each safety level is merely the cost of carrying a unit of inventory over the 13-week inventory period, $0.308, times the safety stock; for example, the cost of carrying a safety stock of 500 units is $0.308(500) = $154. Finally, we sum the expected shortage cost in Column 6 and the safety stock carrying cost in Column 7 to obtain the total cost figures given in Column 8. Since the 500-unit safety stock has the lowest expected total cost, Cotton Tops should carry this safety level.[5]

Of course, the resulting optimal safety level is highly sensitive to the firm's estimates of the sales probability distribution and shortage costs. Errors here could result in incorrect safety stock levels. Note also that in calculating the $2.04 per unit shortage cost, we implicitly assumed that a lost sale in one period would not result in lost sales in future periods. If shortages cause customer ill-will, this could lead to permanent sales reductions. Then the situation would be much more seri-

---

[5]For a more detailed discussion of safety stocks, see Arthur Snyder, "Principles of Inventory Management," *Financial Executive*, April 1964, 13-21. If we also knew the probability distributions of order and lead times, we could determine joint probabilities of stock-outs with various safety stock levels.

Table 17-3
Safety Stock Analysis

Safety Stock (1)	Sales during Delivery Period (2)	Probability (3)	Shortage[a] (4)	Shortage Cost (Lost Profits): $2.04 × (4) = (5)	Expected Shortage Cost: (3) × (5) = (6)	Safety Stock Carrying Cost: $0.308 × (1) = (7)	Expected Total Cost: (6) + (7) = (8)
0	0	0.1	0	$ 0	$ 0		
	500	0.2	0	0	0		
	1,000	0.4	0	0	0		
	1,500	0.2	500	1,020	204		
	2,000	0.1	1,000	2,040	204		
		1.0		Expected shortage cost =	$408	$0	$408
500	0	0.1	0	$ 0	$ 0		
	500	0.2	0	0	0		
	1,000	0.4	0	0	0		
	1,500	0.2	0	0	0		
	2,000	0.1	500	1,020	102		
		1.0		Expected shortage cost =	$102	$154	$256
1,000	0	0.1	0	$0	$0		
	500	0.2	0	0	0		
	1,000	0.4	0	0	0		
	1,500	0.2	0	0	0		
	2,000	0.1	0	0	0		
		1.0		Expected shortage cost =	$0	$308	$308

[a]Shortage = Actual sales − (1,000 Order point stock + Safety stock); positive values only.

ous, stock-out costs would be far higher, and the firm should consequently carry a larger safety stock.

The stock-out example is just one example of the many judgments required in inventory management—the mechanics are relatively simple, but the inputs are judgmental and difficult to obtain.

Quantity Discounts

Now suppose the T-shirt manufacturer offered Cotton Tops a *quantity discount* of 2 percent on large orders. If the quantity discount applied to orders of 5,000 or more, then Cotton Tops would continue to place the EOQ order of 6,500 shirts and take the quantity discount. However, if the quantity discount required orders of 10,000 or more, then Cotton Tops' inventory manager would have to compare the savings in purchase price that would result if its ordering quantity were increased to 10,000 units with the increase in total inventory costs caused by the departure from the 6,500 unit EOQ.

First, consider the total costs associated with Cotton Tops' EOQ of 6,500 units. We found earlier that total inventory costs are $8,000:

$$TIC = TCC + TOC$$

$$= (C)(P)\left(\frac{Q}{2}\right) + (F)\left(\frac{S}{Q}\right)$$

$$= 0.25(\$4.92)\left(\frac{6,500}{2}\right) + (\$1,000)\left(\frac{26,000}{6,500}\right)$$

$$\approx \$4,000 + \$4,000 = \$8,000.$$

Now, what would the total inventory costs be if Cotton Tops ordered 10,000 units instead of 6,500? The answer is $8,625:

$$TIC = (0.25)(\$4.82)\left(\frac{10,000}{2}\right) + (\$1,000)\left(\frac{26,000}{10,000}\right)$$

$$= \$6,025 + \$2,600 = \$8,625.$$

Notice that when the discount is taken, the price, P, is reduced by the amount of the discount; the new price per unit would be $0.98(\$4.92) = \$4.82$. Also note that when the ordering quantity is increased, carrying costs increase because the firm is carrying a larger average inventory, but ordering costs decrease since the number of orders per year decreases. If we were to calculate total inventory costs at an ordering quantity of 5,000, we would find that carrying costs would be less than $4,000 and ordering costs would be more than $4,000, but the total inventory costs would be more than $8,000, since they are at a minimum when 6,500 units are ordered.[6]

Thus, inventory costs would increase by $8,625 − $8,000 = $625 if Cotton Tops were to increase its order size to 10,000 shirts. However, this cost increase must be compared with Cotton Tops' savings if it takes the discount. Taking the discount would save $0.02(\$4.92) = \$0.0984$ per unit. Over the year, Cotton Tops orders 26,000 shirts, so the annual savings is $0.0984(26,000) \approx \$2,558$. Thus, the net saving to Cotton Tops, if it were to increase its ordering quantity to 10,000 units and take the discount, is $2,558 in discounts less $625 in increased inventory costs, or $1,933. Obviously, the company should order 10,000 units at a time and take advantage of the quantity discount.

Inflation

Moderate inflation—say 3 percent per year—can largely be ignored for purposes of inventory management, but higher rates of inflation must be explicitly considered. If the rate of inflation in the types of goods the firm stocks tends to be

---

[6]At an ordering quantity of 5,000 units, total inventory costs are $8,275:

$$TIC = (0.25)(\$4.92)\left(\frac{5,000}{2}\right) + (\$1,000)\left(\frac{26,000}{5,000}\right)$$

$$= \$3,075 + \$5,200 = \$8,275.$$

relatively constant, it can be dealt with quite easily—simply deduct the expected annual rate of inflation from the carrying cost percentage, C, in Equation 17-7, and use this modified version of the EOQ model to establish the working stock. The reason for making this deduction is that inflation causes the value of the inventory to rise, thus offsetting somewhat the effects of depreciation and other carrying costs factors. Since C will now be smaller, the calculated EOQ, and hence the average inventory, will increase. However, the higher the rate of inflation, the higher are interest rates, and this factor will cause C to increase, thus lowering the EOQ and average inventories.

On balance, there is no evidence that inflation either raises or lowers the optimal inventories of firms in the aggregate. Inflation should still be explicitly considered, however, for it will raise the individual firm's optimal holdings if the rate of inflation for its own inventories is above average (and is greater than the effects of inflation on interest rates), and vice versa.

Seasonal Demand

For most firms, it is unrealistic to assume that the demand for an inventory item is uniform throughout the year. What happens when there is seasonal demand, as would hold true for an ice cream company? Here the standard annual EOQ model is obviously not appropriate. However, it does provide a point of departure for setting inventory parameters, which are then modified to fit the particular seasonal pattern. The procedure here is to divide the year into seasons in which annualized sales are relatively constant, say the summer, spring and fall, and winter. Then, the EOQ model could be applied separately to each period. During the transitions between seasons, inventories would be either run down or built up with special seasonal orders.

EOQ Range

Thus far, we have interpreted the EOQ, and the resulting inventory variables, as single point estimates. It has been demonstrated that small deviations from the EOQ do not appreciably affect total inventory costs and, consequently, that the optimal ordering quantity should be viewed more as a range than as a single value.[7]

To illustrate this point, we can examine the sensitivity of total inventory costs to ordering quantity for Cotton Tops, Inc. Table 17-4 contains the results of our sensitivity analysis. We conclude that the ordering quantity could range from 5,000 to 8,000 units without affecting total inventory costs by more than 3.4 percent. Thus, we see that managers can adjust the ordering quantity within a fairly wide range without fear of significantly increasing total inventory costs.

---

[7]This is somewhat analogous to the optimal capital structure in that small changes in capital structure around the optimum do not have much effect on the firm's weighted average cost of capital. See Snyder, op. cit.

Table 17-4
EOQ Sensitivity Analysis

Ordering Quantity	Total Inventory Costs	Percentage Deviation from Optimal
3,000	$10,512	+31.4%
4,000	8,960	+12.0
5,000	8,275	+3.4
6,000	8,023	+0.3
6,500	8,000	0.0
7,000	8,019	+0.2
8,000	8,170	+2.1
9,000	8,423	+5.3
10,000	8,750	+9.4

INVENTORY CONTROL SYSTEMS

The EOQ model, together with safety stock analysis, can be used to establish the proper inventory level, but inventory management also involves the establishment of an *inventory control system*. Inventory control systems have run the gamut from very simple to extremely complex, depending on the size of the firm and the nature of its inventories. For example, one simple control procedure is the *red-line method*—inventory items are stocked in a bin, a red line is drawn around the inside of the bin at the level of the order point, and the inventory clerk places an order when the red line shows. The *two-bin method* has inventory items stocked in two bins. When the working bin is empty, an order is placed and inventory is drawn from the second bin. These procedures work well for parts such as bolts in a manufacturing process, or for many items in retail businesses.

Computerized Systems

Larger companies employ *computerized inventory control systems*. The computer starts with an inventory count in memory. As withdrawals are made, they are recorded by the computer, and the inventory balance is revised. When the order point is reached, the computer automatically places an order, and when the order is received, the recorded balance is increased. Retail stores have carried this system quite far—each item has a magnetic bar code, and, as an item is checked out, the code is read, a signal is sent to the computer, and the inventory balance is adjusted at the same time the price is fed into the cash register tape. When the balance drops to the order point, an order is placed.

A good inventory control system is dynamic, not static. A company such as IBM or General Motors stocks hundreds of thousands of different items. The sales (or use) of these various items can rise or fall quite separately from rising or falling overall corporate sales. As the usage rate for an individual item begins to rise or fall, the inventory manager must adjust its balance to avoid running short or ending up with obsolete items. If the change in the usage rate appears to be permanent, then the EOQ should be recomputed, the safety stock level should be reconsidered, and the computer model used in the control process should be reprogrammed.

Just-In-Time Systems

A relatively new approach to inventory control called *just-in-time* has been developed by Japanese firms and is gaining popularity in the United States. Toyota provides a good example of the just-in-time system. Eight of Toyota's ten factories, along with most of Toyota's suppliers, dot the countryside around Toyota City. Delivery of components is tied to the speed of the assembly line, and parts are generally delivered no more than a few hours before they are used. The just-in-time system reduces the need for Toyota and other manufacturers to carry inventories, but it requires a great deal of coordination between the manufacturer and its suppliers, both in the timing of deliveries and the quality of the goods.

Not surprisingly, U.S. automobile manufacturers are among the first domestic firms to move toward just-in-time systems. Ford has been restructuring its production system with a goal of increasing its inventory turnover from 20 times a year to 30 or 40 times. Of course, just-in-time systems place considerable pressure on suppliers. GM used to keep a 10-day supply of seats and other parts made by Lear Siegler; now GM sends in orders at four- to eight-hour intervals and expects immediate shipment. A Lear Siegler spokesman stated, "we can't afford to keep things sitting around either," so Lear Siegler has had to be tougher on its own suppliers.

INVENTORY COST HEDGING

In Chapter 15, we discussed the use of financial futures to hedge against changes in interest rate levels. Actually, futures markets were established for many industrial and agricultural commodities long before they began to be used for financial instruments. We can use Porter Electronics, which uses large quantities of copper as well as several precious metals, to illustrate inventory hedging. Suppose that in May 1986, Porter foresaw a need for 100,000 pounds of copper in March 1987 for use in fulfilling a fixed-price contract to supply solar power cells to the U.S. Government. Porter's managers are concerned that a strike by the copper mineworkers' union will occur when the union contract expires in October 1986. A strike would raise the price of copper significantly and possibly turn the expected profit on the solar cell contract into a loss.

Porter could, of course, go ahead and buy the copper now that it will need to fulfill the contract, but if it does, it will incur substantial carrying costs. As an alternative, the company could hedge against increasing copper prices in the futures market. The New York Commodity Exchange trades standard copper futures contracts of 25,000 pounds each. Thus, Porter could buy four contracts (go long) for delivery in March 1987. These contracts were trading on May 21, 1986, for about 64 cents per pound. The spot price at that date was about 62 cents per pound. If copper prices do rise appreciably over the next 10 months, the value of Porter's long position in copper futures would increase, thus offsetting some of the price increase in the commodity itself. Of course, if copper prices fall, Porter would lose money on its hedge, but the company would be buying the copper on the spot market at a cheaper price, so it would make a higher-than-anticipated profit on its sale of solar cells. Thus, hedging in the futures markets locks in the cost of raw materials and removes some uncertanties, or risks, to which the firm would otherwise be exposed.

Some firms have been using the futures markets for speculation, rather than hedging, and this can lead to disastrous results. For example, when the once-stable aluminum ingot market began fluctuating wildly in the early 1980s, aluminum fabricators did what mining companies had been doing for years—they turned to the futures market to lock in prices. That worked well, but then some companies started speculating. One company, National Aluminum Corporation, lost $41.4 million in futures trading. Basically, National Aluminum bought forward contracts to buy 100,000 tons of ingot for 80 cents a pound, which was far in excess of its planned production needs. When the contracts were near expiration, the price of ingots had dropped below 50 cents a pound, resulting in the $41.4 million loss.

SUMMARY

Inventory management centers around the balancing of a set of costs that increase with larger inventory holdings (storage costs, cost of capital, and physical deterioration) and a set of costs that decline with larger holdings (ordering costs, lost sales, and disruptions of production schedules). Inventory management has been quantified to a greater extent than most aspects of business, with the *EOQ model* being one important part of most inventory systems. This model can be used to determine the optimal order quantity, which, when combined with a specified safety stock, determines the average inventory level. Inventory control systems are used to keep track of actual inventories, and to insure that inventory levels are adjusted to changing sales levels. The commodity futures markets can be used to hedge inventory requirements, and hence to lock in future prices.

Good inventory management will result in a relatively high inventory turnover, low write-offs of obsolete or deteriorated inventories, and few instances of work stoppages or lost sales due to stock-outs. All this, in turn, contributes to a high profit margin, a high rate of return on investment, and a strong stock price.

Questions and Problems

17-1 (Inflation adjustments) If a firm calculates its optimal inventory of bolts to be 500 units when the general rate of inflation is 4 percent, is it true that the optimal inventory (in units) will almost certainly rise if the general rate of inflation climbs to 8 percent?

17-2 (Factors influencing inventory levels) Would each of the following events cause average inventories (the sum of the inventories held at the end of each month of the year divided by 12) to rise, fall, or change in an indeterminate manner?

    a. Our suppliers switch from delivery by train to air freight.

    b. We change from seasonal sales production to steady, year-round production. Sales peak at Christmas.

    c. Competition increases in the markets in which we sell.

    d. The rate of general inflation increases.

    e. Interest rates rise; other things are constant.

17-3 (EOQ model) The following relationships for inventory costs have been established for the Zocco Service Corporation:

    (1) Orders must be placed in multiples of 50 units.

    (2) Annual sales are 1,000,000 units.

    (3) The purchase price per unit is $4.

    (4) Carrying cost is 25 percent of the purchase price of goods.

    (5) Cost per order placed is $40.

    (6) Desired safety stock is 10,000 units; this amount is on hand initially.

    (7) Two days are required for delivery.

    a. What is the EOQ?

    b. How many orders should Zocco place each year?

    c. At what inventory level should a reorder be made?

    d. Calculate the total cost of ordering and carrying the working inventory if the order quantity is (1) 8,000 units, (2) 8,950 units, or (3) 10,000 units. What is the cost of carrying the safety stock?

17-4 (Accounting for inventory) Boyles Corporation produces steam turbines used in electric generating plants. Although much of their sales is by special order, the company also maintains a small inventory to meet rush orders for standard units. During 1986, Boyles produced six units for inventory. Raw material prices actually fell during 1986, and concessions by labor resulted in decreased labor costs. The following table contains the cost of each of the six units (in millions of dollars):

Unit Number	Cost
1	$12.4
2	12.0
3	11.6
4	11.2
5	10.8
6	10.6
	$68.6

Boyles had zero inventory at the beginning of 1986, and Units 1, 3, and 5 were sold during the year.

    a. What would be Boyle's cost of goods sold and ending inventory value for 1986 if the firm used (1) specific identification, (2) FIFO, (3) LIFO, and (4) weighted average accounting methods?

    b. Which method provides the greatest net income? The greatest cash flow?

    c. Which method should be used in an inflationary period?

    d. Which method is preferred if costs remain constant throughout the year?

17-5 (Quantity discounts) Koehl Electric Company sells 500,000 standard wall switches a year. Each switch costs the company $2.00. The percentage cost of carrying the switch inventory is 20 percent of inventory value. Koehl can order these switches from either of two competing manufacturers. Manufacturer A delivers in 3 days and requires a fixed ordering cost of $100 per order. Manufacturer B, which would require a fixed ordering cost of $75 per order, takes 5 days to deliver. To begin the analysis, assume that no safety stock is carried.

a. Calculate Koehl's EOQ for wall switches for both suppliers.

b. How many orders a year must be placed with each supplier (assuming that only one supplier is used)?

c. What are the reorder point levels for ordering from each supplier?

d. Considering only inventory costs, should Koehl order its wall switches from Manufacturer A or Manufacturer B?

e. Assume that the firm chose Manufacturer B as its wall switch supplier. Koehl has been offered a 1 percent discount if it orders 20,000 units or more at a time. Should the firm increase the ordering quantity to 20,000 units and take the discount?

17-6 (Safety stocks) Carlson Aircraft has an inventory of over 20,000 items used in the maintenance of small aircraft. One item is a special titanium-alloy rivet. Carlson orders these rivets every month, so it has a 30-day inventory cycle. It takes Carlson 3 days to receive the rivets once an order is placed. Each 3 days' expected usage is 1,000 rivets, but usage could be greater or less, depending on the specific types of aircraft brought in for maintenance. The 3-day usage distribution is:

Probability	Unit Usage
0.05	0
0.20	500
0.50	1,000
0.20	1,500
0.05	2,000
1.00	Expected usage = 1,000

If a shortage occurs, Carlson incurs a cost of $500 in lost maintenance time. Carlson's management is considering safety stock levels of 0; 500; or 1,000 rivets. Each rivet costs $5.00, and the annual inventory carrying cost is estimated to be 10 percent of inventory value.

a. What is the expected shortage cost, safety stock carrying cost, and expected total cost if the safety stock is set at zero?

b. What are the total costs if the safety stock is set at 500 rivets?

c. What are the total costs if the safety stock is set at 1,000 rivets?

d. Which of the three safety stock levels should Carlson adopt?

17-7 (EOQ model) Welch Manufacturing, a large manufacturer of PVC water pipes, uses large quantities of solvents in its production process. Throughout the year, the firm uses 1,000,000 gallons of one particular type of solvent. The fixed costs of placing and receiving an order of this solvent are $2,500, including a $2,000 charge for tank cleaning and inspection required by governmental regulation. The annual carrying cost of this solvent is $0.40 *per unit (gallon)* of inventory, and the solvent costs $2.00 per gallon. Welch maintains a 10,000-gallon safety stock. The solvent supplier requires a 10-day lead time from order to delivery.

    a. What is the EOQ for this inventory item?

    b. What is the average inventory dollar value, including safety stock?

    c. What is the total cost of ordering and carrying the inventory, including safety stocks? (Assume that the safety stock is on hand at the beginning of the year.)

    d. What is Welch's annual carrying cost expressed as a percentage of inventory value?

    e. Using a 360-day year, at what inventory unit level should a reorder be placed? (Again, assume a 10,000-gallon on-hand safety stock.)

17-8 (EOQ model) The following inventory data have been established for the Strassburg Corporation:

    (1) Orders must be placed in multiples of 200 units.

    (2) Annual sales are 750,000 units.

    (3) The purchase price per unit is $10.

    (4) Carrying cost is 20 percent of the purchase price of goods.

    (5) Cost per order placed is $35.

    (6) Desired safety stock is 18,000 units; this amount is on hand initially.

    (7) Five days are required for delivery.

    a. What is the EOQ?

    b. How many orders should Strassburg place each year?

    c. Calculate the total cost of ordering and carrying inventories if the order quantity is (1) 4,000 units, (2) 5,000 units, or (3) 6,000 units. What are the total costs if the order quantity is the EOQ?

    (Do Part d only if you are using the computerized diskette.)

    d. What are the EOQ and total inventory cost if

        1. Sales increase to 1,000,000 units?

        2. Fixed order costs increase to $50? (Sales remain at 750,000 units.)

        3. Purchase price increases to $15? (Leave sales and fixed costs at original values.)

Selected Additional References and Cases

The following articles provide additional insights into the problems of inventory management:

Bierman, H., Jr., C. P. Bonini, and W. H. Hausman, *Quantitative Analysis for Business Decisions* (Homewood, Ill.: Irwin, 1977).

Brooks, L. D., "Risk-Return Criteria and Optimal Inventory Stocks," *Engineering Economist*, Summer 1980, 275-299.

Kallberg, Jarl G., and Kenneth L. Parkinson, *Current Asset Management: Cash, Credit, and Inventory* (New York: Wiley, 1984).

Magee, John F., "Guides to Inventory Policy, I," *Harvard Business Review*, January-February 1956, 49-60.

————, "Guides to Inventory Policy, II," *Harvard Business Review*, March-April 1956, 103-116.

————, "Guides to Inventory Policy, III," *Harvard Business Review*, May-June 1956, 57-70.

Mehta, Dileep R., *Working Capital Management* (Englewood Cliffs, N. J.: Prentice-Hall, 1974).

Shapiro, A., "Optimal Inventory and Credit Granting Strategies under Inflation and Devaluation," *Journal of Financial and Quantitative Analysis*, January 1973, 37-46.

Smith, Keith V., *Guide to Working Capital Management* (New York: McGraw-Hill, 1979).

The Crum-Brigham casebook has a useful case on inventory management:

Case 8, "Good Connections," which focuses on the EOQ model and safety stocks.

18

CASH AND MARKETABLE SECURITIES MANAGEMENT

Approximately 1.5 percent of the average industrial firm's assets are held in the form of cash, which is defined as demand deposits plus currency. In addition, sizable holdings of near-cash short-term marketable securities such as U.S. Treasury bills (T-bills), bank certificates of deposit (CDs), money market funds, and floating rate preferred stock are often reported on corporations' financial statements. Moreover, cash and marketable securities balances vary widely both across industries and between firms within a given industry. In this chapter, we analyze the factors that determine firms' cash and marketable securities balances, and we describe the most commonly used types of marketable securities. The lessons to be learned from this chapter apply to the cash holdings of individuals and nonprofit organizations, including government agencies.

CASH MANAGEMENT

Cash is often called a "nonearning" asset. It is needed to pay for labor and raw materials, to buy fixed assets, to pay taxes, to service debt, to pay dividends, and so on. However, cash itself (and also most commercial checking accounts) earns no interest. Thus, the goal of the cash manager is to minimize the amount of cash held by the firm without adversely affecting its business activities. We begin our discussion of cash management with the cash budget.

THE CASH BUDGET

The firm estimates its needs for cash as a part of its general budgeting, or forecasting, process. First, it forecasts both fixed asset and inventory requirements, along with the times when payments must be made. This information is combined with projections about the delay in collecting accounts receivable, tax payment dates, dividend and interest payment dates, and so on. All of this information is summarized in the *cash budget*, which shows the firm's projected cash inflows and outflows over some specified period. Generally, firms use a monthly cash budget forecasted over the next year, plus a more detailed daily or weekly cash budget for the coming month. The monthly cash budget is used for planning purposes and the daily or weekly budget for actual cash control.

Constructing the Cash Budget

As noted above, cash budgets can be constructed on a monthly, a weekly, or even a daily basis. We shall illustrate the process with a monthly cash budget covering the last six months of 1987 for the Foxcraft Printing Company, a leading producer of greeting cards. Foxcraft's birthday and get-well cards are sold year-round, but the bulk of the company's sales occurs from July through November, with a peak in September, when retailers are stocking up for Christmas and New Years. All sales are made on terms that allow a cash discount for payments made within 10 days, and if the discount is not taken, the full amount is due in 40 days. However, like most other companies, Foxcraft finds that some of its customers delay payment up to 90 days. Experience shows that on 20 percent of the sales, payment is made during the month in which the sale is made; on 70 percent of the sales, payment is made during the first month after the month of the sale; and on 10 percent of the sales, payment is made during the second month after the month of the sale. Foxcraft offers a 2 percent discount for payments received within 10 days of sales. Virtually all payments received in the month of sale are discount sales.

Rather than operate its production lines at a uniform rate throughout the year, Foxcraft prints cards immediately before they are required for delivery. Paper, ink, and other materials amount to 70 percent of sales, and these items are bought the month before the company expects to sell the finished product. Its own purchase terms permit Foxcraft to delay payment on purchases for one month. Accordingly, if July sales are forecast at $10 million, then purchases during June will amount to $7 million, and this amount will actually be paid in July.

Such other cash expenditures as wages and rent are also built into the cash budget, and Foxcraft must make tax payments of $2 million on September 15 and on December 15, while payment for a new plant must be made in October. Assuming that the company's target cash balance is $2.5 million, and that it has $3 million on July 1, what are Foxcraft's monthly cash requirements for the period July through December?[1]

The monthly cash requirements are worked out in Table 18-1. The top part of the table provides a worksheet for calculating both collections on sales and payments on purchases. The first line in the worksheet gives the sales forecast for the period May through December. (May and June sales are necessary to determine collections for July and August.) Next, cash collections are given. The first line of

---

[1]Setting the target cash balance is an important part of cash management. We will discuss this topic in the next section.

Table 18-1
Foxcraft Printing Company:
Worksheet and Cash Budget
(Thousands of Dollars)

	May	June	July	Aug.	Sept.	Oct.	Nov.	Dec.
Worksheet								
Sales (gross)	$5,000	$5,000	$10,000	$15,000	$20,000	$10,000	$10,000	$5,000
Collections:								
During month of sale (20% less 2% discount)	980	980	1,960	2,940	3,920	1,960	1,960	980
During first month after sale month (70%)		3,500	3,500	7,000	10,500	14,000	7,000	7,000
During second month after sale month (10%)			500	500	1,000	1,500	2,000	1,000
Total collections	$ 980	$4,480	$ 5,960	$10,440	$15,420	$17,460	$10,960	$8,980
Purchases (70% of next month's gross sales)	$3,500	$7,000	$10,500	$14,000	$ 7,000	$ 7,000	$ 3,500	
Payments (one-month lag)		$3,500	$ 7,000	$10,500	$14,000	$ 7,000	$ 7,000	$3,500
Cash Budget								
(1) Collections (from worksheet)			$ 5,960	$10,440	$15,420	$17,460	$10,960	$8,980
(2) Payments:								
(3) Purchases (from worksheet)			$ 7,000	$10,500	$14,000	$ 7,000	$ 7,000	$3,500
(4) Wages and salaries			750	1,000	1,250	750	750	500
(5) Rent			250	250	250	250	250	250
(6) Other expenses			100	150	200	100	100	50
(7) Taxes					2,000			2,000
(8) Payment for plant construction						5,000		
(9) Total payments			$ 8,100	$11,900	$17,700	$13,100	$ 8,100	$6,300
(10) Net cash gain (loss) during month (Line 1 - Line 9)			($ 2,140)	($ 1,460)	($ 2,280)	$ 4,360	$ 2,860	$2,680
(11) Cash at start of month if no borrowing is done (start July with $3,000; calculated thereafter)			3,000	860	(600)	(2,880)	1,480	4,340
(12) Cumulative cash (cash at start + gains or – losses = Line 10 + Line 11)			$ 860	($ 600)	($ 2,880)	$ 1,480	$ 4,340	$7,020
(13) Deduct: Target cash balance			2,500	2,500	2,500	2,500	2,500	2,500
(14) Total loans outstanding required to maintain $2,500 target cash balance			$ 1,640	$ 3,100	$ 5,380	$ 1,020	—	—
(15) Surplus cash			—	—	—	—	$ 1,840	$4,520

Notes:
a. The amount shown on Line 11 for the first month, the $3,000 balance on July 1, was on hand initially. The values shown for each of the following months on Line 11 represent the cumulative cash as shown on Line 12 for the preceding month; for example, the $860 shown on Line 11 for August is taken from Line 12 in the July column.
b. When the target cash balance of $2,500 (Line 13) is deducted from the cumulative cash balance (Line 12), if a negative figure results, it is shown on Line 14 as a required loan, while if a positive figure results, it is shown on Line 15 as surplus cash.

this section shows that 20 percent of the sales during any given month are collected that month. However, customers who pay in the first month typically take the discount, so the actual cash collected in the month of a sale is reduced by 2 percent. The second line shows the collections during a given month of sales made the prior month; collections are 70 percent of the preceding month's sales. The third line gives collections from sales two months earlier—10 percent of sales in that month. The collections are summed to find the total cash receipts during each month of the cash budget period.

With the worksheet completed, the cash budget itself can be constructed. Cash from collections is given on Line 1. Next, on Lines 2 through 9, payments during each month are summarized. The difference between cash receipts and cash payments (Line 1 minus Line 9) is the net cash gain or loss during the month; for July there is a net cash loss of $2.14 million. The initial cash on hand at the beginning of the month is added to the net cash gain or loss during the month to obtain the cumulative cash that would be on hand if no financing were done; at the end of July, Foxcraft would have cumulative cash totaling $860,000 if it did no borrowing.

The target cash balance, $2.5 million, is next subtracted from the cumulative cash to determine the firm's borrowing requirements or surplus cash, whichever the case may be. At the end of July, Foxcraft expects to have cumulative cash, as shown on Line 12, of $860,000. It has a target cash balance of $2.5 million, and Foxcraft has arranged a $7 million revolving credit agreement with the Second National Bank of Dayton to meet its temporary cash needs. Thus, to maintain the target cash balance, Foxcraft would borrow $1.64 million on the revolver, and hence loans outstanding are projected to total $1.64 million at the end of July.

This same procedure is used in the following months. Sales will expand seasonally in August. With the increased sales will come increased payments for purchases, wages, and other items. Receipts from sales will also go up, but the firm will still be left with a $1.46 million net cash outflow during the month. The revolving loan balance at the end of August will be $3.10 million, the cumulative cash plus the target cash balance. The $3.10 million is also equal to the $1.64 million needed at the end of July plus the $1.46 million cash deficit for August. Sales peak in September, and the cash deficit during this month will amount to $2.28 million. Thus, the revolving loan balance will increase to $5.38 million in September.

Sales, purchases, and payments for past purchases will fall markedly in October, and collections will be the highest of any month because they reflect the high September sales. As a result, Foxcraft should enjoy a healthy $4.36 million cash surplus during October. This surplus will be used to pay down the revolver, so loans outstanding will decline by $4.36 million, to $1.02 million. In November, Foxcraft will have another cash surplus which will permit it to pay off the entire revolving loan balance. In fact, the company is expected to have $1.84 million in surplus cash by the month's end, while another cash surplus in December will swell the extra cash to $4.52 million. With such a large amount of unneeded funds, Foxcraft's treasurer will doubtless want to invest in interest-bearing securities or to put the funds to use in some other way.

Before concluding our discussion of the cash budget, we should make six additional points:

1. Our cash budget does not reflect interest on the revolving loan or income from the investment of surplus cash. This refinement could be added easily.

2. More important, if cash inflows and outflows are not uniform during the month, we could be seriously understating or overstating our financing requirements. For example, if all payments must be made on the fifth of each month, but collections come in uniformly throughout the month, then we would need to borrow much larger amounts than those shown in Table 18-1. In such a case, we would need to prepare a cash budget centered on the fifth of the month, which would identify the peak borrowing requirements, or, better yet, prepare the statement on a weekly or even daily basis.

3. Since depreciation is a noncash charge, it does not appear on the cash budget other than through its effect on taxes paid.

4. The cash budget represents a forecast, so all the values in the table are *expected* values. If actual sales, purchases, and so on are different from the forecasted levels, then our forecasted cash deficits and surpluses will also be incorrect. This point is explored further in the next section.

5. Computerized spreadsheet models are particularly well suited for constructing and analyzing the cash budget. Such models are especially useful for analyzing the sensitivity of cash flows to changes in sales levels, collection periods, and the like.

6. Finally, we should note that the target cash balance, set here at $2.5 million, would probably be adjusted over time, rising and falling with seasonal patterns and with long-term changes in the scale of the firm's operations. Factors that influence the target cash balance are discussed in the following sections. Also, the firm might even set the target cash balance at zero—this could be done if it carried a portfolio of marketable securities which could be sold to replenish the cash account or if it had an arrangement with its bank that permitted it to borrow the funds it needed on a daily basis. In that event, the cash budget would simply stop with Line 12, and the amounts on that line would represent the projected loans outstanding or surplus cash. Note, though, that most firms would find it difficult to operate with a zero balance bank account, just as you would, and the costs of such an operation would in most instances offset the opportunity cost associated with maintaining a positive cash balance. Therefore, most firms do have a positive target cash balance.

SETTING THE TARGET CASH BALANCE

When we discussed Foxcraft Printing Company's cash budget, we assumed that it has a $2.5 million target cash balance. In this section, we discuss three methods for setting the target cash balance: (1) the Baumol model, (2) the Miller-Orr model, and (3) computer simulation.

The Baumol Model

William Baumol first noted that cash balances are in many respects similar to inventories, and that the EOQ inventory model developed in Chapter 17 can be used to establish the target cash balance.[2] Baumol's model assumes (1) that the firm uses cash at a steady, predictable rate, say $1 million per week, and (2) that the firm's cash inflows from operations also occur at a steady, predictable rate, say $900,000 per week, so (3) its net cash outflows, or net need for cash, also occur at a steady rate, in this case, $100,000 per week.[3] Under these steady-state assumptions, the firm's cash balance will resemble an inventory balance, which is conceptually identical to the inventory position shown in Figure 17-2 in Chapter 17.

If our illustrative firm started at Time 0 with a cash balance of C = $300,000, and if its outflows exceeded its inflows by $100,000 per week, then (1) its cash balance would drop to zero at the end of Week 3, and (2) its average cash balance would be C/2 = $300,000/2 = $150,000. At the end of Week 3, the firm would have to replenish its cash balance, either by selling marketable securities, if it has any, or by borrowing.

If C were set at a higher level, say $600,000, then the cash supply would last longer (six weeks), so the firm would have to sell securities (or borrow) less frequently, but its average cash balance would rise from $150,000 to $300,000. Since a "transactions cost" must be incurred to sell securities (or to borrow), establishing large cash balances will lower the "ordering costs" associated with cash management. On the other hand, cash provides no income, so the larger the average cash balance, the higher the opportunity cost, or the return that could have been earned on marketable securities held in lieu of cash (or the higher the interest expense on borrowings). The situation is analogous to the one for inventories presented in Figure 17-1, and the optimal cash balance is found in the same way as in the EOQ model, but with a different set of variables:

C = amount of cash raised by selling marketable securities or by borrowing. C/2 = average cash balance.

C^* = optimal amount of cash to be raised by selling marketable securities or by borrowing. $C^*/2$ = optimal average cash balance.

F = fixed costs of making a securities trade or of borrowing.

T = total amount of net new cash needed for transactions over the entire period (usually a year, but some other period if cash needs are seasonal).

k = opportunity cost of holding cash (equals the rate of return foregone on marketable securities or the cost of borrowing to hold cash).

---

[2]See William J. Baumol, "The Transactions Demand for Cash: An Inventory Theoretic Approach," *Quarterly Journal of Economics*, November 1952, 545-556.

[3]Although our hypothetical firm is experiencing a $100,000 weekly cash shortfall, it is not necessarily headed toward bankruptcy. The firm could, for example, be highly profitable and have high earnings, but be expanding so rapidly that it is subject to chronic cash shortages that must be made up by borrowing or by selling common stock. Similarly, the firm could be in the construction business and therefore receive major cash inflows at wide intervals, but have net cash outflows of $100,000 per week between major inflows.

The total costs of cash balances consist of a holding, or opportunity, cost plus a transactions cost:[4]

$$\text{Total costs} = \text{Holding cost} + \text{Transactions cost}$$

$$= \frac{C}{2}(k) \quad + \quad \frac{T}{C}(F). \tag{18-1}$$

To minimize total costs, we differentiate Equation 18-1 with respect to C and set the derivative equal to zero:

$$\frac{d(\text{Total costs})}{dC} = \frac{k}{2} - \frac{(T)(F)}{C^2} = 0. \tag{18-2}$$

Finally, we solve for C*, the optimal cash transfer:

$$\frac{k}{2} = \frac{(F)(T)}{C^2}$$

$$C^2 = \frac{2(F)(T)}{k}$$

$$C^* = \sqrt{\frac{2(F)(T)}{k}}. \tag{18-3}$$

Equation 18-3 is the Baumol model for determining optimal cash balances. To illustrate its use, suppose F = $150; T = 52 weeks × $100,000 per week = $5,200,000; and k = 15% = 0.15. Then

$$C^* = \sqrt{\frac{2(\$150)(\$5,200,000)}{0.15}} = \$101,980.$$

Therefore, the firm should sell securities (or borrow) in the amount of $101,980 when its cash balance approaches zero, thus building its cash balance back up to $101,980. If we divide T by C*, we have the number of transactions per year: $5,200,000/$101,980 = 50.99 ≈ 51, or about once a week. The firm's average cash balance would be $101,980/2 = $50,990 ≈ $51,000.

Notice that the optimal transfer amount, and hence the target cash balance, increases less than proportionately with increases in transactions. For example, if the firm's size and consequently its net new cash needs doubled, from $5.2 million to $10.4 million per year, average cash balances would increase by only 41 percent, from $51,000 to $72,000. This suggests that there are economies of scale in the holding of cash balances, and this, in turn, gives larger firms an edge over smaller ones.[5]

---

[4]Total costs can be expressed on a before-tax basis or on an after-tax basis. Both methods lead to the same conclusions regarding target cash balances and comparative costs. Here, for simplicity, we present the model on a before-tax basis.

[5]This edge may, of course, be more than offset by other factors—after all, cash management is only one aspect of running a business.

Note that the lower the value of F, the cost of making a securities trade or of borrowing, the lower the optimal cash balance. Computers, electronic wire transfers, and other technological changes have lowered F in recent years, so required cash balances have been falling.

Also, just as in the case of inventory holdings, firms often find it desirable to hold "safety stocks" of cash designed to reduce the probability of a cash shortage to some specified level. However, if a firm is able to sell securities or to borrow on short notice—and most larger firms can do either in a matter of a couple of hours simply by making a telephone call—then the safety stock of cash can be quite low.

The Baumol model is obviously simplistic in many respects. Most important, it assumes relatively stable, predictable cash inflows and outflows, and it does not take account of any seasonal or cyclical trends. Other models have been developed to deal with uncertainty in the cash flows and with trends. Two of these models are discussed next.

The Miller-Orr Model

Merton Miller and Daniel Orr developed a model for setting the target cash balance which incorporates uncertainty in the cash inflows and outflows.[6] They assumed that the distribution of daily net cash flows is approximately normal. Each day, the net cash flow could be the expected value or some higher or lower value drawn from a normal distribution. Thus, the daily net cash flow follows a trendless random walk.

Figure 18-1 shows how the Miller-Orr model operates over time. The model sets higher and lower control limits, H and L respectively, and a target cash balance, Z. When the cash balance reaches H, such as at Point A, then $(H - Z)$ dollars are transferred from cash to marketable securities, that is, the firm purchases $(H - Z)$ dollars of securities. Similarly, when the cash balance hits L, as at Point B, then $(Z - L)$ dollars are transferred from marketable securities to cash. The lower limit, L, is set by management depending on how much risk of a cash shortfall the firm is willing to accept, and this, in turn, depends both on access to borrowings and to the consequences of a cash shortfall.

Given L as set by management, the Miller-Orr model determines the target cash balance and the upper limit. We will not show their derivations here, but Miller-Orr found these values for Z and H:

$$Z = \left[\frac{3F\sigma^2}{4k}\right]^{1/3} + L,$$

(18-4)

and

$$H = 3\left[\frac{3F\sigma^2}{4k}\right]^{1/3} + L = 3Z - 2L.$$

(18-5)

[6]See Merton H. Miller and Daniel Orr, "A Model of the Demand for Money by Firms," *Quarterly Journal of Economics*, August 1966, 413-435.

Figure 18-1
Concept of the Miller-Orr Model

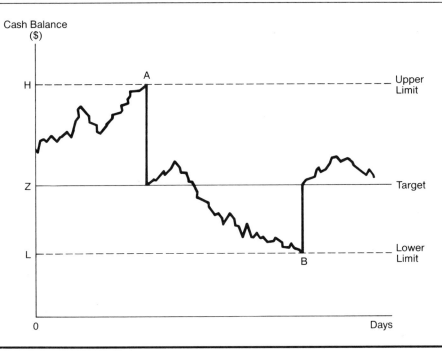

Additionally, the average cash balance is

$$\text{Average cash balance} = \frac{4Z - L}{3}. \qquad (18\text{-}6)$$

Here

Z = target cash balance.
H = upper limit.
L = lower limit.
F = fixed transactions cost.
k = opportunity cost on a daily basis.
σ^2 = variance of net daily cash flows.

To illustrate, suppose F is \$150, the opportunity cost is k = 15 percent annually, and the standard deviation (σ) of daily net cash flows is \$1,000. The daily opportunity cost and variance of daily net cash flows are, thus,

$$(1 + k)^{360} - 1.0 = 0.15$$
$$(1 + k)^{360} = 1.15$$
$$1 + k = 1.00039$$
$$k = 0.00039,$$

and

$$\sigma^2 = (1,000)^2 = 1,000,000.$$

Further, assume that management sets the lower limit, L, at zero because it can arrange transfers quickly. Substituting these values into Equations 18-4, 18-5, and 18-6 gives Z = \$6,607, H = \$19,821, and an average cash balance of \$8,809:

$$Z = \left[\frac{3(150)(1,000,000)}{4(0.00039)} \right]^{1/3} + \$0$$

$$= (288,461,500,000)^{1/3} = \$6,607,$$

and

$$H = 3(\$6,607) - 2(\$0) = \$19,821,$$

and

$$\text{Average cash balance} = \frac{4(\$6,607) - \$0}{3} = \$8,809.$$

Several other points should be noted about the Miller-Orr model:

1. The target cash balance is *not* midway between the upper and lower limits. Therefore, the cash balance will, on average, hit the lower limit more often than the upper limit. Placing the target cash balance midway between the limits would minimize transactions costs, but placing the target cash balance lower than midway decreases opportunity costs. In their derivation of the model, Miller and Orr find, assuming L = \$0, that a target of H/3 minimizes total costs.

2. The target cash balance, and consequently the acceptable range, increases with both F and σ^2; a higher F makes it more costly to hit either limit, and a larger σ^2 causes the firm to hit the limits more frequently.

3. The target cash balance decreases with k, because the higher the value of k, the more costly it is to hold cash.

4. The lower limit need not be set at zero. It could be greater than zero because of compensating balance requirements or because of management's desire to maintain a safety stock.

5. The Miller-Orr model has been tested by several firms. It performed as well or better than intuitive cash management rules. However, it starts to break down when the firm has multiple cash alternatives rather than a single type of marketable security such as T-bills.

6. The Miller-Orr model assumes that the distribution of net cash flows is symmetric about the expected net cash flow. Similar models could be derived with other assumptions concerning the net cash flow distribution. For example, the model could be adjusted for seasonal trends. Here the distribution of cash flows would not be normal, but would reflect a greater probability of either increasing or decreasing the cash balance, depending on whether the firm was moving into or away from the peak season. The target cash balance in these cases would not be one-third of the way between the lower and upper limits.

Simulation

Monte Carlo simulation can also be used to set the target cash balance.[7] To illustrate this concept, we use the Foxcraft Printing Company cash budget presented earlier in Table 18-1.

Sales and collections are the driving forces in the cash budget. In the Table 18-1 cash budget, we used expected values for sales, and these values were used to derive most of the other cash flow forecasts. Now we repeat the cash budget, but we assume that sales are subject to a probability distribution about the expected value. Specifically, we assume that the distribution of sales for each month is normal, with a coefficient of variation (CV) of 0.10 and a standard deviation which varies with the sales level. In effect, we assume that the relative variability of sales is constant from month to month. Thus in May, when expected sales are $5 million, the standard deviation of sales is $500,000:

$$CV = 0.10 = \frac{\sigma_{Sales}}{\text{Expected sales}} = \frac{\sigma_{Sales}}{\$5,000,000}$$

$$\sigma_{Sales} = 0.10(\$5,000,000) = \$500,000.$$

Similarly, the standard deviation of sales in the peak month of September is found to be $2 million, and so forth.

Of course, collections are based on actual sales rather than expected sales, so the collections pattern will reflect realized sales. If we assume that the sales realized in any month will not change Foxcraft's expectations for future sales, then purchases in any month will be based on 70 percent of next month's expected sales, but with upward or downward adjustments to reflect excess inventories on hand due to the current month's sales being less than expected or to inventory shortages that result from above-normal sales. Other payments, such as wages, rent, and so on, are assumed to be fixed for the analysis, although uncertainty could be built into them, too.

Based on these assumptions, we used the *IFPS* modeling system to conduct a Monte Carlo simulation of Foxcraft's cash budget. The simulation analysis focuses on Line 10 of Table 18-1, the net cash gain (loss) during the month. Table 18-2 summarizes the results and compares the range of likely cash gains or losses with the point estimates taken from Line 10 of Table 18-1.

Now suppose Foxcraft's managers want to be 90 percent confident that the firm will not run out of cash during July. They would set the beginning of month balance at $2,855,000 (rather than $2,500,000), because there is a 90 percent probability that the July cash flow will be no worse than a $2,855,000 net outflow.

---

[7]See Eugene M. Lerner, "Simulating a Cash Budget," in *Readings on the Management of Working Capital*, 2nd ed., Keith V. Smith, ed. (St. Paul, Minn.: West, 1980).

Table 18-2
Simulation of Foxcraft Printing Company's Cash Flows
(Thousands of Dollars)

Month	Net Cash Flow from Table 18-1	Net Cash Flow: at Least the Indicated Amount with the Indicated Probability				
		90%	70%	50%	30%	10%
July	($2,140)	($2,855)	($2,432)	($2,275)	($2,157)	($1,952)
August	(1,460)	(2,425)	(1,857)	(1,622)	(1,413)	(859)
September	(2,280)	(3,465)	(2,784)	(2,500)	(2,235)	(1,433)
October	4,360	3,786	4,129	4,334	4,712	5,799
November	2,860	2,140	2,553	2,767	2,991	3,478
December	2,680	2,367	2,567	2,684	2,937	3,464

Notes:
a. The value ($2,855) in the 90% column indicates that there is a 90% probability that the cash flow in July will be at least − $2,855 and a 10% probability that the cash flow will be less than − $2,855.
b. Point estimate values were taken from Line 10 of Table 18-1. These values should, theoretically, equal the values shown in the 50 percent column. The deviations are caused by randomness in the simulation runs.

Thus, with a beginning cash balance of $2,855,000, there would be only a 10 percent probability that the firm would run out of cash during July. This type of analysis could be extended for the other months, and it could be used in lieu of the fixed $2.5 million as the target beginning-of-month cash balance.

Note that in our simulation we assumed that sales are independent from month to month. Alternatively, we could have assumed some type of dependence such that a lower-than-expected sales level in July would signal a trend toward lower sales in the following months. This type of dependency would increase the firm's uncertainty with regard to cash flows in any given month and, consequently, increase the required cash balance needed to provide any prescribed level of confidence regarding running out of cash.

Other Factors Influencing the Target Cash Balance

Firms actually set their target cash balances as the larger of (1) their transactions balances plus precautionary (safety stock) balances or (2) their required compensating balances as determined by their agreements with banks. Transactions balances and precautionary balances depend upon the firm's volume of business, the degree of uncertainty inherent in its forecasts of cash inflows and outflows, and its ability to borrow on short notice to meet cash shortfalls. Consider again the cash budget shown for Foxcraft Printing Company in Table 18-1. The target cash balance is shown on Line 13 of the table. Other factors held constant, the target cash balance would increase if Foxcraft expanded, whereas it would decrease if Foxcraft contracted. Similarly, Foxcraft could afford to operate with a smaller target balance if it could forecast better and thus be more certain that inflows would come in as scheduled and that no unanticipated outflows such as might result from uninsured fire losses, lawsuits, and the like, would occur.

Statistics are not available on whether transactions balances or compensating balances actually control most firms' target cash balances, but compensating balance requirements do often dominate, especially during periods of high interest rates and tight money.[8]

CASH MANAGEMENT TECHNIQUES

Cash management has changed significantly over the last two decades as a result of two factors. First, interest rates have been trending up, pushing up the opportunity cost of holding cash and forcing financial managers to search for more efficient ways of managing the firm's cash. Second, new technology, particularly computerized electronic funds transfer mechanisms, has provided a means to optimize cash transactions on a real-time basis.

Most cash management activities are performed jointly by the firm and its primary bank, but the financial manager is responsible for the effectiveness of the cash management program. Cash management techniques fall generally into three categories: (1) accelerating collections, (2) determining where and when funds are needed, and getting available funds to the right place, and (3) controlling disbursements. Most business is conducted by large firms, many of which operate regionally, nationally, or even worldwide. They collect cash from many sources and make payments from a number of different points. For example, companies like IBM, General Motors, and Hewlett-Packard have manufacturing plants all around the world, even more sales offices, and bank accounts in virtually every city where they do business. Their collections are typically spread out, following sales patterns. Some disbursements are made from local offices, but most disbursements are made in the areas where manufacturing occurs, or from the home office (dividend and interest payments, taxes, debt repayments, and the like). Thus, a major corporation might have hundreds or even thousands of bank accounts, and since there is no reason to think that inflows and outflows will balance in each account, a system must be in place to transfer funds from where they are to where they are needed, to arrange loans to cover net corporate shortfalls, and to invest without delay net corporate surpluses. We discuss the most commonly used techniques for accomplishing these tasks in the following sections.

---

[8]This point is underscored by an incident that occurred at a professional finance meeting. A professor presented a scholarly paper that used operations research techniques to determine "optimal cash balances" for a sample of firms. He then reported that actual cash balances of the firms greatly exceeded their "optimal" balances, suggesting inefficiency and the need for more refined techniques. The discussant of the paper made her comments short and sweet. She reported that she had written and asked the sample firms why they had so much cash. They uniformly replied that their cash holdings were set by compensating balance requirements. The model was useful to determine the optimal cash balance in the absence of compensating balance requirements, but it was precisely those requirements that determined actual balances. Since the model did not include compensating balances as a determinant of cash balances, its usefulness was questionable.

Acceleration of Receipts

Financial managers have searched for faster ways to collect receivables since credit transactions began. Although cash collection is the financial manager's responsibility, the speed with which checks are cleared is dependent on the banking system. Several techniques are now used both to speed collections and to get funds where they are needed. Included are lockbox services, pre-authorized debits, and concentration banking.

Lockboxes

Lockboxes are one of the oldest cash management tools. The concept was first used on a large scale by RCA, but now virtually all banks that offer cash management services also offer lockbox services. In a lockbox system, incoming checks are sent to post office boxes rather than to corporate headquarters. For example, a firm headquartered in New York City might have its West Coast customers send their payments to a box in San Francisco, its customers in the Southwest send their checks to Dallas, and so on, rather than having all checks sent to New York City. Several times a day a local bank will collect the contents of the lockbox and deposit the checks into the company's local account. The bank would then provide the firm with a daily record of the receipts collected, usually via an electronic data transmission system in a format that permits on-line updating of the firm's receivables accounts.

A lockbox system reduces the time required for a firm to receive incoming checks, to deposit them, and to get them cleared through the banking system so that the funds are available for use. This time reduction occurs because mail time and check collection time are both reduced if the lockbox is located in the geographic area where the customer is located. Lockbox services can often increase the availability of funds by one to four days over the "regular" system.

Pre-Authorized Debits

A *pre-authorized debit* allows funds to be automatically transferred from a customer's account to the firm's account on specified dates. These transactions are also called "checkless" or "paperless" transactions since they are accomplished without using traditional paper checks. However, a record of payment does appear on both parties' bank statements. Pre-authorized debiting accelerates the transfer of funds because mail and check-clearing time are totally eliminated. Although pre-authorized debits are efficient, and they appear to be the trend of the future, the pace of acceptance by payers has been much slower than originally predicted. Of course, a payer who uses a pre-authorized debit system loses the disbursement float that is inherent in the paper-based system.

Concentration Banking

Lockbox systems and pre-authorized debits, although efficient in speeding up collections, result in the firm's cash being spread around among many banks. The primary purpose of *concentration banking* is to mobilize funds from decentralized receiving locations, whether they be lockboxes or decentralized company locations, into one or more central cash pools. The cash manager then uses these pools for short-term investing or reallocation among the firm's banks.

In a typical concentration system, the firm's collection banks record deposits received each day. Then, based on disbursement needs, the corporate cash manager transfers the funds from these collection points to a concentration bank. Concentration accounts allow firms to take maximum advantage of economies of scale in cash management and investment.

One of the keys to concentration banking is the ability to quickly transfer funds from collecting banks to concentration banks. One commonly used transfer tool is the *depository transfer check (DTC)*. Here's how it works: Collection banks report the amounts deposited daily to a central data collection service, which operates a nationwide data processing network. This information is then transmitted at a specified time to the firm's concentration bank. The concentration bank, based on preset cash balance targets for the collection accounts, automatically produces DTCs drawn against the collection banks; this transfers funds to the concentration bank.

A relatively new development in funds transfer is the *electronic depository transfer,* sometimes called an *ACH-DTC*. The ACH stands for automated clearinghouse, which is a communications network that provides a means of sending data from one financial institution to another. Instead of using paper checks, magnetic tape files are processed by the ACH, and all entries for a particular bank are placed on a single file which is sent to that bank. Some banks send and receive their data on tapes, while others have direct computer links to the ACH. There are actually 32 regional ACH associations, but all of the ACH facilities, except for the New York ACH, are operated by the Federal Reserve System. All ACHs guarantee one-day clearing regardless of the location of the bank on which the check was written. The ACH network sorts all transactions daily, the entries are then forwarded for processing the following day, and the processing accomplishes the actual transfer.

In addition to the automated clearinghouses, there are two other systems for wire transfer of funds which could be used for cash concentration or for other cash transfers: (1) The Federal Reserve wire service, operated by the Federal Reserve System, and (2) the Bank Wire System, which is operated by a bank member cooperative. These systems are used to move large sums that occur on a sporatic basis, such as would occur if a firm borrowed $10 million in the commercial paper market.

Disbursement Control

Accelerated collections represents one side of cash management, and controlling funds outflow is the flip side of the coin. Of course, efficient cash management can only result if both inflows and outflows are effectively managed.

Payables Centralization

No single action controls cash outflow more effectively than centralization of payables. This permits the financial manager to evaluate the payments coming due for the entire firm and to schedule cash transfers to meet these needs on a company-wide basis. Centralized disbursement also permits more efficient monitoring of payables and float balances. Of course, there are also disadvantages to a centralized disbursement system—regional offices may not be able to make prompt payment for services rendered, which can create ill-will and raise the company's operating costs. More than one firm has saved a few pennies by using a cheaper check-disbursing system but lost far more as a result of higher operating costs caused by ill-will.

Zero-Balance Accounts

Zero-balance accounts (ZBA) are special disbursement accounts having a zero-dollar balance on which checks are written. Typically, a firm establishes several ZBAs in the concentration bank and funds the ZBA from a master account. As checks are presented to a ZBA for payment, funds are automatically transferred from the master account. If the master account goes negative, it is replenished by borrowing from the bank against a line of credit, by borrowing in the commercial paper market, or by selling some T-bills from the marketable securities portfolio. Zero-balance accounts simplify the control of disbursements and cash balances, and hence reduce the amount of idle (non-interest-bearing) cash.

Controlled Disbursement Accounts

Whereas zero-balance accounts are typically established at concentration banks, *controlled disbursement accounts* can be set up at any bank. In fact, controlled disbursement accounts were initially used only in relatively remote banks, and hence this technique was originally called *remote disbursement*. The basic technique is simple: controlled disbursement accounts are not funded until the day's checks are presented against the account. The key to controlled disbursement is the ability of the bank having the account to report the total daily amount of checks received for clearance by 11 in the morning, New York time. This early notification gives financial managers sufficient time (1) to wire funds to the controlled disbursement to cover the checks presented for payment and (2) to invest excess cash at midday, when money market trading is at a peak.

MATCHING THE COSTS AND BENEFITS OF CASH MANAGEMENT

Although a number of techniques have been discussed to hold down cash balance requirements, implementing these procedures is not a costless operation. How far should a firm go in making its cash operations more efficient? As a general rule, the firm should incur these expenses so long as the marginal returns exceed the marginal costs.

For example, suppose that by establishing a lockbox system a firm can reduce its investment in cash by $1 million without increasing the risk of running short of cash. Further, suppose the firm borrows at a cost of 12 percent. The lockbox system will release $1 million, which can be used to reduce bank loans and thus save $120,000 per year. If the costs of setting up and operating the lockbox system are less than $120,000, the move is a good one, but if the costs exceed $120,000, the improvement in efficiency is not worth the cost. It is clear that larger firms, with larger cash balances, can better afford to hire the personnel necessary to maintain tight control over their cash positions. Cash management is one element of business operations in which economies of scale are present.

Very clearly, the value of careful cash management depends upon the costs of funds invested in cash, which in turn depend upon the current rate of interest. In the 1980s, with interest rates at relatively high levels, firms have been devoting a great deal of care to cash management.[9]

MARKETABLE SECURITIES MANAGEMENT

Realistically, cash and marketable securities management cannot be separated— management of one implies management of the other. In the first part of the chapter, we focused on cash management. Now we turn to marketable securities.

Rationale for Holding Marketable Securities

Marketable securities typically provide much lower yields than firms' operating assets; for example, in 1986 IBM held a $4.7 billion portfolio of marketable securities that yielded about 8 percent, while its operating assets provided a return of about 18 percent. Why would a company such as IBM have such large holdings of low-yielding assets? There are two basic reasons for these holdings: (1) They serve as a substitute for cash balances, and (2) they are used as a temporary investment. These points are considered below.

Marketable Securities as a Substitute for Cash

Some firms hold portfolios of marketable securities in lieu of larger cash balances, liquidating part of the portfolio to increase the cash account when cash outflows exceed inflows. In such situations, the marketable securities could be used as a substitute for transactions balances, for precautionary balances, for speculative balances, or for all three. In most cases, the securities are held primarily for precautionary purposes—most firms prefer to rely on bank credit to make temporary transactions or to meet speculative needs, but they may still hold some liquid assets to guard against a possible shortage of bank credit.

IBM a few years ago had substantially more marketable securities than it does today. Those large liquid balances had been built up primarily as a reserve for possible damage payments resulting from pending antitrust suits. When it became clear that IBM would win most of the suits, its liquidity need declined, and the company spent some of the funds on other assets, including repurchases of its own stock. This is a prime example of a firm's building up its precautionary balances to handle possible emergencies.

---

[9]Banks have also placed considerable emphasis on developing and marketing cash management services. Because of scale economies, banks can generally provide these services to smaller companies at lower costs than companies can operate in-house cash management systems.

Marketable Securities Held as a Temporary Investment
Temporary investments in marketable securities generally occur in one of the following two situations:

1. When the firm must finance seasonal or cyclical operations. If the firm has a conservative policy as we defined it back in Chapter 16, in Panel C of Figure 16-3, then its long-term capital will exceed its permanent assets, and marketable securities will be held when inventories and receivables are low. On the other hand, with an aggressive policy it will never carry any securities, and it will borrow heavily to meet peak needs. With a moderate policy, where maturities are matched, permanent assets will be matched with long-term financing, most seasonal increases in inventories and receivables will be met by short-term loans, and the firm will also carry marketable securities at certain times.

2. When the firm must meet some known financial requirements. Marketable securities are frequently built up immediately preceding quarterly corporate tax payment dates. Further, if a major plant construction program is planned for the near future, or if a bond issue is about to mature, a firm may build up its marketable securities portfolio to provide the required funds. For example, Commonwealth Edison, the electric utility serving Chicago, has a permanent, ongoing construction program, generating a continuous need for new capital. Since there are substantial fixed costs involved in stock or bond flotations, these securities are issued infrequently and in large amounts.

During the 1960s, Commonwealth followed the practice of selling bonds and stock *before* the capital was needed, investing the proceeds in marketable securities, and then liquidating the securities to finance plant construction. Plan A in Figure 18-2 illustrates this procedure. However, during the 1970s and early 1980s, Commonwealth encountered financial stress. It was forced to use up its liquid assets and to switch to its present policy of financing plant construction with short-term bank loans and then selling long-term securities to retire the bank loans when they have built up to some target level. This policy is illustrated by Plan B of Figure 18-2.

Plan A is the more conservative, less risky one. First, the company is minimizing its liquidity problems because it has no short-term debt hanging over its head. Second, it is sure of having the funds available to meet construction payments as they come due. On the other hand, firms generally have to pay higher interest rates when they borrow than the return they receive on marketable securities, so following the less risky strategy has a cost. Again, we are faced with a risk/return trade-off.

Criteria for Selecting Marketable Securities

A wide variety of securities and investment strategies, differing in terms of default risk, interest rate risk, liquidity risk, and expected rate of return, are available to firms that choose to hold marketable securities. In this section, we first consider the characteristics of different securities, and then we discuss how financial managers select the specific instruments held in the marketable securities portfolios.

Figure 18-2
Alternative Methods of Financing a Continuous Construction Program

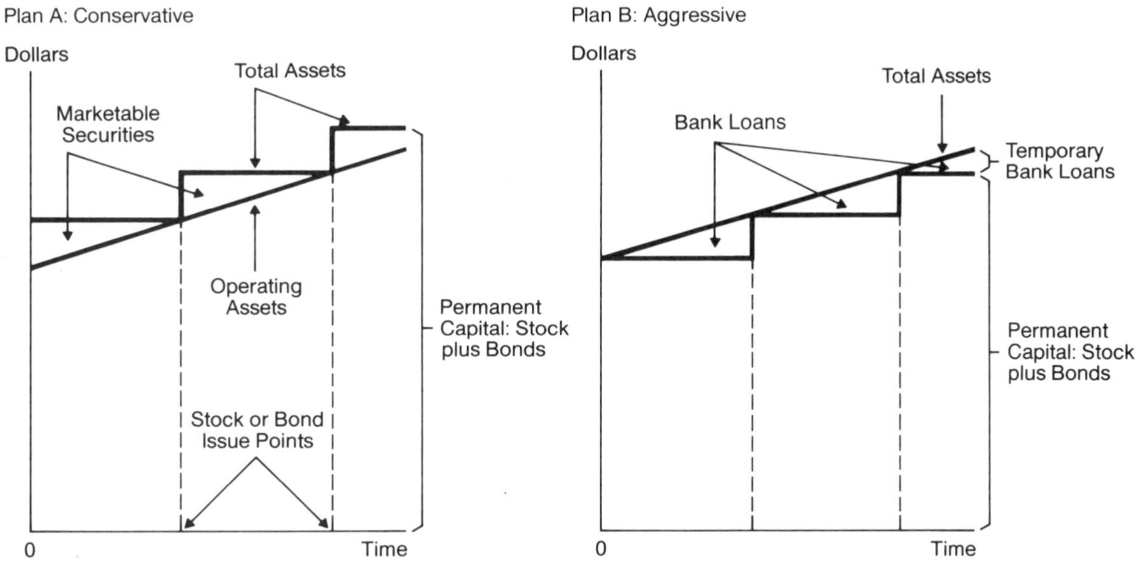

Plan A: Conservative

Dollars

Marketable Securities

Total Assets

Operating Assets

Permanent Capital: Stock plus Bonds

Stock or Bond Issue Points

0   Time

Plan B: Aggressive

Dollars

Bank Loans

Total Assets

Temporary Bank Loans

Permanent Capital: Stock plus Bonds

0   Time

Default Risk

The risk that a borrower will be unable to make interest or principal payments is known as *default risk*. If the borrower is the U.S. Treasury, default risk is essentially zero, so Treasury securities are risk free with regard to default risk. Corporate securities and bonds issued by state and local governments are subject to some degree of default risk, and they are rated with regard to their chances of going into default.

Interest Rate Risk

Bond prices vary with changes in interest rates. Further, the prices of long-term bonds are much more sensitive to shifts in interest rates than are prices of short-term securities—they have much more *interest rate risk*. Therefore, even Treasury securities are not free of all risk; they are subject to risk due to interest rate fluctuations. Thus, if Foxcraft's treasurer purchased at par $1 million of 25-year U.S. government bonds paying 9 percent interest, and if interest rates rose to 14.5 percent, then the market value of the bonds would fall from $1 million to approximately $638,000—a loss of almost 40 percent. (This actually happened from 1980 to 1982.) Had 90-day Treasury bills been held, the capital loss resulting from the change in interest rates would have been negligible.

Purchasing Power Risk

Another type of risk is *purchasing power risk*, or the risk that inflation will reduce the purchasing power of a given sum of money. This risk is important both to

Table 18-3
Securities Available for Investment of Surplus Cash

Security	Typical Maturity at Time of Issue	Approximate Yields		
		6/10/77	2/10/82	5/22/86
Suitable to Hold as Near-Cash Reserve				
U.S. Treasury bills[a]	91 days to 1 year	4.8%	15.1%	6.4%
Commercial paper[a]	Up to 270 days	5.5	15.3	6.7
Negotiable certificates of deposit (CDs) of U.S. banks	Up to 1 year	6.0	15.5	6.8
Money market mutual funds	Instant liquidity	5.1	14.0	6.3
Floating rate and market auction preferred stock[b]	Instant liquidity	N.A.	N.A.	5.0
Eurodollar market time deposits	Up to 1 year	6.1	16.2	7.1
Not Suitable to Hold as Near-Cash Reserve				
U.S. Treasury notes	3 to 10 years	6.8	14.8	7.9
U.S. Treasury bonds	Up to 30 years	7.6	14.6	8.2
Corporate bonds (AAA)[c]	Up to 40 years	8.2	16.0	8.9
State and local government bonds (AAA)[c,d]	Up to 30 years	5.7	12.8	7.8
Preferred stocks (AAA)[c,d]	30 years to perpetual	7.5	14.0	7.7
Common stocks of other corporations	Unlimited	Variable	Variable	Variable
Common stock of the firm in question	Unlimited	Variable	Variable	Variable

[a]Treasury bills and commercial paper are sold at a discount but are paid off at par upon maturity, and hence their returns are quoted on a *discount basis rate*. To obtain an interest rate which can be compared to quoted yields on coupon bonds—called a *yield basis rate*—we use the following formula:

$$\frac{\text{Yield basis rate}}{(\text{Effective annual rate})} = \frac{365(\text{Discount basis rate})}{360 - (\text{Discount basis rate})(\text{Days to maturity})}.$$

To illustrate, if we assume a 3-month (91-day) maturity, the T-bill's 6.4 percent discount basis rate on May 22, 1986, translates into a yield basis rate (or effective annual rate) of 6.6 percent:

$$\text{Yield basis rate} = \frac{365(0.064)}{360 - 0.064(91)}$$
$$= 0.0660 = 6.6\%.$$

See Robert C. Radcliffe, *Investment Concepts, Analysis, and Strategy* (Glenview, Ill.: Scott, Foresman, 1986), for a further discussion.

[b]Floating rate and market auction preferred stock is a recent innovation in near-cash securities. It is held by corporations (often through money funds designed for this purpose) because of the 80 percent dividend tax exclusion. (See Footnote 11.)

[c]Rates shown for corporate and state/local government bonds, and for preferred stock, are for longer maturities rated AAA. Lower-rated securities have higher yields. The slope of the yield curve determines whether shorter- or longer-term securities of a given rating would have higher yields.

[d]Rates are lower on state/municipal government bonds because the interest they pay is exempt from federal income taxes, and for preferred stocks because 80 percent of the dividends paid on them is exempt from federal taxes for corporate owners, who own most preferred stocks.

firms and to individual investors during times of inflation, and it is generally regarded as being lower on assets whose returns can be expected to rise during inflation than on assets whose returns are fixed. Thus, real estate and common stocks are often thought of as being better "hedges against inflation" than are bonds and other long-term fixed income securities.

Liquidity, or Marketability, Risk

An asset that can be sold on short notice for close to its quoted market price is defined as being highly *liquid*. If Foxcraft purchased $1 million of infrequently traded bonds issued by a relatively obscure company, it would probably have to accept a price reduction to sell the bonds on short notice. On the other hand, if Foxcraft bought $1 million worth of U.S. Treasury bonds, or bonds issued by AT&T, General Motors, or Exxon, it would be able to dispose of them almost instantaneously at close to the current market price. These latter bonds are said to have very little *liquidity risk*. Note, though, that although Treasury bonds and AT&T bonds may be liquid, their value will decline if they have long maturities and interest rates rise.

Returns on Securities

As we know from earlier chapters, the higher a security's risk, the higher is its expected and required rate of return. Thus, corporate treasurers, like other investors, must make a trade-off between risk and return when choosing investments for their marketable securities portfolios. Since the liquidity portfolio is generally held for a specific known need, or else for use in emergencies, the firm might be financially embarrassed should the portfolio decline in value. Accordingly, the marketable securities portfolio is generally confined to safe, highly liquid, short-term securities issued by either the U.S. government or the very strongest corporations. However, the cash managers of larger firms with substantial marketable security holdings often use sophisticated hedging strategies which permit them to take low risk positions in risky assets. We will discuss such strategies shortly.

Types of Marketable Securities

Table 18-3 lists the major types of securities available for investment, with yields as of June 10, 1977, February 10, 1982, and May 22, 1986. Depending on how

---

[11]We discussed adjustable rate and market auction preferred stock in Chapter 12. Note that the 1984 Tax Act contained provisions which reduce the dividend tax advantage previously enjoyed by corporations. Prior to this act, firms could borrow money, use the proceeds to buy preferred or common stock, and then deduct their full interest payments while paying reduced taxes on the dividend income, resulting in what was called "tax arbitrage." For example, in 1983, if a firm with a 46 percent marginal tax rate borrowed $1 million at 12.5 percent and then invested the proceeds in preferred stock with a 9 percent dividend yield, then its after-tax cost for the loan would be $12.5\%(1 - T) = 12.5\%$ $(0.54) = 6.75\%$, or $67,500, while its after-tax return on the preferred would be $9\%[1 - T(0.15)] =$ $9\%(1 - 0.069) = 9\%(0.931) = 8.38\%$, or $83,800. (Note that the dividend exclusion was reduced from 85 percent to 80 percent by the Tax Reform Act of 1986.) Thus, the firm would gain 1.63 percentage points, or $16,300, on the transaction. However, since 1984 the dividend exclusion is reduced by the amount of funds borrowed to buy the stock—the higher the percentage of funds borrowed, the lower the percentage that can be excluded.

long they will be held, the financial manager decides upon a suitable set of securities and maturity pattern for the firm's portfolio. Because the securities' characteristics change with shifts in financial market conditions, it would be misleading to attempt to give detailed descriptions of them here.

It should be noted that larger corporations, with large amounts of surplus cash, tend to own directly Treasury bills, commercial paper, and CDs, as well as Euromarket securities. Smaller firms, on the other hand, are more likely to invest through a money market or preferred stock mutual fund, because the small firm's volume of investment simply does not warrant its hiring specialists to manage the portfolio and to make sure that the securities held mature (or can be sold) at the same time cash is required. Firms can use a mutual fund and then literally write checks on the fund to meet cash needs as they arise. Interest rates on mutual funds are somewhat lower than rates on direct investments of equivalent risk because of management fees, but for smaller companies net returns may well be higher on money funds.

Aggressive Cash Investments

Traditionally, investing excess cash meant investing in Treasury securities, certificates of deposit, money funds, and so on. However, in 1986 rates on such investments yielded less than seven percent, the lowest in eight years, and these low rates caused some financial managers to be more aggressive with their cash investments.

For example, Foote, Cone & Belding Communications, Inc., an advertising agency with $2 billion in annual billings, employs specialized brokers and cash managers who use highly creative techniques to maximize the yield on the firm's liquid asset portfolio. One such technique is to write covered options—buying stocks and then selling (or writing) call options on them and pocketing the premium. However, if the stock takes a nose dive, this strategy can result in real losses. For this reason, Foote, Cone, & Belding's investment managers must constantly keep abreast of the situation and also diversify over many stocks. Even so, this technique is far from riskless.

Dividend capture is another aggressive strategy used by some firms. Here a firm such as Foxcraft Printing buys the stock of a high-dividend-yield company such as Commonwealth Edison just before the ex-dividend date and then sells the stock at least 46 days later—the minimum holding period required to get the dividend tax exclusion. Table 18-4 gives an example of an actual dividend capture strategy executed in the fall of 1985. The firm in question had $10 million of funds which would be available for at least a year, and it could afford to invest those funds fairly aggressively. It began by buying 10,000 shares of Exxon stock for $517,500 just before the holder-of-record date. The firm also hedged its dividend-capture portfolio by selling call options on the Exxon stock. The income from writing the call option, $25,625, reduced the net cost of the stock by a like amount, and that provided some protection against a drop in stock price. (Other hedging techniques could also be used.) The firm then "captured" $8,500 in dividend payments from Exxon, and finally closed its position. In this case, the stock was actually called,

Table 18-4
Dividend Capture Strategy

August 5	Buy 10,000 shares of Exxon at 51¾.	($517,500)
August 5	Sell 100 October Exxon call options (strike price = $50) at 2⁹⁄₁₆.	25,625
August 7	Holder of record date for quarterly dividend of $0.85, payable September 10.	
September 10	Dividend payment.	8,500
October 18	Exxon is trading at 52⅝. The option expires, and stock is called at $50 per share.	500,000
Net gain		$16,625
Less commissions		1,450
Pretax profit		$15,175

$$\text{Taxes} = \text{Tax on dividends} + \text{Tax on net gain from stock and options}$$

$$= 0.46(0.15)(\$8,500) + 0.46[\$25,625 - (\$517,500 - \$500,000) - \$1,450]$$

$$= \$586 + \$3,070 = \$3,656.$$

$$\text{Net profit after tax} = \$15,175 - \$3,656 = \$11,519.$$

$$\text{Annualized after-tax rate of return} = \left(1 + \frac{\$11,519}{(\$517,500 - \$25,625)}\right)^{365/74} - 1.0$$

$$= (1.0234)^{365/74} - 1.0 = 12.1\%.$$

but in other situations the firm would merely sell the stock in the secondary market.

The strategy employed in Table 18-4 certainly has its risks. If Exxon's stock price had dropped below 49³⁄₁₆, a trading loss would have occurred. But this did not happen, and the firm realized a $15,175 pre-tax profit. Taxes of $3,070 were paid on the net proceeds from the stock and option transactions, but the effective tax rate on the dividend income was only 46%(0.15) = 6.9%, and hence taxes on the dividends amounted to only $586. The end result was an after-tax profit of $11,519, which translates into a 12.1 percent effective after-tax annual rate of return. During the same period, the after-tax return on Treasury bills was only about 4 percent.[12]

---

[12]There are many other nontraditional cash investment techniques. For example, some firms are now getting into the most exotic money management game in town, "programmed trading," whereby stock index futures are hedged against a portfolio consisting of the stocks in the index, and trades are executed by a computer. A description of this procedure, which is essentially riskless and thus suitable as an investment for the liquidity portfolio, would go beyond the scope of this book, but we mention it to illustrate the point that cash and liquidity management can be a highly sophisticated process.

Of course, these more aggressive cash investment strategies carry more risk than the more traditional instruments. We suspect that large firms with increasingly sophisticated cash managers will accept the risk and go for the higher returns on at least part of their portfolios, while smaller firms will continue to park their excess cash in more conservative securities.

SUMMARY

The first topic covered in this chapter was *cash management*. We saw that the key element in any cash management system is the *cash budget*, which is a forecast of cash inflows and outflows during a given planning period. The cash budget shows whether the firm can expect a cash deficit, in which case plans must be made to obtain external capital, or a cash surplus, in which case plans should be made to invest the available funds. The next section of the chapter dealt with three models designed to determine the target cash balance. The *Baumol model*, based on the standard EOQ inventory model, balances the opportunity cost of holding cash against the transactions costs associated with replenishing the cash account either by selling off marketable securities or by borrowing. The other models discussed were the *Miller-Orr model* and *simulation*.

Our study of marketable securities began with a discussion of why securities are held. Primarily, they are held (1) as a reserve for future contingencies; (2) to meet seasonal needs, with holdings being built up during the slack season and then liquidated when cash requirements are high; (3) to meet known future cash requirements such as construction progress payments or taxes; and (4) immediately after the sale of long-term securities. Given the motives for holding risky securities, treasurers generally do not want to gamble by holding them—safety is the watchword, and rarely will a treasurer sacrifice safety for the higher yields offered on risky securities. However, if a firm is in a position to take a bit of risk, it may be able to get a significantly higher return on its short-term portfolio by such aggressive strategies as *dividend capture programs*.

Questions and Problems

18-1   (Cash budgeting) Neil and Terry Sicherman recently leased space in the Southside Mall and opened a new business, Sicherman's Coin Shop. Business has been good, but the Sichermans have frequently run out of cash. This has necessitated late payment on certain orders, and this, in turn, is beginning to cause a problem with suppliers. The Sichermans plan to borrow money from the bank to have cash ready as needed, but first they need a forecast of just how much they must borrow. Accordingly, they have asked you to prepare a cash budget for the critical period around Christmas, when needs will be especially high.

Sales are made on a *cash basis only*. The Sichermans' purchases must be paid for the following month. The Sichermans pay themselves a salary of $4,800 per month, and the rent is $2,000 per month. In addition, the Sichermans must make a tax payment of $12,000 in December. The current cash on hand (on December 1) is $400, but the Sichermans have agreed to maintain an end-of-month bank balance of $6,000, their target cash balance. (Disregard till cash, which is insignificant because the Sichermans keep only a small amount on hand in order to lessen the chances of robbery.)

The estimated sales and purchases for December, January, and February are shown next. Purchases during November amounted to $140,000.

	Sales	Purchases
December	$160,000	$40,000
January	40,000	40,000
February	60,000	40,000

a. Prepare a cash budget for December, January, and February.

b. Now suppose the Sichermans were to start selling on a credit basis on December 1, giving customers 30 days to pay. All customers accept these terms, and all other facts in the problem are unchanged. What would the company's loan requirements be at the end of December in this case?

18-2 **(Target cash balance)** Explain how each of the following factors would probably affect a firm's target cash balance if all other factors are held constant.

a. The firm institutes a new billing procedure which better synchronizes its cash inflows and outflows.

b. The firm develops a new sales forecasting technique which improves its forecasts.

c. The firm reduces its portfolio of U.S. Treasury bills.

d. The firm arranges to use an overdraft system for its checking account.

e. The firm borrows a large amount of money from its bank, and it also begins to write far more checks than it did in the past.

f. Interest rates on Treasury bills rise from 5 to 10 percent.

18-3 **(Cash budgeting)** The Torrence Company is planning to request a line of credit from its bank. The following sales forecasts have been made for 1987 and 1988:

May 1987	$150,000
June	150,000
July	300,000
August	450,000
September	600,000
October	300,000
November	300,000
December	75,000
January 1988	150,000

Collection estimates were obtained from the credit and collection department as follows: collected within the month of sale, 10 percent; collected the month following the month of sale, 85 percent; and collected the second month following the month of sale, 5 percent. Payments for labor and raw materials are typically made during the month following the month in which these costs are incurred. Total labor and raw materials costs are estimated for each month as follows (payments are made the following month):

May 1987	$ 75,000
June	75,000
July	105,000
August	735,000
September	255,000
October	195,000
November	135,000
December	75,000

General and administrative salaries will amount to approximately $29,250 a month; lease payments under long-term lease contracts will be $9,750 a month; depreciation charges will be $39,000 a month; miscellaneous expenses will be $2,925 a month; income tax payments of $68,250 will be due in both September and December; and a progress payment of $195,000 on a new research laboratory must be paid in October. Cash on hand on July 1 will amount to $143,000, and a minimum cash balance of $97,500 should be maintained throughout the cash budget period.

a. Prepare a monthly cash budget for the last six months of 1987. How much money will Torrence need to borrow (or how much will it have available to invest) each month?

b. Suppose receipts from sales come in uniformly during the month—that is, cash payments come in 1/30 each day—but all outflows are paid on the fifth of the month. Would this have an effect on the cash budget— in other words, would the cash budget you have prepared be valid under these assumptions? If not, what could be done to make a valid estimation of financing requirements? No calculations are required, although calculations can be used to illustrate the effects.

c. Torrence produces on a seasonal basis, just ahead of sales. Without making any calculations, discuss how the company's current ratio and debt ratio would vary during the year assuming all financial requirements were met by short-term bank loans. Could changes in these ratios affect the firm's ability to obtain bank credit?

d. If you prepared the cash budget in Part a correctly, you would show a surplus at the end of July, which increases by the end of August. Suggest some alternative investments for this money. Be sure to consider the pros and cons of long-term versus short-term debt instruments, and the appropriateness of investing in common stock.

e. Would your choice of securities in Part d be affected if the cash budget showed continuous cash surpluses versus alternating surpluses and deficits?

(Do Parts f, g, and h only if you are using the computerized diskette.)

f. By offering a 2 percent cash discount for paying within the month of sale, the credit manager has revised the collection percentages to 50 percent, 35 percent, and 15 percent, respectively. How will this affect the loan requirements?

g. Return the payment percentages to their base case values and the discount to zero. Now suppose sales fall to only 70 percent of the forecasted level. Production is maintained, so cash outflows are unchanged. How does this affect Torrence's financial requirements?

h. Return sales to the forecasted level (100%), and suppose collections slow down to 5%, 20%, and 75% for the three months, respectively. How does this affect financial requirements? If Torrence went to a cash-only sales policy, how would that affect requirements, other factors held constant?

18-4 (Baumol model) You have just been hired as the cash manager of the Broske Company. Your first task is to determine the target cash balance. Broske expects to need

$1,000,000 of net new cash during the coming year. This requirement occurs at a relatively constant rate over the year. The firm plans to meet this cash requirement by borrowing from Bank A at an annual interest rate of 10 percent. The fixed cost of transferring funds from the bank is $50 per transfer.

    a. Assume that the firm will not carry a cash "safety stock." What average cash balance is indicated by the Baumol model? How many cash transfers are expected over the year?

    b. Suppose the firm wants to maintain a $5,000 cash "safety stock," which is currently on hand. What would be the new average cash balance?

18-5 (Baumol model) The Upton Company has accumulated $100,000 in excess cash. However, it is expected that the firm will need the entire amount to cover cash outflows anticipated to occur evenly over the coming year. Upton has the funds invested in commercial paper that pays 10 percent annually. The cost of transferring funds is $50 per transaction.

    a. What is Upton's target cash balance according to the Baumol model? What is Upton's total cost of cash balances?

    b. As Upton's cash manager, you are concerned about whether the Baumol model is on a before-tax or after-tax basis. Upton's federal-plus-state tax rate is 40 percent. What is Upton's target cash balance and total costs of cash balances on an *after-tax* basis?

    c. Upton is considering putting its excess cash in a floating rate preferred stock mutual fund. The fund pays 10 percent annually, but only 20 percent of its dividends are taxable. What affect would this decision have on Upton's target cash balance and cost of cash balances?

18-6 (Miller-Orr model) The Taussig Corporation has estimated that the standard deviation of its daily net cash flows is $2,500. The firm pays $50 in transaction costs to transfer funds into and out of commercial paper that pays 7.465 percent annual interest. Taussig uses the Miller-Orr model to set its target cash balance. Additionally, the firm has decided to maintain a $10,000 minimum cash balance (lower limit).

    a. What is Taussig's target cash balance?

    b. What are the upper and lower limits?

    c. What are Taussig's decision rules? (That is, when is a transaction called for, and what is the transaction?)

    d. What is Taussig's expected average cash balance?

18-7 (Cash budgeting) Piedmont Furniture Company, a prominent manufacturer of Early American style furniture, expects gross sales of $120,000 in January, $140,000 in February, $150,000 in March, $160,000 in April, and $180,000 in May. Piedmont has found, on average, that 50 percent of its customers take the 2 percent discount, and these customers are assumed to pay in the month of sale. Another 25 percent pay the month following the sale, while the remaining 20 percent pay in the second month following the sale. Piedmont's bad debt losses are currently running at 5 percent.

    The furniture is produced one month prior to sale. Wages, which are 30 percent of sales, are paid in the month of manufacture. The materials must be purchased two months prior to sale, but Piedmont's terms with its suppliers allows it to pay one month after the materials are purchased. Materials amount to 50 percent of sales.

    Piedmont's fixed assets are being depreciated using the appropriate ACRS tables. Depreciation expense is forecast to be $10,000 in March and $9,800 in April. Administrative and selling expenses run $7,000 per month. The plant site is leased, with before-tax lease payments running at $2,000 per month. Piedmont is in the 40 percent federal-plus-state tax bracket.

Estimated taxes are paid in the first month of each calendar quarter. Piedmont's tax liability for the next whole year is estimated at $50,000.

a. Construct Piedmont's cash budget for March and April. What are the net cash flows for March and April?

b. Piedmont's target cash balance is $5,000, which it has on March 1. In order to maintain this balance, Piedmont borrowed $6,400 in January and $3,800 in February against its $50,000 line of credit at the bank. What are Piedmont's cumulative borrowings at the end of April? Is the line of credit sufficient up to this point?

Additional References and Cases

Perhaps the best way to get a good feel for the current state of the art in cash management is to look through recent issues of The Journal of Cash Management, *a relatively new publication aimed at professionals in the field.*

For more information on cash management in general, see

Beehler, Paul J., *Contemporary Cash Management* (New York: Wiley, 1983).

Discoll, Mary C., *Cash Management: Corporate Strategies for Profit* (New York: Wiley, 1983).

Key references on cash balance models include the following:

Daellenbach, Hans G., "Are Cash Management Optimization Models Worthwhile?" *Journal of Financial and Quantitative Analysis*, September 1974, 607-626.

Miller, Merton H., and Daniel Orr, "The Demand for Money by Firms: Extension of Analytic Results," *Journal of Finance*, December 1968, 735-759.

Mullins, David Wiley, Jr., and Richard B. Homonoff, "Applications of Inventory Cash Management Models," in *Modern Developments in Financial Management*, Stewart C. Myers, ed. (New York: Praeger, 1976).

Stone, Bernell K., "The Use of Forecasts for Smoothing in Control-Limit Models for Cash Management," *Financial Management*, Spring 1972, 72-84.

For more information on float management, see

Batlin, C. A., and Susan Hinko, "Lockbox Management and Value Maximization," *Financial Management*, Winter 1981, 39-44.

Gitman, Lawrence J., D. Keith Forrester, and John R. Forrester, Jr., "Maximizing Cash Disbursement Float," *Financial Management*, Summer 1976, 32-41.

Nauss, Robert M., and Robert E. Markland, "Solving Lockbox Location Problems," *Financial Management*, Spring 1979, 21-31.

The following articles provide more information on cash concentration systems:

Stone, Bernell K., and Ned C. Hill, "Cash Transfer Scheduling for Efficient Cash Concentration," *Financial Management*, Autumn 1980, 35-43.

———, "The Design of a Cash Concentration System," *Journal of Financial and Quantitative Analysis*, September 1981, 301-322.

For greater insights into compensating balance requirements, see

Campbell, Tim S., and Leland Brendsel, "The Impact of Compensating Balance Requirements on the Cash Balances of Manufacturing Corporations," *Journal of Finance*, March 1977, 31-40.

Frost, Peter A., "Banking Services, Minimum Cash Balances, and the Firm's Demand for Money," *Journal of Finance*, December 1970, 1029-1039.

For more information on marketable securities, see any of the investment textbooks referenced in Chapter 2, or see

Brown, Keith C., and Scott L. Lummer, "A Reexamination of the Covered Call Option Strategy for Corporate Cash Management," *Financial Management*, Summer 1986, 13-17.

Kamath, Ravindra R. et al, "Management of Excess Cash: Practices and Developments," *Financial Management*, Autumn 1985, 70-77.

Stigum, M., *The Money Market: Myth, Reality, and Practice* (Homewood, Ill.: Dow Jones-Irwin, 1978).

Van Horne, J. C., *Financial Market Rates and Flows* (Englewood Cliffs, N. J.: Prentice-Hall, 1984).

Zivney, Terry L., and Michael J. Alderson, "Hedged Dividend Capture with Stock Index Options," *Financial Management*, Summer 1986, 5-12.

The following cases focus on cash management:

Case 6, "Bollinger Corporation," in the Crum-Brigham casebook, which illustrates the mechanics of the cash budget and the rationale behind its use.

"Austin, Limited," in the Harrington casebook, which examines changes in a firm's cash disbursement system.

19

RECEIVABLES MANAGEMENT AND CREDIT POLICY

Firms would, in general, rather sell for cash than on credit, but competitive pressures force most firms to offer credit. Thus, goods are shipped, inventories are reduced, and an account receivable is created. Eventually, the customer will pay the account, at which time (1) the firm will receive cash and (2) its receivables will decline. Managing receivables has both direct and indirect costs, but it also has an important benefit—granting credit will increase sales. The optimal credit policy is the one which maximizes the firm's profits over time, giving consideration to the risk assumed.

RECEIVABLES MANAGEMENT

Receivables management begins with the decision of whether or not to grant credit. In this section, we discuss the manner in which a firm's receivables build up, and we also present several alternative means of monitoring receivables. A monitoring system is important, because without it, receivables will build up to excessive levels, cash flows will decline, and bad debts will offset the profits on sales. Corrective action is often needed, and the only way to know whether the situation is getting out of hand is to set up and then follow a good receivables control system.

The Accumulation of Receivables

The total amount of accounts receivable outstanding at any given time is determined by two factors: (1) the volume of credit sales and (2) the average length of time between sales and collections. For example, suppose the Boston Lumber Company (BLC), a wholesale distributor of lumber products, opens a warehouse on January 1 and, starting the first day, makes sales of $1,000 each day. (For simplicity, we assume that all sales are on credit.) Customers are given 10 days in which to pay. At the end of the first day, accounts receivable will be $1,000; they will rise to $2,000 by the end of the second day; and by January 10, they will have risen to $10(\$1,000) = \$10,000$. On January 11, another $1,000 will be added to receivables, but payments for sales made on January 1 will reduce receivables by $1,000, so total accounts receivable will remain constant at $10,000. In general, once the firm's operations have stabilized, this situation will exist:

$$\frac{\text{Accounts}}{\text{receivable}} = \frac{\text{Credit sales}}{\text{per day}} \times \frac{\text{Length of}}{\text{collection period}}$$

$$= \quad \$1,000 \quad \times \quad 10 \quad \text{days} = \$10,000.$$

If either credit sales or the collection period changes, such changes will be reflected in accounts receivable.

Notice that the $10,000 investment in receivables must be financed. To illustrate, suppose that when the store opened on January 1, BLC's shareholders had put up $800 as common stock and used this money to buy the goods sold the first day. The $800 worth of inventory will be sold for $1,000; thus, BLC's gross margin is $200 or 25 percent. In this situation, the initial balance sheet would be as follows:[1]

Inventories	$800	Common equity	$800
Total assets	$800	Total claims	$800

At the end of the day, the balance sheet would look like this:

Accounts receivable	$1,000	Common equity	$ 800
Inventories	0	Retained earnings	$ 200
Total assets	$1,000	Total claims	$1,000

In order to remain in business, BLC must replenish inventories. To do so requires that $800 of goods be purchased, and this requires $800 in cash. Assuming that BLC borrows the $800 from the bank, the balance sheet at the start of the second day will be as follows:

Accounts receivable	$1,000	Notes payable to bank	$ 800
Inventories	800	Common equity	800
		Retained earnings	200
Total assets	$1,800	Total claims	$1,800

At the end of the second day, the inventories will have been converted to receivables, and the firm will have to borrow another $800 to restock for the third day.

---

[1] Note that the firm would need other assets such as cash, fixed assets, and a permanent stock of inventory. Also, overhead costs would have to be deducted, so retained earnings would be less than the figures shown here. We abstract from these details here so that we may focus on receivables.

This process will continue, provided the bank is willing to lend the necessary funds, until the beginning of the eleventh day, when the balance sheet reads as follows:

Accounts receivable	$10,000	Notes payable to bank	$ 8,000
Inventories	800	Common equity	800
		Retained earnings	2,000
Total assets	$10,800	Total claims	$10,800

From this point on, $1,000 of receivables will be collected every day, and $800 of these funds can be used to purchase new inventories.

This example should make it clear (1) that accounts receivable depend jointly on the level of credit sales and the collection period, (2) that any increase in receivables must be financed in some manner, but (3) that the entire amount of receivables does not have to be financed because the profit portion ($200 of each $1,000 of sales) does not represent a cash outflow. In our example, we assumed bank financing, but, as noted in Chapter 16, there are many alternative ways to finance current assets.

Monitoring the Receivables Position

The optimal credit policy, and hence the optimal level of accounts receivable, depends on the firm's own unique operating conditions. For example, a firm with excess capacity and low variable production costs should extend credit more liberally and carry a higher level of receivables than a firm operating at full capacity on a slim profit margin. However, even though optimal credit policies vary among firms, or even for a single firm over time, it is still useful to analyze the effectiveness of the firm's credit policy in an overall, aggregate sense. Investors—both stockholders and bank loan officers—should pay close attention to accounts receivable management, for otherwise they could be misled by reported financial statements and later suffer serious losses on their investments.

When a credit sale is made, the following events occur: (1) Inventories are reduced by the cost of goods sold, (2) accounts receivable are increased by the sales price, and (3) the difference is profit which is added to retained earnings. If the sale is for cash, the profit is definitely earned, but if the sale is on credit, the profit is not actually earned unless and until the account is collected. Firms have been known to encourage "sales" to very weak customers in order to inflate reported profits. This could boost the firm's stock price, at least until credit losses begin to lower earnings, at which time the stock price will fall. Analyses along the lines suggested in the following sections would detect any such questionable practice, as well as any unconscious deterioration in the quality of accounts receivable. Such early detection could help both investors and bankers avoid losses.[2]

---

[2]Accountants are increasingly interested in these matters. Investors have sued several of the Big Eight accounting firms for substantial damages when (1) profits were overstated and (2) it could be shown that the auditors should have conducted an analysis along the lines described here and then should have reported the results to stockholders on the audited financial statements.

Average Collection Period

Suppose Super Sets, Inc., a television manufacturer, sells 200,000 television sets a year at a sales price of $198 each. Further, assume that all sales are on credit, with terms of 2/10, net 30. Finally, assume that 70 percent of the customers take discounts and pay on Day 10, while the other 30 percent pay on Day 30.

Super Sets' *average collection period (ACP)* is 16 days:

$$\text{ACP} = 0.7(10 \text{ days}) + 0.3(30 \text{ days}) = 16 \text{ days}.$$

The ACP is sometimes called *days sales outstanding (DSO)*.

Super Sets' *average daily sales (ADS)*, assuming a 360-day year, is $110,000:

$$\text{ADS} = \frac{\text{Annual sales}}{360} = \frac{200,000(\$198)}{360}$$

$$= \frac{\$39,600,000}{360} = \$110,000.$$

If the company had made cash as well as credit sales, we would have concentrated on credit sales only, and calculated average daily *credit* sales.

Super Sets' accounts receivable, assuming a constant, uniform rate of sales all during the year, will at any point in time be $1,760,000:[3]

$$\text{Receivables} = (\text{ADS})(\text{ACP}) = (\$110,000)(16) = \$1,760,000.$$

Finally, note that its ACP is a measure of the average length of time it takes Super Sets' customers to pay off their credit purchases, and the ACP is often compared with an industry average ACP. For example, if all television manufacturers sell on the same credit terms, and if the industry average ACP is 25 days versus Super Sets' 16-day ACP, then Super Sets either has a higher percentage of discount customers or else its credit department is exceptionally good at ensuring prompt payment.

The ACP can also be compared with the firm's own credit terms. For example, suppose Super Sets' ACP had been running at a level of 35 days versus its 2/10, net 30, credit terms. With a 35-day ACP, some customers would obviously be taking more than 30 days to pay their bills. In fact, if some customers were paying within 10 days to take advantage of the discount, the others would, on average, have to be taking much longer than 35 days. One way to check this possibility is to use an aging schedule as described in the next section.

Aging Schedules

An *aging schedule* breaks down a firm's receivables by age of account. Table 19-1 contains the December 31, 1986 aging schedules of two television manufacturers, Super Sets and Wonder Vision. Both firms offer the same credit terms, 2/10, net

---

[3]Note that the ACP can be calculated, given a firm's accounts receivable balance and its average daily credit sales, as follows:

$$\text{ACP} = \frac{\text{Receivables}}{\text{ADS}} = \frac{\$1,760,000}{\$110,000} = 16 \text{ days}.$$

Table 19-1
Aging Schedules

Age of Account (Days)	Super Sets		Wonder Vision	
	Value of Account	Percentage of Total Value	Value of Account	Percentage of Total Value
0-10	$1,232,000	70%	$ 825,000	47%
11-30	528,000	30	460,000	26
31-45	0	0	265,000	15
46-60	0	0	179,000	10
Over 60	0	0	31,000	2
Total receivables	$1,760,000	100%	$1,760,000	100%

30, and both show the same total receivables. Note that Super Sets' aging schedule indicates that all of its customers pay on time—70 percent pay on Day 10 while 30 percent pay on Day 30. However, Wonder Vision's schedule shows that many of its customers are not abiding by its credit terms—some 27 percent of its receivables are more than 30 days due, even though Wonder Vision's credit terms call for full payment by Day 30.

Aging schedules cannot be constructed from the type of summary data that are reported in financial statements; data must be extracted from the firm's accounts receivable ledger. However, well-run firms have computerized their accounts receivable records, so it is easy to determine the age of each invoice, to sort electronically by age categories, and thus to generate an aging schedule. Note, though, that although changes in aging schedules over time do provide more information than does the corporate ACP taken alone, we discuss a better way to monitor the performance of the credit department in the next section.

The Payments Pattern Approach

Both the ACP and aging schedules are affected by a firm's pattern of sales. Thus, changes in sales levels, including seasonal or cyclical changes, can change a firm's ACP and aging schedule even though its customers' payment behavior has not changed. For this reason, a procedure called the *payments pattern approach* has been developed to measure any changes that might be occurring in customers' payment behavior.[4] To illustrate the payments pattern approach, consider the credit sales of Hanover Manufacturing Company, a small manufacturer of hand tools which commenced operations in January 1986. Table 19-2 contains Hanover's credit sales and receivables data for 1986. Column 2 shows that Hanover's credit sales are seasonal, with the lowest sales in the fall and winter months and the highest sales during the summer.

---

[4]See Wilbur G. Lewellen and Robert W. Johnson, "A Better Way to Monitor Accounts Receivable," *Harvard Business Review*, May-June 1972, 101-109; and Bernell Stone, "The Payments-Pattern Approach to the Forecasting and Control of Accounts Receivable," *Financial Management*, Autumn 1976, 65-82.

Table 19-2
Hanover Manufacturing Company:
Receivables Data for 1986
(Thousands of Dollars)

Month (1)	Credit Sales (2)	Receivables (3)	Quarterly		Cumulative (Year to date)	
			ADS[a] (4)	ACP[b] (5)	ADS (6)	ACP (7)
January	$ 60	$ 54				
February	60	90				
March	60	102	$2.00	51 days	$2.00	51 days
April	60	102				
May	90	129				
June	120	174	3.00	58 days	2.50	70 days
July	120	198				
August	90	177				
September	60	132	3.00	44 days	2.67	49 days
October	60	108				
November	60	102				
December	60	102	2.00	51 days	2.50	41 days

[a]ADS = Average daily sales.
[b]ACP = Average collection period.

Now assume that 10 percent of Hanover's customers pay in the same month that the sale is made, that 30 percent pay in the first month following the sale, that 40 percent pay in the second month, and that the remaining 20 percent pay in the third month. Further, assume that Hanover's customers have the same payment behavior throughout the year; that is, they always take the same length of time to pay. On the basis of this payment pattern, Column 3 of Table 19-2 contains Hanover's receivables balance at the end of each month. For example, during January, Hanover has $60,000 in sales. Ten percent of the customers paid during the month of sale, so the receivables balance at the end of January was $60,000 − 0.1($60,000) = (1.0 − 0.1)($60,000) = 0.9($60,000) = $54,000. By the end of February, 10% + 30% = 40% of the customers had paid for January's sales, and 10 percent had paid for February's sales. Thus, the receivables balance at the end of February was 0.6($60,000) + 0.9($60,000) = $90,000. By the end of March, 80 percent of January's sales had been paid, 40 percent of February's had been paid, and 10 percent of March's sales had been paid, so the receivables balance was 0.2($60,000) + 0.6($60,000) + 0.9($60,000) = $102,000. And so on.

Columns 4 and 5 give Hanover's average daily sales (ADS) and average collection period (ACP) respectively, as these measures would be calculated from quarterly financial statements. For example, in the April-June quarter, ADS = ($60,000 + $90,000 + $120,000)/90 = $3,000, and the end-of-quarter (June 30) ACP = $174,000/$3,000 = 58 days. Columns 6 and 7 also show ADS and ACP, but here

Table 19-3
Hanover Manufacturing Company:
Aging Schedules for 1986
(Thousands of Dollars)

Age of Accounts (Days)	Value and Percentage of Total Value of Accounts Receivable at the End of Quarter Ending							
	March 31		June 30		September 30		December 31	
0–30	$ 54	53%	$108	62%	$ 54	41%	$ 54	53%
31–60	36	35	54	31	54	41	36	35
61–90	12	12	12	7	24	18	12	12
	$102	100%	$174	100%	$132	100%	$102	100%

they are calculated on the basis of the semiannual report, using accumulated sales data for the first six months. For example, at the end of June, ADS = $450,000/180 = $2,500 and ACP = $174,000/$2,500 = 70 days. (For the entire year, sales are $900,000; ADS = $2,500, and ACP at year-end = 41 days. These last two figures are shown in the lower right corner of the table.)

The data in Table 19-2 illustrate two major points. First, the ACP is changing, which suggests that customers are paying faster or slower, even though we know that customer payment patterns are actually not changing at all. The rising monthly sales trend causes the calculated ACP to rise, whereas falling sales (as in the third quarter) cause the calculated ACP to fall, even though nothing is changing with regard to when customers pay. Second, we see that the ACP depends on an aver-aging procedure, and results can change depending on whether quarterly, semian-nual, or annual data are used. Therefore, it is difficult to use the ACP as a monitor-ing device for a firm whose sales exhibit seasonal or cyclical patterns, and it is also difficult to make comparisons between different firms.

Seasonal or cyclical variations also make it difficult to interpret aging schedules. Table 19-3 contains Hanover's aging schedules at the end of each quarter of 1986. At the end of June, Table 19-2 showed that Hanover's receivables balance is $174,000. Eighty percent of April's $60,000 of sales have been paid, 40 percent of May's $90,000 sales have been paid, and 10 percent of June's $120,000 sales have been paid. Thus, the end-of-June receivables balance consists of 0.2($60,000) = $12,000 of April sales, 0.6($90,000) = $54,000 of May sales, and 0.9($120,000) = $108,000 of June sales. Note again that Hanover's customers have not changed their payment patterns. However, rising sales during the second quarter create the impression of faster payments when judged by the percentage aging schedule, and falling sales after July create the opposite appearance. Thus, neither the ACP nor the aging schedule provides the financial manager with an accurate picture of cus-tomers' payment patterns in this instance, which is, unfortunately, typical.

With this background, we can now examine another basic tool, the *uncollected balances schedule*. Table 19-4 contains Hanover's quarterly uncollected balances schedules. At the end of each quarter, the dollar amount of receivables remaining from each month's sales is divided by that month's sales to obtain the receivables-to-sales ratio. For example, at the end of the first quarter, $12,000 of the $60,000

Table 19-4
Hanover Manufacturing Company:
End-of-Quarter Uncollected Balances Schedules for 1986
(Thousands of Dollars)

Quarter	Sales	Remaining Receivables	Receivables/Sales
Quarter 1:			
January	$ 60	$ 12	20%
February	60	36	60
March	60	54	90
		$102	170%
Quarter 2:			
April	$ 60	$ 12	20%
May	90	54	60
June	120	108	90
		$174	170%
Quarter 3:			
July	$120	$ 24	20%
August	90	54	60
September	60	54	90
		$132	170%
Quarter 4:			
October	$ 60	$ 12	20%
November	60	36	60
December	60	54	90
		$102	170%

January sales, or 20 percent, are still outstanding; 60 percent of February sales are still out; and 90 percent of March sales are uncollected. Exactly the same situation is revealed at the end of the next three quarters. Thus, Table 19-4 shows Hanover's financial manager that customers' payment behavior has not changed over the year.

Of course, in the example we assumed the existence of a constant payments pattern at the very beginning. In a normal situation, the firm's customers' payments patterns would probably vary somewhat over time. Such variations would be shown in the last column of the uncollected balances schedule. For example, suppose the May purchasers paid their accounts slower than assumed initially. That might cause the second quarter uncollected balances schedule to look like this (in thousands of dollars):

Quarter 2, 1986	Sales	Receivables	Receivables/Sales
April	$ 60	$ 12	20%
May	90	70	78
June	120	108	90
		$190	188%

We see that the receivables-to-sales ratio was higher in May than in February, the corresponding month in the first quarter. This caused the total uncollected balances percentage to rise from 170 to 188 percent, which in turn would alert Hanover's managers that customers are paying slower than they did earlier in the year.

The uncollected balances schedule not only permits a firm to monitor its receivables better, but it can also be used to forecast future receivables balances. When Hanover's pro forma 1987 quarterly balance sheets are constructed, management can use the receivables-to-sales ratios, coupled with 1987 sales estimates, to project each quarter's receivables balance. For example, with projected sales as given below, and using the same payments pattern as in 1986, Hanover's projected end-of-June 1987 receivables balance would be as follows:

Quarter 2, 1987	Projected Sales	Receivables/Sales	Projected Receivables
April	$ 70,000	20%	$ 14,000
May	100,000	60	60,000
June	140,000	90	126,000
		Total projected receivables =	$200,000

The payment patterns approach permits us to remove the effects of seasonal and/or cyclical sales variation and hence construct an accurate measure of customers' payment patterns. Thus, it provides financial managers with better information than such crude measures as the average collection period or the aging schedule. Managers should use the payments pattern approach to monitor collection performance as well as to project future receivables requirements.

Use of Computers in Receivables Management

Except possibly in the inventory and cash management areas, nowhere in the typical firm have computers had more of an impact than in accounts receivable management. A well-run business will use a computer system to record sales, to send out bills, to keep track of when payments are made, to alert the credit manager when an account becomes past due, and to ensure that actions are taken to collect past due accounts (for example, to prepare form letters requesting payment) automatically. Additionally, the payment history of each customer can be summarized and used to help establish credit limits for customers and classes of customers, and the data on each account can be aggregated and used for the firm's accounts receivable monitoring system. Finally, historical data can be stored in the firm's data base and used to develop inputs for studies related to credit policy changes as discussed in the next section.

Technological developments in the computer area are causing fundamental changes in receivables management. Firms that use the new technology in an intelligent manner will be the winners in the new business environment.

CREDIT POLICY

The success or failure of a business depends primarily on the demand for its products—as a rule, the higher its sales, the larger its profits and the higher the value of its stock. Sales, in turn, depend on a number of factors, some exogenous but others under the control of the firm. The major controllable variables which affect demand are sales prices, product quality, advertising, and *the firm's credit policy*. Credit policy, in turn, consists of these four variables:

1. The *credit period*, which is the length of time allowed buyers to pay for their purchases.
2. The *credit standards*, which refer to the minimum financial strength of acceptable credit customers.
3. The firm's *collection policy*, which is measured by its toughness or laxity in following up on slow-paying accounts.
4. Any *discounts* given for early payment.

The credit manager has the responsibility for administering the firm's credit policy. However, because of the pervasive importance of credit, the credit policy itself is normally established by the executive committee, which usually consists of the president and the vice presidents in charge of finance, marketing, and production.

SETTING THE CREDIT PERIOD AND STANDARDS

A firm's regular credit terms, which include the *credit period*, might call for sales on a 2/10, net 30 basis to all "acceptable" customers. Its *credit standards* would be applied to determine which customers are qualified for the regular credit terms, and the amount of credit available to each customer. The focal point when considering credit standards is the likelihood that a given customer will pay slowly or even end up as a bad debt loss. This requires a measurement of *credit quality*, which is defined in terms of the probability of default. The probability estimate for a given customer is, for the most part, a subjective judgment, but credit evaluation is a well-established practice, and a good credit manager can make reasonably accurate judgments regarding the probability of default by different classes of customers.

Credit-Scoring Systems

Although most credit decisions are subjective, many firms are starting to use a sophisticated statistical method called *multiple discriminant analysis (MDA)* to assess credit quality. MDA is very similar to multiple regression analysis. The dependent variable is, in essence, the probability of default, and the independent variables are various factors associated with financial strength and the ability to pay off the debt if credit is extended. For example, if a firm such as Sears evaluated consumers' credit quality, then the independent variables in the credit scoring system would be such factors as these: (1) Does the credit applicant own his or her own home? (2) How long has the applicant worked on his or her current job? (3) What is the applicant's outstanding debt in relation to his or her annual income? (4) Does the potential customer have a history of paying his or her debts on time?

One major advantage of an MDA credit-scoring system is that a customer's credit quality is expressed in a single numerical value, rather than as a subjective assessment of various factors. This is a tremendous advantage for a large firm which must evaluate many customers in many different locations using many different credit approvers, for without an automated procedure, the firm would have a hard time applying equal standards to all credit applicants. Therefore, most credit card companies, department stores, oil companies, and the like use credit-scoring systems to determine who gets how much credit, as do the larger building supply chains and manufacturers of electrical products, machinery, and so on.

Multiple discriminant analysis will be discussed in detail in Chapter 20 in connection with financial statement analysis. For now, we will briefly describe the concept. Suppose Hanover Manufacturing has historical information on 500 of its customers, all of whom are retail businesses. Of these 500, assume that 400 have always paid on time, but the other 100 either paid late or, in some cases, went bankrupt and did not pay at all. Further, the firm has historic data on each customer's quick ratio, times-interest-earned ratio, debt ratio, years in existence, and so on. Multiple discriminant analysis relates the experienced record (or historic probability) of late payment or nonpayment with various measures of a firm's financial condition, and MDA assigns weights for the critical factors. In effect, MDA produces an equation that looks much like a regression equation, and when data on a customer are plugged into the equation, then a credit score for that customer is produced.

For example, suppose Hanover's multiple discriminant analysis indicates that the critical factors affecting prompt payment are its customers' times-interest-earned ratio (TIE), quick ratio, debt/assets ratio, and number of years in business. Here is the discriminant function:

$$\text{Credit score} = 3.5(\text{TIE}) + 10.0(\text{Quick ratio}) - 25.0(\text{Debt/Assets}) + 1.3(\text{Years in business}).$$

Further, assume that a score less than 40 indicates a poor credit risk, 40-50 indicates an average credit risk, and a score above 50 signifies a good credit risk. Now, suppose a firm with the following conditions applies for credit:

$$\text{Times-interest-earned} = 4.2$$
$$\text{Quick ratio} = 3.1$$
$$\text{Debt/assets} = 0.30$$
$$\text{Years in business} = 10$$

This firm's credit score would be $3.5(4.2) + 10.0(3.1) - 25.0(0.30) + 1.3(10) = 51.2$. Therefore, it would be considered a good credit risk, and consequently it would be offered favorable credit terms.

Sources of Credit Information

Two major sources of external information are available. The first is the work of the *credit associations*, which are local groups that meet frequently and which correspond with one another to exchange information on credit customers. These local groups have also banded together to create Credit Interchange, a system developed by the National Association of Credit Management for assembling and distributing information about debtors' past performance. The interchange reports show the paying records of different debtors, the industries from which they are buying, and the geographic areas in which they are making purchases. The second source of external information is the work of the *credit-reporting agencies*, which collect credit information and sell it for a fee. The best known of these agencies are Dun & Bradstreet (D&B) and TRW, Incorporated. D&B, TRW, and other agencies provide factual data that can be used in credit analysis; they also provide ratings similar to those available on corporate bonds.[5]

Managing a credit department requires fast, accurate, up-to-date information, and to help get such information, the National Association of Credit Management (a group with 43,000 member firms) persuaded TRW, Inc., to develop a computer-based telecommunication network for the collection, storage, retrieval, and distribution of credit information. The TRW system contains credit data on over 120 million individuals, and it electronically transmits credit reports which are available within seconds to its thousands of subscribers. Dun & Bradstreet has a similar electronic system which covers businesses, plus another service which provides more detailed reports through the U.S. mail.

A typical business credit report would include the following pieces of information:

1. A summary balance sheet and income statement.

2. A number of key ratios, with trend information.

3. Information obtained from the firm's suppliers telling whether it has been paying promptly or slowly, and whether it has recently failed to make any payments.

4. A verbal description of the physical condition of the firm's operations.

5. A verbal description of the backgrounds of the firm's owners, including any previous bankruptcies, lawsuits, divorce settlement problems, and the like.

6. A summary rating, ranging from A for the best credit risks down to F for those that are deemed likely to default.

Although a great deal of credit information is available, it must still be processed in a judgmental manner. Computerized information systems can assist in making better credit decisions, but, in the final analysis, most credit decisions are really exercises in informed judgment. Even credit scoring systems require judgment in deciding where to draw the lines, given the set of derived scores.

---

[5]For additional information, see Christie and Bracuti, *Credit Management*, a publication of the National Association of Credit Management; and also, see Peter Nulty, "An Upstart Takes on Dun & Bradstreet," *Fortune*, April 9, 1979, 98-100.

SETTING THE COLLECTION POLICY

Collection policy refers to the procedures the firm follows to collect past-due accounts. For example, a letter may be sent to customers when a bill is 10 days past due; a more severe letter, followed by a telephone call, may be used if payment is not received within 30 days; and the account may be turned over to a collection agency after 90 days.

The collection process can be expensive in terms of both out-of-pocket expenditures and lost goodwill, but at least some firmness is needed to prevent an undue lengthening of the collection period and to minimize outright losses. Again, a balance must be struck between the costs and benefits of different collection policies.

Changes in collection policy influence sales, the collection period, the bad debt loss percentage, and the percentage of customers who take discounts. The effects of a change in collection policy, along with changes in the other credit policy variables, will be analyzed later in the chapter.

CASH DISCOUNTS

The last element in the credit policy decision, the use of *cash discounts* for early payment, is also analyzed by balancing the costs and benefits of different cash discounts. For example, a firm might decide to change its credit terms from "net 30," which means that customers must pay within 30 days, to "2/10, net 30," which means that it will allow a 2 percent discount if payment is received within 10 days, while the full invoice price must otherwise be paid within 30 days. This change should produce two benefits: (1) It should attract new customers who consider discounts to be a type of price reduction, and (2) the discounts should cause a reduction in the average collection period, since some established customers will pay more promptly in order to take advantage of the discount. Offsetting these benefits is the dollar cost of the discounts taken.[6] The optimal discount is established at the point where the marginal costs and benefits are exactly offsetting. The methodology for analyzing changes in the discount is developed later in the chapter.

If sales are seasonal, a firm may use *seasonal dating* on discounts. For example, Slimware, Inc., a swimsuit manufacturer, sells on terms of 2/10, net 30, May 1 dating. This means that the effective invoice date is May 1, even if the sale was made back in January. The discount may be taken up to May 10; otherwise, the full amount must be paid on May 30. Slimware produces throughout the year, but retail sales of bathing suits are concentrated in the spring and early summer, and by offering seasonal dating, the company induces some of its customers to stock up early, saving Slimware storage costs and also "nailing down sales."

---

[6]Note that some firms offer discounts only to customers who pay cash on the spot, because the cost of giving such discounts is offset by the reduction in receivables accounting costs. Also, in certain types of businesses, cash sales are kept off the books and hence profits on them out of reach of the tax collectors.

OTHER FACTORS INFLUENCING CREDIT POLICY

In addition to the factors discussed above, several other conditions also influence a firm's overall credit policy.

Profit Potential

Thus far, we have emphasized the costs of granting credit. *However, if it is possible to sell on credit and also to assess a carrying charge on the receivables that are outstanding, then credit sales can actually be more profitable than cash sales.* This is especially true for consumer durables (autos, appliances, clothing, and so on), but it is also true for certain types of industrial equipment. Thus, GM's General Motors Acceptance Corporation (GMAC) unit, which finances automobiles, is highly profitable, as is Sears Roebuck's credit subsidiary.[7] Some encyclopedia companies are even reported to lose money on cash sales but to more than make up these losses from the carrying charges on their credit sales; obviously, such companies would rather sell on credit than for cash!

The carrying charges on outstanding credit are generally about 18 percent on a nominal interest rate basis: 1.5 percent per month, so $1.5\% \times 12 = 18\%$. This is equivalent to an effective rate of $(1.015)^{12} - 1.0 = 19.6\%$. Except in the early 1980s, when short-term interest rates rose to unprecedented levels, having receivables outstanding that earn over 18 percent is highly profitable.

Legal Considerations

It is illegal, under the Robinson-Patman Act, for a firm to charge prices that discriminate between customers unless these differential prices are cost-justified. The same holds true for credit—it is illegal to offer more favorable credit terms to one customer or class of customers than to another, unless the differences are cost-justified.

Credit Instruments

Most credit is offered on *open account*, which means that the only formal evidence of credit is an invoice which accompanies the shipment and which the buyer signs to indicate that goods have been received. Then, the buyer and the

---

[7]Companies that do a large volume of sales financing typically set up subsidiary companies called *captive finance companies* to do the actual financing. Thus, General Motors, Chrysler, and Ford all have captive finance companies, as do Sears Roebuck and Montgomery Ward. The reason for this is that consumer finance companies, because their assets are highly liquid, tend to use far more debt, and especially short-term debt, than manufacturers or retailers. Thus, if GM did not use a captive finance company, its balance sheet would show an exceptionally high debt ratio and a very low current ratio. By setting up GMAC as a separate but wholly owned corporation, and then reporting only its equity investment in the subsidiary rather than a fully consolidated balance sheet which included the subsidiary's debt, GM avoids distorting its own balance sheet, presumably helping it to raise capital on more favorable terms.

seller each record the purchase on their books of account. Under certain circumstances, the selling firm may require the buyer to sign a *promissory note* evidencing the credit obligation. Promissory notes are useful (1) if the order is very large; (2) if the seller anticipates the possibility of having trouble collecting, because a note is a stronger legal claim than a simple signed invoice; or (3) if the buyer wants a longer-than-usual time in which to pay for the order, because in that case interest should be charged, and interest charges can be built into a promissory note.

Another instrument used in trade credit, especially in international trade, is the *commercial draft*. Here the seller draws up a draft—which is a sort of combination check and a promissory note—calling for the buyer to pay a specific amount to the seller by a specified date. This draft is then sent to the buyer's bank, along with the shipping invoices necessary to take possession of the goods. The bank forwards the draft to the buyer, who signs it and returns it to the bank. The bank then delivers the shipping documents to its customer, who at this point can claim the goods. If the draft is a *sight draft*, then upon delivery of the shipping documents and acceptance of the draft by the buyer, the bank actually withdraws money from the buyer's account and forwards it to the selling firm. If the draft is a *time draft*, payable on a specific future date, then the bank returns it to the selling firm. In this case, the draft is called a *trade acceptance*, and it amounts to a promissory note that the seller can hold for future payment or use as collateral for a loan. The bank, in such a situation, has served as an intermediary, making sure that the buyer does not receive title to the goods until the note (or draft) has been executed for the benefit of the seller.

A seller who lacks confidence in the ability or willingness of the buyer to pay off a time draft may refuse to ship without a guarantee of payment by the buyer's bank. Presumably, the bank knows its customer, and for a fee, the bank will guarantee payment of the draft. In this instance, the draft is called a *banker's acceptance*. Such instruments are widely used, especially in foreign trade. They have a low degree of risk if guaranteed by a strong bank, and there is a ready market for acceptances, making it easy for the seller of the goods to sell the instrument to raise immediate cash. (Banker's acceptances are sold at a discount below face value, and then paid off at face value when they mature, so the discount amounts to interest on the acceptance. The effective interest rate on a strong banker's acceptance is a little above the Treasury bill rate of interest.)

A final type of credit instrument that should be mentioned is the *conditional sales contract*. With a conditional sales contract, the seller retains legal ownership of the goods until the buyer has completed payment. Conditional sales contracts are used primarily for such items as machinery, dental equipment, and the like, which are often purchased on an installment basis over a period of two or three years. The significant advantage of a conditional sales contract is that it is easier for the seller to repossess the equipment in the event of default than it would be if title had passed. This feature makes possible some credit sales that otherwise would not be feasible. Conditional sales contracts generally have a market interest rate built into their payment schedules.

ANALYZING CHANGES IN A FIRM'S CREDIT POLICY

If the firm's credit policy is *eased* by such actions as lengthening the credit period, relaxing credit standards, following a less tough collection policy, or offering cash discounts, then sales should increase: *Easing the credit policy stimulates sales.* Of course, if credit policy is eased and sales rise, then costs will also rise because more labor, materials, and so on will be required to produce the additional goods. Additionally, receivables outstanding will also increase, which will increase carrying costs, and bad debt and/or discount expenses may also rise. Thus, the key question when deciding on a credit policy change is this: Will sales revenues rise more than costs, including credit-related costs, causing net income to increase, or will the increase in sales revenues be more than offset by the higher costs?

Table 19-5 illustrates the general idea behind credit policy analysis. Suppose, in late 1986, a firm is considering easing its credit policy—the proposed change includes lengthening the credit period, offering larger discounts, relaxing credit standards, and relaxing collection efforts. Column 1 shows the projected 1987 income statement under the assumption that the current credit policy is maintained throughout the year. Column 2 shows the projected 1987 income statement incorporating the expected effects of the easing in credit policy. The generally looser policy would increase sales, but discounts and several other types of costs would rise. Column 3 shows the expected incremental effects of easing the credit policy. The overall, bottom line effect is a $6 million expected increase in projected profits.

There would, of course, be corresponding changes on the projected balance sheet—the higher sales would necessitate somewhat larger cash balances, inven-

Table 19-5
Analysis of a Proposed Change in Credit Policy (Millions of Dollars)

	Projected 1987 Income Statement under Current Credit Policy (1)	Projected 1987 Income Statement under New Credit Policy (2)	Effect of Credit Policy Change (3)
Gross sales	$1,000	$1,200	+ $200
Less discounts	10	30	+ 20
Net Sales	$ 990	$1,170	+ $180
Production costs, including overhead	700	820	+ 120
Gross profit before credit costs	$ 290	$ 350	+ $ 60
Credit-related costs:			
Cost of carrying receivables	40	70	+ 30
Bad debt losses	25	45	+ 20
Gross profit	$ 225	$ 235	+ $ 10
Taxes (40%)	90	94	+ 4
Net income	$ 135	$ 141	+ $ 6

tories, and perhaps (depending on the existence of excess capacity) more fixed assets. Accounts receivable would, of course, also increase. Those increases in assets would have to be financed, so certain liabilities and/or equity would also have to be increased.

Whether or not the $6 million expected increase in net income would be deemed sufficient to warrant the credit policy change would require a substantial amount of analysis, and, in the end, some judgments. In the first place, there would be some uncertainty, perhaps quite a lot of uncertainty, about the projected $200 million increase in sales. Conceivably, if the firm's competitors match its changes, sales might not rise at all. Similar uncertainties would be attached to the number of customers who would take discounts, to production costs at higher or lower sales levels, to the costs of carrying additional receivables, and to bad debt losses. Perhaps, in view of all the uncertainties, and also considering the effects on the balance sheet ratios, management would deem the projected $6 million increase in net income insufficient to justify the change.

Incremental Analysis

To evaluate a proposed change in credit policy, one could compare alternative projected income statements, as we did in Table 19-5. Alternatively, one could develop the data in Column 3, which shows the incremental effect of the proposed change without first developing the pro forma income statements. This second approach is often preferable—because firms usually change their credit policies in specific divisions or on specific products, and not across the board, it may not be feasible to develops complete corporate income statements. Of course, the two approaches are based on exactly the same data, so they should produce identical results.

In an incremental analysis, we attempt to determine the increase or decrease in both sales and costs associated with a given easing or tightening of credit policy. The difference between incremental sales and incremental costs is defined as *incremental profit*. If the expected incremental profit is positive, and if it is sufficiently large to compensate for the risks involved, then the proposed credit policy change should be accepted.

The Basic Equations

To ensure that all relevant factors are considered, it is useful to set up some equations to analyze changes in credit policy. We begin by defining the following terms and symbols:

S_0 = current gross sales.

S_N = new gross sales, after the change in credit policy. Note that S_N can be greater or less than S_0.

$S_N - S_0$ = incremental, or change in, gross sales.

V = variable costs as a percentage of gross sales. V includes production costs, inventory carrying costs, the cost of administering the credit department, and all other variable costs except bad debt losses, financing costs associated with carrying the investment in receivables, and costs of giving discounts.

$1 - V$ = contribution margin, or the percentage of each gross sales dollar that goes toward covering overhead and increasing profits. The contribution margin is sometimes called the gross profit margin.

k = cost of financing the investment in receivables.

ACP_0 = average collection period prior to the change in credit policy.

ACP_N = new average collection period, after the credit policy change.

B_0 = average bad debt loss at the current sales level as a percentage of current gross sales.

B_N = average bad debt loss at the new sales level as a percentage of new gross sales.

P_0 = percentage of total customers who take discounts under the current credit policy.

P_N = percentage of total customers who will take discounts under the new credit policy.

D_0 = discount percentage offered at the present time.

D_N = discount percentage offered under the new credit policy.

With these definitions in mind, we can calculate values for the incremental change in the level of the firm's investment in receivables, ΔI, and the incremental change in pre-tax profits, ΔP. The formula for calculating ΔI differs depending on whether the change in credit policy results in an increase or decrease in sales. Here we simply present the equations; we discuss and explain them shortly, through use of examples, once all the equations have been set forth.

If the change is expected to *increase* sales—either additional sales to old customers or sales to newly attracted customers, or both—then we have this situation:

Formula for ΔI if sales increase:

$$\Delta I = \begin{bmatrix} \text{Increased investment in} \\ \text{receivables associated with} \\ \text{original sales} \end{bmatrix} + \begin{bmatrix} \text{Increased investment in} \\ \text{receivables associated} \\ \text{with incremental sales} \end{bmatrix}$$

$$= \begin{bmatrix} \text{Change in} \\ \text{collection period} \end{bmatrix}\begin{bmatrix} \text{Old sales} \\ \text{per day} \end{bmatrix} + V\begin{bmatrix} (ACP_N)\begin{pmatrix} \text{Incremental} \\ \text{sales per day} \end{pmatrix} \end{bmatrix}$$

$$= [(ACP_N - ACP_0)(S_0/360)] \qquad + V[(ACP_N)(S_N - S_0)/360]. \qquad (19\text{-}1)$$

However, if the change in credit policy is expected to *decrease* sales, then the change in the level of investment in receivables is calculated as follows:

Formula for ΔI if sales decrease:

$$\Delta I = \begin{bmatrix} \text{Decreased investment in} \\ \text{receivables associated with} \\ \text{remaining original customers} \end{bmatrix} + \begin{bmatrix} \text{Decreased investment in} \\ \text{receivables associated with} \\ \text{customers who left} \end{bmatrix}$$

$$= \begin{bmatrix} \text{Change in} \\ \text{collection} \\ \text{period} \end{bmatrix}\begin{bmatrix} \text{Remaining} \\ \text{sales} \\ \text{per day} \end{bmatrix} + V\begin{bmatrix} (ACP_0)\begin{pmatrix} \text{Incremental} \\ \text{sales} \\ \text{per day} \end{pmatrix} \end{bmatrix}$$

$$= [(ACP_N - ACP_0)(S_N/360)] \qquad + V[(ACP_0)(S_N - S_0)/360]. \qquad (19\text{-}2)$$

With the change in receivables investment calculated, we can now analyze the pre-tax profitability of the proposed change:

Formula for ΔP:

$$\Delta P = \begin{bmatrix} \text{Change in} \\ \text{gross} \\ \text{profit} \end{bmatrix} - \begin{bmatrix} \text{Change in} \\ \text{cost of} \\ \text{carrying} \\ \text{receivables} \end{bmatrix} - \begin{bmatrix} \text{Change in} \\ \text{bad debt} \\ \text{losses} \end{bmatrix} - \begin{bmatrix} \text{Change in} \\ \text{cost of} \\ \text{discounts} \end{bmatrix}$$

$$= (S_N - S_0)(1 - V) - k(\Delta I) - (B_N S_N - B_0 S_0) - (D_N S_N P_N - D_0 S_0 P_0). \quad \textbf{(19-3)}$$

Thus, changes in credit policy are analyzed by using either Equation 19-1 or 19-2, depending on whether the proposed change is expected to increase or decrease sales, and Equation 19-3. The rationale behind these equations will become clear as we work through several illustrations. Note that all the terms in Equation 19-3 need not be used in a particular analysis. For example, a change in credit policy might not affect discount sales or bad debt losses, in which case the last two terms of Equation 19-3 would both be zero. Note also that the form of the equations depends on the way in which the variables are first defined.[8]

Changing the Credit Period

In this section, we examine the effects of changing the credit period, while in the following sections, we consider changes in credit standards, collection policy, and cash discounts. Throughout, we illustrate the situation with data on Stylish Fashions, Inc.

Lengthening the Credit Period

Stylish Fashions currently sells on a cash-only basis. Since it extends no credit, the company has no funds tied up in receivables, has no bad debt losses, and has no credit expenses of any kind. On the other hand, its sales volume is lower than it would be if credit terms were offered. Stylish is now considering offering credit on 30-day terms. Current sales are $100,000 per year; variable costs are 60 percent of sales; excess production capacity exists (so no new fixed costs will be incurred as a result of expanded sales); and the cost of capital invested in receivables is 10 percent. Stylish estimates that sales would increase to $150,000 per year if credit were extended, and that bad debt losses would be 2 percent of total sales. Thus,

---

[8]For example, P_0 and P_N are defined as the percentage of *total* customers who take discounts. If P_0 and P_N were defined as the percentage of *paying* customers (as opposed to bad debts) who take discounts, then Equation 19-3 would become

$$\Delta P = (S_N - S_0)(1 - V) - k(\Delta I) - (B_N S_N - B_0 S_0) - [D_N S_N P_N(1 - B_N) - D_0 S_0 P_0(1 - B_0)].$$

Similarly, changing the definitions of B_0 and B_N would affect the third term of Equation 19-3, as we discuss later.

$S_0 = \$100,000.$

$S_N = \$150,000.$

$V = 60\% = 0.6.$

$1 - V = 1 - 0.6 = 0.4.$

$k = 10\% = 0.10.$

$ACP_0 = 0$ days.

$ACP_N = 30$ days. Here we assume that all customers will pay on time, so ACP = specified credit period. Generally, some customers pay late, so in most cases ACP is greater than the specified credit period.

$B_0 = 0\% = 0.00.$ There are currently no bad debt losses.

$B_N = 2\% = 0.02.$ These losses apply to the $150,000 new level of sales.

$D_0 = D_N = 0\%.$ No discounts are given under either the current or the proposed credit policies.

Since sales are expected to increase, Equation 19-1 is used to determine the change in the investment in receivables:

$$\Delta I = [(ACP_N - ACP_0)(S_0/360)] + V[(ACP_N)(S_N - S_0)/360]$$
$$= [(30 - 0)(\$100,000/360)] + 0.6[30(\$150,000 - \$100,000)/360]$$
$$= \$8,333 + \$2,500 = \$10,833.$$

Note that the first term, the increased investment in accounts receivable associated with *old sales*, is based on the full amount of the receivables, whereas the second term, the investment associated with *incremental sales*, consists of incremental receivables multiplied by V, the variable cost percentage. This difference reflects the facts (1) that the firm invests only its variable cost in *incremental* receivables, but (2) that it would have collected the *full sales price* on the old sales earlier had it not made the credit policy change. There is an *opportunity cost* associated with the $8,333 additional investment in receivables from old sales and a *direct financing cost* associated with the $2,500 investment in receivables from incremental sales.

Looking at this another way, *incremental* sales will generate an actual increase in receivables of $(ACP_N)(S_N - S_0)/360 = 30(\$50,000/360) = \$4,167$. However, the only part of that increase which has to be financed (by bank borrowing or from other sources) and reported as a liability on the right side of the balance sheet is the cash outflow generated by the incremental sales, that is, the variable costs, $V(\$4,167) = 0.6(\$4,167) = \$2,500$. The remainder of the receivables increase, $1,667 of accrued before-tax profit, is reflected on the balance sheet not as some type of credit used to finance receivables, but as an increase in retained earnings generated by the sales. On the other hand, the old receivables level was zero, meaning that the original sales produced cash of $\$100,000/360 = \$277.78$ per day, which was immediately available for investing in assets or for reducing capital from other sources. The change in credit policy will cause a delay in the collection of these funds, and hence will require the firm (1) to borrow to cover the variable costs of the sales and (2) to forego a return on the retained earnings portion, which would have been available immediately had the credit policy change not been made.

Given ΔI, we may now determine the incremental profit, ΔP, associated with the proposed credit period change, using Equation 19-3:

$$\Delta P = (S_N - S_0)(1 - V) - k(\Delta I) - (B_N S_N - B_0 S_0) - (D_N S_N P_N - D_0 S_0 P_0)$$
$$= (\$50,000)(0.4) - 0.10(\$10,833) - [0.02(\$150,000) - 0.00(\$100,000)] - \$0$$
$$= \$20,000 - \$1,083 - \$3,000 = \$15,917.$$

Since pre-tax profits are expected to increase by $15,917, the credit policy change appears to be desirable.

Two simplifying assumptions which were made in our analysis should be noted: We assumed (1) that all customers paid on time (ACP = credit period), and (2) that there were no current bad debt losses. The assumption of prompt payment can be relaxed quite easily—we can simply use the actual average collection period (say 40 days), rather than the 30-day credit period, to calculate the investment in receivables, and then use this new (and higher) value of ΔI in Equation 19-3 to calculate ΔP. Thus, if ACP_N were 40 days, then the increased investment in receivables would be

$$\Delta I = [(40 - 0)(\$100,000/360)] + 0.6[40(\$50,000/360)]$$
$$= \$11,111 + \$3,333 = \$14,444,$$

and the change in pre-tax profits would be

$$\Delta P = \$50,000(0.4) - 0.10(\$14,444) - 0.02(\$150,000)$$
$$= \$20,000 - \$1,444 - \$3,000 = \$15,556.$$

The longer collection period causes incremental profits to fall slightly, but they are still positive, so the credit policy should probably still be relaxed.

If the company had been selling on credit initially and therefore incurring some bad debt losses, then we would have had to include this information in Equation 19-3. In our example, $B_0 S_0$ was equal to zero because Stylish Fashions did not previously sell on credit; therefore, the change in bad debt losses was equal to $B_N S_N$.

Notice that B_N is defined as the average credit loss percentage on total sales, and not just on incremental sales. Bad debts might be higher for new customers attracted by the credit terms than for old customers who take advantage of them, but B_N is an average of these two groups. However, if one wanted to keep the two groups separate, it would be easy enough to define B_N as the bad debt percentage of the incremental sales only.

Other factors could be introduced into the analysis. For example, the company could consider a further easing of credit by extending the credit period to 60 days, or it could analyze the effects of a sales expansion so great that fixed assets, and hence additional fixed costs, had to be added. Or the variable cost ratio might change as sales increased, falling if economies of scale were present or rising if diseconomies were present. Adding such factors complicates the analysis, but the basic principles are the same—just keep in mind that we are seeking to determine the *incremental sales revenues*, the *incremental costs*, and consequently the *incremental before-tax profit* associated with a given change in credit policy.

Shortening the Credit Period

Suppose that one year after Stylish Fashions began offering 30-day credit terms, management decided to consider the possibility of shortening the credit period from 30 to 20 days. It was believed that sales would decline by $20,000 per year from the current level, $150,000, so S_N = $130,000. It was also believed that the bad debt percentage on these lost sales would be 2 percent, the same as on other sales, and that all other values would remain as given in the last section.

We first calculate the incremental investment in receivables. Since the change in credit policy is expected to decrease sales, Equation 19-2 is used:

$$\Delta I = [(ACP_N - ACP_0)(S_N/360)] + V[(ACP_0)(S_N - S_0)/360]$$
$$= [(20 - 30)(\$130,000/360)] + 0.6[30(\$130,000 - \$150,000)/360]$$
$$= (-10)(\$361.11) + 0.6[(30)(-\$55.56)]$$
$$= -\$3,611 - \$1,000 = -\$4,611.$$

With a shorter credit period there is a shorter collection period, so sales are collected sooner. There is also a smaller volume of business, and hence a smaller investment in receivables. The first term captures the speedup in collections, while the second reflects the reduced sales, and hence the lower receivables investment (at variable cost).

Notice that V is included in the second term but not in the first one. The logic here is parallel to that with regard to Equation 19-1. V is included in the second term because, by shortening the credit period, Stylish Fashions will drive off some customers and lose sales of $20,000 per year, or $55.56 per day. The firm's investment in those sales was only 60 percent of the average receivables outstanding, or $0.6(30)(\$55.56)$ = $1,000. However, the situation is different for the remaining customers. They would have paid their full purchase price—variable cost plus profit—after 30 days. Now, however, they will have to pay this amount 10 days sooner, so those funds will be available to meet operating costs or for investment. Thus, the first term should not be reduced by the variable cost factor. Therefore, in total, reducing the credit period would result in a $4,611 reduction in the investment in receivables, consisting of a $3,611 decline in receivables associated with continuing customers and a further $1,000 decline in investment as a result of the reduced sales volume.

With the change in investment calculated, we can now analyze the profitability of the proposed change using Equation 19-3:

$$\Delta P = (S_N - S_0)(1 - V) - k(\Delta I) - (B_N S_N - B_0 S_0) - (D_N S_N P_N - D_0 S_0 P_0)$$
$$= (\$130,000 - \$150,000)(0.4) - 0.10(-\$4,611)$$
$$- [(0.02)(\$130,000) - (0.02)(\$150,000)] - \$0$$
$$= -\$8,000 + \$461 + \$400 = -\$7,139.$$

Since the expected incremental pre-tax profits are negative, the firm should not reduce its credit period from 30 to 20 days.

Changing the Discount Policy

To illustrate how a change in cash discount policy should be analyzed, suppose, sometime after Stylish started using terms of net 30, it decided to consider offering a 2 percent discount for payments made within 10 days, which would represent a change in credit terms to 2/10, net 30. The following conditions currently exist or are expected to occur if the change is made:

S_0 = current gross sales = \$150,000.

S_N = new gross sales level if a discount is offered = \$160,000.

D_0 = original discount percentage = 0%.

D_N = new discount percentage = 2%.

ACP_0 = old average collection period = 30 days.

ACP_N = new average collection period = 20 days. The new ACP is based on the assumption that 49 percent of the customers will take discounts and pay on the tenth day, another 49 percent will pay on the thirtieth day, and 2 percent will end up as bad debt losses.

P_0 = proportion of total customers who took discounts previously = 0.0.

$B_0 = B_N$ = bad debt losses as a proportion of gross sales = 0.02.

P_N = proportion of total customers who will take discounts under the new policy = 0.49.

V = 60%.

k = 10%.

Since sales are expected to increase, the incremental investment in receivables is found by using Equation 19-1:

$$\Delta I = [(ACP_N - ACP_0)(S_0/360)] + V[(ACP_N)(S_N - S_0)/360]$$
$$= (20 - 30)(\$150,000/360) + 0.6[20(\$160,000 - \$150,000)/360]$$
$$= -\$4,167 + \$333 = -\$3,834.$$

Thus, offering discounts will speed up collections and reduce the investment in receivables by \$3,834.

The expected change in profits may now be analyzed by using Equation 19-3:

$$\Delta P = (S_N - S_0)(1 - V) - k(\Delta I) - (B_N S_N - B_0 S_0) - (D_N S_N P_N - D_0 S_0 P_0)$$
$$= (\$160,000 - \$150,000)(0.4) - (0.1)(-\$3,834)$$
$$\quad - [0.02(\$160,000) - 0.02(\$150,000)]$$
$$\quad - [(0.02)(\$160,000)(0.49) - (0.00)(\$150,000)(0.0)]$$
$$= \$4,000 + \$383 - \$200 - \$1,568 = \$2,615.$$

Since expected incremental pre-tax profits are positive, Stylish should consider offering discounts.

Changes in Other Credit Policy Variables

In the preceding sections, we examined the effects of changes in the credit and discount periods. Changes in other credit policy variables may be analyzed similarly. In general, we would follow these steps:

Step 1. Estimate the effect of the policy change on sales, on ACP, on bad debt losses, and so on.

Step 2. Determine the change in the firm's investment in receivables. If the change will increase sales, then use Equation 19-1 to calculate ΔI. Conversely, if the change will decrease sales, then use Equation 19-2.

Step 3. Use Equation 19-3, or one of its variations, to calculate the effect of the change on pre-tax profits. If profits are expected to increase, the policy change should be made, unless it is judged to increase the firm's risk by a disproportionate amount.

Simultaneous Changes in Policy Variables

In the preceding discussion we considered the effects of changes in credit policy one variable at a time. The firm could, of course, change several or even all policy variables simultaneously. An almost endless variety of equations could be developed, depending on which policy variables are manipulated and on the assumed effects on sales, discounts taken, the collection period, bad debt losses, the existence of excess capacity, changes in credit department costs, changes in the variable cost percentage, and so on. The analysis would get "messy," and the incremental profit equation would be complex, but the principles we have developed could be used to handle any type of policy change.

SUMMARY

The investment in receivables is dependent on the firm's *credit policy*, and the four credit policy variables are these: (1) the *credit standards*, or the financial strength that customers must exhibit in order to be granted credit; (2) the *credit period*, or the length of time for which credit is extended; (3) *cash discounts*, which are designed to encourage rapid payment; and (4) *collection policy*, which helps determine how long accounts remain outstanding. Credit policy has an important impact on the volume of sales, and the optimal credit policy involves a tradeoff between the costs inherent in various credit policies and the profits generated by higher sales. From a practical standpoint, it is impossible to determine the optimal credit policy in a mathematical sense—good credit management involves a blending of quantitative analysis and business judgment.

Monitoring receivables is an important part of credit management. Firms often use the *average collection period* and *aging schedules* to monitor collections, but these summary measures do not always provide a clear picture of changes in payment behavior. A better method of receivables monitoring is the *payments pattern approach*.

Questions and Problems

19-1 (Investment in receivables) Stevens, Inc., sells on terms of 2/10, net 30. Total sales for the year are $800,000. Sixty percent of the customers pay on the tenth day and take discounts, while 40 percent pay, on average, 40 days after their purchases.
  a. What is the average collection period?
  b. What is the average investment in receivables?
  c. What would happen to the average investment in receivables if Stevens toughened up on its collection policy, with the result that all nondiscount customers paid on the 30th day?

19-2 (Monitoring of receivables) The Damon Company, a small manufacturer of cordless telephones, began operations on January 1, 1986. Its credit sales for the first six months of operations were as follows:

Month	Credit Sales
January	$ 50,000
February	100,000
March	120,000
April	105,000
May	140,000
June	160,000

Throughout this entire period, Damon's credit customers maintained a constant payments pattern: 20 percent paid in the month of sale, 30 percent paid in the month following the sale, and 50 percent paid in the second month following the sale.
  a. What was Damon's receivables balance at the end of March and at the end of June?
  b. Assume 90 days per calendar quarter. What was the average daily sales (ADS) and average collection period (ACP) for the first quarter and for the second quarter? What was the cumulative ADS and ACP for the first half-year?
  c. Construct an aging schedule as of June 30. Use 0-30, 31-60, and 61-90 day account ages.
  d. Construct the uncollected balances schedule for the second quarter as of June 30.

19-3 (Credit policy changes) Indicate by a +, −, or 0 whether each of the following events would probably cause accounts receivable (A/R), sales, and profits to increase, decrease, or be affected in an indeterminate manner.

	A/R	Sales	Profits
a. The firm tightens its credit standards.	——	——	——
b. The terms of trade are changed from 2/10, net 30, to 3/10, net 30.	——	——	——
c. The terms are changed from 2/10, net 30, to 3/10, net 40.	——	——	——
d. The credit manager gets tough with past due accounts.	——	——	——

19-4 (Incremental analysis) Celec Distributors, Inc., currently sells on terms of 1/10, net 30, with bad debt losses at 1 percent of gross sales. Of the 99 percent of the customers who pay, 50 percent take the discount and pay on Day 10, while the remaining 50 percent pay on Day 30.

Celec's gross sales are currently $2,000,000 per year, with variable costs amounting to 75 percent of sales. The firm finances its receivables with a 10 percent line of credit, and there are sufficient fixed assets to support a doubling in sales.

Celec's credit manager has proposed that credit terms be changed to 2/10, net 40. He estimates that these terms would boost sales to $2,500,000 per year. However, bad debt losses would double to 2 percent of the new sales level. It is expected that 50 percent of the paying customers will continue to take the discount and pay on Day 10, while 50 percent will pay on Day 40.

   a. What are the old and new average collection periods?

   b. Find ΔI, the incremental change in Celec's receivables investment, and ΔP, the incremental change in pre-tax profits. Should the change in credit terms be made?

   c. Assume that Celec's credit terms are currently 2/10, net 40, and it is considering a change to terms of 1/10, net 30. Assume that all the variables for these two credit policies hold at the levels set forth previously. In other words, reverse the analysis.

   d. Assume that Celec's competitors react to the change as originally stated in the problem by also granting more liberal credit terms. This causes Celec's sales to remain at the original level of $2,000,000. Additionally, bad debt losses remain at the original 1 percent. What is the effect on Celec's profits?

19-5 (Alternative credit policy changes) The Settle Company expects to have sales of $20 million this year under current operating policies. Its variable costs as a proportion of sales is 0.8, and its cost of receivables financing is 8 percent. Currently, Settle's credit policy is net 25. However, its average collection period is 30 days, indicating that some customers are paying late, and its bad debt losses are 3 percent of sales.

Settle's credit manager is considering two alternative credit policies:

Proposal 1. Lengthen the credit period to net 40. If this were done, it is estimated that sales would increase to $20,500,000, that the average collection period would increase to 45 days, and that the bad debt losses on the *incremental sales* would be 5 percent. Existing customer bad debt losses would remain at 3 percent.

Proposal 2. Shorten the credit period to net 20. Under these terms, sales would be expected to decrease to $18 million, the average collection period would drop to 22 days, and bad debt losses would decrease to 1 percent of the new sales level.

   a. Evaluate Proposal 1. What is the expected change in investment in receivables and the expected change in before-tax profit?

   b. Evaluate Proposal 2. What is the expected change in investment in receivables and the expected change in before-tax profit?

   c. Should either proposal be adopted? If so, which one? Why?

19-6 (Additional alternatives) This problem extends Problem 19-5. Read the basic problem and Proposals 1 and 2, and then analyze Proposals 3, 4, and 5.

Proposal 3. Relax credit standards and sell to less creditworthy customers. It is estimated that this action would increase sales by $2,000,000. The *incremental sales* would have bad debt losses of 6 percent and an average collection period of 40 days. (Note that current customers would continue to have an average collection period of 30 days and bad debt losses of 3 percent.)

Proposal 4. Tighten credit collection policy. The estimated impact of this change is to decrease sales by $1,500,000, decrease the bad debt losses on total sales to 1.5 percent, and decrease the average collection period on total sales to 25 days.

Proposal 5. Offer a 2 percent discount for payment within 10 days, that is, offer terms of 2/10, net 25. It is estimated that 50 percent of the paying customers would take the discount. Further, the new terms would increase sales by $2,000,000, decrease bad debt losses to 2 percent of the new sales level, and decrease the average collection period to 20 days.

19-7 (Incremental analysis) Rzasa Industries, Inc., currently sells on terms of 2/10, net 40, with bad debt losses running at 2 percent of gross sales. Of the 98 percent of the customers who pay, 60 percent take the discount and pay on Day 10, while 40 percent pay on Day 40. The firm's gross sales are currently $1,000,000 per year, with variable costs amounting to 60 percent of sales. The firm finances its receivables with a 10 percent line of credit, and there are sufficient fixed assets to support a doubling in sales.

The firm's credit manager has proposed that credit terms be changed to 2/20, net 60, and she estimates that this change would increase sales to $1,100,000. However, bad debt losses at the new sales level would be 3 percent, compared with only 2 percent at the old sales level. It is expected that 75 percent of the paying customers would take the discount under the new terms, paying on Day 20, while 25 percent would now pay on Day 60.

a. What are the old and new average collection periods?

b. Find ΔI, the incremental change in the firm's investment in receivables.

c. Find ΔP, the incremental change in pre-tax profits. Should the change in credit terms be made?

d. Assume that the firm's competitors immediately react to the change in credit terms by easing their own terms. This causes Rzasa to gain no new customers; however, of the existing buyers who pay (2 percent continue as bad debt losses), 75 percent now take the discount and pay on Day 20, while 25 percent pay on Day 60. What is the effect on the firm's pre-tax profits?

(Do Parts e and f only if you are using the computerized diskette.)

e. The responsiveness of sales to a proposed change in credit terms is, of course, uncertain. Suppose that the firm implemented the credit manager's policy, but sales only rose to $1,025,000. (Assume that all other aspects of her forecast actually occur.) What change in pre-tax profits will this generate? What if sales are $1,050,000?

f. Refer back to the firm's original terms, collection experience, and level of sales. Suppose that the firm's credit manager decides to shorten the collection period by tightening the credit terms to 2/10, net 30. Bad debt losses would remain at 2 percent of gross sales and collection percentages are expected to remain at 60 and 40 percent. However, this tightening of credit terms is expected to reduce gross sales to $900,000. Would this decision be advisable?

Selected Additional References and Cases

Recent articles which address credit policy and receivables management include the following:

Atkins, Joseph C., and Yong H. Kim, "Comment and Correction: Opportunity Cost in the Evaluation of Investment in Accounts Receivable," *Financial Management*, Winter 1977, 71-74.

Ben-Horim, Moshe, and Haim Levy, "Management of Accounts Receivable under Inflation," *Financial Management*, Spring 1983, 42-48.

Dyl, Edward A., "Another Look at the Evaluation of Interest in Accounts Receivable," *Financial Management*, Winter 1977, 67-70.

Gentry, James A., and Jesus M. De La Garza, "A Generalized Model for Monitoring Accounts Receivable," *Financial Management*, Winter 1985, 28-38.

Hill, Ned C., and Kenneth D. Riener, "Determining the Cash Discount in the Firm's Credit Policy," *Financial Management*, Spring 1979, 68-73.

Kim, Yong H., and Joseph C. Atkins, "Evaluating Investments in Accounts Receivable: A Wealth Maximizing Framework," *Journal of Finance*, May 1978, 403-412.

Oh, John S., "Opportunity Cost in the Evaluation of Investment in Accounts Receivable," *Financial Management*, Summer 1976, 32-36.

Roberts, Gordon S., and Jeremy A. Viscione, "Captive Finance Subsidiaries: The Manager's View," *Financial Management*, Spring 1981, 36-42.

Sachdeva, Kanwal S., and Lawrence J. Gitman, "Accounts Receivable Decisions in a Capital Budgeting Framework," *Financial Management*, Winter 1981, 45-49.

Walia, Tinlochan S., "Explicit and Implicit Cost of Changes in the Level of Accounts Receivable and the Credit Policy Decision of the Firm," *Financial Management*, Winter 1977, 75-78.

Weston, J. Fred, and Pham D. Tuan, "Comment on Analysis of Credit Policy Changes," *Financial Management*, Winter 1980, 59-63.

The following cases focus on the credit policy decision:

Case 7, "Englehardt Kitchens," in the Crum-Brigham casebook, which demonstrates how the various credit policy variables interact to determine (1) the firm's level of accounts receivable and (2) its risk and rate of return.

"Zukowski Meats, Inc.," in the Harrington casebook, which stresses forecasting the effect of a credit policy change on the working capital accounts.

VI
FINANCIAL ANALYSIS AND PLANNING

649

20

FINANCIAL STATEMENT ANALYSIS

Financial analysis is of vital concern to corporate managers, security analysts, investors, and lenders, all of whom use it for a variety of purposes. As an indication of its importance, a recent U.S. Commerce Department survey showed that the highest salaries for corporate employees in the 25 to 30 age group went to people engaged in financial analysis and control—they beat out engineers, marketers, and all the rest. Further, this situation extends on up the ladder—throughout the United States and indeed the world, efficiency and cost control are the keys to success, so people with those skills are increasingly taking over the top spots in industry.

The scope of any financial analysis depends on its purpose, which may range from a total analysis of a firm's strengths and weaknesses to a relatively simple analysis of its short-term liquidity. Since the foundation of most types of financial analysis is the firm's financial statements, we focus on statement analysis in this chapter. Note, though, that its financial statements reflect what has happened in the past, yet the really interesting question is where the firm will go in the future. Therefore, analysts invariably use the types of analysis discussed in this chapter as a springboard for predicting and planning for the future, the subject of the next chapter.

FINANCIAL STATEMENTS AND REPORTS

A corporate *annual report* provides a verbal description of the firm's operating results during the past year and a discussion of new developments that will affect its future operations. More important, the report presents several financial statements, including three basic financial statements—the *income statement*, the *balance sheet*, and the *statement of changes in financial position*. Taken together, these statements give an accounting picture of the firm's operations and its financial position. Detailed data are provided for the two most recent years, along with brief historical summaries of key operating statistics for the past 5 or 10 years.[1]

Table 20-1 contains the 1985 and 1986 income statements for Southern Metals Company, a major producer of fabricated aluminum products, and Table 20-2 presents its balance sheets for those same years.

Some points about the income statement and balance sheet are worth noting:

1. **Earnings and dividends.** Southern earned $110 million for its common stockholders in 1986, and it paid out $90 million in common dividends. EPS was $2.20, and DPS was $1.80.

2. **Cash flows.** Southern's cash flow from operations is equal to net income plus any noncash expenses. In 1986, the cash flow after preferred dividends was $110 million net income plus $100 million depreciation expense, for a total cash flow of $210 million. Depreciation does not really *provide* funds; it is simply a noncash charge which is added back to net income to obtain an estimate of the cash flow from operations. However, if the firm made no sales and hence paid no taxes, then depreciation would certainly not provide cash flows.

3. **Cash versus other assets.** Although the assets are all stated in terms of dollars, only cash represents actual money. We see from Table 20-2 that Southern can write checks at present for a total of $50 million (versus current liabilities of $300 million due within a year). The noncash current assets will presumably be converted to cash eventually, but they do not represent cash-in-hand.

4. **Liabilities versus stockholders' equity.** The claims against assets are of two types—liabilities, or money the company owes, and the stockholders' ownership position.[2] The equity, or net worth, is a residual; for 1986,

$$\text{Assets} \quad - \quad \text{Liabilities} \quad = \text{Stockholders' equity.}$$
$$\$2,000,000,000 \ - \ \$1,100,000,000 \ = \quad \$900,000,000.$$

Suppose assets decline in value. For example, suppose some of the accounts receivable are written off as bad debts. Liabilities remain constant, so the value of the equity declines. Therefore, the risk of asset value fluctuations is borne largely by the stockholders, and specifically by the common stockholders. Note, however, that if asset values rise, these benefits accrue exclusively to the common stockholders.

5. **Breakdown of the stockholders' equity account.** Note that the equity section is divided into four accounts—preferred stock, common stock, paid-in capital,

---

[1]Firms also provide quarterly reports, but these are much less comprehensive than the annual reports. In addition, larger firms file even more detailed statements, giving the particulars of each major division or subsidiary, with the Securities and Exchange Commission (SEC). These reports, called *10-K reports*, are made available to stockholders upon request to a company's secretary. Finally, many larger firms also publish *statistical supplements*, which give financial statement data and key ratios going back about 10 years. Like the 10-K, statistical supplements may be obtained from the corporate secretary.

[2]One could divide liabilities into (1) debts owed to specific firms or individuals and (2) other items such as deferred taxes and reserves. We do not make this distinction, so the terms *debt* and *liabilities* are used synonymously.

Table 20-1
Southern Metals Company:
Income Statements for the Years Ended December 31
(Millions of Dollars, Except for Per Share Data)

	1986	1985
Net sales	$3,000	$2,850
Costs and expenses:		
Labor and materials	2,544	2,413
Depreciation	100	90
Selling	22	20
General and administrative	40	35
Lease payments	28	28
Total costs	$2,734	$2,586
Net operating income, or earnings before interest and taxes (EBIT)	$ 266	$ 264
Less interest expense:		
Interest on notes payable	8	2
Interest on first mortgage bonds	40	42
Interest on debentures	18	3
Total interest	$ 66	$ 47
Earnings before taxes	$ 200	$ 217
Taxes (at 40%)	80	87
Net income before preferred dividends	$ 120	$ 130
Dividends to preferred stockholders	10	10
Net income available to common stockholders	$ 110	$ 120
Disposition of net income:		
Dividends to common stockholders	$ 90	$ 80
Addition to retained earnings	$ 20	$ 40
Per share of common stock:		
Stock price	$28.50	$29.00
Earnings per share (EPS)[a]	$ 2.20	$ 2.40
Dividends per share (DPS)[a]	$ 1.80	$ 1.60

[a]There are 50 million common shares outstanding; see Table 20-2. EPS is based on earnings after preferred dividends, that is, on net income available to common stockholders. Calculations of EPS and DPS for 1986 are as follows:

$$EPS = \frac{\text{Net income available to common stockholders}}{\text{Shares outstanding}} = \frac{\$110,000,000}{50,000,000} = \$2.20.$$

$$DPS = \frac{\text{Dividends paid to common stockholders}}{\text{Shares outstanding}} = \frac{\$90,000,000}{50,000,000} = \$1.80.$$

and retained earnings. The retained earnings account is built up over time by the firm's "saving" a part of its earnings rather than paying all earnings out as dividends. The other three accounts arose from the sale of stock by the firm to raise capital. Accountants generally assign a *par value* to common stock—Southern's stock has a par value of $1. Now suppose Southern were to sell 1 million additional shares at a price of $30 per share. The company would raise $30 million, and the cash

Table 20-2
Southern Metals Company:
December 31 Balance Sheets
(Millions of Dollars)

Assets	1986	1985	Liabilities and Equity	1986	1985
Cash	$ 50	$ 55	Accounts payable	$ 60	$ 30
Marketable securities	0	25	Notes payable	100	60
Accounts receivable	350	315	Accrued wages	10	10
Inventories	300	215	Accrued taxes	130	120
Total current assets	$ 700	$ 610	Total current liabilities	$ 300	$ 220
Gross plant and equipment	1,800	1,470	First mortgage bonds	500	520
Less depreciation	500	400	Debentures	300	60
Net plant and equipment	$1,300	$1,070	Total long-term debt	$ 800	$ 580
			Stockholders' equity:		
			Preferred stock (1,000,000 shares, 10% preferred, $100 par value)	100	100
			Common stock (50,000,000 shares, $1 par value)	50	50
			Additional paid-in capital	90	90
			Retained earnings	660	640
			Total common equity	$ 800	$ 780
			Total stockholders' equity	900	880
Total assets	$2,000	$1,680	Total claims	$2,000	$1,680

Notes:
a. The first mortgage bonds have a sinking fund requirement of $20 million a year.

b. Southern had $28 million in uncapitalized lease payments in both 1985 and 1986; see Table 20-1.

account would go up by this amount. Of the total, $1 million would be added to common stock, and $29 million would be added to paid-in capital. Thus, after the sale, common stock would show $51 million, paid-in capital would show $119 million, and there would be 51 million shares outstanding.

6. The time dimension. The balance sheet may be thought of as a snapshot of the firm's financial position *at a point in time*—for example, on December 31, 1986. The income statement, on the other hand, reports on operations *over a period of time*—for example, during the calendar year 1986.

7. Retained earnings. The balance sheet account retained earnings indicates how much of its past earnings the firm has reinvested. Further, firms retain earnings primarily to expand the business, which means investing in plant and equipment, inventories, and so on, and *not* in a bank account. *Thus, retained earnings as reported on the balance sheet do not represent cash and are not "available" for the payment of dividends or anything else.*[3]

---

[3]Also, recall from your accounting course the difference between accrual and cash accounting. Even though a company reports record earnings and shows an increase in the retained earnings account, it may still be short of cash.

Statement of Changes in Financial Position

Twenty years ago, most annual reports contained a statement called the "Sources and Uses of Funds Statement." The purpose of the statement was to report where the firm had obtained funds during the past year and how it had used them. For example, had it obtained most of its funds as bank loans, as retained earnings, or what, and had it used those funds to retire bonds, to build new plants, to build up inventories, or what? One could look at the statement and see the total sources and total uses (which were equal), and how funds were obtained and used, but there was no summary figure which could be used to judge whether the company ended the year in a stronger or weaker position.

Gradually, companies changed the name of the statement to "Statement of Changes in Financial Position." The same basic sources and uses were listed, but a focal point, or bottom line, was provided—the statement was prepared to show not just total sources and uses but also the change in net working capital (current assets minus current liabilities). It was believed—generally correctly—that if its net working capital increased, then the firm's financial position was strengthened.

Within the last year or two, a number of companies have begun to use a new format for the statement, one that focuses on cash rather than net working capital. These firms were still in the minority in 1986 (when the 1985 annual reports came out), but they included trend-setters such as IBM and Xerox. Our prediction is that the new format will soon dominate, not because IBM uses it but because it provides information in the most useful way for financial analysis. Accordingly, in this section we discuss the statement of changes in financial position with a focus on cash and cash equivalents (marketable securities).

The starting point in preparing a statement of changes in financial position is to determine the change in each balance sheet item, and then to record it as either a source or a use of funds in accordance with the following rules:

Sources: **1.** Any increase in a liability or equity account. Borrowing and issuing common stock are examples.
2. Any decrease in an asset account. Selling some inventories is an example.

Uses: **1.** Any decrease in a liability or equity account. Paying off a loan is an example.
2. Any increase in an asset account. Buying fixed assets is an example.

Thus, sources of funds include bank loans, retained earnings, and new issues of stock, as well as money generated by selling assets, collecting receivables, and even drawing down the cash account. Uses include acquiring fixed assets, building up inventories, paying off debts, and repurchasing stock.

Table 20-3 shows the changes in Southern Metals' balance sheet accounts during the calendar year 1986, with each change designated as a source or a use. Sources and uses each total $470 million.[4] Note that Table 20-3 does not contain

---

[4]Adjustments must normally be made if fixed assets were sold or retired during the year. Southern had no sales of fixed assets or major retirements during 1986.

Table 20-3
Southern Metals Company:
Changes in Balance Sheet Accounts during 1986
(Millions of Dollars)

	12/31/86	12/31/85	Change	
			Source	Use
Cash	$ 50	$ 55	$ 5	
Marketable securities	0	25	25	
Accounts receivable	350	315		$ 35
Inventories	300	215		85
Gross plant and equipment	1,800	1,470		330
Accumulated depreciation[a]	500	400	100	
Accounts payable	60	30	30	
Notes payable	100	60	40	
Accrued wages	10	10		
Accrued taxes	130	120	10	
Mortgage bonds	500	520		20
Debentures	300	60	240	
Preferred stock	100	100		
Common stock	50	50		
Paid-in capital	90	90		
Retained earnings	660	640	20	
			$470	$470

[a]Depreciation is a *contra-asset*, and not an asset. Hence, an increase in depreciation is a source of funds.

any summary accounts such as total current assets or net plant and equipment. If we included summary accounts in Table 20-3, and then used these accounts to prepare the statement of changes in financial position, we would be "double counting."

The data contained in Table 20-3 are next used as inputs to the formal statement of changes in financial position. As noted above, several formats are used, but we focus on the cash format as shown in Table 20-4. Note that every item in the "change" columns of Table 20-3 is carried over to Table 20-4 except retained earnings: The statement of changes in financial position reports net income as a source and dividends as a use, rather than netting these items out and just reporting the increase in retained earnings. Also, cash and marketable securities are combined in Table 20-4. Like most large companies, Southern regards its marketable securities as cash equivalents, so with regard to financial position, they are not distinguished.

Table 20-4 pinpoints the sources and uses of Southern's funds, *funds* being defined as cash and marketable securities. The top part shows funds generated by and used in operations—for Southern, operations provided $260 million but required the use of $450 million, so $190 million of new funds were required to support operations. By far the heaviest use of funds was to increase fixed assets.

Table 20-4

Southern Metals Company:
1986 Statement of Changes in Financial Position (Cash Basis)
(Millions of Dollars)

Funds Provided by and Used in Operations

Sources:

Net income before preferred dividends	$120.00
Depreciation	100.00
Increase in accounts payable	30.00
Increase in accrued taxes	10.00
Total sources from operations	$260.00

Uses:

Increase in accounts receivable	$ 35.00
Increase in inventories	85.00
Increase in fixed assets	330.00
Total uses for operations	$450.00
Net funds from operations	($190.00)

Financing Activities

Increase in notes payable	$ 40.00
Increase in debentures	240.00
Repayment of mortgage bonds	(20.00)
Net funds from financing	$260.00
Total funds from operations and financing	$ 70.00
Less common and preferred dividends	100.00
Increase (decrease) in cash and equivalents	($ 30.00)

Southern's financing activities included borrowing from banks (notes payable) and the sale of debentures, while it paid off part of its mortgage bonds through sinking fund operations. In net, Southern raised $260 million from the capital markets during 1986. However, Southern also paid $100 million of dividends on its common and preferred stock.

When all these items are totaled, we see that Southern had a $30 million cash shortfall during 1986, which was met by selling off marketable securities ($25 million) and reducing cash balances ($5 million).

Southern is a strong, well-managed company, and its statement of changes in financial position shows nothing unusual or alarming. It does show a $190 million net cash drain from operations, but that is entirely attributable to its expansion of net fixed assets. Had it showed an operating cash drain in a situation where fixed assets did not increase (that is, where the addition to gross fixed assets equaled depreciation charges), then we would have had something to worry about, because such a drain would be much more likely to continue and to bleed the company to death unless the problem was corrected.

Sophisticated security analysts, loan officers, and corporate raiders pay close attention to the statement of changes in financial position. Finance is, after all, a cash flow oriented discipline, and this statement gives a good picture of the annual cash flows generated by the business. A bank loan officer could examine Table 20-4 (or, better yet, a series of such tables going back for perhaps the last 5 years and projected out several years into the future) to get an idea of whether or not the business could generate the cash necessary to pay off a requested loan. If projected cash flows appear sufficient, then the loan will be granted. If the cash flows are questionable, then the banker will pay close attention to the balance sheet, attempting to determine whether the assets would bring enough in a liquidation to satisfy the loan.

Cash flow analysis has always been important, but perhaps raiders such as T. Boone Pickens have done more than anyone to highlight the importance of such analysis. Pickens and others have made a science of looking at a company such as Gulf Oil, analyzing each of its many parts on a separate basis to determine the cash flows attributable to each part, setting values on those parts, and then adding up the calculated values of each part to determine the *break-up value* of the firm. Pickens and the other raiders work with investment banking houses like Drexel Burnham Lambert, who use the cash flow projections to ascertain how much debt the operation can support, and then line up purchasers of such debt to provide the funds needed to enable the raiders to make offers for the target companies.

Managers have, of course, always been interested in their companies' cash flows, but the actions of Pickens and the other raiders has heightened that interest enormously. Companies now know (1) that their values are very much dependent on cash flows (as well as reported accounting profits), because the higher the cash flows, the more someone can bid for the company, and (2) that if their assets are not providing as much cash flow as they could under more efficient management, then again, raiders will attempt to take over the company and either install better managers or break up the company and sell its assets to companies who can operate those assets better.

We will consider the takeover phenomena in more depth in Chapter 22, but first, in the remainder of this chapter, we shall discuss techniques for analyzing a firm's financial statements in order to pinpoint its strengths and weaknesses.

RATIO ANALYSIS

Table 20-5 presents 15 commonly used ratios and illustrates them with data on Southern Metals. The ratios are broken down into five categories: liquidity, asset management, debt management, profitability, and market value. Since ratios are discussed in most introductory finance courses, we will not go over them in detail. Still, the following points are worth repeating:

1. Inventory turnover is sales divided by inventory. Note that sales occur over the entire year, whereas the inventory figure is for one point in time. This makes it better to use an average inventory figure. The average inventory could be calculated by adding beginning and ending figures and dividing by 2, but it would be

Table 20-5
Southern Metals Company:
Summary of Financial Ratios

Ratio	Formula for Calculation	1985	1986	1986 Industry Average	Comment
I. Liquidity					
1. Current	$\dfrac{\text{Current assets}}{\text{Current liabilities}}$	2.8×	2.3×	2.5×	Slightly low; bad trend
2. Quick, or acid test	$\dfrac{\text{Current assets} - \text{Inventories}}{\text{Current liabilities}}$	1.8×	1.3×	1.1×	OK, but bad trend
II. Asset Management					
3. Inventory turnover	$\dfrac{\text{Sales}}{\text{Inventory}}$	13.3×	10.0×	9.3×	OK, but bad trend
4. Average collection period (ACP)	$\dfrac{\text{Receivables}}{\text{Sales}/360}$	39.8 days	42.0 days	36.2 days	Poor; bad trend
5. Fixed asset turnover	$\dfrac{\text{Sales}}{\text{Fixed assets}}$	2.7×	2.3×	3.1×	Low; bad trend
6. Total asset turnover	$\dfrac{\text{Sales}}{\text{Total assets}}$	1.7×	1.5×	1.8×	Low; bad trend
III. Debt Management					
7. Debt to total assets (D/A)	$\dfrac{\text{Total debt}}{\text{Total assets}}$	47.6%	55.0%	40.1%	Very high; bad trend
8. Times interest earned (TIE)	$\dfrac{\text{EBIT}}{\text{Interest charges}}$	5.6×	4.0×	6.2×	Very low; bad trend
9. Fixed charge coverage	$\dfrac{\text{EBIT} + \text{Lease payments}}{\text{Interest charges} + \text{Lease payments} + \dfrac{\text{Sinking fund payments}}{(1-T)}}$	2.7×	2.3×	4.0×	Very low; bad trend
IV. Profitability					
10. Profit margin on sales	$\dfrac{\text{Net income}^{a}}{\text{Sales}}$	4.2%	3.7%	5.1%	Low; bad trend
11. Basic earning power (BEP)	$\dfrac{\text{EBIT}}{\text{Total assets}}$	15.7%	13.3%	17.2%	Very low; bad trend
12. Return on total assets (ROA)	$\dfrac{\text{Net income}^{a}}{\text{Total assets}}$	7.1%	5.5%	9.0%	Very low; bad trend
13. Return on equity (ROE)	$\dfrac{\text{Net income}^{a}}{\text{Common equity}}$	15.4%	13.8%	15.0%	Low; bad trend
V. Market Value					
14. Price/earnings (P/E)	$\dfrac{\text{Price per share}}{\text{Earnings per share}}$	12.1×	13.0×	13.5×	Slightly low
15. Market/book (M/B)	$\dfrac{\text{Market price per share}}{\text{Book value per share}}$	1.9×	1.8×	2.1×	Low

[a]Net income after preferred dividends.

preferable to sum the monthly inventory figures and divide by 12. If it were determined that the firm's business is highly seasonal, or if there has been a strong upward or downward sales trend during the year, it becomes essential to make some such adjustment. To maintain comparability with industry averages, however, the figures shown in Table 20-5 are based on year-end data.

2. It would be better to base the average collection period (ACP) on credit sales rather than total sales. However, since information on credit sales is generally unavailable, total sales must be used. Also, note that the financial community generally uses 360 rather than 365 as the number of days in the year for purposes such as this, but as long as consistency is maintained, this makes no difference. Note too that it would be better to use *average* receivables = (beginning + ending)/2 = ($315 + $350)/2 = $332.5 (or else a 12-month average) in the formula. Had this been done, Southern's ACP would have been $332.5/$8.333 = 40.0 days. Finally, as we know from our discussion in Chapter 19, the ACP does have weaknesses from the standpoint of appraising a company's credit management program, so keep these problems in mind when using this ratio.

3. Potential problems exist with the fixed asset and total asset turnover ratios because of differences in accounting methods (inventory valuation and depreciation for fixed assets), the effects of inflation as discussed later in the chapter, and leasing (one company may lease many of its assets and hence report high fixed asset and total asset turnover ratios).

4. In this book, we generally focus on the ratio of total debt to total assets, because we are concerned with how assets have been financed. However, one often sees two other debt ratios: (1) *long-term debt to total capital*, with capital defined as long-term debt, preferred stock, and common equity; and (2) the *debt/ equity ratio*, where debt generally is total debt and equity means common equity. Note that, for a firm with no preferred stock, the debt to assets (D/A) and debt to equity (D/E) ratios are simply transformations of one another:[5]

$$D/A = \frac{D/E}{1 + D/E} \quad \text{and} \quad D/E = \frac{D/A}{1 - D/A}.$$

Thus, given one ratio, it is easy to convert to the other. Note that both ratios increase as a firm of a given size (total assets) uses a greater proportion of debt.

---

[5]The proofs of these two relationships are straightforward:

$$\frac{D}{A} = \frac{D}{E + D} = \frac{D/E}{E/E + D/E} = \frac{D/E}{1 + D/E},$$

and

$$\frac{D}{E} = \frac{D}{A - D} = \frac{D/A}{A/A - D/A} = \frac{D/A}{1 - D/A}.$$

Note that the debt/equity ratio can also be defined in terms of long-term debt only. It is essential that analysts know precisely what definitions are being used when developing ratios for comparative purposes.

However, D/A rises linearly and approaches a limit of 100 percent (for any solvent firm), whereas D/E rises exponentially and approaches infinity.

5. As you know, for purposes of calculating the weighted average cost of capital, the debt ratio should in theory be based on the market value of the firm's assets, that is, the sum of the market values of its debt and equity. Market values are especially important if the accounting values as shown on the balance sheet are significantly different from the market values, as is true of many technology companies and natural resource firms.

6. With regard to the fixed charge coverage ratio, note that whereas interest charges and lease payments are tax deductible, and hence are paid with pre-tax dollars, sinking fund payments must be paid with after-tax dollars. Thus, in the equation, sinking fund payments are "grossed up" by dividing by $(1 - T)$, where T is the firm's marginal tax rate, to find the before-tax income required both to pay taxes and to cover the sinking fund payment. The fixed charge coverage ratio recognizes that failure to meet lease payments or sinking fund payments can result in bankruptcy just as surely as failure to meet interest payments.[6]

7. The basic earning power ratio is useful for comparing firms in different tax situations and with different degrees of financial leverage. Notice, however, that EBIT is earned all during the year, whereas the total assets figure is as of the end of the year. Therefore, it would be conceptually better to calculate the ratio as EBIT/Average assets = EBIT/[(Beginning assets + Ending assets)/2]. We have not made this adjustment because the published ratios used for comparative purposes do not include it. However, when we develop our own comparative industry ratios from basic data, we do make the adjustment. Also, note that the same adjustment would be appropriate for both ROA and ROE.

8. Although the return on total assets is useful for internal purposes, it is not useful for making interfirm comparisons because it is sensitive to differences in capital structures. Therefore, for interfirm profitability comparisons, either the basic earning power ratio or the ROE should be used.

9. The price/earnings (P/E) ratio shows how much investors are willing to pay per dollar of reported profits. Other factors held constant, companies with better

---

[6]For certain purposes, primarily ascertaining whether or not coverage ratios as specified in bond indentures are met before issuing new bonds, companies are required to use a coverage ratio which is prescribed by the SEC:

$$\text{SEC coverage ratio} = \frac{\text{EBIT} + (1/3)(\text{Lease payments})}{\text{Interest charges} + (1/3)(\text{Lease payments})}.$$

There is no particular reason for using one-third of the lease payments, but the formula is a rule-of-thumb that has been used since the 1930s. Another ratio that is frequently used is the following:

$$\frac{\text{Rate of return on}}{\text{investors' capital}} = \frac{\text{Interest charges} + \text{Net income}}{\text{Long-term debt} + \text{Equity}}.$$

This ratio is especially important in the public utility industries, where regulators are concerned about the companies' using their monopoly positions to earn excessive returns on investors' capital. In fact, regulators try to set utility prices (service rates) at levels that will force the rate of return on investors' capital to equal the company's cost of capital.

growth prospects have higher P/E ratios. Similarly, the lower a company's risk, the higher is its P/E ratio, other factors held constant.[7]

10. The ratio of a stock's market price to its book value (M/B) gives another indication of how investors regard the company. Companies with high rates of return on equity in relation to their cost of equity sell at higher multiples of book value than those with low returns. Note also that the degree of conservatism used by the company's accountants can affect the market/book ratio: The more conservative the accountants, the higher the market/book ratio will be, other factors held constant. The same holds true for the P/E ratio.

Analyzing the Ratios

Financial ratios are analyzed (1) by comparing a firm's ratios with the industry average ratios and (2) by comparing the trends in a firm's ratios over time.[8] Industry comparisons provide an indication of the comparative financial condition of the firm being analyzed, while trend analysis gives clues as to whether the financial condition is improving or deteriorating. We will use both techniques to assess Southern Metals' financial condition.

Liquidity

Southern's *current ratio* is slightly below the industry average, but not enough to cause concern. Since current assets are scheduled to be converted to cash in the near future, it is highly probable that they could be liquidated at close to their stated value. With a current ratio of 2.3, Southern could liquidate current assets at only 43 percent of book value and still pay off current creditors in full.[9]

The industry average *quick ratio* is 1.1, so Southern's 1.3 compares favorably with other firms in the industry. If the accounts receivable could be collected, the company could pay off current liabilities even without selling any inventory. However, it should be noted that the trend is downward for both the current and quick ratios. In summary, Southern's liquidity position is adequate, but it bears watching in the future.

---

[7]Since earnings per share are generally somewhat volatile, a high or low "spot" P/E ratio may simply reflect the fact that investors expect a change in earnings, that is, that this year's earnings are different from "normalized" or "trend line" earnings on which market prices are based. Thus, General Motors sold at a P/E of 21 in 1982, when earnings were depressed, but at a P/E of only 3.7 in 1984, when earnings were inflated as a result of a combination of "catch-up demand," restrictions on Japanese imports, and the effects of labor union give-backs carried over from the 1982 recession. GM's P/E based on "normalized" earnings is about 8.

We should also note that the EPS used to calculate the P/E ratio can be either EPS over the *past* year, as in our example, or the EPS projected for the *next* 12 months. Projected P/E ratios are often used by security analysts. For comparison purposes, either definition is suitable, so long as one maintains consistency.

[8]These two analytical techniques are often called (1) *cross-sectional analysis* and (2) *time-series analysis*, respectively.

[9]$1/2.3 = 0.43 = 43\%$. Note that $0.43(\$700) \approx \$300$, the amount of current liabilities.

Asset Management

Southern's *inventory turnover* of 10.0 times compares favorably with an industry average of 9.3 times. This suggests that the company does not hold excessive stocks of inventory; excess stocks are, of course, unproductive and represent an investment with a low or zero rate of return. This high inventory turnover ratio also reinforces our faith in the current ratio. If the turnover were low—say 3 or 4 times—one might wonder whether the firm was holding damaged or obsolete materials not actually worth their stated value.

Southern's *average collection period* is almost 6 days longer than the industry average, indicating either poor collection procedures or credit terms that are more lenient than the industry in general. Moreover, Southern's credit terms call for payment within 30 days, so the 42-day collection period indicates that customers, on the average, are not paying their bills on time. Also, note that the ACP has been rising over the past two years. If the credit policy has not been changed, this would be evidence that steps should be taken to expedite the collection of accounts receivable. Recall from Chapter 19, though, that if sales are seasonal or cyclical, the ACP could be misleading, so care must be taken when analyzing this ratio.

Southern's *fixed asset turnover* ratio of 2.3 times compares poorly with the industry average of 3.1 times, indicating that the firm is not using its fixed assets to as high a percentage of capacity as are the other firms in the industry. The financial manager should bear this fact in mind when production people request funds for new capital investments.

Southern's *total asset turnover* ratio is also below the industry average—the company is not generating a sufficient volume of business for the size of its asset investment. Sales should be increased, some assets should be disposed of, or both steps should be taken.

Debt Management

Southern's *debt ratio* is 55.0 percent, meaning that creditors have supplied more than half of its capital. Since the average debt ratio for this industry—and for manufacturing generally—is about 40 percent, Southern would find it difficult to borrow additional funds at a reasonable cost without first raising more equity capital. Creditors would be reluctant to lend the firm more money, and management would probably be subjecting the company to the risk of bankruptcy if it sought to increase the debt ratio still more by borrowing. Also, note that Southern had obtained 5 percent of its 1986 capital as preferred stock. If we classify preferred as debt because of its fixed-charge nature, then the firm's 1986 fixed charge capital ratio would be 60.0 percent.

Southern's *interest coverage (TIE)* is 4.0 times. Since the industry average is 6.2 times, the company is covering its interest charges by a relatively low margin of safety and deserves a poor rating. Additionally, Southern's *fixed charge coverage* ratio is even further below the industry average (on a proportional basis). These ratios reinforce our conclusion, based on the debt ratio, that Southern would face difficulties if it attempted to borrow additional funds, and a small decrease in earnings would place the company in jeopardy of bankruptcy.

Profitability

Southern's *profit margin* is below the industry average of 5.1 percent, indicating that its sales prices are relatively low, that its costs are relatively high, or both. Additionally, Southern's *basic earning power* ratio is well below the industry average. Thus, because of its low turnover ratios and its low profit margin on sales, the company is not getting as much operating income out of its assets as is the average metals company.

Southern's 5.5 percent *return on total assets* is well below the 9.0 percent average for the industry. This low rate results in part from Southern's low basic earning power and in part from its above average use of debt, which causes its interest payments to be high and its profits to be correspondingly low. Southern's 13.8 percent *return on equity* is also below the 15 percent industry average, but not as far below as the return on total assets. This results from Southern's greater use of debt, a point analyzed in detail later in the chapter.

Southern's *P/E ratio* is slightly below the average of other large metal fabricators, suggesting that the company is regarded as being somewhat riskier than most, as having poorer growth prospects, or both. The *M/B* ratio also indicates that investors are willing to pay slightly less for Southern's book value than for that of an average metals company.

COMMON SIZE ANALYSIS

In a common size analysis, all income statement items are divided by sales, and all balance sheet items are divided by total assets. Thus, a *common size income statement* shows each item as a percentage of sales, and a *common size balance sheet* shows each item as a percentage of total assets. The significant advantage of common size statements is that they facilitate comparisons of balance sheets and income statements over time and across companies.

Table 20-6 contains Southern's common size income statements, along with the composite statement for the industry. Southern's labor and materials costs are somewhat above average, as is its depreciation. However, Southern's selling expenses are lower than average, which could be one reason why it is not generating sales commensurate with its asset base, and hence has low asset turnover ratios. Thus, Southern's marketing people may not be sufficiently aggressive. Note also that Southern's interest expenses are relatively high, but its taxes are relatively low because of its low EBIT. The net effect of all these forces is a relatively low profit margin.

Table 20-7 contains Southern's common size balance sheets, along with the industry average. Three striking differences are revealed: (1) Southern's receivables are significantly higher than the industry average, (2) its inventories are significantly lower, and (3) Southern uses far more fixed charge capital (debt and preferred) than the average metals firm.

The conclusions reached in a common size analysis generally parallel those derived from ratio analysis. However, occasionally a serious deficiency is highlighted

Table 20-6
Southern Metals Company:
Common Size Income Statements

	1985	1986	1986 Industry Average
Net sales	100%	100%	100%
Costs and expenses:			
Labor and materials	85	85	83
Depreciation	3	3	2
Selling	1	1	2
General and administrative	1	1	1
Lease payments	1	1	1
Total costs	91%	91%	89%
Earnings before interest and taxes	9%	9%	11%
Interest expense:			
Interest on notes payable	0	0	0
Interest on first mortgage bonds	1	1	1
Interest on debentures	0	1	0
Total interest	1%	2%	1%
Earnings before taxes	8%	7%	10%
Taxes	3	3	5
Net income (profit margin)	5%	4%	5%

only by one of the two analytical techniques. Thus, a thorough financial statement analysis will include both ratio and common size analyses, as well as a Du Pont analysis, our next topic.

DU PONT ANALYSIS

Figure 20-1, which is called a *modified Du Pont chart* because that company's managers developed the general approach, shows how the profit margin on sales, asset turnover, and financial leverage combine to determine the rate of return on equity. The left-hand side of the chart develops the profit margin on sales. The various expense items are listed, and then summed to obtain Southern's total costs. Subtracting costs from sales yields the company's net income, which when divided by sales indicates that 3.7 percent of each sales dollar is left over for stockholders.

The right-hand side of the chart lists the various categories of assets, which are summed, and then sales are divided by the sum to find the number of times Southern "turns its assets over" each year. Southern's total asset turnover ratio is 1.5 times.

The profit margin times the total asset turnover ratio is defined as the *Du Pont equation*, which gives the rate of return on total assets (ROA):

Table 20-7
Southern Metals Company:
Common Size Balance Sheets

	1985	1986	1986 Industry Average
Assets			
Cash	3%	2%	2%
Marketable securities	1	0	1
Accounts receivable	19	18	13
Inventories	13	15	20
Total current assets	36%	35%	36%
Gross plant and equipment	88	90	85
Less: Depreciation	24	25	21
Net plant and equipment	64%	65%	64%
Total assets	100%	100%	100%
Liabilities and Equity			
Accounts payable	2%	3%	4%
Notes payable	4	5	3
Accrued wages	1	0	0
Accrued taxes	7	6	7
Total current liabilities	13%	15%	14%
First mortgage bonds	31	25	17
Debentures	4	15	9
Total long-term debt	35%	40%	26%
Preferred equity	6	5	0
Common equity	46	40	60
Total equity	52%	45%	60%
Total claims	100%	100%	100%

$$\frac{\text{Return on}}{\text{total assets}} = (\text{Profit margin})(\text{Total asset turnover})$$

$$\text{ROA} = \left(\frac{\text{Net income}}{\text{Sales}}\right)\left(\frac{\text{Sales}}{\text{Total assets}}\right) \qquad (20\text{-}1)$$

$$= (3.7\%)(1.5) = 5.5\%.$$

Southern made 3.7 percent, or 3.7 cents, on each dollar of sales, and assets were "turned over" 1.5 times during the year, so Southern earned a return of 5.5 percent on its assets.

If Southern used only equity, the 5.5 percent return on assets would equal the rate of return on equity. However, 60 percent of the firm's capital was supplied by creditors and preferred stockholders. Since the 5.5 percent return on total assets all goes to common stockholders, who put up only 40 percent of the capital, the return on equity is higher than 5.5 percent. Specifically, the rate of return on assets (ROA) must be multiplied by the *equity multiplier*, which shows the total assets

Figure 20-1
**Modified Du Pont Chart Applied to
Southern Metals Company (Millions of Dollars)**

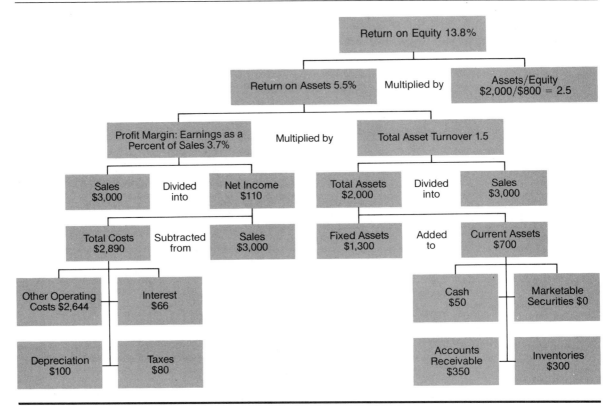

working for each dollar of common equity, to obtain the rate of return on equity
(ROE):

$$
\begin{aligned}
\text{ROE} &= \quad (\text{ROA}) \quad (\text{Equity multiplier}) \\
&= \left(\frac{\text{Net income}}{\text{Total assets}}\right)\left(\frac{\text{Total assets}}{\text{Common equity}}\right) \qquad \textbf{(20-2)} \\
&= (5.5\%)(\$2,000/\$800) \\
&= (5.5\%)(2.5) = 13.8\%.
\end{aligned}
$$

We can combine Equations 20-1 and 20-2 to form the *extended Du Pont equation*:

$$ROE = \left(\begin{array}{c}\text{Profit}\\\text{margin}\end{array}\right)\left(\begin{array}{c}\text{Total asset}\\\text{turnover}\end{array}\right)\left(\begin{array}{c}\text{Equity}\\\text{multiplier}\end{array}\right)$$

$$= \left(\frac{\text{Net income}}{\text{Sales}}\right)\left(\frac{\text{Sales}}{\text{Total assets}}\right)\left(\frac{\text{Total assets}}{\text{Common equity}}\right) \qquad \textbf{(20-3)}$$

$$= \frac{\text{Net income}}{\text{Common equity}}.$$

For Southern Metals, we thus have

$$ROE = (3.7\%)(1.5)(2.5) \approx 13.8\%.$$

This 13.8 percent return on equity could, of course, be calculated directly: Net income/Common equity = $110/$800 = 13.8%. However, the extended Du Pont equation shows how the profit margin, turnover, and leverage interact to determine the return on equity.[10]

Management can use the Du Pont system to analyze ways of improving the firm's performance. On the left, or "profit margin," side of the chart, marketing people can study the effects of raising sales prices (or lowering them to increase volume), of moving into new products or markets with higher margins, and so on, and cost accountants can study the expense items and, working with engineers, purchasing agents, and other operating personnel, seek ways to hold down costs. On the "turnover" side, financial analysts, working with both production and marketing people, can investigate ways of reducing investments in various types of assets. At the same time, the treasurer can analyze the effects of alternative financing strategies, seeking to hold down interest expenses and the risks of debt while still using debt to increase the rate of return on equity.

Equation 20-3 provides a useful comparison between a firm's performance as measured by ROE and the performance of an average firm in the industry:

$$\text{Southern Metals: } ROE = (3.7\%)(1.5)(2.50) \approx 13.8\%.$$
$$\text{Metals industry: } ROE = (5.1\%)(1.8)(1.67) \approx 15.3\%.$$

We see (1) that the average metal company has a significantly higher profit margin, and thus better control over expenses; (2) that the average firm has a higher total asset turnover, and thus is using its assets more productively; but (3) that Southern has offset some of these advantages with its higher financial leverage, although this increased use of leverage increases Southern's risk.

---

[10]Note that in our Du Pont analysis, we have treated preferred stock as debt. Thus, the relevant net income is that available to common stockholders, and the relevant equity multiplier is Total assets/Common equity. The resulting ROE is, therefore, a measure of return to common stockholders. This treatment is consistent with the facts (1) that the common stockholders have voting control of the firm and (2) that preferred stock, with its fixed dividend payments, is really closer to debt financing than to common stock for purposes of performance analysis.

DIVISIONAL ANALYSIS

Thus far we have discussed ratio analysis, and financial analysis generally, on a total corporation basis. Such a consolidated analysis is useful for security analysts and lending officers, but financial managers in large corporations utilize the procedures described in this chapter primarily on a divisional basis. Most U.S. businesses have a large number of *profit centers*; indeed, the 1,000 largest U.S. companies, which produce over half the private sector's goods and services, each have an average of 25 profit centers. Each profit center has its own asset investments, and each is expected to contribute to the corporation's overall profitability. Each profit center can utilize the Du Pont system to monitor its performance, and these data can be transmitted (often electronically) to corporate headquarters, where financial analysts can keep tabs on the various divisions. If the divisions are all performing well, then the corporation's ROE and market value ratios will also look good. If not, then top management should see to it that corrective actions are taken.

Such a *financial control system*, used with good judgment, is absolutely essential for the proper management of any corporation with sales over a few million dollars. Companies like Du Pont, IBM, GM, and GE, which have had excellent performance over a long period, rely heavily upon such systems. Conversely, when larger companies get into trouble, their difficulties can usually be traced either to a breakdown in their control system or a failure to heed the signals the system was giving.[11]

SOURCES OF INDUSTRY DATA

The preceding analysis pointed out the need to compare the company in question with other firms in its industry. In this section, we describe some of the sources of industry data.

External Sources

One useful set of comparative data is Dun & Bradstreet (D&B), which, in its *Key Business Ratios,* provides 14 ratios for a large number of industries. Useful ratios

---

[11]An extended discussion of financial controls would go beyond the scope of this book, but we should point out a few problems with such systems: (1) Different divisions will have assets of different ages. This will affect depreciation, hence profits, and also the investment base, hence ROA and ROE. (2) Frequently, one division sells to another, and the transfer price used in such intercorporate sales will have a major effect on the divisions' relative profitability. (3) The allocation of corporate overheads will affect relative profitability. (4) Certain types of investments may have no payoff for a number of years, and if divisional managers are rewarded only on the basis of short-term results, this may bias decisions against long-run projects. (5) Certain divisions have more debt capacity than others, yet borrowing is generally done at the corporate level; this must be taken into account.

These are just a few of the problems that arise when one attempts to utilize a system of divisional financial controls. Some top managers, when faced with these problems, have just given up and let their division managers operate autonomously. However, this is a sure path to corporate destruction. Well-run corporations recognize and deal with the problems.

can also be found in the *Annual Statement Studies* published by Robert Morris Associates, which is the national association of bank loan officers. The Federal Trade Commission's *Quarterly Financial Report* gives a set of ratios for manufacturing firms by industry group and size of firm. Trade associations and individual firms' credit departments also compile industry average financial ratios. Finally, financial statements for thousands of corporations are available on magnetic tapes, and since most of the larger brokerage houses, banks, and other financial institutions have access to these tapes, security analysts and loan officers can and do generate comparative ratios tailored to their own individual needs.

Each of the listed organizations uses a somewhat different set of ratios, designed for its own purposes. For example, D&B deals mainly with small firms, many of which are proprietorships, and it is concerned largely with the creditors' viewpoint. Accordingly, D&B's ratios emphasize current assets and liabilities, and it provides no market value ratios whatever. Therefore, when you select a comparative data source, be sure that your emphasis is similar to that of the organization whose data you use, or else recognize the limitations of its ratios for your purposes. Additionally, there are often minor definitional differences in the ratios presented by different sources—for example, one may report ROE as net income divided by year-end common equity (Value Line does this) while another may divide by average common equity (Salomon Brothers does this). Therefore, before mixing ratios from different sources, be sure to verify the exact definitions of the ratios used.

Internal Sources

Larger firms will generally create their own comparative data using a data base on magnetic tape supplied by a financial services firm. For example, Standard and Poor's Compustat Services, Inc., markets a number of data tapes and diskettes, covering several thousand industrial and nonindustrial companies.

To illustrate, the *Compustat* primary industry file consists of data on approximately 900 companies. For most companies, annual data are available for the past 20 years, and quarterly data for the last 20 quarters. The data, which are picked up from reports filed with the SEC, are in the form of annual report statements, and the records are updated on a weekly basis to reflect new data as companies report them. Firms which subscribe to the *Compustat* service can use this data base to create up-to-date, tailor-made statistics that best serve their individual needs.

PROBLEMS IN FINANCIAL STATEMENT ANALYSIS

In our discussion of the ratios in Table 20-5, we mentioned some problems one encounters in financial statement analysis. In this section, we discuss some additional problems and limitations.

Development of Comparative Data

Many large firms operate a number of different divisions in quite different industries, and in such cases, it is difficult to develop meaningful industry averages. This tends to make financial statement analysis more useful for small firms with single product lines than for large, multiproduct companies.

Additionally, most firms want to be better than average (although half will be above and half below the median), so merely attaining average performance is not necessarily good. As a target for high-level performance, it is preferable to look at the industry leaders' ratios. Compilers of ratios such as D&B and Robert Morris Associates generally report industry ratios in quartiles. For example, D&B might report that 25 percent of the firms in the aluminum industry have a current ratio above 4.8, that the median is 2.5, and that 25 percent are below 1.6. This gives the analyst an idea of the distribution of ratios within an industry, and he or she can make better judgments about how the firm in question compares with the top firms in its industry.

Distortion of Comparative Data

Inflation has badly distorted firms' balance sheets. Further, reported profits are affected because past inflation affects both depreciation charges and the cost of inventory included in the cost of goods sold. Thus, a financial statement analysis for one firm over time, or a comparative analysis of firms of different ages or which use different accounting methods, must be interpreted with caution and judgment. Inflation's effects are discussed in detail later in this chapter.

Seasonal factors can also distort ratio analysis. For example, the inventory turnover ratio for a food processor will be radically different if the balance sheet figure used for inventory is the one just before versus just after the close of the canning season. Receivables, and also current liabilities, are often affected similarly. These problems can be minimized by using 12-month average figures for balance sheet items.

Notes to Financial Statements

Information which can significantly impact a firm's financial condition is often contained in the notes to its financial statements. These notes contain information on the firm's pension plan, on its noncapitalized lease agreements, on recent acquisitions and divestitures, on its accounting policies, and so on. For example, the notes to Southern's financial statements contain the following information: (1) Inventories are valued at the lower of cost or market, with cost determined by the last-in, first-out (LIFO) method. (2) Receivables have been reduced by $51.3 million in 1986 and by $42.7 million in 1985 to allow for doubtful accounts. (3) Noncancellable operating lease commitments are $26.8 million for 1987, $23.3 million for 1988, and $21.1 million for 1989. (4) As of December 31, 1986, the firm had a $968.2 million actuarial present value of vested pension benefits and $881.6 million in pension fund assets, so its unfunded pension liability was $86.6 million.

Clearly, this information affects Southern's financial position, and it should be considered, either directly or indirectly, by the financial analyst. The decreasing lease commitment means that, other factors held constant, Southern's fixed charge coverage ratio will improve in the future unless it signs new lease contracts. The unfunded pension liability means that the book value of the equity is in a sense overstated, so the general creditors' position is weaker than it would appear at first glance. Other potential problems might be revealed in a more detailed analysis. Indeed, professional analysts occasionally use the footnote information to recast financial statements on a common basis before they even begin to develop and compare ratios, and to these analysts the notes are especially vital.

Interpretation of Results

It is difficult to generalize about whether a particular ratio is "good" or "bad." For example, a high quick ratio may show a strong liquidity position, which is good, or an excessive amount of cash, which is bad because cash is a nonearning asset. Similarly, a high asset turnover ratio may denote either a firm that uses its assets efficiently or one that is undercapitalized and simply cannot afford to buy enough assets. Also, firms often have some ratios which look "good" and others which look "bad," making it difficult to tell whether the firm is, on balance, in a strong or a weak position. For this reason, ratio analysis is normally used as an input to judgmental decisions. However, later in the chapter we shall discuss multiple discriminant analysis, a procedure which can be used to assign weights to different ratios and which can thus permit us to quantify a company's overall financial strength.

Differences in Accounting Treatment

Different accounting practices can distort ratio comparisons. For example, consider the effect of different inventory valuation methods. In Chapter 17, we discussed four inventory valuation methods: (1) specific identification, (2) first-in, first-out (FIFO), (3) last-in, first-out (LIFO), and (4) weighted average. Here we will focus on the effects of using FIFO versus LIFO.

During inflationary periods, LIFO produces a higher cost of goods sold and a lower end-of-period inventory valuation. Table 20-8 contains the simplified financial statements for two firms: Firm L, which uses LIFO inventory accounting, and Firm F, which uses FIFO accounting. The footnotes to Table 20-8 explain how the costs of goods sold and ending inventories were calculated. We assume that neither firm pays any dividends, and that cash flows not needed for taxes or inventory maintenance go into the cash account.

Here is what a Du Pont analysis would indicate about the two firms:

	Profit Margin		Total Asset Turnover		Equity Multiplier		ROE
Firm L:	20.0%	×	1.43	×	1.40	=	40.0%
Firm F:	30.0%	×	1.28	×	1.34	=	51.5%

Table 20-8
LIFO Versus FIFO Financial Statements

	Both Firms at Beginning of Year	End of Year	
		Firm L	Firm F
Balance Sheet			
Assets:			
Cash	$ 10	$ 60	$ 35
Inventories	50[a]	50[d]	100[d]
Net plant	100	100	100
Total assets	$160	$210	$235
Claims on assets:			
Current liabilities	10	10	10
Long-term debt	50	50	50
Common equity	100	150	175
Total claims	$160	$210	$235
Income Statement			
Revenues[b]		$300	$300
Cost of goods sold[c]		150	100
Gross profit		$150	$200
Other expenses		50	50
Earnings before tax		$100	$150
Tax (40%)		40	60
Net income		$ 60	$ 90

[a]Beginning inventory for both firms is 200 units, valued at $0.25 per unit for a total of $50. Each firm adds to its inventory by purchasing 300 units at $0.50 each, or a total of $150.
[b]Each firm sells 300 units at a price of $1.00 per unit to produce sales revenues of $300.
[c]Cost of goods sold = (Units sold)(Appropriate inventory unit price)

$$L = 300(\$0.50) = \$150.$$
$$F = 200(\$0.25) + 100(\$0.50) = \$100.$$

[d]Ending inventory = Beginning inventory + Purchases − Cost of goods sold

$$L = \$50 + \$150 - \$150 = \$50.$$
$$F = \$50 + \$150 - \$100 = \$100.$$

An analyst would be tempted to conclude that the firms are reasonably similar in asset and debt utilization, but that Firm F has better expense control and is, therefore, more profitable. But that would be misleading. The firms are identical from an operating standpoint. However, Firm L, the one which looks worse on a superficial analysis, is actually in better shape because it paid $20 less in taxes. Thus, Firm L is the stronger and more profitable of the two in a cash flow sense, yet this fact is disguised by the difference in inventory accounting methods. Note, though, that the distortions in our example result from a 100% inflation rate in the purchase price. At more typical inflation rates, the problem would appear much less severe. Also, the problem would disappear (or be greatly reduced) if the firms being compared used the same accounting policies. Fortunately, most firms in a given industry normally do use similar procedures.

Other accounting practices can also create distortions. For example, if one firm uses short-term, noncapitalized leases to obtain a substantial amount of its productive equipment, then its reported assets may be low relative to its sales. At the same time, if the lease liability is not shown as a debt, then leasing may artificially improve the debt and turnover ratios. Again, this problem has been reduced but not eliminated by the accountants' requirement that firms capitalize most large nonoperating leases.

Window Dressing

Firms sometimes employ "window dressing" techniques to make their financial statements look better to analysts. To illustrate, a Chicago builder borrowed on a two-year note on December 29, 1986, held the proceeds of the loan as cash for a few days, and then paid off the loan ahead of time on January 4, 1987. This improved his current and quick ratios, and made his year-end 1986 balance sheet look good. However, the improvement was strictly temporary; a week later, the balance sheet was back at the old level.

On an even larger scale, E. F. Hutton and several other brokerage houses follow the practice of recording checks they have written, but which have not yet been cleared through the banking system, as current liabilities rather than simply deducting them from reported cash balances. Hutton had been systematically overdrawing its bank accounts, and the question was raised, during investigations into this practice, why its negative cash balances did not alert its bankers that something was amiss. It turned out that, presumably to avoid having to report negative cash, Hutton recorded checks received as cash, but it recorded checks written as current liabilities rather than as deductions from cash.

Financial statement analysis is useful, but analysts should be aware of the problems discussed in this section and make adjustments as necessary. Financial statement analysis conducted in a mechanical, unthinking manner is dangerous; however, used intelligently and with good judgment, it can provide useful insights into a firm's operations.

EFFECTS OF INFLATION

Our recent high inflation rates have drawn increased attention to the need to assess both the impact of inflation on business and the success of management in coping with it. Numerous reporting methods have been proposed to adjust accounting statements for inflation, but no consensus has been reached either on how to do this or even on the practical usefulness of the resulting data. Nevertheless, the Financial Accounting Standards Board (FASB) issued Statements 33 and 82, which require large businesses to disclose supplementary data to reflect the effects of general inflation.

Financial Statement Effects

Traditionally, financial statements have been prepared on the basis of historical costs, that is, the actual number of dollars paid for each asset purchased. However, inflation has caused the purchasing power of dollars to change over time, and as a result financial statements can be badly distorted. To illustrate, a $100,000 expenditure on industrial land in 1986 would, in general, purchase far less acreage than a $100,000 expenditure in 1946, so adding 1986 dollars and 1946 dollars is much like adding apples and oranges. Nevertheless, this is done when the typical balance sheet is constructed. To help eliminate this disparity, the assets acquired in different years may be restated in *constant* dollars, each of which has equal purchasing power.

To reflect the effects of inflation, and thus to express operating results in dollars of comparable purchasing power, FASB requires a company to show what it characterizes as "income from continuing operations" calculated as if all its depreciable assets had been purchased with current-year dollars, and consequently its depreciation were based on higher-valued assets. Such an adjustment comes closer to showing what profits might be in the long-run, when the old, undervalued assets have been replaced with new, inflated-value assets, and depreciation is correspondingly higher. Table 20-9 contains the adjusted amounts as reported in the 1985 annual report of American Brands, a consumer products conglomerate which owns such companies as American Tobacco, Sunshine Biscuit, Beam Distilling, and Pinkerton's. It is clear from the data that American Brands' reported income would

Table 20-9
American Brands:
Financial Data Adjusted for Inflation, December 31, 1985
(Millions of Dollars, Except for per Share Amounts)

	As Reported in the Basic Financial Statements (Historical Costs) (1)	Adjusted for General Inflation (Constant Dollars) (2)
Net sales	$7,308	$7,308
Expenses:		
Depreciation	110	148*
Cost of products sold	5,403	5,433*
Operating expenses	1,070	1,070
Interest charges	117	117
Provision for taxes	330	330
Other income	(143)	(143)
Total expenses	$6,887	$6,955
Net income	$ 421	$ 353
Income per common share	$ 7.34	$ 6.15

*Item affected by inflation.

Table 20-10
American Brands:
Supplementary Five-Year Comparison of Selected Financial Data
Adjusted for the Effects of Changing Prices
(Millions of Dollars, Except for per Share Amounts)

	1985	1984	1983	1982	1981
Net sales:					
As reported	$7,308	$6,995	$7,093	$6,505	$6,538
In 1985 dollars	7,308	7,247	7,661	7,247	7,735
Cash dividends declared per common share:					
At historical cost	$3.90	$3.71	$3.55	$3.50	$3.21
In 1985 dollars	3.90	3.85	3.83	3.90	3.80
Market price per common share at year end:					
At historical cost	$ 66.00	$ 64.25	$ 58.25	$ 45.37	$ 35.50
In 1985 dollars	64.94	65.60	62.92	50.55	42.08
Consumer Price Index	322.2	311.1	298.4	289.1	272.4

have been much lower had depreciation and cost of products and services sold been based on inflated asset values rather than on the historical values, with other factors held constant.

FASB also requires firms to present a supplementary five-year comparison of selected financial data in current dollars. This type of comparison is shown in Table 20-10, where selected financial data are given for American Brands for the years 1981 through 1985. Operating revenues, net income, and cash dividends per common share have all been restated in constant 1985 dollars. The effect of these calculations is to increase the number of dollars shown in previous years as compared to the actual number of dollars received or spent. On a comparable dollar basis, it becomes clear that American Brands' sales growth was caused entirely by rising prices, not by increases in unit sales. Indeed, on a constant dollar basis, sales fell. Also, it is clear that American Brands' stockholders have not done as well, considering inflation, as the raw data would indicate. Based on unadjusted data, we see that dividends have grown from $3.21 to $3.90, or by 5 percent per year. However, the real value of those dividends has actually increased by less than 1 percent per year. Further, the historical stock price data suggest that the value of American Brands' stock increased on average, by 16.8 percent per year, but the inflation-adjusted data reveal an increase of only 11.5 percent.

Effects of Inflation on Ratio Analysis

If a ratio analysis is based on "regular" financial statements, unadjusted for inflation, then distortions can creep in. Obviously, there will be a tendency for the value of the fixed assets to be understated, and inventories will also be understated if the firm uses last-in, first-out (LIFO) accounting. At the same time, increasing rates of inflation will lead to increases in interest rates, which in turn will cause the value of the outstanding long-term debt to decline. Further, profits will vary from year to year as the inflation rate changes, and these variations will be especially severe if inventory is charged to cost of goods sold based on the first-in, first-out (FIFO) method.

These factors tend to make ratio comparisons over time for a given company, and across companies at any point in time, less reliable than would be the case in the absence of inflation. This is especially true if a company changes its accounting procedures (say, from straight-line to accelerated depreciation, or from FIFO to LIFO), or if various companies in a given industry use different accounting methods. Analysts can attempt to restate financial statements to put everything on a common basis, but at best, this can only reduce the problem, not eliminate it. Indeed, with the present state of the art, financial analysts cannot do much more than base their financial statement analysis of a firm on its existing accounting data. However, analysts ought to recognize that there are weaknesses in this approach, and they should apply judgment in interpreting the data.

MULTIPLE DISCRIMINANT ANALYSIS

As we discussed earlier, one of the problems with ratio analysis is the interpretation of results—some ratios might look "good" while other ratios look "bad," and it might thus be difficult to reach a conclusion on an action such as approving or denying a loan for the company. *Multiple discriminant analysis (MDA)* is a statistical procedure that can help one interpret ratios and use them for decision purposes. Discriminant analysis is similar to regression analysis, and it identifies those factors which seem to have an important bearing on the likelihood of some future event. For example, when we first discussed MDA in Chapter 19, we listed several factors associated with an individual's being a good or bad credit risk. In this section, we discuss MDA in more detail, and we illustrate its application to bankruptcy prediction.[12]

The Basics of Multiple Discriminant Analysis

Suppose a bank loan officer wants to segregate corporate loan applicants into those likely to default or not default. Assume that data for some past period are available on a group of firms which includes both companies that went bankrupt and companies that did not. For simplicity, we assume that only the current ratio and the debt/assets ratio are analyzed. These ratios for our sample of firms are given in

---

[12]This section is based largely on the work of Edward I. Altman, especially these two papers: (1) "Financial Ratios, Discriminant Analysis, and the Prediction of Corporate Bankruptcy," *Journal of Finance*, September 1968, 589-609; and (2) with Robert G. Haldeman and P. Narayanan, "Zeta Analysis: A New Model to Identify Bankruptcy Risk of Corporations," *Journal of Banking and Finance*, June 1977, 29-54.

Columns 2 and 3 at the bottom of Figure 20-2. The X's in the graph represent firms that went bankrupt, while the dots represent firms that remained solvent. For example, Point A in the upper left section is the point for Firm 2, which had a current ratio of 3.0, a debt ratio of 20 percent, and a dot to indicate that the firm did not go bankrupt. Point B, in the lower right section, represents Firm 19, which had a current ratio of 1.0, a debt ratio of 60 percent, and an X to indicate that it did go bankrupt.

The objective of discriminant analysis is to construct a boundary line through the graph such that, if the firm is to the left of the line, it is not likely to become insolvent, whereas it is likely to go bankrupt if it falls to the right. This boundary line is called the *discriminant function*, and in our example it takes this form:

$$Z = a + b_1(\text{Current ratio}) + b_2(\text{Debt ratio}).$$

Here Z is called the *Z score*, a is a constant term, and b_1 and b_2 indicate the effect of the current ratio and the debt ratio on the probability of a firm's going bankrupt.

Although a full discussion of discriminant analysis would go well beyond the scope of this book, some useful insights may be gained by observing these points:

1. The discriminant function is fitted (that is, the values of a, b_1, and b_2 are obtained) using historical data for a sample of firms that either went bankrupt or did not during some past period. When the data in the lower part of Figure 20-2 were fed into a "canned" discriminant analysis program (the computing centers of most universities and large corporations have such programs), the following discriminant function was obtained:

$$Z = -0.3877 - 1.0736(\text{Current ratio}) + 0.0579(\text{Debt ratio}).$$

2. This equation was plotted on Figure 20-2 as the locus of points for which Z = 0. All combinations of current ratios and debt ratios shown on the line result in Z = 0.[13] Companies that lie to the left of the line (and also have Z values greater than zero) are not likely to go bankrupt, while those to the right (and have Z less than zero) are likely to fail. It may be seen from the graph that one X, indicating a failing company, lies to the left of the line, while two dots, indicating nonbankrupt companies, lie to the right of the line. Thus, the discriminant analysis failed to classify properly three companies.

---

[13]To plot the boundary line, let D/A = 0% and 80%, and then find the current ratio that forces Z = 0 at those two values. For example, at D/A = 0,

$$Z = -0.3877 - 1.0736(\text{Current ratio}) + 0.0579(0) = 0$$
$$0.3877 = -1.0736(\text{Current ratio})$$
$$\text{Current ratio} = 0.3877/(-1.0736) = -0.3611.$$

Thus, -0.3611 is the vertical axis intercept. Similarly, the current ratio at D/A = 80% is found to be 3.9533. Plotting these two points on Figure 20-2, and then connecting them, provides the discriminant boundary line, which is the line that best partitions the companies into bankrupt and nonbankrupt. It should be noted that nonlinear discriminant functions may also be used.

Figure 20-2
Discriminant Boundary between Bankrupt and Solvent Firms

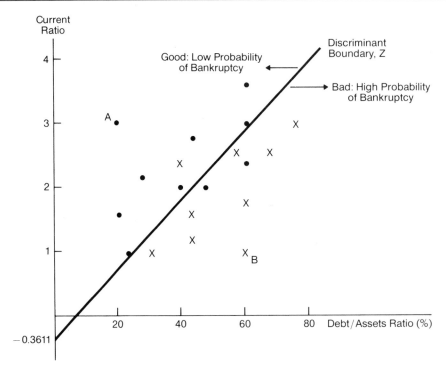

Firm Number (1)	Current Ratio (2)	Debt/Assets Ratio (3)	Did Firm Go Bankrupt? (4)	Z Score (5)	Probability of Bankruptcy (6)
1	3.6	60%	No	−0.780	17.2%
2(A)	3.0	20	No	−2.451	0.8
3	3.0	60	No	−0.135	42.0
4	3.0	76	Yes	0.791	81.2
5	2.8	44	No	−0.847	15.5
6	2.6	56	Yes	0.062	51.5
7	2.6	68	Yes	0.757	80.2
8	2.4	40	Yes[a]	−0.649	21.1
9	2.4	60	No[a]	0.509	71.5
10	2.2	28	No	−1.129	9.6
11	2.0	40	No	−0.220	38.1
12	2.0	48	No[a]	0.244	60.1
13	1.8	60	Yes	1.153	89.7
14	1.6	20	No	−0.948	13.1
15	1.6	44	Yes	0.441	68.8
16	1.2	44	Yes	0.871	83.5
17	1.0	24	No	−0.072	45.0
18	1.0	32	Yes	0.391	66.7
19(B)	1.0	60	Yes[a]	2.012	97.9

3. If we have determined the parameters of the discriminant function, then we can calculate the Z score for other companies, say loan applicants at a bank. The Z scores for our hypothetical companies, along with their probabilities for going bankrupt, are given in Columns 5 and 6 of Figure 20-2. The higher the Z score, the worse the company looks from the standpoint of bankruptcy. Here is an interpretation:

Z = 0:   50-50 probability of future bankruptcy (say within two years). The company lies exactly on the boundary line.

Z < 0:   If Z is negative, there is less than a 50 percent probability of bankruptcy. The smaller (more negative) the Z score, the lower is the probability of bankruptcy. The computer output from MDA programs gives this probability, and it is shown in Column 6 of Figure 20-2.

Z > 0:   If Z is positive, the probability of bankruptcy is greater than 50 percent, and the larger Z is, the greater the probability of bankruptcy.

4. The mean Z score of the companies that did not go bankrupt is -0.583, while that for the bankrupt firms is $+0.648$. These means, along with approximations of the Z score probability distributions of the two groups, are shown in Figure 20-3. We may interpret this graph as indicating that if Z is less than about -0.3, there is a very small probability that the firm will go bankrupt, whereas if Z is greater than $+0.3$, there is only a small probability that it will remain solvent. If Z is in the range ± 0.3, called the *zone of ignorance*, we are uncertain about how the firm should be classified.

5. The signs of the coefficients of the discriminant function are logical. Since its coefficient is negative, the larger the current ratio, the lower is a company's Z score, and the lower the Z score, the smaller is the probability of failure. Similarly, high debt ratios produce high Z scores, and this is directly translated into a higher probability of bankruptcy.

6. Our illustrative discriminant function has only two variables, but other characteristics could be introduced. For example, we could add such variables as the rate of return on assets, the times-interest-earned ratio, the average collection period,

---

Table footnote:
[a]Denotes a misclassification. Firm 8 had Z $= -0.649$, so MDA predicted no bankruptcy, but it did go bankrupt. Similarly, MDA predicted bankruptcy for Firms 9 and 12, but they did not go bankrupt. The following tabulation shows bankruptcy and solvency predictions versus actual results:

	Z Positive: MDA Predicts Bankruptcy	Z Negative: MDA Predicts Solvency
Went bankrupt	8	1
Remained solvent	2	8

The model did not perform perfectly, as two predicted bankruptcies remained solvent, and one firm that was expected to remain solvent went bankrupt. Thus, the model misclassified 3 out of 19 firms, or 16 percent of the sample. Its success rate was 84 percent.

Figure 20-3
Probability Distributions of Z Scores

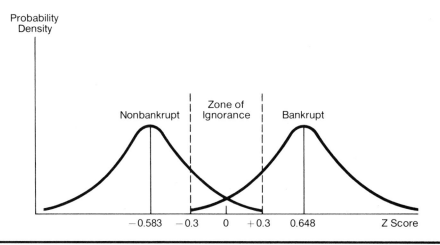

the quick ratio, and so forth.[14] Had the rate of return on assets been introduced, it might have turned out that Firm 8 (which failed) had a low ROA, while Firm 9 (which did not fail) had a high ROA. A new discriminant function would be calculated:

$$Z = a + b_1(\text{Current ratio}) + b_2(\text{D/A}) + b_3(\text{ROA}).$$

Firm 8 might now have a positive Z, while Firm 9's Z might become negative. Thus, it is likely that by adding more characteristics we could improve the accuracy of our bankruptcy forecasts. In terms of Figure 20-3, this would cause each probability distribution to become tighter, would narrow the zone of ignorance, and would lead to fewer misclassifications.

Altman's Model

In a classic paper, Edward Altman applied MDA to a sample of corporations, and he developed a discriminant function that has seen wide use in actual practice. Altman's function was fitted as follows:

$$Z = 0.012X_1 + 0.014X_2 + 0.033X_3 + 0.006X_4 + 0.999X_5.$$

---

[14]With more than two variables, it is difficult to graph the function, but this presents no problem in actual usage because graphs are only used to explain MDA.

Here

X_1 = net working capital/total assets.

X_2 = retained earnings/total assets.[15]

X_3 = EBIT/total assets.

X_4 = market value of common and preferred stock/book value of debt.[16]

X_5 = sales/total assets.

The first four variables are expressed as percentages rather than as decimals. Also, Altman's 50-50 point was 2.675, and not 0.0 as in our hypothetical example; his zone of ignorance was from Z = 1.81 to Z = 2.99; and the *larger* the Z score, the less the probability of bankruptcy.[17]

Altman's function can be used to calculate a Z score for Southern Metals Company based on the data presented previously in Tables 20-1 and 20-2. This calculation, ignoring the small amount of preferred stock, is shown below for 1986:

$$X_1 = \$400/\$2,000 = 20.0\% \qquad\qquad\qquad \times 0.012 = 0.240$$

$$X_2 = \$660/\$2,000 = 33.0\% \qquad\qquad\qquad \times 0.014 = 0.462$$

$$X_3 = \$266/\$2,000 = 13.3\% \qquad\qquad\qquad \times 0.033 = 0.439$$

$$X_4 = (50)(\$28.50)/(\$300 + \$800) = 129.5\% \times 0.006 = 0.777$$

$$X_5 = \$3,000/\$2,000 = 1.5 \qquad\qquad\qquad \times 0.999 = \underline{1.499}$$

$$Z = \underline{\underline{3.417}}$$

Since Southern's Z score of 3.417 is above the 2.99 upper limit of Altman's zone of ignorance, the data indicate that there is virtually no chance that Southern will go bankrupt within the next two years. (Altman's model predicts bankruptcy reasonably well for about two years into the future.)

Altman and his colleagues' later work updated and improved his original study. In their more recent work, they explicitly considered such factors as capitalized lease obligations, and they applied smoothing techniques to level out random fluctuations in the data. The new model was able to predict bankruptcy with a high degree of accuracy for two years into the future, and with a slightly lower but still reasonable degree of accuracy (70 percent) for about five years.

MDA has been used with success to quantify ratio analysis, by credit analysts to establish default probabilities for both consumer and corporate loan applicants, and by portfolio managers considering both stock and bond investments. It can also be used to evaluate a set of pro forma ratios as developed in Chapter 21, or to gain insights into the feasibility of a reorganization plan filed under the Bank-

---

[15]Retained earnings is the balance sheet figure, not the addition to retained earnings for the year.

[16][(Shares of common outstanding)(Price per share) + (Shares of preferred)(Price per share of preferred)]/Balance sheet value of total debt.

[17]These differences reflect the software package he used to generate the discriminant function. Altman's program operated from a base of 2.675 rather than 0.0, and his program simply reversed the sign of Z from ours.

ruptcy Act. Altman's model has also been used by Morgan Stanley and other investment banking houses to appraise the quality of "junk bonds" used to finance takeovers and leveraged buyouts. The technique is described in detail in many statistics texts, while several articles cited at the end of the chapter discuss financial applications of MDA. The interested reader is urged to study this literature, for MDA has many potentially valuable applications in finance.

SUMMARY

The primary purposes of this chapter were (1) to describe the basic financial statements and (2) to discuss techniques used by investors and managers to analyze these statements. Three basic statements were covered: the *income statement*, the *balance sheet*, and the *statement of changes in financial position*.

Financial analysis is designed to determine the relative strengths and weaknesses of a company—whether the firm is financially sound and profitable in relation to other firms in its industry, and whether its position is improving or deteriorating over time. Investors need such information in order to estimate a firm's future profits and the riskiness inherent in those profits. Managers need to be aware of their firms' financial positions in order to detect actual or potential weaknesses.

Our study of financial analysis concentrated on a set of ratios designed to highlight the key aspects of a firm's operations. These ratios were broken down into five categories: (1) *liquidity ratios*, (2) *asset management ratios*, (3) *debt management ratios*, (4) *profitability ratios*, and (5) *market value ratios*. The ratios for a given firm are calculated, and then compared with those of other firms in the same industry to judge the relative strength of the firm in question. Trends in the ratios are also analyzed. Another technique is *common size analysis*. Here financial statements are expressed as percentages, and comparative and trend analyses are performed. Additionally, a *Du Pont analysis* may be used to gain insights into how a company compares with the average firm in the industry in the areas of expense control, total asset utilization, and debt utilization, and consequently in its relative return on equity.

We also discussed some of the problems encountered in financial statement analysis: Financial statement analysis has limitations, but, used with care and judgment, it can be most helpful. Finally, we discussed the use of *Multiple Discriminant Analysis (MDA)* in financial analysis. MDA develops a summary statistic which nets out the favorable and unfavorable ratios and provides a single number which can be used as an estimate of a firm's probability of bankruptcy over the next year or two.

Questions and Problems

20-1 (Financial ratios) The following data apply to Fisher & Company (in millions of dollars):

Cash and marketable securities	$100.00
Fixed assets	$283.50
Sales	$1,000.00

Net income	$50.00
Quick ratio	2.0×
Current ratio	3.0×
ACP	40 days
ROE	12%

Fisher has common equity, current liabilities, and long-term debt, but no preferred stock.

a. Find Fisher's (1) accounts receivable, (2) current liabilities, (3) current assets, (4) total assets, (5) ROA, (6) common equity, and (7) long-term debt.

b. If Fisher should reduce its ACP from 40 days to 30 days while holding other factors constant, how much cash would it generate? If this cash were used to buy back common stock (at book value), and thus to reduce the amount of common equity, how would this affect (1) the ROE, (2) the ROA, and (3) the total debt/ total assets ratio?

20-2 (Du Pont analysis) Data for the Pettijohn Company, and its industry averages, are given next.

a. Calculate the indicated ratios for Pettijohn.

b. Construct the extended Du Pont equation for both Pettijohn and the industry.

c. Outline Pettijohn's strengths and weaknesses as revealed by your analysis.

d. Suppose the firm had doubled its sales and also its inventories, accounts receivable, and common equity during 1986. How would that information affect the validity of your ratio analysis?

Balance Sheet as of December 31, 1986

Cash	$ 220,000	Accounts payable	$ 165,000
Receivables	275,000	Notes payable	220,000
Inventory	825,000	Other current liabilities	110,000
Total current assets	$1,320,000	Total current liabilities	$ 495,000
Net fixed assets	605,000	Long-term debt	220,000
		Common equity	1,210,000
Total assets	$1,925,000	Total claims	$1,925,000

Income Statement and Industry Averages for Year Ended December 31, 1986

Sales		$2,750,000
Cost of goods sold:		
Materials	$1,045,000	
Labor	660,000	
Heat, light, and power	99,000	
Indirect labor	165,000	
Depreciation	60,500	$2,029,500
Gross profit		$ 720,500
Selling expenses		275,000
General and administrative expenses		316,800
Earnings before interest and taxes		$ 128,700
Less interest expense		13,200
Net profit before taxes		$ 115,500
Less income taxes (40%)		46,200
Net income		$ 69,300

	Ratios	
	Pettijohn	Industry Average
Current assets/current liabilities	————	2.4×
Average collection period	————	43 days
Sales/inventories	————	9.8×
Sales/total assets	————	2×
Net income/sales	————	3.3%
Net income/total assets	————	6.6%
Net income/net worth	————	18.1%
Total debt/total assets	————	63.5%

20-3 **(Ratio analysis)** The Flint Furniture Company, a manufacturer and wholesaler of high-quality home furnishings, has been experiencing low profitability in recent years. As a result, the board of directors has replaced the president of the firm with a new president, John Stockwell, who asks you to make an analysis of the firm's financial position. The most recent industry average ratios, and Flint's financial statements, are reproduced next.

Industry Average Ratios

Current ratio	2×	Sales/fixed assets	6×
Debt/total assets	30%	Sales/total assets	3×
Times interest earned	7×	Net profit on sales	3%
Sales/inventory	10×	Return on total assets	9%
Average collection period	24 days	Return on common equity	12.8%

Balance Sheet as of December 31, 1986 (Millions of Dollars)

Cash	$ 30	Accounts payable	$ 30
Marketable securities	22	Notes payable	30
Net receivables	44	Other current liabilities	14
Inventories	106	Total current liabilities	$ 74
Total current assets	$202	Long-term debt	16
Gross fixed assets	150	Total liabilities	$ 90
Less depreciation	52	Common stock	76
Net fixed assets	$ 98	Retained earnings	134
		Total stockholder equity	$210
Total assets	$300	Total claims	$300

Income Statement for Year Ended December 31, 1986 (Millions of Dollars)

Net sales	$530
Cost of goods sold	440
Gross profit	$90
Operating expenses	49
Depreciation expense	8
Interest expense	3
Total expense	$60
Net income before tax	$30
Taxes (40%)	12
Net income	$18

a. Calculate those ratios which you feel would be useful in this analysis.

b. Do the balance sheet accounts or the income statement figures seem to be primarily responsible for the low profits?

c. Which specific accounts seem to be most out of line in relation to other firms in the industry?

d. If Flint had a pronounced seasonal sales pattern, or if it grew rapidly during the year, how might this affect the validity of your ratio analysis? How might you correct for such potential problems?

20-4 **(Sources and uses of funds)** The consolidated balance sheets for the Maese Lumber Company at the beginning and end of 1986 follow. The company bought $75 million worth of fixed assets during the year. The charge for depreciation in 1986 was $15 million. Earnings after taxes were $38 million, and the company paid out $10 million in dividends.

Balance Sheet at the Beginning and End of 1986 (Millions of Dollars)

	Jan. 1	Dec. 31	Change Source	Change Use
Cash	$ 15	$ 7	_____	_____
Marketable securities	11	0	_____	_____
Net receivables	22	30	_____	_____
Inventories	53	75	_____	_____
Total current assets	$101	$112	_____	_____
Gross fixed assets	75	150	_____	_____
Less accumulated depreciation	26	41	_____	_____
Net fixed assets	$ 49	$109	_____	_____
Total assets	$150	$221	_____	_____
Accounts payable	$ 15	$ 18	_____	_____
Notes payable	15	3	_____	_____
Other current liabilities	7	15	_____	_____
Long-term debt	8	26	_____	_____
Common stock	38	64	_____	_____
Retained earnings	67	95	_____	_____
Total claims	$150	$221	_____	_____

a. Fill in the amount of source or use in the appropriate column.

b. Prepare a statement of changes in financial position.

c. Briefly summarize your findings.

20-5 **(Transaction effects)** Indicate the effects of the transactions listed below on each of the following: total current assets, net working capital, current ratio, and net profit. Use + to indicate an increase, − to indicate a decrease, and 0 to indicate no effect or an indeterminate effect. State any necessary assumptions and assume an initial current ratio of more than 1.0. Note: A good accounting background is necessary to answer some of these questions; if your background is not strong, just answer the parts you can handle.

	Total Current Assets	Net Working Capital	Current Ratio	Effect on Net Income
a. Cash is acquired through issuance of additional common stock.	____	____	____	____
b. Merchandise is sold for cash.	____	____	____	____
c. Federal income tax due for the previous year is paid.	____	____	____	____
d. A fixed asset is sold for less than book value.	____	____	____	____
e. A fixed asset is sold for more than book value.	____	____	____	____
f. Merchandise is sold on credit.	____	____	____	____
g. Payment is made to trade creditors for previous purchases.	____	____	____	____
h. A cash dividend is declared and paid.	____	____	____	____
i. Cash is obtained through short-term bank loans.	____	____	____	____
j. Short-term notes receivable are sold at a discount.	____	____	____	____
k. Marketable securities are sold below cost.	____	____	____	____
l. Advances are made to employees.	____	____	____	____
m. Current operating expenses are paid.	____	____	____	____
n. Short-term promissory notes are issued to trade creditors for prior purchases.	____	____	____	____
o. Ten-year notes are issued to pay off accounts payable.	____	____	____	____
p. A fully depreciated asset is retired.	____	____	____	____
q. Accounts receivable are collected.	____	____	____	____
r. Equipment is purchased with short-term notes.	____	____	____	____
s. Merchandise is purchased on credit.	____	____	____	____
t. The estimated taxes payable are increased.	____	____	____	____

20-6 (Du Pont and MDA analyses) The Hill Corporation's balance sheets for 1986 and 1985 are as follows (in millions of dollars):

	1986	1985
Cash	$ 21	$ 45
Marketable securities	0	33
Receivables	90	66
Inventories	225	159
Total current assets	$336	$303
Gross fixed assets	450	225
Less accumulated depreciation	123	78
Net fixed assets	$327	$147
Total assets	$663	$450

Accounts payable	$ 54	$ 45
Notes payable	9	45
Accruals	45	21
Total current liabilities	$108	$111
Long-term debt	78	24
Common stock	192	114
Retained earnings	285	201
Total long-term capital	$555	$339
Total claims	$663	$450

Additionally, Hill's 1986 income statement is as follows (in millions of dollars):

Sales	$1,365
Cost of goods sold	888
General expenses	282
EBIT	$ 195
Interest	10
EBT	$ 185
Taxes (40%)	74
Net income	$ 111

a. What was Hill's dividend payout ratio in 1986?

b. Here is the industry average extended Du Pont equation for 1986:

Profit Margin		Asset Turnover		Equity Multiplier		ROE
6.52%	×	1.82	×	1.77	=	21.00%.

Construct Hill's 1986 extended Du Pont equation. What does the Du Pont analysis indicate about Hill's expense control, asset utilization, and debt utilization? What is the industry's assets-to-debt ratio?

c. Construct Hill's 1986 statement of changes in financial position.

d. Use Altman's discriminant function to assess Hill's potential for bankruptcy in 1986. (Assume that Hill's stock is selling at book value.)

20-7 (Ratio trend analysis) The Kiernan Corporation's forecasted 1987 financial statements are given next, along with some industry average ratios.

a. Calculate Kiernan's 1987 forecasted ratios, compare them with the industry average data, and comment briefly on the firm's projected strengths and weaknesses.

(Do Part b only if you are using the computerized diskette.)

b. Suppose Kiernan is considering installing a new computer system which would provide tighter control of inventory, accounts receivable, and accounts payable. If the new system is installed, the following data are projected rather than the data now given in certain balance sheet and income statement categories (in dollars except P/E ratio):

Cash	$ 81,000
Receivables	400,000
Inventories	750,000
Other fixed assets	91,000
Accounts payable	300,000
Accruals	133,000
Retained earnings	279,710
Cost of goods sold	3,510,000
Administrative and selling expenses	228,320
P/E ratio	6×

(1) How does this affect the projected ratios and the comparison to the industry averages?

(2) If the new computer system were either more efficient or less efficient, and caused the cost of goods sold to increase or decrease by $150,000 from the new projections, what effect would that have on the company's position?

Pro Forma Balance Sheet as of December 31, 1987

Cash	$ 72,000
Accounts receivable	439,000
Inventories	894,000
Total current assets	$1,405,000
Land and building	238,000
Machinery	132,000
Other fixed assets	61,000
Total assets	$1,836,000
Accounts and notes payable	$ 432,000
Accruals	170,000
Total current liabilities	$ 602,000
Long-term debt	404,290
Common stock	575,000
Retained earnings	254,710
Total liabilities and equity	$1,836,000

Pro Forma Income Statement for 1987

Sales	$4,290,000
Cost of goods sold	3,580,000
Gross operating profit	$ 710,000
General administrative and selling expenses	236,320
Depreciation	159,000
Miscellaneous	134,000
Taxable income	$ 180,680
Taxes (40%)	72,272
Net income	$ 108,408
Number of shares outstanding	23,000
Per share data:	
EPS	$4.71
Cash dividends	$0.95
P/E ratio	5×
Market price (average)	$23.57

Industry Financial Ratios (1986)[a]

Quick ratio	$1.0\times$
Current ratio	$2.7\times$
Inventory turnover[b]	$7\times$
Average collection period	32 days
Fixed assets turnover[b]	$13.0\times$
Total assets turnover[b]	$2.6\times$
Return on total assets	9.1%
Return on equity	18.2%
Debt ratio	50%
Profit margin on sales	3.5%
P/E ratio	$6\times$
M/B ratio	1.40

[a]Industry average ratios have been constant for the past four years.

[b]Based on year-end balance sheet figures.

Selected Additional References and Cases

The effects of alternative accounting policies on both financial statements and ratios based on these statements are discussed in the investment textbooks referenced in Chapter 2, and also in the many excellent texts on financial statement analysis. For example, see

Gibson, Charles H., and Patricia A. Frishkoff, *Financial Statement Analysis* (Boston: Kent, 1986).

Hawkins, David F., *Corporate Financial Reporting and Analysis* (Homewood, Ill.: Irwin, 1986).

For further information on the relative usefulness of various financial ratios, see

Chen, Kung H., and Thomas A. Shimerda, "An Empirical Analysis of Useful Financial Ratios," *Financial Management*, Spring 1981, 51-60.

Considerable work has been done to establish the relationship between bond ratings and financial ratios. For one example, see

Belkaoui, Ahmed, *Industrial Bonds and the Rating Process* (London: Quorum Books, 1983).

For sources of ratios and common size statements, see the following:

Dun & Bradstreet, *Key Business Ratios* (New York: Updated annually).

Financial Research Associates, *Financial Studies of the Small Business* (Arlington, Va.: Updated annually).

Robert Morris Associates, *Annual Statement Studies* (Philadelphia: Updated annually).

For a better understanding of multiple discriminant analysis and its use in financial analysis, see

Collins, Robert A., "An Empirical Comparison of Bankruptcy Prediction Models," *Financial Management*, Summer 1980, 52-57.

Eisenbeis, Robert A., "Pitfalls in the Application of Discriminant Analysis in Business Finance and Economics," *Journal of Finance*, June 1977, 875-900.

Joy, O. Maurice, and John O. Tollefson, "On the Financial Application of Discriminant Analysis," *Journal of Financial and Quantitative Analysis*, December 1975, 723-739.

Pinches, George E., "Factors Influencing Classification Results from Multiple Discriminant Analysis," *Journal of Business Research*, December 1980, 429-456.

Scott, Elton, "On the Financial Application of Discriminant Analysis: Comment," *Journal of Finance and Quantitative Analysis*, March 1978, 201-205.

Tollefson, John O., and O. Maurice Joy, "Some Clarifying Comments on Discriminant Analysis," *Journal of Financial and Quantitative Analysis*, March 1978, 197-200.

The following cases focus on financial analysis:

Case 1, "Silver River Manufacturing Company," in the Crum-Brigham casebook illustrates the use of ratio analysis in the evaluation of a firm's existing and potential financial positions, and Case 2, "Crescent Beach Sportswear," focuses on breakeven analysis.

21
FINANCIAL PLANNING AND CONTROL

In the last chapter, we saw how to analyze financial statements in order to identify a firm's strengths and weaknesses. Now we consider the actions a firm can take to exploit its strengths and to overcome its weaknesses. As we shall see, managers are vitally concerned with projected, or pro forma, financial statements, and with the effects of alternative policies on these statements. An analysis of such effects is indeed the key ingredient of financial planning. However, a good financial plan cannot, by itself, ensure that the firm's goals will be met; the plan must be backed up by a financial control system for monitoring the situation both to ensure that the plan is carried out properly and to facilitate rapid adjustments if economic and operating conditions change from projected levels.

STRATEGIC PLANS

Financial planning must occur within the framework of the firm's overall strategic and operating plans. Thus, we begin our discussion with an overview of the strategic planning process.[1]

Corporate Purpose

The long-run strategic plan should begin with a statement of the *corporate purpose*, which defines the overall mission of the firm. The purpose can be defined either specifically or in general terms. For example, one firm might state that its corporate purpose is "to increase the intrinsic value of the firm's common stock." Another might say that its purpose is "to maximize the growth rate in earnings and dividends per share while avoiding excessive risk." Yet another might state that its principal goal is "to provide our customers with state-of-the-art computing systems at the lowest attainable cost, which in our opinion will also maximize benefits to our employees and stockholders."

---

[1] One can take many approaches to corporate planning. For more insights into the corporate planning process, see Benton E. Gup, *Guide to Strategic Planning* (New York: McGraw-Hill, 1980).

There should be no conflict between sound operations and stockholders' benefits, but occasionally there is. For example, Varian Associates, Inc., a NYSE company with 1986 sales of about $1 billion, was for years regarded as one of the most technologically advanced companies in the electronics devices and semiconductor fields. However, Varian's management was reputed to be more concerned with developing new technology than with marketing it, and the stock price was lower in 1979 than it had been 10 years earlier. Some of the larger stockholders were intensely unhappy with the state of affairs, and management was faced with the threat of a proxy fight or a forced merger. At that point, management announced a conscious change in policy and stated that it would, in the future, emphasize both technological excellence *and* profitability, rather than focus primarily on technology. Earnings improved dramatically, and the stock price rose from a low of $6.75 in 1979 to over $60 in 1983.

The Varian example illustrates both the importance of the corporate purpose as viewed by management and also the discipline of the market. Well-run companies need to define an area and then develop competence with regard to meeting the needs of their customers, but they will be forced by the market to translate that competence into earnings.

Corporate Scope

The *corporate scope* defines a firm's lines of business and geographic area of operations. Again, the corporate scope can be spelled out in great detail or put merely in general terms. Here is Western Electronics' statement of corporate scope:

> Our current operations are concentrated in the manufacture and sales of electronic components. We expect to continue this emphasis, primarily because the electronics industry offers above-average growth opportunities.
>
> The company is not confined to any geographical area of operations, but, for now, international expansion is not envisioned. However, domestic expansion will continue until the firm fully realizes its marketing potential.
>
> In order to accomplish our corporate purpose, it may be necessary or desirable to provide products which supplement, complement, or enhance our principal lines of business. Any such activities will be consistent with our responsibilities to our investors, customers, employees, suppliers, and the public in general.

Corporate Objectives

The corporate purpose and scope outline the general philosophy and approach of the business, but they do not provide managers with operational objectives. The *corporate objectives* set forth specific goals that management strives to attain. Corporate objectives can be quantitative, such as specifying a target market share, a target ROE, or a target earnings per share growth rate, or they can be qualitative, such as "keeping the firm's research and development efforts at the cutting edge of the industry." Multiple goals are often established, and these goals are not static—they should be and are changed when conditions change. The goals should also be challenging, yet realistically attainable, and it is appropriate that management compensation be based on the extent to which objectives are met.

Corporate Strategies

Once a firm has defined its purpose, scope, and objectives, it should develop a strategy designed to help it achieve its stated objectives. *Corporate strategies* are broad approaches rather than detailed plans. For example, one airline may have a strategy of offering "no frills" service between a limited number of cities, while another may plan to offer "staterooms in the sky." Strategies must be attainable and compatible with the firm's purpose, scope, and objectives.

Perhaps the most interesting and important set of strategies that has been developed in recent years is that of AT&T and the Bell operating companies in the wake of the breakup of AT&T. The seven regional telephone holding companies which emerged from the breakup all provide basic local telephone service, but beyond that, they appear to be developing different strategies which will take them in different directions. Some now sell a broad array of telecommunications equipment, while others have more limited offerings. Some are rapidly diversifying into nonregulated lines of business—Bell Atlantic has spent over $300 million for this purpose—while others are diversifying at a much slower pace.

The surviving AT&T faces perhaps even greater challenges in setting its corporate strategy. On the one hand, it faces increasing competition in its two major markets, long-distance transmission and telephone equipment manufacturing. Currently, it has most of the industry's capacity in these areas, so to some extent, it can price high and enjoy high short-run profits, but at the expense of a rapid erosion of its share of the business. Alternatively, it can price low and maintain a large market share, but not maximize short-run (and perhaps also long-run) profits. Also, AT&T must decide on the extent of its foray into the computer business. Its PC6300 clone of the IBM PC has not done very well, and its other computer ventures, such as its Unix operating system, have done poorly. IBM, meanwhile, has invested heavily in the telecommunications business (both manufacturing and satellite transmissions), and is thus attacking AT&T on its own turf. At the same time, the new Bell companies are all trying to get permission to compete with their former parent in the businesses of long distance service and equipment manufacturing.

The AT&T/Bell companies' strategic decisions are more dramatic than most, but they do illustrate the kinds of issues that arise when companies develop their strategic plans.

OPERATING PLANS

Operating plans can be developed for any time horizon, but most companies use a five-year horizon, and thus the name *five-year plan* has become common. In a five-year plan, the plans are most detailed for the first year, with each succeeding

---

Table 21-1
Century Electronics Corporation:
Annual Planning Schedule

Months	Action
April-May	Planning department analyzes environmental and industry factors. Marketing department prepares sales forecast for each product group.
June-July	Engineering department prepares cost estimates for new manufacturing facilities and plant modernization programs.
August-September	Financial analysts evaluate proposed capital expenditures, divisional operating plans, and proposed sources and uses of funds.
October-November	Five-year plan is finalized by planning department, reviewed by divisional officers, and put into "semi-final" form.
December	Five-year plan is approved by the executive committee and then submitted to the board of directors for final approval.

---

year's plan becoming less specific. The operating plan is intended to provide detailed implementation guidance, based on the corporate strategy, in order to meet the corporate objectives. The five-year plan explains in considerable detail who is responsible for what particular function, and when specific tasks are to be accomplished.

Table 21-1 contains the annual planning schedule of Century Electronics Corporation, a leading manufacturer of telecommunications equipment. This schedule illustrates the fact that for larger companies, the planning process is essentially continuous. Next, Table 21-2 outlines the key elements of Century's five-year plan. A full outline would require several pages, but Table 21-2 does at least provide insights into the format and content of a five-year plan. It should be noted that Century, like other large, multidivisional companies, breaks down its operating plan by divisions. Thus, each division has its own goals, mission, and plan for meeting its objectives, and these plans are then consolidated to form the corporate plan.

THE FINANCIAL PLAN

The financial planning process can be broken down into five steps:

1. Set up a system of projected financial statements which can be used to analyze the effects of the operating plan on projected profits and other financial condition indicators. This system can also be used to monitor operations after the plan has been finalized and put into effect. Rapid awareness of deviations from plans is essential to a good control system, which in turn is essential to corporate success in a changing world.

2. Determine the specific financial requirements needed to support the company's five-year plan. This includes funds for plant and equipment as well as for inventory and receivables buildups, for R&D programs, and for major advertising campaigns.

Table 21-2
Century Electronics Corporation:
Five-Year Operating Plan Outline

A. Corporate mission
B. Corporate scope
C. Corporate objectives
D. Projected business environment
E. Corporate strategies
F. Summary of projected business results
G. Product line plans and policies
   1. Marketing
   2. Manufacturing
   3. Finance
      a. Working capital
         (1) Overall working capital policy
         (2) Cash and marketable securities management
         (3) Inventory management
         (4) Credit policy and receivables management
      b. Dividend policy
      c. Financial forecast
         (1) Capital budget
         (2) Cash budget
         (3) Pro forma financial statements
         (4) External financing requirements
         (5) Financial condition analysis
      d. Accounting plan
      e. Control plan
   4. Administrative and personnel
   5. Research and development
   6. New products
H. Consolidated corporate plan

---

3. Forecast the financing sources to be used over the next five years. This involves estimating the funds which will be generated internally as well as those which must be obtained from external sources. Any constraints on operating plans imposed by financial limitations which would limit the use of total and/or short-term debt should be incorporated into the plan; examples include debt ratio, current ratio, and coverage restrictions.

4. Establish and maintain a system of controls governing the allocation and use of funds within the firm. Essentially, this involves making sure that the basic plan is carried out properly.

5. Develop procedures for adjusting the basic plan if the forecasted economic conditions upon which the plan was based do not materialize. For example, if the economy turns out to be stronger than was forecasted when the basic plan was drawn up, then these new conditions must be recognized and reflected in higher production budgets, larger marketing quotas, and the like as rapidly as possible. Thus, Step 5 is really a "feedback loop" which triggers modifications to the plan.

The principal components of the financial plan are (1) an analysis of the firm's current financial condition as indicated by an analysis of its most recent statements, (2) a sales forecast, (3) the capital budget, (4) the cash budget, (5) a set of pro forma (or projected) financial statements, and (6) the external financing plan. We have in previous chapters discussed the capital budget, the cash budget, and financial statement analysis. In the remainder of this chapter, we focus on the other elements—the sales forecasts, the pro forma financial statements, and the external financing plan.

SALES FORECASTS

The first, and perhaps the most critical, step in the financial planning process is the sales forecast. Actually, the marketing department generally has primary responsibility for the sales forecast, but it is of such pervasive importance that we need to discuss it here. The sales forecast generally starts with a review of sales over the past 5 to 10 years, expressed in a graph such as Figure 21-1. The first part of the graph shows actual sales for Century Electronics Corporation from 1977 through 1986. During this period, sales grew from $200 million to $500 million, or at a compound annual growth rate of 10.7 percent. However, the growth rate has accelerated sharply in recent years, primarily as a result of regulatory changes in the telecommunications market which forced the major national telephone companies to start buying from companies such as Century when they had products that were competitive with those of the telephone companies' own captive manufacturing companies. Also, Century's R&D program had been especially successful, so when the telecommunications market broke open, Century was ready.

On the basis of the recent trend in sales, on new product introductions, and on a forecast by Century's economics staff that the national economy will be strong during the coming year, Century's planning group projects a 50 percent growth rate during 1987, to a sales level of $750 million.

Of course, a great deal of work lies behind all good sales forecasts. Companies must project the state of the national economy, economic conditions within their own geographic areas, and conditions in the product markets they serve. Further, they must consider their own pricing strategies, credit policies, advertising programs, capacity limitations, and the like. They must also consider the strategies and policies of their competitors—the introduction of new products by IBM, AT&T, or the Japanese, or more aggressive pricing by these and other companies, could seriously affect Century's 1987 sales forecast.

If the sales forecast is off, the consequences could be serious. If the market expanded *more* than Century expected and geared up for, then it would not be able to meet its customers' needs. Orders would back up, delivery times would lengthen, repair and installations would be harder to schedule, and customer unhappiness would increase. Customers would go elsewhere, Century would lose

Figure 21-1
Century Electronics Corporation:
1987 Sales Projection

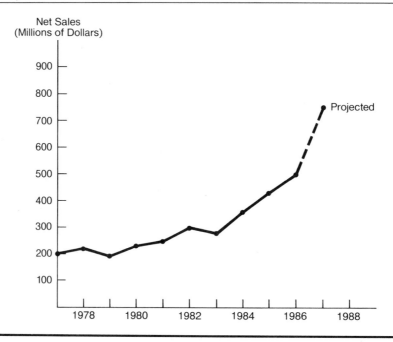

market share, and it would have missed a major opportunity. On the other hand, if its projections are overly optimistic, Century would end up with too much plant, equipment, and inventories, resulting in unneeded capital costs, low turnover ratios, high costs for depreciation and storage, and, possibly, write-offs of obsolete inventory and equipment. All of this would result in a low rate of return on equity, which in turn would depress the company's stock price. If Century had financed the expansion with debt, its problems would, of course, be compounded. Thus, an accurate sales forecast is critical to the well-being of the firm.

Note that the $750 million sales forecast for 1987 is actually the expected value of a probability distribution of possible levels of sales. Thus, we are interested not only in the expected sales level, but also the distribution about the expected value. If the probability distribution is relatively tight, then the company will have more confidence in its sales projection. In that event, its operating plans can be relatively firm—for example, it can sign fixed purchase contracts for materials on a long-term basis, it can make long-run commitments to its labor force, and so on. On the other hand, if the sales projections are "iffy," then the company will want to build flexibility into its operating plans, to monitor sales trends very closely, and to cut back production immediately if demand falls below the forecasted level.

PERCENTAGE OF SALES FORECASTING

Several procedures are used to forecast financial statements, and in this chapter, we present five of them: (1) the percentage of sales method, (2) linear regression, (3) curvilinear regression, (4) multiple regression, and (5) specific item forecasting. We begin with the *percentage of sales* method, a simple but often practical technique for forecasting financial statement variables. The procedure is based on two assumptions: (1) that all variables are tied directly to sales, and (2) that the current levels of most balance sheet items are optimal for the current level of sales. We illustrate the method with Century Electronics Corporation, whose 1986 financial statements are given in Table 21-3. Century operated its fixed assets at full capacity to support the $500 million in sales in 1986; it had no excess manufac-

---

Table 21-3
Century Electronics Corporation:
Financial Statements
(Millions of Dollars)

Income Statement	For the Year Ended December 31, 1986
Net sales	$500
Cost of goods sold	400
Selling and administrative expenses	52
Earnings before interest and taxes	$ 48
Interest expense	8
Earnings before taxes	$ 40
Taxes (40%)	16
Net income	$ 24
Dividends (payout: 33%)	$ 8
Addition to retained earnings	$ 16

Balance Sheet	As of December 31, 1986
Cash	$ 10
Receivables	85
Inventories	100
Total current assets	$195
Net fixed assets	150
Total assets	$345
Accounts payable	$ 40
Notes payable (8%)	10
Accrued wages and taxes	25
Total current liabilities	$ 75
Mortgage bonds (10%)	72
Common stock	150
Retained earnings	48
Total claims	$345

turing capacity. Also, its stocks of inventories and its cash balances were in line with sales of $500 million. Since it was operating at full capacity in 1986, if sales are to increase in 1987, Century will need to increase all its assets.

Century's 1986 profit margin was 4.8 percent, and it distributed one-third of its net income to stockholders as dividends. If Century's sales increase to $750 million in 1987, what will its pro forma 1987 income statement, balance sheet, and statement of changes in financial position look like, and how much external financing will the company require during 1987?

The first step in the percentage of sales method is to isolate those income statement and balance sheet items that vary directly with sales. Regarding the income statement, increased sales are expected to bring direct increases in all of the variables except interest expense. That is, cost of goods sold and selling and administrative expenses are assumed to be tied directly to sales, but interest expense is a function of financing decisions. Further, Century's federal, state, and local taxes are expected to continue to amount to 40 percent of pre-tax income.

Turning to its balance sheet, since Century was operating at full capacity, fixed assets as well as current assets must increase if sales are to rise. Thus, each asset item must increase if the higher level of sales is to be attained. More cash will be needed for transactions, receivables will be higher, additional inventory must be stocked, and new plant must be added.[2]

If Century's assets are to increase, its liabilities and/or equity must likewise rise—the balance sheet must balance, and increases in assets must be financed in some manner. Accounts payable and accruals will rise *spontaneously* with sales: As sales increase, so will purchases, and larger purchases will result in higher levels of accounts payable. Thus, if sales double, accounts payable will also double. Similarly, a higher level of operations will require more labor, so accrued wages will increase, and, assuming profit margins are maintained, an increase in profits will pull up accrued taxes. Retained earnings should also increase, but not in direct proportion to the increase in sales. Neither notes payable, mortgage bonds, nor common stock will rise spontaneously with sales—higher sales do not automatically trigger increases in these items.

We can construct pro forma financial statements for December 31, 1987, proceeding as outlined in the following paragraphs.

Step 1. In Table 21-4, Column 1, we express those income statement and balance sheet items that vary directly with sales as a percentage of 1986 sales. An item such as interest expense that does not vary directly with sales is designated n.a., or "not applicable."

Step 2. Next, we multiply these percentages (their fractions, really) by the $750 million projected 1987 sales to obtain the projected 1987 amounts. These figures are shown in Column 2 of the table.

---

[2]Some assets, such as marketable securities, are not tied directly to operations, and hence do not vary directly with sales. In fact, marketable securities, if they were held, could be run down to zero, thus reducing external funding requirements.

Table 21-4
Century Electronics Corporation:
Pro Forma Financial Statements
(Millions of Dollars)

Income Statement	Percentage of 1986 Sales (1)	1987 Projections[a] (2)
Net sales	100.0%	$750
Cost of goods sold	80.0	600
Selling and administrative expenses	10.4	78
Earnings before interest and taxes	9.6%	$ 72
Interest expense	n.a.[b]	8[c]
Earnings before taxes	n.a.	$ 64
Taxes (40%)	n.a.	26
Net income	n.a.	$ 38
Dividends	n.a.	$ 8[c]
Addition to retained earnings	n.a.	$ 30

Balance Sheet	Percentage of 1986 Sales (1)	1987 Projections (2)
Cash	2.0%	$ 15
Receivables	17.0	128
Inventories	20.0	150
Total current assets	39.0%	$293
Net fixed assets	30.0	225
Total assets	69.0%	$518
Accounts payable	8.0%	$ 60
Notes payable (8%)	n.a.	10[c]
Accrued wages and taxes	5.0	38
Total current liabilities	n.a.	$108
Mortgage bonds (10%)	n.a.	72[c]
Common stock	n.a.	150[c]
Retained earnings	n.a.	78[d]
Total claims	n.a.	$408

$$\begin{array}{l}\text{External funds} \\ \text{needed}\end{array} = \begin{array}{l}\text{Projected} \\ \text{total assets}\end{array} - \begin{array}{l}\text{Projected} \\ \text{claims}\end{array}$$

$$= \$518 \text{ million} - \$408 \text{ million} = \$110 \text{ million}.$$

[a]1987 projection = Column 1 fraction × $750 projected 1987 sales, rounded to the nearest million.
[b]Not applicable (item does not vary spontaneously with sales).
[c]Initially projected at the 1986 level. Later financing decisions might change this level.
[d]1986 retained earnings balance plus projected 1987 addition to retained earnings = $48 million + $30 million = $78 million.

Step 3. Now, as a first approximation, we insert figures for interest expense, dividends, notes payable, mortgage bonds, and common stock from 1986. Several of these accounts will have to be changed later in the analysis.

Step 4. We next add the addition to retained earnings estimated for 1987 to the December 31, 1986, balance sheet figure to obtain the December 31, 1987, projected retained earnings. Ignoring any additional interest expense, Century would have a net income of $38 million in 1987. If the firm does not increase its dividend in 1987, the total dividend payment would be $8 million, leaving $38 million − $8 million = $30 million of new retained earnings.[3] Thus, the 1987 balance sheet account retained earnings would be $48 million + $30 million = $78 million.

Step 5. Next, we sum the balance sheet asset accounts, obtaining a projected total assets figure of $518 million, and we also sum the projected liability and equity items to obtain $408 million. At this point, the balance sheet does not balance: Assets total $518 million, but only $408 million of liabilities and equity is projected. Thus, we have a shortfall of $110 million, which will presumably be raised by bank borrowings and/or by selling securities. (For simplicity, we disregard depreciation by assuming that cash flows generated by depreciation are used to replace worn-out fixed assets.)

Financing the External Requirements

Century could use short-term notes, mortgage bonds, common stock, or a combination of these securities to make up the $110 million shortfall. Ordinarily, it would base this choice on its target capital structure, the relative costs of different types of securities, maturity matching considerations, and so on. However, in Century's case, the company's mortgage bond indenture requires it to keep total debt at or below 50 percent of total assets, and also to keep the current ratio at a level of 2.5 or greater. These provisions restrict the financing choices as follows (in millions of dollars):

1. Restriction on additional debt:

Maximum debt permitted = (0.5)(Total assets) = (0.5)($518) =		$259
Subtract debt already projected for December 31, 1987:		
Current liabilities	$108	
Mortgage bonds	72	$180
Maximum additional debt		$ 79

2. Restriction on additional current liabilities to maintain 2.5 × current ratio:

$$\frac{\text{Projected current assets}}{\text{Maximum current liabilities}} = 2.5$$

Maximum current liabilities $= \dfrac{\text{Projected current assets}}{2.5} = \$293/2.5 =$		$117
Subtract current liabilities already projected		108
Maximum additional current liabilities		$ 9

---

[3] Normally, companies attempt to "grow" their dividends at a relatively stable rate, and they also have a long-run target payout ratio in mind which is reasonably consistent with the targeted growth rate. However, dividend policy is invariably reviewed as a part of the financial planning process. In its planning, Century begins by holding constant the dollar dividend per share at the earlier year level, but it may modify this figure at a later stage in the process. An alternative first approximation would be to assume the 1986 payout ratio ($8/$24 = 0.33) will be maintained, in which case dividends would be projected at 0.33($38) = $12.7 million as a first approximation.

3. Common equity requirements:

Total external funds needed	$110
Maximum additional debt permitted	79
Common equity funds required	$ 31

From Table 21-4, we saw that, as a first approximation, Century needs a total of $110 million from external sources. Its bond indenture limits new debt to $79 million, and of that amount, only $9 million can be short-term debt. Thus, assuming that Century wants to make maximum use of debt financing, it must plan to sell common stock in the amount of $31 million, in addition to its debt financing, to cover its financial requirements.

However, the use of external funds will change the forecasted income statement for 1987 as set forth in Table 21-4. First, the issuance of new debt will increase the firm's 1987 interest expense. Second, the sale of new common stock will increase the total dividend payment, assuming that dividends per share are not to be reduced. Century is forecasting that new short-term debt will cost 10 percent, and that new long-term debt will cost 12 percent. Additionally, Century has 10 million shares of common stock outstanding, and it currently sells for $25 per share. Thus, Century's shareholders received $8 million/10 million = $0.80 of dividends per share in 1986, and management has stated that the dividend is not to be cut.

If Century financed in 1987 as outlined previously, and if the external financing occurred on January 1, 1987, then its income statement expenses and dividends would increase by the following amounts:

1. Additional interest requirements:

Short-term interest = 0.10($9,000,000)	=	$ 900,000
Long-term interest = 0.12($70,000,000)	=	8,400,000
Total additional interest		$9,300,000 ≈ $9 million

2. Additional dividend requirements:

New shares = $31,000,000/$25 per share = 1,240,000.
Additional dividends = $0.80(1,240,000) = $992,000 ≈ $1 million.

The projected 1987 income statement and balance sheet, including financing feedback effects, are contained in Table 21-5. We see that Century is still $6 million short in meeting its financing requirements, because interest and dividends associated with external financing reduced the addition to retained earnings from $30 million, before feedback effects were considered, to $24 million. Century's managers could repeat the preceding process with an additional $6 million of external financing. In this case, the additional $6 million would have to be raised as equity, because Century has already issued debt up to its limit. The addition to retained earnings would be further reduced by additional dividend requirements, but the balance sheet would be closer to being in balance. Successive iterations would continue to reduce the discrepancy. If the budget process were computerized, as would be true for most firms, an exact solution could be reached very rapidly. (We discuss this point later in the chapter.) Otherwise, firms would go

---

Table 21-5
Century Electronics Corporation:
Pro Forma Financial Statements
Including Feedback Effect
(Millions of Dollars)

Income Statement	1987 Projection
Net sales	$750
Cost of goods sold	600
Selling and administrative expense	78
Earnings before interest and taxes	$ 72
Interest expense	17[a]
Earnings before taxes	$ 55
Taxes (40%)	22
Net income	$ 33
Dividends	9[b]
Addition to retained earnings	$ 24

Balance Sheet	1987 Projection
Cash	$ 15
Receivables	128
Inventories	150
Total current assets	$293
Net fixed assets	225
Total assets	$518
Accounts payable	$ 60
Notes payable (8% and 10%)	19[c]
Accrued wages and taxes	38
Total current liabilities	$117
Mortgage bonds (10% and 12%)	142[d]
Common stock	181[e]
Retained earnings	72[f]
Total claims	$512

External financing requirements = $518 million − $512 million = $6 million.

[a] $8 million on beginning debt plus $9 million on new debt.
[b] $8 million on old shares plus $1 million on new shares.
[c] $10 million of old 8% notes payable plus $9 million of new 10% notes.
[d] $72 million of old 10% mortgage bonds plus $70 million of new 12% bonds.
[e] $150 from 1986 plus $31 million from sale of new stock.
[f] 1986 retained earnings balance plus projected 1987 additions = $48 million + $24 million = $72 million.

---

through two or three iterations and then stop. At this point, the projected statements would generally be very close to being in balance, and they would certainly be close enough for practical purposes, given the uncertainty inherent in the projections themselves.

For Century, the additional $6 million of new equity would have a minimal feedback effect. Thus, we could use Table 21-5, with $187 million in common

Table 21-6
Century Electronics Corporation:
Pro Forma Statement of Changes in Financial Position
for the Year Ending December 31, 1987
(Millions of Dollars)

Funds Provided by and Used in Operations

Sources:[a]

Net income	$ 33
Increase in accounts payable	20
Increase in accruals	13
Total sources from operations	$ 66

Uses:

Increase in receivables	43
Increase in inventories	50
Increase in net fixed assets	75
Total uses in operations	$168
Net funds from operations	($102)

Financing Activities

Increase in notes payable	$ 9
Sale of bonds	70
Sale of common stock	37
Net funds from financing	$116
Total funds from operations and financing	$ 14
Less common dividends	9
Increase (decrease) in cash and equivalents	$ 5

Key Ratios Projected for December 31, 1987[b]

1.	Current ratio	2.5 times
2.	Total debt/total assets	50%
3.	Rate of return on equity	13.0%

[a]Normally, funds from operations would include depreciation. Here we have assumed that depreciation is reinvested in fixed assets; that is, depreciation is netted out against fixed asset additions.
[b]Other ratios could also be calculated and analyzed, and a Du Pont chart could be developed.

stock, as the projected 1987 income statement and balance sheet. These statements could then be used (1) to create the pro forma statement of changes in financial condition and (2) to check Century's critical financial ratios. This is done in Table 21-6.

FACTORS INFLUENCING EXTERNAL FINANCING REQUIREMENTS

The five factors which have the greatest influence on a firm's external funding requirements are (1) its projected sales growth, (2) its initial fixed asset utilization rate, or excess capacity situation, (3) its capital intensity, (4) its profit margin, and (5) its dividend policy. We discuss these factors next.

Sales Growth

The faster Century's sales grow, the greater will be its need for external financing. At very low growth rates, Century will need no external financing; indeed, all required funds can be obtained by spontaneous increases in current liability accounts plus retained earnings, and the company may even generate surplus capital. However, if the company's projected sales growth rate increases beyond a certain level, then it must seek outside financing, and the faster the projected growth rate, the greater will be its outside capital requirements. The reasoning here is as follows:

1. Increases in sales normally require increases in assets. If sales were not projected to grow, no new assets would be needed.

2. Any projected asset increases require financing of some type. Some of the required financing will come from spontaneously generated liabilities. Also, assuming a positive profit margin and a payout ratio of less than 100 percent, the firm will generate some retained earnings.

3. If the sales growth rate is low enough, spontaneously generated funds plus retained earnings will be sufficient to support the asset growth. However, if the sales growth rate exceeds a certain level, then external funds will be needed. If management foresees difficulties in raising this capital—perhaps because the current owners do not want to sell additional stock—then the feasibility of expansion plans may have to be reconsidered.

Excess Capacity

In determining Century's external financing requirements for 1987, we assumed that its fixed assets were being fully utilized.[4] Thus, any significant increase in sales would require an increase in fixed assets. What would be the effect if Century had been operating its fixed assets at only 70 percent of capacity? Under this condition, fixed assets could remain constant until sales reach that level at which fixed assets were being fully utilized, defined as *capacity sales*, which is calculated as follows:

$$\text{Utilization rate (\% of capacity)} = \frac{\text{Actual sales}}{\text{Capacity sales}},$$

so

$$\text{Capacity Sales} = \frac{\text{Actual sales}}{\text{Utilization rate}}.$$

If Century had been operating in 1986 at 70 percent of capacity, then its capacity sales without new fixed assets would be $714 million:

---

[4]We also assumed that depreciation-generated funds were being used to replace worn-out assets, and that no excess stocks of current assets existed.

$$\text{Capacity sales} = \frac{\$500 \text{ million}}{0.70} = \$714 \text{ million.}$$

Thus, Century could have increased sales to $714 million with no increase in fixed assets, and to reach its projected sales of $750 million in 1987, it would require only enough new fixed assets to support the sales increase from $714 million to $750 million, or $36 million of new sales.

Operating at less than full capacity can be incorporated into the pro forma balance sheet as follows:

1. Calculate a new target fixed assets percentage of sales based on capacity sales rather than on actual sales. If Century had been operating at 70 percent of capacity in 1986, then its target fixed assets percentage of sales would be $150/$714 = 0.21 rather than the $150/$500 = 0.30 that we calculated earlier and used in Table 21-4 to determine the 1987 fixed assets requirement.

2. Use the new percentage of sales to forecast the 1987 level of fixed assets. For Century, the 1987 level would be 0.21($750) = $158 million, rather than the $225 million originally projected. Thus, operating at only 70 percent of capacity in 1986 reduces 1987 projected net fixed assets by $225 million − $158 million = $67 million. This decrease in projected assets, in turn, reduces external funding requirements by a like amount. Obviously, operating at less than full capacity has a significant impact on the need for external funds.

Capital Intensity

The amount of assets required per dollar of sales (total assets/sales) is often called the *capital intensity ratio*. Notice that the capital intensity ratio is the reciprocal of the total asset turnover ratio. This factor has a major effect on capital requirements to support any level of sales growth. If the capital intensity ratio is low, then sales can grow rapidly without much outside capital. However, if the firm is capital intensive, then even a small growth in output will require a great deal of outside capital.

If a company anticipates that it might have trouble financing its projected capital requirements, then it might, as a part of its strategic planning, consider a reduction in its capital intensity ratio. For example, when they were faced with a funds shortage in the early 1980s, several U.S. automakers began a policy of purchasing rather than manufacturing certain parts, thus eliminating the need for facilities to manufacture those parts.

Profit Margin

The profit margin is also an important determinant of external funds requirements—the higher the profit margin, the lower the external financing requirement, other factors held constant. Century's profit margin in 1986 was 4.8 percent. Now suppose its profit margin increased to 10 percent through higher sales prices and better expense control. This would increase net income, and hence retained earnings (assuming a constant payout), which in turn would decrease the requirement for external funds.

Because of the relationship between profit margin and external capital requirements, some very rapidly growing firms do not need much external capital. For example, for many years Xerox grew rapidly with very little borrowing or stock sales. However, as the company lost patent protection, and as competition intensified in the copier industry, Xerox's profit margin declined, its needs for external capital rose, and it began to borrow from banks and other sources. IBM and a number of other companies have had similar experiences.

Dividend Policy

Dividend policy also affects external capital requirements, so if Century foresees difficulties in raising capital, it might want to consider a reduction in its dividend payout ratio. However, before making this decision, management should consider the possible effects of changes in dividends on stock prices.[5]

PROBLEMS WITH THE PERCENTAGE OF SALES APPROACH

For the percentage of sales method to produce accurate forecasts, the financial statement ratios must remain constant over time, and for the ratios to remain constant, each asset item must increase in the same proportion as sales. In graph form, this assumption suggests the existence of the type of relationship indicated in Panel A of Figure 21-2, where we graph inventory versus sales. Here the plotted relationship is linear and passes through the origin. Thus, if the company grows and sales expand from $200 million to $400 million, inventories will increase proportionately, from $100 million to $200 million.

The assumption of constant ratios is appropriate at times, but there are times when it is incorrect. Three such conditions are described in the following sections.

Economies of Scale

There are economies of scale in the use of many kinds of assets, and when they occur, the ratios are likely to change over time as the size of the firm increases. Often, for example, firms need to maintain base stocks of different inventory items, even if sales levels are quite low. Then, as sales expand, inventories tend to grow less rapidly than sales, so the ratio of inventory to sales declines. This situation is depicted in Panel B of Figure 21-2. Here we see that the inventory/sales ratio is 1.5, or 150 percent, when sales are $200 million, but the ratio declines to 1.0 when sales climb to $400 million.

---

[5]Dividend policy was discussed in detail in Chapter 11. Note that if management believes that dividends are irrelevant, Century could adopt a residual dividend policy and use retained earnings to the maximum extent to meet equity financing requirements. However, if dividends are considered to be relevant, then changes in dividend policy must be assumed to affect stock prices, and the tradeoff between retained earnings financing and new stock financing becomes more complex.

Figure 21-2
Four Possible Ratio Relationships
(Millions of Dollars)

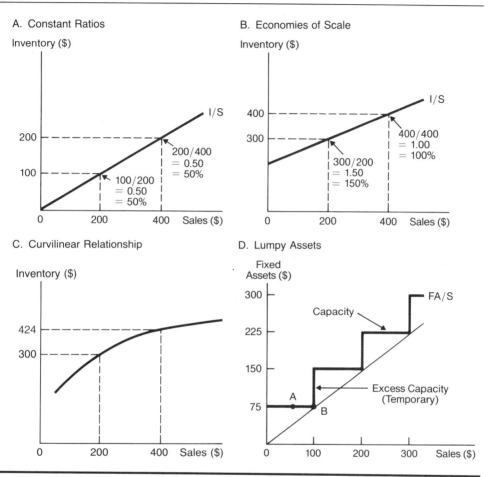

A. Constant Ratios

B. Economies of Scale

C. Curvilinear Relationship

D. Lumpy Assets

Panel B still shows a linear relationship between inventories and sales, but even this is not necessarily the case. Indeed, as we saw in Chapter 19, if a firm employs the EOQ model to establish inventory levels, then inventory will rise with the square root of sales. This type of situation is illustrated in Panel C.

Lumpy Assets

In many industries, technological considerations dictate that if a firm is to be competitive, it must add fixed assets in large, discrete units. For example, in the paper industry, there are strong economies of scale in basic paper mill equipment, so when paper companies expand capacity, they must do so in large increments. This type of situation is depicted in Panel D of Figure 21-2. Here we assume that the minimum-sized feasible plant has a cost of $75 million, and that such a plant can produce enough output to attain a sales level of $100 million per year. If the firm is to be competitive, it simply must have at least $75 million of fixed assets.

This situation has a major effect on the fixed assets/sales (FA/S) ratio at different sales levels, and consequently on financial requirements. At Point A in Panel D, which represents a sales level of $50 million, the fixed assets are $75 million, so the ratio FA/S = $75/$50 = 1.5. However, sales can expand by $50 million, out to $100 million, with no required increase in fixed assets. At that point, represented by Point B, the ratio FA/S = $75/$100 = 0.75. If the firm is operating at full capacity, even a small increase in sales would require the firm to double its plant capacity, so a small projected sales increase would bring with it very large financial requirements.[6]

Cyclical Changes

All the panels in Figure 21-2 focus on target, or projected, relationships between sales and assets. Actual sales, however, are often different from projected sales, and the actual asset/sales ratio for a given period might be quite different from the planned ratio. To illustrate, the firm depicted in Panel B might, when its sales are at $200 million and its inventories at $300 million, predict a sales expansion to $400 million and then increase its inventories to $400 million in anticipation of the sales expansion. But suppose an unforeseen economic downturn holds sales to only $300 million. In this case, actual inventories would be $400 million versus only about $350 million needed to support sales of $300 million. In this situation, if the firm were forecasting its financial requirements, it should recognize that sales can be expanded by $100 million with no increase in inventories, but that any sales expansion beyond $100 million would require additional financing to build inventories.

If any of the ratios is subject to any of the conditions noted here, the simple percentage of sales method of forecasting financial requirements should not be used. Rather, other techniques must be used to forecast financial statement item levels and the resulting external financing requirements. Some of these methods are discussed in the following sections.

---

[6]Several other points should be noted about Panel D of Figure 21-2. First, if the firm is operating at a sales level of $100 million or less, then any expansion that calls for a sales increase above $100 million would require a *doubling* of fixed assets. Much smaller percentage increases would be involved if the firm were large enough to be operating a number of plants. Second, firms generally go to multiple shifts and take other actions to minimize the need for new fixed asset capacity as they approach Point B. However, these efforts can go only so far, and eventually a fixed asset expansion is required. Third, firms often make arrangements to purchase excess capacity output from other firms in their industry, or to sell excess capacity to other firms. For example, the situation in the electric utility industry is very much like that depicted in Panel D. As a result, when Tampa Electric brought a new base load coal-fired plant on line in 1985, it had arranged ahead of time to sell half of the plant's output to Florida Power & Light in 1985 and one-fourth of the output in 1986. By 1987, Tampa Electric projected that its own demand would have grown enough to fully utilize the plant.

REGRESSION ANALYSIS

Regression analysis is often used to estimate asset requirements. For example, Century's selling and administrative expenses, receivables, inventories, and net fixed assets over the last 10 years are given in the lower section of Figure 21-3 and plotted as scatter diagrams against sales in the upper section. Estimated regression equations as found using *Lotus 1-2-3* Release 2 are also shown in the figure. For

Figure 21-3
Century Electronics Corporation:
Linear Regression Models
(Millions of Dollars)

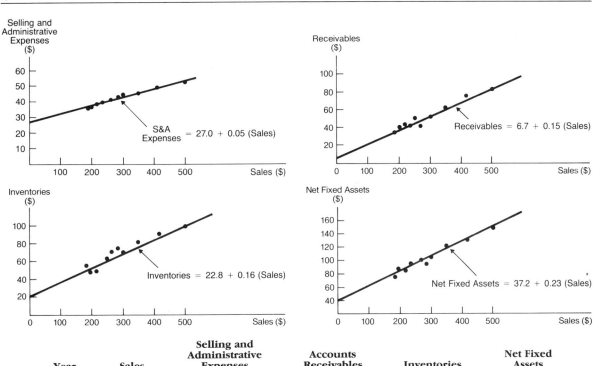

Year	Sales	Selling and Administrative Expenses	Accounts Receivables	Inventories	Net Fixed Assets
1977	$200	$37	$38	$48	$83
1978	215	38	44	53	86
1979	185	36	35	57	79
1980	235	39	43	60	91
1981	265	42	45	66	98
1982	300	45	52	73	106
1983	280	43	47	70	101
1984	350	46	61	78	118
1985	420	49	71	90	135
1986	500	53	85	100	150

example, the estimated relationship between inventories and sales (in millions of dollars) is

$$\text{Inventories} = \$22.8 + 0.16(\text{Sales}).$$

The plotted points are quite close to the regression line. In fact, the correlation coefficient between inventories and sales is 0.98, indicating that there is a very strong linear relationship between these two variables. Why might this be the case for Century? According to the EOQ model, inventories should increase with the square root of sales, which would cause the scatter diagram to be nonlinear—the true regression line would rise at a decreasing rate. However, Century has greatly expanded its product line over the last decade, and the base stocks associated with these new products have caused inventories to rise. These two influences—economies of scale in existing products and base stocks for new products—are offsetting, resulting in the observed linear relationship between inventories and sales.

We can use the estimated relationship between inventories and sales to forecast 1987 inventory levels. Since 1987 sales are projected at $750 million, 1987 inventories should be $142.8 million:

$$\text{Inventories} = \$22.8 + 0.16(\$750) = \$142.8 \text{ million.}$$

This is $7.2 million less than our earlier forecast based on the percentage of sales method. The difference occurs because the percentage of sales method assumes that the ratio of inventories to sales remains constant, but the ratio actually declines because the inventory regression line in Figure 21-3 does not pass through the origin.

The other panels in Figure 21-3 illustrate the use of the regression method for forecasting the relationships between sales and (1) selling and administrative expenses, (2) receivables, and (3) net fixed assets. We will use these relationships later in the chapter, when we develop a computerized forecasting model for Century. We could actually use the same process for all appropriate financial statement items, but first, in the next section, we discuss several other forecasting techniques.

OTHER FORECASTING METHODS

In this section, we discuss three additional forecasting methods that are commonly used in practice: curvilinear regression, multiple regression, and specific item forecasting using such procedures as the EOQ model.

Simple Curvilinear Regression

Simple linear regression as discussed previously is based on the assumption that a straight-line relationship exists. Although linear relationships between financial statement variables and sales do exist frequently, this is not a universal rule. For example, if the EOQ relationship had dominated the inventory-sales relationship, the plot of inventory versus sales would have been a concave curve such as the one depicted back in Panel C of Figure 21-2. If we forecasted the inventory level needed to support sales of $400 million using the linear relationship, our forecast would be too high.

Firms have in their data bases historical data on their own company by divisions, by product lines, and by individual products. They also have or can easily obtain certain types of data for other firms in their industry. These data can be analyzed using computer programs based on advanced statistical techniques (1) to help determine whether a relationship is curvilinear or linear and (2) to estimate the curvilinear relationship should one exist. Once the best-fit relationship has been estimated, it can be used to project future levels of items such as inventories, given the sales forecast.[7]

Multiple Regression

If the relationship between a variable such as inventories and sales is such that the individual points are widely scattered about the regression line, and hence the correlation coefficient is low, then there is a good chance that other factors, in addition to sales, affect the level of that variable. For example, inventory levels might be a function of both sales level and number of different products sold. In this case, we would obtain the best forecast for inventory level by using multiple regression techniques, where inventories would be regressed against both sales and the number of products sold. Then, the projected inventories would be based on forecasts of number of products in addition to total sales. Most computer installations now have complete regression software packages, making it easy to apply multiple and curvilinear regression techniques. One can even do multiple regression analysis with up to 12 independent variables on a PC with Release 2 of *Lotus 1-2-3*.

Specific Item Forecasting

A final approach to financial forecasting is to develop a specific model for each variable. For example, inventories could be forecasted by using the EOQ model; target cash balances could be forecasted by using the Baumol model; receivables could be forecasted by using the payments pattern approach; and fixed assets could be forecasted on the basis of the firm's capital budget and depreciation schedule. Of course, projected sales demand is still the driving force behind each of these specific forecasts, but given the sales forecast, each item could be analyzed by its own unique forecasting method. Similarly, on the income statement side, a firm could forecast its cost of goods sold by conducting an engineering/production analysis of each major product. Specific item analysis is likely to provide the most accurate forecasts, but it is also the most expensive and time consuming technique.

---

[7]Often, a plot of the data will suggest a nonlinear relationship. The data—inventories in this case—can then be converted to logarithms if it appears that the regression line slopes down, or raised to a power if the slope seems to be increasing. We often use the graphics capabilities of *Lotus 1-2-3* for such analyses. However, for an important forecast such as demand for the output of a power plant, we would use more powerful statistical procedures.

COMPARISON OF FORECASTING METHODS

The percentage of sales method assumes that different financial statement items vary directly with sales. It is the easiest and least expensive method, but often its forecasts are of questionable accuracy. Regression analysis differs from the percentage of sales method in that regression does not assume constant ratios. This technique can improve on the forecasts for many financial statement items. Note too that curvilinear and multiple regression techniques can provide especially accurate forecasts when relationships (1) are not linear or (2) depend on other variables in addition to sales. Finally, specific item forecasting that utilizes various decision models can be used.

As we move down the list of forecasting methods, accuracy increases, but so do costs. The need to employ more complicated, and consequently more costly, methods varies from situation to situation. As in all applications, the costs of using more refined techniques must be balanced against the benefits of increased accuracy.

COMPUTERIZED FINANCIAL PLANNING MODELS

Although the types of financial forecasting described thus far in the chapter can be done with a hand calculator, most well-managed firms with sales greater than a few hundred thousand dollars have at least a PC and can employ some type of computerized financial planning model. Such models can be programmed to show the effects of different sales levels, different relationships between sales and operating assets, and even different assumptions about sales prices and input costs (labor, materials, and so forth). Plans are then made regarding how projected financial requirements are to be met—through short-term bank loans, by selling long-term bonds, or by selling new common or preferred stock. Pro forma balance sheets and income statements are generated under the different financing plans, and earnings per share are projected, along with such risk and profitability measures as the current ratio, the debt/assets ratio, the times-interest-earned ratio, return on assets, and return on equity.

Depending on how these projections look, management may need to modify the initial plan. For example, management might conclude that the projected growth rate must be cut because external capital requirements exceed the firm's ability to raise money. Or management could decide to reduce dividends and thus generate more funds internally. Alternatively, the company might investigate production processes that require fewer fixed assets, or it might consider the possibility of buying rather than manufacturing certain components, thus eliminating some raw materials and work-in-process inventories, as well as certain manufacturing facilities.

The Basic Forecasting Model

To illustrate how computerized forecasting models work, we have constructed a financial statement forecasting model for Century Electronics Corporation using

Lotus 1-2-3. In the model, we defined the key variables' relationships with sales as shown in Table 21-7; these relationships were developed from historical data using linear regression analysis. Further, we assumed (1) that sales will grow at an annual rate of 50 percent in 1987, at a 25 percent rate in both 1988 and 1989, and at a 15 percent rate in 1990 and 1991; (2) that dividends per share will be increased by 10 percent per year over the next five years; (3) that the stock price will grow at an annual rate of 20 percent during the next five years; (4) that the state-plus-federal income tax rate will be 40 percent for the next five years; (5) that the current ratio cannot fall below 2.5, (6) that the debt ratio cannot exceed 50 percent; (7) that all new financing will occur on January 1 of the year in which it is needed; (8) that new short-term debt will cost 10 percent and new long-term debt will cost 12 percent; and (9) that flotation costs are insignificant and thus can be ignored.

The *Lotus* model automatically performs the financing feedback iterations and generates the 5-year pro forma financial statements along with selected ratios and other information. Section A of Table 21-8 presents the following selected output from the model under the assumptions set forth: (1) forecasted earnings per share (EPS), (2) the times-interest-earned (TIE) ratio, (3) the return on assets (ROA), (4) the rate of return on equity (ROE), and (5) the external funds needed (EFN) in each year from 1987 through 1991. We could have displayed the full set of statements as well as more financial ratios, but Table 21-8 is sufficient to show that, under the above assumptions, Century's financial condition will be strong and will actually improve over the next five years. However, to support the growth in sales, Century must raise a total of over $144 million through external funding over the next three years.

The forecasted situation could look good or bad. In this case, it looks almost too good. Rising earnings could attract new entry into Century's markets, and this new competition could drive down prices, profit margins, EPSs, and ROEs. Thus, Century might want to reexamine its basic assumptions and to rerun the model using more conservative forecasts as discussed next.

Table 21-7
Variable to Sales Relationships
(Millions of Dollars)

Variable	Relationship to Sales
Cost of goods sold	0.80(Sales)
Administrative and selling expenses	$27.0 + 0.05(Sales)
Cash	0.02(Sales)
Receivables	$6.7 + 0.15(Sales)
Inventories	$22.8 + 0.16(Sales)
Net fixed assets	$37.2 + 0.23(Sales)
Accounts payable	0.08(Sales)
Accrued wages and taxes	0.05(Sales)

Table 21-8
Century Electronics Corporation:
Selected Model Output

	1987	1988	1989	1990	1991
A. Base Case					
EPS	$4.12	$5.50	$7.29	$8.84	$10.66
TIE	5.45×	5.97×	6.40×	7.65×	9.38×
ROA	8.61%	9.59%	10.42%	11.12%	11.79%
ROE	17.22%	19.18%	20.84%	20.73%	20.49%
EFN[a]	$74	$34	$36	($4)	($10)
B. Low-Growth Case					
EPS	$3.50	$4.53	$5.79	$6.73	$7.44
TIE	5.83×	6.20×	6.71×	8.30×	9.31×
ROA	8.14%	8.99%	9.80%	10.45%	10.92%
ROE	15.22%	17.03%	18.49%	18.24%	16.90%
EFN[a]	$38	$20	$20	($15)	($22)

[a]In millions of dollars. Note that, for 1990 and 1991, the external funds needed are negative, indicating that operations are generating excess funds.

Changing Assumptions and Policies

The most important benefit of computerized financial modeling is that it permits financial managers to see the effects of changing both basic assumptions and specific financial policies. For example, what would Century's financial condition be if competition lowered its growth rate over the next five years to 30 percent for 1987, to 20 percent for both 1988 and 1989, and then to 10 percent for 1990 and 1991? Section B of Table 21-8 contains selected output data based on these lower sales growth estimates. All other assumptions and financial policies remain as defined by the base case. Here we see that Century's general financial condition and profitability still improve over the next five years, but not as dramatically as in the base case. However, external funding requirements are significantly reduced, to only $78 million over the five years versus $144 million in the base case.

The pro forma financial statements could be rerun over and over, each time changing one or more assumptions regarding sales growth rates, cost relationships, profit margins, future interest rates, and so on. We could also rerun the model with changes in financial policies, such as increasing or decreasing the dividend growth rate, changing the external financing mix, and so on. Thus, the results of differing assumptions and financial policies could be compared.[8] It is important, however,

---

[8]See Problem 21-6 for an extension of this example. For students with access to *Lotus 1-2-3,* this problem provides an excellent introduction to computerized financial forecasting.

to note (1) that the financial manager still must interpret the results of alternative financial policies and (2) that the analysis could encompass virtually hundreds of combinations of assumptions and policies, and thus we could generate hundreds of different sets of pro forma financial statements.

One way to reduce the number of different possible scenarios is to perform a sensitivity analysis on the assumptions—those assumptions that have little effect on the key financial integrity and profitability ratios need not be changed from their base case levels. Another approach to reducing the number of scenarios is to perform a Monte Carlo simulation analysis. For example, instead of specifying sales growth rates, costs of goods sold, and so on at discrete levels, probability distributions could be specified. Then, the key results would be presented as distributions rather than as point estimates.[9]

FINANCIAL CONTROLS

Financial forecasting and planning is vital to corporate success, but planning is for nought unless the firm has a control system (1) that insures implementation of the planned policies and (2) that provides an information feedback loop which permits rapid adjustments if the market conditions upon which the plan is based change. In a financial control system, the key question is not "How is the firm doing in 1987 as compared with 1986?" Rather, it is "How is the firm doing in 1987 as compared with our forecasts, and if actual results differ from the budget, what can we do to get back on track?"

The basic tools of financial control are budgets and pro forma financial statements. These documents set forth expected performance, and, hence, they express management's targets. These targets are then compared with actual corporate performance—on a daily, weekly, or monthly basis—to determine the variances, which are defined here as the difference between actual values and target values. Thus, the control system identifies those areas where performance is not meeting target levels. If a division's actuals are better than its targets, this could signify that its manager should be given a raise, but it could also mean that the targets were set too low and thus should be raised in the future. Conversely, failure to meet the financial targets could mean that market conditions are changing, that some managers are not performing up to par, or that the targets were set initially at unrealistic, unattainable levels. In any event, some action should be taken, and perhaps quickly, if the situation is deteriorating rapidly. By focusing on variances, managers

---

[9]This is a good time to mention the basic axiom of computer modeling: GIGO, which means "garbage in, garbage out." Stated another way, the output of a financial model is no better than the assumptions and other inputs used to construct it. So, when you build models, proceed with caution. Note, though, that one advantage of computer modeling is that it does bring the key assumptions out into the open, where their realism can be examined. One strong advocate of models made this statement: "Critics of our models generally attack our assumptions, but they forget that in their own forecasts, they simply assume the answer."

can "manage by exception," concentrating on those variables that are most in need of improvement and leaving alone those operations that are running smoothly.[10]

SUMMARY

This chapter has focused on the financial planning and control process. Financial planning must be performed within the overall context of the firm's *strategic* and *operating plans.* The heart of financial planning is the construction of *pro forma financial statements*, and the accuracy of these statements rests both on sales forecasts and on the estimates of the relationships between the financial statement variables and sales. There are five basic methods for estimating these relationships: (1) *percentage of sales*, (2) *linear regression*, (3) *curvilinear regression*, (4) *multiple regression*, and (5) *specific item forecasting.*

Pro forma financial statements help financial managers (1) evaluate the expected future financial health of the firm, (2) determine financing requirements, and (3) determine how alternative financial policies affect financial condition and financing requirements. Because of financing feedback effects and the usefulness of sensitivity analysis, the pro forma financial statements are best constructed by computer programs such as *Lotus 1-2-3.*

Financial planning is of little value if the firm does not have a control system to monitor the plan's implementation and to provide information needed to develop future financial plans. However, financial planning and control is a costly process, in terms of both human and financial resources. Thus, in designing the process, one must balance the costs against the benefits to be gained.

Questions and Problems

21-1 (External funding requirements) Suppose a firm makes the following policy changes. If the change means that external, nonspontaneous financial requirements for any rate of growth will increase, indicate this by a +, indicate decreases by a −, and indicate indeterminate and/or no effect by a 0. Think in terms of the immediate, short-run effect on funds requirements.

    a. The dividend payout ratio is increased.

    b. The firm contracts to buy rather than make certain components used in its products.

    c. The firm decides to pay all suppliers on delivery, rather than after a 30-day delay, in order to take advantage of discounts for rapid payment.

    d. The firm begins to sell on credit; previously, all sales had been on a cash basis.

    e. The firm's profit margin is eroded by increased competition; sales are steady.

    f. Advertising expenditures are stepped up.

---

[10]Of course, entire textbooks have been written on financial controls, and much of the subject of financial control overlaps with managerial, or cost, accounting. Here, we want only to emphasize that financial controls are as critical to financial performance as are financial planning and forecasting. We must also add that financial control systems are not costless. Thus, the control system must balance its costs against the savings it is intended to produce.

g. A decision is made to substitute long-term mortgage bonds for short-term bank loans.

h. The firm begins to pay employees on a weekly basis; previously, it paid them at the end of each month.

21-2 (Pro forma balance sheet) A group of investors is planning to set up a new company to manufacture and distribute a novel type of running shoe. To help plan the new operation's financial requirements, you have been asked to construct a pro forma balance sheet for December 31, 1987, the end of the first year of operations. Sales for 1987 are projected at $20 million, and the following are industry average ratios for athletic shoe companies.

Sales to common equity	$5 \times$
Current debt to equity	50%
Total debt to equity	80%
Current ratio	$2.2 \times$
Net sales to inventory	$9 \times$
Accounts receivable to sales	10%
Fixed assets to equity	70%
Profit margin	3%
Dividend payout ratio	30%

a. Complete the pro forma balance sheet below, assuming that the firm maintains industry average ratios.

Cash	$_____	Current debt	$_____
Accounts receivable	_____	Long-term debt	_____
Inventories	_____	Total debt	$_____
Total current assets	$_____	Equity	_____
Fixed assets	_____		
Total assets	$_____	Total claims	$_____

b. If the investor group supplies all of the new firm's equity, how much capital will the group be required to put up during 1987?

21-3 (Percentage of sales method) Lamm Textile's 1986 sales were $72 million. The percentage of sales of each balance sheet item except notes payable, mortgage bonds, and common stock is given below:

Cash	4%
Receivables	25
Inventories	30
Net fixed assets	50
Accounts payable	15
Accruals	5
Profit margin	5

The dividend payout ratio is 60 percent; the December 31, 1985, balance sheet account for retained earnings was $41.80 million; and both common stock and mortgage bonds are constant and equal to the amounts shown on the following balance sheet.

a. Complete the firm's December 31, 1986, balance sheet below (in thousands of dollars).

Cash	$		Accounts payable	$
Receivables			Notes payable	6,840
Inventories	_____		Accruals	
Total current assets	$		Total current liabilities	$
Net fixed assets			Mortgage bonds	10,000
			Common stock	4,000
			Retained earnings	
	_____			_____
Total assets	$ _____		Total claims	$ _____

b. Assume that the company was operating at full capacity in 1986 with regard to all items *except* fixed assets. If the fixed assets had been used to full capacity, the fixed assets/sales ratio would have been 40 percent in 1986. By what percentage could 1987 sales increase over 1986 sales without the need for an increase in fixed assets?

c. Now suppose that 1987 sales increase over 1986 sales by 20 percent. How much additional external capital will be required? Assume that Part b conditions hold and that any required financing is borrowed as notes payable.

d. Suppose the industry percentage of sales averages for receivables and inventories are 20 percent and 25 percent, respectively, and that Lamm matches these figures in 1987 and then uses the funds released to reduce equity. (It could pay a special dividend out of retained earnings.) What would this do to the rate of return on year-end 1987 equity? (Assume that Part c conditions hold.)

21-4 (Pro forma financial statements) The 1986 income statement and balance sheet for Muscarella Industries are given below (in thousands of dollars):

Net sales	$10,000
Cost of goods sold	6,500
Gross profit	$ 3,500
Administrative expenses	1,000
Miscellaneous expenses	500
EBIT	$ 2,000
Interest expense	200
EBT	$ 1,800
Taxes (48%)	864
Net income	$ 936
Dividends	$ 468
Addition to retained earnings	$ 468

Cash	$ 50		Accounts payable	$ 250
Accounts receivable	423		Notes payable	200
Inventory	513		Accruals	50
Total current assets	$ 986		Total current liabilities	$ 500
Net plant	4,014		Long-term debt	1,500
			Common stock	1,500
			Retained earnings	1,500
Total assets	$5,000		Total claims	$5,000

As the financial manager, you want to construct a pro forma income statement, balance sheet, and statement of changes in financial position for 1987. As a first step, you develop the following relationships between the financial statement variables and sales (in thousands of dollars):

Variable	Relationship to Sales
Cost of goods sold	0.65(Sales)
Administrative expenses	$500 + 0.05(Sales)
Miscellaneous expenses	0.05(Sales)
Cash	0.005(Sales)
Accounts receivable	0.0423(Sales)
Inventory	$200 + 0.03(Sales)
Net plant	0.40(Sales)
Accounts payable	0.025(Sales)
Accruals	0.005(Sales)

Taxes are expected to continue at 48 percent (the firm operates in a very high state and local tax jurisdiction); sales in 1987 are forecast to increase over 1986 by 30 percent; and fixed assets were fully utilized in 1986. Any external funding required for 1987 will be financed in the proportion of 4 percent notes payable, 36 percent long-term debt, and 60 percent new equity. The firm's stock currently sells for $25 per share, and there are 1,000,000 shares outstanding. Thus, the 1986 DPS was $468,000/ 1,000,000 = $0.468. However, the firm wants to increase the dividend in 1987 to $0.50 per share. New short-term debt is expected to cost 12 percent, while new long-term debt will cost 14 percent.

a. Construct the initial 1987 pro forma income statement and balance sheet. What is the external funding requirement? How will it be met? (For now, ignore financing feedback effects.)

b. Recast the 1987 pro forma income statement and balance sheet considering financing feedback effects. How much of an external financing shortfall still exists?

c. Perform one more iteration on the pro forma income statement and balance sheet. Construct the pro forma 1987 statement of changes in financial position. (You should still have a shortfall of $1,000 after the second iteration. Use $1,000 worth of new equity to balance the balance sheet.)

d. The firm's current bond indenture limits the firm to a minimum current ratio of 1.5, a maximum debt ratio of 35 percent, and a minimum times-interest-earned ratio of 8.0. Are any of these restrictions violated in the pro forma statements? If so, how must the financing program be modified to meet these restrictions?

e. What would be the effect on external financing requirements if the firm had been operating at only 80 percent of capacity in 1986? (Note that the net plant account is forecast using the percentage of sales technique.)

21-5 (Pro forma financial statements) The 1986 income statement and balance sheet for O'Brien Pulp and Paper are shown below (in thousands of dollars):

Sales	$500
Operating expenses	320
General expenses	80
EBIT	$100
Interest expense	20
EBT	$ 80
Taxes (50%)	40
Net income	$ 40

Cash	$ 30	Accounts payable	$ 40
Receivables	50	Accruals	20
Inventories	420	Notes payable	20
Net fixed assets	500	Long-term debt	180
		Common stock	200
		Retained earnings	540
Total assets	$1,000	Total claims	$1,000

The firm, which operates in a high-tax environment, has 40,000 shares outstanding, and next year's dividend is forecast at $0.55 per share. O'Brien has fixed assets sufficient to support a sales level of $750,000. Next year's sales are forecast to be $700,000. The stock is currently selling at $2.86 per share, and the stock price is expected to be flat over the next year. Any external financing would be met with a mix of 60 percent long-term debt, at an estimated cost of 12.82 percent and 40 percent common equity. No new short-term debt would be used, but the old short-term debt would be rolled over at the current rate.

The relationships between certain financial statement variables and sales are given below (in thousands of dollars):

Variable	Relationship to Sales
General expenses	$30 + 0.10(Sales)
Inventories	$200 + 0.44(Sales)

All other variables are forecast using the percentage of sales method. The 1986 levels of these variables are appropriate for a sales level of $500,000.

a. Construct the initial 1987 pro forma income statement and balance sheet, excluding financial feedback effects. What amount of external financing is required? How will it be obtained?

b. Construct the first iteration pro forma income statement and balance sheet; that is, the statements which include financing feedback effects. What is the additional interest expense resulting from external financing? What is the additional dividend payment? How much external financing is still required after this iteration?

21-6 (Financial forecasting) Century Electronics Corporation's 1986 financial statements are given below (in millions of dollars):

Income Statement	For the Year Ended December 31, 1986
Net sales	$500
Cost of goods sold	400
Selling and administrative expenses	52
Earnings before interest and taxes	$ 48
Interest expense	8
Earnings before taxes	$ 40
Taxes (40%)	16
Net income	$ 24
Dividends (payout: 33%)	$ 8
Addition to retained earnings	$ 16

Balance Sheet	As of December 31, 1986
Cash	$ 10
Receivables	82
Inventories	103
Total current assets	$195
Net fixed assets	152
Total assets	$347
Accounts payable	$ 40
Notes payable (8%)	8
Accrued wages and taxes	25
Total current liabilities	$ 73
Mortgage bonds (10%)	70
Common stock	150
Retained earnings	54
Total claims	$347

Note: Century's 1986 balance sheet has been recast slightly to reflect the variable relationships given below. Thus, this balance sheet is not an exact duplicate of Table 21-3.

Assume (1) that sales will grow at an annual rate of 50 percent in 1987, at a 25 percent rate in both 1988 and 1989, and at a 15 percent rate in 1990 and 1991; (2) that dividends per share will be increased by 10 percent per year over the next 5 years; (3) that the stock price will grow at an annual rate of 20 percent over the next 5 years; (4) that the state-plus-federal income tax rate will remain at 40 percent; (5) that the current ratio cannot fall below 2.5 and the debt ratio cannot exceed 50 percent; (6) that all new financing will occur on January 1 of the year in which it is needed; (7) that new short-term debt will cost 10 percent and new long-term debt will cost 12 percent; and (8) that 10 million common shares are outstanding and selling at $25 per share.

Further, Century uses the following relationships in its financial forecasting (in millions of dollars):

Variable	Relationship to Sales
Cost of goods sold	0.80(Sales)
Selling and administrative expenses	$27.0 + 0.05(Sales)
Cash	0.02(Sales)
Receivables	$6.7 + 0.15(Sales)
Inventories	$22.8 + 0.16(Sales)
Net fixed assets	$37.2 + 0.23(Sales)
Accounts payable	0.08(Sales)
Accrued wages and taxes	0.05(Sales)

a. Construct Century's 1987 pro forma income statement and balance sheet. *(Do Parts b, c, d, e, and f only if you are using the computerized diskette.)*
b. How much will the firm require in external funds each year from 1987 through 1991? How will the firm raise the needed external funds in order to maintain the current ratio and debt ratio requirements given in the problem?
c. What effect will the use of external funds have upon the firm's ROE? Why? (Hint: Think about the three main components of return on equity—that is, asset efficiency, expense control, and debt utilization.)

d. Suppose that management's growth forecasts include the possibility of higher sustained growth in the early years than originally given in the problem. They foresee the possibility of a 35 percent growth rate in Years 2 and 3 followed by a 20 percent growth rate in Years 4 and 5. How does this affect the firm's external funds requirements for 1987-1991?

e. Return to the original scenario. Suppose now that the firm is no longer constrained by a 2.5 current ratio requirement, but rather by a 1.5 current ratio. How does this affect the composition of the firm's external funds financing? What effect does this have upon ROA? ROE? Why?

f. The firm's financial management is considering increasing dividends at the rate of 25 percent per year. What effect does this have upon the firm's key financial ratios? (Assume a 1.5 current ratio requirement.)

Selected Additional References and Cases

The heart of successful financial planning is the sales forecast. On this key subject, see

Pan, Judy, Donald R. Nichols, and O. Maurice Joy, "Sales Forecasting Practices of Large U.S. Industrial Firms," *Financial Management,* Fall 1977, 72-77.

Pappas, James L., Eugene F. Brigham, and Mark Hirschey, *Managerial Economics* (Hinsdale, Ill.: Dryden, 1983).

Computer modeling is becoming increasingly important. For general references, see

Carleton, Willard T., Charles L. Dick, Jr., and David H. Downes, "Financial Policy Models: Theory and Practice," *Journal of Finance*, December 1973, 691-709.

Francis, Jack Clark, and Dexter R. Rowell, "A Simultaneous Equation Model of the Firm for Financial Analysis and Planning," *Financial Management*, Spring 1978, 29-44.

Grinyer, P. H., and J. Wooller, *Corporate Models Today—A New Tool for Financial Management* (London: Institute of Chartered Accountants, 1978).

Pappas, James L., and George P. Huber, "Probabilistic Short-Term Financial Planning," *Financial Management*, Autumn 1973, 36-44.

Traenkle, J. W., E. B. Cox, and J. A. Bullard, *The Use of Financial Models in Business* (New York: Financial Executives' Research Foundation, 1975).

Considerable effort has been expended to develop integrated financial planning models that identify optimal policies. For one example, see

Myers, Stewart C., and Gerald A. Pogue, "A Programming Approach to Corporate Financial Management," *Journal of Finance*, May 1974, 579-599.

The Crum-Brigham casebook contains the following applicable cases:

Case 3, "Ceramic Structures Engineering, Inc.," which focuses on the importance and mechanics of financial planning.

Case 4, "Moseley Vault and Alarm Company," which illustrates some of the basic problems involved in maintaining financial control.

The following classic case is available from Harvard Business School (HBS) Case Services:

"The O. M. Scott & Sons Company," which illustrates financial forecasting and analysis as well as working capital management.

VII

SPECIAL TOPICS

22

MERGERS, DIVESTITURES, AND HOLDING COMPANIES

Most corporate growth occurs through *internal expansion*, which takes place when the firm's existing divisions grow through normal capital budgeting activities. However, the most dramatic examples of growth, and often the largest increases in firms' stock prices, are the result of mergers, the first topic covered in this chapter.[1] On the other hand, the conditions of corporate life do change over time, and, as a result, firms occasionally find it desirable to *divest*, or sell off, major divisions to other firms that can better utilize the divested assets. Divestitures are also discussed in the chapter. Finally, we discuss the *holding company* form of organization, wherein one corporation owns the stock of one or more other companies.

RATIONALE FOR MERGERS

Many reasons have been proposed by both financial managers and theorists to account for the high level of merger activity in the United States. In this section, we present some of the motives behind corporate mergers.

Synergy

The primary motivation for most mergers is to increase the value of the combined enterprise. If Companies A and B merge to form Company C, and if C's value exceeds that of A and B taken separately, then *synergy* is said to exist. Such a merger should be beneficial to both A's and B's stockholders.[2] Synergistic effects

---

[1]As we use the term, *merger* means any combination that forms one economic unit from two or more previous ones. For legal purposes, there are distinctions among the various ways these combinations can occur, but our emphasis is on the fundamental business and financial aspects of mergers.

[2]If synergy exists, then the whole is greater than the sum of the parts. Synergy is also called the "2 plus 2 equals 5 effect." The distribution of the synergistic gain between A's and B's stockholders is determined by negotiation. This point is discussed later in the chapter.

can arise from four sources: (1) *operating economies*, which result from economies of scale in management, production, or distribution; (2) *financial economies*, including a lower cost of debt and/or a greater debt capacity; (3) *differential efficiency*, which implies that the management of one firm is inefficient, and that the firm's assets will be more productive after the merger; and (4) *increased market power* due to reduced competition. Operating and financial economies are socially desirable, as are mergers that increase managerial efficiency, but mergers that reduce competition are both undesirable and illegal.[3]

Tax Considerations

Tax considerations have stimulated a number of mergers. For example, a firm which is highly profitable and is therefore in the highest corporate tax bracket could acquire a firm with large accumulated tax losses. These losses could then be turned into immediate tax savings rather than carrying them forward and hoping to use them in the future.[4] Also, mergers can provide an outlet for excess cash. If a firm has a shortage of internal investment opportunities compared to its cash flow, it could (1) pay an extra dividend, (2) invest in marketable securities, (3) repurchase its own stock, or (4) purchase another firm. If the firm pays an extra dividend, the stockholders would have to pay immediate taxes on the distribution. Marketable securities often provide a good temporary parking place for money, but generally the rate of return on such securities is less than that required by stockholders. A stock repurchase would result in a capital gain for the remaining stockholders, but (1) a repurchase might push up the firm's stock price to a level which is temporarily above the equilibrium price, so the company would have to pay too much for the repurchased shares, which would be disadvantageous to remaining stockholders, and (2) a repurchase designed solely to avoid dividend payment might be challenged by the IRS. However, using surplus cash to acquire another firm has no immediate tax consequences to the acquiring firm or its stockholders, and this fact has motivated a number of mergers.

Purchase of Assets below Their Replacement Cost

Sometimes a firm will be touted as a possible acquisition candidate because the cost of replacing its assets is considerably higher than its market value. For example, in the early 1980s oil companies could acquire reserves cheaper by buying

---

[3]In the 1880s and 1890s, many mergers occurred in the United States, and some of them were rather obviously directed toward gaining market power rather than increasing operating efficiency. As a result, Congress passed a series of acts designed to insure that mergers are not used as a method of reducing competition. The principal acts include the Sherman Act (1890), the Clayton Act (1914), and the Celler Act (1950). These acts make it illegal for firms to combine in any manner if the combination tends to lessen competition. The acts are administered by the antitrust division of the Justice Department and by the Federal Trade Commission.

[4]Mergers undertaken only to use accumulated tax losses would probably be challenged by the IRS. However, because many factors are present in any given merger, it is hard to prove that a merger was motivated only, or even primarily, by tax considerations.

out other oil companies than by exploratory drilling. Thus, in 1984 Chevron Corporation acquired Gulf Oil in order to augment its reserves. Similarly, steel companies have stated that it is cheaper to buy an existing steel company than to construct a new mill, and in 1984, LTV (the fourth largest steel company) acquired Republic Steel (the sixth largest) for $700 million in a merger that created the second largest firm in the industry.

At the time the LTV-Republic merger was announced, Republic was selling for less than one-third of its book value. However, the market value of a firm should be based on its earnings power, which sets the economic value of its assets. If a firm is fairly valued (that is, if markets are efficient), then its market value, rather than book value, will reflect the economic value of its assets. The real question, then, was this: Could LTV operate the merged company more efficiently than the two companies had been operating before the merger? LTV argued that sufficient economies of scale existed to make the merger synergistic. The least efficient plants of both companies would be closed; plants that make similar products (say sheet steel for autos or oil drilling pipe) would be consolidated, and distribution systems would be integrated. If these moves resulted in sizable cost savings, then the merger could be successful. Otherwise, the fact that LTV bought Republic's assets at below their replacement value would be immaterial. To date, the merger appears to have done little for LTV—it has reported losses consistently over the last several years and, in July 1986 it filed for protection from its creditors under Chapter 11 of the Bankruptcy Act.

Diversification

Managers often claim that diversification is a reason for mergers. They contend that diversification helps to stabilize the firm's earnings stream and thus benefits its owners. Stabilization of earnings is certainly beneficial to employees, suppliers, and customers, but its value is questionable from the standpoint of stockholders. If a stockholder is worried about the variability of a firm's earnings, he or she could probably diversify more easily than could the firm. Why should Firms A and B merge to stabilize earnings when a stockholder in Firm A could sell half of his or her stock in A and use the proceeds to purchase stock in Firm B? Stockholders can generally create diversification more easily than can the firm.

Of course, if you were the owner-manager of a closely held firm, it might be well nigh impossible for you to sell part of your stock to diversify, because this would dilute your ownership and perhaps also generate a large capital gains tax liability. In this case, a diversification merger might well be the best way to achieve personal diversification.

We can use option pricing theory to gain some insights into the ways stockholders and debtholders are affected by mergers. In Appendix 15A, we discussed the Galai and Masulis application of option pricing theory to corporate decisions.[5] If we view stock ownership as a call option, then the value of the stock is increased

---

[5]See Dan Galai and Ronald W. Masulis, "The Option Pricing Model and the Risk Factor of Stock," *Journal of Financial Economics*, January/March 1976, 53-82.

by an increase in earnings variability, but lowered by a decrease in variability. Assume that two firms have the same variability of earnings. If these two firms merge, and their earnings are not perfectly positively correlated, then the earnings of the combined firm will have less variability than the pre-merger earnings. This decrease in earnings variability would, according to option theory, lower the value of the combined firm's equity. Conversely, the value of the debt would increase, because the probability of default would lessen. According to Galai and Masulis, using mergers for diversification results in a transfer of wealth from stockholders to debtholders, leaving the total value of the combined firm at the sum of the pre-merger values, assuming no synergistic effects.

However, it is possible for the stockholders to avoid these theoretical losses by financing the merger with debt, or to recoup them by issuing additional debt based on the increased debt capacity of the combined firm, and then using the proceeds to repurchase equity. Also, note that the Galai-Masulis results depend on the CAPM assumption that only market risk is relevant to stockholders, and that corporate stability has no beneficial effects on operating income. To the extent that these assumptions are not correct, then corporate diversification could benefit stockholders.

Managers' Personal Incentives

Financial economists like to think that business decisions are based only on economic considerations. However, there can be no question but that some business decisions are based more on managers' personal motivations than on economic analysis. Many people, business leaders included, like power, and more power is attached to running a larger corporation than a smaller one. Obviously, no executive would ever admit that his or her ego was the primary reason behind a series of mergers, but knowledgeable observers are convinced that egos do play a role in some mergers.

It has also been observed that executive salaries are highly correlated with company size—the bigger the company, the higher the salaries of its top officers. This too could play a role in the aggressive acquisition programs of some corporations.

Managers' personal incentives as a basis for mergers constitute another example of a potential agency problem. Of course, there is nothing wrong with executives feeling good about increasing the size of their firms, or of their getting paid a higher salary as a result of growth through mergers—provided the mergers make economic sense from the stockholders' viewpoint. There have been quite a few stockholder suits against managers who resisted hostile takeovers. Perhaps there should be a few such suits against managers who paid too high a price for target companies.

TYPES OF MERGERS

Economists classify mergers into four groups: (1) horizontal, (2) vertical, (3) congeneric, and (4) conglomerate. A *horizontal merger* occurs when one firm combines with another in its same line of business. Bank of Montreal's acquisition of

Harris Bankcorp in 1984 is an example. An example of a *vertical merger* is a steel producer's acquisition of one of its own suppliers, such as an iron or coal mining firm (an "upstream merger"), or an oil producer's acquisition of a company which uses its products, such as a petrochemical company (a "downstream merger"). *Congeneric* means "allied in nature or action"; hence, a *congeneric merger* involves related enterprises, but not producers of the same product (horizontal) or firms in a producer-supplier relationship (vertical). Examples of congeneric mergers would be American Express's takeover of Shearson Hammill and R. J. Reynolds' acquisition of Nabisco in 1985. A *conglomerate merger* occurs when unrelated enterprises combine; Mobil Oil's acquisition of Montgomery Ward is an example.

Operating economies (and also anticompetitive effects) are at least partially dependent on the type of merger involved. Vertical and horizontal mergers generally provide the greatest operating benefits, but they are also the ones most likely to be attacked by the U.S. Department of Justice. In any event, it is useful to think of these economic classifications when analyzing the feasibility of a prospective merger.

LEVEL OF MERGER ACTIVITY

There have been four major periods of merger activity in the United States. The first was in the late 1800s, when consolidations occurred in oil, steel, tobacco, and other basic industries. The second was in the 1920s, when the stock market boom helped financial promoters consolidate firms in a number of industries, including utilities and communication companies. The third was in the 1960s, when conglomerate mergers were the rage. And the fourth began in the early 1980s and is still going strong.

The "merger mania" of the 1980s has been sparked by four factors: (1) the relatively depressed condition of the stock market in the early 1980s (for example, the Dow Jones Industrial Index in early 1982 was below its 1968 level); (2) the unprecedented level of inflation that existed during the 1970s and early 1980s; (3) the Reagan administration's stated view that "bigness is not necessarily badness" and its generally more tolerant attitude toward mergers; and (4) the general belief among major natural resource companies that it is cheaper to "buy reserves on Wall Street" than to explore and find them in the field. As illustrated in Table 22-1, the top five mergers of all time in terms of dollar value occurred in the 1980s. Brief descriptions of some different types of recent mergers will help explain how the deals are worked out:

Getty Oil

Getty Oil, the fourteenth largest U.S. oil company, was acquired by Texaco, the fourth largest, in February 1984 at a cost of $10.1 billion. Prior to the merger activity, Getty's shares were selling at around $65, and the descendants of J. Paul Getty, the founder, were complaining of inefficient management. Then the controlling trustees of the Sarah C. Getty Trust, together with Pennzoil Company,

Table 22-1
The Five Largest Mergers
(Billions of Dollars)

Companies	Year	Value	Percent of Book Value	Type of Transaction
Chevron-Gulf	1984	$13.3	136%	Acquisition for cash
Texaco-Getty	1984	10.1	191	Acquisition for cash and notes
Du Pont-Conoco	1981	7.2	156	Acquisition for cash and common stock
GE-RCA	1986	6.4	200	Acquisition for cash
KKR-Beatrice[a]	1986	6.2	212	Acquisition for cash and preferred stock

[a]The KKR-Beatrice deal was actually a leveraged buyout (LBO) rather than a merger. We will discuss LBOs shortly.

announced plans to take the firm private through an offering to buy the shares which they did not already control at a price of $112.50 per share. Texaco then jumped in with an offer of $125 per share.

The merger doubled Texaco's domestic oil and gas reserves, and, with Getty's retail outlets, gave Texaco a larger share of the gasoline market. Some analysts claim that Texaco, with its sprawling network of refineries and rapidly dwindling reserves, made the correct decision by acquiring Getty, with its large reserves and minimal refining operations. Other analysts contend that Texaco paid too much for Getty. Whether Texaco will get its money's worth remains to be seen. For Texaco, acquiring Getty's reserves may be cheaper than finding new oil, but the value of these reserves depends on the price of oil, which in 1986 fell by about 50 percent.

A side issue that arose at the end of the merger concerned the Bass Brothers of Texas, an immensely wealthy family which had acquired over $1 billion of Texaco stock during all the action. Texaco's management was afraid the Basses planned to try to take over Texaco, so they bought out the Bass interests at a premium of about 20 percent over the market value. Some of Texaco's stockholders argued that the payment amounted to *greenmail* and that it was made with stockholders' money just to ensure that Texaco's managers could keep their jobs. This situation, along with several others that were similar, has led to the introduction of bills in Congress to limit the actions that a management group can take in its efforts to avoid being taken over.

A second side issue to the Texaco-Getty merger is still ongoing. Shortly after Getty accepted Texaco's offer, Pennzoil filed a suit charging that Texaco had improperly seized ownership of Getty from Pennzoil. Although Pennzoil acknowledged that it never signed a formal agreement with Getty, the Getty board agreed to the deal, a joint news release was issued, handshakes were exchanged, and a champagne toast was made. Pennzoil claimed that these acts constituted a valid contract, and, in November 1985, a Texas state court agreed. Pennzoil was awarded the largest civil judgment in history, a whopping $10.5 billion, but, of course, Texaco has appealed the decision. The case is still in the courts, and it will probably take years before a final decision is reached. However, the suit has made deal makers much more cautious in their public announcements. Said one takeover expert, "It (the decision) will reinforce the notion that you don't announce any kind of agreement until all the papers are signed."

Bendix

Bendix, after one of the most dramatic merger fights of all time, was acquired in 1982 by Allied Corporation. A four-way takeover battle began when Bendix, directed by William Agee and Mary Cunningham, made an unfriendly takeover offer for Martin Marietta. However, Martin Marietta responded with a "Pac Man" bid to buy Bendix. Additionally, Martin Marietta enlisted the aid of United Technologies, which also made a separate bid for Bendix. While this three-way struggle was going on, it looked as though Bendix would own 70 percent of Martin Marietta, but Martin Marietta would own over 50 percent of Bendix. Then, who controlled whom would depend on who could vote the other's shares first in the annual election of directors. Naturally, this led to lawsuits regarding the two companies' voting of each other's shares.

This co-ownership situation would probably have meant a stalemate which would drag on in the courts for years, with both companies essentially paralyzed in the meantime. At this point, Allied Corporation entered the fray with a bid for Bendix. The final agreement found Allied acquiring Bendix for over $1.8 billion, and Bendix and Martin Marietta swapping the shares each held of the other on the basis of the shares' market values. This left Allied with 8.8 million shares of Martin Marietta, which it got when it completed the purchase of Bendix. Martin Marietta retained its independence, but at a heavy price: The company had taken on $892 million of new debt to buy its Bendix stock, and then it had to issue $346 million of new stock to the public to buy back Allied's shares. Wall Street analysts predicted that it would take Martin Marietta seven years to straighten out its balance sheet.

This monumental struggle between corporate giants has been characterized as more of a battle of personal egos than a battle to increase shareholder wealth. Even so, it demonstrated once more that the threat of a takeover is one of the best incentives to a manager to run his or her firm at its best.

Beatrice Companies

In 1986, Kohlberg Kravis Roberts & Company (KKR), a New York investment partnership, engineered a *leveraged buyout (LBO)* which took Beatrice Companies private. In a leveraged buyout, a small group of equity investors acquires a firm in a transaction financed largely by borrowing. Ultimately, the debt is paid with funds generated by the acquired company's operations or by sale of its assets.

Beatrice, a consumer products conglomerate with such brands as Tropicana, Playtex, and Hunt Foods, already carried $1.8 billion in debt, which amounted to 64 percent of total capitalization. The $6.2 billion takeover, the largest LBO on record, added another $4 billion in debt. Drexel Burnham Lambert, the major supplier of takeover capital, raised $2.5 billion through junk bonds for KKR, and some banks, including Bankers Trust, Citibank, and Manufacturers Hanover, put up most of the rest. The lenders were convinced that Beatrice could make the estimated $480 million annual interest payments, and they were especially impressed with the stability of the cash flows generated by Beatrice's food subsidiaries—the same kind of stable earnings that enabled Philip Morris and R. J. Reynolds to borrow billions to buy General Foods and Nabisco Brands. KKR's financing required no principal repayments for two years, and by that time, $1 to $1.5 billion of the debt should be retired through a mixture of operating cash flow and asset sales. (Indeed, less than six months after the LBO, Beatrice had already arranged over $1.5 billion of asset sales.)

Assuming it is not overwhelmed by the debt, Beatrice will enjoy several advantages as a private company. It will be free of (almost mandatory) dividend payments, which amounted to $170 million in 1985. Further, without stockholders to please, acquisitions and divestitures should be easier. But the most important change, according to KKR, will be a new management team which owns about 15 percent of the new company. That, says KKR, makes all the difference: "They have the same interest we have. They'll run the company for the long-term." Generally, in LBOs the firm is restructured and operations are whipped into shape, and then, after a few years, the company again goes public and the owner-managers and investors get their returns. KKR has specialized in LBOs, and they have been very successful—over the period 1980 to 1986, their investors received a 47 percent compounded annual rate of return.

RCA

On December 11, 1985, the boards of directors of General Electric and RCA announced that RCA agreed to be acquired by GE in a friendly, all-cash transaction for $66.50 a share. The total price was $6.4 billion, the largest ever non-oil merger. The two companies, which together had 1985 revenues exceeding $40 billion, had common interests in commercial and consumer electronics, defense, broadcasting, and satellite communications. However, to effect the transaction, the merger required approval by RCA's shareholders and federal regulators, including the Federal Communications Commission and the Justice Department.

The RCA shareholders voted overwhelmingly in favor of the merger in February 1986. Of course, they would receive $66.50 per share for stock that had been trading at $47.50 several days before the merger announcement. Later in 1986, the merger was approved by the FCC and Justice Department, but GE had to agree to sell (1) five radio stations, since a company cannot own radio and television stations which serve the same market, and (2) a small part of its defense businesses.

Finally, in June 1986, GE completed the acquisition. Although the merger process itself went smoothly, it prompted criticism in two areas. First, some critics claimed that the acquisition was largely funded by U.S. taxpayers. Because it owns what has been described as the world's largest tax shelter, General Electric Credit Corporation, the parent GE paid no federal income taxes from 1981 through 1983, despite total earnings of $5.5 billion during that period. Further, its tax bill was only $185 million in 1984 on earnings of $3.4 billion. GE may well be generating more future tax shelters than it can use, making the purchase of a highly taxed TV network, like RCA's NBC, viable. The taxes for the combined company will likely be less than the total for the two separately.

A second controversy involves possible illegal insider trading, and circumstantial evidence that such trading did occur appears convincing. The merger was announced on a Wednesday evening, after the close of trading, but the price of RCA stock had started moving up the preceding Monday, and by Wednesday the trading activity had turned into an avalanche. During those three days, the stock jumped almost $16 a share, or by 33 percent. The price soared 20 percent on Wednesday alone, closing at $63.50 a share, just $3 shy of GE's bid. The action on RCA's call options was even more dramatic. The price of the December 50s (the right to buy 100 shares at $50 a share until December 20) leaped from $100 on Monday to $1,100 on Wednesday. Both RCA and GE insisted that leaks could not have come from their merger teams or employees, but the sources of leaks are almost unlimited. Each side in a merger deal hires lawyers and advisers, and these players have secretaries, paralegals, and other support troops. *Arbitrageurs* and other speculators cultivate sources who might be in the know, and even without direct tips are often able to pick up telltale signs.[6] One analyst recently stated, "The thing about Wall Street is they all talk—everybody has a friend."

Union Carbide

The friendly GE-RCA merger was put together successfully in six days, but hostile merger attempts are often never consummated. A good example is the ill-fated attempt by GAF to acquire Union Carbide. The story begins in the summer of 1985 when Carbide's stock was depressed because of lawsuits stemming from the tragedy in Bhopal, India, where, in 1984, poisonous gas escaping from a Carbide plant killed an estimated 2,000 people. In early September 1985, GAF announced that it had purchased nearly 10 percent of Carbide's stock. Carbide's management felt hamstrung by the GAF ownership. It knew that GAF's chairman, Samuel J. Heyman, had won control of GAF in 1983 through a proxy fight. Any strong anti-takeover measures that depressed Carbide's stock could help Mr. Heyman if he chose to wage a proxy fight. But, if Carbide did nothing, it might invite a tender offer.

---

[6]Arbitrageurs, or "arbs," are individuals and firms that speculate in the stocks of companies that are likely takeover candidates. Most of the large investment banking houses have arb groups, and they are allocated vast sums of money to use in their operations. To be successful, arbs need to be able to sniff out likely targets, assess the probability of offers reaching fruition, and move in and out of the market quickly and with low transactions costs.

At this point, Carbide turned to its investment banker, Morgan Stanley, and it also hired a prominent law firm with substantial takeover experience. The advisers pressed one point home: Because of the Bhopal disaster, Carbide had lost practically all of its insurance protection for its directors. If found guilty of any breach of shareholder obligations, directors might be personally liable for large damages. On December 7, 1985, GAF announced a $68-per-share, all-cash tender offer. On Friday, December 13, the Carbide board met to consider the offer. At that meeting, Morgan Stanley representatives stated that Carbide was at least worth $85 a share as an operating company and, if the company were liquidated, its assets could be worth as much as $100 a share. With these estimates in mind, the board voted unanimously to reject the GAF bid, and issued a statement denouncing the offer as "grossly inadequate."

Then, the board considered its strategic alternatives: (1) taking the company private, (2) mounting a "Pac Man" defense (in which Carbide would gobble up its would-be acquirer), or (3) making an exchange offer, in which shareholders would receive $85 a share in cash and debt securities for 35 percent of their holdings, to induce stockholders to reject GAF's tender offer. The directors quickly dismissed the first two alternatives: (1) Although Kohlberg Kravis Roberts & Company indicated a willingness to top GAF's bid in a leveraged buyout, the board, which was dominated by outside directors, was not enthusiastic about entrenching current management. (2) GAF's stock had risen so sharply since the offer that the board considered GAF overvalued. Thus, on December 15, Carbide made a $2 billion exchange offer of $85 a share for 35 percent of its stock. The exchange offer consisted of $20 in cash and $65 worth of debentures and notes.

Then, the day after Christmas, GAF upped its offer to $74 a share cash. Further, GAF said it would up it to $78 a share if Carbide's directors accepted the offer. The board quickly rejected the new offers, but it still faced a difficult situation: Carbide was bidding for only 35 percent of its stock while GAF, by seeking all Carbide shares, was offering to put much more money, and all cash, into shareholders' pockets. The board's problem was how to make its offer more attractive. Carbide was already heavily indebted, and it would have to use even more debt in its initial exchange offer. The answer lay in the sale of Carbide's consumer products division, which manufactured and marketed such name-brand products as Glad trash bags, Eveready batteries, and Prestone automotive products. This was a tough decision because Carbide's consumer products division had the most growth potential of all its operations.

Nevertheless, after almost eight hours of discussion, the Carbide board reluctantly concluded that it had no alternative. It agreed to sell the consumer products division, to offer to buy back 55 percent of the shares instead of 35 percent, and to raise the dividend on the remaining stock. This was too much for GAF to counter and, on January 8, 1986, it withdrew its tender offer.

Carbide's successful defense is considered a landmark in takeover battles: It was the first time a company had defeated an all-cash bid for its shares. It was also believed to be the first battle in which independent, outside directors took control of the defense and acted to enhance shareholder value. To survive, Carbide doubled its debt and cut the common equity to one-quarter of its book value prior to the fight. However, Carbide's shareholders saw the stock rise from $48 to a high of $76. In defeat, GAF walked away with 3.1 million Carbide shares and a potential pre-tax profit of $135 million. Also, the investment bankers and lawyers profited from the fight: GAF's investment bankers and lawyers garnered about $60 million in fees, while Carbide's bankers took in at least $14 million. It appears that Carbide's forced restructuring actually created value, and this value was shared by all the parties involved.

PROCEDURES FOR COMBINING FIRMS

In the vast majority of merger situations, one firm (generally the larger of the two) simply decides to buy another company, negotiates a price, and then acquires the target company. Occasionally, the acquired firm will initiate the action, but it is much more common for a firm to seek acquisitions than to seek to be acquired.[7] Following convention, we shall call a company that seeks to acquire another the *acquiring company* and the one which it seeks to acquire the *target company*.

Once an acquiring company has identified a possible target, it must establish a suitable price, or range of prices, that it is willing to pay. With this in mind, the acquiring firm's managers must decide how to approach the target company's managers. If the acquiring firm has reason to believe that the target company's management will approve the merger, then it will simply propose a merger and try to work out some suitable terms. If an agreement can be reached, then the two management groups will issue statements to their stockholders recommending that they approve the merger. Assuming that the stockholders do approve, the acquiring firm will simply buy the target company's shares from its stockholders, paying for them either with its own shares (in which case the target company's stockholders become stockholders of the acquiring company) or with cash. This is exactly what happened in the GE-RCA merger.

Under other circumstances, the target company's management may resist the merger. Perhaps it feels that the price offered for the stock is too low, or perhaps the target firm's managers simply want to maintain their jobs. In either case, the target firm's management is said to be *hostile* rather than *friendly*, and the acquiring firm must make a direct appeal to the target firm's stockholders. In hostile mergers, the acquiring company generally makes a *tender offer*, in which it asks the stockholders of the firm it is seeking to control to submit, or "tender," their shares in exchange for a specified price. The price is generally stated as so many dollars per share of the stock to be acquired, although it can be stated in terms of shares of stock in the acquiring firm. The tender offer is a direct appeal to stock-

---

[7]However, if a firm is in financial difficulty, if its managers are elderly and do not feel that suitable replacements are on hand, or if it needs the support (often the capital) of a larger company, then it may seek to be acquired. Thus, when a number of Texas banks were in trouble in 1986, they lobbied to persuade the Texas legislature to pass a law that would make it easier for troubled Texas banks to be acquired by out-of-state banks. Similar actions have been taken recently in Ohio, Illinois, and Maryland.

holders, so it need not be approved by the management of the target firm. This is how GAF approached the aborted attempt at a hostile takeover of Union Carbide. Tender offers are not new, but the frequency of their use has increased greatly in recent years.

MERGER ANALYSIS

In theory, merger analysis is quite simple. The acquiring firm simply performs a capital budgeting analysis to determine whether the present value of the expected future income from the merger exceeds the price it must pay for the target company. The target company's stockholders, on the other hand, should accept the proposal if the price offered exceeds the present value of its expected future cash flows, assuming that it continues to operate independently. However, some difficult issues are involved: (1) The acquiring company must estimate the cash flow benefits that will be obtained from the acquisition. (2) The acquiring firm must determine what effect, if any, the merger will have on its required rate of return on equity. (3) The acquiring company will have to decide how to pay for the merger if it is not done on an exchange-of-stock basis. (4) Having estimated the benefits of the merger, the acquiring and target firms' managers and stockholders must bargain over how to share these benefits.

Operating Mergers Versus Financial Mergers

From the standpoint of financial analysis, there are two basic types of mergers:

1. One is an *operating merger*, in which the operations of two companies are integrated with the expectation of obtaining synergistic effects. The Chevron-Gulf combination is a good example of an operating merger.

2. The other extreme is a *pure financial merger*, in which the merged companies will not be operated as a single unit and from which few operating economies are expected. The 1982 acquisition of Columbia Pictures by Coca-Cola is an example of a pure financial merger.

Of course, mergers may actually combine these two features. The GE-RCA merger resulted in some operations being integrated, while others remained independent.

Estimating Postmerger Cash Flows

In a pure financial merger, the postmerger cash flows are simply the sum of the expected cash flows of the two companies if they were to continue to operate independently. However, if the two firms' operations are to be integrated, or if the acquiring firm plans to change the target firm's management and expects to get better results, then accurate projected cash flow estimates, which are absolutely essential to sound merger decisions but difficult to construct, must be developed.

Del Monte Corporation provides a good example of a series of well thought out, favorable operating mergers. Del Monte successfully merged and integrated numerous small canning companies into a very efficient, highly profitable organization. It used standardized production techniques to increase the efficiency of all its plants, a national brand name and national advertising to develop customer loyalty, a consolidated distribution system, and a centralized purchasing office that obtained substantial discounts from volume purchases. Because of these economies, Del Monte became the most efficient and profitable U.S. canning company, and its merger activities helped make possible the size that produced these economies. Consumers also benefited, because Del Monte's efficiency enabled the company to sell high-quality products at relatively low prices.

An example of poor pro forma analysis that resulted in a disastrous merger was the consolidation of the Pennsylvania and New York Central railroads. The premerger analysis was grossly misleading, failing to reveal the fact that certain key elements in the two rail systems were incompatible, and hence could not be meshed together. Rather than gaining synergistic benefits, the combined system actually incurred additional overhead costs that helped lead to its bankruptcy. *Thus, in planning operating mergers, the development of pro forma statements is the single most important aspect of the merger analysis.*[8]

Merger Terms

The terms of a merger include two important elements: (1) Who will control the combined enterprise? (2) How much will the acquiring firm pay for the acquired company? These points are discussed next.

Postmerger Control
The employment/control situation is often of vital interest. First, consider the situation where a small, owner-managed firm sells out to a larger concern. The owner-manager may be anxious to retain a high-status position, and he or she may also have developed a camaraderie with the employees and thus be concerned about keeping operating control of the organization after the merger. Thus, these points are likely to be stressed during the merger negotiations.[9] When a publicly

---

[8]It should be noted that firms heavily engaged in mergers have "acquisition departments" whose functions include (1) seeking suitable merger candidates and (2) taking over and integrating acquired firms into the parent corporation. The first step involves the development of both pro forma statements and a plan for making the projections materialize. The second step involves (1) streamlining operations of the acquired firm, if necessary, and (2) instituting a system of controls that will permit the parent to manage the new division effectively and to coordinate its operations with those of other units.

[9]The acquiring firm may also be concerned about this point, especially if the acquired firm's management is quite good. A condition of the merger may be that the management team agrees to stay on for a period, such as five years, after the merger. Also, the price paid may be contingent on the acquired firm's performance subsequent to the merger. For example, when International Holdings acquired Walker Products, the price set was 100,000 shares of International Holdings stock at the time the deal was closed plus an additional 30,000 shares each year for the next three years, provided Walker earned at least $500,000 during each of these years. Since Walker's managers owned the stock and would receive the bonus, they had incentive to stay on and to help the firm meet its targets.

If the managers of the target company are highly competent but do not wish to remain on after the merger, the acquiring firm will often build into the merger contract a noncompetitive agreement with the old management. Typically, the acquired firm's principal managers must agree not to affiliate with a new business which is competitive with the business they sold for a period, such as five years. Such agreements are especially important with service-oriented businesses.

owned firm not controlled by its managers is merged into another company, the acquired firm's management also is worried about its postmerger position. If the acquiring firm agrees to keep the old management, then management may be willing to support the merger and to recommend its acceptance to the stockholders. If the old management is to be removed, then it will probably resist the merger.[10]

The Price Paid

The second key element in a merger is the price to be paid for the target company—the cash or shares of stock to be given in exchange for the firm. The analysis is similar to a regular capital budgeting analysis: The incremental cash flows are estimated; a discount rate is applied to find the present value of those flows; and, if the present value of the future incremental cash flows exceeds the price to be paid for the target firm, then the merger is approved. Thus, only if the target firm is worth more to the acquiring firm than its market value as a separate entity will the merger be feasible. Obviously, the acquiring firm tries to buy at as low a price as possible, while the target firm tries to sell out at the highest possible price. The final price is determined by negotiations, with the side that negotiates better capturing most of the incremental value. *The larger the synergistic benefits, the more room there is for bargaining, and the higher the probability that the merger will actually be consummated.*[11]

VALUING THE TARGET FIRM

To determine the value of the target firm, we need two key items: (1) a set of pro forma incremental financial statements, and (2) a discount rate, or cost of capital, to apply to the projected cash flows.

The Pro Forma Cash Flow Statements

Table 22-2 contains the projected cash flow statements for Southwest Express, an acquisition candidate being considered by Transcon Trucking, a large national transportation company. The projected data are postmerger, so all synergistic effects are included. Southwest currently uses 30 percent debt, but, if acquired, Transcon would increase Southwest's debt ratio to 50 percent. Both Transcon and Southwest have 40 percent federal-plus-state marginal tax rates.

---

[10]The managers of firms that are thought to be attractive merger candidates occasionally arrange *golden parachutes* for themselves. These are extremely lucrative retirement plans which take effect if a merger is consummated. Thus, when Bendix was acquired by Allied, Bill Agee, Bendix's chairman, pulled the ripcord of his golden parachute and walked away with $4 million. Congress is currently considering controls on golden parachutes as a part of its greenmail legislative proposals. In fact, recent tax law changes have made golden parachutes more expensive for firms to grant by disallowing tax deductibility on amounts above a certain limit.

[11]It has been estimated that of all merger negotiations seriously begun, only about one-third actually results in merger. Also, note that in contested merger situations the company that offers the most will usually make the acquisition, and the company that will gain the greatest synergistic benefits should bid the most.

Table 22-2
Southwest Express:
Projected Postmerger Cash Flow Statements
(Millions of Dollars)

	1987	1988	1989	1990	1991
Net sales	$105	$126	$151	$174	$191
Cost of goods sold	80	94	111	127	137
Selling/administrative costs	10	12	13	15	16
EBIT	$ 15	$ 20	$ 27	$ 32	$ 38
Interest[a]	3	4	5	6	6
EBT	$ 12	$ 16	$ 22	$ 26	$ 32
Taxes[b]	5	6	9	10	13
Net income	$ 7	$ 10	$ 13	$ 16	$ 19
Retentions for growth[c]	2	2	4	6	8
Cash available to Transcon	$ 5	$ 8	$ 9	$ 10	$ 11
Terminal value[d]					121
Net cash flow[e]	$ 5	$ 8	$ 9	$ 10	$132

[a]Interest payment estimates are based on currently outstanding debt plus additional debt to increase the debt ratio up to 50 percent, plus additional debt after the merger to finance asset expansion. Note also that all amounts are rounded to the nearest million.

[b]Transcon will file a consolidated tax return after the merger. Thus, the taxes shown here are the full corporate taxes attributable to Southwest's operations; there will be no additional taxes on the cash flowing from Southwest to Transcon because a consolidated tax return will be filed.

[c]Some of the net income generated by Southwest after the merger will be retained to finance asset growth, while some will be transferred to Transcon and will be available to pay dividends on its stock or for redeployment in the corporation. It is assumed that depreciation-generated funds are used to replace worn-out and obsolete plant and equipment.

[d]Southwest's earnings are expected to grow at a constant 8.3 percent after 1991. The value of all post-1991 dividends to Transcon, as of December 31, 1991, is estimated by use of the constant growth model to be $121 million: $V_{1991} = \$11(1.083)/(0.1815 - 0.083) = \$121$ million. In the next section, we discuss the estimation of the 18.15 percent cost of equity.

[e]These are the estimated net cash flows that will be available to Transcon if it acquires Southwest Express. They may be used for dividend payments to Transcon's stockholders or to finance asset expansion in Transcon's other divisions.

In the analysis, we focus on the net cash flows that would be available to Transcon's stockholders.[12] Of course, the postmerger flows attributable to the target firm are extremely difficult to estimate. In a complete merger valuation, just as in a complete capital budgeting analysis, distributions for the cash flow components should be specified, and sensitivity, scenario, and simulation analyses should be conducted. Indeed, in friendly mergers, the acquiring firm will often send a team consisting of literally dozens of accountants, engineers, and so forth, to the target

---

[12]We purposely keep the cash flows relatively simple to help focus on the key valuation issues. In an actual merger analysis, the cash flow statements would be much more complex, normally including such items as additional capital furnished by the acquiring firm and tax loss carry-forwards. Also, note that we are using the equity residual method for valuing Southwest's postmerger flows; this approach was introduced in Chapter 8.

firm's headquarters to go over its books, estimate required maintenance expenditures, set values on assets such as petroleum reserves, and the like.

Estimating the Discount Rate

The bottom line net cash flows shown in Table 22-2 are equity flows, so they should be discounted at the cost of equity rather than at the overall cost of capital. Further, the cost of equity used should reflect the riskiness of the net cash flows in Table 22-2; thus, the appropriate discount rate should be based on Southwest's own cost of equity, not that of either Transcon or the consolidated postmerger firm. Southwest's market-determined premerger beta was 1.28. However, this beta reflects the firm's premerger 30 percent debt ratio, whereas Southwest's postmerger debt ratio will increase to 50 percent. The Hamada equations, which were developed in Chapter 9, can be used to approximate the effects of the leverage change on beta. First, we obtain the unlevered beta of Southwest's assets:

$$b_U = \frac{b_L}{1 + (1 - T)(D/E)} = \frac{1.28}{1 + (1 - 0.40)(0.30/0.70)} = \frac{1.28}{1.26} = 1.02.$$

Next, we recalculate Southwest's beta to reflect the new 50 percent debt ratio:

$$b_L = b_U[1 + (1 - T)(D/E)]$$
$$= 1.02[1 + (1 - 0.40)(0.50/0.50)] = 1.02(1.6) = 1.63.$$

Finally, we use the Security Market Line to estimate Southwest's postmerger cost of equity. If the risk-free rate is 10 percent and the market risk premium is 5 percent, then Southwest's cost of equity, k_s, after the merger with Transcon, would be 18.15 percent:[13]

$$k_s = k_{RF} + b(RP_M) = 10\% + 1.63(5\%) = 18.15\%.$$

Valuing the Cash Flows

The value of Southwest to Transcon at the end of 1986 is the present value of the expected cash flows accruing to Transcon, discounted at 18.15 percent (in millions of dollars):

---

[13]In this example, we used the Capital Asset Pricing Model to estimate Southwest's cost of equity. This assumes that investors require a premium for market risk only. We could have also conducted a total risk analysis, in which the relevant total risk would be the contribution of Southwest's cash flows to the total risk of the postmerger firm. That is, the postmerger firm's cash flows could be more risky or less risky than the premerger flows, or have the same risk.

In actual merger situations, companies almost always hire investment banking firms to help develop valuation estimates. For example, when General Electric acquired Utah International in the late 1970s, the largest merger up to that time, GE hired Morgan Stanley to determine Utah's value. We discussed the valuation process with the Morgan Stanley analyst in charge of the appraisal. Morgan Stanley considered using the CAPM, but chose instead to base the discount rate on DCF methodology. However, other analysts, and Morgan Stanley people in other situations, have used a CAPM analysis as we describe it here. Merger analysis, like the analysis of any other complex issue, requires judgment, and people's judgment differs as to which method is most appropriate for any given situation.

$$V_{1986} = \frac{\$5}{(1.1815)^1} + \frac{\$8}{(1.1815)^2} + \frac{\$9}{(1.1815)^3} + \frac{\$10}{(1.1815)^4} + \frac{\$132}{(1.1815)^5} = \$78.$$

Thus, if Transcon could acquire Southwest for $78 million or less, the merger would appear to be acceptable from Transcon's standpoint.

THE ROLE OF THE INVESTMENT BANKER

The investment banking community is directly involved in mergers in a number of ways: (1) helping to arrange and finance mergers, (2) aiding target companies resist mergers, and (3) helping to value target companies. These merger-related activities have been quite profitable. For example, in the 1985 acquisition of General Foods by Philip Morris, First Boston, which backed Philip Morris, received over $10 million in fees, while the fees to Goldman Sachs and Shearson Lehman, which assisted General Foods, amounted to over $14 million. By some estimates, the merger departments at three leading firms, Goldman Sachs, First Boston, and Morgan Stanley, *each* pulled in about $200 million in fees in 1985, not counting commissions for helping raise the funds to finance the deals. Drexel Burnham, whose forte is financing mergers and LBOs, earned $86 million on the Beatrice deal alone. No wonder investment banking houses are able to make top offers to finance graduates![14]

Arranging Mergers

The major investment banking firms have merger and acquisition groups which operate within their corporate finance departments. (Corporate finance departments offer advice, as opposed to underwriting services, to business firms.) Members of these groups strive to identify firms with excess cash that might want to buy other firms, firms that might be willing to be bought, and firms that may for a number of reasons be attractive to others. Also, if a firm, say an oil company, decided to expand into coal mining, then it might enlist the aid of an investment banker to help it locate and then negotiate with a target coal company. Similarly, dissident stockholder groups of firms with poor track records may work with investment bankers to oust management through a merger.

Fighting Off Mergers

Target firms that do not want to be acquired generally enlist the help of an investment banking firm, along with a law firm that specializes in helping to block mergers. Defenses include such tactics as (1) changing the by-laws so that only one-

---

[14]*Business Week*, on July 7, 1986, reported that the president of Drexel Burnham earned a salary of over $3.2 million in 1985, yet "two dozen or so Drexel employees took home paychecks fatter than the boss's." Heading the list is Mike Milken (a finance MBA who runs Drexel's junk bond business), who reportedly earned $40 million.

third of the directors are elected each year and/or so that a 75 percent approval versus a simple majority is required to approve a merger, (2) trying to convince the target firm's stockholders that the price being offered is too low, (3) raising antitrust issues in hopes that the Justice Department will intervene, (4) repurchasing stock in the open market in an effort to push the price above that being offered by the potential acquirer, and (5) getting a "white knight" (a company that is more acceptable to the target firm's management) to compete with the potential acquirer. More extreme measures are also available.

The most common tactic being used today is the issuance of stock purchase rights. For example, in 1986, J. C. Penney distributed to shareholders one purchase right for each common share outstanding. The rights become exercisable on the 10th day following the public announcement of a takeover attempt. If the takeover offer is friendly, Penney can redeem the rights for $0.10 per right. However, the rights would not be redeemed if the takeover were hostile, and each right entitles the holder to purchase $300 worth of stock of the acquiring company for $150. This action would seriously dilute the equity value and ownership position of the acquiring company's shareholders and hence makes the unfriendly acquisition of Penney prohibitively expensive. A number of companies, including Household International, Colgate-Palmolive, McDonald's, and United Technologies, have issued similar rights. Household International's issue was challenged in the courts, but the tactic was upheld by the Delaware Supreme Court. Since more than half of U.S. companies are incorporated in Delaware, it appears that this tactic is here to stay. However, the use of such extreme tactics, known as *poison pills*, is somewhat constrained by directors' awareness that blatant use of them will trigger personal suits by stockholders against directors who vote for them and, perhaps in the near future, by laws that will limit their use.[15]

Establishing a Price

If a friendly merger is being worked out between two firms' managements, it is important to be able to prove that the agreed-upon price is a fair one. Otherwise, the stockholders of either company may sue to block the merger. Therefore, in many larger mergers, each side will engage an investment banking firm to evaluate the target company and to help establish the fair price. For example, General Electric employed Goldman Sachs to determine a fair price for RCA in their merger, while RCA engaged Lazard Freres. Royal Dutch used Morgan Stanley to help establish the price it paid for Shell Oil in 1984. (Royal Dutch owned 70 percent of Shell Oil's stock, and in 1984 it sought to buy the remaining 30 percent and to then merge Shell into Royal Dutch. With a 70 percent ownership, it could have forced a merger anyway, but the controlling ownership position would ensure a stock-

---

[15]It has become extremely difficult and expensive for companies to buy "directors' insurance" which protects the board from losses from such contingencies as stockholders' suits, and even where insurance is available, it often does not pay for losses if the directors did not exercise due caution and judgment. This exposure is making directors extremely leery of actions that might trigger stockholder suits.

holder suit charging an unfairly low price. At any rate, Morgan Stanley worked with Royal Dutch to establish an offer price and then to defend this price in the courts.) Even if the merger is not friendly, investment bankers may still be asked to help establish a price. If a surprise tender offer is to be made, the acquiring firm will want to know the lowest price at which it might be able to acquire the stock, while the target firm may seek help in "proving" that the price being offered is too low.

Financing Mergers and LBOs

Many mergers are financed with the acquiring company's excess cash. At other times, however, the acquiring company has no excess cash, and hence requires a source of funds to pay for the target company. Perhaps the single most important factor behind the 1980s merger wave has been the development of a new financing vehicle, junk bonds, and the system that has been developed to market these bonds.

As noted earlier, Drexel Burnham Lambert was the primary developer of junk bonds, defined as bonds rated below investment grade (BBB/Baa) at the time of issue. Prior to Drexel's entry on the scene, it was almost impossible to sell low-grade bonds to raise new capital. Drexel then pioneered a procedure wherein a target firm's situation would be appraised very closely, and a cash flow projection similar to that in Table 22-2 (but much more detailed) would be developed. Part of the cash flow projection would generally include cash flows from major asset sales.

With the cash flows having been forecasted, Drexel's analysts would figure out a debt mix—amount of debt, maturity structure, and interest rate—that could be serviced by the cash flows. With this information, Drexel's junk bond people, operating out of Beverly Hills with a high degree of independence from the New York headquarters, would approach financial institutions (savings and loans, insurance companies, and mutual funds) and wealthy individuals with a financing plan and an offer of a rate of return several percentage points above the rate on more conservative investments. Drexel's early deals worked out well, and the institutions that bought the bonds were quite pleased. These results enabled Drexel to expand its network of investors, and to commit to finance larger and larger mergers and LBOs. T. Boone Pickens, who went after a number of oil giants, was an early Drexel customer.

At the present time (1986), to be a successful investment banker in the mergers and acquisitions (M&A) business, a banker must be able to offer a financing package to clients, whether they are acquirers like Pickens who need capital to take over companies like Phillips Petroleum, or target companies like Union Carbide or CBS trying to finance stock repurchase plans or other defenses against takeovers. Drexel is the leading player in the merger financing game, but all the other major investment banking houses are jumping into the game with both feet. All of this has created some extremely interesting and lucrative jobs for finance students who are able to develop accurate cash flow data, to structure debt packages that can be serviced from these cash flows, and then to make convincing presentations of the data to potential (and sophisticated) investors.

ACCOUNTING TREATMENT FOR MERGERS

Although a detailed discussion of accounting is best left to accounting courses, at least some mention should be made of the accounting implications of mergers. Mergers are handled in either of two basic ways: (1) as a pooling of interests or (2) as a purchase. The method used can have a significant effect on postmerger reported profits, and this, in turn, can influence the desirability of the merger.

Pooling of Interests Accounting

A *pooling of interests* is, in theory, a merger among equals, and hence the consolidated balance sheet is constructed by simply adding together the balance sheets of the merged companies. The top section of Table 22-3 shows the essential elements of the consolidated balance sheet after Firms A and B have merged under a pooling of interests. This final balance sheet holds regardless of how many shares Firm A (the survivor) gave up to acquire Firm B. (In a pooling, shares, not cash, must be exchanged.)

Table 22-3
Accounting for Mergers

Pooling of Interests

	Firm A	Firm B	Postmerger: Firm A
Current assets	$ 50	$25	$ 75
Fixed assets	50	25	75
Total assets	$100	$50	$150
Debt	$ 40	$20	$ 60
Common equity	60	30	90
Total claims	$100	$50	$150

Purchase Accounting

	Firm A (1)	Firm B (2)	$20 Paid (3)	$30 Paid[a] (4)	$50 Paid (5)
Current assets	$ 50	$25	$ 75[b]	$ 75	$ 80
Fixed assets	50	25	65[b]	75	80
Goodwill[c]	0	0	0	0	10
Total assets	$100	$50	$140	$150	$170
Debt	$ 40	$20	$ 60	$ 60	$ 60
Equity	60	30	80[d]	90	110[e]
Total claims	$100	$50	$140	$150	$170

[a]The price paid is the *net asset value,* that is, total assets minus debt.
[b]Here we assume that Firm B's fixed assets are written down to $15 before constructing the consolidated balance sheet.
[c]*Goodwill* refers to the excess paid for a firm above the appraised value of the physical assets purchased. Goodwill represents payment both for intangibles such as patents and for "organization value" that might arise from having an effective sales force.
[d]Firm B's common equity is reduced by $10 prior to consolidation to reflect the fixed asset write-off.
[e]Firm B's equity is increased prior to consolidation to reflect the above-book purchase price.

Purchase Accounting

The lower section of Table 22-3, which uses the same data as for the pooled companies, illustrates purchase accounting. Here the acquiring firm is assumed to have "bought" the acquired company in much the same way it would buy any capital asset, paying for it with cash, debt, or stock of the acquiring company. If the price paid is exactly equal to the acquired firm's *net asset value*, which is defined as its total assets minus its liabilities, then the consolidated balance sheet will be identical to that under pooling. Otherwise, there is an important difference. If the price paid exceeds the net asset value, then asset values will be increased to reflect the price actually paid, whereas if the price paid is less than the net asset value, then assets must be written down when preparing the consolidated balance sheet.

Note that Firm B's net asset value is $30, which is also its reported common equity value. This $30 book value could be equal to the market value (which is determined by the firm's earning power), but book value could also be more or less than the market value. Three situations are considered in the lower section of Table 22-3. First, in Column 3 we assume that Firm A gives cash or stock worth $20 for Firm B. Thus, B's assets as reported on its balance sheet were overvalued, and A pays less than B's net asset value. The overvaluation could be in either fixed or current assets; an appraisal would be made, but we assume that it is fixed assets which are overvalued. Accordingly, we reduce B's fixed assets and also its common equity by $10 before constructing the consolidated balance sheet shown in Column 3. Next, in Column 4, we assume that A pays exactly the net asset value for B. In this case, pooling and purchase accounting would produce identical balance sheets.

Finally, in Column 5 we assume that A pays more than the net asset value for B: $50 is paid for $30 of net assets. This excess is assumed to be partly attributable to undervalued assets (land, buildings, machinery, and inventories), so to reflect this undervaluation, current and fixed assets are each increased by $5. In addition, we assume that $10 of the $20 excess of market value over book value is due to a superior sales organization, or some other intangible factor, and we post this excess as *goodwill*. B's common equity is increased by $20, the sum of the increases in current and fixed assets plus goodwill, and this markup is also reflected in A's postmerger equity account.[16]

Income Statement Effects

Significant differences can also arise in reported profits under the two accounting methods. If asset values are increased, as they often are under a purchase, this must be reflected in higher depreciation charges (and also in a higher cost of goods sold if inventories are written up). This, in turn, will reduce future reported profits.

---

[16]This example assumes that additional debt was not issued to help finance the acquisition. If the acquisition were totally debt financed, the postmerger balance sheet would show increases in the debt account rather than increases in the equity account. If it were financed by a mix of debt and equity, both accounts would be changed.

Table 22-4
Income Effects of Pooling versus Purchase Accounting

	Premerger		Postmerger: Firm A	
	Firm A (1)	Firm B (2)	Pooling (3)	Purchase (4)
Sales	$100.0	$50.0	$150.0	$150.0
Operating costs	72.0	36.0	108.0	109.0[a]
Operating income	$ 28.0	$14.0	$ 42.0	$ 41.0[a]
Interest (10%)	4.0	2.0	6.0	6.0
Taxable income	$ 24.0	$12.0	$ 36.0	$ 35.0
Taxes (40%)	9.6	4.8	14.4	14.0
Earnings after tax	$ 14.4	$ 7.2	$ 21.6	$ 21.0
Goodwill write-off	0	0	0	1.0[b]
Net income	$ 14.4	$ 7.2	$ 21.6	$ 20.0
EPS[c]	$ 2.40	$2.40	$ 2.40	$ 2.22

[a]Operating costs are $1 higher than they otherwise would be to reflect the higher reported costs (depreciation and cost of goods sold) caused by the physical asset markup at the time of purchase.
[b]($10 of increased goodwill)/10 years = $1 write-off per year.
[c]Firm A had six shares and Firm B had three shares before the merger. A gives one of its shares for each of B's, so A has nine shares outstanding after the merger.

Also, goodwill represents the excess paid for a firm over its adjusted net asset value. This excess is presumably paid because of the acquired firm's superior earning power, which will probably be eroded over time as patents expire, as new firms enter the industry, and so forth. Thus, the accountants (in Accounting Principles Board Opinion #17) require that goodwill be written off, or "amortized," over a period corresponding to the expected life of the superior earning power but in no case more than 40 years. Goodwill is certainly not a trivial issue. For example, when Philip Morris acquired Seven-Up for a price of $520 million, approximately $390 million of the purchase price represented goodwill.

Table 22-4 illustrates the income statement effects of the higher current and fixed assets, and also the write-off of goodwill, under pooling versus purchase. For the purchase, we assume that A purchased B for $50, creating $10 of goodwill and $10 of higher physical asset value. Further, we assume that this $20 will be written off over 10 years.[17] As Column 4 indicates, the writing off of goodwill and asset markups under purchase accounting causes reported profits to be lower than they would be under pooling.

The write-off of goodwill is also reflected in earnings per share. In our hypothetical merger, we assume that nine shares exist in the consolidated firm. (Six of these shares went to A's stockholders, and three to B's.) Under pooling, EPS =

---

[17]The write-off of goodwill is not a deduction for income tax purposes, but the other excess write-offs (fixed assets and inventories) were deductible prior to the Tax Reform Act of 1986.

$2.40, while under purchase, EPS = $2.22. Further, the greater the amount of goodwill, the larger is the write-off and the more significant is the dilution in reported earnings per share. This fact causes managers to prefer pooling to purchase accounting.

Several conditions must be met to use the pooling method, the most important of which is that the acquisition must be paid for with common stock of the acquiring firm.[18] This, coupled with other conditions, greatly restricts the use of pooling in practice, and hence the vast majority of recent mergers have used purchase accounting.

The 1986 Tax Reform Act

Prior to the Tax Reform Act of 1986, the acquired company could pay more than book value for a target firm's assets, write up those assets, depreciate the marked up value for tax purposes, and thus lower the postmerger firm's taxes vis-à-vis the taxes of the two firms operating separately. At the same time, the target firm would not have to pay any taxes on the capital gains at the time of the merger, although its stockholders would be subject to a capital gains liability on their profits if and when they are realized.

Under the new law, if the acquiring company writes up the target company's assets for tax purposes, then the target company must pay capital gains taxes in the year the merger occurs. (These immediate capital gains taxes can be avoided if the acquiring company elects not to write up acquired assets and hence depreciates them on their old basis.) So, under the new law, the entities will have to pay more taxes than under the old law, and this fact will make mergers less profitable.

Note also that the maximum personal capital gains tax rate rose from 20 percent to 28 percent under the new law, a 40 percent increase. This, of course, means that target companies' stockholders will generally net out less after a merger now than they would have under the old law.

When we considered the joint effects of the corporate and the personal tax changes, it is clear that mergers in which the target company sells for more than its book value are much less favorable today than they were prior to 1987. First, either the target company will have to pay capital gains taxes, thus netting less, or else the acquiring company will have a lower depreciable basis, which will reduce its cash flows and thus lower the target's value. Either way, the target firm's stockholders will realize less before their personal taxes. Second, the target firm's stockholders will have a 40 percent higher tax liability on any gains they make, which will further reduce their after-tax net from the merger. The combined effect is a lot less money in the pockets of selling stockholders, so they will be much less anxious to sell out. We predict that this will lead to a dropoff in merger activity after 1986.

---

[18]See Accounting Principles Board Opinions #16 and #17.

JOINT VENTURES

A merger is not the only way in which the resources of two firms can be combined. In contrast to mergers, in which all the resources of two firms are combined under a single management, joint ventures involve the joining together of parts of companies to accomplish specific, limited objectives.[19] Joint ventures are controlled by the combined management of the two (or more) parent companies.

In one widely publicized joint venture, General Motors and Toyota, the first and third largest automakers in the world, combined resources in 1984 to produce the new Chevrolet Nova at an idle GM plant in Fremont, California. Toyota contributed an estimated $150 million to the venture, while GM put up $20 million in cash in addition to the California plant. Although both firms appointed an equal number of directors, Toyota named the chief executive. GM is reported to have sought the venture in order to gain better insights into the reason the Japanese can produce higher quality cars at a substantially lower cost than do U.S. automakers, while Toyota wanted to increase its production in the United States to help offset import quota limitations on its cars produced in Japan.

DIVESTITURES

Although corporations do more buying than selling of productive facilities, a good bit of selling does occur. In this section, we briefly discuss the major types of divestitures, after which we present some recent examples and rationales for divestitures.

Types of Divestitures

There are three primary types of divestitures: (1) sale of an operating unit to another firm, (2) setting up the business to be divested as a separate corporation and then giving (or "spinning off") its stock on a pro rata basis to the divesting firm's stockholders, and (3) outright liquidation of assets.

Sale to another firm generally involves the sale of an entire division or unit, usually for cash but sometimes for stock of the acquiring firm. In a *spin-off*, the firm's existing stockholders are given new stock representing separate ownership rights in the division which was divested. The division establishes its own board of directors and officers, and it becomes a separate company. The stockholders end up owning shares of two firms instead of one, but no cash has been transferred. Finally, in a *liquidation* the assets of a division are sold off piecemeal, rather than as a single entity. To illustrate the different types of divestitures, we present some recent examples in the next section.

---

[19]Cross-licensing, consortia, joint bidding, and franchising are still other ways for firms to combine resources. For more information on joint ventures, see Sanford V. Berg, Jerome Duncan, and Phillip Friedman, *Joint Venture Strategies and Corporate Innovation* (Cambridge, Mass.: Oelgeschlager, Gunn and Hain, 1982).

Divestiture Illustrations

1. ITT, in a move to streamline and rationalize its holdings, recently divested itself of 27 separate companies, with a value of $1.2 billion. Some of these divisions were suffering losses and were holding down the parent company's earnings, while others simply no longer fitted into ITT's corporate strategy. Also, ITT had a debt ratio that many regarded as excessive, and it used the proceeds from its asset sales to reduce debt.

2. In 1985, prior to its acquisition by GE, RCA sold its Hertz rental car subsidiary to UAL, Inc., the parent of United Airlines. RCA had been trying to sell Hertz for three years because it just didn't fit into its basic business lines of electronics and broadcasting. UAL, on the other hand, was trying to build a travel-oriented conglomerate, with hotels, rental cars, an airline, and a reservation system to tie the whole works together.

3. IU International, a multimillion dollar conglomerate listed on the NYSE, recently spun off or sold three major subsidiaries—Gotaas-Larson, an ocean shipping company involved in petroleum products transportation; Canadian Utilities, an electric utility; and Echo Bay Mines, a gold mining company. The Gotaas-Larson and Echo Bay stock was distributed to IU's own stockholders, while Canadian Utilities was sold for cash, which IU then used to repurchase its own shares. IU also owned (and retained) some major trucking companies (Ryder and PIE), several manufacturing businesses, and some large agribusiness operations. IU's management originally planned to combine highly cyclical businesses such as ocean shipping and gold mining with stable ones such as utilities, thereby gaining overall corporate stability through diversification. The strategy worked reasonably well from an operating standpoint, but it failed in the financial markets. According to its management, IU's very diversity kept it from being assigned to any particular industrial classification, so security analysts tended not to follow the company and therefore did not recommend it to investors. (Analysts tend to concentrate on an industry, and they do not like to recommend, and investors do not like to invest in, a company they do not understand.) As a result, IU had a low P/E ratio and a low market price. After the divestitures, IU's stock price rose from $10 to $25.

4. In 1984, AT&T was broken up to settle a Justice Department antitrust suit. For almost 100 years, AT&T had operated as a holding company which owned Western Electric (its manufacturing subsidiary), Bell Labs (its research arm), a huge long distance network system which was operated as a division of the parent company, and 22 Bell operating companies such as Pacific Telephone, New York Telephone, Southern Bell, and Southwestern Bell. Under the settlement, AT&T was reorganized into eight separate companies—a slimmed down AT&T, which kept Western Electric, Bell Labs, and all interstate long distance operations, plus seven new regional telephone holding companies which were created from the 22 old operating telephone companies. The stock of the seven new telephone companies was spun off to AT&T's stockholders. A person who held 10 shares of AT&T stock owned, after the divestiture, 10 shares of the new AT&T plus one share in each of the seven new operating companies. The 17 shares were backed by the same assets that had previously backed 10 shares of AT&T common.

The AT&T divestiture occurred at the insistence of the Justice Department, which wanted to break up the Bell System into a regulated monopoly segment (the telephone companies) and a segment which would be subjected to competition and which would not have a huge captive market (the surviving AT&T). The breakup was designed to strengthen competition in those parts of the telecommunications industry which are not natural monopolies.

5. In late 1982 Woolworth liquidated every one of its 336 Woolco discount stores in the United States. This reduced the company, which had 1981 sales of $7.2 billion, by 30 percent. Woolco had posted operating losses of $19 million in 1981, and losses in the first half of 1982 had climbed to an alarming $21 million. Woolworth's CEO, Edward F. Gibbons, was quoted as saying: "How many losses can you take?" Woolco's demise cost the parent company some $325 million, taken as a one-time, after-tax write-off.

6. Continental Illinois, once one of the largest U.S. bank holding companies, was struggling to avoid bankruptcy in 1984 as a result of imprudent loans to oil companies, real estate developers, and developing nations. Continental sold off several profitable divisions, such as its leasing and credit card operations, in an effort to raise the funds it needed to cover its bad loan losses and deposit withdrawals. Thus, Continental's asset sales were part of an effort to stay alive. Ultimately, Continental was bailed out by the Federal Deposit Insurance Corporation and the Federal Reserve, which arranged a $7.5 billion rescue package and which gave a blanket guarantee for Continental's entire $40 billion of liabilities.

The preceding examples illustrate the varied reasons for divestitures. Sometimes, the market does not appear to properly recognize the value of a firm's assets when they are held as part of a conglomerate. Also, if IU International's management is correct, there are cases in which a company becomes so complex and so diverse that analysts and investors just do not understand it and consequently ignore it.

Often, a company will need cash, and divestitures can be used to raise cash, as illustrated earlier by Union Carbide's sale of its consumer products division in its successful defense against GAF's hostile tender offer, and by Continental Illinois, which sold off operations in a desperate effort to get the cash needed to stay alive. The ITT example illustrates that business is dynamic—conditions change, corporate strategies change in response, and, as a result, firms alter their asset portfolios by both acquisitions and divestitures. Some divestitures, such as Woolworth's liquidation of its Woolco stores, occur to unload losing assets that cannot be divested by another method. The AT&T example illustrates one of the many instances in which a divestiture is the result of an antitrust settlement.

HOLDING COMPANIES

Holding companies date from 1889, when New Jersey became the first state to pass a law permitting corporations to be formed for the sole purpose of owning the stocks of other companies. Many of the advantages and disadvantages of holding companies are identical to those large-scale operations already discussed in connection with mergers and consolidations. Whether a company is organized on a divisional basis or with the divisions kept as separate companies does not affect the basic reasons for conducting a large-scale, multiproduct, multiplant operation. However, as we show next, the use of holding companies to control large-scale operations has some distinct advantages and disadvantages over those of completely integrated divisionalized operations.

Advantages of Holding Companies

1. Control with fractional ownership. Through a holding company operation, a firm may buy 5, 10, or 50 percent of the stock of another corporation. Such fractional ownership may be sufficient to give the acquiring company effective working control or substantial influence over the operations of the company in which it has acquired stock ownership. Working control is often considered to entail more than 25 percent of the common stock, but it can be as low as 10 percent if the stock is widely distributed. One financier says that the attitude of management is more important than the number of shares owned: "If they think you can control the company, then you do." In addition, control on a very slim margin can be held through relationships with large stockholders outside the holding company group.

2. Isolation of risks. Because the various operating companies in a holding company system are separate legal entities, the obligations of any one unit are separate from those of the other units. Catastrophic losses incurred by one unit of the holding company system are therefore not transmitted as claims on the assets of the other units. However, we should note that while this is a customary generalization, it is not always valid. First, the parent company may feel obligated to make good on the subsidiary's debts, even though it is not legally bound to do so, in order to keep its good name and to retain customers. Examples of this include American Express's payment of over $100 million in connection with a swindle that was the responsibility of one of its subsidiaries, and United California Bank's coverage of its Swiss affiliate's multimillion dollar fraud loss in the 1970s. Second, a parent company may feel obligated to supply capital to an affiliate in order to protect its initial investment; General Public Utilities' continued support of its subsidiaries' Three Mile Island nuclear plant is an example. And, third, when lending to one of the units of a holding company system, an astute loan officer may require a guarantee by the parent holding company. To some degree, therefore, the assets in the various elements of a holding company are joined. Still, a catastrophic loss, as could occur if a drug company's subsidiary distributed a batch of toxic medicine, may be avoided.[20]

---

[20]Note, though, that the parent company will still be held accountable for such losses if it is deemed to exercise operating control over the subsidiary. Thus, Union Carbide was held responsible for its subsidiary's Bhopal disaster.

Disadvantages of Holding Companies

1. Partial multiple taxation. Provided the holding company owns at least 80 percent of a subsidiary's voting stock, the IRS permits the filing of consolidated returns, in which case dividends received by the parent are not taxed. However, if less than 80 percent of the stock is owned, then returns cannot be consolidated and only 80 percent of the dividends received by the holding company may be excluded. With a tax rate of 34 percent, this means that the effective tax rate on intercorporate dividends is 6.8 percent. This partial double taxation somewhat off-sets the benefits of holding company control with limited ownership, but whether the penalty of 6.8 percent of dividends received is sufficient to offset other possible advantages is a matter that must be decided in individual situations.

2. Ease of enforced dissolution. It is relatively easy for the U.S. Department of Justice to require dissolution by disposal of stock ownership of a holding company operation it finds unacceptable. For instance, in the 1950s Du Pont was required to dispose of its 23 percent stock interest in General Motors Corporation, acquired in the early 1920s. Because there was no fusion between the corporations, there were no difficulties, from an operating standpoint, in requiring the separation of the two companies. However, if complete amalgamation had taken place, it would have been much more difficult to break up the company after so many years, and the likelihood of forced divestiture would have been reduced.

Holding Companies as a Leveraging Device

The holding company vehicle has been used to obtain huge degrees of financial leverage. In the 1920s, several tiers of holding companies were established in the electric utility and other industries. In those days, an operating company at the bottom of the pyramid might have $100 million of assets, financed by $50 million of debt and $50 million of equity. Then, a first-tier holding company might own the stock of the operating firm as its only asset and be financed with $25 million of debt and $25 million of equity. A second-tier holding company, which owned the stock of the first-tier company, might be financed with $12.5 million of debt and $12.5 million of equity. Such systems were extended to five or six levels, but with only four holding companies, we see that $100 million of operating assets could be controlled at the top by $3.125 million of equity, and that the operating assets would have to provide enough cash income to support $96.875 million of debt. *Such a holding company system is highly leveraged—its consolidated debt ratio is 96.875 percent, even though the individual components only have 50 percent debt/assets ratios.* Because of this consolidated leverage, even a small decline in profits at the operating company level could bring the whole system down like a house of cards.[21]

---

[21]Excessive leverage through holding companies caused problems for the electric utilities during the 1930s. Accordingly, Congress passed the Holding Company Act, which specifically forbids electric utility holding companies from issuing debt for the purpose of buying the stock of operating electric utilities. The same situation does not exist in the telephone industry. Therefore, telephone holding companies can and do sell bonds and use the proceeds to buy stock in their operating subsidiaries.

Cost of Capital Implications

A question arises as to the cost of capital to the subsidiaries of a holding company system. To see the problem, consider Table 22-5, which shows the balance sheets of a pure holding company, H, its two operating subsidiaries, A and B, and the consolidated corporation. H's only asset is the stock of A and B. Each of the operating companies has issued its own debt, and the parent company, H, has also issued debt. All of the operating companies' equity is owned by the parent.

Here are some points to note:

1. The holding company's debt interest must be paid out of dividend income paid by the operating companies after they have paid interest on their own debt. Similarly, the operating companies' debt has first claim on the assets in the event of bankruptcy. Therefore, the debt of the operating companies is less risky than that of the holding company. Conceivably, if there were many operating companies, diversification would cause the debt of the holding company to be better regarded than that of the operating companies, but this is unlikely.

2. Equity investors in the market see only the consolidated balance sheet—this is the one in the annual report. Thus, in the illustrative situation, stockholders would think of the debt ratio as being ($100 + $50)/$200 = 75%, and the risk associated with a 75 percent debt ratio would be incorporated into the cost of equity. (Bond investors, on the other hand, would see the balance sheets of the entities whose bonds they bought—A, B, or H—but if H, they would certainly know that operating company debt stood between them and physical assets and operating cash flows.)

3. If the two operating companies had equally risky assets, then the cost of capital for capital budgeting purposes should be based on the marginal cost of capital at

---

Table 22-5
Holding Company System Balance Sheets

	Operating Company A				Operating Company B		
		Debt	$ 50			Debt	$ 50
		Equity	50			Equity	50
Total		Total		Total			
assets	$100	claims	$100	assets	$100	Total claims	$100

	Holding Company H				Consolidated Balance Sheet		
Stock A	$ 50	Debt	$ 50	Operating		Operating	
Stock B	50	Equity	50	assets	$200	company debt	$100
						Holding	
						company debt	50
						Holding	
						company equity	50
Total		Total		Total			
assets	$100	claims	$100	assets	$200	Total claims	$200

the *consolidated* level. For example, if the after-tax debt cost to the operating companies were 5 percent, the cost of debt to the holding company were 6 percent, and the cost of common equity to the holding company were 15 percent, then the cost of capital for capital budgeting at the subsidiary level would be

$$k_a(A\&B) = 0.5(5\%) + 0.25(6\%) + 0.25(15\%) = 7.75\%.$$

Alternatively, one could calculate the cost of capital to the *unconsolidated* holding company and then use that cost as the cost of equity to the operating companies:

$$k_a(H) = 0.5(6\%) + 0.5(15\%) = 10.5\%.$$

$$k_a(A\&B) = 0.5(5\%) + 0.5(10.5\%) = 7.75\%.$$

Either way, we see that the cost of capital to the operating companies is 7.75 percent.

The situation would become much more complicated if the debt ratios of Companies A and B were not identical, if A and B operated in different industries and consequently had different business risks, or if the holding company owned operating assets as well as the stock of A and B. In any of these cases, it becomes difficult to determine the appropriate cost of capital for either the operating companies or for the holding company. We can estimate a cost of equity, and hence an overall cost of capital, at the consolidated level, but it is difficult to "unscramble the egg" to determine the separate units' capital costs. The cost of capital estimating process in such a case is conceptually identical to that described in Chapter 9 for multidivisional firms, and it should be approached in the same way.

SUMMARY

A *merger* involves the consolidation of two or more firms. Mergers can provide economic benefits through economies of scale or through the concentration of assets in the hands of more efficient managers, but they also have the potential for reducing competition, and for this reason, they are carefully regulated by governmental agencies.

In most mergers, one company (the acquiring firm) initiates action to take over another (the target firm). As a first step, the acquiring company must analyze the situation and determine the value of the target company. Often there will be operating economies, or *synergistic benefits*, which will raise the earnings of the combined enterprise over the sum of the earnings of the two separate companies. In this circumstance, the merger is potentially beneficial to both sets of stockholders, but the two firms' managers and stockholders must agree on how the net benefits will be shared. This all boils down to how much the acquiring company is willing to pay, either in cash or in shares of its own stock, for the target company.

Although mergers are more common, firms do on occasion get rid of assets—this is called a *divestiture*. Sometimes divestitures involve a firm's *selling* one of its divisions to some other firm. At other times, the divestiture involves setting up a separate corporation and then *spinning off* the stock of the new company to the stockholders of the old company. The reasons for divestitures vary from antitrust to cleaning up a company's image to raising capital needed for strengthening the corporation's core business.

In a merger, one firm disappears. However, an acquiring firm may wish to buy all or a majority of the common stock of another and to run the acquired firm as an operating subsidiary. When this occurs, the acquiring firm is said to be a *holding company*. Holding company operations have both advantages and disadvantages. The major advantage is the fact that control can often be obtained for a smaller cash outlay. The disadvantages include tax penalties and, perhaps, incomplete ownership.

Questions and Problems

22-1 (Diversification motive) Two large, publicly owned firms are contemplating a merger. No operating synergy is expected, but returns on the two firms are not perfectly positively correlated, so σ_{EBIT} would be reduced for the combined corporation. One group of consultants argues that this risk reduction is sufficient grounds for the merger. Another group thinks that this type of risk reduction is irrelevant because stockholders could already hold the stock of both companies, and thus gain the risk reduction benefits of a merger. Whose position is correct?

22-2 (Accounting for mergers) The Tallman Company is being acquired by the Garlington Corporation for $2 million. In addition to the $2 million paid to Tallman's stockholders, Garlington will also assume Tallman's debt. No synergistic effects are expected. The two companies' premerger balance sheets and income statements are as follows (in thousands of dollars except EPS):

Tallman

Current assets	$ 750	Debt	$ 875
Fixed assets	1,125	Common equity	1,000
Total assets	$1,875	Total claims	$1,875

Garlington

Current assets	$1,500	Debt	$2,000
Fixed assets	1,625	Common equity	1,125
Total assets	$3,125	Total claims	$3,125

	Tallman	Garlington
Sales	$750	$1,300
Operating costs	488	830
EBIT	$262	$ 470
Interest expense	100	200
EBT	$162	$ 270
Taxes (40%)	65	108
Net income	$ 97	$ 162
Common shares	60,000	100,000
EPS	$1.62	$1.62

a. Construct Garlington's postmerger balance sheet assuming that the acquisition is treated as a pooling of interests.

b. Assume that the merger is treated as a purchase rather than a pooling of interests, and that any excess paid above net asset value will be recorded as goodwill. Now, what would be the postmerger balance sheet?

c. Construct the postmerger income statements for both pooling of interests and purchase, assuming a one-for-one exchange of stock. Goodwill will be written off over 25 years. What would be the postmerger EPS under each accounting method?

d. What are the postmerger cash flows under each accounting method assuming that the postmerger depreciation expense, which is an operating cost, is $300,000? Now suppose that Tallman's fixed assets will be written up by $500,000, and $500,000 will be recorded as goodwill. What impact would this have on the postmerger income statement and cash flow under both old and new tax laws?

22-3 (Merger analysis) Masson, Inc., a large building materials manufacturer, is evaluating the possible acquisition of the Rolf Company, a small aluminum window manufacturer. Masson's analysts project the following postmerger data for Rolf (in thousands of dollars):

	1987	1988	1989	1990
Net sales	$250	$288	$312	$338
Selling and administrative expense	25	31	38	40
Interest	12	15	16	18

Cost of goods sold as a percentage of sales: 65%
Terminal growth rate of cash flow available to Masson: 8%

If the acquisition is made, it will occur on January 1, 1987. All cash flows are assumed to occur at end-of-year. Rolf currently has a market value capital structure of 40 percent debt, but Masson would increase that to 50 percent if the acquisition were made. Rolf, if independent, would pay taxes at 30 percent, but its income would be taxed at 40 percent if it were consolidated. Rolf's current market-determined beta is 1.50, and its investment bankers think that its beta would rise to 1.68 if the debt ratio were increased to 50 percent. Depreciation-generated funds would be used to replace worn-out equipment, so they would not be available to Masson's shareholders. The risk-free rate is 8 percent, and the market risk premium is 6 percent.

a. What is the appropriate discount rate for valuing the acquisition?

b. What is the terminal value? What is the value of the Rolf Company to Masson?

(Do Parts c, d, and e only if you are using the computerized diskette.)

c. If sales in each year were $100,000 higher than the base case amounts, and if the cost of goods sold/sales ratio were 60 percent, what would Rolf be worth to Masson?

d. With sales and the cost of goods sold ratio at the Part c levels, what would Rolf's value be if its postmerger beta were 1.8, k_{RF} rose to 10 percent, and RP_M rose to 7 percent?

e. Leaving all values at the Part d levels, what would the value of the acquisition be if the terminal growth rate rose to 20 percent or dropped to 3 percent?

22-4 (Merger analysis) Hoffmeister Electric Corporation is considering a merger with the Cary Lamp Company. Cary is a publicly traded company, and its current beta is 1.40. Cary has barely been profitable, so it has paid only 20 percent in taxes over the last several years. Additionally, Cary uses little debt, having a market value debt ratio of just 25 percent.

If the acquisition is made, Hoffmeister plans to operate Cary as a separate, wholly owned subsidiary. Hoffmeister would pay taxes on a consolidated basis, and thus the federal-plus-state tax rate would increase to 40 percent. Additionally, Hoffmeister would increase the debt capitalization in the Cary subsidiary to a market value of 40 percent of assets. Hoffmeister's acquisition department estimates that Cary, if acquired, would produce the following net cash flows to Hoffmeister's shareholders (in millions of dollars):

Year	Net Cash Flow
1	$1.20
2	1.40
3	1.65
4	1.80
5 and beyond	Constant growth at 5%

These cash flows include all acquisition effects. Hoffmeister's cost of equity is 16 percent, its beta is 1.0, and its cost of debt is 12 percent. The risk-free rate is 10 percent.

a. What discount rate should be used to discount the above cash flows?

b. What is the dollar value of Cary to Hoffmeister?

c. Cary has 1.2 million common shares outstanding. What is the maximum price per share that Hoffmeister should offer for Cary? If the tender offer is accepted at this price, what would happen to Hoffmeister's stock price?

22-5 (Greenmail and poison pills) In the spring of 1984, Disney Productions' stock was selling for about $50 per share. Then Saul Steinberg, a New York financier, began acquiring it, and after he had 12 percent, he announced a tender offer for another 37 percent of the stock, which would bring his holdings up to 49 percent, at a price of $67.50 per share. Disney's management then announced plans to buy Gibson Greeting Cards and Arvida properties, paying for them with stock, and Disney also lined up bank credit and (according to Steinberg) was prepared to borrow up to $2 billion and use the funds to repurchase shares at a higher price than Steinberg was offering. All of these efforts were designed to prevent Steinberg from taking control. In June, Disney's management agreed to pay Steinberg $77.45 per share, which gave him a gain of about $60 million on a two-month investment of about $26.5 million.

When Disney's buyback of Steinberg's shares was announced, the stock price fell almost immediately from $68 to $46. Many Disney stockholders were irate, and they sued to block the buyout. Also, the Disney affair added fuel to a fire in a Congressional committee that was holding hearings on some proposed legislation that would (1) prohibit someone from acquiring more than 10 percent of a firm's stock without making a tender offer for all the remaining shares, (2) prohibit "poison pill" tactics such as those Disney's management used to fight off Steinberg, (3) prohibit buybacks such as the deal eventually offered to Steinberg unless there were an approving vote by stockholders, and (4) prohibit (or significantly curtail) the use of "golden parachutes" (the one thing Disney's management did not try).

Set forth a set of arguments for and against the type of legislation discussed above. What provisions, if any, should be in such legislation?

22-6 (Holding companies) Suppose a holding company has subsidiaries which have issued preferred stock and bonds to public investors (all of the subsidiaries' common stock is owned by the holding company). The holding company's major asset is its stock in its subsidiaries, but the parent company does own in its own right certain operating assets. The holding company also issues its own bonds and preferred stock.

Given this information, describe the relative riskiness of investments in the common, preferred, and bonds both of the holding company itself (the parent) and of the operating subsidiaries. Assume that all the operating assets are equally risky.

22-7 (Accounting for mergers) Philip Morris, Inc., recently acquired Seven-Up Corporation for $520 million. Seven-Up had a book value of $130 million. Do you think Philip Morris's management would prefer to treat the merger as a pooling or a purchase? Would your reaction be the same if the book value had been $520 million and the price paid $130 million? Explain.

Selected Additional References and Cases

Considerable empirical investigation has been conducted to determine whether stockholders of acquiring or acquired companies benefit most from corporate mergers. One of the classic works in this field is

Mandelker, Gershon, "Risk and Return: The Case of Merging Firms," *Journal of Financial Economics*, December 1974, 303-335.

One of the more recent works is

Wansley, James W., William R. Lane, and Ho C. Yang, "Abnormal Returns to Acquired Firms by Type of Acquisition and Method of Payment," *Financial Management*, Autumn 1983, 16-22.

For a comprehensive review of the empirical literature on mergers, see

Elgers, Pieter T., and John J. Clark, "Merger Types and Shareholder Returns: Additional Evidence," *Financial Management*, Summer 1980, 66-72.

Mueller, Dennis C., "The Effects of Conglomerate Mergers," *Journal of Banking and Finance*, December 1977, 315-347.

For an interesting test of the existence of synergy in mergers, see

Haugen, Robert A., and Terence C. Langetieg, "An Empirical Test for Synergism in Merger," *Journal of Finance*, September 1975, 1003-1014.

For more insights into the likelihood of acceptance of a cash tender offer, see

Hoffmeister, J. Ronald, and Edward A. Dyl, "Predicting Outcomes of Cash Tender Offers," *Financial Management*, Winter 1981, 50-58.

Some additional works on tender offers include

Dodd, Peter, and Richard Ruback, "Tender Offers and Stockholder Returns," *Journal of Financial Economics*, November 1977, 351-373.

Kummer, Donald R., and J. Ronald Hoffmeister, "Valuation Consequences of Cash Tender Offers," *Journal of Finance*, May 1978, 505-516.

The following article examines the effect of merger accounting on stock price:

Hong, Hai, Gershon Mandelker, and R. S. Kaplan, "Pooling versus Purchase: The Effects of Accounting for Mergers on Stock Prices," *Accounting Review*, January 1978, 31-47.

The Summer 1984 issue of the Midland Corporate Finance Journal *contains these relevant articles:*

DeAngelo, Harry, Linda DeAngelo, and Edward M. Rice, "Going Private: The Effects of a Change in Corporate Ownership Structure," 35-44.

Hite, Gailen L., and James E. Owers, "The Restructuring of Corporate America: An Overview," 6-16.

Linn, Scott C., and Michael S. Rozeff, "The Corporate Sell-Off," 17-26.

Schipper, Katherine, and Abbie Smith, "The Corporate Spin-Off Phenomenon," 27-34.

Stern, Joel (Moderator), "A Discussion of Corporate Restructuring," 44-79.

For a very interesting discussion of many of the important merger issues, see

"A Discussion of Mergers and Acquisitions," *Midland Corporate Finance Journal*, Summer 1983, 21-47.

The following case in the Crum-Brigham casebook illustrates merger analysis:

Case 36, "Dustain Industries," which examines the effects of different types of mergers on EPS, P/E ratios, and stock prices.

The following cases in the Harrington casebook focus on Chapter 22 material:

"Philip Morris," which describes the firm's acquisition goals and its success in the acquisition of Miller Brewing Company.

"Kennecott Copper," which illustrates how management's attempt to maintain its position can conflict with shareholder interests.

"Diamond Shamrock," which illustrates divestiture analysis.

23

PENSION PLAN MANAGEMENT

Most companies—and practically all governmental units—have some type of employee pension plan. Typically, the chief financial officer administers the plan, and he or she has these three specific responsibilities: (1) deciding on the general nature of the plan, (2) determining the required annual payments into the plan, and (3) managing the plan's assets. Obviously, the company does not have total control over these decisions—employees, primarily through their unions, have a major say about the plan's structure, and the federal government imposes strict rules on certain aspects of all plans. Still, companies do have considerable latitude regarding several key decisions, and these decisions can materially affect both the firm's profitability and its employees' welfare.

Although a few firms have provided pensions for many years, the real start of large-scale pension plans dates from 1949, when the United Steelworkers negotiated a comprehensive plan in their contract with the steel companies. Other industries followed, and the plans grew rapidly thereafter. Under a typical pension plan, the company (or governmental unit) agrees to provide some type of retirement payments for employees. These promised payments constitute a liability, and the employer is required to establish a *pension fund* and place money in it each year, with the idea being to have sufficient assets to meet the pension payments as they come due.

In 1986, private pension funds constituted the largest and fastest growing major class of investors: These funds had assets of roughly $1 trillion; they owned about one-third of all the stock of U.S. corporations; they accounted for approximately one-half of all trading in the stock market; and they owned about half of all outstanding corporate bonds. In 1986, General Motors had over $20 billion in its fund, and GE and IBM each had about $12 billion. For these companies, and most other NYSE firms, pension fund assets were equal to about 30 percent of operating assets. If the pension fund is managed well and produces relatively high returns, the firm's contributions—which are a cost and hence reduce earnings—can be minimized. If the fund does not do well, or if its assets are not sufficient to cover the retire-

---

This chapter was coauthored by H. Russell Fogler of the University of Florida.

ment benefits promised to employees, then the firm will be required to increase contributions, which will have a negative effect on profits.

Pension plans can also affect mergers and leveraged buyouts (LBOs). On the one hand, a number of mergers that otherwise made good sense have been abandoned because one of the prospective partners had large unfunded pension liabilities which the other partner was unwilling to assume. On the other hand, overfunded pension plans have made other companies attractive merger and LBO candidates, because excess funds in the pension plans could be removed to help pay for the merger or LBO.

It is clear that pension fund management is an important but complex job. Indeed, pension fund administration requires so much specialized technical knowledge that companies typically hire specialists as consultants to help design, modify, and administer their plans. Still, because the plans are under the general supervision of the financial staff, and because the plans have such significant implications for the firm as a whole, it is important that students of financial management understand the basics of pension plan management.

KEY DEFINITIONS

Certain terms are used frequently in pension plan management, and it is useful to define them at the outset.

Defined Benefit Plan

Under any pension plan, the employer agrees to give something to the employees when they retire. Under a *defined benefit plan*, the employer agrees to give retirees a specifically defined benefit, such as $500 per month, 80 percent of his or her average salary over the five years preceding retirement, or 2.5 percent of his or her highest annual salary for each year of employment. The payments could be set in final form as of the retirement date, or they could be indexed to increase as the cost of living increases, but they are defined prior to retirement.

Defined Contribution Plan

Rather than specifying exactly how much each retiree will receive, companies can agree to make specific payments into a retirement fund, and then have retirees receive benefits from the plan depending on the investment success of the plan. This is called a *defined contribution plan*. For example, a trucking firm might agree to make payments equal to 15 percent of all union members' wages each year into a pension fund administered by the Teamsters' Union, and the fund would then dispense benefits to retirees. Such plans do not have to be administered by unions—they could be administered by a bank's trust department, or the monthly payments applicable to each employee could simply be paid into a mutual fund and credited to the employee's account.

Profit Sharing Plan

A third procedure also calls for the employer to make payments into the retirement fund, but this time with the payments varying with the level of corporate profits; this is a *profit sharing plan*. For example, a computer manufacturer might agree to pay 10 percent of its pre-tax profits into a fund which would then invest the proceeds and pay benefits to employees upon their retirement. Profit sharing plans can be operated separately or be used in conjunction with defined benefit or defined contribution plans. For example, a drug company might have a defined benefit plan which pays employees 1½ percent of their final average salary for each year of employment and, in addition, have a profit sharing plan which calls for putting 5 percent of pre-tax profits into an account for retired employees. Under most profit sharing plans, a separate account is maintained for each employee, and each employee gets a "share" of the contribution each year based upon his or her salary. The employee's account builds up over time just as if he or she were putting money into a mutual fund.

Vesting

If employees have a right to receive pension benefits even if they leave the company prior to retirement, then their pension rights are said to be *vested*. If the employee loses his or her pension rights if he or she leaves the company prior to retirement, the rights are said to be *nonvested*. Most plans today have *deferred vesting*; that is, pension rights are nonvested for the first few years, but become fully vested if the employee remains with the company for a prescribed period, say five years. The costs to the company are clearly lower for plans with nonvested rights, because such plans do not cover employees who leave prior to retirement. Moreover, nonvested plans tend to reduce turnover, which in turn lowers training costs. However, it is much easier to recruit employees if the plan offers some type of vesting. Also, many argue that vesting is socially desirable, and as a result there has been a tendency over time for Congress to require vesting for more and more employees, and with a shorter period of deferral before vesting takes effect. The Tax Reform Act of 1986 requires that employees be fully vested within five years.

Portability

Portable means "capable of being carried," and a *portable pension plan* is one that an employee can carry from one employer to another. Portability is extremely important in occupations such as construction, where workers move from one employer to another fairly frequently. However, for a plan to be portable, both the old and the new employer must be part of the same plan—it would simply not be feasible for an IBM employee to leave IBM and go to work for Delta Airlines and take along a share of the IBM plan. (Note, however, that if the employee's rights under the IBM plan were vested, then he or she could receive payments from both Delta's and IBM's plans upon retirement.) Where job changes are frequent—as in trucking, construction, and coal mining—union-administered plans are used to make portability possible.

Funding

Under either a defined contribution or a profit sharing plan, the company's obligation is satisfied when it makes its required annual contributions to the plan. However, under a defined benefit plan, the company promises to give employees pensions for some unknown number of future years. Pension fund actuaries can determine the present value of the expected future benefits under a defined benefit plan, and this present value constitutes a liability of the plan. This liability may be measured (1) by the present value of *all projected* benefits accrued by present workers or (2) by the present value of *vested* benefits earned to date. The vested amount is obviously smaller, and it represents the expected present value of the benefits that would be paid to workers if the firm went out of business today, or if all workers resigned today. The value of the fund's assets can easily be determined: It is the current market value of the fund's assets. If the present value of expected retirement benefits is equal to assets on hand, then the plan is said to be *fully funded*. If assets exceed the present value of benefits, the plan is *overfunded*, but if the present value of benefits exceeds assets, the plan is *underfunded*, and an *unfunded pension liability* exists.

Actuarial Rate of Return

The discount rate used to determine the present value of future benefits under a defined benefit plan is called the *actuarial rate of return*. The actuarial rate is also, in theory, the rate of return at which the fund's assets are assumed to be invested.

ERISA

The *Employee Retirement Income Security Act of 1974 (ERISA)* is the basic federal law governing the administration and structure of corporate pension plans. ERISA requires that companies fully fund their pension plans, although it gives them up to 30 years to correct for underfunding of past service benefits such as would exist if a company agreed in 1986 to double payments to all employees who retire in the future. This "retroactive benefit" would create an immediate and large under-funding problem. The prolonged adjustment period is especially important in such a situation. Relevant provisions of ERISA are discussed throughout the chapter.

Contributions to the Plan

Actuaries calculate each year how much a company must pay into a defined benefit pension fund in order to keep it fully funded (or to move it toward full funding). These contributions are a tax-deductible expense, just as are wages. Obviously, if a company agrees to an increase in benefits, this increases its required contribution and consequently lowers its reported profits and cash flow to stockholders. Also, if pension benefits are tied to wages, then any wage increase will also require an increase in payments to the pension plan. Payments also depend on the investment performance of the pension fund—if the fund's managers do a good job of investing its assets, then required annual contributions will be reduced, and vice versa if the fund's investment performance is poor.

FASB

The Financial Accounting Standards Board (FASB), together with the SEC, establishes the rules under which a firm reports its financial results, including its income and its balance sheet position, to stockholders. In December 1985, the FASB issued Statement 87, "Employers' Accounting for Pension Plans," which provided new guidance for reporting pension costs and liabilities. Under the old rule, pension plan funding information was given only in the notes to the financial statements, and firms could choose almost any actuarial rate of return when computing the present value of their plan liabilities. However, FASB Statement 87 made three major changes in the old rules: (1) Some pension plan information will in the future have to be shown directly on the balance sheet. This provision was opposed strongly by firms with large underfunding. For example, if the rule were applied today, GM would have to report a liability of over $2 billion directly on its balance sheet. (2) The new rule requires a uniform method for determining a firm's actuarial rate of return based on prevailing market rates, rather than permitting it to use arbitrarily chosen values. (3) Additional information must now be provided in the notes to the financial statements. For example, firms must now show a breakdown of the pension contribution reported in the income statement.[1]

PENSION FUND MATHEMATICS

It is clear from the preceding definitions that the calculation of the present value of expected future benefits is of primary importance in pension plan operations. This calculation determines both the required contribution to the fund for the year and also the reported unfunded liability or surplus. Thus, it is essential that financial managers understand the basic mathematics which underlies the benefits calculation.[2]

To illustrate the process, let us begin with the following assumptions:

1. A firm has only one employee, age 40, who will retire 25 years from now, at age 65, and die at age 80. There is no uncertainty about these facts.

---

[1]FASB Statement 87 is very complex, and hence we cannot discuss its provisions in detail in this text. Also, note that firms need not immediately comply with the provisions of Statement 87, but full implementation must take place by the end of 1989.

[2]For a detailed treatment of pension fund mathematics, see C. L. Trowbridge and C. E. Farr, *The Theory and Practice of Pension Funding* (Homewood, Ill.: Irwin, 1976).

2. The firm has promised a benefit of $10,000 at the end of each year following retirement until death. For accounting purposes, 1/25 of this $10,000 payment will be vested each year the employee works for the company.

3. No uncertainty regarding the contribution stream exists; that is, the company will definitely make the required payments, in equal annual installments over the next 25 years, in order to build the fund up to the level needed to make the payments of $10,000 per year during the employee's 15-year retirement life.

4. The pension fund will earn 8 percent on its assets; this rate is also known with certainty.

The problem is to find (1) the present value of the future benefits and (2) the company's required annual contributions. We find these values as follows:

Step 1. Find the present value (at retirement) of a 15-year regular annuity of $10,000 per year:

$$\text{PV of an annuity of \$10,000 per year for 15 years at 8\%} = \$10,000(\text{PVIFA}_{8\%,15}) = \$85,594.79.$$

Figure 23-1
Pension Fund Cash Flows and Value under Certainty

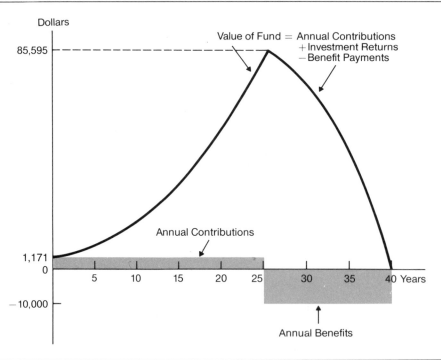

Step 2. Find the set of equal annual cash contributions required to accumulate $85,594.79 over 25 years:

$$\frac{\text{Annual cash contribution to establish a fund of \$85,594.79 over a 25-year period at 8\%}}{} = \frac{\$85,594.79}{\text{FVIFA}_{8\%,25}} = \$1,170.83.$$

Thus, the company must contribute $1,170.83 per year to satisfy its pension requirements. If it makes these payments each year, it will be able to report a fully funded position.

A graphical representation of the contribution and benefit cash flows and fund value is presented in Figure 23-1. The "Value of Fund" line is drawn continuously, although in reality, it would be a step function. Note also that setting up a pension plan for this worker requires analysis over a 40-year horizon.

The assumed rate of return can make a substantial difference to the annual contribution. If we had assumed a 9 percent return rather than 8 percent, the annual contributions would have dropped from $1,170.83 to $951.67. Thus, annual contributions would have fallen by 18.7 percent from only a one percentage point change in the assumed investment rate. Conversely, if we had assumed a 7 percent return, the annual contributions would have increased to $1,440.01, a 23 percent increase. Assumptions about how long the worker will live, years before retirement, and, if the payment is based on salary, annual raises, will have similarly large effects on the annual contribution.

RISKS INHERENT IN PENSION PLANS

Different types of plans differ with regard to the certainty of cash contributions, investment earnings, and promised benefits at retirement. In a *defined contribution plan*, the corporation, or *plan sponsor*, contributes a guaranteed amount which will be invested for eventual retirement payments to the beneficiaries of the plan. No guarantee, however, is made about either the rate of return earned on funds or the final payments. Thus, the beneficiaries assume the risk of fluctuations in the rate of return on the invested money, so they must bear a corresponding risk regarding the level of their retirement incomes.

A *profit sharing plan* is similar to a defined contribution plan, except that the sponsor's cash contributions are also uncertain. This uncertainty regarding contributions, along with uncertainty about the fund's earned rate of return, increases the risks to the beneficiaries. The value of the fund at retirement, and hence retirees' incomes, could be quite large or quite small, depending on how profitable the corporation is and how well the plan's assets are managed.

Finally, in a *defined benefit plan*, which guarantees to pay a stated amount from retirement to death, the corporate sponsor assumes all risks of unexpected variations in rates of return on investment. Note too that the required level of the fund, and the resulting annual contributions, could vary if the defined benefits are based on some average of the final years' salaries, for salaries can grow at a rate different from the assumed level. Thus, the future cash contribution requirements are relatively uncertain. Further, these contributions cannot be reduced if the corporation's profits fall, as they could be with a profit sharing plan. *Therefore, a defined benefit plan is by far the riskiest from the standpoint of the sponsoring corporation, but the least risky from the standpoint of the employees.*

Large corporations generally use defined benefit plans, while smaller ones typically use profit sharing and/or defined contribution plans. As a result, approximately 71 percent of current pension plans are defined contribution plans, but those plans include only 35 percent of the total number of employees participating in pension plans. The reason for this situation lies in the relative ability to bear risk—large firms such as GM, GE, and IBM can afford to take the risks inherent in defined benefit plans better than their employees, but many small firms simply do not have the stability required to assume such long-term risks, and consequently both they and their employees are better off under a defined contribution and/or a profit sharing plan.

Risks to the Corporation

From the foregoing discussion, we see that the risks inherent in pension fund operations depend on how the plans are structured. Under a defined benefit plan, the risks fall primarily on the corporation (through the uncertainty of its future contributions). If the plan calls for defined contributions, then risks are shared, whereas under a profit-sharing plan, almost all the risk falls on the beneficiaries. Risk to the corporation under a defined benefit plan can be further subdivided into (1) uncertainty about the annual cash contribution and (2) uncertainty about the firm's obligations in the event it goes bankrupt.

Risks of Annual Cash Contributions

The *minimum annual cash contribution* is the sum of (1) the amount needed to fund projected future benefit payments that were accrued during the current period, (2) the amount (which could be zero) that must be contributed to make up for not having funded all benefits for service that occurred prior to the current period, and (3) an additional amount (which could be zero or negative) required to offset unexpected deviations from the plan's actuarial assumptions, especially deviations in the earned rate of return and in employee turnover and wage rates. This minimum cash contribution can be expressed by the following equation:

$$\text{Minimum cash contribution} = NC + PS + AG,$$

where

NC = normal contribution, which is a figure based on funding the present value of benefits earned for service during the current period, discounted at the actuarial rate. NC can vary widely depending on the assumptions made about the return on pension plan assets, future employee turnover, and future salary increases.

PS = past service, which is the make-up contribution for unfunded past service. The minimum PS make-up under ERISA is the amount required to amortize the unfunded liability on a straight line basis over 30 years. The company can, if it has the cash and chooses to do so, set PS equal to the full unfunded liability, and hence immediately bring the plan up to full funding. However, for tax purposes, the IRS will allow as a deduction only amounts based on amortization over a 10-year or longer period.

AG = actuarial gains and losses from the assumed actuarial forecast, amortized over 15 years at the plan's assumed rate of interest. These actuarial gains or losses could occur because of deviations in employees' turnover, final salaries, life expectancy, and so on, and also because of deviations between actual and expected investment performance for the fund's assets.

In our Figure 23-1 illustration of pension fund mathematics, the annual cash contributions were known with certainty. In actual plans, there are three key types of actuarial assumptions which reflect real-world risks: (1) *decrement assumptions*, which allow the actuary to adjust annually for the probability that any employee will leave the company (that is, terminate employment, become disabled, retire, or die); (2) *future salary assumptions*, which take into account expected future average wage increases, which will, of course, affect the final salary and hence defined benefit payments based on the final salary; and (3) *discount rate assumptions*, which explicitly forecast the portfolio's expected future rate of return, which is used both to compound the fund's growth from investment and also to discount and thus find the present value of future benefits.

At the end of each year, the assumptions are examined and modified if necessary, and actuaries determine the present value of expected future benefits. Then the deviation between this value and the actual value of the fund's assets is calculated, and it becomes part of an account called "total cumulative actuarial gains and losses." Then the annual cash contribution is adjusted by an amount sufficient to amortize this cumulative amount over a 15-year period. For example, suppose a fund were set up on January 1, 1986, and money were deposited based on a set of actuarial assumptions. Then, at the end of the year, the actual actuarial conditions were examined and compared with the assumed conditions, and the actual value of the fund were compared with the money that would be needed for full funding under the revised actuarial assumptions. Any difference between the actual and required fund balance would be added to the cumulative gains and losses account, and the required annual contribution would be increased or decreased by an amount sufficient to amortize this account's balance over a 15-year period. The same method would be used at the end of 1987; the cumulative gains and losses account would be adjusted, and a new 15-year amortization payment for actuarial gains and losses would be determined. To illustrate, suppose the cumulative amount in the actuarial gains and losses account at the end of 1986 were a $15 million shortfall, and the actuarial earnings rate were 8 percent. Under these conditions, in 1987 the value of AG would be about $1.75 million because this level of AG would gradually eliminate the deficiency over 15 years. If everything else remained constant, then AG would remain at $1.75 million for 15 years. However, in future years new deviations are bound to occur, and the cumulative amount of actuarial gains and losses will rise or fall, requiring new calculations and new values for AG. All of this is designed to build the fund up to its required level but, at the same time, to smooth out the annual cash contribution charge, and hence to smooth out the firm's reported profits and cash flows.

Bankruptcy Liens

Prior to the passage of ERISA in 1974, employees had no claim against a corporation's assets in the event of bankruptcy. Of course, if a plan were fully funded, bankruptcy would present no problem for employees, but bankruptcy would impose a serious hardship on members of plans that were not fully funded. When it passed ERISA, Congress elevated the priority of unfunded vested pension liabilities in the event of bankruptcy. Today, in the event of a pension plan termination due to bankruptcy, unfunded vested liabilities have a lien on a par with federal taxes on up to 30 percent of the stockholders' equity. Thus, the pension fund ranks above the unsecured creditors for up to 30 percent of common and preferred equity, and any unsatisfied pension claims rank on a par with the general creditors. The rights of the pension fund are enforced by the *Pension Benefit Guarantee Corporation (PBGC),* which was created by ERISA to guarantee beneficiaries of their vested pension benefits.[3] PBGC is funded by an annual "head tax" of $2.60 per beneficiary. However, because of the high level of bankruptcies that occurred in the early 1980s, it is now clear that $2.60 is not sufficient, and drawdowns from PBGC have been exceeding inflows. Thus, higher taxes are likely in the future.[4]

Note also that if one of the subsidiaries of a holding company had been operating at a loss, and consequently had a low net worth, and if the subsidiary also had an unfunded pension liability which was greater than its net worth, then the parent company would probably be better off without the subsidiary than with it. This situation has undoubtedly led some companies to spin off or otherwise dispose of some subsidiaries. Such spinoffs have a detrimental effect on the PBGC, which in fact sued International Harvester (IH) for having sold its Wisconsin Steel subsidiary three years before the subsidiary went bankrupt and turned its underfunded pension plan over to the PBGC. PBGC claimed that the purpose of the divestiture was to rid IH of its subsidiary's pension liability. Several recent leveraged buyouts of divisions of corporations may also have been motivated in part by the pension situation.

---

[3]Actual benefit payments to employees are subject to a maximum limit. Thus, when bankruptcy occurs, highly paid employees would obtain less from the PBGC than they would had the company survived. Note also that if a company has been suffering losses prior to bankruptcy, which is generally the case, its equity will be low, and 30 percent of a low number is lower yet. Nevertheless, PBGC must still make full payments as specified in the company's plan to all vested pension holders, subject to the limits noted previously.

[4]The shortfall between PBGC's assets and the present value of its liabilities was over $550 million in 1985, and thus in 1986 its directors asked for an increase in the head tax. (PBGC has estimated that it needs a premium increase to $8.10 to cover known future obligations.) Critics argue that the flat tax currently being used is unfair to plans which are fully funded, and that the tax rate ought to penalize underfunded plans. As with any issue in the political arena, there are many contradictory opinions. Experience to date suggests that approximately 97 percent of terminating plans have assets sufficient to cover their current vested benefits. However, the 1986 bankruptcy of LTV may effectively bankrupt PBGC itself, in which case the federal government will doubtless bail out the system, at a potentially huge cost to taxpayers. As we write this chapter, Congress is considering a bill that would (1) increase the insurance premium and (2) increase PBGC's claim against the firm in the event of bankruptcy. For a theoretical discussion of the insurance features of the PBGC, see William F. Sharpe, "Corporate Pension Funding Policy," *Journal of Financial Economics,* June 1976, 183-193.

Stock Market Effects

The value of a firm's stock is obviously affected by the financial condition of its pension plan, but because of the uncertainties inherent in pension plan calculations, devising a reasonable set of accounting procedures for reporting both the annual pension expense and the corporation's pension liabilities has proved to be quite difficult. FASB Statement 87 was designed to increase the disclosure of information about a firm's pension fund condition, as well as mandate more uniformity in choosing the actuarial rate of return used to calculate the present value of benefits. However, because of the vast variety of funding techniques and the great difficulty involved in forecasting future pension liabilities, reported pension plan data must still be viewed with a certain amount of skepticism.[5]

Can investors make sense of pension fund accounting data? To help answer this question, Martin Feldstein and Randall Morck examined the relationship between corporations' market values and their pension fund liabilities, and they concluded that investors recognize the existence of unfunded pension liabilities and lower the firm's value accordingly.[6] This and other evidence indicates that investors are well aware of the condition of companies' pension funds, and that unfunded pension liabilities do reduce corporate value. FASB statement 87 will make it even easier for investors to assess the impact of a firm's pension fund on its value, and hence stock prices should be even more affected in the future.

Risks to Beneficiaries

Although the preceding section might suggest that all the risks inherent in a defined benefit pension plan are borne by the PBGC or the corporate sponsor, this is not entirely true. For example, suppose that in 1986 a corporation went bankrupt and its employees were laid off. It is true that the PBGC will provide the promised retirement payments when the employees actually retire. But suppose an employee is 50 years old now, his or her benefits are $10,000 per year, and retirement is 15 years away. If the firm is in an industry where employment is contracting, such as steel or auto production, the worker will have a hard time finding a new job offering comparable wages. Moreover, even if the worker could get another job that provides the same salary and an equivalent pension plan, his or her benefits will still be adversely affected. The benefits under the bankrupt company's plan will be frozen—the past benefits from the now-bankrupt firm will not be increased as a result of pay increases over the worker's remaining employment life, as they probably would have been had the original employer not gone bankrupt. The worker's benefits under his or her new plan, assuming he or she does get a new job, would rise with inflation, but the worker's retirement income will be the sum of payments under the old frozen plan and the new one, and these benefits

---

[5]FASB Statement 87, the new rule on pension fund accounting, was passed by a 4-3 vote, which reflects the lack of consensus regarding the proper accounting treatment for pension plans.

[6]See Martin Feldstein and Randall Morck, "Pension Funds and the Value of Equities," *Financial Analysts Journal*, September-October 1983, 29-39.

will almost certainly be lower than they would have been had no bankruptcy occurred. Thus, bankruptcy still imposes hardships on workers, and a realization of this fact has been a major factor in unions' acceptance of reduced wages and benefits in situations where corporate bankruptcy with corresponding layoffs would otherwise have occurred.

It should also be recognized (1) that prior to the 1930s, most people had to depend on personal savings (and their children) to support them in their old age, (2) that Social Security was put into effect in 1933 to provide a formalized retirement system for workers, (3) that corporate pension plans did not really "take off" until after World War II, and (4) that even today many workers, especially those employed by smaller firms, have no formal retirement plan other than Social Security. Also, when the Social Security Act was passed in 1933, it was supposed to be based on insurance principles in the sense that each person would pay into the system and then receive benefits which, actuarially, were equivalent to what he or she had paid in. Thus, Social Security was designed to help workers provide for their own future. Today, Social Security has become an income transfer mechanism in the sense that workers with high salaries get less out of the system than they pay in, while low salaried workers get more out than they pay in. In a sense, the Social Security system, including Medicare, is becoming a "safety net" for all older Americans, irrespective of their payments into the system. Even so, few people want to have to live on the income provided by Social Security, so private pension plans are still a vital part of the American economic scene.

ILLUSTRATION OF A DEFINED BENEFIT VERSUS A DEFINED CONTRIBUTION PLAN

Many corporations and governmental units give their employees a choice between a defined benefit plan and a defined contribution plan. The implications of these plans ought to be understood both by employees and by the agencies responsible for paying the prescribed benefits. Although pension plan status would rarely be the primary factor when choosing a job, it still should be given at least some consideration. Our example does not correspond (to our knowledge) exactly with the plan of any university, but the University of Florida and UCLA do have plans that are similar to our hypothetical University DB (for defined benefit), while the University of Wisconsin and many private colleges have plans similar to our University DC (for defined contribution).

Here are the assumptions used in the illustration:

1. It is now 1987.

2. The employee is 30 years old, earns $30,000 per year, and plans to retire in 35 years, at age 65.

3. Both universities provide for immediate vesting. (This is not always the case.)

4. The rate of inflation is expected to be 6 percent per year. Salaries will also increase at this same rate.

5. Pension fund assets are expected to earn a return of 10 percent.

6. The employee is expected to live for 15 years past retirement at age 65, or to age 80.

University DB: Defined Benefit

This school has a defined benefit plan which offers 2 percent of the average salary paid during the last year the employee works for the university for each year of service at the university. Thus, if the employee worked for one year and then resigned, we would have the following situation:

1. The annual benefit at age 65 would be 0.02($30,000) = $600.

2. The amount needed to establish an annuity of $600 per year for 15 years (assuming payment at the end of each year) would be

$$\text{PV of the annuity} = \$600(\text{PVIFA}_{10\%,15}) = \$4,564.$$

3. The university will have to put up $162 today to provide the required annuity 35 years from now:[7]

$$\text{PV of the PV of the annuity} = \$4,564(\text{PVIF}_{10\%,35}) = \$162.$$

Thus, the cost to the university is $162. (The cost to the university would have been $4,564 had the employee been 64 years old instead of 30; this helps explain why older workers sometimes have a hard time landing jobs.)

4. Given an inflation rate of 6 percent, the real (1987) value of the income for the employee from this pension would be $78 in the first year of retirement:

$$\text{Real income} = \$600(\text{PVIF}_{6\%,35}) = \$78.$$

If the person remained at University DB until retirement, and if his or her salary increased with inflation, then the final salary would be $30,000(\text{FVIF}_{6\%,35})$ = $230,583 per year, and his or her retirement income would be 0.02(35)($230,583) = $161,408, which, in 1987 dollars, would be $21,000, or 70 percent of the 1987 employment income.

University DC: Defined Contribution

This school has a defined contribution plan under which an amount equal to 6 percent of each employee's salary is put into a pension fund account. The fund keeps track of the dollar amount of the contribution attributable to each employee, just as if the university had put the money into a bank time deposit or mutual fund

---

[7]We have assumed that inflation in wages is not built into the funding requirement. If a 6 percent wage inflation were built in, then the cost would rise from $162 to $1,245 (as determined by a simple *Lotus 1-2-3* spreadsheet model).

for the employee. Here is the situation that would exist if the employee worked for one year and then resigned:

1. The university would contribute 0.06($30,000) = $1,800 to the employee's account in the pension fund. This is the university's cost, and it would be the same irrespective of the professor's age.

2. The fund's assets would earn 10 percent per year, so when the employee retired, the value of his or her share of the fund would be

$$\text{Value in fund} = \$1,800(\text{FVIF}_{10\%,35}) = \$50,584.$$

3. At a 10 percent rate of return, this $50,584 would provide an annuity of $6,650 per year for 15 years:

$$\text{Annuity} = \frac{\$50,584}{\text{PVIFA}_{10\%,15}} = \$6,650.$$

4. The real (1987) retirement income for this person would be

$$\text{Real income} = \$6,650(\text{PVIF}_{6\%,35}) = \$865.$$

If the person remained at University DC, his or her retirement fund would accumulate to $1,024,444 over the 35-year employment period (we worked this amount out on a personal computer using *Lotus 1-2-3*). This would provide a retirement income of $134,688, or 58 percent of the $230,583 final salary. The real (1987 dollar) retirement income would be $17,524.

Conclusions

1. A young professor, who has a high probability of moving, would be better off under a defined contribution plan such as the one offered by University DC.

2. A worker who planned to spend his or her entire career at one school would be better off at University DB, with its defined benefit plan.

3. The economic consequences of changing jobs are much worse under the defined benefit plan because benefits are frozen rather than increased with inflation. Therefore, defined benefit plans contribute to lower employee turnover, other factors held constant.

4. It is much more costly to a university (or to a company) to hire older workers if it operates under a defined benefit plan than if it operates under a defined contribution plan. In our example, the 1987 cost to provide pension benefits to a 30-year-old employee under the defined benefit plan would be $162 versus $4,564 for a 64-year-old employee earning the same salary. The average cost per employee to the university would depend on the age distribution of employees. However, the cost would be $1,800 per employee, irrespective of age, under the defined contribution plan. Thus, defined benefit plans carry with them economic incentive to discriminate against older workers in hiring, while defined contribution plans are neutral in this regard.

5. If one were to vary the assumptions, it would be easy to show that employees are generally exposed to more risks under a defined contribution plan, while employers face more risks under a defined benefit plan. In particular, the pension benefits of the defined contribution plan are highly sensitive to changes in the actuarial rate of return on the pension fund's investments. Likewise, the costs to University DB would vary greatly depending on investment performance, but University DC's costs would not vary with respect to changes in investment performance.

6. We could have changed the facts of the example to deal with an "average man" with a life expectancy of 70.6 years and an "average woman" with a 78.2-year life expectancy. Obviously, an average woman would receive benefits over a longer period and thus would need a larger accumulated sum in the plan upon retirement, and hence would have a higher actuarial annual required cost to the university than an average man under the defined benefit plan. Thus, other factors held constant, there is an economic incentive for employers to discriminate against women in their hiring practices if they use defined benefit plans. Defined contribution plans are again neutral in this regard.

DEVELOPING A PLAN STRATEGY

The actual choice of a plan type is often dictated by competitive conditions in the labor market. For example, unions generally seek defined benefit plans in order to cushion the beneficiaries from the investment risks that would exist under a defined contribution or a profit sharing plan. Even if a firm has the economic power to resist a defined benefit plan, it may still agree to one on the grounds that such a plan would, for the reasons set forth above, reduce its turnover rate. However, this advantage must be weighed against the fact that the use of a defined contribution plan would relieve the corporation of the risks of both underfunding and accounting interpretations. In practice, defined contribution and/or profit sharing plans are often used by small firms when they first agree to offer corporate retirement plans to their employees, while larger and more stable firms generally have defined benefit plans.

Assuming that a firm has decided on a defined benefit plan, proper strategic planning requires integrating the plan's funding and investment policies into the company's general corporate policies. The *funding strategy* involves two decisions: (1) How fast should any unfunded liability be reduced, and (2) what rate of return should be assumed in the actuarial calculations? The *investment strategy* also involves two decisions: (1) What rate of return should be targeted, given investment risk considerations, and (2) how should a portfolio that minimizes the risk of not achieving that return be structured?

Pension fund managers use *asset allocation models* to help plan funding and investment strategies. These models examine the risk/return relationships of portfolios with various mixes of assets, including stocks, bonds, T-bills, real estate, international assets, and so on, under different economic scenarios. Several conclusions emerge from such model runs. First, the very nature of pension funds suggests that safety of principal is a paramount consideration, so pension fund managers ought not to "reach" for the highest possible return levels. Second, as we discussed in Chapter 2, for a given level of return, the inclusion of more types of assets generally reduces the portfolio's standard deviation, because asset types are not perfectly correlated. And third, choices among the possible portfolios are limited by the introduction of managerial constraints, such as (1) that the portfolio should not drop more than 30 percent if a 1930s-level depression occurs, and (2) that the portfolio should earn at least 10 percent if a 1970s-level inflation occurs.

Pension fund managers must also consider the impact of portfolio selection and actuarial assumptions on required contributions. First, note that the most commonly used measure of pension plan cost is the ratio of pension contributions to payroll. Now suppose salary inflation heats up to 15 percent, and therefore the company's projected benefit payments under a final pay plan are growing at 15 percent per year for active participants. Such a situation might not affect the percentage of pension costs to payroll costs, because payroll costs inflate rapidly during such times. However, if a company has a large number of retirees, relative to actives, and if the payments to retirees are raised at a rate lower than the inflation rate, while the reinvestment rate rises on those assets held for retirees (because inflation pushes up interest rates), then pension costs as a percentage of payroll might even decline. On the other hand, in a 1930s-style depression, a company with a lot of retirees on defined benefits might be in substantial trouble. For example, suppose production cutbacks caused employees to be laid off, and many of them elected to take early retirement. This would simultaneously reduce payroll expenses but increase retirement benefit expenses. At the same time, the pension fund, if it was heavily invested in stocks, would also decline substantially in price, which in turn would lead to higher required contributions to the fund. For such a company, the pension expenses could become an extremely high percentage of the reduced payroll and operating income.

These examples illustrate the interdependence of business policies, economic conditions, and pension fund planning. Understanding these relationships under alternative economic scenarios requires that managers have information regarding actuarial forecasts of plan liabilities under different scenarios. Pension fund consultants have developed "asset-liability simulators" which produce (1) probability distributions for the plan under different portfolio mixes and (2) probability distributions for plan contributions over time, assuming different investment strategies.[8] These models are helpful, but it is often difficult to develop reasonable assumptions about asset and liability interrelationships under different economic scenarios.

In summary, it is important to understand how a plan's liabilities will change under alternative economic scenarios, and to combine this understanding with projected asset returns under the same scenarios. The use of asset allocation models has resulted in a widespread recognition that portfolios consisting of between

---

[8]An excellent description of several such simulation models is found in the May 1982 *Journal of Finance.* Included are articles by Louis Kingsland, Howard E. Winklevoss, and Alice B. Goldstein and Barbara G. Markowitz, plus excellent discussions of these articles by William F. Sharpe and Irwin Tepper.

25 to 50 percent bonds, and 50 to 75 percent stocks, provide adequate diversification for safety along with a satisfactory expected return. Additionally, it is now recognized that further benefits can be gained by investing in assets other than stocks and bonds. Indeed, many pension funds make minimum commitments to at least four asset categories. A typical minimum commitment might be 25 percent in bills and bonds, 30 percent in domestic stocks, 15 percent in real estate, and 10 percent in international assets, with the remaining 20 percent of the portfolio being available for discretionary investment in whichever category seems best at a particular time.

PENSION FUND INVESTMENT TACTICS

Three characteristics have a major influence on pension funds' investment tactics: (1) the dollar size of a fund's investable assets, (2) the mix of the funds' liabilities between those attributable to active workers and those attributable to retired beneficiaries, and (3) the tax situation facing the corporate sponsor. To show how these characteristics affect funds' investment tactics, we next discuss four topics: (1) performance measurement, (2) equity portfolio risk, (3) bond portfolio risk, and (4) procedures for controlling management fees and transactions costs.

Performance Measurement

Pension fund sponsors need to evaluate the performance of their portfolio managers on a regular basis, and then to use this performance evaluation information as a basis for allocating the fund's assets among portfolio managers. Suppose a fund's common stock portfolio provided a total return of 16 percent during a recent year—is this good, bad, or average performance? To answer this question, the portfolio's market risk (beta) should be estimated, and then the portfolio's return should be compared to the Security Market Line (SML). Suppose, for example, that the "market" portfolio, say the S&P 500, returned 15 percent, that 20-year Treasury bonds returned 9 percent, and that our fund's equity portfolio had a beta of 0.9 (that is, it was invested in stocks that had lower systematic risk than the market). An SML analysis would lead to the visual comparison shown in Figure 23-2, which indicates that the portfolio did better than expected—it is said to have an *alpha* (α) of 1.6 percentage points. Alpha measures the vertical distance of a portfolio's return above or below the Security Market Line. Looked at another way, alpha is the portfolio's extra return (positive or negative) after adjustment for the portfolio's market risk.[9]

---

[9]The Jensen alpha, so-called because this performance measure was first suggested by Professor Michael Jensen, is very popular because of its ease of calculation. Theoretically, its purpose was to measure the performance of a single portfolio versus the market portfolio, after adjusting for the portfolio's beta. However, this measure is not useful in comparing the performance of two portfolios which include real estate and other assets which do not trade actively on the market. This fact has led to the development of a number of other portfolio performance measures. For a discussion of these measures, see Jack L. Treynor and Fischer Black, "How to Use Security Analysis to Improve Portfolio Selection," *Journal of Business*, January 1973, 66-86.

Figure 23-2
SML Analysis

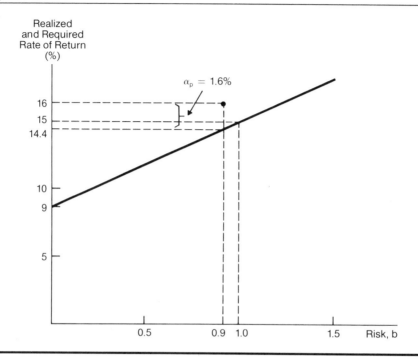

Alpha analysis adds substantially to a pension manager's knowledge about his or her equity portfolio's results, but several shortcomings must be recognized. First, alpha analysis relies on the CAPM, which, as we discussed in Chapter 2, is an ex ante equilibrium concept which in theory requires that all risky assets be included in the market portfolio (for example, human capital and residential real estate), so market proxies such as the Standard and Poor's 500 Index result in some degree of measurement error.[10] Second, the statistical significance of alpha is often too low to make strong statements about the portfolio's relative performance. And third, all of our measurements are based on ex post results which contain both expected returns plus unanticipated returns that resulted from unexpected random economic events. Thus, a large positive alpha may indicate good luck rather than good management, and vice versa.

---

[10]Although managerial performance statistics exhibit about 80 to 90 percent correlation regardless of the index used, Richard Roll presents some interesting examples which show how easily rankings can be changed by measurement procedures. See Richard Roll, "Ambiguity When Performance Is Measured by the Securities Market Line," *Journal of Finance*, September 1978, 1051-1069.

Equity Portfolio Risk

In Chapter 2, we saw that the standard deviation of returns on a portfolio is reduced when assets with less than perfect positive correlation are combined. The
same principle applies to combining portfolios under different management. Further, it is common practice to classify portfolio managers by their stated investment objectives. For example, some managers specialize in emerging high-growth
firms, others specialize in energy-related companies, and still others invest in well-
established, large-capitalization firms. One pension fund consulting firm divides all
managers into five groups, depending on the types of firms included in their portfolios: Group A: high-quality growth firms; Group B: high-yield, low-price volatility
firms; Group C: small, aggressive growth companies; Group D: broadly diversified
companies; and Group E: a mix of all types of firms. Since the groups' returns are
not perfectly correlated, a pension fund manager could, by diversification among
portfolio managers within different groups, control the pension fund's expected
risk/return relationship. If a pension fund manager targets on equaling a specific
index, such as the S&P 500, then the weights assigned to each group would be
chosen to correspond to the weightings of these groups in the index. If a pension
fund manager wants to try to "beat the market," then he or she should attempt to
forecast which groups will perform best, and then "tilt" the allocation to favor
those particular groups.

Fund administrators can manage their funds' assets with company employees
(in-house management) or with external managers (out-of-house management).
Insurance companies and bank trust departments are often used as external managers, but "boutique" managers, who have more flexibility than the major institutions, have had strikingly better performance and are capturing an ever increasing
share of the money management market. Regardless of whether a fund is using
internal or external managers, if different managers specialize in different types of
stocks, then it will be necessary to diversify among managers.

Bond Portfolio Risk

By diversifying broadly to eliminate diversifiable risk, and by selecting stocks with
low betas, a firm can reduce the riskiness inherent in its stock portfolio. Several
devices are also available to help reduce the riskiness of a pension fund's bond
portfolio. First, there is obviously some credit (or default) risk inherent in any
bond other than those issued by the U.S. Treasury (foreign government bonds have
exchange rate risk to U.S. investors), so some type of credit analysis is obviously
required. To a large extent, fund managers restrict their bond holdings to selected
bond ratings: The most conservative plans hold only Treasury bonds, or perhaps
Treasuries plus triple A's, but as the corporate sponsor's tolerance for risk and
quest for returns increases, the fund will purchase lower and lower rated bonds.

In addition to default risk, pension plans' bond portfolios are also exposed to
interest rate risk. To illustrate, consider the situation in which a firm is obligated
to pay a worker a lump sum retirement benefit of $10,000 at the end of 10 years.

Assume that the yield curve is horizontal, so the current interest rate on all Treasury securities is 9 percent, and the fund is restricted to Treasury debt. The present value of $10,000 discounted back 10 years at 9 percent is $10,000(0.4224) = $4,224. Therefore, the firm could invest $4,224 in Treasury bonds and expect to be able to meet its obligation 10 years hence.

Suppose, however, that interest rates change from the current 9 percent rate immediately after the firm has funded its pension plan. How would this affect the situation? The answer is, "It all depends." If rates fall, then the value of the bonds in the portfolio will rise, but this benefit will be offset to a greater or lesser degree by a decline in the rate at which the coupon payment of 0.09($4,224) = $380.16 can be reinvested. The reverse would hold if interest rates rise above 9 percent. Here are some examples (for simplicity, we assume annual coupons):

1. *The fund buys $4,224 of 9 percent, 10-year maturity bonds; rates fall to 7 percent immediately after the purchase and remain at that level:*

$$\text{Portfolio value at the end of 10 years} = (0.09)(\$4,224)(\text{FVIFA}_{7\%,10}) + \$4,224$$

$$= \$5,252 + \$4,224 = \$9,476.$$

Therefore, the fund cannot meet its $10,000 obligation, and the corporation must contribute additional funds.

2. *The fund buys $4,224 of 9 percent, 40-year bonds; rates fall to 7 percent immediately after the purchase and remain at that level:*

$$\text{Portfolio value at the end of 10 years} = \$5,252 + \frac{\text{Value of 30-year, 9\% bonds}}{\text{when } k_d = 7\%}$$

$$= \$5,252 + \$5,272 = \$10,524.$$

In this situation, the fund has excess capital and can return money to the sponsor at the end of the 10-year period.

3. *The fund buys $4,224 of 9 percent, 10-year bonds; rates rise to 12 percent immediately after the purchase and remain at that level:*

$$\text{Portfolio value at the end of 10 years} = (0.09)(\$4,224)(\text{FVIFA}_{12\%,10}) + \$4,224$$

$$= \$6,671 + \$4,224 = \$10,895.$$

This situation also produces a funding surplus.

4. *The fund buys $4,224 of 9 percent, 40-year bonds; rates rise to 12 percent immediately after the purchase and remain at that level:*

$$\text{Portfolio value at the end of 10 years} = \$6,671 + \frac{\text{Value of 30-year, 9\% bonds}}{\text{when } k_d = 12\%}$$

$$= \$6,671 + \$3,203 = \$9,874.$$

This time, a shortfall occurs.

Here are some generalizations we can draw from the examples:

1. If interest rates *fall*, and the portfolio is invested in relatively short-term bonds, then the reinvestment rate penalty exceeds the capital gains, so a net shortfall occurs. However, if the portfolio had been invested in relatively long-term bonds, a drop in rates would produce capital gains which would offset the shortfall caused by low reinvestment rates.

2. If interest rates *rise*, and the portfolio is invested in relatively short-term bonds, then gains from high reinvestment rates will more than offset capital losses, and the final portfolio value will exceed the required amount. However, if the portfolio had been invested in long-term bonds, then capital losses would more than offset reinvestment gains, and a net shortfall would result.

If a company has many employees who are expected to retire at varying times in the future, and if benefits are to be paid on an annual (or monthly) basis from retirement to death rather than as lump sums, the complexity of estimating the effects of interest rate changes is obviously expanded. Still, methods have been devised to help deal with interest rate risk in the management of pension funds. Two methods are discussed in the following sections.

Zero Coupon Bonds and Stripped Treasuries

We discussed zero coupon bonds and stripped Treasury bonds in Chapter 13, where we indicated that they were devised for and are primarily held by pension funds. In our example, in which the fund manager needs $10,000 in 10 years, the purchase of a 10-year zero coupon corporate bond, or a bond due in 10 years that is backed by coupons stripped from Treasury bonds, would eliminate all risks associated with changes in interest rates. The fund manager would, in our example, simply purchase for $4,224 a zero coupon bond which promised to pay $10,000 in 10 years. Note also that if a fund had many employees who were likely to retire at different future dates and who would take annuities rather than lump sum payments, and if the actuaries could make accurate forecasts of cash requirements for each future date, then the fund manager could simply buy many different zero coupon bonds whose maturities matched the fund's cash flow requirements. Thus, zero coupon bonds and bonds backed by stripped Treasuries can be used to take a lot of the uncertainty out of pension fund management.

Immunization

Bond portfolios can be *immunized* against interest rate risk. The details of immunization are best left to investments courses, but, in brief, the process involves selecting maturities for the bonds in a portfolio such that gains or losses from reinvestment exactly match capital gains or losses. To see what is involved, refer to the example in which the fund bought $4,224 of 9 percent Treasury bonds to meet an obligation due 10 years hence. Where interest rates fell from 9 to 7 percent, we saw that a shortfall occurred if the fund bought 10-year bonds, but a surplus arose if the fund bought 40-year bonds. There is some maturity between 10 and 40 years where a breakeven would have occurred. Similarly, in the example where rates rose, there also exists a breakeven maturity within the range from 10 to 40 years.

In investments terminology, what we are seeking is a bond whose *duration* is 10 years, because that is when the $10,000 benefit is due. A bond's duration can be thought of as the "average date" that a holder will receive cash flows (interest and principal repayment) on the bond. For a zero coupon bond, with only one cash inflow, the duration is the same as the maturity. For coupon bonds, the duration is less than the years to maturity. Duration is calculated by use of this formula:

$$\text{Duration} = \sum_{t=1}^{n} \frac{t(\text{PVCF}_t)}{\sum_{t=1}^{n} \text{PVCF}_t} = \sum_{t=1}^{n} \frac{t(\text{PVCF}_t)}{\text{Value}}.$$

Here n is the bond's years to maturity, t is the year each cash flow occurs, and PVCF_t is the present value of the cash flow at Year t discounted at the current rate of interest. Note that the denominator of the equation is merely the current value of the bond.

To illustrate the process, consider a 20-year, 9 percent bond bought at its par value of $4,224. It provides cash flows of 0.09($4,224) = $380.16 per year for 19 years, and $380.16 + $4,224 = $4,604.16 in the twentieth year. For calculating duration, we use the following format:

t	CF	PVCF (9%)	PVCF/Value = PVCF/$4,224	t(PVCF/Value)
1	$ 380.16	$348.77	0.08257	0.08257
2	380.16	319.97	0.07575	0.15150
.	.	.	.	.
.	.	.	.	.
.	.	.	.	.
19	380.16	73.94	0.01750	0.33258
20	4,604.16	821.52	0.19449	3.88979
			Duration =	9.95011

Since this 20-year bond's duration is close to that of the pension fund's liability, if the fund manager bought it and reinvested the coupons as they came in, the accumulated interest payments, plus the value of the bond after 10 years, would be close to $10,000 irrespective of whether interest rates rose, fell, or remained constant at 9 percent. A bond with a maturity slightly over 20 years would have exactly the 10-year duration needed to exactly immunize the fund from interest rate risk.

It is not very difficult to find a bond with a 10-year duration, purchase it, and thus immunize the fund from changes in interest rates with respect to this one future benefit claim. However, the problem becomes vastly more complex when we bring in multiple beneficiaries with nonlump sum claims. Still, it is possible to view a series of future liabilities as a series of separate, single payments, and for a fund manager to immunize each of them by appropriate bond selection.

Unfortunately, other complications arise. Our simple example looked at a single interest rate change which occurred immediately after funding. In reality, interest rates change every day; this causes a bond's duration to change; and this, in turn, requires that bond portfolios be *rebalanced* periodically to maintain immunization. Still, this can be done, and computer programs are available to assist in the rebalancing process, but there is yet another critical requirement for immunization to work for the entire pension fund: The future liabilities must be fixed. However, for most pension liabilities, inflation indexing causes future payments to be variable, not fixed. Such indexing is, of course, clearly inherent in plans with liabilities that are defined in terms of future salaries, which includes most plans. One class of pension liabilities, however, is relatively constant—the benefits owed to those employees who are already retired (termed *retired lives*). Because benefits to present retirees are relatively constant, a recent practice has been to set aside a *dedicated asset pool* in an immunized bond portfolio to provide for these liabilities. Such a practice can reduce and stabilize unfunded liabilities, especially if a company has a large portion of retirees in its plan.

Management of Pension Fund Managers

As indicated in the section on equity portfolio risk, large pension funds usually employ more than one investment manager. The use of multiple managers can help a firm achieve better diversification and earn higher returns by utilizing different managers' specialized knowledge of particular segments of the market. In general, the fund's assets are invested on either an *active* or a *passive* basis. Active managers select stocks with the idea of "beating the market," while passive management is based on the idea of achieving average returns while minimizing transactions costs and management fees.

The simplest method of passive management is to utilize an *index fund*, which is a portfolio whose securities are selected and rebalanced periodically to achieve a rate of return that will be nearly the same as that of an index such as the S&P 500. The goal is to minimize transactions costs and management fees while achieving average returns. The hypothesis underlying this approach is market efficiency, for *if the market is efficient, then all costs and fees associated with active management merely reduce the fund's return*. In practice, index funds often concentrate their purchases on a subset of the securities in the broad index. Recall from our discussion of working capital that an increase in "order size" produces a corresponding reduction in transaction costs. This principle also applies in portfolio management, and it leads to "S&P-like portfolios" which actually have fewer stocks than the S&P 500. Selection of securities for the proxy portfolio is usually done by matching the industrial sector percentages of the portfolio to the mix of the target index.[11]

---

[11]For an excellent discussion of constructing passive portfolios, see Andrew Rudd, "Optimal Selection of Passive Portfolios," *Financial Management*, Spring 1980, 57-66.

Some fund administrators have employed what is called the *active-passive* concept in an attempt to have the pension fund earn more than an index such as the S&P 500. The fund would be set up as follows. First, the plan administrator selects a series of managers with expertise in different segments of the market, and each manager is required to confine his or her purchases to the type of stocks in which the respective managers specialize. Second, each manager is allocated a percentage of the pension fund's equity assets equal to the percentage of the particular group to the index. For example, if a particular manager specializes in energy stocks, and if energy stocks represent 20 percent of the capitalization of the S&P 500 Index, then this manager would be given 20 percent of the pension fund's equity assets to invest. Each manager's allocation would be based on this same principle, and any remaining assets of the fund would be invested on a pro rata basis in those stocks that are not on any manager's list. These residual assets would thus be invested in a passive fund that merely buys and holds the required stocks. Thus, every stock in the index (say the S&P 500) would either be available for purchase by one of the active managers or else held in the passive fund. If the active managers are indeed superior stock-pickers in their specialized areas, then the overall portfolio's excess risk-adjusted return (or "alpha") will be positive.[12]

The effectiveness of the active-passive approach to fund management depends on (1) whether the active managers can produce positive alphas net of fees and transactions costs and (2) the management and transactions costs associated with the passive fund. Thus, the keys to success in using this approach are to select the best active managers and to limit passive funds' costs.

"Tapping" Pension Fund Assets

Corporate sponsors administer defined benefit plans which have assets running into the hundreds of billions of dollars. To what extent should a corporation be able to invest its fund's assets to the corporation's own advantage? Or, if the plan is overfunded because, for example, investment results were better than the actuaries had assumed, or for any other reason, should the company be able to take assets out of the plan? (Obviously, we are talking about defined benefit plans only; companies clearly should not tinker with the assets of a defined contribution or profit sharing plan.) Here are some examples of recent actions which have been called to question:

1. Occidental Petroleum recently acquired Cities Service. The combined pension plans had assets of $700 million, but the vested funding requirement was only $300 million. Occidental terminated the two old plans, replaced them with a new one, and took $400 million out of the fund's assets. Similarly, in 1985, FMC Cor-

---

[12]Robert Monks has argued that it is impossible for pension funds to "beat the market," because they are, in effect, the market. He goes on to assert that pension plan sponsors should replace the active management of securities with active involvement in the long-term operations of the companies that they own. Instead of trying to add value by juggling stocks, he argues that sponsors should add value through active, informed ownership. See the September 2, 1985, issue of *Fortune*, 97-99.

poration filed an application to restructure its plan to recoup about $325 million from it. FMC stated that the benefits of retirees would not be affected by the change in pension plans. FMC's pension investments have earned an average return of about 16 percent over the past 10 years, placing it near the top in performance ratings. FMC has used outside advisors and investment funds for its plan, and the vast bulk of the plan's assets have been invested in stocks. Recent estimates suggest that, in total, corporate pension funds are overfunded by about $300 billion, so there is a lot of scope for actions such as those of Occidental and FMC.[13] Incidentally, the old Occidental plan was a defined benefit plan; the new one is a defined contribution plan.

2. Some cash-short companies have been making required payments to their funds by using their own stock, bonds, and real property used in their operations, rather than cash. This is legal under ERISA provided that a fund has no more than 10 percent of its sponsor's own securities and assets, and provided that the Department of Labor agrees that the transaction is made at a fair price. Thus, Exxon recently contributed a $5.4 million office complex to its plan; Boise Cascade sold timberland worth $16 million to its plan; and U.S. Steel, Alcoa, Armco, Reynolds Metals, and Republic Steel all contributed their own newly issued securities rather than cash.

3. Grumman Corporation, Bendix Corporation, and others have tried to use their pension funds to help thwart hostile takeover attempts, or to help the sponsoring company take over another firm. For example, Grumman's pension fund bought 1.2 million of its shares, paying a 43 percent premium over the pre-bid price, to help fend off a takeover attempt by LTV. The takeover failed, but the fund incurred an immediate $16 million paper loss on these shares.[14] Similarly, Bendix tried (unsuccessfully) to stop its fund's trustee from tendering 4.5 million shares of its stock to Martin Marietta.

These examples raise some interesting issues: Do the excess assets in a defined benefit plan belong to the sponsoring company or to the employees? Legally, they belong to the company, but a number of union leaders have argued that they ought to belong to the workers. Should the PBGC get involved in reversions such as Occidental's? Since Occidental switched from a defined benefit to a defined contribution plan, it left the PBGC's jurisdiction (and also eliminated the $2.60 per employee per year "head tax"), but if it had simply reduced the funding level of a defined benefit plan from overfunded to fully funded, the plan would have been exposed to more risk after assets were removed. Should companies be able to use fund assets to help fight off takeovers? There are no easy answers to these ques-

---

[13]We should point out that this type of action can be taken only (1) when approved by the plan's beneficiaries, (2) in conjunction with the establishment of a new pension plan, and (3) after approval by the Labor Department, Internal Revenue Service, and PBGC if the new plan is a defined benefit plan.

[14]Although the Grumman pension fund eventually made a $13.2 million profit on the Grumman stock it purchased, a lawsuit brought against the plan's trustees resulted in a ruling which held that trustees are liable for actions in using the fund to counter takeover attempts. This ruling sends a clear signal that plan assets must be managed, according to ERISA, for the "sole and exclusive benefit" of beneficiaries.

tions. Obviously, actions which would either violate existing laws or jeopardize the safety of the plan should not be permitted, but many actions are not at all clear-cut. Given the importance of pension plans, it is safe to assume that the debate will continue.

SUMMARY

Because the management of pension fund assets and liabilities has major long-term implications for both corporations and workers, financial managers must plan carefully their strategies for pension fund management. The development of a good strategy requires both a basic knowledge of actuarial concepts and a knowledge of the operating and financial characteristics of the firm. Additionally, an investment strategy must be developed based on (1) the portfolio's average volatility and (2) its relationship to both future pension liabilities and corporate profitability under alternative economic scenarios. The development of such strategies is complex, but extremely important to both workers and investors.

Questions and Problems

23-1 (Benefits and contributions) The Certainty Company (CC) operates in a world of certainty. It has just hired Mr. Jones, age 20, who will retire at age 65, draw retirement benefits for 15 years, and die at age 80. Mr. Jones's salary is $20,000 per year, but wages are expected to increase at the 5 percent annual rate of inflation. CC has a defined benefit plan in which workers receive 1 percent of the final year's wage for each year employed. The retirement benefit, once started, does not have a cost of living adjustment. CC earns 10 percent annually on its pension fund assets. Assume that pension contribution and benefit cash flows occur at year end.

    a. How much will Mr. Jones receive in annual retirement benefits?

    b. What is CC's required annual contribution to fully fund Mr. Jones's retirement benefits?

    c. Assume now that CC hires Mr. Smith at the same $20,000 salary as Mr. Jones. However, Mr. Smith is 45 years old. Repeat the analysis in Parts a and b under the same assumptions used for Mr. Jones. What do the results imply about the costs of hiring older versus younger workers?

    d. Now assume that CC hires Ms. Brown, age 20, at the same time that it hires Mr. Smith. Ms. Brown is expected to retire at age 65 and to live to age 90. What is CC's annual pension cost for Ms. Brown? If Mr. Smith and Ms. Brown are doing the same work, are they truly doing it for the same pay? Would it be "reasonable" for CC to lower Ms. Brown's annual retirement benefit to a level that would mean that she received the same present value as Mr. Smith?

23-2 (Performance measurement) Mitchell Metals, Inc., has a small pension fund which is managed by a professional portfolio manager. All of the fund's assets are invested in corporate equities. Last year, the portfolio manager realized a rate of return of 18 percent. The risk-free rate was 10 percent and the market risk premium was 6 percent. The portfolio's beta was 1.2.

    a. Compute the portfolio's alpha.

b. What does the portfolio alpha imply about the manager's performance last year? What can Mitchell Metal's financial manager conclude about the portfolio manager's performance next year?

23-3 **(Plan funding)** Vanderheiden Industries is planning to operate for 10 more years and then cease operations. At that time (in 10 years), it expects to have the following pension benefit obligations:

Years	Annual Total Payment
11-15	$2,500,000
16-20	2,000,000
21-25	1,500,000
26-30	1,000,000
31-35	500,000

The current value of Vanderheiden's pension fund is $6 million. Assume that all cash flows occur at year end.

a. Vanderheiden's actuarial rate of return is 10 percent. What is the present value of the firm's pension fund benefits?

b. Is the plan underfunded or overfunded?

23-4 **(Duration)** A small corporation wishes to provide a lump sum retirement benefit to its founder and president, Dan Smith. Dan will retire in 10 years; his benefit at that time will be $100,000. His firm plans to fully fund this benefit now through the purchase of high grade bonds. As an outside consultant, you have been asked to assist in choosing among available alternatives.

a. Dan would like the firm to purchase a new Treasury issue which will mature at the time of his retirement 10 years hence. The issue is selling at par, with a 7.5 percent coupon, paid semiannually. The firm's treasurer, Jim Yoder, feels that an issue he has chosen is better suited for the purpose. He has located a T-bond which is also selling at a 7.5 percent yield. The bond carries a coupon rate of 9.25 percent (also paid semiannually). It was issued one year ago with an original maturity of 20 years. Dan thinks that Jim has lost his financial acumen and has obviously made a mistake, since he will need the funds in 10 years, rather than 19. Which of the two alternatives given do you recommend? Why?

b. What assumptions were necessary to make your recommendation for Part a?

c. What other bond investment might you suggest for Dan? (No calculation is necessary.)

d. Suppose that Dan changes his mind about retirement in 10 years and decides to work 20 more years until retirement. Would the bonds originally purchased to fund his retirement still be appropriate? Why or why not?

(Do Parts e and f only if you are using the computerized diskette.)

e. Suppose the bond suggested by Mr. Yoder had an annual coupon. Now what would its duration be? Explain why duration is affected by the type of coupon.

f. Assume that semiannual Treasury bonds with a 9.25 percent coupon and 7.5 percent yield are available in any maturity. Which maturity should be chosen if Dan decides to retire in 5 years?

23-5 **(Pension plan reporting)** Examine the annual report of any large U.S. corporation. Where are the pension fund data located? What effect does this information have on the firm's financial condition?

23-6 (Diversification) A firm's pension fund assets are currently invested only in domestic stocks and bonds. The outside manager recommends that assets such as precious metals, real estate, and foreign financial assets be added to the fund. What effect would the addition of these assets have on the fund's risk/return trade-off?

23-7 (Pension fund types) How does the type of pension fund a company uses influence each of the following:
    a. The likelihood of age discrimination in hiring?
    b. The likelihood of sex discrimination in hiring?
    c. Employee training costs?
    d. The likelihood that union leaders will be "flexible" if a company faces a changed economic environment such as have faced the airline, steel, and auto industries in recent years?

23-8 (Insurance premiums) Should employers be required to pay the same "head tax" to PBGC irrespective of the financial condition of their plans?

Selected Additional References

For more information on how pension fund management has been affected by the Employee Retirement Income Security Act of 1974 (ERISA), including the establishment of the Pension Benefit Guarantee Corporation (PBGC), see

Treynor, Jack L., W. Priest, and Patrick J. Regan, *The Financial Reality of Pension Funding Under ERISA* (Homewood, Ill.: Dow Jones-Irwin, 1976).

The following articles provide additional insights into the relationship between pension plan funding and capital costs:

Malley, Susan L., "Unfunded Pension Liabilities and the Cost of Equity Capital," *Financial Review*, May 1983, 133-145.

Regan, Patrick J., "Pension Fund Perspective: Credit Ratings and Pension Costs," *Financial Analysts Journal*, September-October 1983, 19-23.

Other pertinent works include

Black, Fischer, "The Tax Consequences of Long-Run Pension Policy," *Financial Analysts Journal*, July-August 1980, 25-31.

Bodie, Zvi, and J. Shoren, eds., *Financial Aspects of the United States Pension System* (Chicago: University of Chicago Press, 1983).

Copeland, Thomas E., "An Economic Approach to Pension Fund Management," *Midland Corporate Finance Journal*, Spring 1984, 26-39.

Munnell, Alicia H., "Guaranteeing Private Pension Benefits: A Potentially Expensive Business," *New England Economic Review*, March-April 1982, 24-47.

Oldfield, G. S. "Financial Aspects of the Private Pension System," *Journal of Money, Credit and Banking*, February 1977, 48-54.

For an excellent discussion of the relationship between pension funding policy and the firm's overall financial policy, see

Bodie, Zvi, Jay O. Light, Randall Morck, and Robert A. Taggart, Jr., "Funding and Asset Allocation in Corporate Pension Plans: An Empirical Investigation," National Bureau of Economic Research Working Paper #1315.

For more information on duration and immunization, see any of the investment textbooks referred to in Chapter 2, or see

Schaefer, Stephen M., "Immunisation and Duration: A Review of Theory, Performance and Applications," *Midland Corporate Finance Journal*, Fall 1984, 41-58.

A

REVIEW OF
DISCOUNTED CASH
FLOW ANALYSIS

This appendix provides a brief review of the principles of discounted cash flow analysis, and it also contains interest factor tables and the values of the areas under the normal distribution function.[1]

FUTURE VALUES

In general, FV_n, the future value of a lump sum at the end of n periods, is found as follows:

$$FV_n = PV(1 + k)^n. \tag{A-1}$$

Here PV = present value, k = interest rate per period, and n = number of periods. The period may be one year, but it may also be six months, one quarter, one month, or one day. If the period is one month, the interest rate will be approximately 1/12 the annual rate. We define the term *future value interest factor for k,n ($FVIF_{k,n}$)* to equal $(1 + k)^n$. Therefore, Equation A-1 can be written as follows:

$$FV_n = PV(FVIF_{k,n}). \tag{A-1a}$$

---

[1]Most people who use this book will have covered discounted cash flow analysis and the "math of finance" in other courses. This appendix is designed for those who have not, or those who need a review of DCF concepts.

A set of future value interest factors is given in Table A-1.[2]

PRESENT VALUES

In general, the present value of a sum due n periods in the future is the amount which, if it were on hand today, would grow to equal the future sum. Finding present values (or *discounting*, as it is commonly called) is simply the reverse of finding future values, or *compounding*, and Equation A-1 can be solved for PV to transform it into a present value formula:

$$PV = \frac{FV_n}{(1 + k)^n} = FV_n(1 + k)^{-n} = FV_n(PVIF_{k,n}). \qquad \text{(A-2)}$$

Tables have been constructed for $(1 + k)^{-n}$ for various values of k and n; see Table A-2. We define $(1 + k)^{-n} = PVIF_{k,n}$ as the *present value interest factor*.

FUTURE VALUE VERSUS PRESENT VALUE

The present value interest factor ($PVIF_{k,n}$) developed from Equation A-2, the basic equation for discounting, was found as the *reciprocal* of the future value interest factor ($FVIF_{k,n}$) for the same k,n combination. In other words,

$$PVIF_{k,n} = \frac{1}{FVIF_{k,n}}.$$

The reciprocal nature of the relationship between present value and future value permits us to find present values in two ways—by multiplying or by dividing. Thus, the present value of a lump sum may be found as

$$PV = FV_n(PVIF_{k,n}) = FV_n\left(\frac{1}{1 + k}\right)^n,$$

or as

$$PV = \frac{FV_n}{FVIF_{k,n}} = \frac{FV_n}{(1 + k)^n}.$$

---

[2]Note that the interest factors given in the tables can be determined with greater accuracy using a financial calculator. For example, to find the future value interest factor for 10 periods at 10 percent, enter PV = 1, i = 10%, n = 10, and then determine the future value (FV). The answer is 2.593742460, which is the appropriate future value interest factor. We could also calculate the factor by finding the solution to $(1.10)^{10}$, using the exponential function on a calculator.

FUTURE VALUE OF AN ANNUITY

An *annuity* is defined as a series of payments of a fixed amount for a specified number of periods. If payments, which are given the symbol PMT, occur at the end of each period, as they typically do, then we have an *ordinary annuity*, or a *deferred annuity* as it is sometimes called. If payments are made at the beginning of each period, then we have an *annuity due*.

Ordinary Annuities

If we define FVA_n = future value of an annuity, PMT = periodic payment, n = length of the annuity, and $FVIFA_{k,n}$ as the future value interest factor for an annuity, then

$$FVA_n = PMT(1 + k)^{n-1} + PMT(1 + k)^{n-2} + \ldots + PMT(1 + k)^1 + PMT(1 + k)^0$$

$$= PMT[(1 + k)^{n-1} + (1 + k)^{n-2} + \ldots + (1 + k)^1 + (1 + k)^0]$$

$$= PMT\sum_{t=1}^{n} (1 + k)^{n-t} = PMT(FVIFA_{k,n}). \tag{A-3}$$

The expression in parentheses, $FVIFA_{k,n}$, has been calculated for various combinations of k and n. A set of these future value annuity interest factors is given in Table A-3.[3]

A look at Table A-3 will show that for all positive interest rates, $FVIFA_{k,n}$ is always equal to or greater than the number of periods the annuity runs. Also note that the entry for each value of n in Table A-3 is equal to the sum of 1.0000 plus the entries in Table A-1 up to and including Period n − 1. For example, the FVIFA for 4 percent, 3 periods, as shown in Table A-3, could have been calculated from Table A-1 as follows:

$$1.0000 + 1.0400 + 1.0816 = 3.1216.$$

Annuities Due

If payments are made at the beginning of the year, the annuity is an *annuity due*. We can modify Equation A-3 to handle annuities due as follows:

$$FVA_n(\text{Annuity due}) = PMT(FVIFA_{k,n})(1 + k). \tag{A-3a}$$

---

[3]The equation given with Table A-3 recognizes that an FVIFA factor is the sum of a geometric progression. The proof of this equation is given in all college algebra texts. Notice that it is easy to use the equation to develop annuity factors. This is especially useful if you need the FVIFA for some interest rate not given in the tables, for example, 6.5 percent, or if you must find the factor for a fractional period—for example, $2\frac{1}{2}$ years. However, one needs a calculator with an exponential function for either calculation. Note also that annuity interest factors can be found using a financial calculator in a fashion similar to that described in Footnote 2.

Each payment is compounded for one extra year, and multiplying $PMT(FVIFA_{k,n})$ by $(1 + k)$ takes care of this extra compounding.

PRESENT VALUE OF AN ANNUITY

Ordinary Annuities

The present value of an annuity is found as the sum of the PVs of the periodic payments. The present value of the first payment is $PMT[1/(1 + k)]$, the second is $PMT[1/(1 + k)]^2$, and so on. Defining the present value of an annuity of n years as PVA_n, and with $PVIFA_{k,n}$ defined as the present value interest factor for an annuity, we may write the following equation in its several equivalent forms:

$$PVA_n = PMT\left(\frac{1}{1 + k}\right)^1 + PMT\left(\frac{1}{1 + k}\right)^2 + \ldots + PMT\left(\frac{1}{1 + k}\right)^n$$

$$= PMT\left[\frac{1}{(1 + k)^1} + \frac{1}{(1 + k)^2} + \ldots + \frac{1}{(1 + k)^n}\right]$$

$$= PMT \sum_{t=1}^{n}\left(\frac{1}{1 + k}\right)^t = PMT(PVIFA_{k,n}). \qquad \text{(A-4)}$$

Again, tables such as Table A-4 have been worked out for $PVIFA_{k,n}$. Notice that the entry for each value of n in Table A-4 is equal to the sum of the entries in Table A-2 up to and including Period n. For example, the PVIFA for 4 percent, 3 periods, as shown in Table A-4, could have been calculated by summing values from Table A-2:

$$0.9615 + 0.9246 + 0.8890 = 2.7751.$$

Observe also from Table A-4 that for all positive interest rates, $PVIFA_{k,n}$ is always less than the number of periods the annuity runs, whereas $FVIFA_{k,n}$ is equal to or greater than the number of periods.

Annuities Due

If the payments occur at the beginning of each year, the annuity is an annuity due. To account for the earlier payment pattern, we modify Equation A-4 as follows:

$$PVA_n(\text{Annuity due}) = PMT(PVIFA_{k,n})(1 + k). \qquad \text{(A-4a)}$$

Since each payment comes earlier, an annuity due is worth more than an ordinary annuity.

COMPOUNDING PERIODS OTHER THAN ANNUAL

Thus far, we have assumed that compounding occurs on an annual basis. However, this is not always the case. When compounding periods are more frequent than once a year, we use a modified version of Equation A-1:

$$\text{Annual compounding: } FV_n = PV(1 + k)^n. \tag{A-1}$$

$$\text{More frequent compounding: } FV_n = PV\left(1 + \frac{k_{Nom}}{m}\right)^{mn}. \tag{A-1b}$$

Here k_{Nom} is the nominal, or stated, annual rate; m is the number of times per year compounding occurs; and n is the number of years. When banks compute daily interest, the value of m is set at 365, and Equation A-1b is applied.

The interest tables can be used when compounding occurs more than once a year. Simply divide the nominal interest rate by the number of times compounding occurs, and multiply the years by the number of compounding periods per year. The same procedure is applied in all the cases covered—compounding, discounting, single payments, and annuities. However, note that for annuities, the corresponding period must match the payment period.

CONTINUOUS COMPOUNDING AND DISCOUNTING

By letting m approach infinity, Equation A-1b can be modified to the special case of *continuous compounding*. Continuous compounding is extremely useful in theoretical finance, and it also has practical applications. For example, some financial institutions pay interest on a continuous basis.

Continuous Compounding

For some purposes, it is better to assume instantaneous, or *continuous*, growth. Equation A-1b, developed earlier, allows for any number of compounding periods per year:

$$\text{More frequent compounding: } FV_n = PV\left(1 + \frac{k_{Nom}}{m}\right)^{mn}. \tag{A-1b}$$

Here m could equal 1 (annual compounding), 2 (semiannual compounding), 12 (monthly compounding), or 365 (daily compounding). We could keep going, compounding every hour, every minute, every second, every 1/1000th of a second, and so on. At the limit, we could compound every instant, or continuously. The equation for the future value of a lump sum at the end of n periods under continuous compounding is

$$FV_n = PV(e^{kn}), \tag{A-5}$$

where e is the value 2.7183···. This equation must be evaluated with a calculator that has an exponential or an antilogarithm function.

Continuous Discounting

Equation A-5 can be transformed into Equation A-6 and used to determine present values under continuous discounting:

$$PV = \frac{FV_n}{e^{kn}} = FV_n(e^{-kn}). \tag{A-6}$$

AMORTIZED LOANS

One important application of compound interest concepts involves loans that are to be paid off in installments over time. Examples include automobile loans, home mortgage loans, and business term loans. If a loan is to be repaid in equal periodic amounts (monthly, quarterly, or annually), it is said to be an *amortized loan*.[4]

To illustrate, suppose a firm borrows $1,000 to be repaid in three equal payments at the end of each of the next 3 years. The bank is to receive 6 percent interest on the funds that are outstanding at each point in time. The first task is to determine the amount the firm must repay each year, or the annual payment. To find this amount, recognize that the $1,000 represents the present value of an annuity of PMT dollars per year for 3 years, discounted at 6 percent:

$$\$1,000 = \text{PV of annuity} = \text{PMT}(\text{PVIFA}_{6\%,3 \text{ years}}). \tag{A-4}$$

The PVIFA is 2.6730, so

$$\$1,000 = \text{PMT}(2.6730).$$

Solving for PMT, we obtain

$$\text{PMT} = \$1,000/2.6730 = \$374.11.$$

If the firm pays the bank $374.11 at the end of each of the next 3 years, the percentage cost to the borrower, and the rate of return to the lender, will be 6 percent.

---

[4]The word *amortize* comes from the Latin *mort*, meaning "dead," so an amortized loan is one that is "killed off" over time.

Each payment consists partly of interest and partly of a repayment of principal. This breakdown is given in the *amortization schedule* shown below:

Year	Payment (1)	Interest (2)	Repayment of Principal (3)	Remaining Balance (4)
1	$ 374.11	$ 60.00	$ 314.11	$685.89
2	374.11	41.15	332.96	352.93
3	374.11	21.18	352.93	0
	$1,122.33	$122.33	$1,000.00	

The interest component is largest in the first year, and it declines as the outstanding balance of the loan goes down. Note that interest is calculated by multiplying the loan balance at the beginning of the year by the interest rate. Therefore, interest in Year 1 is $1,000(0.06) = $60; in Year 2, interest is $685.89(0.06) = $41.15; and in Year 3, interest is $352.93(0.06) = $21.18. Also notice that the repayment of principal is equal to the payment of $374.11 minus the interest charge in each year.

AREAS UNDER THE NORMAL CURVE

Although not related directly to discounted cash flow analysis, Table A-5 contains the values of areas under the standard normal distribution function. The values are required (1) to determine probabilities of occurrence when the random variable has a normal distribution and (2) to calculate the value of a call option using the Black-Scholes Option Pricing Model (OPM).[5]

---

[5]Normal distributions are discussed in Appendix 2A, while the Black-Scholes Option Pricing Model is discussed in Chapter 15.

Table A-1
Future Value of $1 at the End of n Periods

$FVIF_{k,n} = (1 + k)^n$

Period	1%	2%	3%	4%	5%	6%	7%	8%	9%	10%
1	1.0100	1.0200	1.0300	1.0400	1.0500	1.0600	1.0700	1.0800	1.0900	1.1000
2	1.0201	1.0404	1.0609	1.0816	1.1025	1.1236	1.1449	1.1664	1.1881	1.2100
3	1.0303	1.0612	1.0927	1.1249	1.1576	1.1910	1.2250	1.2597	1.2950	1.3310
4	1.0406	1.0824	1.1255	1.1699	1.2155	1.2625	1.3108	1.3605	1.4116	1.4641
5	1.0510	1.1041	1.1593	1.2167	1.2763	1.3382	1.4026	1.4693	1.5386	1.6105
6	1.0615	1.1262	1.1941	1.2653	1.3401	1.4185	1.5007	1.5869	1.6771	1.7716
7	1.0721	1.1487	1.2299	1.3159	1.4071	1.5036	1.6058	1.7138	1.8280	1.9487
8	1.0829	1.1717	1.2668	1.3686	1.4775	1.5938	1.7182	1.8509	1.9926	2.1436
9	1.0937	1.1951	1.3048	1.4233	1.5513	1.6895	1.8385	1.9990	2.1719	2.3579
10	1.1046	1.2190	1.3439	1.4802	1.6289	1.7908	1.9672	2.1589	2.3674	2.5937
11	1.1157	1.2434	1.3842	1.5395	1.7103	1.8983	2.1049	2.3316	2.5804	2.8531
12	1.1268	1.2682	1.4258	1.6010	1.7959	2.0122	2.2522	2.5182	2.8127	3.1384
13	1.1381	1.2936	1.4685	1.6651	1.8856	2.1329	2.4098	2.7196	3.0658	3.4523
14	1.1495	1.3195	1.5126	1.7317	1.9799	2.2609	2.5785	2.9372	3.3417	3.7975
15	1.1610	1.3459	1.5580	1.8009	2.0789	2.3966	2.7590	3.1722	3.6425	4.1772
16	1.1726	1.3728	1.6047	1.8730	2.1829	2.5404	2.9522	3.4259	3.9703	4.5950
17	1.1843	1.4002	1.6528	1.9479	2.2920	2.6928	3.1588	3.7000	4.3276	5.0545
18	1.1961	1.4282	1.7024	2.0258	2.4066	2.8543	3.3799	3.9960	4.7171	5.5599
19	1.2081	1.4568	1.7535	2.1068	2.5270	3.0256	3.6165	4.3157	5.1417	6.1159
20	1.2202	1.4859	1.8061	2.1911	2.6533	3.2071	3.8697	4.6610	5.6044	6.7275
21	1.2324	1.5157	1.8603	2.2788	2.7860	3.3996	4.1406	5.0338	6.1088	7.4002
22	1.2447	1.5460	1.9161	2.3699	2.9253	3.6035	4.4304	5.4365	6.6586	8.1403
23	1.2572	1.5769	1.9736	2.4647	3.0715	3.8197	4.7405	5.8715	7.2579	8.9543
24	1.2697	1.6084	2.0328	2.5633	3.2251	4.0489	5.0724	6.3412	7.9111	9.8497
25	1.2824	1.6406	2.0938	2.6658	3.3864	4.2919	5.4274	6.8485	8.6231	10.835
26	1.2953	1.6734	2.1566	2.7725	3.5557	4.5494	5.8074	7.3964	9.3992	11.918
27	1.3082	1.7069	2.2213	2.8834	3.7335	4.8223	6.2139	7.9881	10.245	13.110
28	1.3213	1.7410	2.2879	2.9987	3.9201	5.1117	6.6488	8.6271	11.167	14.421
29	1.3345	1.7758	2.3566	3.1187	4.1161	5.4184	7.1143	9.3173	12.172	15.863
30	1.3478	1.8114	2.4273	3.2434	4.3219	5.7435	7.6123	10.063	13.268	17.449
40	1.4889	2.2080	3.2620	4.8010	7.0400	10.286	14.974	21.725	31.409	45.259
50	1.6446	2.6916	4.3839	7.1067	11.467	18.420	29.457	46.902	74.358	117.39
60	1.8167	3.2810	5.8916	10.520	18.679	32.988	57.946	101.26	176.03	304.48

Table A-1
Continued

Period	12%	14%	15%	16%	18%	20%	24%	28%	32%	36%
1	1.1200	1.1400	1.1500	1.1600	1.1800	1.2000	1.2400	1.2800	1.3200	1.3600
2	1.2544	1.2996	1.3225	1.3456	1.3924	1.4400	1.5376	1.6384	1.7424	1.8496
3	1.4049	1.4815	1.5209	1.5609	1.6430	1.7280	1.9066	2.0972	2.3000	2.5155
4	1.5735	1.6890	1.7490	1.8106	1.9388	2.0736	2.3642	2.6844	3.0360	3.4210
5	1.7623	1.9254	2.0114	2.1003	2.2878	2.4883	2.9316	3.4360	4.0075	4.6526
6	1.9738	2.1950	2.3131	2.4364	2.6996	2.9860	3.6352	4.3980	5.2899	6.3275
7	2.2107	2.5023	2.6600	2.8262	3.1855	3.5832	4.5077	5.6295	6.9826	8.6054
8	2.4760	2.8526	3.0590	3.2784	3.7589	4.2998	5.5895	7.2058	9.2170	11.703
9	2.7731	3.2519	3.5179	3.8030	4.4355	5.1598	6.9310	9.2234	12.166	15.917
10	3.1058	3.7072	4.0456	4.4114	5.2338	6.1917	8.5944	11.806	16.060	21.647
11	3.4785	4.2262	4.6524	5.1173	6.1759	7.4301	10.657	15.112	21.199	29.439
12	3.8960	4.8179	5.3503	5.9360	7.2876	8.9161	13.215	19.343	27.983	40.037
13	4.3635	5.4924	6.1528	6.8858	8.5994	10.699	16.386	24.759	36.937	54.451
14	4.8871	6.2613	7.0757	7.9875	10.147	12.839	20.319	31.691	48.757	74.053
15	5.4736	7.1379	8.1371	9.2655	11.974	15.407	25.196	40.565	64.359	100.71
16	6.1304	8.1372	9.3576	10.748	14.129	18.488	31.243	51.923	84.954	136.97
17	6.8660	9.2765	10.761	12.468	16.672	22.186	38.741	66.461	112.14	186.28
18	7.6900	10.575	12.375	14.463	19.673	26.623	48.039	85.071	148.02	253.34
19	8.6128	12.056	14.232	16.777	23.214	31.948	59.568	108.89	195.39	344.54
20	9.6463	13.743	16.367	19.461	27.393	38.338	73.864	139.38	257.92	468.57
21	10.804	15.668	18.822	22.574	32.324	46.005	91.592	178.41	340.45	637.26
22	12.100	17.861	21.645	26.186	38.142	55.206	113.57	228.36	449.39	866.67
23	13.552	20.362	24.891	30.376	45.008	66.247	140.83	292.30	593.20	1178.7
24	15.179	23.212	28.625	35.236	53.109	79.497	174.63	374.14	783.02	1603.0
25	17.000	26.462	32.919	40.874	62.669	95.396	216.54	478.90	1033.6	2180.1
26	19.040	30.167	37.857	47.414	73.949	114.48	268.51	613.00	1364.3	2964.9
27	21.325	34.390	43.535	55.000	87.260	137.37	332.95	784.64	1800.9	4032.3
28	23.884	39.204	50.066	63.800	102.97	164.84	412.86	1004.3	2377.2	5483.9
29	26.750	44.693	57.575	74.009	121.50	197.81	511.95	1285.6	3137.9	7458.1
30	29.960	50.950	66.212	85.850	143.37	237.38	634.82	1645.5	4142.1	10143.
40	93.051	188.88	267.86	378.72	750.38	1469.8	5455.9	19427.	66521.	*
50	289.00	700.23	1083.7	1670.7	3927.4	9100.4	46890.	*	*	*
60	897.60	2595.9	4384.0	7370.2	20555.	56348.	*	*	*	*

*FVIF > 99,999.

Table A-2
Present Value of $1 Due at the End of n Periods

$$PVIF_{k,n} = \frac{1}{(1 + k)^n}$$

Period	1%	2%	3%	4%	5%	6%	7%	8%	9%	10%
1	.9901	.9804	.9709	.9615	.9524	.9434	.9346	.9259	.9174	.9091
2	.9803	.9612	.9426	.9246	.9070	.8900	.8734	.8573	.8417	.8264
3	.9706	.9423	.9151	.8890	.8638	.8396	.8163	.7938	.7722	.7513
4	.9610	.9238	.8885	.8548	.8227	.7921	.7629	.7350	.7084	.6830
5	.9515	.9057	.8626	.8219	.7835	.7473	.7130	.6806	.6499	.6209
6	.9420	.8880	.8375	.7903	.7462	.7050	.6663	.6302	.5963	.5645
7	.9327	.8706	.8131	.7599	.7107	.6651	.6227	.5835	.5470	.5132
8	.9235	.8535	.7894	.7307	.6768	.6274	.5820	.5403	.5019	.4665
9	.9143	.8368	.7664	.7026	.6446	.5919	.5439	.5002	.4604	.4241
10	.9053	.8203	.7441	.6756	.6139	.5584	.5083	.4632	.4224	.3855
11	.8963	.8043	.7224	.6496	.5847	.5268	.4751	.4289	.3875	.3505
12	.8874	.7885	.7014	.6246	.5568	.4970	.4440	.3971	.3555	.3186
13	.8787	.7730	.6810	.6006	.5303	.4688	.4150	.3677	.3262	.2897
14	.8700	.7579	.6611	.5775	.5051	.4423	.3878	.3405	.2992	.2633
15	.8613	.7430	.6419	.5553	.4810	.4173	.3624	.3152	.2745	.2394
16	.8528	.7284	.6232	.5339	.4581	.3936	.3387	.2919	.2519	.2176
17	.8444	.7142	.6050	.5134	.4363	.3714	.3166	.2703	.2311	.1978
18	.8360	.7002	.5874	.4936	.4155	.3503	.2959	.2502	.2120	.1799
19	.8277	.6864	.5703	.4746	.3957	.3305	.2765	.2317	.1945	.1635
20	.8195	.6730	.5537	.4564	.3769	.3118	.2584	.2145	.1784	.1486
21	.8114	.6598	.5375	.4388	.3589	.2942	.2415	.1987	.1637	.1351
22	.8034	.6468	.5219	.4220	.3418	.2775	.2257	.1839	.1502	.1228
23	.7954	.6342	.5067	.4057	.3256	.2618	.2109	.1703	.1378	.1117
24	.7876	.6217	.4919	.3901	.3101	.2470	.1971	.1577	.1264	.1015
25	.7798	.6095	.4776	.3751	.2953	.2330	.1842	.1460	.1160	.0923
26	.7720	.5976	.4637	.3604	.2812	.2198	.1722	.1352	.1064	.0839
27	.7644	.5859	.4502	.3468	.2678	.2074	.1609	.1252	.0976	.0763
28	.7568	.5744	.4371	.3335	.2551	.1956	.1504	.1159	.0895	.0693
29	.7493	.5631	.4243	.3207	.2429	.1846	.1406	.1073	.0822	.0630
30	.7419	.5521	.4120	.3083	.2314	.1741	.1314	.0994	.0754	.0573
35	.7059	.5000	.3554	.2534	.1813	.1301	.0937	.0676	.0490	.0356
40	.6717	.4529	.3066	.2083	.1420	.0972	.0668	.0460	.0318	.0221
45	.6391	.4102	.2644	.1712	.1113	.0727	.0476	.0313	.0207	.0137
50	.6080	.3715	.2281	.1407	.0872	.0543	.0339	.0213	.0134	.0085
55	.5785	.3365	.1968	.1157	.0683	.0406	.0242	.0145	.0087	.0053

Table A-2
Continued

Period	12%	14%	15%	16%	18%	20%	24%	28%	32%	36%
1	.8929	.8772	.8696	.8621	.8475	.8333	.8065	.7813	.7576	.7353
2	.7972	.7695	.7561	.7432	.7182	.6944	.6504	.6104	.5739	.5407
3	.7118	.6750	.6575	.6407	.6086	.5787	.5245	.4768	.4348	.3975
4	.6355	.5921	.5718	.5523	.5158	.4823	.4230	.3725	.3294	.2923
5	.5674	.5194	.4972	.4761	.4371	.4019	.3411	.2910	.2495	.2149
6	.5066	.4556	.4323	.4104	.3704	.3349	.2751	.2274	.1890	.1580
7	.4523	.3996	.3759	.3538	.3139	.2791	.2218	.1776	.1432	.1162
8	.4039	.3506	.3269	.3050	.2660	.2326	.1789	.1388	.1085	.0854
9	.3606	.3075	.2843	.2630	.2255	.1938	.1443	.1084	.0822	.0628
10	.3220	.2697	.2472	.2267	.1911	.1615	.1164	.0847	.0623	.0462
11	.2875	.2366	.2149	.1954	.1619	.1346	.0938	.0662	.0472	.0340
12	.2567	.2076	.1869	.1685	.1372	.1122	.0757	.0517	.0357	.0250
13	.2292	.1821	.1625	.1452	.1163	.0935	.0610	.0404	.0271	.0184
14	.2046	.1597	.1413	.1252	.0985	.0779	.0492	.0316	.0205	.0135
15	.1827	.1401	.1229	.1079	.0835	.0649	.0397	.0247	.0155	.0099
16	.1631	.1229	.1069	.0980	.0708	.0541	.0320	.0193	.0118	.0073
17	.1456	.1078	.0929	.0802	.0600	.0451	.0258	.0150	.0089	.0054
18	.1300	.0946	.0808	.0691	.0508	.0376	.0208	.0118	.0068	.0039
19	.1161	.0829	.0703	.0596	.0431	.0313	.0168	.0092	.0051	.0029
20	.1037	.0728	.0611	.0514	.0365	.0261	.0135	.0072	.0039	.0021
21	.0926	.0638	.0531	.0443	.0309	.0217	.0109	.0056	.0029	.0016
22	.0826	.0560	.0462	.0382	.0262	.0181	.0088	.0044	.0022	.0012
23	.0738	.0491	.0402	.0329	.0222	.0151	.0071	.0034	.0017	.0008
24	.0659	.0431	.0349	.0284	.0188	.0126	.0057	.0027	.0013	.0006
25	.0588	.0378	.0304	.0245	.0160	.0105	.0046	.0021	.0010	.0005
26	.0525	.0331	.0264	.0211	.0135	.0087	.0037	.0016	.0007	.0003
27	.0469	.0291	.0230	.0182	.0115	.0073	.0030	.0013	.0006	.0002
28	.0419	.0255	.0200	.0157	.0097	.0061	.0024	.0010	.0004	.0002
29	.0374	.0224	.0174	.0135	.0082	.0051	.0020	.0008	.0003	.0001
30	.0334	.0196	.0151	.0116	.0070	.0042	.0016	.0006	.0002	.0001
35	.0189	.0102	.0075	.0055	.0030	.0017	.0005	.0002	.0001	*
40	.0107	.0053	.0037	.0026	.0013	.0007	.0002	.0001	*	*
45	.0061	.0027	.0019	.0013	.0006	.0003	.0001	*	*	*
50	.0035	.0014	.0009	.0006	.0003	.0001	*	*	*	*
55	.0020	.0007	.0005	.0003	.0001	*	*	*	*	*

*The factor is zero to four decimal places.

Table A-3
Future Value of Annuity of $1 per Period for n Periods

$$\text{FVIFA}_{k,n} = \sum_{t=1}^{n} (1 + k)^{n-t} = \frac{(1 + k)^n - 1}{k}$$

Number of Periods	1%	2%	3%	4%	5%	6%	7%	8%	9%	10%
1	1.0000	1.0000	1.0000	1.0000	1.0000	1.0000	1.0000	1.0000	1.0000	1.0000
2	2.0100	2.0200	2.0300	2.0400	2.0500	2.0600	2.0700	2.0800	2.0900	2.1000
3	3.0301	3.0604	3.0909	3.1216	3.1525	3.1836	3.2149	3.2464	3.2781	3.3100
4	4.0604	4.1216	4.1836	4.2465	4.3101	4.3746	4.4399	4.5061	4.5731	4.6410
5	5.1010	5.2040	5.3091	5.4163	5.5256	5.6371	5.7507	5.8666	5.9847	6.1051
6	6.1520	6.3081	6.4684	6.6330	6.8019	6.9753	7.1533	7.3359	7.5233	7.7156
7	7.2135	7.4343	7.6625	7.8983	8.1420	8.3938	8.6540	8.9228	9.2004	9.4872
8	8.2857	8.5830	8.8923	9.2142	9.5491	9.8975	10.260	10.637	11.028	11.436
9	9.3685	9.7546	10.159	10.583	11.027	11.491	11.978	12.488	13.021	13.579
10	10.462	10.950	11.464	12.006	12.578	13.181	13.816	14.487	15.193	15.937
11	11.567	12.169	12.808	13.486	14.207	14.972	15.784	16.645	17.560	18.531
12	12.683	13.412	14.192	15.026	15.917	16.870	17.888	18.977	20.141	21.384
13	13.809	14.680	15.618	16.627	17.713	18.882	20.141	21.495	22.953	24.523
14	14.947	15.974	17.086	18.292	19.599	21.015	22.550	24.215	26.019	27.975
15	16.097	17.293	18.599	20.024	21.579	23.276	25.129	27.152	29.361	31.772
16	17.258	18.639	20.157	21.825	23.657	25.673	27.888	30.324	33.003	35.950
17	18.430	20.012	21.762	23.698	25.840	28.213	30.840	33.750	36.974	40.545
18	19.615	21.412	23.414	25.645	28.132	30.906	33.999	37.450	41.301	45.599
19	20.811	22.841	25.117	27.671	30.539	33.760	37.379	41.446	46.018	51.159
20	22.019	24.297	26.870	29.778	33.066	36.786	40.995	45.762	51.160	57.275
21	23.239	25.783	28.676	31.969	35.719	39.993	44.865	50.423	56.765	64.002
22	24.472	27.299	30.537	34.248	38.505	43.392	49.006	55.457	62.873	71.403
23	25.716	28.845	32.453	36.618	41.430	46.996	53.436	60.893	69.532	79.543
24	26.973	30.422	34.426	39.083	44.502	50.816	58.177	66.765	76.790	88.497
25	28.243	32.030	36.459	41.646	47.727	54.865	63.249	73.106	84.701	98.347
26	29.526	33.671	38.553	44.312	51.113	59.156	68.676	79.954	93.324	109.18
27	30.821	35.344	40.710	47.084	54.669	63.706	74.484	87.351	102.72	121.10
28	32.129	37.051	42.931	49.968	58.403	68.528	80.698	95.339	112.97	134.21
29	33.450	38.792	45.219	52.966	62.323	73.640	87.347	103.97	124.14	148.63
30	34.785	40.568	47.575	56.085	66.439	79.058	94.461	113.28	136.31	164.49
40	48.886	60.402	75.401	95.026	120.80	154.76	199.64	259.06	337.88	442.59
50	64.463	84.579	112.80	152.67	209.35	290.34	406.53	573.77	815.08	1163.9
60	81.670	114.05	163.05	237.99	353.58	533.13	813.52	1253.2	1944.8	3034.8

Table A-3
Continued

Number of Periods	12%	14%	15%	16%	18%	20%	24%	28%	32%	36%
1	1.0000	1.0000	1.0000	1.0000	1.0000	1.0000	1.0000	1.0000	1.0000	1.0000
2	2.1200	2.1400	2.1500	2.1600	2.1800	2.2000	2.2400	2.2800	2.3200	2.3600
3	3.3744	3.4396	3.4725	3.5056	3.5724	3.6400	3.7776	3.9184	4.0624	4.2096
4	4.7793	4.9211	4.9934	5.0665	5.2154	5.3680	5.6842	6.0156	6.3624	6.7251
5	6.3528	6.6101	6.7424	6.8771	7.1542	7.4416	8.0484	8.6999	9.3983	10.146
6	8.1152	8.5355	8.7537	8.9775	9.4420	9.9299	10.980	12.136	13.406	14.799
7	10.089	10.730	11.067	11.414	12.142	12.916	14.615	16.534	18.696	21.126
8	12.300	13.233	13.727	14.240	15.327	16.499	19.123	22.163	25.678	29.732
9	14.776	16.085	16.786	17.519	19.086	20.799	24.712	29.369	34.895	41.435
10	17.549	19.337	20.304	21.321	23.521	25.959	31.643	38.593	47.062	57.352
11	20.655	23.045	24.349	25.733	28.755	32.150	40.238	50.398	63.122	78.998
12	24.133	27.271	29.002	30.850	34.931	39.581	50.895	65.510	84.320	108.44
13	28.029	32.089	34.352	36.786	42.219	48.497	64.110	84.853	112.30	148.47
14	32.393	37.581	40.505	43.672	50.818	59.196	80.496	109.61	149.24	202.93
15	37.280	43.842	47.580	51.660	60.965	72.035	100.82	141.30	198.00	276.98
16	42.753	50.980	55.717	60.925	72.939	87.442	126.01	181.87	262.36	377.69
17	48.884	59.118	65.075	71.673	87.068	105.93	157.25	233.79	347.31	514.66
18	55.750	68.394	75.836	84.141	103.74	128.12	195.99	300.25	459.45	700.94
19	63.440	78.969	88.212	98.603	123.41	154.74	244.03	385.32	607.47	954.28
20	72.052	91.025	102.44	115.38	146.63	186.69	303.60	494.21	802.86	1298.8
21	81.699	104.77	118.81	134.84	174.02	225.03	377.46	633.59	1060.8	1767.4
22	92.503	120.44	137.63	157.41	206.34	271.03	469.06	812.00	1401.2	2404.7
23	104.60	138.30	159.28	183.60	244.49	326.24	582.63	1040.4	1850.6	3271.3
24	118.16	158.66	184.17	213.98	289.49	392.48	723.46	1332.7	2443.8	4450.0
25	133.33	181.87	212.79	249.21	342.60	471.98	898.09	1706.8	3226.8	6053.0
26	150.33	208.33	245.71	290.09	405.27	567.38	1114.6	2185.7	4260.4	8233.1
27	169.37	238.50	283.57	337.50	479.22	681.85	1383.1	2798.7	5624.8	11198.0
28	190.70	272.89	327.10	392.50	566.48	819.22	1716.1	3583.3	7425.7	15230.3
29	214.58	312.09	377.17	456.30	669.45	984.07	2129.0	4587.7	9802.9	20714.2
30	241.33	356.79	434.75	530.31	790.95	1181.9	2640.9	5873.2	12941.	28172.3
40	767.09	1342.0	1779.1	2360.8	4163.2	7343.9	22729.	69377.	*	*
50	2400.0	4994.5	7217.7	10436.	21813.	45497.	*	*	*	*
60	7471.6	18535.	29220.	46058.	*	*	*	*	*	*

*FVIFA > 99,999.

Table A-4
Present Value of an Annuity of $1 per Period for n Periods

$$PVIFA_{k,n} = \sum_{t=1}^{n} \frac{1}{(1 + k)^t} = \frac{1 - \dfrac{1}{(1 + k)^n}}{k} = \frac{1}{k} - \frac{1}{k(1 + k)^n}$$

Number of Periods	1%	2%	3%	4%	5%	6%	7%	8%	9%
1	0.9901	0.9804	0.9709	0.9615	0.9524	0.9434	0.9346	0.9259	0.9174
2	1.9704	1.9416	1.9135	1.8861	1.8594	1.8334	1.8080	1.7833	1.7591
3	2.9410	2.8839	2.8286	2.7751	2.7232	2.6730	2.6243	2.5771	2.5313
4	3.9020	3.8077	3.7171	3.6299	3.5460	3.4651	3.3872	3.3121	3.2397
5	4.8534	4.7135	4.5797	4.4518	4.3295	4.2124	4.1002	3.9927	3.8897
6	5.7955	5.6014	5.4172	5.2421	5.0757	4.9173	4.7665	4.6229	4.4859
7	6.7282	6.4720	6.2303	6.0021	5.7864	5.5824	5.3893	5.2064	5.0330
8	7.6517	7.3255	7.0197	6.7327	6.4632	6.2098	5.9713	5.7466	5.5348
9	8.5660	8.1622	7.7861	7.4353	7.1078	6.8017	6.5152	6.2469	5.9952
10	9.4713	8.9826	8.5302	8.1109	7.7217	7.3601	7.0236	6.7101	6.4177
11	10.3676	9.7868	9.2526	8.7605	8.3064	7.8869	7.4987	7.1390	6.8052
12	11.2551	10.5753	9.9540	9.3851	8.8633	8.3838	7.9427	7.5361	7.1607
13	12.1337	11.3484	10.6350	9.9856	9.3936	8.8527	8.3577	7.9038	7.4869
14	13.0037	12.1062	11.2961	10.5631	9.8986	9.2950	8.7455	8.2442	7.7862
15	13.8651	12.8493	11.9379	11.1184	10.3797	9.7122	9.1079	8.5595	8.0607
16	14.7179	13.5777	12.5611	11.6523	10.8378	10.1059	9.4466	8.8514	8.3126
17	15.5623	14.2919	13.1661	12.1657	11.2741	10.4773	9.7632	9.1216	8.5436
18	16.3983	14.9920	13.7535	12.6593	11.6896	10.8276	10.0591	9.3719	8.7556
19	17.2260	15.6785	14.3238	13.1339	12.0853	11.1581	10.3356	9.6036	8.9501
20	18.0456	16.3514	14.8775	13.5903	12.4622	11.4699	10.5940	9.8181	9.1285
21	18.8570	17.0112	15.4150	14.0292	12.8212	11.7641	10.8355	10.0168	9.2922
22	19.6604	17.6580	15.9369	14.4511	13.1630	12.0416	11.0612	10.2007	9.4424
23	20.4558	18.2922	16.4436	14.8568	13.4886	12.3034	11.2722	10.3711	9.5802
24	21.2434	18.9139	16.9355	15.2470	13.7986	12.5504	11.4693	10.5288	9.7066
25	22.0232	19.5235	17.4131	15.6221	14.0939	12.7834	11.6536	10.6748	9.8226
26	22.7952	20.1210	17.8768	15.9828	14.3752	13.0032	11.8258	10.8100	9.9290
27	23.5596	20.7069	18.3270	16.3296	14.6430	13.2105	11.9867	10.9352	10.0266
28	24.3164	21.2813	18.7641	16.6631	14.8981	13.4062	12.1371	11.0511	10.1161
29	25.0658	21.8444	19.1885	16.9837	15.1411	13.5907	12.2777	11.1584	10.1983
30	25.8077	22.3965	19.6004	17.2920	15.3725	13.7648	12.4090	11.2578	10.2737
35	29.4086	24.9986	21.4872	18.6646	16.3742	14.4982	12.9477	11.6546	10.5668
40	32.8347	27.3555	23.1148	19.7928	17.1591	15.0463	13.3317	11.9246	10.7574
45	36.0945	29.4902	24.5187	20.7200	17.7741	15.4558	13.6055	12.1084	10.8812
50	39.1961	31.4236	25.7298	21.4822	18.2559	15.7619	13.8007	12.2335	10.9617
55	42.1472	33.1748	26.7744	22.1086	18.6335	15.9905	13.9399	12.3186	11.0140

Table A-4
Continued

Number of Periods	10%	12%	14%	15%	16%	18%	20%	24%	28%	32%
1	0.9091	0.8929	0.8772	0.8696	0.8621	0.8475	0.8333	0.8065	0.7813	0.7576
2	1.7355	1.6901	1.6467	1.6257	1.6052	1.5656	1.5278	1.4568	1.3916	1.3315
3	2.4869	2.4018	2.3216	2.2832	2.2459	2.1743	2.1065	1.9813	1.8684	1.7663
4	3.1699	3.0373	2.9137	2.8550	2.7982	2.6901	2.5887	2.4043	2.2410	2.0957
5	3.7908	3.6048	3.4331	3.3522	3.2743	3.1272	2.9906	2.7454	2.5320	2.3452
6	4.3553	4.1114	3.8887	3.7845	3.6847	3.4976	3.3255	3.0205	2.7594	2.5342
7	4.8684	4.5638	4.2883	4.1604	4.0386	3.8115	3.6046	3.2423	2.9370	2.6775
8	5.3349	4.9676	4.6389	4.4873	4.3436	4.0776	3.8372	3.4212	3.0758	2.7860
9	5.7590	5.3282	4.9464	4.7716	4.6065	4.3030	4.0310	3.5655	3.1842	2.8681
10	6.1446	5.6502	5.2161	5.0188	4.8332	4.4941	4.1925	3.6819	3.2689	2.9304
11	6.4951	5.9377	5.4527	5.2337	5.0286	4.6560	4.3271	3.7757	3.3351	2.9776
12	6.8137	6.1944	5.6603	5.4206	5.1971	4.7932	4.4392	3.8514	3.3868	3.0133
13	7.1034	6.4235	5.8424	5.5831	5.3423	4.9095	4.5327	3.9124	3.4272	3.0404
14	7.3667	6.6282	6.0021	5.7245	5.4675	5.0081	4.6106	3.9616	3.4587	3.0609
15	7.6061	6.8109	6.1422	5.8474	5.5755	5.0916	4.6755	4.0013	3.4834	3.0764
16	7.8237	6.9740	6.2651	5.9542	5.6685	5.1624	4.7296	4.0333	3.5026	3.0882
17	8.0216	7.1196	6.3729	6.0472	5.7487	5.2223	4.7746	4.0591	3.5177	3.0971
18	8.2014	7.2497	6.4674	6.1280	5.8178	5.2732	4.8122	4.0799	3.5294	3.1039
19	8.3649	7.3658	6.5504	6.1982	5.8775	5.3162	4.8435	4.0967	3.5386	3.1090
20	8.5136	7.4694	6.6231	6.2593	5.9288	5.3527	4.8696	4.1103	3.5458	3.1129
21	8.6487	7.5620	6.6870	6.3125	5.9731	5.3837	4.8913	4.1212	3.5514	3.1158
22	8.7715	7.6446	6.7429	6.3587	6.0113	5.4099	4.9094	4.1300	3.5558	3.1180
23	8.8832	7.7184	6.7921	6.3988	6.0442	5.4321	4.9245	4.1371	3.5592	3.1197
24	8.9847	7.7843	6.8351	6.4338	6.0726	5.4509	4.9371	4.1428	3.5619	3.1210
25	9.0770	7.8431	6.8729	6.4641	6.0971	5.4669	4.9476	4.1474	3.5640	3.1220
26	9.1609	7.8957	6.9061	6.4906	6.1182	5.4804	4.9563	4.1511	3.5656	3.1227
27	9.2372	7.9426	6.9352	6.5135	6.1364	5.4919	4.9636	4.1542	3.5669	3.1233
28	9.3066	7.9844	6.9607	6.5335	6.1520	5.5016	4.9697	4.1566	3.5679	3.1237
29	9.3696	8.0218	6.9830	6.5509	6.1656	5.5098	4.9747	4.1585	3.5687	3.1240
30	9.4269	8.0552	7.0027	6.5660	6.1772	5.5168	4.9789	4.1601	3.5693	3.1242
35	9.6442	8.1755	7.0700	6.6166	6.2153	5.5386	4.9915	4.1644	4.5708	3.1248
40	9.7791	8.2438	7.1050	6.6418	6.2335	5.5482	4.9966	4.1659	3.5712	3.1250
45	9.8628	8.2825	7.1232	6.6543	6.2421	5.5523	4.9986	4.1664	3.5714	3.1250
50	9.9148	8.3045	7.1327	6.6605	6.2463	5.5541	4.9995	4.1666	3.5714	3.1250
55	9.9471	8.3170	7.1376	6.6636	6.2482	5.5549	4.9998	4.1666	3.5714	3.1250

Table A-5
Values of the Areas under the Standard Normal Distribution Function

z	0.00	0.01	0.02	0.03	0.04	0.05	0.06	0.07	0.08	0.09
0.0	.0000	.0040	.0080	.0120	.0160	.0199	.0239	.0279	.0319	.0359
0.1	.0398	.0438	.0478	.0517	.0557	.0596	.0636	.0675	.0714	.0753
0.2	.0793	.0832	.0871	.0910	.0948	.0987	.1026	.1064	.1103	.1141
0.3	.1179	.1217	.1255	.1293	.1331	.1368	.1406	.1443	.1480	.1517
0.4	.1554	.1591	.1628	.1664	.1700	.1736	.1772	.1808	.1844	.1879
0.5	.1915	.1950	.1985	.2019	.2054	.2088	.2123	.2157	.2190	.2224
0.6	.2257	.2291	.2324	.2357	.2389	.2422	.2454	.2486	.2517	.2549
0.7	.2580	.2611	.2642	.2673	.2704	.2734	.2764	.2794	.2823	.2852
0.8	.2881	.2910	.2939	.2967	.2995	.3023	.3051	.3078	.3106	.3133
0.9	.3159	.3186	.3212	.3238	.3264	.3289	.3315	.3340	.3365	.3389
1.0	.3413	.3438	.3461	.3485	.3508	.3531	.3554	.3577	.3599	.3621
1.1	.3643	.3665	.3686	.3708	.3729	.3749	.3770	.3790	.3810	.3830
1.2	.3849	.3869	.3888	.3907	.3925	.3944	.3962	.3980	.3997	.4015
1.3	.4032	.4049	.4066	.4082	.4099	.4115	.4131	.4147	.4162	.4177
1.4	.4192	.4207	.4222	.4236	.4251	.4265	.4279	.4292	.4306	.4319
1.5	.4332	.4345	.4357	.4370	.4382	.4394	.4406	.4418	.4429	.4441
1.6	.4452	.4463	.4474	.4484	.4495	.4505	.4515	.4525	.4535	.4545
1.7	.4554	.4564	.4573	.4582	.4591	.4599	.4608	.4616	.4625	.4633
1.8	.4641	.4649	.4656	.4664	.4671	.4678	.4686	.4693	.4699	.4706
1.9	.4713	.4719	.4726	.4732	.4738	.4744	.4750	.4756	.4761	.4767
2.0	.4773	.4778	.4783	.4788	.4793	.4798	.4803	.4808	.4812	.4817
2.1	.4821	.4826	.4830	.4834	.4838	.4842	.4846	.4850	.4854	.4857
2.2	.4861	.4864	.4868	.4871	.4875	.4878	.4881	.4884	.4887	.4890
2.3	.4893	.4896	.4898	.4901	.4904	.4906	.4909	.4911	.4913	.4916
2.4	.4918	4920	.4922	.4925	.4927	.4929	.4931	.4932	.4934	.4936
2.5	.4938	.4940	.4941	.4943	.4945	.4946	.4948	.4949	.4951	.4952
2.6	.4953	.4955	.4956	.4957	.4959	.4960	.4961	.4962	.4963	.4964
2.7	.4965	.4966	.4967	.4968	.4969	.4970	.4971	.4972	.4973	.4974
2.8	.4974	.4975	.4976	.4977	.4977	.4978	.4979	.4979	.4980	.4981
2.9	.4981	.4982	.4982	.4982	.4984	.4984	.4985	.4985	.4986	.4986
3.0	.4987	.4987	.4987	.4988	.4988	.4989	.4989	.4989	.4990	.4990

 # B

ANSWERS TO SELECTED END-OF-CHAPTER PROBLEMS

We present here some of the intermediate steps and final answers to selected end-of-chapter problems. These are provided to aid the student in determining whether he or she is on the right track in the solution process. The primary limitation of this approach is that some of the problems may have more than one correct solution, depending upon which of several equally appropriate assumptions are made in the solution. Furthermore, there are often differences in answers due to rounding errors or other computational differences. Many of the problems involve some verbal discussion as well as numerical calculations. This verbal material is not presented here.

2-1   a. $1 million.
      d. (1) 15%.

2-3   a. $\hat{k}_A = 13.5\%; \sigma_A^2 = 4.75; \sigma_A = 2.2\%; CV_A = 0.16.$
      $\hat{k}_B = 13.25\%; \sigma_B^2 = 10.19; \sigma_B = 3.2\%; CV_B = 0.24.$
      $\hat{k}_C = 12.0\%; \sigma_C^2 = 2.0; \sigma_C = 1.4\%; CV_C = 0.12.$
      b. A dominates B.

2-4   a. 12.9%.
      b. $\sigma_p^2 = 1.69; \sigma_p = 1.3\%.$
      c. Cov(AB) = 6.63; $r_{AB} = 0.94.$
         Cov(AC) = $-3.00; r_{AC} = -0.97.$
      d. $b_B = 1.4; b_C = -0.6.$

2-5   a. $\hat{k}_A = 10.0\%; \sigma_A^2 = 0.0; \sigma_A = 0.0\%; CV_A = 0.0.$
      $\hat{k}_B = 14.0\%; \sigma_B^2 = 76.0; \sigma_B = 8.7\%; CV_B = 0.62.$
      $\hat{k}_C = 12.0\%; \sigma_C^2 = 73.6; \sigma_C = 8.6\%; CV_C = 0.72.$
      $\hat{k}_M = 15.0\%; \sigma_M^2 = 40.0; \sigma_M = 6.3\%; CV_M = 0.42.$

      d. $b_A = 0.0; b_B = 1.25; b_C = -1.30; b_M = 1.0.$
         $k_A = 10.0\%; k_B = 16.3\%; k_C = 3.5\%; k_M = 15.0\%.$

2-6   a. $\hat{k}_M = 14.5\%; \hat{k}_p = 16.25\%.$
      b. $b_M = 1.0; b_p = 1.43.$
      c. 17.3%.

2-8   a. $\bar{k}_A$ (Avg) = $\bar{k}_B$ (Avg) = $\bar{k}_p$ (Avg) = 11.4%.
      b. $\sigma_A = 21.9\%; \sigma_B = 21.9\%; \sigma_p = 21.3\%.$
      c. 0.9.

2-9   a. 15.6%.
      b. (1) $k_M = 15\%; k_A = 16.6\%.$
         (2) $k_M = 13\%; k_A = 14.6\%.$
      c. (1) $k_A = 17.0\%.$
         (2) $k_A = 12.8\%.$
      d. (1) $k_A = 16.4\%.$
         (2) $k_A = 13.0\%.$

2-10 a. $k_i = 7\% + b_i (5\%).$
      b. $b_p = 1.75; k_p = 15.75\%.$
      c. No, k = 19.5%, but $\hat{k}$ = 16.0%; $\hat{k}$ = 19.5%.

2-11 a. 0.56.
  b. $\bar{k}_X$ (Avg) = 10.6%; $\bar{k}_M$ (Avg) = 12.1%.
   σ_X = 13.1%; σ_M = 22.6%.
  c. 8.6%.
2-12 a. 0.62.
2-16 a. $\hat{k}_A$ = 15.0%; σ_A = 12.8%.
  b. 71.5%.
  h. b_A = 0.74; b_B = 1.47.

3-1 a. (1) $1,392.01.
   (2) $1,081.44.
   (3) $862.35.
  b. (1) $1,038.27.
   (2) $1,009.36.
   (3) $981.67.
3-2 a. 12%.
  b. $1,182.56.
  c. 10.15; −0.15%.
  d. 14%; 14.49%.
  e. 13.38%; 0.62%.
  f. 8.52%.
3-3 a. 3.40%.
  b. 6.98%.
  c. $853.13.
  d. $1,000 plus accrued interest.
  f. CY(74) = 5.23%; CY(86) = 3.99%.
   CGY(74) = 1.75%; CGY(86) = 2.99%.
   TY(74) = TY(86) = 6.98%.
3-4 a. YTM = 9.00%; YTC = 7.73%.
  d. YTM = 8.20%; YTC = 4.58%.
  e. YTM = 13.23%; YTC = 23.13%.
3-5 a. $1,487 to $1,730.
  b. Closer to $1,487, call is likely.
  c. 7.76%, the YTC.
3-6 a. 13.28%.
  b. 13.72%.
  c. (1) 9.51%.
   (2) 9.61%.
3-7 a. 11.76%.
  b. 12.29%.
  c. (1) 8.47%.
   (2) 10.96%.
  d. 14.41%.
3-9 a. $21.60.
3-10 a. $22.22.
  b. $23.44.
3-12 a. $0; $0; $0.50; $0.515; $0.530; $0.562.
  b. $3.99.
  c. 0.0%, 15.0%, 15.0%; 0.0%, 15.0%, 15.0%; 9.5%, 5.5%, 15.0%.

3-13 a. $36.46; 6.86%; 7.16%.
  c. 8.0%; 6.0%.
3-14 a. $1.95; $2.54; $3.30; $4.28; $5.57; $6.01.
  b. $97.32.
  c. 2.0%, 10.0%, 12.0%; 4.0%, 8.0%, 12.0%.
  d. 1991.
  e. $1.73; $1.98; $2.28; $2.62; $3.02; $3.20; $38.37.
  f. $25.17; $15.79; $11.40.
3-15 a. $22.26.
  b. $888.07; 9.74%.
  d. $863.
  e. 13.55% vs. 10.38% as compared to 10.39% vs. 9.74%.
3-16 a. 7.03%.
  b. 6.90%.
  c. 6.61%.
  d. (1) (a) 11.93%.
     (b) 11.68%.
     (c) 10.59%.
   (2) (a) 10.94%.
     (b) 6.90%.
     (c) 6.61%.

4-1 a. 8.0%.
  b. EPS = $2.16; DPS = $0.86.
  c. 12.0%.
  d. 15.0%; 12.7%.
4-2 a. 14.0%.
  b. 14.4%.
  c. (1) 11.1%.
   (2) 11.4%.
4-3 a. 9.08%.
  b. 11.4%.
  c. 8.27%.
  d. Average = 8.44%, 7.76%; log-linear = 7.71%, 7.09%.
  e. 10.80%; 10.40%; 9.94%.
  f. k_e = 13.43%, 12.85%, 12.20%; WACC = 10.99%, 10.58%, 10.12%.
4-4 STD = 11%; LTD = 22%; CE = 67%.
4-7 a. k_d (1 − T) = 7.92%; k_p = 11.58%; k_s = 15.5%; k_e = 16.3%.
  b. With retained earnings, 13.0%; new common stock, 13.5%.
4-8 With retained earnings, 15.3%; new common stock, 15.7%.

5-1 a. $20,000,000.
  b. 10%; 15%.
  c. $10,000,000.
  d. 10%; 10%.

5-2   a. V_U = \$12,000,000; V_L = \$16,000,000.
       b. k_{sU} = 10%; k_{sL} = 15%.
       c. \$6,000,000.
       d. 10%; 7.5%.
       e. COR_U = 10%; COR_L = 7.5%.

5-3   a. 9.6 million.
       b. \$12.93 million.
       c. \$3.33 million vs. \$4 million.
       d. \$20 million; \$0.
       e. \$16 million; \$4 million.
       f. \$12.64 million; \$4 million.

5-4   a. \$14,545,455; \$14,545,455.
       b. \$0 debt: k_a = 11%, k_s = 11%; \$6 million debt: k_a = 11%, k_s = 14.51%; \$10 million debt: k_a = 11%, k_s = 22%.
       c. \$0 debt: \$8,727,273; \$6 million debt: \$11,127,273.
       d. \$0 debt: k_a = 11%, k_s = 11%; \$6 million debt: k_a = 8.63%, k_s = 14.51%; \$10 million debt: k_a = 7.54%, k_s = 22.0%.
       e. \$14,545,455; \$14,545,455; 11%.

5-6   a. Project A: \$32.5 million; Project B: \$30 million.
       b. Project B.
       c. Project B.
       d. Project A.

5-8   a. \$10 million.

5-10 a. \$15 million.
       b. \$7.5 million debt; \$6.7 million equity.
       d. \$7.5 million debt; \$9.7 million equity.
       e. \$10.0 million debt; \$2.0 million equity.
       f. \$10.0 million debt; \$4.75 million equity.

6-1   a. ROE_C = 15.0%; σ_C = 11.0%.

6-2   a. 1.13.
       b. 15.65%; 5.65%.
       c. (1) 16.65%; 1.0%.
          (2) 18.07%; 2.42%.
          (3) 20.27%; 4.62%.
       d. 20.27%; 4.62%.

6-3   a. Yes.
       b. \$2 million.
       c. \$20.28; \$17.96.
       d. \$2.10; \$2.33; \$2.69.

6-4   a. Yes.
       b. Increase, 47.17% vs. 44.44%; Increase, 45.45 units vs. 40 units.

6-5   a. S = \$16.72 million; P_0 = \$27.87; V = \$18.72 million.
       b. 14.1%.
       c. Yes; V = \$20,870,588; P_0 = \$31.45; k_a = 12.65%.
       d. V = \$20,692,549; P_0 = \$31.71.
       e. 20× vs. 3.33×.

6-6   a. V = \$3,283,636.
       b. P_0 = \$16.42.
       c. EPS_{OLD} = \$1.50; EPS_{NEW} = \$1.81.
       d. \$900,000 debt distribution.
       e. 10%.

6-7   a. 14.0%.
       b. Yes, \$30 million debt.
       c. \$38.85.
       d. Yes, \$70 million debt.
       e. P_0 = \$51.03.
       f. (1) EPS = \$10.62; σ_{EPS} = \$8.84.
          (2) TIE = 2.03×; σ_{TIE} = 0.85×.

6-8   a. \$2.25; \$2.70.

7-1 NPV_S = \$814.33; NPV_L = \$1,675.34; IRR_S = 15.24%; IRR_L = 14.67%; PI_S = 1.081; PI_L = 1.067.

7-2   a. $Payback_X$ = 2.17 yrs.; $Payback_Y$ = 2.86 yrs.; ARR_X = 31.9%; ARR_Y = 33.3%; NPV_X = \$966.01; NPV_Y = \$630.72; IRR_X = 18.0%; IRR_Y = 15.0%; PI_X = 1.10; PI_Y = 1.06.
       b. X and Y.
       c. X.
       D. Crossover rate: 6.2%.

7-6   b. IRR_A = 18.1%; IRR_B = 24.0%.
       c. k = 10%: A; k = 17%: B.
       d. 14.53%.
       e. Worst: IRR_A = 16.67%; IRR_B = 19.86%.
          Best: IRR_A = 19.30%; IRR_B = 26.54%.
          Worst: k = 10%: A; k = 17%: B.
          Best: k = 10%: A; k = 17%: B.
       f. k = 0%: NPV_A = \$890; NPV_B = \$399; k = 5%: NPV_A = \$540; NPV_B = \$275; k = 20%: NPV_A = −\$49; NPV_B = −\$41; k = 400%: NPV_A = −\$385; NPV_B = −\$372.

7-7   a. Yr. 1: −\$10,250,000; Yrs. 2–20: \$1,750,000.
       b. 16.07%.
       d. IRR_A = 20%; IRR_B = 16.7%; Crossover = 16.07%.

7-8   a. NPV_A = \$18,108,510; NPV_B = \$13,946,117; IRR_A = 15.03%; IRR_B = 22.26%.
       b. NPV = \$4,162,393; IRR = 11.71%.

7-9   b. No; Yes.

7-10 $<13\%$ or $>76\%$.

7-11   a. Undefined.
      b. PV cost$_C$ = $-$ \$911,067; PV cost$_F$ = $-$ \$838,834; Forklifts.

8-1   \$784,785.

8-2   a. $-$ \$62,000.
      b. \$20,160; \$19,920; \$19,920.
      c. \$14,000.
      d. No, NPV = $-$ \$1,725.

8-3   a. $-$ \$212,500.
      b. \$73,198; \$72,501; \$72,501.
      c. \$60,300.
      d. Yes, NPV = \$13,737.
      e. \$5,178; \$22,856.
      f. $-$ \$1,139; \$18,696; \$52,000.
      g. \$4,555.
      h. $-$ \$621; \$199,100.

8-4   a. $-$ \$88,400.
      b. \$47,280; \$46,770; \$46,770; \$29,940; \$29,940.
      c. $-$ \$10,000.
      d. NPV = \$45,862; Yes.

8-5   a. $-$ \$880,000.
      b. Change in depreciation: \$140,000; \$284,000; \$140,000; \$68,000; \$68,000.
      c. \$221,000; \$278,600; \$221,000; \$192,200; \$192,200.
      d. \$105,000.
      e. NPV = \$33,011; Buy.
      g. NPV = \$16,366.
      h. NPV = $-$ \$2,262.
      i. NPV = \$37,967.

8-6   a. NPV$_{190-3}$ = \$11,982; NPV$_{360-6}$ = \$22,256; EAA$_{190-3}$ = \$5,161; EAA$_{360-6}$ = \$5,723.
      b. Yrs. 1-6: Model 360-6; Yrs. 7-9: Model 190-3.

8-7   a. 3 yrs.; NPV = \$1,307.

8-8   a. \$397; \$1,669.60.

8-9   a. Yes, NPV = \$106,537.

8-10 a. 11.6%; 5.28%.
      b. \$7,657; \$7,582; \$7,582; real WACC.
      c. \$1,811; Accept.
      d. \$7,963; \$8,213; \$8,556; \$1,085.
      e. \$7,769; \$7,799; \$7,895; NPV = $-$ \$283.

9-1   a. \$1,463.35.
      b. \$1,541.93.

9-2   a. \$24,900.19.
      c. \$24,900.19; \$29,904; 1.20.
      d. 12%; Accept, NPV = \$18,356.97.

9-3   a. 0.72.
      b. 1.04.
      c. Yes, k$_s$ = 15.2%, k$_a$ = 12.8%.

9-4   Oil; PV cost$_C$ = $-$ \$5,137,930; PV cost$_O$ = $-$ \$4,645,190.

9-5   a. NPV = \$117,779.
      b. σ_{NPV} = \$445,060; CV$_{NPV}$ = 3.78.

9-7   a. 16.5%.
      b. k$_{TD}$ = 18%; k$_{RD}$ = 12%; NPV$_{TD}$ = $-$ \$10,118.27; NPV$_{RD}$ = \$13,004.46.

9-8   a. NPV$_4$ = $-$ \$1,734; NPV$_5$ = \$1,843; NPV$_8$ = \$11,107.
      b. NPV$_{8\%}$ = \$3,539; NPV$_{12\%}$ = \$280.

9-9   a. 15.3%.
      b. \$38,589.36.
      c. NPV = $-$ \$2,631,396.40; IRR = $-$31.55%.

10-1   \$10 million.

10-2   \$42,000; Accept A, C, and D.

10-5   a. 2.
      b. \$75,000 (Retained earnings); \$140,000 (Debt).
      c. 9.84%; 10.33%; 11.05%.
      d. IRR$_C$ = 10%; IRR$_E$ = 14%.
      f. E, A, and D.

10-6   a. Debt = \$10 million; Preferred = \$2 million; Common = \$18 million.
      b. \$1,710,000; \$6,710,000; \$9,000,000; \$15,000,000.
      c. 11.71%; 12.05%; 12.86%; 12.93%; 13.40%.
      d. Accept A', B, and C.
      e. A, B, and D.

10-7   a. \$10,000, \$20,000, \$25,000, and \$30,000.
      b. Retained earnings: 15.54%; New common stock: 16.27%, 17.18%; Preferred: 11.58%; 12.22%; Debt: 7.2%; 8.4%, 9.6%.
      c. 12.86%; 13.16%; 13.90%; 14.00%; 14.54%.
      d. 16.0%.
      f. B, E, and C.

10-8   a. Breakpoints: \$3.5 million; \$13 million; MCC: 11.41%; 12.37%; 13.69%.
      c. Projects C, B, and 20% of D; \$13 million.
      d. Projects C and B; \$12.5 million.
      e. A, B, and C; \$15 million.

10-9   a. 3.
      b. \$1,000,000 (Debt); \$1,250,000 (Retained earnings); \$1,875,000 (Debt).

c. 11.64%; 12.17%; 12.80%; 13.33%.
d. $IRR_1 = 16\%$; $IRR_3 = 14\%$.
f. 1, 2, and 3.

11-4 a. $6.
     b. 60%.
     c. $66.67; $100.00.

11-5 Cash = $29.2 million; Common = $52 million (52 million shares outstanding); Paid-in capital = $248 million; Retained earnings = $679.2 million.

11-6 a. 62.22%; $15.45 million; 11.21%; 10.97%.
     b. $24 million.

11-7 Yes; Price with repurchase = $36.40 vs. $36.00 without repurchase.

12-2 a. $4.
12-3 a. $3.
12-7 a. $EPS_{81} = \$8,160$; $DPS_{81} = \$4,200$; $EPS_{86} = \$12,000$; $DPS_{86} = \$6,000$; $BVS_{86} = \$90,000$.
     d. $EPS_{81} = \$2.04$; $DPS_{81} = \$1.05$; $EPS_{86} = \$3.00$; $DPS_{86} = \$1.50$; $BVS_{86} = \$22.50$.
     e. Teweles: $g_{EPS} = 8.0\%$; $g_{DPS} = 7.4\%$; $g_{Avg} = 7.7\%$.
     f. Teweles: $PO_{81} = 51\%$; $PO_{86} = 50\%$.
     g. $ROE_G = 15\%$; $ROE_S = 13.64\%$; $ROE_T = 13.33\%$.
     h. $D/A_G = 43\%$; $D/A_S = 37\%$; $D/A_T = 55\%$.
     i. $P/E_G = 8.00\times$; $P/E_S = 8.67\times$.
     j. Earnings: $24.00, $26.01; Dividends: $24.000, $26.000; Book: $27.00, $26.55.
     k. $k_G = 15.18\%$; $k_S = 12.54\%$; $21.60; $33.38.
     n. $7,360,000.

13-4 a. $10 million.
     c. $7,586,796.
     d. $15,586,796; 9.01%.

13-5 c. (1) Wait 5 yrs., PV = $80.04.
        (2) YTM = 24.23%.
     d. 7.15%: $41.96; 2%: $150.00.

13-6 a. Zero coupon = 1,037,506; Annual coupon = 400,000.
     b. (1) Zero = 10%; Annual = 11%.
        (2) Zero = 7.2%; Annual = 7.92%.
     c. Zero = 6.6%; Annual = 7.26%.

13-7 a. NPV = $2,846,818.
13-8 a. NPV = $16,520,618.
     b. 13.08%.
     c. NPV = $15,871,773; refund this year.

14-5 a. Lease; NAL = $28,335.
     c. $337,033.
     d. Lease; NAL = $122,083.

14-6 a. $392.
     b. 5.94%; yes.
     c. − $1,713.
     d. $11,302.50.
     e. $2,823; − $2,039; 12.727%.
     f. Yes, NPV = $812, but total NPV = $3,127.
     g. − $32; No.
     h. Yes, $1,070; Yes, $697; No, $320.

14-7 a. Purchase, $77,375 vs. $77,587.
     b. <15.1855% buy; >15.1855% lease.
     c. Lease, $77,587 vs. $78,005.
     e. Lease, $76,315 vs. $77,375.
     f. NAL = − $2,742; NAL = $148; <45.49% purchase; >45.49% lease.

15-1 a. $1.41.
     b. $1.14.
     c. $5.65.
     d. $0.18.
15-3 a. $0; $0; $5; $75.
     d. 10%; $100.
15-5 a. 14.1%.
     b. $12,000,000.
15-6 a. (1) Common = $162,500; Total claims = $800,000.
        (2) Common = $150,000; Total claims = $800,000.
        (3) LT debt = $500,000; Total claims = $1,300,000.
     b. 49%; 53%; 53%.
     c. $0.59; $0.64; $0.88.
     d. 19%; 19%; 50%.
15-7 b. 11.65%.

16-1 a. $83,333.
     c. 36.7%, effective cost = 43.8%.
     d. 24.5%, effective cost = 27.4%.
16-2 a. Expand payables, effective cost = 7.5%.
16-3 a. $200,000.
16-7 a. 81 days.
     b. $194,775.
16-8 a. $5,104; $10,824; $5,075; $6,417.

17-3 a. 8,950.
      b. 112.
      c. 15,556.
      d. $9,000; $8,944; $9,000; $10,000.
17-4 a. (1) $34.8 million; $33.8 million.
         (2) $36 million; $32.6 million.
         (3) $32.6 million; $36 million.
         (4) $34.3 million; $34.3 million.
17-5 a. EOQ_A = 15,811; EOQ_B = 13,693.
      b. 32; 37.
      c. 4,167; 6,945.
      d. B; TIC_A = $6,324; TIC_B = $5,478.
17-6 a. $125; $0; $125.
      b. $45.83.
      c. $41.67.
      d. 1,000 units.
17-7 a. 111,803.4.
      b. $131,803.40.
      c. $48,721.36.
      d. 20%.
      e. 37,777.78.
17-8 a. 5,200.
      b. 144.
      c. $46,563; $46,250; $46,375; $46,248.
      d. 6,000, $47,833; 6,200, $48,248; 4,200, $66,550.

18-1 b. $164,400.
18-3 a. $93,575; $254,150; − $133,525; − $62,950; $15,125; $47,450.
      f. Oct: − $64,450; Dec: − $17,800.
      g. Dec: − $578,050.
      h. Dec: − $12,550.
18-4 a. $15,811; 32.
      b. $20,811.
18-5 a. $10,000; $1,000.
      b. $10,000; $600.
      c. $8,076.
18-6 a. $20,543.
      b. $41,629; $10,000.
      d. $24,057.
18-7 a. − $4,500; − $21,600.
      b. $36,300; LOC sufficient.

19-1 a. 22 days.
      b. $48,888.89.
      c. $40,000.
19-2 a. $146,000; $198,000.
      b. ADS_1 = $3,000, ACP_1 = 48.7 days; ADS_2 = $4,500, ACP_2 = 44 days; ADS = $3,750, ACP = 52.8 days.
19-4 a. 20 days; 25 days.
      b. ΔI = $53,820; ΔP = $75,018.
      c. ΔI = − $53,820; ΔP = − $75,018.
      d. ΔP = − $12,678.

19-5 a. ΔI = $883,333; ΔP = $4,333.
      b. ΔI = − $533,333; ΔP = $62,667.
19-6 ΔI_3 = $177,778, ΔP_3 = $265,778; ΔI_4 = − $356,944, ΔP_4 = $51,056; ΔI_5 = − $466,667, ΔP_5 = $381,733.
19-7 a. 22 days; 30 days.
      b. ΔI = $27,222.
      c. ΔP = $20,033.
      d. ΔI = $22,222; ΔP = − $5,162.
      e. − $6,251; $2,510.
      f. ΔI = − $13,667; ΔP = − $35,457.

20-1 a. $111.11 million, $105.56 million, $316.67 million, $600.17 million, 8.33%, $416.67 million, $77.94 million.
      b. $27.78 million; 12.86%; 8.74%; 32.1%.
20-2 a. CA/CL = 2.67×, ACP = 36 days, S/INV = 3.33×, S/TA = 1.43×, PM = 2.5%, ROA = 3.6%, ROE = 5.7%, D/A = 37.1%.
20-3 a. CA/CL = 2.73×; D/A = 30%; TIE = 11×; S/INV = 5×; ACP = 30 days; S/FA = 5.41×; S/TA = 1.77×; PM = 3.4%; ROA = 6%; ROE = 8.6%.
20-4 a. Sources = Uses = $117 million.
20-6 a. 24.3%.
      b. 8.13% × 2.06 × 1.39 = 23.27%; A/D = 2.30.
      d. 5.58.
20-7 a. Quick = 0.8×; CA/CL = 2.3×; S/INV = 4.8×; ACP = 37 days; S/FA = 10×; S/TA = 2.3×; ROA = 5.9%; ROE = 13.1%; D/A = 54.8%; PM = 2.5%; M/B = 0.65×.

21-2 a. Cash = $200,000; A/R = $2,000,000; CS = $4,000,000; LTD = $1,200,000.
      b. $3,580,000.
21-3 b. 25%.
      d. ROE = 10.7%.
21-4 a. $489,000; STD = $20,000; LTD = $176,000; CS = $293,000.
      b. $20,000.
21-5 a. $52,000; LTD = $31,200; CS = $20,800.
      b. $4,000; $4,000; $6,000.
21-6 b. $74 million; $34 million; $37 million; − $4 million; − $10 million.
      c. Increases from 11.76% to 20.50%.
      d. $74 million; $61 million; $74 million; $17 million; $13 million.

22-2   a. CA = \$2,250,000; CS =
             \$2,125,000; TA = \$5,000,000.
       b. GW = \$1,000,000; TA =
             \$6,000,000; CS = \$3,125,000.
       c. EPS_{Pool} = \$1.62; $EPS_{Purchase}$ = \$1.37.
22-3   a. 18.1%.
       b. \$386,875; \$286,806.
       c. \$563,439.
       d. \$391,444.
       e. \$1,597,764; \$324,768.
22-4   a. 19.3%.
       b. \$10.37 million.
       c. \$8.64; remain at current price.

23-1   a. \$80,865.
       b. \$856.
       c. \$10,613; \$1,409.
       d. \$1,021.
23-2   a. 0.8%.
23-3   a. \$6,772,460.
23-4   e. 10.3 yrs.
       f. 6.5 yrs.

INDEX